Mastercam 2027 Black Book

By

Gaurav Verma

Matt Weber

(CADCAMCAE Works)

Edited by

Kristen

ISBN # 978-1-77459-230-4

DEDICATION

To teachers, who make it possible to disseminate knowledge
to enlighten the young and curious minds
of our future generations

To students, who are the future of the world

THANKS

To my friends and colleagues

To my family for their love and support

Training and Consultant Services

At CADCAMCAE Works, we provide effective and affordable one to one online training on various software packages in Computer Aided Design(CAD), Computer Aided Manufacturing(CAM), Computer Aided Engineering (CAE), Computer programming languages(C/C++, Java, .NET, Android, Javascript, HTML, and so on). The training is delivered through remote access to your system and voice chat via Internet at any time, any place, and at any pace to individuals, groups, students of colleges/universities, and CAD/CAM/CAE training centers. The main features of this program are:

Training as per your need

Highly experienced Engineers and Technician conduct the classes on the software applications used in the industries. The methodology adopted to teach the software is totally practical based, so that the learner can adapt to the design and development industries in almost no time. The efforts are to make the training process cost effective and time saving while you have the comfort of your time and place, thereby relieving you from the hassles of traveling to training centers or rearranging your time table.

Software Packages on which we provide basic and advanced training are:

CAD/CAM/CAE: CATIA, Creo Parametric, Creo Direct, SolidWorks, Autodesk Inventor, Solid Edge, UG NX, AutoCAD, AutoCAD LT, EdgeCAM, MasterCAM, SolidCAM, DelCAM, BOBCAM, UG NX Manufacturing, UG Mold Wizard, UG Progressive Die, UG Die Design, SolidWorks Mold, Creo Manufacturing, Creo Expert Machinist, NX Nastran, Hypermesh, SolidWorks Simulation, Autodesk Simulation Mechanical, Creo Simulate, Gambit, ANSYS and many others.

Computer Programming Languages: C++, VB.NET, HTML, Android, Javascript and so on.

Game Designing: Unity.

Civil Engineering: AutoCAD MEP, Revit Structure, Revit Architecture, AutoCAD Map 3D and so on.

We also provide consultant services for Design and development on the above mentioned software packages

For more information you can mail us at:
cadcamcaeworks@gmail.com

Table of Contents

Training and Consultant Services iv
Preface xvi
About Authors xviii

Chapter 1 : Introduction

Introduction to manufacturing 1-2
Roughing Process 1-2
Finishing Process 1-3
Types of Machines 1-3
Turning Machines 1-3
Milling Machines 1-4
Drilling Machines 1-4
Shaper 1-4
Planer 1-4
Electric Discharge Machine 1-4
Electro Chemical Machine 1-5
Laser Beam Machine 1-5
NC Machines 1-5
Applications of Computer Aided Manufacturing 1-6
Downloading Student Version of Mastercam 1-7
Installing Mastercam 1-8
License Activation 1-9
Basic approach in Mastercam 1-12
User Interface 1-13
Quick Access Toolbar 1-13
Ribbon 1-17
Selection Toolbar 1-17
Quick Masks Toolbar 1-25
Managers 1-26
Viewsheet Tiles 1-27
GView Controls 1-27
Status Bar 1-29
File Menu 1-30
Project Manager 1-30
Comparing Models 1-31
Tracking Changes 1-32
AutoSave 1-33
Repairing File 1-33
Starting a New File 1-34
Opening a File 1-34
Opening File in Editor 1-35
Merging Entities in Existing File 1-36
Saving File 1-38
Saving Partial File 1-38
Compressing and Sharing Files 1-39
Conversion Tools 1-39
Printing File 1-40
Help and Community Options 1-41

System Configuration 1-41
Navigation Shortcuts 1-46
Mouse Functions 1-47
Self-Assessment 1-47
Review Questions 1-48

Mastercam Design Section

Chapter 2 : Wireframe Design

Introduction 2-2
Creating Points 2-2
Creating Point by Position 2-2
Creating Point Dynamically 2-3
Creating Point Segments 2-4
Creating Points at End Points 2-4
Creating Points at Nodes 2-5
Creating Points at Circles/arcs 2-5
Creating Bolt Circle 2-5
Creating Lines 2-7
Creating Lines by Endpoints 2-7
Creating Parallel Lines 2-8
Creating Perpendicular Line 2-9
Creating Closest Line 2-10
Creating Bisector Line 2-10
Creating Circles and Arcs 2-11
Creating Center Point Circle 2-11
Creating 3 Point Arc 2-12
Creating Tangent Arc 2-13
Creating Circle using Edge Points 2-15
Creating Arc using Endpoints 2-16
Creating Polar Arc 2-17
Creating Arcs Using Polar Endpoints 2-18
Creating Splines 2-18
Creating Spline Manually 2-19
Creating Blended Spline 2-20
Creating Spline from Curves 2-21
Creating Spline using Points 2-22
Converting Curves to NURBS Spline 2-23
Creating a Rectangle 2-23
Creating Rectangular Shapes 2-24
Creating Polygon 2-25
Creating Ellipse 2-26
Creating Helix Curve 2-27
Creating Spiral Curve 2-28
Creating Letters 2-29
Creating Bounding Box 2-31
Converting Raster Graphic to Vector File 2-33
Creating Stair Geometry 2-36
Creating Door Geometry 2-37
Creating Curves 2-38
Creating Curve using Single Edge 2-39

Creating Curve using Slicing Plane 2-39
Modifying Entities Dynamically 2-40
Dynamically Trimming 2-41
Trimming Entities 2-42
Trimming using Entities 2-42
Trimming Entity at Desired Point 2-43
Trimming Multiple Entities 2-43
Modifying Entities at Intersection 2-44
Breaking Entities 2-45
Breaking Entity at Specified Point 2-45
Break at Intersection 2-46
Breaking Multiple Entities 2-46
Break at Points 2-47
Dividing Curves 2-47
Joining Entities 2-48
Modifying Length of Entities 2-49
Modifying Direction Vector 2-49
Applying Fillet 2-50
Fillet Entities Tool 2-50
Applying Fillets to Chained Entities 2-51
Applying Chamfers 2-53
Applying Chamfer to Selected Entities 2-53
Offsetting Entities 2-55
Offsetting an Entity 2-55
Projecting Entities 2-56
Closing an Arc 2-58
Breaking Circle to Segments 2-59
Combining Views 2-59
Refitting Splines 2-59
Untrimming Spline 2-60
Simplifying Spline 2-60
Editing Spline 2-61
Practical 1 2-62
Practical 2 2-65
Practice 1 2-71
Self-Assessment 2-71
Review Questions 2-72

Chapter 3 : Surface Design

Introduction 3-2
Creating Cylinder 3-2
Creating Surface Block 3-3
Creating Surface Sphere 3-4
Creating Surface Cone 3-5
Creating Torus Surface 3-7
Creating Surface Using Face of Solid 3-8
Creating Flat Boundary Surface 3-9
Creating Lofted Surface 3-10
Creating Extruded Surface 3-11
Creating Sweep Surface 3-13

Creating Revolve Surface 3-14
Creating Draft Surface 3-15
Creating Net Surface 3-16
Creating Offset Surface 3-17
Creating Fence Surface 3-19
Creating Power Surface 3-20
Trimming Surfaces 3-21
Trimming Surfaces using Curves 3-21
Trimming Surface using Surface 3-23
Trimming Surfaces to Plane 3-25
Filling Holes 3-26
Extending Surface 3-27
Extending Trimmed Edges 3-28
Applying Fillets to Surfaces 3-29
Creating Fillet at Intersection of Surfaces 3-29
Applying Surface Fillet to Plane 3-32
Applying Surface Fillet at Curves 3-33
Creating Two Surfaces Blend 3-34
Creating Three Surface Blend 3-35
Creating Three Fillet Blend 3-36
Untrimming 3-37
Untrimming Boundary of Surface 3-37
Splitting Surface 3-38
Editing Surface 3-39
Editing UV Flowline of Surface 3-40
Overflowing UV Flowlines 3-40
Rotating Flowlines 3-42
Changing Surface Normal 3-42
Practice 1 3-43
Practice 2 3-44
Self-Assessment 3-44
Review Questions 3-45

Chapter 4 : Solid Design

Introduction 4-2
Placing Solid Cylinder 4-2
Creating Solid Extrusion Feature 4-2
Planes Manager 4-4
Creating Planes Using Geometry 4-5
Creating Plane Using Solid Face 4-6
Creating Plane parallel to Current View Screen 4-6
Creating Plane Normal to Selected Entity 4-6
Creating Plane Relative to WCS 4-7
Importing Plane 4-8
Creating Quick Construction Plane 4-8
Creating Plane Dynamically 4-9
Creating Lathe Planes 4-9
Adding Group Folder 4-10
Finding a Plane 4-10
Setting WCS, Tool Plane, and Construction Plane to Current Plane 4-11

Resetting WCS, Construction Plane, and Tool Plane 4-11
Display options 4-11
Follow rules 4-13
Creating Revolve Solid Feature 4-13
Creating Solid Loft Feature 4-15
Creating Solid Sweep Feature 4-16
Performing Boolean Operations 4-18
Creating Negative Impression 4-19
Creating Hole in Solid 4-21
Creating Rectangular Pattern 4-23
Creating Circular Pattern 4-25
Creating Manual Pattern 4-26
Creating Solid from Surfaces 4-27
Creating Fillets 4-27
Creating Constant Fillet 4-27
Creating Face to Face Fillet 4-28
Creating Chamfers 4-31
Creating One Distance Chamfer 4-32
Creating Two Distance Chamfer 4-33
Applying Distance and Angle Chamfer 4-34
Creating Shell Feature 4-35
Thicken 4-35
Applying Draft Angle 4-35
Applying Draft Angle to Faces 4-36
Applying Draft Angle Referenced to Edge 4-37
Applying Draft to Extrude Feature 4-38
Applying Draft using Reference Plane 4-40
Trimming a Solid 4-41
Trimming Solid by Plane 4-41
Trimming Solid Using Surface/Sheet 4-42
Generating Layout of Solid 4-43
Adding View 4-45
Removing a View 4-45
Changing View 4-46
Transforming View 4-46
Adding Section View 4-46
Practice 1 to 4 4-47
Self-Assessment 4-49
Review Questions 4-50

Chapter 5 : Model Preparation and Mesh Design

Introduction 5-2
Creating Hole Axis 5-2
Performing Push-Pull Editing 5-3
Performing Move Operation (Direct Editing) 5-4
Splitting Solid Faces 5-5
Modifying Feature 5-7
Modifying Fillets 5-7
Removing Faces 5-8
Removing Fillets 5-9

Finding Holes 5-10
Removing History 5-11
Adding History 5-12
Simplifying Solid 5-13
Optimizing Imported Model 5-13
Repairing Small Faces of Solid Body 5-13
Disassembly of Solid Bodies 5-14
Aligning Solid to Plane 5-15
Aligning Face of Selected Solid to Another Solid Face 5-17
Aligning Solid Body along Z 5-18
Color Tools 5-18
Clearing All Colors 5-18
Changing Colors of Faces 5-19
Mesh Designing 5-19
Creating Cylinder Mesh 5-20
Creating Mesh from Entity 5-20
Offsetting Mesh 5-21
Smoothening Free Edges 5-22
Filling Holes 5-23
Smoothening Mesh Region 5-24
Refining Mesh 5-25
Decimation 5-26
Exploding Mesh 5-27
Modifying Mesh Facets 5-27
Trimming Mesh using Planar Entity 5-28
Trimming Mesh using Surface/Sheet Object 5-29
Trimming Mesh Using Curve Chain 5-30
Checking Mesh Quality 5-31
Self-Assessment 5-31
Review Questions 5-32

Chapter 6 : Drafting

Introduction 6-2
Smart Dimensioning 6-2
Applying Horizontal Dimension 6-6
Creating Vertical Dimension 6-7
Applying Circular Dimension 6-7
Applying Dimension to a Point 6-8
Applying Angular Dimension 6-8
Applying Perpendicular Dimension 6-9
Creating Baseline Dimension 6-10
Creating Chained Dimension 6-10
Creating Tangent Dimension 6-11
Creating Horizontal Ordinate Dimension 6-11
Creating Vertical Ordinate Dimension 6-12
Adding Ordinate Dimensions to Existing Ordinate Dimension 6-12
Creating Multiple Sets of Ordinate Dimensions 6-13
Aligning Ordinate Dimensions 6-14
Creating Note Annotations 6-14
Creating Hole Tables 6-16

Creating Cross Hatch 6-17
Creating Leader and Witness Lines 6-18
Creating Leader 6-18
Creating Witness Lines 6-19
Regenerate Tools 6-20
Aligning Notes 6-21
Converting Legacy Notes 6-21
Editing Parameters of Draft Entities 6-21
Breaking Drafting Elements into Lines 6-22
Self-Assessment 6-22
Review Questions 6-23

Chapter 7 : Transform and View Tools

Introduction 7-2
Transformation Tools 7-2
Dynamically Transforming Objects 7-2
Translating Objects in 3 Dimension 7-3
Translating Objects Along a Plane 7-4
Rotating Objects 7-4
Projecting Entities 7-5
Moving Objects to New WCS 7-6
Mirroring Objects 7-6
Wrapping Geometry about an Axis 7-7
Creating Copies Between Points 7-8
Stretching Line Segments 7-9
Scaling Entities 7-10
View Tools 7-11
Zoom Tools 7-11
Graphics View Tools 7-11
Setting Appearances of Model 7-13
Advanced Display Options for Toolpaths 7-14
Showing/Hiding Managers 7-15
Showing/Hiding Axes 7-17
Showing/Hiding Gnomons 7-18
Grid Setting 7-18
Specifying View Rotation Position 7-19
Viewsheet Options 7-19
Self-Assessment 7-20
Review Questions 7-21

Machining Section

Chapter 8 : Starting with Mastercam Machining

Introduction 8-2
CNC Machine Structure 8-2
Tool Spindle 8-2
Tool Changer or Turret 8-3
Translational and Rotational Limits 8-3
Tail Stock 8-3
Setting up a Milling Machine 8-4

Modifying Machine Definition **8-5**
Machine Parameters 8-6
Kinematic Tree Configuration 8-7
Axis Combinations 8-12
Control Definition Parameters 8-12
Options 8-16
Replacing Machine Definition **8-17**
New Machine Definitions **8-17**
Managing Control Definition **8-17**
Applying Material to Workpiece **8-18**
Tool Manager **8-18**
Creating New Tool 8-19
Editing Tool 8-23
Tools Used in CNC Milling and Lathe Machines **8-24**
Milling Tools 8-24
Lathe Tools or Turning Tools 8-31
Creating Stock for Model **8-36**
Creating Stock using Stock Model Tool 8-36
Exporting the Stock Model **8-40**
Self Assessment **8-41**
Review Questions **8-42**

Chapter 9 : Milling Toolpaths

Introduction **9-2**
2D Toolpaths **9-2**
Creating 2D Contour Toolpath 9-2
Creating Drill Toolpath 9-15
Dynamic Mill Toolpath 9-18
Creating Facing Toolpath 9-24
Dynamic Contour Toolpath 9-25
Creating Pocket Toolpath 9-27
Creating Peel Mill Toolpaths 9-31
Creating Area Mill Toolpath 9-32
Creating Blend Mill Toolpath 9-34
Creating Slot Mill Toolpath 9-36
Creating Model Chamfer Toolpath 9-38
Creating Engrave Toolpath 9-40
Feature Based Milling 9-44
Creating Swept 2D Toolpath 9-50
Creating Swept 3D Toolpath 9-52
Creating Revolve Toolpath 9-54
Creating Lofted Toolpath 9-55
Creating Ruled Toolpath 9-57
Creating Chamfer Drill Toolpath 9-58
Creating Advanced Drill Toolpaths 9-60
Creating Circular Mill Toolpath 9-61
Creating Helix Bore Toolpath 9-64
Creating Thread Mill Toolpath 9-66
Creating FBM Drill Toolpath 9-68
Creating Auto Drill Toolpath 9-70

Creating Start Hole Toolpath 9-70
Point Toolpaths 9-73
Creating Manual Entry Toolpath 9-74
Self Assessment 9-76
Review Questions 9-77

Chapter 10 : 3D Milling Toolpaths

Introduction 10-2
3D Roughing Toolpaths 10-2
OptiRough Toolpaths 10-2
Pocket Surface Rough Toolpath 10-8
Project Rough Surface Toolpath 10-11
Parallel Rough Surface Toolpath 10-13
Plunge Rough Surface Toolpath 10-18
Creating Multisurface Pocket Toolpath 10-20
Creating Area Rough Toolpath 10-21
3D Finishing Toolpaths 10-24
Creating Waterline Toolpath 10-25
Creating Raster Toolpath 10-29
Creating Scallop Surface Finish Toolpath 10-29
Creating Equal Scallop Toolpath 10-32
Hybrid Toolpath 10-32
Pencil Surface Finish Toolpath 10-33
Blend Surface Finish Toolpath 10-33
Creating Surface Finish Contour Toolpath 10-35
Creating Horizontal Area Toolpath 10-37
Flowline Surface Finish Toolpath 10-38
Spiral Toolpath 10-41
Creating Radial Surface Finish Toolpath 10-42
3-axis Deburring Toolpath 10-44
Self Assessment 10-47
Review Questions 10-48

Chapter 11 : Multiaxis Milling Toolpaths

Introduction 11-2
Creating Curve Toolpath 11-2
Creating Swarf Milling Toolpath 11-5
Creating Unified Multiaxis Toolpath 11-10
Patterns for Unified Toolpath 11-11
Creating Parallel Multiaxis Toolpaths 11-14
Collision Control Options 11-17
Linking Parameters for Unified Toolpath 11-18
Creating Multiaxis Morph Toolpath 11-19
Creating Multiaxis Flow Toolpath 11-20
Creating Multiaxis Multisurface Toolpath 11-22
Creating Multiaxis Port Expert Toolpath 11-23
Creating Multiaxis Triangular Mesh Toolpath 11-25
Creating Multiaxis Deburr Toolpath 11-27
Creating Multiaxis Pocketing Toolpath 11-29
Creating 3+2 Automatic Roughing Toolpath 11-30

Creating Multiaxis Project Curve Toolpath 11-31
Creating Multiaxis Rotary Toolpath 11-33
Creating Multiaxis Rotary Advanced Toolpath 11-34
Creating Multiaxis Blade Expert Toolpath 11-36
Self Assessment 11-40
Review Questions 11-40

Chapter 12 : Advanced Milling Tools
Introduction 12-2
Multiaxis Linking 12-2
Toolpath Transformation 12-4
Mirror Transformation 12-6
Rotation Transformation 12-7
Translate Transformation 12-8
Converting Toolpath to 5-axis Toolpath 12-8
Converting to 5 axis 12-10
Dropping 5 Axis Toolpath 12-11
Trimming a Toolpath 12-12
Nesting Toolpaths 12-13
Sheets tab 12-14
Parts tab 12-15
Parameters tab 12-16
Additions tab 12-19
Checking Tool Holder 12-21
Checking Reach of Tool in Model 12-22
Art Machining (Image Based) 12-24
Self Assessment 12-28
Review Questions 12-29

Chapter 13 : Milling Operations Practical and Practice
Practical 1 13-2
Practice 1 13-12
Practical 2 13-13
Practice 2 13-21

Chapter 14 : Lathe Machining and Toolpaths
Introduction 14-2
Lathe Machine Setup 14-2
Defining Stock For Lathe Operation 14-2
Aligning Model with Machining Plane 14-2
Creating Stock of Model 14-4
Lathe Tool Manager 14-13
Inserts tab 14-13
Type tab 14-15
Holders tab 14-16
Parameters tab 14-18
Creating Turn Profile 14-19
General Lathe Toolpaths 14-20
Creating Rough Machining Toolpath 14-21

Toolpath parameters 14-22
Rough parameters 14-24
Finish Toolpath on Lathe 14-30
Lathe Drill 14-31
Face Toolpath 14-32
Lathe Cutoff toolpath 14-33
Groove Toolpath 14-35
Groove shape parameters tab 14-37
Groove rough parameters tab 14-38
Groove finish parameters tab 14-39
Dynamic Rough Toolpath 14-39
Thread Toolpath 14-42
Thread shape parameters tab 14-42
Thread cut parameters 14-44
Plunge Turn Toolpath 14-45
Plunge turn shape parameters tab 14-48
Plunge turn rough parameters tab 14-48
Contour Rough Toolpath 14-50
PrimeTurning Toolpath 14-52
Rough Parameters Tab 14-53
Custom Threading Toolpath 14-55
Toolpath through points 14-59
Canned Toolpaths 14-60
Practical 1 14-62
Self Assessment 14-74
Review Questions 14-74

Chapter 15 : Advanced Lathe Tools and Toolpaths

Introduction 15-2
Face Contour 15-2
Cross Contour 15-5
Pickoff/Pull/Cutoff Operation 15-6
Preparing for Pickoff/Pull/Cutoff Operation 15-6
Performing Pickoff, bar pull, cutoff Operation 15-7
Stock Transfer 15-9
Stock Flip 15-11
Stock Advance 15-12
Undoing Stock related Operations in Mastercam 15-13
Chuck 15-14
Tail Stock 15-15
Backplot and Verifying Toolpath 15-16
Back plotting Toolpath 15-16
Verifying Toolpaths 15-17
Practical 1 15-18
Self Assessment 15-27
Review Questions 15-28

Index I-1
Ethics of an Engineer I-8

Preface

Mastercam is one of the world's most widely used CAM software for creating NC program for most complex part. Mastercam provides toolpaths and machining strategies preferred by most of the manufacturing firms around the world. Mastercam offers CAD/CAM software tools for a variety of CNC programming needs, from basic to complex. Mastercam CAD/CAM software controls CNC machines like mills, routers, lathes, and wire EDMs.

The **Mastercam 2027 Black Book** is the 7th edition of our series on Mastercam. The book is authored to help professionals as well as learners in creating some of the most complex NC toolpaths. The book follows a step by step methodology. In this book, we have tried to give real-world examples with real challenges in designing. We have tried to reduce the gap between university use of Mastercam and industrial use of Mastercam. The book covers almost all the information required by a learner to master Mastercam. The book starts with basics of machining and ends at advanced topics like Multiaxis Machining Toolpaths. This book covers Mastercam Designing tools, Milling Machine Tools, Lathe Machine tools, and Art Machining technique. Some of the salient features of this book are :

In-Depth explanation of concepts

Every new topic of this book starts with the explanation of the basic concepts. In this way, the user becomes capable of relating the things with real world.

Topics Covered

Every chapter starts with a list of topics being covered in that chapter. In this way, the user can easy find the topic of his/her interest easily.

Instruction through illustration

The instructions to perform any action are provided by maximum number of illustrations so that the user can perform the actions discussed in the book easily and effectively. There are about 1070 small and large illustrations that make the learning process effective.

Tutorial point of view

At the end of concept's explanation, tutorials make the understanding of users firm and long lasting. Almost each chapter of the book related to machining has tutorials that are real world projects. Moreover most of the tools in this book are discussed in the form of tutorials.

For Faculty

If you are a faculty member, then you can ask for video tutorials on any of the topic, exercise, tutorial, or concept. As faculty, you can register on our website to get electronic desk copies of our latest books, self-assessment, and solution of practical. Faculty resources are available in the **Faculty Member** page of our website (**www.cadcamcaeworks.com**) once you login. Note that faculty registration approval is manual and it may take two days for approval before you can access the faculty website.

Formatting Conventions Used in the Text

All the key terms like name of button, tool, drop-down etc. are kept bold.

Free Resources

Link to the resources used in this book are provided to the users via email. To get the resources, mail us at ***cadcamcaeworks@gmail.com*** with your contact information. With your contact record with us, you will be provided latest updates and informations regarding various technologies. The format to write us mail for resources is as follows:

Subject of E-mail as ***Application for resources of ________book***.
Also, given your information like
Name:
Course pursuing/Profession:
E-mail ID:

Note: We respect your privacy and value it. If you do not want to give your personal informations then you can ask for resources without giving your information.

About Authors

The author of this book, Gaurav Verma, has authored and assisted in more than 16 titles in CAD/CAM/CAE which are already available in market. He has authored **AutoCAD Electrical Black Books** which are available in both **English** and **Russian** language. He has also authored **Creo Manufacturing 13.0 Black Book** which covers Machining module of Creo Parametric and **Mastercam 2023 for SolidWorks Black Book**. He has provided consultant services to many industries in US, Greece, Canada, and UK. He has assisted in preparing many Government aided skill development programs. He has been speaker for Autodesk University. He has assisted in preparing AutoCAD Electrical course for Autodesk Design Academy. He has worked on Sheetmetal, Forging, Machining, and Casting in Design and Development department.

The author of this book, Matt Weber, has authored many books on CAD/CAM/CAE available already in market. The author has hands on experience on almost all the CAD/CAM/CAE packages. Besides that he is a good person in his real life, helping nature for everyone. If you have any query/doubt in any CAD/CAM/CAE package, then you can contact the author by writing at cadcamcaeworks@gmail.com

For Any query or suggestion

If you have any query or suggestion, please let us know by mailing us on ***cadcamcaeworks@gmail.com***. Your valuable constructive suggestions will be incorporated in our books and your name will be addressed in special thanks area of our books on your confirmation.

Chapter 1

Introduction

Topics Covered

The major topics covered in this chapter are:

- ***Introduction to manufacturing.***
- ***Types of Machines.***
- ***Applications of CAM.***
- ***Installing Mastercam.***
- ***General Approach in Mastercam.***
- ***Walkthrough of Mastercam.***

INTRODUCTION TO MANUFACTURING

Manufacturing is the process of creating a useful product by using a machine, a process, or both. For manufacturing a product, there are some steps to be followed:

- Generating Layout of final product.
- Raw material/Work piece; selection of raw material depending on the application of the product.
- Forging, Casting, or any other pre-machining method for creating outlines of final shape.
- Roughing Processes.
- Finishing Processes.
- Quality Control.

As the "Generating Layout of final product" is above all the steps, it is the most important step. One should be very clear about the final product because all the other steps are totally dependent on the first step. The layout of final product can be a drawing or a model created by using any modeling software like SolidWorks, Inventor, Solid Edge, and so on. You can also use the Design environment of Mastercam software to create the model.

The next step is "Selection of Raw material/Workpiece". This step is solely dependent on the first step. Our final product defines what should be the raw material and the workpiece shape. Here, workpiece is the piece of raw material of desired shape to be used for the next step or process.

The next step is "Forging, Casting, or any other process for creating outline of the final shape". The outline created for the final shape is also called Blank in industries. In this step, various machines like Press, Cutter, or Moulding machines are used for creating the blank. In some cases of Casting, there is no requirement of machining processes. For example, in case of Investment casting, most of the time there is no requirement of machining process. Machining processes can be divided further into two processes:

- Roughing Processes
- Finishing Processes

These processes are the main discussion area of this book. An introduction to these processes is given next.

Roughing Process

Roughing process is the first step of machining process. Generally, roughing process is the removal of large amount of stock material in comparison to finishing process. In a roughing process, the quantity of material removed from the workpiece is more important than the quality of the machining. There are no close tolerances for roughing process so the main areas of concern are maximum limit of material that can be removed without harming the cutting tool life. So, these processes are relatively cheaper than the finishing process.

In manufacturing industries, there are three principle machining processes called Turning, Milling, and Drilling. In case of roughing process, there can be turning, milling, drilling, combination of any two, or all the processes. Along with these machining processes, there are various other processes like shaping, planing, broaching, reaming, and so on. But these processes are used in special cases.

Finishing Process

Finishing process can include all the machining processes discussed in case of roughing processes but in close tolerances. Also, the quality of machining at required accuracy level is very important for finishing. Along with the above discussed machining processes, there are a few more machining processes like Electric Discharge Machining(EDM), Laser Beam Machining, Electrochemical Machining, and so on. These processes are called unconventional machining processes because of their cutting method. In unconventional machining processes, the cutting is not performed by mechanical pull/push of tool in the workpiece. In these machining processes, electrical discharge, chemical reaction, laser beams, and other sources are used for cutting. Some of the common machines used for machining processes are discussed next.

TYPES OF MACHINES

There are various types of machines for different type of machining process. For example- for turning process, there are machines like conventional lathe and CNC Turner. Similarly for milling process, there are machines called Milling machine, VMC, or HMC. Some of the machines are discussed next with details of their functioning.

Turning Machines

Turning machine is a category of machines used for turning process (cutting cylindrical parts). In this machine, the workpiece is held in a chuck (collet in case of small workpieces). This chuck revolves at a defined rotational speed. Note that the workpiece can revolve in either CW(Clockwise) or CCW(Counter-Clockwise) direction but cannot translate in any direction. The cutting tool used for removing material can translate in X and Y directions. The most basic type of turning machine is a lathe. But now a days, lathes are being replaced by CNC Turning machines, which are faster and more accurate than the traditional lathes. The CNC Turning machines are controlled by numeric codes. These codes are interpreted by machine controller attached in the machine and then the controller commands various sections of the machine to do a specific job like asking the motor of cutting tool to rotate in clockwise direction by 10 degree. The basic operations that can be done on turning machines are:

- Taper turning
- Spherical generation
- Facing
- Grooving
- Parting (in few cases)
- Drilling
- Boring
- Reaming
- Threading

Milling Machines

Milling machine is a category of machines used for removing material by using a perpendicular tool relative to the workpiece. In this type of machine, workpiece is held on a bed with the help of fixtures. The tool rotates at a defined speed. This tool can move in X, Y, and Z directions. In some machines, the bed can also translate and rotate like in Turret milling machines, 5-axis machines, and so on. Milling machines are of two types; horizontal milling machine and vertical milling machine. In Horizontal milling machine, the tool is aligned with the horizontal axis (X-axis). In Vertical milling machine, the tool is aligned with the vertical axis (Y-axis). The Vertical milling machine is generally used for complex cutting processes like contouring, engraving, embossing, and so on. The Horizontal milling machines are used for cutting slots, grooves, gear teeth, and so on. In some Horizontal milling machines, table can move up-down by motor mechanism or power system. By using the synchronization of table movement with the rotation of rotary fixture, we can also create spiral features. The tools used in both milling machine types have cutting edge on the sides as well as at the tip.

Drilling Machines

Drilling machine is a category of machines used for cutting holes in the workpiece. In Drilling machine, the tool (drill bit) is fixed in a tool holder and the tool can move up-down. The workpiece is fixed on the bed. The tool goes down, by motor or by hand, penetrating through the workpiece. There are various types of Drilling machine available like drill presses, cordless drills, pistol grip drills, and so on.

Shaper

Shaper is a category of machines, which is used to cut material in a linear motion. Shaper has a single point cutting tool, which goes back-forth to create linear cut in the workpiece. This type of machine is used to create flat surface of the workpiece. You can create dovetail slot, splines, key slot, and so on by using this machine. In some operation, this machine can be an alternative for EDM.

Planer

Planer is a category of machines similar to Shaper. The only difference is that, in case of Planer machine, the workpiece reciprocates and the tool is fixed.

There are various other special purpose machines (SPMs), which are used for some uncommon requirements. The machines discussed above are conventional machines. The unconventional machines are discussed next.

Electric Discharge Machine

Electric Discharge Machine is a category of machines used for creating desired shapes on the workpiece with the help of electric discharges. In this type of machines, the tool and the workpiece act as electrodes and a dielectric fluid is passed between them. The workpiece is fixed in the bed and tool can move in X, Y, and Z direction. During the machining process, the tool is brought near to the workpiece. Due to this, a spark is generated between them. This spark causes the material on the workpiece to melt and get separated from the workpiece. This separated material is drained with the help of dielectric fluid. There are two types of EDMs which are listed next.

Wire-cut EDM

In this type of EDM, a brass wire is commonly used to cut the material from the workpiece. This wire is held in upper and lower diamond shaped guides. It is constantly fed from a bundle. In this machine, the material is removed by generating sparks between tool and workpiece. A Wire-cut EDM can be used to cut a plate having thickness up to 300 mm.

Sinker EDM

In this type of EDM, a metal electrode is used to cut the material from the workpiece. The tool and the workpiece are submerged in the dielectric fluid. Power supply is connected to both the tool and the workpiece. When tool is brought near the workpiece, sparks are generated randomly on their surfaces. Such sparks gradually create impression of tool on the workpiece.

Electro Chemical Machine

Electro Chemical Machine is a category of machines used for creating desired shape by using the chemical electrolyte. This machining works on the principles of chemical reactions.

Laser Beam Machine

Laser Beam Machine is a category of machines that uses a beam, a highly coherent light. This type of light is called laser. A laser can output a power of up to 100MW in an area of 1 square mm. A laser beam machine can be used to create accurate holes or shapes on a material like silicon, graphite, diamond, and so on.

The machines discussed till now are the major machines used in industries. Some of these machines can be controlled by numeric codes and are called NC machines. NC Machines and their working are discussed next.

NC MACHINES

An NC Machine is a manufacturing tool that removes material by following a predefined command set. An NC Machine can be a milling machine or it can be a turning center. NC stands for Numerical Control so, these machines are controlled by numeric codes. These codes are dependent on the controller installed in the machines. There are various controllers available in the market like Fanuc controller, Siemens controller, Heidenhain controller, and so on. The numeric codes change according to the controller used in the machine. These numeric codes are compiled in the form of a program, which is fed in the machine controller via a storage media. The numeric codes are generally in the form of G-codes and M-codes. For understanding purpose, some of the G-codes and M-codes are discussed next with their functions for a Fanuc controller.

Code		**Function**
G00	-	Rapid movement of tool.
G01	-	Linear movement while creating cut.
G02	-	Clockwise circular cut.
G03	-	Counter-clockwise circular cut.
G20	-	Starts inch mode.

G21 - Starts mm mode.
G96 - Provides constant surface speed.
G97 - Constant RPM.
G98 - Feed per minute
G99 - Feed per revolution

M00 - Program stop
M02 - End of program
M03 - Spindle rotation Clockwise.
M04 - Spindle rotation Counter Clockwise.
M05 - Spindle stop
M08 - Coolant on
M09 - Coolant off
M98 - Subprogram call
M99 - Subprogram exit

These codes as well as the other codes will be discussed in the subsequent chapters according to their applications.

As there is a long list of codes which are required in NC programs to make machine cut workpiece in desired size and shape, it becomes a tedious job to create programs manually for each operation. Moreover, it take much time to create a program for small operations on a milling machine. To solve this problem and to reduce the human error, Computer Aided Manufacturing (CAM) comes in light. Various applications of CAM are discussed next.

APPLICATIONS OF COMPUTER AIDED MANUFACTURING

Computer Aided Manufacturing (CAM) is a technology which can be used to enhance the manufacturing process. In this technology, the machines are controlled by a workstation. This workstation can serve more than one machines at a time. Using CAM, you can create and manage the programs being fed in the workstation. Some of the applications of CAM are discussed next.

1. CAM with the combination of CAD can be used to create complex shapes by machining in a small time.
2. CAM can be used to manage more than one machines at the same time with less human power.
3. CAM is used to automate the manufacturing process.
4. CAM is used to generate NC programs for various types of NC machines.
5. 5-Axis Machining

CAM is generally the next step after CAD (Computer Aided Designing). Sometimes CAE (Computer Aided Engineering) is also required before CAM. There are various software companies that provide the CAM software solutions. CNC Software is one of those companies which publishes Mastercam software. Mastercam is one of the most popular software for CAM programming.

DOWNLOADING STUDENT VERSION OF MASTERCAM

- Open your internet browser and reach the link :

https://signup.mastercam.com/demo-hle

- On reaching the link, a web-page will be displayed. Scroll down on this page and you will find fields as shown in Figure-1.

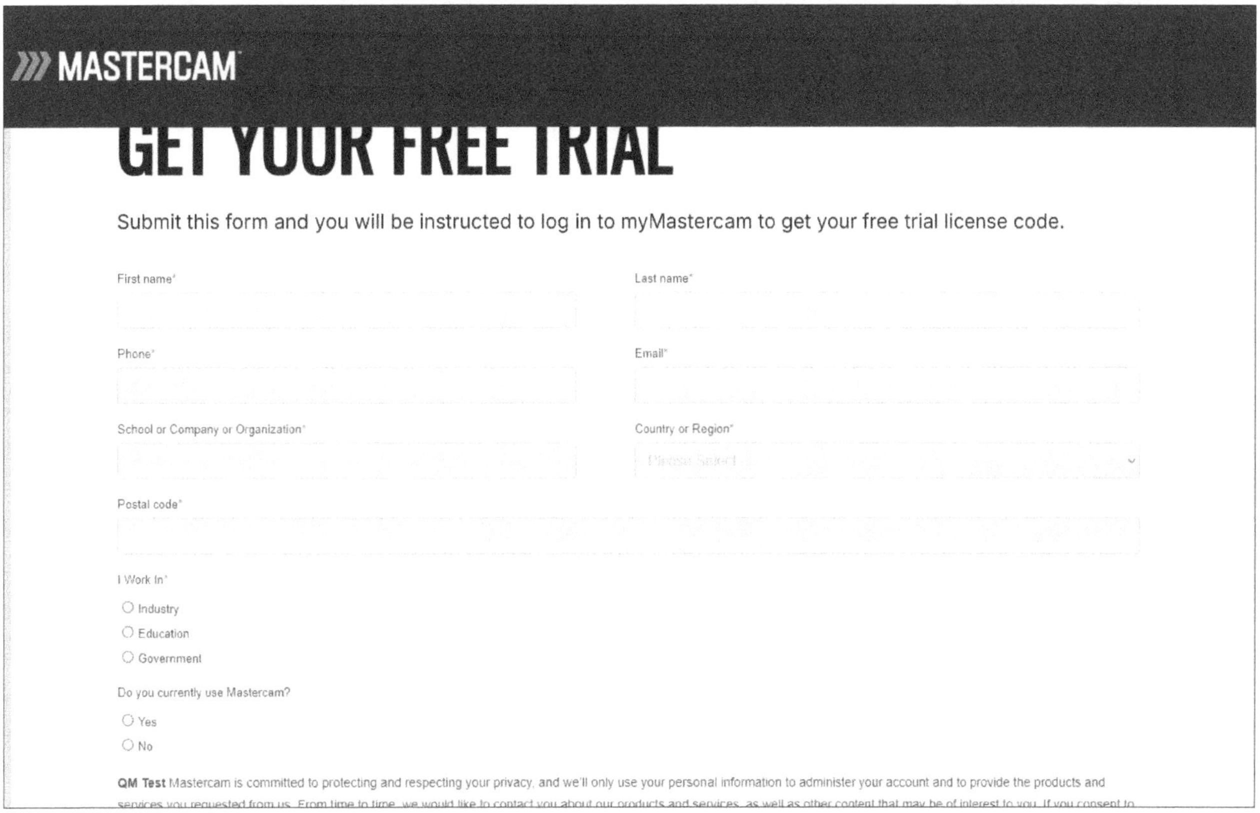

Figure-1. Mastercam Home Learning Edition web page

- Enter your student/educator information in the fields and click on the **Access Learning Edition via myMastercam** button. The **CREATE YOUR ACCOUNT** page will be displayed in the web browser. Set desired password and other details for new account and click on the **Create Account** button. An E-mail will be sent to your E-mail box for validating account. Click on the link in E-mail to validate account and log in to your account. After login, click on the Get a License button to get a new learning edition license for the software The web page to download software will be displayed; refer to Figure-2.

- Click on **Mastercam Learning Edition** button from Mastercam 2027 Learning Edition area and click on the. A file of approximately 1.96 GB will start downloading. (You can also use direct link: *https://downloads.mastercam.com/latest/mastercam2027-web.exe* to download the installation file after login.)

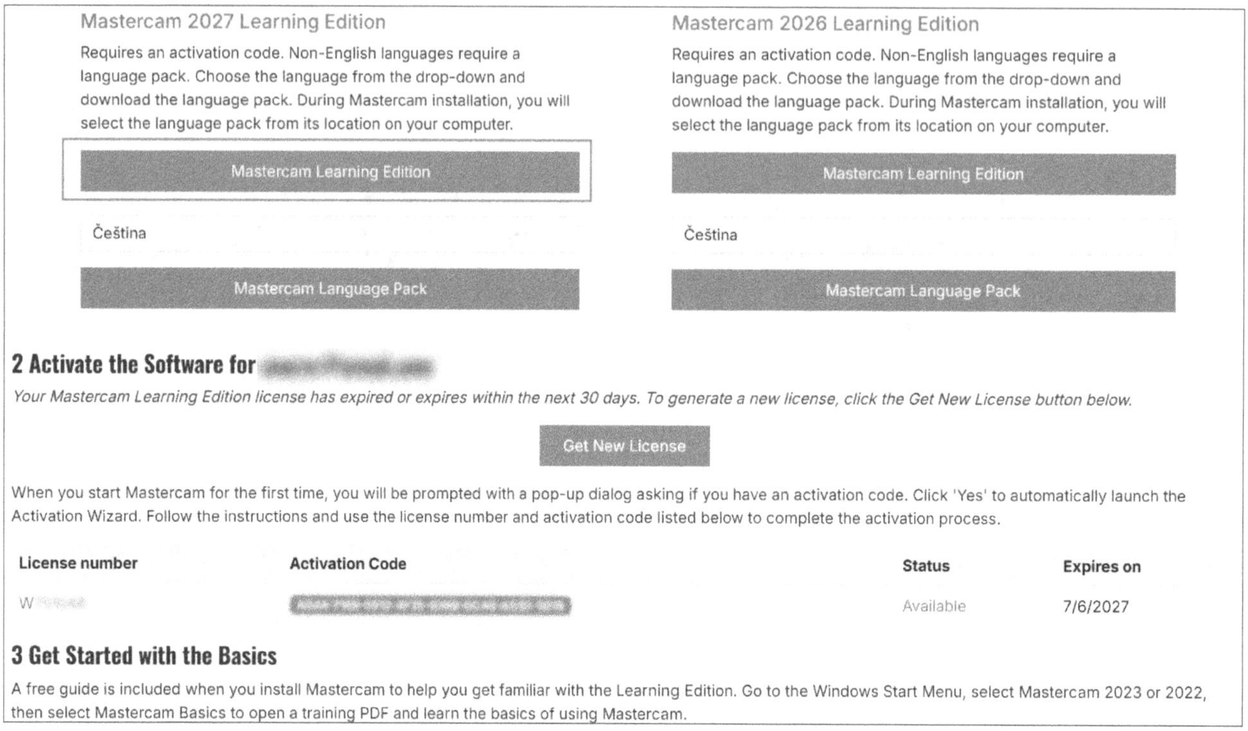

Figure-2. Download page for Mastercam HLE

INSTALLING MASTERCAM

- After downloading the setup file of Mastercam from the Mastercam website, right-click on the setup file (**mastercam2027-web.exe**) file from the location where you downloaded the file and select the **Run as Administrator** option from the shortcut menu. Follow the instructions to install as displayed.
- The Learning Edition of software will automatically pick the license. Make sure CodeMeter application is running in the Taskbar Icons when running software for the first time. When asked for license detail then you need to provide License number and Activation Code provided to you via email using online activation during the setup. Connect the adapter having license or start the license server in your system as directed by your reseller if you are using standard version of Mastercam.
- Click on the **Mastercam 2027** option from the **Mastercam** folder in the **Start** menu. You can also search the app in **Start** menu. On first start of application, you will be asked to accept a user agreement. Select the check box and click on the **Continue** button from agreement dialog box. The Mastercam Design application window will be displayed; refer to Figure-3.

There are mainly two environments in Mastercam, one for CAD and other for CAM. By default, CAD environment is active. In this book, we will first discuss the CAD environment tools and then we will discuss the CAM environment tools.

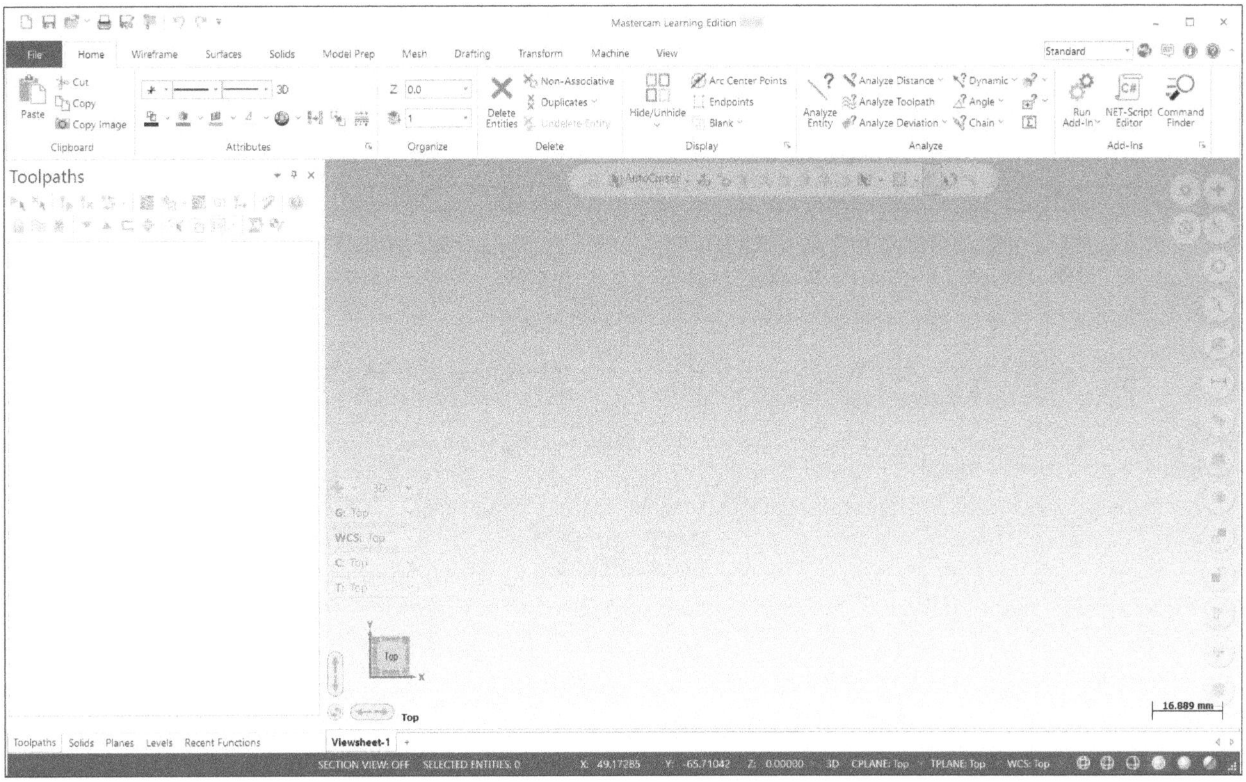

Figure-3. Mastercam Design application window

License Activation

If you have installed earlier versions of the software and your learning license has expired then you can use following steps to renew and activate your learning license.

- Open the link *https://my.mastercam.com/* in your web browser and login with your credentials earlier created.
- Hover the cursor on **DOWNLOADS** link button at top right corner of the web page and select the **Learning Edition** option from the menu; refer to Figure-4. You will reach at page to download learning edition of software; refer to Figure-2.

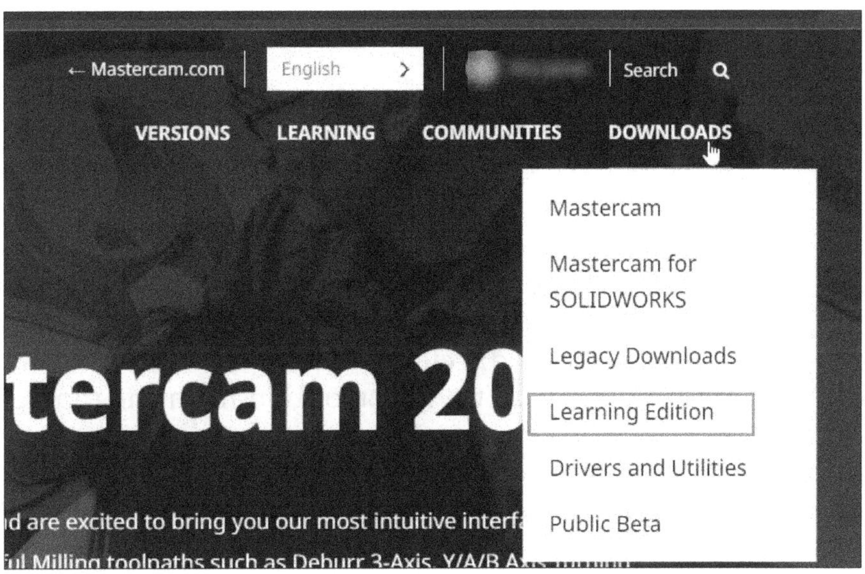

Figure-4. Learning Edition option

- If your earlier license has expired or will expire within 30 days then the **Get New License** button will be displayed on this page; refer to Figure-5.

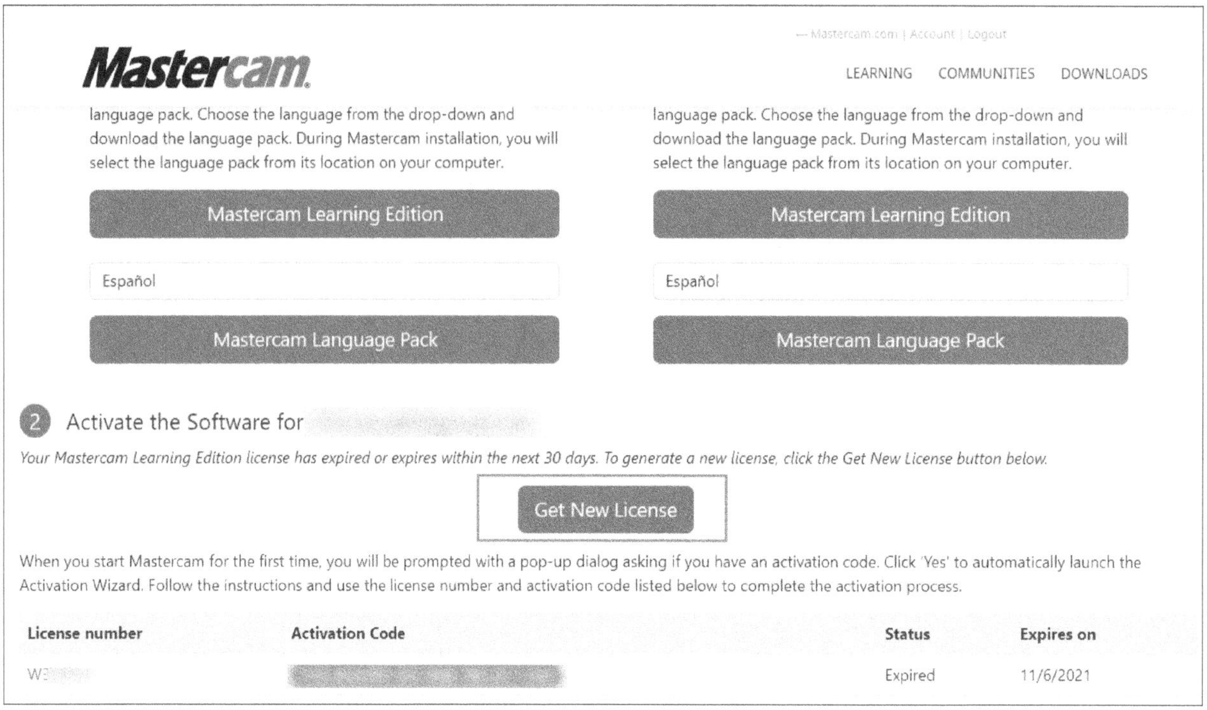

Figure-5. Get New License button

- Click on the **Get New License** button from the page and click on the **OK** button from Popup displayed. A new license number will be added in the list with activation code; refer to Figure-6.

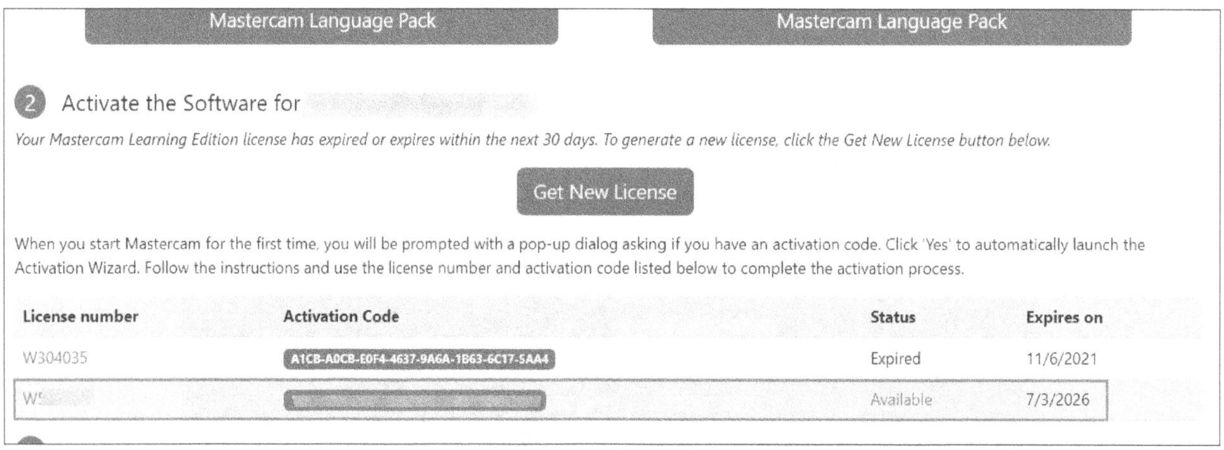

Figure-6. New license added in list

- Keep this page open because we will need the license number and activation code.
- Click on the **Activation Wizard** tool from the **Mastercam Licensing Utilities** folder in the **Start** menu; refer to Figure-7. The **Mastercam Product Activation Wizard** dialog box will be displayed; refer to Figure-8.
- Select the **Online Activation/Deactivation** option from the dialog box and then select the **Activate a New License** option from the dialog box. The **Terms and Conditions** page will be displayed in the dialog box. Select the “I agree to the terms and conditions listed above” check box and click on the **Next** button. The **Product Activation Code** page will be displayed; refer to Figure-9.

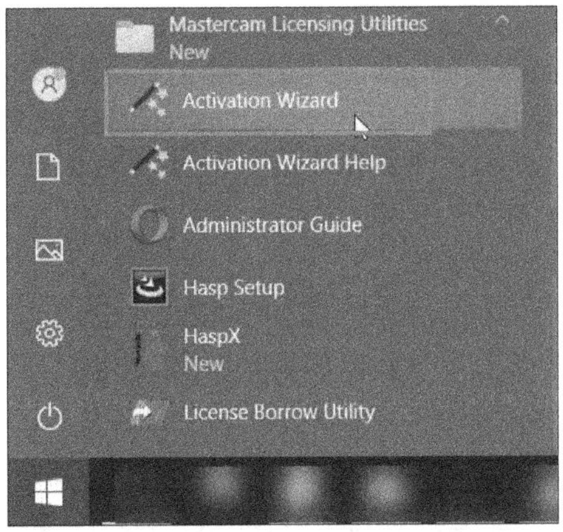

Figure-7. Activation Wizard application

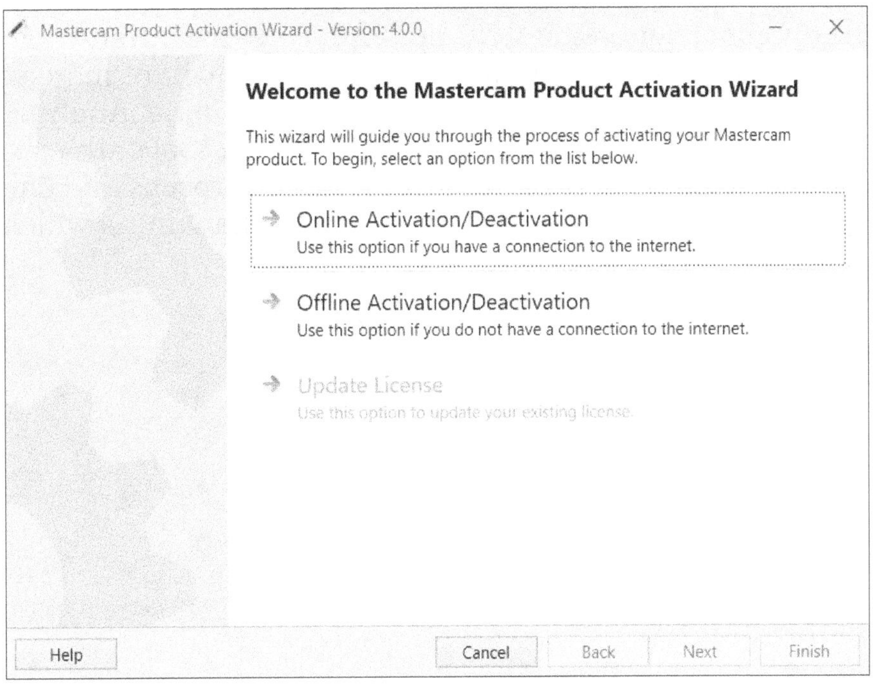

Figure-8. Mastercam Product Activation Wizard dialog box

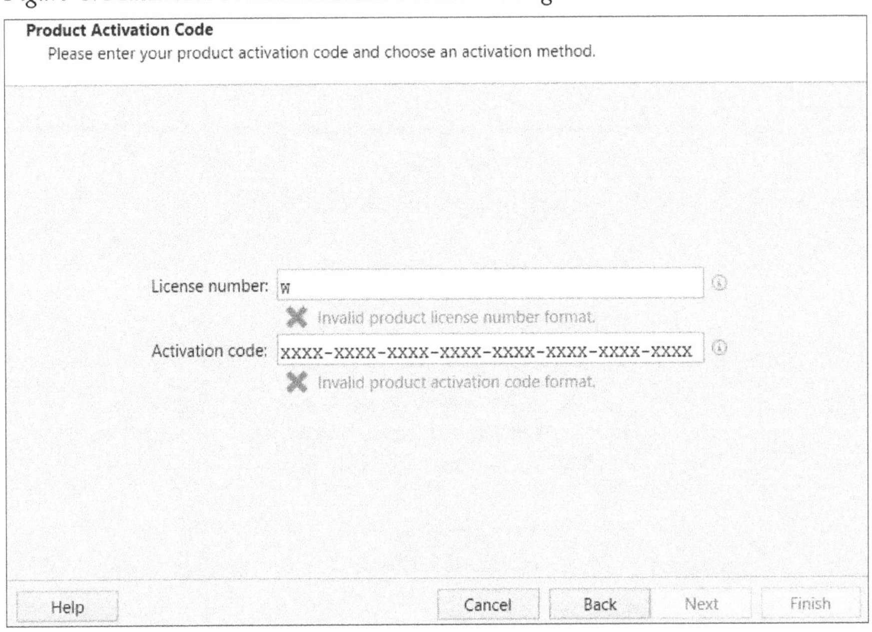

Figure-9. Product Activation Code page

- Copy the License number and Activation code from web page, and paste them in designated fields of the dialog box. The indications of valid format will be displayed below the fields in the dialog box if you have input correct license number and activation codes. Click on the **Next** button from the dialog box and follow next prompts to activate your new license.

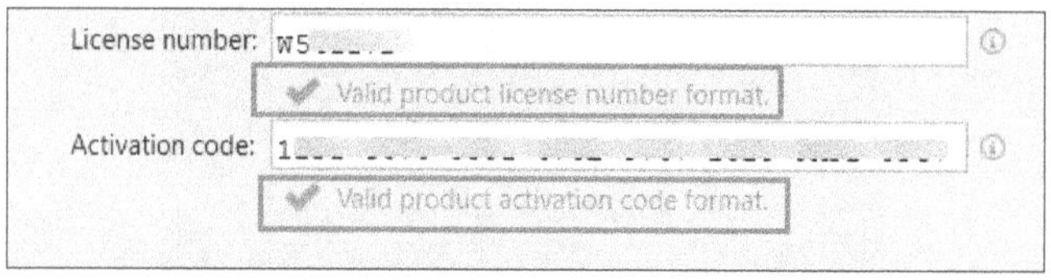

Figure-10. Valid format notifications

BASIC APPROACH IN MASTERCAM

Whether you use the stand-alone program of Mastercam or the integrated one with SolidWorks, the approach for creating NC programs is same. First, you need to import or create the CAD model of the product. Then, create stock of material (workpiece) from which the product will be manufactured after machining. Apply settings related to machine. Apply parameters related to tools. Create the tool paths for operations to be performed on the machine. Simulate the machining process and check whether it is as per the requirement. Generate the output of the machining which is NC codes. Refer to Figure-11.

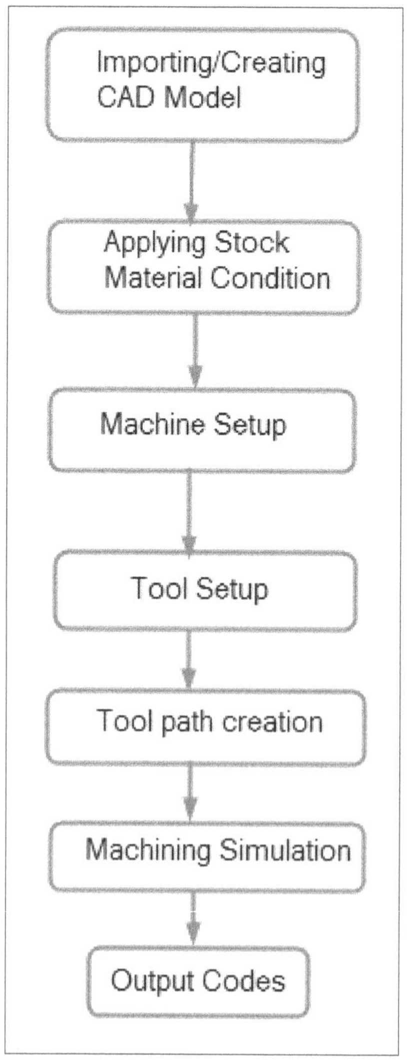

Figure-11. Workflow in Mastercam

USER INTERFACE

The user interface of Mastercam can be divided into various elements like Ribbon, Quick Access Toolbar, Managers, and so on. Various elements of interface are marked in Figure-12. These interface elements are discussed next.

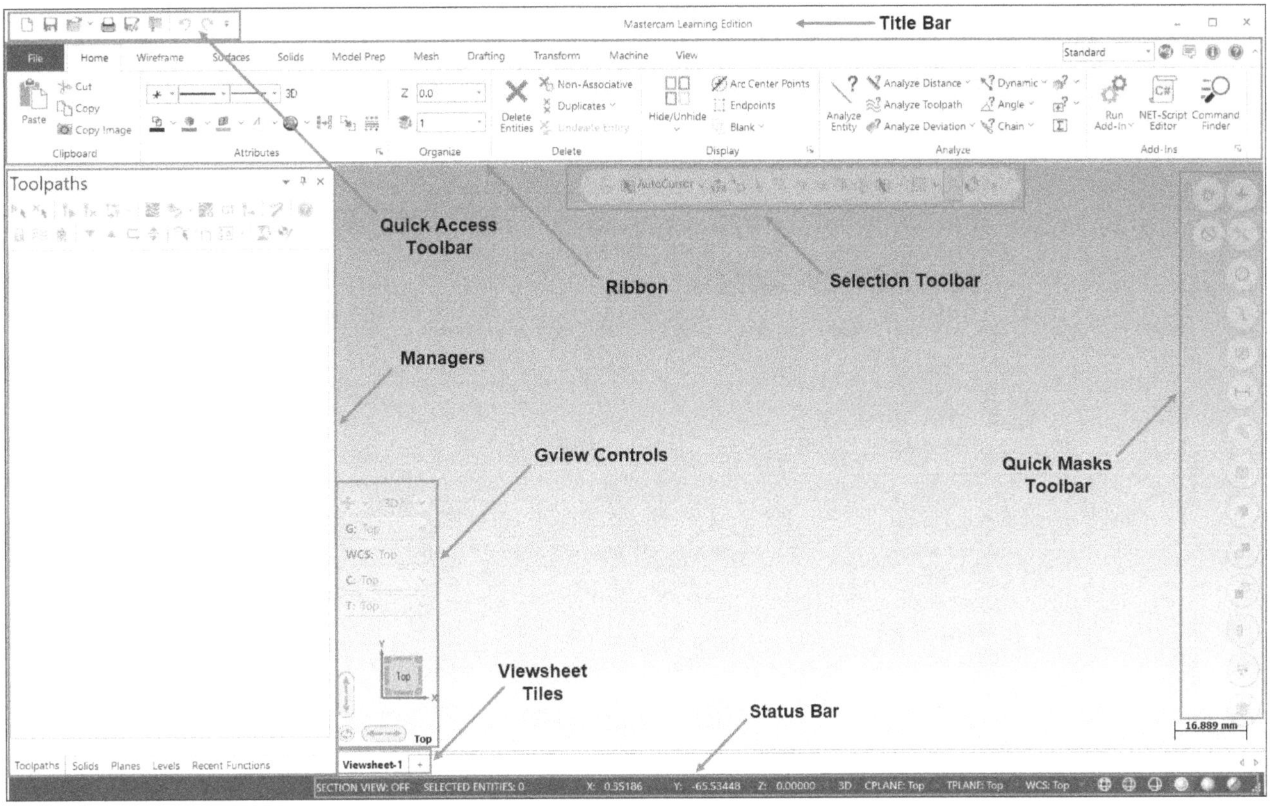

Figure-12. Mastercam interface

Quick Access Toolbar

The **Quick Access Toolbar** contains some of the most common tools used for file handling, Undo & Redo, and other customized tools; refer to Figure-12. The **Quick Access Toolbar** (QAT) is available at the top left corner of the application window as shown in previous figure. You can add or remove any tool from the **Quick Access Toolbar** by following the procedure given next.

Customizing Quick Access Toolbar

- Click on the **Customize Quick Access Toolbar** ( ) tool in the **Quick Access Toolbar**. The customization drop-down will be displayed; refer to Figure-13.

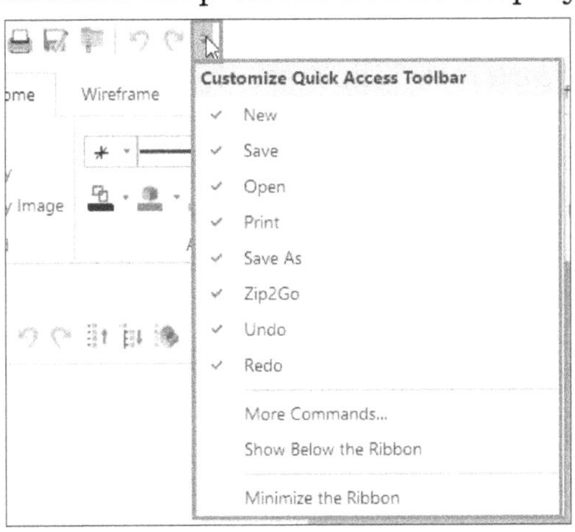

Figure-13. Customize Quick Access Toolbar drop-down

- Select the tools in the drop-down to display them in **Quick Access Toolbar**. If you click on an earlier selected tool then it will be removed from the **Quick Access Toolbar**.
- Click on the **More Commands** tool from the drop-down to add more tools in the **Quick Access Toolbar**. The **Options** dialog box will be displayed; refer to Figure-14.

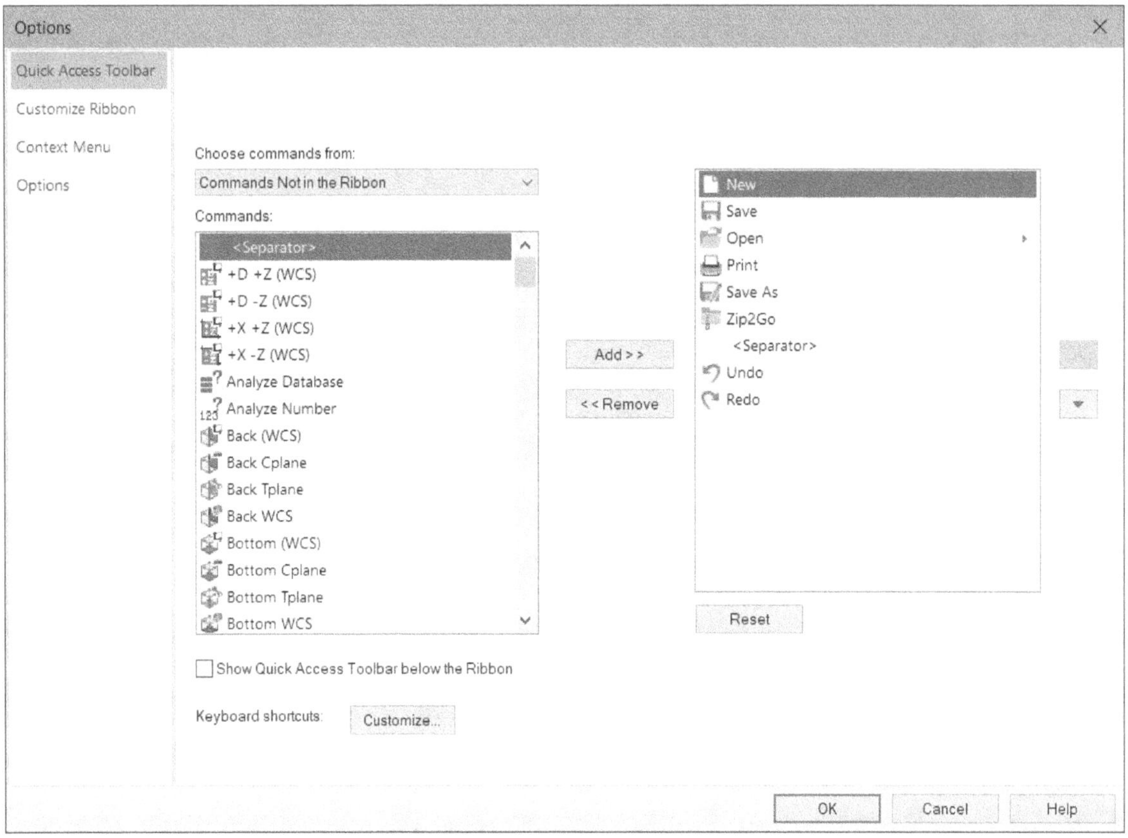

Figure-14. Options dialog box

- Select desired option from the **Choose commands from** drop-down in the dialog box to specify category of tools from which you want to add tool in **Quick Access Toolbar**. Selecting the **All Commands** option from the **Choose commands from** drop-down will display all the tools available in Mastercam.
- Select desired tool from the **Commands** list box in the left of dialog box and click on the **Add>>** button. The selected tool will be added in **Quick Access Toolbar**. Using the Up and Down buttons in the dialog box, you can move selected tool to desired position in the **Quick Access Toolbar**.
- Select the **Show Quick Access Toolbar below the Ribbon** check box to display **Quick Access Toolbar** below the **Ribbon** in application window.
- After setting desired parameters, click on the **OK** button from the dialog box to apply changes.

Customizing Ribbon

- Select the **Customize Ribbon** option from the left area in the dialog box. The options in the dialog box will be displayed as shown in Figure-15. You can also get the options to customize **Ribbon** by selecting **Customize the Ribbon** option from shortcut menu displayed on right-clicking on any **Ribbon** option; refer to Figure-16.

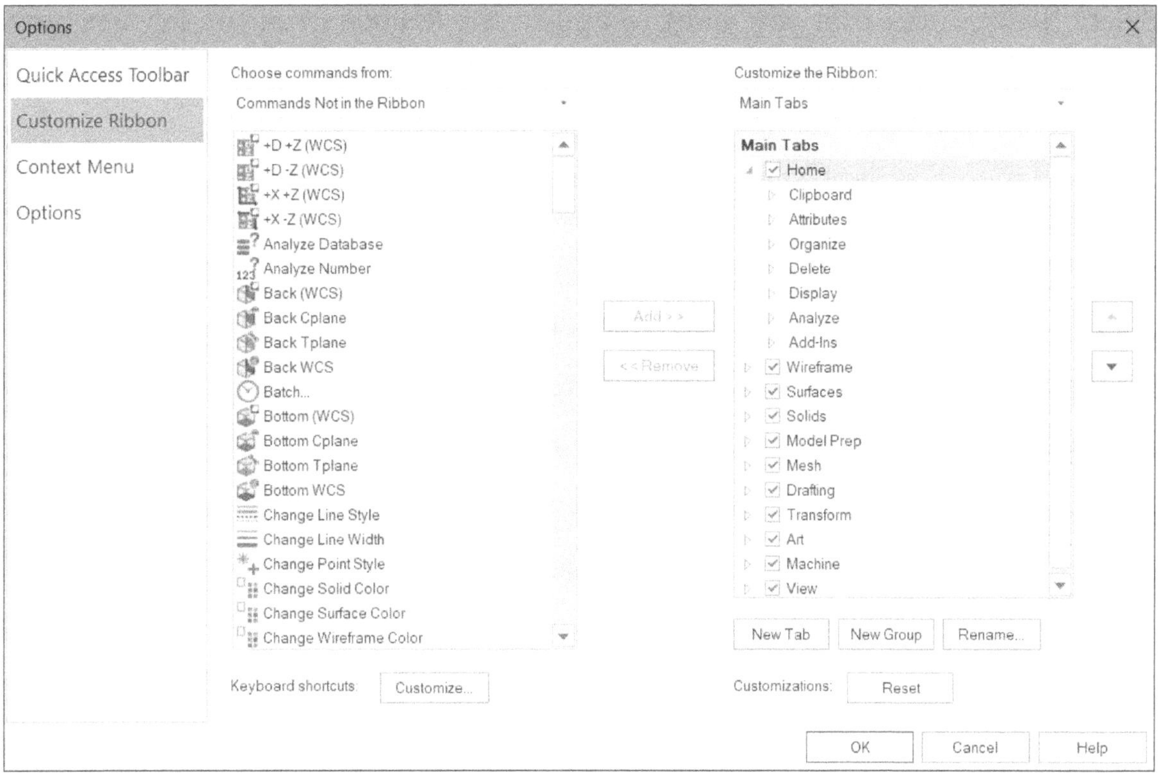

Figure-15. Customize Ribbon options

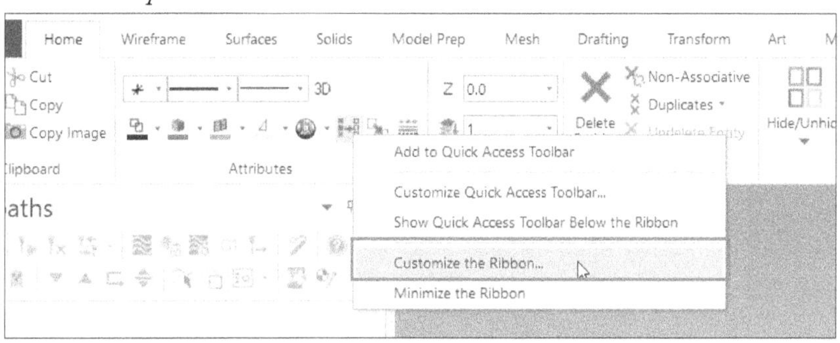

Figure-16. Customize the Ribbon option

- Select desired tab from the right list box and click on the **New Group** button to add a custom group for adding tools. A new group will be added in the selected tab; refer to Figure-17. Note that you can add new tools only in custom groups.

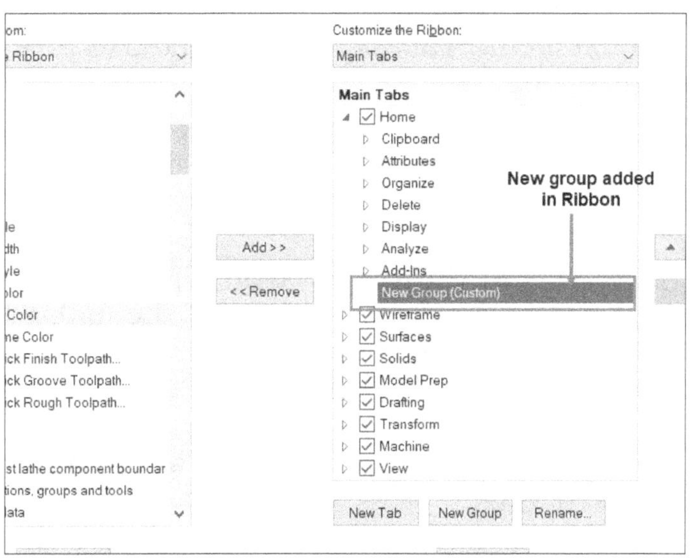

Figure-17. New group for customization

- Select desired tool that you want to add in the **Ribbon** from the left list box and click on **Add>>** button. The selected tool will be added in the new group.

Customizing Context Menu

The context menu is displayed when you right-click on an element in the model. The procedure to customize context menu is given next.

- Click on the **Context Menu** option from the left side of **Options** dialog box. The options to customize context menu will be displayed; refer to Figure-18.

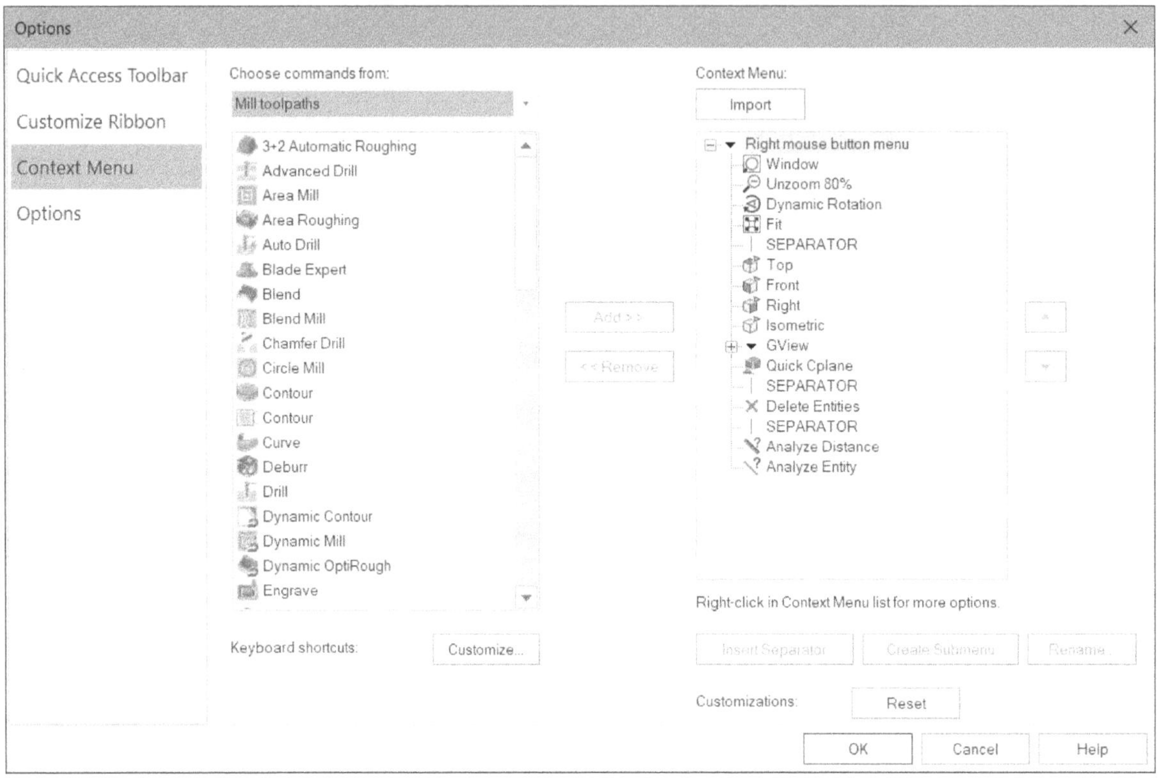

Figure-18. Context Menu options

- Select desired option from the **Context Menu** list box before which you want to place the new option.
- Select desired option from the **Category** drop-down to define category of tools to be added in the context menu. The tools of selected category will be displayed in the left list box of the dialog box.
- Select desired tools from the left list box and click on the **Add>>** button. The selected tools will be added in the context menu. Note that you can select multiple tools while holding the **CTRL** key.

General Customization Options

- Click on the **Options** option from the left area of the dialog box. The options in the dialog box will be displayed as shown in Figure-19.
- Select the **Large icons** check box from the dialog box to display large icons in the **Managers**.
- Select the **Top** or **Bottom** radio button from the **Tab position** area of the dialog box to change position of tabs.
- Select desired options from the **Theme** and **Accent color** drop-downs to change colors of application interface.

- Select the **Enable ribbon access keys** check box to use **ALT** key shortcuts for accessing **Ribbon** tools.

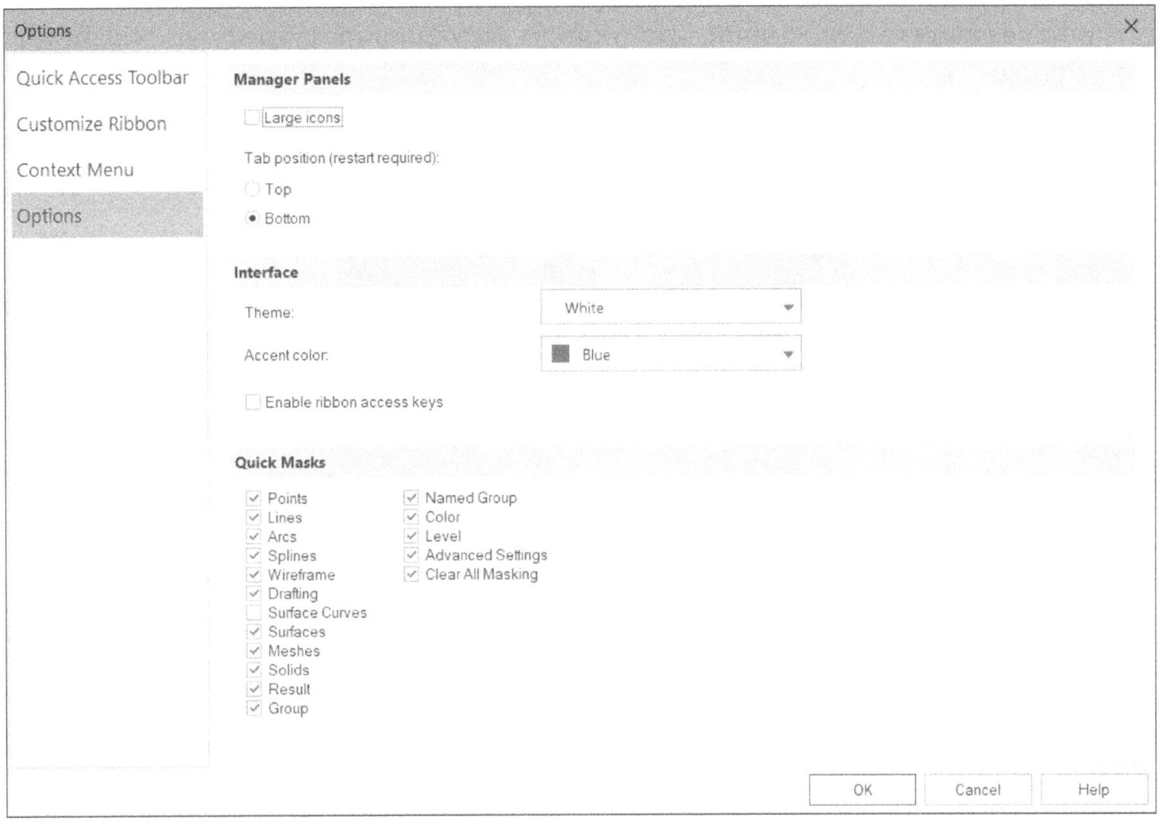

Figure-19. Options option in dialog box

- Select desired check boxes from the **Quick Masks** area of the dialog box to display them in interface. Quick Masks are used for selection filtering.
- After setting desired parameters, click on the **OK** button from the dialog box.

Ribbon

Ribbon is the area of the application window that holds all the tools for designing and editing; refer to Figure-20.

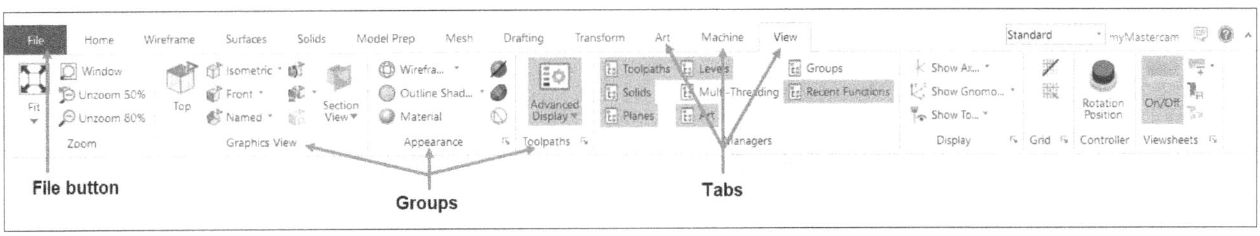

Figure-20. Ribbon

The procedure to customize **Ribbon** has been discussed earlier. You will learn about various tools of **Ribbon** in subsequent chapters.

Selection Toolbar

The tools in the **Selection Toolbar** are used to select various entities of model with different selection filters. These tools are discussed next.

AutoCursor drop-down

The options in the **AutoCursor** drop-down are available when you are creating a sketch entity or other features. For example, on selecting the **Line Endpoints** tool from the **Wireframe** tab of **Ribbon**, the tools in **AutoCursor** drop-down will be active; refer to Figure-21.

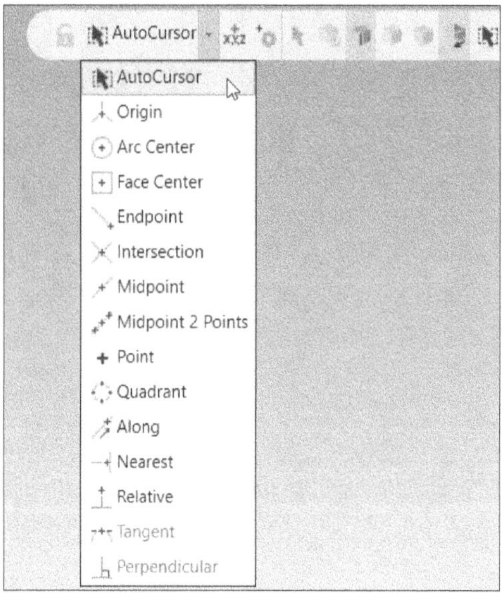

Figure-21. AutoCursor drop-down

- Select the **Origin** option from the drop-down to select origin of model as point for creating an entity.
- Select the **Arc Center** option from the drop-down to select center of arc as point for creating entity; refer to Figure-22.
- Select the **Face Center** option from the drop-down to select center of a face; refer to Figure-23.

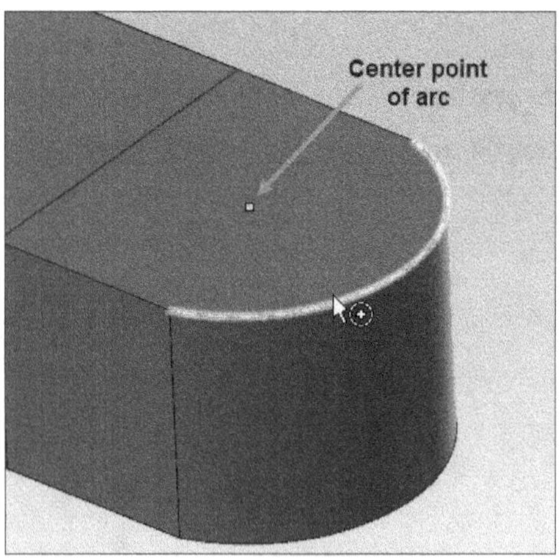

Figure-22. Selecting center point of arc

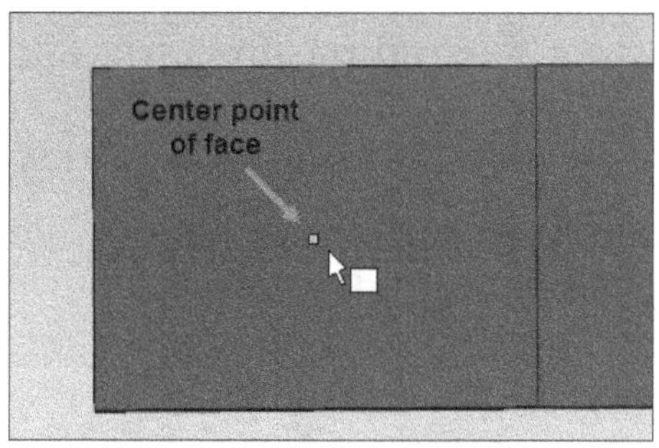

Figure-23. Selecting center point of face

- Select the **Endpoint** option from the drop-down to select end point of selected entity; refer to Figure-24.
- Select the **Intersection** option from the drop-down to select intersection point of two selected entities; refer to Figure-25.

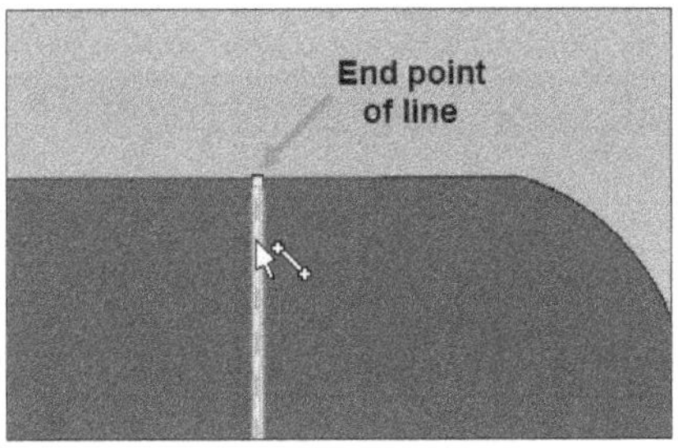

Figure-24. Selecting end point of entity

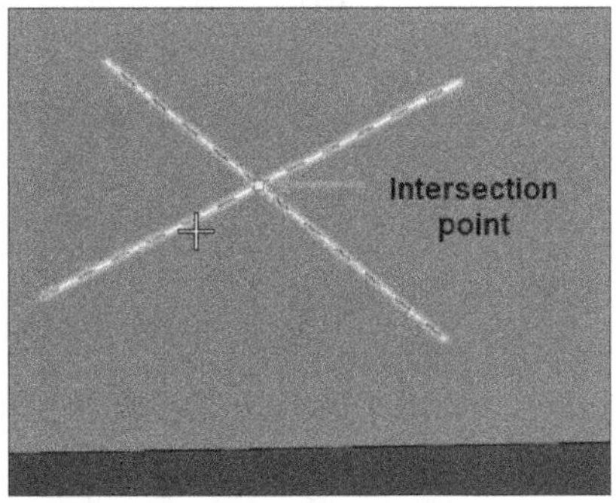

Figure-25. Selecting intersection point of entities

- Select the **Midpoint** option from the drop-down to select mid point of selected entity; refer to Figure-26.

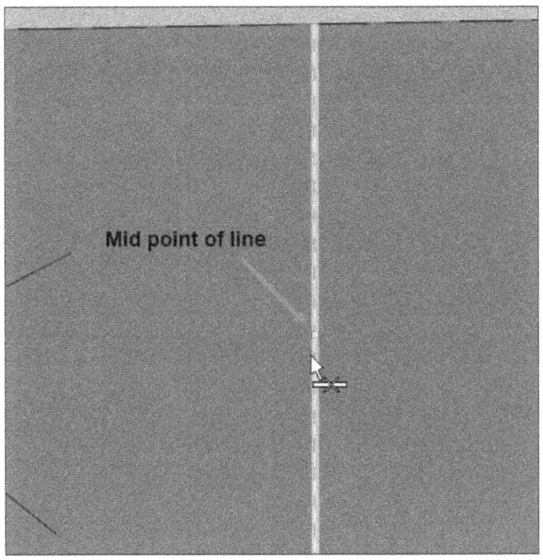

Figure-26. Selecting mid point of line

- Select the **Midpoint 2 Points** option from the drop-down to select mid point between two selected points; refer to Figure-27.

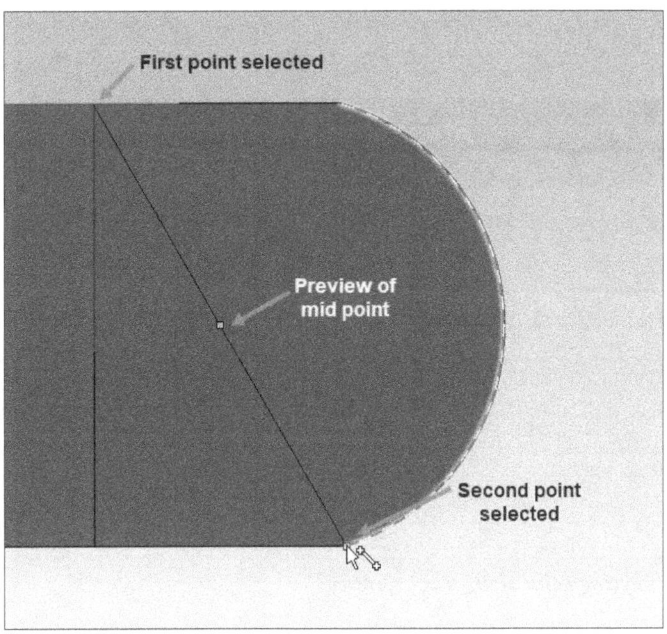

Figure-27. Selecting mid point between two points

- Select the **Point** option from the drop-down to select sketch points from the model; refer to Figure-28.

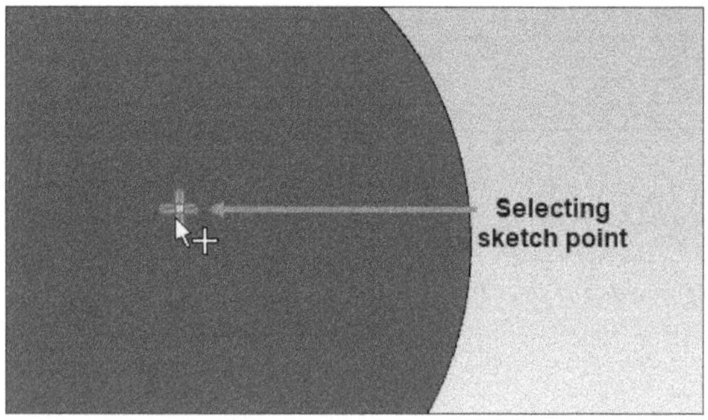

Figure-28. Selecting sketch point

- Select the **Quadrant** option from the drop-down to select quadrant points of circles, ellipses, and arcs; refer to Figure-29.

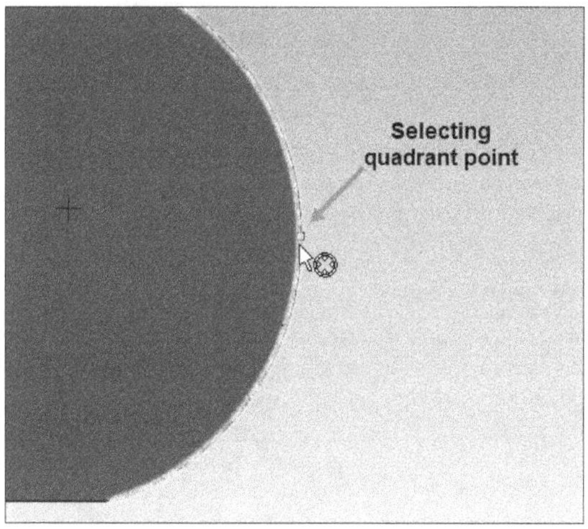

Figure-29. Selecting quadrant point

- Select the **Along** option from the drop-down to select a point at specified distance along selected entity. After selecting the entity, enter desired distance in the **Length** edit box of **Along Relative Position Manager**; refer to Figure-30.

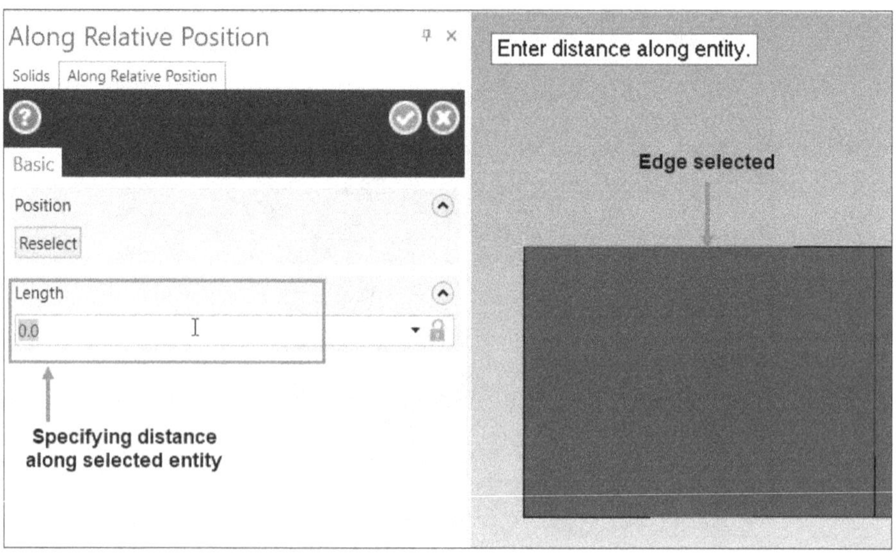

Figure-30. Selecting point along selected entity

- Select the **Nearest** option from the drop-down to select a point near selected entity; refer to Figure-31.

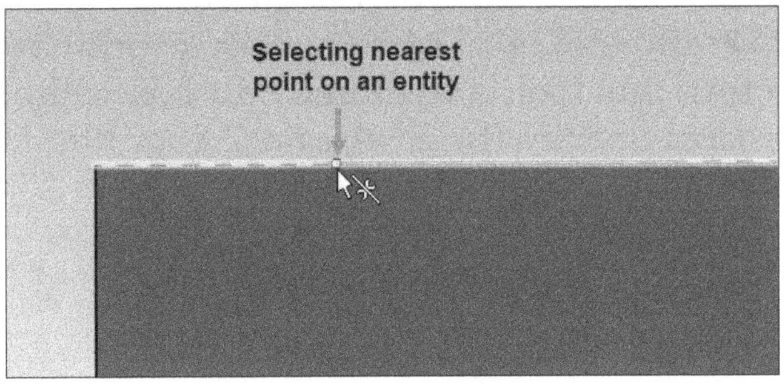

Figure-31. Selecting nearest point on an entity

- Select the **Relative** option from the **AutoCursor** drop-down to select a point relative to another known point. On selecting the reference point, the **Dynamic Gnomon** will be displayed; refer to Figure-32. Select desired direction line from **Gnomon** and drag to move the point. After setting desired location of point, press **ENTER** to complete selection.

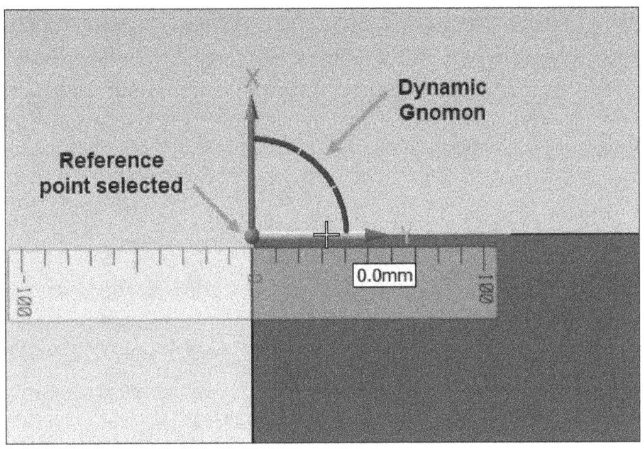

Figure-32. Selecting relative point

- Similarly, you can use the **Tangent** and **Perpendicular** options from the drop-down to select tangent and perpendicular points, respectively. After selecting desired autocursor option, you can select the **Toggle AutoCursor Lock** toggle button from the **Selection** toolbar to keep the selected snap method active.

Note that when you are selecting a specific type of point then the shape of cursor also changes. This shape change is called visual cue. Various visual cues display in Mastercam during selection are shown in Figure-33.

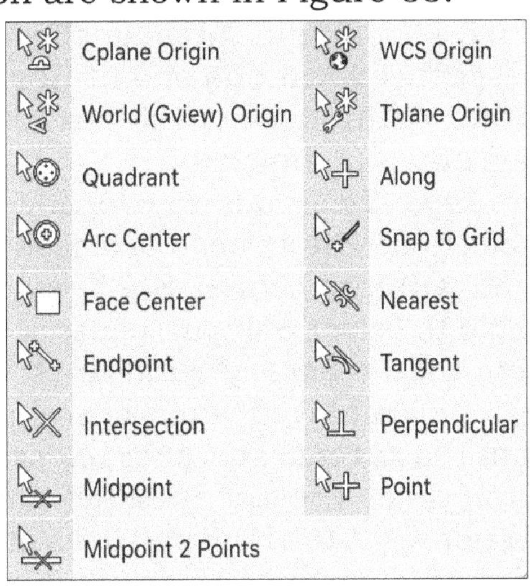

Figure-33. Visual cues

AutoCursor Fast Point

The **AutoCursor Fast Point** tool is used to specify coordinates for the point; refer to Figure-34. On selecting this tool, a dynamic edit box will be displayed at top left corner of the drawing area. Specify the X, Y, and Z coordinates of point using "," to separate and then press **ENTER** to select the point.

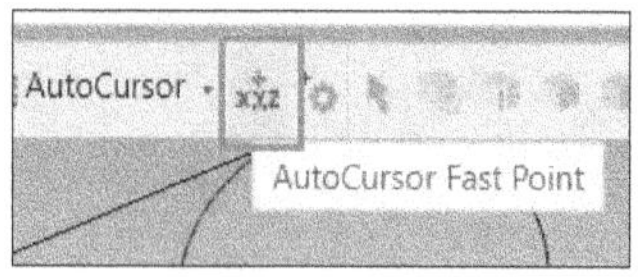

Figure-34. AutoCursor Fast Point tool

Selection Settings

The **Selection Settings** tool is used to define settings related to Selection and AutoCursor. On clicking the **Selection Settings** tool from the **Selection** toolbar, the **Selection** dialog box will be displayed; refer to Figure-35.

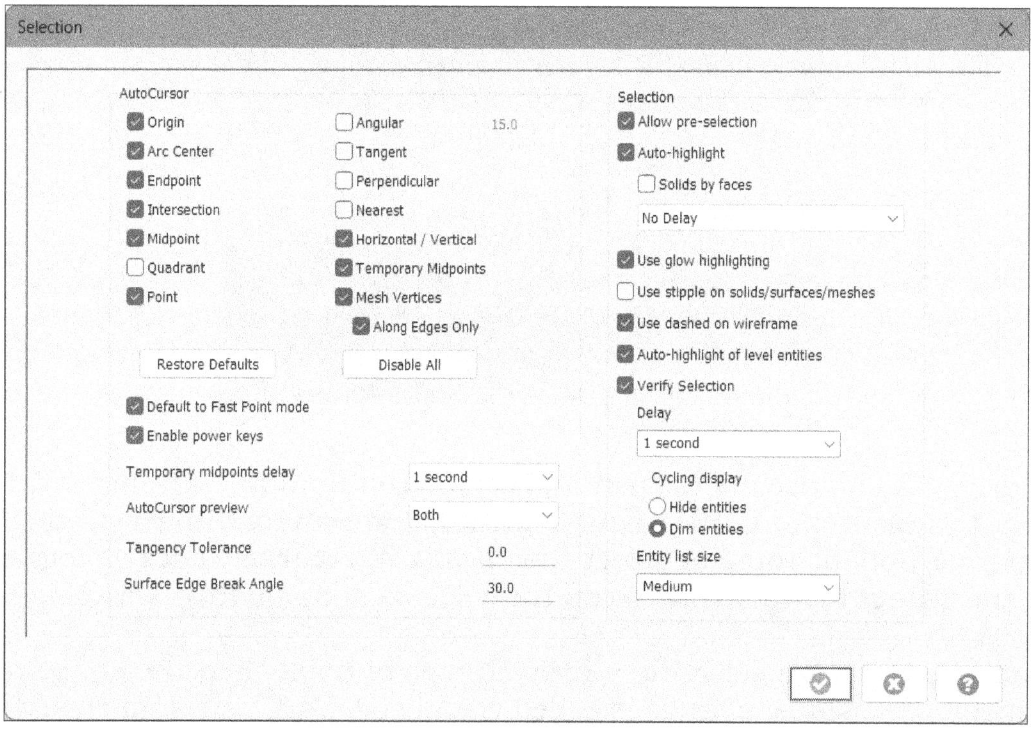

Figure-35. Selection dialog box

- Select desired check boxes from the **AutoCursor** area of the dialog box to automatically snap to respective locations on entities during selection.
- Select the **Default to Fast Point mode** check box to allow input of coordinates by default when you start creating an entity.
- Select the **Enable power keys** check box to override **AutoCursor** when a power key is pressed during selection. Power keys are associated with specific type of points like C is associated with arc center. So, if you press **C** while selecting an entity then you will be able to select only arc centers.
- Select desired option from the **Temporary midpoints delay** drop-down to define seconds before midpoints are displayed when hovering over an entity.
- Select desired option from the **AutoCursor preview** drop-down to define whether you want to display auto cursor preview in Wireframe mode (sketching), Solid mode, in both, or you do not want to show previews of auto cursors. Auto cursor preview is the highlighting of key points when you hover cursor on wireframe or solid edge when creating objects; refer to Figure-36.

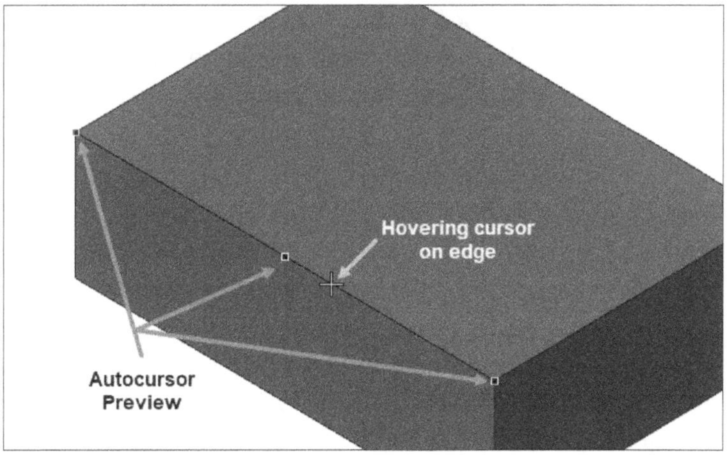

Figure-36. Autocursor preview

- Select the **Allow pre-selection** check box to select the entities before choosing any tool to perform an operation.
- Select the **Auto-highlight** check box to automatically highlight the entity when you hover cursor on it.
- Select the **Solids by faces** check box to select highlighted faces of solid body rather than selecting the complete solid body. You can specify the delay after which full solid will be selected in the drop-down below this check box.
- Select the **Use glow highlighting** check box to highlight the entities under cursor by glow effect.
- Select the **Use stipple on solids/surfaces/meshes** check box to highlight the selected objects with pattern of dots.
- Select the **Use dashed on wireframe** check box to display dashed edges of wireframe model on selecting or highlighting it.
- Select the **Auto-highlight of level entities** check box to highlight entities in same level at which you are working. (You will learn about Levels later in the book).
- Select the **Verify Selection** check box to allow graphical verification of entity to be selected. For example, when you hold cursor on an edge near multiple edges of model then a box will display to verify selection. Specify desired value in the **Delay** drop-down to define amount of time after which selection will be verified. Select desired radio button from **Cycling display** section to define whether you want to hide rest of the entities or you want to dim the display of other entities when select an entity from model.
- Specify desired value in **Tangency Tolerance** edit box to define maximum diversion from tangency which will still be considered tangent.
- Specify desired value in the **Surface Edge Break Angle** edit box to define the angle value after which a consecutive edge will be counted as separate edge instead of continuous edge.
- After setting desired parameters, click on the **OK** button. The **System Configuration** dialog box will be displayed.
- Select the **Yes** button if you want to save the specified settings as default for Mastercam or select the **No** button to use specified settings for current session only.

Selection Filters

The tools in the middle section of **Selection** toolbar are used to set selection filter for specific type of objects. Select the **Solid Selection** tool if you want to select full solid body. Select the **Edge Selection** tool if you want to select edges of selected body. Select the **Face Selection** tool if you want to select face of a body. Select the **Body Selection** tool if you want to select full surface/solid/wireframe body. Select the **From Back** tool if you want to select back side of desired faces.

Selection Method drop-down

The tools in the **Selection Method** drop-down are used to define the method of selecting objects; refer to Figure-37. You can use windows selection, chain selection, single object selection, and so on. Select the **Chain** option from the drop-down if you want to select all the entities falling in continuous tangency. Select the **Window** option from the drop-down if you want to select the objects by drawing a window around the objects. Select the **Polygon** option from the drop-down to select objects by drawing a polygon around the objects. Select the **Single** option from the drop-down if you want to select a single object in one selection move. Select the **Area** option from the drop-down if you want to select multiple nested shapes with a single mouse click. Select the **Vector** option from the drop-down if you want to select all the objects intersecting with drawn vector. Specify the start and end points of vector, and then press **ENTER** to select all the objects through which the vector passes. Select the **Freehand** option from the drop-down to draw an enclosure boundary around the objects to be selected by clicking and dragging the mouse.

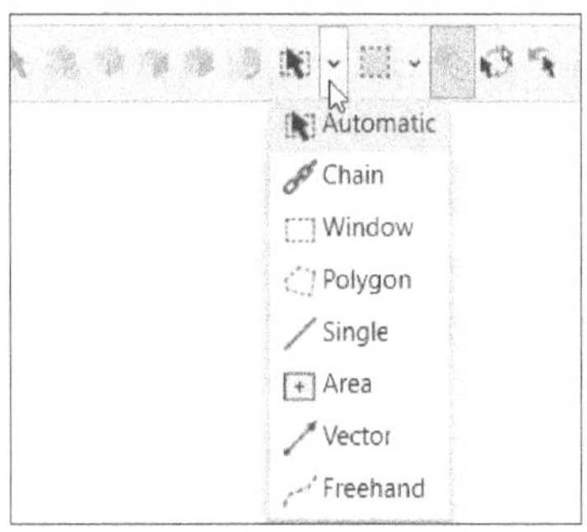

Figure-37. Selection Method drop-down

Selection Mode

The options in the **Selection Mode** drop-down are used to define the mode in which objects will be selected; refer to Figure-38. For example, you can select objects falling inside or outside of window/polygon, intersecting with the window/polygon, and so on. Select the **In** option from the drop-down if you want to select the objects falling completely inside the drawn window/polygon. Select the **Out** option from the drop-down to select objects falling completely outside the window/polygon. Select the **In+** option from the drop-down to select objects falling inside the selection window/ polygon as well as intersecting the window/polygon. Select the **Out+** option from the drop-down to select objects falling outside the selection window/polygon as well as intersecting the window/polygon. Select the **Intersect** option from the drop-down to select all the objects that intersect with selection window/polygon.

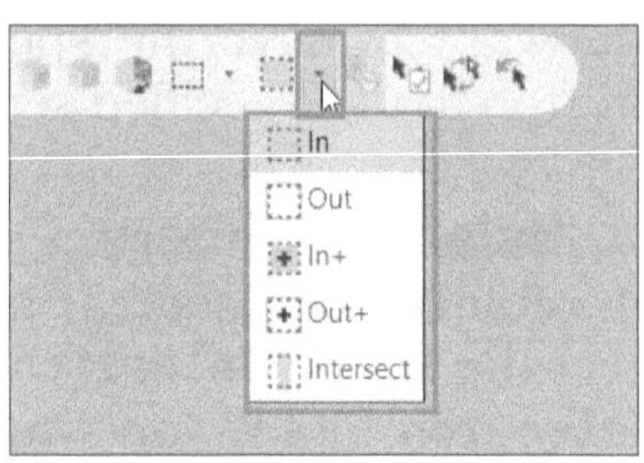

Figure-38. Selection Mode drop-down

Verify Selection

When you are selecting an entity (a face/edge/wireframe) from the model and there are multiple related entities in the vicinity then a multiple selection available indicator will be displayed; refer to Figure-39. Right-click in the graphics area when this indicator is being shown, the **Verify Selection** box will be displayed; refer to Figure-40. Select desired entity from the **Verify Selection** box or right-click in the empty area, current selection will be highlighted in graphics area to show your selection. After confirming selection, left-click in the empty area to select respective entity.

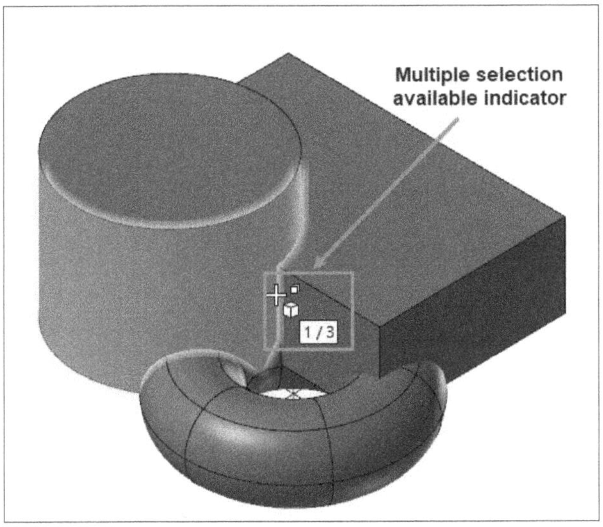

Figure-39. Indicator for multiple selection availability

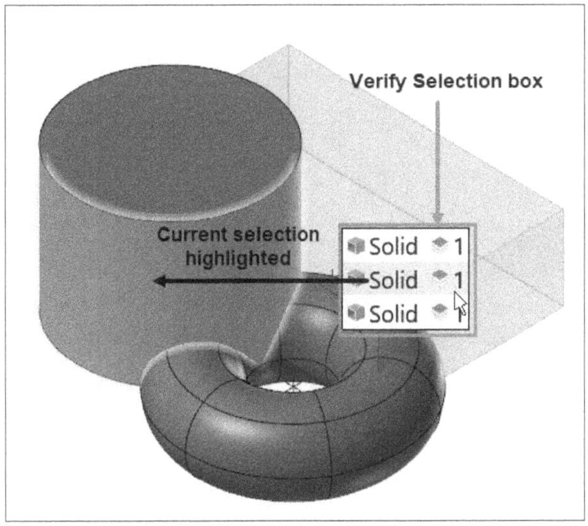

Figure-40. Verify selection box

Inverting Selection

The **Invert Selection** tool in the toolbar is used to reverse the selection. It means all the objects which are selected will get de-selected and all the other objects which have not been selected will get selected.

Selecting Last Object

The **Select Last** tool in the toolbar is used to select the previous selected object.

Quick Masks Toolbar

The tools in the **Quick Masks Toolbar** are used to select different type of entities from the model; refer to Figure-41. Note that most of the tools in this toolbar are divided into two sections. The upper section of tool is used to select all the entities related to the tool whereas lower section of tool is used to select single entity of type related to the tool; refer to Figure-42.

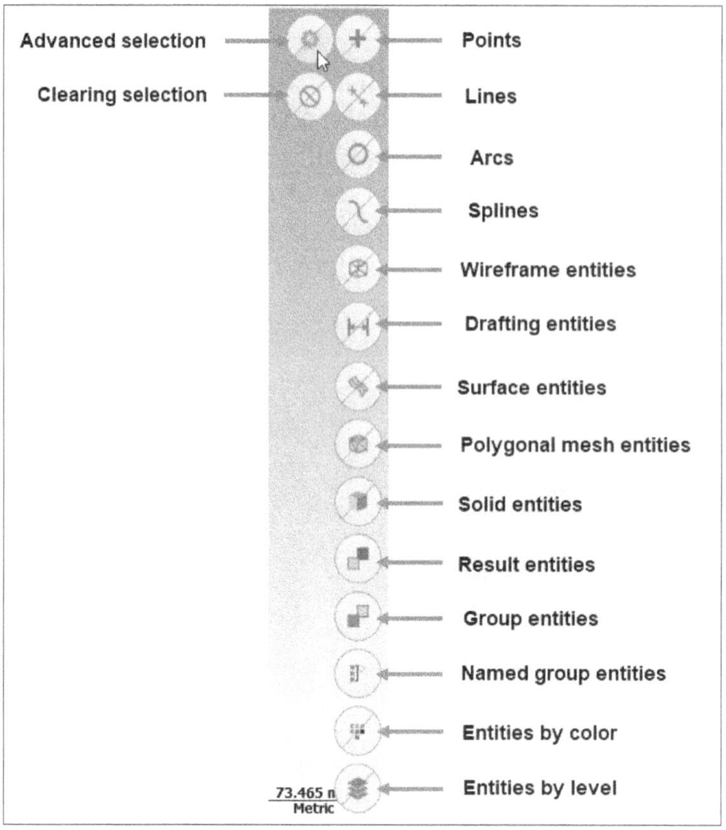

Figure-41. Quick Masks Toolbar

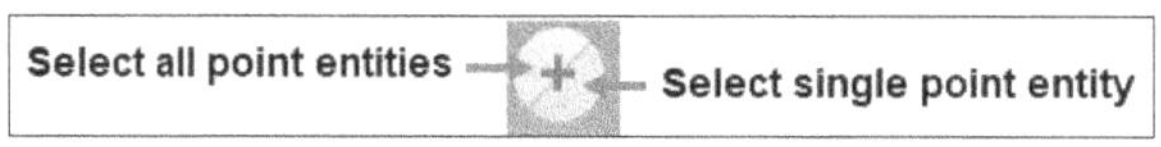

Figure-42. Point Quick Mask button

Managers

The **Managers** are displayed in the left area of application window. The options in the **Managers** are used to manage features of model like toolpaths, solid creation features, groups, levels, and so on; refer to Figure-43. You can display or hide any Manager by selecting/clearing respective button from **Managers** group in the **View** tab of **Ribbon**; refer to Figure-44. The tabs to toggle the managers are available at the bottom in Managers area of application window; refer to Figure-45.

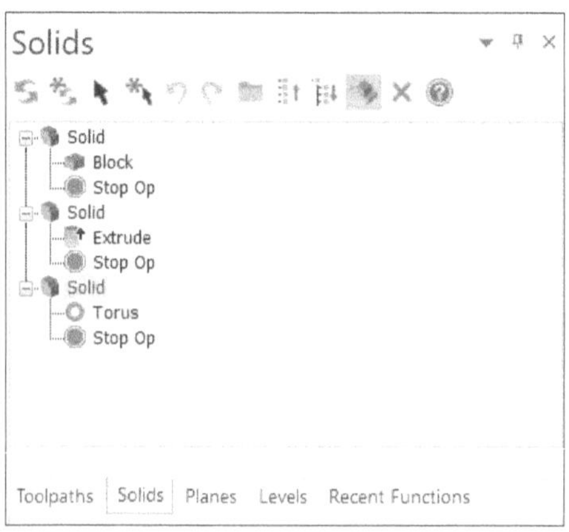

Figure-43. Solids Manager

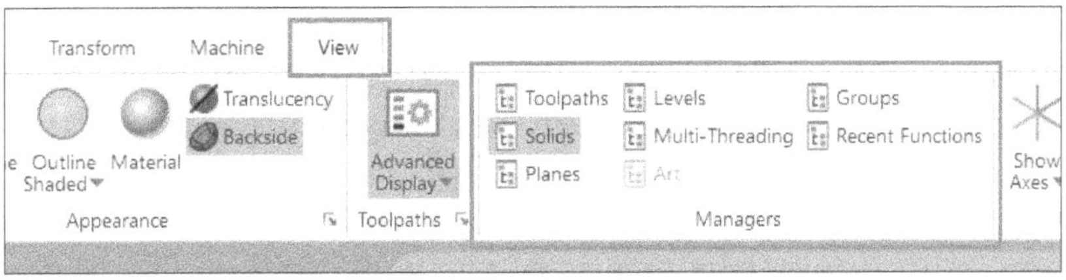

Figure-44. Managers group

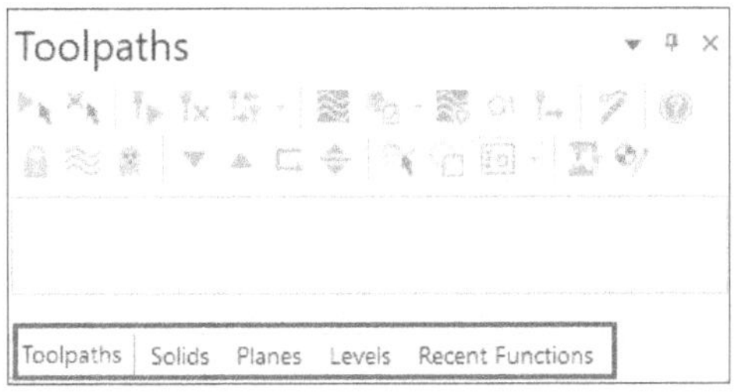

Figure-45. Tabs in Manager

Viewsheet Tiles

Viewsheets are used to store orientation, scale, and section views of the model. You can also store level settings and view states using the view sheets. View sheets are available in the form of tiles at the bottom of drawing area; refer to Figure-46. Click on the **+** button next to **Viewsheet** tile, to create a new viewsheet.

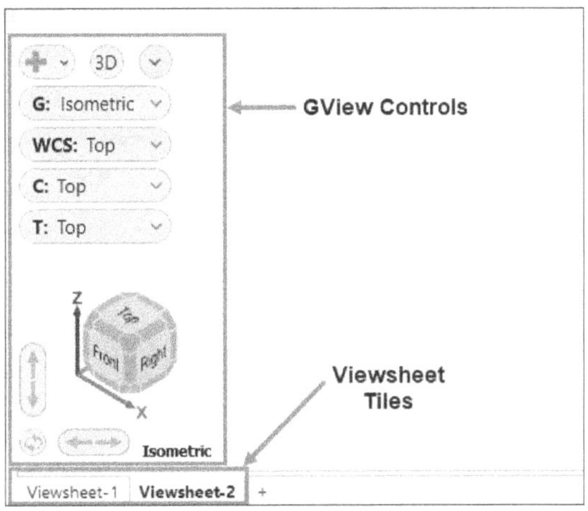

Figure-46. Viewsheet tiles

GView Controls

By default, the **GView Controls** is available at the bottom left corner of drawing area in the application window; refer to Figure-46. Click on desired face of GView cube to orient the model accordingly. For example, click on the Front face of GView cube to orient the model to front plane.

Click on the **+** button to create a new plane. Click on the down arrow next to **+** button in **GView Controls** to use other options for creating new planes. You will learn about creating new planes later in the book.

Select the **3D/2D** button from the **GView Controls** to toggle between 2 dimensional and 3 dimensional construction plane so that you can create 2D sketch or 3D sketch respectively.

Click on the **Settings** button in the **GView Controls** to modify settings related to **GView Controls** like display of GView, binding different planes with each other and so on; refer to Figure-47. Select the **Screen settings** option from the menu to modify how the **GView Controls** are displayed in graphics area. The **Screen** dialog box will be displayed; refer to Figure-48. Set desired parameters in the dialog box to modify the size and other related graphic details of Cube as well as Gnomons at the right in the application window. Note that changes are reflected live in graphics area. Click on the **OK** button from the dialog box to apply the changes.

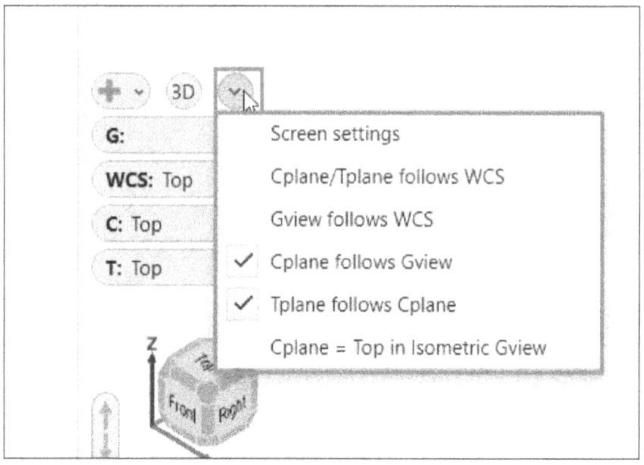

Figure-47. GView settings menu

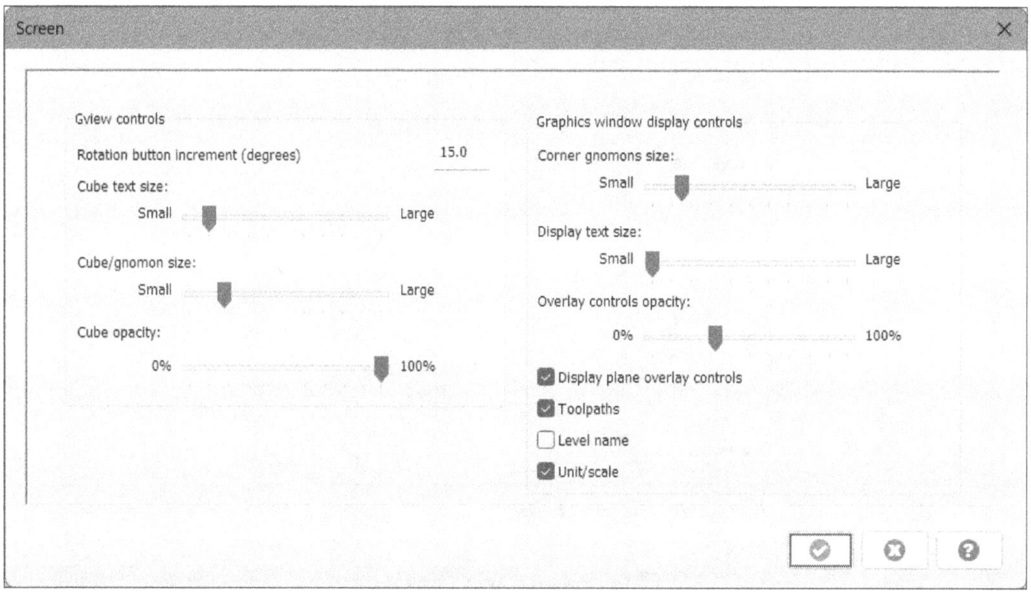

Figure-48. Screen dialog box

Click on the Up/Down arrow buttons and Left/Right arrow buttons from the GView cube to pan the model in vertical and horizontal directions, respectively. Click on the **Flip** button to rotate the model view by 180 degree. To rotate the model by 90 degree, click on the **Flip** button while holding the **SHIFT** key. To reverse flip the model by 90 degree, click on the **Flip** button while holding **ALT+SHIFT** key. Similarly, you can use **CTRL+Click** on **Flip** button to rotate the model about current GView and **CTRL+ALT+Click** on **Flip** button to reverse rotate the model about current GView. You will learn about other tools and parameters of the **GView Controls** later in the book.

Status Bar

The **Status Bar** displays some common information about the model like coordinates, selected entities, section view status, visual style, and so on; refer to Figure-49.

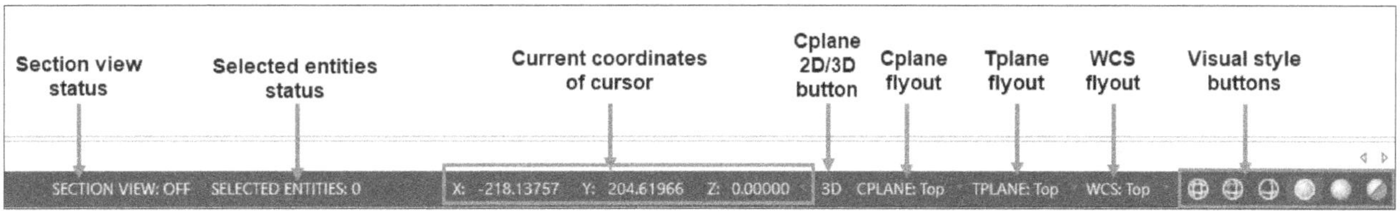

Figure-49. Status Bar

- The **Section view status** area of **Status Bar** shows whether the section view is active or not in the drawing area.
- The **Selected entities status** area of **Status Bar** shows the total number of entities selected from the model.
- The **Coordinates** area of the **Status Bar** shows the current coordinates of cursor.
- Click on the **Cplane 2D/3D** button from the **Status Bar** to use 2D plane for creating objects or 3D environment to create objects.
- Click on the **CPLANE** button from the **Status Bar** to switch between various planes to use as construction plane of 2D objects. A flyout will be displayed; refer to Figure-50. Select desired plane for construction from the flyout.
- Click on the **TPLANE** button from the **Status Bar** to switch between various planes for current cutting tool. A flyout will be displayed; refer to Figure-51. Select desired plane to be used as cutting plane.
- Click on the **WCS** button from the **Status Bar** to switch between different orientations of work coordinate systems. A flyout will be displayed; refer to Figure-52.

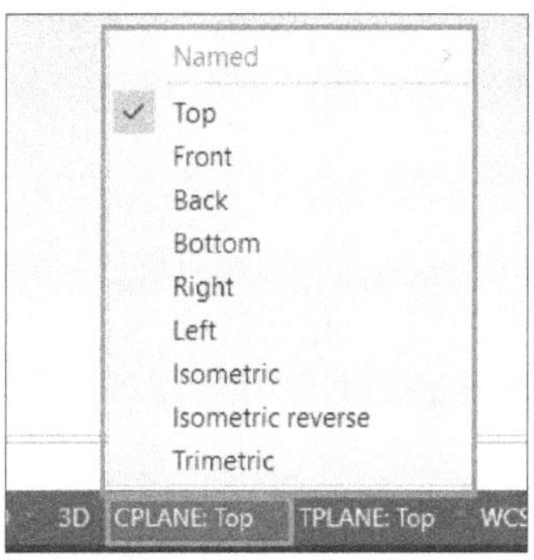

Figure-50. CPLANE flyout

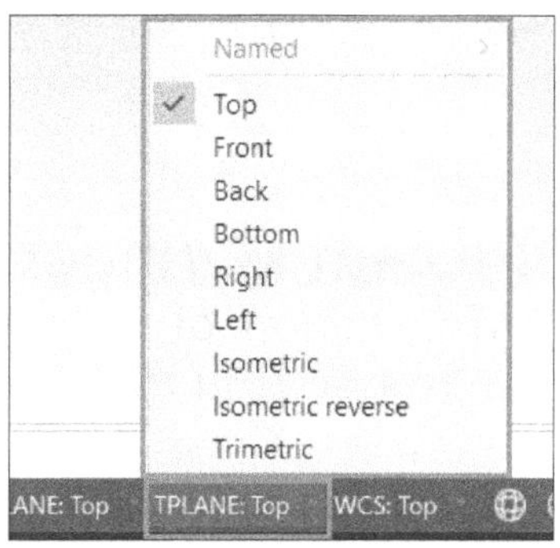

Figure-51. TPLANE flyout

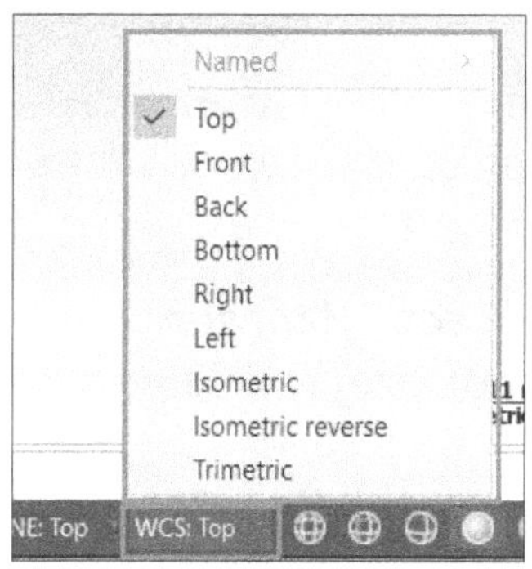

Figure-52. WCS flyout

- Select desired button from the **Visual styles** area of the **Status Bar** to change the visual style of model. Select the **Wireframe** button to display model in the form of lines and curves. Note that in wireframe style, the hidden edges are also displayed dark lines. Select the **Dimmed** button to display hidden edges as dimmed lines in wireframe model. Select the **No Hidden** button to hide non-visible edges of model in wireframe style. Select the **Outline Shaded** button to display shaded model with dark edges. Select the **Shaded** button to display shaded model without dark edges. Select the **Translucency** button to display faces of model transparent so that inner of model can be checked.

FILE MENU

The tools in the **File** menu are used to manage various operations related to files like opening a file, starting a new file, saving a file, and so on; refer to Figure-53.

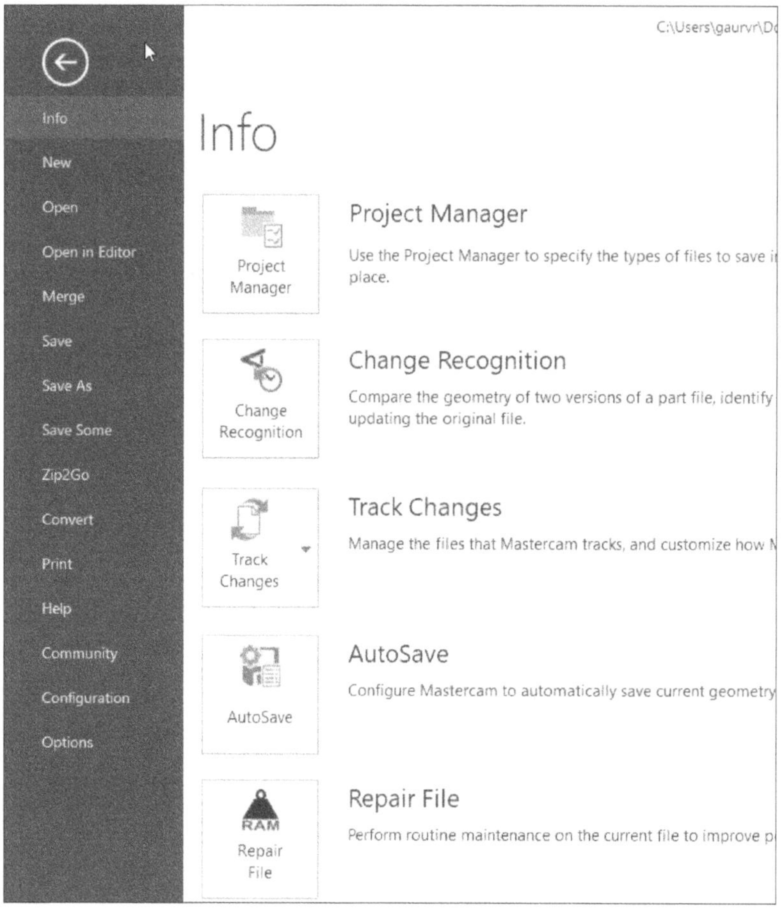

Figure-53. File menu

Project Manager

The **Project Manager** tool in **Info** section of **File** menu is used to specify basic settings of project. The procedure to use this tool is given next.

- Click on the **Project Manager** tool from the **Info** section of **File** menu. The **Project File Manager** dialog box will be displayed; refer to Figure-54.

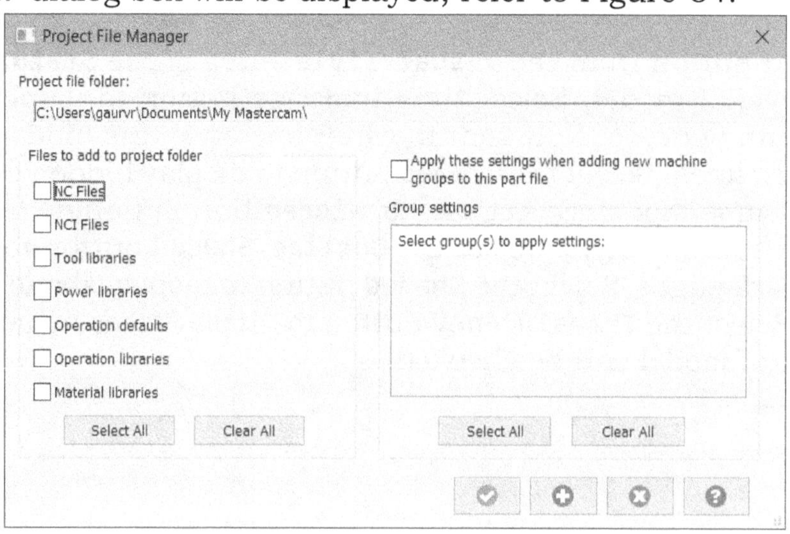

Figure-54. Project File Manager dialog box

- Select the check boxes for files to be added in the project folder from the **Files to add to project folder** area of the dialog box. Note that selecting more files will increase the size of project folder.
- Select the **Apply these settings when adding new machine groups to this part file** check box to automatically apply specified settings to new groups in project.
- Select desired groups of the **Group settings** area to which you want to apply the project settings.
- After setting desired parameters, click on the **OK** button from the dialog box.

Comparing Models

The **Change Recognition** tool in **File** menu is used to compare two models for differences in model or toolpaths. The procedure to use this tool is given next.

- Click on the **Change Recognition** tool from the **File** menu. If there are no toolpaths in the current file then a message box will be displayed; refer to Figure-55.

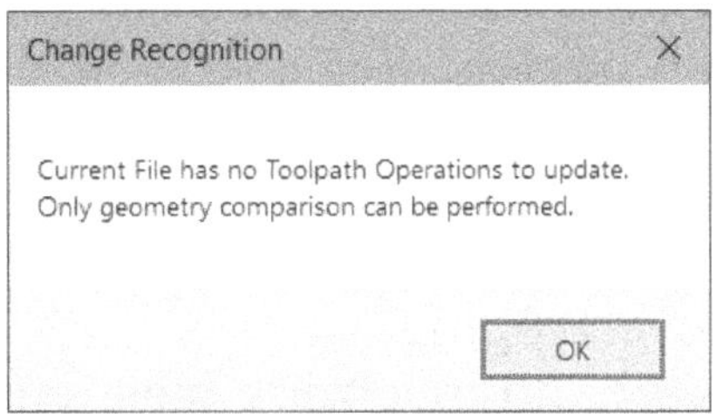

Figure-55. Change Recognition dialog box

- Click on the **OK** button to allow geometry comparison. The **Open** dialog box will be displayed; refer to Figure-56.

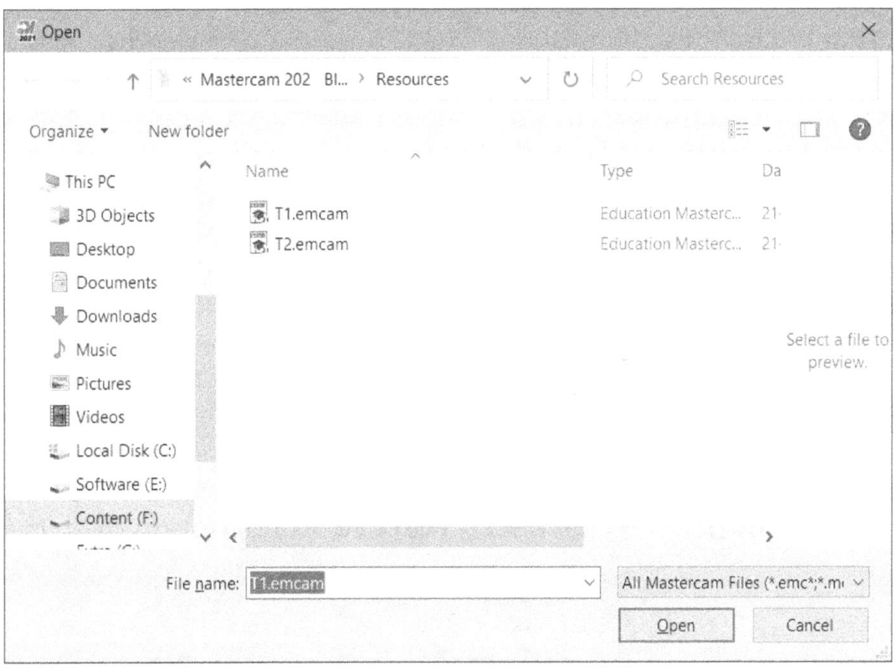

Figure-56. Open dialog box

- Select desired model file with which you want to compare current model and click on the **Open** button. The **Change Recognition - Geometry Only** dialog box will be displayed with preview of comparison; refer to Figure-57.

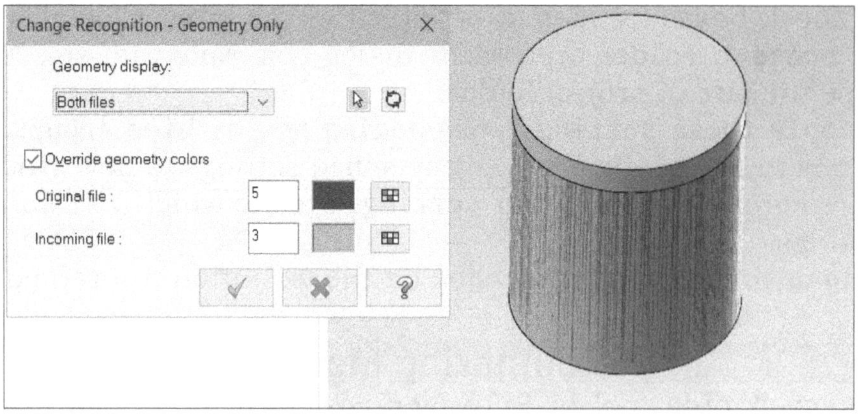

Figure-57. Change Recognition-Geometry Only dialog box

- Select desired option from the **Geometry display** drop-down to specify which type of comparison you want to perform. Select the **Original file** option from the drop-down to check main file. Select the **Incoming file** option from the drop-down to check incoming file. Select the **Common** option from the drop-down to check which features are common in two models. Select the **Unique to Original** option from the drop-down to check which properties are unique to main model. Similarly, select the **Unique to Incoming** option from the drop-down to check the properties unique to incoming model file. Select the **Both files** option from the drop-down to check both the models overlapping.
- Set desired colors for original and incoming files using respective buttons in the dialog box.
- Click on the **OK** button from the dialog box to exit.

Tracking Changes

The tools in **Track Changes** drop-down of **File** menu are used to track changes in the current file(s) open in application. Click on the **Check Current File** option from the drop-down to track changes in current file after it was earlier. On selecting this option, the **File Tracking Options** dialog box will be displayed; refer to Figure-58. Select desired check boxes and click on the **OK** button to apply tracking. If you want to track changes in multiple files then click on the **Tracking Options** option from the **Track Changes** drop-down of **File** menu. The **File Tracking** dialog box will be displayed; refer to Figure-59. Select the **Tracking** check box from the top in the dialog box to enable tracking of the file. The table below the check box will become active. Right-click in the table and select the **Add** option to add a file to be tracked; refer to Figure-60. The **Open** dialog box will be displayed and you will be asked to select the file. Add desired files and select check boxes from the dialog box as discussed earlier to enable tracking. After setting parameters, click on the **OK** button from the dialog box. Similarly, you can use the **Check All Tracked Files** option from the drop-down.

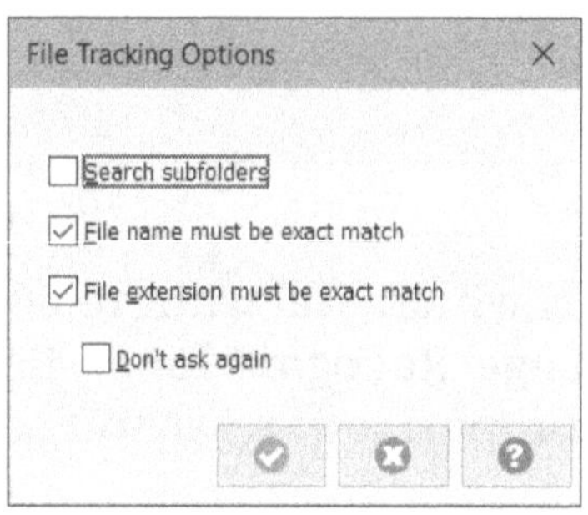

Figure-58. File Tracking Options dialog box

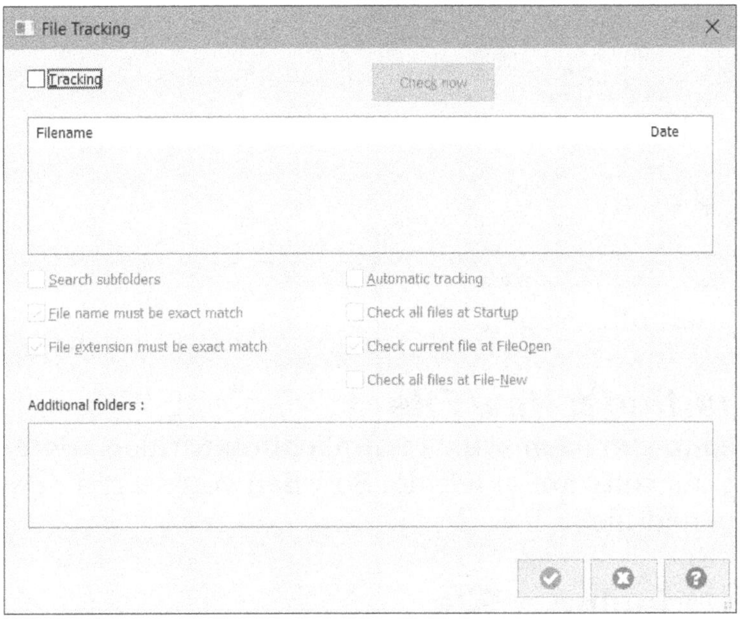

Figure-59. File Tracking dialog box

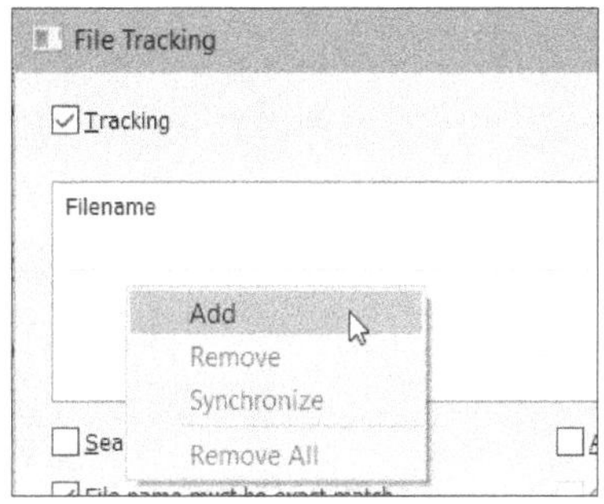

Figure-60. Add option

AutoSave

The **AutoSave** tool in **File** menu is used to set the time interval for automatically saving the model and define related parameters. On clicking this tool, the **AutoSave/ Backup** dialog box will be displayed; refer to Figure-61. Select the **AutoSave** check box to define parameters for automatically saving file. Set desired parameters to define interval, method for saving existing file, and so on below the check box. Select the **Mastercam Backup Files** check box to automatically create backup files of mastercam model at regular intervals. Click on the **OK** button from the dialog box to apply changes.

Figure-61. AutoSave/Backup dialog box

Repairing File

The **Repair File** tool in **File** menu is used to perform routine check of model file to improve file integrity. On clicking this tool, the **Repair File** dialog box will be displayed; refer to Figure-62. Select the **Yes** button to compact the files and database for reducing file size. After using this tool, only those files which are needed in project will be included.

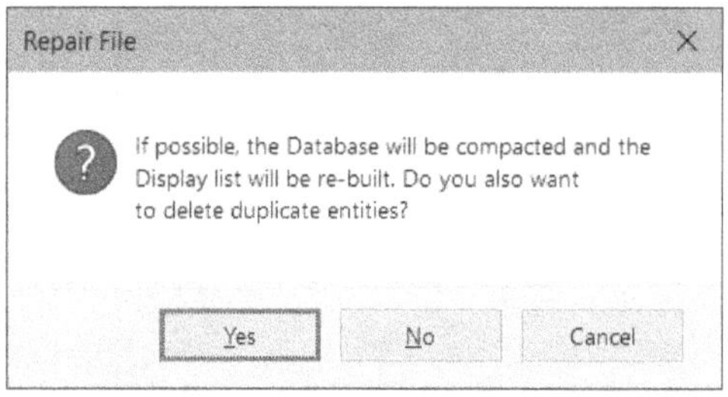

Figure-62. Repair File dialog box

Save the new file at desired location after repair.

Starting a New File

The **New** tool in **File** menu is used to start a new file in application window. Note that only one file can be kept open in the software at a time. So when you start a new file, software will close the earlier opened file.

Opening a File

The **Open** tool in **File** menu is used to open an existing file. The procedure to use this tool is given next.

- Click on the **Open** tool from the **File** menu. The options to open files will be displayed; refer to Figure-63.

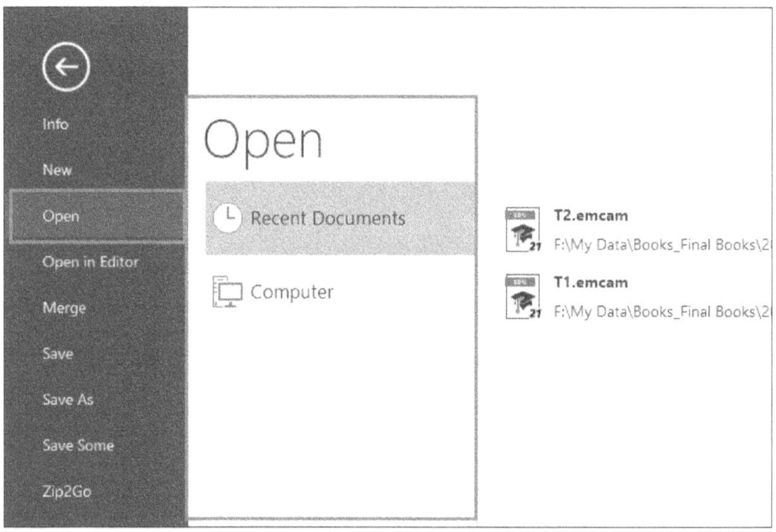

Figure-63. Options for opening files

- Select the **Recent Documents** option from the menu to open recently visited documents.
- Select the **Computer** option from the menu and then click on the **Browse** button. The **Open** dialog box will be displayed; refer to Figure-64.

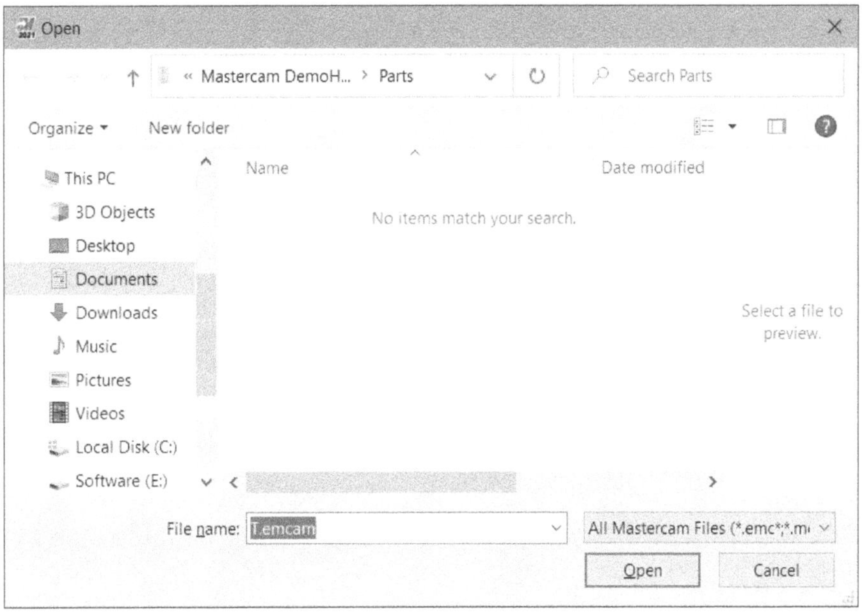

Figure-64. Open dialog box

- Select desired file from the dialog box and click on the **Open** button. The file will open in application window.

Opening File in Editor

The **Open in Editor** tool is used to edit currently open file in **Mastercam Code Expert**. The procedure to use this tool is given next.

- Click on the **Open in Editor** tool from the **File** menu. The **Open** dialog box will be displayed; refer to Figure-65.

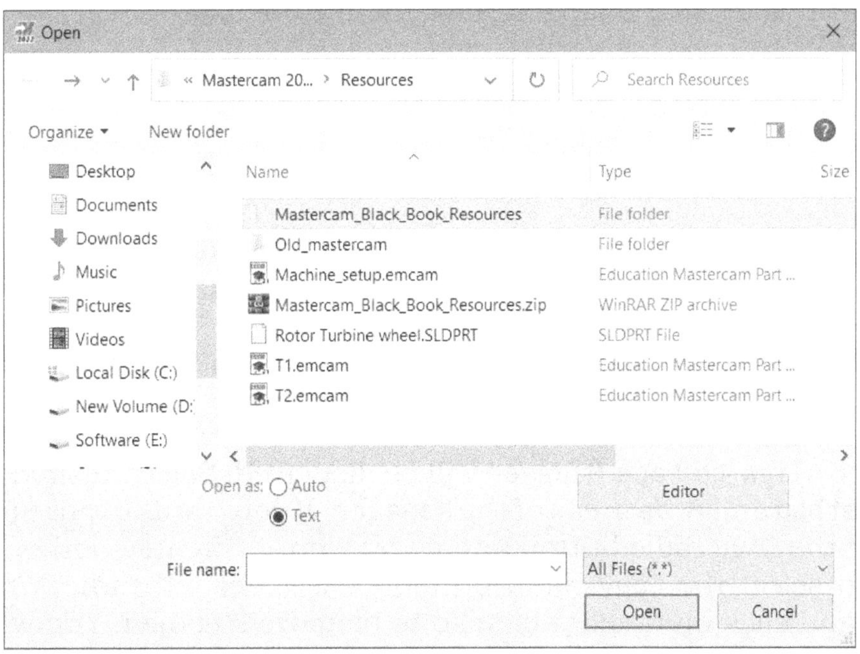

Figure-65. Open dialog box for editor

- Select desired NC code file to be edited and click on the **Open** button. The **Mastercam Code Expert** application window will be displayed with file opened; refer to Figure-66.

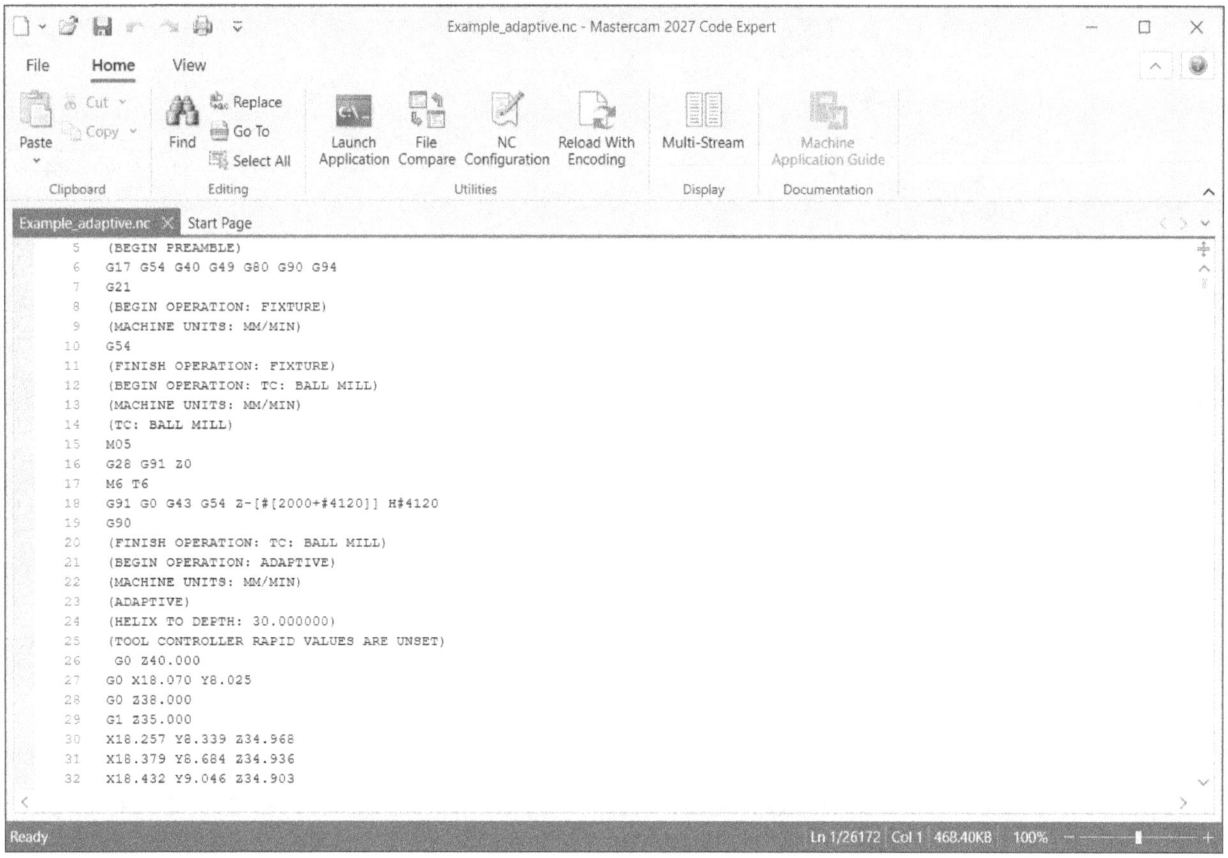

Figure-66. Mastercam Code Expert application window

- You can edit the code of file in the Editor by using simple text operations as in any word processor application.
- After performing desired changes, save the file and exit.

Merging Entities in Existing File

The **Merge** tool in **File** menu is used to merge entities of other files into existing file. The procedure to use this tool is given next.

- Click on the **Merge** tool from the **File** menu. The **Open** dialog box will be displayed.
- Select desired file from the dialog box and click on the **Open** button. The **Merge Pattern Manager** will be displayed; refer to Figure-67.
- Click on the **Select** button from the **Position** rollout in **Manager** and click at desired location to specify position of merging objects.
- Click on the **Align** button from the **Position** rollout to set alignment of incoming objects. The **Align to Face Manager** will be displayed. Select desired radio buttons from the **Method** and **Mode** areas of the **Manager**. If you want to move merging object then select the **Move** radio button and if you want to create another copy merging object then select the **Copy** radio button. Select desired radio button from the **Mode** area and click on the face of solid to be moved/copied. You will be asked to select a line/edge or draw a line along which you want to move/copy the merging object. Select/draw desired reference line. Gnomon will be displayed on the object to be moved/copied; refer to Figure-68. Move the Gnomon to desired location and press **ENTER** to create copy.

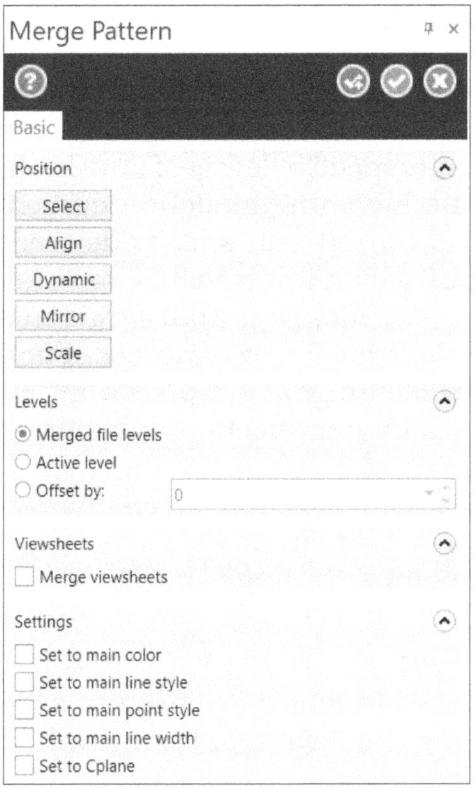

Figure-67. Merge Pattern Manager

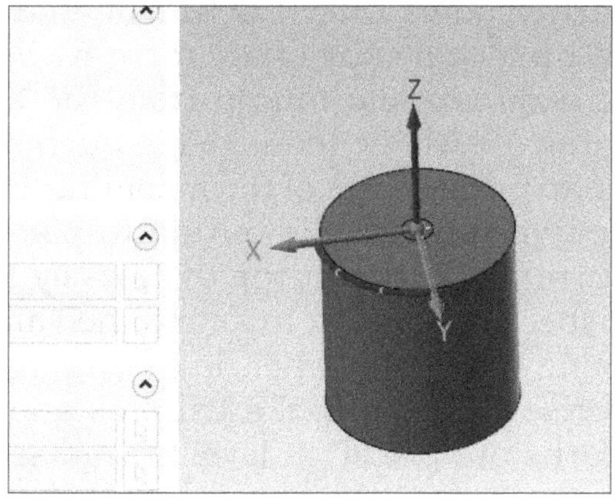

Figure-68. Gnomon on body

- Click on the **Dynamic** button from the **Manager** to dynamically move/copy objects. You will be asked to select entities to be copied/moved. Select desired objects and click on the **End Selection** button. The gnomon will get attached to cursor and you will be asked to place it at desired location for specifying origin. Click at desired location to specify origin. The **Dynamic Manager** will be displayed; refer to Figure-69. Select desired radio buttons from the **Method** and **Type** section of **Entity** rollout. If you want to create multiple copies then set desired number of instances in the **Instances** spinner. Using the axes of gnomon, move the copies to desired location and click to place copies; refer to Figure-70. Click on the **OK** button from the **Manager** to create dynamic copies.

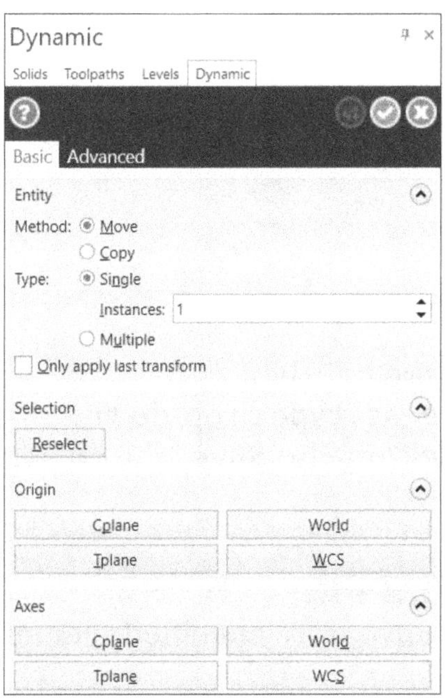

Figure-69. Dynamic Manager

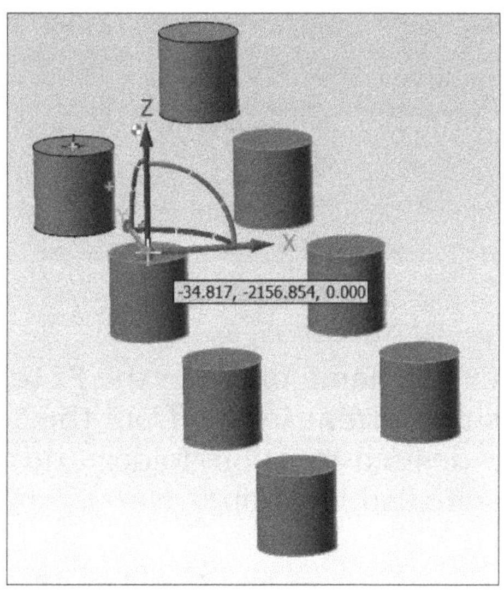

Figure-70. Copies of merging objects

- Similarly, you can use the **Mirror** and **Scale** buttons to create mirror copy and scaled up/down copy of the merging body, respectively.
- Select desired radio button from the **Levels** section to define how the levels of incoming file will be managed in current file. Select the **Merged file levels** radio button to merge parts of the incoming file on respective levels of current file. Select the **Active level** radio button to place the incoming model on current level of the current file. Select the **Offset by** radio button and specify desired value in the respective edit box to define the value by which levels will be increased in the incoming model file when inserting in current file. Note that levels are used to categorise values model attributes and properties for easy access. For example, tool paths are placed at level xx and surfaces of model are placed xy level.
- Select the **Merge viewsheets** check box to add viewsheets of incoming model in current file.
- Select the check boxes of **Settings** rollout to set color, line style, line weight, and other parameters of merging (incoming) body to main body.
- Click on the **OK** button from the **Manager** to apply settings.

Saving File

The **Save**, **Save As**, and **Save Some** tools in the **File** menu are used to save the file. If you are saving the file for the first time using the **Save** tool then it will behave as **Save As** tool. The procedure to save files is given next.

- Click on the **Save** tool from the **File** menu. The **Save As** dialog box will be displayed; refer to Figure-71.

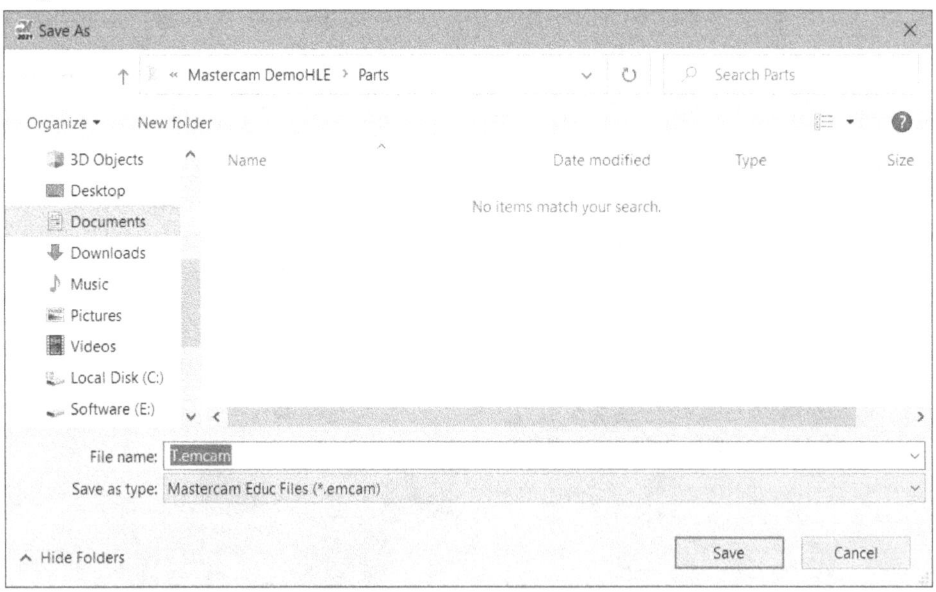

Figure-71. Save As dialog box

- Specify desired name of file in the **File name** edit box.
- Select desired format for file from the **Save as type** drop-down.
- Browse to desired location/folder and click on the **Save** button. The file will be saved at specified location.

Saving Partial File

The **Save Some** tool in **File** menu is used to save only specified elements of model. The procedure to use this tool is given next.

- Click on the **Save Some** tool from the **File** menu. You will be asked to select the entities to be saved.
- One by one select the entities to be saved and click on the **End Selection** button. The **Save As** dialog box will be displayed.
- Specify new name of the file in the **File name** edit box, format of file in the **Save as type** drop-down, and click on the **Save** button to save the file.

Compressing and Sharing Files

The **Zip2Go** tool in **File** menu is used to compress the current file in WinZip compatible file. This tool is not available in educational/demo version of the software. On clicking this tool, the **Zip2Go Wizard** dialog box will be displayed. Select **Create** button from the dialog box to select objects to be compressed and shared. The **File Options** page will be displayed in the dialog box; refer to Figure-72. Select the check boxes for file types to be included in the zip file and click on the **Next** button. The list of files to be added in zip file will be displayed. Set the other parameters and click on the **Finish** button from the dialog box. The **Save As** dialog box will be displayed. Specify desired file type, name of file, and click on the **Save** button to save file.

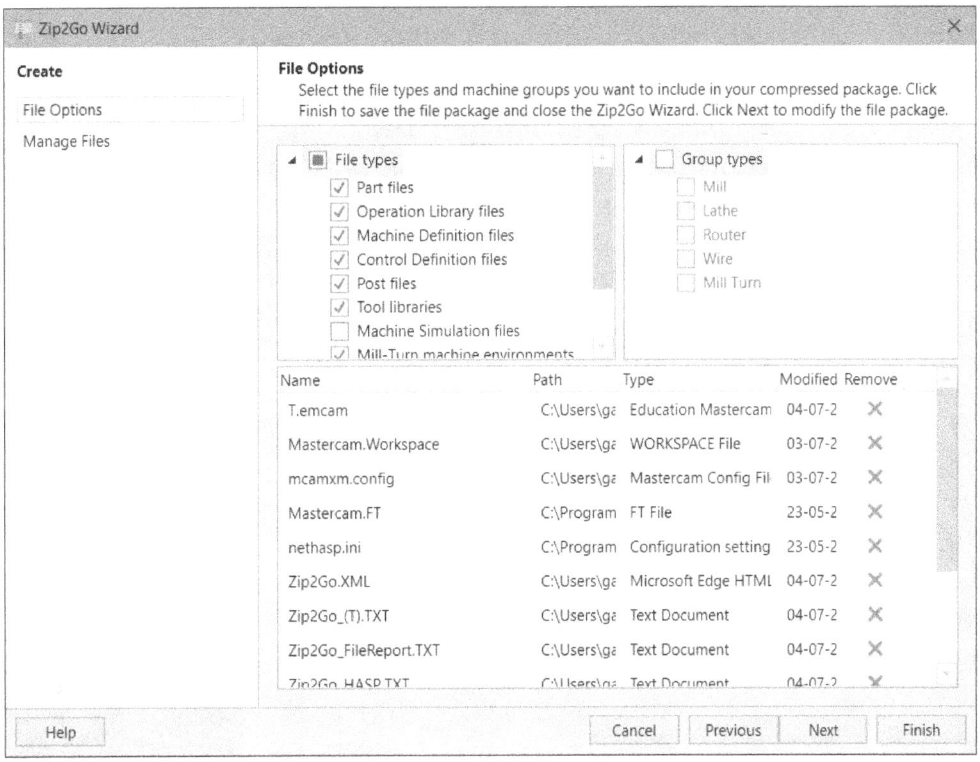

Figure-72. Zip2Go Wizard dialog box

Conversion Tools

The tools in the **Convert** cascading menu of **File** menu are used to import, export, and migrate files; refer to Figure-73. The tools in this cascading menu are also available in home learning/demo version of the software. Using the **Migration Wizard** tool, you can migrate files saved in previous version to the current latest version of the files. Using the **Import Folder** tool, you can import files from another folder and convert them in Mastercam files. Similarly, you can use the **Export Folder** tool to convert Mastercam model files to CAD files of supported formats.

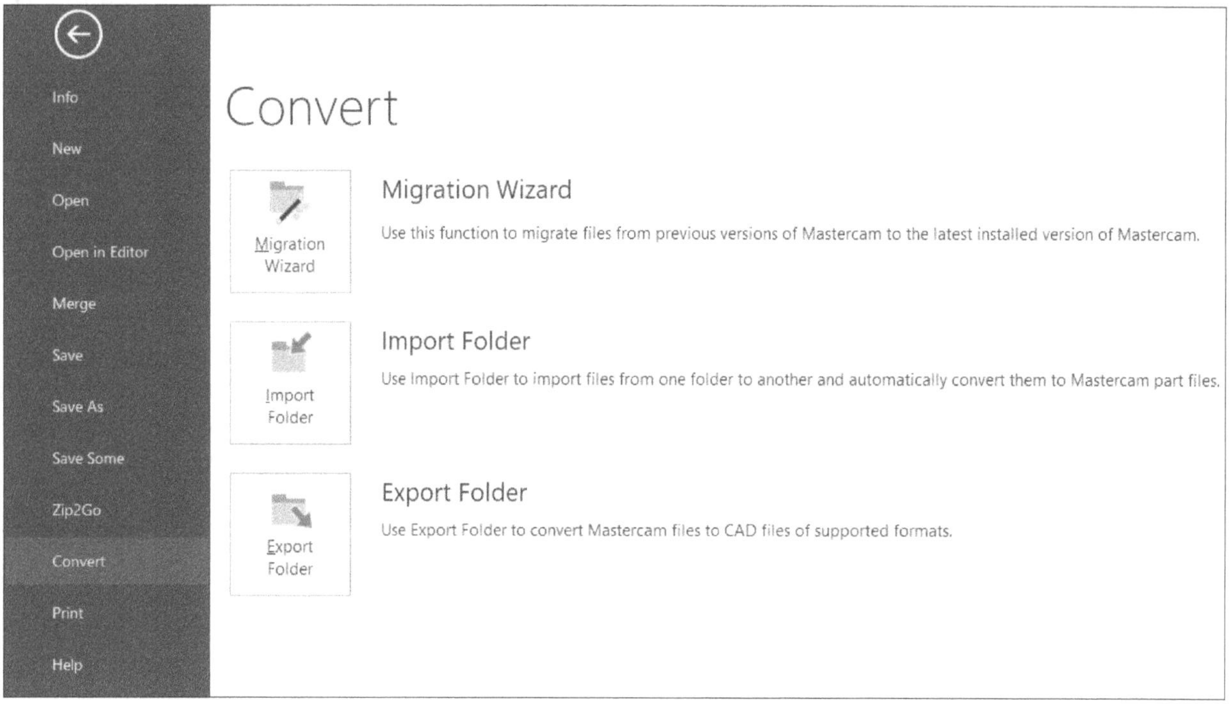

Figure-73. Convert cascading menu

Printing File

The **Print** tool is used to print the model displaying in drawing area to paper or file. The procedure to use this tool is given next.

- Click on the **Print** tool from the **File** menu. The options to print model will be displayed with preview of the model; refer to Figure-74.

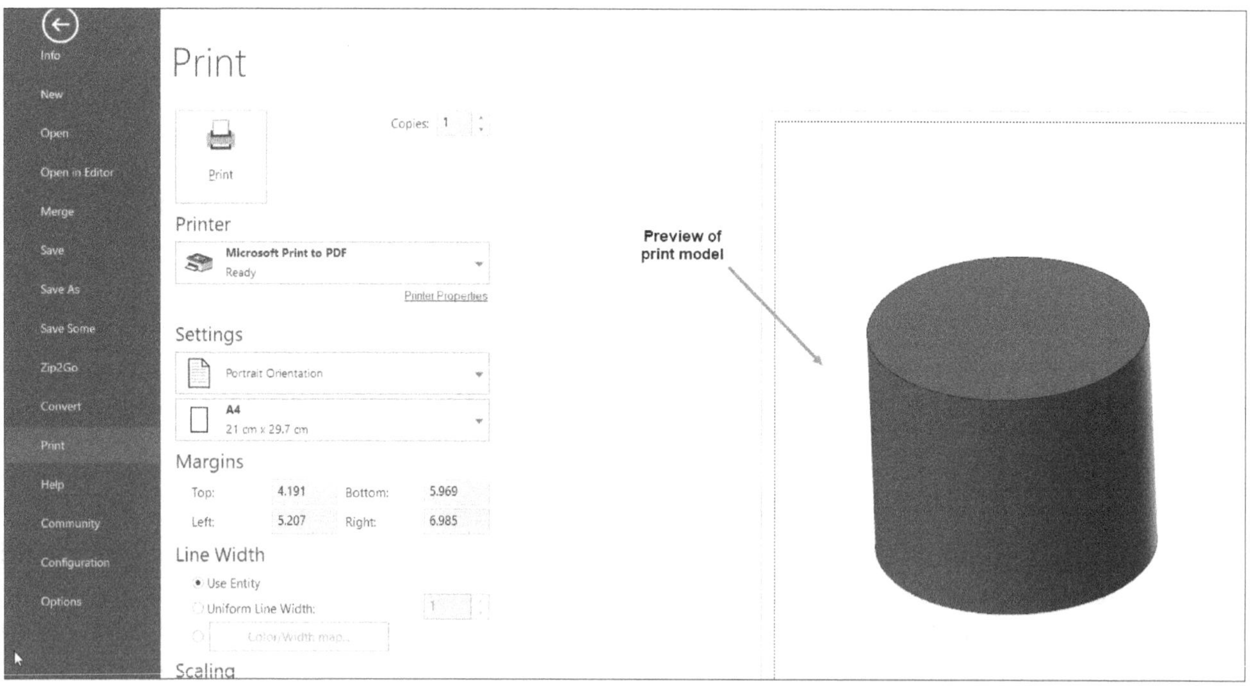

Figure-74. Options for printing

- Set desired number of copies to be printed in the **Copies** spinner.
- Select desired option from the **Printer** drop-down to select desired printer.
- Select desired paper size and orientation of paper from respective drop-downs in the **Settings** section of **Print** cascading menu.

- Similarly, set the other parameters in the **Print** cascading menu as desired and click on the **Print** button.

Help and Community Options

- Click on the **Help** menu to access help resources. The options to access help content from Mastercam website will be displayed along with licensing information of software; refer to Figure-75.

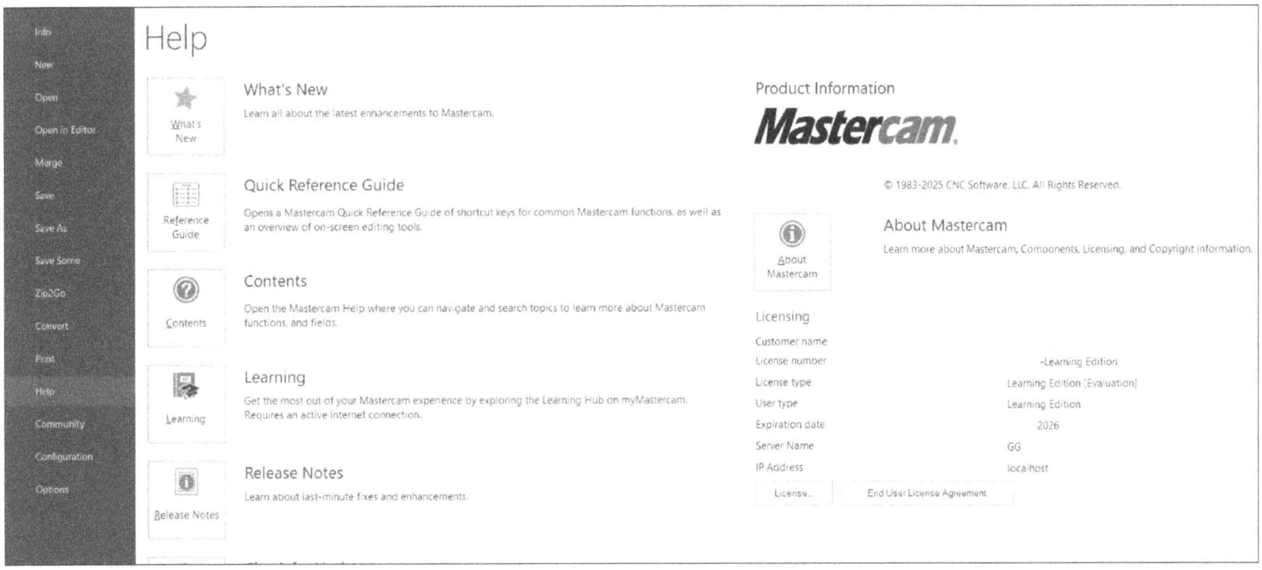

Figure-75. Help cascading menu

- Click on the **Community** menu to access community of Mastercam users for sharing knowledge; refer to Figure-76. You can also access Mastercam university for certification.

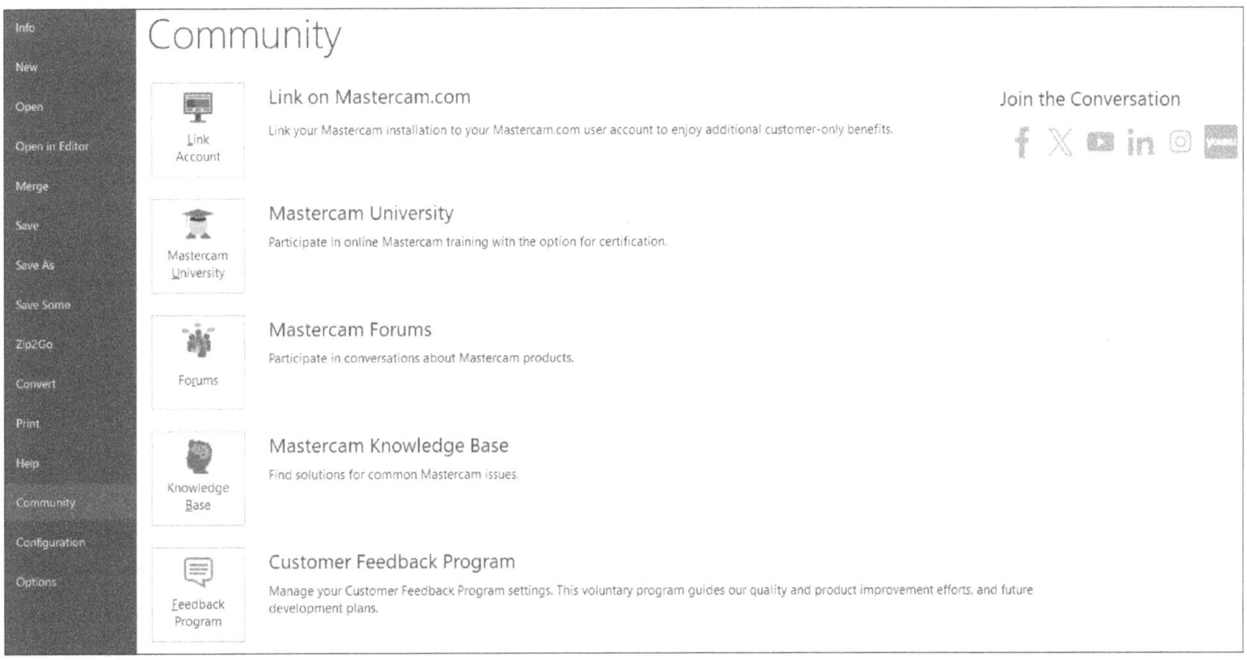

Figure-76. Community cascading menu

System Configuration

The **Configuration** tool is used to set system configurations for Mastercam. The procedure to use this tool is given next.

- Click on the **Configuration** tool from the **File** menu. The **System Configuration** dialog box will be displayed; refer to Figure-77.

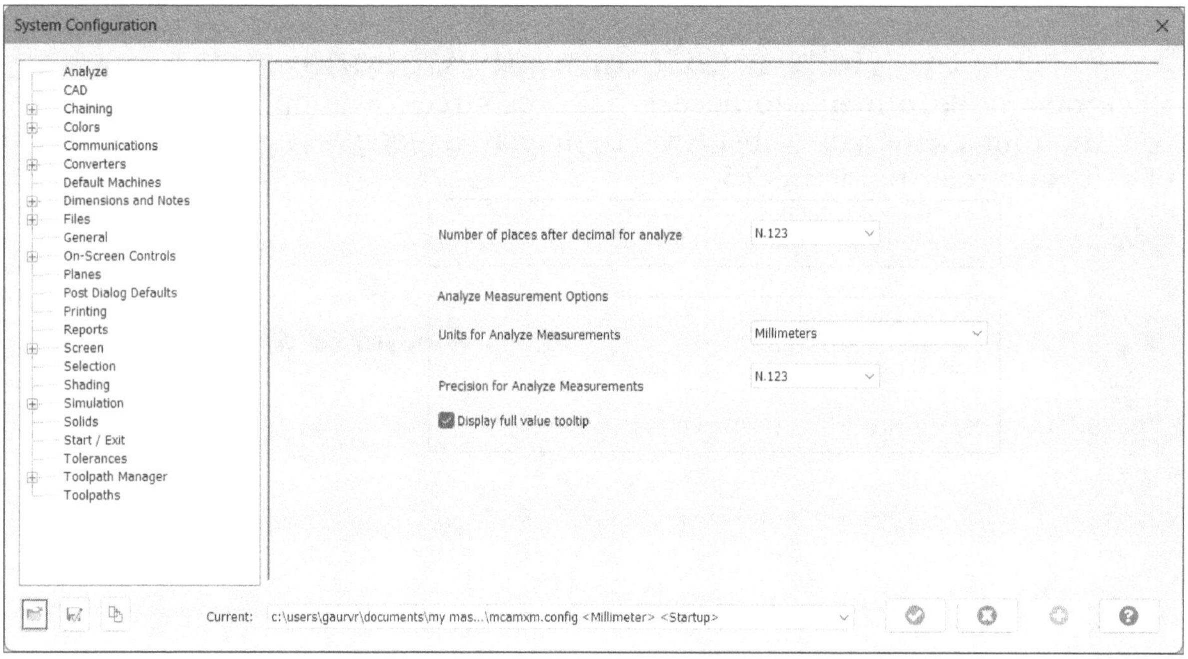

Figure-77. System Configuration dialog box

Analyze Options

- Click on the **Analyze** option from the left area of the dialog box to define settings related to analyze measurement.
- Select desired option from the **Number of places after decimal for analyze** drop-down to define up to how many decimal places, the measurement will be performed.
- Select desired option from the **Units for Analyze Measurements** drop-down to set unit for measuring objects using measurement tools.
- Select desired option from the **Precision for Analyze Measurements** drop-down to specify up to what precision, the objects will be measured.
- Select the **Display full value tooltip** check box to display full value of a number in **Analyze** dialog box ignoring the precision set by you.

CAD Options

- Click on the **CAD** option from the left area of the dialog box. The options to set parameters for CAD objects will be displayed; refer to Figure-78.
- Select the **Point** radio button from the **Type of center line** area to automatically create center lines in CAD model using series of points. Set the color and level options from the **Color** and **Level** areas of the dialog box.
- Select the **Lines** radio button from the **Type of center line** area to mark center lines as lines. Specify desired value for defining length of arc center mark in the **Line Length** area. Select desired type of line from the **Style** area of the dialog box.
- Set desired parameters in **Default attributes** area to define line style, line width, and point style for model edges and vertices.

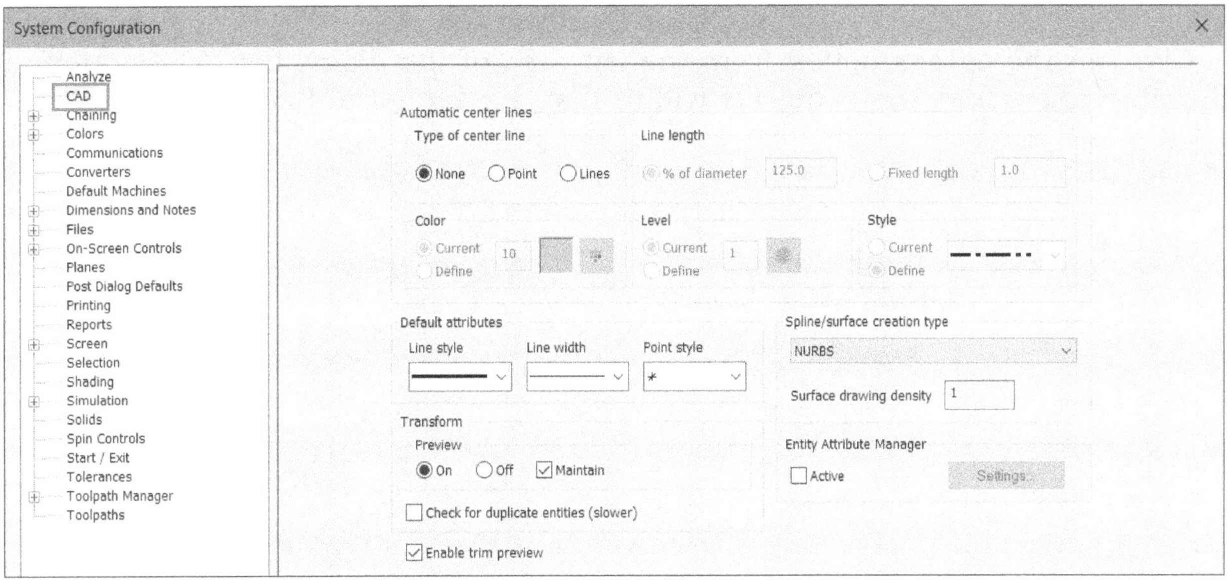

Figure-78. CAD options

- Select the **On** radio button from **Preview** area of **Transform** section to check preview of transformation in graphics area while performing operation. Select **Off** radio button if you do not want to see preview. Select the **Maintain** check box so that Mastercam remember last preview settings for transformation.
- Select desired option from the **Spline/surface creation type** drop-down to define what type of surfaces/splines will be created/imported.
- Specify desired value in **Surface drawing density** edit box to define how much dense, the surfaces will be displayed as wireframe. Value **1** means least dense and value **15** means most dense.
- Select the **Active** check box from the **Entity Attribute Manager** area to apply attributes to entities. On selecting this check box, the **Settings** button next to it will be active. Click on the **Settings** button and specify desired parameters.

Chaining Options

- Select desired check boxes from the **Mask** area of the dialog box to specify parameters for masking (filtering).
- Select the **Use entity Masking** check box to chain only entities that are the same type as the first entity when selecting.
- Select the **Use color Masking** check box to chain only entities that are assigned the same color as the first entity when selecting.
- Select the **Use level Masking** check box to chain only entities that are on the same level as the first entity when selecting.
- Select the **Open chains** check box to select open chains and select **Closed chains** check box to select closed chains.
- Specify desired value in the **Section angle** edit box to define maximum angle up to which the entities will be selected in chain selection.
- Similarly, set the other parameters for chaining in the **Chaining** and **Chain Similar** pages of the dialog box. You will learn more about the options when working later.

Color Options

- Click on the **Colors** option from the left area of the dialog box. The options to define colors for various objects will be displayed; refer to Figure-79.

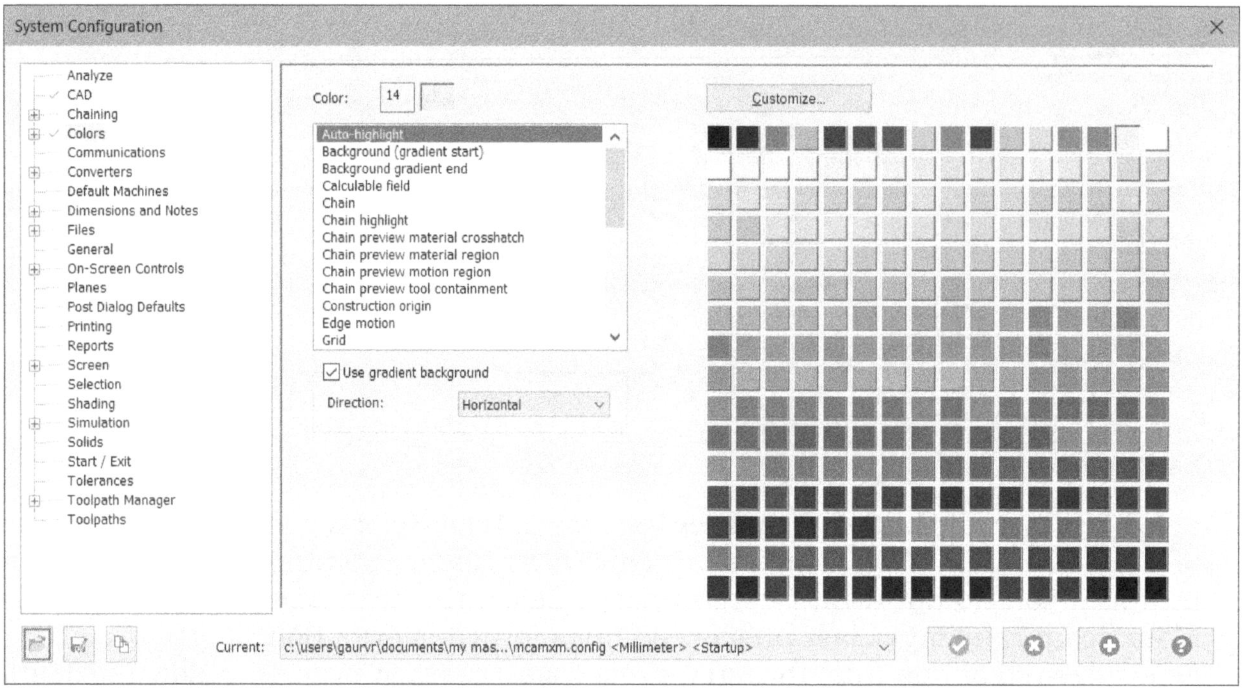

Figure-79. Colors page of System Configuration dialog box

- Select desired software interface from the list box to change color and then select desired color from the **Color Palette**.
- If you have selected **Use gradient background** check box then you can define the direction of gradient border in the **Direction** drop-down.

Communication Options

Select the **Communications** option from the left area of the dialog box to define communication channel between software and CNC machines; refer to Figure-80. Select desired communication channel from the **Communications** drop-down. If you want to use a custom channel for communication then select the **Browse** button from the drop-down and select the execution file for communication software.

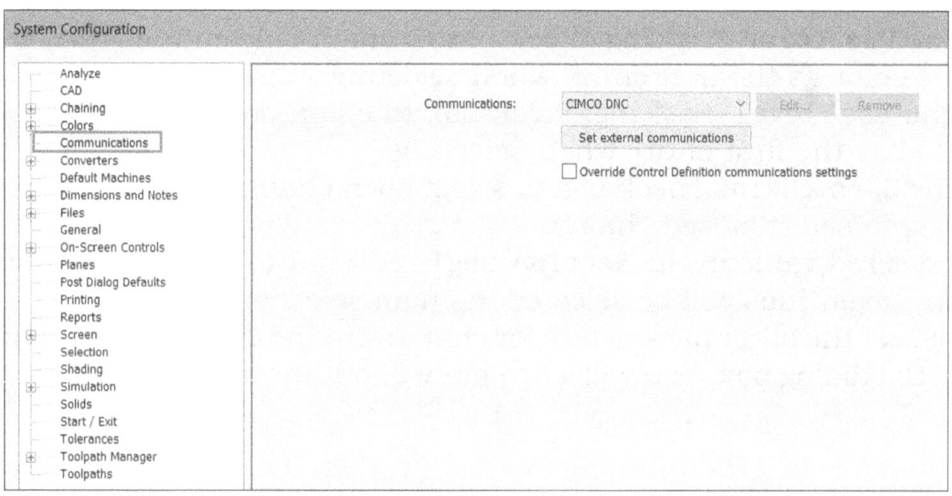

Figure-80. Communications options

Conversion (Import) Options

- Click on the **Converters** option from the left area of the dialog box. The options to define parameters for importing files will be displayed; refer to Figure-81.

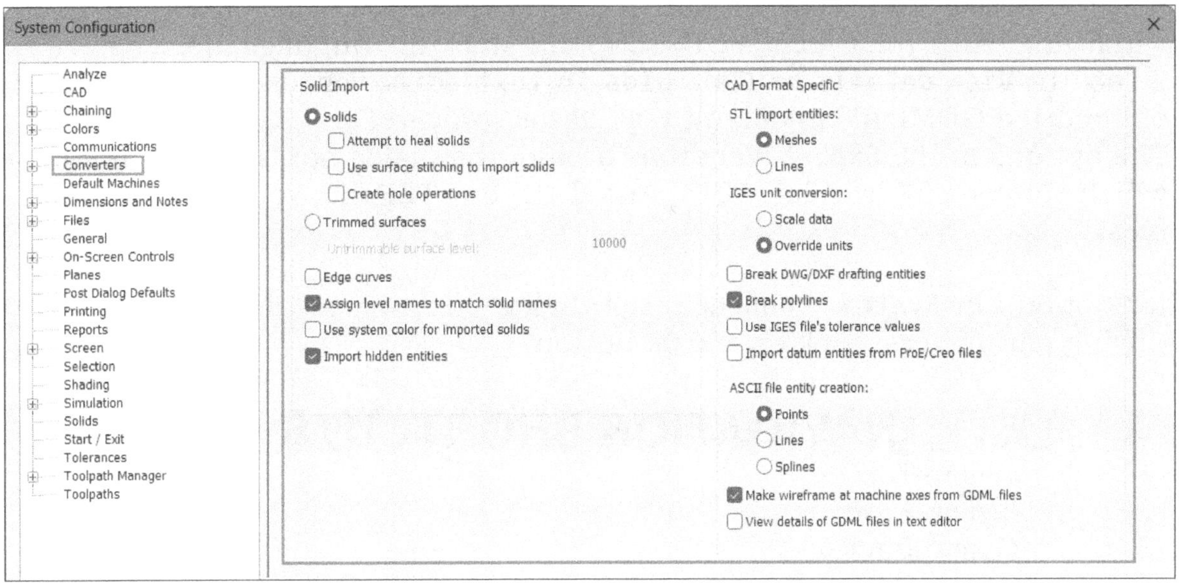

Figure-81. Converters options

- The options in the **Solid import** area are used to define how solids will be imported in the model.
- Select the **Solids** radio button to import solid objects as solids. The check boxes below the radio button will be active. Select the **Attempt to heal solids during import** check box to repair edges of model. Select the **Use surface stitching to import Solids** check box to stitch surfaces for forming solids while importing model. Select the **Create hole operations** check box to identify and create holes in converted model.
- Select the **Trimmed surfaces** radio button to import the model as trimmed surfaces.
- Select the **Edge curves** check box to import model with separate edge curves.
- Select the **Assign Level names to match Solid names** check box to create levels in Mastercam with names matching to names of Solids from imported files.
- Select the **Use System Color for imported Solids** check box to use system color for imported solids.
- Select the **Import hidden entities** check box to include hidden objects of model/ body to be imported.
- Select desired radio button from the **STL import entities** section to define whether you want to import mesh from STL file or you want to import only lines.
- Select **Scale data** radio button from the **IGES unit conversion** section to convert units of importing IGES model as per current model setup. Select the **Override units** radio button to change the units of current model to importing model.
- Select the **Break DWG/DXF Drafting Entities** check box to break drafting entities into segments before importing them into Mastercam.
- Select the **Use IGES files tolerance values** check box to use tolerance values specified in IGES file as tolerance for model.
- Select the **Import Datum entities from ProE/Creo files** check box to also import datum objects while importing ProE or Creo file.
- Similarly, you can select the other check boxes in the dialog box to import various parameters from the files.

- Select desired radio button from the **ASCII file entity creation** section to define what type of entities will be imported using ASCII file. You can import points, lines, and splines.
- Select the **Make wireframe at machine axis from GDML files** check box to create wireframe using the Geometry Description Markup Language file.
- Select the **View details of GDML files in text editor** check box to check details of imported GDML file in default text editor software.
- The options in the **Export versions** area of the dialog box are used to define to which version of Parasolid, ACIS, AutoCAD, or STEP file, you want to export the files.

Other options in **System Configuration** dialog box will be discussed later. After specifying parameters, click on the **OK** button.

NAVIGATION SHORTCUTS

Alt+1	Gview–Top
Alt+2	Gview–Front
Alt+3	Gview–Back
Alt+4	Gview–Bottom
Alt+5	Gview–Right
Alt+6	Gview–Left
Alt+7	Gview–Isometric
Alt+A	AutoSave
Alt+B	Art Model
Alt+C	Open
Alt+D	Drafting global parameters
Alt+E	Hide/unhide geometry
Alt+G	Selection grid parameters
Alt+H	On-line help
Alt+O	Operations Manager
Alt+P	Previous View
Alt+S	Full-time shading on/off
Alt+V	Mastercam version number and SIM serial number
Alt+X	Set main color, level, line style, and width from selected entity
Alt+Z	Set visible levels
Alt+F1	Fit geometry to screen
Alt+F2	Unzoom by 0.8
Alt+F4	Exit Mastercam
Alt+F8	System configuration
Alt+F9	Display all axes
F1	Zoom
F2	Unzoom
F3	Analyze Toolpath
F4	Analyze Entities
F5	Show Delete menu
F9	Show Axes
Esc	System interrupt or menu backup
Page Up	Zoom in by 0.8
Page Down	Zoom out by 0.8
Arrow Keys	Pan

Mouse Functions

- Scroll the Middle Mouse Button downward/upward to zoom out or zoom in, respectively. Note that this function can be reversed by using options in **System Configuration** dialog box; refer to Figure-82.

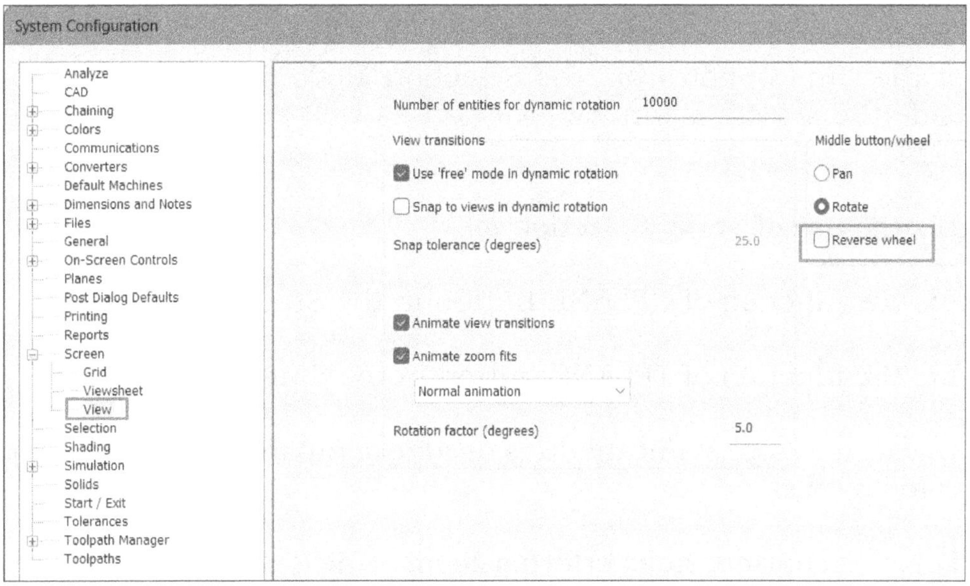

Figure-82. Reverse Wheel check box

- Click and drag the Middle Mouse Button to orbit the view.
- Use the **Shift** + Middle Mouse Button to pan the view.
- Press the left mouse button to select any object or tool.
- Press right mouse button (right-click) to access shortcut menus in the software.

SELF-ASSESSMENT

Q1. Manufacturing is the process of creating a useful product by using a machine, a process, or both. (T/F)

Q2. Discuss the difference between roughing process and finishing process.

Q3. Which of the following is an unconventional machine?

a. Electric Discharge Machine (EDM) b. Vertical Milling Machine
c. Shaper Machine d. Planar Machine

Q4. Discuss the applications of CAM in manufacturing.

Q5. Draw the flow chart basic approach for CAM program generation.

Q6. Post processor is used to translate the codes generated by CAM program to machine readable codes based on machine controller. (T/F)

Q7. Define the term “stock” for machining.

Q8. What is the function of options in **AutoCursor** drop-down?

Q9. Which of the following is not an option for Selection Filters?
a. From Back
b. Body Selection
c. From Side
d. Solid Selection

Q10. Select the Out+ option from the Selection Mode drop-down to select objects falling outside the selection window/polygon as well as intersecting the window/polygon. (T/F)

Q11. What is the use of Verify Selection tool?

Q12. What is the function of CPLANE button in the Status Bar?

Q13. What is the function of TPLANE button in the Status Bar?

Q14. The .... tool in File menu is used to compare two models for differences in model or toolpaths.

Q15. The Page Up shortcut key performs zoom in by 0.8 (T/F)

REVIEW QUESTIONS

Q1. What is the first and most important step in the manufacturing process?
A. Quality Control
B. Roughing Process
C. Generating Layout of Final Product
D. Raw Material Selection

Q2. What determines the selection of raw material in manufacturing?
A. Cost of the product
B. Size of the machine
C. Layout of final product
D. Power availability

Q3. In manufacturing terminology, what is a "Blank"?
A. Finished component
B. Raw material
C. Tool
D. Outline of the final shape

Q4. Which process removes a large amount of material with low concern for tolerance?
A. Finishing Process
B. Forging
C. Casting
D. Roughing Process

Q5. Which of the following is NOT typically part of roughing operations?
A. Turning
B. EDM
C. Drilling
D. Milling

Q6. What distinguishes finishing processes from roughing processes?
A. Speed of material removal
B. Quality and precision
C. Number of tools used
D. Manual intervention

Q7. What is the primary characteristic of unconventional machining processes?
A. High cost
B. Cutting without mechanical contact
C. Low accuracy
D. Use of lathes and drills

Q8. Which machine is used primarily for cutting cylindrical parts?
A. Milling Machine
B. Shaper
C. Turning Machine
D. Planer

Q9. Which movement is not possible for the workpiece in a turning machine?
A. Clockwise rotation
B. Counter-clockwise rotation
C. Translation
D. Rotation

Q10. In which type of milling machine is the tool aligned with the X-axis?
A. Vertical Milling Machine
B. Turret Milling Machine
C. Horizontal Milling Machine
D. 5-axis Milling Machine

Q11. What is the primary function of a drilling machine?
A. Cutting grooves
B. Making holes
C. Cutting threads
D. Contouring

Q12. In a Shaper machine, which of the following moves?
A. Tool in circular path
B. Workpiece in circular motion
C. Tool in linear motion
D. Workpiece in linear motion

Q13. What is the key difference between Planer and Shaper?
A. Planer uses multiple tools
B. Shaper reciprocates workpiece
C. Planer has fixed tool, moving workpiece
D. Shaper is used only for metals

Q14. What is the tool material commonly used in Wire-cut EDM?
A. Tungsten carbide rod
B. Copper tube
C. Brass wire
D. Stainless steel bar

Q15. What is used as medium between electrodes in EDM?
A. Air
B. Dielectric Fluid
C. Water
D. Lubricating oil

Q16. What is the cutting principle of Electro Chemical Machining?
A. Electrical discharge
B. Chemical reaction
C. Frictional heating
D. Tool vibration

Q17. Which process is suitable for cutting silicon and graphite with high precision?
A. Planer
B. Laser Beam Machining
C. Shaper
D. Turning

Q18. What does NC stand for in NC Machines?
A. Numerical Control
B. Non-Centralized
C. Normal Code
D. None of the above

Q19. Which of the following G-codes represents rapid movement of tool?
A. G01
B. G20
C. G00
D. G99

Q20. Which M-code stops the spindle rotation?
A. M03
B. M05
C. M02
D. M08

Q21. What does CAM primarily help in?
A. Improving design quality
B. Creating NC programs
C. Surface finishing
D. Tool sharpening

Q22. What is Mastercam?
A. A type of CNC machine
B. A manual cutting tool
C. CAM software
D. Programming language

Q23. Which software environment is active by default in Mastercam?
A. CAM
B. Simulation
C. CAD
D. Licensing

Q24. What feature in Mastercam allows adding frequently used tools for quick access?
A. Ribbon
B. Context Menu
C. Quick Access Toolbar
D. Custom Panels

Q25. What tool is used to customize the Ribbon in Mastercam?
A. Customize QAT
B. Ribbon Designer
C. Options Dialog Box
D. Add-ins Manager

Q26. What is the primary purpose of the Ribbon in the Mastercam interface?
A. To display the current coordinates of the cursor
B. To manage toolpaths and levels
C. To provide access to design and editing tools
D. To preview the AutoCursor snap points

Q27. Which tool would you use to select the origin point while creating an entity?
A. Midpoint
B. Origin
C. Tangent
D. Quadrant

Q28. Which AutoCursor option allows you to select the point at a specified distance along an entity?
A. Relative
B. Along
C. Endpoint
D. Midpoint 2 Points

Q29. What is a visual cue in Mastercam?
A. A pop-up help box
B. A change in status bar text
C. A change in cursor shape indicating snap mode
D. A blinking toolbar icon

Q30. What does the AutoCursor Fast Point tool allow you to do?
A. Automatically detect all midpoints
B. Specify coordinates for a point manually
C. Select arc centers quickly
D. Highlight selected entities with glow

Q31. What does enabling the "power keys" option in Selection Settings allow you to do?
A. Display hidden edges
B. Pre-select entities
C. Override AutoCursor using keyboard shortcuts
D. Switch viewsheets

Q32. Which setting highlights selected objects using a dot pattern?
A. Use dashed on wireframe
B. Use glow highlighting
C. Use stipple on solids/surfaces/meshes
D. Auto-highlight

Q33. What does the "Auto-highlight of level entities" checkbox do?
A. Highlights all objects in the graphics area
B. Highlights entities in the current working level
C. Highlights entities that are tangent
D. Highlights only selected edges

Q34. Which option lets you define the maximum deviation allowed from tangency?
A. Tangency Tolerance
B. Power Keys
C. Visual Style
D. Chain Selection

Q35. What does the Invert Selection tool do?
A. Selects last used object
B. Selects entities based on type
C. Swaps selected and unselected entities
D. Changes view orientation

Q36. What is the purpose of the Quick Masks Toolbar?
A. To apply transparency to objects
B. To select different types of entities quickly
C. To highlight toolpaths
D. To toggle between construction planes

Q37. What is the function of the GView Controls?
A. Edit part geometry
B. Orient and manipulate the model view
C. Manage toolpath groups
D. Configure Selection Settings

Q38. What is the default position of the GView Controls in the Mastercam interface?
A. Top-right corner
B. Bottom-left corner
C. Middle of screen
D. Below the Ribbon

Q39. Which combination flips the model by 180 degrees in GView?
A. SHIFT + Click
B. CTRL + ALT + Click
C. ALT + SHIFT + Click
D. Click Flip button only

Q40. What does the "Dimmed" visual style in the Status Bar do?
A. Displays only shaded view
B. Hides all entities
C. Displays hidden edges as dim lines
D. Makes model faces translucent

Q41. Which button allows switching between construction planes in the Status Bar?
A. CPLANE
B. TPLANE
C. WCS
D. Visual Style

Q42. What is shown in the Coordinates area of the Status Bar?
A. Number of selected entities
B. Cursor's X, Y, Z position
C. Number of hidden entities
D. Construction plane

Q43. Which Selection Method option selects all entities in continuous tangency?
A. Window
B. Chain
C. Area
D. Vector

Q44. What does the "Out+" option in Selection Mode do?
A. Selects objects inside selection only
B. Selects objects intersecting the selection only
C. Selects objects outside or intersecting selection boundary
D. Selects all entities within the full model

Q45. How do you activate graphical confirmation when multiple selection candidates are near the cursor?
A. By toggling the Ribbon
B. By clicking View tab
C. By using Verify Selection
D. By switching GView mode

Q46. What is the function of the View Sheets panel in Mastercam?
A. To store tool libraries
B. To preview CAM operations
C. To manage saved screen views of the part
D. To set origin points

Q47. Which of the following is not a function of the View Manager in Mastercam?
A. Store named views
B. Configure AutoCursor
C. Toggle visibility of viewports
D. Save WCS, TPlane, and CPlane orientations

Q48. What does the shortcut F9 do in Mastercam?
A. Opens Level Manager
B. Toggles wireframe visibility
C. Displays coordinate axes
D. Regenerates all toolpaths

Q49. How do you access the View Manager?
A. From the Quick Masks Toolbar
B. Using ALT + V
C. By right-clicking the graphics area and choosing "View Manager"
D. By pressing CTRL + Shift + M

Q50. Which Mastercam function is primarily used to create named construction views?
A. Level Manager
B. View Manager
C. GView Controls
D. Status Bar

Q51. What is the purpose of the AutoCursor option "Midpoint 2 Points"?
A. Finds midpoint between two selected endpoints
B. Snaps to the nearest axis-aligned midpoint
C. Snaps to midpoint of a single line
D. Creates a new midpoint entity

Q52. What is the significance of enabling "Highlight when selected" in Selection settings?
A. Shows object details in a tooltip
B. Highlights entities as you hover the mouse over them
C. Only highlights after confirmation
D. Shows axis colors on selection

Q53. In the GView Controls, what does the Red Arrow icon represent?
A. Show construction plane
B. Apply changes
C. Rotate model view
D. Indicates active construction orientation

Q54. What does the "Verify Selection" option do in Mastercam?
A. Simulates toolpath
B. Confirms and shows names of multiple overlapping entities
C. Refreshes all selected viewsheets
D. Validates file integrity

Q55. What is the function of the "Fast Point" feature when sketching?
A. Automatically selects multiple points
B. Calculates geometric center
C. Lets you enter exact coordinates of a point
D. Displays selection priority

Q56. Which selection option is most appropriate when selecting a closed loop of connected lines and arcs?
A. Rectangular window
B. Single
C. Chain
D. Area fill

Q57. What happens when "Auto-highlight of level entities" is disabled?
A. The geometry from the current level won't be selectable
B. Entities will still exist but won't glow when hovered
C. You can't switch between levels
D. Level names won't be displayed

Q58. What does the blue highlight typically indicate during entity selection in Mastercam?
A. Final selection confirmed
B. Entity is being hovered for selection
C. Error in selection
D. Toolpath is pending regeneration

Q59. What is the use of the "Power keys" feature in Mastercam's Selection Settings?
A. To assign shortcut keys to viewports
B. To override standard snapping behavior with keyboard
C. To open the Operations Manager
D. To enable fast geometry copying

Q60. Which of the following is a valid way to flip the part 180° in the graphics view?
A. Double-click CPLANE
B. Use View Manager and select "Mirror"
C. Use the Flip icon in GView Controls
D. Press CTRL + Spacebar

For Student Notes

Mastercam Design Section

Chapter 2

Wireframe Design

Topics Covered

The major topics covered in this chapter are:

- ***Introduction to Wireframe.***
- ***Sketch Creation Tools.***
- ***Curve Creation Tools.***
- ***Sketch Modification Tools.***
- ***Turn Profile Creation***

INTRODUCTION

The first step to create any 3D model is creating base sketches. Using the sketch curves, you can draw profile for turn machining. The points specified using sketch tools can act as reference for various machining features. The tools to create sketch entities are available in the **Wireframe** tab of the **Ribbon**; refer to Figure-1. These tools are discussed next.

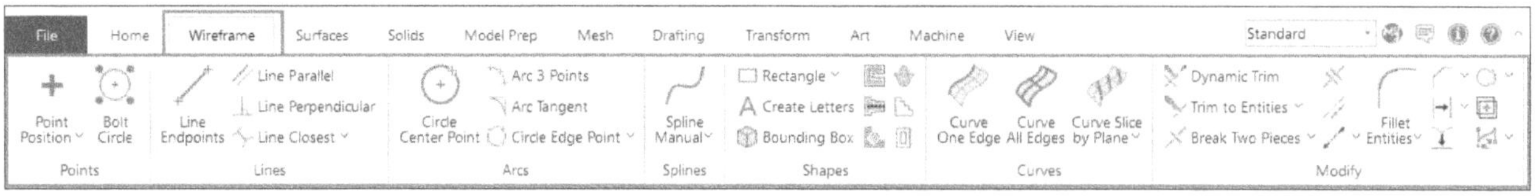

Figure-1. Wireframe tab of Ribbon

CREATING POINTS

The tools to create points are available in the **Point Position** drop-down of the **Points** group in the **Wireframe** tab of the **Ribbon**; refer to Figure-2. Various tools in this drop-down are discussed next.

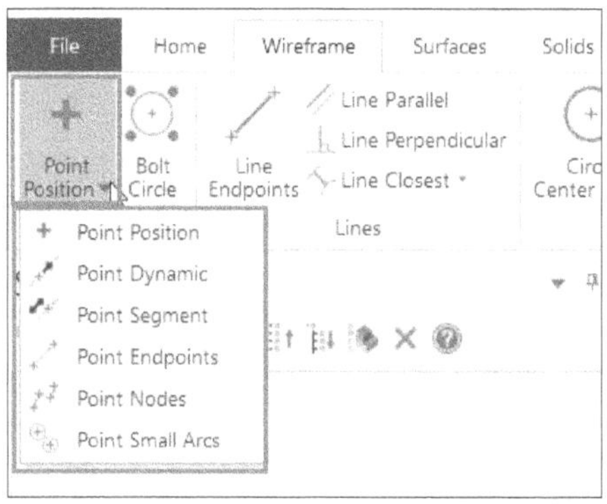

Figure-2. Point Position drop-down

Creating Point by Position

The **Point Position** tool is used to create point by specifying its position. The procedure to use this tool is given next.

- Click on the **Point Position** tool from the **Points** group in the **Wireframe** tab of the **Ribbon**. The **Point Position Manager** will be displayed; refer to Figure-3.

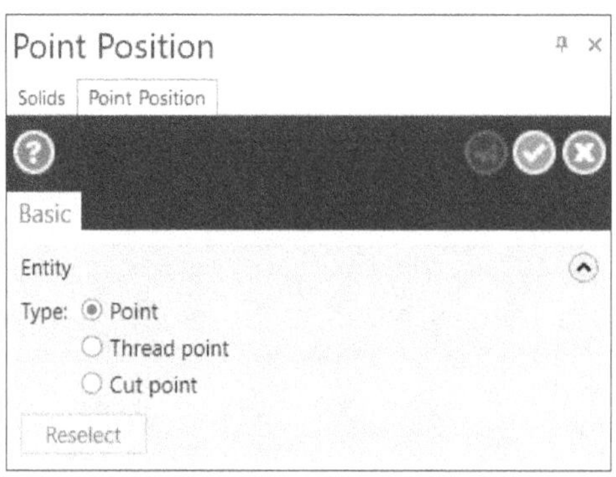

Figure-3. Point Position Manager

- Select desired radio button from the **Type** area to define what type of point you want to create.

- Select the **Point** radio button to create simple point at specified location to use as reference location. Select the **Thread point** radio button to specify point where Wire cut machine will start creating thread. The wire moves from the thread position to the start of the toolpath chain based on the lead in/out parameters. Select the **Cut point** radio button to specify point where Wire cut machine will stop cutting and start a new toolpath.
- After setting desired parameters, click at desired location. The point will be created.
- Click on the **OK** button from the **Manager** to create points and exit the tool.

Creating Point Dynamically

The **Point Dynamic** tool is used to create point along selected line, arc, surface, or solid face. The procedure to use this tool is given next.

- Click on the **Point Dynamic** tool from the **Point Position** drop-down in the **Points** group of **Wireframe** tab in the **Ribbon**. The **Point Dynamic Manager** will be displayed; refer to Figure-4 and you will be asked to select a line, arc, surface, or solid face.

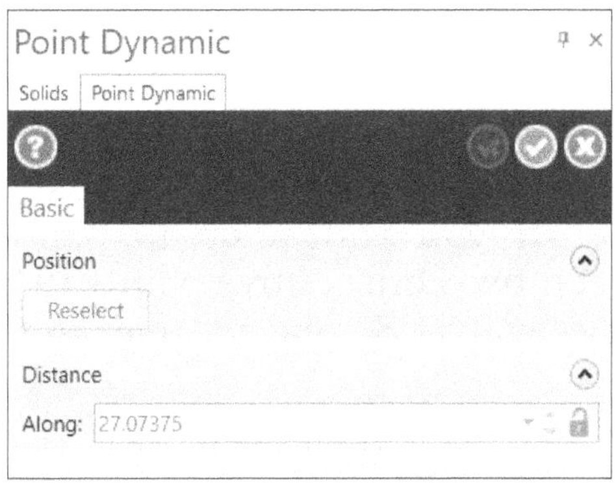

Figure-4. Point Dynamic Manager

- Select desired line, arc, curve, surface, or solid face. The point will get attached to cursor and you will be asked to specify distance of point along the selected curve; refer to Figure-5.

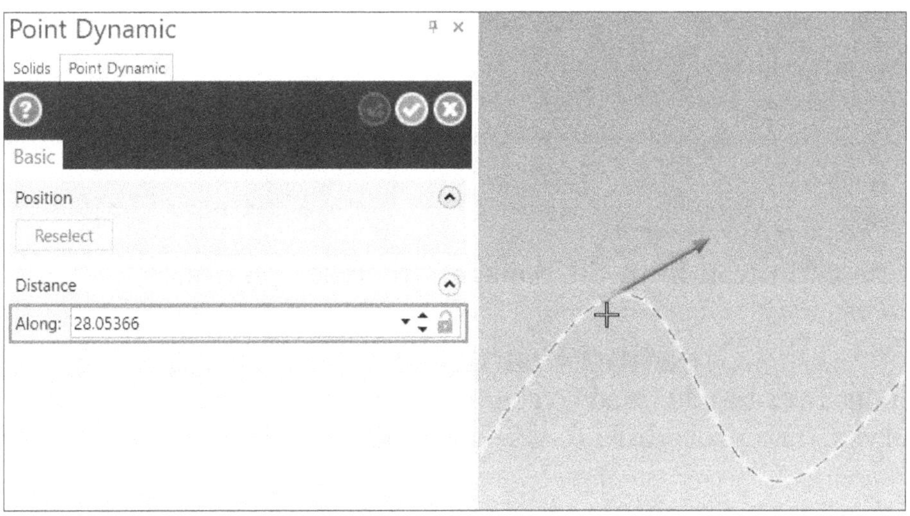

Figure-5. Specifying point dynamically

- Specify desired value in the **Along** edit box or click at desired location. You can create multiple points by clicking on the curve.
- After setting desired parameters, click on the **OK** button to create the points.

Creating Point Segments

The **Point Segment** tool is used to create specified number of points along selected curve. The procedure to use this tool is given next.

- Click on the **Point Segment** tool from the **Point Position** drop-down in the **Points** group of **Wireframe** tab in the **Ribbon**. The **Point Segment Manager** will be displayed; refer to Figure-6.

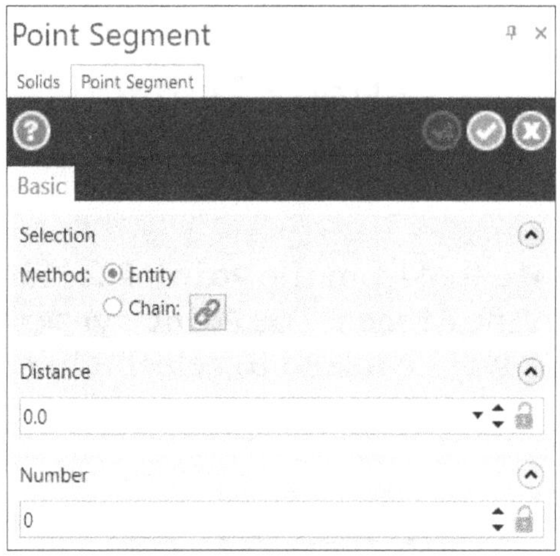

Figure-6. Point Segment Manager

- Select the curve along which you want to create points and enter the number of points or distance between two consecutive points in respective edit boxes of the **Manager**. Preview of points will be displayed; refer to Figure-7.

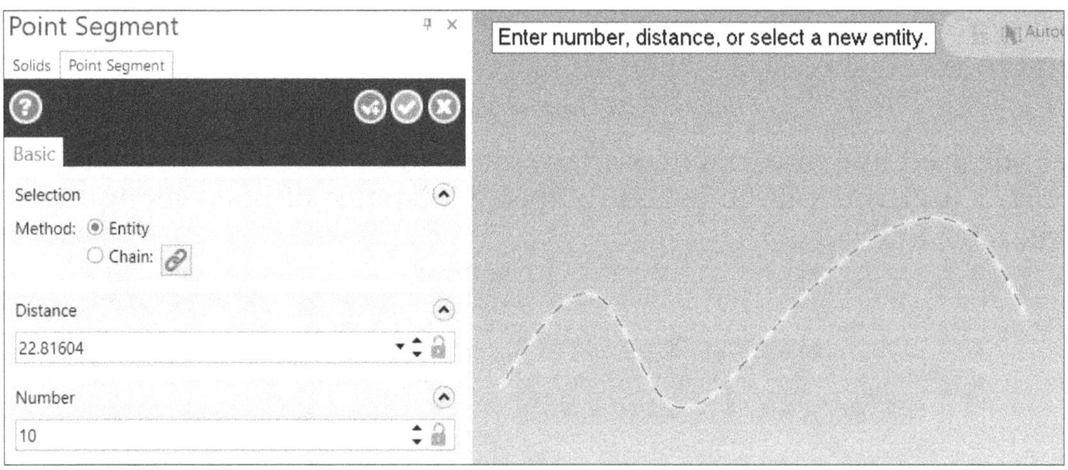

Figure-7. Preview of point segment

- Click on the **OK** button from the **Manager** to create points.

Creating Points at End Points

The **Point Endpoints** tool is used to create points at the end points of selected lines, arcs, and curves. The procedure to use this tool is given next.

- Click on the **Point Endpoints** tool from the **Point Position** drop-down in the **Points** group of **Wireframe** tab in the **Ribbon**. The end points of all the curves will be displayed.
- If you want to create end points of specific curves then select them before using the tool.

Creating Points at Nodes

The **Point Nodes** tool is used to create points at the nodes of existing spline. The procedure to use this tool is given next.

- Click on the **Point Nodes** tool from the **Point Position** drop-down in the **Points** group of the **Wireframe** tab in the **Ribbon**. You will be asked to select a spline.
- Select desired spline. The points will be displayed; refer to Figure-8.

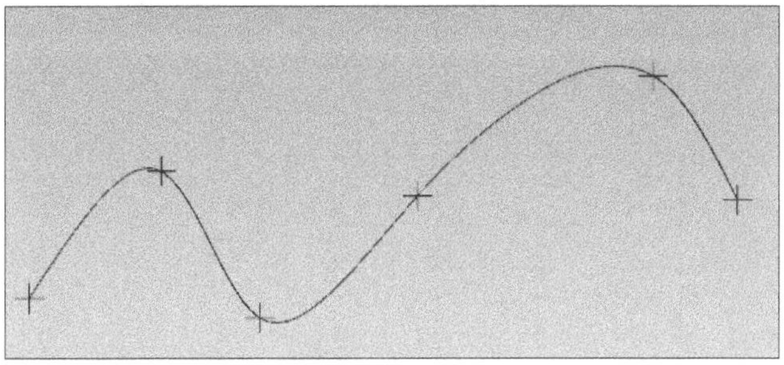

Figure-8. Node points of spline

Creating Points at Circles/arcs

The **Point Small Arcs** tool is used to generate points on arcs and circles which have radius lesser than specified value. The procedure to use this tool is given next.

- Click on the **Point Small Arcs** tool from the **Point Position** drop-down in the **Points** group of the **Wireframe** tab in the **Ribbon**. The **Small Arcs Manager** will be displayed; refer to Figure-9.

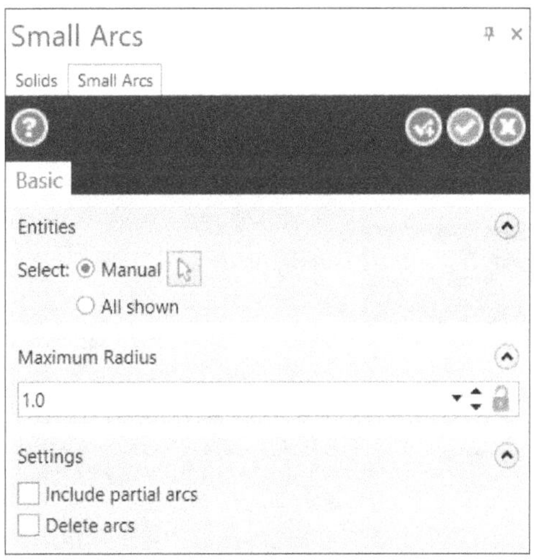

Figure-9. Small Arcs Manager

- Specify desired value of radius in the **Maximum Radius** edit box to define up to how much value of radius, the circles and arcs will be used for generating points.
- Select the **All shown** radio button to generate points on all the circles/arcs which have radius less than specified maximum radius value. Select the **Manual** radio button and click on the **Select** button next to it for selecting circles/arcs.
- After the selection, click on the **OK** button from the **Manager**. The center points of selected arcs/circles will be displayed.

CREATING BOLT CIRCLE

The **Bolt Circle** tool is used to create points and arcs in circular pattern. The procedure to use this tool is given next.

- Click on the **Bolt Circle** tool from the **Points** group in the **Wireframe** tab of **Ribbon**. The **Bolt Circle Manager** will be displayed; refer to Figure-10 and you will be asked to specify base point of circular pattern.

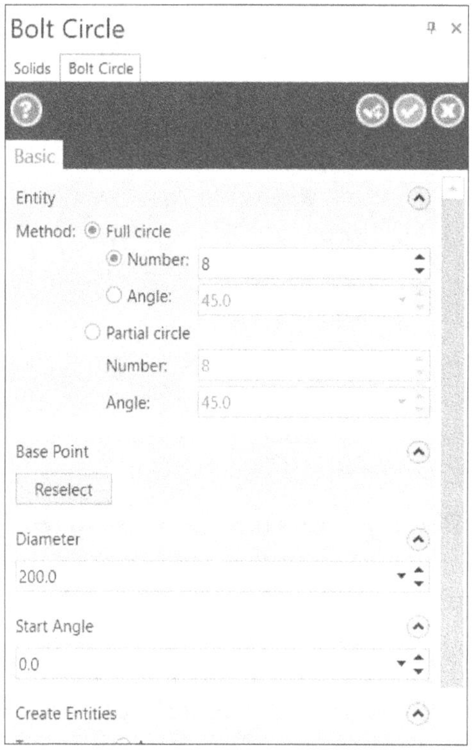

Figure-10. Bolt Circle Manager

- Click at desired location to specify base point of pattern. Preview of pattern will be displayed; refer to Figure-11.

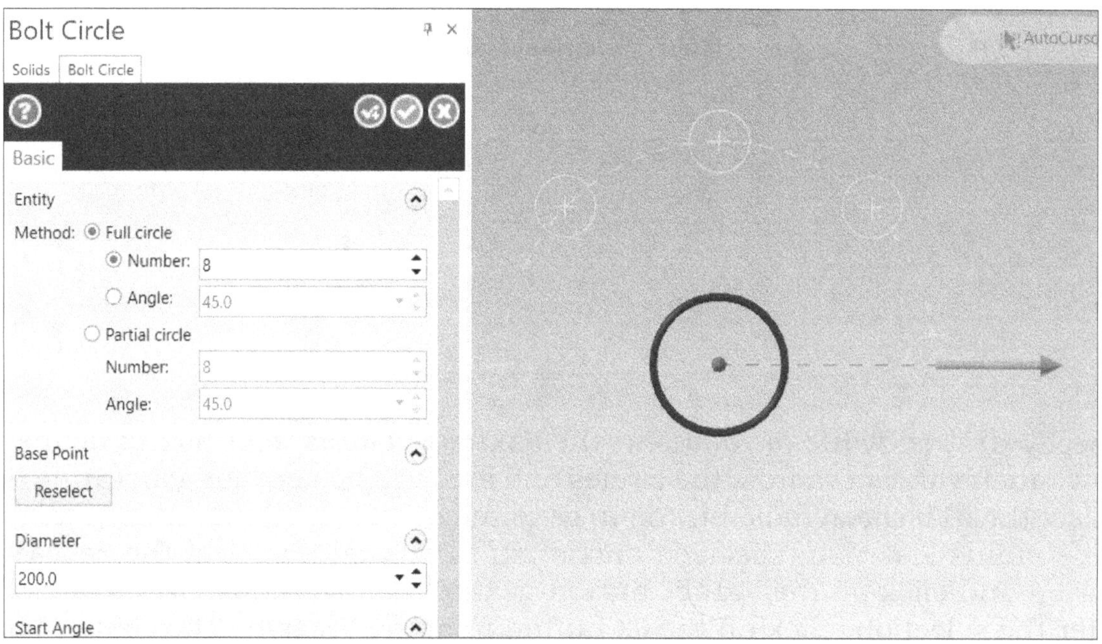

Figure-11. Preview of circular pattern

- Select desired option from the **Method** section of **Manager** to define whether you want to create pattern on full 360 degree circle or partial circle.
- Specify desired value in the **Number** edit box to define total number of arcs/circles to be created.

- Specify desired value in the **Angle** edit box to define angular gap between two consecutive instances of the arcs/circles on pattern.
- Click in the **Diameter** edit box to specify diameter of construction circle along which you want to create arcs/circles in pattern.
- Select desired radio button from the **Type** area of **Create Entities** rollout to define what type of entities are to be created in the pattern. Select the **Arcs** radio button to create arcs and **Points** radio button to create points. If you want to create both arcs and points in pattern then select the **Both** radio button.
- Similarly, set the other parameters in the **Manager** and click on the **OK** button. The bolt circle pattern will be created.

CREATING LINES

The tools to create lines are available in the **Lines** group of **Wireframe** tab in the **Ribbon**. Various tools in this group are discussed next.

Creating Lines by Endpoints

The **Line Endpoints** tool is used to create lines by specifying their start and end points. The procedure to use this tool is given next.

- Click on the **Line Endpoints** tool from the **Lines** group in the **Wireframe** tab of **Ribbon**. The **Line Endpoints Manager** will be displayed; refer to Figure-12.

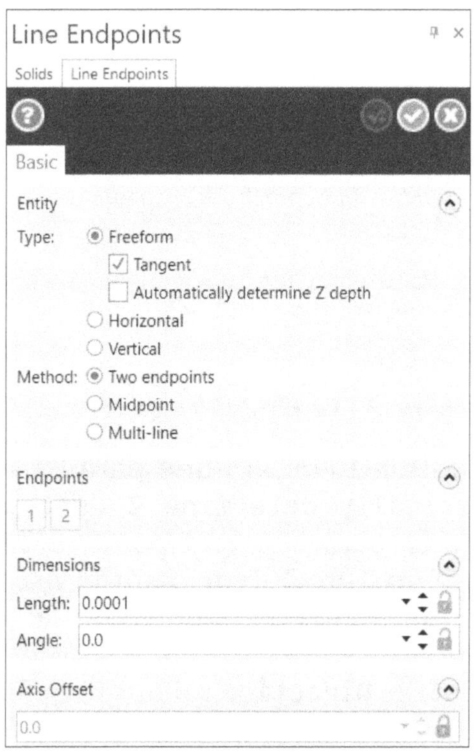

Figure-12. Line Endpoints Manager

- Select the **Freeform** radio button to create line at any specified angle. Select the **Tangent** check box to create lines tangent to selected objects. Select the **Automatically determine Z depth** check box to keep same AutoCursor Z level as previous while creating line in 3D.
- Select the **Horizontal** radio button to create a horizontal line.
- Select the **Vertical** radio button to create a vertical line.

- The options in the **Method** area are used to define the method of creating line. Select the **Two endpoints** radio button to specify start and end points of line for creating it. Select the **Midpoint** radio button to create a line starting from the mid point of line. After specifying midpoint, you will be asked to specify end point of the line. Select the **Multi-line** radio button to create chain of lines.
- Click at desired locations to create the line(s). Note that cursor automatically snaps to various keypoints in the model like mid point, end point, and intersection point. You can also create a line by specifying length and angle in the respective edit boxes of **Dimensions** rollout.
- Press **ESC** to exit the tool.

Creating Parallel Lines

The **Line Parallel** tool is used to create line parallel to selected line. The procedure to use this tool is given next.

- Click on the **Line Parallel** tool from the **Lines** group in the **Wireframe** tab of **Ribbon**. The **Line Parallel Manager** will be displayed; refer to Figure-13 and you will be asked to select the line.

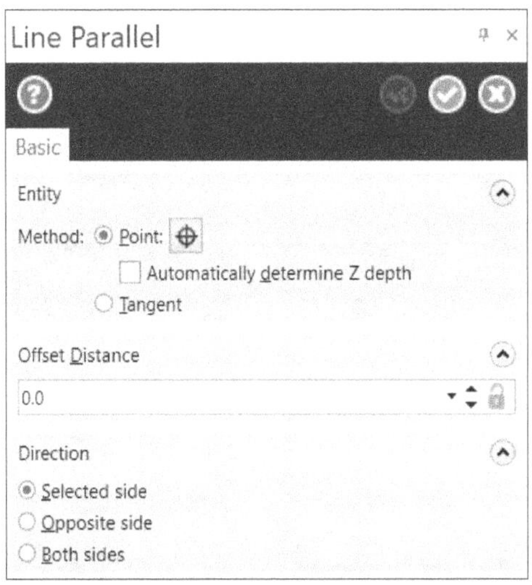

Figure-13. Line Parallel Manager

- Select the **Point** radio button to create line parallel to selected line at specified point. Select the **Automatically determine Z depth** check box to keep height/ depth of point along Z axis same for end point and start point of parallel line based on selected point if no AutoCursor point is used.
- Select the **Tangent** radio button to create line parallel to selected line and tangent to selected circle/arc.
- Select desired option from the **Direction** rollout to define on which side of selected line will the new line be created, if **Point** radio button is selected. If the **Tangent** radio button is selected in the **Manager** then the lines will be created on the sides of selected arc/circle.
- After setting desired parameters in **Manager**, select the line to which you want the new line to be parallel and then specify the placement point for line or select the circle/arc to use its center point. Preview of line will be displayed; refer to Figure-14.
- Click on the **OK** button from the **Manager** to create lines.

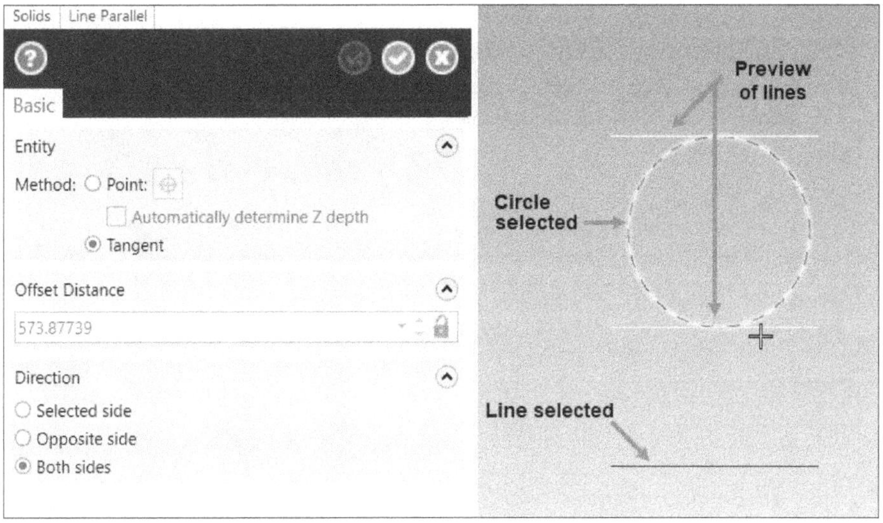

Figure-14. Preview of parallel lines

Creating Perpendicular Line

The **Line Perpendicular** tool is used to create a line perpendicular to selected entity. The procedure to use this tool is given next.

- Click on the **Line Perpendicular** tool from the **Lines** group in the **Wireframe** tab of the **Ribbon**. The **Line Perpendicular Manager** will be displayed; refer to Figure-15.

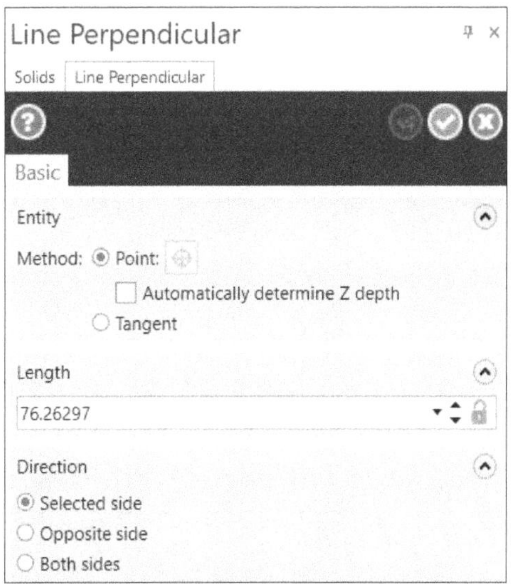

Figure-15. Line Perpendicular Manager

- Select desired radio button from the **Method** section as discussed earlier and select the entity to which you want to create perpendicular line. Preview of perpendicular line will be displayed; refer to Figure-16.
- Click at desired location to place the line and click on the **OK** button from the **Manager**.

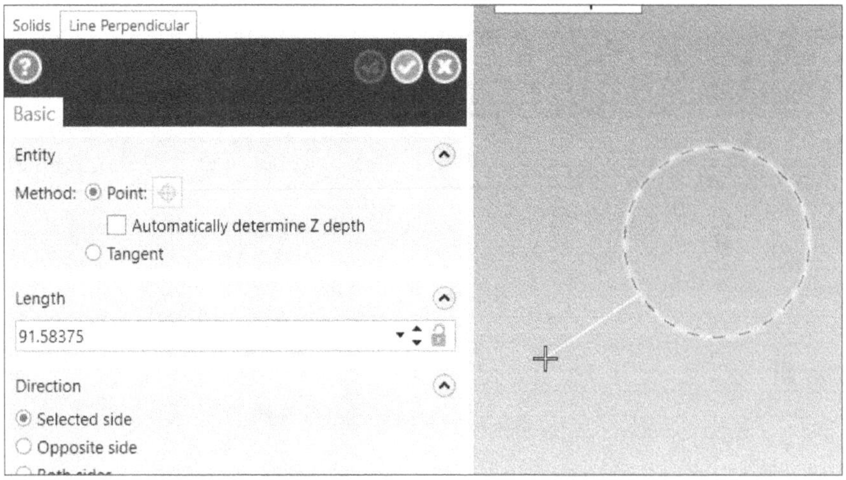

Figure-16. Preview of perpendicular line

Creating Closest Line

The **Line Closest** tool is used to create shortest line between two selected entities. The procedure to use this tool is given next.

- Click on the **Line Closest** tool from the **Line Closest** drop-down in the **Lines** group of **Wireframe** tab in the **Ribbon**. You will be asked to select two lines, arcs, or splines for creating lines.
- Select desired entities. The line will be created between the points on selected entities which are closest; refer to Figure-17.

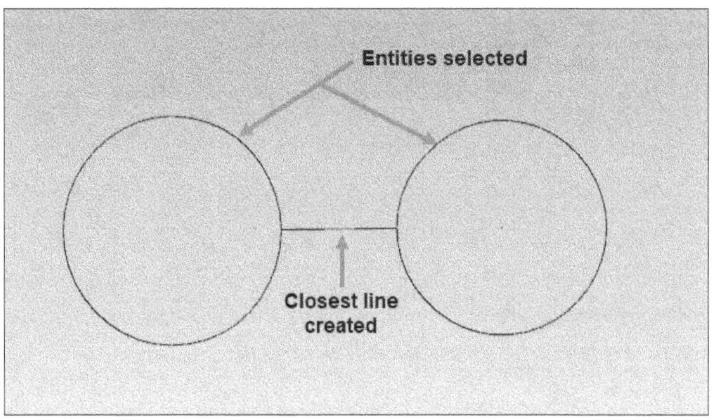

Figure-17. Creating closest line

Creating Bisector Line

The **Line Bisect** tool is used to create bisector of two lines. The procedure to use this tool is given next.

- Click on the **Line Bisect** tool from the **Line Closest** drop-down in the **Lines** group of **Wireframe** tab in the **Ribbon**. The **Line Bisect Manager** will be displayed; refer to Figure-18.
- Select desired radio button from the **Manager** to define whether single or multiple bisector lines are to be created.
- Specify desired length of bisector line in the **Length** edit box.
- Select two lines to create bisector line. Preview of line will be displayed; refer to Figure-19.

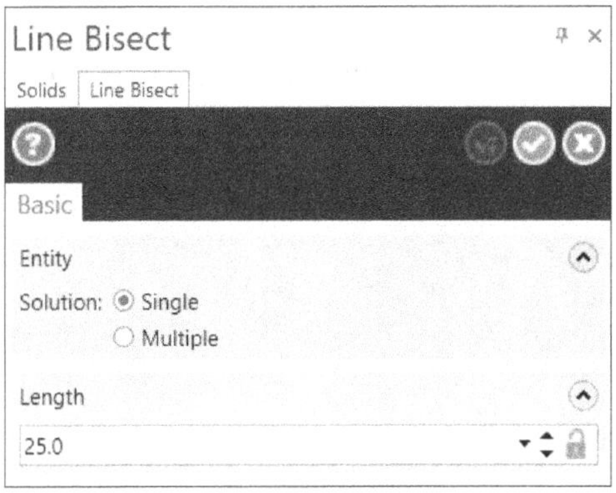

Figure-18. Line Bisect Manager

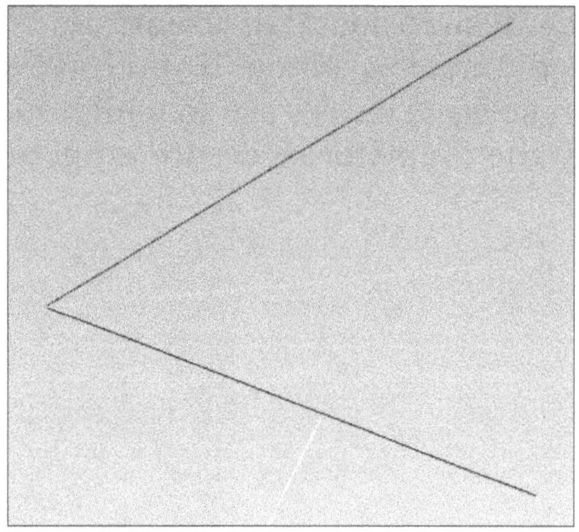
Figure-19. Preview of bisector line

- Click on the **OK** button from the **Manager** to create bisector line.

Similarly, you can use the **Line Tangent Through Point**, **Line Normal to Point**, and other tools from the **Line Closest** drop-down.

CREATING CIRCLES AND ARCS

The tools to create circles and arcs are available in the **Arcs** group of the **Wireframe** tab in the **Ribbon**. These tools are discussed next.

Creating Center Point Circle

The **Circle Center Point** tool is used to create circle by specifying center point and diameter. The procedure to use this tool is given next.

- Click on the **Circle Center Point** tool from the **Arcs** group in the **Wireframe** tab of the **Ribbon**. The **Circle Center Point Manager** will be displayed; refer to Figure-20.

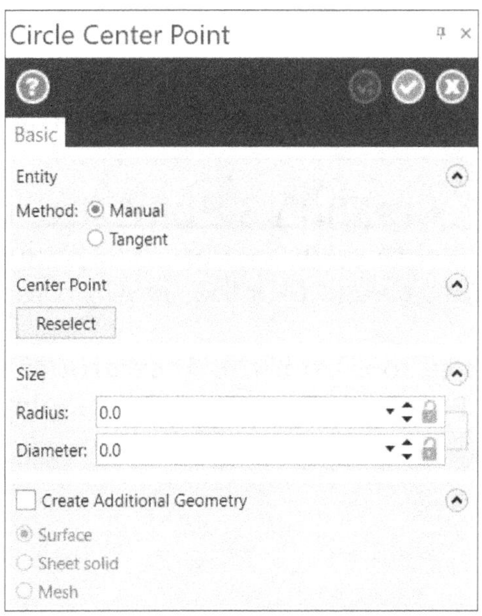

Figure-20. Circle Center Point Manager

- Select desired radio button from the **Method** section. Select the **Manual** radio button to manually specify diameter of circle. Select the **Tangent** radio button to create circle tangent to another circle or arc.

- Click at desired location to specify center point of circle. You will be asked to specify diameter of circle. If you have selected the **Tangent** radio button then you need to select a circle/arc to which new circle will be tangent.
- Specify the diameter or create tangent circle; refer to Figure-21.

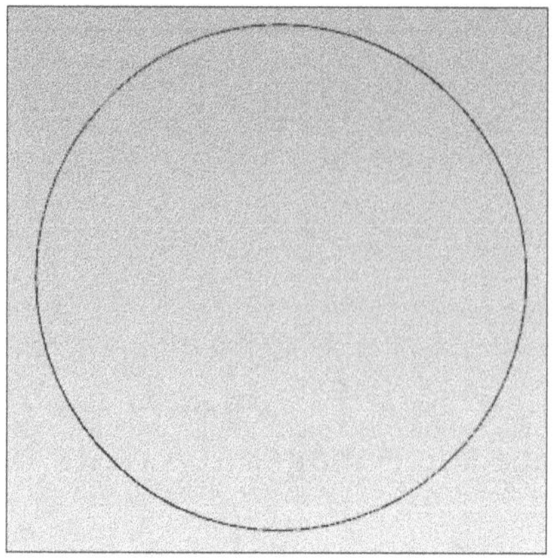

Figure-21. Preview of circle

- Select the **Create Additional Geometry** check box if you want to create surface/ sheet solid/mesh body using boundary of circle; refer to Figure-22.

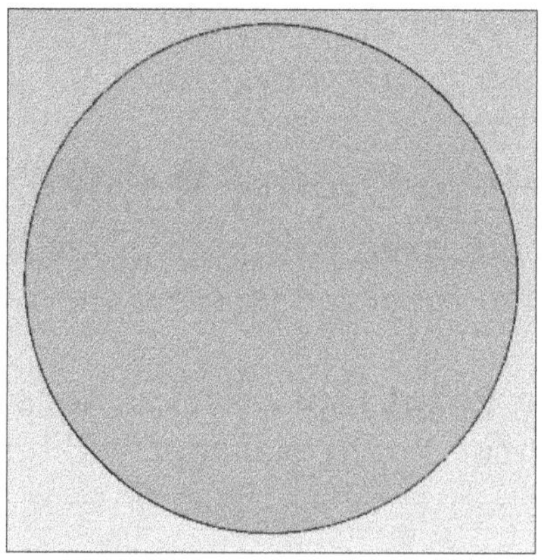

Figure-22. Circular surface created

- Click on the **OK** button from the **Manager** to create the circle/surface.

Creating 3 Point Arc

The **Arc 3 Points** tool is used to create an arc by specifying start point, mid point, and end point. The procedure to use this tool is given next.

- Click on the **Arc 3 Points** tool from the **Arcs** group in the **Wireframe** tab of the **Ribbon**. The **Arc Three Points Manager** will be displayed; refer to Figure-23 and you will be asked to specify start point of the arc.

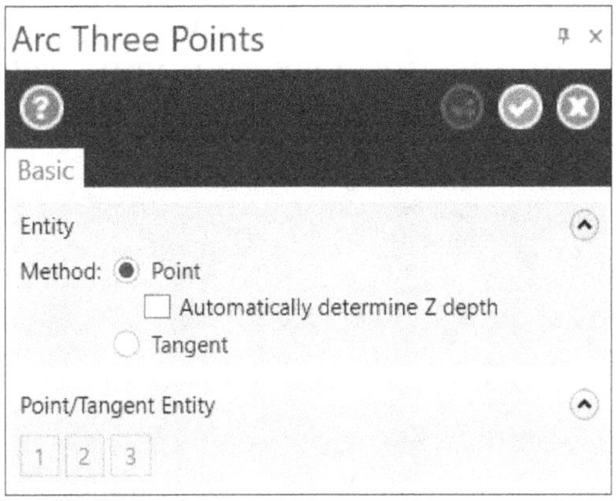

Figure-23. Arc Three Points Manager

- Click at desired location to specify start point of arc. You will be asked to specify second point (mid point) arc.
- Click at desired locations to specify the midpoint and end point of the arc.
- After specifying the points, click on the **OK** button.

Creating Tangent Arc

The **Arc Tangent** tool is used to create an arc tangent to selected arcs/circles. The procedure to use this tool is given next.

- Click on the **Arc Tangent** tool from the **Arcs** group in the **Wireframe** tab of the **Ribbon**. The **Arc Tangent Manager** will be displayed; refer to Figure-24.

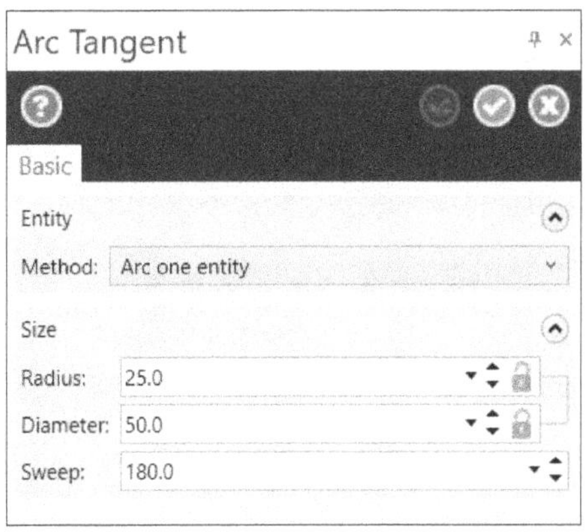

Figure-24. Arc Tangent Manager

- Select the **Arc one entity** option from the **Method** drop-down if you want to create an arc tangent single selected entity. You will be asked to select entity to which arc will be tangent. Select the entity and then click at desired location on earlier selected entity to define the tangency point. Preview of possible tangent arcs will be displayed; refer to Figure-25. Click on desired side of preview to generate the arc.

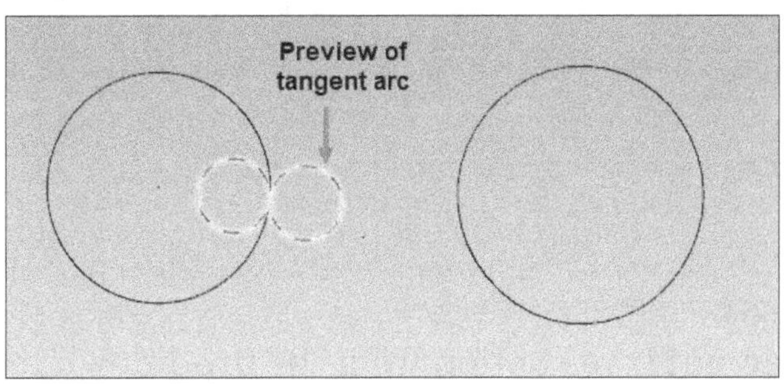

Figure-25. Preview of tangent arc

- Select the **Arc one point** option from the drop-down to create an arc tangent to selected entity and passing through selected point; refer to Figure-26.

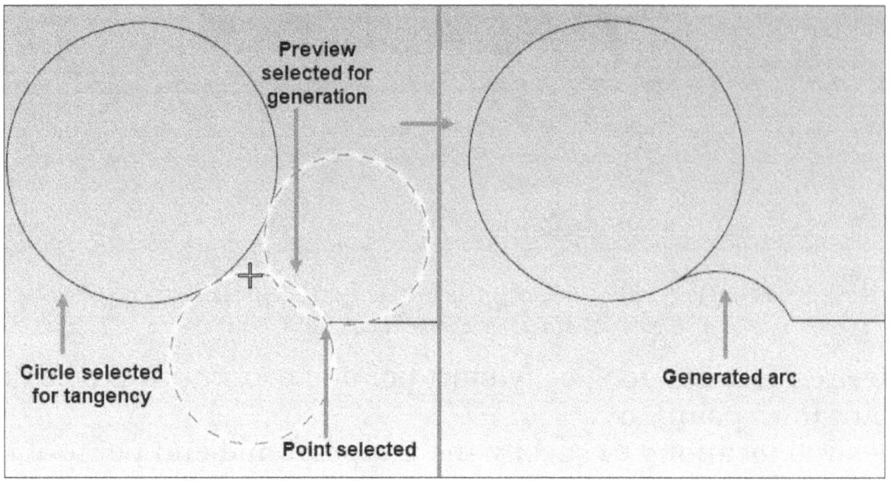

Figure-26. Tangent arc using single point

- Select the **Arc centerline** option to use first selected line as tangent reference and second selected line as center point reference for tangent arc; refer to Figure-27. Preview of arc will be displayed. Select desired arc to create it.

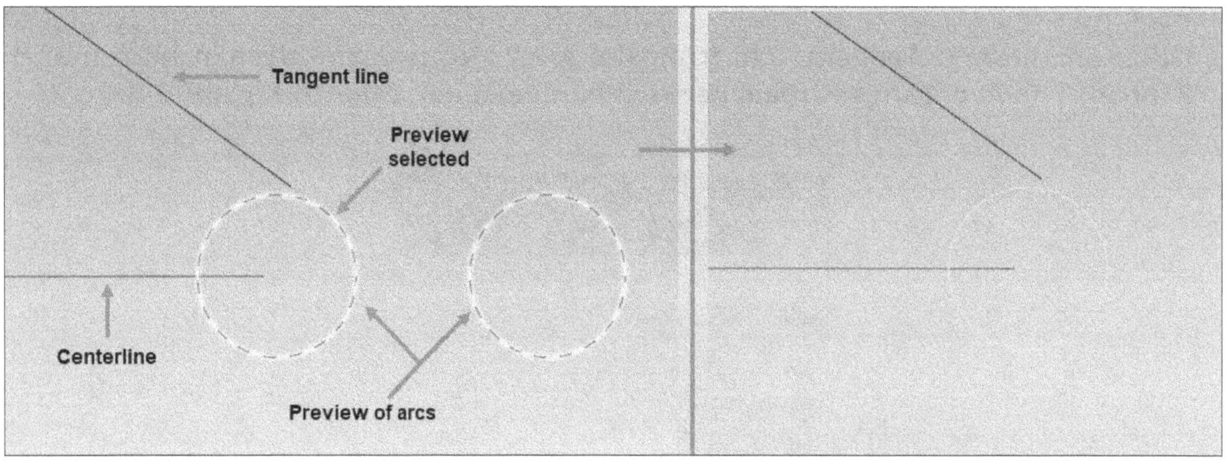

Figure-27. Tangent arc created using Arc centerline

- Select the **Arc dynamic** option from the drop-down to select the tangency object, start point, and end point of the tangent arc. The tangent arc will be created; refer to Figure-28.

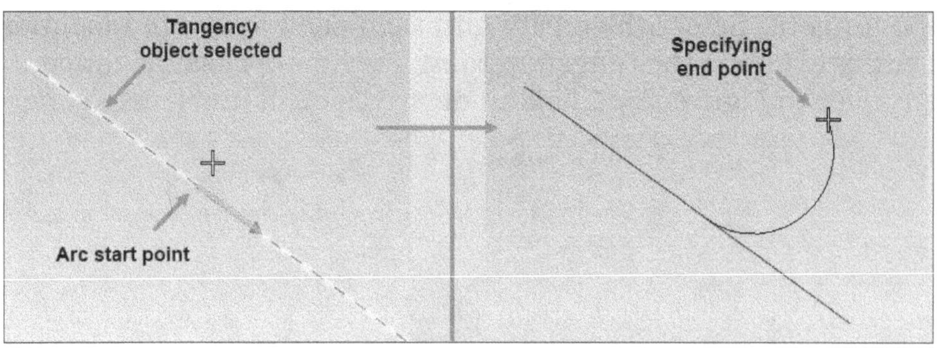

Figure-28. Creating tangent arc dynamically

- Select the **Arc three entities** option from the drop-down to create an arc tangent to three selected entities; refer to Figure-29.

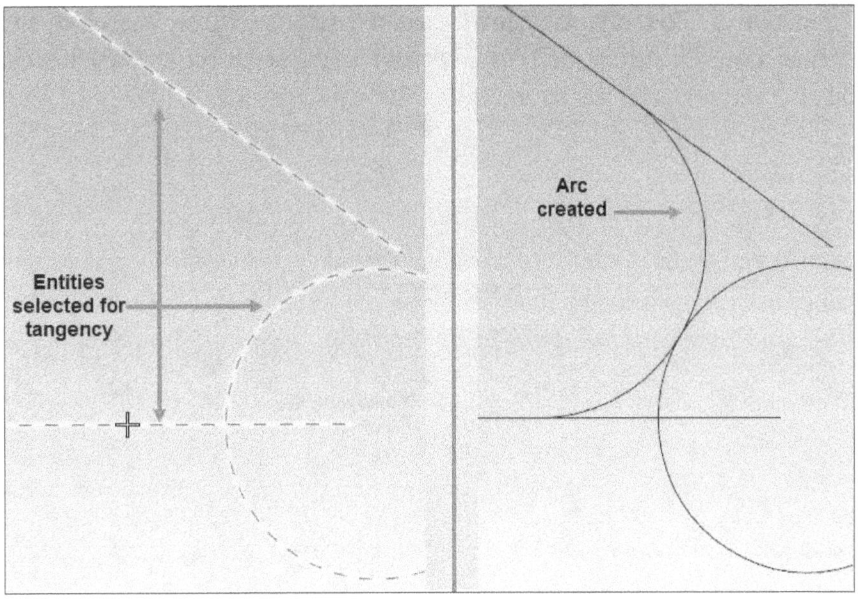

Figure-29. Creating 3 entities tangent arc

- Similarly, you can use **Circle three entities** and **Arc two entities** options to create tangent arcs.
- After setting desired parameters, click on the **OK** button to create the arc.

Creating Circle using Edge Points

The **Circle Edge Point** tool is used to create circle by using 2 points and 3 points. The procedure to use this tool is given next.

- Click on the **Circle Edge Point** tool from the **Circle Edge Point** drop-down in the **Arcs** group of **Wireframe** tab in the **Ribbon**. The **Circle Edge Point Manager** will be displayed; refer to Figure-30.

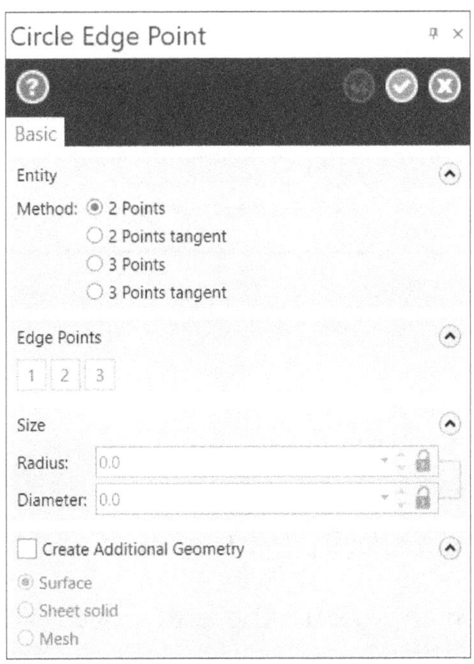

Figure-30. Circle Edge Point Manager

- Select desired radio button from the **Method** area to define how many points you want to use for creating circle. We are using **3 Points tangent** radio button to create circle tangent to three entities.

- After selecting the **3 Points tangent** radio button, click on three entities one by one to create circle. Preview of the 3 point tangent circle will be displayed; refer to Figure-31.

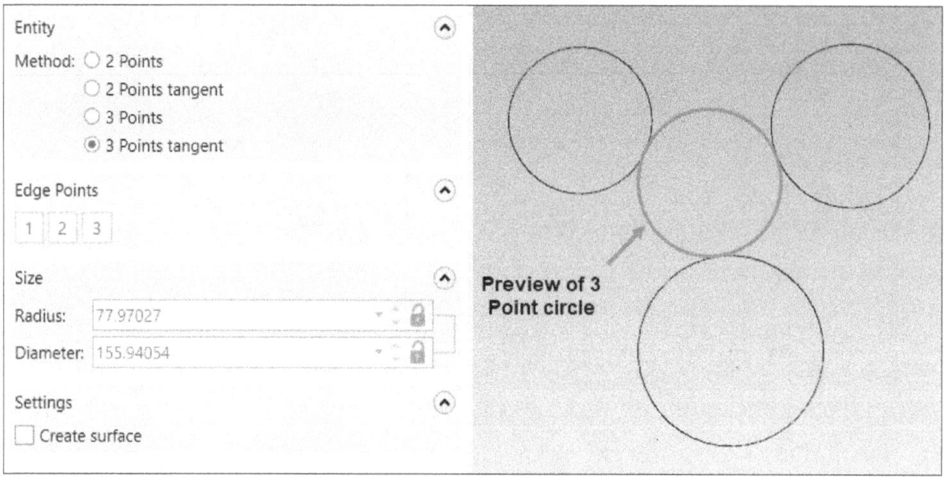

Figure-31. Preview of 3 points tangent circle

- Set the parameters as desired and click on the **OK** button.

Creating Arc using Endpoints

The **Arc Endpoints** tool is used to create an arc by specifying end points. The procedure to use this tool is given next.

- Click on the **Arc Endpoints** tool from the **Circle Edge Point** drop-down in the **Arcs** group of the **Wireframe** tab in the **Ribbon**. The **Arc Endpoints Manager** will be displayed; refer to Figure-32.

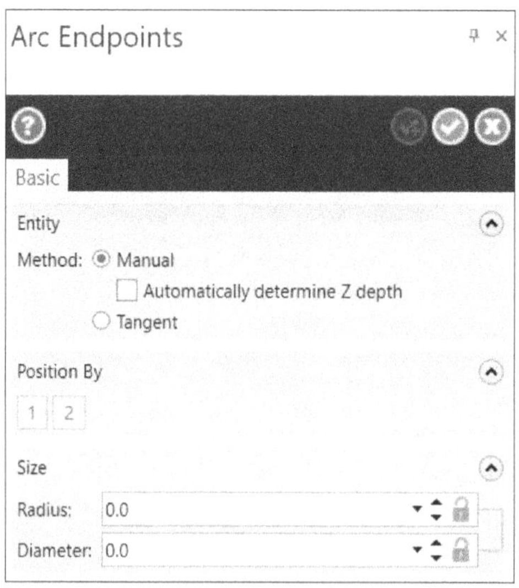

Figure-32. Arc Endpoints Manager

- Click at desired location to specify start point of arc. You will be asked to specify end point of the arc.
- Click at desired location to specify the end point. You will be asked to specify circumferential point of the arc.
- Click at desired location to specify circumferential point. The options to specify radius/diameter of arc will be displayed in the **Manager**.
- Enter desired value of radius/diameter in respective edit box of the **Manager**. Preview of the arc will be displayed; refer to Figure-33.

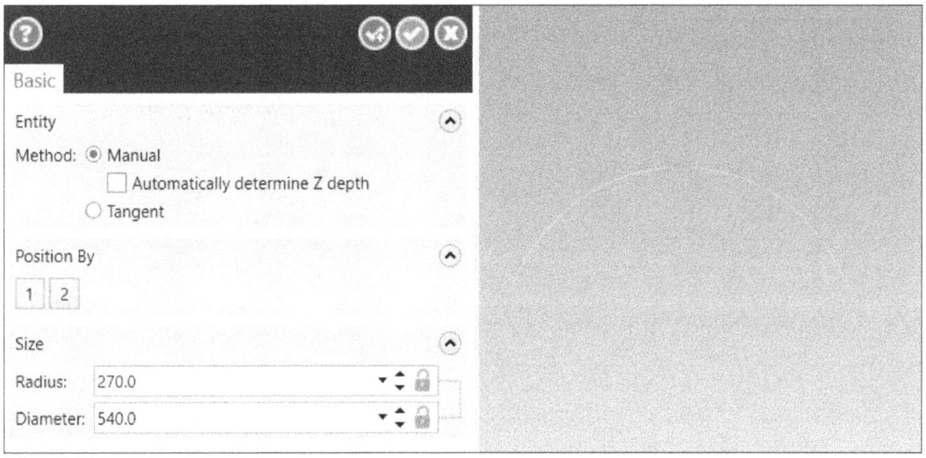

Figure-33. Preview of arc using end points

- Click on the **OK** button from the **Manager** to create the arc.

Creating Polar Arc

The **Arc Polar** tool is used to create arc of specified angular span. The procedure to use this tool is given next.

- Click on the **Arc Polar** tool from the **Arcs** group in the **Wireframe** tab of **Ribbon**. The **Arc Polar Manager** will be displayed; refer to Figure-34.

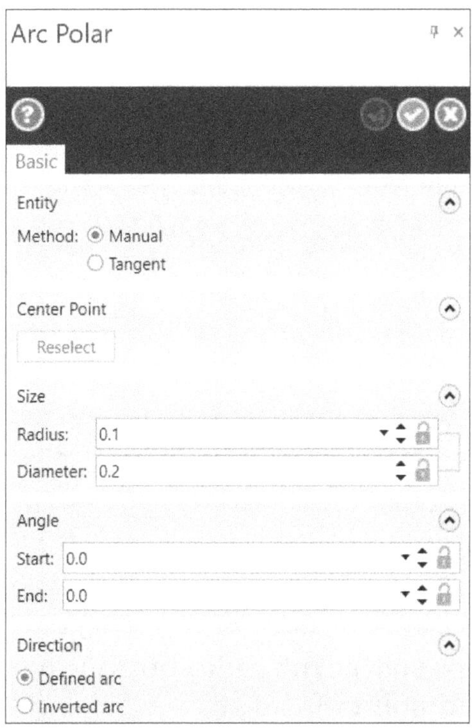

Figure-34. Arc Polar Manager

- Specify desired value in the **Radius** or **Diameter** edit box to define radius/diameter of arc, respectively.
- Similarly, specify the start point angle and end point angle of arc in **Angle** rollout of the **Manager**.
- Click at desired location to specify center point of the arc. Preview of the arc will be displayed; refer to Figure-35.

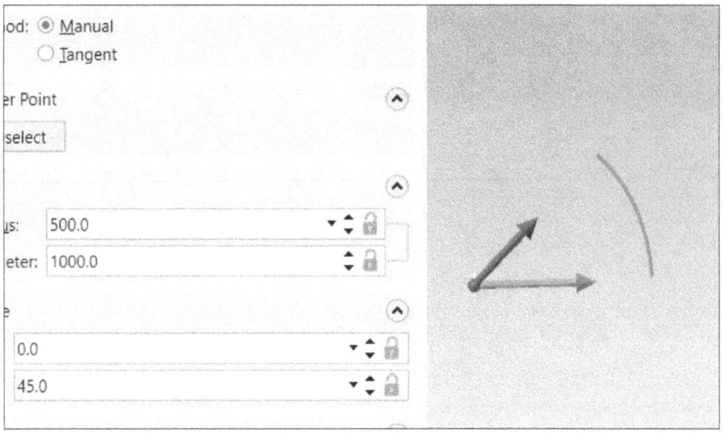

Figure-35. Preview of polar arc

- Click on the **OK** button from the **Manager** to create the arc.

Creating Arcs Using Polar Endpoints

The **Arc Polar Endpoints** tool is used to create an arc by specifying start point/end point of arc and angles. The procedure to use this tool is given next.

- Click on the **Arc Polar Endpoints** tool from the **Circle Edge Point** drop-down in the **Arcs** group of **Wireframe** tab in the **Ribbon**. The **Arc Polar Endpoints Manager** will be displayed; refer to Figure-36.

Figure-36. Arc Polar Endpoints Manager

- Select the **Start point** or **End point** radio button to specify whether you want to specify start point or end point of the arc.
- Set desired parameters as discussed earlier and click in the drawing area to place the arc.
- Click on the **OK** button from the **Manager** to create the arc.

CREATING SPLINES

The tools to create splines are available in the **Spline Manual** drop-down of **Splines** group in the **Wireframe** tab of **Ribbon**; refer to Figure-37. These tools are discussed next.

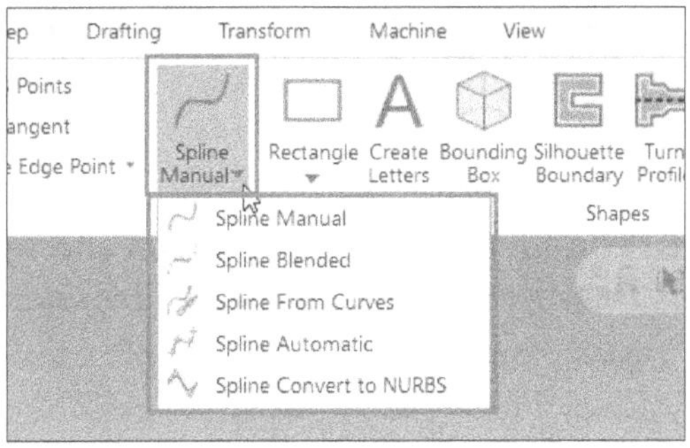

Figure-37. Spline Manual drop-down

Creating Spline Manually

The **Spline Manual** tool is used to create splines manually by specifying the vertices. The procedure to use this tool is given next.

- Click on the **Spline Manual** tool from the **Splines** group in the **Wireframe** tab of **Ribbon**. The **Spline Manual Manager** will be displayed; refer to Figure-38.

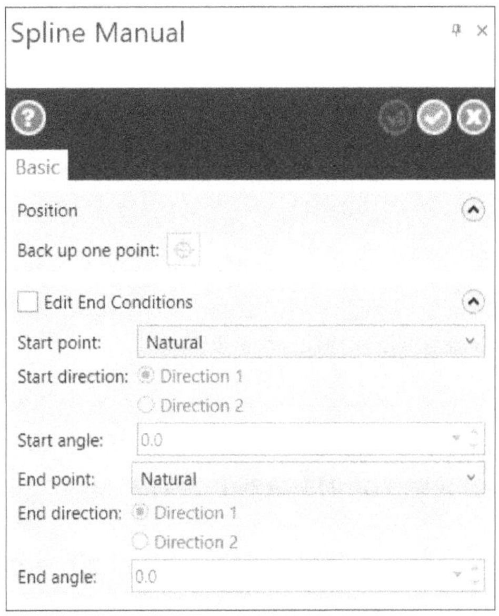

Figure-38. Spline Manual Manager

- Set desired parameters in the **Manager** and click in the drawing area to specify start point, mid point, and end point of the spline.
- After specifying desired points, press **ENTER**. Preview of the spline will be displayed; refer to Figure-39.
- Click on the **OK** button to create the spline and exit the tool.

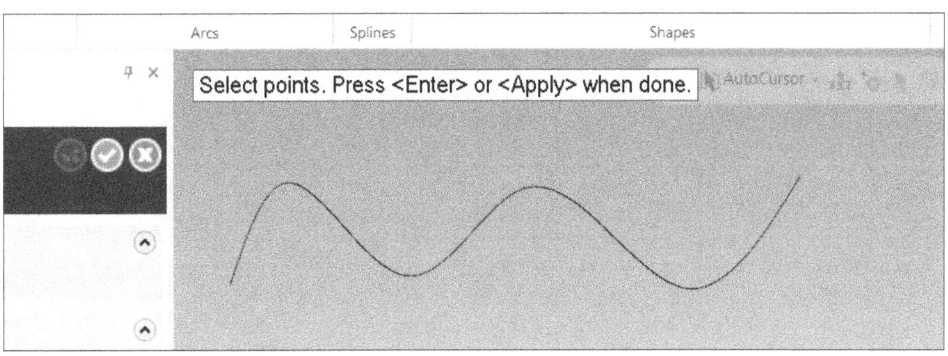

Figure-39. Preview of spline

Creating Blended Spline

The **Spline Blended** tool is used to join two curves by a spline. The procedure to use this tool is given next.

- Click on the **Spline Blended** tool from the **Spline Manual** drop-down in the **Splines** group of **Wireframe** tab in the **Ribbon**. The **Spline Blended Manager** will be displayed; refer to Figure-40.

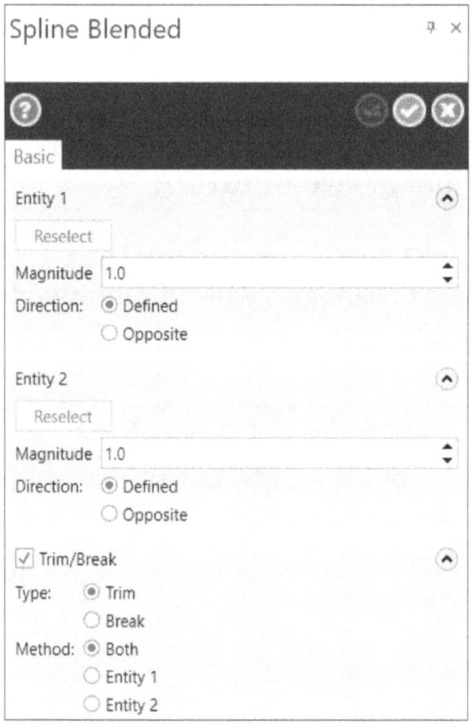

Figure-40. Spline Blended Manager

- Specify desired parameters in the **Manager**. Note that generally, direction of second entity is set to opposite.
- After setting desired parameters, select the two entities. Preview of blended spline will be displayed; refer to Figure-41.

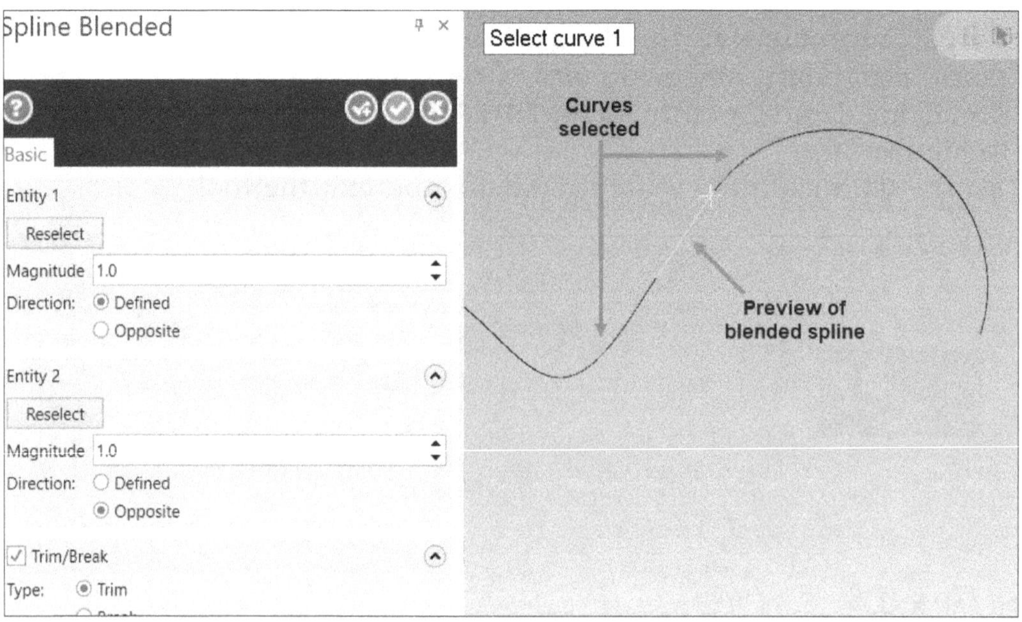

Figure-41. Preview of blended spline

- Click on the **OK** button to create the spline.

Creating Spline from Curves

The **Spline From Curves** tool is used to create spline based on geometry of other curves. The procedure to use this tool is given next.

- Click on the **Spline From Curves** tool from the **Spline Manual** drop-down in the **Splines** group of **Wireframe** tab in the **Ribbon**. The **Spline Curves Manager** will be displayed with **Wireframe Chaining** selection box; refer to Figure-42.

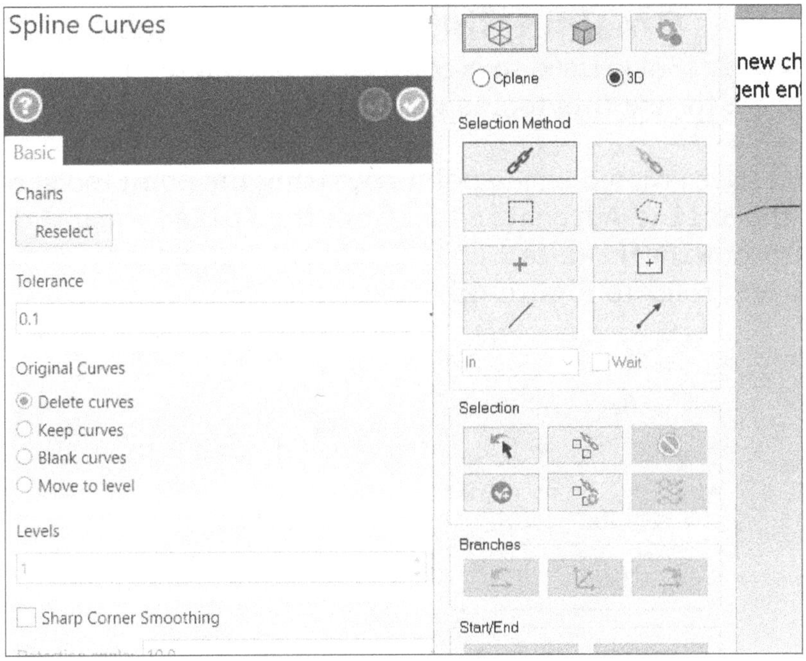

Figure-42. Spline Curves Manager with Wireframe Chaining selection box

- Select a curve from the curve chain and then use the buttons in **Start/End** area of the **Wireframe Chaining** box to select complete chain; refer to Figure-43.

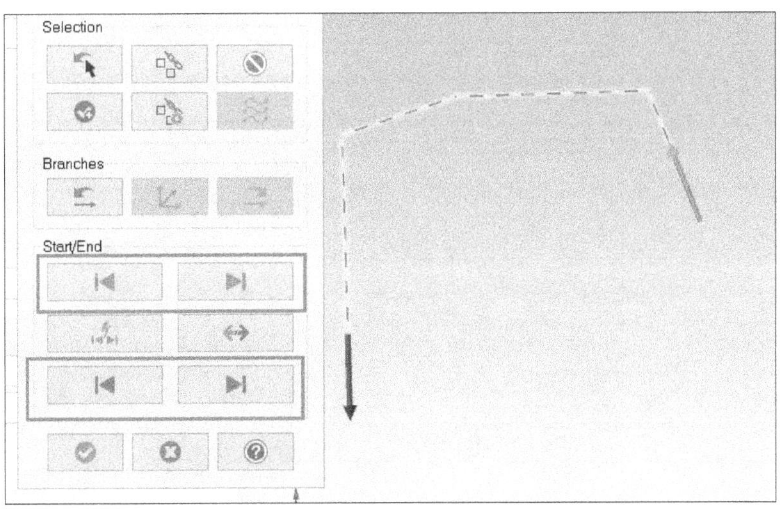

Figure-43. Chain selection of geometry

- After selecting desired geometry chain, click on the **OK** button from the **Wireframe Chaining** selection box. The options of **Spline Curves Manager** will be activated.

- Select desired radio button from the **Original Curves** rollout of **Manager** to define what will happen to original curve after creating spline. Generally, we select the **Delete curves** radio button to delete original curves after creating spline.
- Set desired value of deviation allowed in spline from original curves in the **Tolerance** edit box.
- Select the **Sharp Corner Smoothing** check box to smoothen sharp corners in the curve and specify desired parameters in the edit boxes below it.
- After specifying the parameters, click on the **OK** button from the **Manager**. The spline curve will be created.

Creating Spline using Points

The **Spline Automatic** tool is used to create spline through string of points in drawing area. The procedure to use this tool is given next.

- Make sure you have created string points by using the point tools; refer to Figure-44 and click on the **Spline Automatic** tool from the **Spline Manual** drop-down in the **Splines** group of **Wireframe** tab in the **Ribbon**. The **Spline Automatic Manager** will be displayed; refer to Figure-45.

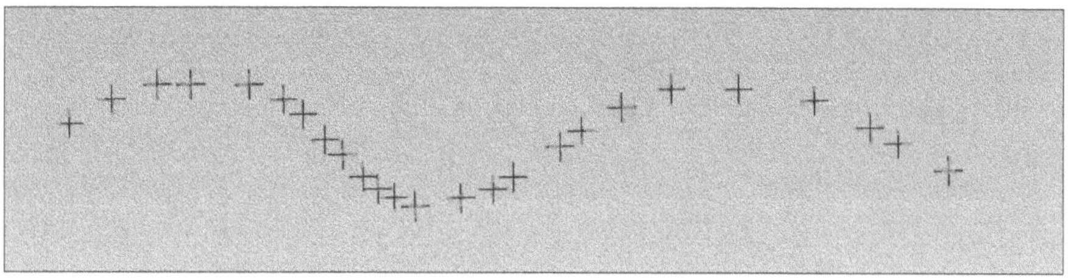

Figure-44. String of points

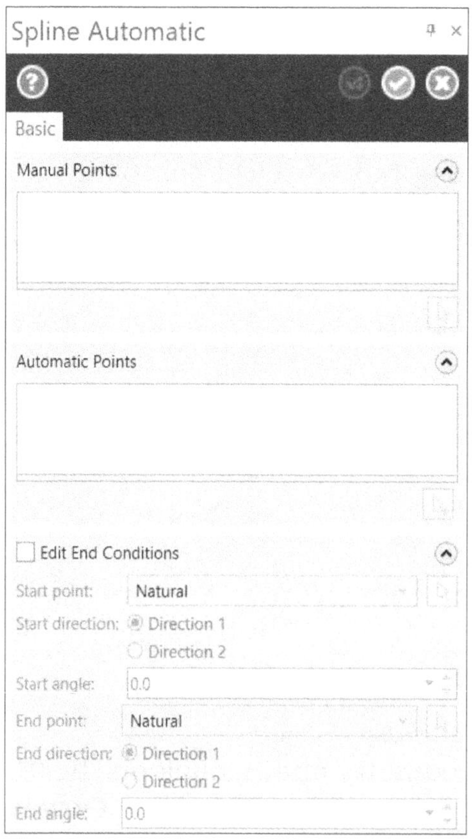

Figure-45. Spline Automatic Manager

- Select the first point of point string. You will be asked to select second point.
- Select the point next to first point in string. You will be asked to select the last point of string.
- Select the last point in point string. The spline will be created; refer to Figure-46.
- Click on the **OK** button from the **Manager** to create spline and exit.

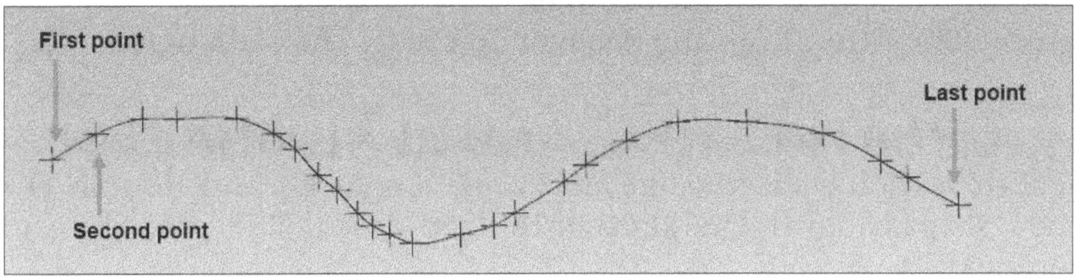

Figure-46. Spline created automatically

Converting Curves to NURBS Spline

The **Spline Convert to NURBS** tool is used to convert parametric curves like line, circle, and arc to NURBS (Non-uniform rational basis spline) splines. The procedure to use this tool is given next.

- Click on the **Spline Convert to NURBS** tool from the **Spline Manual** drop-down in the **Splines** group of **Wireframe** tab in the **Ribbon**. You will be asked to select a line, arc, spline, or surface to be converted to NURBS.
- Select desired curves and click on the **End Selection** button. The selected curves will be converted to NURBS splines.

CREATING A RECTANGLE

The **Rectangle** tool is used to create rectangle of desired dimension. The procedure to create a rectangle is given next.

- Click on the **Rectangle** tool from the **Rectangle** drop-down in the **Shapes** group of **Wireframe** tab in the **Ribbon**. The **Rectangle Manager** will be displayed; refer to Figure-47 and you will be asked to specify position of first corner point.

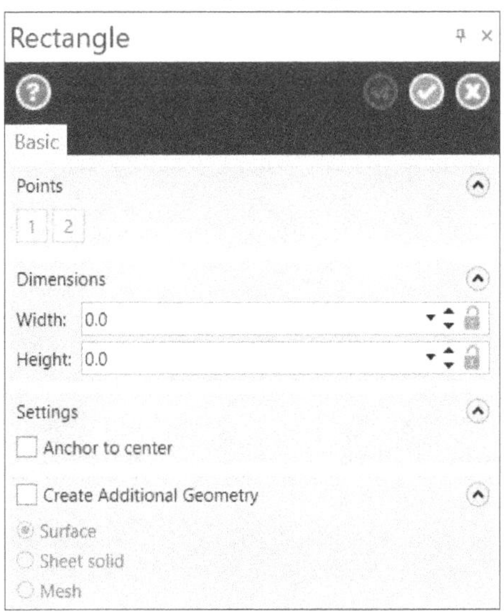

Figure-47. Rectangle Manager

- Click in the drawing area to specify first corner point of rectangle. You will be asked to specify position of second corner point.
- Specify desired value of width and height of rectangle in the **Width** and **Height** edit boxes of the **Manager**, respectively and press **ENTER** to create the rectangle. Preview of rectangle will be displayed. You can also click in the drawing area to specify second corner point of rectangle.
- Click on the **OK** button from the **Manager** to create the rectangle.

CREATING RECTANGULAR SHAPES

You can create various shapes like obround, single D, and double D using the **Rectangular Shapes** tool in the **Rectangle** drop-down. The procedure to use this tool is given next.

- Click on the **Rectangular Shapes** tool from the **Rectangle** drop-down in the **Shapes** group of **Wireframe** tab in the **Ribbon**. The **Rectangular Shapes Manager** will be displayed; refer to Figure-48.
- Select desired radio button from the **Type** area to define shape of rectangular object to be created.
- Select the **Base point** or **2 points** radio button to define how the points of rectangle will be specified.
- Set the other parameters as desired and click in the drawing area to create rectangular shape; refer to Figure-49.
- Click on the **OK** button from the **Manager** to create rectangular shape and exit the tool.

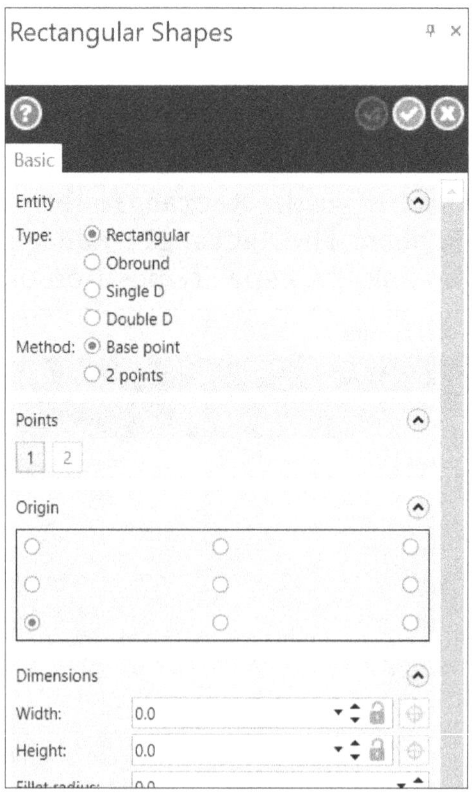

Figure-48. Rectangular Shapes Manager

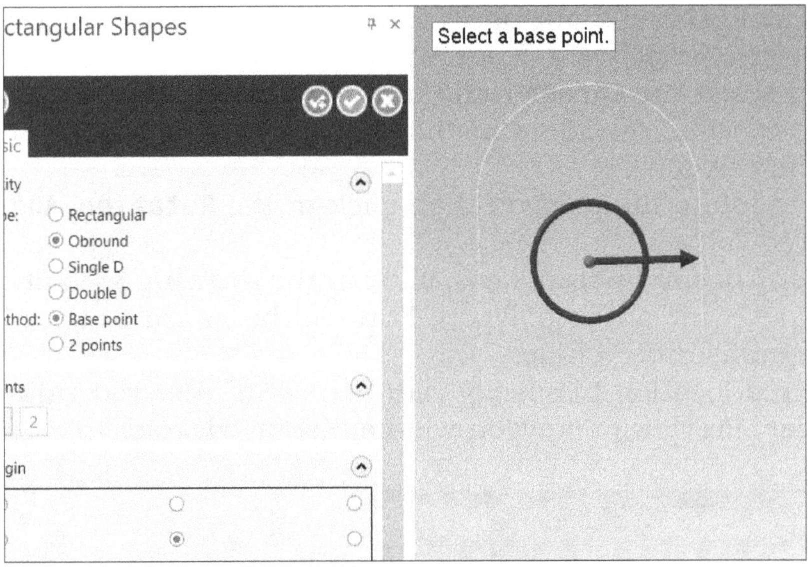

Figure-49. Preview of rectangular shape

CREATING POLYGON

The **Polygon** tool is used to create a polygon of desired number of sides. The procedure to use this tool is given next.

- Click on the **Polygon** tool from the **Rectangle** drop-down in the **Shapes** group of **Wireframe** tab in the **Ribbon**. The **Polygon Manager** will be displayed; refer to Figure-50.

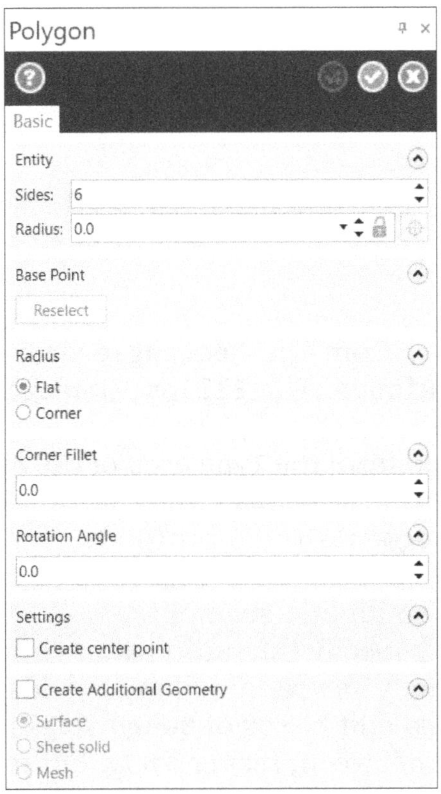

Figure-50. Polygon Manager

- Specify desired number of sides to be created for polygon in the **Sides** edit box of **Manager**.

- By default, the **Flat** radio button is selected, so you are asked to specify radius of inscribed circle for polygon. If you want to use circumscribed circle for creating polygon then select the **Corner** radio button in **Radius** rollout of **Manager**.
- Specify desired value of radius in the **Corner Fillet** edit box to apply fillet at corners in the polygon.
- If you want to rotate the polygon then click in the **Rotation Angle** edit box and specify desired value.
- After specifying desired parameters, click in the drawing area at desired location to specify base point of the polygon. You will be asked to specify radius of the inscribed/circumscribed circle.
- Click at desired location to specify radius or enter desired value in **Radius** edit box of **Manager**. Preview of polygon will be displayed; refer to Figure-51.

Figure-51. Preview of polygon

- Using the drag handle displayed in drawing area, you can rotate the polygon.
- Click on the **OK** button from the **Manager** to create the polygon and exit the tool.

Creating Ellipse

The **Ellipse** tool is used to create the ellipses in sketch. The procedure to use this tool is given next.

- Click on the **Ellipse** tool from the **Rectangle** drop-down in the **Shapes** group of **Wireframe** tab in the **Ribbon**. The **Ellipse Manager** will be displayed; refer to Figure-52.
- Select desired radio button from the **Type** area of the **Manager** to define what type of ellipse will be created. Select the **NURBS** radio button to create ellipse using NURBS splines. Select the **Arc segments** radio button to create ellipse as combination of multiple arc segments. Select the **Line segments** radio button to create ellipse as combination of multiple small line segments.
- Click in the **A** edit box and specify the radius along horizontal axis. Similarly, click in the **B** edit box and specify the radius along vertical axis.
- Click in the **Start** and **End** edit boxes of **Sweep Angle** rollout of **Manager** to define start and end point angle of sweep, respectively. For example, if you want to create only upper quadrant of ellipse then specify **0** as start point and **90** as end point of the ellipse.
- After specifying desired parameters, click on desired location. Preview of the ellipse will be displayed; refer to Figure-53.
- Click on the **OK** button from the **Manager** to create the ellipse.

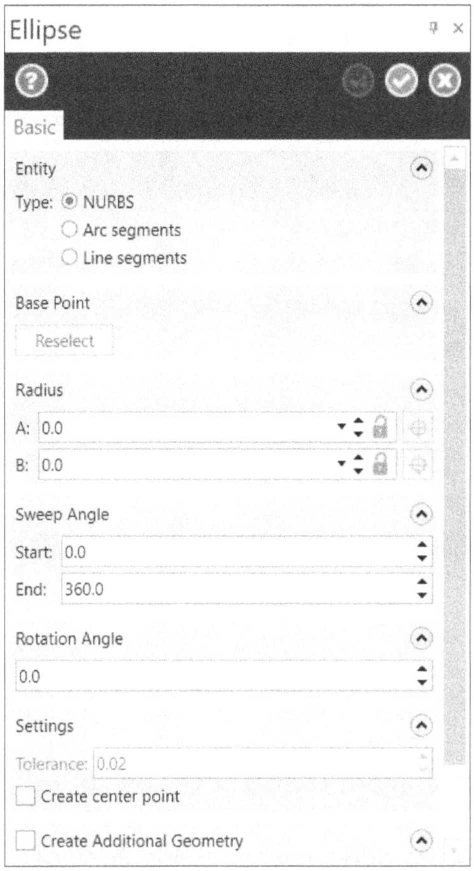

Figure-52. Ellipse Manager

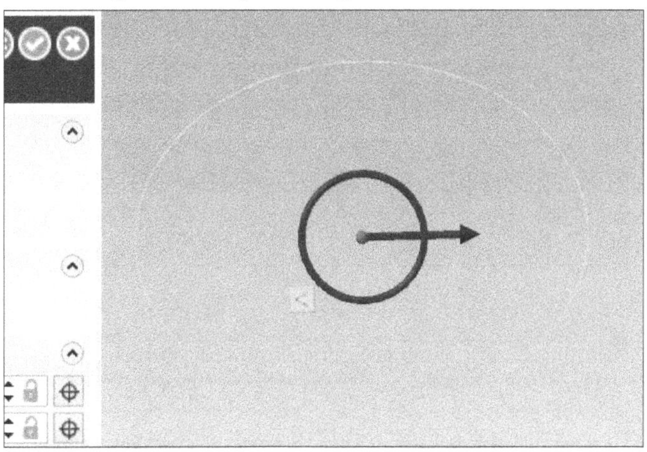

Figure-53. Preview of ellipse

CREATING HELIX CURVE

The **Helix** tool is used to create 3D helix curve of specified parameters. The procedure to use this tool is given next.

- Click on the **Helix** tool from the **Rectangle** drop-down in the **Shapes** group of **Wireframe** tab in the **Ribbon**. The **Helix Manager** will be displayed; refer to Figure-54.
- Specify the base radius of helix in the **Radius** edit box.
- Specify total height of helix in the **Height** edit box.
- Specify the total number of turns in the helix in **Revolutions** edit box.

- Specify the distance between two consecutive turns of helix in the **Pitch** edit box.
- You can also create tapered helix by specifying angle in the **Taper angle** edit box.

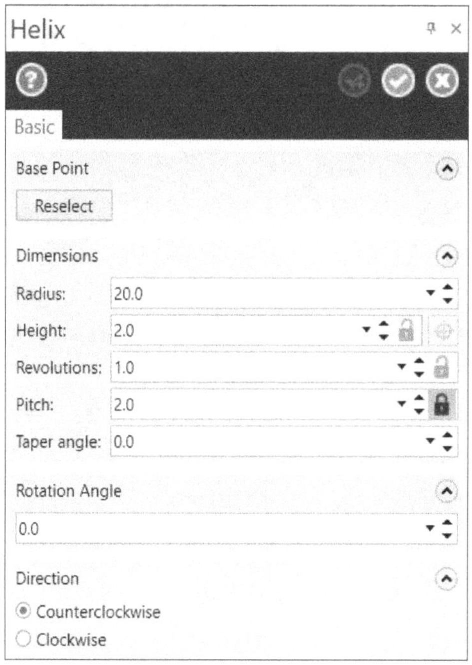

Figure-54. Helix Manager

- Select desired radio button from the **Direction** rollout to define direction of turns in the helix curve.
- Click at desired location to place the curve. Preview of helix curve will be displayed.
- Click on the **OK** button from the **Manager**. The helix curve will be created; refer to Figure-55.

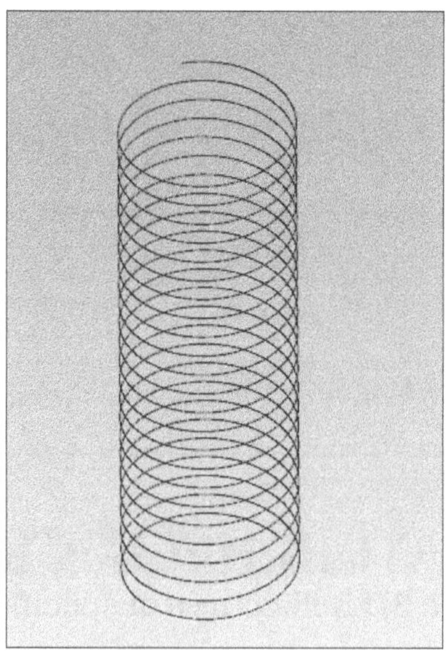

Figure-55. Helix curve created

CREATING SPIRAL CURVE

The **Spiral** tool is used to create spiral curve of specified diameter and number of turns. The procedure to use this tool is given next.

- Click on the **Spiral** tool from the **Rectangle** drop-down in the **Shapes** group of **Wireframe** tab in the **Ribbon**. The **Spiral Manager** will be displayed; refer to Figure-56.

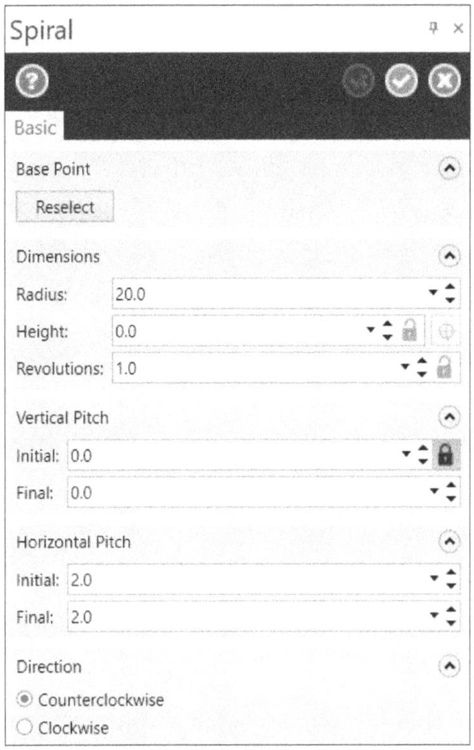

Figure-56. Spiral Manager

- Specify the parameters in **Manager** as discussed earlier for helix curve. Note that in case of spiral curve, you need to specify horizontal pitch also for creating the curve.
- After specifying parameters, click at desired location to place the curve. The preview of curve will be displayed.
- Click on the **OK** button from the **Manager** to create the curve; refer to Figure-57.

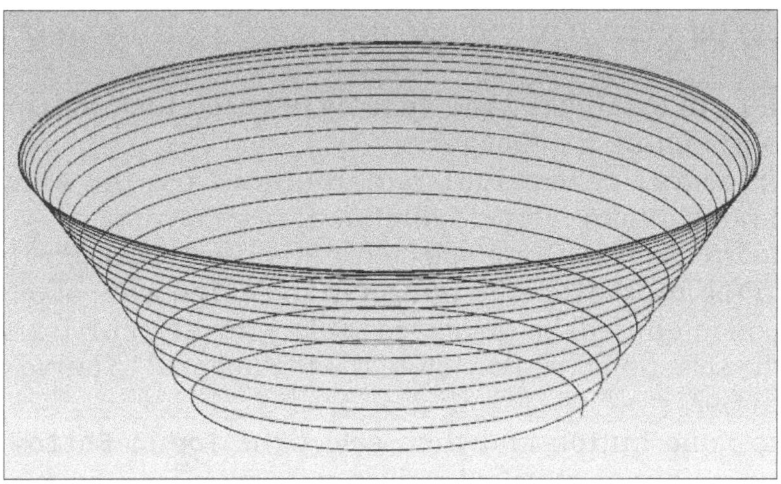

Figure-57. Spiral curve created

CREATING LETTERS

The **Create Letters** tool is used to create machinable geometry from text. The procedure to use this tool is given next.

- Click on the **Create Letters** tool from the **Shapes** group in the **Wireframe** tab of **Ribbon**. The **Create Letters Manager** will be displayed; refer to Figure-58.

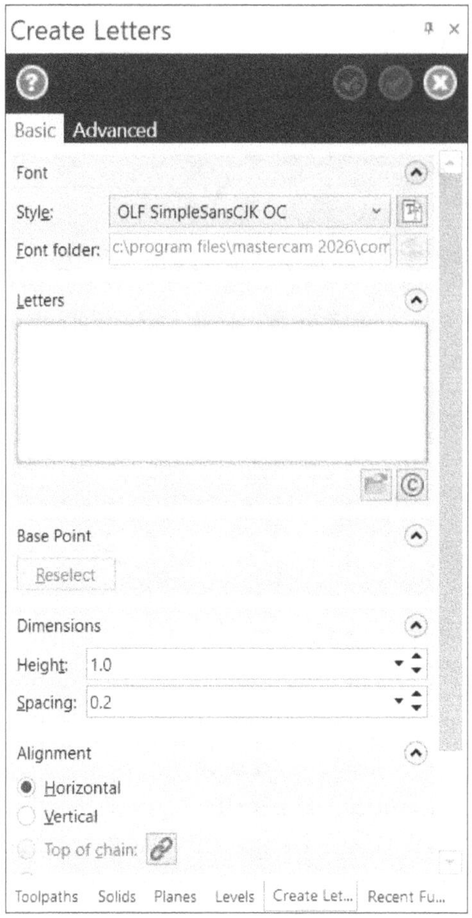

Figure-58. Create Letters Manager

- Select desired option from the **Style** drop-down to define font of text to be used for machining.
- Click in the **Letters** edit box and specify desired text. The text will get attached to cursor.
- Set desired value of text height and spacing between text in respective edit boxes of **Dimensions** rollout in the **Manager**.
- Select the **Horizontal** or **Vertical** radio button from the **Alignment** rollout to create text in horizontal or vertical direction, respectively.
- If you want to create text along selected curve then click on the **Select Chain** button next to **Top of chain** radio button in the **Alignment** rollout. The **Wireframe Chaining** selection box will be displayed. Select desired curve and click on the **OK** button from the selection box. Preview of the text aligned to curve will be displayed; refer to Figure-59.
- Select the **Arc** radio button and then select the **Top** or **Bottom** radio button to create text around arc of specified radius.
- Click on the **Advanced** tab from the **Manager** to create text note using old style and click on the **Note text** button. The **Note Text (Legacy)** dialog box will be displayed; refer to Figure-60.
- Set desired parameters in the dialog box and click on the **OK** button.
- After setting all the parameters for text, click at desired location to place the text and click on the **OK** button from the **Manager**.

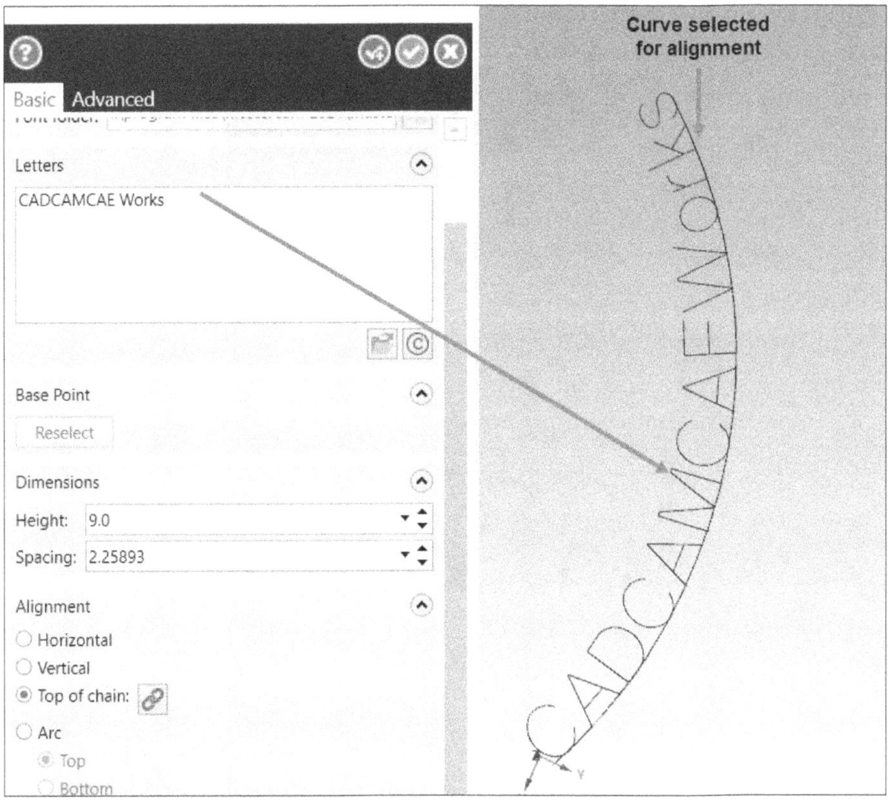

Figure-59. Text aligned to curve

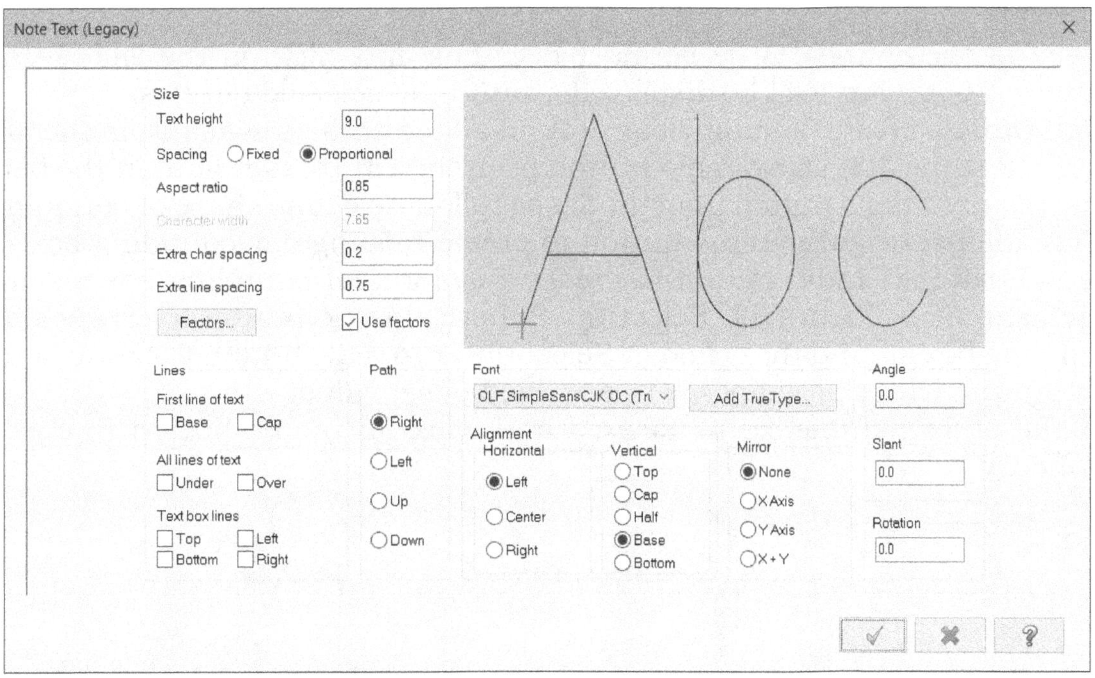

Figure-60. Note Text (Legacy) dialog box

CREATING BOUNDING BOX

The **Bounding Box** tool is used to create a rectangular or cylindrical 3 dimensional bounding box around selected objects. The procedure to use this tool is given next.

- Click on the **Bounding Box** tool from the **Shapes** group in the **Wireframe** tab of the **Ribbon**. The **Bounding Box Manager** will be displayed; refer to Figure-61 and you will be asked to select objects to be bound.

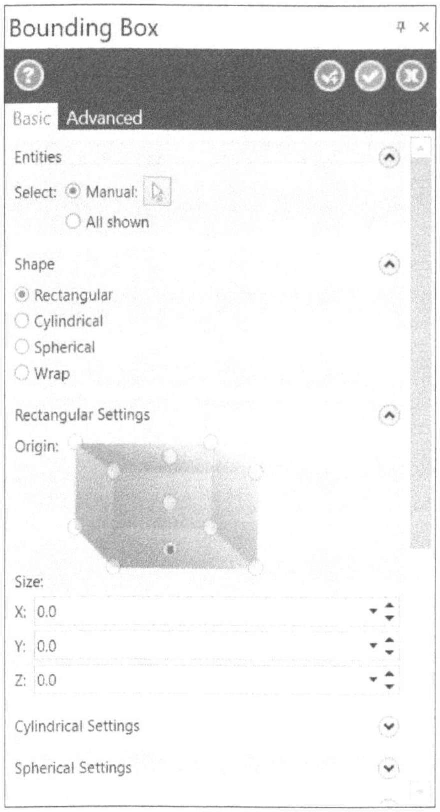

Figure-61. Bounding Box Manager

- Select all the entities to be bound by 3D box and click on the **End Selection** button. A boundary will be displayed around the selected entities.
- If you want to create bounding box around all the entities available in the 3D view then select the **All shown** radio button from the **Entities** rollout in the **Manager**.
- Select desired radio button from the **Shape** rollout to define shape of bounding box. Select the **Rectangular** radio button to create rectangular bounding box. Select the **Cylindrical** radio button to create a cylindrical bounding box around the entities; refer to Figure-62. Select the Spherical radio button to create a sphere bounding box around the cylinder. Select the **Wrap** radio button to create bounding box around irregular shapes with specified offset value.
- Set the other parameters as desired and click on the **OK** button to create the boundary.

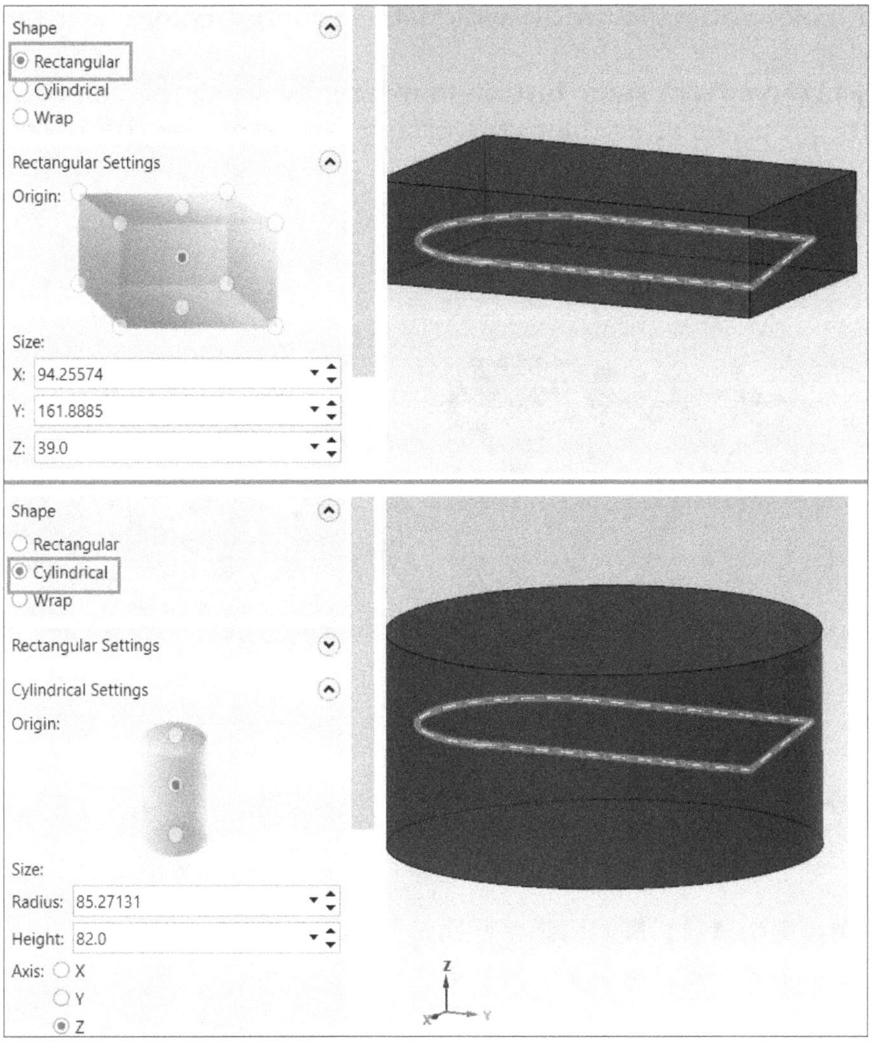

Figure-62. Rectangular or cylindrical bounding box examples

Similarly, you can use **Silhouette Boundary** tool to create boundary curves on selected solid, surface, or mesh body. You will learn about the **Turn Profile** and **Relief Groove** tools later in this book.

CONVERTING RASTER GRAPHIC TO VECTOR FILE

The **Raster to Vector** tool is used to convert raster graphic displayed in 3D view to vector graphic file. The procedure to use this tool is given next.

- Click on the **Raster to Vector** tool from the **Shapes** group in the **Wireframe** tab of the **Ribbon**. A message box will be displayed asking whether you want to merge new geometry with existing geometry.
- Select the **Yes** button to merge geometries and **No** button if you want to reinitialize the graphic screen.
- On selecting the **Yes** button, the **Open** dialog box will be displayed and you will be asked to select the raster image file to be converted to vector file.
- Select desired image file of format BMP, JPEG/JPG, or PNG from the dialog box and click on the **OK** button. The **Black/White conversion** dialog box will be displayed; refer to Figure-63.
- Select the **Linear Black/White conversion** radio button to linearly convert colored image to black & white vector graphic file. Using the **Threshold** slider, you can

specify the color intensity up to which the original colors will be converted to black or white.

- Select the **Filter colors** radio button to manually select the colors to be generated in the vector graphics after color conversion. You can use the **Tolerance** slider to set intensity of selected filter colors.

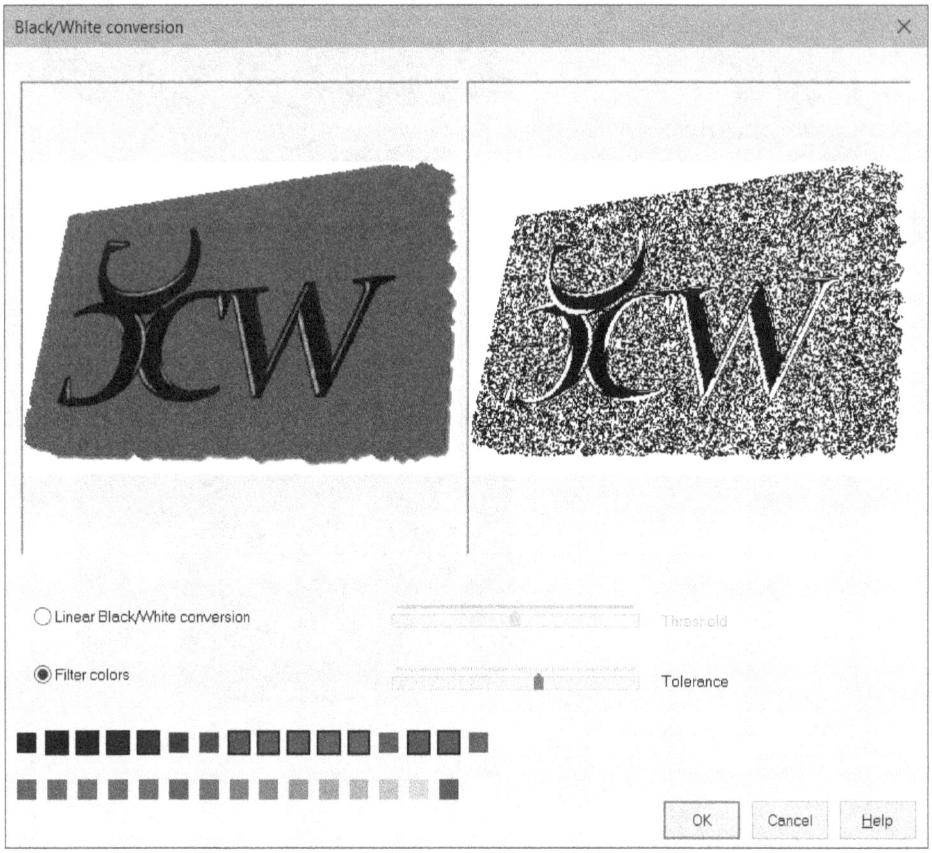

Figure-63. Black White conversion dialog box

- After setting desired parameters, click on the **OK** button. The **Raster to Vector** dialog box will be displayed with preview of converted graphics; refer to Figure-64.
- Set desired resolution of image file in the **Resolution DPI** drop-down. The DPI value defines the quality of image. Higher the value of DPI, better the quality of image. Note that high DPI also means more data size of file and finer machining.
- Select the **Create outlines** radio button to generate only outlines in the image. This option is useful when you are creating toolpath for vector graphics which is large enough for tool movement. Select the **Manually trace bitmap image** radio button to place actual image file in the background of 3D view for manual tracing. Select the **Create center lines** radio button to create arcs and lines for vector graphics. Note that this radio button is not available for spline fit curves.
- Select the **Background bitmap** check box to set desired color at the background of image. After selecting check box, click on the button next to the check box for defining background color.
- Select desired options from the **Optimize for** and **Accuracy** drop-downs in the **Spline Parameters** area of the dialog box.
- After setting desired parameters, click on the **OK** button from the dialog box. Preview of outlines will be displayed; refer to Figure-65 (if **Create outlines** radio button has been selected).

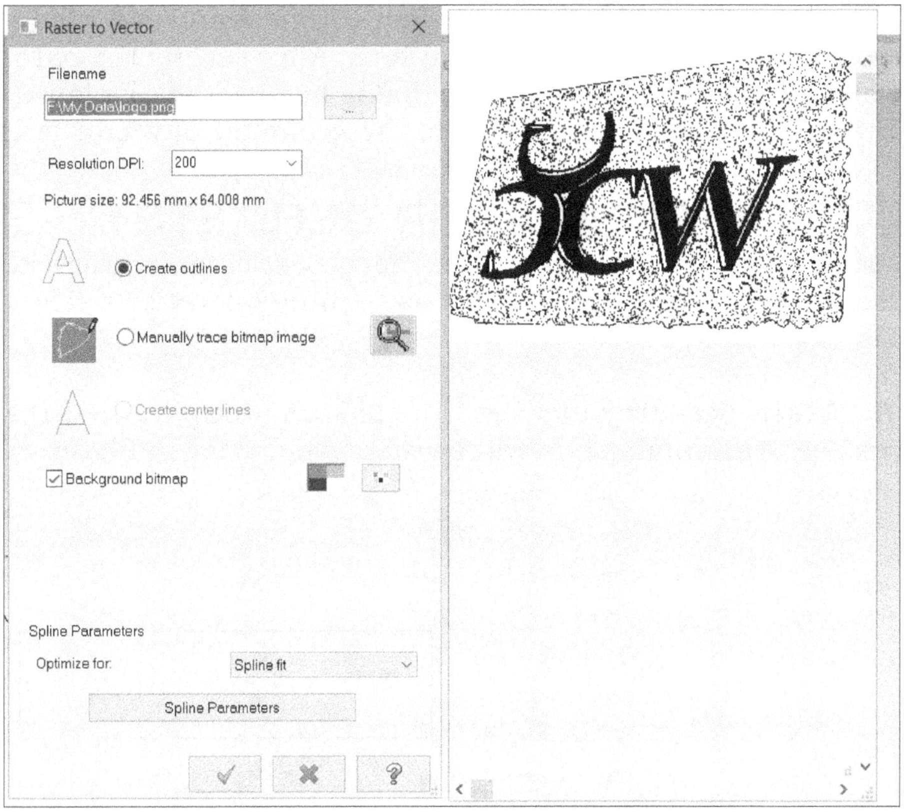

Figure-64. Raster to Vector dialog box

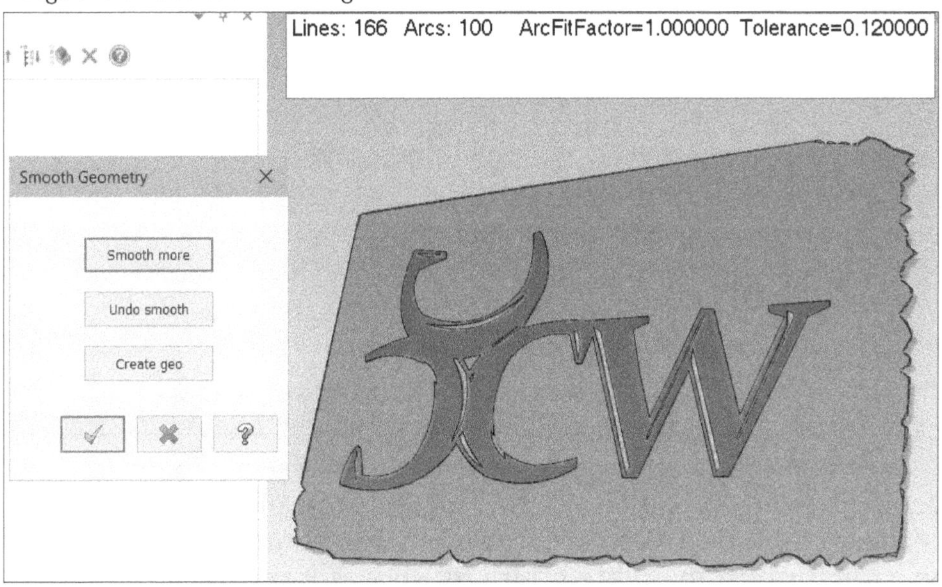

Figure-65. Preview of vector graphics outlines

- Select the **Smooth more** button to smoothen the vector graphics. The **Smooth** dialog box will be displayed; refer to Figure-66.

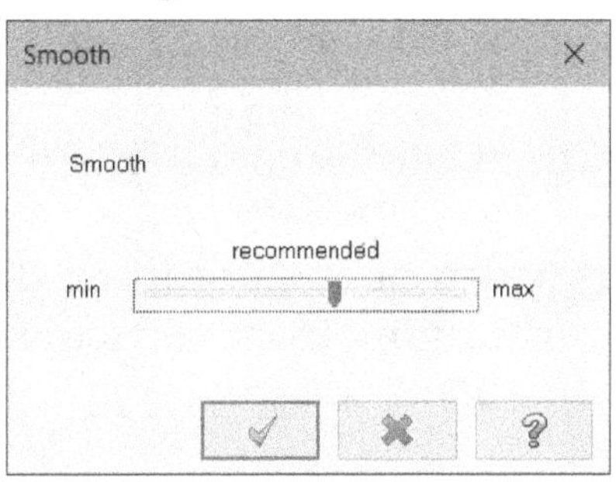

Figure-66. Smooth dialog box

- Move the slider towards right for increasing smoothness and move the slider towards left to decrease smoothness of vector graphics. After setting the parameters, click on the **OK** button. The **Smooth Geometry** dialog box will be displayed again.
- Click on the **Create geo** button to create the geometry of vector graphics.

CREATING STAIR GEOMETRY

The **Stair Geometry** tool is used to create geometry of stair with specified parameters. The tool is useful for woodworking as well as turning operations. The procedure to use this tool is given next.

- Click on the **Stair Geometry** tool from the **Shapes** group in the **Wireframe** tab of the **Ribbon**. The **Stair** dialog box will be displayed; refer to Figure-67.

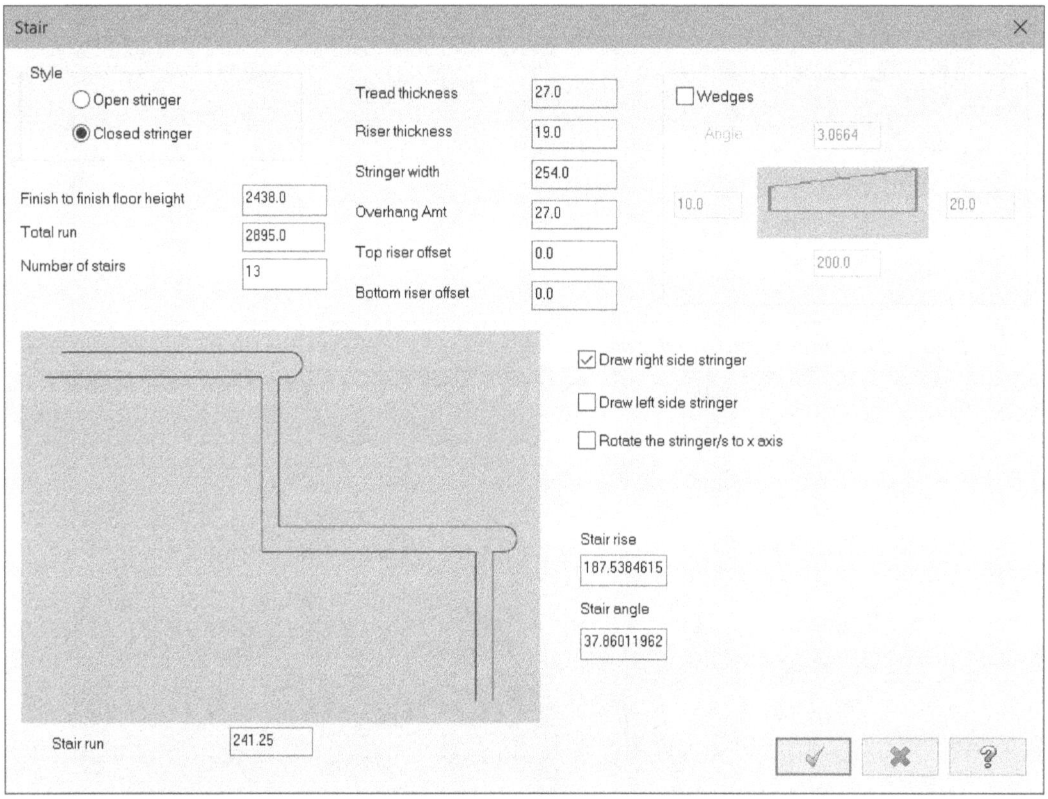

Figure-67. Stair dialog box

- Select desired radio button from the **Style** area of the dialog box. Select the **Open stringer** radio button to create single line steps of stairs. Select the **Closed stringer** radio button to create stairs as shown in preview of Figure-67.
- Specify total height of stairs in the **Finish to finish floor height** edit box.
- Specify the total width of stairs in the **Total run** edit box.
- Specify total number of stairs in the **Number of stairs** edit box.
- Specify the thickness of horizontal section of each stair in the **Tread thickness** edit box.
- Specify the thickness of vertical section of each stair in the **Riser thickness** edit box.
- Specify the total horizontal width of each stair in the **Stringer width** edit box.
- Specify the width of stair overhanging from vertical section of stair in the **Overhang Amt** edit box.

- Specify desired values in the **Top riser offset** and **Bottom riser offset** edit boxes to define offset distance for top riser and bottom riser, respectively.
- Specify desired height of each stair in the **Stair run** edit box.
- Select the **Wedges** check box to create stairs in the form of wedges; refer to Figure-68. Specify desired parameters in the **Wedges** area of the dialog box.

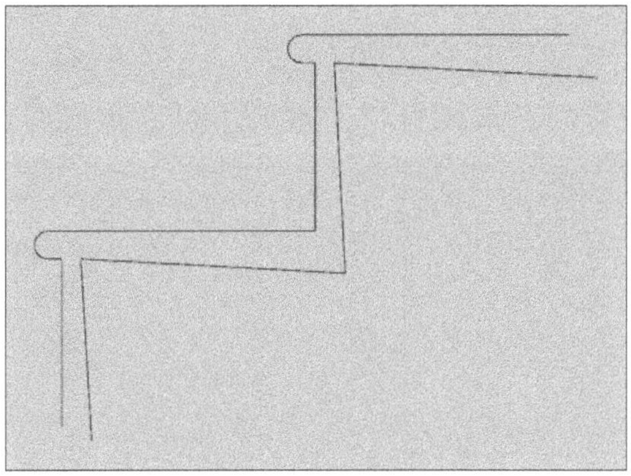

Figure-68. Stairs in the form of wedges

- Select the **Draw right side stringer** check box to make right-sided stairs.
- Select the **Rotate the stringer/s to x axis** check box to rotate stringers about x axis.
- Click on the **OK** button from the dialog box. You will be asked to specify location of stair's lower corner point.
- Click at desired location to place the stairs; refer to Figure-69.

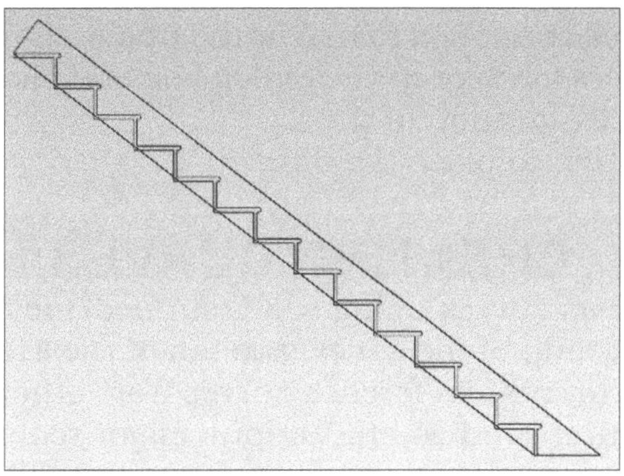

Figure-69. Stairs created

CREATING DOOR GEOMETRY

The **Door Geometry** tool is used to create door geometry in the 3D view. The procedure to use this tool is given next.

- Click on the **Door Geometry** tool from the **Shapes** group in the **Wireframe** tab of **Ribbon**. The **Door** dialog box will be displayed; refer to Figure-70.

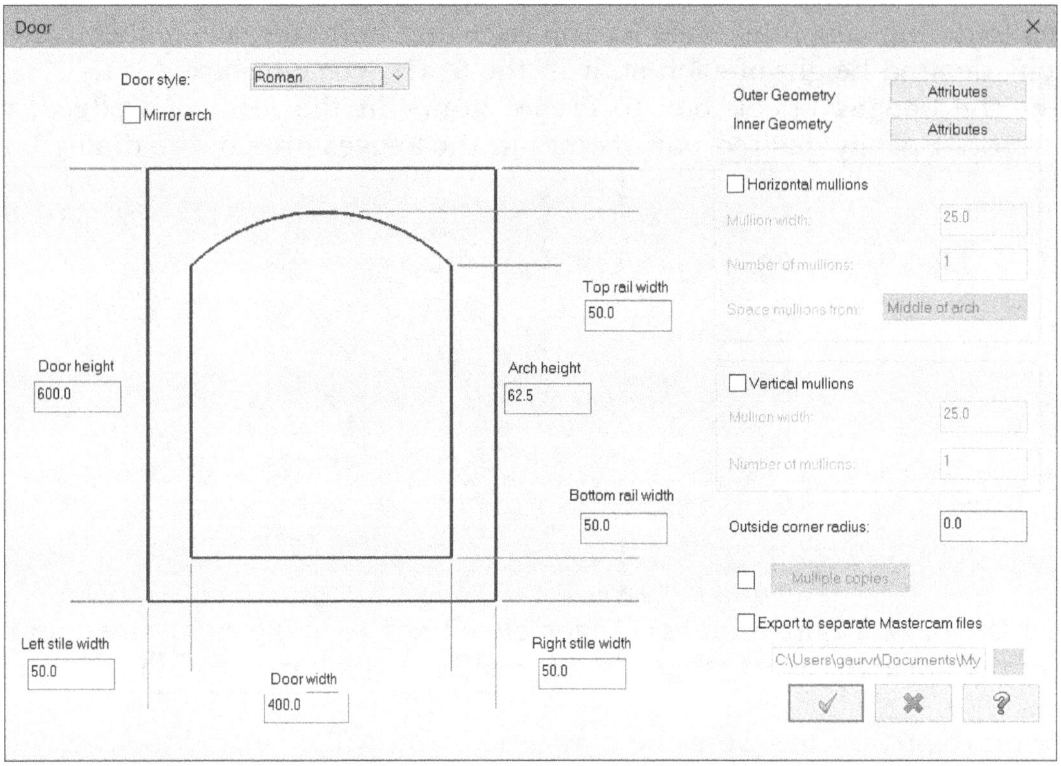

Figure-70. Door dialog box

- Select desired option from the **Door style** drop-down to modify style of doors.
- Select the **Mirror arch** check box to mirror the upper shape of door at the bottom.
- Set desired parameters for door in the dialog box and click on the **OK** button. You will be asked to specify location of door.
- Click at desired location to place the door.

CREATING CURVES

The tools to create various curves using solid/surface/mesh body as reference are available in the **Curves** group of the **Wireframe** tab of the **Ribbon**; refer to Figure-71. You can use these tools to create reference curves from other objects to use them for creating toolpaths, features, and so on. Various major tools of this group are given next.

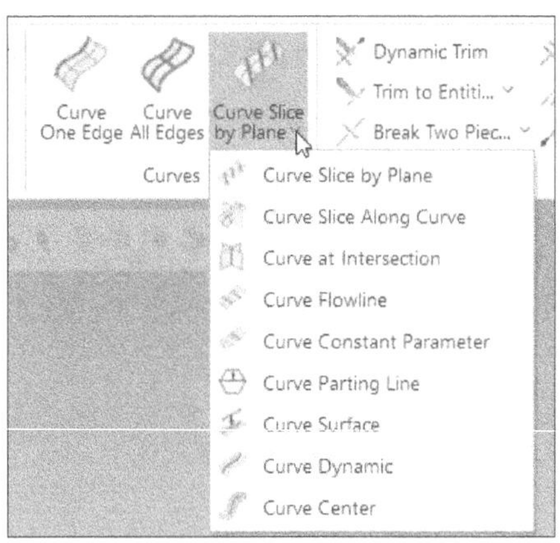

Figure-71. Curves group

Creating Curve using Single Edge

The **Curve One Edge** tool is used to generate curve using selected edge of solid, surface, or mesh model. The procedure to use this tool is given next.

- Click on the **Curve One Edge** tool from the **Curves** group in the **Wireframe** tab of the **Ribbon**. The **Curve On One Edge Manager** will be displayed; refer to Figure-72.

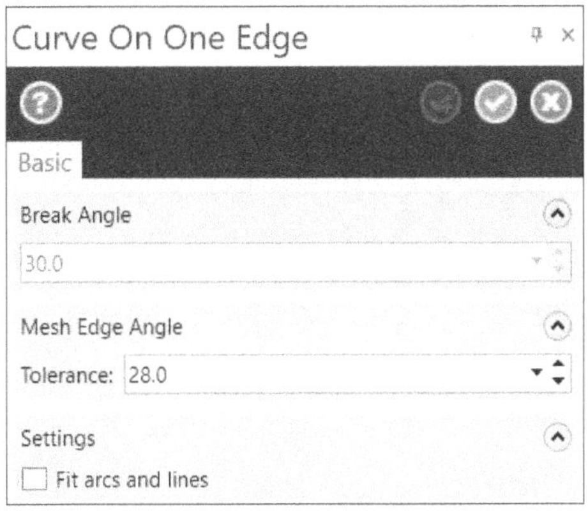

Figure-72. Curve On One Edge Manager

- Select desired edge from the model to generate a new wireframe curve; refer to Figure-73.

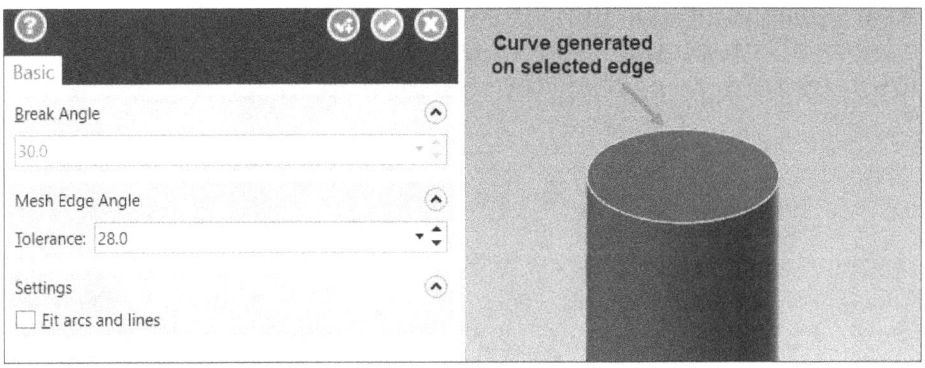

Figure-73. Curve generated from one edge

- Select the **Fit arcs and lines** check box if you want to include arcs and lines expected to be created after trimmed boundary of selected surface.
- Specify desired value in the **Break Angle** edit box to define the angle limit for trimmed surface edge. When angle of edge goes above this value then software defines that point as end point of curve generated from edge.
- Click on the **OK** button from the **Manager** to create the curve.

Similarly, you can use the **Curve All Edges** tool from the **Curves** group to generate curves from all the edges of the model.

Creating Curve using Slicing Plane

The **Curve Slice by Plane** tool is used to create curve at the intersection of selected plane and surface. The procedure to use this tool is given next.

- Click on the **Curve Slice by Plane** tool from the **Curve Slice by Plane** drop-down in the **Curves** group of the **Ribbon**. The Curve Slice by Plane Manager will be displayed; refer to Figure-74.

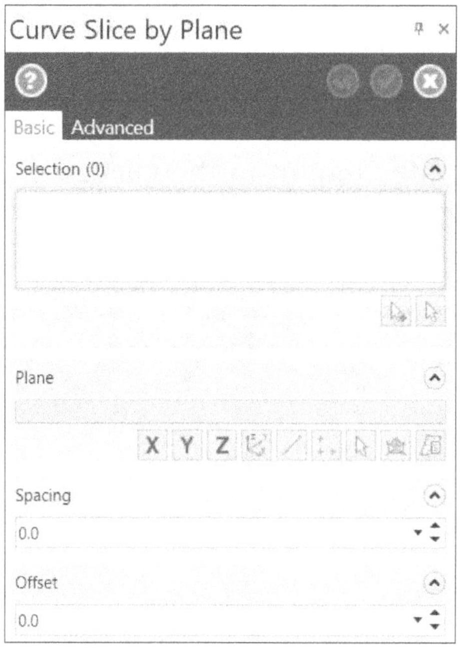

Figure-74. Curve Slice by Plane Manager

- Select the face(s)/surface(s) to be used for creating curve and click on the End Selection button from graphics area. You will be asked to select a slicing plane.
- Select the plane which is passing through selected face(s)/surface(s). You can select **X**, **Y**, **Z**, **Dynamic**, and other buttons in the **Plane** rollout to define plane. You will learn more about planes later in the book.
- After defining parameters, click on the **OK** button to create the curve; refer to Figure-75.

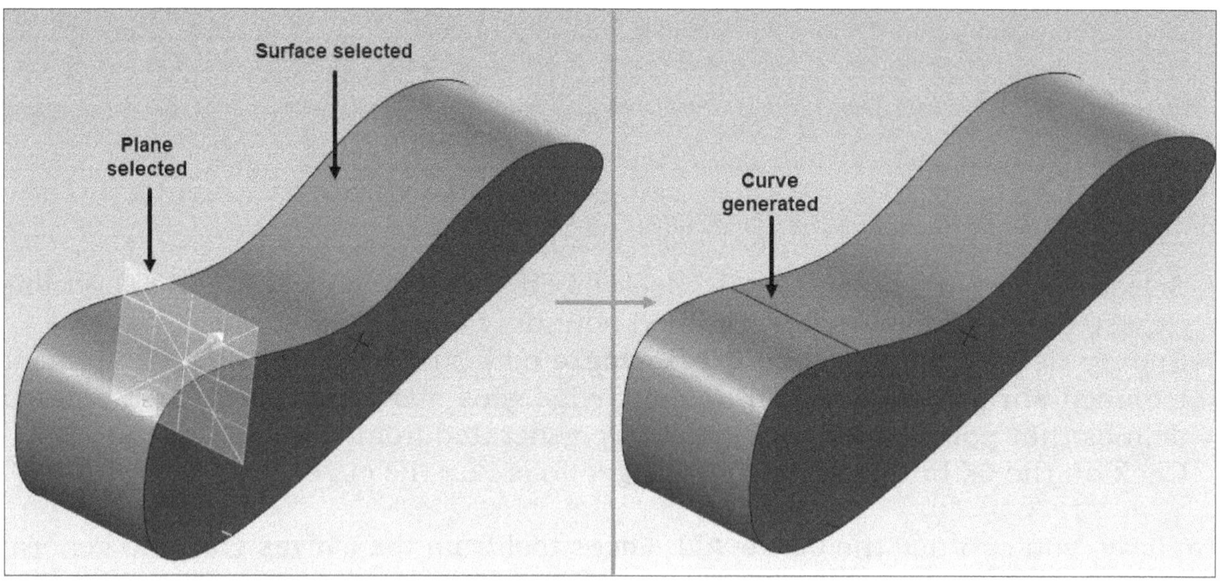

Figure-75. Curve by plane slicing

Similarly, you can use other tools of the Curves group to create reference curves for modeling and toolpath generation.

MODIFYING ENTITIES DYNAMICALLY

You can modify parameters of any wireframe entity by double-clicking on it and then using the key points to change parameters. On double-clicking the entity, key points will be displayed as shown in Figure-76.

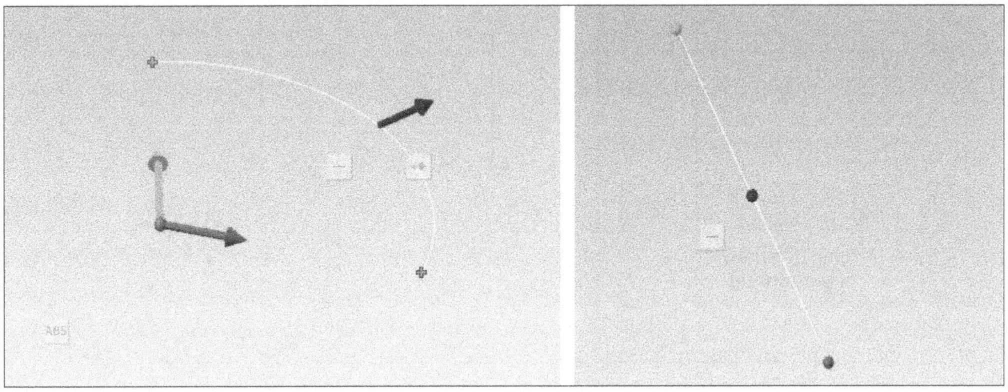

Figure-76. Dynamic keypoints

DYNAMICALLY TRIMMING

The **Dynamic Trim** tool is used to trim entities based on various dynamic methods like trimming single entity or multiple entity. The procedure to use this tool is given next.

- Click on the **Dynamic Trim** tool from the **Modify** group in the **Wireframe** tab of the **Ribbon**. The **Dynamic Trim Manager** will be displayed; refer to Figure-77.

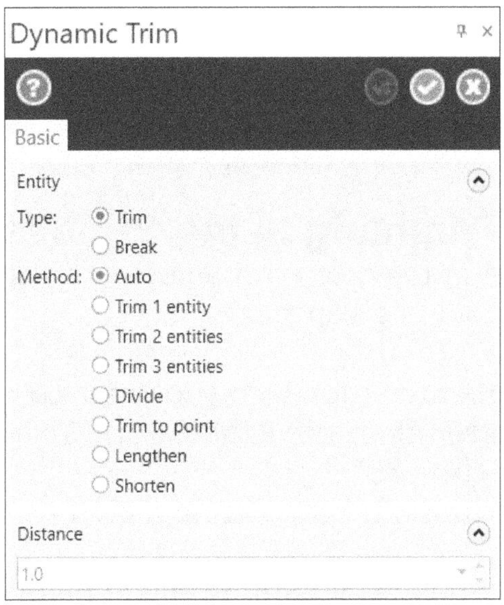

Figure-77. Dynamic Trim Manager

- Select the **Trim** radio button from **Type** section of **Manager** to trim selected entities. Select the **Break** radio button to split the entities at intersection point.
- Select the **Auto** radio button from the **Method** section to automatically select method for dynamically trimming based on selected entities. Select the **Trim 1 entity**, **Trim 2 entities**, or **Trim 3 entities** radio button to trim respective number of entity(s) using one reference trimming tool. Select the **Divide** radio button to delete segment of selected entity based on two nearest intersection points. Select the **Trim to point** radio button to trim/extend selected entity at specified point; refer to Figure-78. Select the **Lengthen** radio button from the **Manager** to increase the length of selected entity by value specified in the **Distance** edit box. Select the **Shorten** radio button to decrease the length of selected entity by specified value.
- Select desired entity(s) from the drawing area based on selected options in the **Manager** to trim/break/extend the entities.
- Click on the **OK** button from the **Manager** to apply changes and exit.

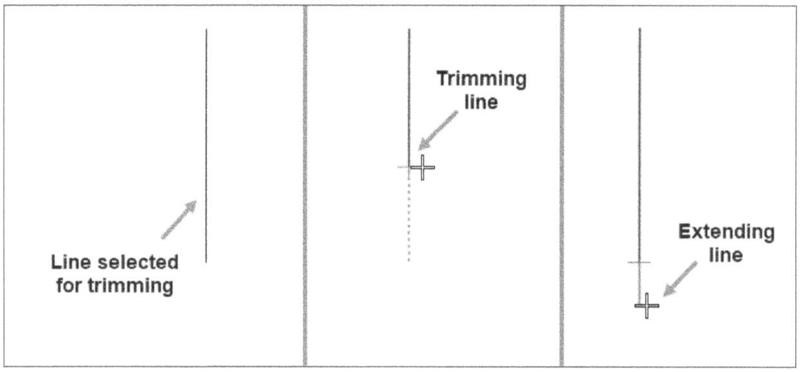

Figure-78. Using Trim to point option

TRIMMING ENTITIES

The tools to perform trimming are available in the **Trim to Entities** drop-down of the **Ribbon**; refer to Figure-79. Various tools of this drop-down are discussed next.

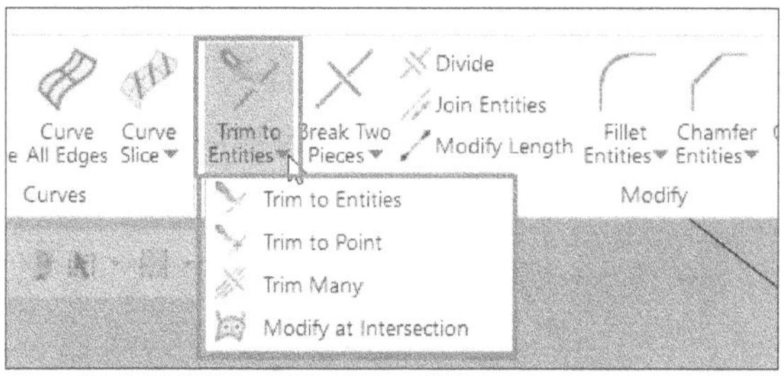

Figure-79. Trim to Entities drop-down

Trimming using Entities

The **Trim to Entities** tool is used to trim selected entity using the trimming tool. The procedure to use this tool is given next.

- Click on the **Trim to Entities** tool from the **Trim to Entities** drop-down in the **Modify** group of **Wireframe** tab in the **Ribbon**. The **Trim to Entities Manager** will be displayed; refer to Figure-80.
- Select the entity to be trimmed. You will be asked to select the entity to be used as cutting tool.
- Click on desired entity. Preview of trimming will be displayed; refer to Figure-81.

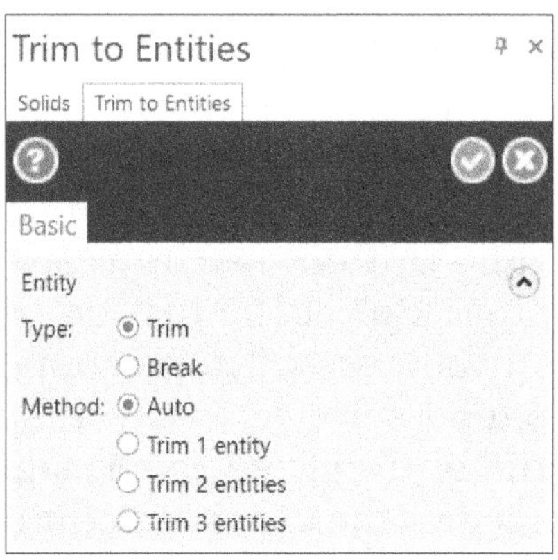

Figure-80. Trim to Entities Manager

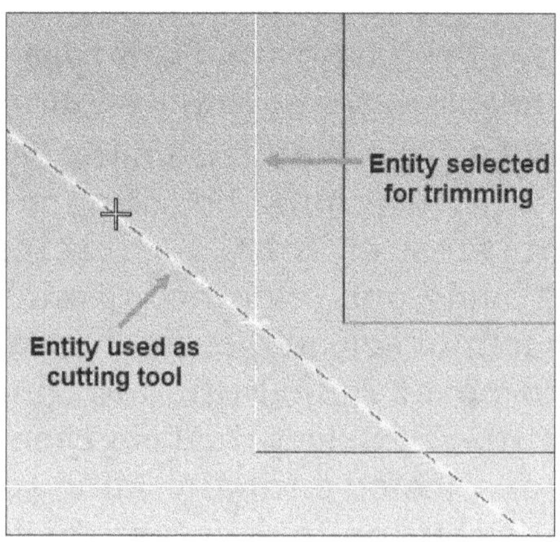

Figure-81. Entities selected for trimming

- Click on the **OK** button from the **Manager** to perform trimming.

Trimming Entity at Desired Point

The **Trim to Point** tool is used to trim selected entity at desired point. The procedure to use this tool is given next.

- Click on the **Trim to Point** tool from the **Trim to Entities** drop-down in the **Modify** group of **Wireframe** tab in the **Ribbon**. The **Trim to Point Manager** will be displayed; refer to Figure-82.
- Select the **Trim** radio button to trim selected entity. If you want to break selected entity at desired point then select the **Break** radio button.
- Select the entity that you want to trim. You will be asked to specify a point on the entity at which entity will be trimmed or broken.
- Click at desired location on the entity. The selected entity will be trimmed; refer to Figure-83.

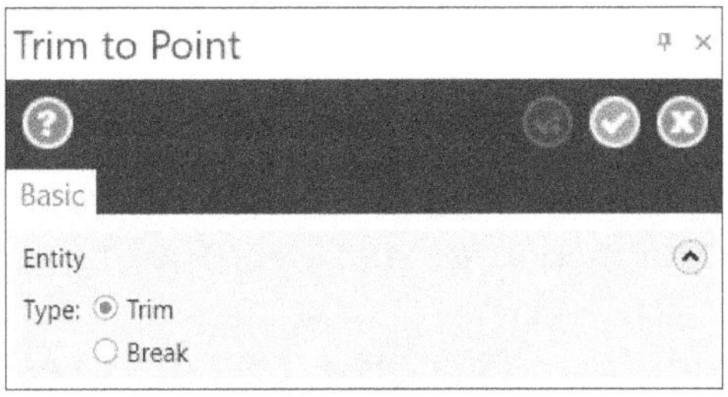

Figure-82. Trim to Point Manager

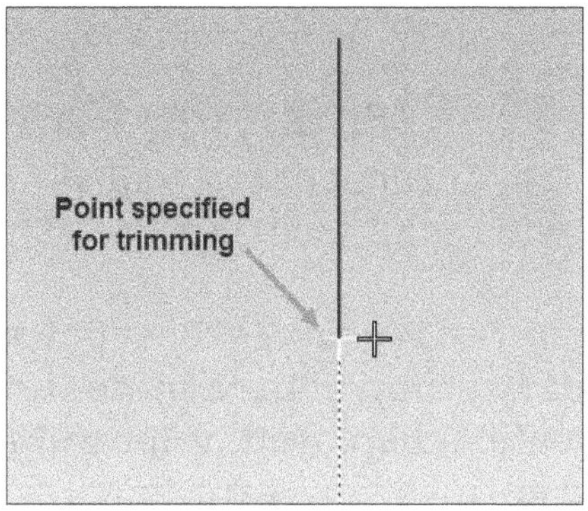

Figure-83. Specifying point for trimming

- Click on the **OK** button from the **Manager**.

Trimming Multiple Entities

The **Trim Many** tool is used to trim multiple entities using selected trimming curve. The procedure to use this tool is given next.

- Click on the **Trim Many** tool from the **Trim to Entities** drop-down in the **Modify** group of **Wireframe** tab in the **Ribbon**. The **Trim Many Manager** will be displayed; refer to Figure-84.

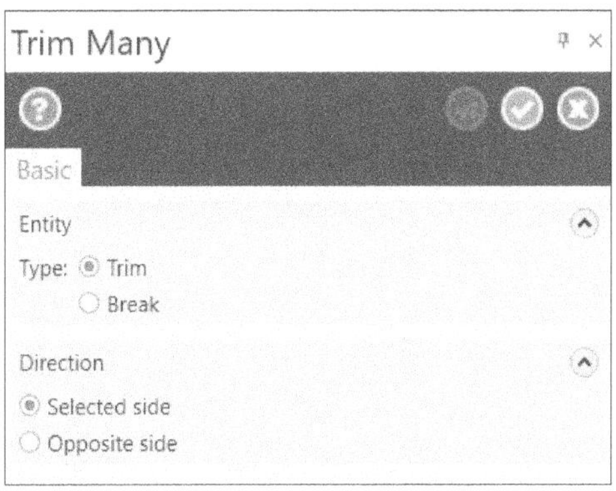

Figure-84. Trim Many Manager

- Set the parameters as discussed earlier in the **Manager**.
- Select all the entities to be trimmed and click on the **End Selection** button. You will be asked to select the entity to be used as trimming curve.
- Select desired intersecting curve. You will be asked to specify which side is to be trimmed saved after trimming.

- Click on desired side, the selected entities will be trimmed; refer to Figure-85.
- Click on the **OK** button from the **Manager** to perform trimming.

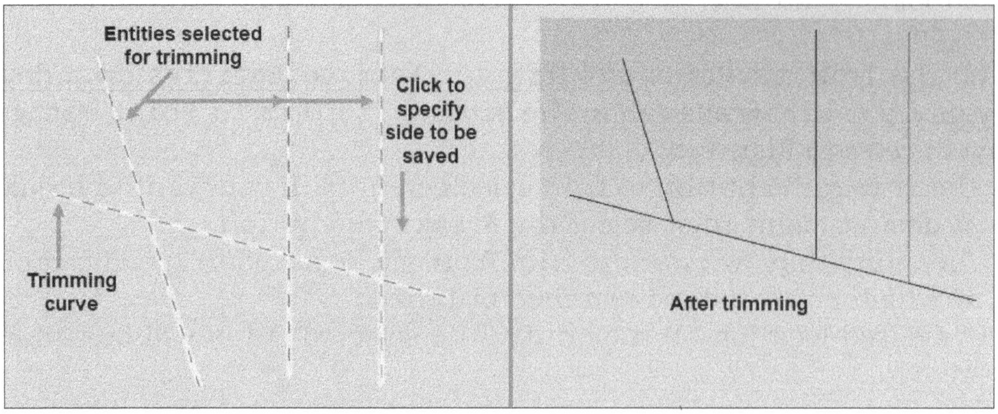

Figure-85. Trimming multiple curves

Modifying Entities at Intersection

The **Modify at Intersection** tool is used to trim/break selected entities at their intersection with solid face/surface. The procedure to use this tool is given next.

- Click on the **Modify at Intersection** tool from the **Trim to Entities** drop-down in the **Modify** group of **Wireframe** tab in the **Ribbon**. The **Modify at Intersection Manager** will be displayed; refer to Figure-86.
- Select the entities you want to trim/break from the 3D view and click on the **End Selection** button. You will be asked to select the surface/face used as trimming tool.
- Select desired face/surface intersecting with the curves. Preview of the trim operation will be displayed; refer to Figure-87.

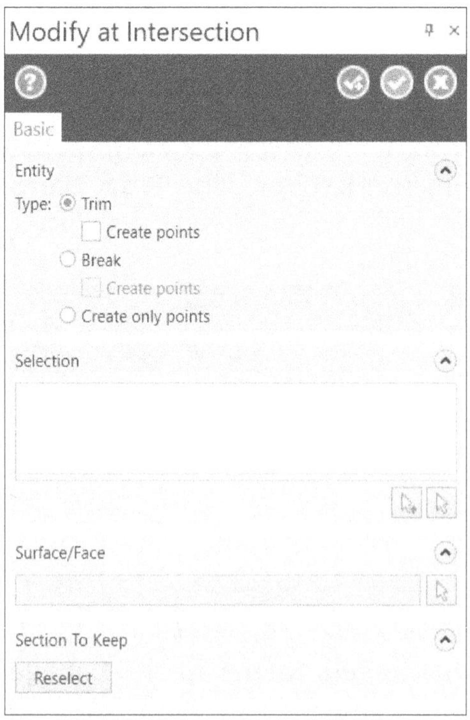

Figure-86. Modify at Intersection Manager

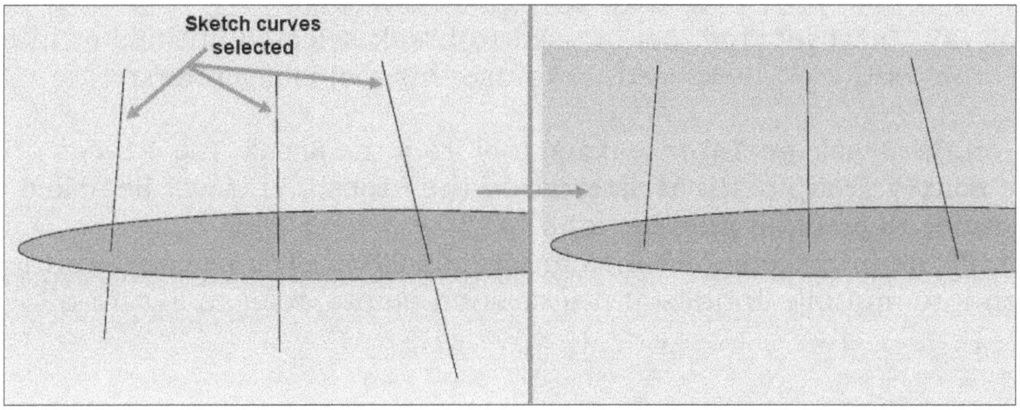

Figure-87. Trimming curves at intersection

- Select desired radio button from the **Entity** rollout in the **Manager**. If you want to trim the portion of entities then select the **Trim** radio button. If you want to break the entities at intersection point then select the **Break** radio button. Select the **Create points** check box below the radio button to create points also at the intersection points. Select the **Create only points** radio button to create only points at intersection locations.
- If you have selected the **Trim** radio button then click on the **Reselect** button from the **Section To Keep** rollout of **Manager** to change which side is to be kept after trimming.
- After setting desired parameters, click on the **OK** button from the **Manager** to complete the operation.

BREAKING ENTITIES

The tools to break entities are available in the **Break Two Pieces** drop-down of the **Ribbon**; refer to Figure-88. Various tools in this drop-down are discussed next.

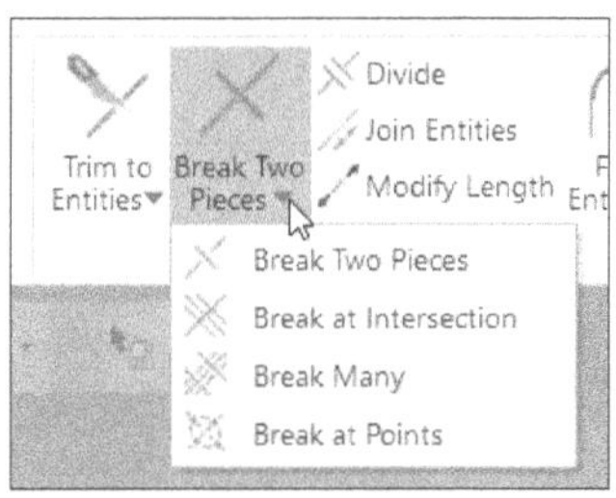

Figure-88. Break Two Pieces drop-down

Breaking Entity at Specified Point

The **Break Two Pieces** tool is used to break the selected entity at specified point. The procedure to use this tool is given next.

- Click on the **Break Two Pieces** tool from the **Modify** group in the **Wireframe** tab of the **Ribbon**. You will be asked to select the entity.
- Select desired entity which you want to break. You will be asked to specify point on the entity where you want to create breaking point.
- Click at desired location on the entity. The selected entity will break into two.

Break at Intersection

The **Break at Intersection** tool is used to break selected entities at intersection with the other entities. The procedure to use this tool is given next.

- Click on the **Break at Intersection** tool from the **Break Two Pieces** drop-down in the **Modify** group of **Wireframe** tab in the **Ribbon**. You will be asked to select the entities to break at intersections.
- Select all the intersecting entities and press **ENTER**. The selected entities will be broken into multiple entities at intersection points; refer to Figure-89.

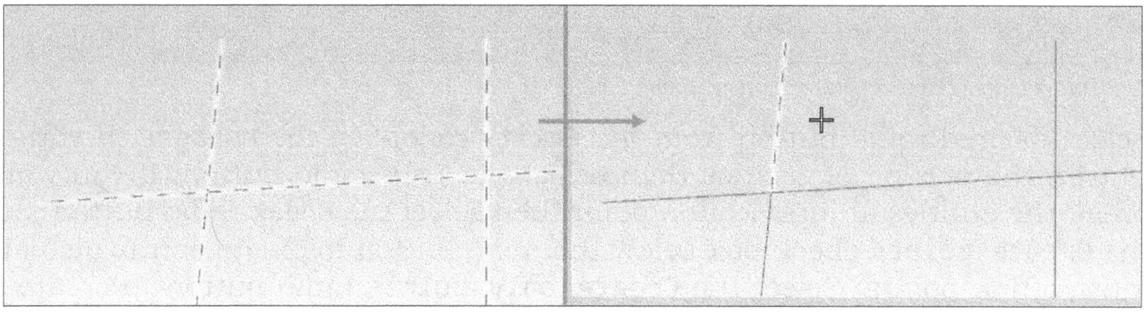

Figure-89. Entities broken at intersections

Breaking Multiple Entities

The **Break Many** tool is used to break selected entities into multiple segments of specified numbers. The procedure to use this tool is given next.

- Click on the **Break Many** tool from the **Break Two Pieces** drop-down in the **Modify** group of **Wireframe** tab in the **Ribbon**. You will be asked to select the entities to be broken.
- Select desired entities and click on the **End Selection** button or press **ENTER**. The **Break Many Pieces Manager** will be displayed with preview of broken entities; refer to Figure-90.

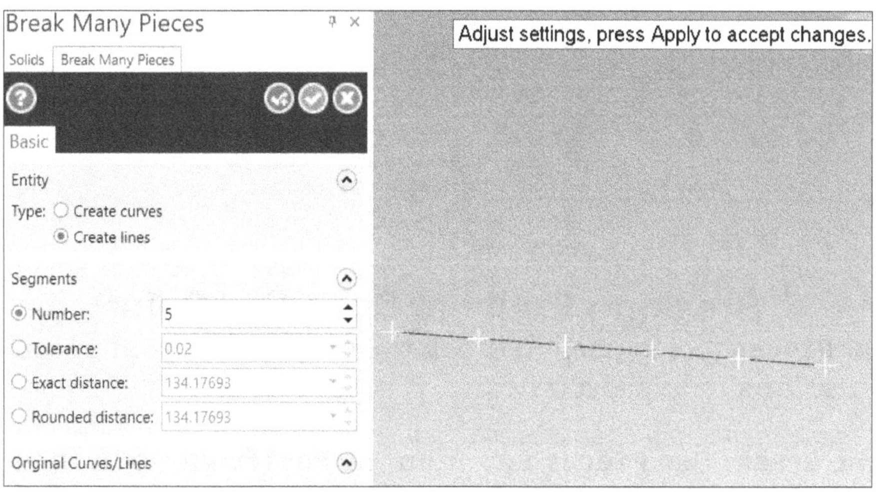

Figure-90. Break Many Pieces Manager

- Select desired radio button from the **Type** section of **Manager**. Select the **Create curves** radio button to create multiple curves after breaking entities. Select the **Create lines** radio button to create multiple lines after breaking entities.

- Select the **Number** radio button from the **Segments** rollout to specify total number of segments to be created in each selected curve. Set the other parameters as desired in the **Segments** rollout.
- Select desired radio button from the **Original Curves/Lines** rollout of **Manager** to define what will happen to original curves/lines after creating segments.
- Click on the **OK** button from the **Manager** to create the segments.

Break at Points

The **Break at Points** tool is used to break selected entities at specified points. The procedure to use this tool is given next.

- Click on the **Break at Points** tool from the **Break Two Pieces** drop-down in the **Modify** group of **Wireframe** tab in the **Ribbon**. You will be asked to select lines, arcs, or splines to be broken.
- Select desired curves with points created on them where you want to break the entities; refer to Figure-91 and click on the **End Selection** button. The entities will be broken at selected points; refer to Figure-92.

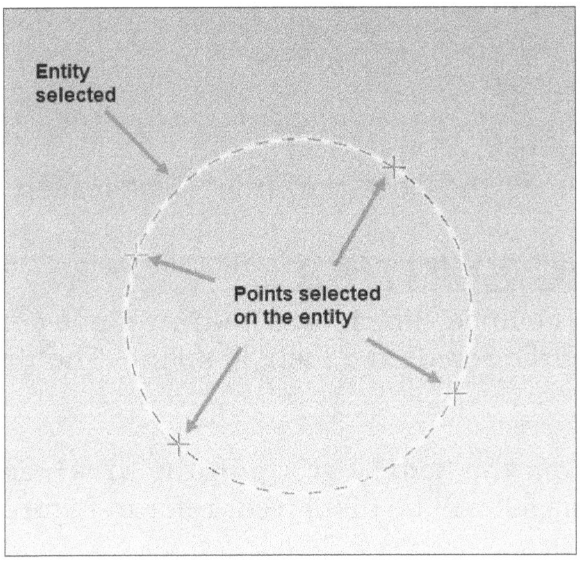

Figure-91. Selecting entities

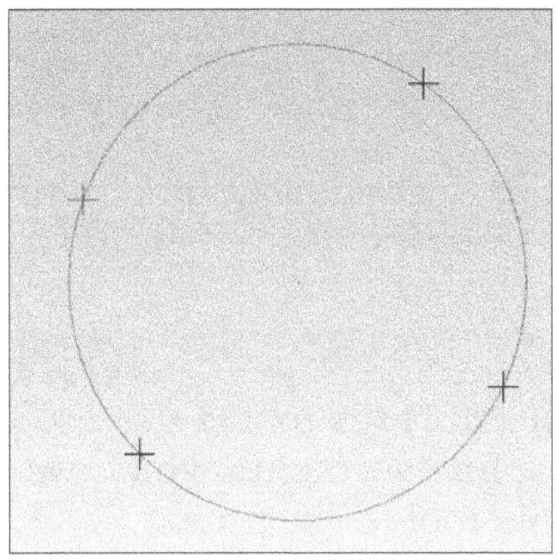

Figure-92. Broken entity

DIVIDING CURVES

The **Divide** tool is used to break or trim selected curves at intersection points of intersecting curves. The procedure to use this tool is given next.

- Click on the **Divide** tool from the **Modify** group in the **Wireframe** tab of the **Ribbon**. The **Divide Manager** will be displayed and you will be asked to select the entities; refer to Figure-93.

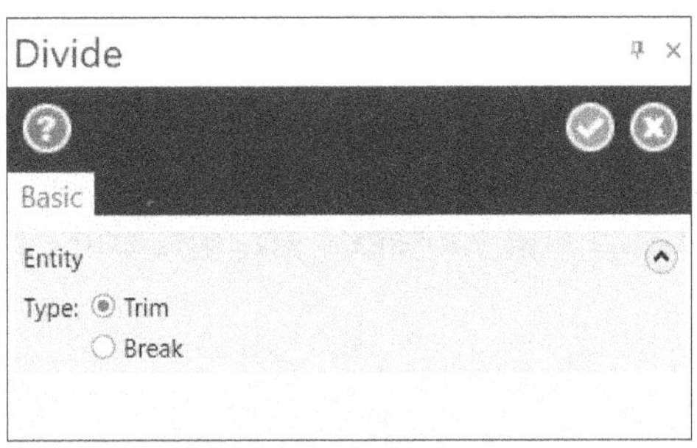

Figure-93. Divide Manager

- Select the **Trim** radio button to delete a section of curve or select the **Break** radio button to split the curve.
- Hover the cursor on the entity to be trimmed or split. Preview of section which will be trimmed or split will be displayed in dashed lines; refer to Figure-94.

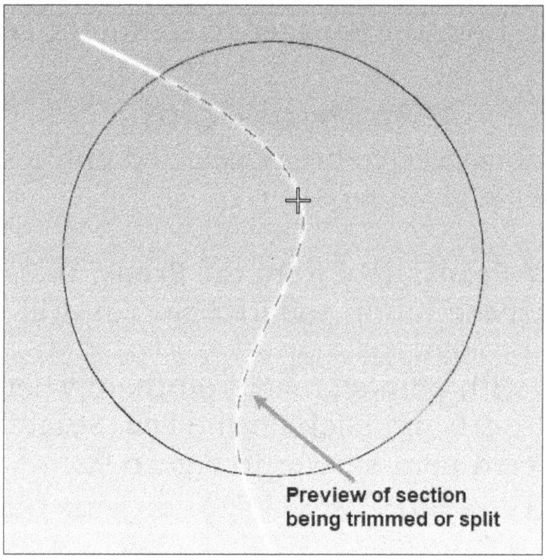

Figure-94. Preview of divide

- Click at desired location on curve to trim or split it.
- After selecting desired entities, click on the **OK** button from the **Manager**.

JOINING ENTITIES

The **Join Entities** tool is used to join collinear lines, arcs sharing same center and radius, spline segments which were earlier created as single spline. The procedure to use this tool is given next.

- Click on the **Join Entities** tool from the **Modify** group in the **Wireframe** tab of the **Ribbon**. The **Join Entities Manager** will be displayed; refer to Figure-95 and you will be asked to select the entities.

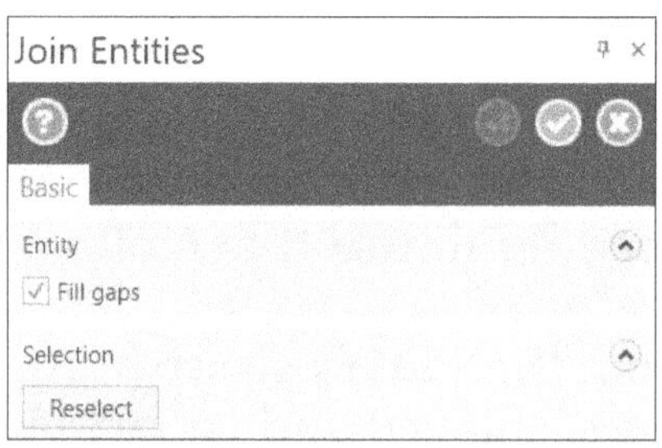

Figure-95. Join Entities Manager

- Select the **Fill gaps** check box if you want to fill gap between two entities while joining them.
- Select desired entities from the 3D view and click on the **End Selection** button. The selected entities will be joined; refer to Figure-96.
- Click on the **OK** button from the **Manager** to join the entities.

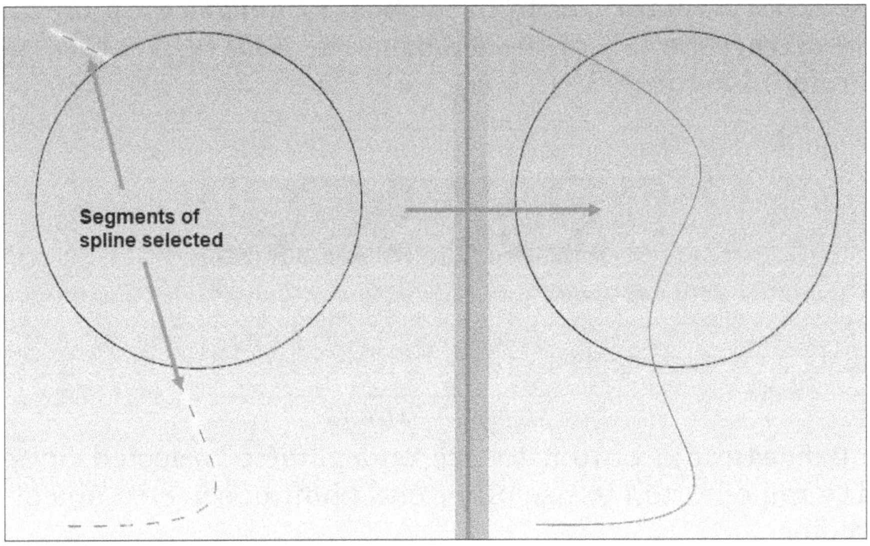

Figure-96. Spline created by joining segments

MODIFYING LENGTH OF ENTITIES

The **Modify Length** tool is used to trim, break, or extend the entities by specified length. The procedure to use this tool is given next.

- Click on the **Modify Length** tool from the **Modify** group in the **Wireframe** tab of the **Ribbon**. The **Modify Length Manager** will be displayed; refer to Figure-97 and you will be asked to select the entity.

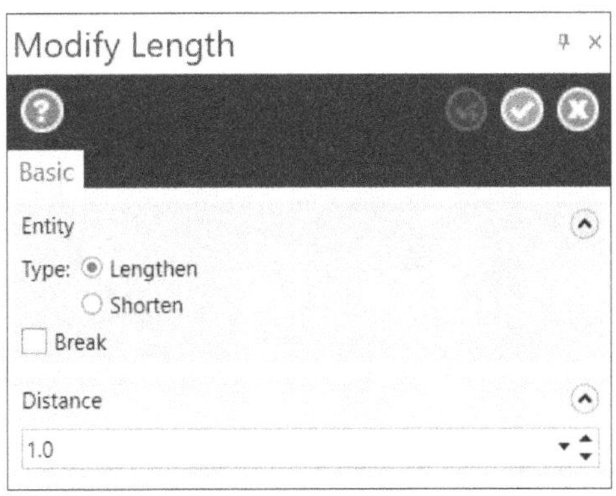

Figure-97. Modify Length Manager

- Select the **Lengthen** or **Shorten** radio button to increase or decrease the length of selected entity.
- Specify the distance by which you want to increase or decrease the length in the **Distance** edit box.
- Click at desired open end of the entity that you want to extend or shorten. The selected end will be extended/shortened.
- After performing extension or shortening, click on the **OK** button from the **Manager**.

MODIFYING DIRECTION VECTOR

The **Modify Vector** tool is used to change the orientation vector of selected entity. In simple words, you can change the orientation of selected entity. The procedure to sue this tool is given next.

- Click on the **Modify Vector** tool from the **Modify Length** drop-down in the **Modify** panel of the **Wireframe** tab of the **Ribbon**. The **Modify Vector Manager** will be displayed; refer to Figure-98.

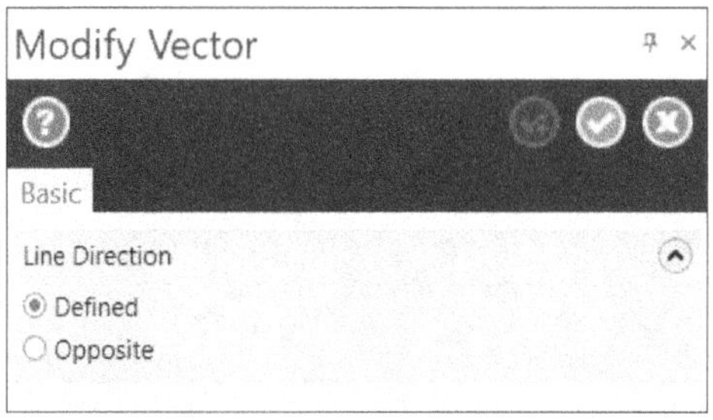

Figure-98. Modify Vector Manager

- Select the **Defined** radio button to use end point of selected line/curve. Select the **Opposite** radio button to use other end point of selected object for modifying direction vector.
- Click on the object whose orientation is to be modified. Drag handles will be displayed on selected object.
- Select desired rotation handle, move it in desired angle, and click to set the vector direction; refer to Figure-99. Click on the **OK** button from the **Manager** to apply the operation.

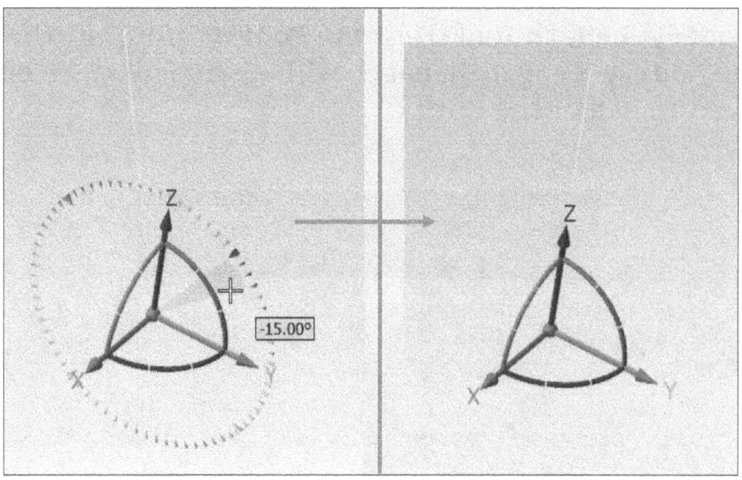

Figure-99. Modifying vector

APPLYING FILLET

The tools to apply fillet are available in the **Fillet Entities** drop-down of the **Ribbon**; refer to Figure-100. These tools are discussed next.

Fillet Entities Tool

The **Fillet Entities** tool is used to apply round/fillet at the intersection of two entities. The procedure to use this tool is given next.

- Click on the **Fillet Entities** tool from the **Modify** group in the **Wireframe** tab of the **Ribbon**. The **Fillet Entities Manager** will be displayed; refer to Figure-101.

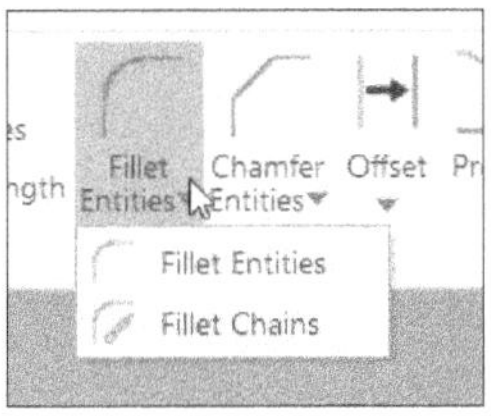

Figure-100. Fillet Entities drop-down

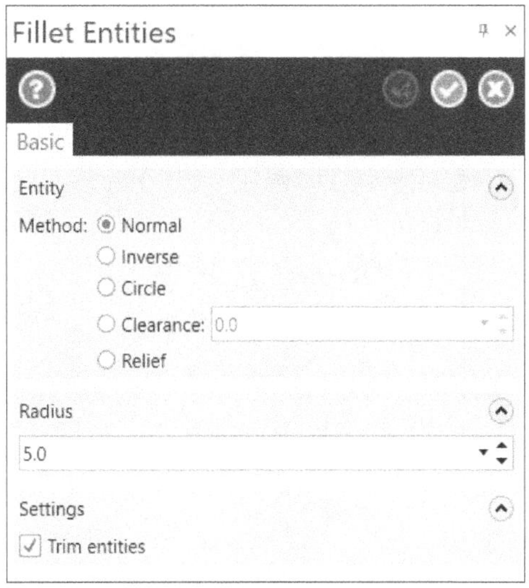

Figure-101. Fillet Entities Manager

- Select the **Normal** radio button to create normal fillet of specified radius. Select the **Inverse** radio button to apply round on the opposite side of normal fillet. Select the **Circle** radio button to create circle at intersection of selected entities. Select the **Clearance** radio button to provide clearance round for movement of cutting tool at the corners. Select the **Relief** radio button to provide cutting tool clearance on one entity at the intersection. The various types of fillet are shown in Figure-102.

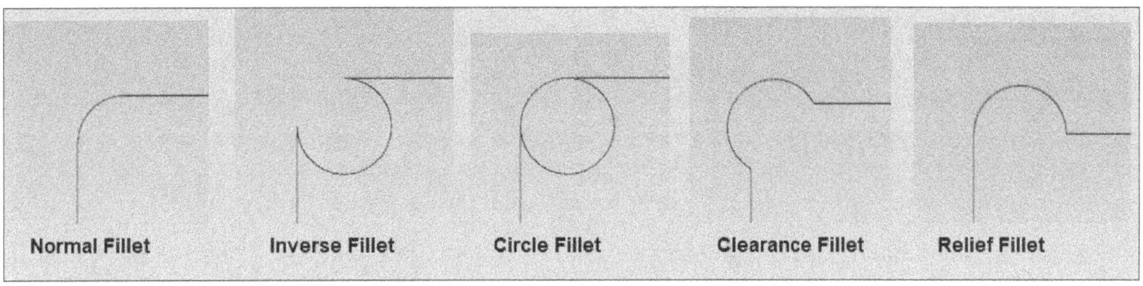

Figure-102. Fillet types

- Specify desired value in **Radius** edit box to define radius of fillet.
- Select the **Trim entities** check box to delete extra segments of entities after creating fillet.
- After specifying desired parameters, click on the two intersecting entities. The fillet will be applied.
- Click on the **OK** button from the **Manager** to create fillet.

Applying Fillets to Chained Entities

The **Fillet Chains** tool is used to automatically apply fillets at intersection points in selected chained entity. The procedure to use this tool is given next.

- Click on the **Fillet Chains** tool from the **Fillet Entities** drop-down in the **Modify** group of **Wireframe** tab in the **Ribbon**. The **Wireframe Chaining** selection box will be displayed with **Fillet Chains Manager**; refer to Figure-103.

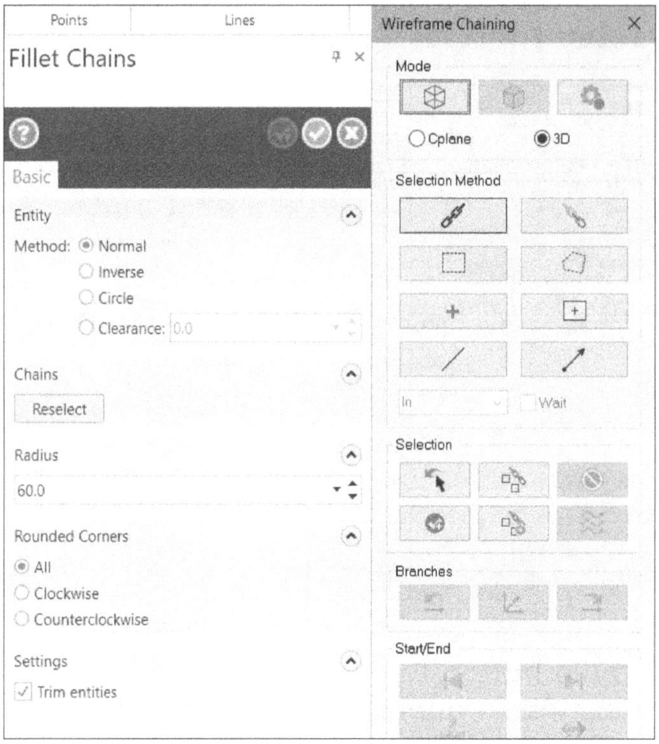

Figure-103. Fillet Chains Manager

- Select first entity of the chain. Two arrows will be displayed on the entity showing the start and end of selected chain; refer to Figure-104.

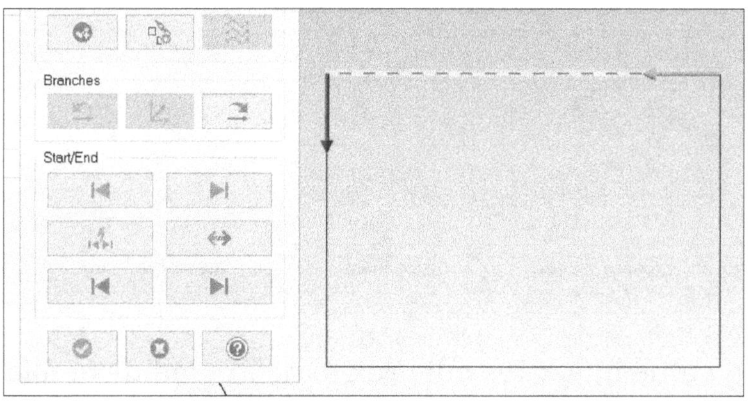

Figure-104. Preview of chain selection

- Click on the **End Point Forward** button multiple times from the **Wireframe Chaining** selection box until all desired entities are selected in the chain.
- After selecting the chain, click on the **OK** button from the selection box.
- Set the parameters as discussed earlier in the **Fillet Chains Manager**. Preview of fillets will be displayed; refer to Figure-105.

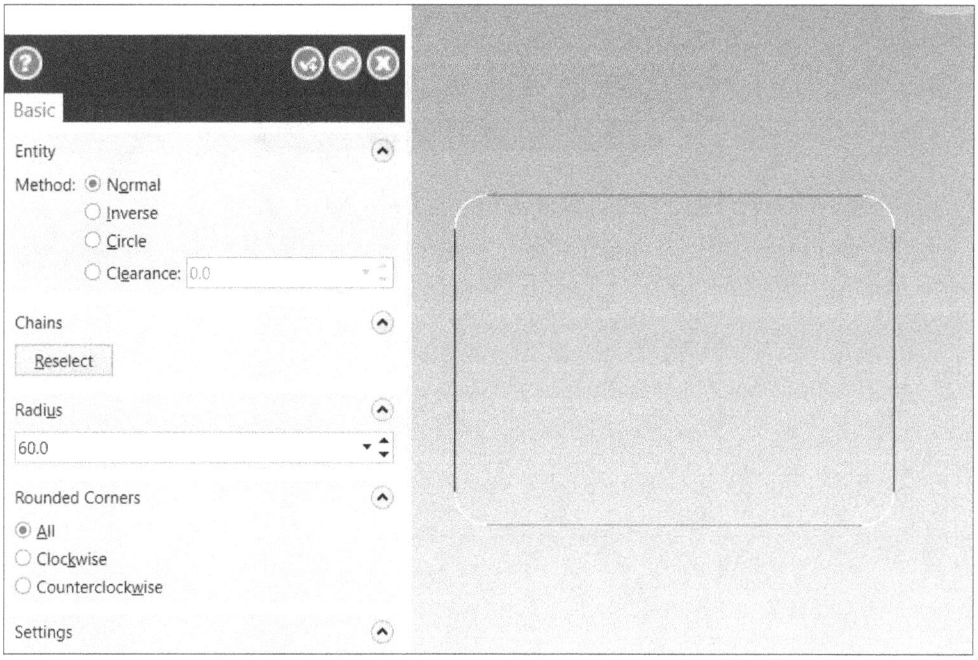

Figure-105. Preview of fillet chain

- Click on the **OK** button from the **Manager** to create fillets.

APPLYING CHAMFERS

The tools to apply chamfer are available in the **Chamfer Entities** drop-down of the **Wireframe** tab in the **Ribbon**; refer to Figure-106. Various tools of this drop-down are discussed next.

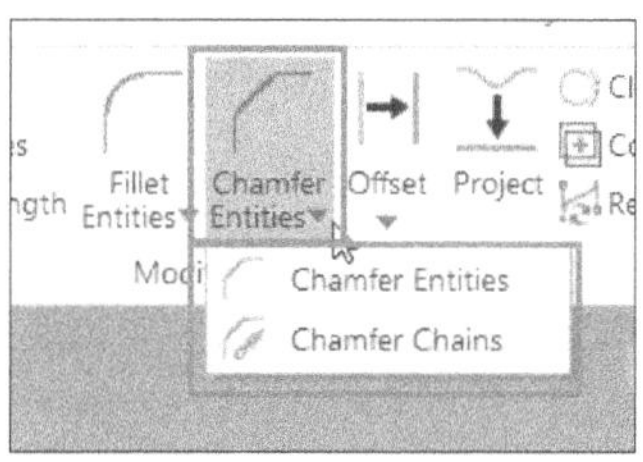

Figure-106. Chamfer Entities drop-down

Applying Chamfer to Selected Entities

The **Chamfer Entities** tool is used to apply chamfer at intersection of selected entities. The procedure to use this tool is given next.

- Click on the **Chamfer Entities** tool from the **Chamfer Entities** drop-down in the **Modify** group of **Wireframe** tab in the **Ribbon**. The **Chamfer Entities Manager** will be displayed; refer to Figure-107 and you will be asked to select the entities.

Figure-107. Chamfer Entities Manager

- Select desired radio button from the **Method** section of the **Manager** to define how the chamfer width and angle will be defined. Select the **1 Distance** radio button to define distance of chamfer from 1st selected entity. Select the **2 Distance** radio button to define distance of chamfer along both the selected entities. Select the **Distance and angle** radio button to define chamfer distance along first entity and angle. Select the **Width** radio button to define total width of chamfer equal on both sides of selected entities. Refer to Figure-108.

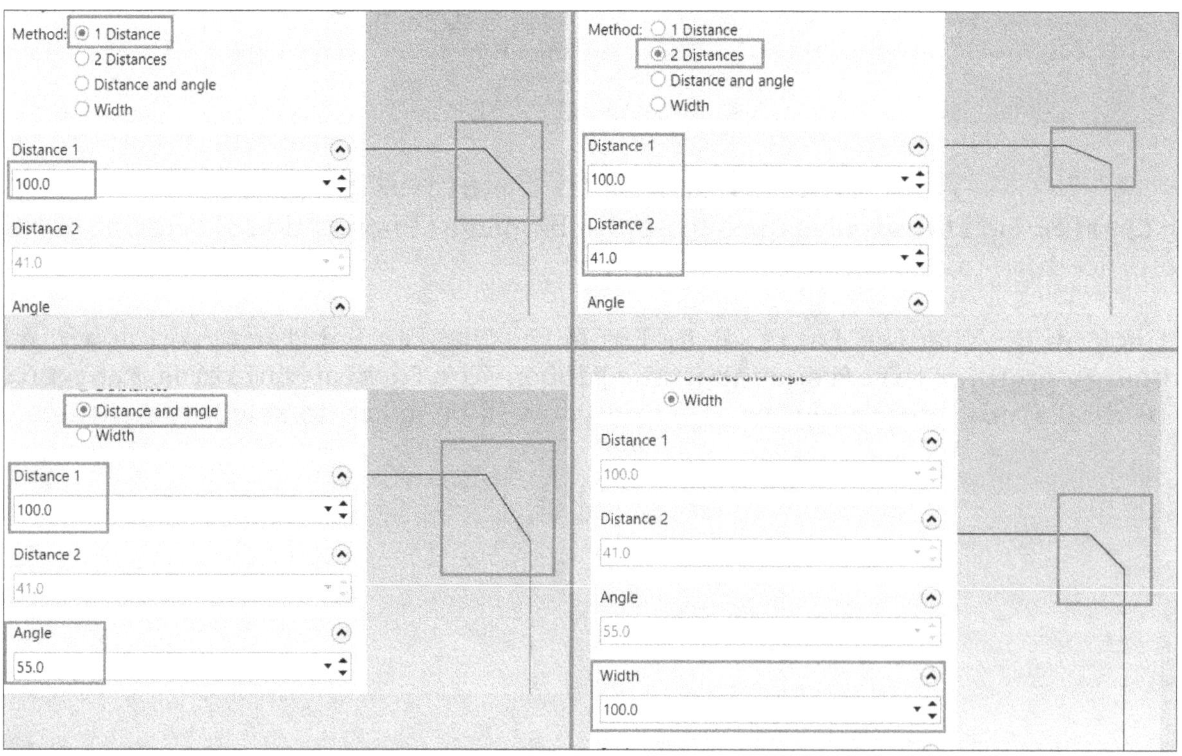

Figure-108. Chamfer types

- Set the parameters as desired in the **Manager** and click on the **OK** button.

The **Chamfer Chains** tool works in the same way as discussed for **Fillet Chains** tool; refer to Figure-109.

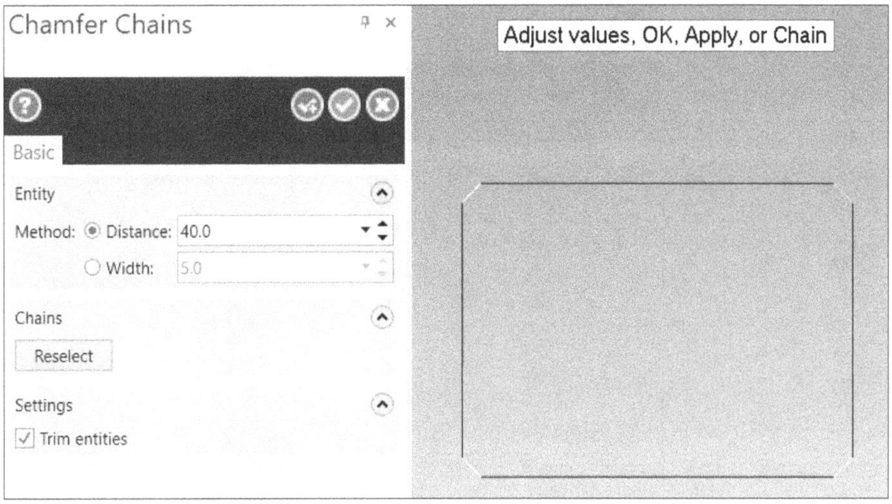

Figure-109. Chamfer chains preview

OFFSETTING ENTITIES

The tools to offset selected entities or chain of entities are available in the **Offset Entity** drop-down of the **Modify** group in the **Ribbon**; refer to Figure-110. Various tools of the drop-down are discussed next.

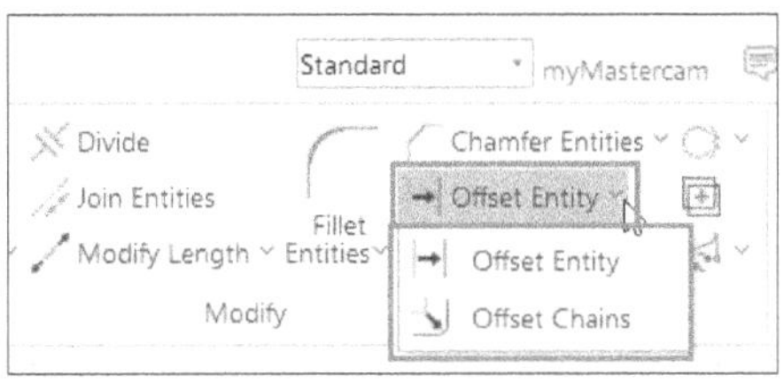

Figure-110. Offset drop-down

Offsetting an Entity

The **Offset Entity** tool is used to move/copy an entity parallel to selected entity. The procedure to use this tool is given next.

- Click on the **Offset Entity** tool from the **Offset** drop-down in the **Modify** group of **Wireframe** tab in the **Ribbon**. The **Offset Entity Manager** will be displayed; refer to Figure-111.
- Select desired radio button from the **Method** section of **Manager**. Select the **Copy** radio button to create a copy of selected entity while offsetting. Select the **Move** radio button to move selected entity while offsetting. Select the **Join** radio button to join the entity with previously connected entities. Select the **Slot** radio button from the **Method** section to create slot using offsetted line.
- Set desired number of entities to be created by offsetting in the **Number** edit box.
- Specify the distance between two consecutive offsetted entities in **Distance** edit box of **Manager**.
- Select desired radio button from the **Direction** rollout in the **Manager** to define direction for offsetting.

- Select the line, arc, spline, or curve from the 3D view to create offset copy. You will be asked to click in the direction where you want to place offset copies.
- Click in desired direction. The preview of offset copies will be displayed; refer to Figure-112.

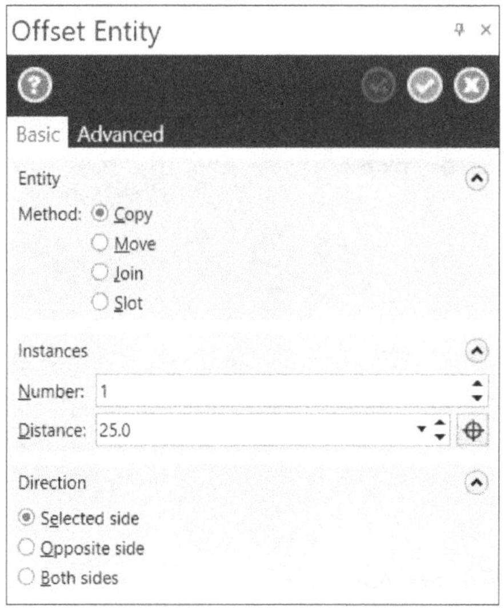

Figure-111. Offset Entity Manager

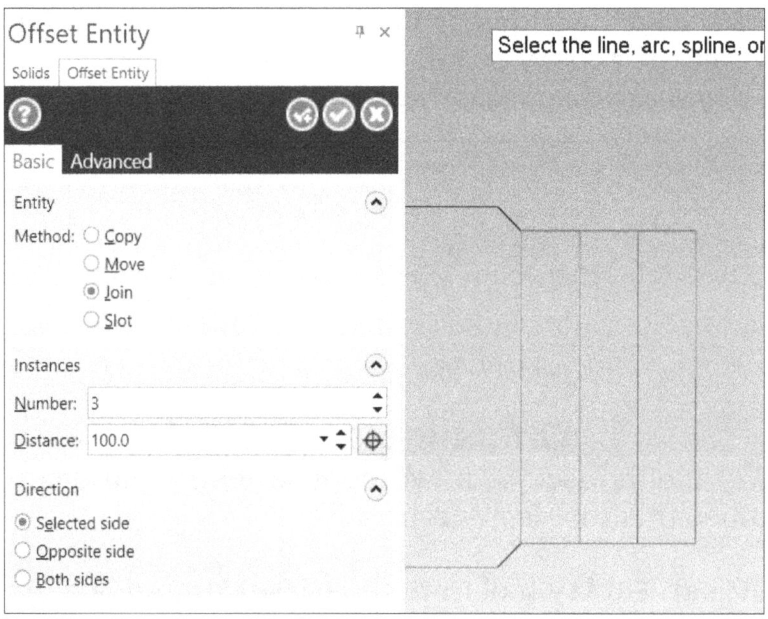

Figure-112. Preview of offsetting

- Click on the **OK** button from the **Manager** to complete offsetting operation.

Similarly, you can use the **Offset Chains** tool in the **Offset** drop-down to offset chain of selected entities.

PROJECTING ENTITIES

The **Project** tool in **Modify** group of **Ribbon** is used to project selected entities on to a plane, surface, or specified depth. The procedure to use this tool is given next.

- Click on the **Project** tool from the **Modify** group in the **Wireframe** tab of the **Ribbon**. The **Project Manager** will be displayed; refer to Figure-113 and you will be asked to select entities to be projected.

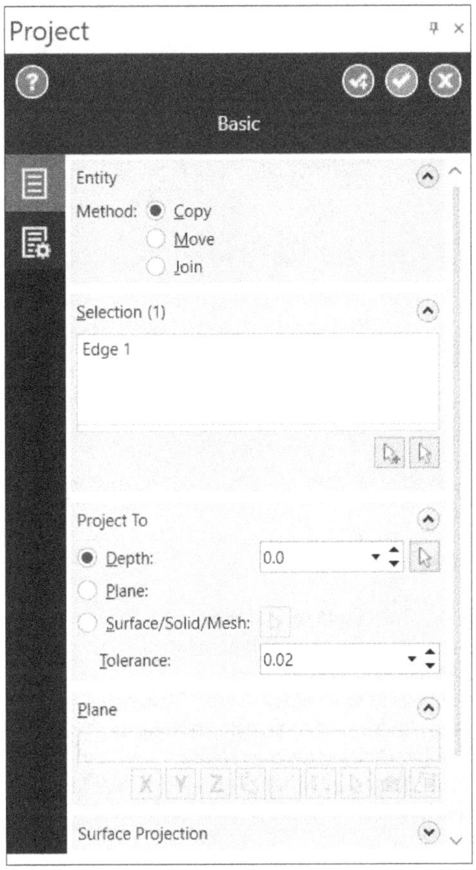

Figure-113. Project Manager

- Select desired entities and click on the **End Selection** button. The options in the **Manager** will become active.
- Select the **Copy** radio button to copy all the selected entities while projecting. Select the **Move** radio button to move all the selected entities while projecting. Select the **Join** radio button to join projected entities with previously attached entities.
- Select the **Depth** radio button to project entities at specified depth value and specify desired depth value in the **Depth** edit box of **Project To** rollout.
- Select the **Plane** radio button to project entities to selected plane. After selecting the radio button, options to define/select plane will become active in **Plane** rollout of the **Manager**. Select the **Entities** button from the rollout to select an entity (face, surface, plane etc.) to be used as plane. Similarly, you can select other buttons to use respective plane option.
- Click on the **OK** button from the dialog box. Preview of projected entities will be displayed; refer to Figure-114.
- Select the **Surfaces/Solids** radio button to select a face or surface on which you want to project the entities. You will be asked to select the surface/face and various selection methods will be displayed; refer to Figure-115.
- Select desired face(s) or surface(s) and click on the **End Selection** button. Preview of projected entities will be displayed; refer to Figure-116. Set the other parameters as desired in the **Manager** and click on the **OK** button.

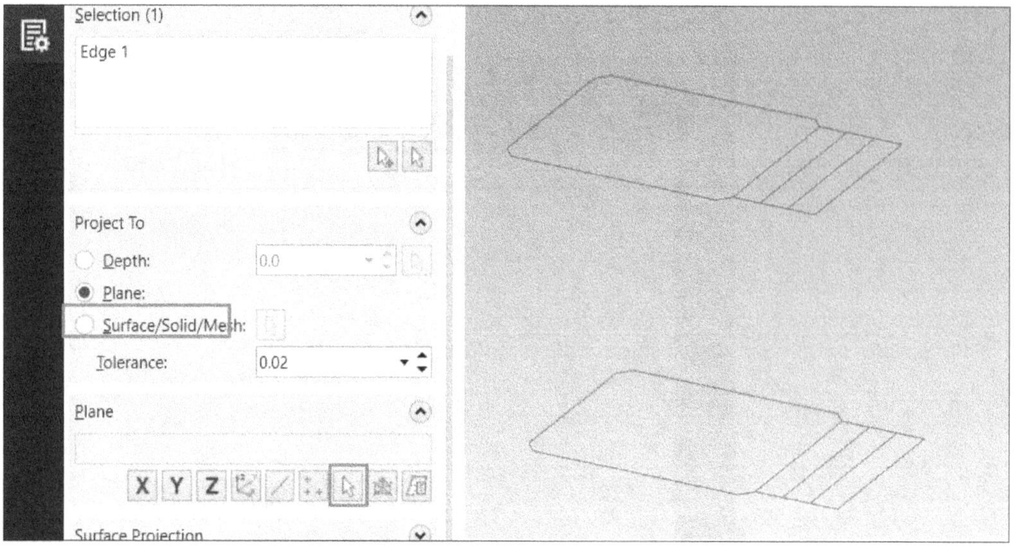

Figure-114. Preview of offsetted entity on plane

Select Solid Face or Surface:
- [Shift+click] to select tangent faces.
- [Alt+click] to vector select.
- [Ctrl+click] to select matching fillets/holes.
- [Ctrl+Shift+click] to select similar faces.
- Double-click to select a feature.
- [Ctrl+Shift+double-click] to select similar features.
- Triple-click to select the solid body.

Figure-115. Selection methods for surface or face projection

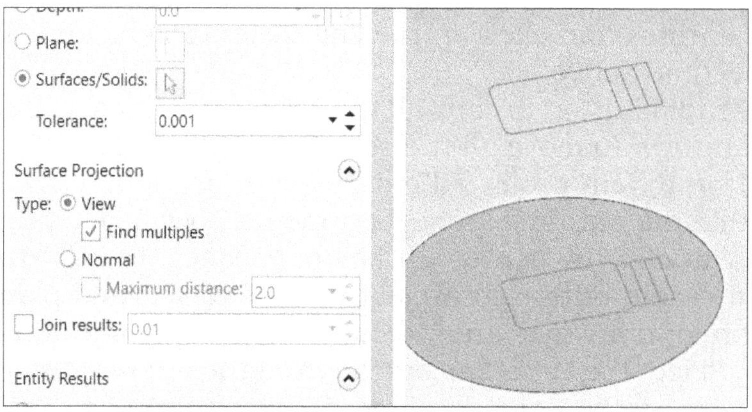

Figure-116. Preview of entities projected on surface

CLOSING AN ARC

The **Close Arc** tool is used to close an open arc to form a full circle. The procedure to use this tool is given next.

- Click on the **Close Arc** tool from the **Close Arc** drop-down in the **Modify** group of **Wireframe** tab in the **Ribbon**. You will be asked to select an arc to be used for forming circle.
- Select desired arc and click on the **End Selection** button. A circle will be created using the arc.

BREAKING CIRCLE TO SEGMENTS

The **Break Circles** tool is used to split selected circle into multiple segments. The procedure to use this tool is given next.

- Click on the **Break Circles** tool from the **Close Arc** drop-down in the **Modify** group of **Wireframe** tab in the **Ribbon**. You will be asked to select the circle to be broken into segments.
- Select desired circle(s) and click on the **End Selection** button. Desi**red number of arcs** input box will be displayed; refer to Figure-117.

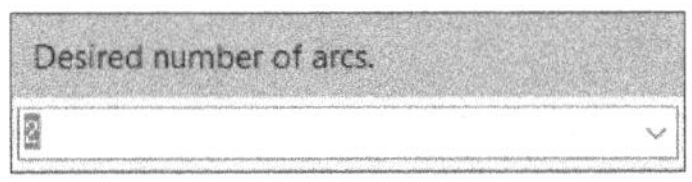

Figure-117. Desired number of arcs input box

- Specify desired number of segments to be created in the input box and press **ENTER**. The specified number of segments will be created in selected circles.

COMBINING VIEWS

The **Combine Views** tool is used to combine multiple parallel views into a single view. Click on the **Combine Views** tool from the **Modify** group in the **Wireframe** tab of the **Ribbon**. All the parallel views will be combined into a single view.

REFITTING SPLINES

The **Refit Spline** tool is used to repair poorly created splines with so many nodes. The procedure to use this tool is given next.

- Click on the **Refit Spline** tool from the **Modify** group in the **Wireframe** tab of the **Ribbon**. The **Refit Spline Manager** will be displayed; refer to Figure-118 and you will be asked to select the splines to be repaired.

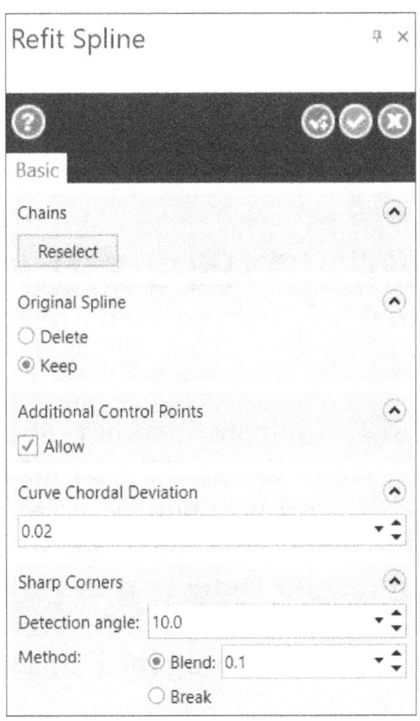

Figure-118. Refit Spline Manager

- Select one or more splines to be refitted and click on the **End Selection** button. The options in the **Manager** will become active.
- Select the **Delete** radio button from the **Original Spline** rollout of **Manager** to delete original splines after making repair. Select the **Keep** radio button to keep original spline as well after creating repaired spline.
- Select the **Allow** check box from the **Additional Control Points** rollout to add more control points as needed for repairing.
- Set desired value in the **Curve Chordal Deviation** edit box to specify maximum deviation allowed from the original spline.
- Specify desired value for angle to be used as sharp corner in spline in the **Detection angle** edit box.
- Select the **Blend** radio button if you want to add a new segment at sharp point in spline for smoothening curve.
- Select the **Break** radio button if you want to split spline at sharp corner points.
- After setting desired parameters, click on the **OK** button from the **Manager**.

UNTRIMMING SPLINE

The **Untrim Spline** tool is used to reverse the effect of trim operation earlier performed on the spline. The procedure to use this tool is given next.

- Click on the **Untrim Spline** tool from the **Refit Spline** drop-down in the **Modify** group of **Wireframe** tab in the **Ribbon**. You will be asked to select the spline or NURBS curve to be untrimmed.
- Select desired spline or NURBS curve to be untrimmed and click on the **End Selection** button. The trimmed portion of spline will get untrimmed; refer to Figure-119.

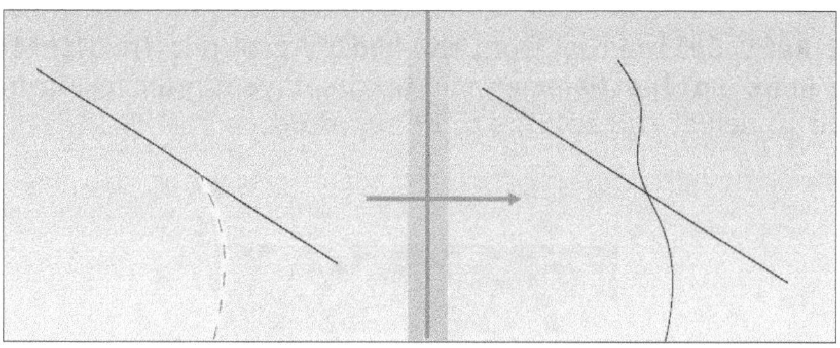

Figure-119. Untrimming spline

SIMPLIFYING SPLINE

The **Simplify Spline** tool is used to convert closed arc spline to circles. The procedure to use this tool is given next.

- Click on the **Simplify Spline** tool from the **Refit Spline** drop-down in the **Modify** group of **Wireframe** tab in the **Ribbon**. The **Simplify Spline Manager** will be displayed; refer to Figure-120 and you will be asked to select the splines.
- Select desired spline from 3D view and click on the **End Selection** button.
- Specify desired angle value in the Detection angle edit box above which corner will be considered a sharp corner and it will be smoothen.
- Select desired radio button from the **Original Spline** rollout to define what will happen to original spline.

- Set desired value in the **Tolerance** edit box to specify maximum deviation allowed in spline from the circular shape for converting spline into circle.
- Click on the **OK** button from the **Manager** to perform conversion.

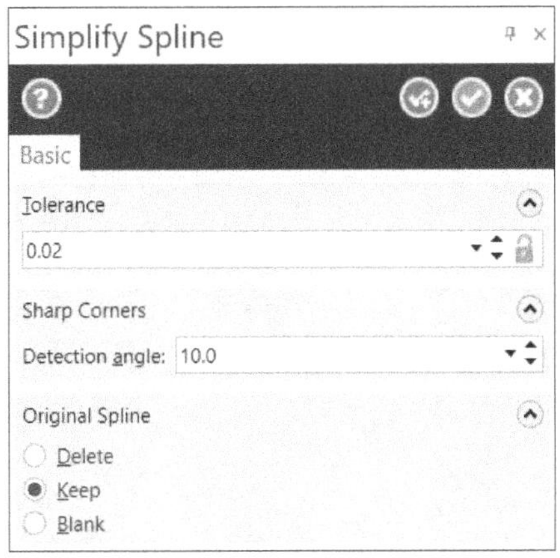

Figure-120. Simplify Spline Manager

EDITING SPLINE

The **Edit Spline** tool is used to modify a spline using nodes or control points. The procedure to use this tool is given next.

- Click on the **Edit Spline** tool from the **Refit Spline** drop-down in the **Modify** group of **Wireframe** tab in the **Ribbon**. The **Edit Spline Manager** will be displayed; refer to Figure-121 and you will be asked to select a line, arc, or spline.

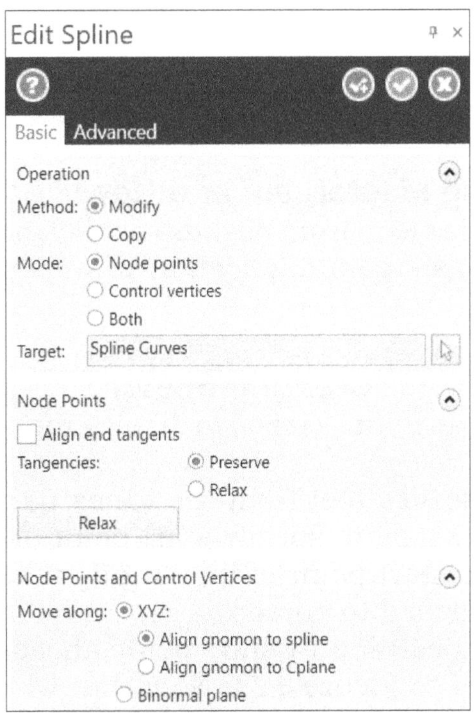

Figure-121. Edit Spline Manager

- Select desired entity to be modified. You will be asked to specify node point to be used for modifying spline/curve.
- Click at desired location to select node point. The gnomon to modify shape of spline/curve will be displayed.
- Drag the handles of gnomon to modify shape of spline/curve.

- If you want to use control vertices in place of nodes then select the **Control vertices** radio button and select control vertex of curve from the 3D view.
- Set the other parameters as discussed earlier and click on the **OK** button from the **Manager**.

Practical 1

Create wireframe sketch as shown in Figure-122 and apply the dimensions.

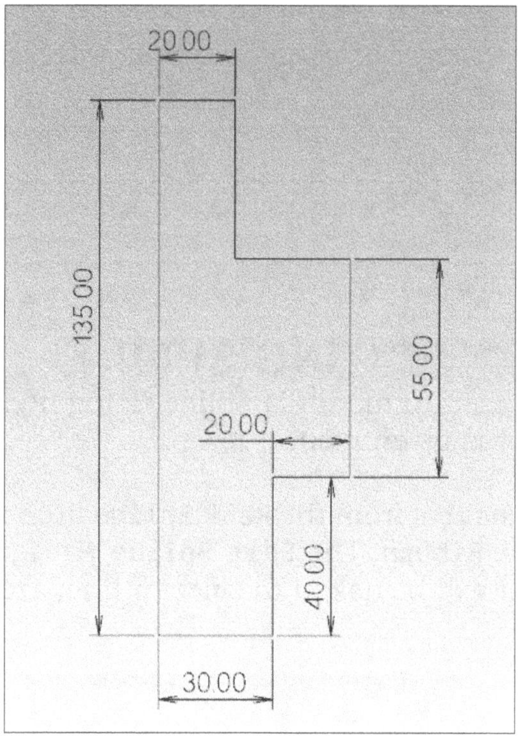

Figure-122. Practical 1 for Wireframe design

Starting Mastercam and New Document

- Double-click on **Mastercam** icon from desktop or click on the **Mastercam** application icon in **Start** menu. Mastercam application will open with a new document by default.

Creating Sketch

- Click on the **Wireframe** tab in the **Ribbon** to display tools for creating and managing wireframe entities.
- Click on the **Line Endpoints** tool from the **Lines** panel in the **Wireframe** tab of the **Ribbon**. You will be asked to specify start point of line.
- Type **0,0,0** to place the start point of line at origin and press **ENTER**. Other end point of line will get attached to cursor.
- Move the cursor in vertical line to start point and click when length of line is approximately **150**; refer to Figure-123. Note that when you click to specify end point of line, it will still be selected and highlighted in cyan color.
- Click in the **Length** edit box of **Dimension** rollout in the **Line Endpoints Manager** and specify the value as **150**; refer to Figure-124.
- After specifying the length value, click on the **OK and Create New Operation** tool from the **Line Endpoints Manager**. You will be asked to specify start point of next line.

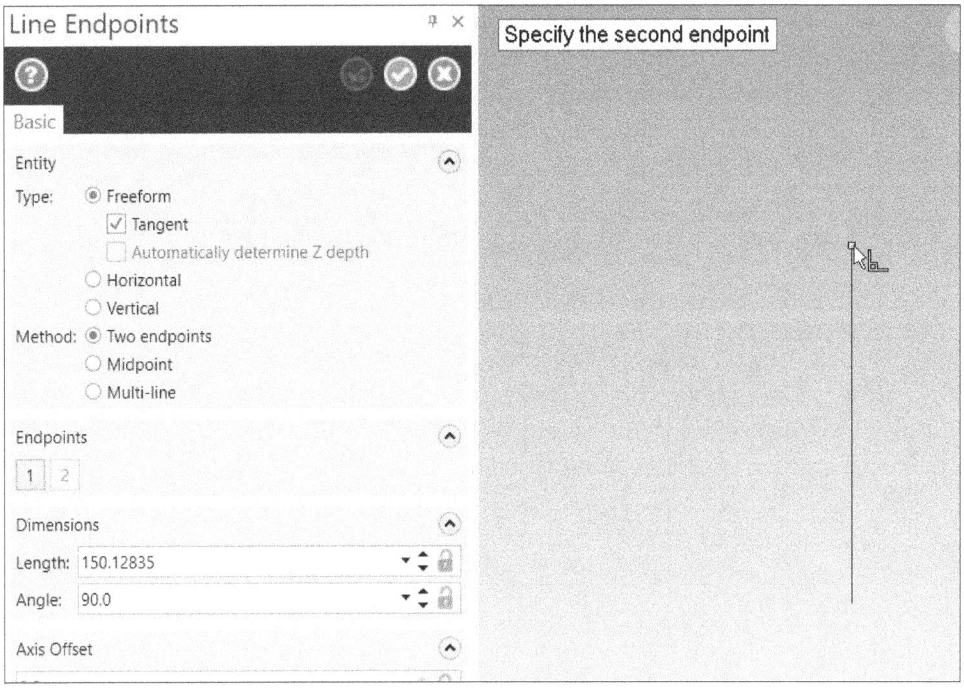

Figure-123. Specifying second point of line

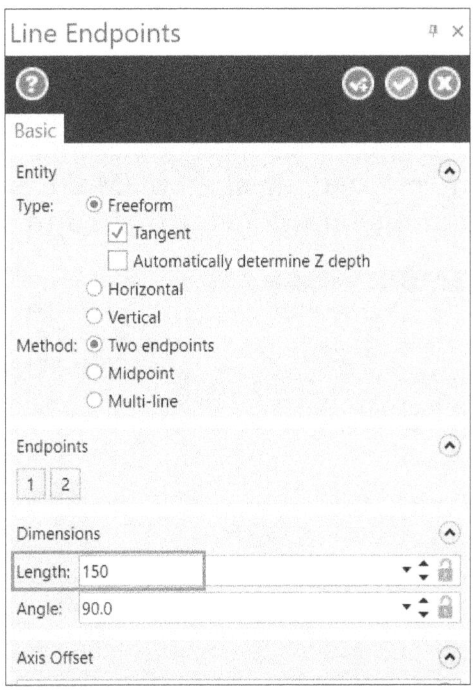

Figure-124. Specifying length of line

- Click at the start point of previous line to define start point of second line. The other end point will get attached to cursor.
- Specify the length value as **30** and angle value as **0** in the respective edit boxes of the **Line Endpoints Manager**. Press **TAB** to check the preview; refer to Figure-125.
- Click on the **OK and Create New Operation** tool from the **Manager**. You will be asked to specify start point of next line.
- Similarly, create other line segments; refer to Figure-126.
- Click on the **Smart Dimension** tool from the **Dimension** panel in the **Drafting** tab of the **Ribbon** to activate tool for dimensioning (You will learn about Drafting tools later in Chapter 6). The **Drafting Manager** will be displayed and you will be asked to select entities to be dimensioned.

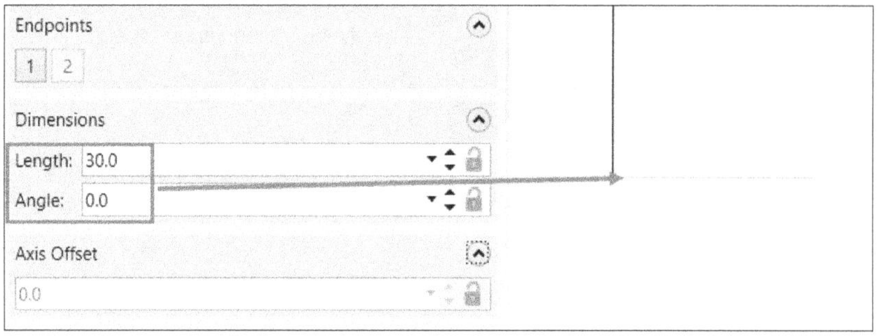

Figure-125. Preview of line

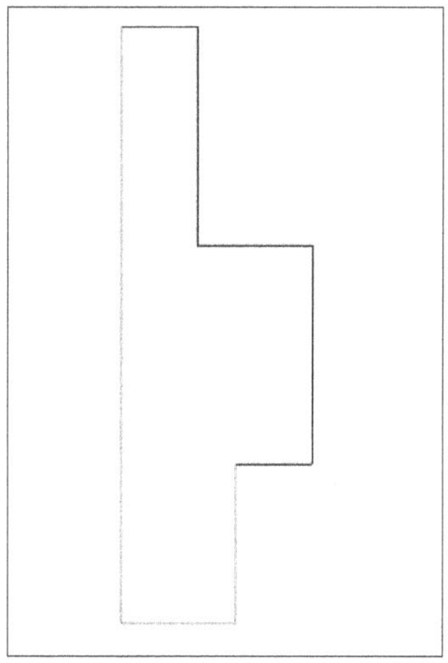

Figure-126. Sketch for Practical 1

- Click on a line segment created in sketch (Make sure you are not selecting keypoints of line). The dimension will get attached to cursor; refer to Figure-127.

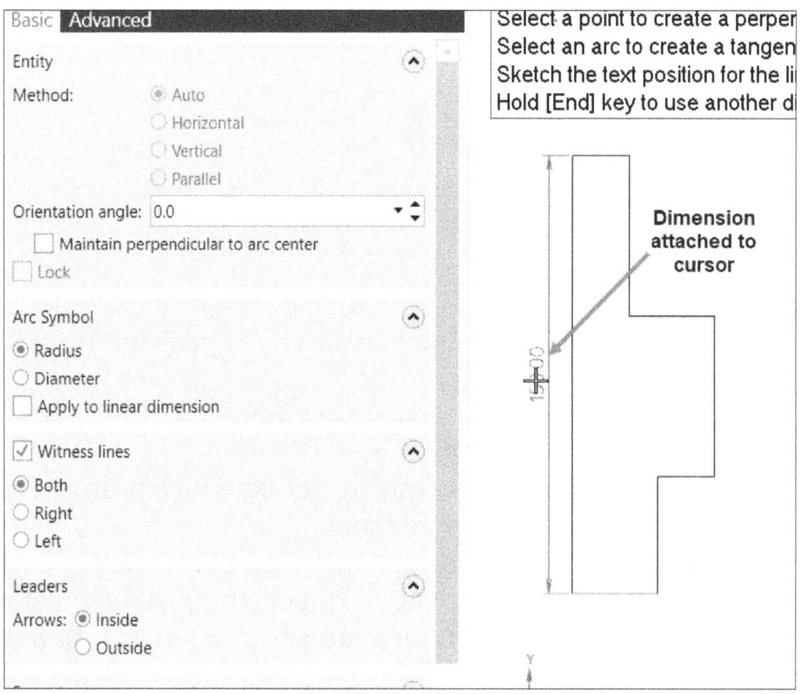

Figure-127. Placing dimension

- Click at desired location to place the dimension. Similarly, you can dimension other lines in the sketch.

PRACTICAL 2

In this practical, you will create the sketch as shown in Figure-128.

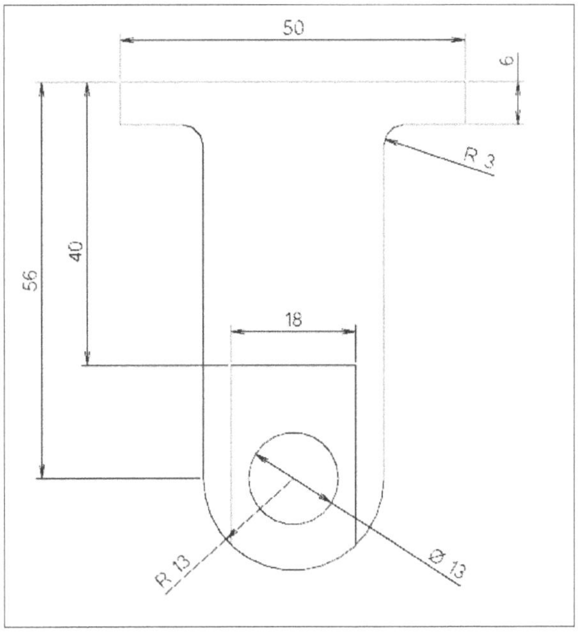

Figure-128. Sketch for Practical 2

- Start Mastercam if not started yet and switch to **Wireframe** tab in the **Ribbon**.
- Click on the **Line Endpoints** tool from the **Lines** panel in **Wireframe** tab of the **Ribbon** and select the **Midpoint** option from the **Method** section in the **Line Endpoints Manager**; refer to Figure-129.

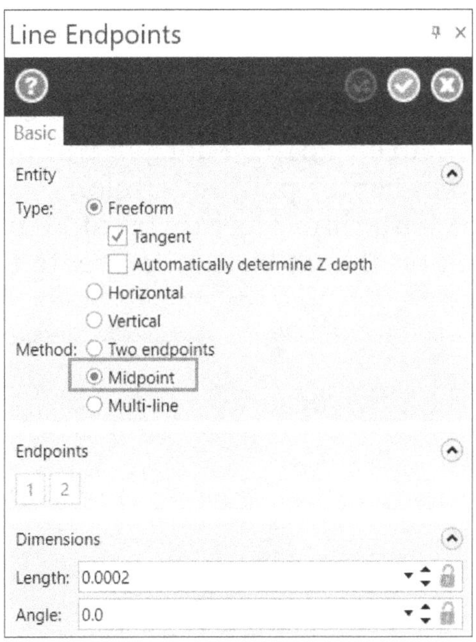

Figure-129. Selecting midpoint option

- Specifying the coordinates of starting point (which is midpoint in this case) as **0,0,0** and press **ENTER**.
- Specify the length of line as **50** and angle as **0** in respective edit boxes of **Manager**. Click on the **OK** button in **Manager** to create the line.
- Create a vertical line of **6** in downward direction starting from endpoint of previous line; refer to Figure-130.

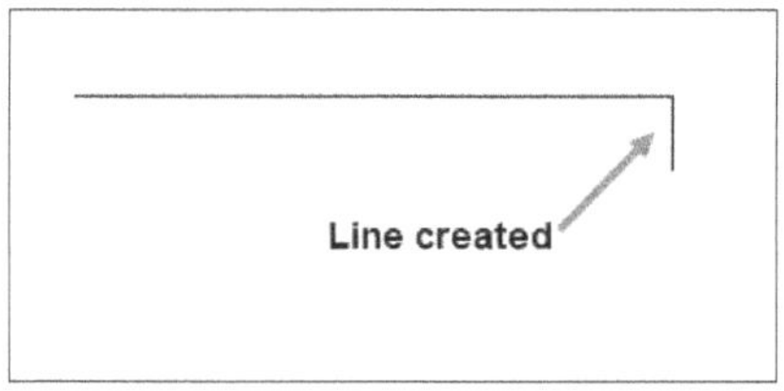

Figure-130. Line created

- Create a line of length **56** starting from mid point of first line created; refer to Figure-131.

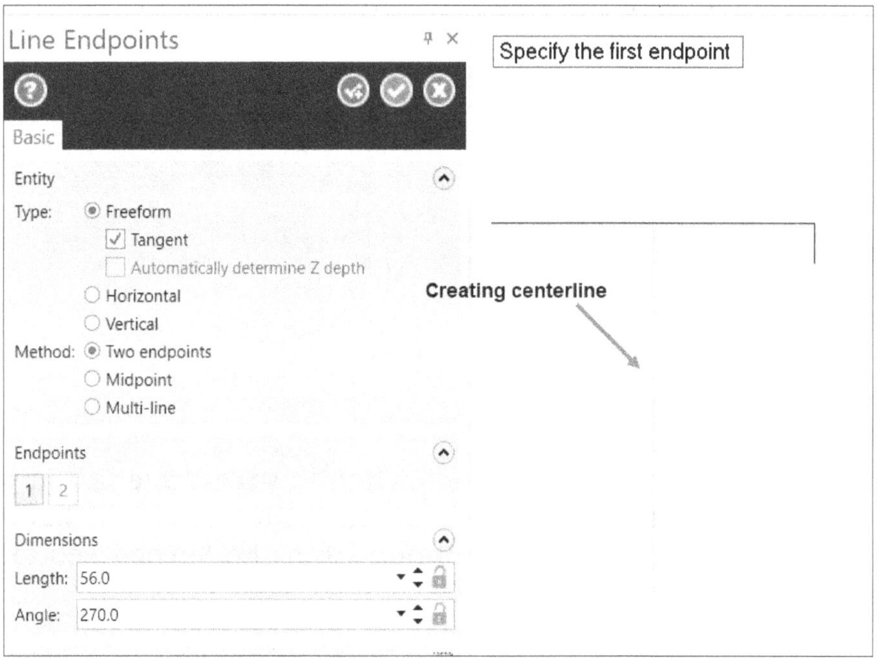

Figure-131. Creating centerline

- Click on the **Circle Center Point** tool from the **Arcs** panel in **Wireframe** tab of the **Ribbon**. The **Circle Center Point Manager** will be displayed and you will be asked to specify location of center point of circle.
- Click on the end point of centerline recently created and specify the radius as **13**; refer to Figure-132. Click on the **OK** button to create the circle.

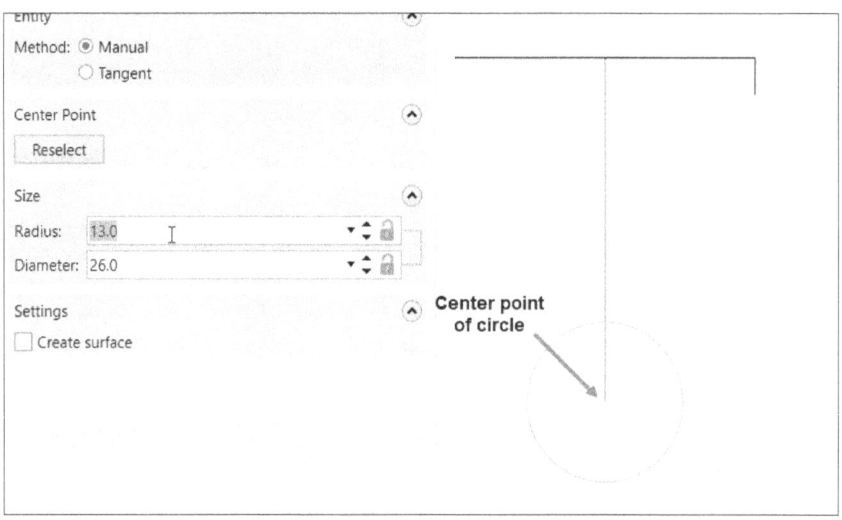

Figure-132. Specifying parameters for circle

- Create two intersecting lines as shown in Figure-133.

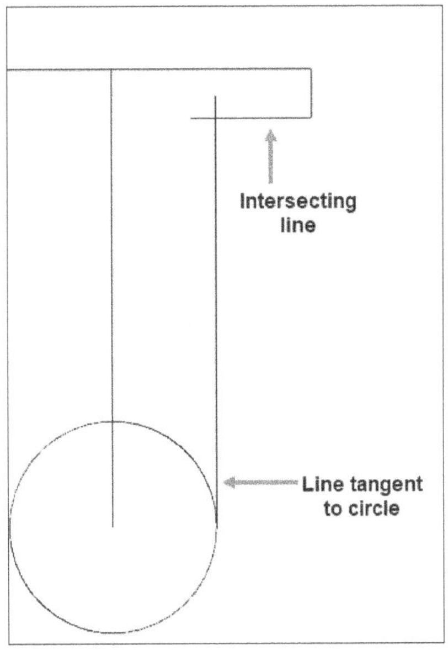

Figure-133. Intersecting lines created

- Click on the **Trim to Point** tool from the **Trim to Entities** drop-down in the **Modify** panel of **Wireframe** tab in the **Ribbon**. You will be asked to select entity to be trimmed.
- Click on the side of line which you want to keep and then click at the point where you want to trim the line; refer to Figure-134. Similarly, trim other intersecting line and click on the **OK** button from **Manager**.
- Select the lines as shown in Figure-135 and click on the **Mirror** tool from **Position** panel in **Tools** contextual tab of **Ribbon**. The **Mirror Manager** will be displayed.

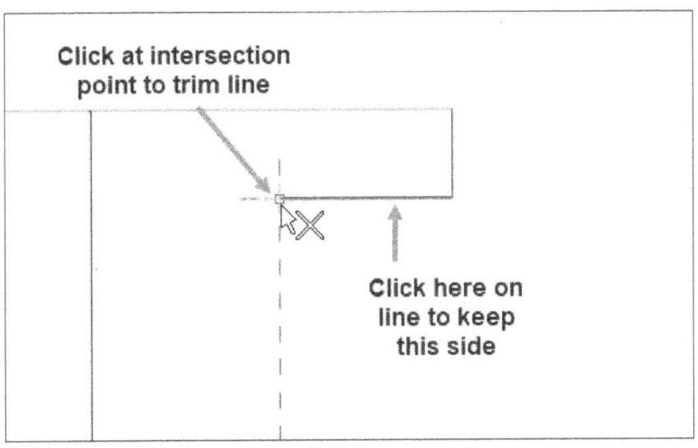

Figure-134. Trimming line

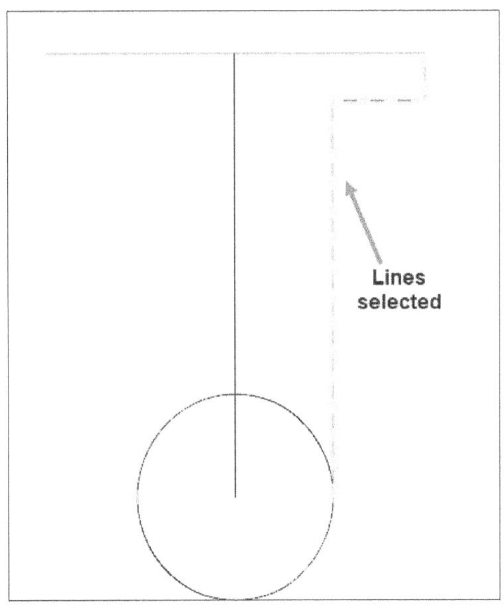

Figure-135. Lines to be selected

- Select the **Vector** radio button from **Axis** rollout in the **Manager** and select the centerline earlier created. Preview of mirror feature will be displayed; refer to Figure-136.

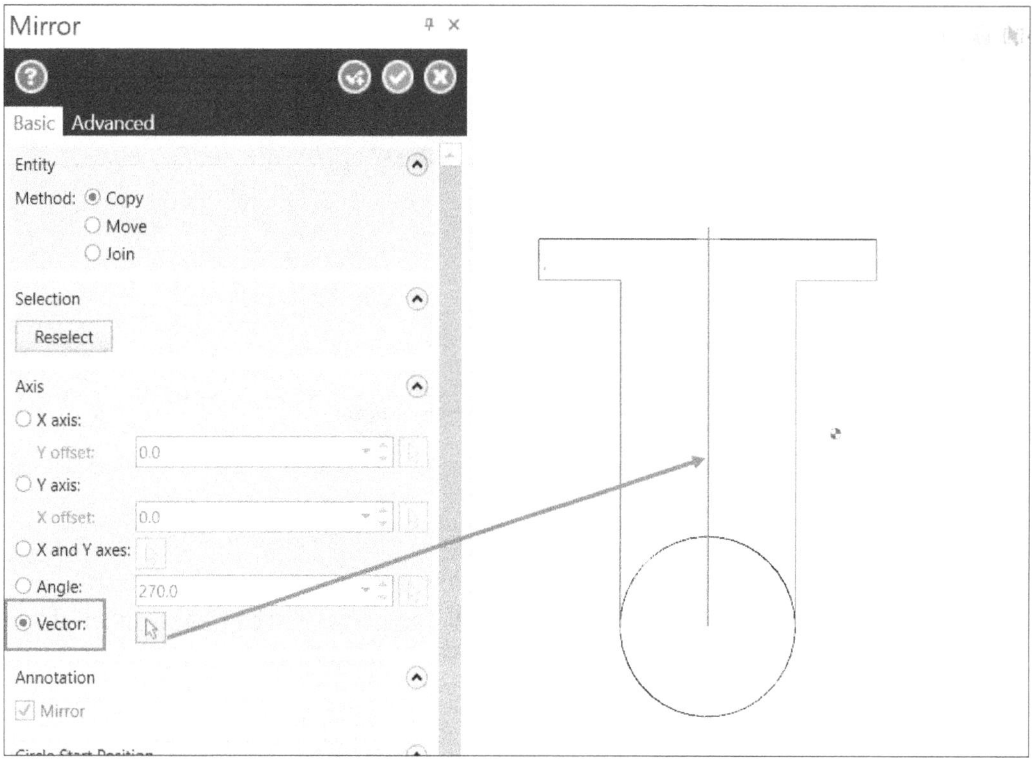

Figure-136. Preview of mirror feature

- Click on the **OK** button from the **Manager** to create mirror feature. Press **ESC** to exit selection.
- Click on the **Trim Many** tool from the **Trim to Entities** drop-down in the **Modify** panel of the **Ribbon**. The **Trim Many Manager** will be displayed and you will be asked to select curves to be trimmed.
- Select the circle and click on the **End Selection** button from graphics area. You will be asked to select curve to be used as trimming tool.
- Select left vertical line created by using **Mirror** tool; refer to Figure-137. You will be asked to select the side of curve (which is circle in this case) to be trimmed.
- Click above the circle to remove upper portion of circle. After trimming, circle will be displayed as shown in Figure-138. Click on the **OK** button from **Trim Many Manager** to exit the tool.

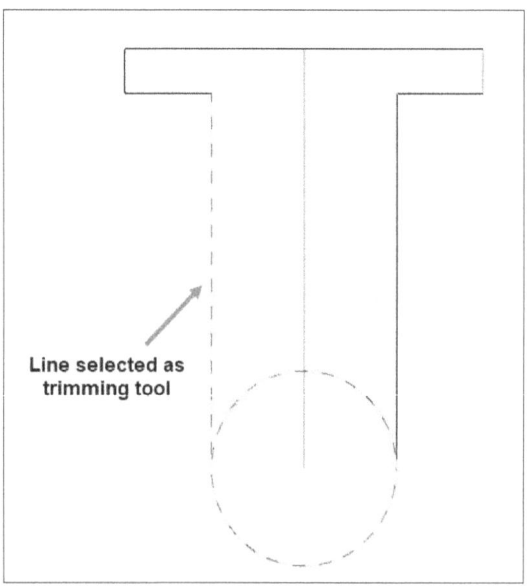

Figure-137. Line selected as trimming tool

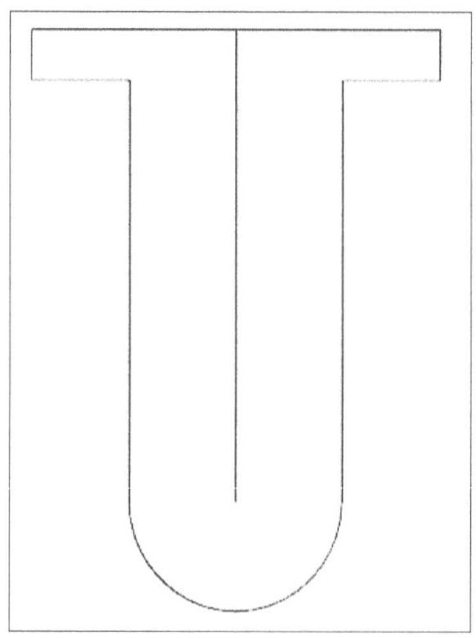

Figure-138. After trimming circle

- Select the center line in the sketch and click on the **Entity** tool from **Offset** panel in **Tools** contextual tab of **Ribbon**. The **Offset Entity Manager** will be displayed.
- Specify the parameters as shown in Figure-139 and click on the **OK** button from **Manager** to create offset copies.

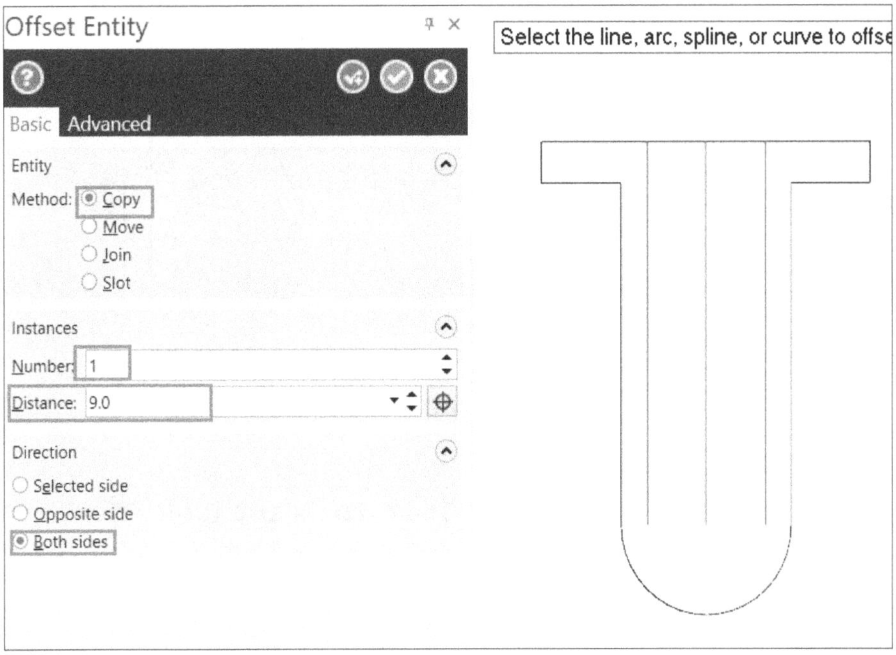

Figure-139. Creating offset copies

- Click on the **Trim to Entities** tool from the **Modify** panel in the **Wireframe** tab of **Ribbon**. The **Trim to Entities Manager** will be displayed and you will be asked to select the entity to be trimmed/extended.
- Select one of the offset line earlier created and then click on the trimmed circle. The offset line will extend automatically up to the trimmed circle; refer to Figure-140.
- Similarly, extend the other offset line; refer to Figure-141.

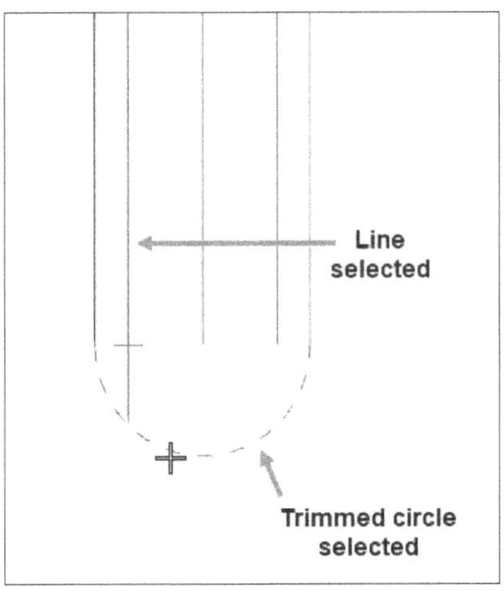

Figure-140. Extending line

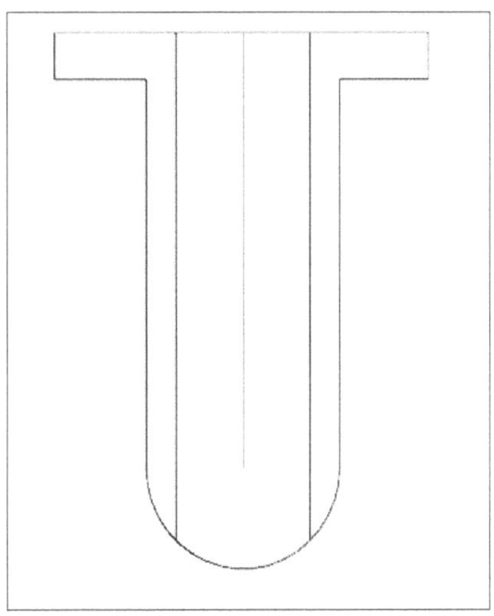

Figure-141. After extending lines

- Offset the horizontal line created at the beginning by a distance of **40**; refer to Figure-142 and click on the **OK** button.

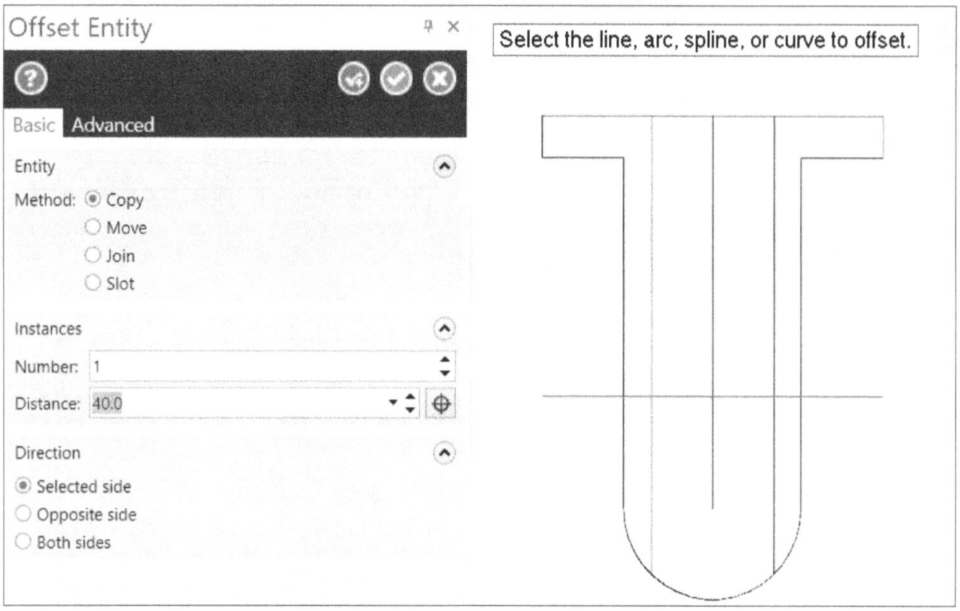

Figure-142. Offsetting horizontal line

- Trim extra segment of lines using the **Trim to Point** tool; refer to Figure-143.

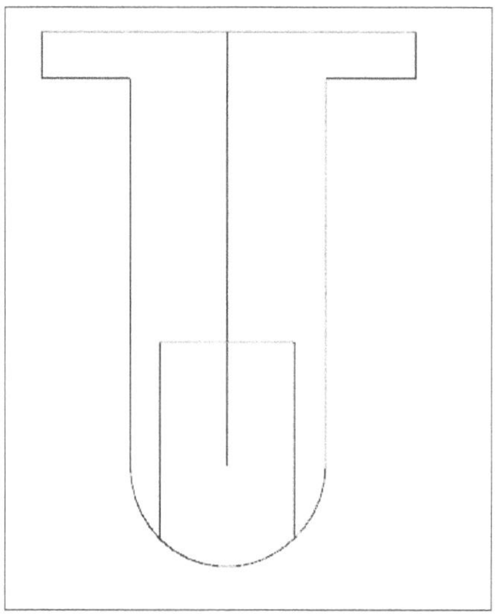

Figure-143. After trimming lines

- Create a circle of diameter **13** at the center of trimmed circle and delete the centerline. Final sketch will be displayed as shown in Figure-144.

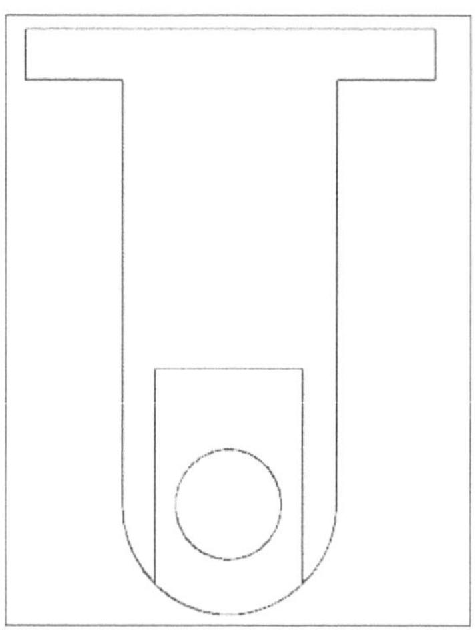

Figure-144. Final sketch

PRACTICE 1

Create the sketch as shown in Figure-145.

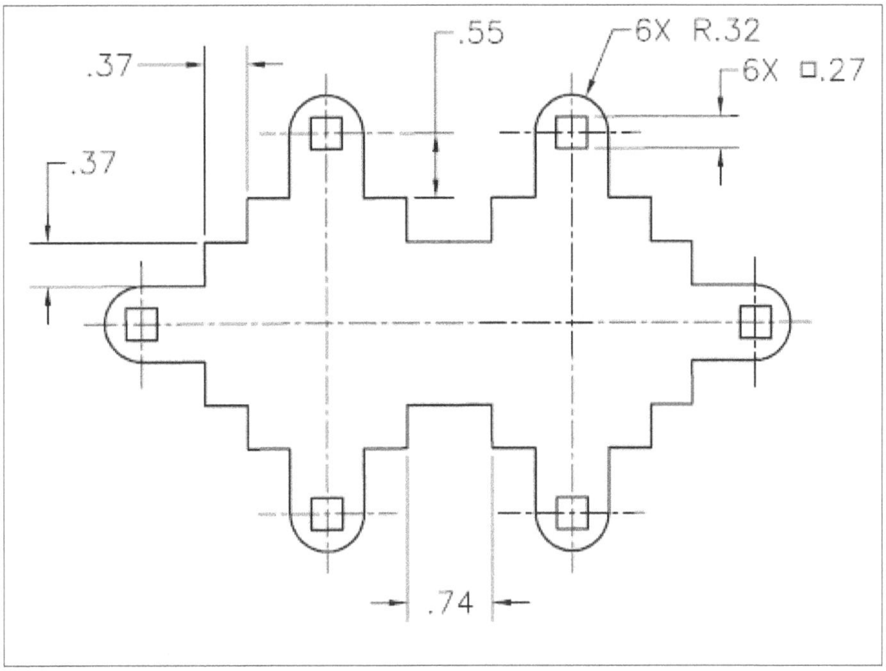

Figure-145. Practice 1

SELF-ASSESSMENT

Q1. Which of the following tools is used to create point by specifying coordinates?

a. Point Position
b. Point Dynamic
c. Point Segment
d. Point Endpoints

Q2. Which of the following tools is used to create a point along selected curve?

a. Point Position
b. Point Dynamic
c. Point Segment
d. Point Endpoints

Q3. The .... tool is used to create an arc by specifying end points.

Q4. The .... tool is used to create arc of specified angular span.

Q5. The Spline Manual tool is used to create splines manually by specifying the ....

a. vertices
b. control points

Q6. What is the function of Spline Blended tool?

Q7. The Spline Automatic tool is used to create spline through string of points in drawing area. (T/F)

Q8. Which of the following shapes cannot be created by using the Rectangular Shapes tool in Mastercam?

a. Obround
b. Single D
c. Double D
d. Parallelogram

Q9. The Bounding Box tool is used to create a rectangular or cylindrical 3-D bounding box around selected objects. (T/F)

Q10. The Break at Intersection tool is used to break the selected entity at specified point. (T/F)

Q11. The Break Two Pieces tool is used to break selected entities at intersection with the other entities. (T/F)

Q12. The Break Circles tool is used to split selected circle into multiple segments. (T/F)

REVIEW QUESTIONS

Q1. Which tool is used to create a point by specifying its exact coordinates?
A. Point Dynamic
B. Point Segment
C. Point Position
D. Point Endpoints

Q2. What is the purpose of the 'Thread point' option in the Point Position Manager?
A. To create a simple reference point
B. To mark the end point of the toolpath
C. To indicate where the wire starts creating thread
D. To create a chain of points

Q3. Which tool allows creation of a point dynamically along an arc, line, or surface?
A. Point Nodes
B. Point Segment
C. Point Dynamic
D. Point Small Arcs

Q4. What parameter must be specified in the Point Segment tool to generate equidistant points?
A. Radius
B. Diameter
C. Number of points or distance
D. Angle

Q5. What does the Point Endpoints tool do?
A. Creates points on small arcs
B. Creates points at spline nodes
C. Creates points at end points of selected curves
D. Creates points at midpoints of lines

Q6. Which tool is used to create points at the nodes of a spline?
A. Point Endpoints
B. Point Small Arcs
C. Point Nodes
D. Point Dynamic

Q7. In the Point Small Arcs tool, what does the Maximum Radius parameter define?
A. Minimum arc length
B. Arc color
C. Maximum radius of arcs for point creation
D. Maximum number of points

Q8. What can be created using the Bolt Circle tool?
A. Spline through curves
B. Circle tangent to three points
C. Points/arcs in a circular pattern
D. Lines perpendicular to arcs

Q9. What method can be selected in the Line Endpoints Manager to create a horizontal line?
A. Freeform
B. Tangent
C. Vertical
D. Horizontal

Q10. What is the purpose of the Line Parallel tool?
A. To draw bisectors
B. To draw perpendicular lines
C. To create lines parallel to selected entities
D. To create concentric arcs

Q11. Which tool creates the shortest line between two selected entities?
A. Line Parallel
B. Line Endpoints
C. Line Bisect
D. Line Closest

Q12. Which tool creates a bisector of two lines?
A. Line Normal to Point
B. Line Tangent Through Point
C. Line Bisect
D. Line Closest

Q13. What is the primary function of the Circle Center Point tool?
A. Create arc tangent to three entities
B. Create spline using curves
C. Create circle by specifying center and diameter
D. Create line through two points

Q14. Which method does the Arc 3 Points tool use to create an arc?
A. Start, midpoint, endpoint
B. Center, radius, angle
C. Start point, radius, tangent
D. Endpoint, midpoint, angle

Q15. What is the function of the Arc Tangent tool?
A. Create arc based on polar coordinates
B. Create arc tangent to selected entity
C. Create a 3-point tangent arc
D. Create arc using endpoints

Q16. Which tool is used to create a circle tangent to three selected entities?
A. Arc Tangent
B. Circle Center Point
C. Circle Edge Point
D. Arc Endpoints

Q17. What is specified first when using the Arc Endpoints tool?
A. Radius
B. Center
C. Start point
D. Midpoint

Q18. Which parameters are required in the Arc Polar tool?
A. Only start and end angles
B. Radius/diameter and start/end angles
C. Diameter and number of segments
D. Midpoint and radius

Q19. The Arc Polar Endpoints tool allows creation of arc using:
A. Center and midpoint
B. Start or end point and angles
C. Radius and three points
D. Midpoint and tangent lines

Q20. What is the function of the Spline Manual tool?
A. Create arc using curves
B. Create spline manually by defining vertices
C. Create 3D arc
D. Join circles with a line

Q21. What is the main use of the Spline Blended tool?
A. Create a spline using points
B. Create circle tangent to curves
C. Join two curves with a spline
D. Create arc by angle

Q22. What option in the Spline From Curves tool deletes original geometry after spline creation?
A. Smooth Corners
B. Delete curves
C. Keep Original
D. Fit Tolerance

Q23. What parameter in Spline From Curves controls deviation from original curves?
A. Z-depth
B. Tangent distance
C. Tolerance
D. Chord length

Q24. Which tool is used to create a spline through a string of predefined points in the drawing area?
A. Spline From Curves
B. Spline Blended
C. Spline Automatic
D. Spline Manual

Q25. What is the function of the Spline Convert to NURBS tool?
A. Create spline through arcs
B. Convert spline into curve
C. Convert lines, arcs, and circles into NURBS splines
D. Create spline tangent to surfaces

Q26. How is the width and height of a rectangle specified using the Rectangle tool?
A. By selecting 3 corner points
B. Using Width and Height edit boxes in the Manager
C. By defining midpoint and radius
D. Using angle and length parameters

Q27. What shapes can be created using the Rectangular Shapes tool?
A. Only rectangles
B. Circle and polygon
C. Obround, single D, and double D
D. Triangle and square

Q28. Which radio button defines whether a polygon is based on an inscribed or circumscribed circle?
A. Flat and Corner
B. Square and Obround
C. Arc and Line
D. Fit and Offset

Q29. What is the purpose of the Arc segments option in the Ellipse tool?
A. Create elliptical splines
B. Create ellipse using single radius
C. Create ellipse from multiple arc segments
D. Create ellipse from multiple line segments

Q30. Which tool is used to create a 3D helix curve in the drawing area?
A. Spiral
B. Circle Edge Point
C. Helix
D. Arc Polar

Q31. What additional parameter must be specified in the Spiral tool compared to the Helix tool?
A. Number of revolutions
B. Base radius
C. Height
D. Horizontal pitch

Q32. What is the purpose of the Create Letters tool?
A. To convert spline to text
B. To insert title block
C. To create machinable geometry from text
D. To write code

Q33. What does the Raster to Vector tool convert?
A. Curves into splines
B. Vector to raster graphics
C. Raster images into vector geometry
D. Spline into text

Q34. What is the function of the Threshold slider in the Raster to Vector tool?
A. Defines number of revolutions
B. Sets color intensity for black & white conversion
C. Adjusts line thickness
D. Defines arc smoothing

Q35. Which radio button in Raster to Vector allows generation of only outlines in the image?
A. Create center lines
B. Create outlines
C. Manually trace bitmap image
D. Background bitmap

Q36. What does the Smooth more button do in the Raster to Vector workflow?
A. Adds sharp corners
B. Increases color saturation
C. Smoothens vector geometry
D. Converts outline to spline

Q37. Which tool is used to create stairs with parameters such as tread thickness and number of steps?
A. Ladder Tool
B. Stair Geometry Tool
C. Step Creator
D. Profile Extruder

Q38. What does the Overhang Amt parameter define in Stair Geometry?
A. Number of risers
B. Width of base
C. Height of stair
D. Width of stair overhanging from vertical section

Q39. Which tool is used to generate door profiles in the 3D view?
A. Wall Builder
B. Curve One Edge
C. Door Geometry
D. Slot Generator

Q40. What does the Curve One Edge tool do?
A. Creates a curve through three points
B. Creates a curve using selected model edge
C. Converts raster image into curve
D. Creates a circle from spline

Q41. In the Curve Slice by Plane tool, what defines the cutting reference?
A. Line length
B. Text height
C. Slicing plane
D. Bounding box

Q42. What happens when you double-click a wireframe entity?
A. It gets deleted
B. It opens a new dialog box
C. Key points are shown for dynamic modification
D. It converts to NURBS

Q43. What is the function of the Dynamic Trim tool?
A. Trim only single arcs
B. Dynamically trim entities using various methods
C. Join broken curves
D. Create toolpaths from wireframe

Q44. Which radio button in the Dynamic Trim Manager is used to increase the length of an entity?
A. Divide
B. Break
C. Shorten
D. Lengthen

Q45. What does the Trim to Entities tool require for trimming?
A. A vector file
B. Start and end points
C. Entity to be trimmed and trimming entity
D. Reference line and arc

Q46. What is the purpose of the Trim to Point tool?
A. Create arcs
B. Trim selected entity at a user-defined point
C. Extend lines
D. Split closed shapes

Q47. What additional selection is required in Trim Many tool after selecting entities to be trimmed?
A. Corner radius
B. Bounding box
C. Cutting curve
D. DPI resolution

Q48. What is the function of the Modify at Intersection tool?
A. To offset selected entities
B. To apply fillets between entities
C. To trim or break entities at intersection with surfaces/faces
D. To join multiple entities together

Q49. Which radio button should be selected in the Modify at Intersection Manager to only create points at intersections?
A. Trim
B. Break
C. Create points
D. Create only points

Q50. What tool is used to break an entity at a user-specified location?
A. Break Many
B. Break at Intersection
C. Break Two Pieces
D. Break at Points

Q51. Which tool breaks multiple selected entities into equal segments?
A. Break Two Pieces
B. Break Many
C. Divide
D. Modify Length

Q52. In the Break Many Pieces Manager, which option creates multiple lines after breaking entities?
A. Create curves
B. Create lines
C. Trim
D. Join

Q53. Which tool splits selected curves at already placed points?
A. Break at Intersection
B. Divide
C. Break at Points
D. Break Circles

Q54. What does the Divide tool do?
A. Joins two arcs
B. Offsets the selected entities
C. Trims or splits curves at intersection points
D. Modifies direction vector

Q55. Which condition must be met to join lines using the Join Entities tool?
A. They must be intersecting
B. They must be collinear
C. They must have same endpoints
D. They must be concentric

Q56. Which tool changes the length of an entity by a defined value?
A. Modify Vector
B. Offset Entity
C. Modify Length
D. Break Many

Q57. What is the function of the Modify Vector tool?
A. Trim entities at surface
B. Change orientation of selected entity
C. Create offset curves
D. Apply chamfer

Q58. Which of the following is NOT a fillet type available in the Fillet Entities Manager?
A. Clearance
B. Relief
C. Taper
D. Circle

Q59. What does the Fillet Chains tool do?
A. Fillets individual points only
B. Applies fillet to the outermost corners only
C. Applies fillets automatically on all intersections of selected chained entities
D. Applies chamfer in chained entities

Q60. In the Chamfer Entities tool, which method allows setting different distances along two intersecting entities?
A. 1 Distance
B. 2 Distance
C. Width
D. Circle

Q61. What does the Offset Entity tool do when "Copy" is selected?
A. Moves selected entity
B. Joins selected entity
C. Creates copy parallel to original
D. Deletes selected entity

Q62. In the Project tool, which radio button projects entities to a specified depth value?
A. Plane
B. Surfaces/Solids
C. Depth
D. Join

Q63. Which tool is used to convert an arc into a complete circle?
A. Refit Spline
B. Close Arc
C. Break Circles
D. Edit Spline

Q64. Which tool splits a circle into multiple arc segments?
A. Break Circles
B. Divide
C. Break Many
D. Trim

Q65. What is the purpose of the Combine Views tool?
A. Join views with different orientations
B. Apply symmetry to views
C. Combine multiple parallel views into one
D. Create section views

Q66. Which option in the Refit Spline tool keeps the original spline after repair?
A. Break
B. Blend
C. Delete
D. Keep

Q67. In the Refit Spline Manager, which option smooths the curve by adding a segment at a sharp point?
A. Blend
B. Break
C. Tolerance
D. Simplify

Chapter 3

Surface Design

Topics Covered

The major topics covered in this chapter are:

- ***Introduction to Surface Design.***
- ***Placing Predefined Surface Blocks.***
- ***Creating Surface Features.***
- ***Modifying Surface Features.***
- ***Setting Surface Direction.***
- ***Modifying Flow Lines.***

INTRODUCTION

Surfaces are used to define shape of top layer of objects. Surfaces are geometric objects with zero thickness, so they do not exist in real world. For creating objects using surfaces, you need to apply thickness to surfaces or solidify them. In Mastercam, surfaces are used as reference for machining faces of the workpiece. The tools to create and manage surfaces are available in the **Surfaces** tab of the **Ribbon**; refer to Figure-1. Various tools of the **Surfaces** tab are discussed next.

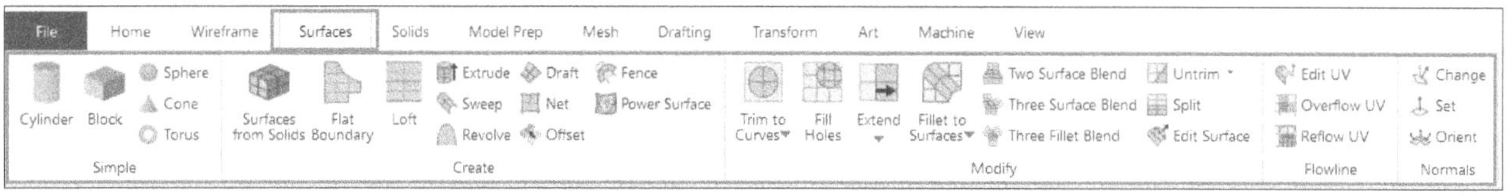

Figure-1. Surfaces tab

CREATING CYLINDER

The **Cylinder** tool is used to place cylindrical surface of specified parameters in 3D view. The procedure to use this tool is given next.

- Click on the **Cylinder** tool from the **Simple** drop-down in the **Surfaces** tab of the **Ribbon**. The **Primitive Cylinder Manager** will be displayed; refer to Figure-2.

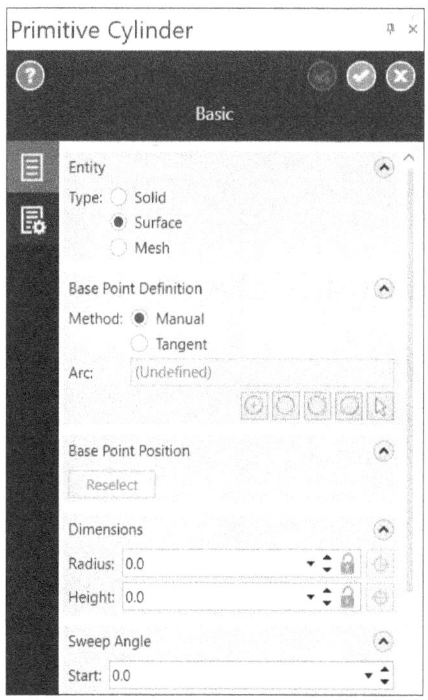

Figure-2. Primitive Cylinder Manager

- By default, the **Surface** radio button is selected in the **Entity** rollout of **Manager** so you will be able to create surface primitives. Select the **Solid** radio button if you want to create solid primitive. Select the **Mesh** radio button to create mesh object.
- By default, **Manual** radio button is selected in the **Base Point Definition** rollout, so you need to specify location of center point and circumferential point manually without constraints. Select the **Tangent** radio button if you want to create base circle tangent to selected entity. You can also select desired button from the rollout to use respective selection filter. For example, select the **Three edges** button to use three selected edges from graphics area as reference for defining base circle of cylinder.

- Set desired parameters in the **Radius** and **Height** edit boxes of **Dimensions** rollout in the **Manager** to define the radius and height of cylinder.
- Specify desired values in **Start** and **End** edit boxes to define start and end angle of cylinder.
- Select desired radio button from the **Axis** rollout to define axis direction of cylinder.
- After setting desired parameters, click at desired location. Preview of primitive cylinder surface will be displayed; refer to Figure-3.

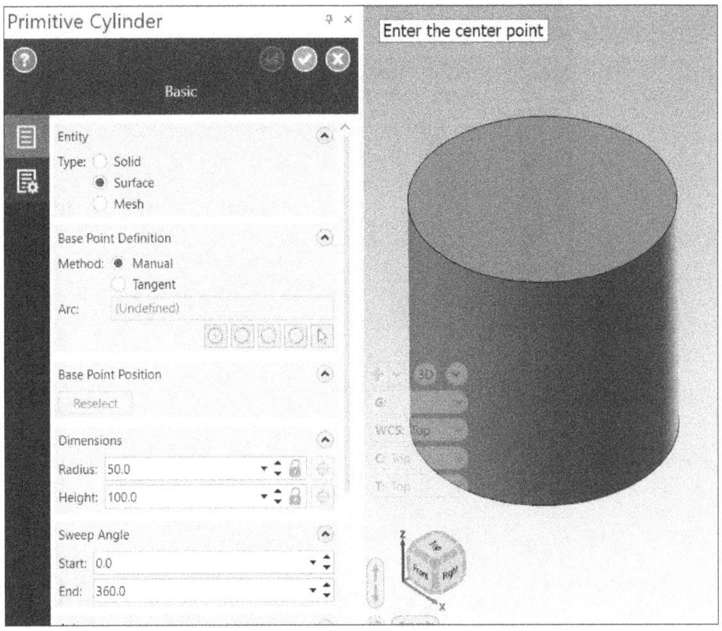

Figure-3. Preview of primitive cylinder

- Select the **Do not create model history** check box to create primitive body without model history.
- Click on the **OK** button from the **Manager** to create the primitive surface body.

CREATING SURFACE BLOCK

The **Block** tool in **Surfaces** tab is used to create rectangular block of surface. The procedure to use this tool is given next.

- Click on the **Block** tool from the **Simple** group in the **Surfaces** tab of the **Ribbon**. The **Primitive Block Manager** will be displayed; refer to Figure-4 and you will be asked to specify base point for block.
- Select desired corner point of the **Origin** rollout to define which point of block is to be used for placing surface block.
- Set desired angle value in the **Rotation Angle** edit box to rotate the surface block about selected placement point.
- Select desired radio button to define axis to be used for defining height of block. Select the **Vector** radio button to use selected direction reference for defining height of block.
- Set desired values in the **Length**, **Width**, and **Height** edit boxes of **Dimensions** rollout to define size of the block.
- After setting desired parameters, click in the drawing area to place the block.
- Click on the **OK** button from the **Manager** to create the block.

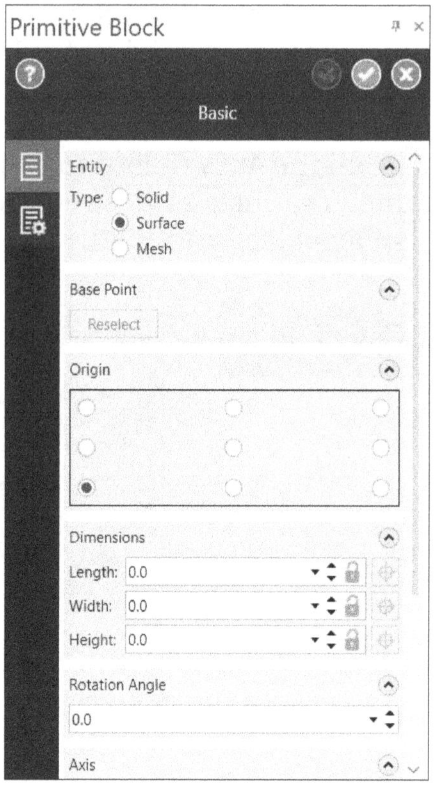

Figure-4. Primitive Block Manager

CREATING SURFACE SPHERE

The **Sphere** tool is used to create surface sphere of specified parameters. The procedure to use this tool is given next.

- Click on the **Sphere** tool from the **Simple** group in the **Surfaces** tab of the **Ribbon**. The **Primitive Sphere Manager** will be displayed; refer to Figure-5.

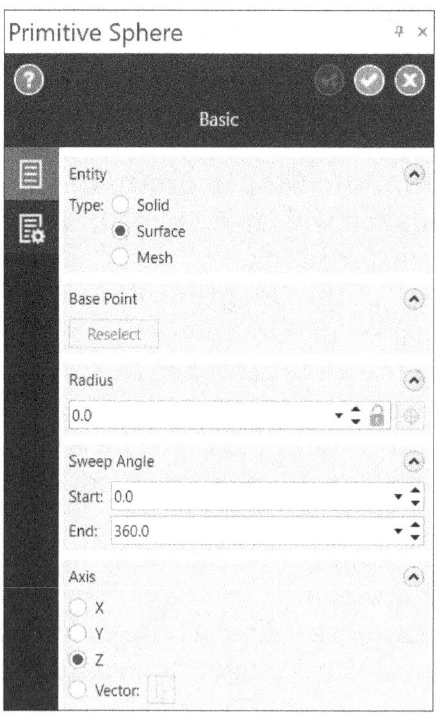

Figure-5. Primitive Sphere Manager

- Select the **Solid** radio button if you want to create a solid sphere. Select the **Surface** radio button to create a surface sphere. Select **Mesh** radio button to create mesh sphere.
- Click in the **Radius** edit box of the **Manager** and specify radius of sphere.
- Specify the values in the **Start** and **End** edit boxes of **Sweep Angle** rollout to define angular span of sphere.
- Specify the other parameters as discussed earlier and click at desired location to place the sphere; refer to Figure-6.

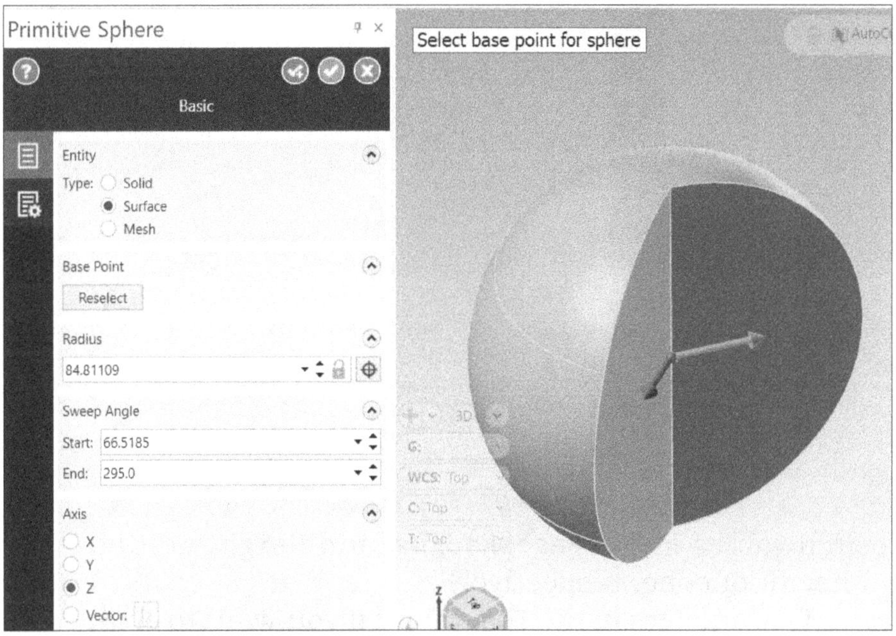

Figure-6. Preview of sphere surface

- Click on the **OK** button from the **Manager** to create the sphere.

CREATING SURFACE CONE

The **Cone** tool in **Surface** group is used to create surface of conical shape. The procedure to use this tool is given next.

- Click on the **Cone** tool from the **Simple** group in the **Surfaces** tab of the **Ribbon**. The **Primitive Cone Manager** will be displayed; refer to Figure-7 and you will be asked to specify the base point of surface cone.

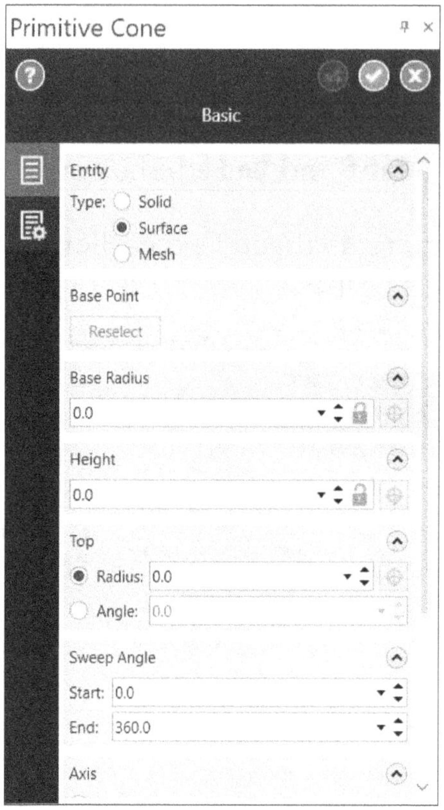

Figure-7. Primitive Cone Manager

- Specify desired values in the **Base Radius** and **Height** edit boxes to define base radius and height of cone, respectively.
- Specify desired parameters in the **Top** rollout if you want to create conical frustum. Specify desired value in the **Radius** edit box of **Top** rollout to specify radius of top face of conical frustum. Select the **Angle** radio button and specify angle of the top of conical frustum.
- Set the other parameters as discussed earlier and click in the 3D view to place the cone. Preview of cone will be displayed; refer to Figure-8.

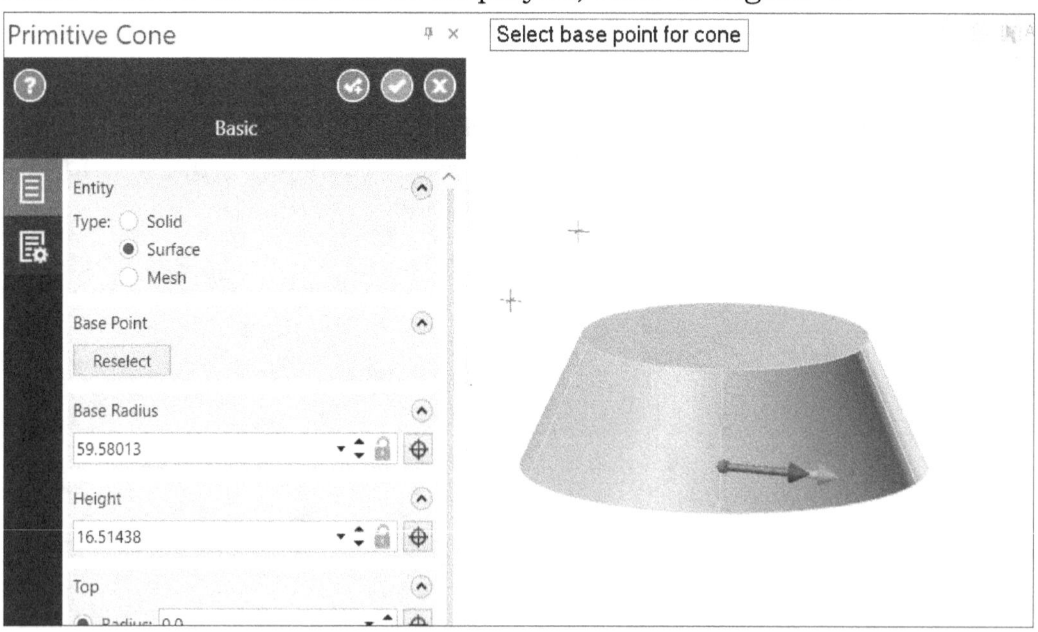

Figure-8. Preview of cone

- Click on the **OK** button from the **Manager** to create the cone.

CREATING TORUS SURFACE

The **Torus** tool is used to create surface torus of specified parameters. The procedure to use this tool is given next.

- Click on the **Torus** tool from the **Simple** group in the **Surfaces** tab of the **Ribbon**. The **Primitive Torus Manager** will be displayed; refer to Figure-9 and you will be asked to specify the base point of torus.
- Specify desired values in the **Major** and **Minor** edit boxes to define major and minor radii of torus, respectively.
- Set the other parameters as desired and click in the 3D view to place torus. Preview of torus will be displayed; refer to Figure-10.

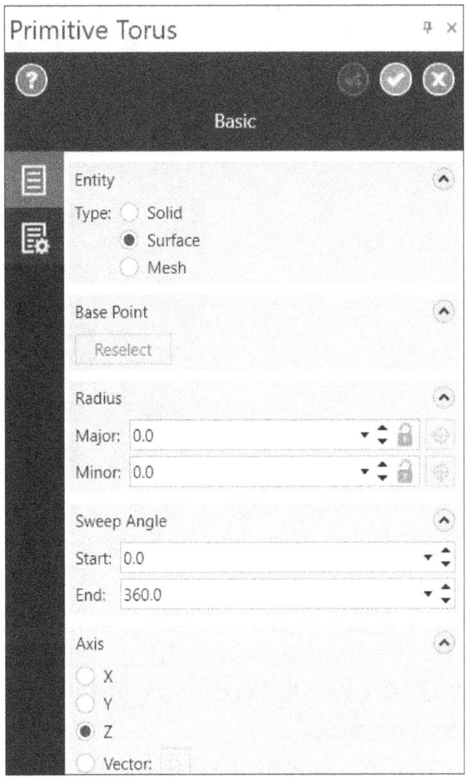

Figure-9. Primitive Torus Manager

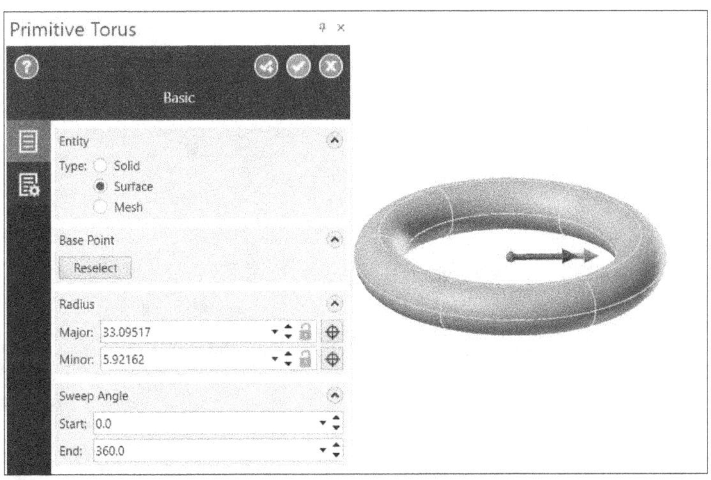

Figure-10. Preview of torus

- Click on the **OK** button from the **Manager** to create the torus.

CREATING SURFACE USING FACE OF SOLID

The **Surfaces from Solid** tool is used to create surface using selected face of solid. The procedure to use this tool is given next.

- Click on the **Surfaces From Solid** tool from the **Create** group in the **Surfaces** tab of the **Ribbon**. You will be asked to select faces of solid for creating surfaces.
- Select desired faces of solid and click on the **End Selection** button. Preview of surfaces will be displayed with **Surface From Solids Manager**; refer to Figure-11.

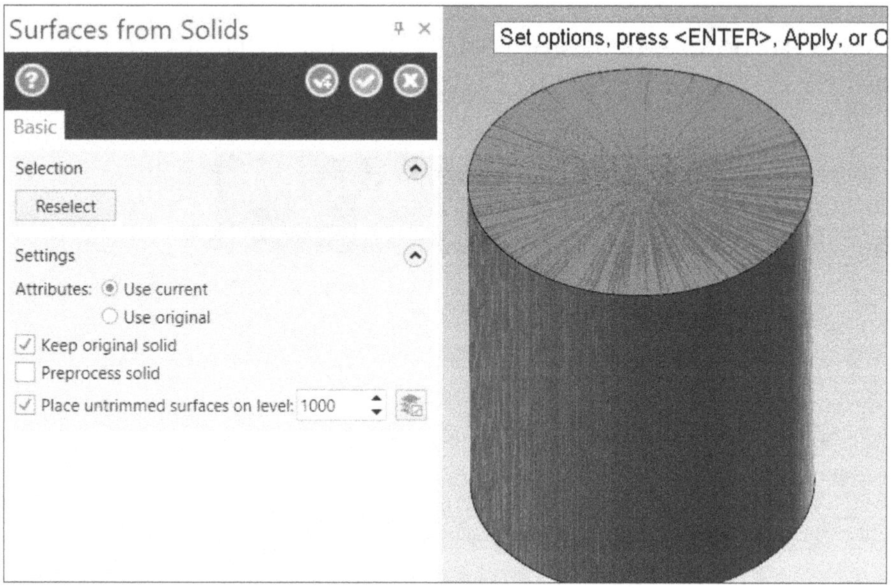

Figure-11. Preview of surfaces created from solid

- Select desired radio button from the **Attributes** section to specify whether you want to use attributes of original solid body or surface body.
- Clear the **Keep original solid** check box if you want to delete the solid body after creating surface.
- Select the **Preprocess solid** check box to repair the surface if there is problem in solid face to surface conversion.
- After setting desired parameters, click on the **OK** button from the **Manager**. The surface will be created; refer to Figure-12.

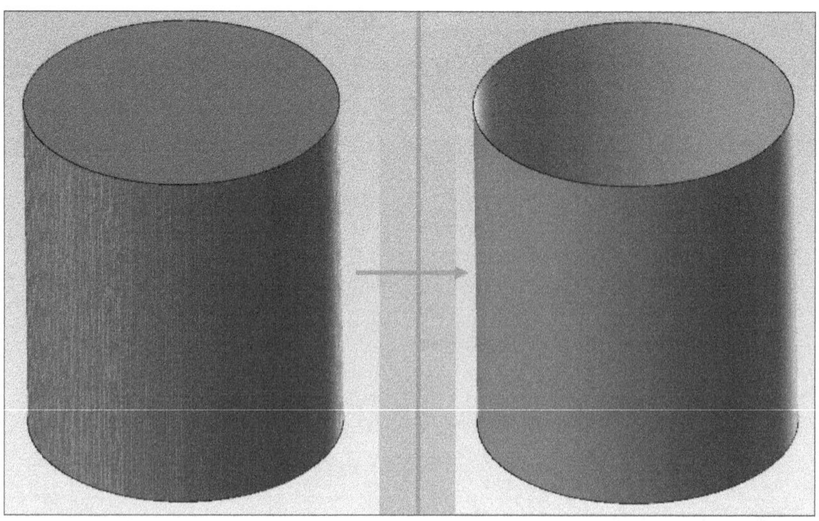

Figure-12. Preview of surface from solid

CREATING FLAT BOUNDARY SURFACE

The **Flat Boundary** tool is used to create flat surface using selected closed chain boundary. The procedure to use this tool is given next.

- Click on the **Flat Boundary** tool from the **Create** group in the **Surfaces** tab of the **Ribbon**. The **Flat Boundary Surface Manager** will be displayed with **Wireframe Chaining** selection box; refer to Figure-13.

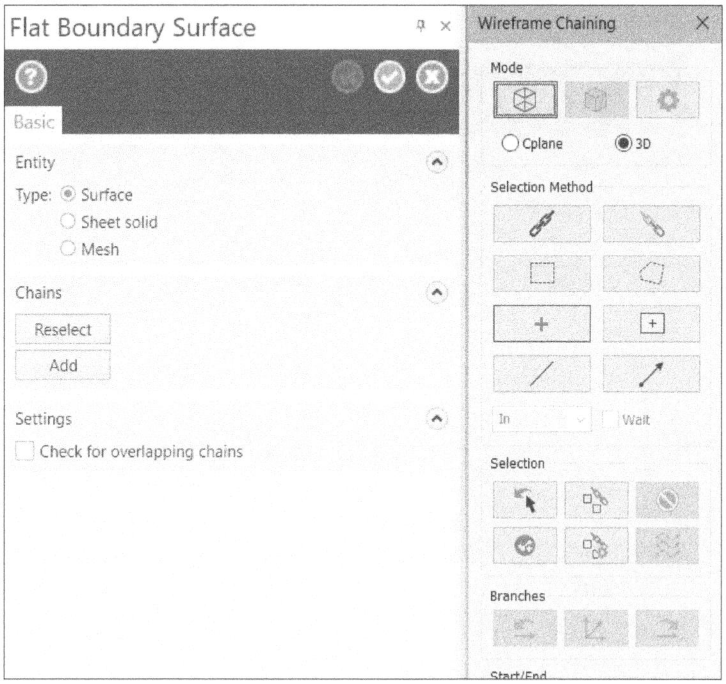

Figure-13. Flat Boundary Surface Manager

- Select the chain of entities and click on the **OK** button from the **Wireframe Chaining** selection box. Preview of flat boundary surface will be displayed; refer to Figure-14.

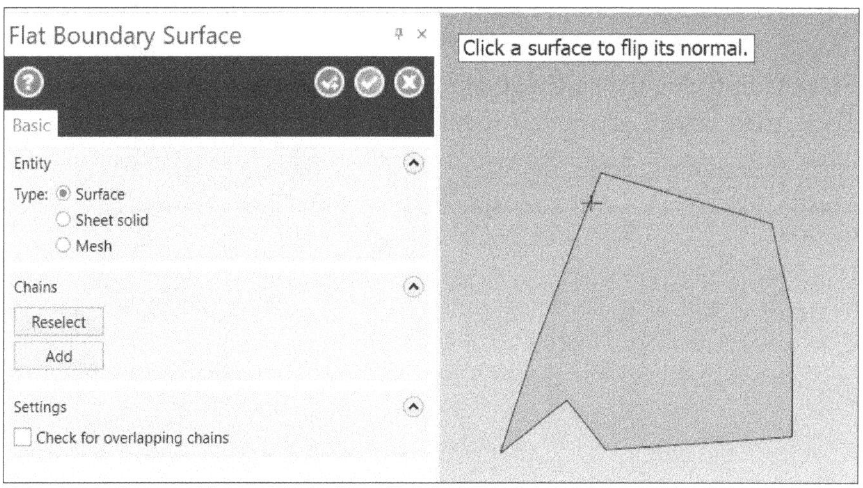

Figure-14. Preview of flat boundary surface

- Select the **Check for overlapping chains** check box to use nested chains for creating surface.
- Click on the **OK** button from the **Manager** to create the surface.

CREATING LOFTED SURFACE

The **Loft** tool is used to create surface by blending two chains. The procedure to use this tool is given next.

- Click on the **Loft** tool from the **Create** group in the **Surfaces** tab of **Ribbon**. The **Surface Ruled/Lofted Manager** will be displayed with **Wireframe Chaining** selection box; refer to Figure-15.

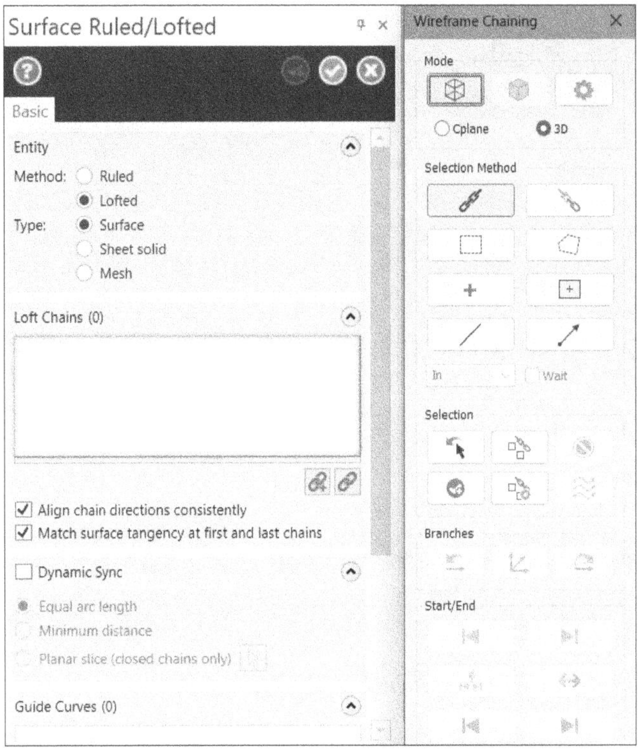

Figure-15. Surface Ruled Lofted Manager

- Select the chains to be used for loft surface; refer to Figure-16 and click on the **OK** button. Note that you can change the position of start point using the **Dynamic** button in **Start/End** section of **Wireframe Chaining** selection box. Preview of loft surface will be displayed; refer to Figure-17.

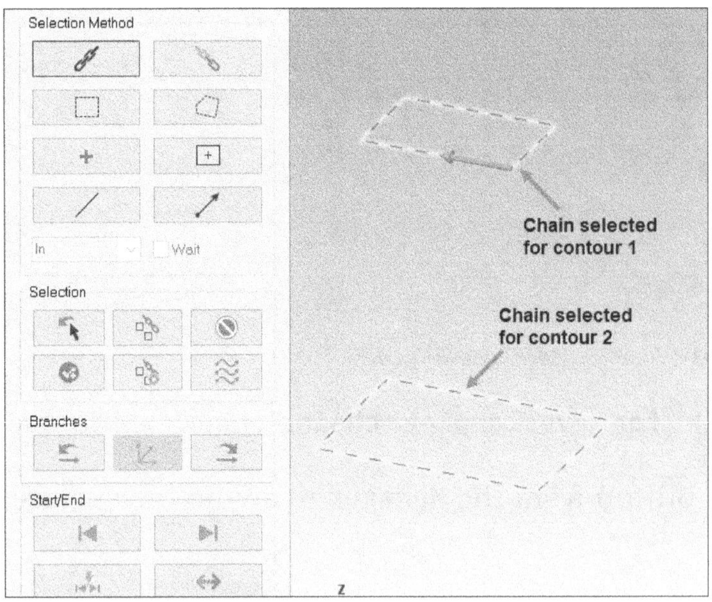

Figure-16. Wireframe chains selected for loft feature

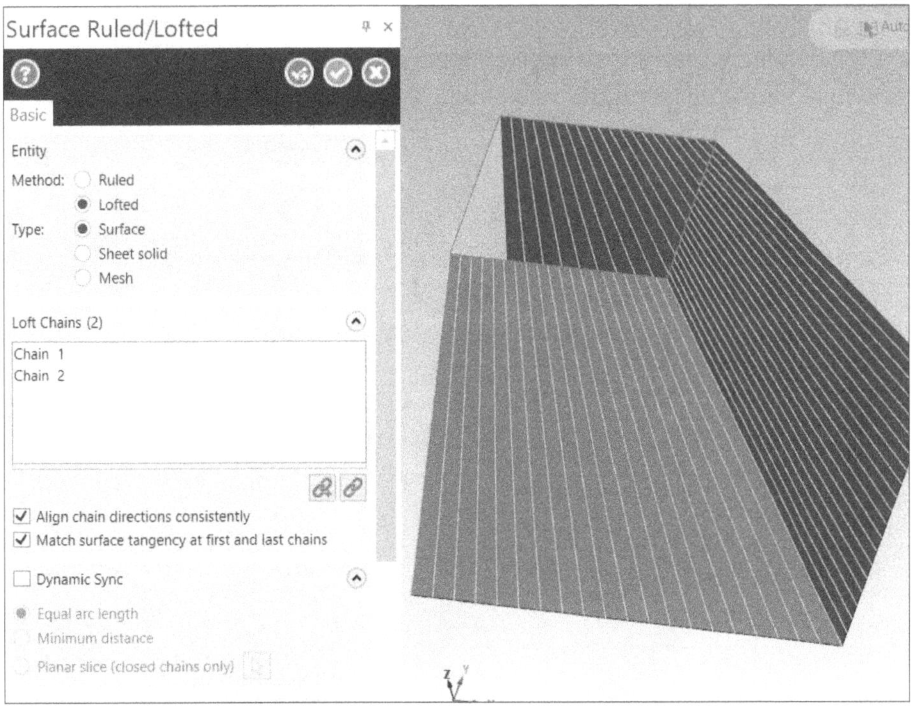

Figure-17. Preview of loft surface

- Select the **Align chain direction consistently** check box to match directions of each selected chain automatically for consistency.
- Select the **Match surface tangency at first and last chains** check box to keep the curvature of joining surfaces in accordance with surfaces connected to selected chains.
- Select the **Dynamic Sync** check box to redefine spacing of points. Note that multiple points are automatically selected on chained geometries for smoothing loft feature. On selecting this check box, the options to manually define space between these points will become active. Select the **Average** radio button to equally space points on chains. Select the **Entity** radio button to use selected entity as spine for loft feature. Select the **Minimum distance** radio button to make sure that points on multiple chains are at minimum distance from each other. For example, point on chain 1 is at minimum distance to in-line point on chain 2.
- Select the **U flowlines** and **V flowlines** check boxes to change curvature of surface along u and v directions. You can specify desired number of flow lines in the edit boxes next to these check boxes.
- Click on the **OK** button from the **Manager** to create the surface.

CREATING EXTRUDED SURFACE

The **Extrude** tool in **Surfaces** tab of **Ribbon** is used to create extruded surface using closed chain curve. The procedure to use this tool is given next.

- Click on the **Extrude** tool from the **Create** group in the **Surfaces** tab of the **Ribbon**. The **Surface Extrude Manager** will be displayed with **Wireframe Chaining** selection box; refer to Figure-18.

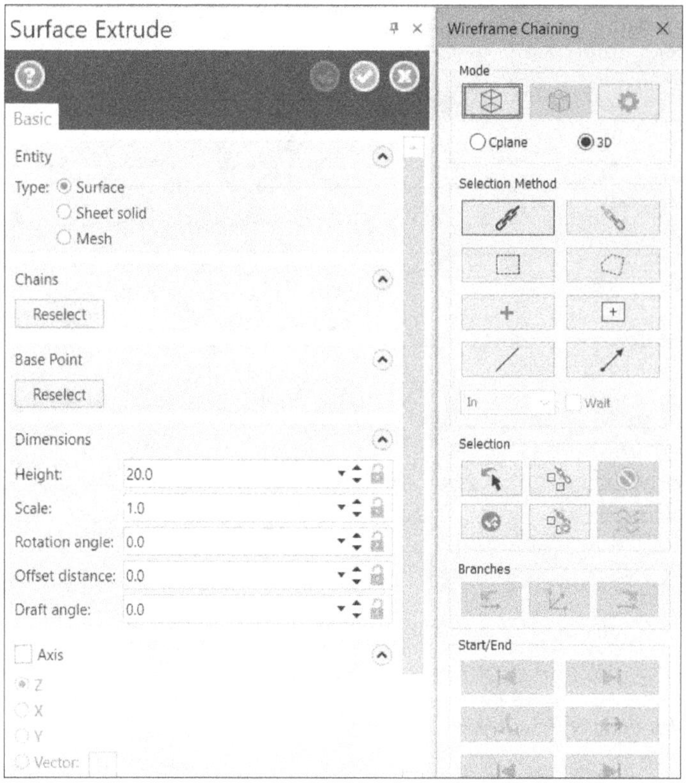

Figure-18. Surface Extrude Manager

- Select desired sketch chain and click on the **OK** button. Preview of extruded surface will be displayed; refer to Figure-19.

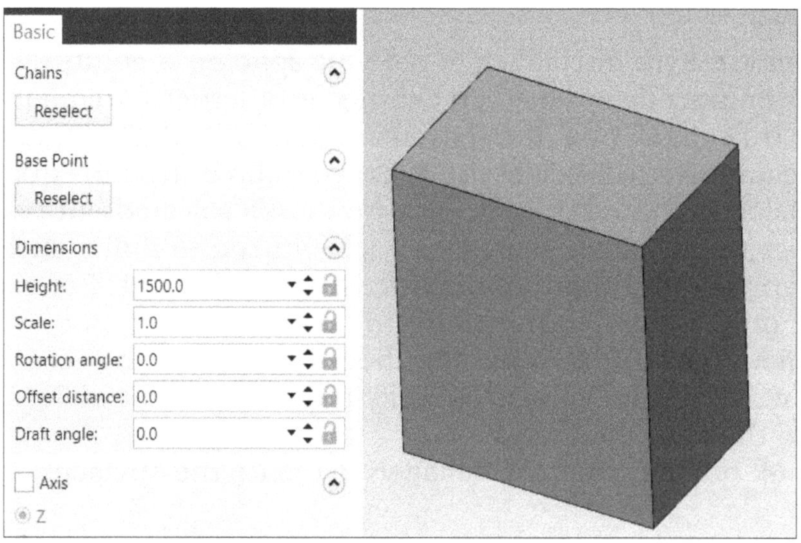

Figure-19. Preview of extrude surface

- Set the parameters as desired in the **Dimensions** rollout.
- Select the **Axis** check box and select desired radio button to define direction of extruded surface.
- Select desired radio button from the **Direction** rollout to define on which side of selected direction will the extrude feature be created.
- After setting desired parameters, click on the **OK** button from the **Manager** to create the feature.

CREATING SWEEP SURFACE

The **Sweep** tool in **Surfaces** tab is used to create surface by moving a closed or open section along selected contour. The procedure to use this tool is given next.

- Click on the **Sweep** tool from the **Create** group in the **Surfaces** tab of **Ribbon**. The **Surface Sweep Manager** will be displayed with **Wireframe Chaining** selection box; refer to Figure-20.

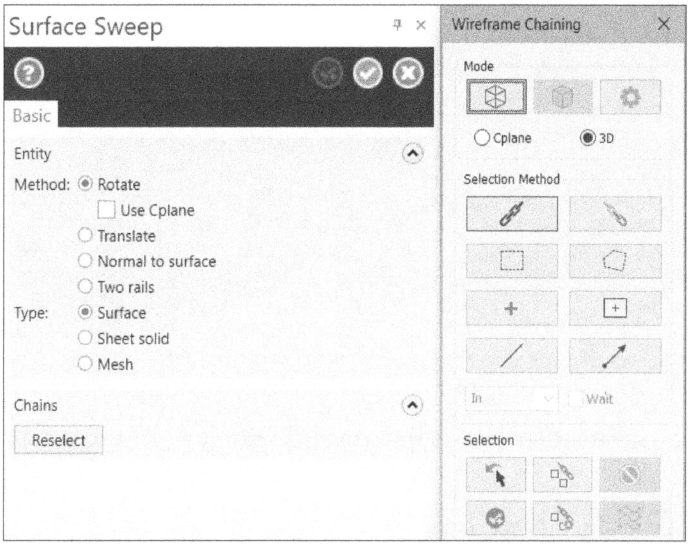

Figure-20. Surface Sweep Manager

- Select desired section to be swept along the contour; refer to Figure-21 and click on the **OK** button from the **Wireframe Chaining** selection box. You will be asked to select the path curve for sweep.

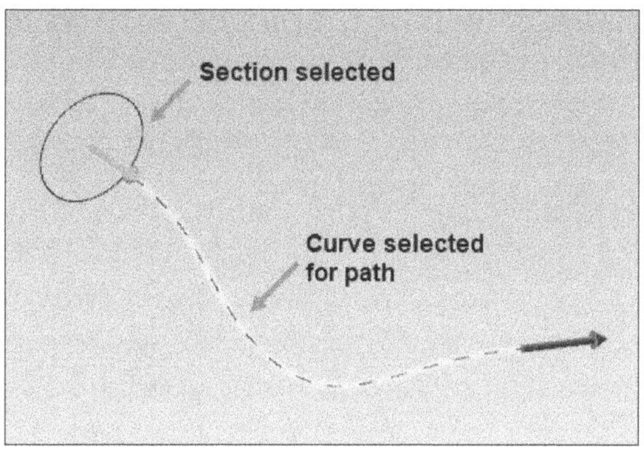

Figure-21. Selecting curves for sweep feature

- Select desired curve for path and click on the **OK** button from the **Wireframe Chaining** selection box. Preview of surface sweep feature will be displayed; refer to Figure-22.

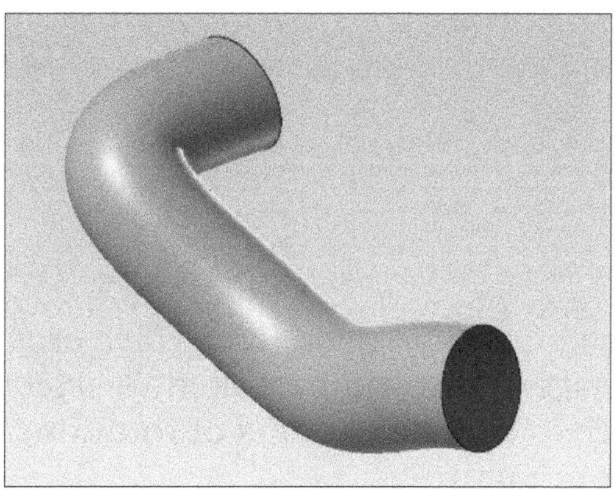

Figure-22. Preview of sweep surface feature

- Select the **Use Cplane** check box to use construction plane as axis for the rotation of section.
- Select the **Translate** radio button from the **Method** section of **Manager** if you do not want the section to rotate along the curve.
- Select the **Normal to surface** radio button from the **Manager** if you want to use a surface for defining direction of sweep feature.
- Select the **Two rails** radio button if you want to use two path curves for defining curvature of sweep feature. Preview of two rail sweep is shown in Figure-23.

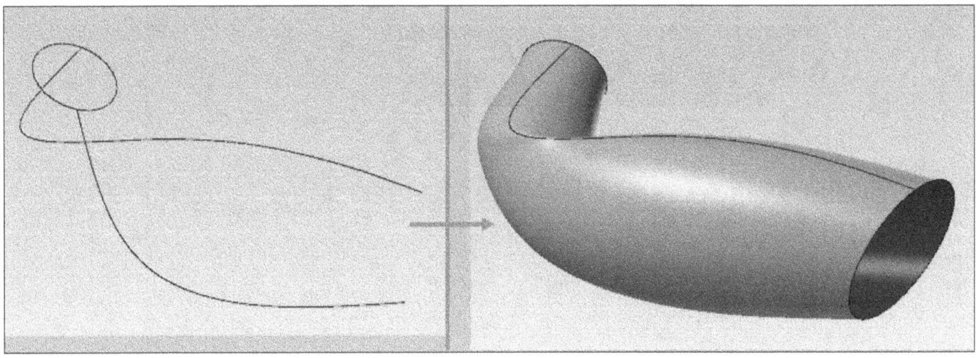

Figure-23. Preview of two rail sweep

- Specify the other parameters as discussed earlier, click on the **OK** button.

CREATING REVOLVE SURFACE

The **Revolve** tool in **Surfaces** tab of **Ribbon** is used to revolve selected sketch section about selected axis. The procedure to create revolve surface is given next.

- Click on the **Revolve** tool from the **Create** group in the **Surfaces** tab of **Ribbon**. The **Surface Revolve Manager** will be displayed with **Wireframe Chaining** selection box; refer to Figure-24.

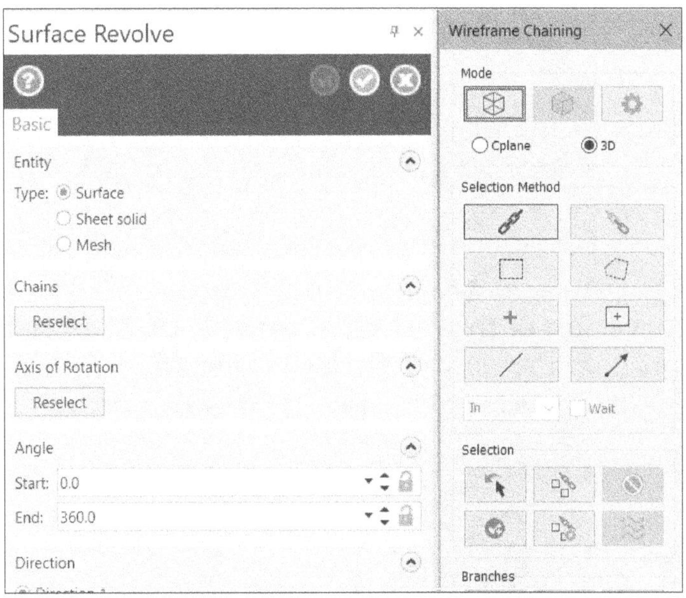

Figure-24. Surface Revolve Manager with Wireframe Chaining

- Select desired sketch section to be used for revolve cross-section and click on the **OK** button from the **Manager**. You will be asked to select an axis of rotation.
- Select desired line/edge to be used as axis of rotation. Preview of revolve surface will be displayed; refer to Figure-25.

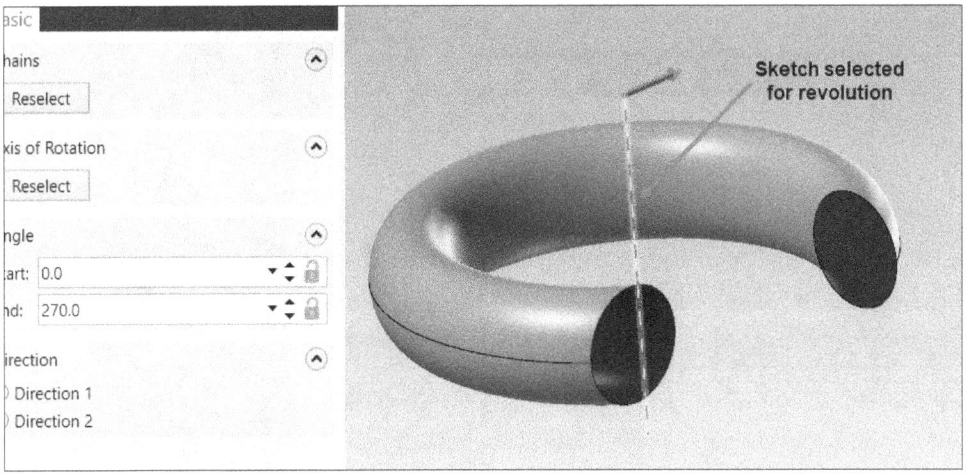

Figure-25. Preview of revolve surface

- After setting desired parameters, click on the **OK** button from the **Manager** to create the surface.

CREATING DRAFT SURFACE

The **Draft** tool is used to create planar surface using selected line, arc, or spline. The procedure to use this tool is given next.

- Click on the **Draft** tool from the **Create** group in the **Surfaces** tab of the **Ribbon**. The **Surface Draft Manager** with **Wireframe Chaining** selection box will be displayed; refer to Figure-26.
- Select desired curve chain and click on the **OK** button from the selection box. Preview of draft surface will be displayed; refer to Figure-27.

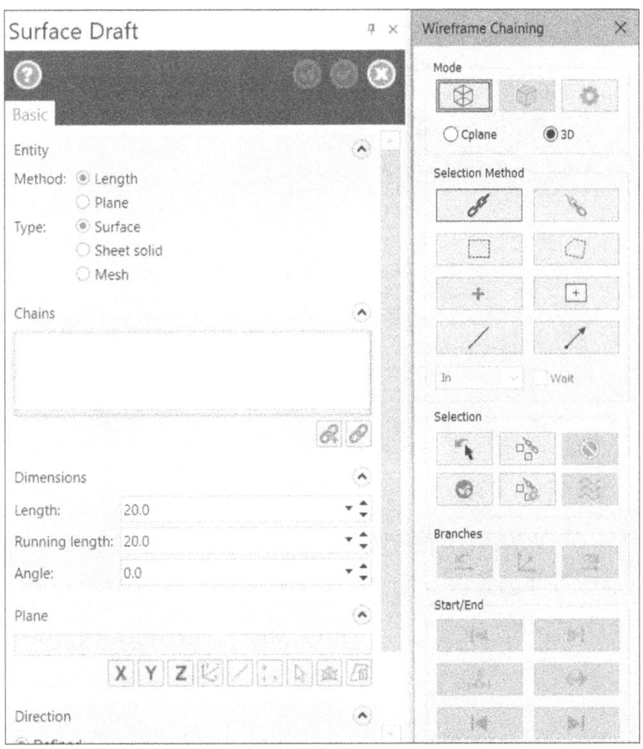

Figure-26. Surface Draft Manager with Wireframe Chaining selection box

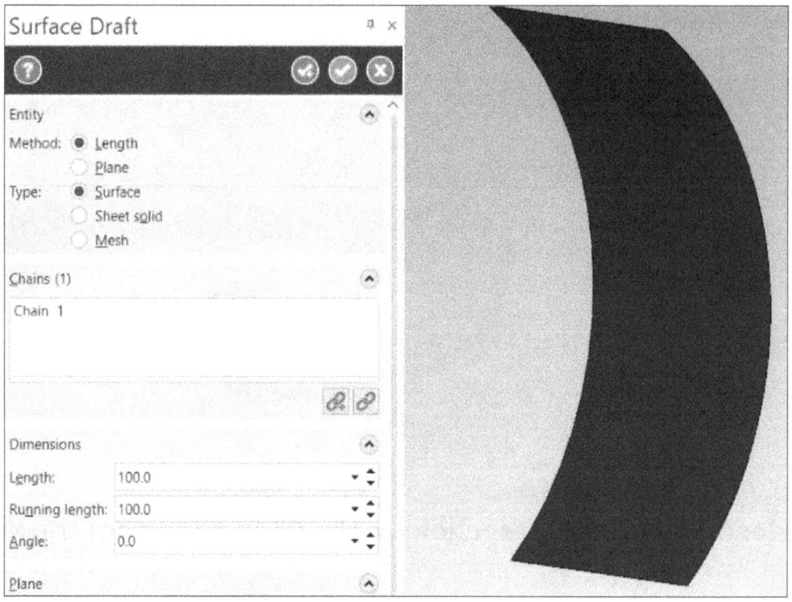

Figure-27. Preview of draft surface

- Set desired parameters in the **Manager** and click on the **OK** button. The surface will be created.

CREATING NET SURFACE

The **Net** tool is used to create surface using intersection curves. The procedure to use this tool is given next.

- Click on the **Net** tool from the **Create** group in the **Surfaces** tab of the **Ribbon**. The **Surface Net Manager** will be displayed with **Wireframe Chaining** selection box; refer to Figure-28.

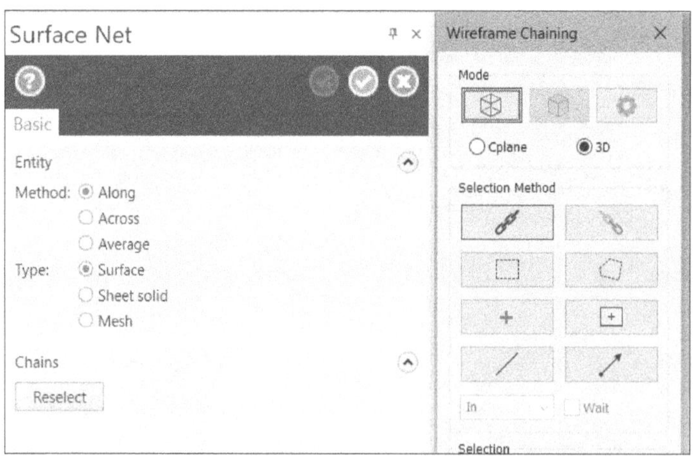

Figure-28. Surface Net Manager

- Select at least two parallel curves and minimum two intersecting curves for defining surface; refer to Figure-29.

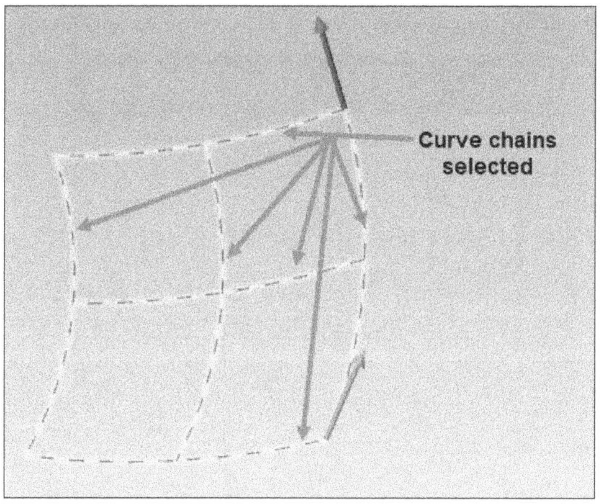

Figure-29. Chains selected for net surface

- Click on the **OK** button from the selection box after selecting the curves. Preview of the surface will be displayed; refer to Figure-30.

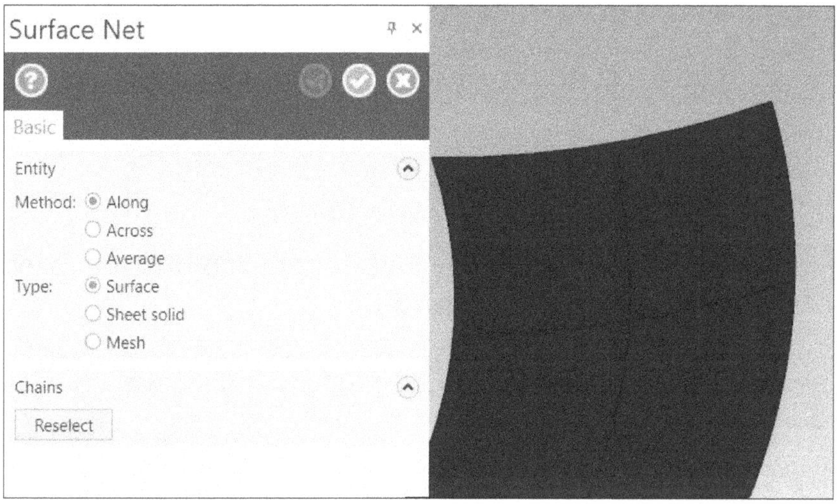

Figure-30. Preview of surface net

- Select desired radio button from the **Method** section of **Manager** and click on the **OK** button to create the surface.

CREATING OFFSET SURFACE

The **Offset** tool is used to offset selected surface by specified distance. The procedure to use this tool is given next.

- Click on the **Offset** tool from the **Create** group in the **Surfaces** tab of the **Ribbon**. The **Surface Offset Manager** will be displayed; refer to Figure-31.

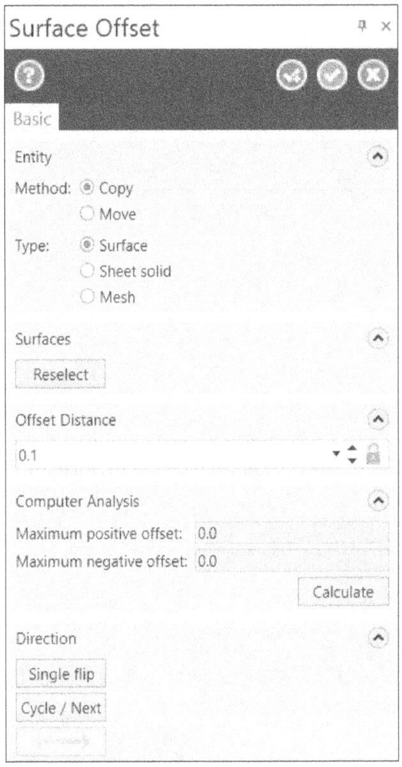

Figure-31. Surface Offset Manager

- Select desired surface and click on the **End Selection** button. Preview of offsetted surface will be displayed; refer to Figure-32.

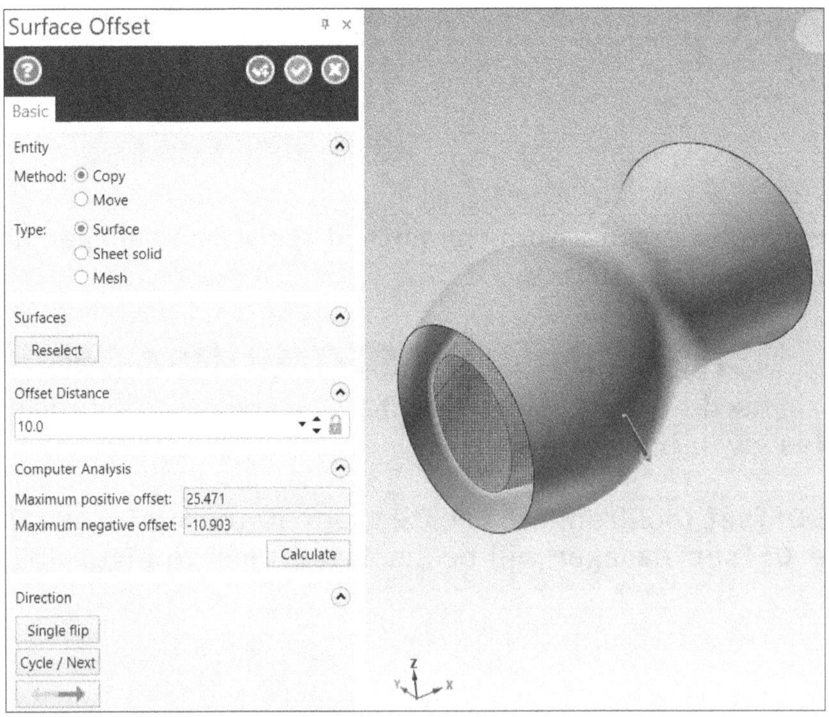

Figure-32. Preview of offset surface

- Specify the distance by which you want to offset the surface in **Offset Distance** edit box. Note that you can specify negative value to reverse offset direction.
- Select the buttons in **Direction** rollout to change direction of offset surface.
- Set the other parameters as discussed and click on the **OK** button. The offset surface will be created.

CREATING FENCE SURFACE

The **Fence** tool is used to create perpendicular surfaces to a selected surface using edges. The procedure to use this tool is given next.

- Click on the **Fence** tool from the **Create** group in the **Surfaces** tab of the **Ribbon**. The **Surface Fence Manager** will be displayed; refer to Figure-33 and you will be asked to select the surface to which new surfaces will be perpendicular.

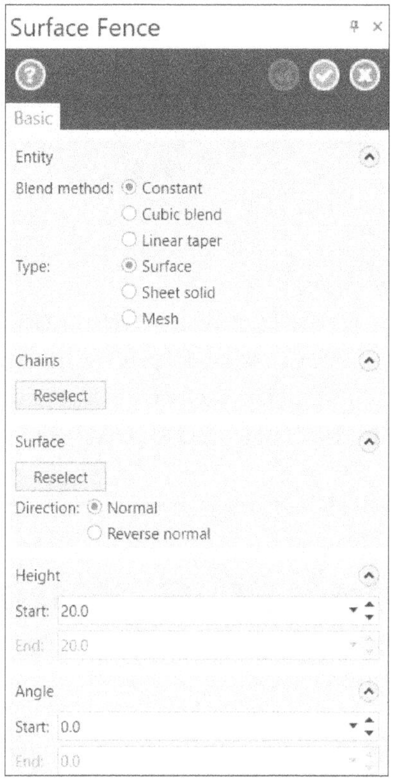

Figure-33. Surface Fence Manager

- Select desired surface to be used as direction reference. The **Wireframe Chaining** selection box will be displayed and you will be asked to select the entities to be used for creating perpendicular surfaces.
- Select desired entities; refer to Figure-34 and click on the **OK** button from the selection box. The preview of fence surface will be displayed; refer to Figure-35.

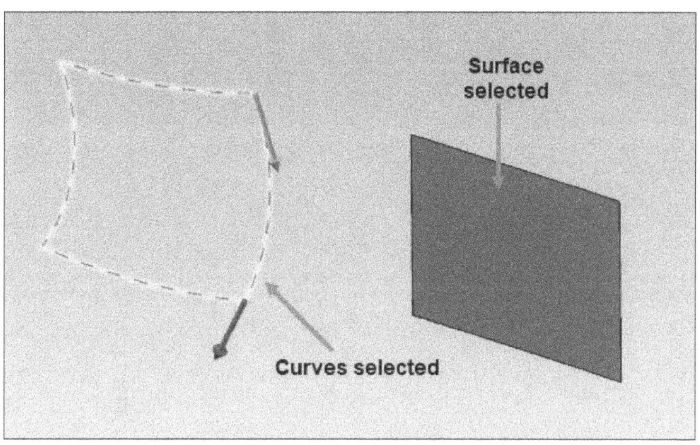

Figure-34. Selecting curves for fence surface

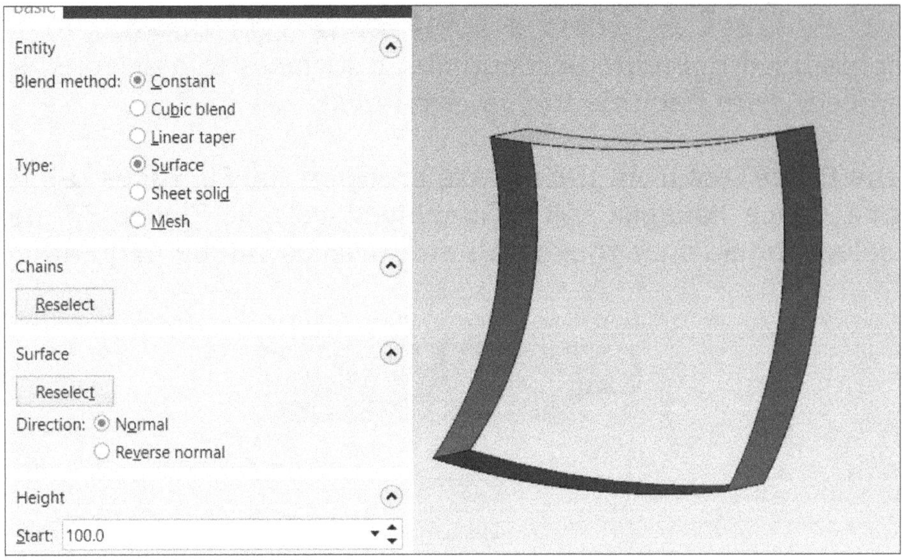

Figure-35. Preview of fence surface

- Select desired radio button from the **Blend method** section to define what type of surface you want to create. Preview of blend will be displayed.
- Select desired radio button from the **Direction** rollout to define direction of fence surface. Select the **Reverse Normal** radio button to flip the direction of surface creation.
- Click on the **OK** button from the **Manager** to create the surfaces.

CREATING POWER SURFACE

The **Power Surface** tool is used to create a surface by selecting chain of curves. The procedure to use this tool is given next.

- Click on the **Power Surface** tool from the **Create** group in the **Surfaces** tab of the **Ribbon**. The **Wireframe Chaining** selection box will be displayed.
- Select the chain of entities to be used for creating surface; refer to Figure-36 and click on the **OK** button from the selection box. Preview of surface will be displayed with **Power Surface Manager**; refer to Figure-37.

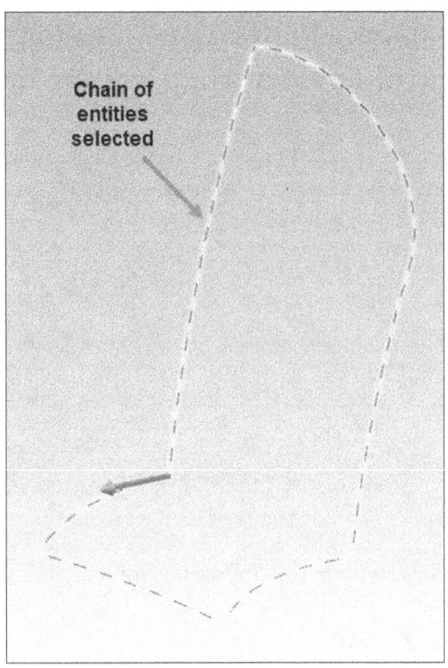

Figure-36. Chain of entities selected

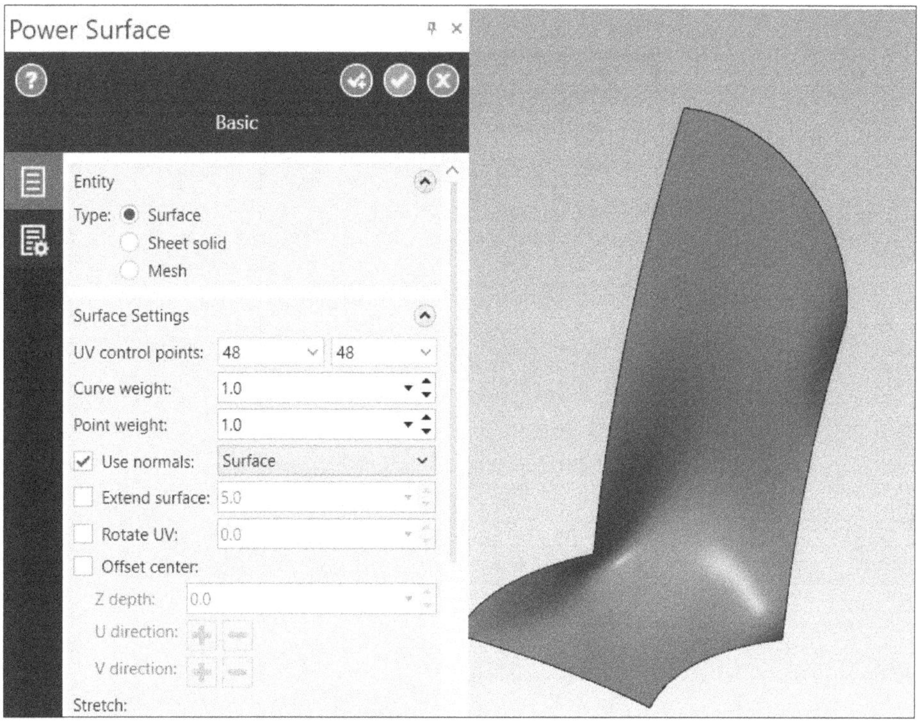

Figure-37. Power Surface Manager with preview

- Set the parameters as desired in the **Manager** and click on the **OK** button.

TRIMMING SURFACES

The tools in the **Trim to Curves** drop-down are used to trim selected surface. Various tools of this drop-down are discussed next.

Trimming Surfaces using Curves

The **Trim to Curves** tool is used to delete portion of surface using wireframe curves. The procedure to use this tool is given next.

- Click on the **Trim to Curves** tool from the **Trim to Curves** drop-down in the **Modify** group of **Surfaces** tab in the **Ribbon**. The **Trim to Curves Manager** will be displayed; refer to Figure-38 and you will be asked to select the surface to be trimmed.
- Select the surface(s) and press **ENTER**. You will be asked to select chain of curves to be used as tool for trimming surface and **Wireframe Chaining** selection box will be displayed.
- Select desired curve chain; refer to Figure-39 and click on the **OK** button from selection box. You will be asked to specify which section of surface is to be kept after trimming.

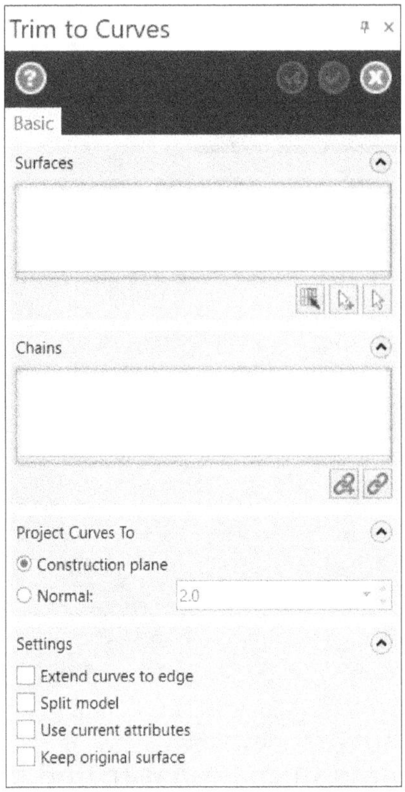

Figure-38. Trim to Curves Manager

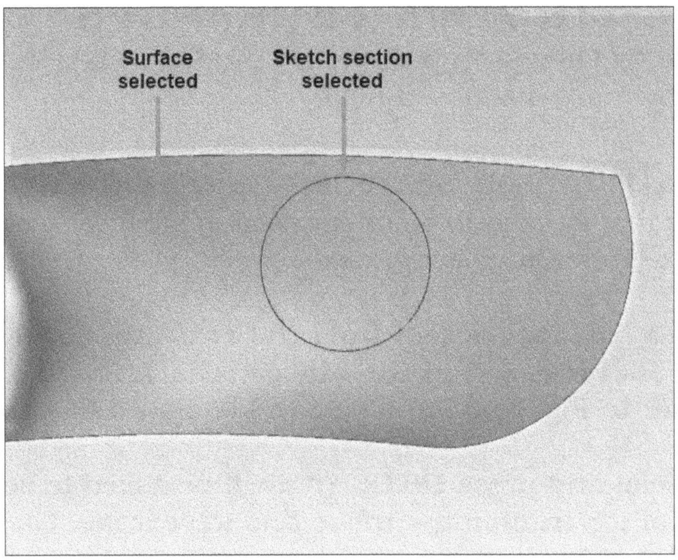

Figure-39. Selecting surface and curve for trimming

- Click on the surface to define which side is to be kept. An arrow will get attached to the cursor.
- Click at desired location to perform trimming; refer to Figure-40.
- If you want to change the area to be kept after trimming then click on the **Area to keep** selection button from **Surfaces** selection section and select desired area as discussed earlier.
- Click on the **Add selection** button from **Surfaces** selection section if you want to select more surface for trimming.

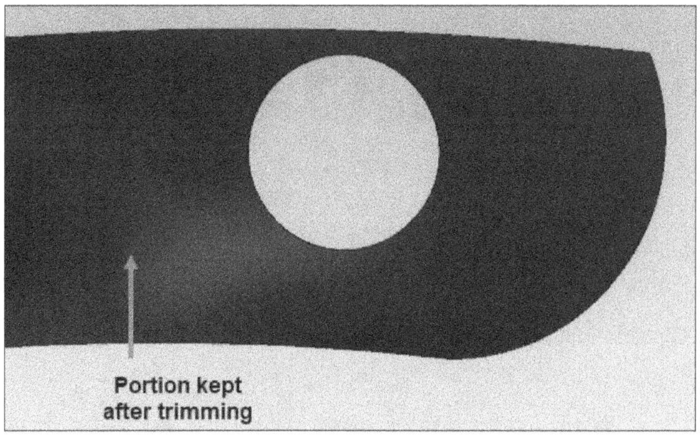

Figure-40. Surface section kept after trimming

- Select the **Extend curves to edge** check box to automatically extend trimming curve up to edge of surface for trimming; refer to Figure-41.

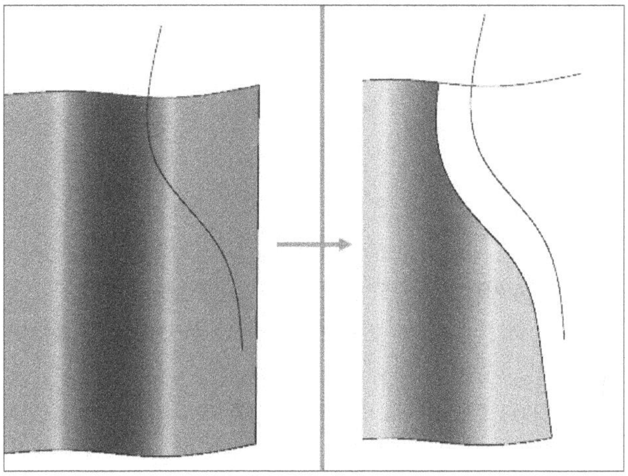

Figure-41. Extending curve for trimming

- Select the **Split model** check box to split the surface by using selected trimming curve.
- Select the **Use current attributes** check box to apply current attributes (color, font, thickness etc.) to the trimmed surfaces.
- Select the **Keep original surface** check box to keep original surface as well as trimmed surfaces.
- Click on the **OK** button from the **Manager** to complete the operation.

Trimming Surface using Surface

The **Trim to Surfaces** tool is used to trim portion of surface intersecting with another surface. The procedure to use this tool is given next.

- Click on the **Trim to Surfaces** tool from the **Trim to Curves** drop-down in the **Modify** group of **Surfaces** tab in the **Ribbon**. The **Trim to Surfaces Manager** will be displayed; refer to Figure-42 and you will be asked to select surfaces for the first set of intersecting surfaces.

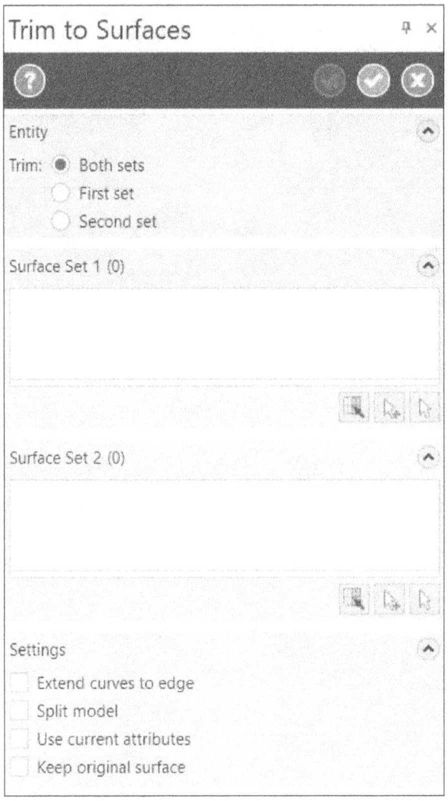

Figure-42. Trim to Surfaces Manager

- Select desired surfaces and press **ENTER**. You will be asked to select surfaces for second set.
- Select the other intersecting surfaces and press **ENTER**. You will be asked to select the portion of surface in first set to be kept safe; refer to Figure-43.

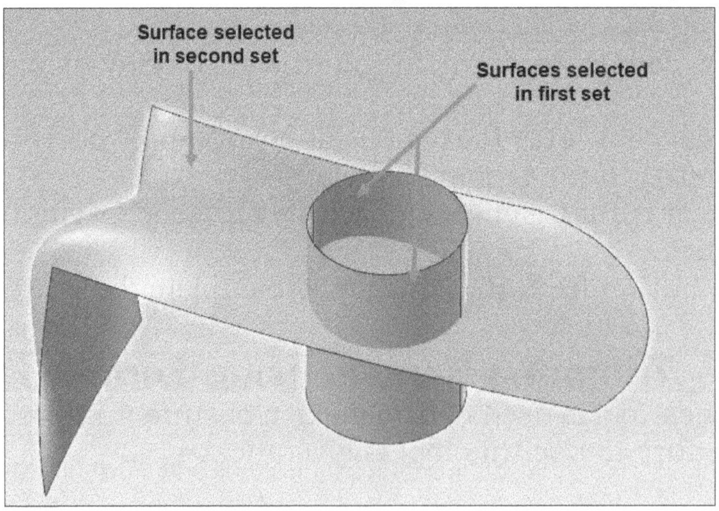

Figure-43. Surfaces selected for trimming

- Note that by default, the **Both sets** radio button is selected from **Trim** section of the **Manager** so you are asked to specify portions to be kept after trimming from both the surface sets. Select the **First set** or **Second set** radio button to trim only respective surface set.
- Click on desired portion of first surface set and then second surface set. Preview of trimmed surface will be displayed; refer to Figure-44.

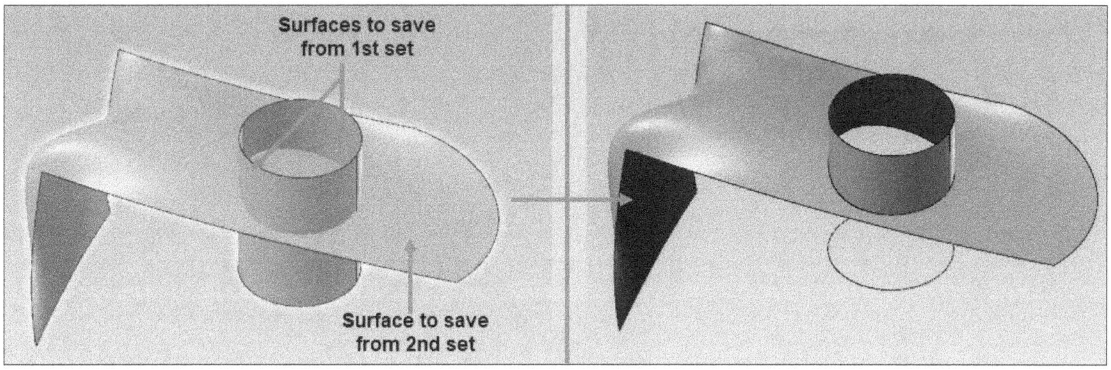

Figure-44. Surfaces selected to keep after trimming

- Set the other parameters as discussed earlier and click on the **OK** button from the **Manager**. The surface will be trimmed.

Trimming Surfaces to Plane

The **Trim to Plane** tool is used to trim selected surfaces using a plane. The procedure to use this tool is given next.

- Click on the **Trim to Plane** tool from the **Trim to Curves** drop-down in the **Modify** group of **Surfaces** tab in the **Ribbon**. You will be asked to select the surfaces to be trimmed.
- Select desired surfaces and press **ENTER**. The **Trim to Plane Manager** will be displayed; refer to Figure-45.
- Click on the **Named Plane** button from the **Plane** rollout in **Manager** to select desired named plane. The **Plane Selection** page will be displayed in **Manager**; refer to Figure-46.
- Select desired plane from the list to check preview of trimming; refer to Figure-47.

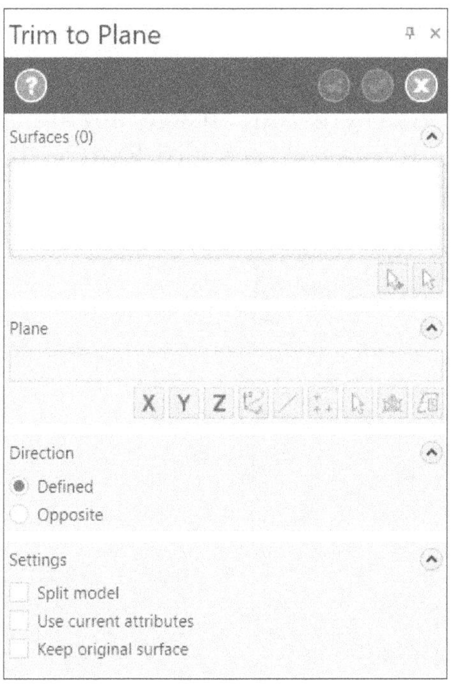

Figure-45. Trim to Plane Manager

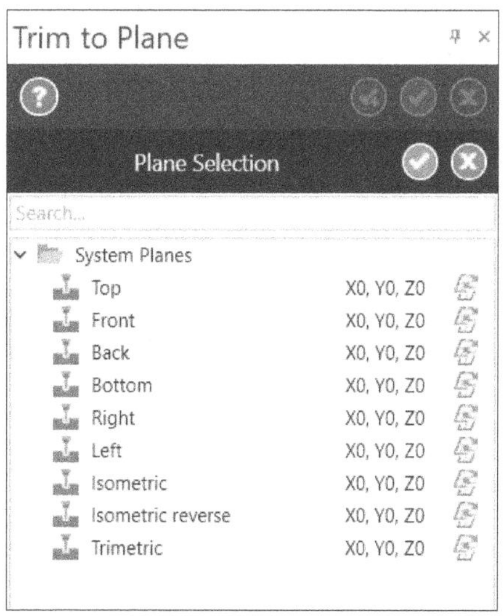

Figure-46. Plane Selection page

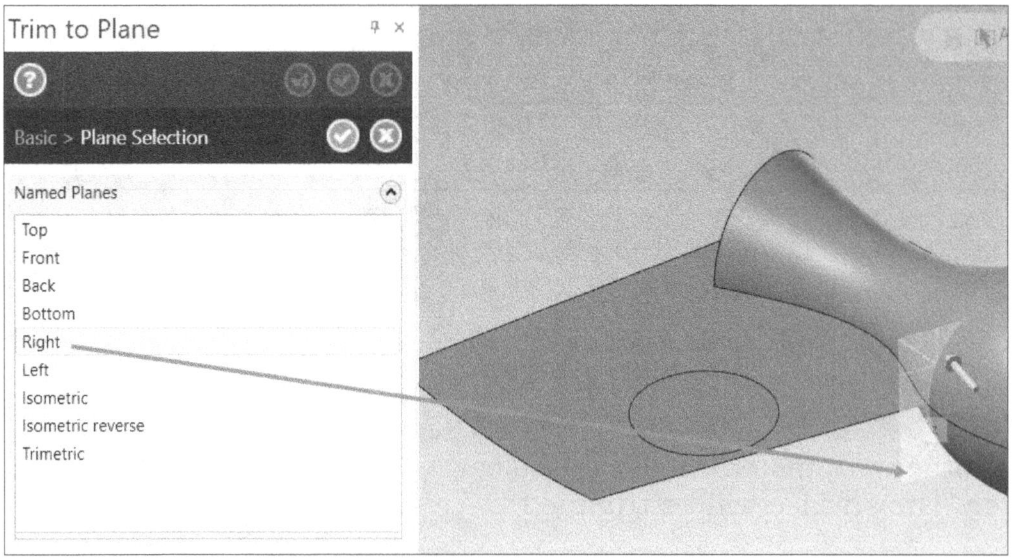

Figure-47. Plane selected or defined for trimming

- Click on the **OK** button from the page in **Manager**. Preview of the trimmed surfaces will be displayed.
- Similarly, you can use other buttons in the **Plane** rollout to use respective planes for trimming the surface.
- Select the **Split model** check box from **Settings** rollout to divide the selected surface at trimming plane.
- Select the **Use current attributes** check box to create each trimmed surface with attributes (color, level, line width etc.) same as current.
- Select the **Keep original surface** check box to keep the main surfaces after trimming. Click on the **OK** button from the **Trim to Plane Manager** to trim surfaces.

FILLING HOLES

The **Fill Holes** tool is used to fill holes created by trimming. The procedure to use this tool is given next.

- Click on the **Fill Holes** tool from the **Modify** group in the **Surfaces** tab of the **Ribbon**. The **Fill Holes Manager** will be displayed; refer to Figure-48.

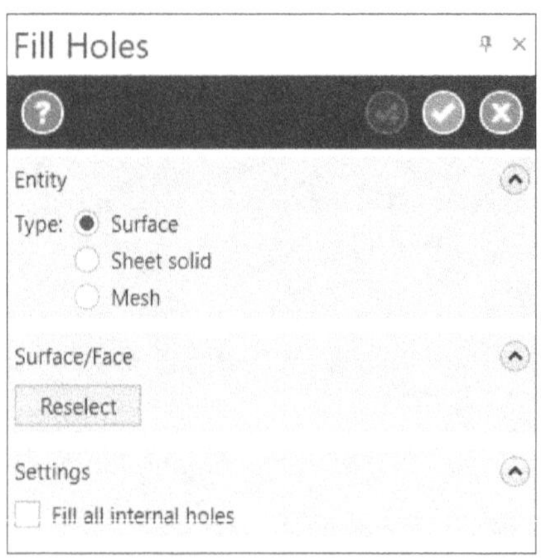

Figure-48. Fill Holes Manager

- Select desired surface or solid face to fill holes created by trimming. You will be asked to place arrow on the boundary of hole.

- Click on the boundary of hole. Preview of filled hole will be displayed; refer to Figure-49.

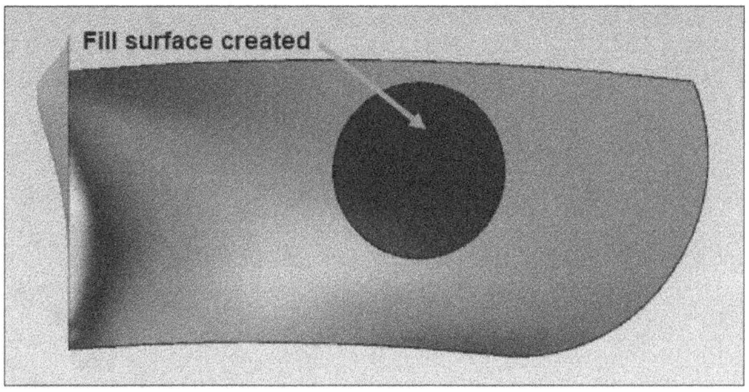

Figure-49. Fill hole surface created

- If you want to fill all the internal holes on the trimmed surface then select the **Fill all internal holes** check box.
- After setting desired parameters, click on the **OK** button from the **Manager**.

EXTENDING SURFACE

The **Extend** tool is used to extend selected surface by specified value. The procedure to use this tool is given next.

- Click on the **Extend** tool from the **Extend** drop-down in the **Modify** group of **Surfaces** tab in the **Ribbon**. The **Surface Extend Manager** will be displayed; refer to Figure-50.

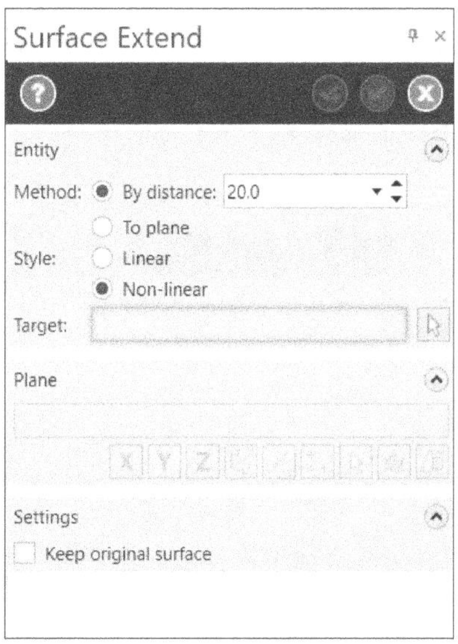

Figure-50. Surface Extend Manager

- Select desired radio button from the **Method** section to define whether you want to extend surface by specified value or by using a plane as reference.
- Select the **Linear** radio button to create linear surface. Select the **Non-linear** radio button from the **Style** section to create extended surface following the curvature of original surface.
- Select desired surface to be extended. You will be asked to specify which end of surface will be extended.
- Slide the arrow at desired edge. The preview of extended surface will be displayed; refer to Figure-51.

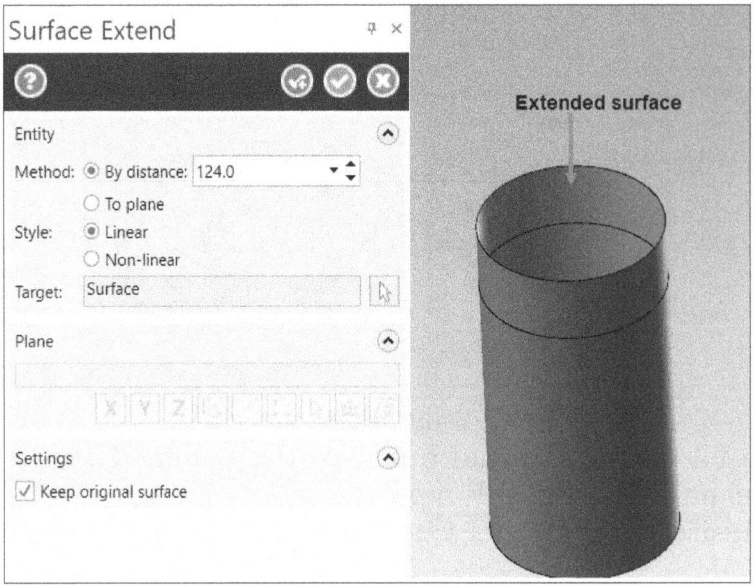

Figure-51. Preview of extended surface

- Set the other options as discussed earlier and click on the **OK** button from the **Manager**. The extended surface will be created.

EXTENDING TRIMMED EDGES

The **Extend Trimmed Edges** tool is used to extend the trimmed surface using edge of trimmed surface. The procedure to use this tool is given next.

- Click on the **Extend Trimmed Edges** tool from the **Extend** drop-down in the **Modify** group of **Surfaces** tab in the **Ribbon**. The **Surface Trimmed Edge Extend Manager** will be displayed; refer to Figure-52.

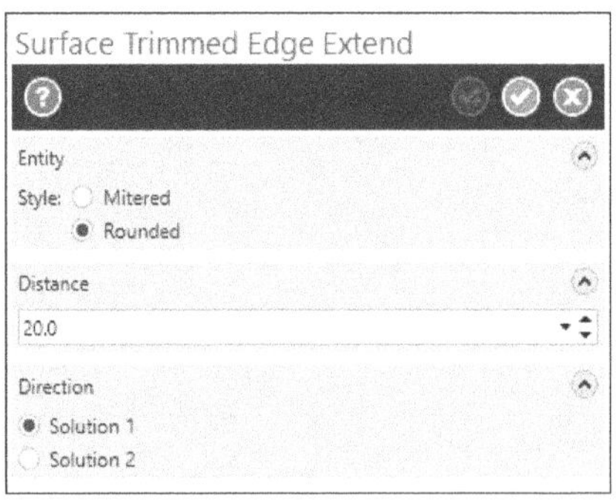

Figure-52. Surface Trimmed Edge Extend Manager

- Select the **Mitered** radio button to create extended surface with mitered corners. Select the **Rounded** radio button to create extended surface with round corners.
- Select the surface which is trimmed to create extended surface. You will be asked to select trimmed surface edge to extend.
- Select desired trimmed edge; refer to Figure-53. You will be asked to specify point on side of edge to be extended.

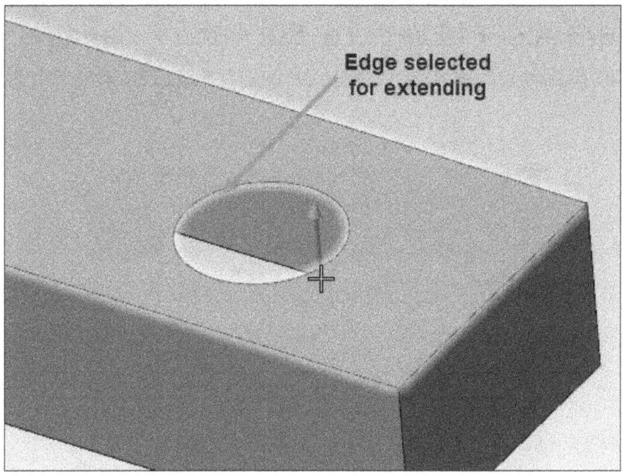

Figure-53. Edge selected for extending

- Click on desired side or press **ENTER** to use full edge. Preview of extended surface will be displayed; refer to Figure-54.

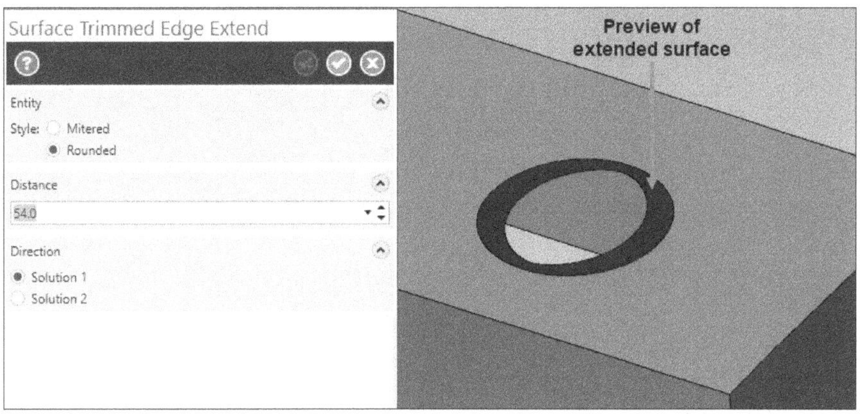

Figure-54. Preview of extended surface at edge

- Specify desired distance value in the **Distance** edit box and click on the **OK** button from the **Manager**.

APPLYING FILLETS TO SURFACES

The tools to apply fillets to surfaces are available in the **Fillet to Surfaces** drop-down in the **Surfaces** tab of **Ribbon**; refer to Figure-55. Various tools of this drop-down are discussed next.

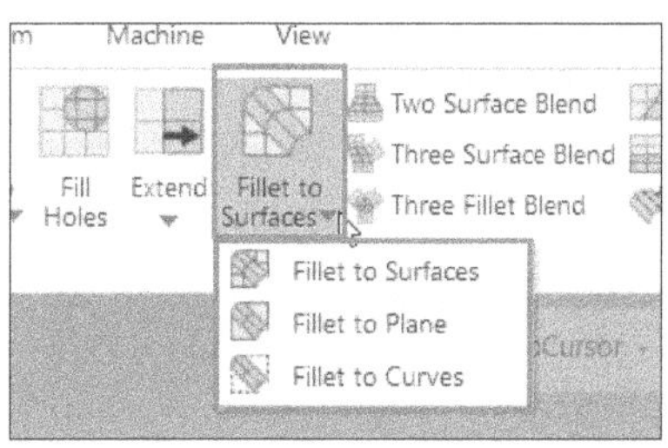

Figure-55. Fillet to Surfaces drop-down

Creating Fillet at Intersection of Surfaces

The **Fillet to Surfaces** tool is used to create fillet at the intersection of set of selected surfaces. The procedure to use this tool is given next.

- Click on the **Fillet to Surfaces** tool from the **Modify** group in the **Surfaces** tab of the **Ribbon**. The **Surface Fillet to Surfaces Manager** will be displayed; refer to Figure-56 and you will be asked to select surfaces of first set.

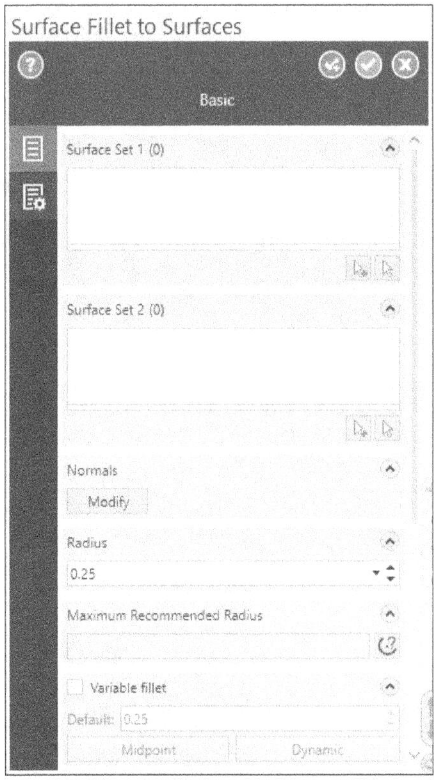

Figure-56. Surface Fillet to Surfaces Manager

- Select desired surfaces for the first set and press **ENTER**. You will be asked to select surfaces for second set.
- Select desired surface(s) and press **ENTER**. Preview of fillet will be displayed; refer to Figure-57.

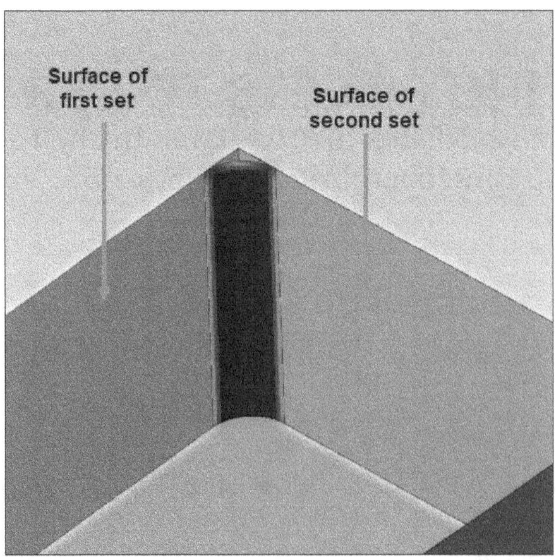

Figure-57. Preview of surface fillet

- If the normals of selected surfaces are not showing correct direction then click on the **Modify** button and select desired surfaces to flip their normal directions. After setting the normal direction, press **ENTER** to accept selection.
- Click in the **Radius** edit box and specify desired value for fillet radius.

- If you want to create a fillet with varying radius then select the **Variable fillet** check box from the **Manager** and specify desired default fillet radius in the **Default** edit box.
- To apply default radius at mid point of the fillet, click on the **Midpoint** button from the **Variable fillet** rollout. You will be asked to specify location of mid point. Click on the top point of fillet and then bottom point of fillet. Preview of variable fillet will be displayed at midpoint; refer to Figure-58.

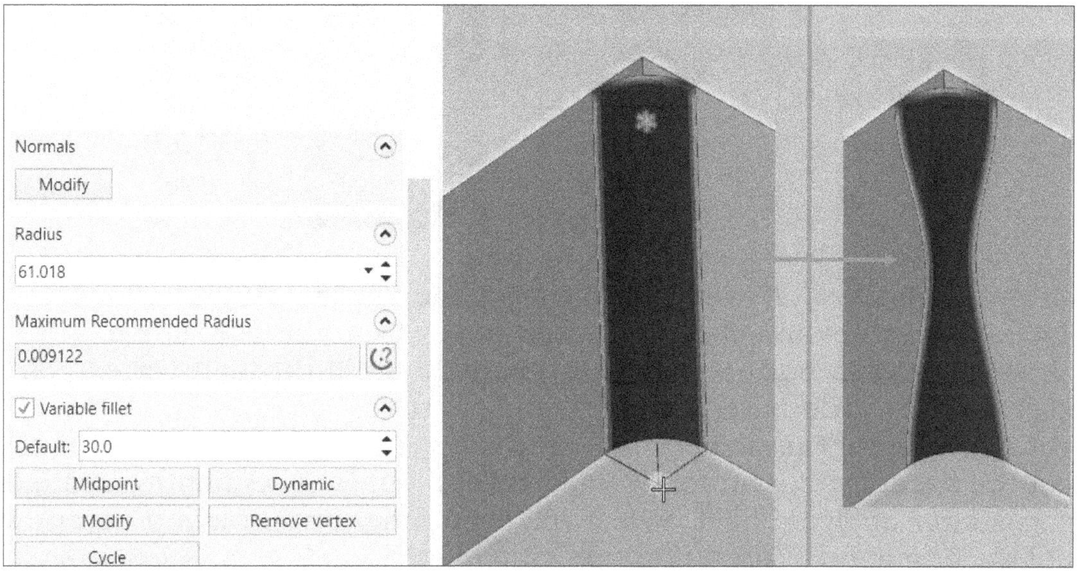

Figure-58. Variable fillet at mid point

- Click on the **Dynamic** button to apply fillet of specified radius at specified dynamic point along the center curve of fillet and select the center curve. You will be asked to specify location of point at which specified radius will be applied; refer to Figure-59. Click at desired location on curve to apply fillet.

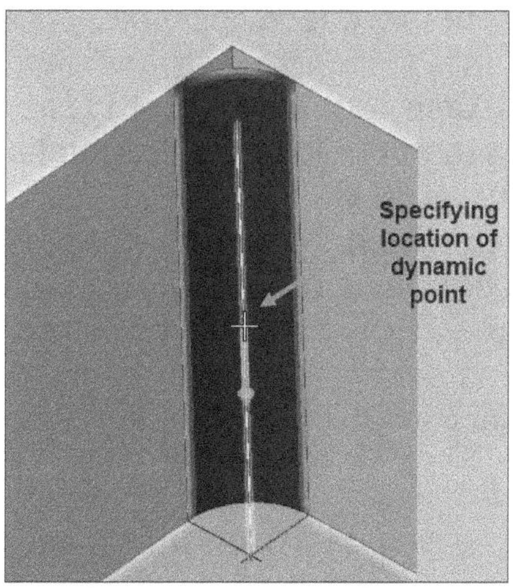

Figure-59. Specifying location of dynamic point

- Click on the **Modify** button from the **Variable fillet** rollout to change radius of selected location. Click on desired radius marker; refer to Figure-60. Specify desired value of radius in the **Default** edit box and press **ENTER**.

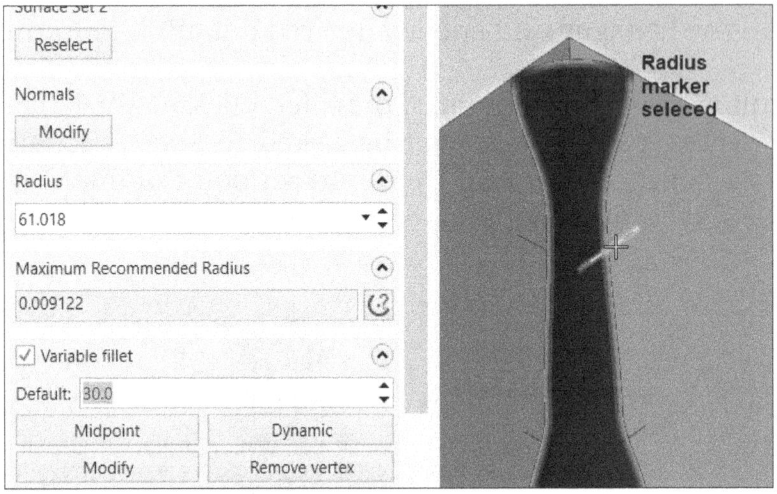

Figure-60. Radius marker selected

- Click on the **Remove Vertex** button from the **Vertex fillet** rollout to remove variable fillet vertex and click at desired vertex from the fillet curve.
- Click on the **Cycle** button from the rollout to cycle through vertex points and specify radii for various vertices on the fillet curve.
- Select the **Trim surfaces** check box to trim base surfaces after creating the fillet. Select the **Delete** radio button from **Original surface** section to create original surfaces after applying fillet. Select the **Keep** radio button if you do not want to delete the original surfaces after applying fillet.
- Set the other parameters as desired and click on the **OK** button from the **Manager**. The fillet will be applied.

Applying Surface Fillet to Plane

The **Fillet to Plane** tool is used to apply fillet at the intersection of surface and plane. The procedure to use this tool is given next.

- Click on the **Fillet to Plane** tool from the **Fillet to Surfaces** drop-down in **Modify** group of **Surfaces** tab in the **Ribbon**. The **Surface Fillet to Plane Manager** will be displayed; refer to Figure-61.
- Select desired surface(s) to which you want to apply fillet and press **ENTER**. You will be asked to specify location of plane.
- Specify the location of plane as discussed earlier and specify desired radius value in the **Radius** edit box.
- You can trim the base surface as discussed earlier. After setting desired parameters, click on the **OK** button.

Figure-61. Surface Fillet to Plane Manager

Applying Surface Fillet at Curves

The **Fillet to Curves** tool is used to create surface fillet at selected curve. The procedure to use this tool is given next.

- Click on the **Fillet to Curves** tool from the **Fillet to Surfaces** drop-down in the **Modify** group of **Surfaces** tab in the **Ribbon**. The **Surface Fillet to Curves Manager** will be displayed; refer to Figure-62 and you will be asked to select surfaces to which you want to apply the fillet.

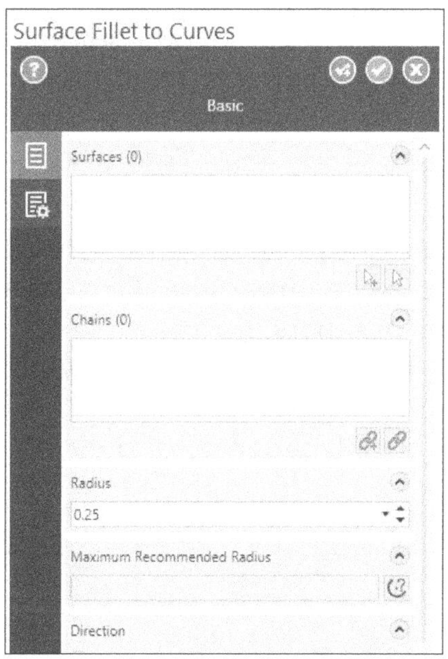

Figure-62. Surface Fillet to Curves Manager

- Select desired surfaces to which you want to apply fillet and press **ENTER**. You will be asked to select wireframe curve chains.

- Select desired wireframe curve intersecting with the surface and click on the **OK** button from the **Wireframe Chaining** selection box. You will be asked to specify whether you want to create fillet inside or outside.
- Click on desired side of surface. Set the other parameters as discussed earlier and click on the **OK** button from the **Manager**.

CREATING TWO SURFACES BLEND

The **Two Surface Blend** tool is used to join two surfaces with a new surface. The procedure to use this tool is given next.

- Click on the **Two Surface Blend** tool from the **Modify** group in the **Surfaces** tab of the **Ribbon**. The **Two Surface Blend Manager** will be displayed; refer to Figure-63.

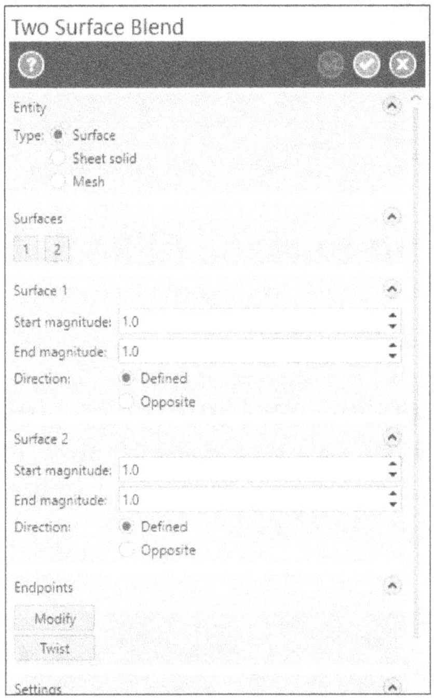

Figure-63. Two Surface Blend Manager

- Select the first surface and click at desired location of surface to define tangent point of surface. Press **F** to flip the direction of blending surface.
- Select the second surface to be blended. (You may need to double-click for specifying normal direction of surface).
- Press **ENTER** key to create blended surface. Preview of blended surface will be displayed; refer to Figure-64.
- Set desired parameters in the **Manager** and click on the **OK** button to create the blending surface.

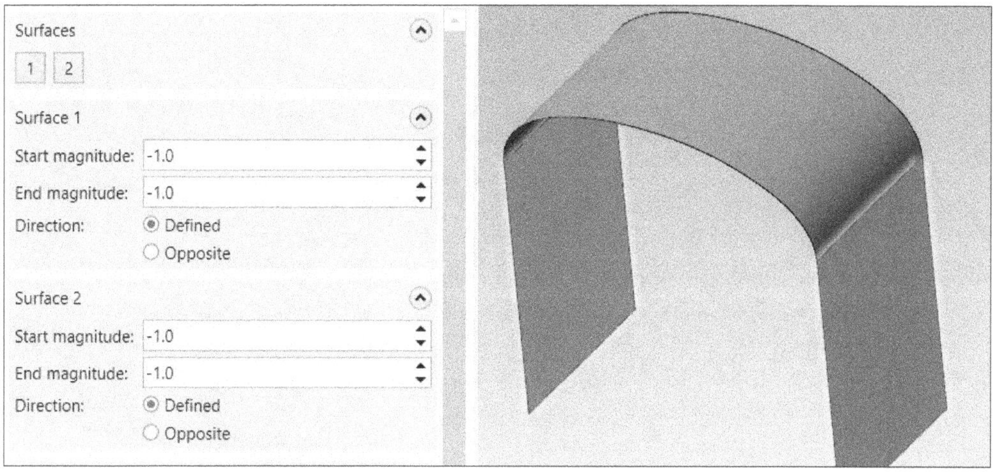

Figure-64. Preview of blended surface

CREATING THREE SURFACE BLEND

The **Three Surface Blend** tool is used to create a blend surface joining three surfaces. The procedure to use this tool is given next.

- Click on the **Three Surface Blend** tool from the **Modify** group of **Surfaces** tab in the **Ribbon**. The **Three Surface Blend Manager** will be displayed; refer to Figure-65.

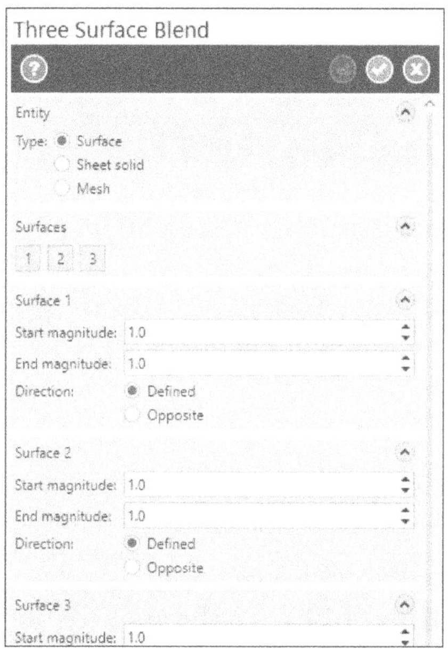

Figure-65. Three Surface Blend Manager

- Select desired surfaces and define spline direction for the three surfaces. Press **ENTER** after selecting surfaces and defining directions. Preview of the surface will be displayed; refer to Figure-66.
- Set desired parameters in the **Manager** and click on the **OK** button.

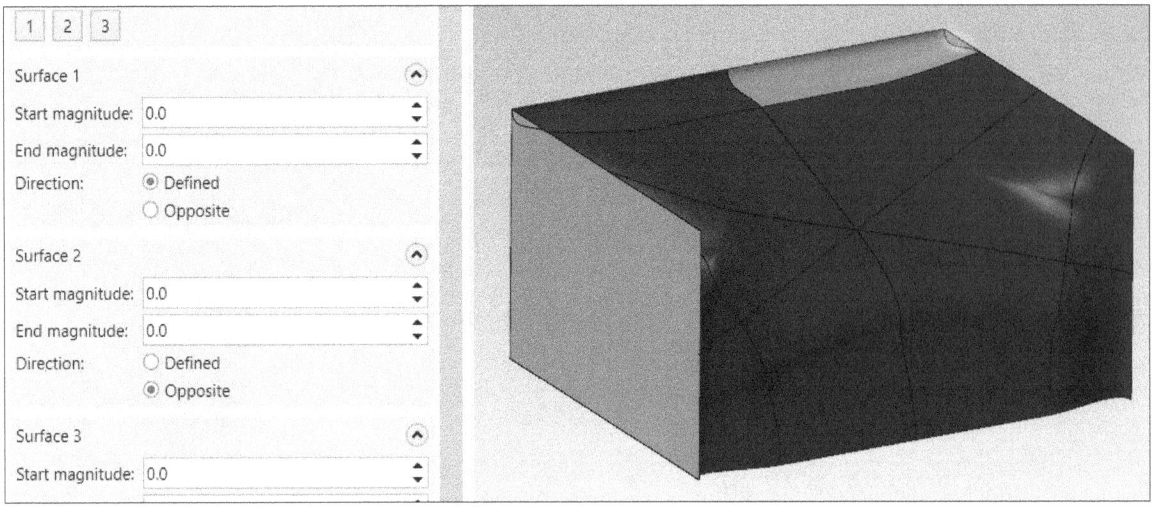

Figure-66. Preview of three surface blend

CREATING THREE FILLET BLEND

The **Three Fillet Blend** tool is used to join three fillets using a surface. The procedure to use this tool is given next.

- Click on the **Three Fillet Blend** tool from the **Modify** group in the **Surfaces** tab of the **Ribbon**. The **Three Fillet Blend Manager** will be displayed; refer to Figure-67.

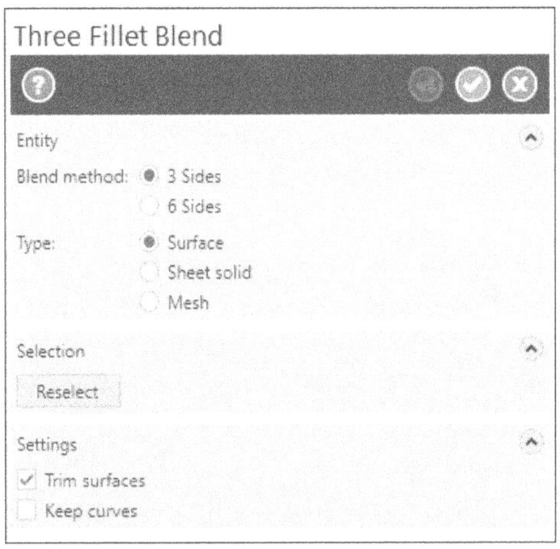

Figure-67. Three Fillet Blend Manager

- One by one select the three fillet surfaces. Preview of blend surface will be displayed; refer to Figure-68.

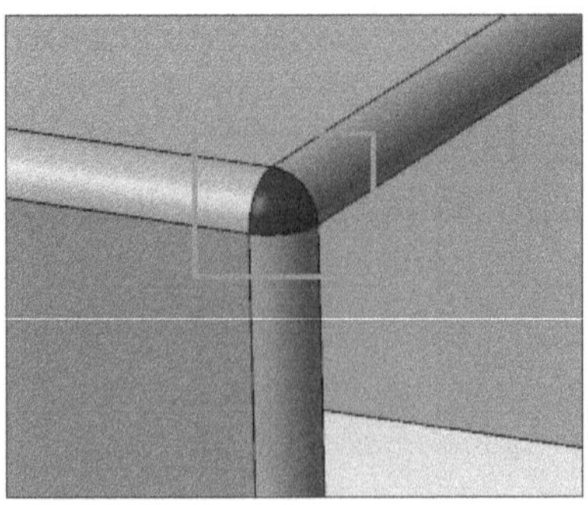

Figure-68. Preview of three fillet blend

- Select desired radio button from the **Blend method** area to specify the type of fillet blend surface to be created. Select **6 Sides** radio button include back sides of fillets when blending.
- Select the **Trim surfaces** check box from the **Settings** rollout to trim original surfaces after creating blend surface.
- Select the **Keep curves** check box to create actual spline curves at the blend.
- Click on the **OK** button from the **Manager** to create the feature.

UNTRIMMING

The **Untrim** tool is used to reverse the effect of trim tool. The procedure to use this tool is given next.

- Click on the **Untrim** tool from the **Modify** group in the **Surfaces** tab of the **Ribbon**. The **Surface Untrim Manager** will be displayed; refer to Figure-69.

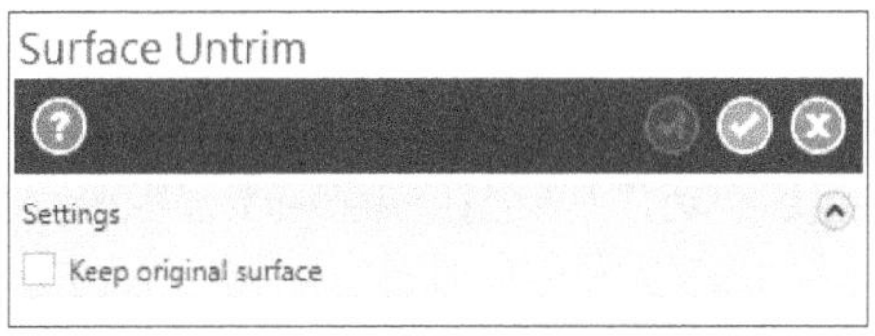

Figure-69. Surface Untrim Manager

- Select the **Keep original surface** check box to keep original trimmed surface after untrimming.
- Select the surface which was trimmed from the 3D view. Preview of untrimmed surface will be displayed; refer to Figure-70.

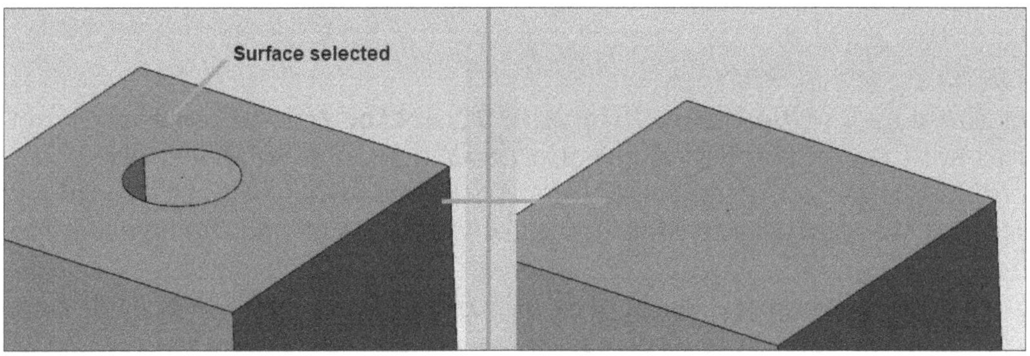

Figure-70. Preview of untrimmed surface

- Click on the **OK** button from the **Manager** to create the untrimmed surface.

UNTRIMMING BOUNDARY OF SURFACE

The **Remove Boundary** tool is used to remove the trimmed section of selected surface. The procedure to use this tool is given next.

- Click on the **Remove Boundary** tool from the **Untrim** drop-down in the **Modify** group of **Surfaces** tab in the **Ribbon**. You will be asked to select the trimmed surface.
- Select desired surface. You will be asked to click on the trimmed boundary to be removed.
- Click on desired side. Preview of removed boundary will be displayed; refer to Figure-71.

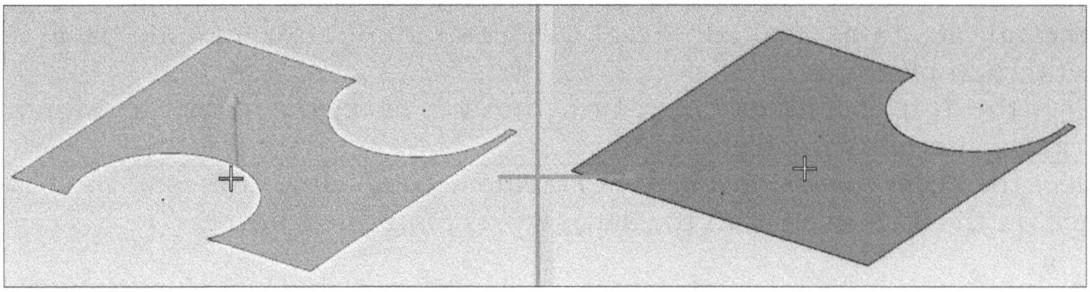

Figure-71. Removing boundary

- Press **ESC** to exit the tool.

SPLITTING SURFACE

The **Split** tool is used to split selected surface at specified location. The procedure to use this tool is given next.

- Click on the **Split** tool from the **Modify** group in the **Surfaces** tab of the **Ribbon**. The **Surface Split Manager** will be displayed; refer to Figure-72.

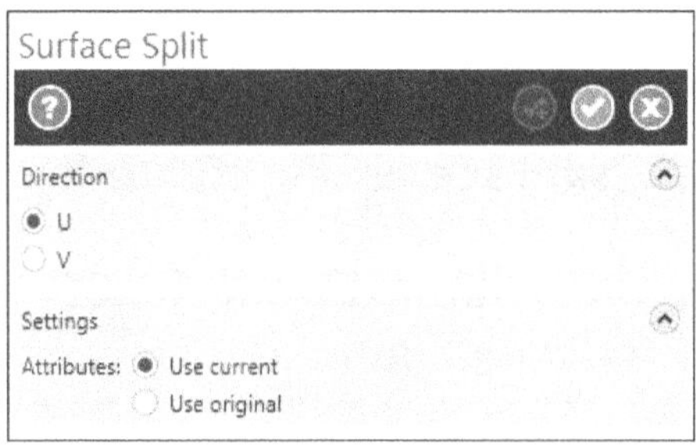

Figure-72. Surface Split Manager

- Select the **U** or **V** radio button from the **Direction** rollout to define whether you want to split the surface in X direction or Y direction, respectively.
- Select desired radio button from the **Attributes** area to define whether you want to use level currently set in Mastercam or you want to use the level set for original surface.
- After setting parameters, click on the surface to be split. You will be asked to specify the location where surface will be split.
- Click at desired location. Preview of the surface split will be displayed; refer to Figure-73.

Figure-73. Surface split along U direction

- You can create multiple split in the surface. After setting desired parameters, click on the **OK** button from the **Manager**.

EDITING SURFACE

The **Edit Surface** tool is used to dynamically modify selected surface using node points or iso-curves. The procedure to use this tool is given next.

- Click on the **Edit Surface** tool from the **Modify** group in the **Surfaces** tab of the **Ribbon**. The **Edit Surface Manager** will be displayed; refer to Figure-74 and you will be asked to select the surface to be modified.

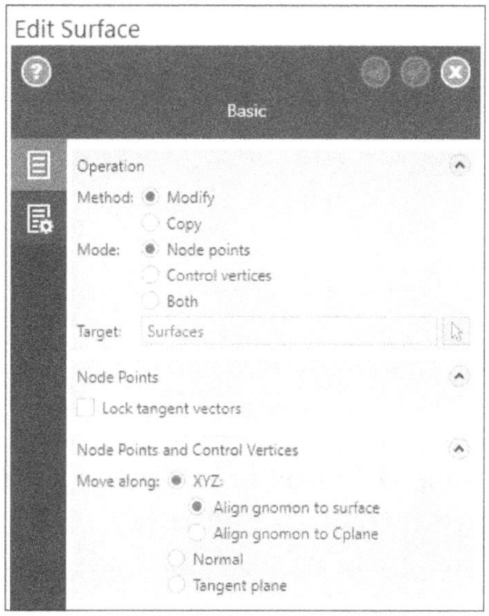

Figure-74. Edit Surface Manager

- Select the surface to be modified. You will be asked to specify the location of node point or isocurve to be used for modification.
- Click at desired location on the surface. A gnomon will be displayed on selected location.
- Drag the gnomon in desired direction to modify surface; refer to Figure-75.

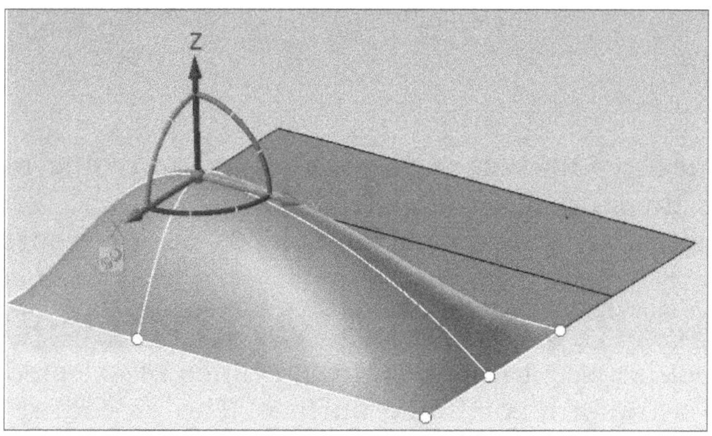

Figure-75. Preview of modified surface

- Press **ENTER** to complete modification by selected node point and select new node point for modification.
- You can delete a node point by selecting it from the model and pressing **DELETE** key.
- After setting desired parameters, click on the **OK** button from the **Manager**.

EDITING UV FLOWLINE OF SURFACE

The **Edit UV** tool in **Flowline** group of **Ribbon** is used to set number of U and V flowlines in the surface. The procedure to use this tool is given next.

- Click on the **Edit UV** tool from the **Flowline** group in the **Surfaces** tab of the **Ribbon**. The **Edit UV Manager** will be displayed; refer to Figure-76 and you will be asked to select the surface.

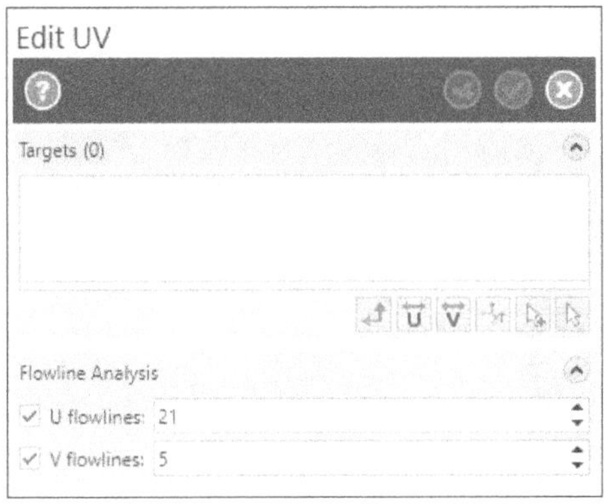

Figure-76. Edit UV Manager

- Select desired surface whose UV lines are to be modified and press **ENTER**. Preview of UV lines will be displayed; refer to Figure-77.

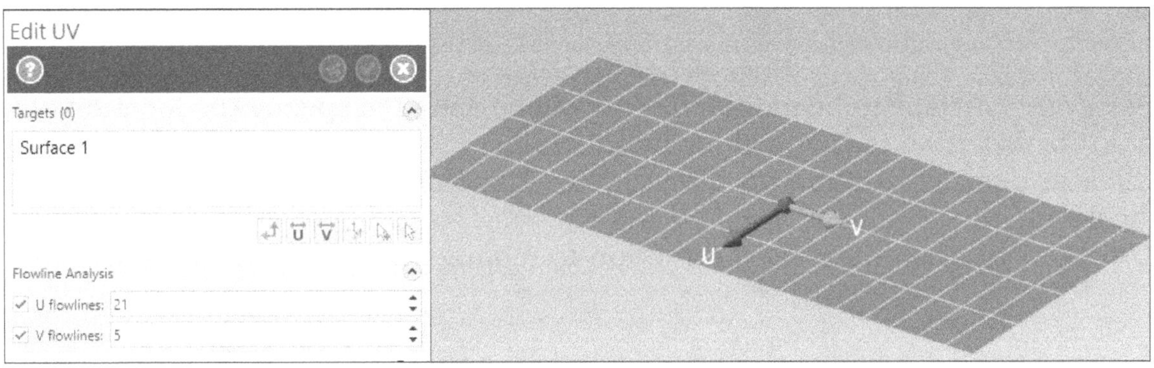

Figure-77. Preview of UV lines

- Set desired values in **Flowline Analysis** rollout to define number of flowlines being created in the surface.
- After setting desired parameters, click on the **OK** button from the **Manager**.

OVERFLOWING UV FLOWLINES

The **Overflow UV** tool is used to project the flowlines of selected surface on target surfaces and form a uniform combined surface. The procedure to use this tool is given next.

- Click on the **Overflow UV** tool from the **Flowline** group in the **Surfaces** tab of the **Ribbon**. The **Overflow UV Manager** will be displayed and you will be asked to select surface whose flowlines will be used to overflow.
- Select desired surface and press **ENTER**. You will be asked to select target surface.
- Select desired surface to be used for UV overflow; refer to Figure-78 and press **ENTER**. Preview of overflow will be displayed; refer to Figure-79.

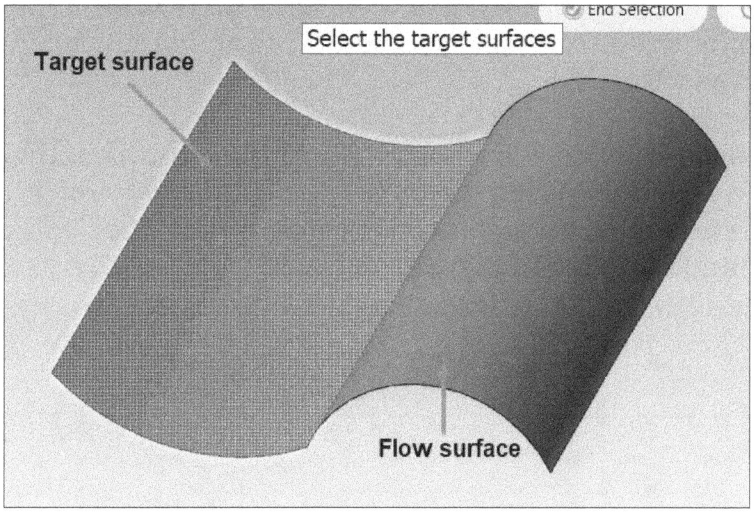

Figure-78. Surfaces selected for UV overflow

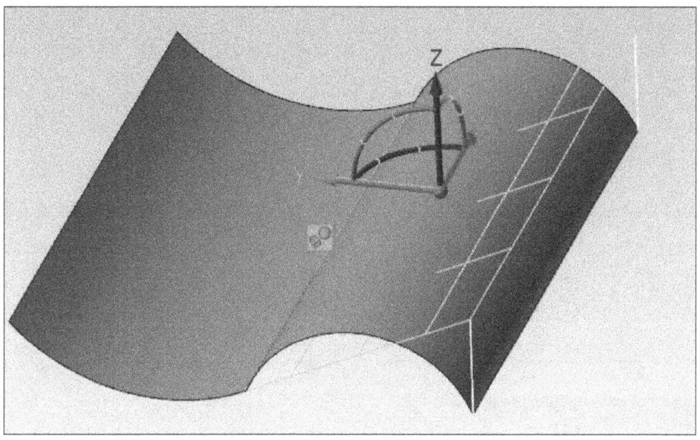

Figure-79. Preview of Overflow UV

- Use the gnomon to modify surface location/orientation. Click on the **OK** button from the **Manager** to create the surface; refer to Figure-80.

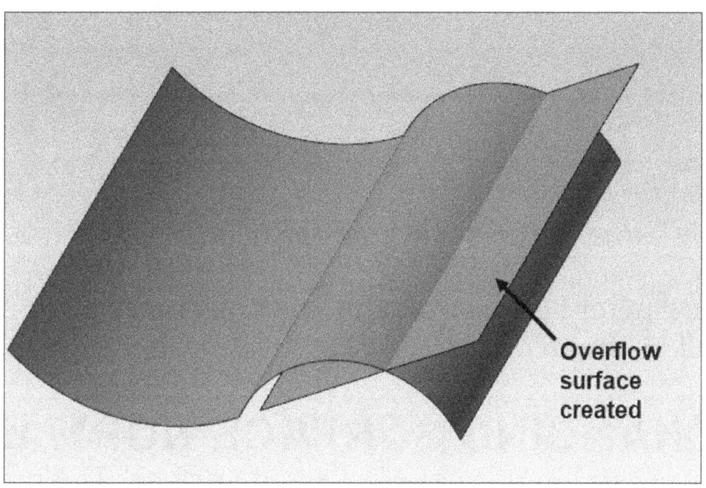

Figure-80. Overflow UV surface created

ROTATING FLOWLINES

The **Reflow UV** tool is used to rotate selected flowlines of surface. The procedure to use this tool is given next.

- Click on the **Reflow UV** tool from the **Flowline** group in the **Surfaces** tab of the **Ribbon**. The **Reflow UV Manager** will be displayed; refer to Figure-81 and select desired surface to be modified. Preview of UV lines will be displayed with modification handles; refer to Figure-82.

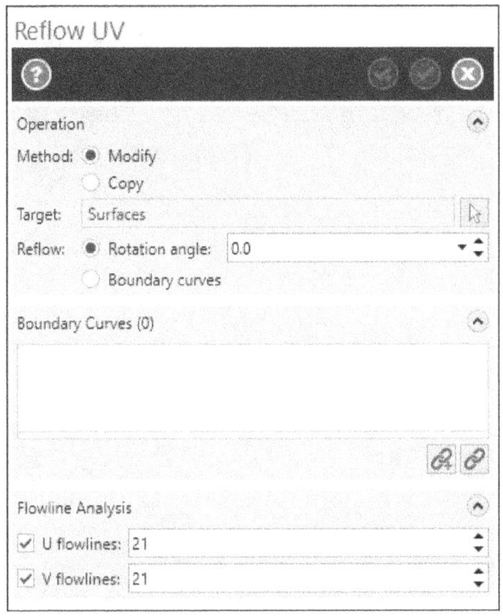

Figure-81. Reflow UV Manager

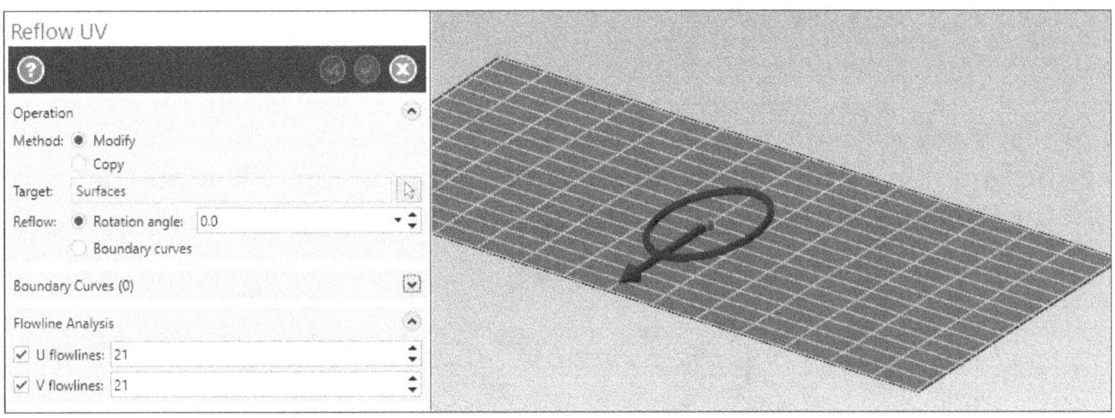

Figure-82. Preview of UV lines for reflow

- Set desired angle value in the **Rotation angle** edit box or use the drag handle to modify UV lines.
- Set the other parameters as desired and click on the **OK** button from the **Manager**. The UV lines will be created.

CHANGING SURFACE NORMAL

The **Change** tool is used to flip normal of selected surface. The procedure to use this tool is given next.

- Click on the **Change** tool from the **Normals** group in the **Surfaces** tab of the **Ribbon**. You will be asked to select the surface whose normal direction is to be flipped.

- Select desired surface to flip its direction; refer to Figure-83.

Figure-83. Flipping direction of surface

- Press **ESC** to exit the tool.

Similarly, you can use the **Set** and **Orient** tools from the **Normals** group in the **Ribbon** to set normal direction of surfaces.

PRACTICE 1

Create the model of helmet glass as shown in Figure-84. The dimensions of the model are given in Figure-85.

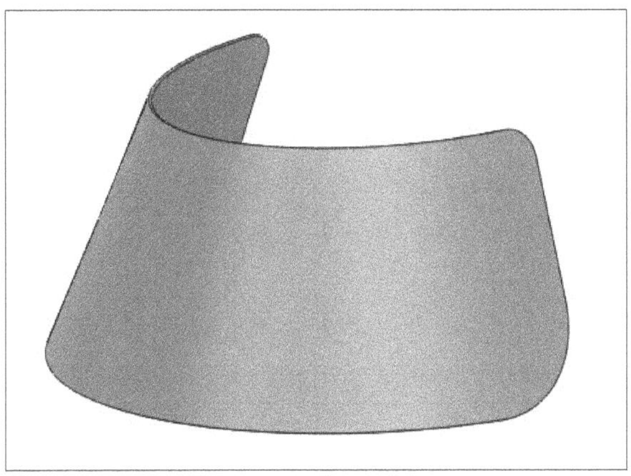

Figure-84. Practice 1 model

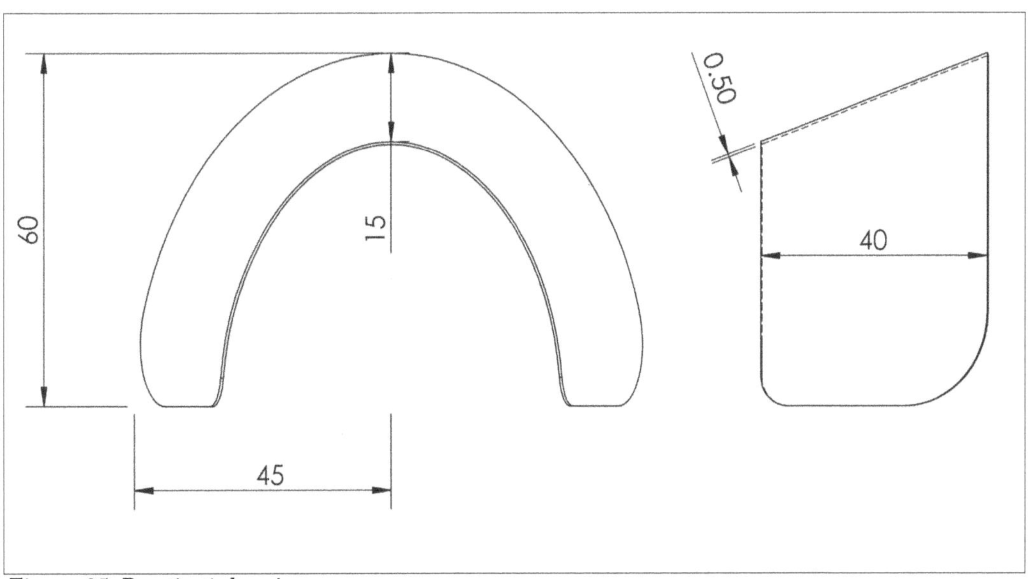

Figure-85. Practice 1 drawing

PRACTICE 2

Create the surface model of tank as shown in Figure-86. The dimensions of the model are given in Figure-87.

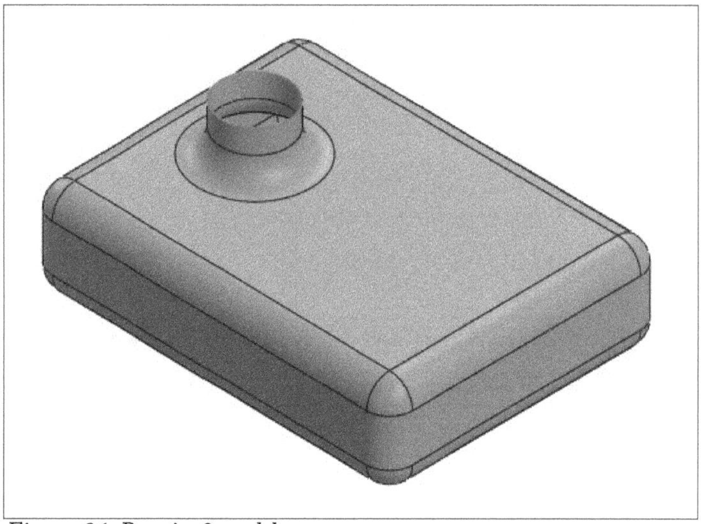

Figure-86. Practice 2 model

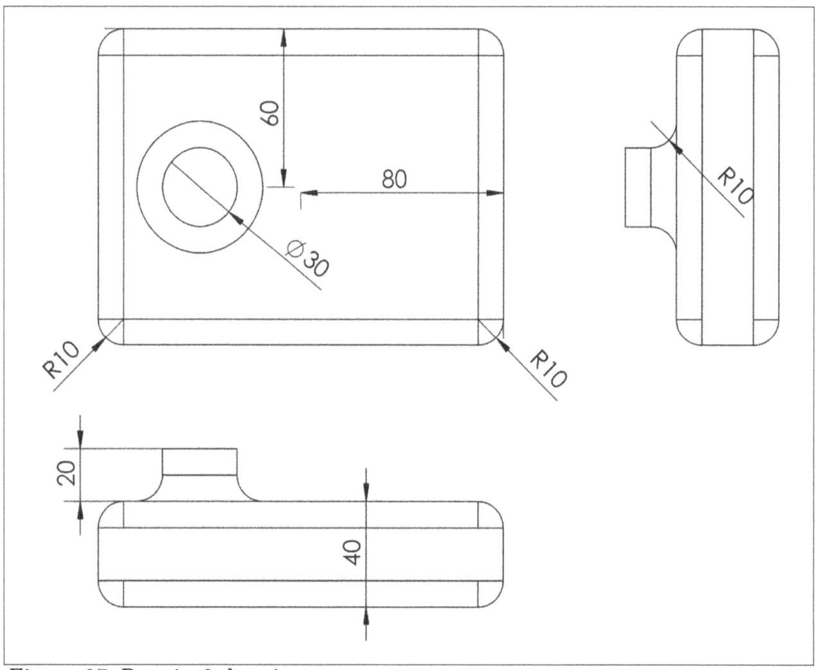

Figure-87. Practice 2 drawing

SELF-ASSESSMENT

Q1. Surfaces are geometric objects with zero thickness, so they do not exist in real world. (T/F)

Q2. The .... tool is used to create surface using selected face of solid.

Q3. Which of the following tools is used to create surface by joining two open chains?

a. Flat Boundary tool
b. Loft tool
c. Extrude tool
d. Sweep tool

Q4. Which of the following tools is used to create surface using set of intersecting curves?

a. Net tool
b. Loft tool
c. Offset tool
d. Sweep tool

Q5. The .... tool is used to create fillet at the intersection of set of selected surfaces.

Q6. The Two Surface Blend tool is used to join two surfaces with a new surface. (T/F)

REVIEW QUESTIONS

Q1. Which tab in the Ribbon contains the Cylinder tool?
A. Solids
B. Transform
C. Wireframe
D. Drafting

Q2. What does selecting the Solid radio button in the Primitive Cylinder Manager do?
A. Creates mesh cylinder
B. Creates surface cylinder
C. Creates a solid primitive
D. Creates a 2D circle

Q3. What is the purpose of the Tangent option under Base Point Definition in Cylinder creation?
A. To place the cylinder at the origin
B. To align cylinder base with axis
C. To create cylinder tangent to a selected entity
D. To apply constraints

Q4. What does checking the Do not create model history option do when creating a cylinder?
A. Prevents rendering
B. Creates a parametric model
C. Prevents storing model history
D. Locks cylinder dimensions

Q5. Which tool is used to create a rectangular block of surface in the Surfaces tab?
A. Prism
B. Loft
C. Block
D. Power Surface

Q6. In surface block creation, what does the Origin rollout help define?
A. Rotation angle
B. Axis alignment
C. Corner placement point
D. Sweep axis

Q7. What does the Vector radio button define in block creation?
A. Volume
B. Direction reference for height
C. Surface texture
D. Chaining of edges

Q8. Which tool is used to create a spherical surface in the Surfaces tab?
A. Sphere
B. Round
C. Ball
D. Dome

Q9. What parameter defines the angular span of a surface sphere?
A. Radius
B. Sweep Angle
C. Axis
D. Length

Q10. What does selecting the Angle radio button in the Cone Top rollout allow?
A. Defines axis length
B. Defines slant height
C. Specifies angle at top of frustum
D. Sets color gradient

Q11. In the Torus creation, what do the Major and Minor values define?
A. Length and Width
B. Outer and inner arc
C. Height and width
D. Major and minor radii

Q12. What is the function of the Surfaces From Solid tool?
A. Extrude 2D sketch
B. Create solid mesh
C. Create surface from selected solid faces
D. Cut solid body

Q13. What does clearing the Keep original solid checkbox do in Surfaces From Solid tool?
A. Hides solid
B. Freezes geometry
C. Deletes original solid after surface creation
D. Locks surface

Q14. Which surface creation tool uses a closed chain boundary?
A. Sweep
B. Net
C. Flat Boundary
D. Revolve

Q15. What option allows creation of surface between two selected chains?
A. Blend
B. Net
C. Loft
D. Extrude

Q16. What does enabling Align chain direction consistently ensure in Loft tool?
A. Adds extra vertices
B. Matches directions of chains
C. Reduces size
D. Offsets curves

Q17. In Loft tool, what does the Dynamic Sync option allow?
A. Aligns surfaces to grid
B. Locks tangency
C. Defines spacing of points
D. Offsets selected surface

Q18. Which method in Loft tool ensures equal spacing of points?
A. Entity
B. Minimum distance
C. Average
D. Uniform Tangency

Q19. What does the Extrude tool require as input?
A. Open surface
B. Closed chain curve
C. Solid edge
D. Tangent edge

Q20. What does the Axis checkbox define in Extrude Manager?
A. Axis of rotation
B. Direction for extrusion
C. Sweep reference
D. Cut reference

Q21. The Sweep tool allows a profile to be moved along a:
A. Arc
B. Grid
C. Contour/path
D. Flat face

Q22. What is the purpose of the Translate radio button in the Sweep method section?
A. Translate the model
B. Avoid section rotation along path
C. Mirror the profile
D. Project geometry

Q23. Which Sweep method uses two path curves to define curvature?
A. Translate
B. Normal to surface
C. Two rails
D. Vector

Q24. What does the Revolve tool require for creating a surface?
A. Solid object
B. Axis and section
C. Mesh selection
D. Net boundary

Q25. Which tool is used to create a planar surface using a line or arc?
A. Offset
B. Power Surface
C. Draft
D. Torus

Q26. What is required for creating a Net Surface?
A. One spline only
B. One closed curve
C. At least two parallel and two intersecting curves
D. One loop

Q27. In the Offset tool, how do you reverse the offset direction?
A. Use mirror option
B. Use a positive value
C. Select Invert tool
D. Enter a negative offset value

Q28. What does the Fence tool create?
A. Shell body
B. Tangent projection
C. Perpendicular surfaces from edges
D. Hole pattern

Q29. What does the Reverse Normal option do in the Fence tool?
A. Converts to mesh
B. Hides surface
C. Flips surface direction
D. Projects in 2D

Q30. Which tool creates a surface from a chain of curves with advanced controls?
A. Sweep
B. Loft
C. Draft
D. Power Surface

Q31. What is the first step when creating a power surface?
A. Select surface to trim
B. Click on the Power Surface tool from Create group in Surfaces tab
C. Select a trimming curve
D. Open Fill Holes Manager

Q32. In the Power Surface tool, what appears after selecting a chain of entities and clicking OK?
A. Trim Manager
B. Extend Manager
C. Power Surface Manager with preview
D. Split Manager

Q33. Which checkbox should be selected to extend a trimming curve up to the edge of surface?
A. Use current attributes
B. Extend curves to edge
C. Split model
D. Keep original surface

Q34. Which tool is used to delete a surface portion using wireframe curves?
A. Trim to Plane
B. Trim to Surfaces
C. Fill Holes
D. Trim to Curves

Q35. What does selecting the “Split model” checkbox in the Trim to Plane tool do?
A. Merge trimmed surfaces
B. Add color to trimmed edge
C. Divide the selected surface at the trimming plane
D. Delete all trimmed surfaces

Q36. What happens when the “Fill all internal holes” checkbox is selected in the Fill Holes Manager?
A. Only the biggest hole is filled
B. External holes are filled
C. Only boundary holes are filled
D. All internal holes on the trimmed surface are filled

Q37. Which style should be selected in the Extend tool to create an extended surface following the original curvature?
A. Linear
B. Rounded
C. Non-linear
D. Mitered

Q38. Which tool is used to extend the trimmed surface using edge of that surface?
A. Extend
B. Extend Trimmed Edges
C. Trim to Curves
D. Fill Holes

Q39. What is the purpose of the "Mitered" radio button in Extend Trimmed Edges tool?
A. Create rounded corners
B. Create smooth transitions
C. Create extended surface with mitered corners
D. Create sharp edges only

Q40. Which tool is used to apply a fillet between two intersecting surfaces?
A. Fillet to Curves
B. Fillet to Plane
C. Two Surface Blend
D. Fillet to Surfaces

Q41. What feature allows creation of a fillet with varying radius?
A. Rounded corners
B. Variable fillet checkbox
C. Fillet to Curves
D. Plane Selection

Q42. Which tool helps apply a fillet at the intersection of surface and a wireframe curve?
A. Fillet to Plane
B. Fillet to Surfaces
C. Fillet to Curves
D. Curve Blend

Q43. What action is required to flip blending direction while creating a Two Surface Blend?
A. Press ENTER
B. Press F
C. Select Modify
D. Click on gnomon

Q44. Which blend tool creates a surface joining three fillet surfaces?
A. Two Surface Blend
B. Three Fillet Blend
C. Three Surface Blend
D. Fillet to Curves

Q45. What does the "Keep curves" checkbox in Three Fillet Blend do?
A. Keeps trimming curves
B. Creates spline curves at the blend
C. Locks original curves
D. Duplicates the blend curves

Q46. What is the purpose of the Untrim tool?
A. Cut surface at edge
B. Fill boundary gaps
C. Reverse the effect of a trim
D. Create blending

Q47. Which tool removes trimmed sections of a surface boundary?
A. Remove Holes
B. Untrim
C. Remove Boundary
D. Split

Q48. What does the Split tool require to define the direction of the split?
A. Fillet radius
B. Gnomon orientation
C. U or V radio button
D. Trimmed surface edge

Q49. What is used to modify surface dynamically using node points or iso-curves?
A. Edit UV
B. Blend Surface
C. Trim Manager
D. Edit Surface

Q50. Which tool allows changing the number of flowlines (U and V) on a surface?
A. Edit Surface
B. Fill Holes
C. Edit UV
D. Blend Curve

For Student Notes

Chapter 4

Solid Design

Topics Covered

The major topics covered in this chapter are:

- ***Introduction to Solid Design.***
- ***Placing Predefined Solid Blocks.***
- ***Creating Solid Features.***
- ***Modifying Solid Features.***
- ***Generating Solid Model Layout.***

INTRODUCTION

In previous chapters, you have learned about wireframe sketching and surface designing. In this chapter, you will learn about creating solid models. The tools to create solid models are available in the **Solids** tab of the **Ribbon**; refer to Figure-1. Various tools of this tab are discussed next.

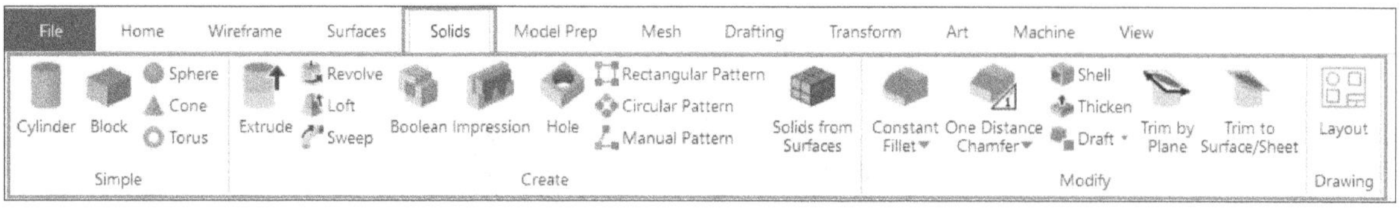

Figure-1. Solids tab

PLACING SOLID CYLINDER

The **Cylinder** tool is used to place solid cylinder of specified parameter at desired location. The procedure to use this tool is given next.

- Click on the **Cylinder** tool from the **Simple** group in the **Solids** tab of the **Ribbon**. The **Primitive Cylinder Manager** will be displayed; refer to Figure-2.

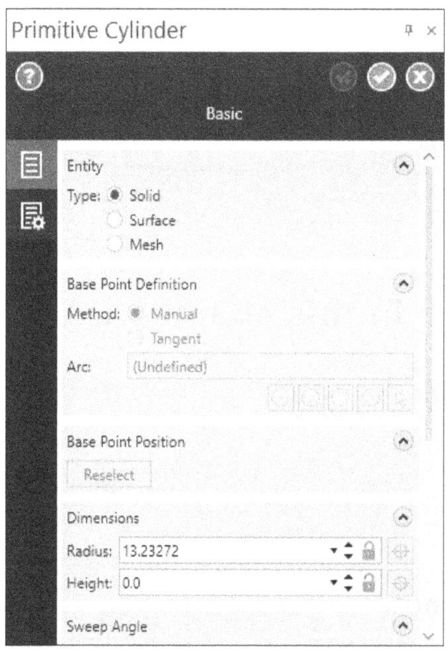

Figure-2. Primitive Cylinder Manager

- Set desired height and radius of cylinder in the **Dimensions** rollout as discussed earlier for surface cylinder.
- Set the other parameters like start and end angle, direction axis, and so on.
- Click at desired location to place the cylinder and click on the **OK** button.

Similarly, you can use the other tools of **Simple** group in the **Solids** tab of **Ribbon** as discussed in **Surface Designing** chapter of this book.

CREATING SOLID EXTRUSION FEATURE

The **Extrude** tool in **Solids** tab is used to create solid extrusion feature similar to the feature discussed in Surface Designing. The procedure to use this tool is given next.

- Click on the **Extrude** tool from the **Create** group in the **Solids** tab of the **Ribbon**. The **Solid Extrude Manager** will be displayed with **Wireframe Chaining** selection box.
- Select desired closed loop curve and click on the **OK** button from the **Wireframe Chaining** selection box. Preview of extrude feature will be displayed; refer to Figure-3.

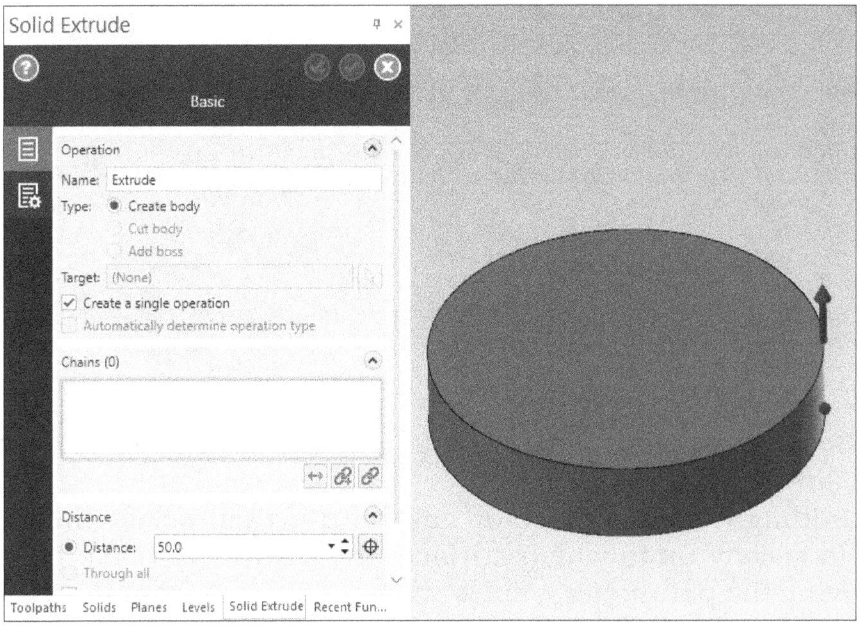

Figure-3. Preview of solid extrude feature

- Select the **Create body** radio button to create a new solid body. Select the **Cut body** radio button to remove material from other solid using extrude feature; refer to Figure-4. Select the **Add boss** radio button to join new solid with another solid.

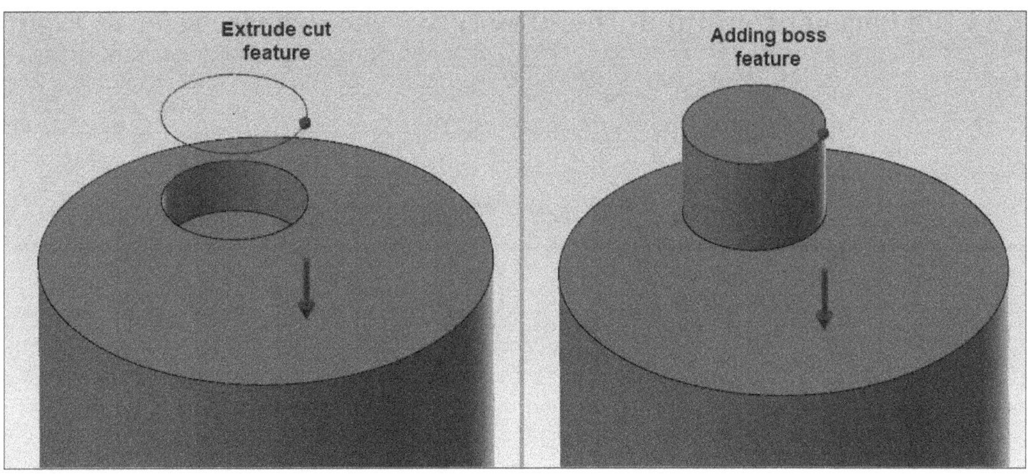

Figure-4. Extrude cut and boss feature preview

- Select the **Create a single operation** check box to create features of multiple wireframe sections as single operation.
- Select the **Automatically determine operation type** check box to automatically select an option from the **Type** section of **Manager** based on selected entities.
- Select the **Distance** radio button from the **Distance** rollout to specify the distance up to which sketch will be extruded.

- Select the **Through all** radio button to extrude the sketch through all the bodies in the extrusion path; refer to Figure-5.

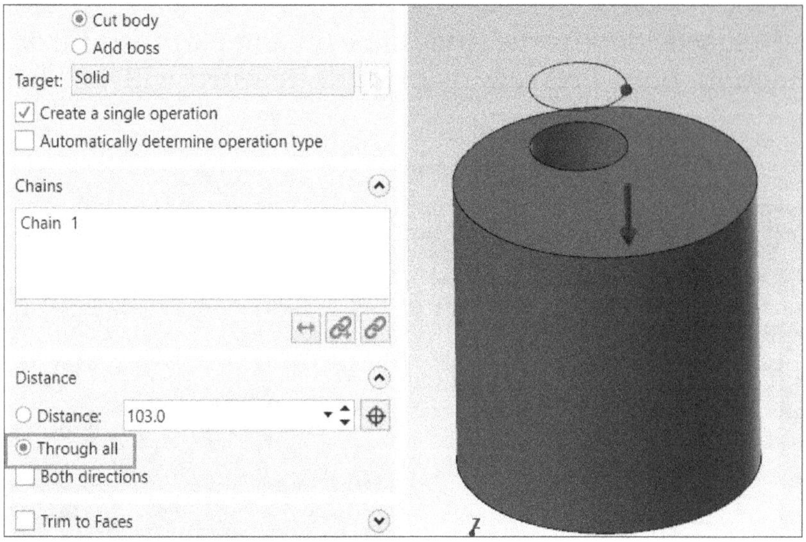

Figure-5. Through all extrusion

- Select the **Both directions** check box to extrude the sketch in both upward and downward directions.
- If you are adding a boss feature or cut feature then select the **Trim to Faces** check box to specify up to which surface, the feature will be created.
- After specifying the parameters, click on the **OK** button from the **Manager** to create the feature.

PLANES MANAGER

The **Planes Manager** is used to create and manage planes of Mastercam; refer to Figure-6. If the **Planes Manager** is not displayed by default then select the **Planes** option from the **Managers** group in the **View** tab of the **Ribbon**; refer to Figure-7.

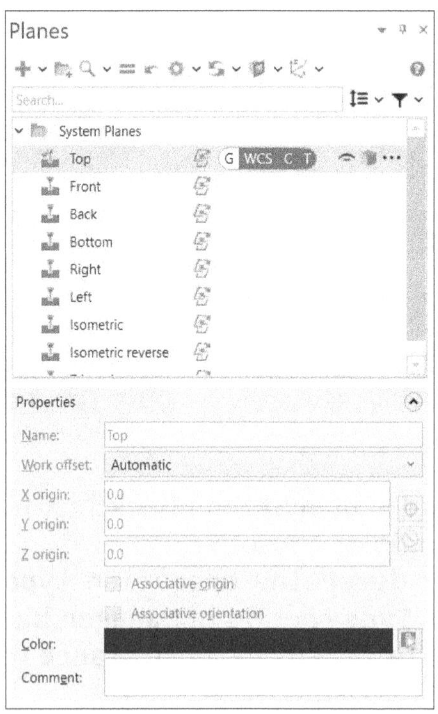

Figure-6. Planes Manager

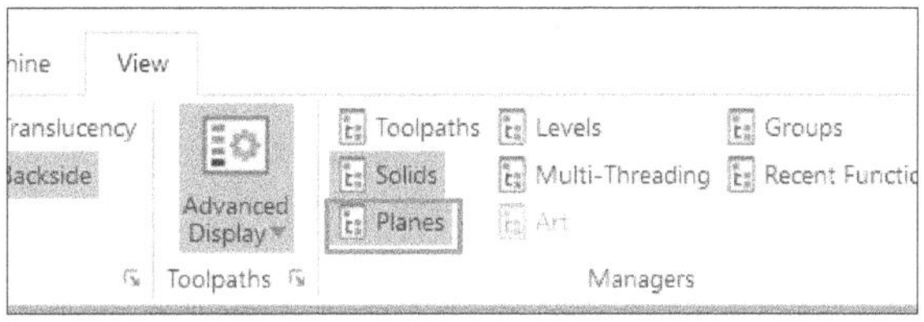

Figure-7. Planes option

Various tools of the **Planes Manager** are discussed next.

Creating Planes Using Geometry

The **From geometry** tool in **Create a new plane** drop-down is used to create a plane using wireframe geometry. The procedure to use this tool is given next.

- Click on the **From geometry** tool from the **Create a new plane** drop-down in the **Planes Manager**. You will be asked to select geometry for creating plane.
- Select three points or two lines from wireframe geometry, or a face of surface feature. The **Select plane** dialog box will be displayed; refer to Figure-8.

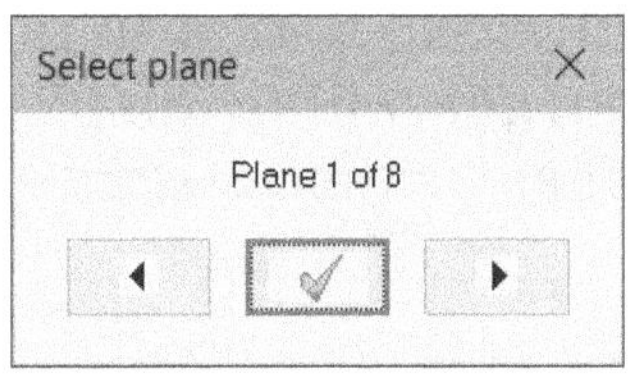

Figure-8. Select plane dialog box

- Click on the **Next** or **Previous** button from the dialog box to switch between planes possible by current selection. Once you get desired plane, click on the **OK** button from the dialog box. Preview of plane will be displayed with **New Plane Manager**; refer to Figure-9.

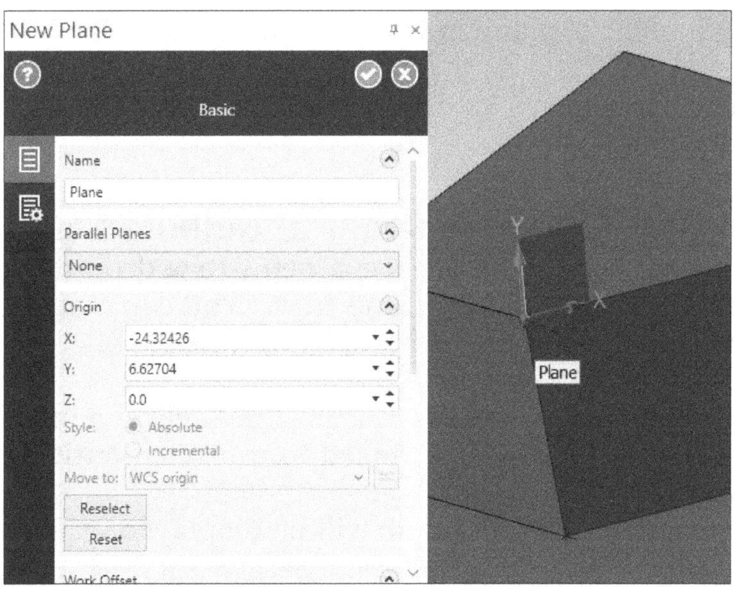

Figure-9. New Plane Manager

- Specify desired name for plane in the **Name** edit box of **Manager**.
- Specify desired values in **X**, **Y**, and **Z** edit boxes of the **Origin** rollout to specify origin point for gnomon of plane.

- Keep the **Work Offset** options to default. We will learn about these options later in the book.
- Select desired check boxes from the **Set As** rollout to set the new plane as tool plane, construction plane, display plane, section plane, and Work coordinate system plane.
- After setting desired parameters, click on the **OK** button from the **Manager** to create the plane. The new plane will be added in the **Planes Manager**.

Creating Plane Using Solid Face

The **From solid face** tool in **Create a new plane** drop-down is used to create a plane using face of solid body. The procedure to use this tool is given next.

- Click on the **From solid face** tool from the **Create a new plane** drop-down in the **Planes Manager**. You will be asked to select a flat solid face.
- Select desired solid face of solid object. Preview of plane will be displayed with **Select plane** dialog box.
- Switch between different plane orientations using the buttons in the dialog box. Click on the **OK** button from the dialog box to accept current displaying plane orientation. The **New Plane Manager** will be displayed.
- Specify the parameters in **Manager** as discussed earlier and click on the **OK** button to create the plane.

Creating Plane parallel to Current View Screen

The **From Gview** tool in the **Create a new plane** drop-down is used to create a plane parallel to current view screen. The procedure to use this tool is given next.

- Click on the **From Gview** tool from the **Create a new plane** drop-down in the **Planes Manager**. The **New Planes Manager** will be displayed as discussed earlier.
- Specify the origin point of plane in the **X**, **Y**, and **Z** edit boxes of the **Origin** rollout in the **Manager**.
- Specify the other parameters as discussed earlier and click on the **OK** button to create the plane.

Creating Plane Normal to Selected Entity

The **From entity normal** tool in the **Create a new plane** drop-down is used to create a plane perpendicular to selected wireframe curve. You can also select two wireframe points to specify normal for plane. The procedure to use this tool is given next.

- Click on the **From entity normal** tool from the **Create a new plane** drop-down in the **Planes Manager**. You will be asked to select an entity to which the plane will be perpendicular.
- Select desired entity. Preview of plane will be displayed; refer to Figure-10.

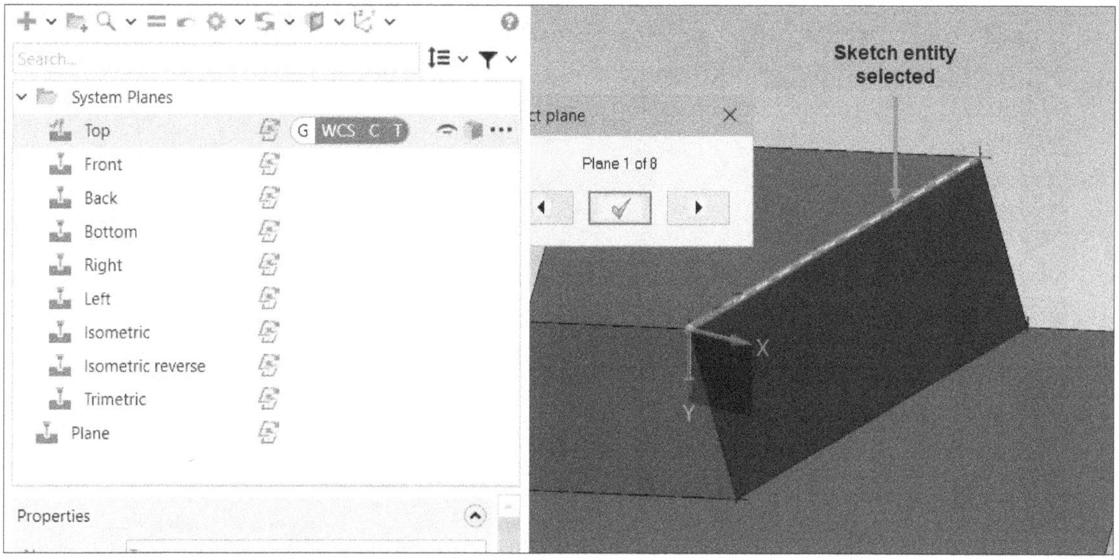

Figure-10. Preview of plane normal to entity

- Switch between various orientations of plane by using the buttons in **Select plane** dialog box to find desired orientation.
- Click on the **OK** button from the dialog box and then click on the **OK** button from the **New Plane Manager** to create the plane.

Creating Plane Relative to WCS

The tools in **Relative to WCS** cascading menu are used to create plane parallel to various WCS planes. The procedure to use these tools is given next.

- Click on desired option from the **Relative to WCS** cascading menu of the **Create a new plane** drop-down in the **Planes Manager**; refer to Figure-11. Preview of the plane parallel to selected WCS plane will be displayed with **New Plane Manager**.

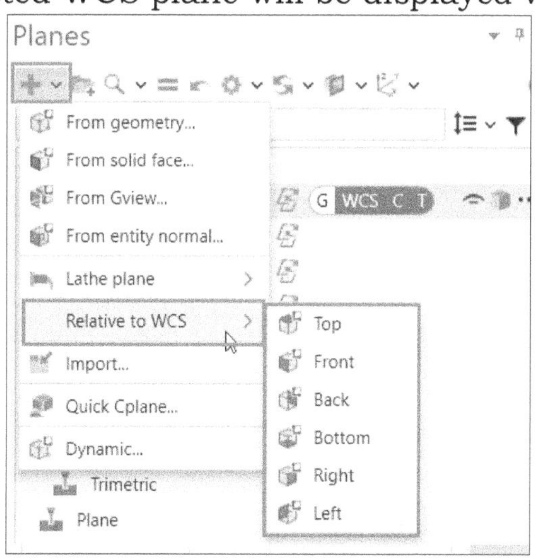

Figure-11. Relative to WCS cascading menu

- Specify desired parameters in the **X**, **Y**, and **Z** edit boxes of **Origin** rollout in **Manager**. The plane will move accordingly; refer to Figure-12.

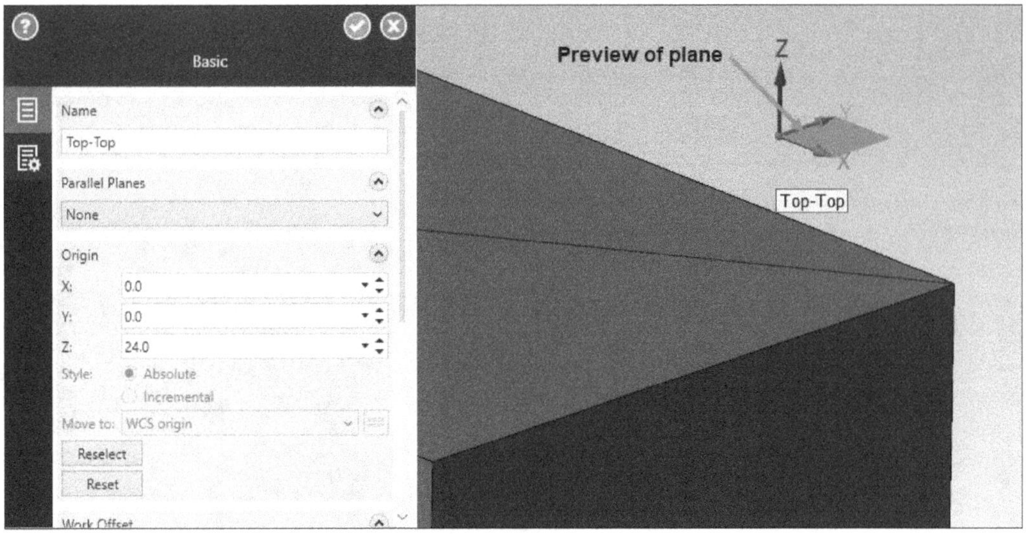

Figure-12. Preview of plane relative to WCS

- Set the other parameters as desired in the **Manager** and click on the **OK** button to create the plane.

Importing Plane

The **Import** tool is used to create planes imported from another Mastercam file. Note that only non-standard planes will be imported. Standard planes are Top, Front, Bottom, Right, Isometric, and so on. The procedure to use this tools is given next.

- Click on the **Import** tool from the **Create a new plane** drop-down in the **Planes Manager**. The **Open** dialog box will be displayed.
- Select desired Mastercam (*.mcam or *.emcam) file from the dialog box and click on the **Open** button. The **Planes Manager** will be displayed with planes available for importing; refer to Figure-13.

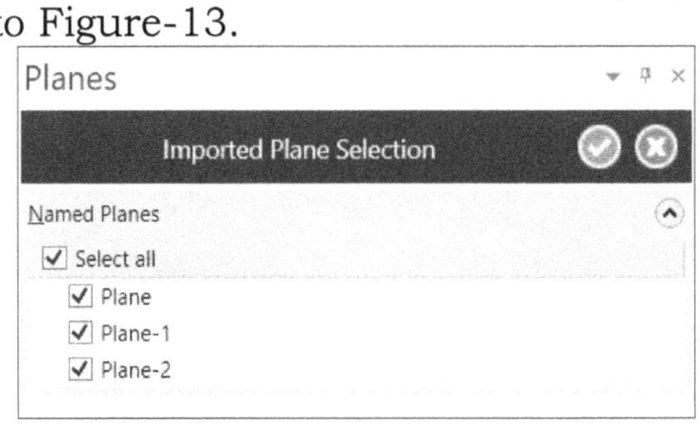

Figure-13. Planes Manager 1

- Select check boxes for planes to be imported and click on the **OK** button. The imported planes will be added in the document.

Creating Quick Construction Plane

The **Quick Cplane** tool is used to create construction plane at desired face. The procedure to use this tool is given next.

- Click on the **Quick Cplane** tool from the **Create a new plane** drop-down in the **Planes Manager**. You will be asked to select a flat face of solid body.
- Select desired face of model. The quick construction plane will be created and set as current construction plane; refer to Figure-14.

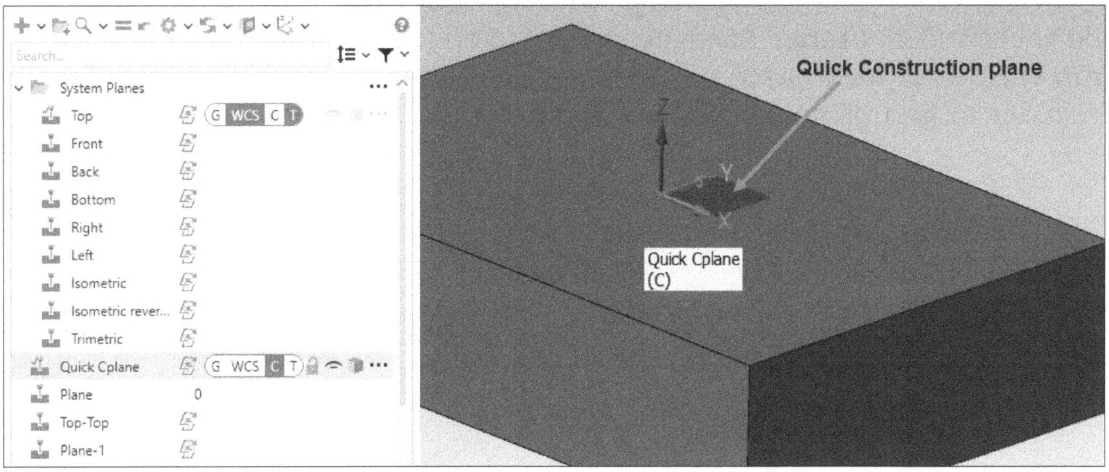

Figure-14. Quick construction plane created

Creating Plane Dynamically

The **Dynamic** tool is used to create plane by specifying its location and orientation. The procedure to use this tool is given next.

- Click on the **Dynamic** tool from the **Create a new plane** drop-down in the **Planes Manager**. A gnomon will get attached to cursor and you will be asked to specify location for placing plane.
- Click at desired location to place gnomon; refer to Figure-15.

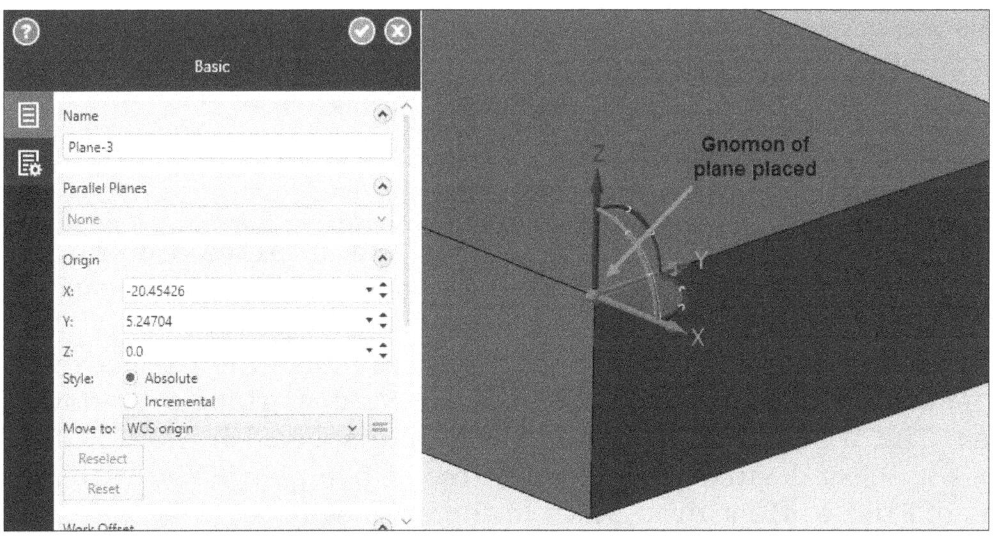

Figure-15. Placing gnomon for plane

- Use the translation and rotation handles of gnomon to specify orientation of plane.
- After setting desired parameters, click on the **OK** button from the **Manager** to create the plane.

Creating Lathe Planes

The tools in the **Select lathe plane** drop-down of **Manager** are used to create planes based on lathe directions (Diameter -D and Depth -Z directions). Select desired tool from the drop-down to create the plane. You will learn more about the lathe planes later in the book.

Adding Group Folder

The **Add group** tool in **Planes Manager** is used to create a new folder in **Planes Manager** to group various planes based on their applications. You can drag and drop planes in this folder to group them; refer to Figure-16.

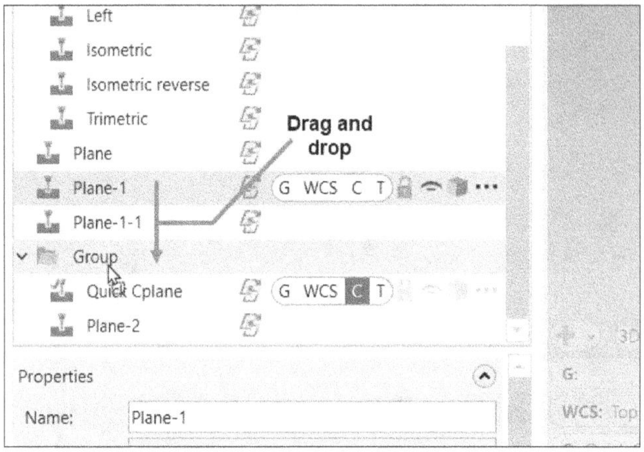

Figure-16. Moving plane to group

Finding a Plane

The tools in the **Find a plane** drop-down are used to display planes created in the model; refer to Figure-17. The procedure to use these tools are discussed next.

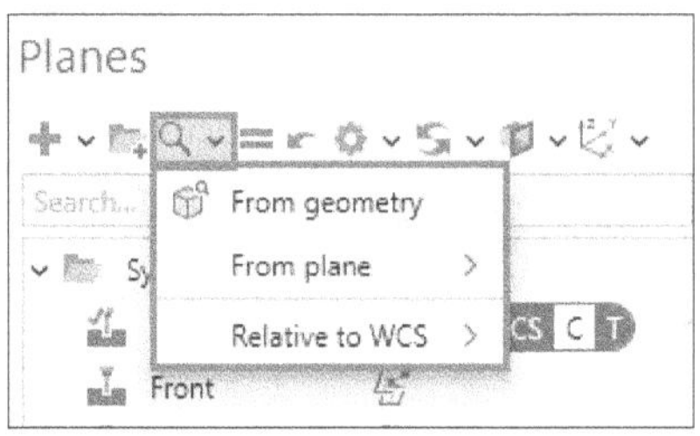

Figure-17. Find a plane drop-down

- Click on the **From geometry** tool from the **Find a plane** drop-down of **Planes Manager**. You will be asked to select the geometry to display associated plane. Select desired geometry. Preview of plane will be displayed.
- If you want to display all the planes created in model then select the **All** option from the **From plane** cascading menu of the **Find a plane** drop-down of **Planes Manager**. The WCSs of all the planes will be displayed in the 3D view; refer to Figure-18. Select desired WCS to select respective plane. You can use the other options of **Find a plane** drop-down in the same way.

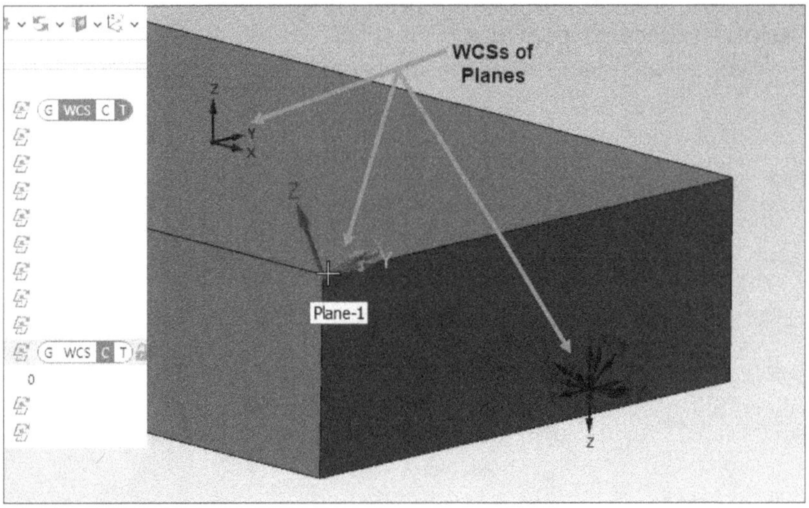

Figure-18. WCSs of planes displayed

Setting WCS, Tool Plane, and Construction Plane to Current Selected Plane

Select desired plane from the **Planes Manager** and click on the **Set your current WCS, construction plane and tool plane** tool from the **Planes Manager**; refer to Figure-19. The selected plane will be set as current WCS, construction plane, and tool plane.

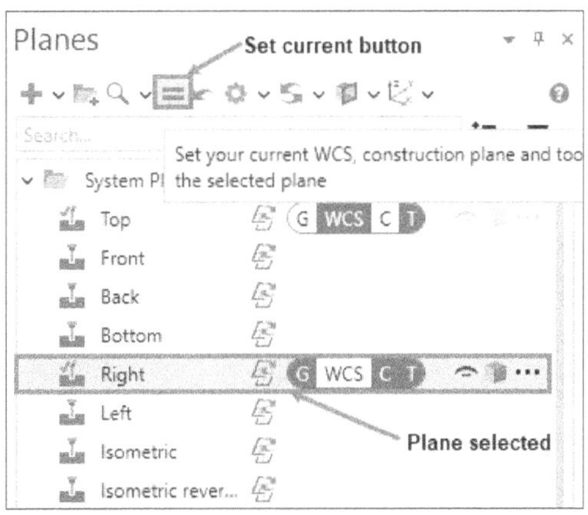

Figure-19. Set current button

Resetting WCS, Construction Plane, and Tool Plane

The **Reset your WCS, construction plane and tool plane to their original state** button is used to reset the planes to default values. Click on this button to reset planes.

Display options

The options in the **Display options** drop-down of **Manager** are used to display or hide various parameters in the **Planes Manager**; refer to Figure-20.

- Select the **List only planes associated with the selected plane** option to display only those planes which are associated with plane selected in **Plane Manager**.

- Select the **Display plane information relative to WCS** option to display information about selected plane.

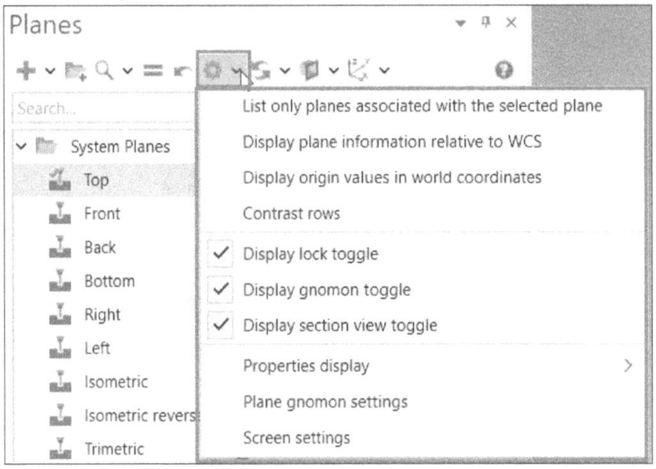

Figure-20. Display options drop-down

- Select the **Display origin values in world coordinates** option from the drop-down to display origin coordinates in world coordinate system rather than in view coordinates.
- Select the **Contrast rows** option from the drop-down to display selected plane row of **Planes Manager** as shaded.
- Select desired check boxes to display respective toggle buttons in the **Planes Manager** for various planes.
- Select desired options from the **Properties display** cascading menu to show respective properties with planes in the **Planes Manager**.
- Click on the **Plane Gnomon settings** option from the drop-down to specify settings related to display of axes and planes. The **Plane Gnomon** dialog box will be displayed; refer to Figure-21.

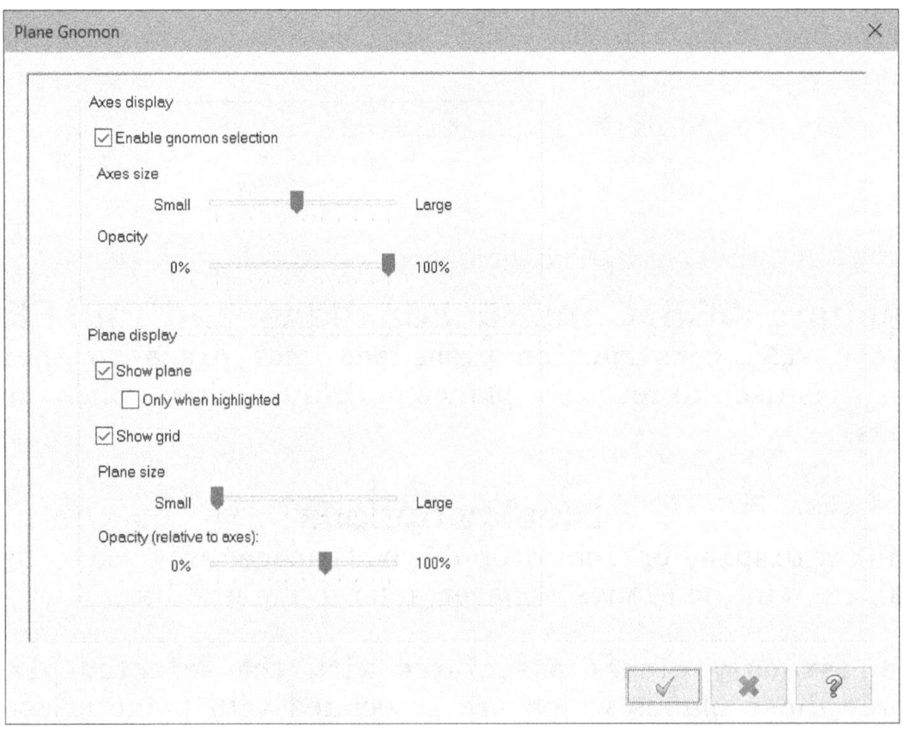

Figure-21. Plane Gnomon dialog box

- Set desired parameters in the dialog box and click on the **OK** button.

Follow rules

The options in the **Follow rules** drop-down are used to define relation between tool plane, construction plane, and WCS; refer to Figure-22. Select desired option to specify relation.

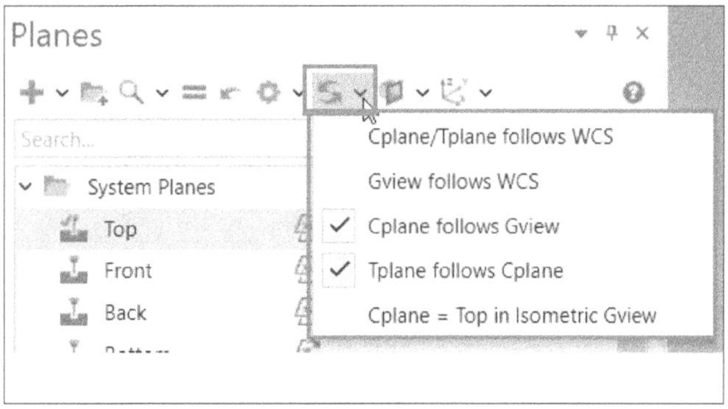

Figure-22. Follow rules drop-down

Similarly, you can use the options of **Section View** and **Show Gnomons** drop-downs in the **Planes Manager**.

CREATING REVOLVE SOLID FEATURE

The **Revolve** tool is used to create a solid revolve feature of specified parameters at desired location. The procedure to use this tool is given next.

- Click on the **Revolve** tool from the **Create** group in the **Solids** tab of the **Ribbon**. The **Solid Revolve Manager** will be displayed with **Wireframe Chaining** selection box; refer to Figure-23. You will be asked to select a closed loop sketch and a line/axis to be used as axis of revolution.
- Select desired closed loop wireframe sketch to be used as revolve profile and click on the **OK** button from the selection box. You will be asked to select a line to be used as axis for revolving sketch.
- Select desired line for axis. Preview of revolve feature will be displayed; refer to Figure-24.

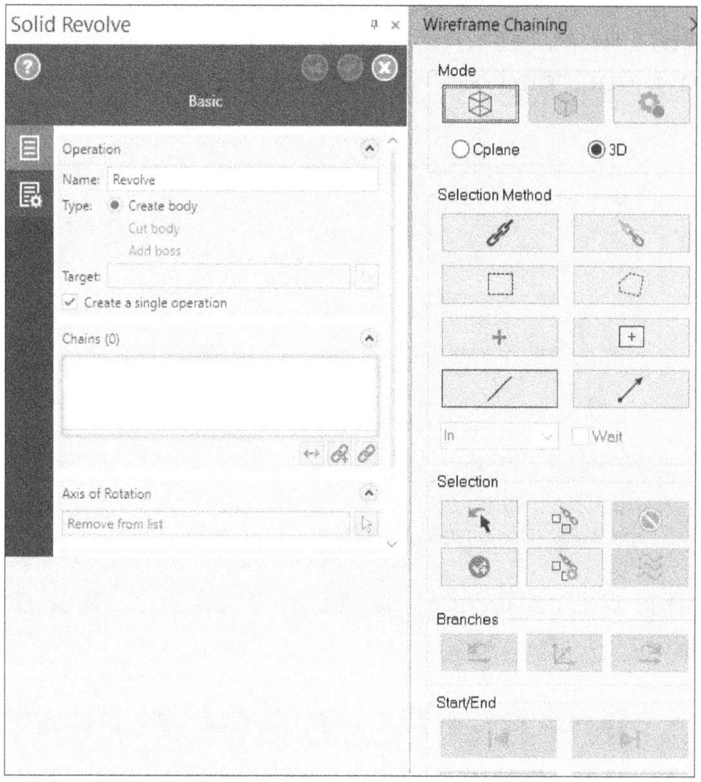

Figure-23. Solid Revolve Manager

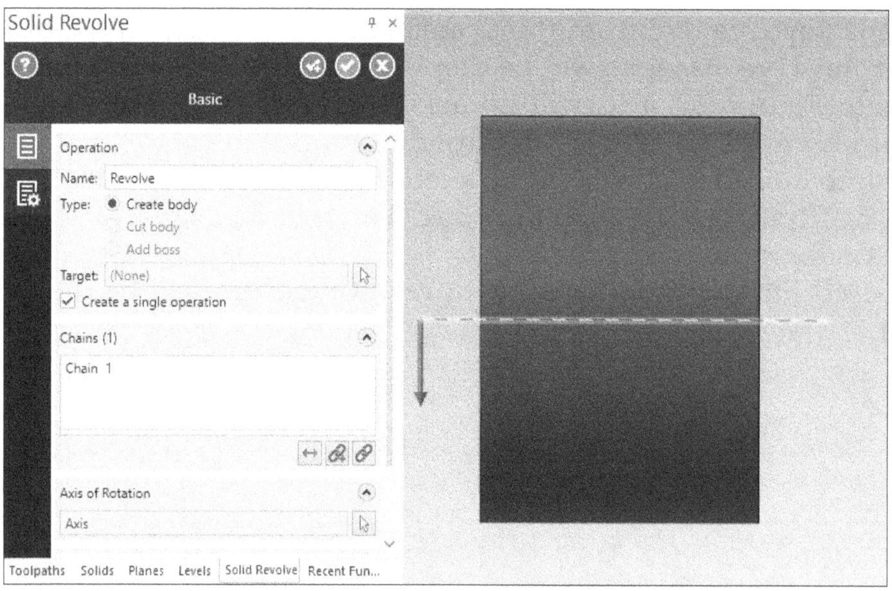

Figure-24. Preview of revolve solid feature

- Click on the **Select Axis** button from the **Axis of Rotation** rollout if you want to select a different axis to define axis of rotation.
- Click on the **Advanced** tab in the **Manager** to specify advanced parameters of revolve solid feature; refer to Figure-25.

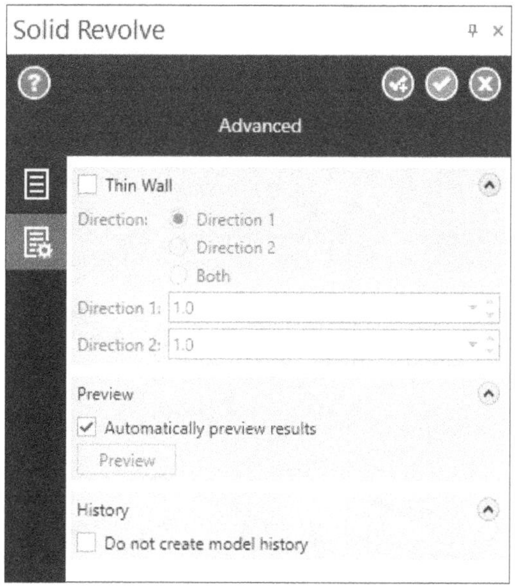

Figure-25. Advanced tab of Solid Revolve Manager

- Select the **Thin Wall** check box if you want to create a tube like feature with specified thickness of walls. On selecting the check box, options below the check box will become active.
- Select desired radio button from the **Direction** rollout and specify the thickness value in the **Direction 1** and **Direction 2** edit boxes based on selected radio button.
- Set the other parameters as desired and click on the **OK** button to create the feature.

CREATING SOLID LOFT FEATURE

The **Loft** tool is used to create a solid loft feature by joining two or more close sketch sections. The procedure to use this tool is given next.

- Click on the **Loft** tool from the **Create** group in the **Solids** tab of the **Ribbon**. The **Loft Manager** will be displayed with **Wireframe Chaining** selection box.
- Select the closed loop sketch chains one by one; refer to Figure-26.
- Note that you can specify the position of start point dynamically at desired location of curve by selecting the **Dynamic** button from the **Start/End** section of **Wireframe Chaining** selection box.
- After selecting desired curve chains, click on the **OK** button from selection box. Preview of the loft feature will be displayed; refer to Figure-27.

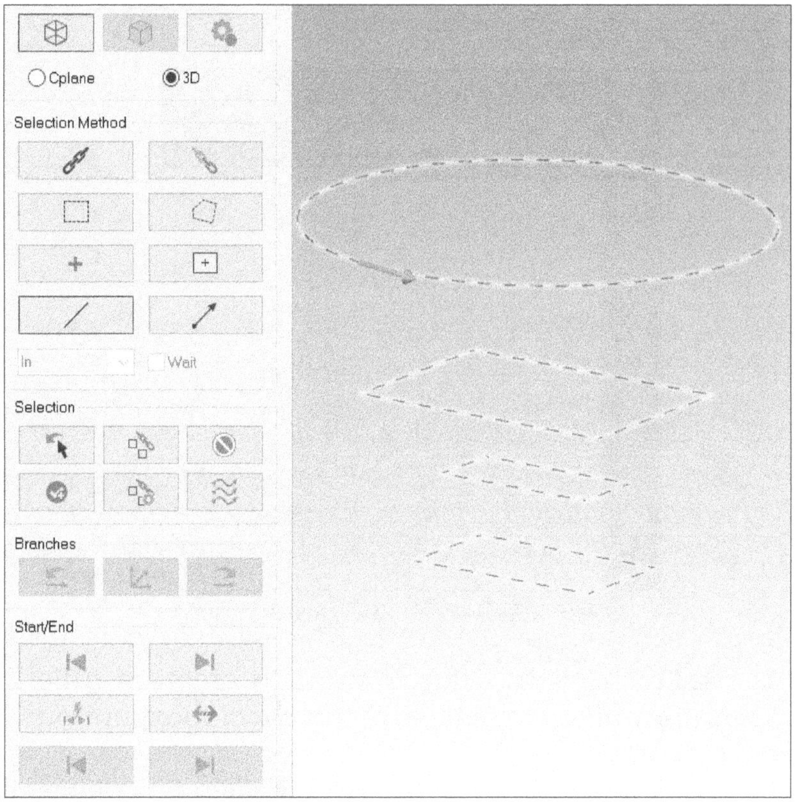

Figure-26. Sketch chains selected for loft feature

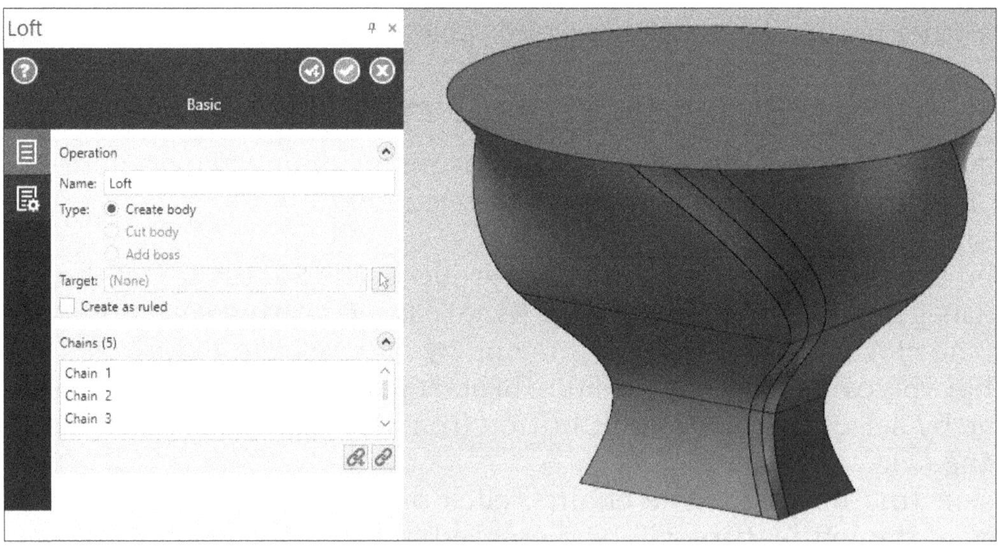

Figure-27. Preview of solid loft feature

- Click on the **OK** button from the **Manager** to create the feature.

CREATING SOLID SWEEP FEATURE

The **Sweep** tool in **Create** group is used to create solid sweep feature using closed loop planar sketch section and an open/closed curve path. The procedure to use this tool is given next.

- Click on the **Sweep** tool from the **Create** group in the **Solids** tab of the **Ribbon**. The **Sweep Manager** will be displayed with **Wireframe Chaining** selection box.

- Select desired closed curve chain for sweep section and click on the **OK** button. You will be asked to select a path curve.
- Select desired curve and click on the **OK** button from the **Wireframe Chaining** selection box. Preview of sweep feature will be displayed; refer to Figure-28.

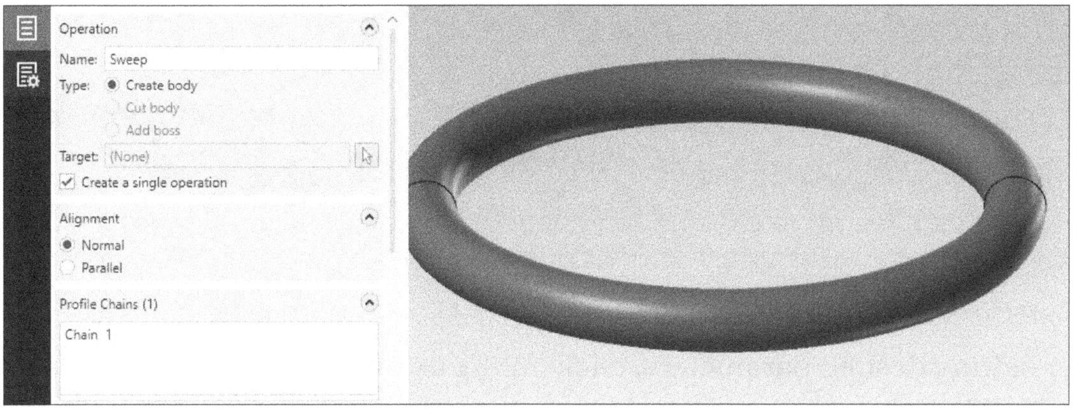

Figure-28. Preview of solid sweep feature

- Click on the **Advanced** tab from the **Manager** to specify advanced parameters of sweep feature; refer to Figure-29.

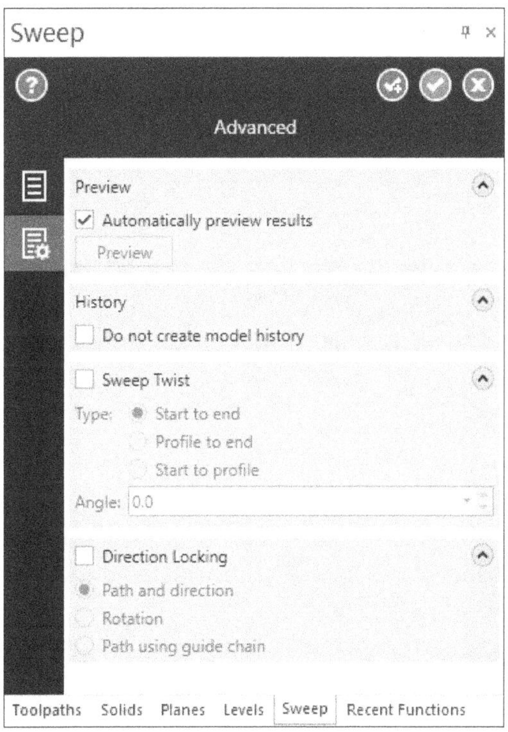

Figure-29. Advanced tab of Sweep Manager

- Select the **Sweep Twist** check box to twist the profile along selected path. Note that the path must be open chain for using twist feature; refer to Figure-30.
- If you are using end profile also then you can specify the direction locking options by selecting **Direction Locking** check box to prevent twisting in sweep.

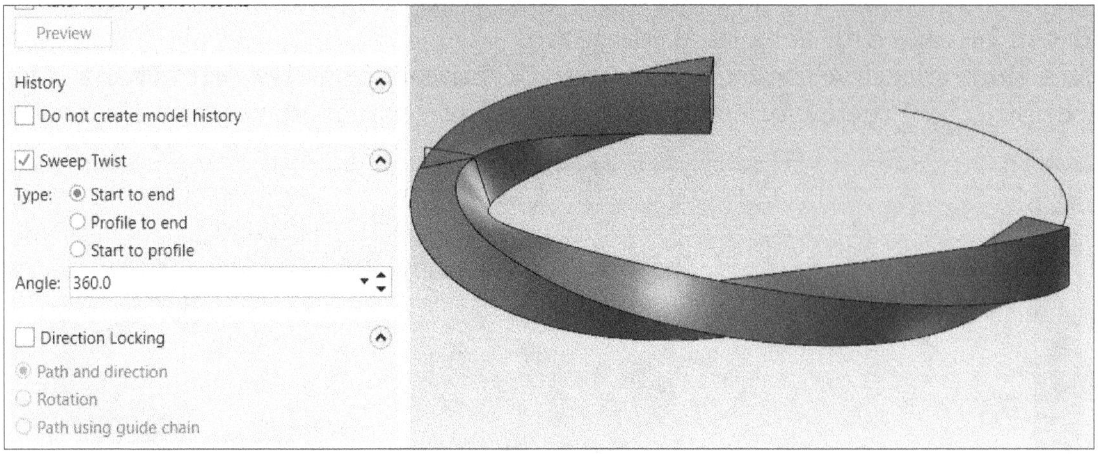

Figure-30. Twisted sweep solid feature

- After setting desired parameters, click on the **OK** button from the **Manager** to create the feature.

PERFORMING BOOLEAN OPERATIONS

The **Boolean** tool is used to perform addition, subtraction, and intersection of selected solid bodies. The procedure to use this tool is given next.

- Click on the **Boolean** tool from the **Create** group in the **Solids** tab of the **Ribbon**. The **Boolean Manager** will be displayed; refer to Figure-31. Also, you will be asked to select the target body.

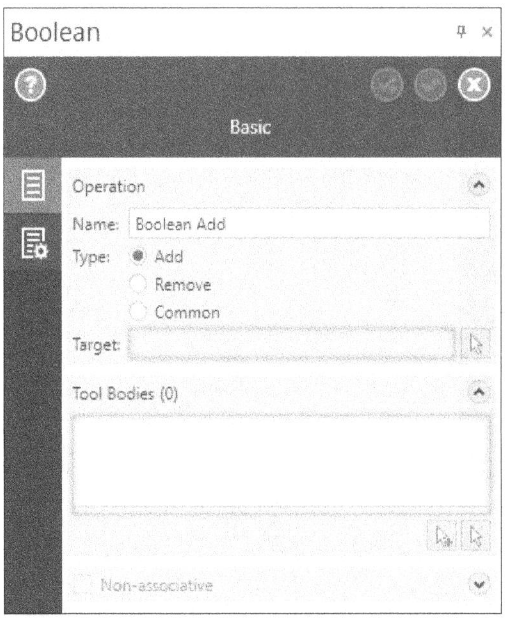

Figure-31. Boolean Manager

- Select desired solid body to be used as base body for operation.
- Select the **Add** radio button to join another selected bodies with the target body. Select the **Remove** radio button to remove selected tool bodies from the target body. Note that after removing material, the tool bodies will disappear. Select the **Common** radio button to keep intersecting portion of both tool bodies and target body, and remove rest of the material.

- Click on the **Add Selection** button from the **Tool Bodies** rollout to select the tool bodies. The **Solid Selection** dialog box will be displayed and you will be asked to select the solid body to be used as tool body.
- Select desired solid body which is intersecting with the target body; refer to Figure-32 and click on the **OK** button from the dialog box. Based on selected radio button in **Type** section of **Manager**, the preview of boolean operation will be displayed; refer to Figure-33.

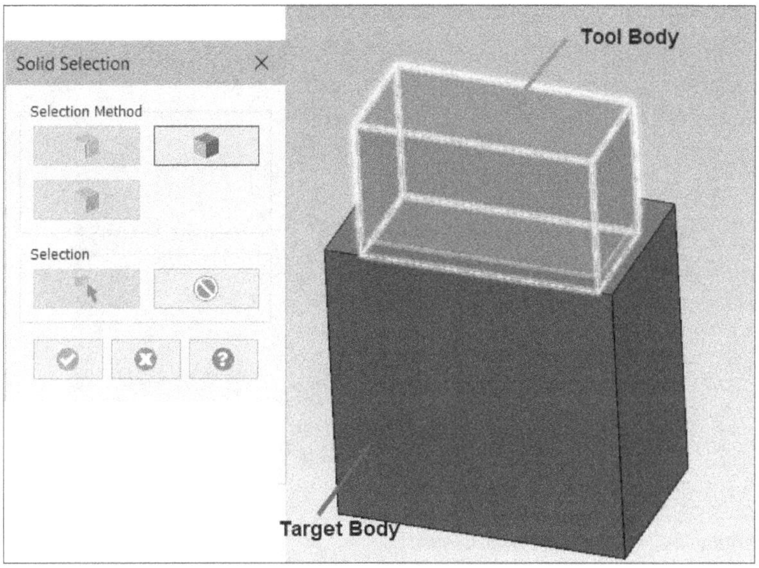

Figure-32. Bodies selected for boolean operation

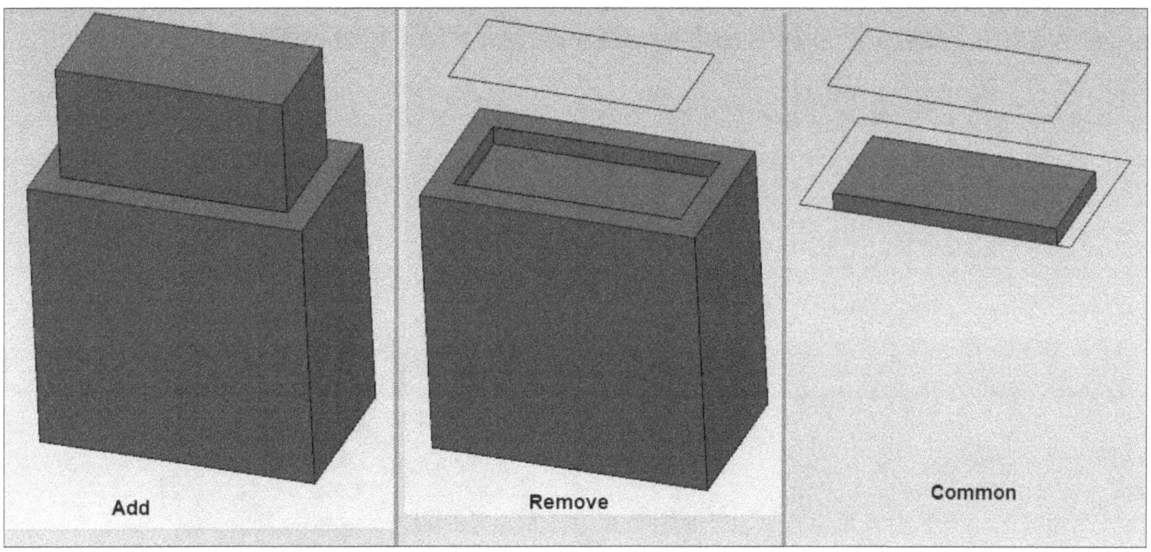

Figure-33. Preview of boolean operation

- Select the **Non-associative** check box from the **Manager** to keep original entities after performing boolean operation. After selecting the **Non-associative** check box, select the other check boxes to save respective objects after operation.
- After setting desired parameters, click on the **OK** button from the **Manager**.

CREATING NEGATIVE IMPRESSION

The **Impression** tool is used to create a negative solid impression of selected closed body. The procedure to use this tool is given next.

- Click on the **Impression** tool from the **Create** group in the **Solids** tab of the **Ribbon**. The **Wireframe Chaining** selection box will be displayed.
- Select the wireframe chain of curves; refer to Figure-34 and click on the **OK** button from the selection box. The **Solid Selection** dialog box will be displayed.

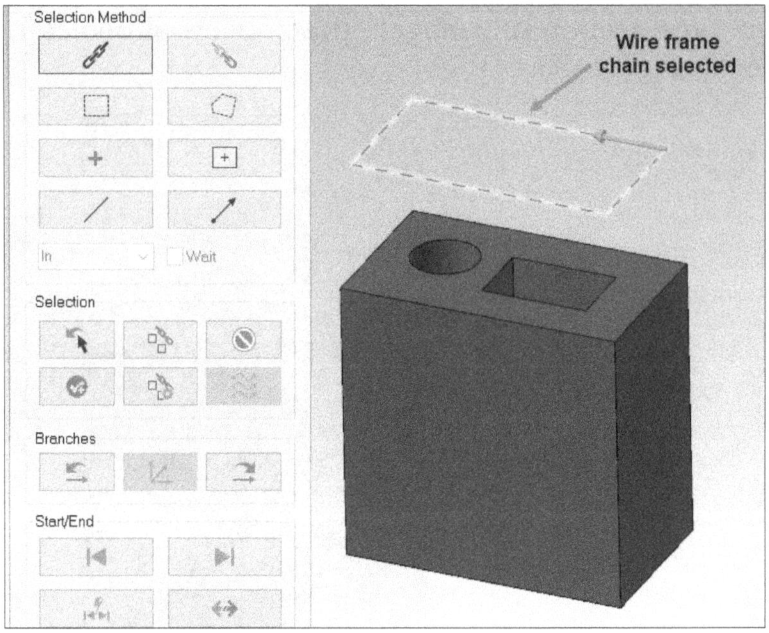

Figure-34. Wireframe chain selected

- Select the solid body with extrude cuts at its top face, directly below wireframe chain; refer to Figure-35 and click on the **OK** button from the dialog box. A solid negative impression body will be created; refer to Figure-36.

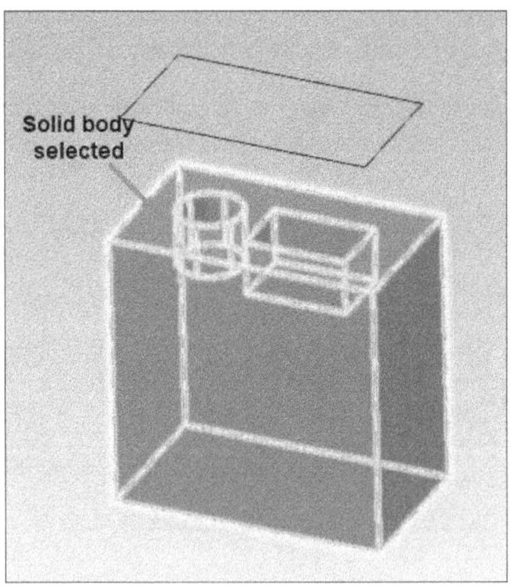

Figure-35. Solid body selected

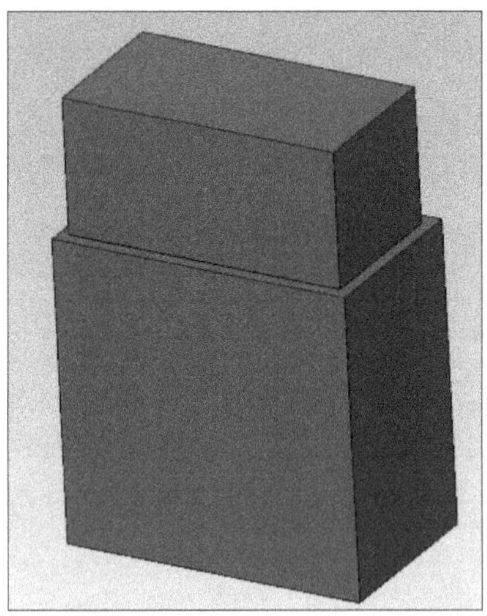

Figure-36. Preview of negative impression body

- Select the base body and delete/hide it. The negative impression body will be displayed; refer to Figure-37.

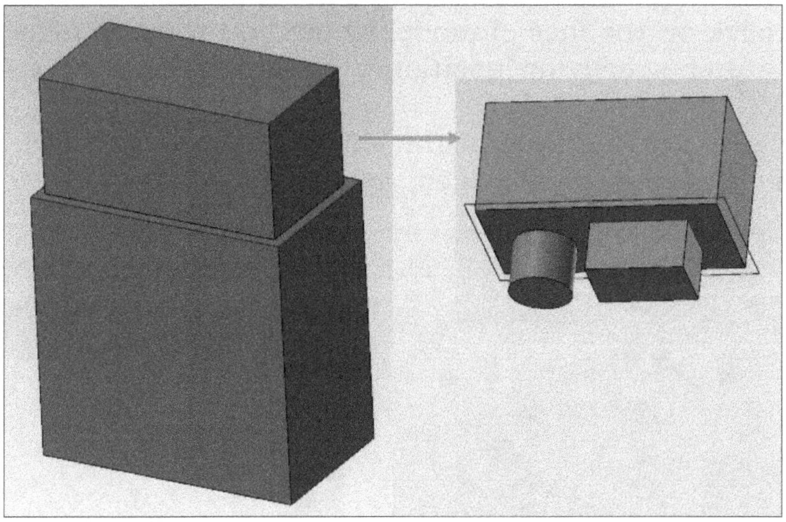

Figure-37. Negative impression of solid created

CREATING HOLE IN SOLID

The **Hole** tool is used to create cylindrical hole through selected solid face. The procedure to use this tool is given next.

- Click on the **Hole** tool from the **Create** group in the **Solids** tab of the **Ribbon**. The **Hole Manager** will be displayed; refer to Figure-38.

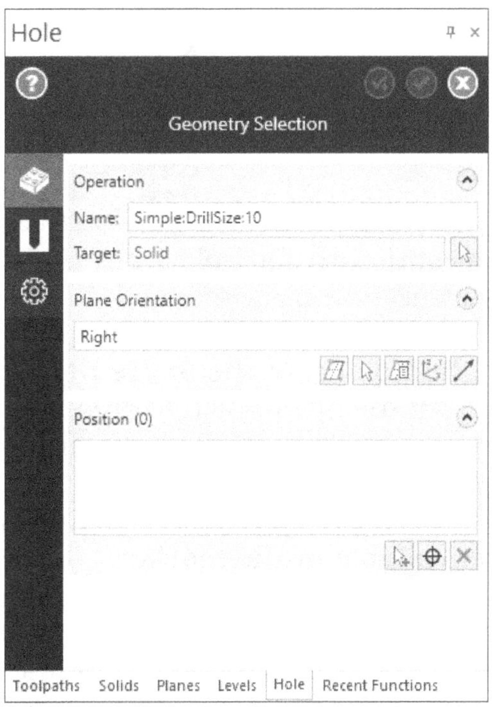

Figure-38. Hole Manager

- Select desired solid body (if there are multiple solid bodies) on which you want to create the hole. The options in **Hole Manager** will become active.
- The options in the **Plane Orientation** rollout are used to define direction of hole axis. Click on the **Select face** button from the rollout and select the top face of model to define vertical direction of hole.

- Click on the **Add AutoCursor position** button from the **Position** rollout of **Manager** and click on the face of model where you want to place the holes; refer to Figure-39. After specifying positions, press **ENTER**. Preview of holes will be displayed.
- Click on the **Hole Style** button at the left in the **Home Manager**. The **Hole Style** page will be displayed in the **Manager**; refer to Figure-40.

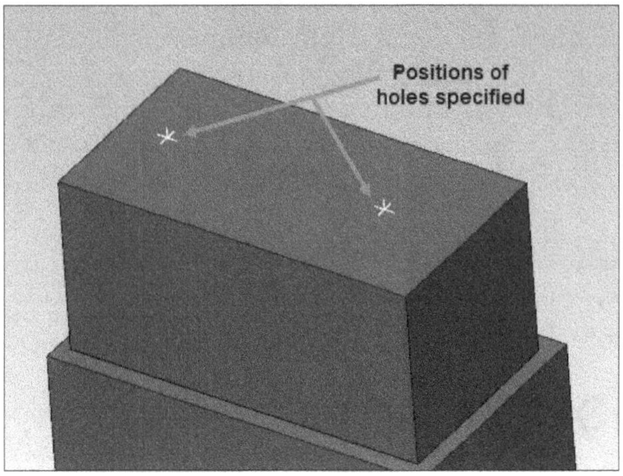

Figure-39. Specifying positions of holes

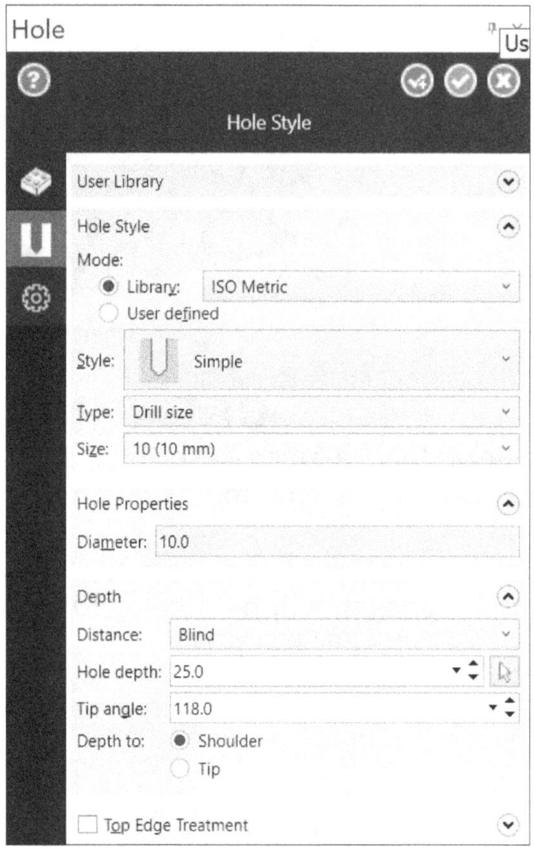

Figure-40. Hole Style page

- Select desired industrial standard for hole from the drop-down next to Library radio button when this radio button is selected. The options in **Style**, **Type**, and **Size** drop-down will be available based on selected library standard.
- Select desired style for the hole from the **Style** drop-down. For example, select the **Counterbore** option from the drop-down to create standard counterbore holes. Based on selected style type, options in the **Type** drop-down will change; refer to Figure-41.
- Select desired size from the **Size** drop-down to define standard hole size for which drill bits are commonly available in the market.
- Select desired option from the **Fit** drop-down in the **Hole Properties** rollout to define whether hole is loose fit, normal fit, or tight fit for the shaft/bolt.
- Set desired parameters in the **Depth** rollout to define depth of hole. Preview of the hole will update based on specified parameters; refer to Figure-42. Select the **Blind** option from the **Distance** drop-down and specify the value of total depth of hole in the **Hole Depth** edit box of the **Depth** rollout.
- Select the **Through all** radio button to create a hole through selected body.

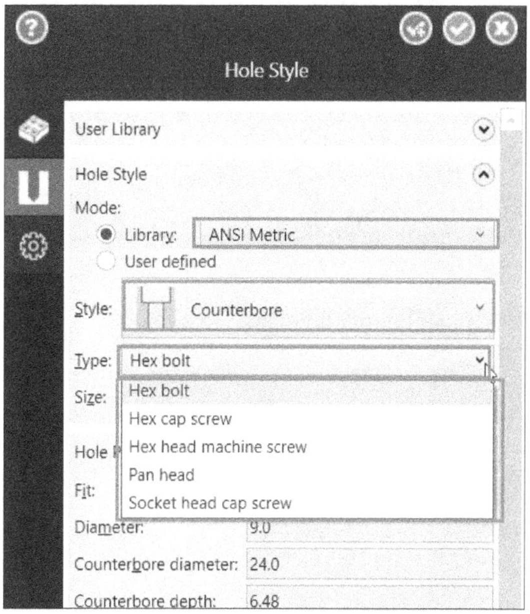

Figure-41. Type options for holes

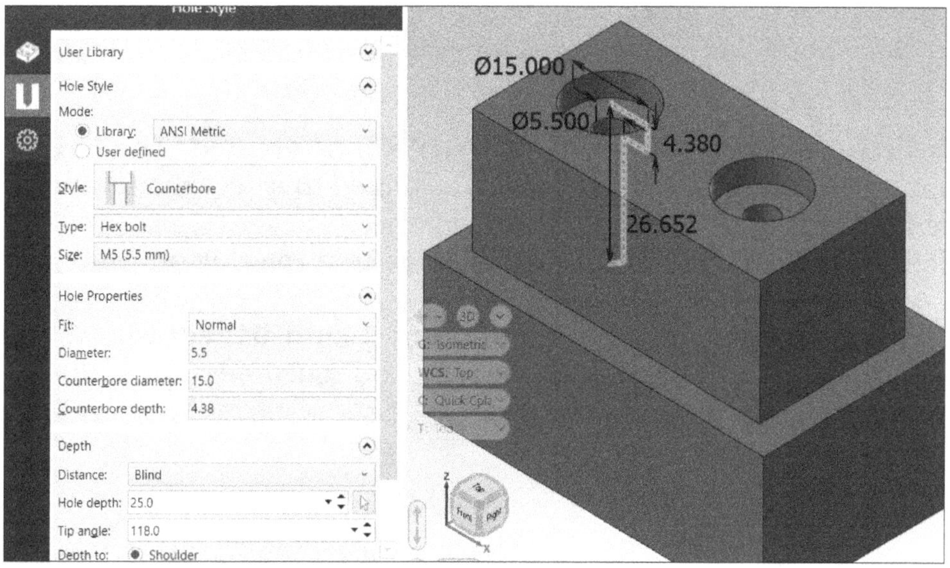

Figure-42. Specifying parameters for counterbore hole

- If you want to chamfer/fillet the edges of holes then select the **Top Edge Treatment** check box and specify the parameters in edit boxes of **Top Edge Treatment** rollout. Similarly, you can define
- If you want to create non-standard custom holes then select the **User defined** radio button from the **Hole Style** rollout at the top in **Hole Manager**. You will be able to modify the values of hole profile like diameter of hole, depth of counterbore, and so on.
- After setting all the parameters, click on the **OK** button from the **Manager**. The holes will be created.

CREATING RECTANGULAR PATTERN

The **Rectangular Pattern** tool is used to create multiple instances of selected feature on a target body in horizontal and vertical directions. The procedure to use this tool is given next.

- Click on the **Rectangular Pattern** tool from the **Create** group in the **Solids** tab of the **Ribbon**. The **Rectangular pattern Manager** will be displayed; refer to Figure-43 and you will be asked to select target body on which pattern will be created.

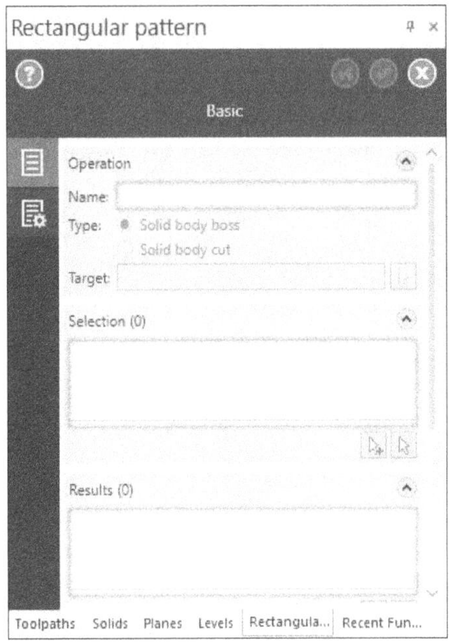

Figure-43. Rectangular Pattern Manager

- Select desired solid body on which pattern will be created. The **Solid Selection** dialog box will be displayed and you will be asked to select the feature to be copied in pattern.
- Select desired feature and click on the **End Selection** button from graphics area. Preview of pattern will be displayed.
- Set desired parameters in the **Direction 1** and **Direction 2** rollouts. The rectangular pattern will be displayed; refer to Figure-44.

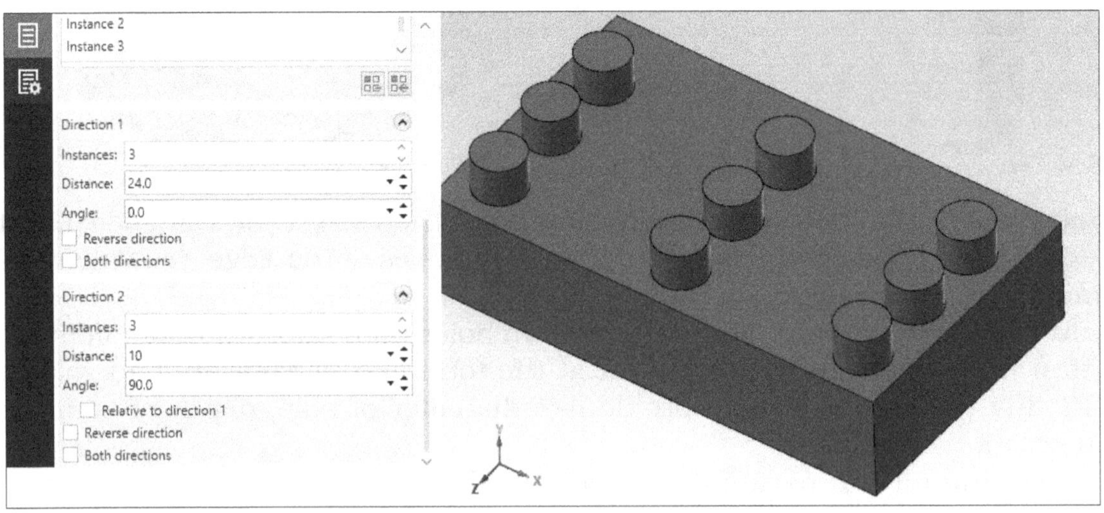

Figure-44. Preview of rectangular pattern

- If you want to remove an instance from the pattern then select desired instance from the list in the **Results** rollout and click on the **Remove Selected Instances** button.
- Click on the **OK** button from the **Manager** to create the pattern.

CREATING CIRCULAR PATTERN

The **Circular Pattern** tool is used to create circular pattern of selected features on selected target body. The procedure to use this tool is given next.

- Click on the **Circular Pattern** tool from the **Create** group in the **Solids** tab of the **Ribbon**. The **Circular pattern Manager** will be displayed and you will be asked to select the target body on which pattern will be created.
- Select desired solid base body. You will be asked to select the feature to be patterned and **Solid Selection** dialog box will be displayed.
- Select the face of desired feature to be patterned and click on the **End Selection** button from graphics area. Preview of pattern will be displayed; refer to Figure-45.
- By default, **Arc** radio button is selected in the **Distribution** section of the **Manager** hence, circular pattern is created with specified angular span between two instances in **Angle** edit box. Select the **Full circle** radio button to create circular pattern in full 360 degree span.
- Click on the **AutoCursor** button next to **Center point** box in the **Location and Distribution** rollout of the **Manager** and select the circular edge of solid base; refer to Figure-46.

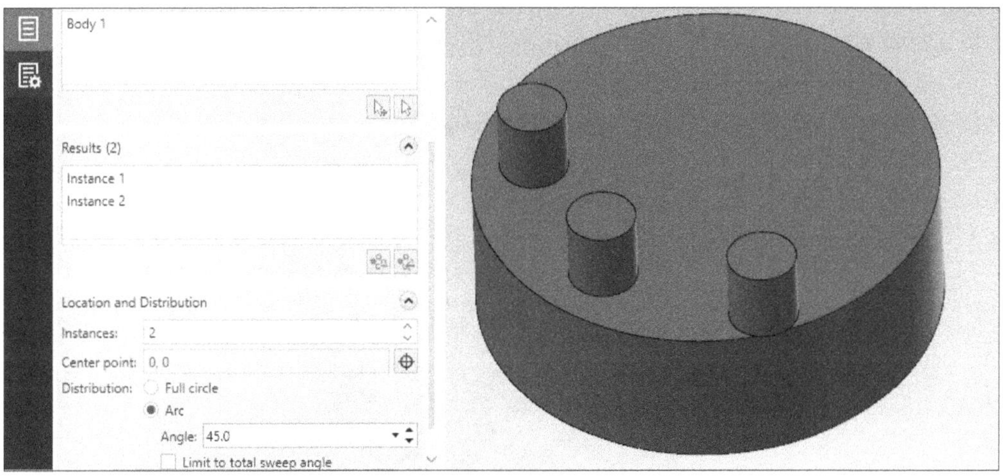

Figure-45. Preview of pattern

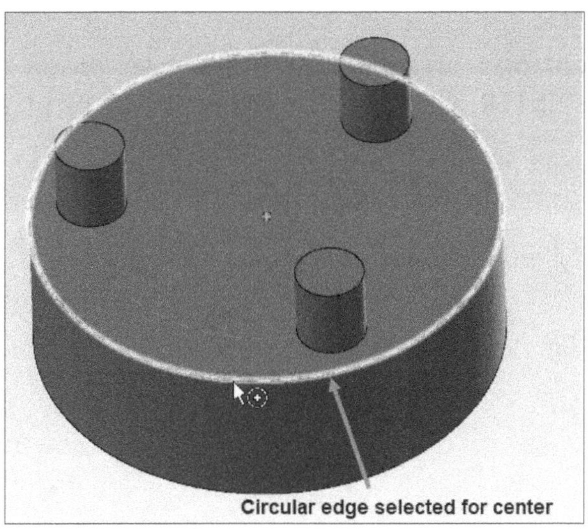

Figure-46. Selecting center for circular pattern

- Specify the number of instances of pattern in the **Instances** edit box.
- If you want to create a cut feature in solid body then select the **Solid body cut** radio button.
- Click on the **OK** button from the **Manager** to create the pattern.

CREATING MANUAL PATTERN

The **Manual Pattern** tool is used to create pattern of selected object on target body. The procedure to use this tool is given next.

- Click on the **Manual Pattern** tool from the **Create** group in the **Solids** tab of the **Ribbon**. The **Manual Pattern Manager** will be displayed and you will be asked to select a target body.
- Select the target body on which pattern will be created. You will be asked to select the body to be patterned.
- Select desired body and click on the **End Selection** button from graphics area. You will be asked to use **Add** button for adding instances in pattern.
- Click on the **Add** button in the **Results** rollout of the **Manual Pattern Manager**. You will be asked to specify base point of pattern.
- Select the base point of feature to be patterned. You will be asked to specify location where you want to place the instances of pattern; refer to Figure-47.

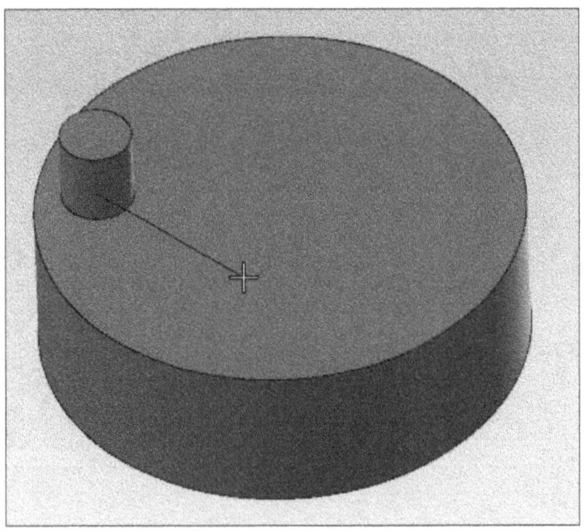

Figure-47. Specifying position of instance

- Click at desired locations on the target body to place the instances; refer to Figure-48 and press **ENTER**. Click on the **OK** button from the **Manager** to create the pattern.

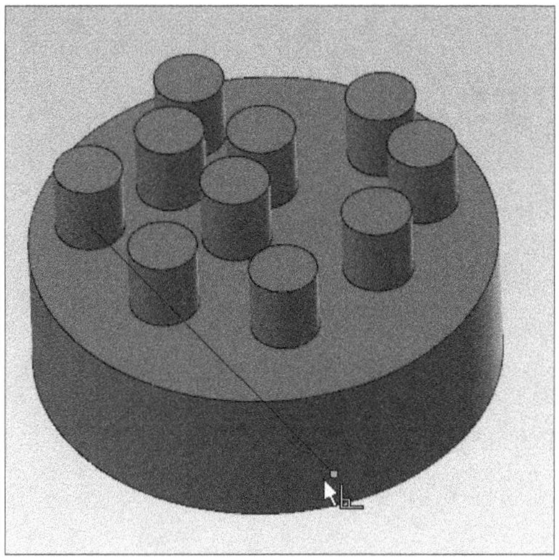

Figure-48. Manual pattern created

CREATING SOLID FROM SURFACES

The **Solids from Surfaces** tool is used to create solid using the surfaces forming a closed region. The procedure to use this tool is given next.

- Click on the **Solids from Surfaces** tool from the **Create** group in the **Solids** tab of the **Ribbon**. The **Solids from Surfaces Manager** will be displayed and you will be asked to select the surfaces for forming solid.
- Select desired surfaces from the 3D view. If you want to select all the visible surfaces then press **CTRL+A** key. After selecting surfaces, press **ENTER** key.
- Select desired radio button from the **Original surface** section of the **Manager** and click on the **OK** button. The solid body will be created.

CREATING FILLETS

The tools in the **Constant Fillet** drop-down are used to create various types of fillets; refer to Figure-49. Various tools in this drop-down are discussed next.

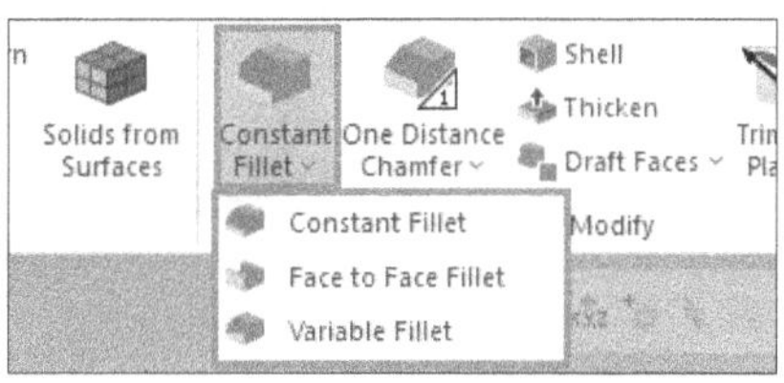

Figure-49. Constant Fillet drop-down

Creating Constant Fillet

The **Constant Fillet** tool is used to create fillets of constant radius value on selected faces. The procedure to use this tool is given next.

- Click on the **Constant Fillet** tool from the **Modify** group in the **Solids** tab of **Ribbon**. The **Constant Radius Fillet Manager** will be displayed with selection filters active in the **Selection** toolbar; refer to Figure-50.

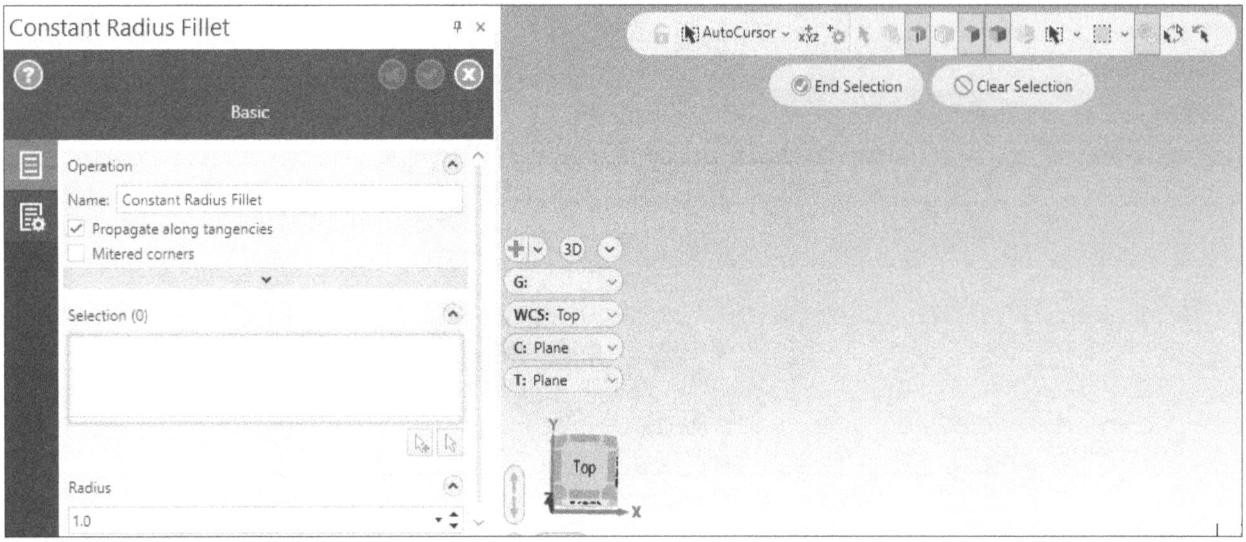

Figure-50. Constant Radius Fillet Manager

- Select desired faces, edges, or bodies to which you want to apply fillet and click on the **End Selection** button from the graphics area. Preview of fillet will be displayed; refer to Figure-51.
- Specify desired value of fillet radius in the **Radius** edit box.
- Select the **Mitered corners** check box to create mitered corners at vertices where three or more fillets meet.
- Click on the **OK** button from the **Manager** to create the fillets.

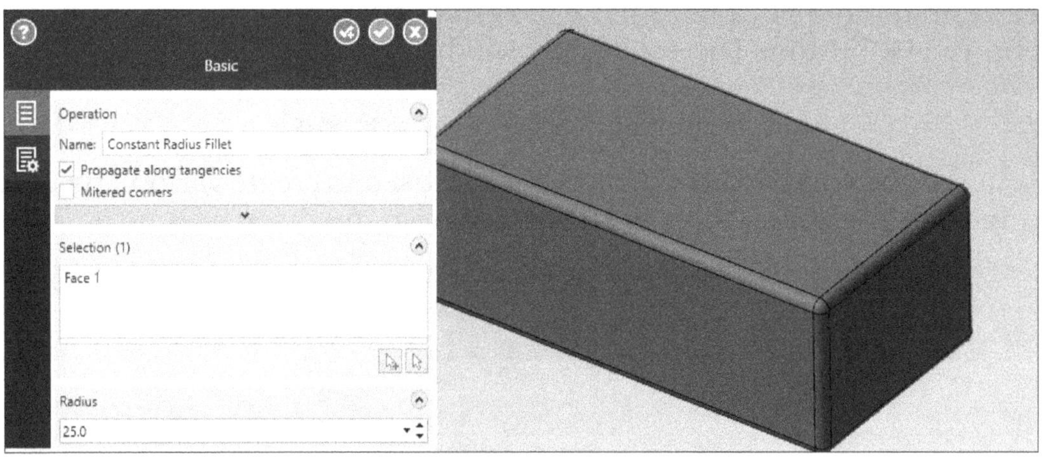

Figure-51. Preview of fillet

Creating Face to Face Fillet

The **Face to Face Fillet** tool is used to create fillet at the edges common to selected faces. The procedure to use this tool is given next.

- Click on the **Face to Face Fillet** tool from the **Constant Fillet** drop-down in the **Modify** group of **Solids** tab in the **Ribbon**. The **Face to Face Fillet Manager** will be displayed and you will be asked to select the faces to which fillet is to be applied; refer to Figure-52 .

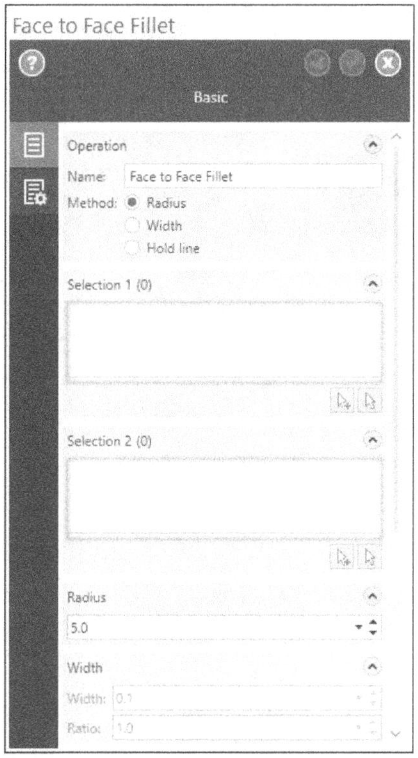

Figure-52. Face to Face Fillet Manager.

- Select the first face or set of faces and press **ENTER**. You will be asked to select faces for the second set. Select desired face and press **ENTER**. Preview of fillet will be displayed; refer to Figure-53.

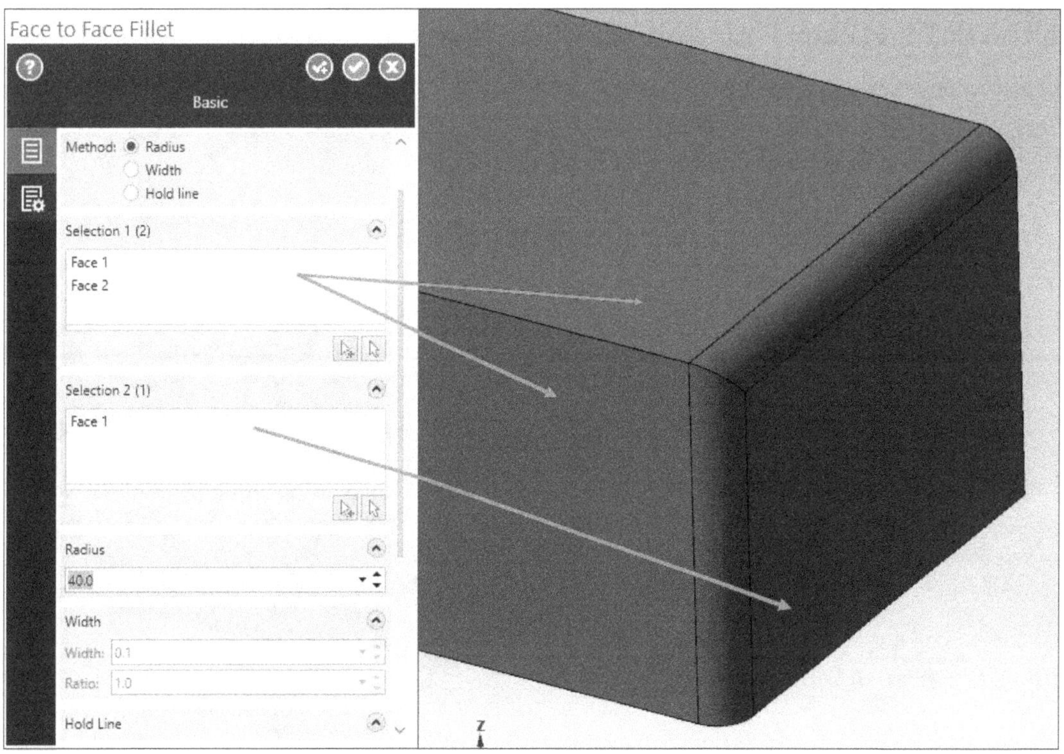

Figure-53. Faces selected for fillet

- Set desired value of radius in the **Radius** edit box.

- Select the **Width** radio button from the **Method** section of the **Manager** if you want to create a fillet of specified chordal width. Set desired values in the **Width** and **Ratio** edit boxes. Preview of fillet will be displayed; refer to Figure-54.

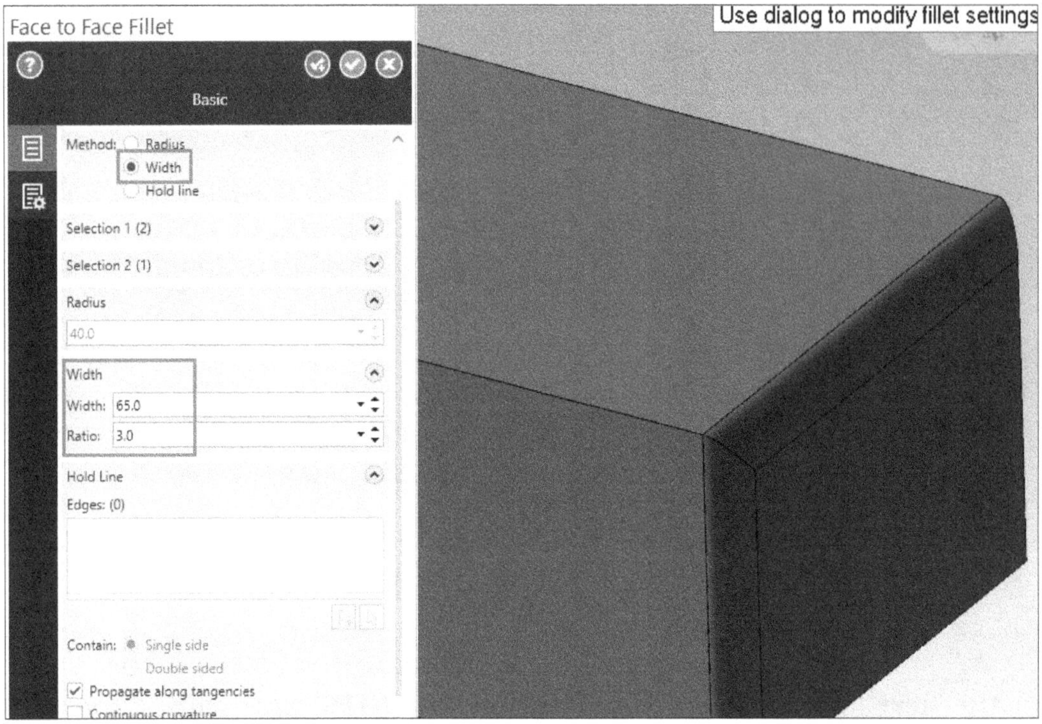

Figure-54. Specifying fillet width

- Select the **Hold line** radio button if you want to join two edges of the solid with fillet. You will be asked to select the edges. Click on the **Add Selection** button from the **Hold Line** rollout and select the two edges; refer to Figure-55.

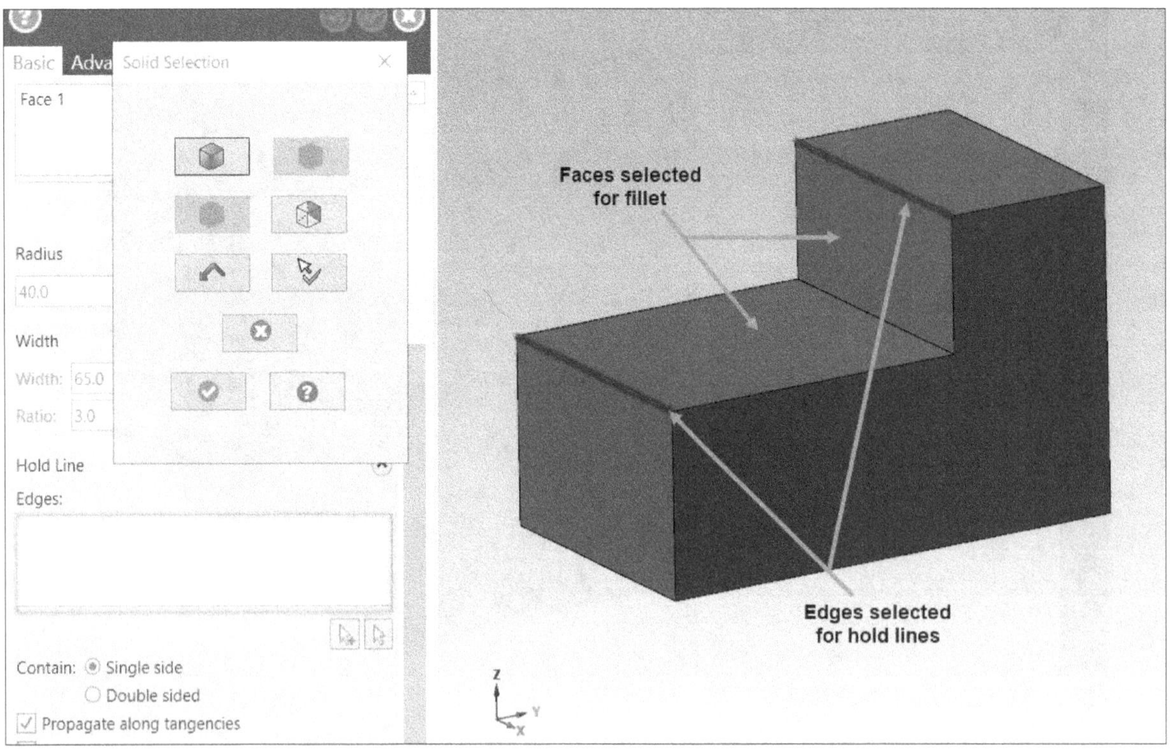

Figure-55. Edges selected for hold line

- Click on the **OK** button from the **Solid Selection** dialog box. Preview of hold line fillet will be displayed; refer to Figure-56. Select the **Double-sided** radio button to create hold line fillet on both sides.

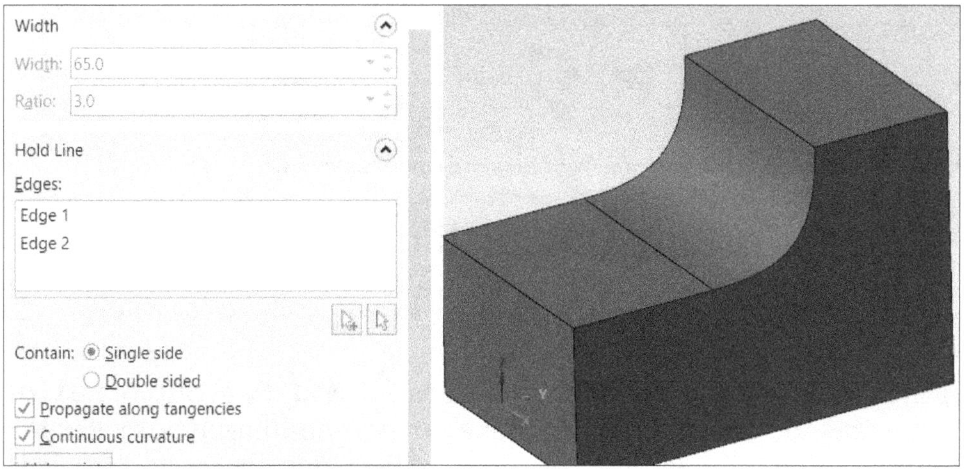

Figure-56. Preview of hold line fillet

- Click on the **OK** button from the **Manager** to create the fillet.

The **Variable Radius Fillet** tool works in the same way as discussed in Surface Designing; refer to Figure-57.

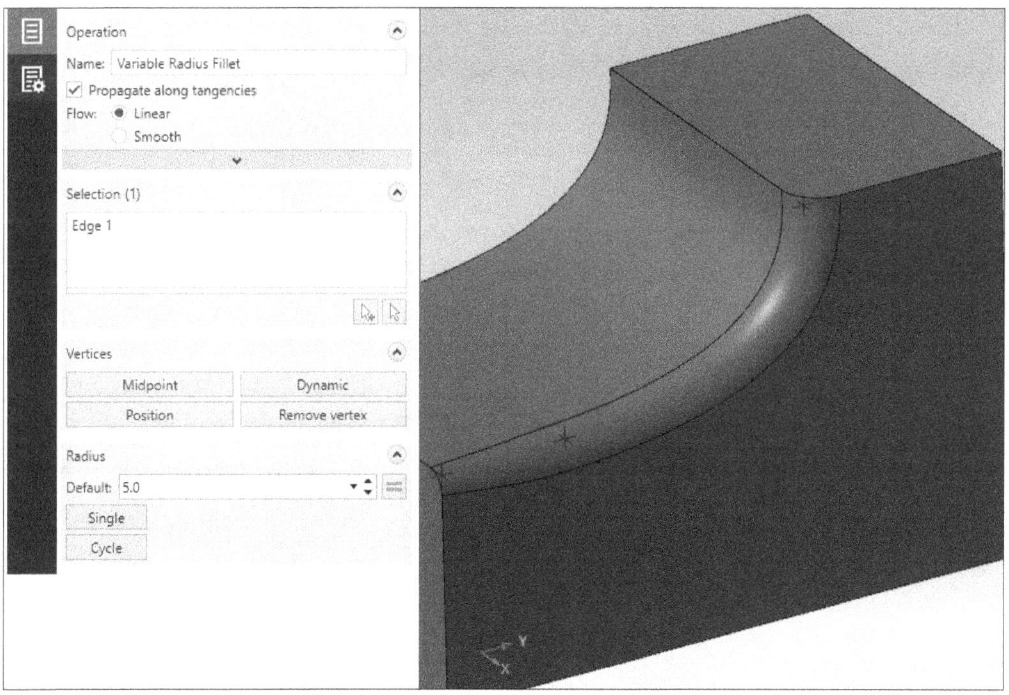

Figure-57. Preview of variable fillet radius

CREATING CHAMFERS

The tools to create chamfers on solid bodies are available in the **One Distance Chamfer** drop-down; refer to Figure-58. Various tools of this drop-down are discussed next.

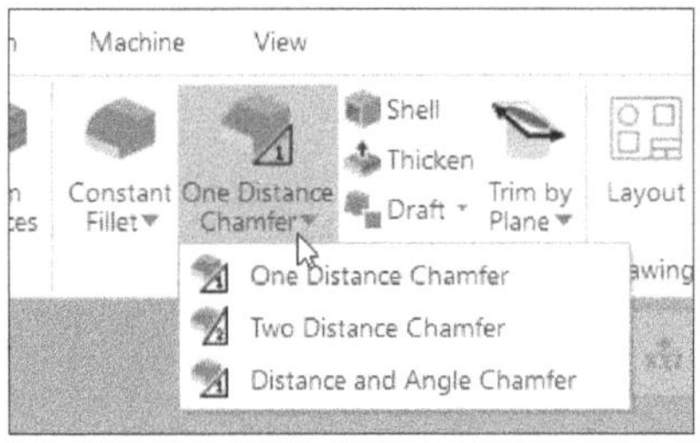

Figure-58. One Distance Chamfer drop-down

Creating One Distance Chamfer

The **One Distance Chamfer** tool is used to create chamfer of value equal on both the sides of selected edges. The procedure to use this tool is given next.

- Click on the **One Distance Chamfer** tool from the **Modify** group of **Solids** tab in the **Ribbon**. The **One Distance Chamfer Manager** will be displayed; refer to Figure-59.
- Select desired edges, faces, and solids to which you want to apply chamfer and click on the **End Selection** button. Preview of the chamfer will be displayed; refer to Figure-60.

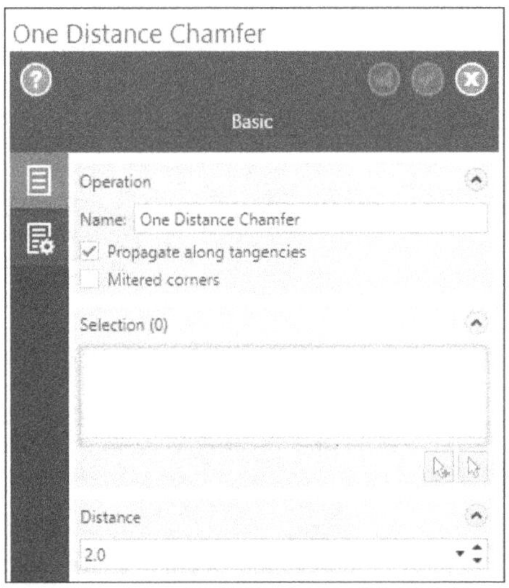

Figure-59. One Distance Chamfer Manager

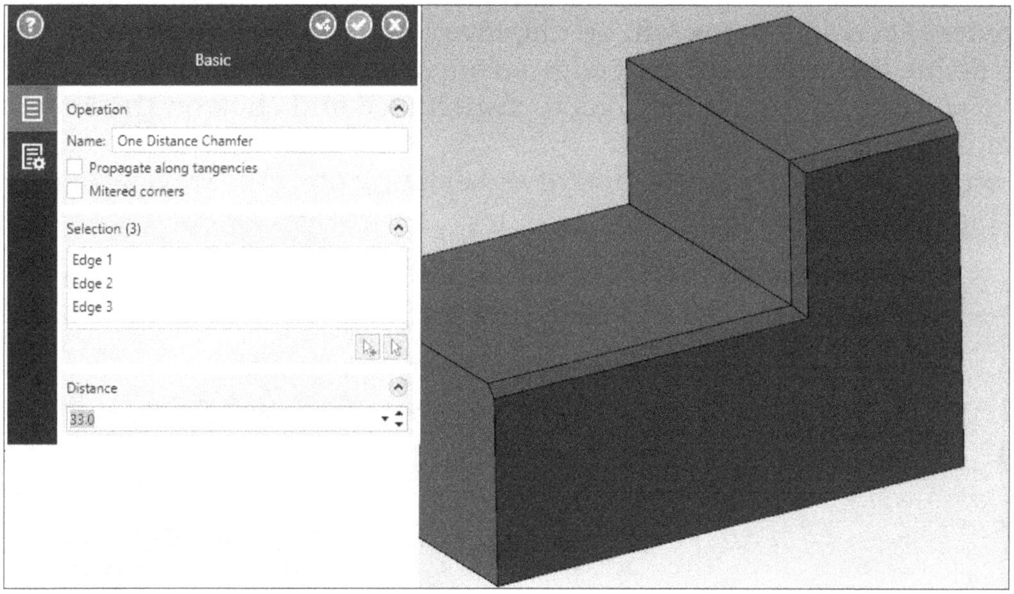

Figure-60. Preview of chamfer

- Set desired value in the **Distance** edit box to specify chamfer distance.
- Set the other parameters as desired and click on the **OK** button from the **Manager** to create the chamfer.

Creating Two Distance Chamfer

The **Two Distance Chamfer** tool is used to create chamfer by specifying distance from two sides of selected edge. The procedure to use this tool is given next.

- Click on the **Two Distance Chamfer** tool from the **One Distance Chamfer** drop-down in the **Modify** group of **Solids** tab in the **Ribbon**. The **Two Distance Chamfer Manager** will be displayed with **Solid Selection** dialog box; refer to Figure-61.

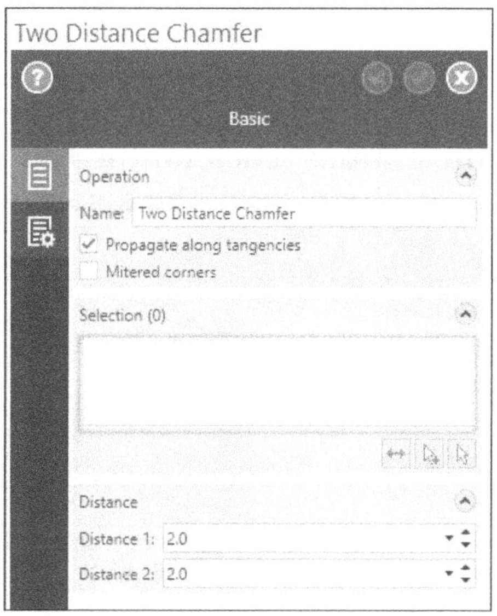

Figure-61. Two Distance Chamfer Manager

- Select the faces, edges, or body to which you want to apply chamfer. The **Pick Reference Face** dialog box will be displayed if you have selected an edge asking you to define the face which that edge belongs to for creating chamfer. Click on the **Other face** button from dialog box to switch face and click on the **End Selection** button from the graphics area.
- Click on the **End Selection** button after selecting objects. Preview of chamfer will be displayed; refer to Figure-62.

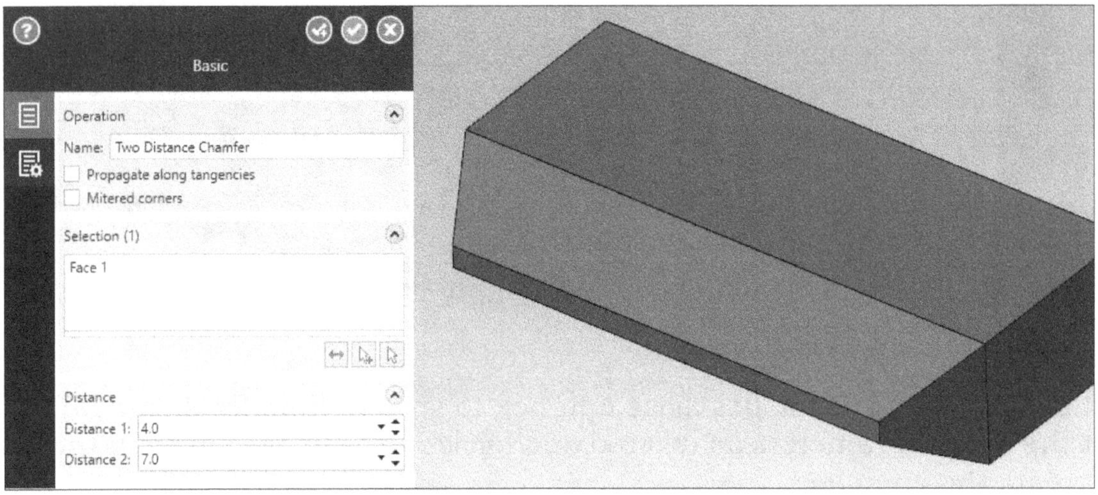

Figure-62. Preview of two distance chamfer

- Set the parameters as discussed earlier in the **Manager** and click on the **OK** button. The chamfers will be created.

Applying Distance and Angle Chamfer

The **Distance and Angle Chamfer** tool is used to apply chamfer of specified distance and chamfer angle. The procedure to use this tool is given next.

- Click on the **Distance and Angle Chamfer** tool from the **One Distance Chamfer** drop-down in the **Modify** group of **Solids** tab in the **Ribbon**. The **Distance and Angle Chamfer Manager** will be displayed.
- Select the edge and reference face or faces on whose edges you want to create chamfer. After selecting the entities, click on the **End Selection** button from the graphics area. Preview of the chamfer will be displayed; refer to Figure-63.

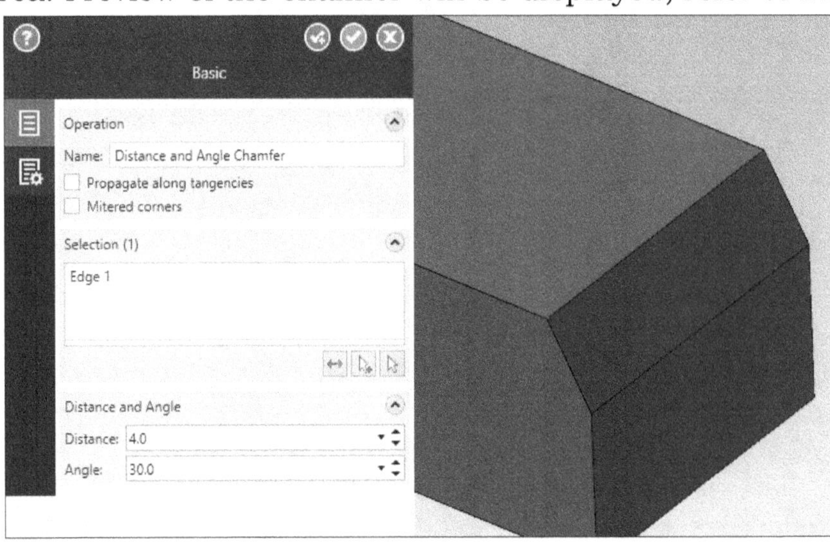

Figure-63. Preview of Distance and Angle chamfer

- Set the parameters as discussed earlier in the **Manager** and click on the **OK** button. The chamfer will be created.

CREATING SHELL FEATURE

The **Shell** tool is used to scoop material from the solid and apply thickness to walls of the solid. The procedure to use this tool is given next.

- Click on the **Shell** tool from the **Modify** group in the **Solids** tab of the **Ribbon**. The **Shell Manager** will be displayed.
- Select the solid body to which you want to apply thickness and remove internal material. After selecting the body, click on the **End Selection** button from the graphics area. The direction of shell thickness will be displayed; refer to Figure-64. Note that if you select a face of solid then the selected face will be removed from shell body. Use the selection filters to select face or body.

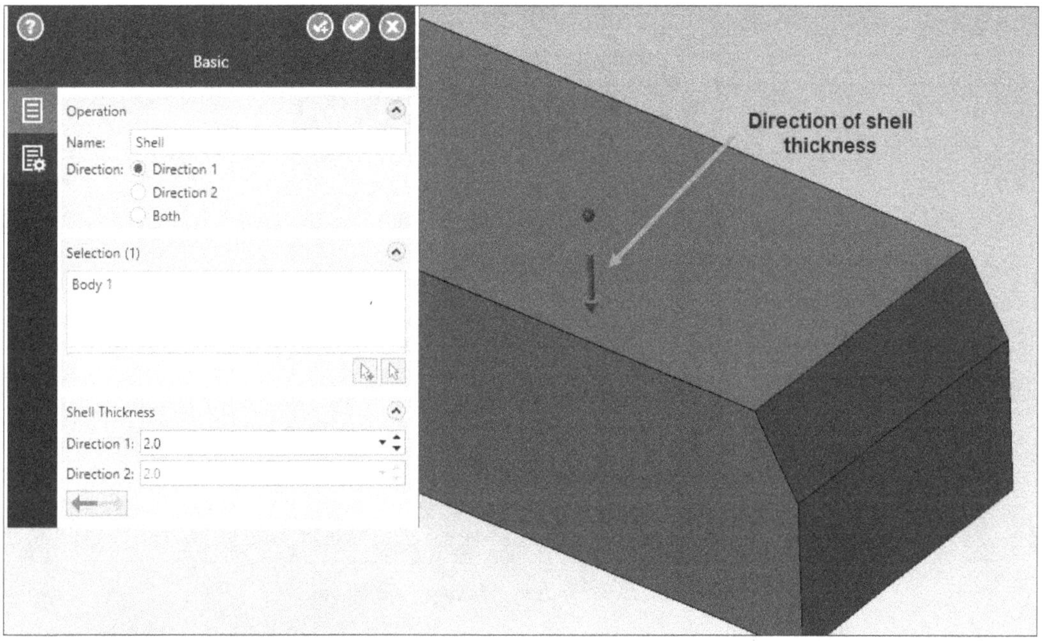

Figure-64. Shell thickness direction

- Select desired radio button from the **Direction** section of the **Manager** to define on which side of selected body, the thickness will be applied.
- Specify desired value in the **Direction 1** and/or **Direction 2** edit boxes to specify thickness of shell.
- Click on the **OK** button from the **Manager** to create the shell feature.

THICKEN

The **Thicken** tool is used to apply thickness to selected sheet solid. The procedure to use this tool is similar to **Shell** tool discussed earlier.

APPLYING DRAFT ANGLE

The tools to apply draft angle are available in the **Draft Faces** drop-down of the **Modify** group in the **Solids** tab of the **Ribbon**; refer to Figure-65. Various tools in this drop-down are discussed next.

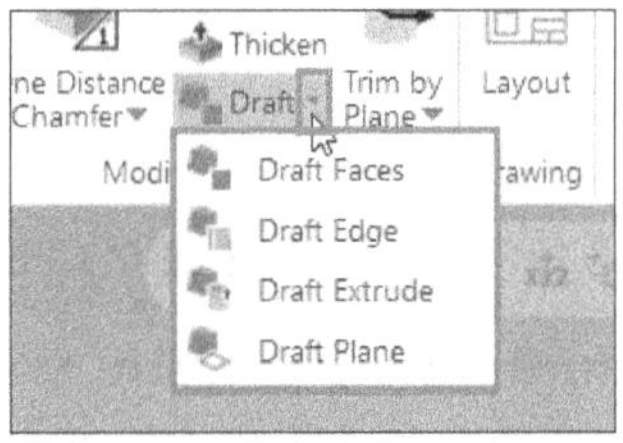

Figure-65. Draft drop-down

APPLYING DRAFT ANGLE TO FACES

The **Draft Faces** tool is used to apply taper angle to the faces of model with respect to selected reference face. The procedure to use this tool is given next.

- Click on the **Draft Faces** tool from the **Draft Faces** drop-down in the **Modify** group of **Solids** tab in the **Ribbon**. The **Draft to Face Manager** will be displayed; refer to Figure-66.

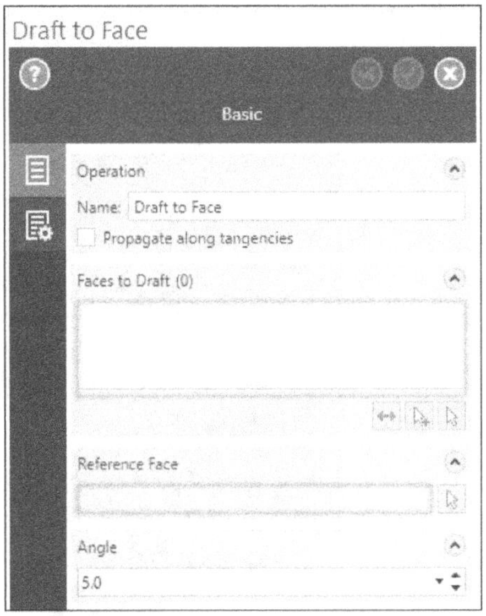

Figure-66. Draft to Face Manager dialog box

- Select the faces to which you want to apply draft angle and click on the **End Selection** button from the graphics area. You will be asked to select planar face to be used as reference for draft angle.
- Select desired planar face; refer to Figure-67. The preview of draft will be displayed.

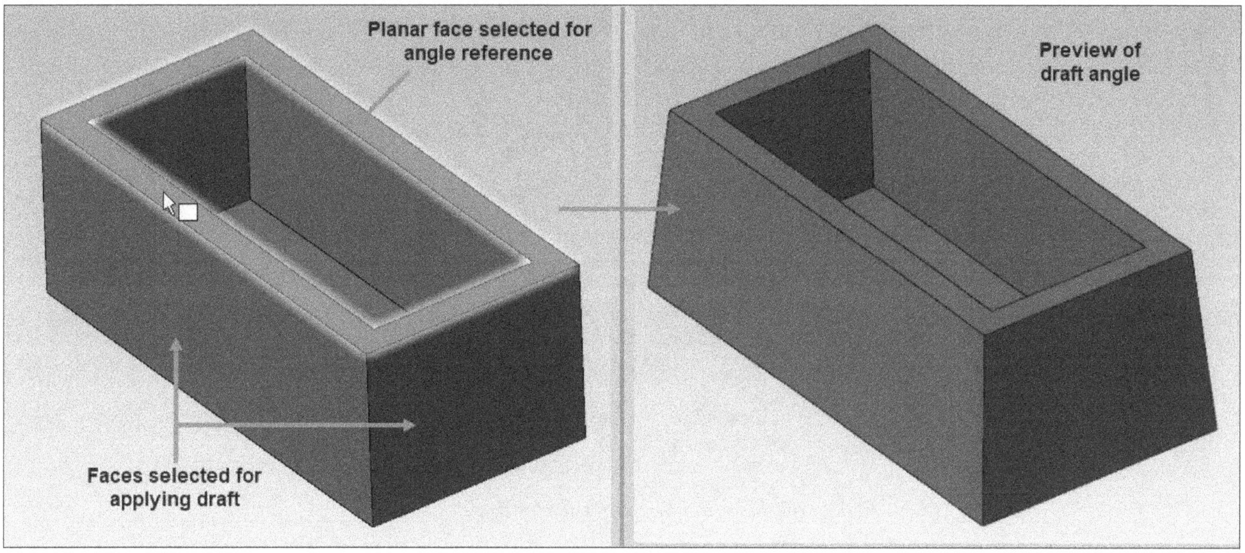

Figure-67. Faces selected for draft

- Set desired angle value in the **Angle** edit box to define draft angle of faces.
- Click on the **OK** button from the **Manager** to apply draft.

Applying Draft Angle Referenced to Edge

The **Draft Edge** tool is used to apply draft angle to selected faces with respect to reference edge. The procedure to use this tool is given next.

- Click on the **Draft Edge** tool from the **Draft Faces** drop-down in the **Modify** group of **Solids** tab in the **Ribbon**. The **Draft to Edge Manager** will be displayed; refer to Figure-68.

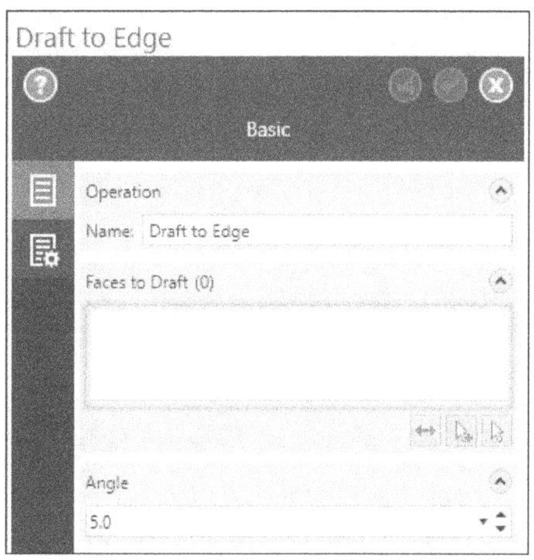

Figure-68. Draft to Edge Manager

- Select desired face to which you want to apply draft angle. You will be asked to select a reference edge with respect to which the angle will be specified.
- Select desired edge from the model; refer to Figure-69. You will be asked to select next set of face and edge for applying draft.

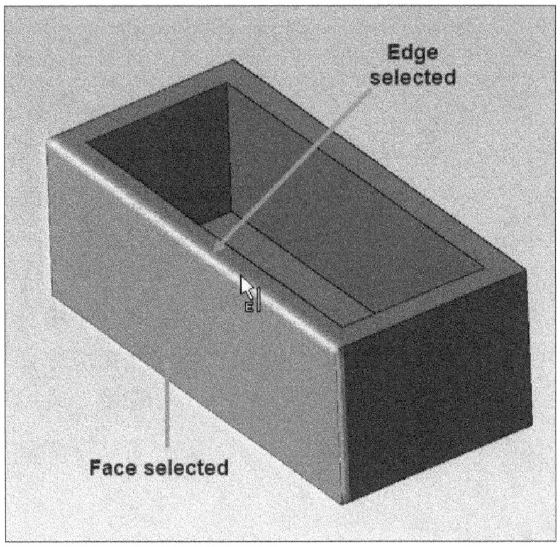

Figure-69. Selecting face and edge for draft

- Select desired set of face and reference edge, or press **ENTER** to complete selection. You will be asked to specify draft direction.
- Select the edge of model parallel to side edge of selected face; refer to Figure-70. The preview of draft feature will be displayed.

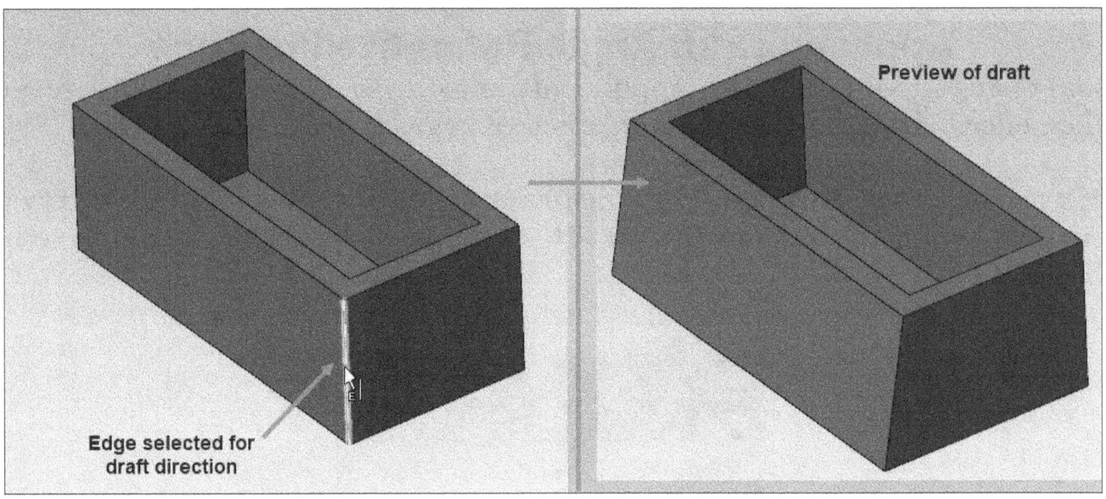

Figure-70. Specifying draft direction

- Specify desired angle value in the **Angle** edit box and click on the **OK** button to apply draft.

Applying Draft to Extrude Feature

The **Draft Extrude** tool is used to apply draft angle to selected faces of extrude feature. The procedure to use this tool is given next.

- Click on the **Draft Extrude** tool from the **Draft Faces** drop-down in the **Modify** group of **Solids** tab in the **Ribbon**. The **Draft to Extrude Manager** will be displayed; refer to Figure-71.

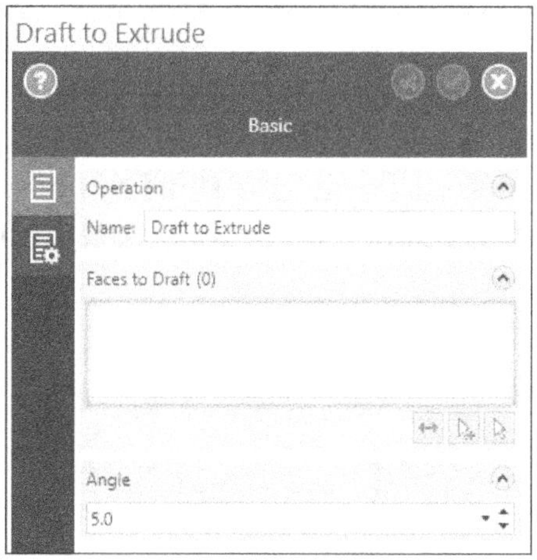

Figure-71. Draft to Extrude Manager

- Select desired side faces of the extrude feature to which you want to apply draft angle; refer to Figure-72 and click on the **End Selection** button from the graphics area.

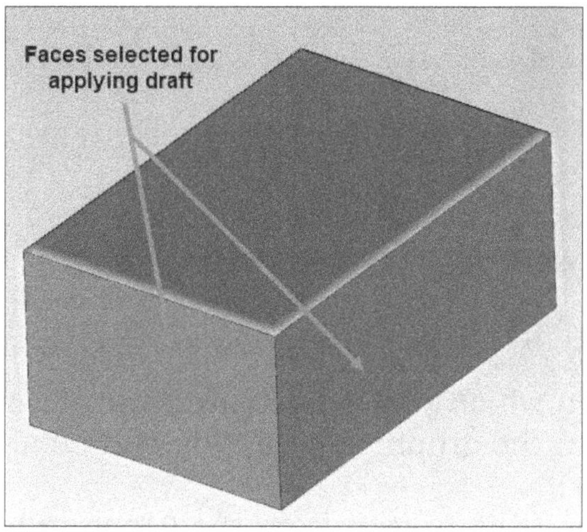

Figure-72. Faces selected for applying draft

- Specify desired draft angle value in the **Angle** edit box. Preview of draft feature will be displayed; refer to Figure-73.
- Click on the **OK** button from the **Manager** to apply draft angle.

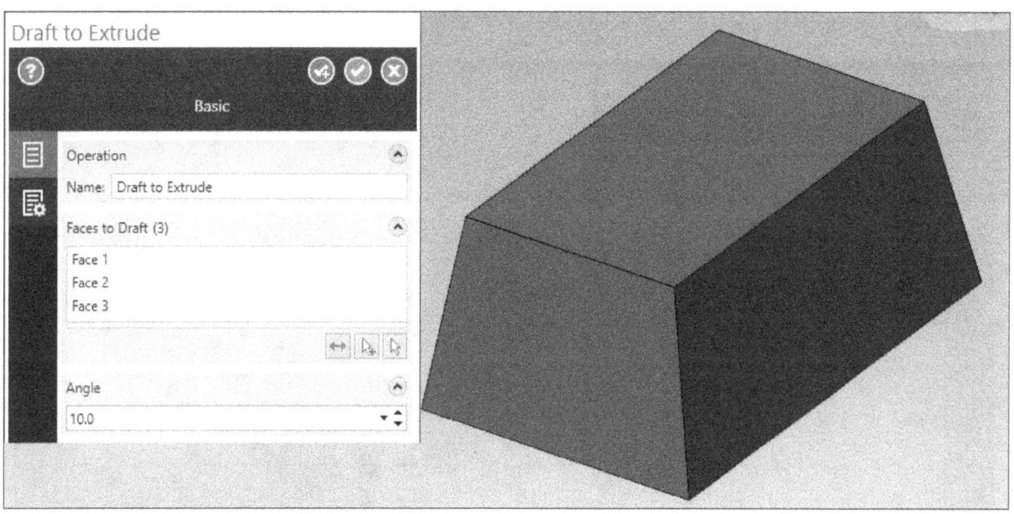

Figure-73. Preview of draft to extrude feature

Applying Draft using Reference Plane

The **Draft Plane** tool is used to apply draft angle to selected faces with respect to selected reference plane. The procedure to use this tool is given next.

- Click on the **Draft Plane** tool from the **Draft Faces** drop-down in the **Modify** group of **Solids** tab in the **Ribbon**. The **Draft to Plane Manager** will be displayed; refer to Figure-74.

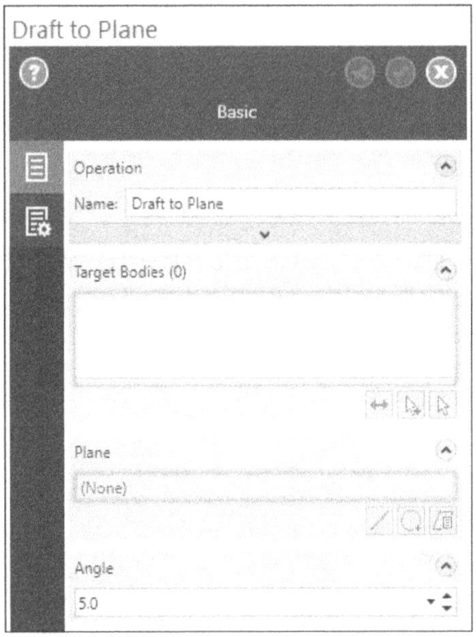

Figure-74. Draft to Plane Manager with Solid Selection dialog box

- Select desired faces on which you want to apply draft angle and click on the **End Selection** button from the graphics area. You will be asked to select a reference plane.
- Click on the **Plane By Line** button from the **Plane** rollout in the **Manager** if you want to use a plane passing through selected line/edge. Click on the **Plane By Entities** button to use a plane passing through a flat face, 2 lines, or 3 points. Click on the **Named Plane** button to select an existing plane from the **Plane Selection** dialog box.
- On selecting the plane, preview of draft feature will be displayed; refer to Figure-75.

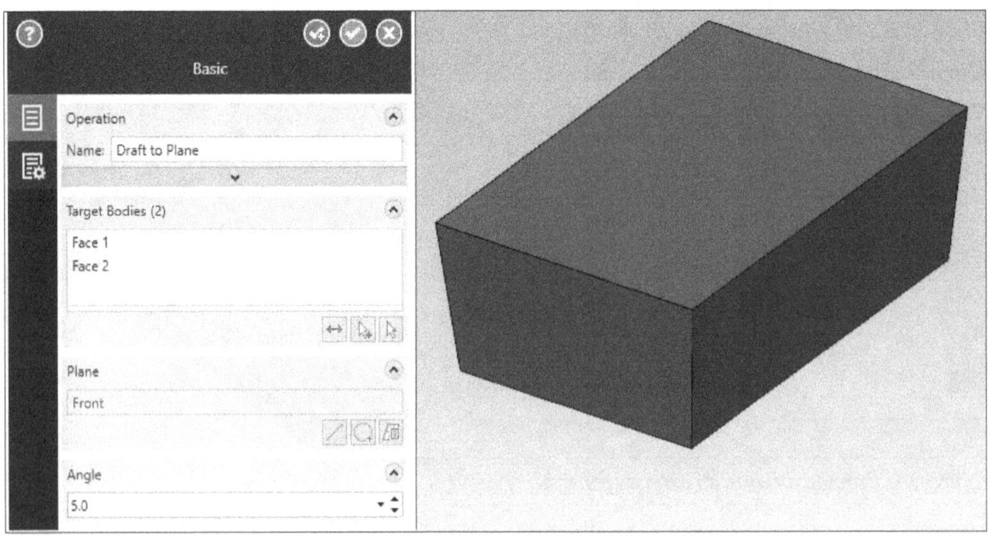

Figure-75. Preview of draft by plane

- Specify desired value of draft angle and click on the **OK** button from the **Manager**.

TRIMMING A SOLID

There are two methods to trim a solid in Mastercam: Using an intersecting plane and using an intersecting surface/sheet. The tools to trim solid are available in the **Modify** group of **Solids** tab in the **Ribbon**; refer to Figure-76. The tools in this drop-down are discussed next.

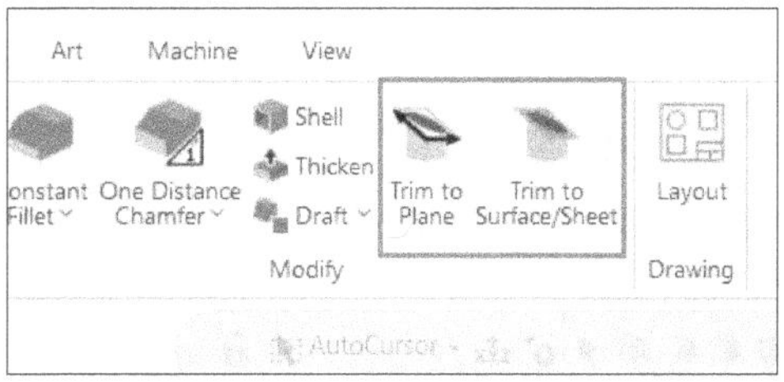

Figure-76. Trim by Plane drop-down

Trimming Solid by Plane

The **Trim to Plane** tool is used to trim selected solid body by an intersecting plane. The procedure to use this tool is given next.

- Click on the **Trim to Plane** tool from the **Modify** group of **Solids** tab in the **Ribbon**. The **Trim to Plane Manager** will be displayed; refer to Figure-77 and you will be asked to select the solid body to be trimmed.
- Select desired solid body from the 3D view and press **ENTER**.

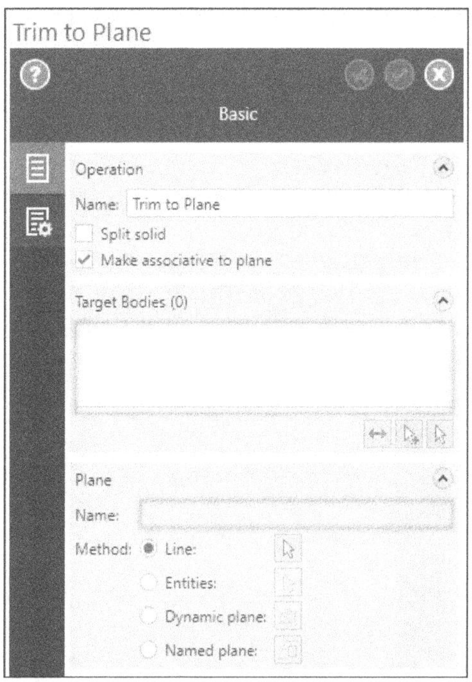

Figure-77. Trim by Plane Manager

- Click on desired radio button from the **Method** section to define which type of plane will be used for trimming. In this case, we are selecting the **Named plane** radio button.
- Select the **Named plane** radio button and select the button next to radio button. The **Plane Selection** dialog box will be displayed and you will be asked to select desired plane by name.

- Select desired intersecting plane from the dialog box and click on the **End Selection** button from graphics area. Preview of trimmed solid body will be displayed; refer to Figure-78.

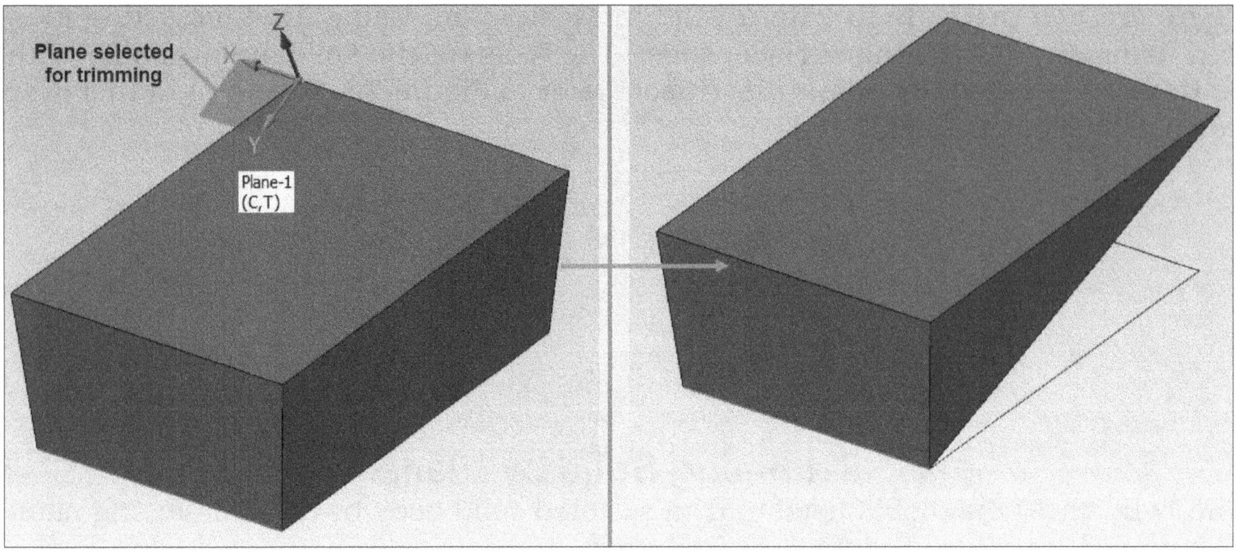

Figure-78. Preview of trimmed solid using plane

- Click on the **OK** button from the **Manager** to apply trim.

Trimming Solid Using Surface/Sheet

The **Trim to Surface/Sheet** tool is used to trim solid body using selected surface/ sheet. The procedure to use this tool is given next.

- Click on the **Trim to Surface/Sheet** tool from the **Trim to Plane** drop-down in the **Modify** group of **Solids** tab in the **Ribbon**. The **Trim to Surface/Sheet Manager** will be displayed; refer to Figure-79.

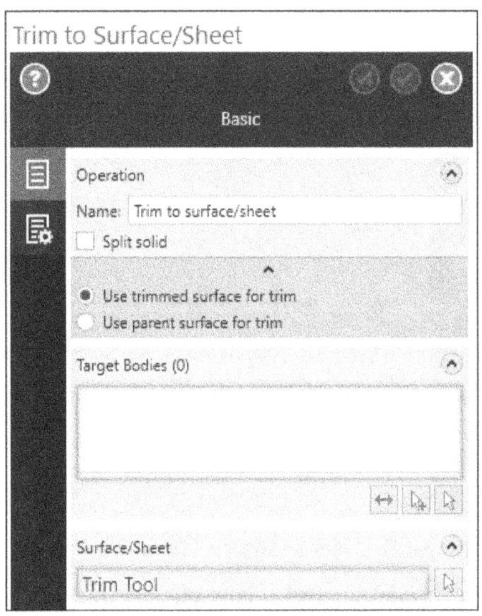

Figure-79. Trim to Surface/Sheet Manager

- Select the solid body which you want to trim and press **ENTER**. You will be asked to select the trim tool (surface).
- Select desired surface. Preview of trimmed solid will be displayed; refer to Figure-80.

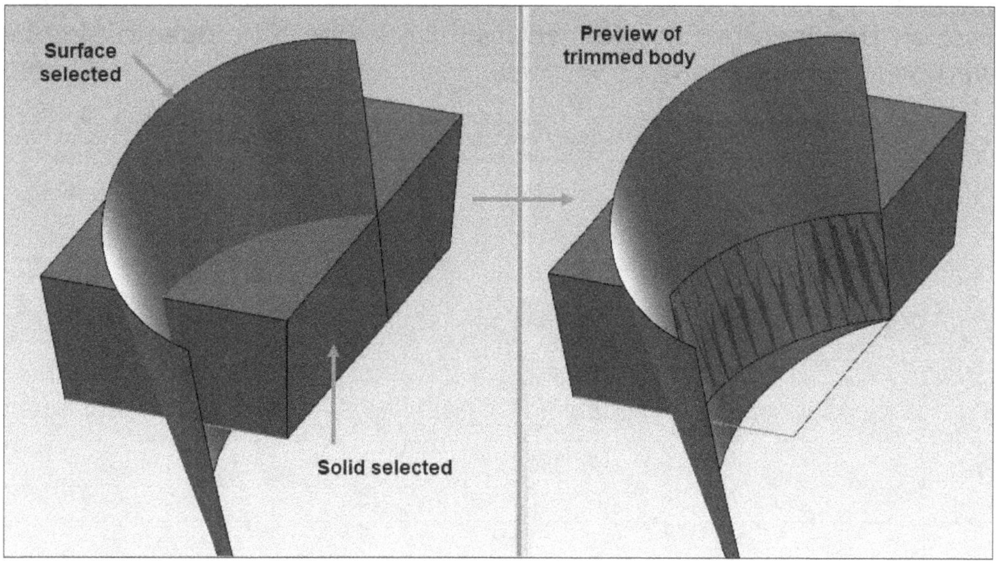

Figure-80. Preview of trimmed body

- Click on the **OK** button from the **Manager** to perform trimming.

GENERATING LAYOUT OF SOLID

The **Layout** tool is used to generate drawing of the part views in specified page template. The procedure to use this tool is given next.

- Click on the **Layout** tool from the **Drawing** group in the **Solids** tab of the **Ribbon**. The **Solid Drawing Layout** dialog box will be displayed; refer to Figure-81.

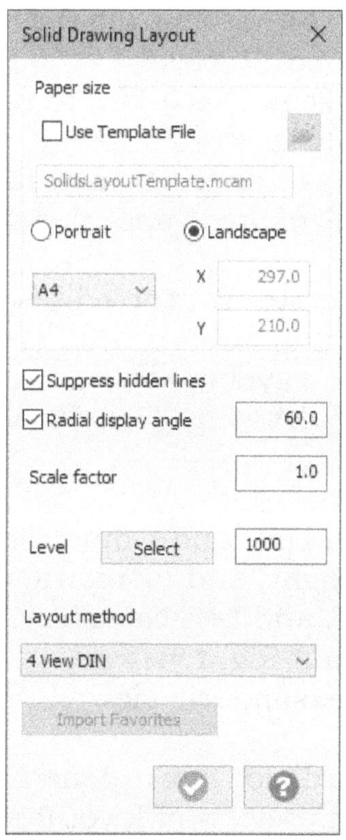

Figure-81. Solid Drawing Layout dialog box

- Select the **Use Template File** check box to select desired drawing layout template and click on the **Open** button next to the check box. The **Open** dialog box will be displayed; refer to Figure-82.

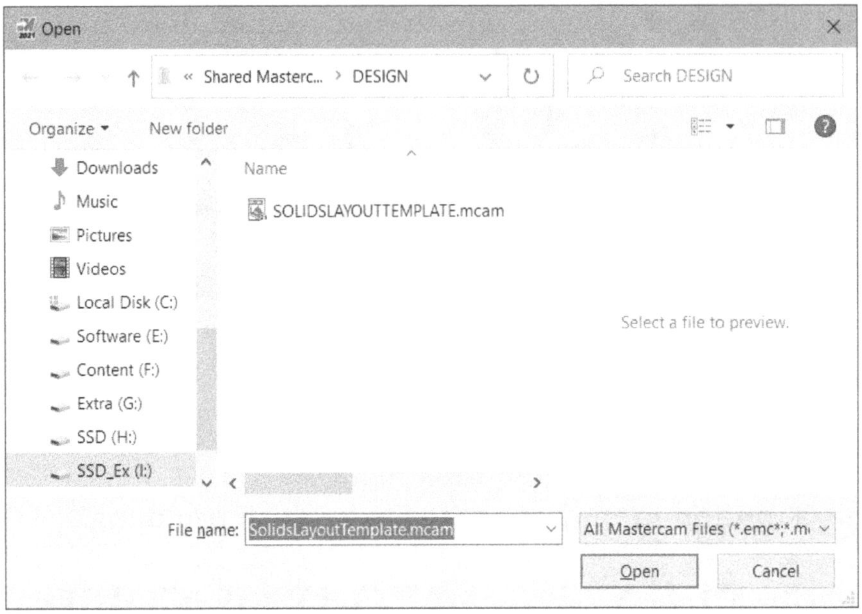

Figure-82. Open dialog box

- Select desired template file and click on the **Open** button. The selected template will be used for generating the layout.
- If you do not want to use a template then select the **Portrait** or **Landscape** radio button to define orientation of page on which views will be placed. Select desired page size from the drop-down below the **Portrait** radio button. You can set custom paper size by selecting the **Custom** option from the drop-down and then specifying desired parameters in **X** and **Y** edit boxes.
- Select the **Suppress hidden lines** check box to remove hidden lines from views in the layout.
- Select the **Radial display angle** check box to add radial lines in surfaces and solid faces. The lower the value of angle specified, the higher the number of lines along a circular face.
- Specify desired value in the **Scale factor** edit box to increase or decrease the view size in layout.
- Select desired option from the **Layout method** drop-down to specify which type of layout will be created in the drawing. The views generated in different layouts are given next.

  4 View DIN: Bottom, Front, Left, and Isometric views
  4 View ANSI: Top, Front, Right, and Isometric views
  3 View DIN: Bottom, Front, and Left views
  3 View ANSI: Top, Front, and Right views
  1 View Isometric: a single isometric view

- Click on the **OK** button from the dialog box to generate the layout. The **Solid Layout Manager** will be displayed with preview of layout; refer to Figure-83.

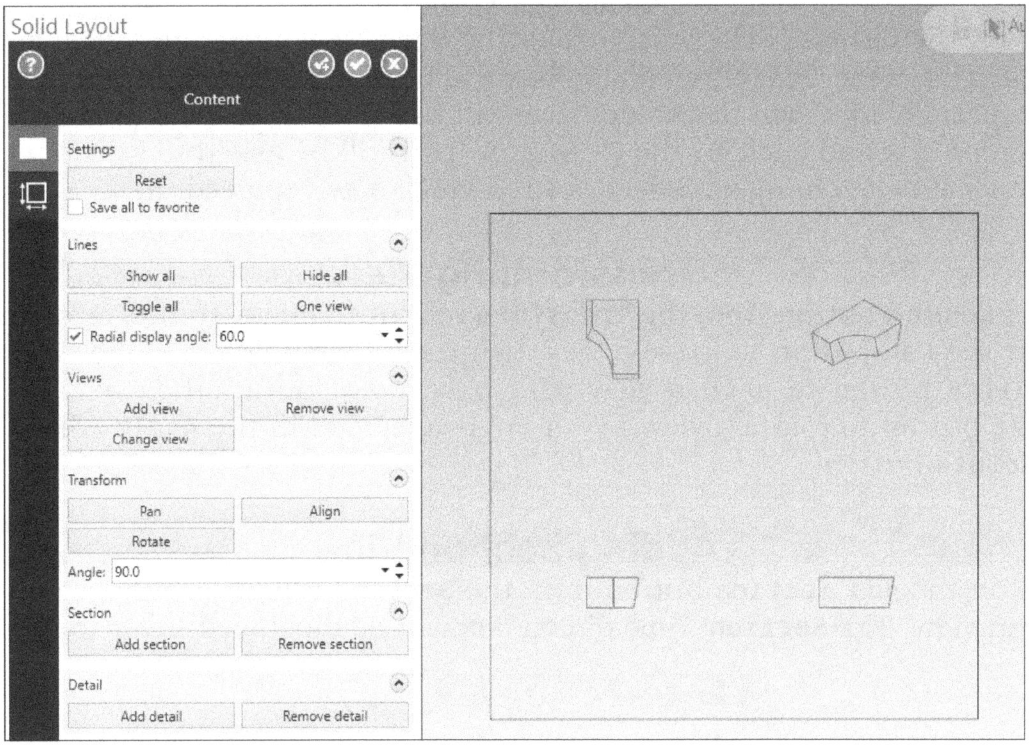

Figure-83. Solid Layout Manager with preview of layout

- Select desired button from the **Lines** rollout to display/hide hidden lines in one or all views.
- Select the **Radial display angle** check box to display lines on round faces of the model in views. After selecting check box, you can specify angle of lines as well in the edit box next to it.

Adding View

- If you want to add a new view then click on the **Add view** button from the **Views** rollout. The **Plane Selection** dialog box will be displayed. Select desired plane and click on the **OK** button. The **Parameters** dialog box will be displayed for specifying scale of view; refer to Figure-84. Specify desired scale value in the edit box and click on the **OK** button. Preview of view will be displayed and you will be asked to specify location of view. Click at desired location to place the view.

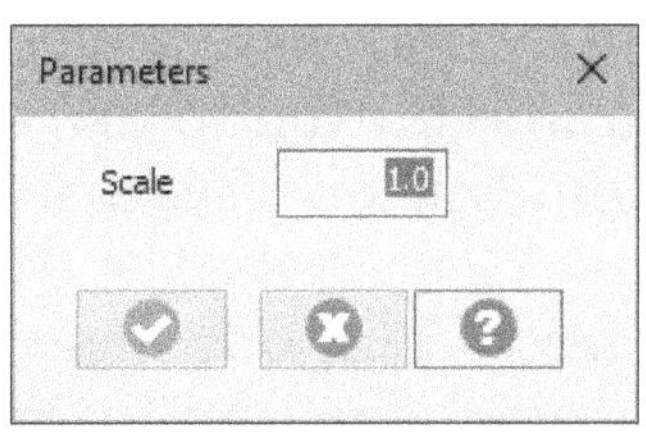

Figure-84. Parameters dialog box

Removing a View

- Click on the **Remove view** button from the **Views** rollout to delete a view. You will be asked to select an element of the view to be removed. The **Solids Drawing Layout** dialog box will be displayed. Click on the **Yes** button from the dialog box to delete the selected view.

Changing View

- Click on the **Change view** button from the **Views** rollout to change a view in the layout. The **Plane Selection** dialog box will be displayed asking you to select the plane parallel to which the model view will be created. Select desired plane from the dialog box and click on the **OK** button. You will be asked to select an element of the view to be changed. Select desired view to be replaced.

Transforming View

- Select desired button from the **Transform** rollout to move, rotate, or align a view. Select the **Pan** button to move a view using its base point in same plane. Select the **Align** button to align a view with base point on another view. Select the **Rotate** button to rotate a view by an angle specified in the **Angle** edit box below the **Rotate** button.

Adding Section View

- Click on the **Add Section** button from the **Section** rollout of **Manager** to create a section view. The **Section Type** dialog box will be displayed; refer to Figure-85.

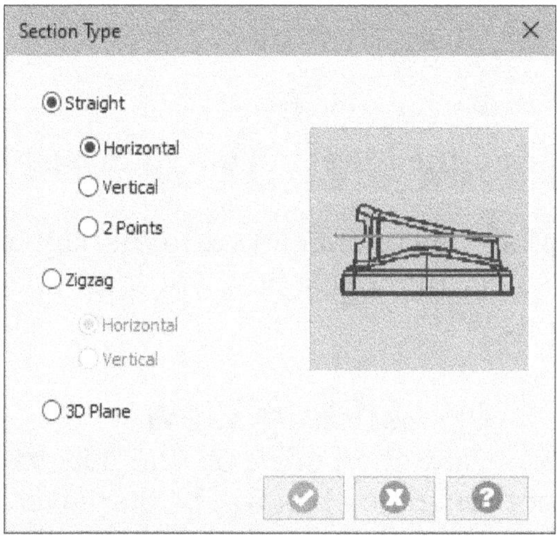

Figure-85. Section Type dialog box

- There are mainly three ways to create section view: using straight lines, using zigzag lines and using a 3D Plane. Select the **Straight** radio button and then **Horizontal**, **Vertical**, or **2 Points** radio button to use a straight line passing through the view for creating section view. Select the **Zigzag** radio button and then **Horizontal** or **Vertical** radio button to use a zigzag line for creating section view. Select the **3D Plane** radio button if you want to use a plane for creating section view.
- After selecting desired radio button (in our case, it is **Zigzag** radio button with **Horizontal** orientation), click on the **OK** button from the dialog box. You will be asked to specify lines of zigzag for section view. Create the zigzag lines as desired and press **ESC** to exit the line creation mode. The **Parameters** dialog box will be displayed.
- Set desired color and scale values in the edit boxes of dialog box and click on the **OK** button. The lines will be displayed and you will be asked to specify location to place section view; refer to Figure-86.

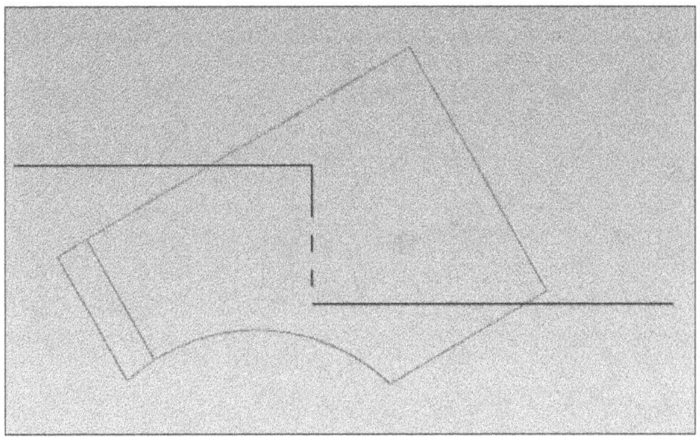

Figure-86. Preview of zigzag section line

- Click at desired location to place the section view.

Similarly, you can use the buttons in **Detail** rollout to add or remove detail view.

After creating desired views, click on the **OK** button from the **Manager**.

PRACTICE 1 TO 4

Create 3D models for drawings shown in Figure-87, Figure-88, Figure-89, and Figure-90.

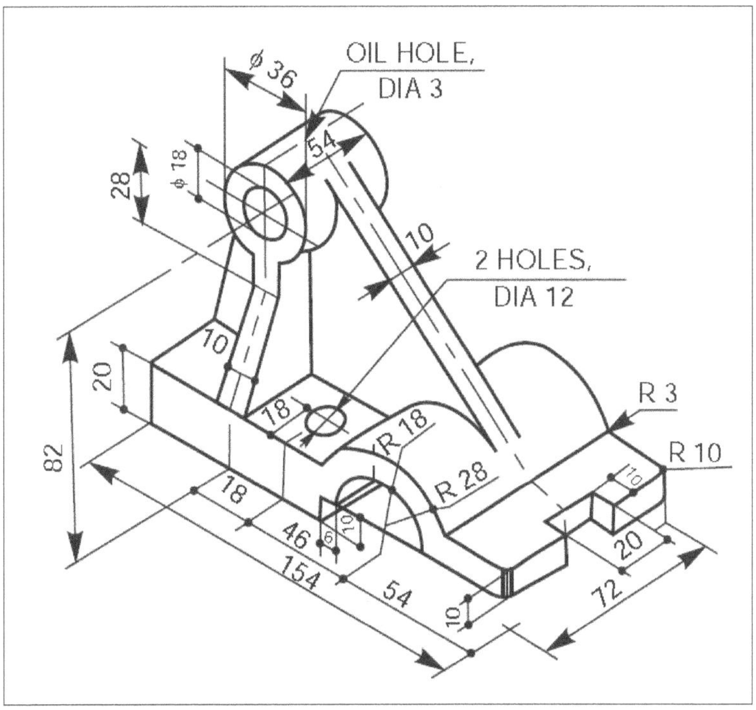

Figure-87. Practice 1

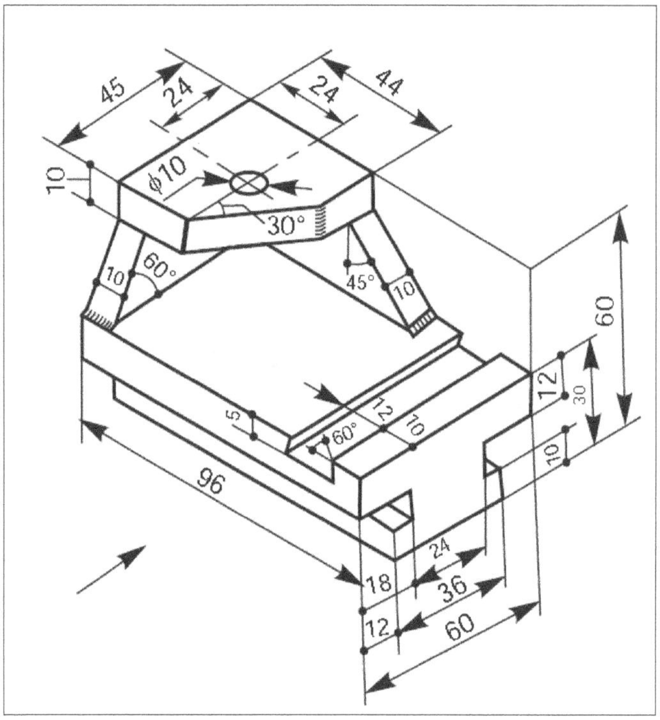

Figure-88. Practice 2

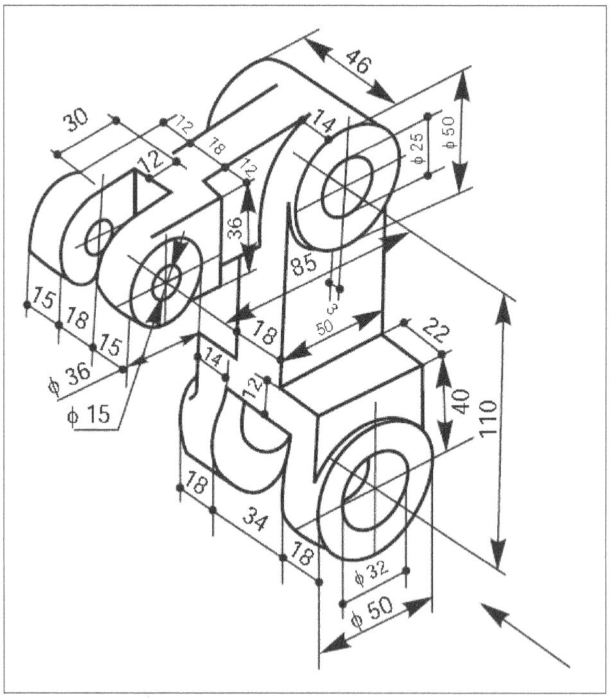

Figure-89. Practice 3

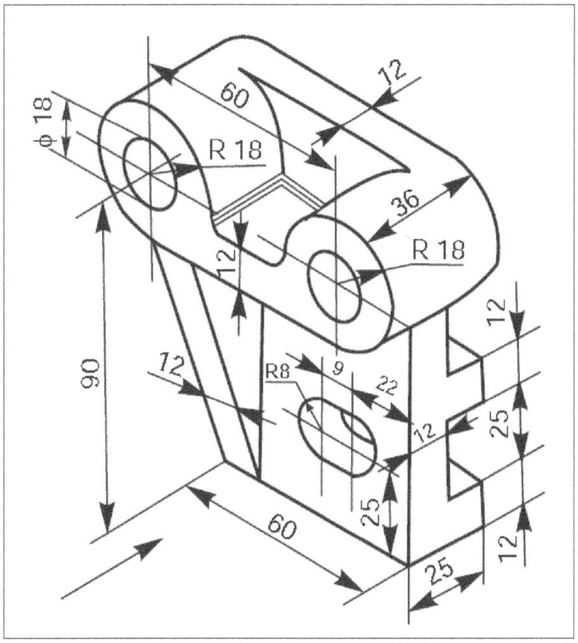

Figure-90. Practice 4

SELF-ASSESSMENT

Q1. Select the Add boss radio button from Solid Extrude Manager to join new solid with another solid. (T/F)

Q2. If you are adding a boss feature or cut feature using Extrude tool then select the .... check box to specify up to which surface, the feature will be created.

Q3. What is the function of Planes Manager?

Q4. Which of the following tools is used to create plane parallel to current view?

a. From entity normal
b. From Gview
c. Relative to WCS
d. Quick Cplane

Q5. What is Gnomon in Mastercam?

Q6. For creating solid loft feature, two or more open wireframe sections are required. (T/F)

Q7. To create solid sweep feature, a closed loop planar sketch section and an open/closed curve path is needed. (T/F)

Q8. The .... tool is used to perform addition, subtraction, and intersection of selected solid bodies.

Q9. The .... tool is used to create a negative solid impression of selected closed body.

Q10. Which of the following tools is used to scoop out material from the solid and apply thickness to walls of the solid?

a. Extrude
b. Revolve
c. Shell
d. Draft

REVIEW QUESTIONS

Q1. What is the purpose of the Cylinder tool in the Solids tab?
A. Create a curved surface
B. Place a solid cylinder at desired location
C. Trim a surface
D. Create a cylindrical hole in a body

Q2. Which group contains the Cylinder tool in the Solids tab?
A. Modify group
B. Create group
C. Simple group
D. Utility group

Q3. What does the Create body radio button do in the Extrude tool?
A. Cuts a body
B. Adds new solid to existing body
C. Creates a new solid body
D. Joins surfaces

Q4. Which radio button should be selected in Extrude tool to cut material from existing solid?
A. Create body
B. Cut body
C. Add boss
D. Distance

Q5. Which option in the Extrude Manager allows extrusion in both directions?
A. Trim to Faces
B. Through all
C. Cut body
D. Both directions

Q6. What is the purpose of the Planes Manager?
A. Create 3D models
B. Render 2D drawings
C. Create and manage planes
D. Manage assemblies

Q7. What kind of geometry can be used in the "From geometry" tool to create planes?
A. Only faces
B. Only edges
C. Three points, two lines, or surface face
D. Only curves

Q8. Which tool is used to create a plane from a solid face?
A. From Gview
B. From geometry
C. From solid face
D. From entity normal

Q9. What does the "From Gview" tool do in Planes Manager?
A. Sets tool plane normal to view
B. Creates a plane parallel to current view screen
C. Sets all views to default
D. Creates an orthographic projection

Q10. What does the "From entity normal" tool in Planes Manager do?
A. Creates a plane parallel to curve
B. Creates a plane perpendicular to selected wireframe
C. Creates 3D point from 2D line
D. Deletes reference plane

Q11. What is the use of "Relative to WCS" options?
A. Rotate planes around solid
B. Move planes randomly
C. Create planes parallel to WCS planes
D. Set planes to ISO standard

Q12. What happens when you use the Import tool in Planes Manager?
A. Exports WCS data
B. Imports only standard planes
C. Imports non-standard planes from other Mastercam files
D. Duplicates all planes

Q13. What does the Quick Cplane tool do?
A. Quick selection of 2D sketch
B. Creates construction plane at selected face
C. Reverses plane direction
D. Creates temporary views

Q14. How is the plane placed using the Dynamic tool?
A. From default templates
B. Using wireframe chaining
C. By specifying location and rotating gnomon
D. By importing from CAD file

Q15. What are Lathe Planes based on?
A. Cartesian axes
B. Isometric projection
C. Diameter and Depth directions
D. Perspective camera

Q16. What does the "Add group" tool do in Planes Manager?
A. Adds new solid
B. Creates section view
C. Groups planes into folder
D. Links planes with mesh

Q17. What is the purpose of "Find a plane" tools?
A. Search planes by file name
B. Display or locate planes in model
C. Remove unused planes
D. Highlight only 3D planes

Q18. Which button sets WCS, Construction Plane, and Tool Plane to selected plane?
A. Reset View
B. Set your current WCS, construction plane and tool plane
C. Fit to View
D. Quick Cplane

Q19. What happens when you click "Reset your WCS, construction plane and tool plane to their original state"?
A. Deletes current planes
B. Restores default values
C. Hides planes
D. Opens geometry manager

Q20. Which display option allows showing origin coordinates in world coordinate system?
A. Contrast rows
B. Display origin values in world coordinates
C. Show gnomon
D. Set display mode

Q21. Which tool creates a revolved solid feature around an axis?
A. Extrude
B. Sweep
C. Revolve
D. Loft

Q22. What is the purpose of the Thin Wall checkbox in Revolve Manager?
A. Remove fillets
B. Create rib-like structure
C. Create tube-like features with wall thickness
D. Offset from axis

Q23. What does the Loft tool require to create a solid loft feature?
A. Mesh surface
B. One sketch and a path
C. Two or more closed sketch sections
D. Two open curves

Q24. What feature does Sweep Twist provide in Sweep Manager?
A. Extrusion control
B. Path alignment
C. Twist the profile along the sweep path
D. Bend surface at joint

Q25. What is the requirement to use the Sweep Twist option?
A. A closed path
B. At least two surfaces
C. Open chain path
D. No sketch required

Q26. What does the Boolean Add operation do?
A. Cuts body from another
B. Creates holes
C. Joins tool bodies with target body
D. Converts to wireframe

Q27. Which Boolean operation keeps only intersecting volume?
A. Remove
B. Subtract
C. Common
D. Add

Q28. What does selecting the Non-associative checkbox do in Boolean Manager?
A. Locks planes
B. Keeps original entities after operation
C. Hides removed material
D. Replaces body

Q29. What does the Impression tool create?
A. 3D sketch
B. Extrude cut
C. Negative solid impression of selected body
D. Animation

Q30. What must be selected to define the area for creating negative impression?
A. Solid face
B. Wireframe sketch and extrude cut body
C. Axis of revolution
D. Sweep section and path

Q31. Which tool is used to create a cylindrical hole through a solid face?
A. Bore Tool
B. Drill Tool
C. Hole Tool
D. Cut Tool

Q32. In the Hole Manager, which rollout defines the direction of the hole axis?
A. Hole Properties
B. Depth
C. Position
D. Plane Orientation

Q33. What happens when you click on the Add AutoCursor position button in the Hole Manager?
A. You define the depth of the hole
B. You place holes on the model face
C. You define chamfer angle
D. You select reference plane

Q34. Which option should you select to create a standard Counterbore hole?
A. Drill
B. Tapered
C. Counterbore from Style drop-down
D. User Defined

Q35. What does the "Fit" drop-down define in Hole Properties?
A. Hole size
B. Hole tolerance (Loose, Normal, Tight)
C. Hole orientation
D. Hole location

Q36. Which option creates a hole completely through the solid body?
A. Blind
B. Full Depth
C. Through all
D. Total Cut

Q37. What should you select to chamfer or fillet the edges of a hole?
A. Fit options
B. Hole Style
C. Top Edge Treatment
D. Hole Position

Q38. Which Hole Style radio button allows creation of custom, non-standard holes?
A. Library
B. User Defined
C. Standard
D. Manual

Q39. Which tool is used to replicate a feature in both horizontal and vertical directions?
A. Linear Copy
B. Manual Pattern
C. Rectangular Pattern
D. Grid Pattern

Q40. How can you remove an instance from a Rectangular Pattern?
A. By deleting the base feature
B. Through the Depth rollout
C. Using Remove Selected Instances button
D. Editing the hole style

Q41. What is the use of the Circular Pattern tool?
A. Create circular holes
B. Pattern features along an arc or circle
C. Add round edges
D. Mirror features along an axis

Q42. What does selecting the Full Circle radio button do in Circular Pattern tool?
A. Creates half circle pattern
B. Applies a radius
C. Creates a 360-degree pattern
D. Removes angles

Q43. Which option is used to define pattern center in the Circular Pattern tool?
A. Fit Option
B. Plane Manager
C. Center point AutoCursor
D. Fillet Manager

Q44. In the Circular Pattern tool, which radio button is selected by default in Distribution section?
A. Full Circle
B. Arc
C. Angle Span
D. Rotate

Q45. What is the first action in Manual Pattern creation?
A. Select a face
B. Select target body
C. Define number of instances
D. Select pattern axis

Q46. Which action allows instance placement in Manual Pattern?
A. Specify radius
B. Select fit
C. Click on target body to place instances
D. Define angle

Q47. Which tool converts closed surface loops into solid bodies?
A. Make Solid
B. Close Surface
C. Solids from Surfaces
D. Fill Surface

Q48. What does selecting CTRL+A do during solid creation from surfaces?
A. Copies all surfaces
B. Highlights visible faces
C. Selects all visible surfaces
D. Opens advanced selection

Q49. Which tool is used to create fillets of uniform radius?
A. Fillet Variable
B. Face to Face Fillet
C. Constant Fillet
D. Uniform Radius

Q50. What happens when you select the Mitered corners checkbox in Constant Fillet?
A. Makes rounded fillet
B. Creates sharp mitered joints
C. Cuts across corner
D. Reduces the fillet radius

Q51. Which fillet tool applies fillets to edges between two selected faces?
A. Edge Blend
B. Two Surface Fillet
C. Face to Face Fillet
D. Uniform Radius

Q52. Which method in Face to Face Fillet allows setting a specific chordal width?
A. Angle Method
B. Radius Fit
C. Width radio button
D. Diameter Fit

Q53. What is the function of the Hold line option in Face to Face Fillet?
A. Creates hole between faces
B. Cuts along edge
C. Joins two edges of the solid
D. Defines reference plane

Q54. Which tool is used to chamfer with equal distances on both sides?
A. Symmetric Chamfer
B. One Distance Chamfer
C. Equal Offset Chamfer
D. Equal Side Chamfer

Q55. Which chamfer tool allows setting different distances from each side of an edge?
A. Distance and Angle Chamfer
B. Equal Chamfer
C. Two Distance Chamfer
D. Variable Radius Chamfer

Q56. In Two Distance Chamfer, what appears after selecting an edge?
A. Face Selection Manager
B. Reference Face dialog box
C. Plane Manager
D. Hole Manager

Q57. Which tool applies chamfer using a specified angle and distance?
A. Distance and Angle Chamfer
B. Angle Blend
C. Tapered Chamfer
D. Custom Cut

Q58. What does the Shell tool do?
A. Thickens entire solid
B. Hollow out solid and apply wall thickness
C. Applies draft
D. Converts surface to solid

Q59. What happens if a face is selected while using the Shell tool?
A. Face is copied
B. Face is thickened
C. Face is removed
D. Face is merged

Q60. Which tool applies draft using a reference face?
A. Draft to Plane
B. Draft Edge
C. Draft Extrude
D. Draft Faces

Q61. How do you apply draft using a reference edge?
A. Use Draft Extrude
B. Select Draft to Face
C. Use Draft Edge
D. Select Axis Manager

Q62. Which tool applies draft angle to faces of an extruded feature?
A. Draft to Plane
B. Draft Extrude
C. Draft Faces
D. Fillet Manager

Q63. Which Draft tool allows selection of a reference plane?
A. Draft Edge
B. Draft to Plane
C. Draft Extrude
D. Draft Faces

Q64. Which tool is used to trim a solid body using an intersecting plane in Mastercam?
A. Trim to Surface
B. Slice Solid
C. Trim to Plane
D. Cut by Line

Q65. In the Trim to Plane method, which radio button is used to select a pre-defined plane?
A. Custom plane
B. Defined face
C. Named plane
D. Sketch plane

Q66. What happens after selecting the intersecting plane in the Trim to Plane tool?
A. Solid body is automatically deleted
B. Tool exits without changes
C. Preview of trimmed solid is shown
D. Solid is split into two parts

Q67. What tool is used to trim a solid using an intersecting surface or sheet?
A. Trim by Line
B. Split Solid
C. Trim to Plane
D. Trim to Surface/Sheet

Q68. After selecting the trim tool in Trim to Surface/Sheet method, what is the next step?
A. Apply chamfer
B. Change view
C. Click OK to perform trimming
D. Create layout

Q69. Which group in the Solids tab contains the Layout tool?
A. Create
B. Draft
C. Drawing
D. Modify

Q70. What must be done to use a custom drawing template in the Layout tool?
A. Choose Landscape orientation
B. Use Custom paper size
C. Check "Use Template File" and click Open
D. Select ISO standard

Q71. What happens when the “Suppress hidden lines” checkbox is selected during layout generation?
A. Views are hidden
B. Solid is hidden
C. Hidden lines are removed from views
D. Layout is not generated

Q72. What does the “Radial display angle” checkbox control in layout generation?
A. Angle of model rotation
B. Display of fillets
C. Display of radial lines on circular surfaces
D. Location of view placement

Q73. Which layout method generates Top, Front, Right, and Isometric views?
A. 4 View DIN
B. 3 View ANSI
C. 1 View Isometric
D. 4 View ANSI

Q74. What is the function of the “Add view” button in the Views rollout?
A. Remove unwanted views
B. Change current view
C. Add a new view by selecting a plane
D. Rotate existing view

Q75. What dialog box appears after clicking “Add view”?
A. Angle Settings dialog
B. Layer Properties dialog
C. Plane Selection dialog
D. View Properties dialog

Q76. What tool is used to delete a specific view from the layout?
A. Change view
B. Remove view
C. Hide view
D. Erase view

Q77. Which rollout contains the Pan, Align, and Rotate buttons for transforming views?
A. Views rollout
B. Modify rollout
C. Section rollout
D. Transform rollout

Q78. What does the Align button do in view transformation?
A. Changes angle of view
B. Rotates view randomly
C. Aligns view with base point of another view
D. Adjusts color of view

Q79. Which type of line can be used in creating a section view using Zigzag method?
A. Curved
B. Horizontal or Vertical
C. Diagonal only
D. Offset line

Q80. What does the Parameters dialog box allow after creating section lines?
A. Specify layout name
B. Set material properties
C. Set color and scale
D. Adjust viewport zoom

Chapter 5

Model Preparation and Mesh Design

Topics Covered

The major topics covered in this chapter are:

- ***Introduction to Model Preparation Tools.***
- ***Creating Hole Axis.***
- ***Direct Editing Tools.***
- ***Modification Tools.***
- ***Layout Tools.***
- ***Color Setting.***
- ***Mesh Primitives***
- ***Mesh creation from entities***
- ***Modifying Mesh***
- ***Analyzing Mesh***

INTRODUCTION

You can create models in Mastercam as well as import CAD models of other software in Mastercam. When you import models of other CAD software, sometimes you need minor changes in the model before performing machining operations. These minor changes can be performed by using the tools in **Model Prep** tab of the **Ribbon**; refer to Figure-1. Various tools in this tab are discussed next.

Figure-1. Model Prep tab

CREATING HOLE AXIS

The **Hole Axis** tool is used to create axis passing through circular holes in the solid body. Note that the hole features may or may not have model history associated. The procedure to use this tool is given next.

- Click on the **Hole Axis** tool from the **Create** group in the **Model Prep** tab of the **Ribbon**. The **Hole Axis Manager** will be displayed; refer to Figure-2 and you will be asked to select the internal hole faces.

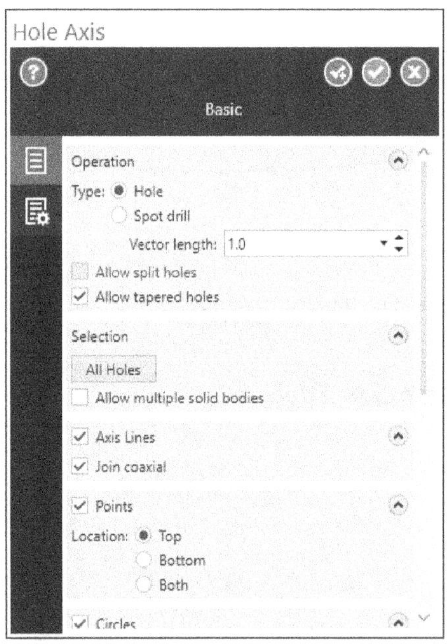

Figure-2. Hole Axis Manager

- Select desired round face from the model; refer to Figure-3, if you want to select all circular faces of same diameter as currently selected.
- Select the **Spot drill** radio button from the **Type** section if you want to create drill mark for creating larger holes later.
- Select the **Allow split holes** check box to create axis of hole which is not full closed.
- Select the **Allow tapered holes** check box to create axis of tapered holes.

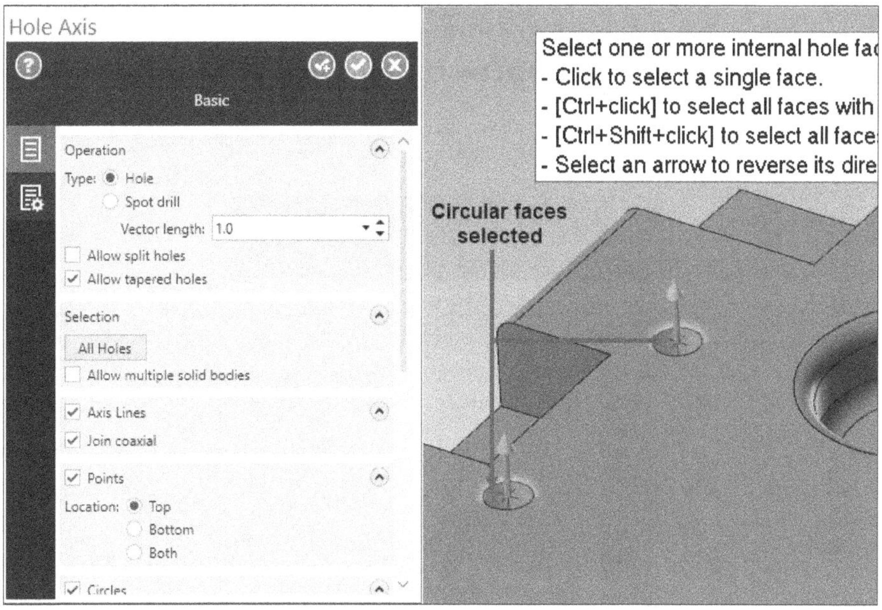

Figure-3. Selecting faces of holes

- Click on the **All Holes** button from the **Selection** rollout if you want to select all holes of the solid body. You will be asked to select the solid body. Click on desired solid body. All the holes will get selected. If the **Allow multiple solid bodies** check box is selected then multiple solid bodies can be selected.
- Select the **Axis Lines** check box to create axis in holes.
- Select the **Join coaxial** check box if you want to join axes of multiple holes which are stacked one over another and are concentric.
- Select the **Points** check box if you want to create wireframe point on the axis and select desired radio button below check box to specify position of point.
- Select the **Circles** check box if you want to create wireframe circle on the axis and select desired radio button to specify position of circle on the axis.
- Set the other parameters as discussed earlier and click on the **OK** button from the **Manager**. The axes and other related entities will be created.

PERFORMING PUSH-PULL EDITING

The **Push-Pull** tool is used to edit extrude, cut, fillet, and other feature directly by moving selected faces. The procedure to use this tool is given next.

- Click on the **Push-Pull** tool from the **Direct Editing** group in the **Model Prep** tab of the **Ribbon**. The **Push-Pull Manager** will be displayed; refer to Figure-4.
- Select the **Move** radio button if you want to move selected face by using arrow handle.
- Select the **Copy** radio button if you want to copy selected features at desired location by dragging arrow handle.
- Select the **Fillet** or **Chamfer** radio button from the **Edge** rollout to apply respective treatment to edges when performing push-pull operation.
- Select the **Maintain fillet radius** check box if you want to keep same radius as original one after apply push-pull editing.
- Select the **Snap to AutoCursor positions** check box to automatically snap the modified feature while performing the operation.

- Select the **Repair faces** check box to automatically repair faces and bodies when you have performed editing.
- Select the **Maintain source surfaces** check box if you want to keep the original surface as well after editing.

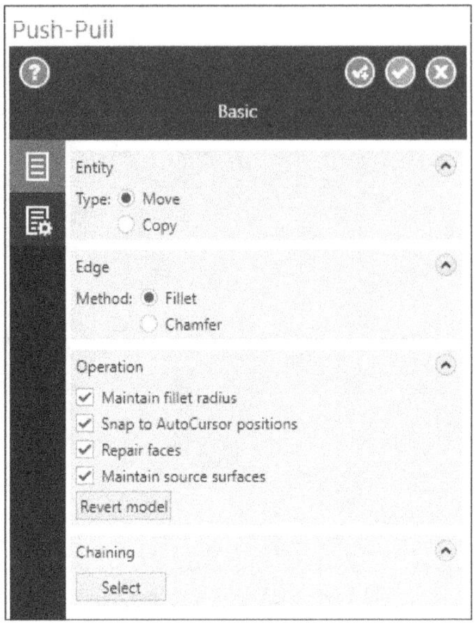

Figure-4. Push-Pull Manager

- Select the **Grow** check box from the **Advanced** tab of **Manager** to increase/decrease the size of features as you move face using direct editing. Select desired radio button from the **Grow** rollout.
- After setting desired parameters, click on the face to be modified using push-pull. An arrow will be displayed on selected face for direct editing; refer to Figure-5.

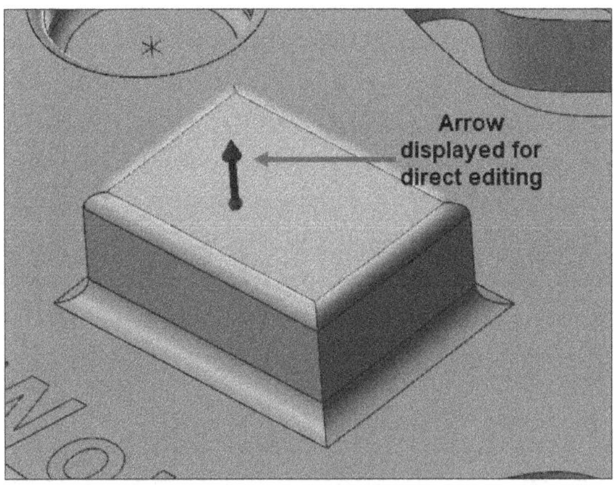

Figure-5. Arrow for direct editing

- Move the arrow handle to desired location for modifying body. Once you have performed desired modification, press **ENTER** to save modification and start a new direct editing operation.
- Click on the **OK** button from the **Manager** to exit the tool.

PERFORMING MOVE OPERATION (DIRECT EDITING)

The **Move** tool is used to move selected faces and features using direct editing method. The procedure to use this tool is given next.

- Click on the **Move** tool from the **Direct Editing** group in the **Model Prep** tab of the **Ribbon**. The **Move Manager** will be displayed; refer to Figure-6.

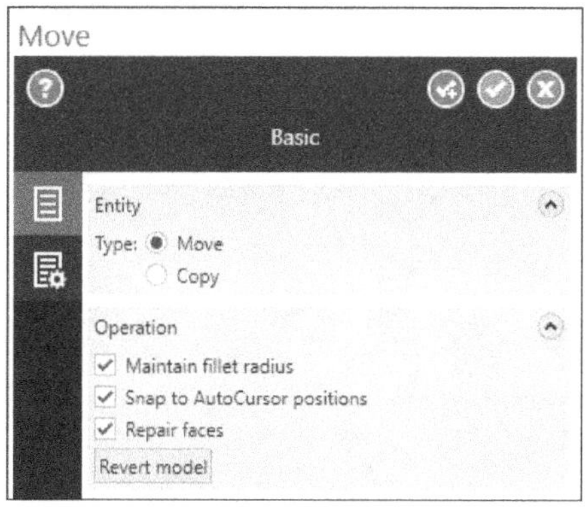

Figure-6. Move Manager

- Select desired radio button from the **Type** section to specify whether you want to move selected faces or copy selected features while moving.
- Set the parameters as discussed earlier for **Push-Pull** tool.
- Select the face you want to move or copy. A gnomon will be displayed attached to the face; refer to Figure-7.

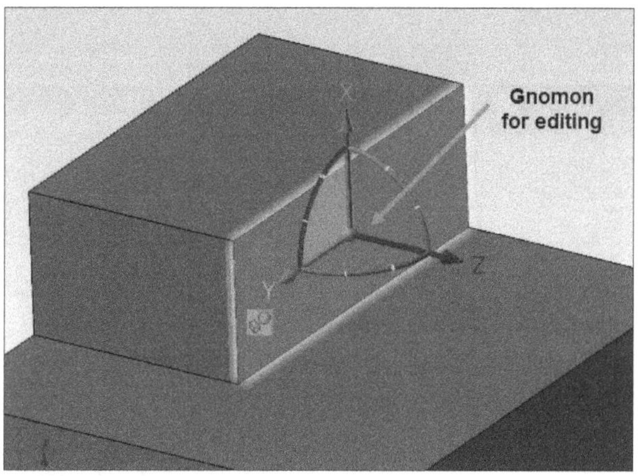

Figure-7. Gnomon for editing

- Select desired linear or rotary handle from the gnomon and drag it to perform editing.
- Press **ENTER** after editing to confirm modification and start a new modification.
- Click on the **OK** button from the **Manager** to exit the tool after modification.

SPLITTING SOLID FACES

The **Split Solid Faces** tool is used to split selected faces of solid by using a geometry, flow lines, or UV. The procedure to use this tool is given next.

- Click on the **Split Solid Faces** tool from the **Direct Editing** group in the **Model Prep** tab of the **Ribbon**. The **Split Solid Face Manager** will be displayed; refer to Figure-8 and you will be asked to select face to be split.

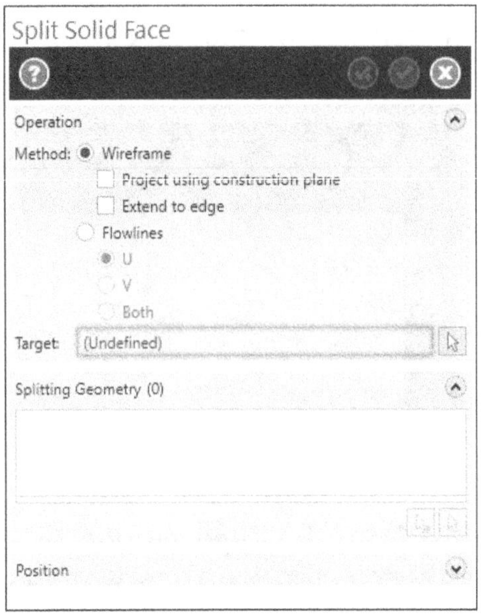

Figure-8. Split Solid Face Manager

- Select desired face of solid body to be split and then select the wireframe curve to be used for splitting. Preview of split faces will be displayed; refer to Figure-9.

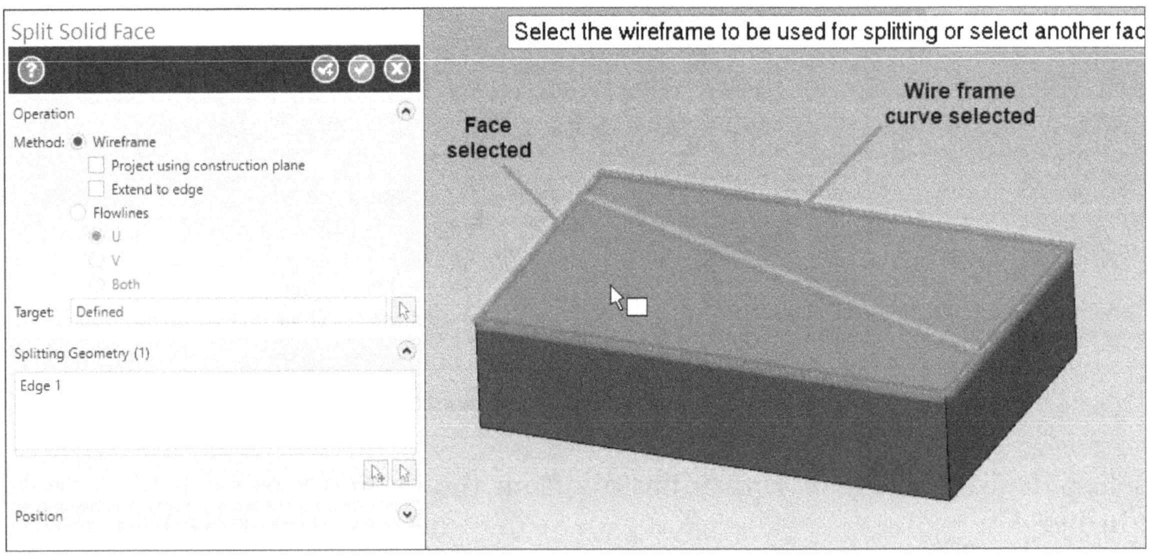

Figure-9. Preview of split faces

- Set desired parameters in the **Manager** as discussed earlier for surface splitting and click on the **OK** button from the **Manager**. The split faces will be generated; refer to Figure-10.

Figure-10. Split faces generated

MODIFYING FEATURE

The **Modify Feature** tool is used to create a body using selected feature or delete the feature. The procedure to use this tool is given next.

- Click on the **Modify Feature** tool from the **Modify** group of **Model Prep** tab in the **Ribbon**. The **Modify Solid Feature Manager** will be displayed; refer to Figure-11.

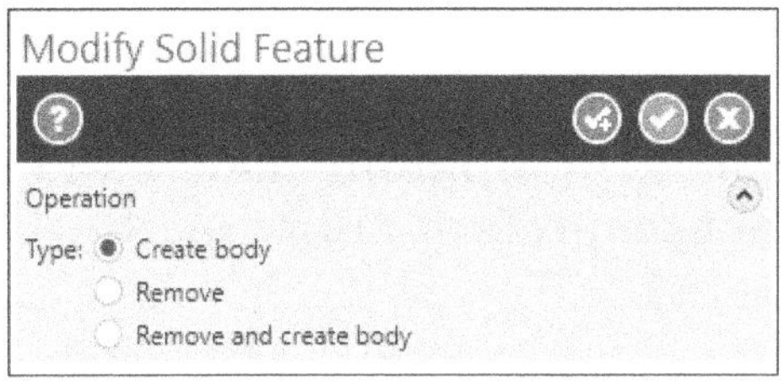

Figure-11. Modify Solid Feature Manager

- Select the **Create body** radio button if you want to create a new body using selected faces.
- Select the **Remove** radio button if you want to delete selected instance of feature.
- Select the **Remove and create body** radio button to delete original instances of feature and create new bodies.
- After selecting desired option from the **Manager**, select desired feature from the model. The **Solids history detected** dialog box will be displayed if the feature is parametric; refer to Figure-12.

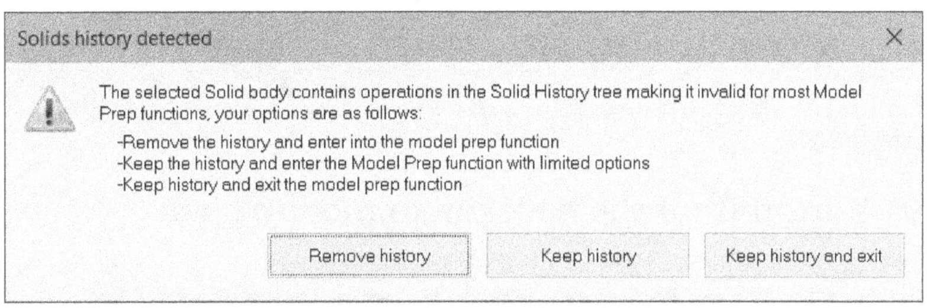

Figure-12. Solids history detected dialog box

- Select the **Remove history** button to remove history and continue creating/ deleting the feature. Keep selecting all the faces of feature to be deleted or used for creating solid body.
- Click on the **OK** button from the **Manager** to perform the operation.

MODIFYING FILLETS

The **Modify Fillet** tool is used to modify radius of fillets in the model. Note that fillet feature may or may not have model history. The procedure to use this tool is given next.

- Click on the **Modify Fillet** tool from the **Modify** group of **Model Prep** tab in the **Ribbon**. The **Modify Solid Fillets Manager** will be displayed; refer to Figure-13.

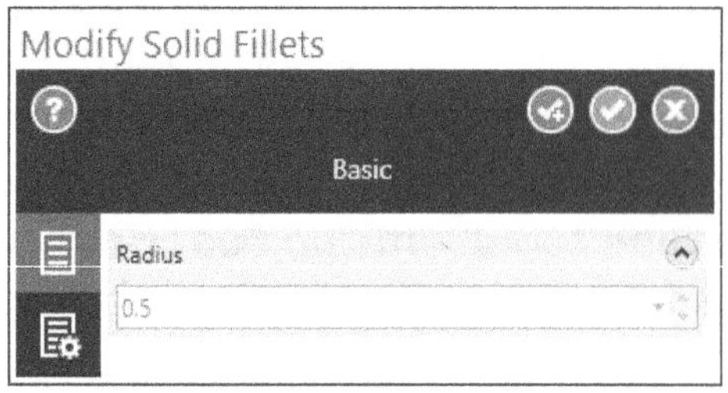

Figure-13. Modify Solid Fillets Manager

- Click on the fillets to be modified from the model and specify desired value in the **Radius** edit box of the **Manager**; refer to Figure-14.

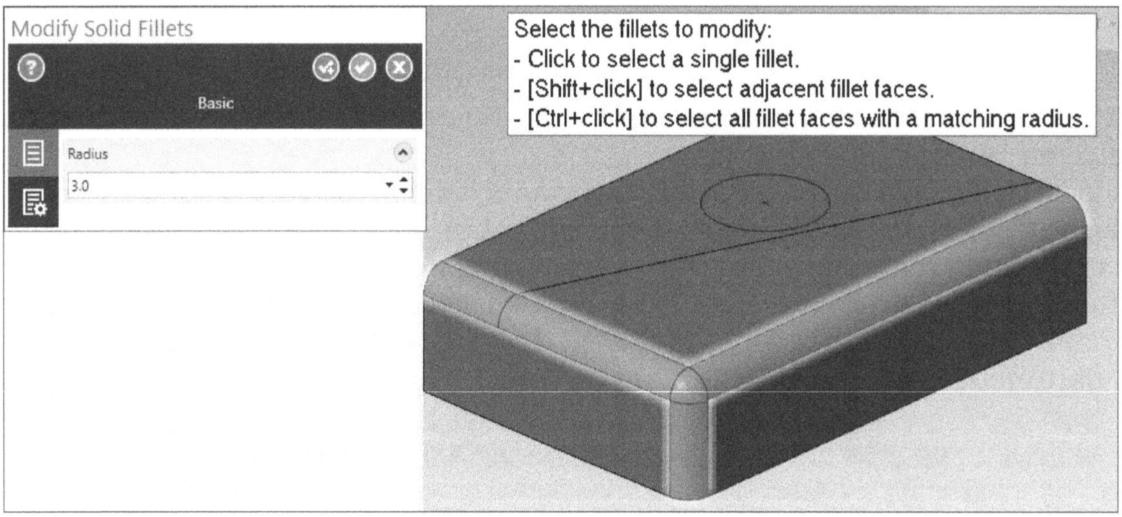

Figure-14. Modifying fillets

- Click on the **OK** button from the **Manager** to modify fillet.

REMOVING FACES

The **Remove Faces** tool is used to remove selected face of solid body. The procedure to use this tool is given next.

- Click on the **Remove Faces** tool from the **Modify** group of **Model Prep** tab in the **Ribbon**. The **Solid Selection** dialog box will be displayed.
- Select desired face(s) from the model and click on the **OK** button. The preview of removed faces will be displayed; refer to Figure-15.
- Select desired radio button from the **Original solid** section of the **Manager** to specify what will happen to original solid body.
- Select the **Create curves on open edges** check box to create wireframe curves on the solid body after deleting faces.
- Click on the **OK** button from the **Manager** to perform the operation.

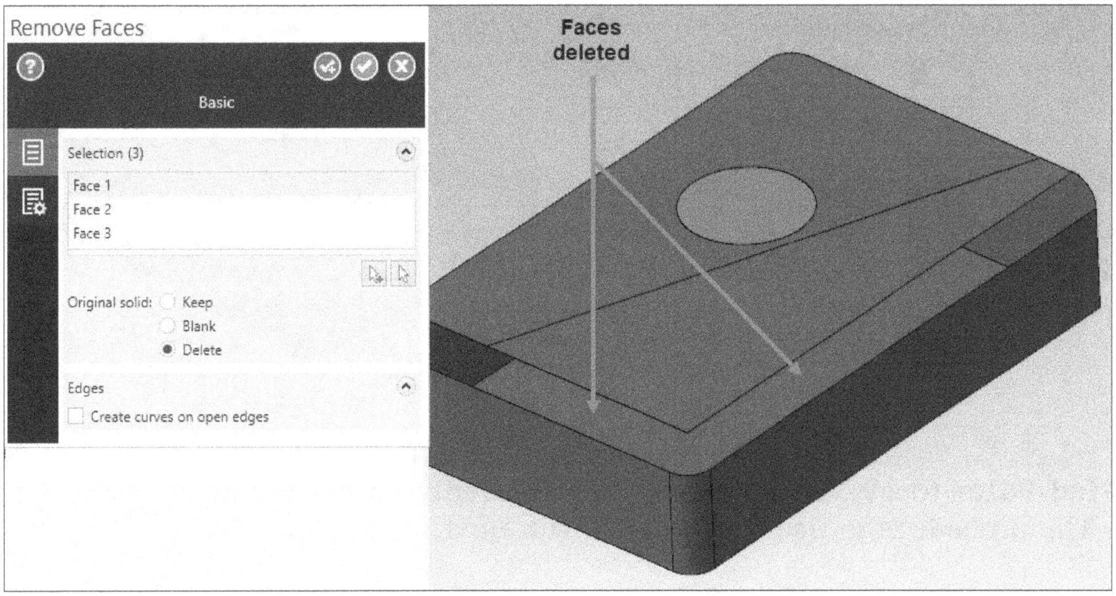

Figure-15. Preview of removed faces

REMOVING FILLETS

The **Remove Fillets** tool is used to remove selected fillets from the body. The procedure to use this tool is given next.

- Click on the **Remove Fillets** tool from the **Modify** group in the **Model Prep** tab of the **Ribbon**. The **Remove Solid Fillets Manager** will be displayed; refer to Figure-16 and you will be asked to select faces of fillets to be removed.

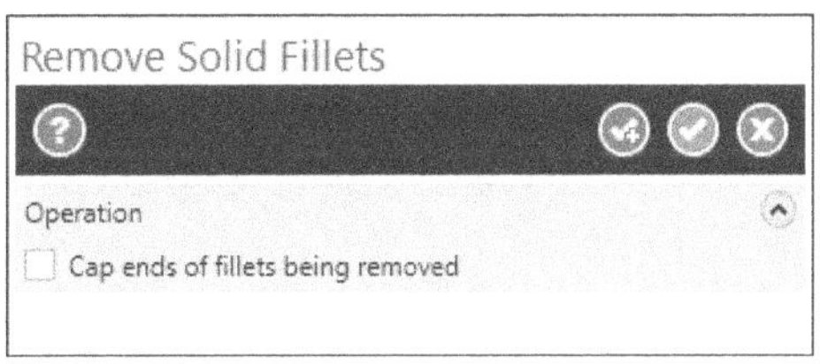

Figure-16. Remove Solid Fillets Manager

- Select desired fillet faces to be removed.
- Select the **Cap ends of fillets being removed** check box to fill the removed fillet face.
- After setting desired parameters, click on the **OK** button from the **Manager**. The fillets will be removed; refer to Figure-17.

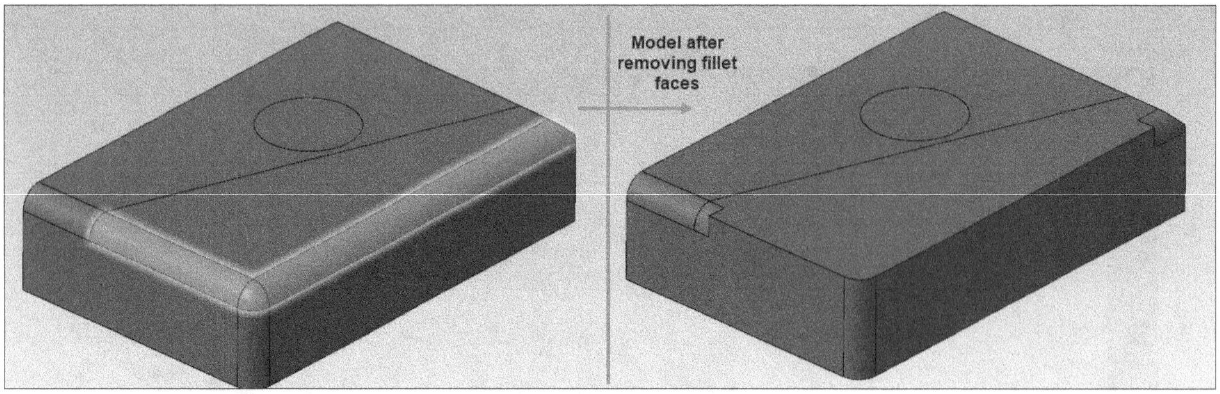

Figure-17. Removing fillets

FINDING HOLES

The **Find Holes** tool is used to automatically identify holes within range of specified radii. The procedure to use this tool is given next.

- Click on the **Find Holes** tool from the **Modify** group in **Model Prep** tab of **Ribbon**. The **Find Holes Manager** will be displayed; refer to Figure-18.

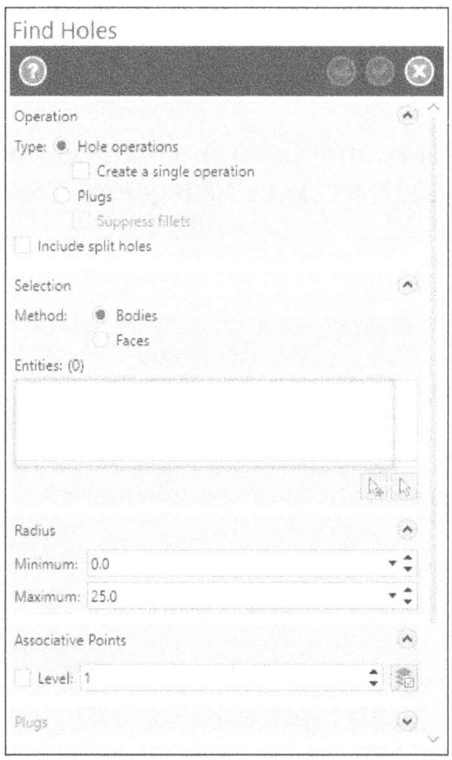

Figure-18. Find Holes Manager

- Select the **Hole Operations** radio button to create hole operations in History for detected holes. If the **Create a single operation** check box is selected below this radio button then the holes of same diameter and depth are combined in single operation.
- Select the **Plugs** radio button if you want to create separate solid bodies for detected holes in place of hole operations. Select the **Suppress fillets** check box below this radio button if you do not want to add detected fillets in the plug solid features.
- Select the **Include Split Holes** check box if you want to include those cuts in body which do not represent full 360 degree hole. This will include cuts like half or quarter holes in the operation.

- Select desired radio button from the **Selection** rollout to define the method to be used for selection. Select the **Bodies** radio button if you want to select bodies for detecting holes. Select the **Faces** radio button if you want to select faces for detection of holes.
- Select desired bodies/faces from the graphics area.
- Specify desired values in the **Minimum** and **Maximum** edit boxes to define the radii range within which holes will be detected. Note that a high range will take more time for processing.
- Specify desired values in the **Associative Points** and **Plugs** edit boxes to define the level at which detected geometry points will be placed.
- Set the other parameters as discussed earlier and click on the **OK** button from **Manager**. A message box will be displayed with number of holes detected; refer to Figure-19. (Note that we have imported a model with holes in our case for this tool).

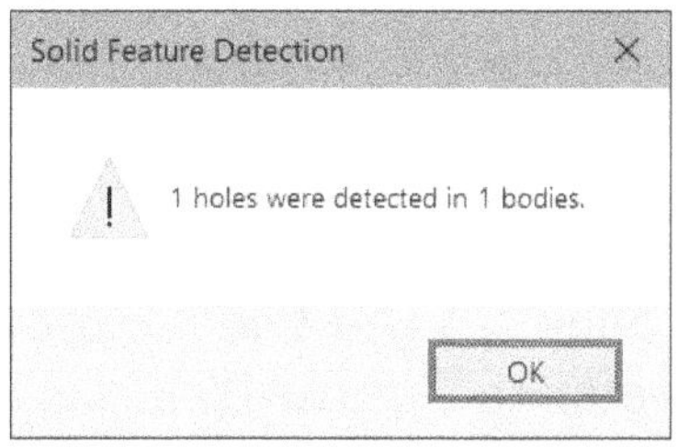

Figure-19. Solid Feature Detection message box

- Click on the **OK** button from the message box. The detected feature will be added in **Solids Manager**; refer to Figure-20.

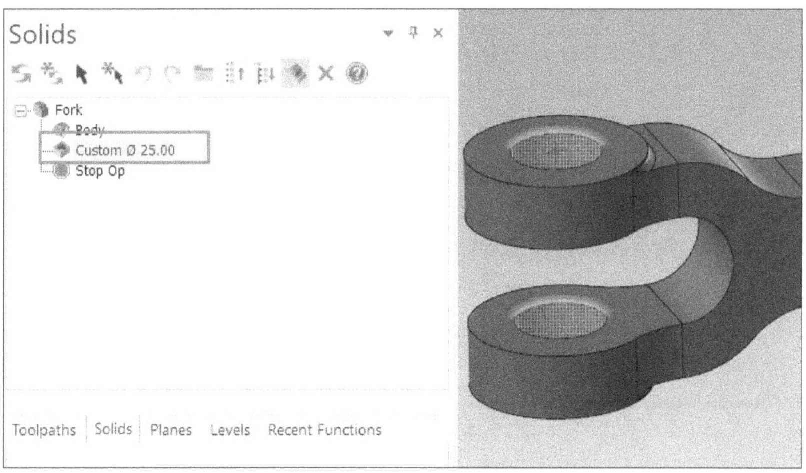

Figure-20. Hole detected

REMOVING HISTORY

The **Remove History** tool is used to remove model history of current model. Removing history of model reduces the file size and convert the model to brick solid body. The procedure to use this tool is given next.

- Click on the **Remove History** tool from the **Modify** group of **Model Prep** tab in the **Ribbon**. You will be asked to select the bodies whose model history is to be removed.
- Select desired solid body(s) and click on the **End Selection** button. The model history of selected bodies will be removed in **Solids Manager**; refer to Figure-21.

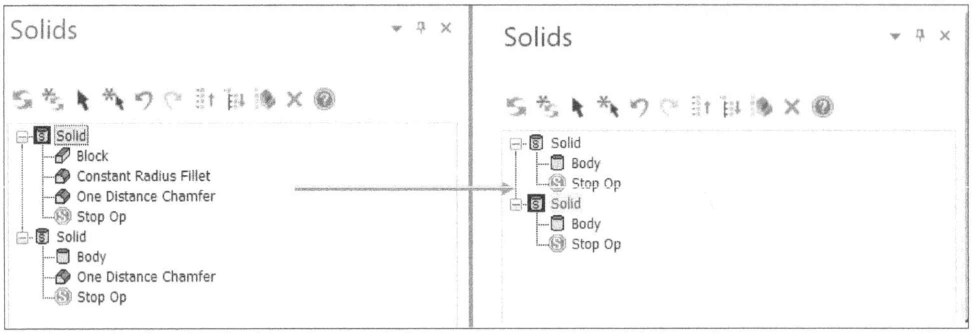

Figure-21. Model after removing history

ADDING HISTORY

The **Add History** tool is used to add model history of holes and fillets automatically by identifying them in the selected solid. The procedure to use this tool is given next.

- Click on the **Add History** tool from the **Modify** group in the **Model Prep** tab of the **Ribbon**. You will be asked to select solid bodies whose fillets and holes are to be identified.
- Select desired body(s) and click on the **End Selection** button. The **Add History Manager** will be displayed; refer to Figure-22.

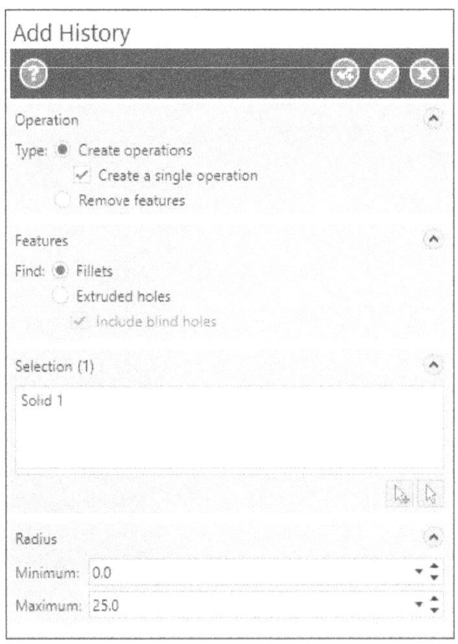

Figure-22. Add History Manager

- Select desired radio button from the **Operation** rollout to define whether you want to create new operations for identified features or you want to delete the identified features. If you want to create a new feature then select the **Create operations** radio button. To create a single operation for all detected features, select the **Create a single operation** check box. If you want to remove the identified features then select the **Remove features** radio button.
- Select desired radio button from the **Find section of Features** rollout to specify which features are to be identified.
- Set desired parameters in the **Minimum** and **Maximum** edit boxes of the **Radius** rollout to define the range of radius for fillets to be identified.
- After setting the parameters, click on the **OK** button. The features will be identified.

SIMPLIFYING SOLID

The **Simplify Solid** tool is used to remove redundant/overlapping faces and edges from the imported model. The procedure to use this tool is given next.

- Click on the **Simplify Solid** tool from the **Simplify Solid** drop-down in the **Modify** group of **Model Prep** tab in the **Ribbon**. You will be asked to select the solid body or its faces and edges to be simplified.
- Select desired body, faces, and edges to be simplified and click on the **End Selection** button from the graphics area. The **Solids history detected** dialog box will be displayed.
- Click on the **Remove history** button from the dialog box. The **Simplify solid** dialog box will be displayed showing the number of faces/edges removed and the redundant edges/faces will be removed.
- Click on the **OK** button from the dialog box displayed.

OPTIMIZING IMPORTED MODEL

The **Optimize** tool is used to repair the imported solid model by improving accuracy of faces and edges. The procedure to use this tool is given next.

- Click on the **Optimize** tool from the **Simplify Solid** drop-down in the **Modify** group of **Model Prep** tab in the **Ribbon**. You will be asked to select solid or its faces.
- Select desired solid body or faces and click on the **End Selection** button from the graphics area. If history is associated with the model then **Solids history detected** dialog box will be displayed. Click on the **Remove history** button from the dialog box to remove history and continue repairing the model. On doing so, the **Optimize solid** dialog box will be displayed showing the number of edges and faces optimized; refer to Figure-23.

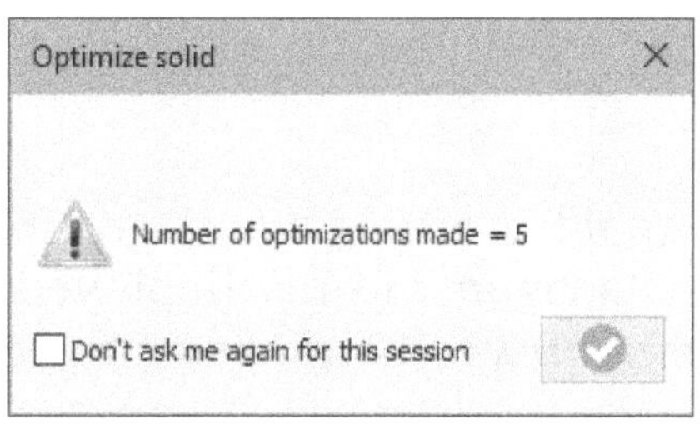

Figure-23. Optimize solid dialog box

- Click on the **OK** button from the dialog box to exit the tool.

REPAIRING SMALL FACES OF SOLID BODY

The **Repair Small Faces** tool is used to repair small faces of a solid body by joining together fragmented faces. The procedure to use this tool is given next.

- Click on the **Repair Small Faces** tool from the **Simplify Solid** drop-down in the **Modify** group of **Model Prep** tab in the **Ribbon**. You will be asked to select the solid body to be analyzed for small faces.
- Select desired solid body. The **Repair Small Faces Manager** will be displayed; refer to Figure-24.

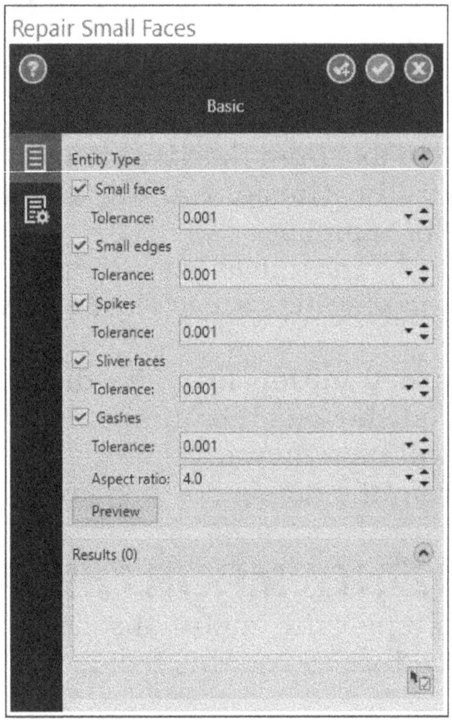

Figure-24. Repair Small Faces Manager

- Select check boxes from the **Entity Type** rollout to select which entities are to be repaired and specify related tolerance value in the **Tolerance** edit boxes.
- Click on the **Preview** button to check preview of changes and click on the **OK** button from the **Manager** to repair entities.

DISASSEMBLY OF SOLID BODIES

The **Disassemble** tool in **Layout** group of **Ribbon** is used to separate the bodies in 3D view and place them at specified distance on a plane. The procedure to use this tool is given next.

- Click on the **Disassemble** tool from the **Layout** group in the **Model Prep** tab of the **Ribbon**. The **Disassemble Manager** will be displayed; refer to Figure-25 and you will be asked to select the bodies to be disassembled.

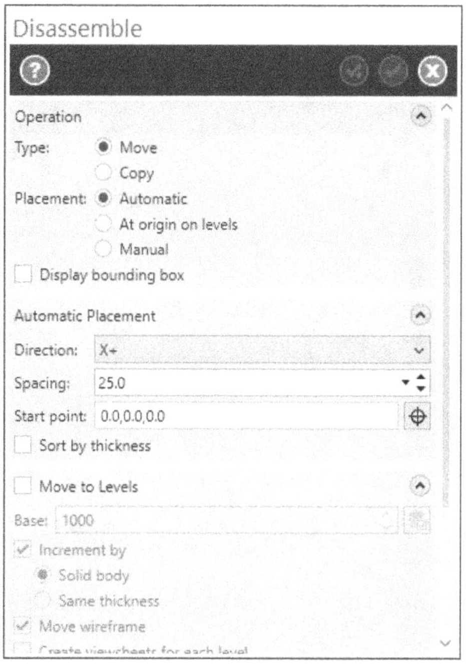

Figure-25. Disassemble Manager

- Select the **Move** radio button if you want to move selected bodies and select the **Copy** radio button from the **Type** section of **Manager** if you want to move copies of selected bodies at desired location.
- Select the **Automatic** radio button from the **Placement** section of **Manager** if you want to move the selected bodies based on parameters specified in the **Automatic Placement** rollout of the **Manager**. Select the **At origin on levels** radio button to place the selected bodies at origin on different levels separated by specified values. Select the **Manual** radio button to place the bodies at desired location specified by clicking.
- Select the **Display bounding box** check box to display bounding box around the selected solid bodies.
- Select the **Move to Levels** check box to move selected bodies to different levels. After selecting the check boxes, specify the base level and other related parameters in the **Move to Levels** rollout.
- After setting desired parameters, click on the body to be disassembled from the 3D view. If you have selected the **Manual** radio button then the body will be attached to cursor and you need to specify the location of solid body. If **Automatic** radio button is selected then the selected bodies will move to specified locations as per parameters in **Automatic Placement** rollout.
- After performing disassembly operation, click on the **OK** button from the **Manager**.

ALIGNING SOLID TO PLANE

The **Align to Plane** tool is used to align face of solid to selected plane. The procedure to use this tool is given next.

- Click on the **Align to Plane** tool from the **Layout** group in the **Model Prep** tab of the **Ribbon**. The **Align to Plane Manager** will be displayed; refer to Figure-26 and you will be asked to select face of the solid body to be aligned.

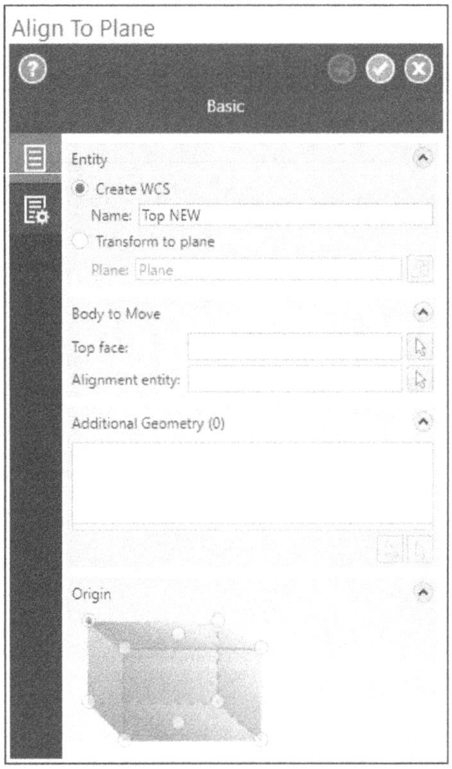

Figure-26. Align To Plane Manager

- Select desired face of the body. You will be asked to specify first point of line for alignment or line/edge to orient the WCS.
- Select desired edge/line or click to specify first and second point of orientation line. Preview of the aligned body will be displayed; refer to Figure-27.

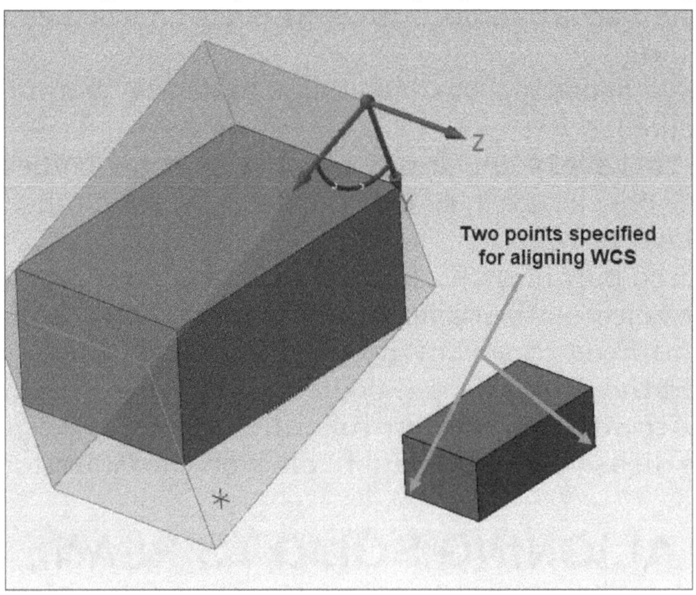

Figure-27. Preview of aligned face

- Select the **Create WCS** radio button to align the body to user specified WCS. Select the **Transform to plane** radio button if you want to align selected face with earlier created plane.
- After setting desired parameters, click on the **OK** button from the **Manager**.

ALIGNING FACE OF SELECTED SOLID TO ANOTHER SOLID FACE

The **Align to Face** tool is used to align selected face of solid to another solid body face. The procedure to use this tool is given next.

- Click on the **Align to Face** tool from the **Layout** group in the **Model Prep** tab of the **Ribbon**. The **Align to Face Manager** will be displayed; refer to Figure-28 and you will be asked to select face of solid to be moved.
- Set desired parameters in the **Method** and **Mode** sections of **Operation** rollout in the **Manager**.
- Select desired face of solid body to be moved. You will be asked to select face of target body to which main solid body will be aligned.
- Select desired face of target body. Preview of aligned body will be displayed; refer to Figure-29.

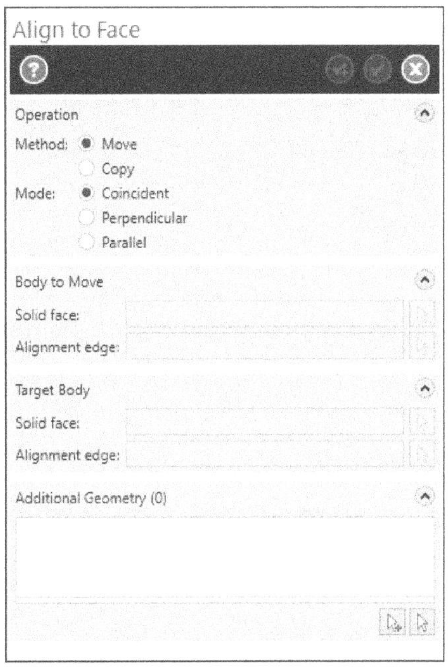

Figure-28. Align to Face Manager

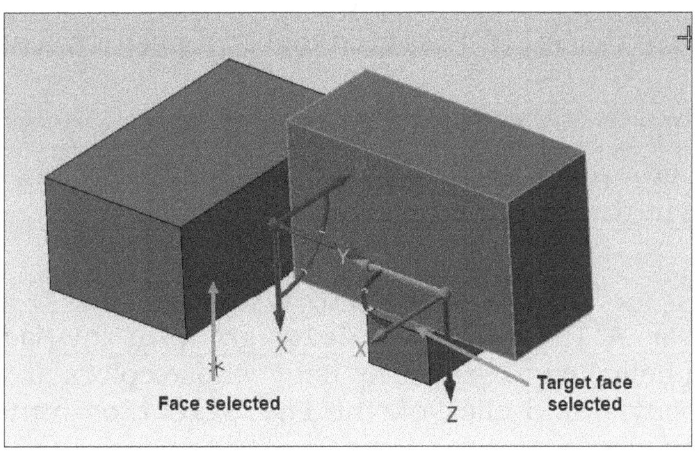

Figure-29. Preview of aligned face

- Click on the **OK** button from the **Manager** to align the body.

ALIGNING SOLID BODY ALONG Z

The **Align to Z** tool is used to align face of selected body to specified value along Z axis. This tool is generally useful when you are performing a turning operation and want to align the workpiece at desired distance along Z axis. The procedure to use this tool is given next.

- Click on the **Align to Z** tool from the **Layout** group in the **Model Prep** tab of the **Ribbon**. The **Align to Z Manager** will be displayed; refer to Figure-30 and you will be asked to select solid body.

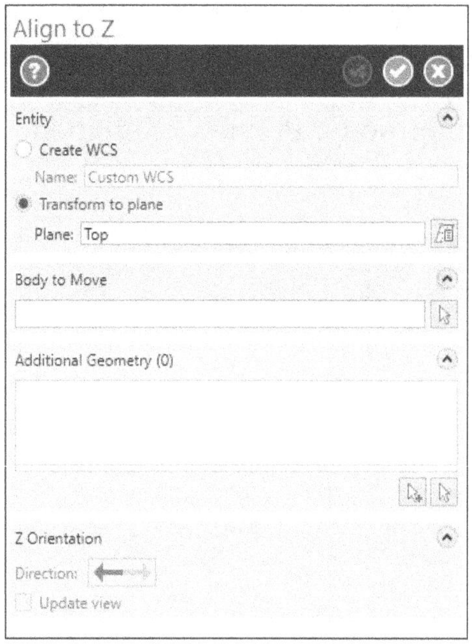

Figure-30. Align to Z Manager

- Click on the solid body to be aligned to Z axis. The body will automatically move along the Z axis.
- Click on the **Direction** button from the **Z Orientation** rollout in the **Manager** to flip orientation of body along Z axis.
- After setting desired parameters, click on the **OK** button from the **Manager**.

Similarly, you can use the **Solid Position** tool to reposition a solid body.

COLOR TOOLS

The tools in **Color** group are used to apply and remove colors from faces of solid body. Various tools in this group are discussed next.

Clearing All Colors

- Click on the **Clear All** tool from the **Color** group in the **Model Prep** tab of the **Ribbon**. You will be asked to select the body whose colors are to be removed.
- Select desired body(s) and click on the **End Selection** button. All the applied colors will be removed.

Changing Colors of Faces

- Click on the **Change Face** tool from the **Color** group in the **Model Prep** tab of the **Ribbon**. The **Modify Solid Face Color Manager** will be displayed and you will be asked to select faces on which color will be applied.
- Click on the **Select Color** button from the **Color** rollout in the **Manager**. The **Colors** dialog box will be displayed; refer to Figure-31.

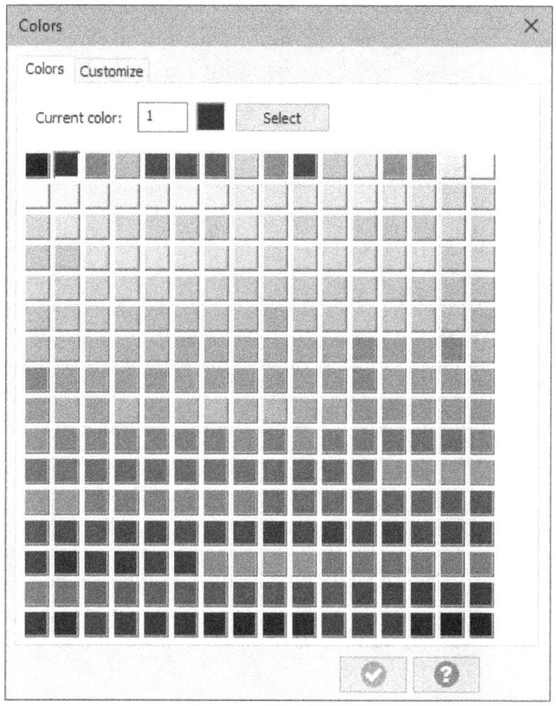

Figure-31. Colors dialog box

- Select desired color from the list and click on the **OK** button. The respective color will be active.
- Select the faces of the model and click on the **OK** button from the **Manager**. Selected colors will be applied to the faces.

Similarly, you can use the other tools in the **Color** group of the **Ribbon**.

MESH DESIGNING

Mesh is a representation of continuous bodies by discrete and topological cells. Meshing is useful in performing tasks like rendering, simulation, and direct editing of model. Generally, meshing breaks the model into triangular cells where each point of triangular cell has separate degree of freedom to move while still attached the body. So, you can freely modify the shape of model using keypoints of these triangular faces(facets). The tools to create and modify mesh model are available in the **Mesh** tab of the **Ribbon**; refer to Figure-32. The tools in this tab are discussed next.

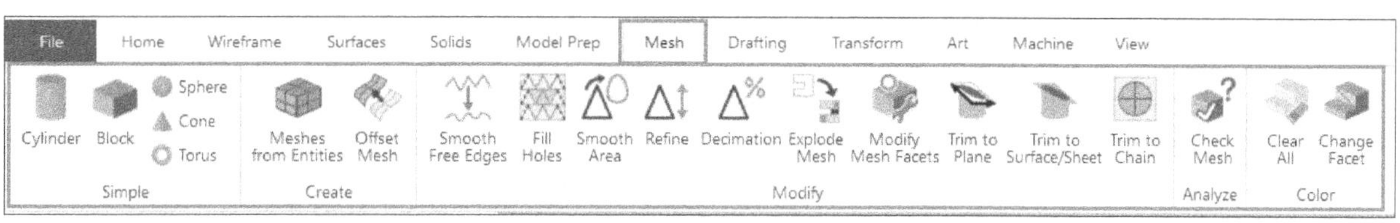

Figure-32. Mesh tab in Ribbon

CREATING CYLINDER MESH

The **Cylinder** tool in **Mesh** tab is used to create cylindrical mesh objects in the graphics area. The procedure to use this tool is given next.

- Click on the **Cylinder** tool from the **Simple** panel in **Mesh** tab of the **Ribbon**. The **Primitive Cylinder Manager** will be displayed; refer to Figure-33.

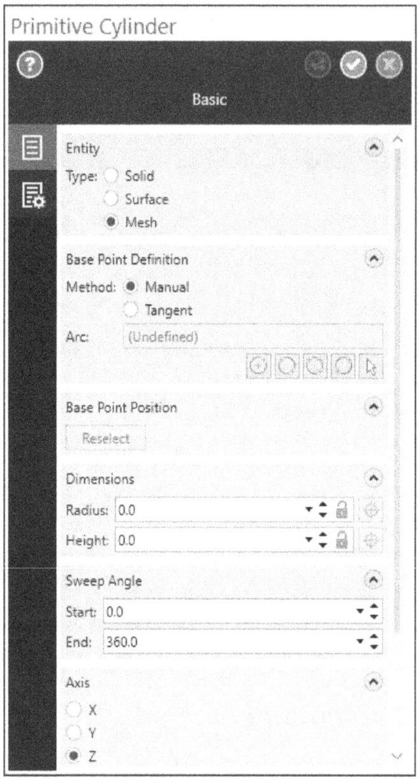

Figure-33. Primitive Cylinder Manager

- Make sure the **Mesh** radio button is selected in **Entity** rollout of the **Manager** and specify the parameters as discussed earlier for Surface and Solid primitive cylinder.
- Click on the **OK** button from the **Manager** to exit the tool.

Similarly, you can use other tools of **Simple** panel in the **Mesh** tab of the **Ribbon** as discussed earlier.

CREATING MESH FROM ENTITY

The **Meshes from Entities** tool is used to create mesh body by using a solid, surface, or mesh entity earlier created. The procedure to use this tool is given next.

- Click on the **Meshes from Entities** tool from the **Create** panel in the **Mesh** tab of the **Ribbon**. The **Meshes from Entities Manager** will be displayed; refer to Figure-34.
- Select the **Entities** radio button to select solid, surface, or mesh body to be used as reference for creating mesh body. Select the **Facets** radio button to select individual faces/facets of solid, surface, or mesh body for creating mesh body.
- Click on the **Add selection** button from the **Selection** rollout and select the object to be used as reference for creating mesh body.

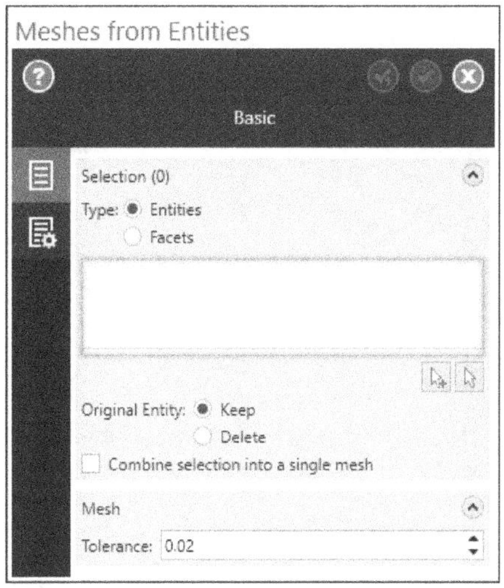

Figure-34. Meshes from Entities Manager

- After selecting objects, click on the **End Selection** button. The options in **Meshes from Entities Manager** will become active.
- Select the **Keep** radio button from the **Original Entity** rollout to keep the original objects after creating mesh body. Select the **Delete** radio button to remove original objects after creating mesh body.
- Select the **Combine selection into a single mesh** check box to make single mesh body by using selected objects.
- Click on the **Advanced** tab in **Manager** and change the color and level of mesh objects to be created.
- After setting desired parameters, click on the **OK** button from the **Manager**. The mesh body will be created.

OFFSETTING MESH

Offset means creating a copy of object at specified distance. Using the **Offset Mesh** tool, you can expand the mesh faces in desired direction at specified distance. The procedure to use this tool is given next.

- Click on the **Offset Mesh** tool from the **Create** group in the **Mesh** tab of the **Ribbon**. The **Offset Mesh Manager** will be displayed; refer to Figure-35.
- Select the mesh to be expanded and click on the **End Selection** button. The options in **Manager** will be activated.
- Select the **Copy** radio button from **Method** section to create offset mesh as copy of original mesh. Select the **Modify** radio button to change the original mesh as offsetted mesh.
- Click on the **Add Selection** button from **Meshes** rollout if you want to add more mesh bodies.
- Specify desired distance value by which the mesh faces will be offsetted in the **Offset Distance** edit box.
- Specify desired value in the **Tolerance** edit box to define the maximum deviation allowed from original mesh curvature.
- Select the **Automatically preview results** check box to display the preview of offset mesh as you modify the parameters in **Manager**.
- Click on the **OK** button from the **Manager** to create the offset feature.

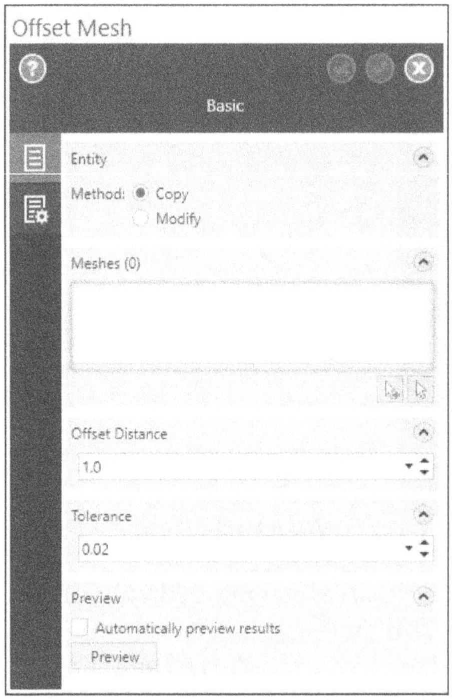

Figure-35. Offset Mesh Manager

SMOOTHENING FREE EDGES

The **Smooth Free Edges** tool is used to smoothen rough edges of the mesh body; refer to Figure-36. The procedure to use this tool is given next.

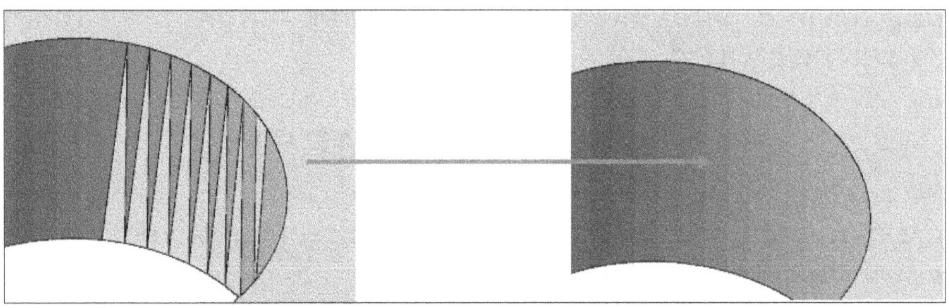

Figure-36. After smoothening edges

- Click on the **Smooth Free Edges** tool after importing/opening a distorted mesh model. The **Smooth Free Edges Manager** will be displayed; refer to Figure-37.
- Set desired value in the **Limiting angle** edit box to define maximum angle between two edges that can be filled by this tool.
- Select the **Automatically preview results** check box to display preview of smoothened edges during operation.
- Select the mesh bodies whose edges are to be smoothened from the graphics area. Preview of filled edges will be displayed.
- Select the **Copy** radio button from the **Method** section in the **Manager** if you want to create a copy of the original mesh model after smoothening. By default, the **Modify** radio button is selected and hence, the original mesh body is modified.
- After setting desired parameters, click on the **OK** button to perform smoothening.

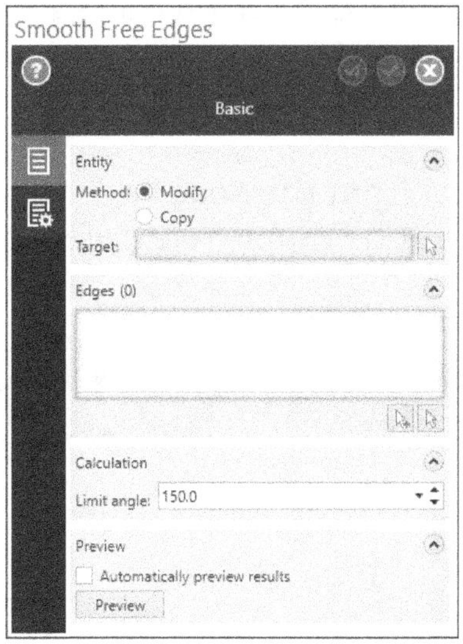

Figure-37. Smooth Free Edges Manager

FILLING HOLES

The **Fill Holes** tool is used to close the holes in mesh body by joining boundary regions is facets. The procedure to use this tool is given next.

- Click on the **Fill Holes** tool from the **Modify** group in the **Mesh** tab of the **Ribbon**. The **Fill Holes Manager** will be displayed; refer to Figure-38.
- Select the **Modify** radio button to modify original body or select the **Copy** radio button to create separate body after filling holes.
- Select the mesh body whose holes are to be filled. The holes/cuts in the mesh body will get highlighted; refer to Figure-39.
- Select the edges of cuts/holes to be filled and click on the **End Selection** button.
- Set the other parameters as discussed earlier in the **Manager** and click on the **OK** button to perform the operation.

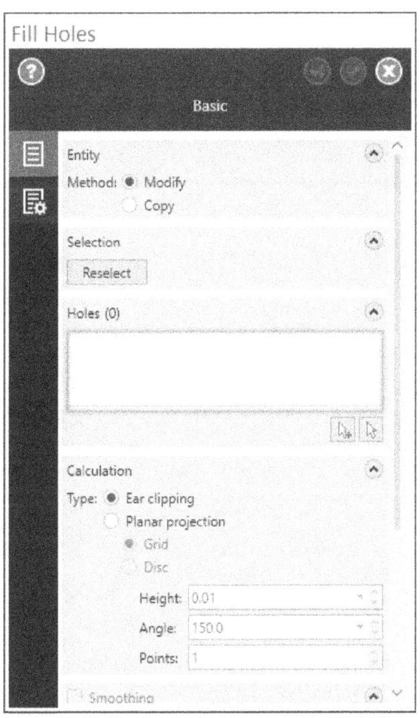

Figure-38. Fill Holes Manager

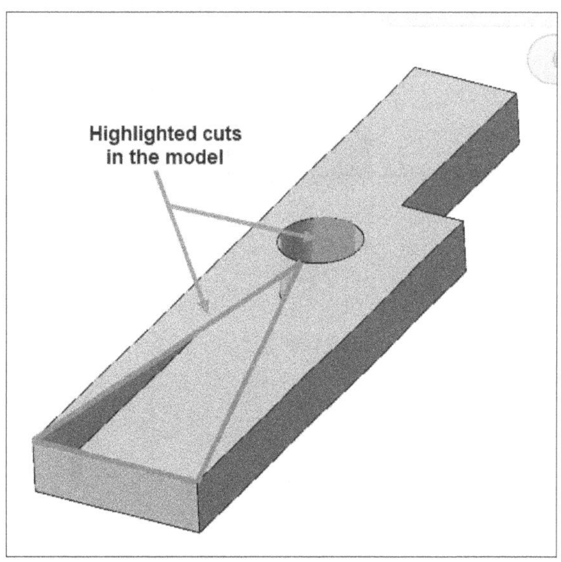

Figure-39. Highlighted cuts in the model

SMOOTHENING MESH REGION

The **Smooth Area** tool is used to smoothen selected region or mesh body. The procedure to use this tool is given next.

- Click on the **Smooth Area** tool from the **Modify** group in the **Mesh** tab of the **Ribbon**. The **Smooth Area Manager** will be displayed; refer to Figure-40.

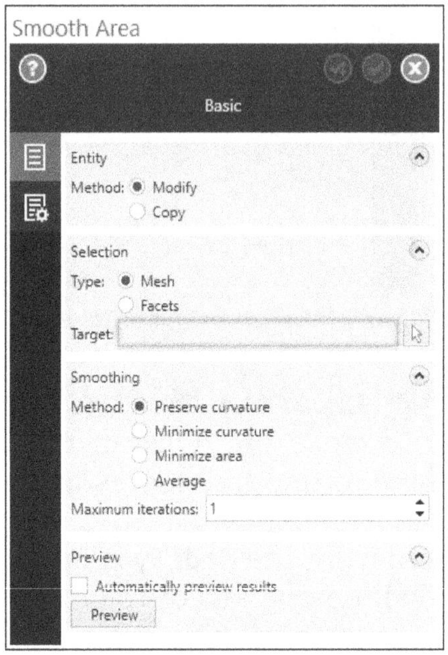

Figure-40. Smooth Area Manager

- Select the **Mesh** radio button from the **Selection** rollout to select the mesh body for smoothening. If you want to smoothen a facet/region of mesh then select the **Facets** radio button. After selecting the **Facets** radio button, click on the **Select mesh** button in the **Selection** rollout. The **Facet Selection Manager** will be displayed; refer to Figure-41.

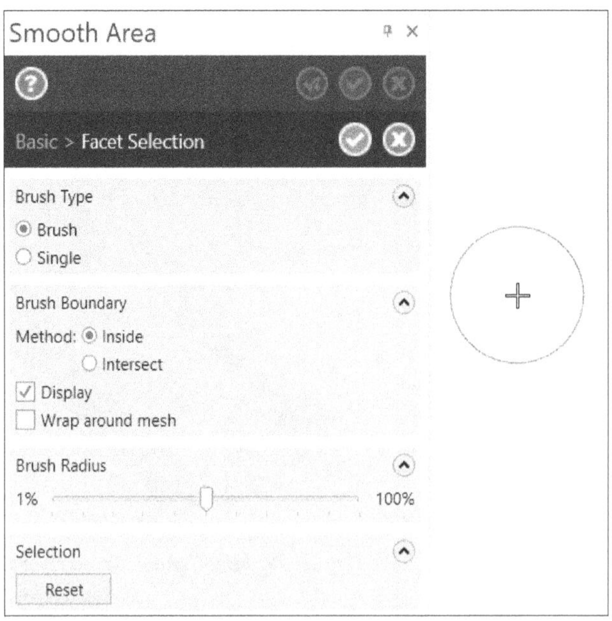

Figure-41. Facet Selection Manager

- Select the **Brush** radio button if you want to select multiple facets by dragging cursor over the facets. All the faces that fall inside the radius of brush will get selected. You can modify the radius of brush by using **Brush Radius** slider. Select the **Single** radio button to select the faces under cursor while dragging. After selecting faces, click on the **OK** button from the **Manager**. The **Smooth Area Manager** will be displayed again.
- Select the **Preserve curvature** radio button to smoothen the mesh without making changes in the curvature of facets. Select the **Minimize curvature** radio button to flatten near by facets when smoothening selected facets. Select the **Minimize area** radio button to reduce the area as well as volume of the mesh by smoothening. Select the **Average** radio button to apply average smoothening to all the nearby vertices.
- Click in the **Maximum iterations** edit box and specify desired value to define number of smoothening iterations to be performed.
- Specify other parameters as discussed earlier and click on the **OK** button from **Manager** to perform the operation.

REFINING MESH

The **Refine** tool is used to add more facets in the mesh to refine detailed areas. The procedure to use this tool is given next.

- Click on the **Refine** tool from the **Modify** group in the **Mesh** tab of the **Ribbon**. The **Refine Manager** will be displayed; refer to Figure-42.

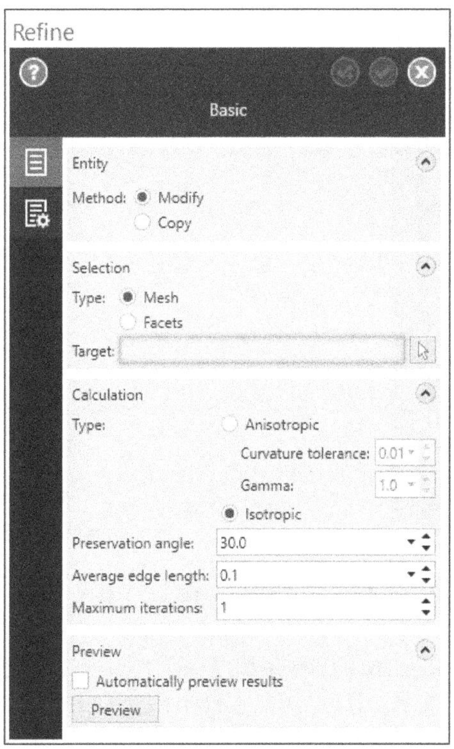

Figure-42. Refine Manager

- Select the mesh you want to refine from the graphics area as discussed earlier.

- Select the **Anisotropic** radio button to apply different size facets to mesh for refining different regions. After selecting this radio button, specify desired value in **Curvature tolerance** edit box to define how much deviation is allowed from original mesh curvature for refinement. Specify desired value in **Gamma** edit box to define weighing factor for increasing/decreasing size of refinement facets as compared to original.
- Select the **Isotropic** radio button to add uniform sized facets for refining mesh.
- Specify other parameters in **Manager** as discussed earlier and click on the **OK** button to apply changes.

DECIMATION

The **Decimation** tool is used to reduce number of facets in the mesh for reducing file size. The procedure to use this tool is given next.

- Click on the **Decimation** tool from the **Modify** group in **Mesh** tab of the **Ribbon**. The **Decimation Manager** will be displayed; refer to Figure-43.

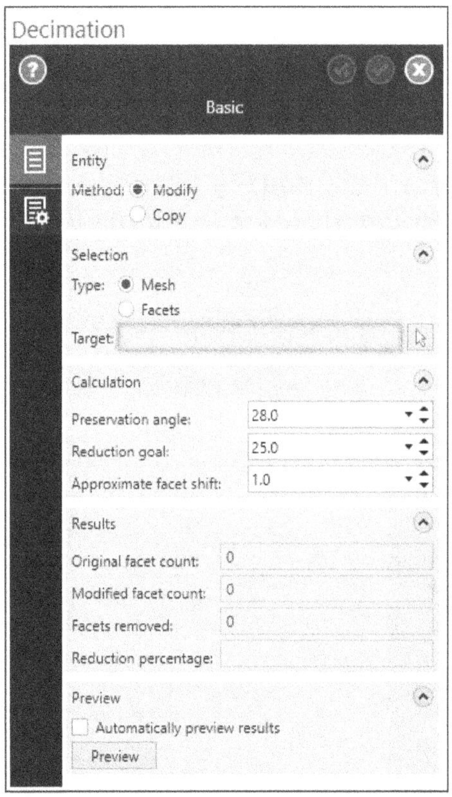

Figure-43. Decimation Manager

- Specify desired value in **Preservation angle** edit box to define range up to which the facets will be preserved.
- Specify desired value in **Reduction goal** edit box to define percentage of facets to be reduced from the mesh model. Note that other constraints are also considered when reducing number of facets.
- Specify desired value in the **Approximate facet shift** edit box to define the amount of alteration allowed in near by facets after removing facets falling under goal.
- After specifying desired parameters, select the mesh to be modified. The details about facet removal will be displayed in the **Results** rollout of the **Manager**.

- Modify the parameters in the **Calculation** rollout to get desired results and click on the **OK** button from the **Manager** to perform decimation.

EXPLODING MESH

The **Explode Mesh** tool is used to break a complex mesh into several simple mesh bodies for easy manipulation. The procedure to use this tool is given next.

- Click on the **Explode Mesh** tool from the **Modify** group in the **Mesh** tab of **Ribbon**. The **Explode Mesh Manager** will be displayed; refer to Figure-44.

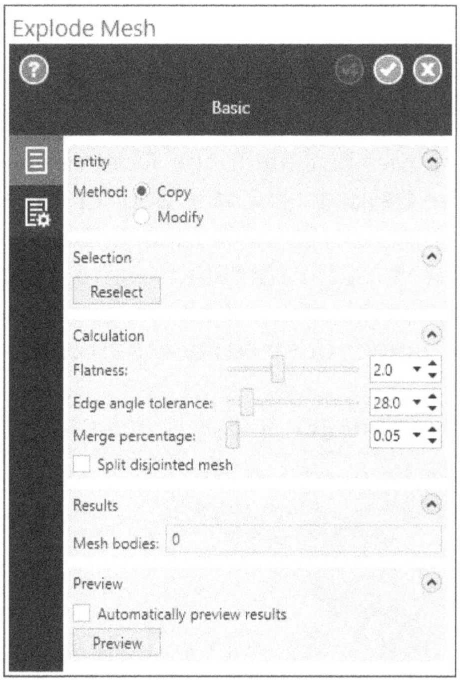

Figure-44. Explode Mesh Manager

- Set desired value using **Flatness** slider to define degree of flatness up to which a section of mesh will be considered as single body. A lower value generally generates more mesh bodies.
- Set desired value using **Edge angle tolerance** slider to define the angle threshold between two facets. If the angle between facets goes above specified value then a new mesh body will be created.
- Set desired value using the **Merge percentage** slider to define size of region to be considered as separate body with respect to total size of mesh. If size of a region is less than specified value then it will be merged with near by facets.
- After setting desired parameters, select the mesh body from graphics area. The number of resulting mesh bodies will be displayed in the **Results** rollout.
- Click on the **OK** button from the **Manager** to explode the mesh.

MODIFYING MESH FACETS

The **Modify Mesh Facets** tool is used to create, remove, and repair mesh facets. The procedure to use this tool is given next.

- Click on the **Modify Mesh Facets** tool from the **Modify** group in **Mesh** tab of **Ribbon**. The **Modify Mesh Facets Manager** will be displayed; refer to Figure-45.

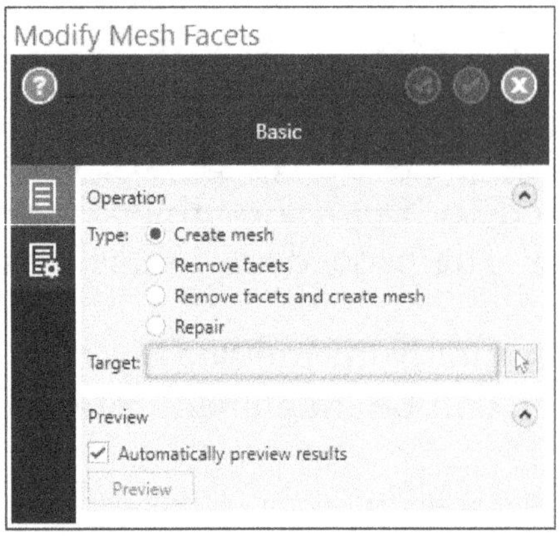

Figure-45. Modify Mesh Facets Manager

- Select the **Create mesh** radio button if you want to create a new mesh using selected facets of another mesh. Select the **Remove facets** radio button to delete selected facets. Select the **Remove facets and create mesh** radio button to split selected facets of a mesh to form a new mesh. Select the **Repair** radio button to delete selected facets and then fill the void using a joining facet.
- After selecting desired radio button, click on the **Select facets** button next to **Target** selection box and select desired facets from the mesh model as discussed earlier.
- Click on the **OK** button from **Manager** to apply selected operation; refer to Figure-46.

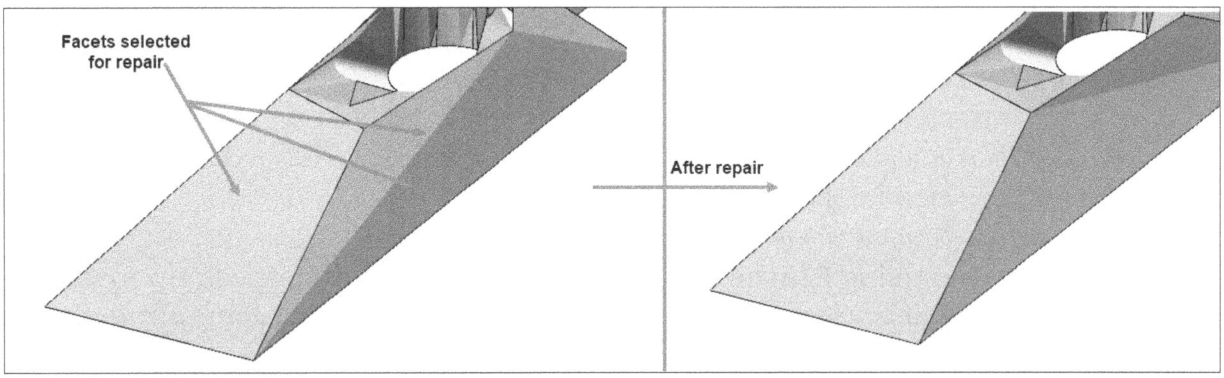

Figure-46. Repairing facets

TRIMMING MESH USING PLANAR ENTITY

The **Trim to Plane** tool is used to trim a mesh by using planar entity or a plane. Note that you will need a wireframe line along with intersecting mesh body to use this tool; refer to Figure-47. The procedure to use this tool is given next.

- Click on the **Trim to Plane** tool from the **Modify** group in the **Mesh** tab of the **Ribbon**. The **Trim to Plane Manager** will be displayed; refer to Figure-48.

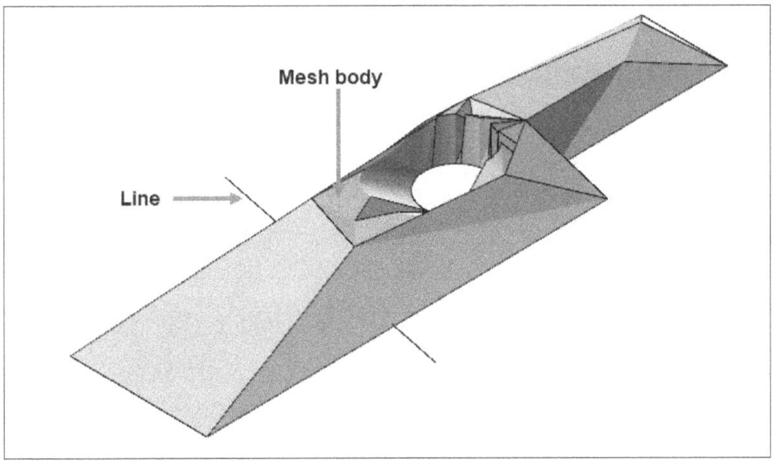

Figure-47. Geometry for mesh trim

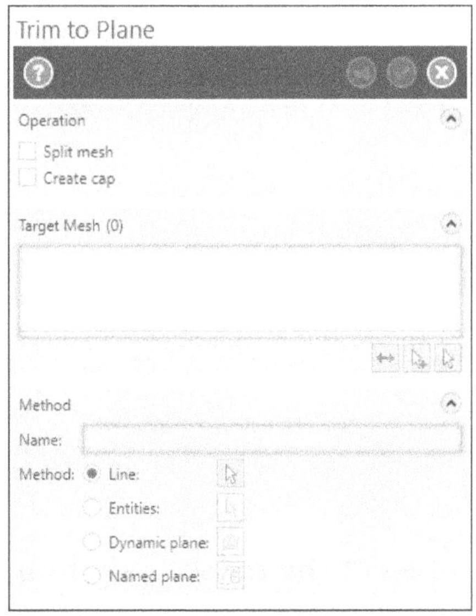

Figure-48. Trim to Plane Manager

- Select the mesh body to be trimmed from the graphics area. You will be asked to select line to be used for trimming plane.
- Select desired trim line. Preview of trimming will be displayed; refer to Figure-49.

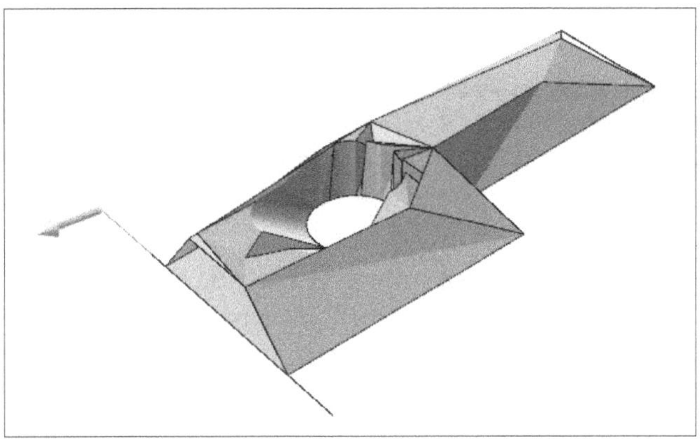

Figure-49. Preview of trimmed mesh body

- Select the **Split mesh** check box to split selected mesh body into two meshes using trimming tool.
- Select the **Create cap** check box to cap trimmed mesh body.
- By default, **Line** radio button is selected hence, the line is used as reference for trimming plane. Select other radio buttons from the **Method** rollout and modify trimming plane as desired.
- After setting desired parameters, click on the **OK** button from the **Manager**.

TRIMMING MESH USING SURFACE/SHEET OBJECT

The **Trim to Surface/Sheet** tool is used to trim selected mesh body by using a surface or sheet geometry as trimming tool. The procedure to use this tool is given next.

- Click on the **Trim to Surface/Sheet** tool from the **Modify** group in the **Mesh** tab of the **Ribbon**. The **Trim to Surface/Sheet Manager** will be displayed; refer to Figure-50.

Figure-50. Trim to Surface Sheet Manager

- Select the mesh body to be trimmed from the graphics area. You will be asked to select the trimming surface/sheet.
- Select an intersecting surface/sheet to be used as trimming tool. Preview of the trimmed body will be displayed.
- Click on the **Reverse all** button in **Target Meshes** rollout to flip the trimmed side of mesh.
- Specify other parameters as discussed earlier and click on the **OK** button.

TRIMMING MESH USING CURVE CHAIN

The **Trim to Chain** tool is used to trim a mesh body using wireframe curve chain. The procedure to use this tool is given next.

- Click on the **Trim to Chain** tool from the **Modify** group in the **Mesh** tab of the **Ribbon**. The **Trim to Chain Manager** will be displayed; refer to Figure-51 and you will be asked to select the mesh body.

Figure-51. Trim to Chain Manager

- Select desired mesh body and click on the **End Selection** button. The **Wireframe Chaining** selection box will be displayed and options in the **Manager** will become active.
- Select the **Split mesh** check box if you want to split the mesh body at intersection with curve chain.

- Select the **Create cap** check box if you want to close the open section of mesh body after trimming.
- Select desired curve chain(s) from graphics area and click on the **OK** button from **Wireframe Chaining** selection box. Preview of trim feature will be displayed; refer to Figure-52. Note that you can use open chain as well as closed chain curves for this tool.

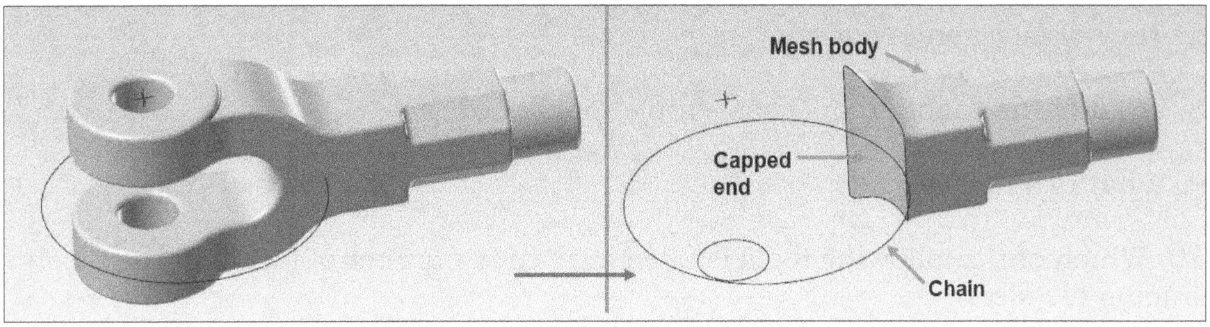

Figure-52. Preview of trim to chain

- Click on the **OK** button from the **Manager** to create feature.

CHECKING MESH QUALITY

The **Check Mesh** tool is used to check quality of mesh. The procedure to use this tool is given next.

- Click on the **Check Mesh** tool from the **Analyze** panel in **Mesh** tab of the **Ribbon**. The **Check Mesh Manager** will be displayed.
- Select the mesh body to be analyzed. Result of mesh analysis will be displayed in the **Manager**; refer to Figure-53. Based on results, you can modify the mesh body. Click on the **OK** button to exit Manager.

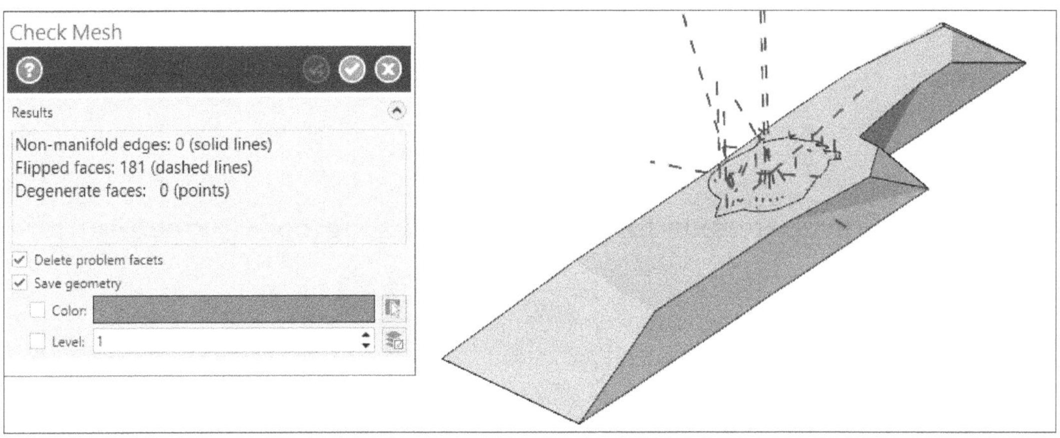

Figure-53. Check Mesh results

SELF-ASSESSMENT

Q1. What is the function of Hole Axis tool?

Q2. The .... tool is used to split selected faces of solid by using a geometry, flow lines, or UV lines.

Q3. The Modify Feature tool is used to create a body using selected feature or delete the feature. (T/F)

Q4. What is the benefit of removing history from the model?

Q5. What is the function of Add History tool?

Q6. What is the use of Simplify Solid tool?

Q7. The .... tool is used to repair the imported solid model by improving accuracy of faces and edges.

Q8. What is the function of Disassemble tool?

Q9. What is a mesh?

Q10. Which of the following tools is used to reduce number of facets in the mesh for reducing file size?

a. Decimation
b. Refine
c. Smooth Area
d. Explode Mesh

REVIEW QUESTIONS

Q1. What is the primary function of the Hole Axis tool?
A. Create fillets along edges
B. Create axis through circular holes
C. Create rectangular extrusions
D. Create chamfers on holes

Q2. Which option allows creation of axis for holes that are not fully closed?
A. Spot drill
B. Join coaxial
C. Allow split holes
D. Circles

Q3. To automatically create axis for all holes in a solid body, which button should be used?
A. Spot Drill
B. All Holes
C. Axis Lines
D. Points

Q4. What is the use of the Push-Pull tool?
A. Create new bodies
B. Move or edit selected faces directly
C. Mesh the geometry
D. Paint the model

Q5. Which checkbox in the Push-Pull Manager allows maintaining the original fillet radius?
A. Maintain source surfaces
B. Maintain fillet radius
C. Repair faces
D. Snap to AutoCursor positions

Q6. What does the Grow option in Push-Pull do?
A. Reduces the model size
B. Repairs surface geometry
C. Increases or decreases size during editing
D. Splits the model into sections

Q7. Which tool is used to split a face of solid using geometry?
A. Hole Axis
B. Push-Pull
C. Split Solid Faces
D. Modify Feature

Q8. What is the function of the Modify Feature tool?
A. Modify dimensions
B. Create mesh
C. Create/delete body using selected feature
D. Apply fillet

Q9. Which tool is used to change fillet radius in a model?
A. Modify Feature
B. Remove Fillet
C. Modify Fillet
D. Push-Pull

Q10. What is the function of the Remove Faces tool?
A. Change the surface color
B. Remove unwanted solid body
C. Remove selected faces from solid
D. Mesh the object

Q11. Which option fills the removed fillet face during Remove Fillets operation?
A. Join coaxial
B. Cap ends of fillets being removed
C. Maintain source surfaces
D. Copy

Q12. In Find Holes tool, which checkbox includes non-complete circular cuts?
A. Suppress fillets
B. Include Split Holes
C. Plugs
D. Hole Operations

Q13. What does the Remove History tool do?
A. Adds new operations
B. Highlights geometry
C. Removes model history
D. Saves file

Q14. Which tool is used to identify holes and fillets automatically and add history?
A. Optimize
B. Remove History
C. Add History
D. Disassemble

Q15. What is the function of the Simplify Solid tool?
A. Add mesh geometry
B. Repair large surfaces
C. Remove redundant faces and edges
D. Add design features

Q16. Which tool is used to improve face and edge accuracy of imported model?
A. Simplify Solid
B. Optimize
C. Push-Pull
D. Add History

Q17. Repair Small Faces tool is used to:
A. Split the model
B. Add radius to small edges
C. Join fragmented small faces
D. Delete small objects

Q18. What does the Disassemble tool do?
A. Break meshes into triangles
B. Separate solid bodies spatially
C. Remove outer edges
D. Add bounding box

Q19. In Align to Plane, which radio button aligns body to custom user WCS?
A. Transform to plane
B. Create WCS
C. Manual
D. Automatic

Q20. Which tool aligns one solid face to another solid's face?
A. Align to Z
B. Align to Plane
C. Align to Face
D. Solid Position

Q21. Align to Z tool is mostly used for:
A. Creating chamfer
B. Painting surface
C. Turning operations
D. Cutting surface

Q22. What is the use of Clear All tool from Color group?
A. Color selected edges
B. Change transparency
C. Remove all face colors
D. Apply textures

Q23. Which tool is used to apply new color to model faces?
A. Clear All
B. Change Face
C. Modify Feature
D. Face Align

Q24. What is mesh primarily composed of?
A. Cubic cells
B. Hexahedrons
C. Triangular cells
D. NURBS

Q25. Which tool is used to create a cylindrical mesh object?
A. Primitive Box
B. Cylinder from Solids
C. Cylinder (Mesh tab)
D. Extrude

Q26. What is the purpose of the Meshes from Entities tool?
A. Detect holes
B. Create fillets
C. Generate mesh from solids/surfaces
D. Paint model

Q27. Which option in Meshes from Entities retains the original object?
A. Delete
B. Keep
C. Snap
D. Add

Q28. What does the Offset Mesh tool do?
A. Offsets color of faces
B. Expands mesh geometry at set distance
C. Aligns mesh with curves
D. Smooths model

Q29. What is the primary function of Smooth Free Edges tool?
A. Create fillets
B. Remove edges
C. Smooth rough edges of mesh
D. Scale mesh model

Q30. What is the primary function of the Fill Holes tool in the Mesh tab?
A. Join two solid bodies
B. Fill holes in mesh body by joining boundary regions
C. Create new mesh from selected region
D. Add facets to mesh

Q31. Which radio button in the Fill Holes Manager allows modifying the original mesh body?
A. Copy
B. Join
C. Modify
D. Smooth

Q32. The Smooth Area tool is used to:
A. Refine curvature
B. Reduce mesh size
C. Smoothen selected region or mesh body
D. Add facets uniformly

Q33. What does the Brush radio button allow in Smooth Area tool?
A. Select faces by clicking individually
B. Select all facets automatically
C. Select multiple facets by dragging cursor
D. Erase selected mesh

Q34. Which smoothing option is used to maintain the shape during smoothening?
A. Minimize area
B. Average
C. Minimize curvature
D. Preserve curvature

Q35. What does the Refine tool do in mesh operations?
A. Removes facets
B. Adds more facets for better detail
C. Applies color
D. Closes mesh holes

Q36. What is the use of the Anisotropic option in the Refine tool?
A. Adds equal-sized facets everywhere
B. Applies mesh smoothing
C. Refines using different sized facets based on curvature
D. Combines two mesh bodies

Q37. In the Refine Manager, what does the Gamma value control?
A. Angle tolerance
B. Brush radius
C. Smoothening strength
D. Weighting factor for facet size

Q38. The Decimation tool is used to:
A. Duplicate the mesh
B. Reduce the number of mesh facets
C. Create mesh from solids
D. Explode mesh into separate parts

Q39. Which parameter in Decimation defines the allowable change in nearby facets?
A. Preservation angle
B. Reduction goal
C. Approximate facet shift
D. Curvature tolerance

Q40. The Explode Mesh tool is used to:
A. Combine two meshes
B. Remove mesh boundaries
C. Break complex mesh into simpler bodies
D. Offset mesh

Q41. What does a lower value of Flatness in Explode Mesh result in?
A. More curved bodies
B. Fewer mesh bodies
C. More mesh bodies
D. Uniform refinement

Q42. In Explode Mesh, what does the Merge percentage slider define?
A. Minimum angle to merge facets
B. Size below which a region is merged
C. Number of iterations for merge
D. Mesh color gradient

Q43. What operation does the Modify Mesh Facets tool support?
A. Adding shell
B. Creating, removing, or repairing mesh facets
C. Meshing solid
D. Mapping UV

Q44. Which radio button in Modify Mesh Facets is used to delete and fill holes in mesh?
A. Create mesh
B. Remove facets
C. Repair
D. Trim

Q45. What is the requirement for using Trim to Plane tool?
A. Circular hole
B. UV curve
C. A wireframe line intersecting mesh
D. Two solid bodies

Q46. What does the Split mesh checkbox do in trimming tools?
A. Joins mesh with solid
B. Splits mesh body into parts
C. Highlights facet boundaries
D. Reduces mesh file size

Q47. Which tool allows trimming mesh using a surface or sheet?
A. Trim to Plane
B. Trim to Chain
C. Trim to Surface/Sheet
D. Explode Mesh

Q48. What is the function of the Reverse all button in Trim to Surface/Sheet Manager?
A. Invert trimming curve
B. Flip the trimmed side of the mesh
C. Apply curvature smoothing
D. Restore deleted facets

Q49. What type of geometry is required for using the Trim to Chain tool?
A. Plane
B. Solid
C. Curve chain
D. Point cloud

Q50. Which checkbox in Trim to Chain allows closing open section of mesh after trimming?
A. Reverse all
B. Create cap
C. Auto connect
D. Join facets

Q51. What is the purpose of the Check Mesh tool?
A. Apply smoothing
B. Add mesh to solid
C. Evaluate mesh quality
D. Convert mesh to surface

Chapter 6

Drafting

Topics Covered

The major topics covered in this chapter are:

- ***Introduction to Drafting.***
- ***Creating Dimensions.***
- ***Creating Ordinate Dimensions.***
- ***Applying Annotations.***
- ***Regenerating and Modifying Dimensions.***

INTRODUCTION

Till this chapter, you have created various wireframe, surface, and solid objects. In this chapter, you will learn to apply various dimensions and coordinates to the model. The tools to apply dimension and annotations are available in the **Drafting** tab of the **Ribbon**; refer to Figure-1. Various tools of this tab are discussed next.

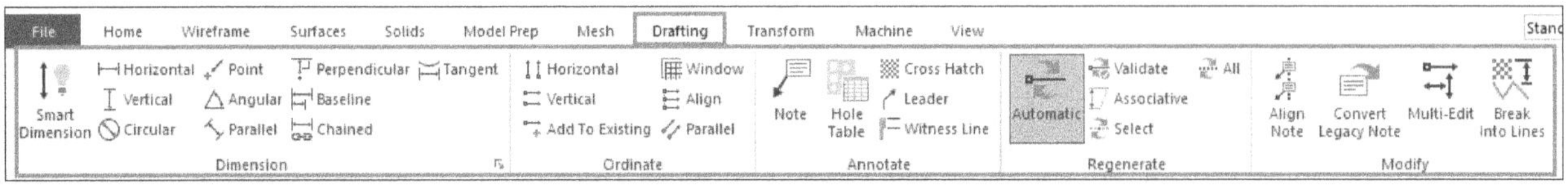

Figure-1. Drafting tab of Ribbon

SMART DIMENSIONING

The **Smart Dimension** tool is used to apply different type of dimensions to entities of the model. The procedure to use this tool is given next.

- Click on the **Smart Dimension** tool from the **Dimension** group in the **Drafting** tab of the **Ribbon**. The **Drafting Manager** will be displayed; refer to Figure-2.

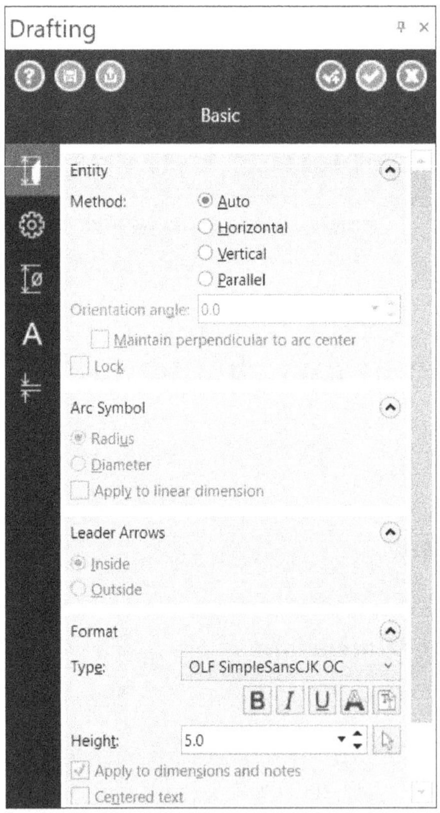

Figure-2. Drafting Manager

- Select desired radio button from the **Method** section to what type of dimensions are to be applied. Select the **Auto** radio button to automatically select whether you are creating horizontal dimension, vertical dimension, or parallel dimension. Select the **Horizontal** radio button to create a horizontal dimension between two selected points or horizontal length of selected line/edge. Select the **Vertical** radio button to create a vertical dimension between two selected points or vertical length of selected line/edge. Select the **Parallel** radio button to create an aligned dimension between two points.

- After selecting desired radio button from the **Method** section, select two points to be dimensioned. The dimension will get attached to cursor and various options will become active in the **Manager**; refer to Figure-3.

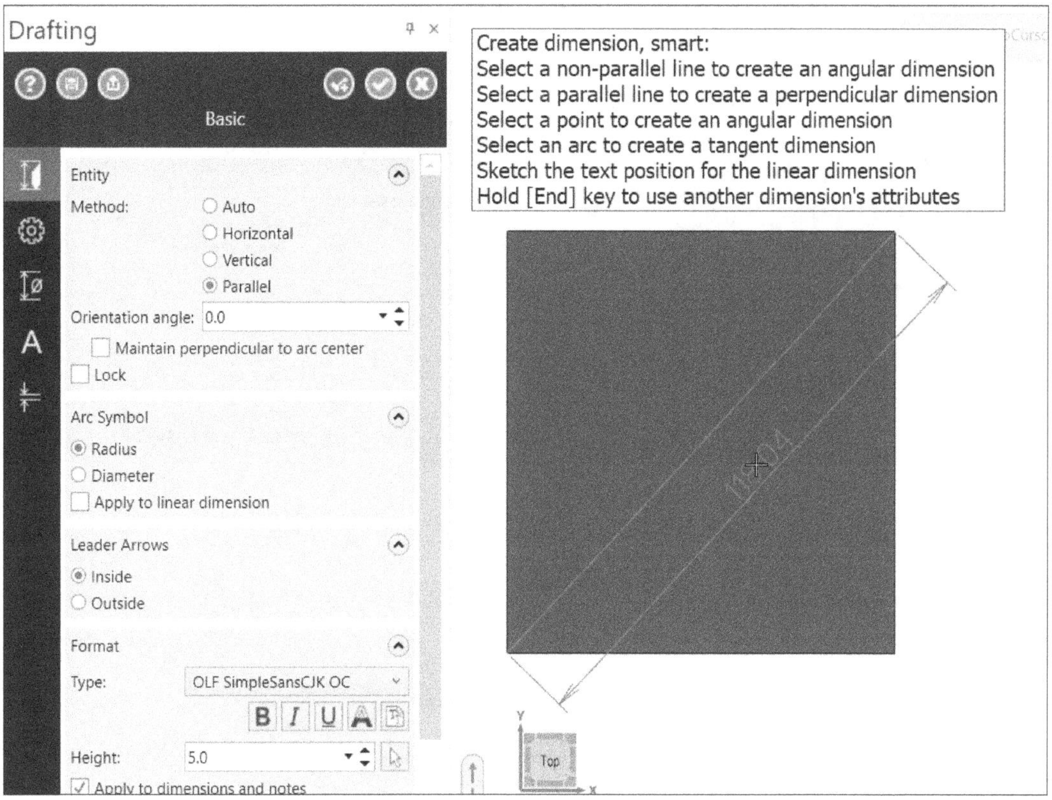

Figure-3. Dimensions attached to cursor

- Set desired angle value in the **Orientation angle** edit box to orient the dimension line at specified angle.
- Select the **Maintain perpendicular to arc center** check box to keep aligned dimension perpendicular to arc center.
- Select the **Lock** check box to lock orientation and location of dimensions.
- Select the **Radius** radio button from the **Arc Symbol** rollout to create a radius dimension between two selected points. Select the **Diameter** radio button from the rollout if you want to create diameter dimension between two points. If you want to apply arc dimensions to linear objects as well then select the **Apply to linear dimension** check box from the rollout.
- Select desired radio button from the **Leader Arrows** rollout to specify the position of leader arrows in dimension. Select the **Inside** radio button to keep arrows inside the witness lines. Select the **Outside** radio button to keep arrows outside the witness lines; refer to Figure-4.
- Select desired font for dimensions from the drop-down in the **Format** rollout. Click on the **Bold**, **Italic**, **Underline**, and **Filled** buttons to change the text style in dimension, accordingly. Click on the **TrueType Font** button from the rollout if desired font is not in the drop-down. The **Font** dialog box will be displayed; refer to Figure-5. Select desired font from the dialog box and click on the **OK** button. The selected font will be added in the drop-down.
- Set desired value in the **Height** edit box to define size of dimension.
- Select the **Apply to dimensions and notes** check box from **Format** rollout to apply the modified dimension format to all the new dimensions and notes as default.

- Select the **Centered text** check box to make the dimension text centered on dimension line.
- Set desired value in the **Decimal places** edit box to define up to how many decimal places, the dimension value will be displayed.

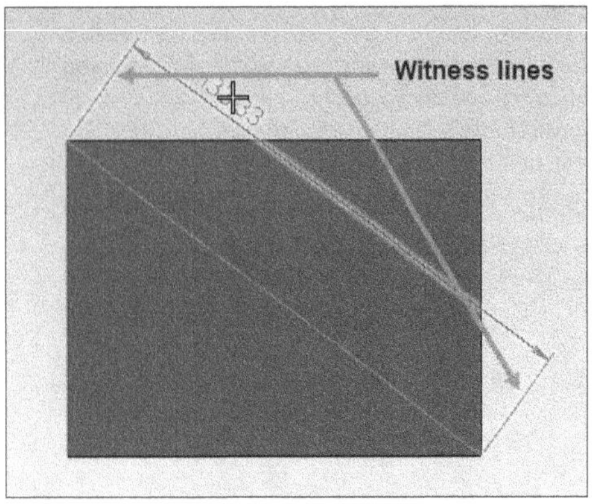

Figure-4. Witness lines in dimension

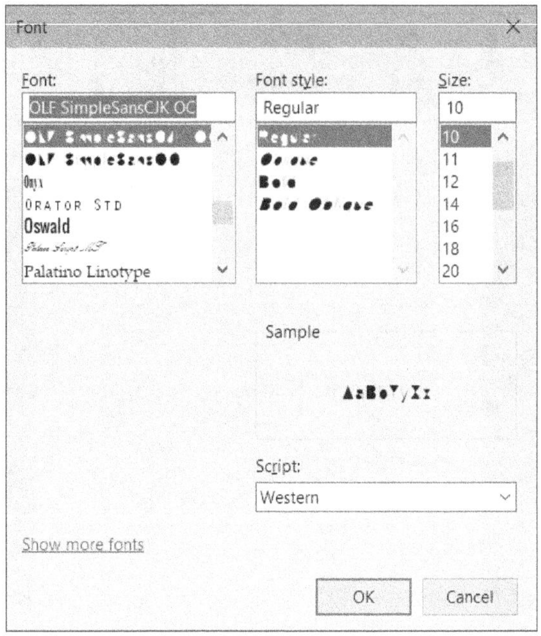

Figure-5. Font dialog box

- Click on the **Show More Options** button at the bottom in **Manager** to expand the **Manager**; refer to Figure-6.

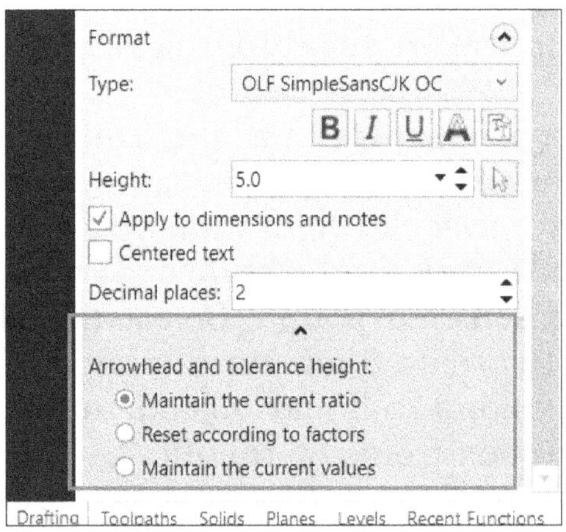

Figure-6. Expanded Manager

- Select the **Maintain the current ratio** radio button if you want to change arrowhead and tolerance height values in same proportion to change in dimension text height value.
- Select the **Reset according to factors** radio button to reset the ratio of change in the height of arrowhead and tolerance text to change in dimension text height.
- Select the **Maintain the current values** radio button to keep the height of arrowhead and tolerance text fixed to current value.
- Click on the **Advanced** option from left side in the **Drafting Manager** to change the value or location of dimension; refer to Figure-7.

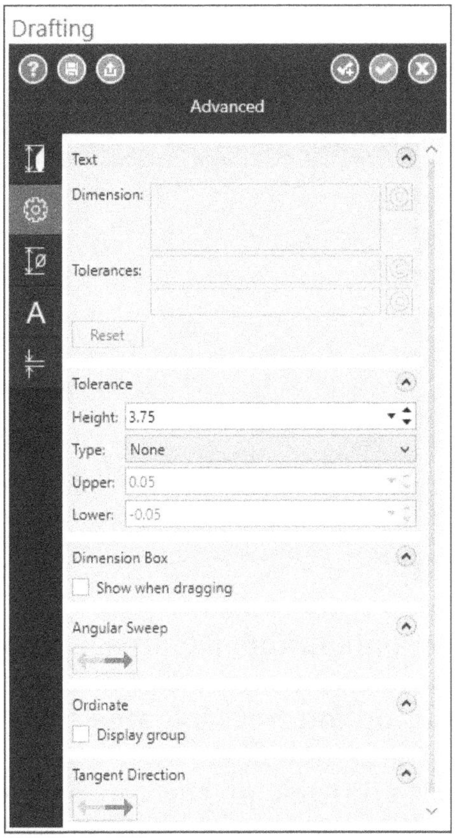

Figure-7. Advanced tab of Drafting Manager

- Specify desired value of dimension in the **Dimension** edit box. Similarly, you can specify tolerance limits in respective edit boxes of **Text** rollout.
- Select the **Show when dragging** check box to show a box around the dimension while moving it.
- Click on the button from the **Angular Sweep** rollout to flip direction of angular dimension.
- If you have created ordinate dimensions then **Display group** check box in **Ordinate** rollout will become active. Select this button to group ordinate dimensions together.
- Click on the **Tangent Direction** button in the **Tangent Direction** rollout to flip direction of tangency for dimension.
- Click on the **Dimension Attributes** option from the left area in the **Manager** to modify attributes of dimension like format, scale, symbols, and so on; refer to Figure-8.
- Select desired option from the **Format** drop-down to define whether you want to display dimensions in decimal format, Scientific format, Engineering format, Fractional, or Architectural format.
- Similarly, set the fractional unit for selected format in the **Fractional units** drop-down and parameters related to symbols in the drop-downs of **Symbols** rollout.

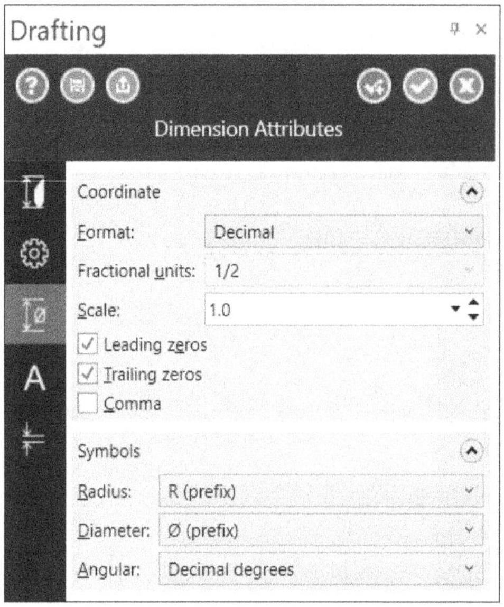

Figure-8. Dimension Attributes page

- Click on the **Dimension Text** option from left area in the **Manager** to tweak character space, alignment, direction, and so on for the dimension text.
- Select the **Leaders/Witness** option from left area in the **Manager** to change leader style and witness lines of the dimension.
- Click on the **Save Defaults** button at the top in the **Manager** to save current specified settings as default for next models to be created.
- Click on the **Load Defaults** button from the top in the **Manager** to load earlier saved default settings.
- After setting desired parameters, click on the **OK** button from the **Drafting Manager**.

APPLYING HORIZONTAL DIMENSION

The **Horizontal** tool of **Dimension** group in the **Manager** is used to create horizontal dimension between two points. The procedure to use this tool is given next.

- Click on the **Horizontal** tool from the **Dimension** group in the **Drafting** tab of the **Ribbon**. The **Drafting Manager** will be displayed as discussed earlier.
- Select two points of the model. The horizontal dimension will get attached to cursor; refer to Figure-9.

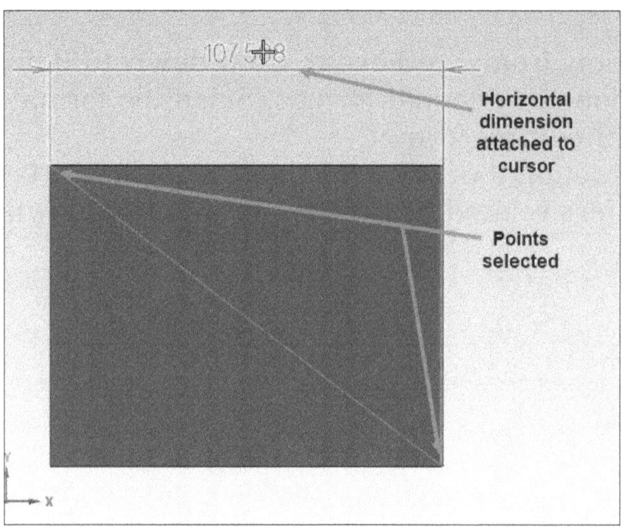

Figure-9. Creating horizontal dimension

- Specify the parameters as discussed earlier in the **Manager** and click at desired location to place the dimension.
- Click on the **OK** button from the **Manager** to exit the tool.

CREATING VERTICAL DIMENSION

The **Vertical** tool is used to create a vertical dimension between two selected points. The procedure to use this tool is given next.

- Click on the **Vertical** tool from the **Dimension** group of **Drafting** tab in the **Ribbon**. The **Drafting Manager** will be displayed and you will be asked to select two points for dimensioning.
- Select desired points. The vertical dimension will get attached to cursor; refer to Figure-10.
- Set the parameters as desired and click at desired location to place the dimension.
- Click on the **OK** button from the **Manager** to exit the tool.

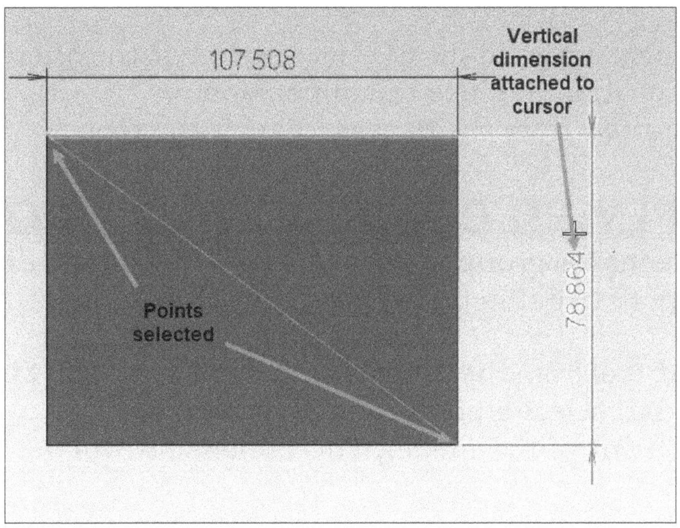

Figure-10. Creating vertical dimension

APPLYING CIRCULAR DIMENSION

The **Circular** tool is used to apply diameter or radius dimension to arcs and circles. The procedure to use this tool is given next.

- Click on the **Circular** tool from the **Dimension** group in the **Drafting** tab of the **Ribbon**. The **Drafting Manager** will be displayed and you will be asked to select circular curve/edge in the model.
- Select desired circular curve/edge. The dimension will get attached to cursor; refer to Figure-11.

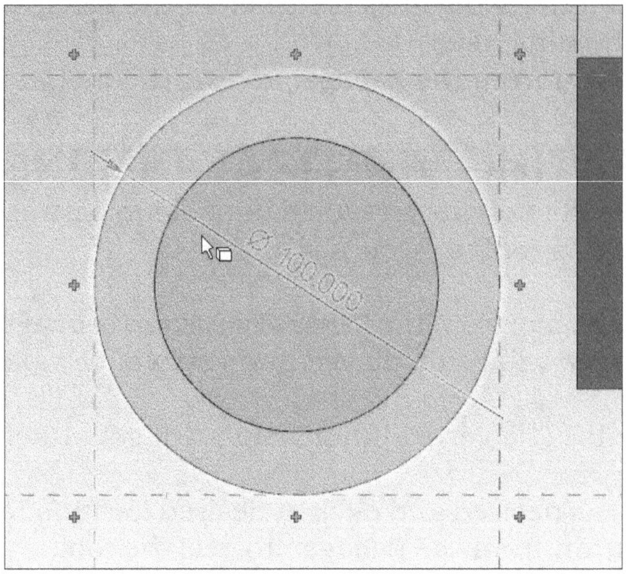

Figure-11. Diameter dimension attached to cursor

- Move the cursor near **+** sign in the 3D view to change the orientation of dimension.
- Click at desired location to place the dimension.
- Click on the **OK** button from the **Manager** to exit the tool.

APPLYING DIMENSION TO A POINT

The **Point** tool in **Dimension** group is used to apply coordinate dimension to selected point. The procedure to use this tool is given next.

- Click on the **Point** tool from the **Dimension** group in the **Drafting** tab of the **Ribbon**. You will be asked to select a point to be dimensioned.
- Click at desired point of the model. The dimension will get attached to cursor; refer to Figure-12.

Figure-12. Point dimension created

- Click at desired location to place the dimension. Press **ESC** twice to exit the tool.

APPLYING ANGULAR DIMENSION

The **Angular** tool in **Dimension** group is used to create angle dimension between two lines/edges using three points. The procedure to use this tool is given next.

- Click on the **Angular** tool from the **Dimension** group in the **Drafting** tab of the **Ribbon**. You will be asked to select three points for creating angle dimension.

- Click at desired location to specify the center point of angle dimension and then click at two end points of lines/edges to be dimensioned by angle. The preview of angle dimension will be displayed; refer to Figure-13.

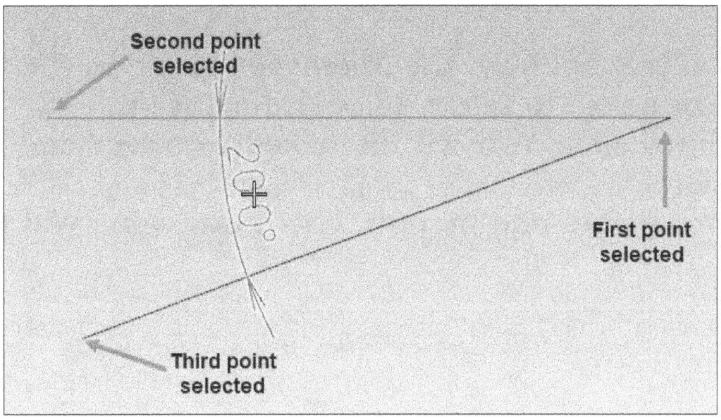

Figure-13. Preview of angle dimension

- Click at desired side of lines/edges to place the dimension.
- Click on the **OK** button from the **Manager** to exit the tool.

The procedure to use **Parallel** tool has been discussed earlier.

APPLYING PERPENDICULAR DIMENSION

The **Perpendicular** tool is used to create perpendicular dimension between two lines. The procedure to use this tool is given next.

- Click on the **Perpendicular** tool from the **Dimension** group in the **Drafting** tab of the **Ribbon**. You will be asked to select the lines to be dimensioned.
- Select the first line and then second line/point parallel to first line. The dimension will get attached to cursor; refer to Figure-14.

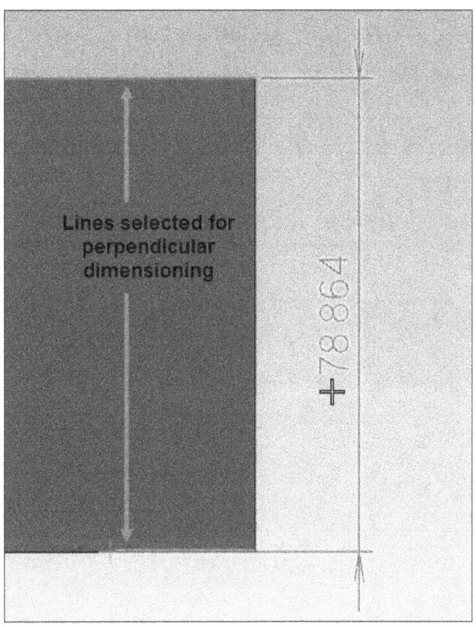

Figure-14. Perpendicular dimension attached to cursor

- Click at desired location to place the dimension. Click on the **OK** button from the **Manager** to exit the tool.

CREATING BASELINE DIMENSION

The **Baseline** tool is used to create linear dimension in reference to selected base dimension. The procedure to use this tool is given next.

- Click on the **Baseline** tool from the **Dimension** group in the **Drafting** tab of the **Ribbon**. You will be asked to select a linear dimension.
- Select desired dimension. You will be asked to select end points for creating baseline dimensions.
- Select desired end points one by one. The dimensions will be created; refer to Figure-15.

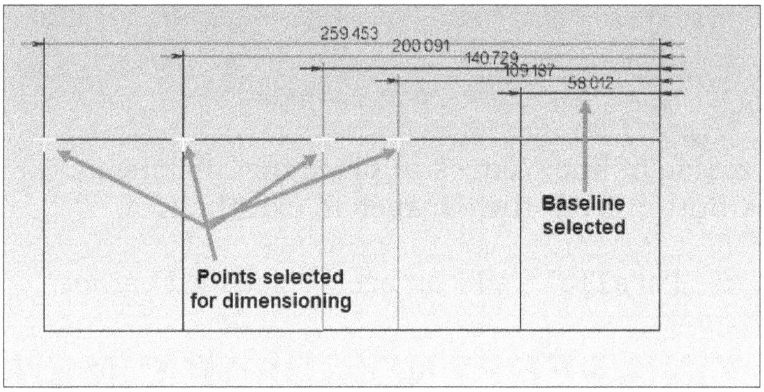

Figure-15. Baseline dimensions created

- After creating dimensions, press **ESC** twice to exit the tool.

CREATING CHAINED DIMENSION

The **Chained** tool is used to create dimensions in the form of a chain with one end point of dimension connected to another. The procedure to use this tool is given next.

- Click on the **Chained** tool from the **Dimension** group in the **Drafting** tab of the **Ribbon**. You will be asked to select a linear dimension as reference for chained dimensions.
- Select desired linear dimension. You will be asked to select end points of lines in chain to create dimensions.
- Select desired end points of lines. The chained dimensions will be created; refer to Figure-16.

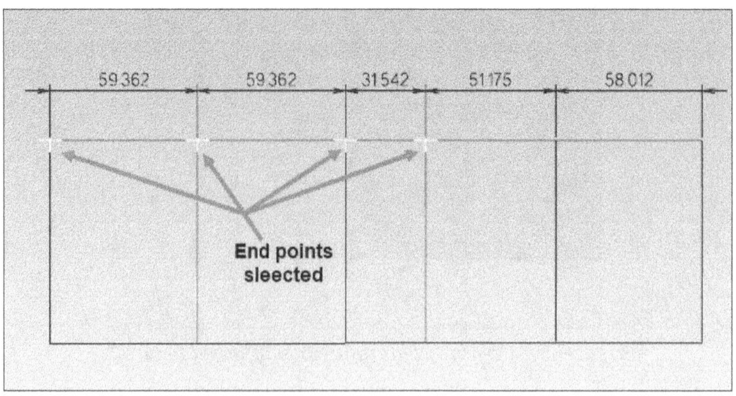

Figure-16. Preview of chained dimensions

- After creating dimensions, press **ESC** twice to exit the tool.

CREATING TANGENT DIMENSION

The **Tangent** tool is used to create dimension between tangency point of an arc or circle and linear/circular objects. The procedure to use this tool is given next.

- Click on the **Tangent** tool from the **Dimension** group in the **Drafting** tab of the **Ribbon**. You will be asked to select linear/circular entities.
- Select desired two entities. The dimension will get attached to cursor; refer to Figure-17.

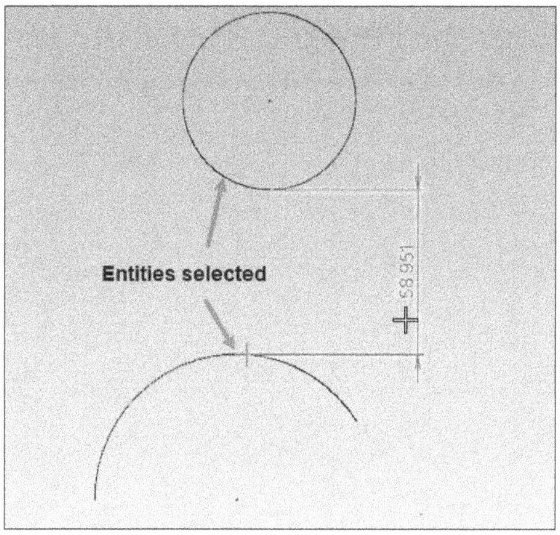

Figure-17. Tangent dimension attached to cursor

- Click at desired location to place the dimension. Press **ESC** twice to exit the tool.

CREATING HORIZONTAL ORDINATE DIMENSION

The **Horizontal** tool in **Ordinate** group is used to create horizontal ordinate dimensions. The procedure to use this tool is given next.

- Click on the **Horizontal** tool from the **Ordinate** group in the **Drafting** tab of the **Ribbon**. You will be asked to select a point on the object to define **0** horizontal point.
- Click at desired location to specify first ordinate point and then click at desired location to place the dimension. You will be asked to specify next points for ordinate dimensioning.
- Click on the next points for dimensioning and place them; refer to Figure-18.

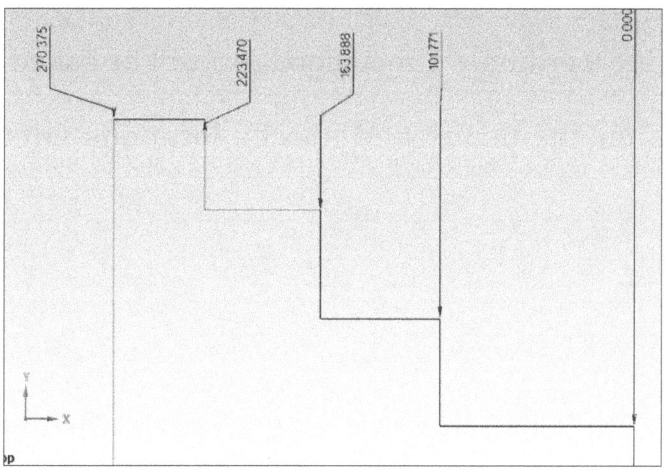

Figure-18. Ordinate dimensions created

- Click on the **OK** button from the **Manager** to create the dimensions.

CREATING VERTICAL ORDINATE DIMENSION

The **Vertical** tool is used to create vertical ordinate dimensions with respect to 0 ordinate dimension. The procedure to use this tool is given next.

- Click on the **Vertical** tool from the **Ordinate** group in the **Drafting** tab of the **Ribbon**. You will be asked to specify vertical **0** ordinate point for dimensioning.
- Click on desired point and specify the location of **0** ordinate dimension. You will be asked to specify other points for dimensioning.
- One by one click on the other points and place the dimensions; refer to Figure-19.
- Click on the **OK** button from the **Manager** to exit the tool.

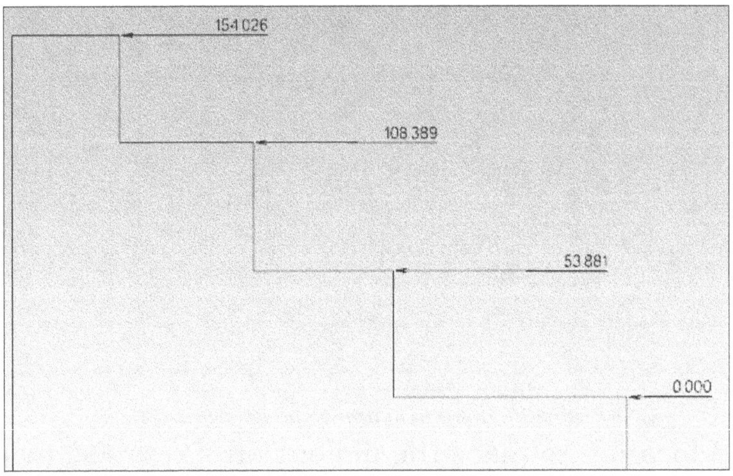

Figure-19. Creating vertical ordinate dimensions

ADDING ORDINATE DIMENSIONS TO EXISTING ORDINATE DIMENSION

The **Add To Existing** tool is used to create ordinate dimensions using existing 0 ordinate reference. The procedure to use this tool is given next.

- Click on the **Add To Existing** tool from the **Ordinate** group in the **Drafting** tab of the **Ribbon**. The **Drafting Manager** will be displayed.
- Select the **Vertical** radio button from the **Manager** if you want to create vertical ordinate dimension and select the **Horizontal** radio button to create horizontal ordinate dimension.
- Click on the existing **0** ordinate dimension. You will be asked to select next points for dimensioning.
- One by one click on the points and specify locations for dimensions; refer to Figure-20.

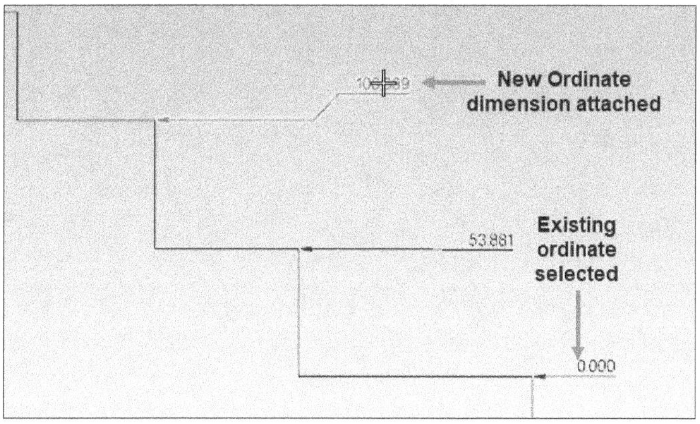

Figure-20. Creating ordinate dimensions

- After setting desired parameters, click on the **OK** button from the **Manager** to exit the tool.

CREATING MULTIPLE SETS OF ORDINATE DIMENSIONS

The **Window** tool is used to create a set of horizontal and vertical ordinates for points of model in window selection. The procedure to use this tool is given next.

- Click on the **Window** tool from the **Ordinate** group in the **Drafting** tab of the **Ribbon**. The **Ordinate Dimension: Automatic** dialog box will be displayed; refer to Figure-21.

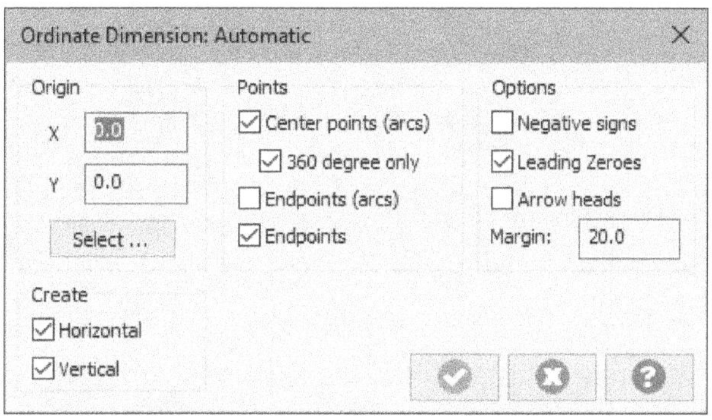

Figure-21. Ordinate Dimension: Automatic dialog box

- Click on the **Select** button from the **Origin** area of dialog box to specify origin point for ordinate dimensioning and click at desired location. All the dimensions will be created with respect to origin point.
- Set the other parameters as desired in the dialog box and click on the **OK** button. You will be asked to create a window or polygon for selecting points.
- Select the entities using window selection. The dimensions will be created; refer to Figure-22.

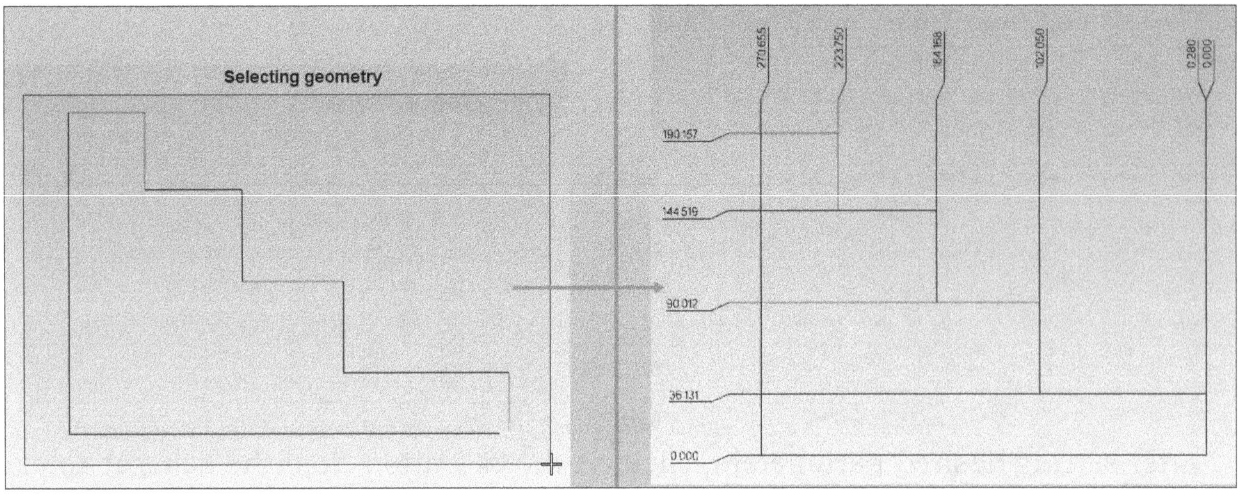

Figure-22. Ordinate window dimensioning

- Press **ESC** to exit the tool.

ALIGNING ORDINATE DIMENSIONS

The **Align** tool is used to align selected ordinate dimensions to a common axis. The procedure to use this tool is given next.

- Click on the **Align** tool from the **Ordinate** group in the **Drafting** tab of the **Ribbon**. You will be asked to select an ordinate dimension.
- Select desired ordinate dimension. The dimension will get attached to cursor.
- Click at desired locations to place the dimensions; refer to Figure-23.

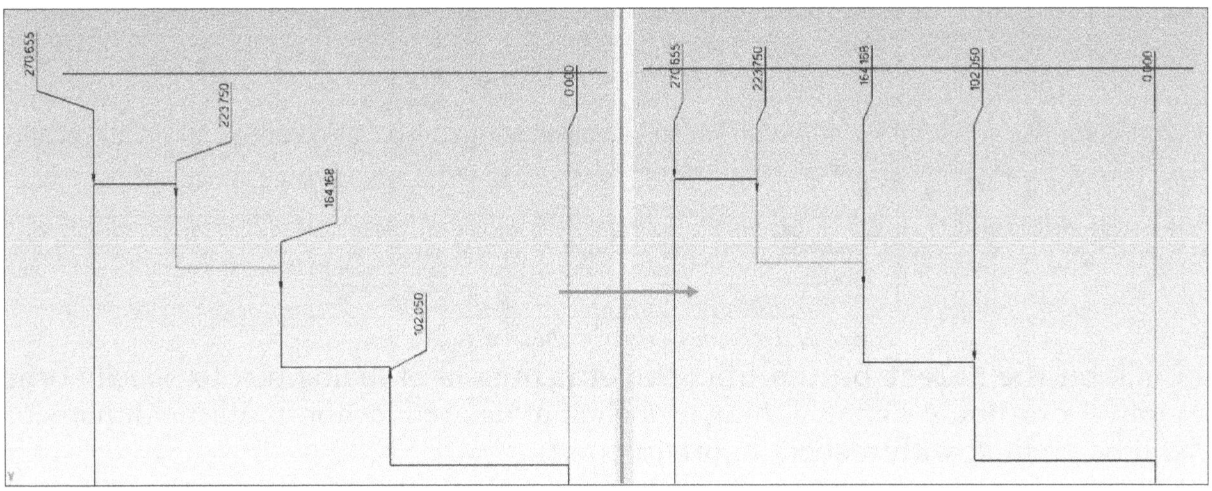

Figure-23. Dimensions after aligning

Similarly, you can use the **Parallel** ordinate dimensioning tool of **Ordinate** group in the **Drafting** tab of **Ribbon** to create ordinate dimensions.

CREATING NOTE ANNOTATIONS

The **Note** tool is used to add a text annotation in the 3D view. The procedure to use this tool is given next.

- Click on the **Note** tool from the **Annotate** group in the **Drafting** tab of **Ribbon**. The **Note Manager** will be displayed; refer to Figure-24.

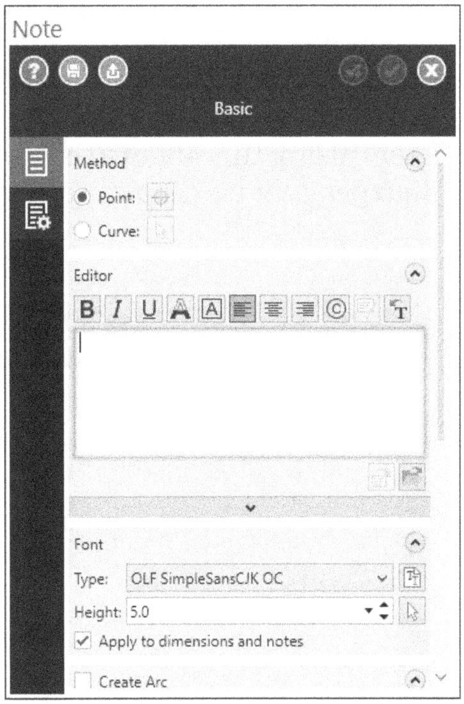

Figure-24. Note Manager

- Select the **Point** radio button to place note text at desired location. Select the **Curve** radio button from the **Manager** to place note text over selected curve.
- Click in the edit box of **Editor** rollout and specify desired text. If you have selected the **Point** radio button then the text will be attached to cursor. If you have selected the **Curve** radio button then you will be asked to select curve.
- Click on desired curve or click at desired location to place the text; refer to Figure-25.

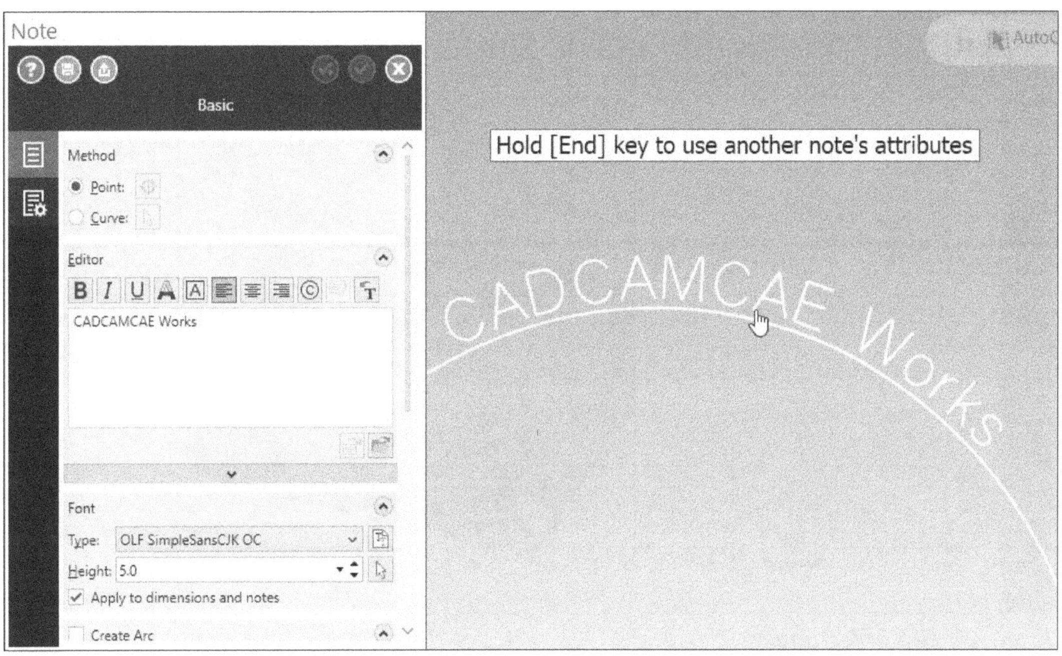

Figure-25. Text placed on curve

- Set the other parameters as desired in the **Manager** and click on the **OK** button.

CREATING HOLE TABLES

The **Hole Table** tool is used to create a table of information about various holes in the model. The procedure to use this tool is given next.

- Click on the **Hole Table** tool from the **Annotate** group of **Drafting** tab in the **Ribbon**. The **Hole Table Manager** will be displayed; refer to Figure-26.

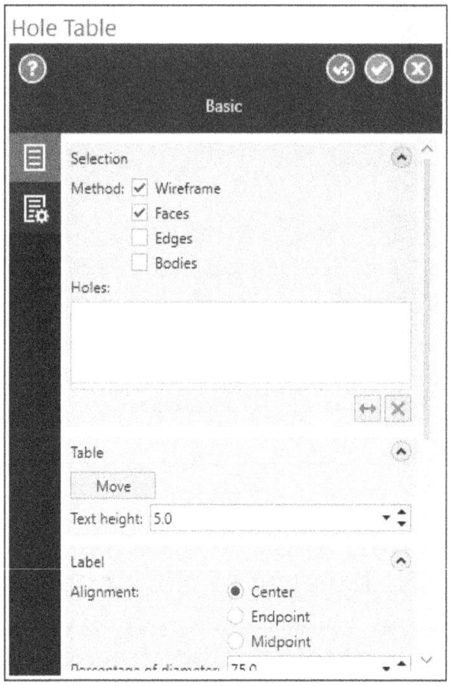

Figure-26. Hole Table Manager

- Select desired check boxes from the **Method** section of **Manager** to define the objects from which holes will be identified for table.
- Select the face, edge, wireframe, or body. A table of holes will be generated; refer to Figure-27.

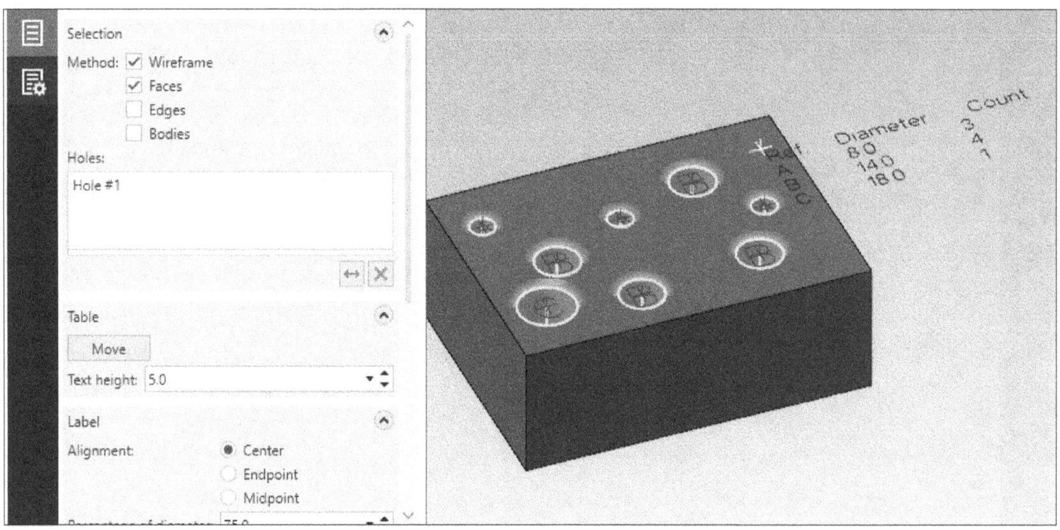

Figure-27. Hole table generated

- Click on the **Move** button from the **Table** rollout to change location of table and click at desired location to place the table.

- Click on the **Create** button from the **Active Reports** rollout of **Manager** to generate a report. The **ActiveReports Viewer** application will be displayed with report of holes; refer to Figure-28. Save the report or print them as desired. Exit the application after generating the reports.

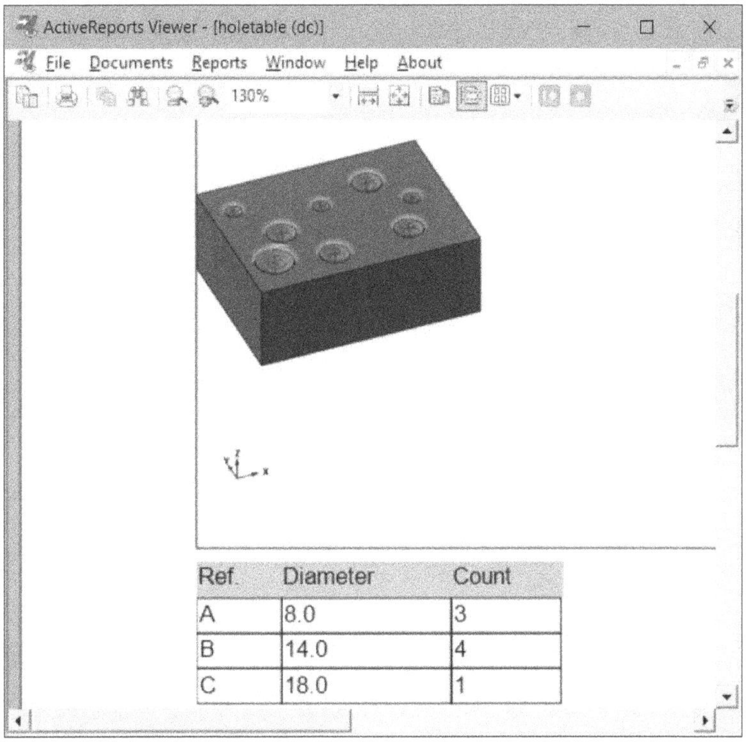

Figure-28. ActiveReports Viewer

- Set the other parameters as desired in the **Manager** and click on the **OK** button to exit the tool.

CREATING CROSS HATCH

The **Cross Hatch** tool is used to create hatching inside closed boundary of wireframe. The procedure to use this tool is given next.

- Click on the **Cross Hatch** tool from the **Annotate** group in the **Drafting** tab of the **Ribbon**. The **Cross Hatch Manager** will be displayed with **Wireframe Chaining** selection box; refer to Figure-29.

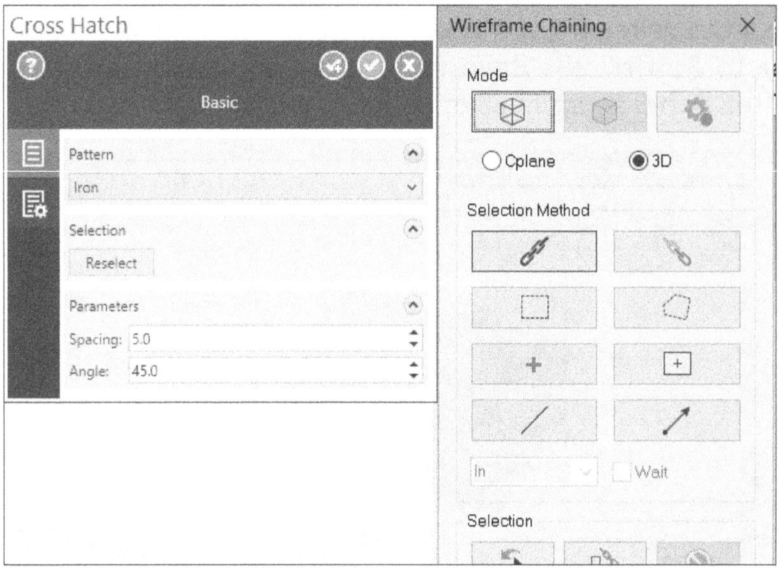

Figure-29. Cross Hatch Manager with Wireframe Chaining selection box

- Select the wireframe entities forming a closed region and click on the **OK** button from the **Wireframe Chaining** selection box. Preview of cross hatching will be displayed; refer to Figure-30.

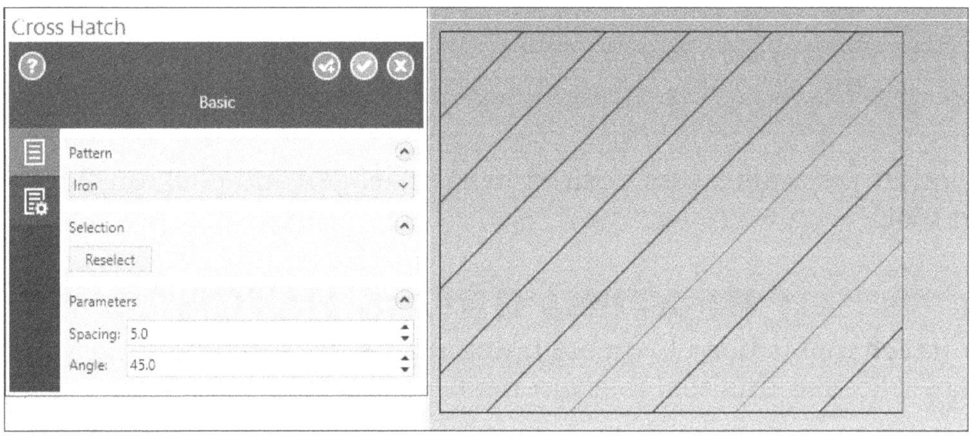

Figure-30. Preview of cross hatch

- Select desired option from the **Pattern** drop-down in the **Manager** to define pattern style.
- Set the other parameters as desired and click on the **OK** button from the **Manager** to apply hatching.

CREATING LEADER AND WITNESS LINES

The leaders are used to mark various notes and objects in the 3D view. The witness lines are used to create guidelines for dimensions. The procedures to create leaders and witness lines are given next.

Creating Leader

- Click on the **Leader** tool from the **Annotate** group in the **Drafting** tab of the **Ribbon**. The **Leader Manager** will be displayed; refer to Figure-31.

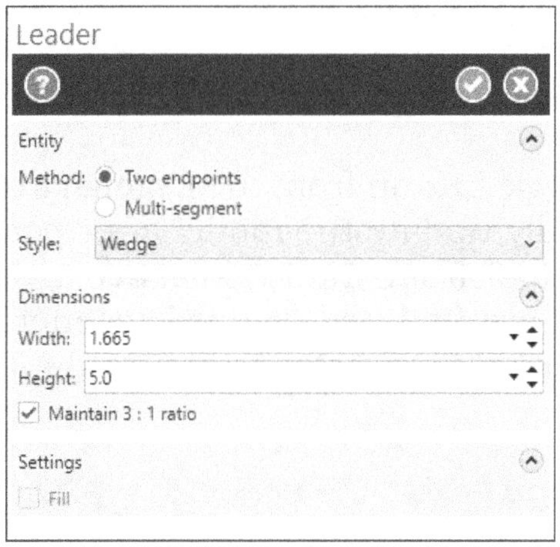

Figure-31. Leader Manager

- Select the **Two endpoints** radio button to create leader by specifying start point and end points. Select the **Multi-segment** radio button to create leader with tail.
- Select desired option from the **Style** drop-down in **Manager** to define shape of leader arrowhead.
- Set the height and width of arrow in the **Dimensions** rollout.
- Click at desired locations in 3D view to specify points for leader. The leader will be created; refer to Figure-32.

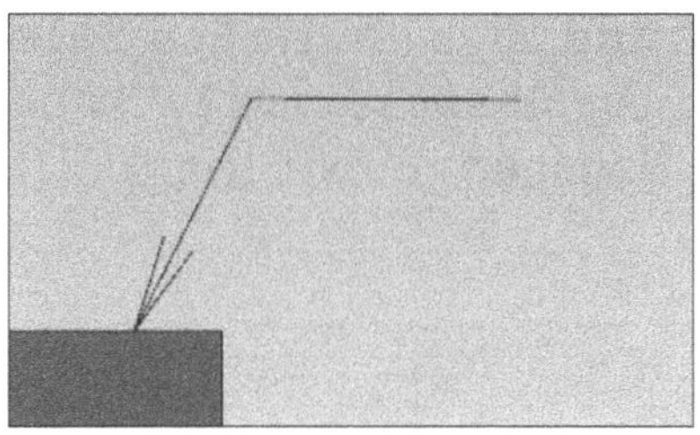

Figure-32. Leader created

- Click on the **OK** button from the **Manager** to exit the tool.

Creating Witness Lines

- Click on the **Witness Line** tool from the **Annotate** group in the **Drafting** tab of the **Ribbon**. You will be asked to specify first point of witness line.
- Click at desired location to specify first point and second point of witness lines; refer to Figure-33. Press **ESC** to exit the tool.

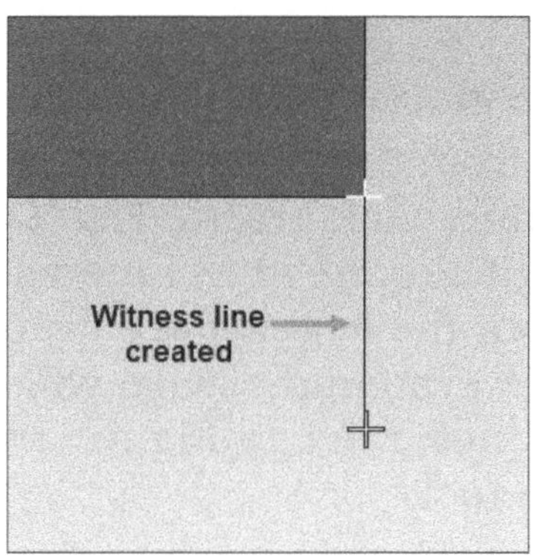

Figure-33. Witness line created

REGENERATE TOOLS

The tools in the **Regenerate** group are used to regenerate the drafting entities after modification. Various tools in this group are discussed next.

- Select the **Automatic** toggle button from the **Regenerate** group in the **Drafting** tab of **Ribbon** to automatically update the model after performing changes.
- Click on the **Validate** tool from the **Regenerate** group in the **Ribbon** to check whether all the entities are updated or need regeneration. The **System Message** information box will be displayed; refer to Figure-34. Click on the **OK** button from the information box.

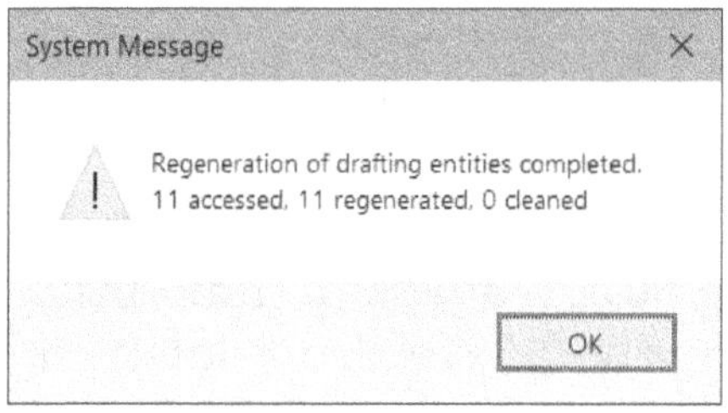

Figure-34. System Message information box

- Click on the **Associative** tool from the **Regenerate** group of **Drafting** tab in the **Ribbon**. You will be asked to select drafting entities to check their association. Select desired draft entities and click on the **End Selection** button. The association status will be displayed in the **Associativity Manager**; refer to Figure-35. Click on the **OK** button from the **Manager** to exit the tool.

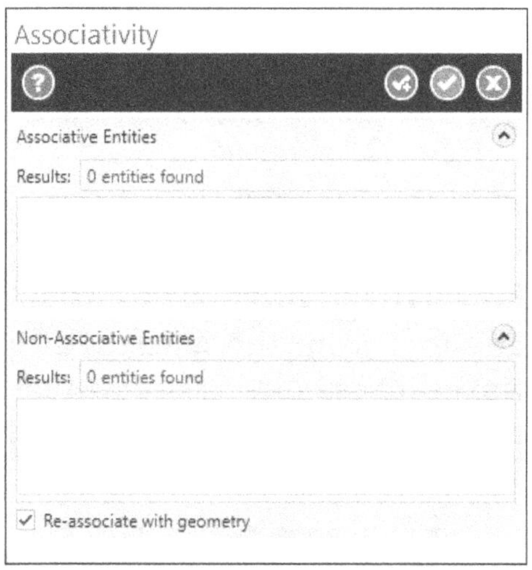

Figure-35. Associativity Manager

- Click on the **Select** button from the **Regenerate** group in the **Ribbon** to select the entities to be regenerated and click on the **End Selection** button to regenerate draft entities based on modifications in the model.
- Click on the **All** button from the **Regenerate** group in **Ribbon** to check if all the draft entities are updated. A system message will be displayed showing whether regeneration is required or not; refer to Figure-36. Click on the **OK** button from the message box to exit the tool.

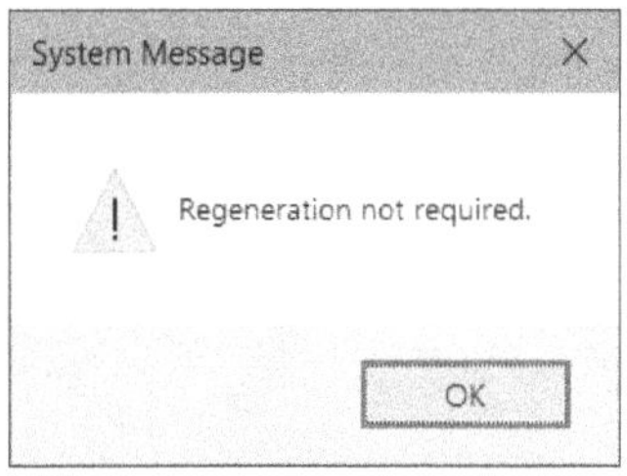

Figure-36. Regeneration system message

ALIGNING NOTES

The **Align Note** tool is used to align selected notes horizontally or vertically. The procedure to use this tool is given next.

- Click on the **Align Note** tool from the **Modify** group in the **Drafting** tab of the **Ribbon**. You will be asked to select the notes and labels to be aligned.
- Select desired notes/labels and click on the **End Selection** button. The options of the **Align Note Manager** will be active.
- Select desired radio button from the **Manager** to define how the notes will be aligned.
- Select desired note from the 3D view to be used as reference note. The notes will be aligned automatically; refer to Figure-37.

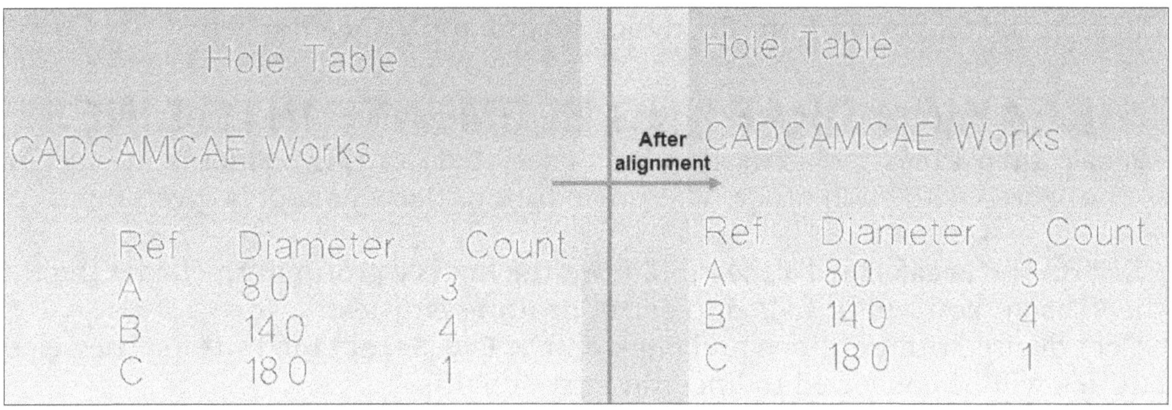

Figure-37. Aligning notes

CONVERTING LEGACY NOTES

The **Convert Legacy Note** tool is used to convert selected notes created in Mastercam 2020 or earlier version to current format. Select the notes and click on this tool from **Modify** group in **Drafting** tab of **Ribbon** to perform the action.

EDITING PARAMETERS OF DRAFT ENTITIES

The **Multi-Edit** tool is used to modify parameters of selected draft entities. The procedure to use this tool is given next.

- Click on the **Multi-Edit** tool from the **Modify** group in the **Drafting** tab of the **Ribbon**. You will be asked to select the draft entities for editing parameters.
- Select desired entities and click on the **End Selection** button. The **Drafting Options** dialog box will be displayed; refer to Figure-38.

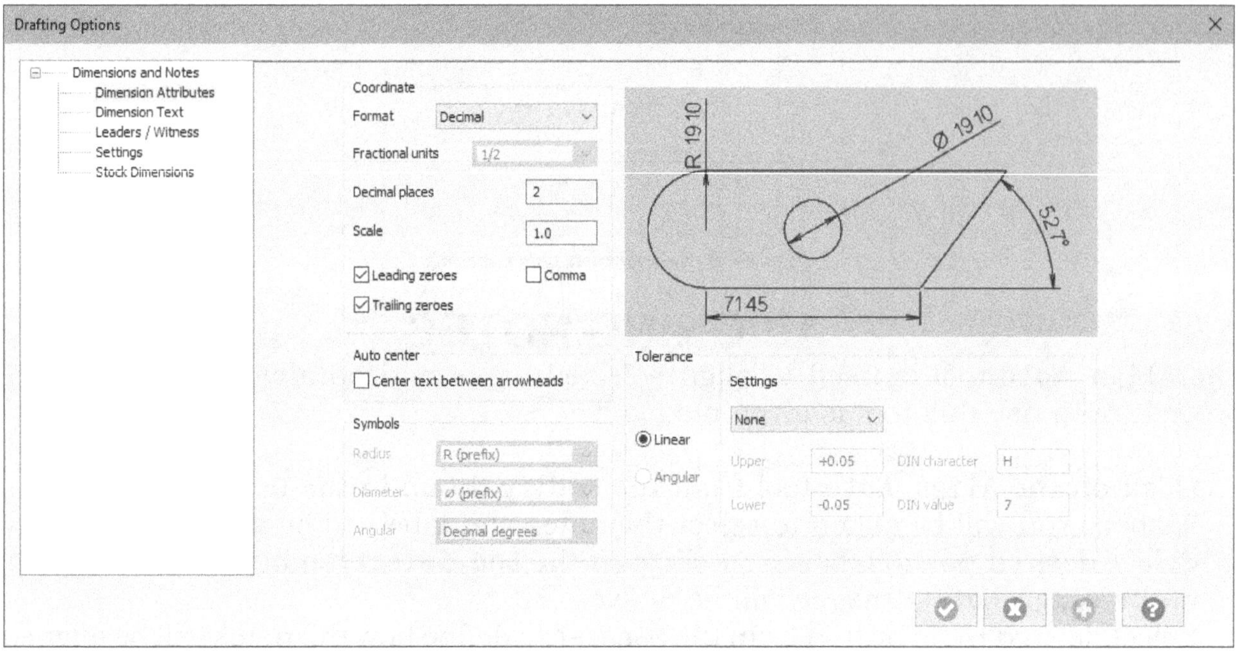

Figure-38. Drafting Options dialog box

- Select desired drafting element from the left box in the dialog box and specify related parameters in the dialog box as discussed earlier.
- Click on the **OK** button from the dialog box to apply the changes.

BREAKING DRAFTING ELEMENTS INTO LINES

The **Break Into Lines** tool is used to break selected drafting elements into separate lines connected with each other. The procedure to use this tool is given next.

- Click on the **Break Into Lines** tool from the **Modify** group in the **Drafting** tab of the **Ribbon**. You will be asked to select drafting entities.
- Select desired draft entities and click on the **End Selection** button. The selected entities will be converted to line and curve chains.

SELF-ASSESSMENT

Q1. Which of the following options for Smart Dimensioning can be used to create aligned dimensions?

a. Horizontal
b. Vertical
c. Parallel
d. Radius

Q2. The Point tool in Dimension group is used to apply coordinate dimension to selected point. (T/F)

Q3. The Angular tool in Dimension group is used to create aligned dimension. (T/F)

Q4. The .... tool in Dimension group is used to create dimensions in the form of a chain with one end point of dimension connected to another.

Q5. The Add to Existing tool is used to create ordinate dimensions using existing 0 ordinate reference. (T/F)

Q6. The .... tool is used to add a text annotation in the 3D view.

REVIEW QUESTIONS

Q1. What is the primary purpose of the Smart Dimension tool?
A. To regenerate the model geometry
B. To apply various types of dimensions to model entities
C. To draw sketches on the model surface
D. To convert 3D models to 2D

Q2. Which option automatically determines the type of dimension to apply in Smart Dimension?
A. Horizontal
B. Vertical
C. Parallel
D. Auto

Q3. What happens when you select the 'Maintain perpendicular to arc center' check box in the Drafting Manager?
A. The text becomes centered
B. The dimension is locked in place
C. Dimension remains perpendicular to the arc center
D. All arrows move inside the witness lines

Q4. To create a dimension that measures the radius between two points, which radio button should be selected?
A. Diameter
B. Radius
C. Parallel
D. Circular

Q5. What does the 'Apply to dimensions and notes' check box do in the Format rollout?
A. Sets font size to zero
B. Applies format only to selected dimension
C. Applies the modified format to all new dimensions and notes
D. Resets format settings to default

Q6. Which radio button in the Symbols rollout allows dimensions to be shown in architectural format?
A. Scientific
B. Decimal
C. Architectural
D. Fractional

Q7. What does the 'Maintain the current values' option do under Show More Options?
A. Changes all settings to default
B. Adjusts values proportionally
C. Keeps arrowhead and tolerance text height fixed
D. Increases font size

Q8. What does the Advanced option in the Drafting Manager allow you to do?
A. Export model
B. Create a drawing sheet
C. Modify dimension values and tolerance limits
D. Open 3D view

Q9. Which tool is used to apply coordinate dimension to a point?
A. Angular
B. Point
C. Circular
D. Perpendicular

Q10. To apply dimension between tangency points of arcs and other entities, which tool should be used?
A. Tangent
B. Chained
C. Baseline
D. Parallel

Q11. What does the Chained dimension tool create?
A. Radial dimensions
B. Angular measurements
C. Sequential dimensions linked by end points
D. Notes for exploded views

Q12. What is the purpose of the Align tool in the Ordinate group?
A. Align 3D objects
B. Convert angular dimensions
C. Align ordinate dimensions to a common axis
D. Align text annotations only

Q13. What does the Window tool in Ordinate group allow you to do?
A. Create 3D windows
B. Define screen resolution
C. Select multiple points to generate ordinate dimensions
D. Import dimension styles

Q14. The Note tool is found under which group in the Drafting tab?
A. Dimension
B. Modify
C. Annotate
D. View

Q15. Which radio button places note text on a curve?
A. Point
B. Curve
C. Style
D. Segment

Q16. What is the function of the Hole Table tool?
A. Lists parts in assembly
B. Creates table of model views
C. Creates tabulated info about holes in the model
D. Defines a section cut

Q17. Which option is used to generate a report in the Hole Table Manager?
A. Print
B. Export
C. Create
D. Save

Q18. What does the Cross Hatch tool require before applying hatch patterns?
A. 3D surface
B. Section view
C. Closed wireframe boundary
D. Solid model

Q19. Which tool allows you to create a multi-segment leader line?
A. Note
B. Witness
C. Multi-Edit
D. Leader

Q20. Which tool breaks drafting entities into connected lines?
A. Split View
B. Break Into Lines
C. Chain Cut
D. Divide

Q21. What is the purpose of the Multi-Edit tool?
A. Edit model sketches
B. Modify drafting parameters for multiple entities
C. Rotate draft entities
D. Switch between drafting tabs

Q22. The Align Note tool is found under which group?
A. Annotate
B. Regenerate
C. Modify
D. Dimension

Q23. What does the Convert Legacy Note tool do?
A. Changes notes to architectural format
B. Converts older version notes to current format
C. Deletes obsolete annotations
D. Adds tolerance limits to notes

Q24. Which tool validates whether entities require regeneration?
A. Select
B. All
C. Validate
D. Associative

Q25. What is the function of the Associative tool in the Regenerate group?
A. Breaks dimension lines
B. Checks entity associations
C. Hides dimension text
D. Locks dimension arrows

Chapter 7

Transform and View Tools

Topics Covered

The major topics covered in this chapter are:

- ***Position Tools***
- ***Offset Tools***
- ***Layout Tools***
- ***Modifying Size of Entities***
- ***Displaying Manager and Interface Elements***
- ***Zooming Model and Graphics View***
- ***Appearance Tools***
- ***Managing View Sheets***

INTRODUCTION

In this chapter, we will work on various tools used for transforming entities like moving the objects, rotating the objects, creating offset copies, creating pattern of objects, increasing/decreasing the objects, and so on. We will also learn to use various tools of **View** tab.

TRANSFORMATION TOOLS

The tools in the **Transform** tab are used to modify position, orientation, and size of the entities; refer to Figure-1. Various tools in this tab are discussed next.

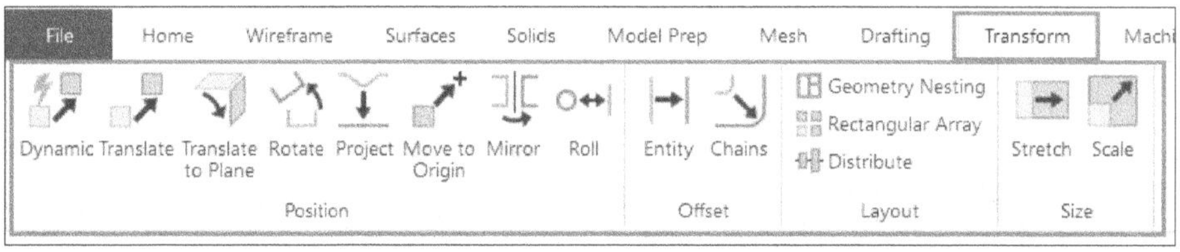

Figure-1. Transform tab

Dynamically Transforming Objects

The **Dynamic** tool is used to change the location and orientation of selected geometry by using dynamic gnomon. The procedure to use this tool is given next.

- Click on the **Dynamic** tool from the **Position** group in the **Transform** tab of the **Ribbon**. You will be asked to select the entities to be repositioned or oriented.
- Select desired entities and click on the **End Selection** button. You will be asked to specify origin position for gnomon.
- Click at desired location to place origin; refer to Figure-2. The **Dynamic Manager** will be displayed; refer to Figure-3.

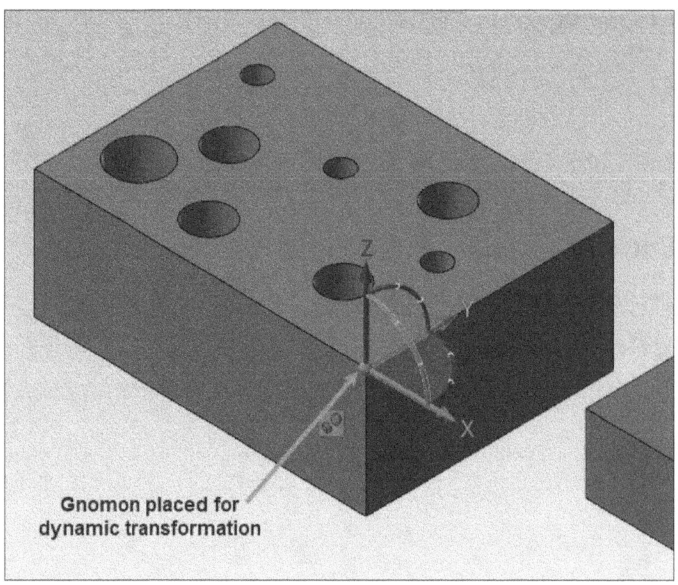

Figure-2. Placing gnomon for transformation

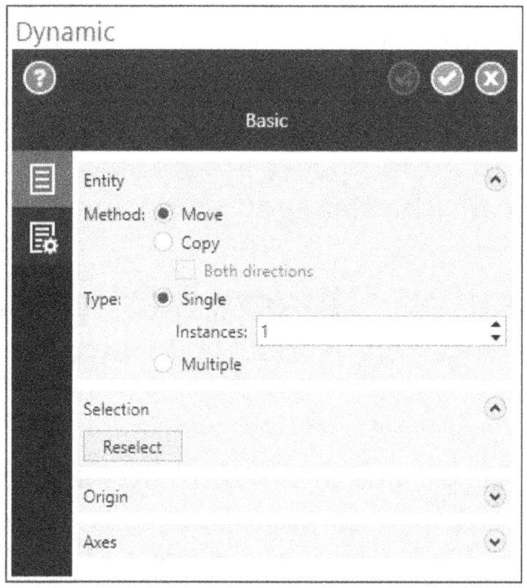

Figure-3. Dynamic Manager

- Set desired parameters in the **Manager** as discussed earlier.
- Use the handles of gnomon to move and rotate the selected objects.
- After performing changes, click on the **OK** button from the **Manager**.

Translating Objects in 3 Dimension

The **Translate** tool is used to move selected object in 3-D direction. The procedure to use this tool is given next.

- Click on the **Translate** tool from the **Position** group in the **Transform** tab of the **Ribbon**. You will be asked to select the objects to be translated.
- Select desired objects and click on the **End Selection** button. The options in **Translate Manager** will be displayed; refer to Figure-4.

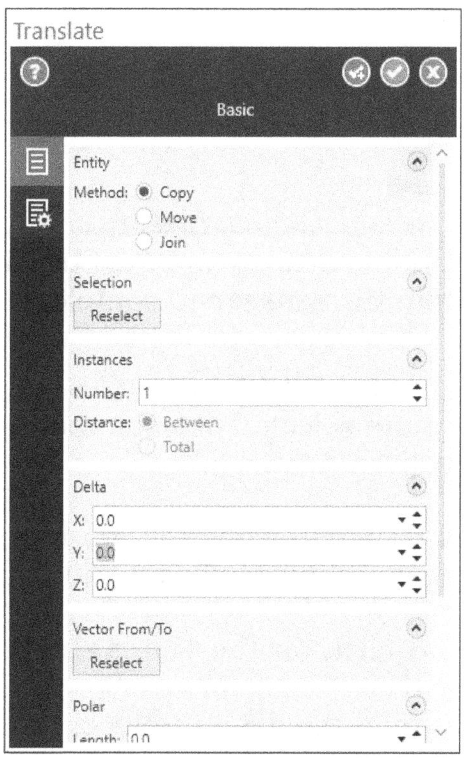

Figure-4. Translate Manager options

- Select desired radio button from the **Method** section to specify whether you want to copy selected objects, move selected objects, or join selected objects at desired location.
- Specify the parameters for moving selected objects in the edit boxes of **Delta** or **Polar** rollouts.
- Click on the **OK** button from the **Manager** to perform translation.

Translating Objects Along a Plane

The **Translate to Plane** tool is used to translate object along a plane. The procedure to use this tool is given next.

- Click on the **Translate to Plane** tool from the **Position** group of **Transform** tab in the **Ribbon**. You will be asked to select objects to be translated.
- Select desired objects and click on the **End Selection** button. The options of **Translate To Plane Manager** will become active; refer to Figure-5.

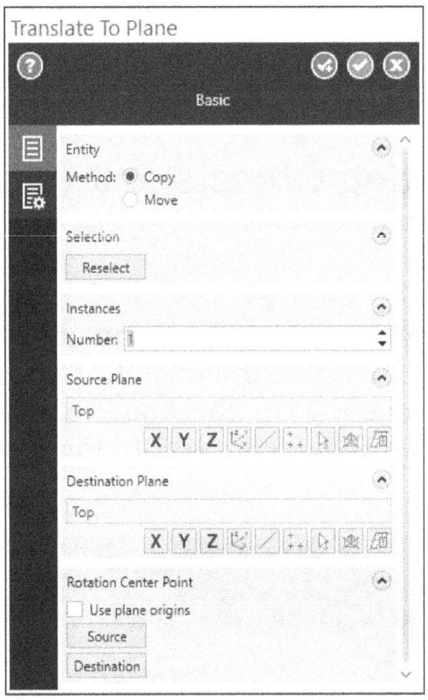

Figure-5. Translate To Plane Manager

- Select desired options from the **Source** and **Destination** rollouts in the **Manager**.
- Click on the **OK** button from the **Manager** to complete translation.

Rotating Objects

The **Rotate** tool is used to rotate selected objects about specified center point. The procedure to use this tool is given next.

- Click on the **Rotate** tool from the **Position** group in the **Transform** tab of the **Ribbon**. The **Rotate Manager** will be displayed and you will be asked to select the objects to be rotated.
- Select desired objects and click on the **End Selection** button. The options of **Rotate Manager** will be active.
- Click on the center of rotation handle and place it at desired location to specify rotation center point; refer to Figure-6.

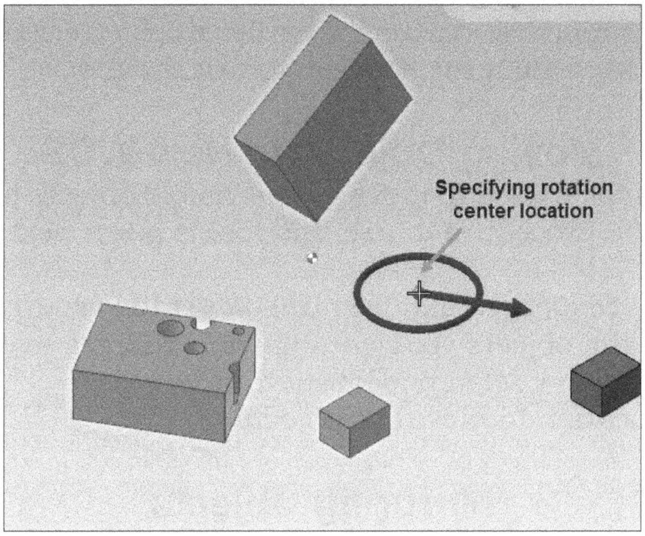

Figure-6. Specifying rotation center point location

- Use the circular handle to rotate the objects at desired location.
- Set the other parameters as desired and click on the **OK** button from the **Manager** to exit the tool.

Projecting Entities

The **Project** tool in **Transform** tab is used to project selected entities on a face, plane, or specified depth. The procedure to use this tool is given next.

- Click on the **Project** tool from the **Position** group in the **Transform** tab of the **Ribbon**. You will be asked to select the entities to be copied on face, plane, or specified depth.
- Select desired entities and click on the **End Selection** button. The options of **Project Manager** will become active; refer to Figure-7.

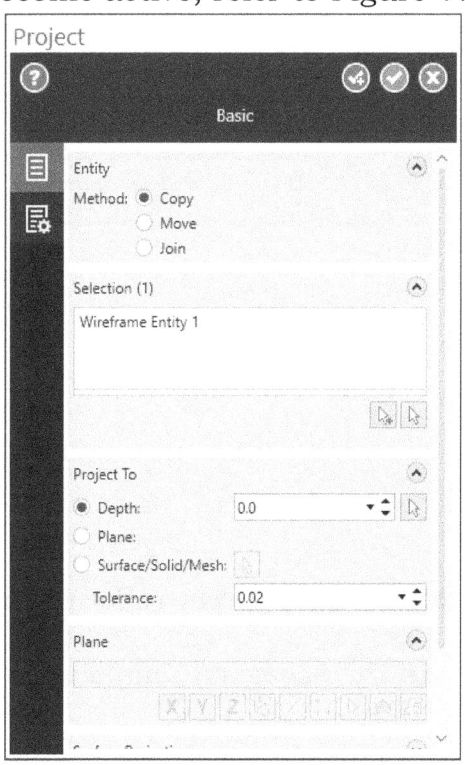

Figure-7. Project Manager

- Select desired radio button from the **Method** section of **Manager**.
- Specify the other options as discussed earlier in chapter related to Wireframe.
- Click on the **OK** button from the **Manager** to exit the tool.

Moving Objects to New WCS

The **Move to Origin** tool is used to move all the visible objects to current WCS based on specified point. The procedure to use this tool is given next.

- Click on the **Move to Origin** tool from the **Position** group in the **Transform** tab of the **Ribbon**. All the objects visible in 3D view will get selected and you will be asked to specify the new reference location for WCS.
- Click at desired location to move the objects.

Mirroring Objects

The **Mirror** tool is used to mirror copy or move selected objects. The procedure to use this tool is given next.

- Click on the **Mirror** tool from the **Position** group in the **Transform** tab of the **Ribbon**. You will be asked to select the objects to be mirrored.
- Select desired objects and click on the **End Selection** button. The options of **Mirror Manager** will become active; refer to Figure-8 and preview of mirror copy will be displayed; refer to Figure-9.

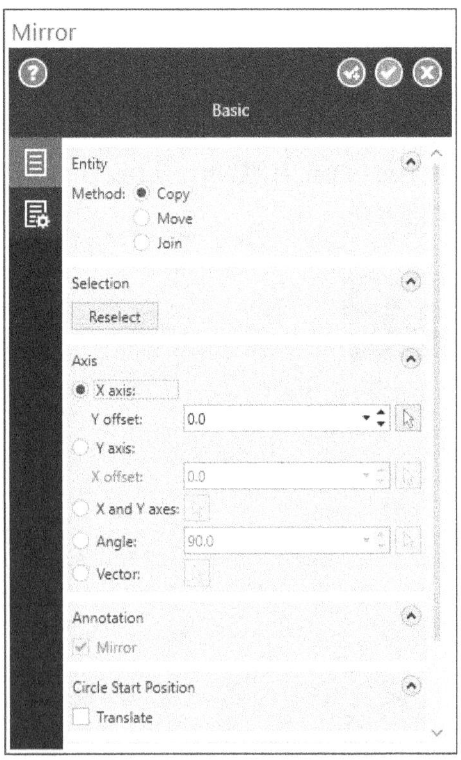

Figure-8. Mirror Manager

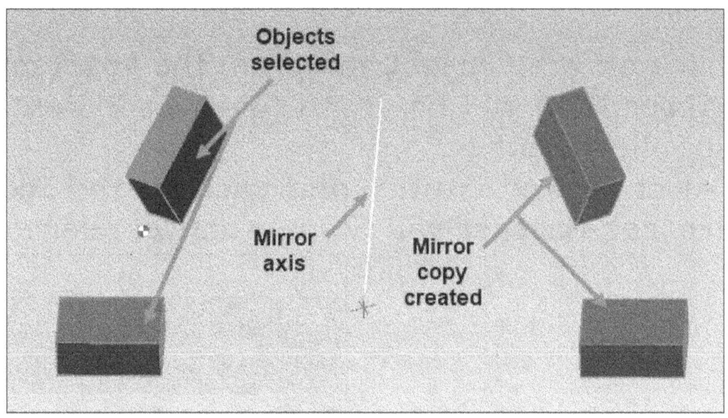

Figure-9. Preview of mirror copy

- Select desired radio button from the **Axis** rollout and specify the offset value if needed.
- Click on the **OK** button from the **Manager** to make a mirror copy and exit the tool.

Wrapping Geometry about an Axis

The **Roll** tool is used to wrap selected chained wireframe geometry about specified axis. The procedure to use this tool is given next.

- Click on the **Roll** tool from the **Position** group in the **Transform** tab of the **Ribbon**. The **Roll Manager** will be displayed with **Wireframe Chaining** selection box; refer to Figure-10.

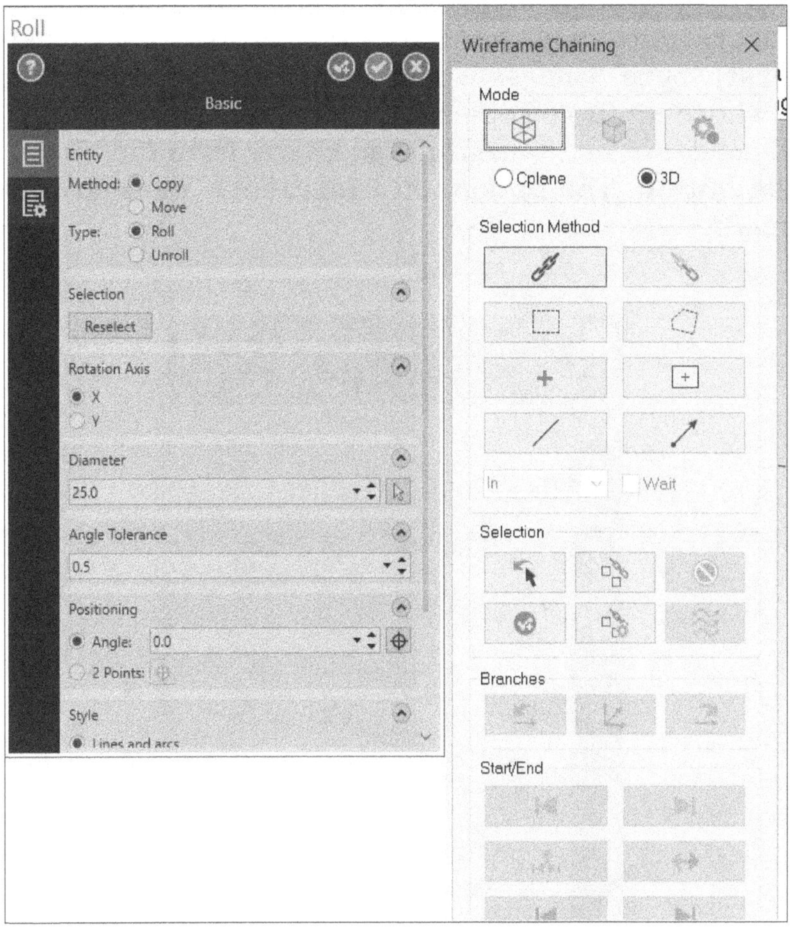

Figure-10. Roll Manager with Wireframe Chaining selection box

- Select desired curve and click on the **OK** button from the **Wireframe Chaining** selection box. Preview of rolled wireframe chain will be displayed; refer to Figure-11.

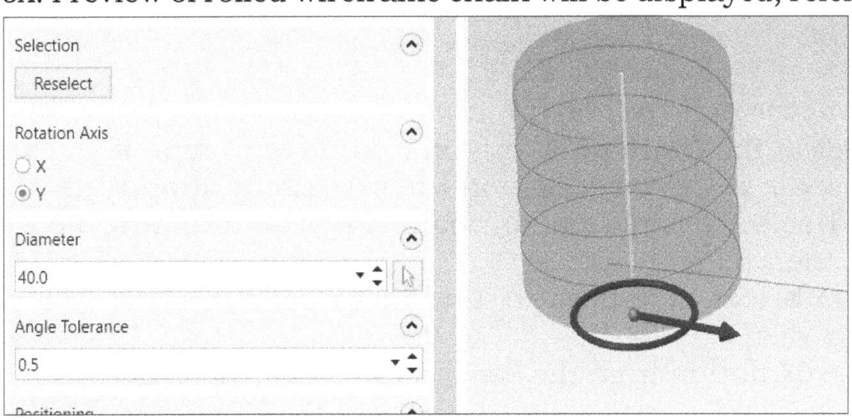

Figure-11. Preview of rolled chain

- Set the parameters as desired in the **Manager** and click on the **OK** button.

The tools in **Offset** group and **Rectangular Array** tool in **Layout** group of **Transform** tab have been discussed earlier. You will learn about **Geometry Nesting** tool in Chapter 12.

Creating Copies Between Points

The **Distribute** tool in **Layout** group is used to create multiple copies of selected body between two points. The procedure to use this tool is given next.

- Click on the **Distribute** tool from the **Layout** group in the **Transform** tab of the **Ribbon**. The **Distribute Manager** will be displayed and you will be asked to select the geometry whose multiple copies are to be created.
- Select desired solid/surface/wireframe geometry from the model and click on the **End Selection** button. The options in **Distribute Manager** will become active; refer to Figure-12.

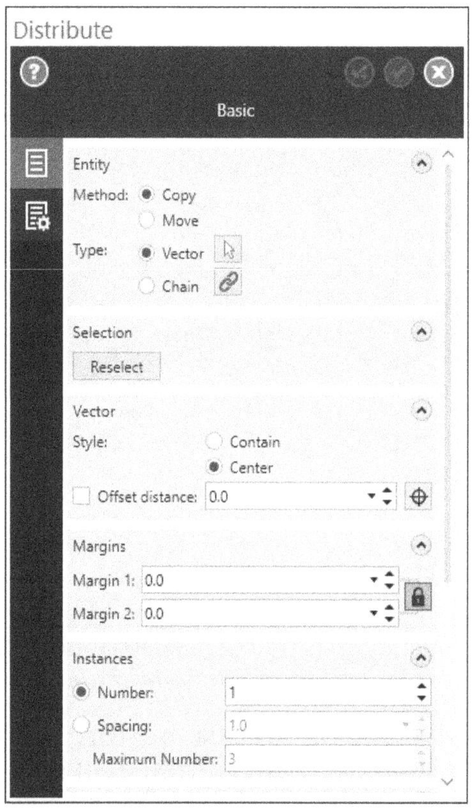

Figure-12. Distribute Manager

- Select the **Vector** radio button if you want to select a single arc/line/edge/cursor position. Select the **Chain** radio button from **Type** section if you want to select a wireframe chain of curves. Click on the selection button next to selected radio button and select desired curve/chain. Preview of distributed copies will be displayed; refer to Figure-13.
- Set the number of instances in **Instances** rollout and other parameters as discussed earlier.
- Click on the **OK** button from the **Manager** to create the copies.

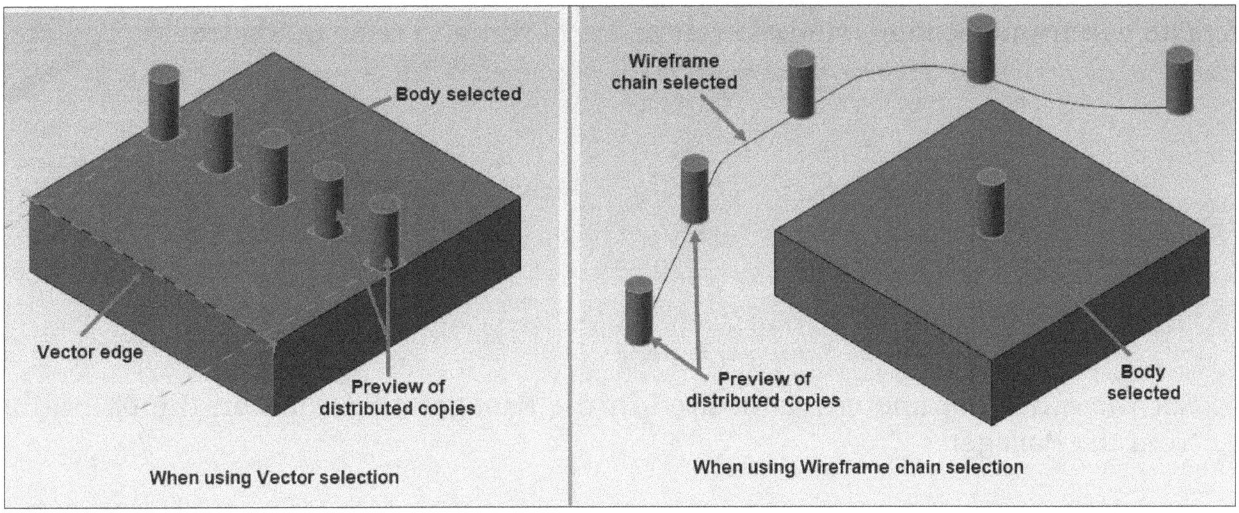

Figure-13. Preview of distributed copy selection

Stretching Line Segments

The **Stretch** tool is used to stretch line segments to specified location. The procedure to use this tool is given next.

- Click on the **Stretch** tool from the **Size** group in the **Transform** tab of the **Ribbon**. You will be asked to select section of geometry to be stretched using the window selection.
- Select the side of wireframe entity to be stretched using windows selection; refer to Figure-14.

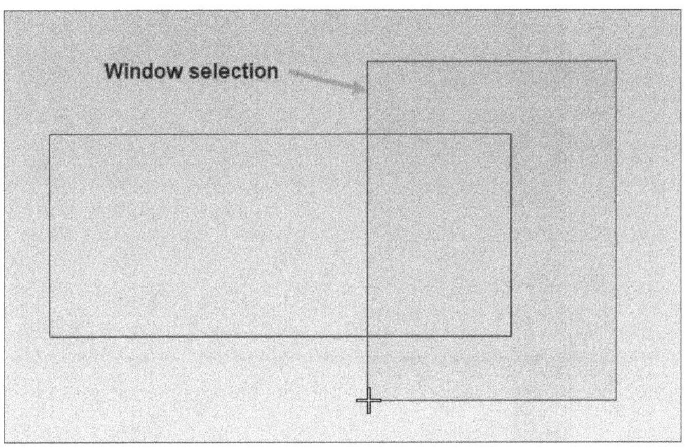

Figure-14. Selecting section of wireframe entities

- After selecting the section, click on the **End Selection** button. A gnomon will be displayed on the sketch section; refer to Figure-15.

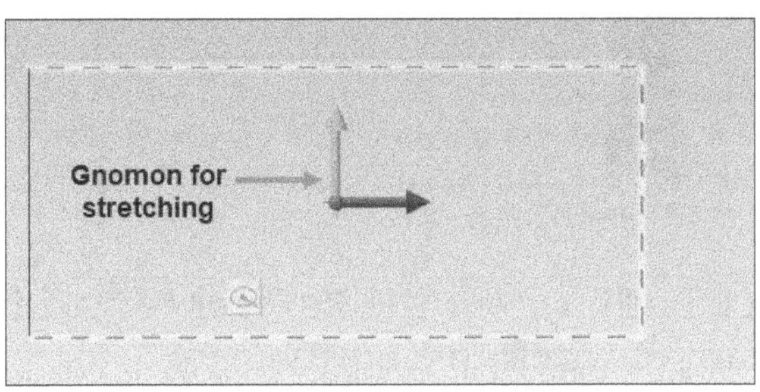

Figure-15. Gnomon handles for stretching

- Use the drag handles or specify desired values in the edit boxes of **Delta** rollout. The wireframe section will be stretched accordingly; refer to Figure-16.

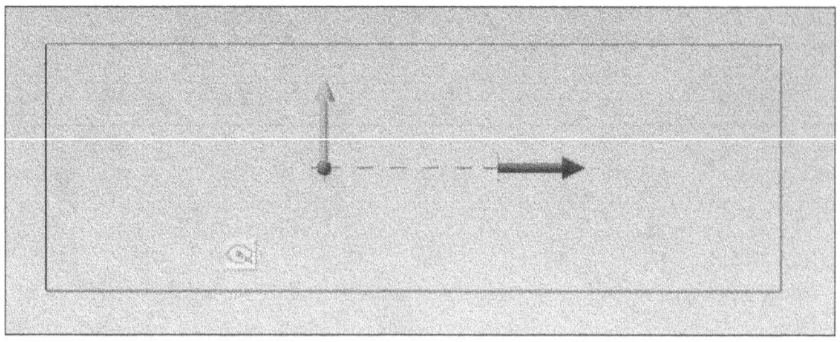

Figure-16. Section after stretching

- Set the other parameters as desired in the **Manager** and click on the **OK** button from the **Manager**.

Scaling Entities

The **Scale** tool is used to increase or decrease the size of entities by specified scale value. The procedure to use this tool is given next.

- Click on the **Scale** tool from the **Size** group in the **Transform** tab of the **Ribbon**. You will be asked to select the entities to be scaled.
- Select desired entities using single selection or window selection and then click on the **End Selection** button. The options of **Scale Manager** will become active; refer to Figure-17.

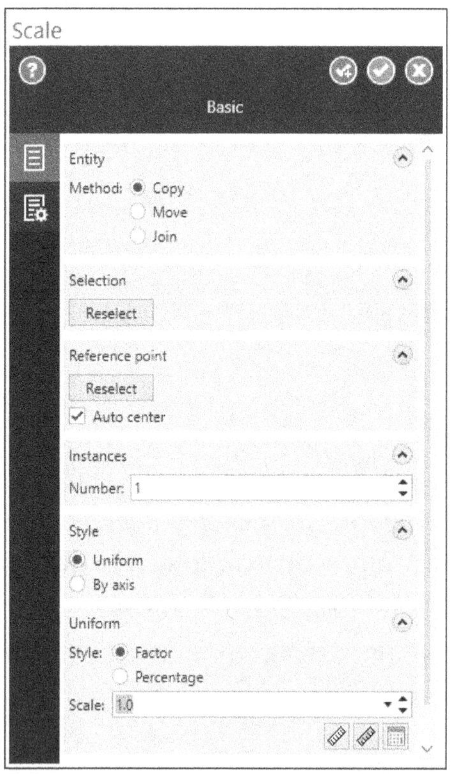

Figure-17. Scale Manager

- Click on the **Reselect** button from the **Reference point** rollout of the **Manager** and select desired point of wireframe entity.
- Click in the **Scale** edit box of the **Uniform** rollout and specify the scale factor by which you want to increase or decrease the size of selected entities.

- Set the other parameters of **Manager** as discussed earlier.
- Click on the **OK** button from the **Manager** to apply scale value and exit the tool.

VIEW TOOLS

The tools to manage graphic views, appearances of model, and interface of elements are available in the **View** tab of the **Ribbon**; refer to Figure-18. Various tools in this tab are discussed next.

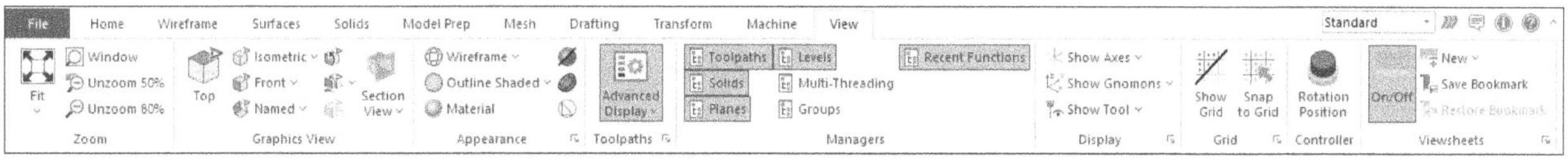

Figure-18. View tab

Zoom Tools

The tools in the **Zoom** group of **View** tab are used to focus on specific region of the 3D view to check model in detail. The tools in this group are discussed next.

Zoom Fit

The **Fit** tool in **Zoom** group of **View** tab is used to display all the visible object in maximum view size possible. To display all the visible objects in current view area, click on the tool.

Zooming Selected Entities

The **Selected** tool in **Fit** drop-down is used to display only selected objects in current view area. To use this tool, select the objects which you want to zoom and then click on the **Selected** tool from the **Fit** drop-down in the **Zoom** group of **View** tab in the **Ribbon**.

Unzooming

There are two tools to perform unzooming in the view area; **Unzoom 50%** and **Unzoom 80%**. Select the **Unzoom 50%** tool from the **Zoom** group to display the current objects as 50% of the original size. Similarly, select the **Unzoom 80%** tool from the **Zoom** group to display current objects as 80% of the original size.

Graphics View Tools

The tools in the **Graphics View** group of **Ribbon** are used to change view orientation of model to standard view orientations like Top view, Right view, and so on. You can select the **Top**, **Isometric Reverse**, **Isometric**, **Trimetric, Right**, **Front**, **Left**, **Back**, and **Bottom** tools to orient the view to respective orientation. The other tools in this group are discussed next.

Rotating the Current View

The **Rotate** tool is used to rotate the current view of model by specified rotation value to change the orientation. Note that this tool does not rotate the model, it rotates the view of user to display different section of model on screen. The procedure to use this tool is given next.

- Click on the **Rotate** tool from the **Graphics View** group of the **View** tab in the **Ribbon**. The **Rotate plane** dialog box will be displayed; refer to Figure-19.

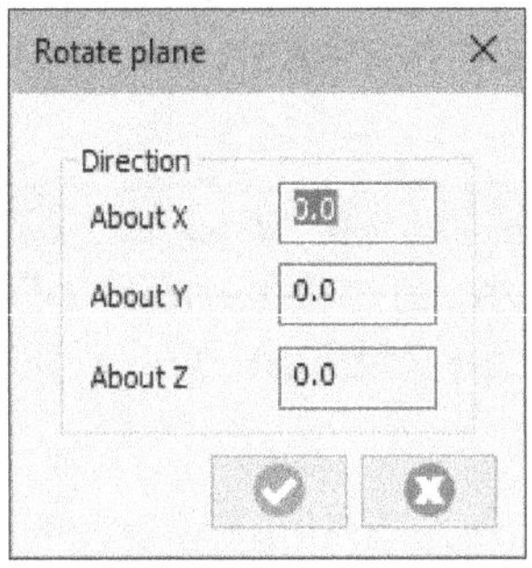

Figure-19. Rotate plane dialog box

- Specify desired angle values in the edit boxes of the dialog box to set the orientation of view plane about different axes.
- After specifying desired values, click on the **OK** button from the dialog box. The view orientation will change accordingly.

Orienting View plane to Construction plane or Tool plane

Click on the **= Cplane** tool in **Graphics View** group of **View** tab in **Ribbon** to make the current view parallel to construction plane. Click on the **= Tplane** tool from the **= Cplane** drop-down in the **Graphics View** group of **View** tab in the **Ribbon** to make current view parallel to current Tool plane.

Saving Current Orientation as Plane

- After setting desired custom orientation, click on the **Save** button from the **Graphics View** group in the **View** tab of the **Ribbon**. The **New Plane Manager** will be displayed; refer to Figure-20.

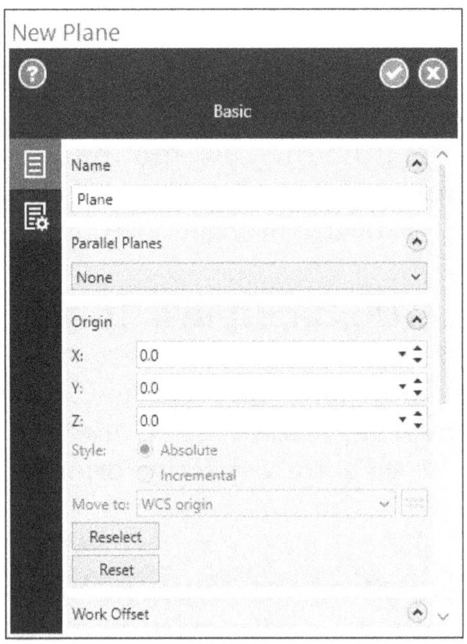

Figure-20. New Plane Manager

- Specify desired parameters in the **Manager** and click on the **OK** button.

Section View Parameters

- Click on the **Section View** button from the **Graphics View** group in the **View** tab of the **Ribbon** to display section view of model for current plane.
- Click on the **Section View** drop-down arrow and select desired options from the drop-down to define which entities will be displayed in section view; refer to Figure-21.

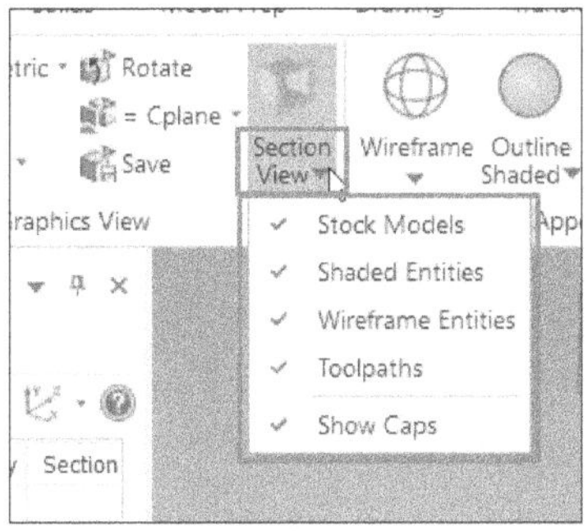

Figure-21. Section View drop-down

Setting Appearances of Model

The tools in the **Appearance** group of **Ribbon** are used to change the display style of model in the 3D view. Various tools in this group are discussed next.

- Select the **Wireframe** tool from the **Appearance** group in the **View** tab of **Ribbon** to display 3D objects as wireframe objects; refer to Figure-22.
- Click on the **Dimmed** tool from the **Wireframe** drop-down in the **Appearance** group of the **Ribbon** to make hidden lines dim in the wireframe view of model; refer to Figure-23.
- Click on the **No Hidden** tool from the **Wireframe** drop-down in the **Appearance** group of **Ribbon** to remove the hidden lines in wireframe model; refer to Figure-24.

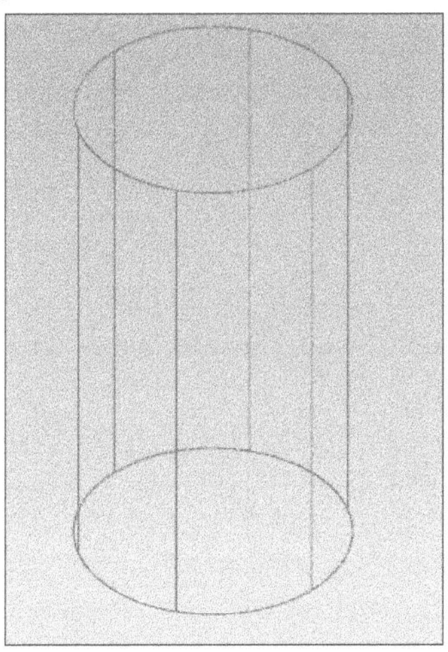

Figure-22. Wireframe model

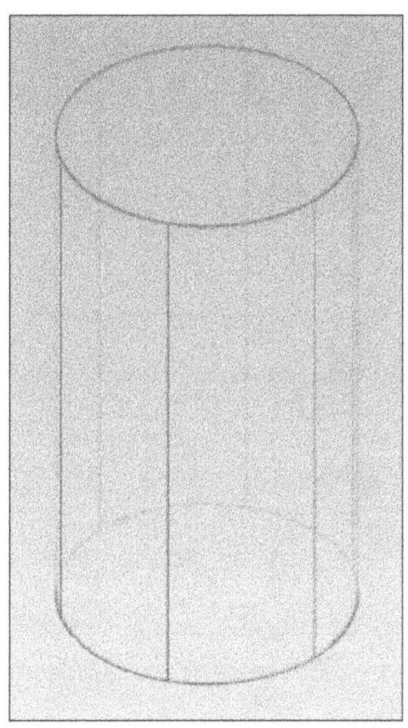

Figure-23. Dimmed wireframe model

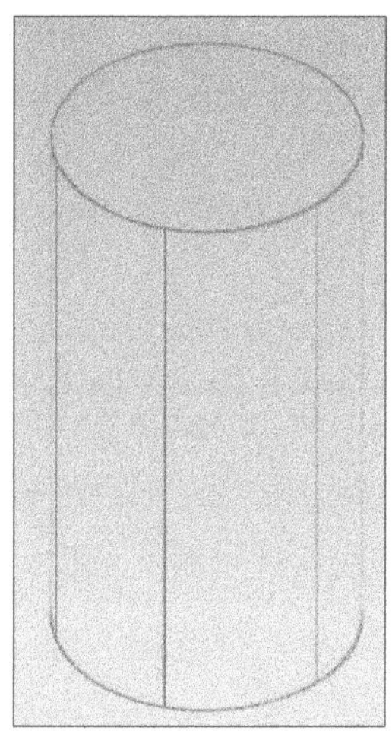

Figure-24. No hidden wireframe model

- Click on the **Outline Shaded** tool from the **Appearance** group in the **View** tab of the **Ribbon** to display 3D shaded model with bold outlines; refer to Figure-25.
- Click on the **Shaded** tool from the **Outline Shaded** drop-down in the **Appearance** group of the **Ribbon** to display the model shaded without outline; refer to Figure-26.

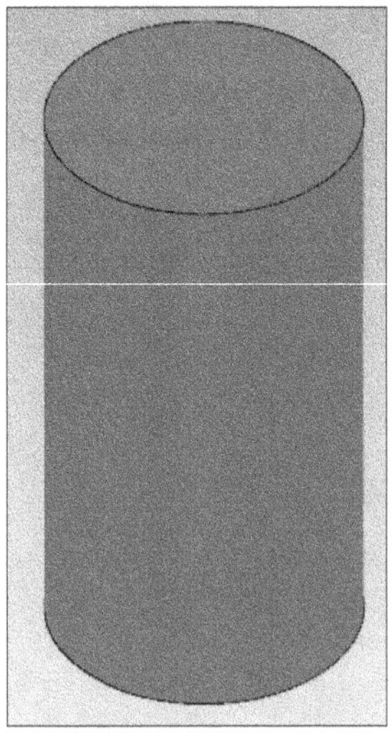

Figure-25. Outline shaded model

Figure-26. Shaded model

- Click on the **Material** button from the **Appearance** group of the **Ribbon** to display texture of the material applied to the model.
- Click on the **Translucency** button from the **Appearance** group of **Ribbon** to display solid model as transparent.
- Click on the **Backside** button from the **Appearance** group of **Ribbon** to display backside of the surfaces with different colors.

Advanced Display Options for Toolpaths

The **Advanced Display** button in the **Toolpaths** group of the **View** tab in the **Ribbon** is used to display various toolpath entities in the 3D view. You can select the toolpath entities to be displayed from the **Advanced Display** drop-down; refer to Figure-27.

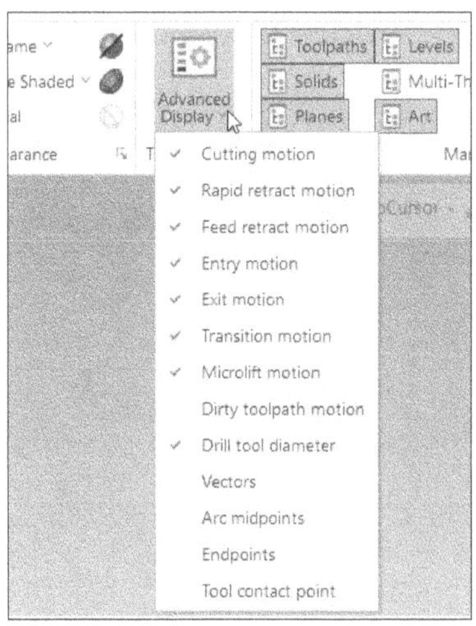

Figure-27. Advanced Display drop-down

You can also change colors of various toolpath entities like cutting motion, rapid retract, and so on. To do so, click on the inclined arrow (**Advanced Toolpath Display Options**) button from the **Toolpaths** group in the **View** tab of **Ribbon**. The **Advanced Toolpath Display** dialog box will be displayed; refer to Figure-28.

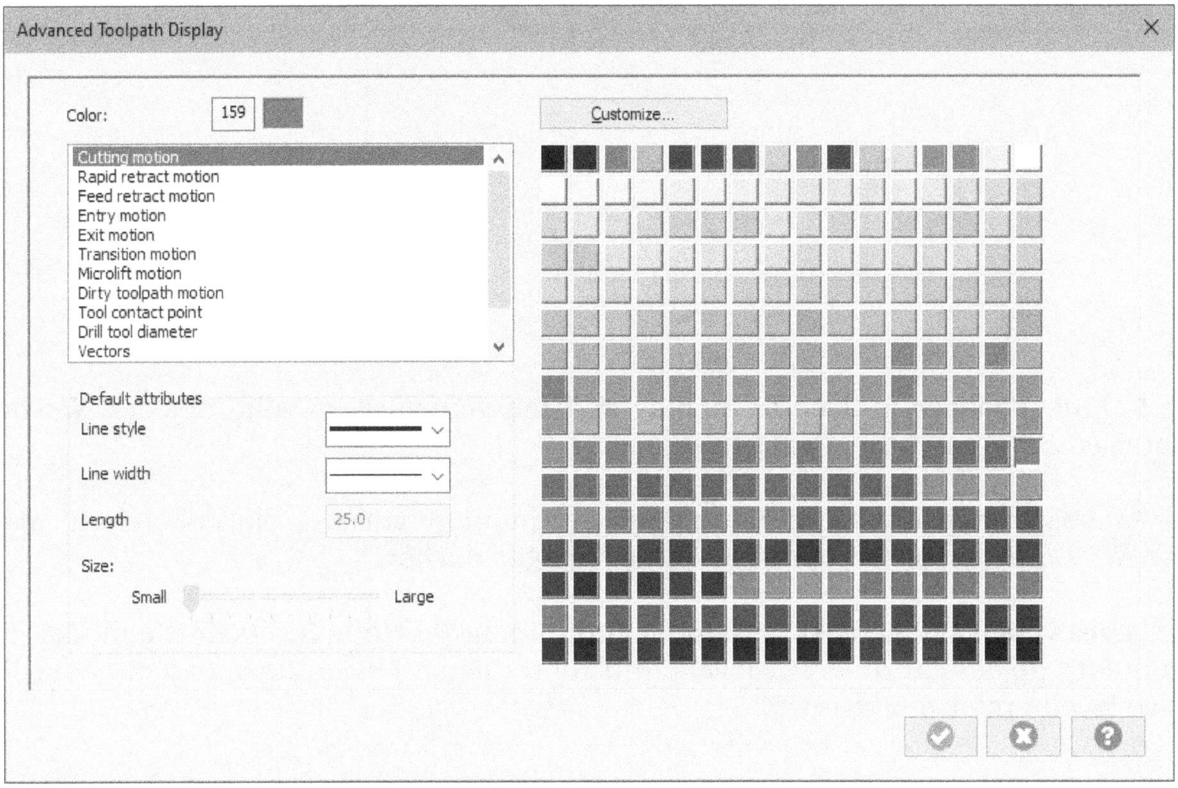

Figure-28. Advanced Toolpath Display dialog box

Select desired toolpath entity from the left box and set desired color from the color palette. You can also set the line style and thickness for various toolpath entities. After setting desired parameters, click on the **OK** button from the dialog box. The **System Configuration** dialog box will be displayed; refer to Figure-29. Click on the **Yes** button if you want to save the settings as standard for all the models in Mastercam. Click on the **No** button if you want to apply settings to current model only.

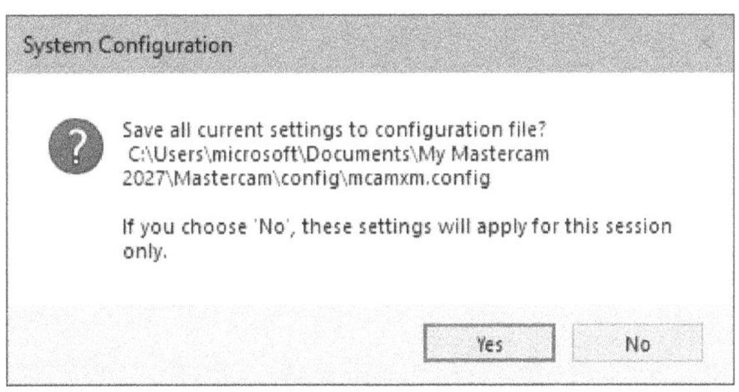

Figure-29. System Configuration dialog box

Showing/Hiding Managers

The buttons in the **Managers** group are used to show or hide various managers from the interface; refer to Figure-30. Select desired toggle buttons from the group to display/hide respective managers.

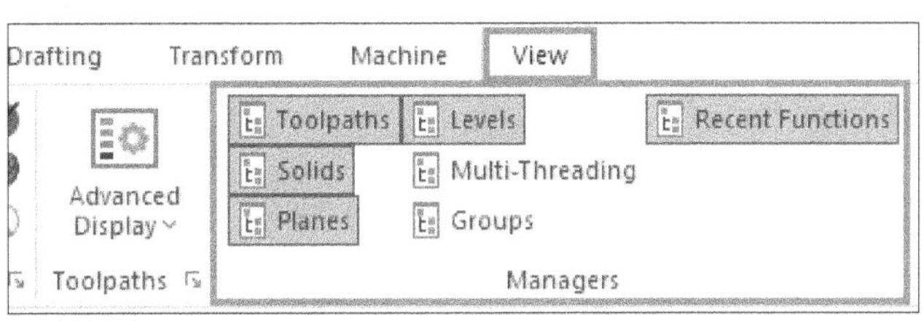

Figure-30. Managers group

The **Toolpaths Manager** is used to display and manipulate toolpaths; refer to Figure-31.

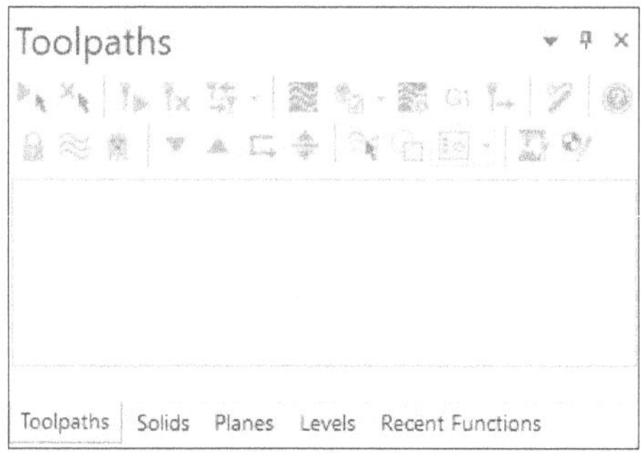

Figure-31. Toolpaths Manager

The **Solids Manager** is used to display and manage various solid objects. We have discussed options of this **Manager** earlier.

The **Planes Manager** is used to display and manage various planes created in 3D view. We have discussed options of this **Manager** earlier.

The **Levels Manager** is used to display and manage various levels of the model. You can create objects at different levels and then display/hide those objects based on active levels; refer to Figure-32.

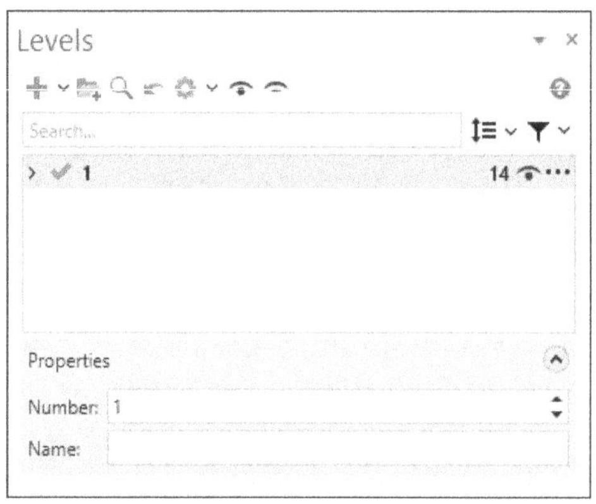

Figure-32. Levels Manager

The **Multi-Threading Manager** is used to display processing of various toolpath threads; refer to Figure-33.

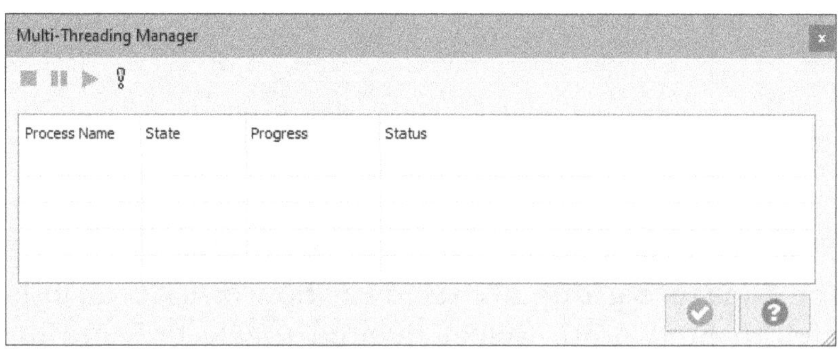

Figure-33. Multi-Threading Manager

The **Groups Manager** is used to create and manage object groups; refer to Figure-34.

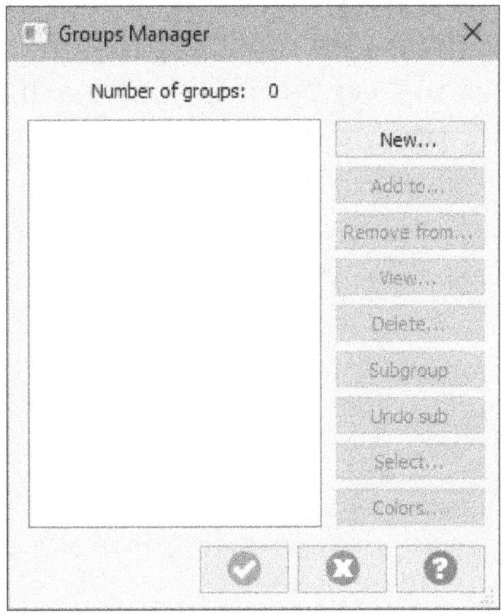

Figure-34. Groups Manager

The **Recent Functions Manager** is used to display and use recently used functions; refer to Figure-35.

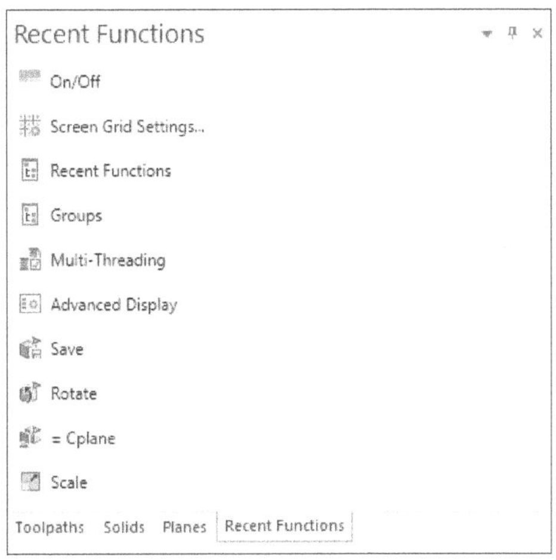

Figure-35. Recent Functions Manager

Showing/Hiding Axes

The tools in **Show Axes** drop-down of the **Display** group in the **View** tab of the **Ribbon** are used to display/hide various standard axes; refer to Figure-36. Select the **World** option from the drop-down if you want to display World axes. Select the **WCS** option from the drop-down to display WCS axes. Select the **Cplane** option from the drop-down to display axes of current construction plane. Select the **Tplane** option from the drop-down to display axes of current tool plane.

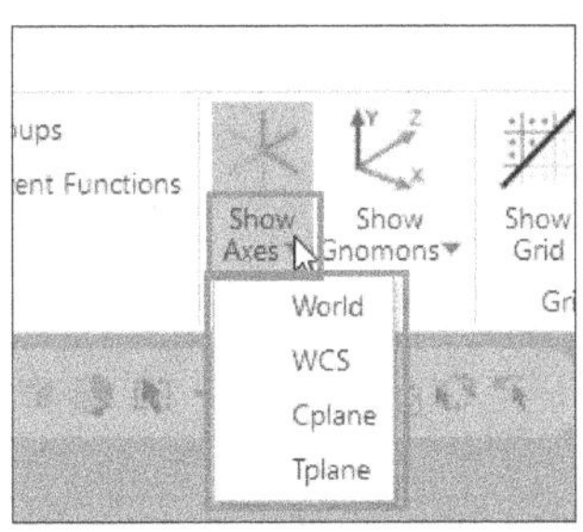

Figure-36. Show Axes drop-down

Showing/Hiding Gnomons

The tools in the **Show Gnomons** drop-down of **Display** group in the **View** tab of the **Ribbon** are used to display/hide various types of Gnomons like WCS, Cplane, Tplane, and so on; refer to Figure-37. The procedure to use these options are same as discussed earlier.

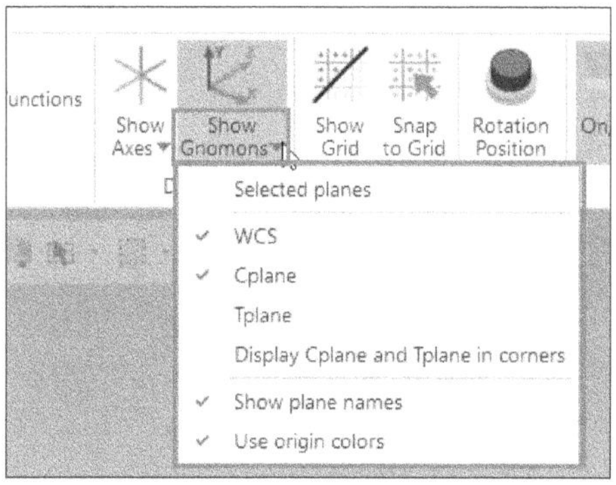

Figure-37. Show Gnomons drop-down

Grid Setting

The tools in the **Grid** group of **View** tab in the **Ribbon** are used to display and manage grid points; refer to Figure-38. Various tools in this group are discussed next.

- Click on the **Show Grid** toggle button from the **Grid** group in **Ribbon** to display grid points on current construction plane.
- Select the **Snap to Grid** toggle button from the **Grid** group of **Ribbon** to automatically snap cursor to nearby grid points.
- Click on the **Grid Settings** (inclined arrow) button from the **Grid** group of **View** tab in the **Ribbon**. The **Grid** dialog box will be displayed; refer to Figure-39.

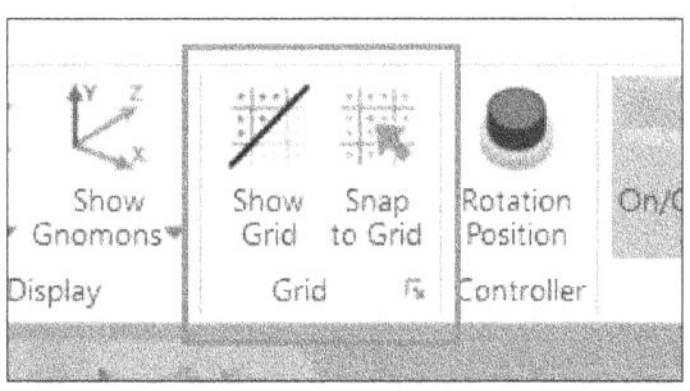

Figure-38. Grid group

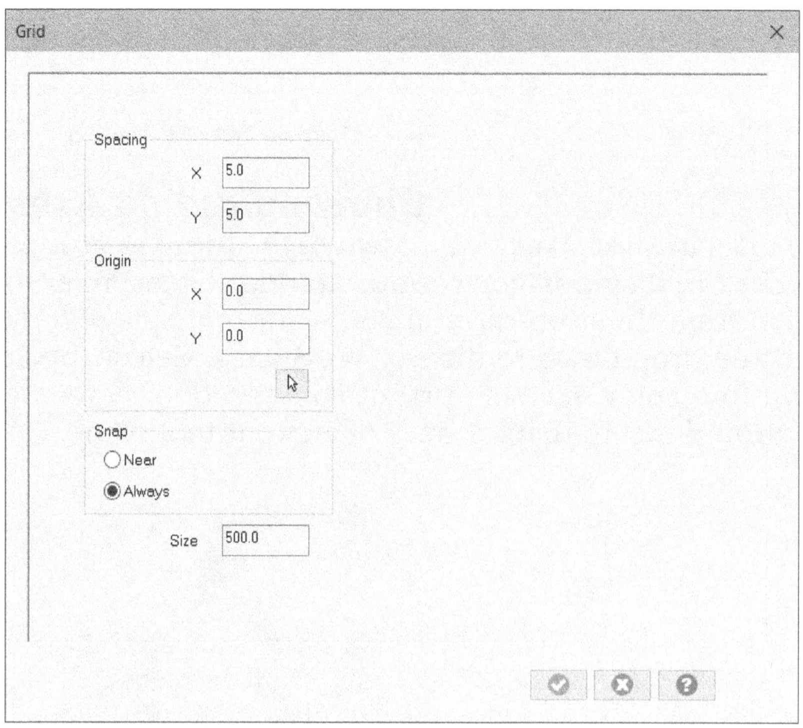

Figure-39. Grid dialog box

- Set desired parameters in the dialog box like gap between two points along X and Y axes. After setting parameters, click on the **OK** button from the dialog box.

Specifying View Rotation Position

The **Rotation Position** tool in **Controller** group of **Ribbon** is used to set location of rotation center point to be used for motion controller. After clicking on this tool, click at desired location to specify position of rotation point.

Viewsheet Options

The tools in the **Viewsheets** group of **View** tab in the **Ribbon** are used to create and manage viewsheets of the model; refer to Figure-40. Various tools of this group are discussed next.

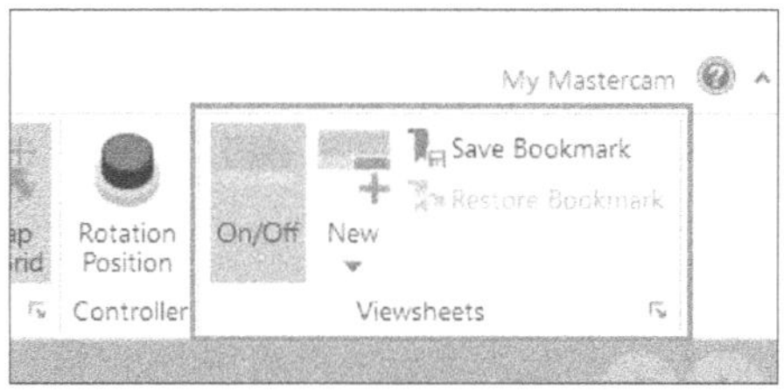

Figure-40. Viewsheets tab

- Click on the **On/Off** button from the **Viewsheets** group of **Ribbon** to display/hide **Viewsheets** bar at the bottom in the 3D view.
- Click on the **New** button from the **Viewsheets** group to create a new view sheet.
- Click on the **Copy** button from the **New** drop-down in the **Viewsheets** group to create copy of the current sheet.
- Click on the **Rename** button from the **New** drop-down in **Viewsheets** group to change the name of current sheet.
- Click on the **Delete** button from the **New** drop-down in **Viewsheets** group to delete current sheet.
- Click on the **Save Bookmark** tool from the **Viewsheets** group to save the current orientation of model book marked. After saving orientation bookmark, if you have modified the orientation of model then click on the **Restore Bookmark** tool from the **Viewsheets** group to restore orientation.
- Click on the **Viewsheet Settings** button (inclined arrow) from the **Viewsheets** group in the **View** tab of **Ribbon** to modify parameters related to viewsheet. The **Viewsheet** dialog box will be displayed; refer to Figure-41.

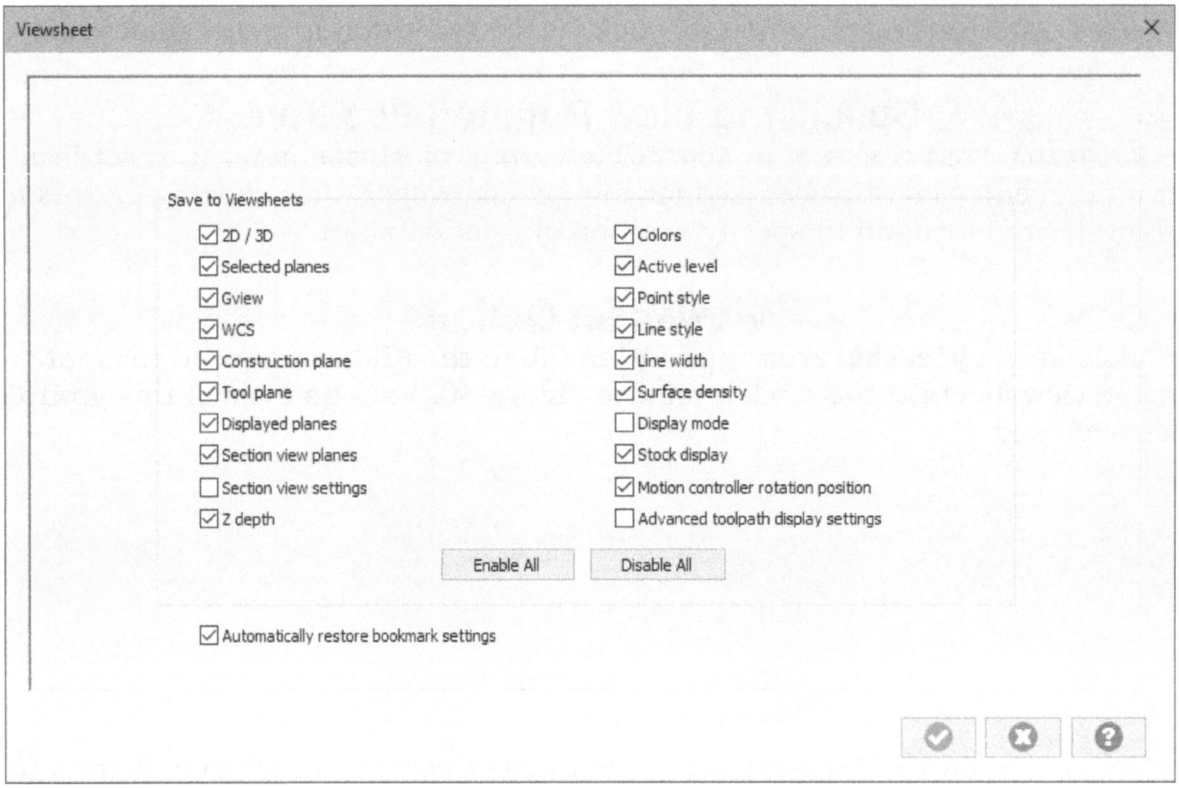

Figure-41. Viewsheet dialog box

- Select desired check boxes from the dialog box and click on the **OK** button to apply changes.

SELF-ASSESSMENT

Q1. What are the functions of tools available in Transform tab of Ribbon?

Q2. The .... tool is used to change the location and orientation of selected geometry by using dynamic gnomon.

Q3. The Translate to Plane tool is used to translate object along a plane. (T/F)

Q4. The Translate tool in Transform tab is used to project selected entities on a face, plane, or specified depth. (T/F)

Q5. The .... tool is used to wrap selected chained wireframe geometry about specified axis.

Q6. The .... Manager is used to display and manage various solid objects.

Q7. The .... Manager is used to display and manage various levels of the model.

REVIEW QUESTIONS

Q1. What is the primary function of the Dynamic tool in the Transform tab?
A. Create copies of selected geometry
B. Rotate objects along a curve
C. Change position and orientation using dynamic gnomon
D. Scale wireframe entities to fit the screen

Q2. Which method allows movement of objects along a 3D direction using Delta or Polar values?
A. Move to Origin
B. Translate
C. Rotate
D. Project

Q3. What does the Translate to Plane tool achieve?
A. Converts wireframe into solid
B. Projects geometry to another plane
C. Moves objects along a defined plane
D. Wraps geometry around an axis

Q4. What is the purpose of the Rotate tool under the Transform tab?
A. Rotate the view
B. Rotate selected objects about a center point
C. Rotate WCS origin
D. Rotate layers

Q5. Which tool is used to project entities on a face, plane, or depth?
A. Roll
B. Project
C. Stretch
D. Translate

Q6. The Move to Origin tool does which of the following?
A. Rotates the model to fit origin
B. Moves all visible objects to new WCS based on a point
C. Creates multiple WCS copies
D. Projects geometry onto the WCS

Q7. What is the function of the Mirror tool in the Transform tab?
A. Create a 2D sketch
B. Copy or move geometry along axis as mirror image
C. Reflect camera view
D. Scale geometry across an axis

Q8. Which tool is used to wrap geometry around a specified axis?
A. Translate
B. Rotate
C. Roll
D. Mirror

Q9. The Distribute tool in the Layout group is used to:
A. Scatter geometry randomly
B. Align points to a plane
C. Create multiple copies of selected geometry between two points
D. Apply grid layout to model

Q10. What is the main use of the Stretch tool in the Size group?
A. Increase layer thickness
B. Resize the complete model
C. Stretch a section of geometry to a new location
D. Move model to origin

Q11. What parameter must be set in the Scale Manager to scale entities?
A. Rotation Axis
B. Reference Depth
C. Translation Point
D. Scale Factor

Q12. What does the Fit tool under the Zoom group in the View tab do?
A. Enlarges grid spacing
B. Fits selected elements in view
C. Displays all visible objects in maximum view size
D. Fits model to background image

Q13. Which tool displays only the selected objects in the current view?
A. Zoom Fit
B. Selected
C. Unzoom 50%
D. View Window

Q14. What is the effect of using the Unzoom 80% tool?
A. Enlarges view by 80%
B. Shrinks view to 80% of original
C. Enlarges grid by 80%
D. Removes 80% of objects from view

Q15. What does the Rotate tool in the Graphics View group allow you to do?
A. Rotate geometry
B. Rotate construction planes
C. Rotate the current view orientation
D. Rotate layers

Q16. Which tool sets the current view to be parallel to the construction plane?
A. = Tplane
B. = Cplane
C. Section View
D. Save Orientation

Q17. What tool displays a section view of the model for the current plane?
A. Grid Settings
B. Section View
C. Advanced Display
D. Hide Gnomon

Q18. Which appearance setting displays the model as wireframe with no hidden lines?
A. Outline Shaded
B. Dimmed
C. No Hidden
D. Shaded

Q19. What does the Translucency tool do in the Appearance group?
A. Changes outline thickness
B. Hides backfaces
C. Makes solid model transparent
D. Sets model color to translucent blue

Q20. Which button is used to modify toolpath display colors and styles?
A. Show Grid
B. Advanced Toolpath Display Options
C. Section View
D. Material

Q21. What does the Multi-Threading Manager display?
A. Layer configurations
B. Artcam objects
C. Toolpath thread processing
D. Memory allocation

Q22. What is the function of the Levels Manager?
A. Manage viewpoints
B. Apply shading
C. Control layers/levels of objects
D. Snap objects to origin

Q23. What can you do using the Show Axes drop-down in the Display group?
A. Display/hide coordinate system axes like WCS, Tplane, etc.
B. Lock model orientation
C. Show internal sketches
D. Highlight measurement axes

Q24. What happens when you enable the Snap to Grid toggle?
A. Objects move along XY curve
B. View zooms to grid
C. Cursor snaps to nearby grid points
D. Grid gets hidden

Q25. What is the use of the Rotation Position tool in the Controller group?
A. Set transparency for model
B. Define location for rotation center in motion controller
C. Set start angle for rotate view
D. Rotate model to fit screen

Q26. What tool is used to create and manage view layouts of the model?
A. View Selector
B. Grid Manager
C. Viewsheets
D. Snap View

Q27. What does the Save Bookmark button in the Viewsheets group do?
A. Save model
B. Save grid layout
C. Save current model orientation
D. Save material setting

Machining Section

Chapter 8

Starting with Mastercam Machining

Topics Covered

The major topics covered in this chapter are:

- ***Introduction***
- ***CNC Machine Structure***
- ***Setting Up a Milling Machine***
- ***Machine Definition Manager***
- ***Managing Control Definitions***
- ***Applying Material to Workpiece***
- ***Tool Manager***
- ***Cutting Tools used in Milling and Lathe Operations***
- ***Creating Stock and Exporting Stock Model***

INTRODUCTION

In the previous section of book, we have discussed the tools related to designing model in Mastercam. In this section of book, we will discuss the tools related to machining. In Mastercam, you can create machining programs for Milling, Lathe, Wire Cut, and Routers. The tools to initiate machining operation are available in the **Machine** tab of the **Ribbon**; refer to Figure-1. We will discuss the tools related to milling first and then we will discuss the other tools of this tab based on their need in subsequent chapters.

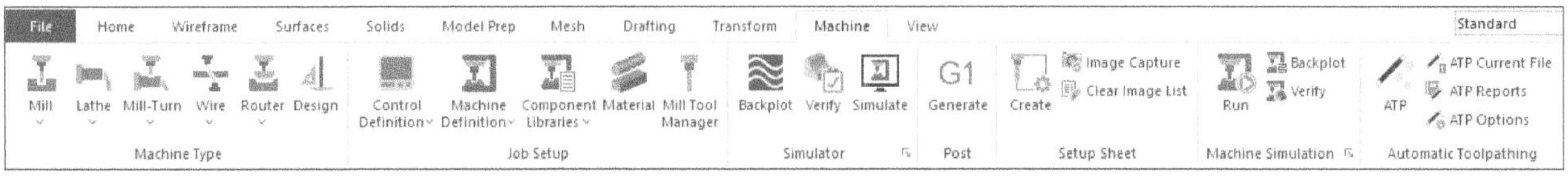

Figure-1. Machine tab

CNC MACHINE STRUCTURE

As discussed in the starting of book, CNC machines are the cutting machines which use numeric codes to perform action. These numeric codes are understood by controller installed on the machine which gives command to various motors in the machine. But, this is not our concern now. Now, we want to know what are the components of machine which should be known before creating or changing a machine in Mastercam. Figure-2 shows a 5 axis VMC with some of the components. Various major components milling and lathe machines are discussed next.

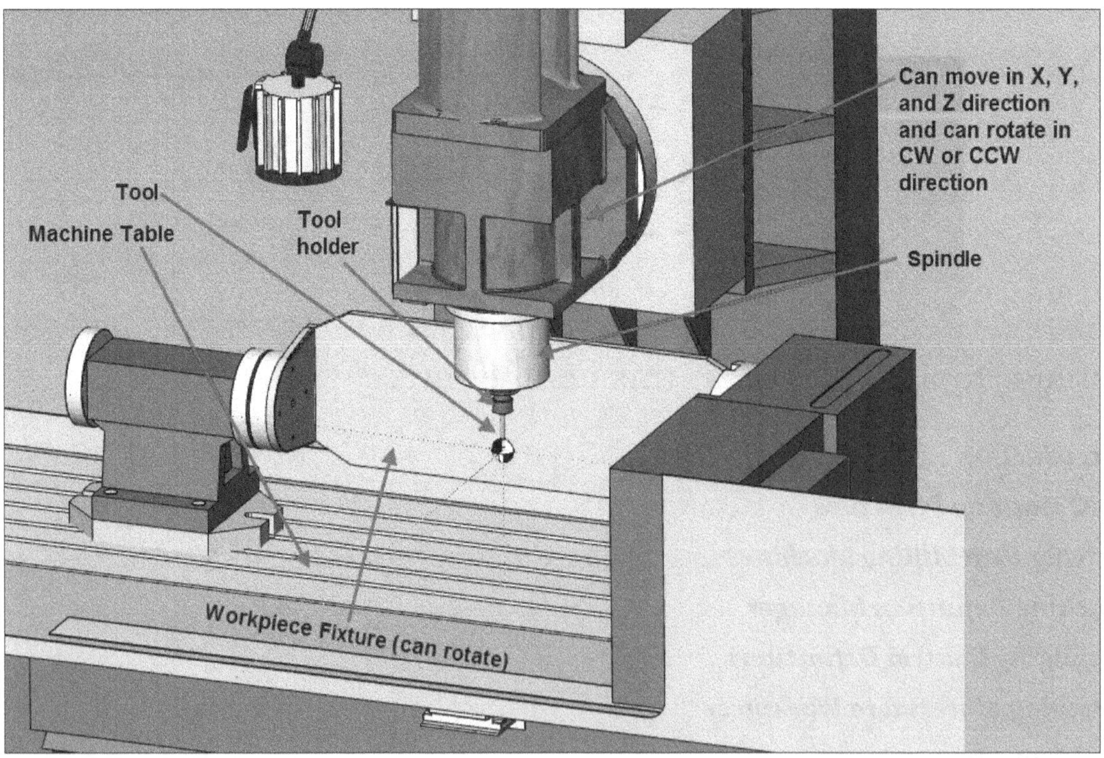

Figure-2. Five axis VMC

Tool Spindle

Machine tool spindles are rotating components that are used to hold and drive cutting tools or work pieces on lathes, milling machines, and other machine tools. They use belt, gear, motorized, hydraulic, or pneumatic drives and are available in a variety of configurations. Various specifications for selecting tool spindle are given next.

- Select spindle as per the required spindle Speed.
- Make sure spindle orientation correct as per your application.
- Consider the gauge length of the tool. Doubling the gauge length of a tool can increase the deflection at the end by a factor of 8. A way to compensate for this would be to go from a 40 taper to a 50 taper spindle and tool holder.
- Choose a spindle that can transmit the required amount of power/torque.
- When boring, select a spindle that has a nose bearing ID larger than the bore being machined.
- Select the nose bearing arrangement suited for the application.

Tool Changer or Turret

Tool changer, tool indexer, or tool turret is used to automatically change the tool in spindle; refer to Figure-3. In some CNC milling and Lathe machines, you can load more than one tool at a time and then use the NC codes to use them in different toolpaths. While purchasing the machine, you should keep a note of time taken by machine to automatically change the tool and direction in which turret can rotate.

Figure-3. Tool Spindle with indexer

Translational and Rotational Limits

The translational and rotational limits are important aspect of cnc machines. You can not make a job which required machining length or angle more than the translational or rotational limits of machine. You can find this information in catalog of machine.

Tail Stock

Tail stock is generally found in lathe machines but can also be seen with rotary table of a milling machine. Tail stock is used to support long workpiece at its end; refer to Figure-4.

Figure-4. Tail Stock in lathe

SETTING UP A MILLING MACHINE

The tools in the **Mill** drop-down of the **Machine Type** group in **Ribbon** are used to select the milling machine to be used for performing milling operations. The procedure to setup a milling machine is given next.

- Click on the **Manage List** option from the **Mill** drop-down in the **Machine Type** drop-down of the **Machine Type** group in the **Machine** tab of **Ribbon**. The **Machine Definition Menu Management** dialog box will be displayed; refer to Figure-5.

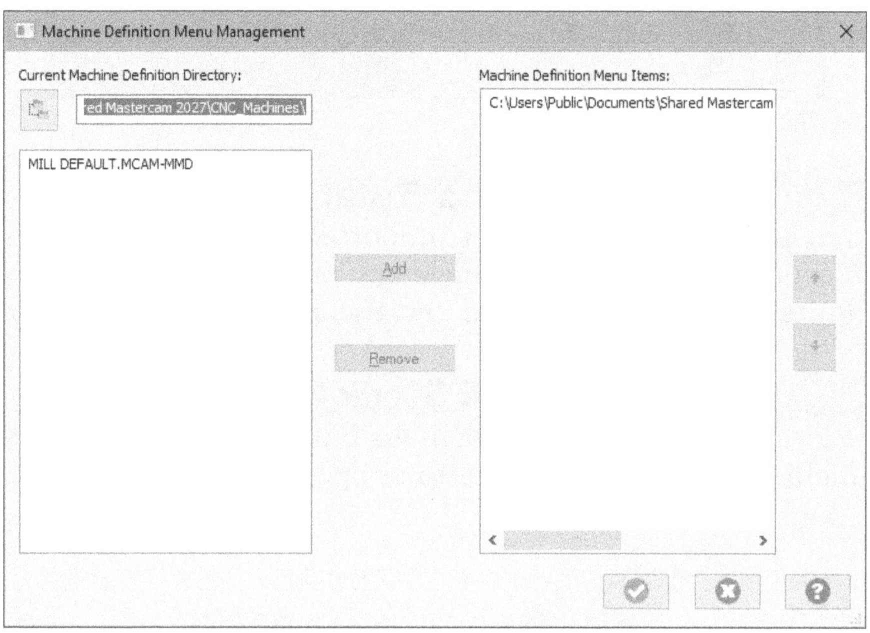

Figure-5. Machine Definition Menu Management dialog box

- Select desired option from the left list box of dialog box and click on the **Add** button. The new machine will be added in the **Machine Definition Menu** list.
- Click on the **OK** button from the dialog box to add selected machines in the list of machines for current project.
- Now, select the newly added machine to be used for current milling operation from the **Mill** drop-down of **Machine Type** group in the **Ribbon**. The **Toolpaths** contextual tab will be added in the **Ribbon**; refer to Figure-6.

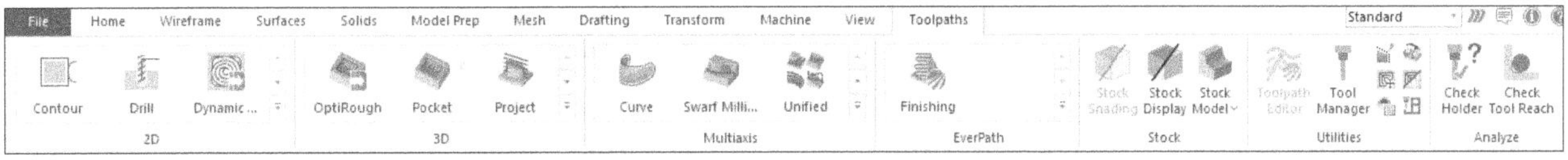

Figure-6. Toolpaths contextual tab

You will learn about the tools of **Toolpaths** contextual tab later in the book.

You can also create new machine definition based on specifications of your machine. The procedure to create a new machine definition is given next.

MODIFYING MACHINE DEFINITION

There are two tools available in **Machine Definition** drop-down of **Job Setup** panel in the **Machine** tab of **Ribbon** to modify machine definition parameters for current machine: **Edit Local** and **Edit Global**. The **Edit Local** tool is used to modify parameters of current machine being used in your model hence modifying only local copy of the machine definition. The **Edit Global** tool is used to modify machine definition parameters at the software level so all the model files (current or earlier created) get affected. We will discuss the procedure to modify machine definition at global level, you can use the same procedure for editing local machine definition. The procedure to modify global machine definition is discussed next.

- Click on the **Edit Global** tool from the **Machine Definition** drop-down in the **Job Setup** panel of the **Machine** tab of the **Ribbon**. A new copy of Mastercam application will open with **Global Machine Definition Manager**; refer to Figure-7.

Figure-7. Global Machine Definition Manager

Machine Parameters

- Click in the **Description** edit box to change the name of the machine.
- Click on the **Edit** button from the **General Machine Parameters** rollout to modify general feed rate and motion control speeds. The **Feed Rates** page will be displayed in the **Manager**; refer to Figure-8.

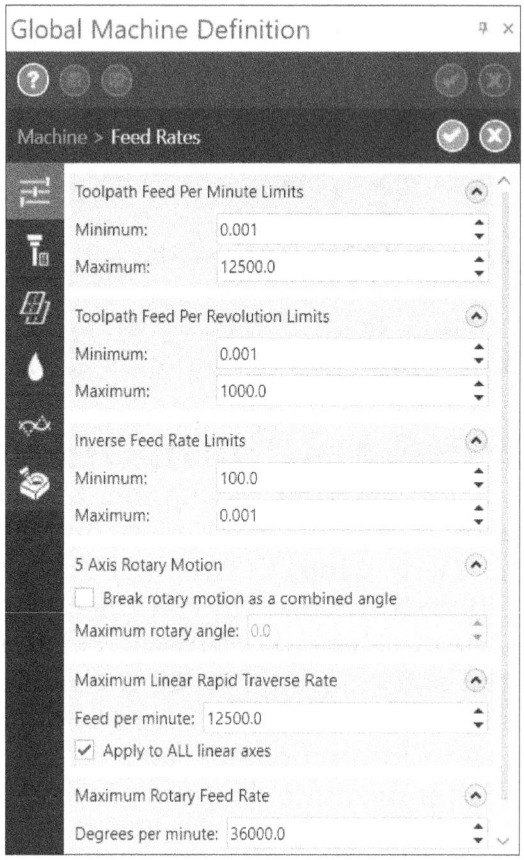

Figure-8. Feed Rates parameters

- Specify minimum and maximum limits for toolpath feed rates and inverse feed rates in respective edit boxes.
- Select the **Break rotary motion as a combined angle** check box to break rotary movement into individual linear movements after specified threshold angle. The threshold angle value is specified in the **Maximum rotary angle** edit box.
- Similarly, specify desired values in the **Maximum Linear Rapid Transverse Rate** and **Maximum Rotary Feed Rate** edit boxes to define rapid movement limits for linear and rotary motion in the machine, respectively.
- Select the **Tool and Material Libraries** tab from left in the **Manager** to select library file of cutting tool and stock material.
- Similarly, use **Planes**, **Coolant Commands**, **Machine Dynamics**, and **Simulation** tabs to define related parameters. Click on the **OK** button from the **Manager** to exit **Feed Rates** page. The **Machine** page will be displayed in **Global Machine Definition Manager**.
- Select desired radio button from the **Display Units** rollout to define whether you want to display only selected system unit in graphics area or you want to show both U.S. inch and metric units.
- Click on the **Security Settings** button from the **File Protection** rollout to apply password to machine definition file. The **Security Settings** page will be displayed in the **Manager**; refer to Figure-9.

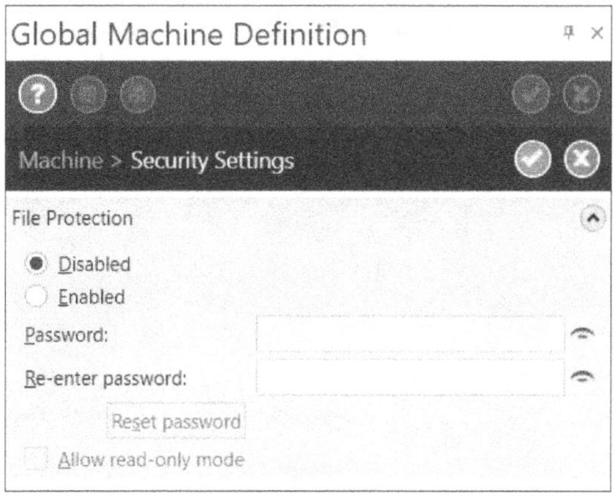

Figure-9. Security Settings page

- Select the **Enabled** radio button to enable file protection.
- Input desired password in **Password** and **Re-enter password** edit boxes.
- Select the **Allow read-only mode** check box to allow users to view machine definition without entering password.
- After setting desired parameters, click on the **OK** button from the page to return to the **Manager**.

Kinematic Tree Configuration

- Select the **Configuration** tab from left in the **Global Machine Definition Manager** to define kinematic structure of machine. The options will be displayed as shown in Figure-10.

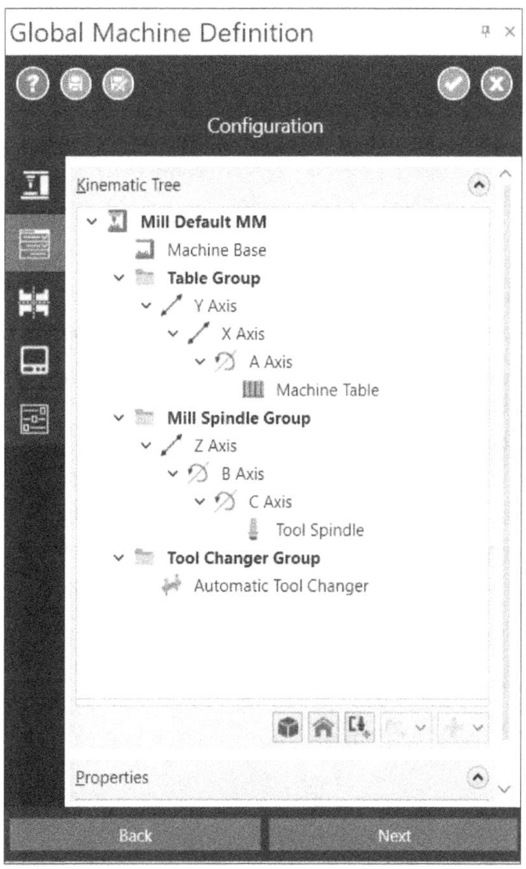

Figure-10. Configuration tab in Global Machine Definition Manager

Editing Linear Axis Components

- Double-click on linear axis moving components like X Axis, Y Axis, or Z Axis in the **Kinematic Tree** rollout. The **Machine Component Manager-Linear Axis** dialog box will be displayed; refer to Figure-11.

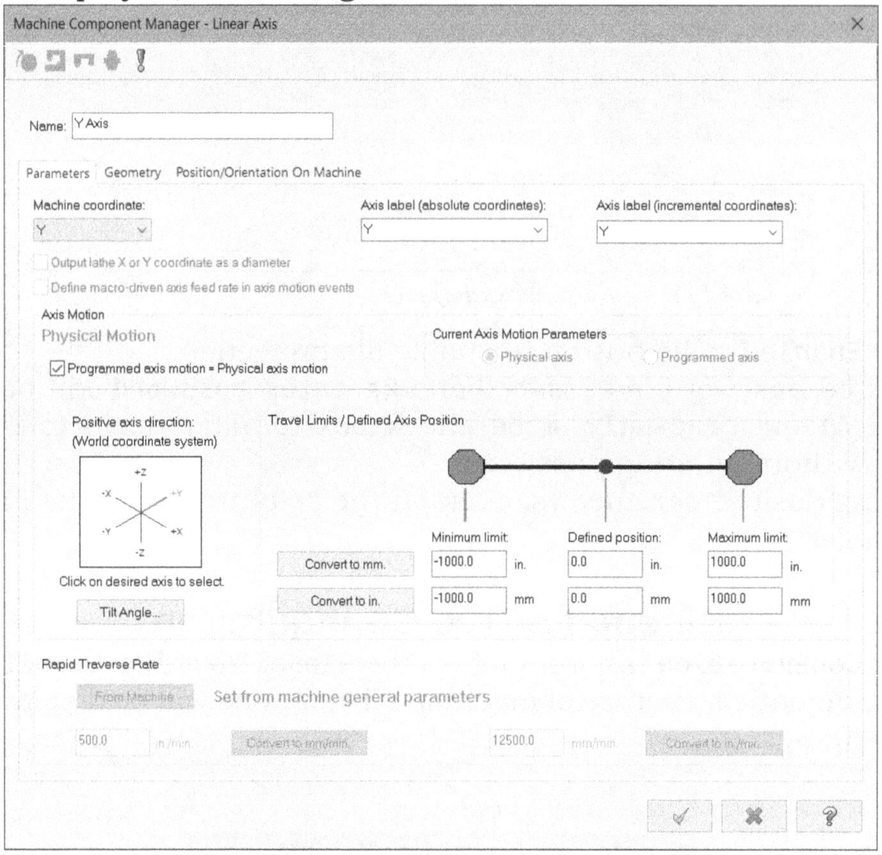

Figure-11. Machine Component Manager-Linear Axis dialog box

- Specify desired name for the axis in the **Name** edit box or you can leave it to its default name.
- Set the machine coordinate, axis label absolute, and axis label relative as required in your programming.
- Enter desired value of minimum limit, defined position, and maximum limit of travel in the respective edit boxes of **Travel Limits/Defined Axis Position** area of the dialog box. If you have specified the values in **inch** edit boxes then click on the **Convert to mm** button to automatically fill the values in **mm** edit boxes in the dialog box or you can do vice-versa.
- Select an axis from the **Position axis** direction box to define the axis of travel in WCS. If you want to tilt the axis then click on the **Tilt Angle** button below **Position axis** direction box in the dialog box; refer to Figure-12. The **Tilt Angle (Linear Axis)** dialog box will be displayed; refer to Figure-13.

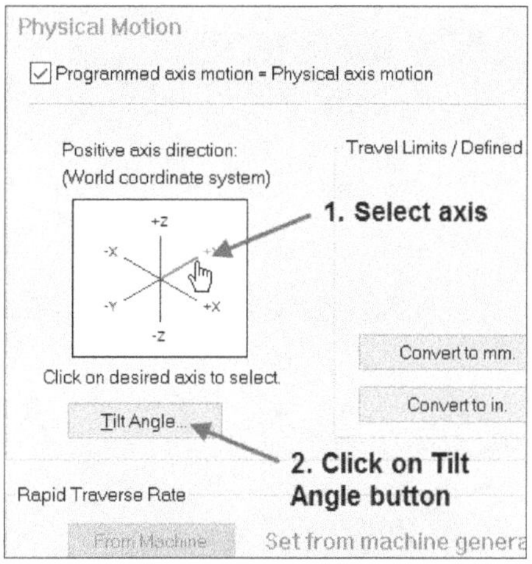

Figure-12. Tilt Angle button

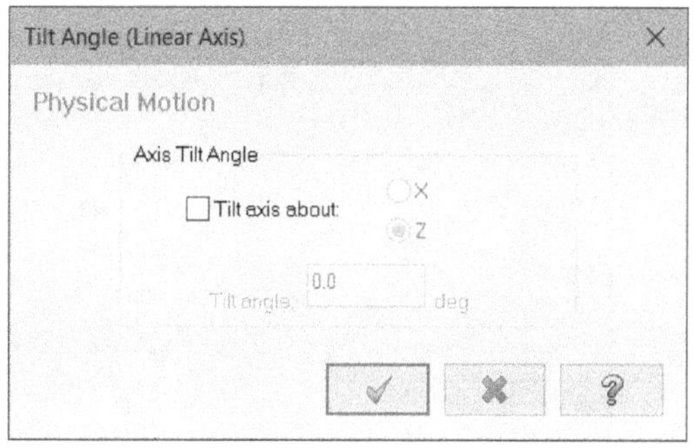

Figure-13. Tilt Angle (Linear Axis) dialog box

- Select the **Tilt axis about** check box and select the radio button for axis about which you want to tilt the current axis.
- Specify desired angle value and click on the **OK** button to tilt the axis.

Editing Rotary Axis Components

- Double-click on the **A Axis**, **B Axis**, or **C Axis** component in the **Kinematic Tree** rollout of the **Global Machine Definition Manager**. The **Machine Component Manager - Rotary Axis** dialog box will be displayed; refer to Figure-14.
- Select desired machine coordinates and axis labels as done for linear axis components in previous topic.
- Select the axis of rotation and **0** degree position from the boxes in the **World coordinate system** area of the dialog box. Specify the tilt angle if required by using the **Tilt Angle** button.
- Set the Counter Clockwise(**CCW**) or Clockwise(**CW**) direction of rotation from the **Direction** area of the dialog box.
- Specify the travel limits in the **Travel Limits** area of the dialog box and position of center of rotation in the **Center of Rotation** area of the dialog box.
- Specify desired value in the **Maximum feed rate** edit box to specify maximum rotation feed allowed by the machine.
- Select the **Break rotary motion** check box to break the rotary motion after specified angular rotation. Select the **Use chordal deviation** check box to allow specified deviation.
- Select desired option from the **Fixed/Continuous Positioning** area to specify the increment angle for rotation or allow smooth rotation of machine in specified direction.
- Click on the **OK** button from the dialog box to apply changes.

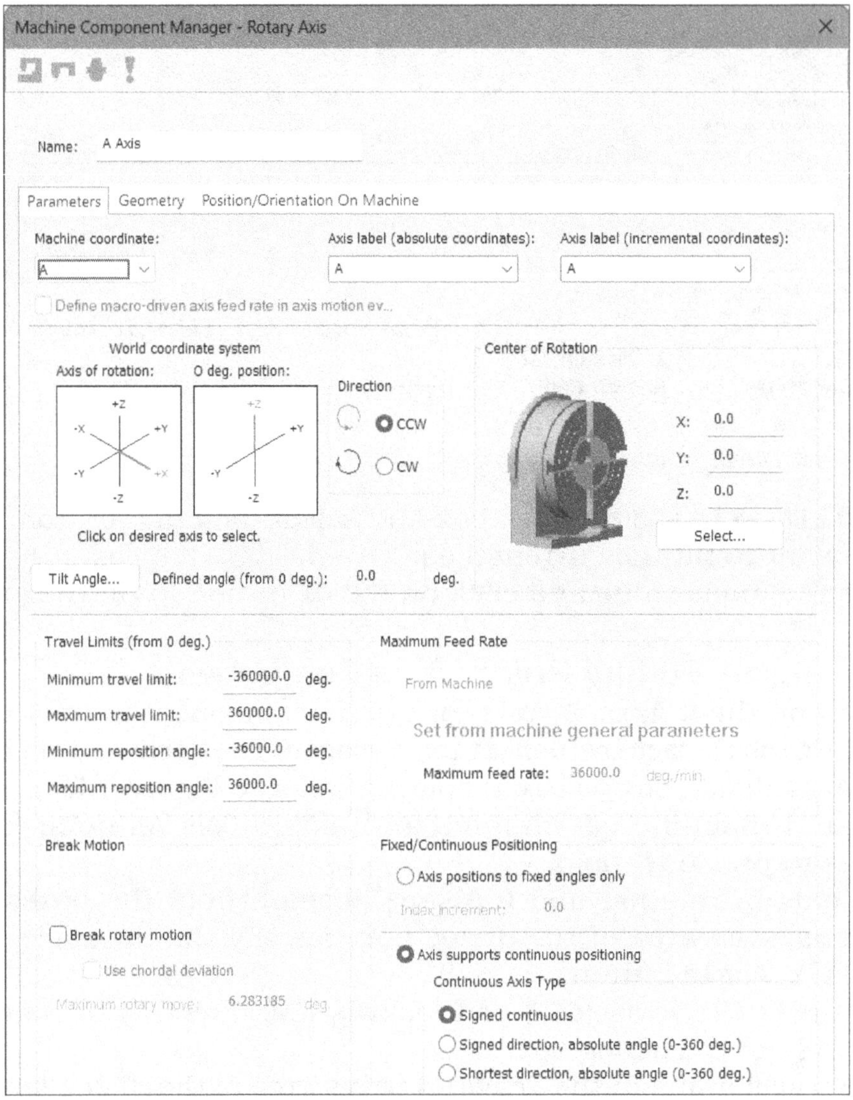

Figure-14. Machine Component Manager-Rotary Axis dialog box

Editing Tool Spindle

- Double-click on **Tool Spindle** from the **Machine** area of the **Machine Definition Manager** dialog box. The **Machine Component Manager - Tool Spindle** dialog box will be displayed; refer to Figure-15.
- Set the minimum and maximum spindle rotation speed in **Minimum spindle speed** and **Maximum spindle speed** edit boxes, respectively.
- Similarly, specify the tool orientation and other parameters of the tool spindle. Click on the **OK** button from the dialog box to apply the changes.

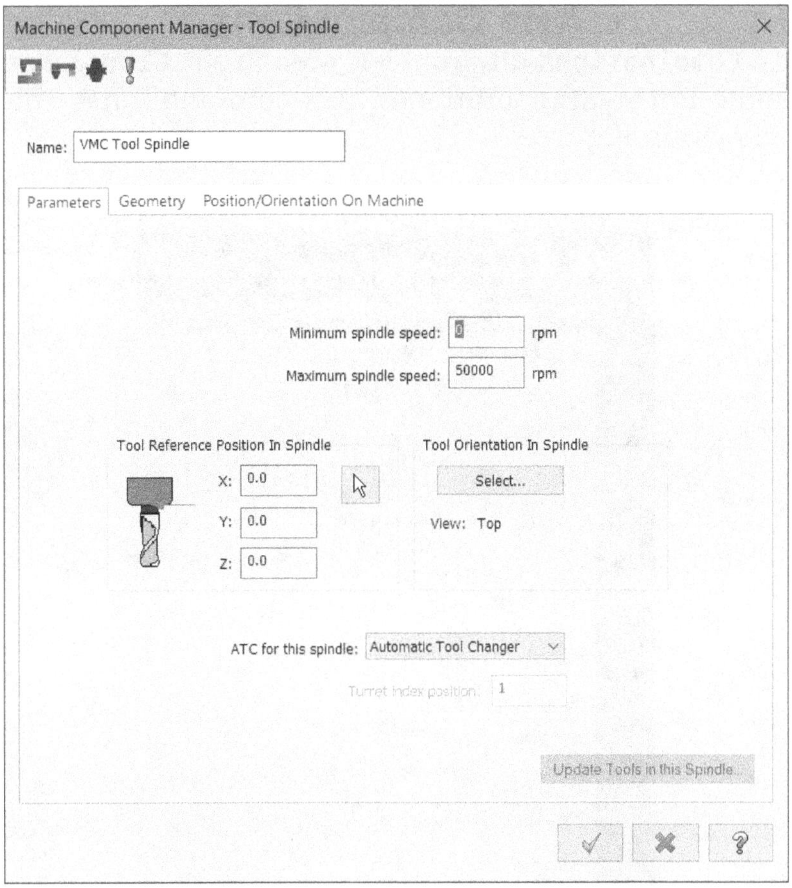

Figure-15. Machine Component Manager-Tool Spindle dialog box

Similarly, you can edit the other components of machine by double-clicking on them in the **Kinematic Tree** rollout.

Adding New Component

- If you want to add a new component to machine structure then click on the **Add Component** button from bottom right section. A flyout will be displayed; refer to Figure-16.

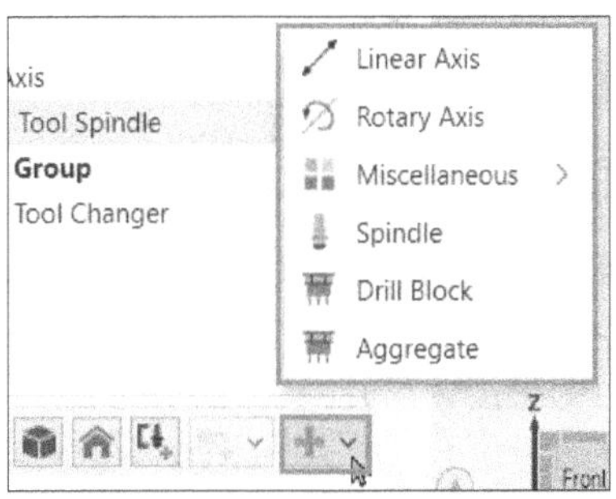

Figure-16. Add Component flyout

- Select desired option from the flyout to add respective component to selected object in **Kinematic Tree**. Related dialog box will be displayed to define parameters. Note that options in this flyout will be active based on selected component in **Kinematic Tree**. The options for added component can be defined as discussed earlier.

Axis Combinations

- Select the **Axis Combinations** tab from left area in the **Global Machine Definition Manager** to define linear and rotational axis combinations. The options will be displayed as shown in Figure-17.

Figure-17. Axis Combinations

- Select check boxes for axes to be used in machining. Note that these axes and their arrangement should match with your physical machine.
- Scroll down in the **Manager** and specify desired values in the edit boxes of **Home position** section to define position of cutting tool tip at the beginning of machining cycle.

Control Definition Parameters

- Select the **Control Definition** tab from left area in the **Global Machine Definition Manager** to define Post Processing controller of the machine. The options in the **Manager** will be displayed as shown in Figure-18.
- Click on the **Open file** button for **File** field to select desired control definition file. The **Control Definition Files** dialog box will be displayed; refer to Figure-19.
- Select the file of desired control system and click on the **Open** button. The control will be applied to the machine.
- Select desired option from the **Control** drop-down to control definition from various definitions available in selected file. The post processor will be selected automatically based on option selected in this drop-down.

Editing Control Definition

- Click on the **Edit control definition** button to modify local copy of control definition. The **Control Definition** dialog box will be displayed; refer to Figure-20. Using this option, you can define how codes will be output for your physical machine components.
- Click on desired topic from the **Control topics** area of the dialog box. The parameters related to the selected topic will be displayed; refer to Figure-21.

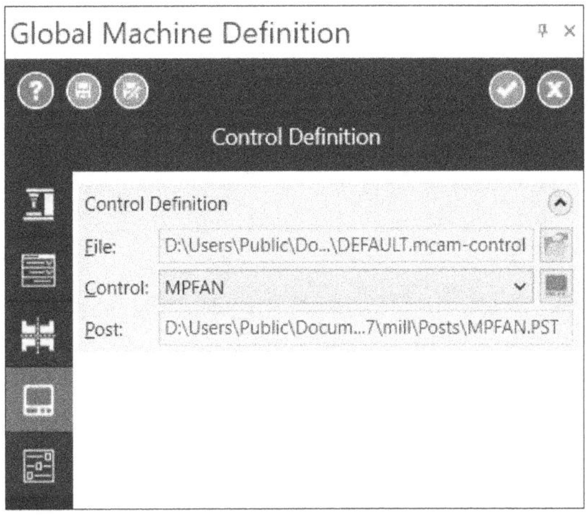

Figure-18. Control Definition tab

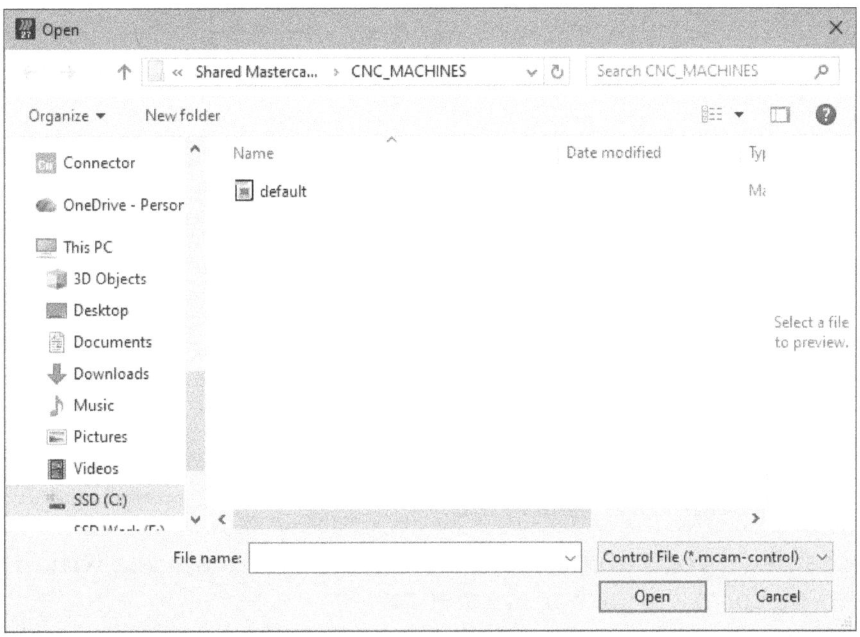

Figure-19. Open dialog box

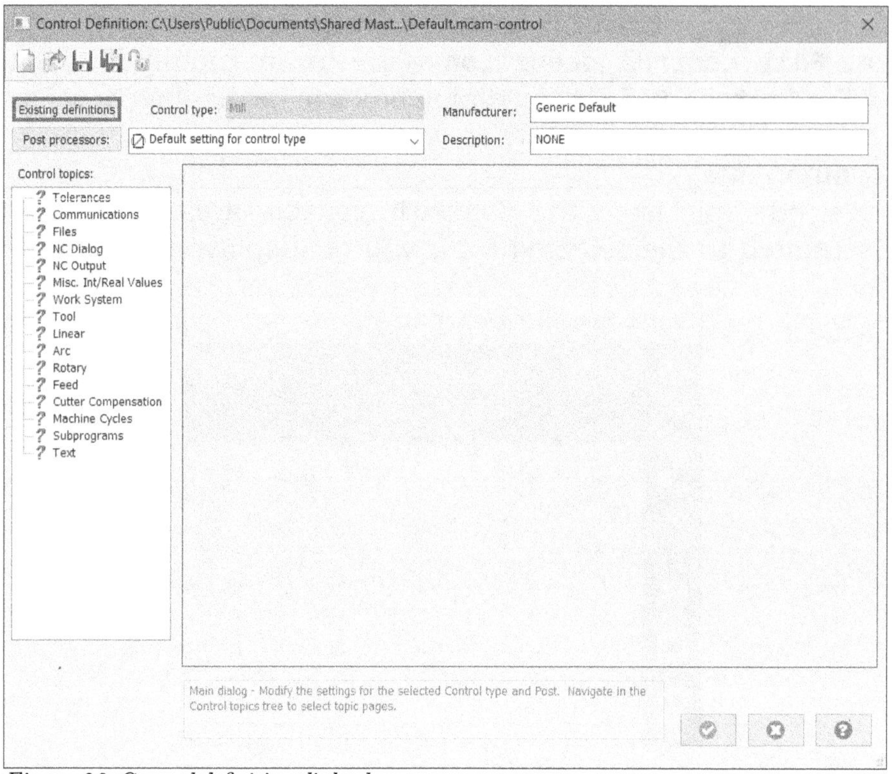

Figure-20. Control definition dialog box

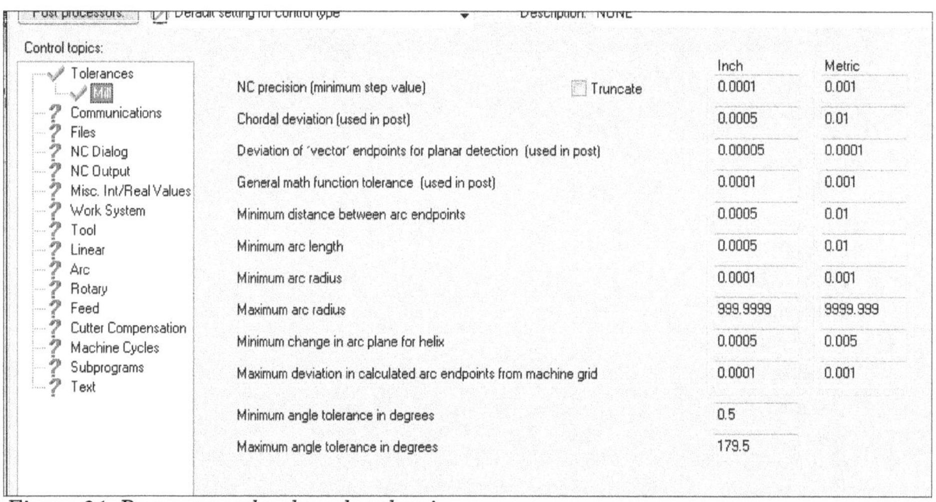

Figure-21. Parameters related to selected topic

- In **Tolerances** page, you can define the tolerance values up to which your machine is capable to perform various movements.
- In **Communications** page, you can define the connection capabilities of your machine. If your machine is capable to connect with computer using **CimcoDNC** then set it in **Communications** drop-down. Similarly, you can define other connection types.
- In the **Files** page, you can set path for various libraries used by machine and directory where output file will be saved. You can also set machine to post error files generated while performing machining operations.
- In the **NC Dialog** page, you can define whether check boxes for **Reference point** and **Tool Display** will be available in **Tool Parameters** dialog box.
- In the **NC Output** page, you can define the NC output capabilities of Machine in the software. You can define various default parameters for output like generate incremental output, add comments in NC output file, starting sequence number and increments in sequence for codes in the file, and so on.

- In the **Misc. Int/Real Values** page, you can set various integers and real numbers to represent different machine functions. For example, you can set 2 to represent G54 code for Work Coordinate system.
- In **Work System** page, you can work coordinate for an operation will be selected for performing an operation in the machine. If you want work coordinates of operations change based on Work offsets then select the option from **Work coordinate selection** drop-down on this page. Similarly, you can set Tool planes to change based on work offsets.
- In **Tool** page, you can define offsets for cutting tools used in the machine. For example, if you have two end mills of 10 mm diameter and one of them is worn out the you can compensate the wear using tool offsets.
- In **Linear** page, you can define how cutting tool will move in linear directions for rapid and feed passes.
- In **Arc** page, you can define parameters related to arc moves (G02 and G03) of the machine. If there is a plane in which your machine does not support arc moves then clear respective check box from this page.
- In **Rotary** page, you can define whether rotary moves of machine will be broken into smaller sections or it will perform large continuous rotary moves.
- In **Feed** page, you can define unit to be used for various feed moves.
- In **Cutter Compensation** page, you can set whether machine supports cutter compensation or not. If machine supports cutter compensation then you can define the modes in which cutter compensation will be applied.
- In **Machine Cycles** page, you can define whether machine supports milling peck cycles and drill cycles or not. If machine supports these cycles then what are the sub types supported by it.
- In **Subprograms** page, you can define if machine supports subprograms (small repeating code blocks which are generally called by reference name in main program).
- In the **Text** page, you can define custom names (values) for various functions which can be performed on the machine.
- Specify desired manufacturer name and description for the control file in respective edit boxes at the top in the dialog box.
- Click on the **Post processors** button at the top in the dialog box to select desired post processor for the machine. The **Control Definition Post List Edit** dialog box will be displayed; refer to Figure-22. Click on the **Add files** button to add more posts in the list that can be used with this machine control definition. Similarly, you can use **Delete files** button to delete posts from list. Click on the **OK** button from the dialog box to apply changes. Note that it is important to add post processors in the list of control definition as they are linked in Mastercam for proper output.

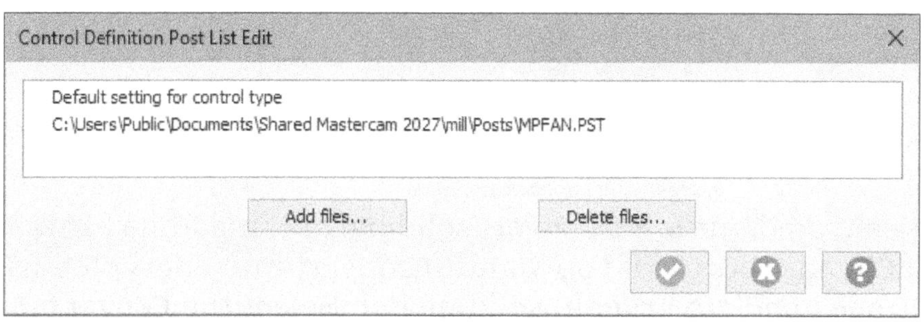

Figure-22. Control Definition Post List Edit dialog box

- Click on the **Save As** button and save your machine control definition by desired name. (Note that this feature is not available in Home Learning Edition of software).
- Click on the **OK** button from the dialog box to use the created control definition. The **Machine Definition Manager** dialog box will be displayed again. Note that the parameters specified in the dialog box are used to specify the limits of your machine controller.

Options

- Click on the **Options** tab from left in the **Global Machine Definition Manager** to define level parameters and mesh conversion settings; refer to Figure-23.

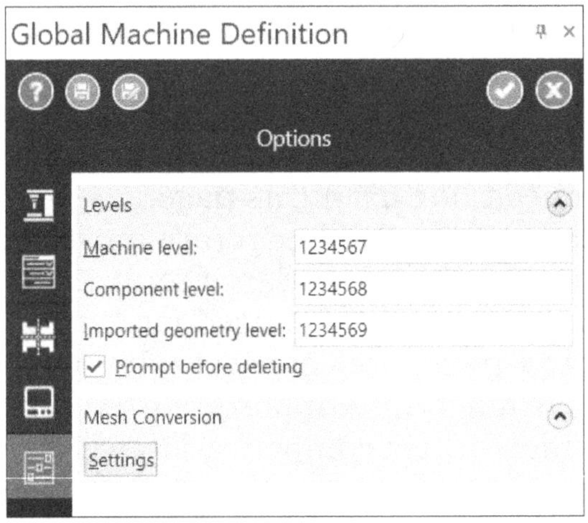

Figure-23. Options tab

- The parameters in the **Levels** section are used to define levels where machine level data, component level data, and imported geometry data will be stored.
- Select the **Prompt before deleting** check box to confirm when you attempt to delete any level defined in this **Manager**.
- Click on the **Settings** button from **Mesh Conversion** rollout to define settings for converting solid parts to mesh models. The **Mesh Conversion** page will be displayed in the **Manager**.

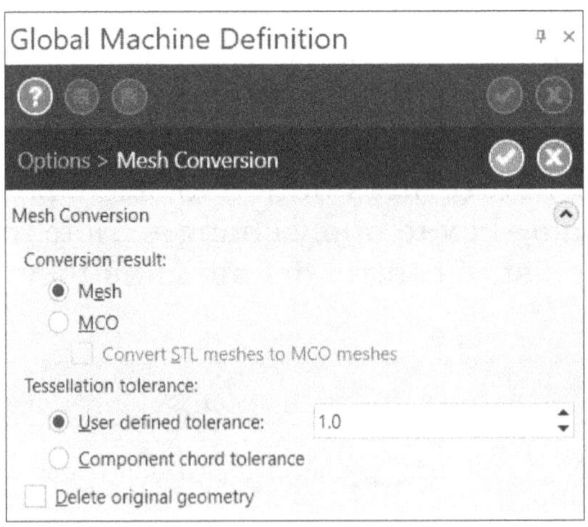

Figure-24. Mesh Conversion page

- Select the **Mesh** radio button to convert solid parts of machine to Mastercam mesh.
- Select the **MCO** radio button if you want to convert into encrypted mesh file which cannot be traced back to original solid model. Select the **Convert STL meshes to MCO meshes** check box to perform conversion of STL mesh files to MCO mesh files if they are present in model.

- Set the other parameters as discussed earlier and click on the **OK** button.
- After setting desired parameters, click on the **Save** button from top left in the **Manager** to overwrite changes to current machine definition file. Click on the **Save as** button to save settings in a new machine definition file.
- Click the **OK** button from the **Global Machine Definition Manager** to apply specified machine settings and exit the tool. Close the current Mastercam application window to return to previous file. Note that you do not need to save current model file when exiting.

REPLACING MACHINE DEFINITION

The **Replace** tool in **Machine Definition** drop-down of **Job Setup** group in **Machine** tab of **Ribbon** is used to replace currently being used Machine definition from selected file. On selecting this tool, the **Open Machine Definition File** dialog box will be displayed as discussed earlier. Select desired file and click on the **Open** button to perform replacement.

Similarly, use the **Reload** tool from **Machine Definition** drop-down to update machine definition being used in current model if there have been changes in the definition file.

NEW MACHINE DEFINITIONS

When you are starting a new machining project and you have not selected any machine from **Machine Type** panel to be assigned for generating toolpath then you will find tools to create new machine definitions in the **Machine Definition** drop-down of **Job Setup** panel in the **Machine** tab of **Ribbon**; refer to Figure-25. Click on the **New Mill** tool to create a new milling machine definition. The **Global Machine Definition Manager** will be displayed which has been discussed earlier. Similarly, you can use other tools in this drop-down to create respective type of machine definitions.

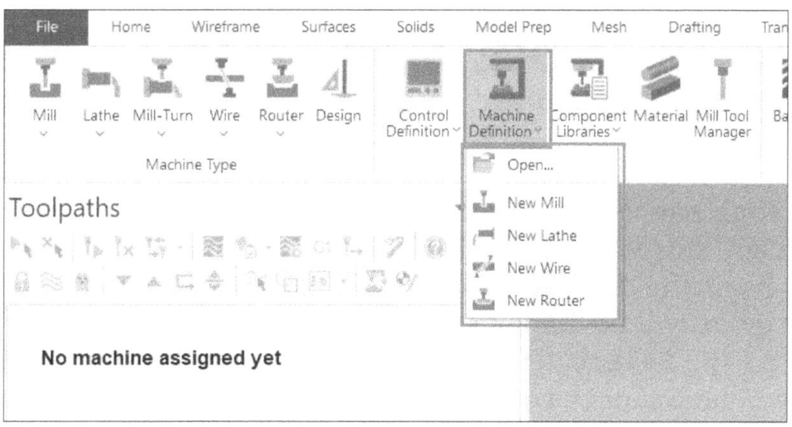

Figure-25. Machine Definition drop-down

MANAGING CONTROL DEFINITION

The **Edit Local** and **Edit Global** tools in **Control Definition** drop-down are used to modify local and global copies of controller definition for current machine. The procedure to use this tool is given next.

- Click on the **Control Definition** tool from the **Job Setup** group of the **Machine** tab in the **Ribbon**. The **Control Definition** dialog box will be displayed. The options of **Control Definition** dialog box have already been discussed.

APPLYING MATERIAL TO WORKPIECE

The **Material** tool is used to apply desired material to the workpiece. Based on the material of workpiece, the feed rate and other cutting parameters are decided while machining. The procedure to use this tool is given next.

- Click on the **Material** tool from the **Job Setup** group in the **Machine** tab of the **Ribbon**. The **Material List** dialog box will be displayed; refer to Figure-26.

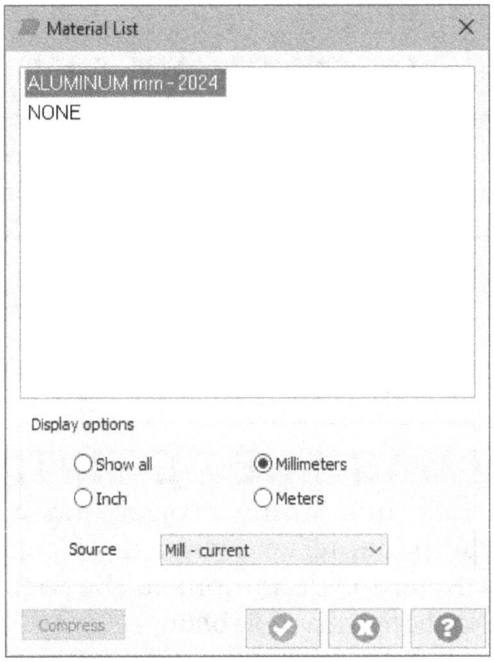

Figure-26. Material List dialog box

- Select desired material from the list and click on the **OK** button.

TOOL MANAGER

The **Tool Manager** is used to manage data related to tools. The procedure to use the **Tool Manager** is given next.

- Click on the **Tool Manager** tool from the **Utilities** group of **Toolpaths** tab in the **Ribbon** while you are working with milling machines or click on the **Mill Tool Manager** tool from the **Job Setup** panel of **Machine** tab in the **Ribbon**. The **Tool Manager** dialog box will be displayed; refer to Figure-27. In case of your dialog box empty, click on the **Select a different tool library button** from the middle in dialog box. The **Select tool library** dialog box will be displayed; refer to Figure-28. Select **mill mm.tooldb** file from the dialog box and click on the **Open** button. Click on the **Tools** tab in the dialog box to display list of tools. The list of tools will be updated.

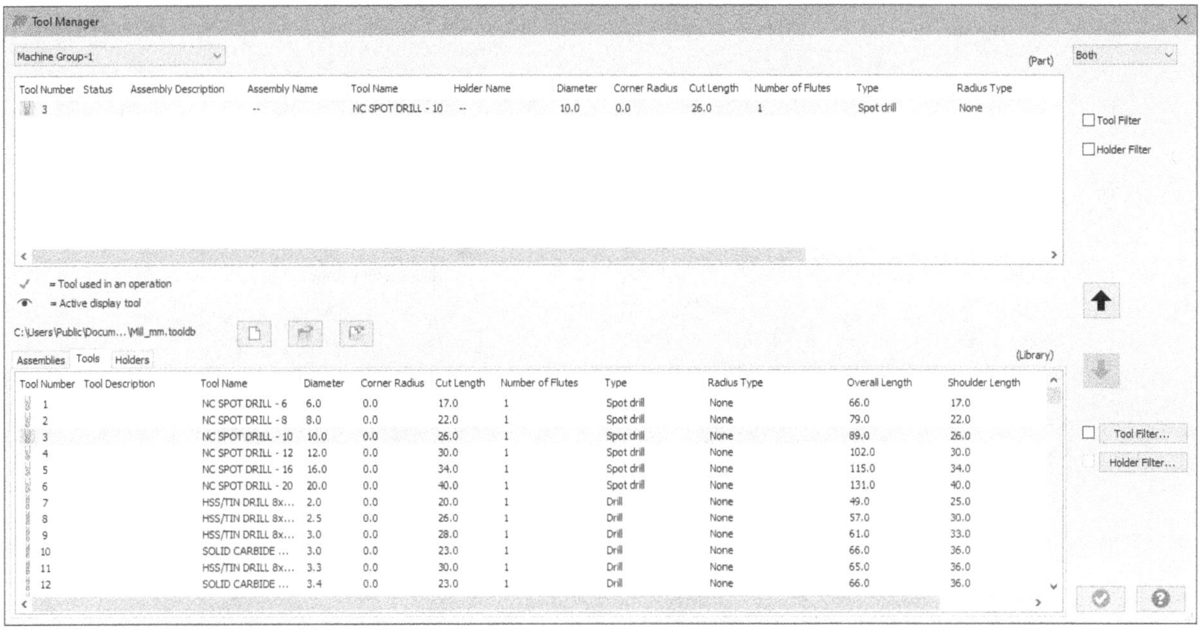

Figure-27. Tool Manager

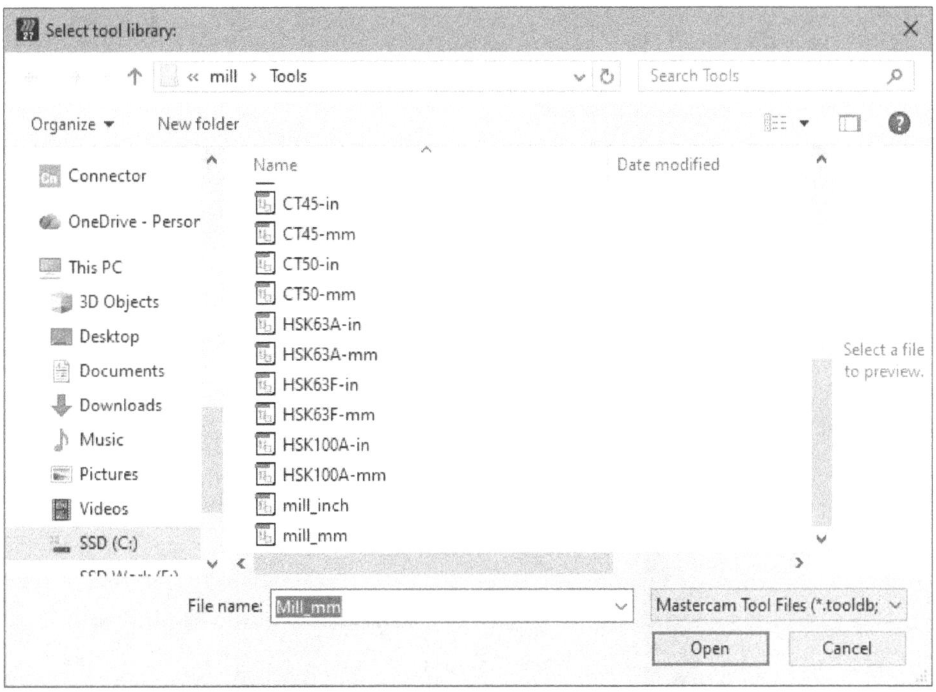

Figure-28. Select tool library dialog box

- Select the tools that you want to include in current machine group. Note that to select multiple tools, you need to press and hold the **CTRL** key while selecting tools.
- Click on the **Up** arrow to include the tools in the current machine group.
- Click on the **OK** button from the dialog box to accept the selected tools.

Creating New Tool

- Right-click in the top area of the dialog box to display shortcut menu; refer to Figure-29.

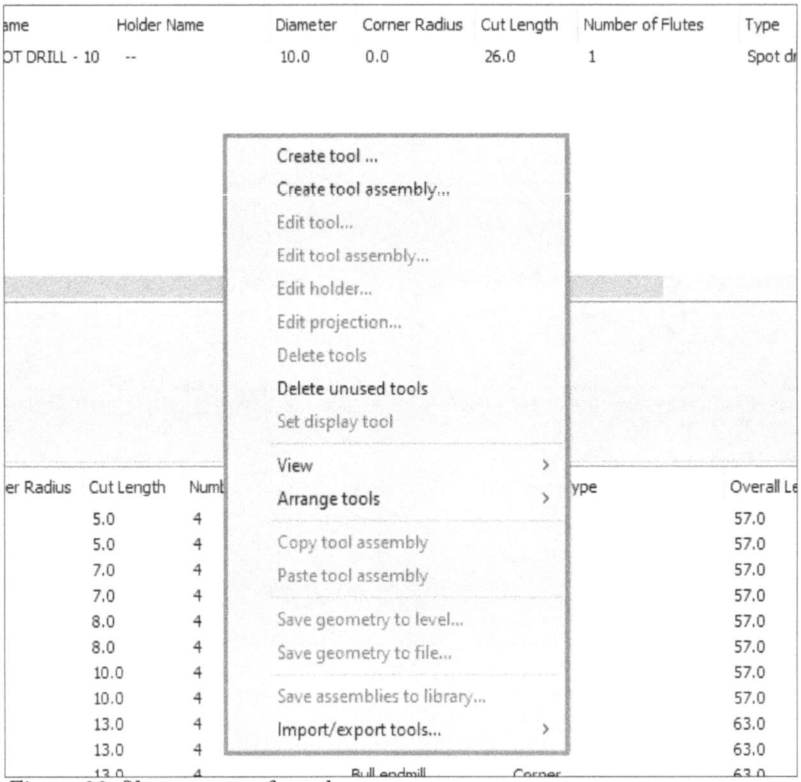

Figure-29. Shortcut menu for tools

- Click on the **Create new tool** option from the shortcut menu. The **Mill Tool Designer Manager** will be displayed; refer to Figure-30.

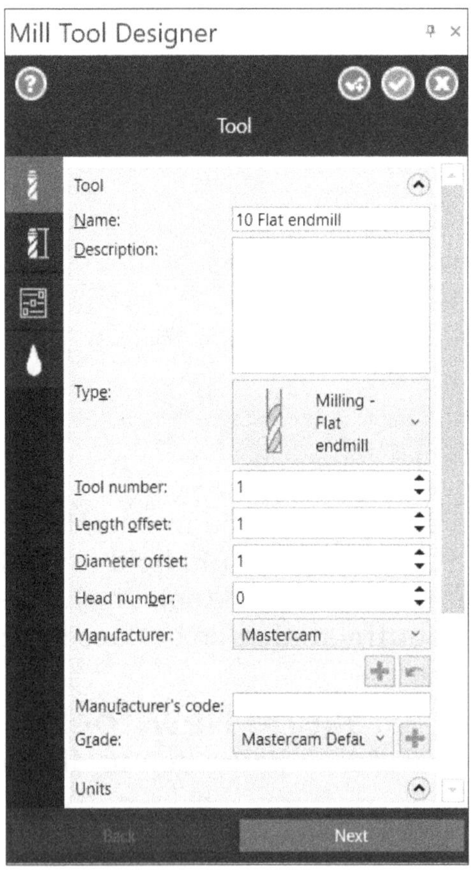

Figure-30. Mill Tool Designer Manager

- Specify desired name of tool in the **Name** edit box and type desired description about the tool in **Description** edit box. You should specify these values in such a way that they are easy to interpret later.
- Select desired option from the **Type** drop-down to define type of cutting tool. (We are using Dove mill).
- Set desired values for **Tool number**, **Length offset**, **Diameter offset**, and **Head number** edit boxes to synchronize it with your physical milling machine.
- Specify manufacturer related data in the **Manufacturer**, **Manufacturer's Code**, and **Grade** fields.
- Select desired radio button from the **Units** rollout to define unit for measurement of cutting tool.
- Specify desired value of angle between cutting edge and horizontal line at the tip of cutting tool in the **Helix angle** edit box of the **Advanced Settings** rollout. Select desired option from the **Helix type** drop-down to define whether cutting edge is moving upward, downward, compression or none. An upward cutting edge will move chips upward and downward cutting edge will move chips downward, while a compression cutting edge will move chips upward upto certain length and then act as downward type.
- Select the **Variable pitch** check box if your cutting tool has varying helix pitch of cutting edge.

Geometry Settings

Click on the **Geometry** option from left in the **Mill Tool Designer Manager**. The **Geometry** page will be displayed as shown in Figure-31.

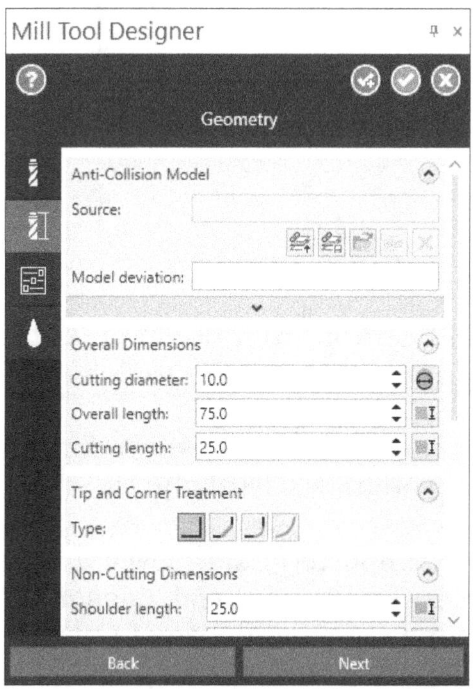

Figure-31. Geometry page in Mill Tool Designer

- In the **Anti-Collision Model** rollout, you can use different options to automatically generate profile of cutting tool using open wireframe sketch (created in Mastercam) or CAD model of cutting tool (created in any CAD software).
- Click on the **Import custom geometry from level** button from the rollout to use sketch drawn in wireframe as profile. The **Select Level** dialog box will be displayed. Select the level on which you have created open profile of cutting tool

(half side; refer to Figure-32), starting from origin and click on the **OK** button from the dialog box to create custom tool; refer to Figure-33.

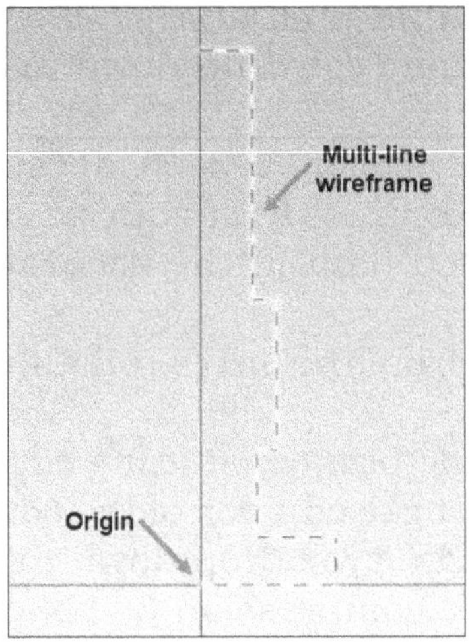

Figure-32. Profile for cutting tool

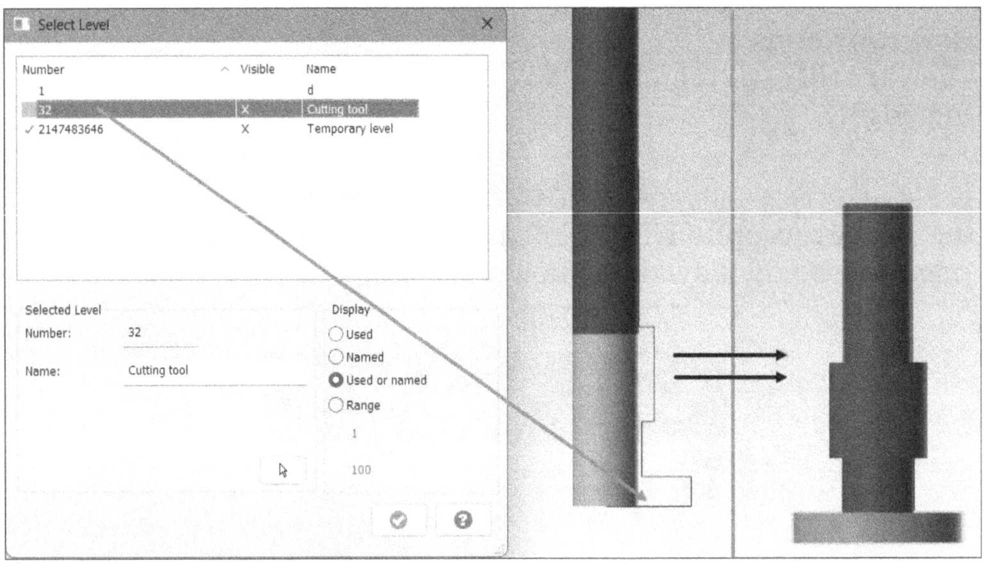

Figure-33. Custom tool using level

- Click on the **Select model** button from the **Anti-Collision Model** rollout to use STEP, DXF, or Mastercam Solid Model file to define cutting tool profile.

Scan the video link to learn how to create custom cutting tool.
https://www.youtube.com/watch?v=xCrInLghb1E

- You can use the geometry imported using level wireframe or model as reference and set desired parameters in the **Tip and Corner Treatment** and **Non-Cutting Dimensions** rollout to define shape and size of cutting tool.
- Use the options in the **Display** and **Opacity** rollouts to control display of tool models during creation.

Parameters

Click on the **Parameters** option from the left to define cutting data and various speed parameters for the tool; refer to Figure-34. This data can be obtained from your cutting tool provider.

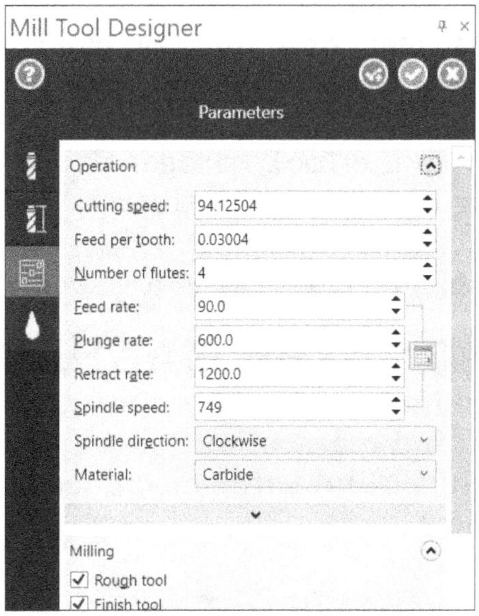

Figure-34. Parameters page

Similarly, set the parameters on **Coolant** page and click on the **OK** button from the **Manager**. The cutting tool will be created.

Editing Tool

- Select the tool from the top list and right-click on it. A shortcut menu will be displayed as discussed earlier.
- Click on the **Edit tool** option from the shortcut menu. The **Mill Assembly Designer** Manager will be displayed; refer to Figure-35.

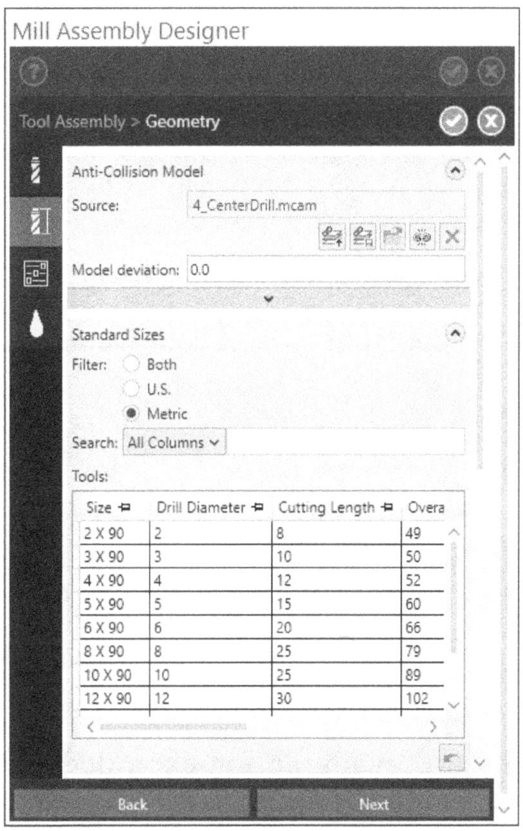

Figure-35. Mill Assembly Designer Manager

- Specify desired parameters related to the tool as discussed earlier and click on the **OK** button from the **Manager**. Note that you can combine various cutting tools in a set using

- Click on the **OK** button from the **Tool Manager** to set the specified settings. Click on the **Yes** button to save changes in the library.

TOOLS USED IN CNC MILLING AND LATHE MACHINES

The tools used in CNC machines are made of cemented carbide, High Speed Steel, Tungsten Alloys, Ceramics, and many other hard materials. The shapes and sizes of tools used in Milling machines and Lathe machines are different from each other. These tools are discussed next.

Milling Tools

There are various type of milling tools for different applications. These tools are discussed next.

End Mill

End mills are used for producing precision shapes and holes on a Milling or Turning machine. The correct selection and use of end milling cutters is paramount with either machining centers or lathes. End mills are available in a variety of design styles and materials; refer to Figure-36.

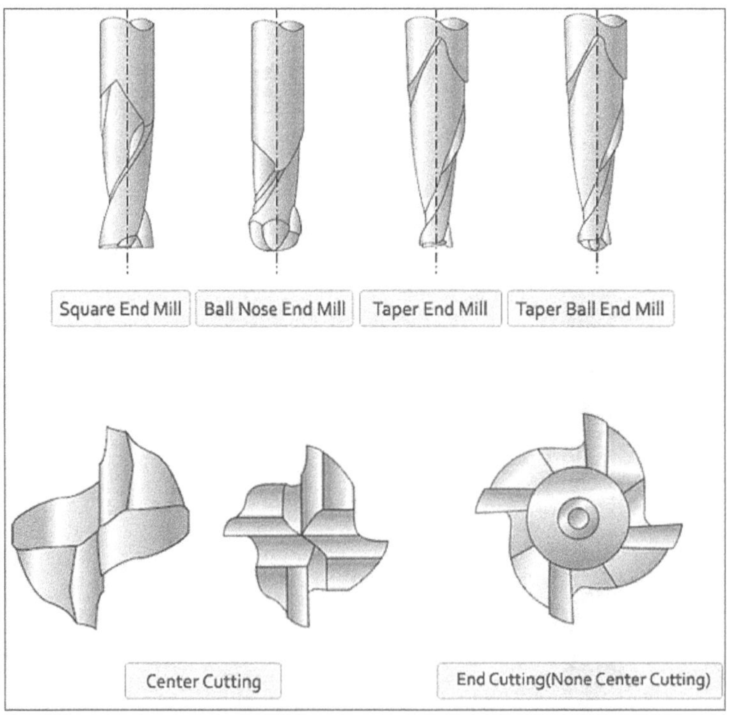

Figure-36. End Mill tool types

Titanium coated end mills are available for extended tool life requirements. The successful application of end milling depends on how well the tool is held (supported) by the tool holder. To achieve best results, an end mill must be mounted concentric in a tool holder. The end mill can be selected for the following basic processes:

FACE MILLING - For small face areas, of relatively shallow depth of cut. The surface finish produced can be 'scratchy".

KEYWAY PRODUCTION - Normally two separate end mills are required to produce a quality keyway.

WOODRUFF KEYWAYS - Normally produced with a single cutter, in a straight plunge operation.

SPECIALTY CUTTING - Includes milling of tapered surfaces, "T" shaped slots & dovetail production.

FINISH PROFILING - To finish the inside/outside shape on a part with a parallel side wall.

CAVITY DIE WORK - Generally involves plunging and finish cutting of pockets in die steel. Cavity work requires the production of three dimensional shapes. A Ball type end mill is used for the finishing cutter with this application.

Roughing End Mills, also known as ripping cutters or hoggers, are designed to remove large amounts of metal quickly and more efficiently than standard end mills; refer to Figure-37. Coarse tooth roughing end mills remove large chips for heavy cuts, deep slotting, and rapid stock removal on low to medium carbon steel and alloy steel prior to a finishing application. Fine tooth roughing end mills remove less material but the pressure is distributed over many more teeth, for longer tool life and a smoother finish on high temperature alloys and stainless steel.

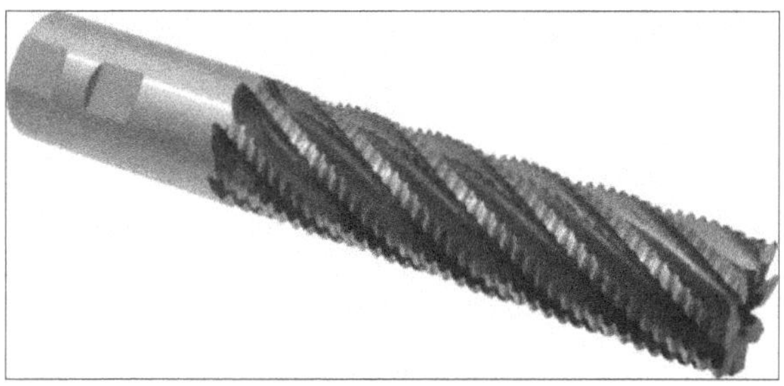

Figure-37. Roughing End Mill

Bull Nose Mill

Bull nose mill look alike end mill but they have radius at the corners. Using this tool, you can cut round corners in the die or mold steels. Shape of bull nose mill tool is given in Figure-38.

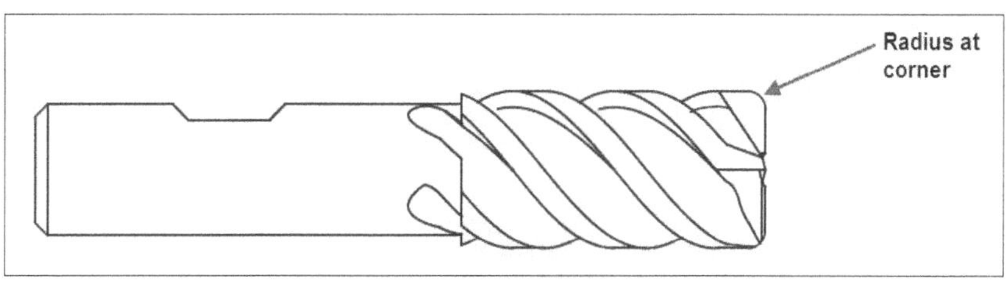

Figure-38. Bull Nose Mill cutter

Ball Nose Mill

Ball nose cutters or ball end mills has the end shape hemispherical; refer to Figure-36. They are ideal for machining 3-dimensional contoured shapes in machining centers, for example in moulds and dies. They are sometimes called ball mills in shop-floor slang. They are also used to add a radius between perpendicular faces to reduce stress concentrations.

Face Mill

The Face mill tool or face mill cutter is used to remove material from the face of workpiece and make it plane; refer to Figure-39.

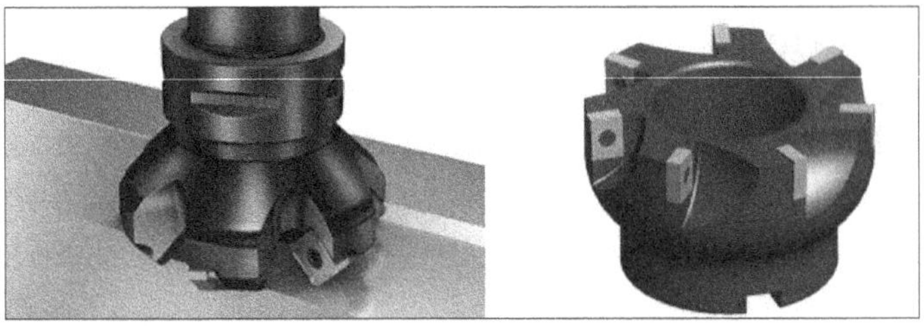

Figure-39. Face milling tool

Radius Mill and Chamfer Mill

The Radius mill tool is used to apply round (fillet) at the edges of the part. The Chamfer mill tool is used to apply chamfer at the edges of the part. Figure-40 shows the radius mill tool and chamfer mill tool.

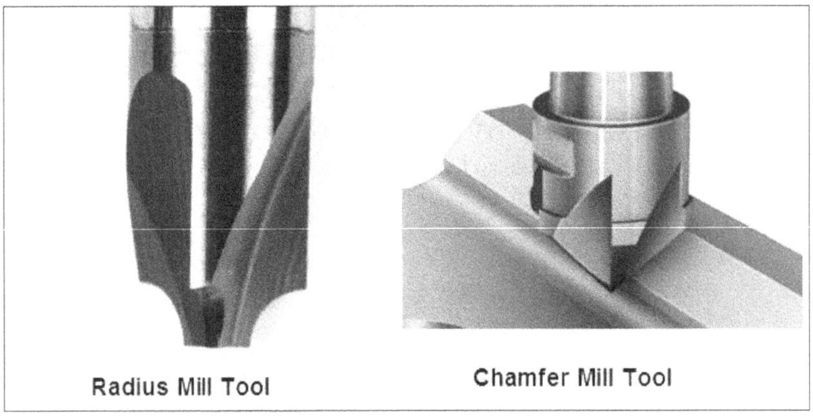

Figure-40. Radius mill and Chamfer mill tool

Slot Mill

The Slot mill tool is used to create slot or groove in the part metal. Figure-41 shows the shape of slot mill tool.

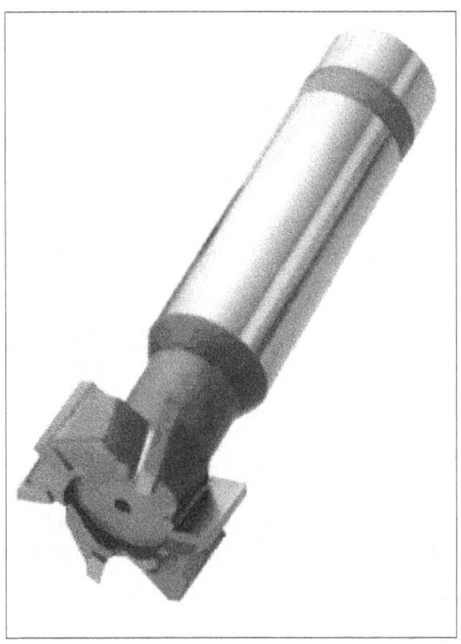

Figure-41. Slot mill tool

Taper Mill

In CNC machining, taper end mills are used in many industries for a large number of applications, such as walls with draft or clearance angle, tool and die work, mold work, even for reaming holes to make them conical. There are mainly two types of taper mills, Taper End Mill and Taper Ball Mill; refer to Figure-36.

Dove Mill

Dove mill or Dovetail cutters are designed for cutting dovetails in a wide variety of materials. Dovetail cutters can also be used for chamfering or milling angles on the bottom surface of a part. Dovetail cutters are available in a wide variety of diameters and in 45 degree or 60 degree angles; refer to Figure-42.

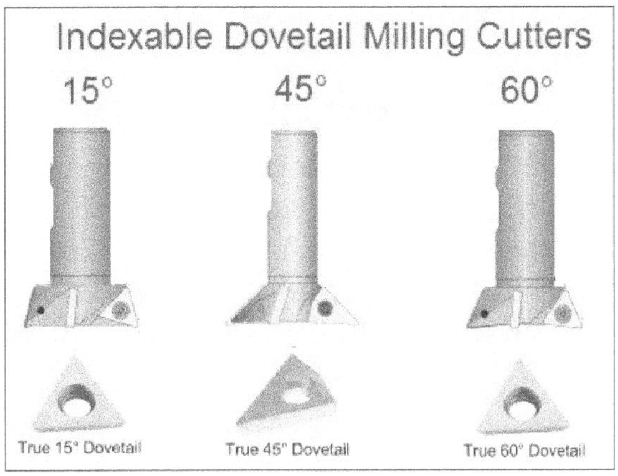

Figure-42. Dovetail milling cutters

Lollipop Mill

The Lollipop mill tool is used to cut round slot or undercuts in workpiece. Some tool suppliers use a name Undercut mill tool in place of Lollipop mill in their catalog. The shape of lollipop mill tool is given in Figure-43.

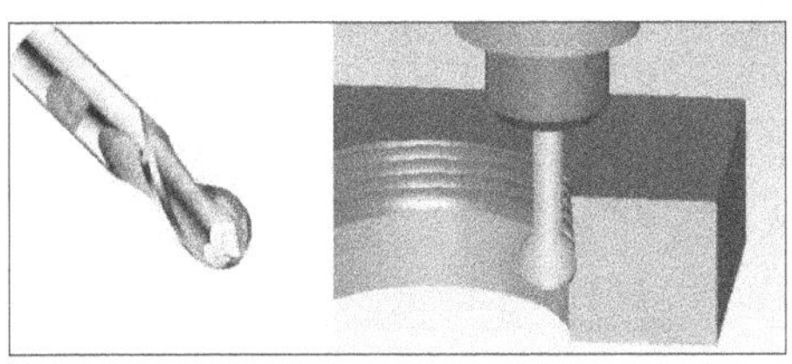

Figure-43. Lollipop mill tool

Engrave Mill

The Engrave mill tool is used to perform engraving on the surface of workpiece. Engraving has always been an art and it is also true for CNC machinist. You can find various shapes of engraving tool that are single flute or multi-flute; refer to Figure-44. You can use ball mill/end mill for engraving or you can use specialized engrave mill tool for engraving. This all depends on your requirement. If you want to perform engraving on softer materials or plastics then it is better to use ball end mill but if you want an artistic shade on the surface then use the respective engrave mill tool. Keep a note of maximum depth and spindle speed mentioned by your engrave mill tool supplier.

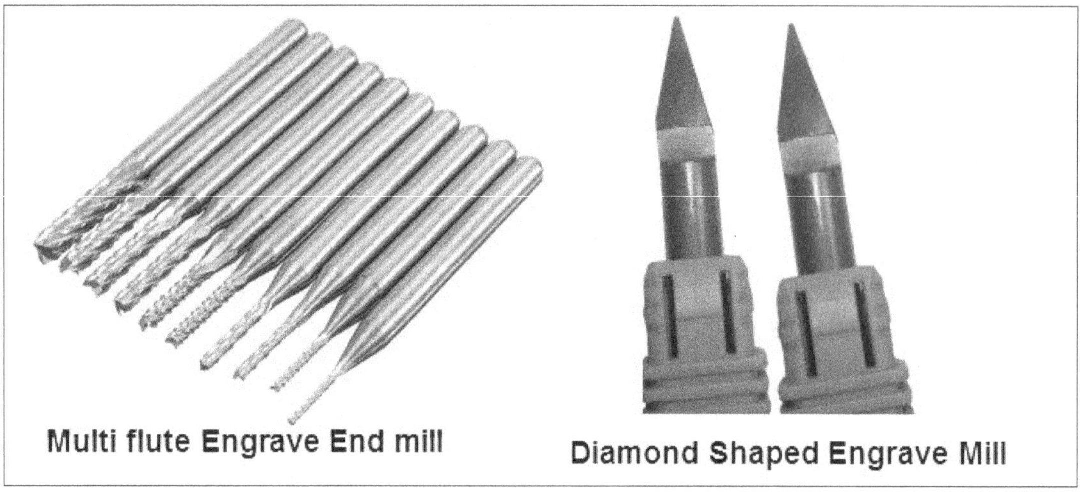

Figure-44. Engrave mill tools

Thread Mill

The Thread mill tool is used to generate internal or external threads in the workpiece. The most common question here is if we have Taps to create thread then why is there need of Thread mill tool. The answer is less machining time on CNC, tool cost saving, more parts per tool, and better thread finish. Now, you will ask why to use tapping. The answer is low machine cost. Figure-45 shows thread mill tools.

Figure-45. Thread Mill

Barrel Mill

Barrel Mill tool is the tool recently being highly used in machining turbine/impeller blades and other 5-axis milling operations. Barrel Mill has conical shape with radius at its end; refer to Figure-46. Note that earlier Ball mill tools were used for irregular surface contouring but Barrel Mill tools give much better surface finish so they are highly in demand for 5-axis milling now a days.

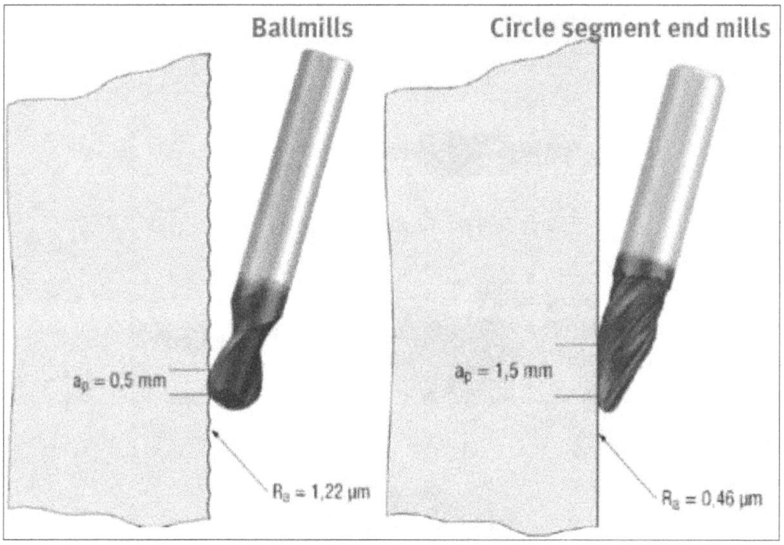

Figure-46. Barrel Mill versus Ball Mill Tool

Drill Bit

Drill bit is used to make a hole in the workpiece. The hole shape depends on the shape of drill bit. Drill bits for various purposes are shown in Figure-47. Note that drill is the machine or holder in which drill bit is installed to make cylindrical holes. There are mainly four categories of drill bit; Twist drill bit, Step drill bit, Unibit (or conical bit), and Hole Saw bit (Refer to Figure-48). Twist drill bits are used for drilling holes in wood, metal, plastic, and other materials. For soft materials, the point angle is 90 degree; for hard materials, the point angle is 150 degree; and general purpose twist drill bits have angle of 150 degree at end point. The Step drill bits are used to make counter bore or countersunk holes. The Unibits are generally used for drilling holes in sheetmetal but they can also be used for drilling plastic, plywood, aluminium, and thin steel sheets. One unibit can give holes of different sizes. The Hole saw bit is used to cut a large hole from the workpiece. They remove material only from the edge of the hole, cutting out an intact disc of material, unlike many drills which remove all material in the interior of the hole. They can be used to make large holes in wood, sheet metal, and other materials.

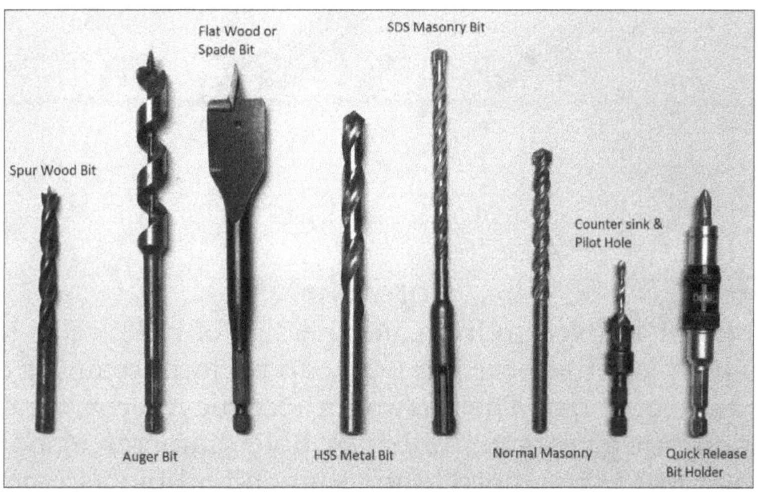

Figure-47. Drill Bits for different purposes

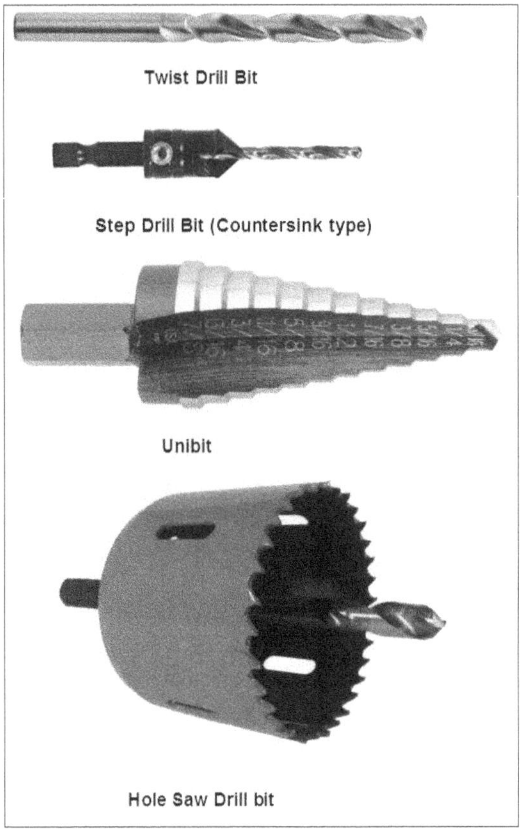

Figure-48. Types of drill bits

Reamer

Reamer is a tool similar to drill bit but its purpose is to finish the hole or increase the size of hole precisely. Figure-49 shows the shape of a reamer.

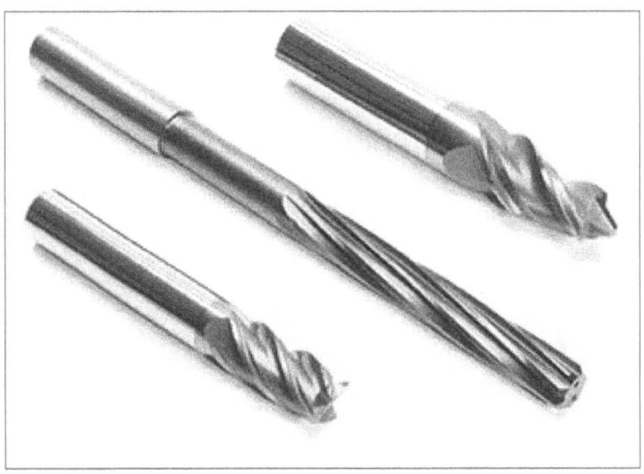

Figure-49. Reamer tool

Bore Bar

Bore Bar or Boring Bar is used to increase the size of hole; refer to Figure-50. One common question is why to use bore bar if we can perform reaming or why to perform reaming when we have bore bar. The answer is accuracy. A reamer does not give tight tolerance in location but gives good finish in hole diameter. A bore bar gives tight tolerance in location but takes more time to machine hole as compared to reamer. The decision to choose the process is on machinist. If you need a highly accurate hole then perform drilling, then boring, and then reaming to get best result.

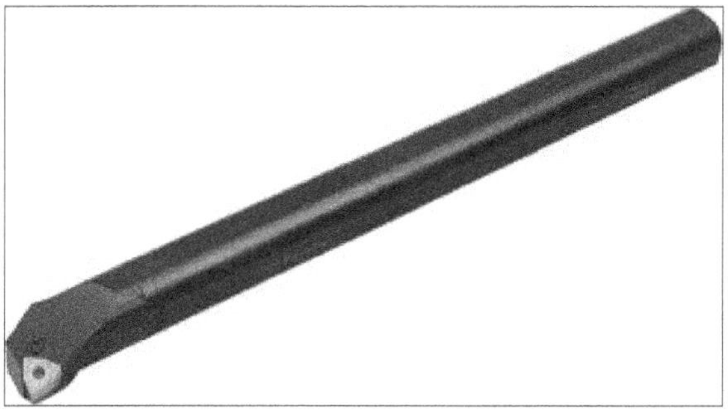

Figure-50. Boring Bar

Lathe Tools or Turning Tools

The tools used in CNC lathe machines use a different nomenclature. In CNC lathe machines, we use insert for cutting material. The Insert Holder and Inserts have a special nomenclature scheme to define their shapes. First, we will discuss the nomenclature of Insert holder and then we will discuss the nomenclature of Inserts.

Insert Holders

Turning holder names follow an ISO nomenclature standard. If you are working on a CNC shop floor with lathes, knowing the ISO nomenclature is a must. The name looks complicated, but is actually very easy to interpret; refer to Figure-51.

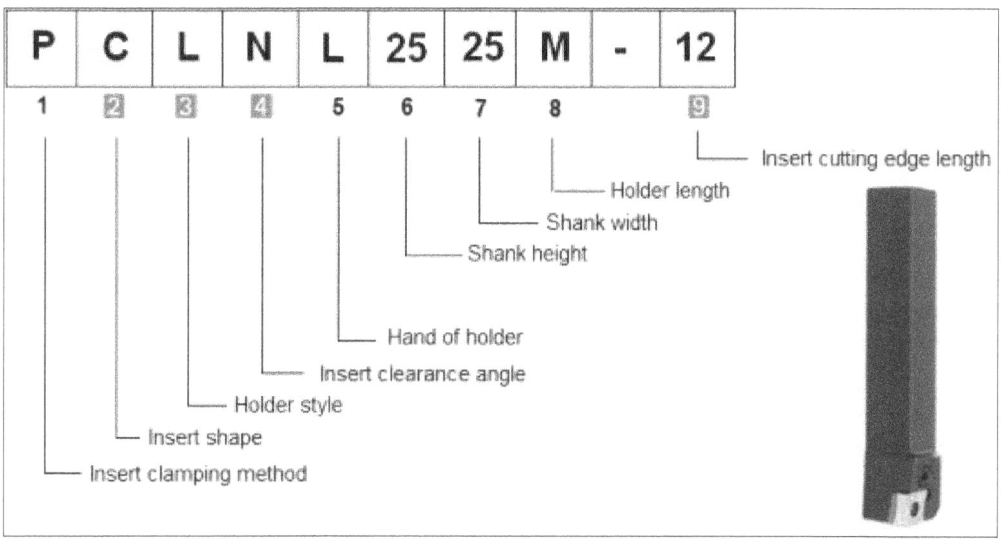

Figure-51. CNC Lathe Insert Holder nomenclature

When selecting a holder for an application, you mainly have to concentrate on the numbers marked in red in the above nomenclature. The others are decided automatically (e.g., the shank width and height are decided by the machine), or require less effort. In Figure-52, the rows with the question mark indicate the parameters that require the decision by machinist based on job.

	Parameter		How is this decided ?
1	Insert clamping method		Select based on cutting forces. Top clamping is the most sturdy, screw clamping the least.
2	Insert shape	?	Decided by the contour that you want to turn.
3	Holder style	?	Decided by the contour that you want to turn.
4	Insert clearance angle	?	Positive / Negative, based on application.
5	Hand of holder		Decided based on whether you want to cut towards the chuck or away from the chuck, and on turret position - turret front / rear
6	Shank height		Decided by holder size.
7	Shank width		Decided by machine.
8	Holder length		Decided by machine.
9	Insert cutting edge length	?	Decide based on depth of cut you want to use.

Figure-52. CNC Lathe Insert Holder nomenclature parameters

Figure-53 and Figure-54 show the options available for each of the parameters.

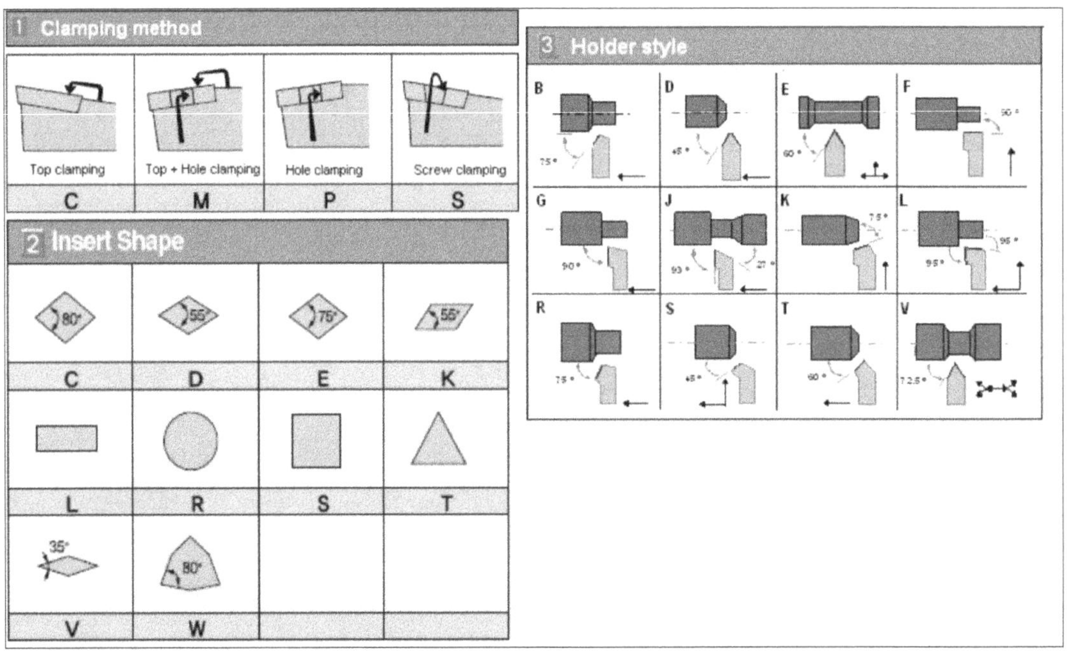

Figure-53. Clamping Method, Insert Shapes, and Holder Style

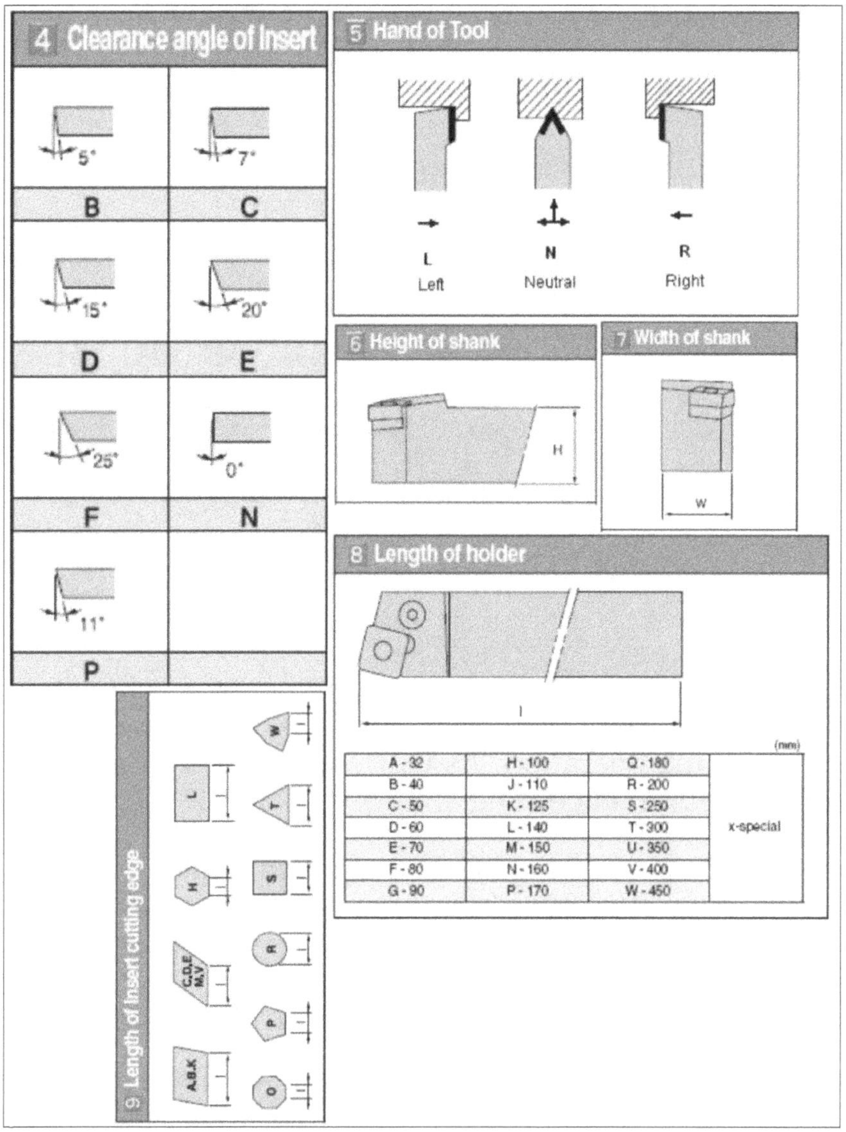

Figure-54. Insert Holder Parameters

CNC Lathe Insert Nomenclature

General CNC Insert name is given as

C	N	M	G	12	04	08
1	2	3	4	5	6	7

Meaning of each box in nomenclature is given next.

1 = Turning Insert Shape

The first letter in general turning insert nomenclature tells us about the general turning insert shape, turning inserts shape codes are like C, D, K, R, S, T, V, W. Most of these codes surely express the turning insert shape like

C = C Shape Turning Insert
D = D Shape Turning Insert
K = K Shape Turning Insert
R = Round Turning Insert
S = Square Turning Insert

T = Triangle Turning Insert
V = V Shape Turning Insert
W = W Shape Turning Insert

Figure-55 shows the turning inserts shapes.

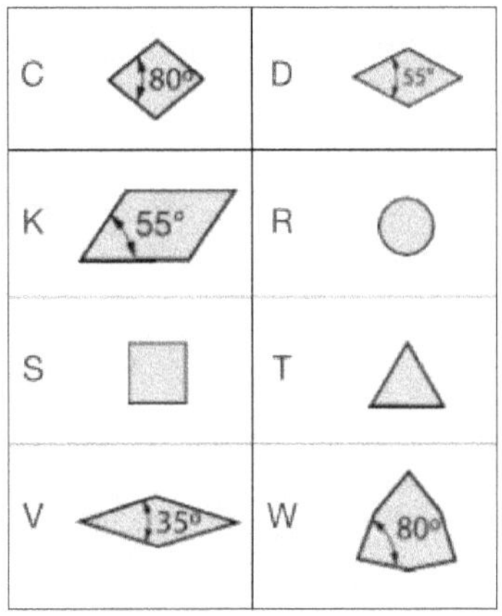

Figure-55. Turning Insert Shapes

The general turning insert shape play a very important role when we choose an insert for machining. Not every turning insert with one shape can be replaced with the other for a machining operation. As C, D, W type turning inserts are normally used for roughing or rough machining.

2 = Turning Insert Clearance Angle

The second letter in general turning insert nomenclature tells us about the turning insert clearance angle.

The clearance angle for a turning insert is shown in Figure-56.

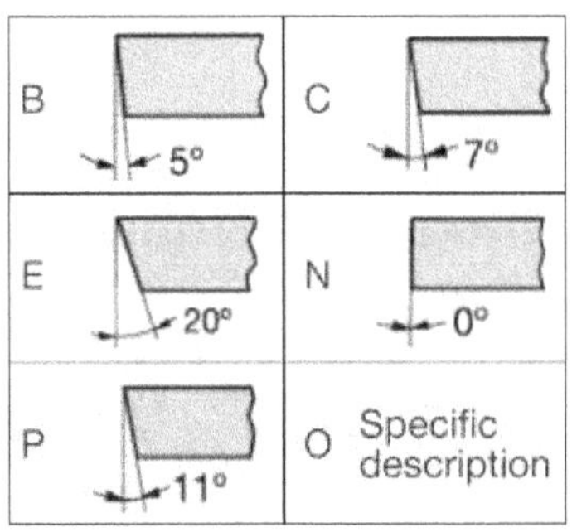

Figure-56. Turning insert clearance angle

Turning insert clearance angle plays a big role while choosing an insert for internal machining or boring small components, because if not properly chosen the insert bottom corner might rub with the component which will give poor machining. On the other hand, a turning insert with 0° clearance angle is mostly used for rough machining.

3 = Turning Insert Tolerances

The third letter of general turning insert nomenclature tells us about the turning insert tolerances. Figure-57 shows the tolerance chart.

Code Letter	Cornerpoint (inches)	Thickness (inches)	Inscribed Circle (in)	Cornerpoint (mm)	Thickness (mm)	Inscribed Circle (mm)
A	.0002"	.001"	.001"	.005mm	.025mm	.025mm
C	.0005"	.001"	.001"	.013mm	.025mm	.025mm
E	.001"	.001"	.001"	.025mm	.025mm	.025mm
F	.0002"	.001"	.0005"	.005mm	.025mm	.013mm
G	.001"	.005"	.001"	.025mm	.13mm	.025mm
H	.0005"	.001"	.0005"	.013mm	.025mm	.013mm
J	.002"	.001"	.002-.005"	.005mm	.025mm	.05-.13mm
K	.0005"	.001"	.002-.005"	.013mm	.025mm	.05-.13mm
L	.001"	.001"	.002-.005"	.025mm	.025mm	.05-.13mm
M	.002-.005"	.005"	.002-.005"	.05-.13mm	.13mm	.05-.15mm
U	.005-.012"	.005"	.005-.010"	.06-.25mm	.13mm	.08-.25mm

Figure-57. Insert tolerance chart

4 = Turning Insert Type

The fourth letter of general turning insert nomenclature tells us about the turning insert hole shape and chip breaker type; refer to Figure-58.

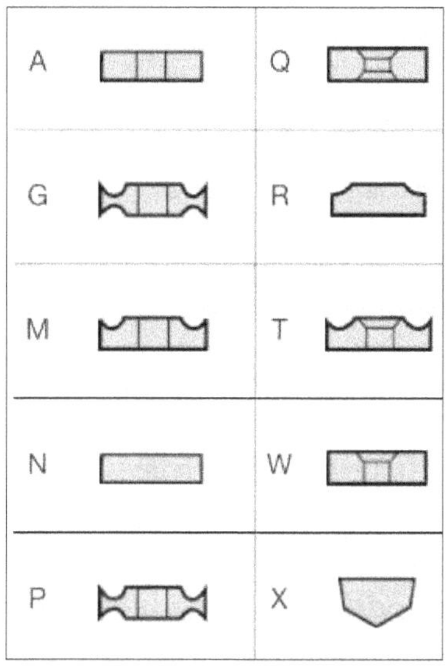

Figure-58. Turning Insert hole shape and chip breaker

5 = Turning Insert Size

This numeric value of general turning insert tells us the cutting edge length of the turning insert; refer to Figure-59.

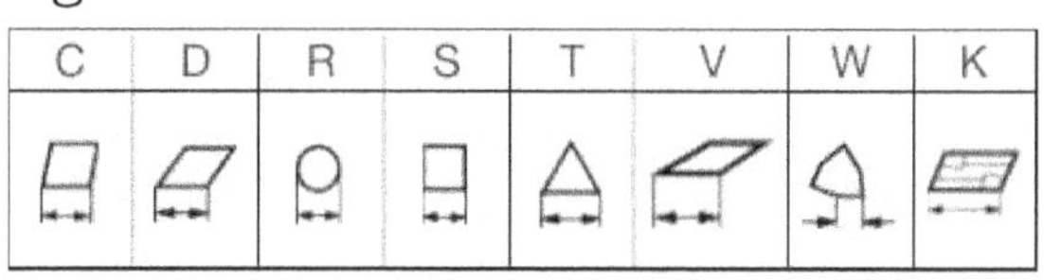

Figure-59. Turning Insert Cutting Edge Length

6 = Turning Insert Thickness

This numeric value of general turning insert tells us about the thickness of the turning insert.

7 = Turning Insert Nose Radius

This numeric value of general turning insert tells us about the nose radius of the turning insert.

Code	=	**Radius Value**
04	=	0.4
08	=	0.8
12	=	1.2
16	=	1.6

You can know more about tooling from your tool supplier manual.

CREATING STOCK FOR MODEL

Stock is the material block from which material will be removed by machining to get the model. The tools to create stock are available in the **Stock Model** drop-down of the **Stock** group in **Toolpaths** tab of the **Ribbon**; refer to Figure-60. Various tools in this drop-down are discussed next.

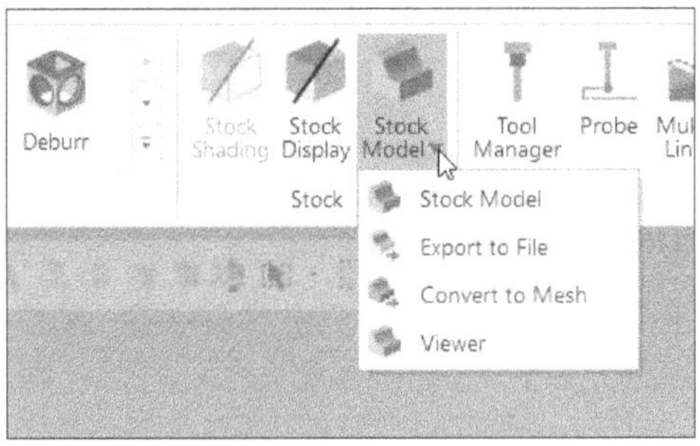

Figure-60. Stock Model drop-down

Creating Stock using Stock Model Tool

The **Stock Model** tool is used to create stock of different shapes by using different shapes and settings. The procedure to use this tool is given next.

- Click on the **Stock Model** tool from the **Stock** group in the **Toolpaths** contextual tab of the **Ribbon**. The **Stock model** dialog box will be displayed; refer to Figure-61.
- Click on the **Stock Plane** button near **Stock plane** check box to specify the plane to be used for aligning stock. The **Plane Selection** dialog box will be displayed; refer to Figure-62.

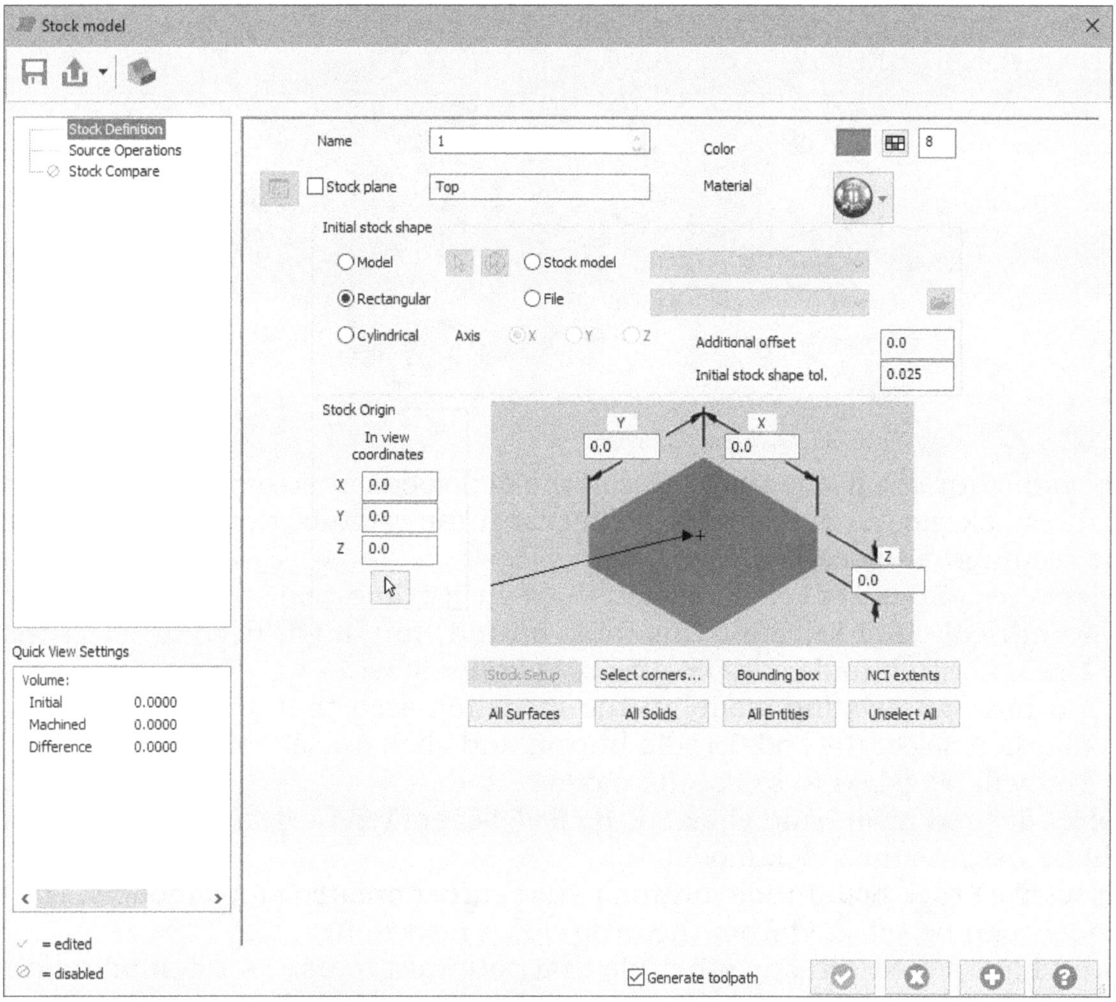

Figure-61. Stock model dialog box

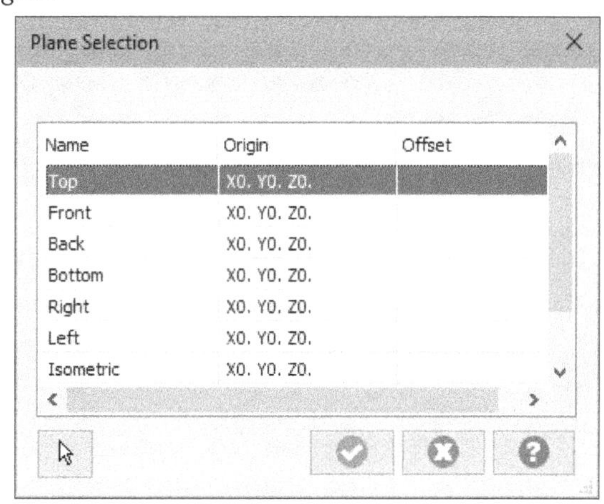

Figure-62. Plane Selection dialog box

- Select desired plane from the dialog box and click on the **OK** button. The selected plane will be used as base plane for creating stock.
- Click on the object selection button from the **Stock origin** area to specify the origin point for stock. You will be asked to select a point from the model to specify origin of stock.
- Click at desired location to specify origin; refer to Figure-63.

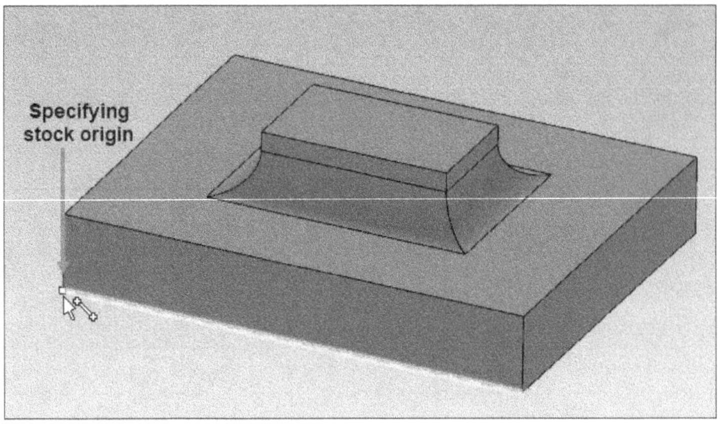

Figure-63. Specifying stock origin

- The radio buttons in the **Shape** area of the dialog box are used to specify the shape of the stock model. By default, the **Rectangular** radio button is selected. Hence, the rectangular block is created.
- Select the **Cylindrical** radio button to create a cylindrical stock if your workpiece is cylindrical. After selecting this radio button, you might need to select the **X**, **Y**, or **Z** radio button to decide the axis of cylinder stock.
- If you have an existing model in the modeling area that you want to define as stock, then select the **Model** radio button and click on selection button next to it. You will be asked to select the model.
- Select desired model and click on the **End Selection** button. The selected model will be used as the stock model.
- Select the **Stock model** radio button to use earlier created stock models. The stock models can be selected from the drop-down next to it.
- If you have a model in any other file that you want to use as stock material, then select the **File** radio button from the dialog box and click on the button. The **Open** dialog box will be displayed; refer to Figure-64.

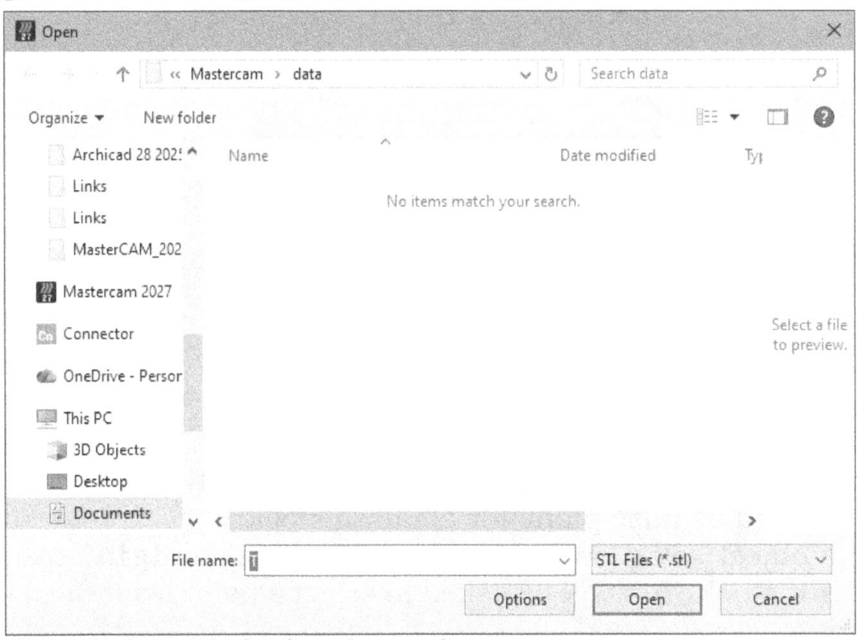

Figure-64. Open dialog box for stock material

- Browse to the location of desired file and double-click on the model file. Note that you can use only STL file format for this. The name of the model will displayed in the field next to the **File** radio button; refer to Figure-65.

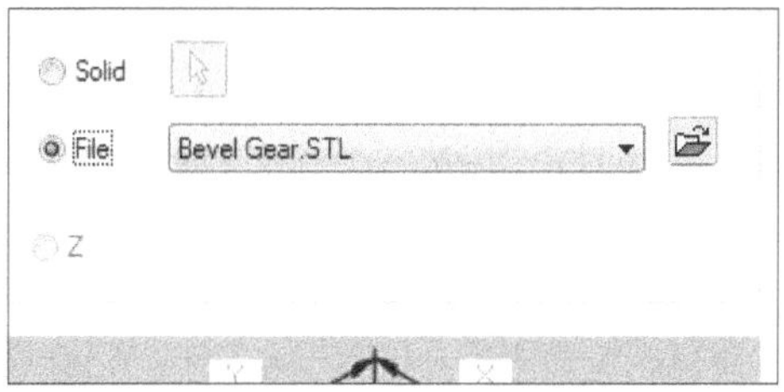

Figure-65. Name of file displayed

- After specifying desired settings, click on the **OK** button from the dialog box.

Creating Bounding Box

- Note that to create a bounding box, you need to select the **Bounding box** button after selecting the **Rectangular** or **Cylindrical** radio button. On selecting the **Bounding box** button, the **Bounding Box Manager** will be displayed; refer to Figure-66.

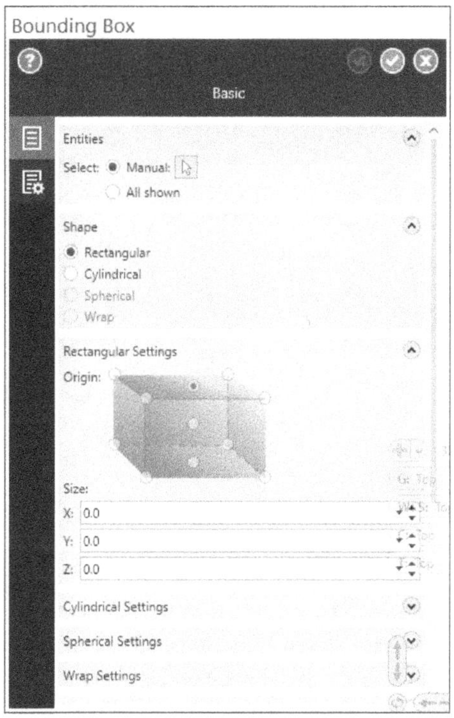

Figure-66. Bounding Box Manager

- Select desired bodies to be used as reference for bounding box and click on the **End Selection** button. Preview of the bounding box will be displayed; refer to Figure-67.

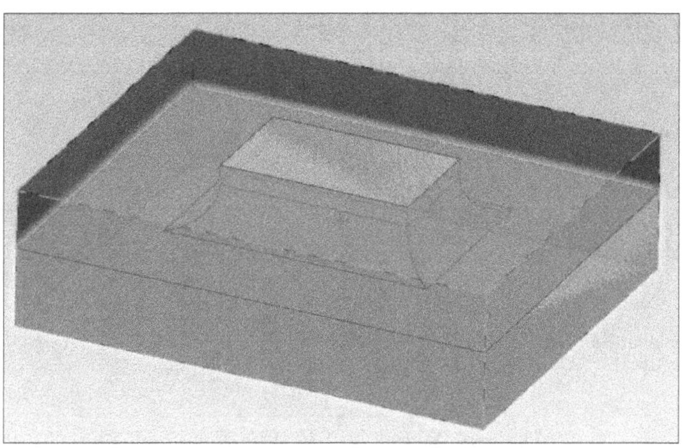

Figure-67. Preview of bounding box

- Select the **All shown** radio button from the **Entities** rollout of the **Manager** to select all the visible objects for creating bounding box.
- Specify desired parameters in the **X**, **Y**, and **Z** edit boxes of **Rectangular Settings** rollout to specify the size of block.
- Set the other parameters as desired and click on the **OK** button to create the bounding box stock. The **Stock model** dialog box will be displayed again. Click on the **OK** button from the dialog box to create stock and exit the dialog box.

EXPORTING THE STOCK MODEL

The **Export to File** tool is used to export current stock model as an STL file or other 3D printable formats. You can use the STL file as model for another machining project as well. The procedure to use this tool is given next.

- Click on the **Export to File** tool from the **Stock Model** drop-down in the **Stock** group of the **Toolpaths** tab in the **Ribbon**. The **Save As** dialog box will be displayed; refer to Figure-68.

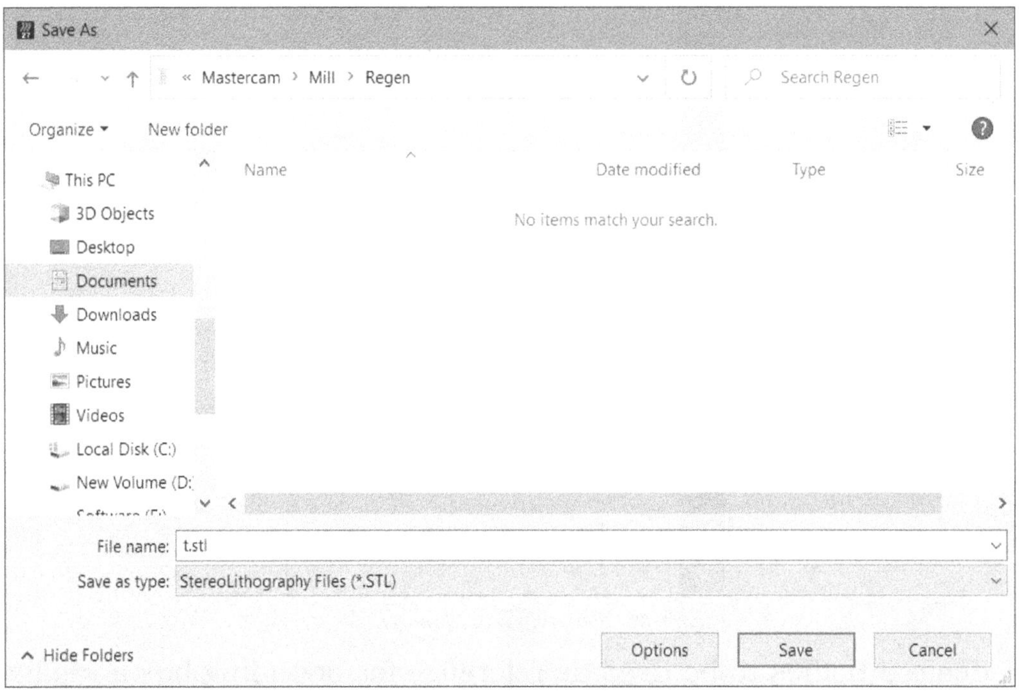

Figure-68. Save As dialog box

- Click on the **Options** button to define format of STL file. The **Save as an STL File** dialog box will be displayed; refer to Figure-69.

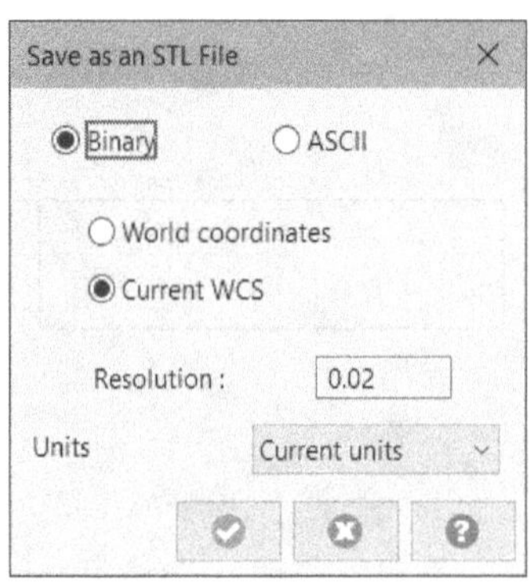

Figure-69. Save as an STL File dialog box

- Select **Binary** radio button to use binary format for conversion of model (generally lower size of output file for 3D printing) and select the **ASCII** radio button to use **ASCII** format if your CAD software supports it. Set the other parameters as desired and click on the **OK** button. The **Save As** dialog box will be displayed again.
- Specify desired name of file in the **File name** edit box and click on the **Save** button.

Using the **Convert to Mesh** tool in the **Stock Model** drop-down, you can convert the stock to mesh.

Using the **Viewer** tool in **Stock Model** drop-down, you can compare the base model and stock.

SELF ASSESSMENT

Q1. What is the full form of CNC?

Q2. What is the function of Machine Tool Spindle in VMC machine?

Q3. What is the function of Tool Turret?

Q4. What is the importance of translational and rotational limits of a CNC machine?

Q5. Tail stock is used to support long workpiece at its end in a lathe. (T/F)

Q6. The Machine Definition Manager is used to edit the parameters related to machine like components of machine. (T/F)

Q7. What is the file extension for Mastercam Machine definition?

Q8. Which of the following is a rotary axis?

a. X
b. Z
c. A
d. Y

Q9. What is the function of Break rotary motion check box?

Q10. What is the file extension for Mastercam controller file?

Q11. The .... tool is used to create and manage controller definitions for various machines.

Q12. Based on the material of workpiece, the feed rate and other cutting parameters are decided while machining. (T/F)

Q13. Discuss the use of End Mill cutting tool.

Q14. Discuss the use of Dovetail cutter in milling.

Q15. Discuss the use of Engrave mill cutting tool.

Q16. Discuss the use of Barrel mill cutting tool.

Q17. Discuss the nomenclature of CNC lathe insert holder and cutting tool insert.

Q18. What is stock?

REVIEW QUESTIONS

Q1. Which component of a CNC machine is responsible for holding and driving the cutting tool or workpiece?
A. Tool changer
B. Tail stock
C. Tool spindle
D. Rotary axis

Q2. When selecting a tool spindle, which factor does not need to be considered?
A. Spindle speed
B. Gauge length of the tool
C. Type of coolant used
D. Power/torque transmission

Q3. What is the primary purpose of a tool changer or turret in CNC machines?
A. To rotate the workpiece
B. To change the machine definition
C. To automatically change the tool
D. To control coolant flow

Q4. Where is the Tail Stock primarily used?
A. Milling machines only
B. Only on 5-axis machines
C. Lathe machines, and sometimes rotary tables of mills
D. In machine simulation only

Q5. What is the purpose of the Machine Definition Manager in Mastercam?
A. To create new toolpaths
B. To import solid models
C. To edit machine-related parameters
D. To define coolant settings

Q6. Which of the following is not a component that can be added through the Machine Definition Manager?
A. Tool spindle
B. Cooling fan
C. Rotary axis
D. Linear axis

Q7. In the Machine Component Manager - Linear Axis dialog box, which of the following parameters can be set?
A. Post processor path
B. Tool diameter

C. Minimum/Maximum axis travel limits
D. Tool number

Q8. What is the role of the Tilt Angle option in Linear Axis configuration?
A. To control coolant angle
B. To define spindle rotation direction
C. To tilt the axis about a specified angle
D. To define tool cutting direction

Q9. Which parameter is unique to rotary axis components and not found in linear axis configuration?
A. Axis label
B. Maximum feed rate (rotation)
C. Minimum travel limit
D. Tool holder length

Q10. What does the Break rotary motion check box do?
A. Stops toolpath creation
B. Breaks motion after a specified angle
C. Turns off rotary axis
D. Switches to linear axis mode

Q11. Which dialog box is used to assign or modify the controller for the machine?
A. Tool Manager
B. Control Definition
C. General Machine Parameters
D. Material List

Q12. In the Control Definition dialog box, which page allows defining machine tolerance values?
A. Feed
B. Files
C. Tolerances
D. Tool

Q13. Which page in Control Definition allows setting parameters for arc moves (G02/G03)?
A. Arc
B. Tool
C. Rotary
D. Misc. Int/Real Values

Q14. Which of the following defines how a machine controller interprets cutter compensation modes?
A. Arc page
B. Rotary page
C. Cutter Compensation page
D. Tool page

Q15. Which dialog box allows you to set the construction and tool planes used in a project?
A. Coolant Commands tab
B. General Machine Parameters – Cplane/Tplane tab
C. Control Definition – Tool page
D. Machine Definition – Tilt Angle tab

Q16. In which tab of General Machine Parameters can you specify machine acceleration and feed rate dynamics?
A. Op. feed rate limits, axis motion
B. Machine Dynamics
C. Axis feed rate limits
D. Simulation

Q17. Which tool in the Machine tab allows you to assign material to a workpiece?
A. Tool Manager
B. Material
C. General Parameters
D. Toolpath Setup

Q18. What is the purpose of the Tool Manager in Mastercam?
A. To define post processors
B. To manage and organize tools
C. To apply machine dynamics
D. To edit NC code output

Q19. What should you do if the Tool Manager dialog box appears empty?
A. Restart Mastercam
B. Create a new toolpath
C. Select a different tool library
D. Reload the NC code

Q20. Which of the following is required to define a new custom tool using wireframe sketch?
A. 3D Solid model from STEP file only
B. Open wireframe profile starting from origin
C. Imported tool library file
D. Fully closed solid sketch

Q21. What does the Variable pitch checkbox represent in tool creation?
A. Constant feed rate
B. Random spindle RPM
C. Varying helix angle along the cutting edge
D. Tool length variation

Q22. What dialog box appears when editing an existing tool?
A. Tool Setup Manager
B. Mill Assembly Designer Manager
C. Control File Dialog Box
D. Linear Axis Configuration

Q23. Which type of file is used for assigning post processors in the control definition?
*A. .nc
*B. .mdf
*C. .control
*D. .post

Q24. What is the purpose of the Coolant Commands tab in General Parameters?
A. Enable coolant sensors
B. Define extra coolant parameters
C. Change NC code format
D. Control work coordinate system

Q25. Which tab is used to define tool and material libraries in the General Machine Parameters dialog box?
A. Files
B. Material
C. Tool/material libraries
D. Libraries

Q26. What is the main material used in manufacturing CNC tools?
A. Mild steel
B. Cemented carbide
C. Aluminum
D. PVC

Q27. Which tool is best suited for machining 3D contoured shapes in molds and dies?
A. End Mill
B. Slot Mill
C. Ball Nose Mill
D. Dove Mill

Q28. What is the main purpose of a Roughing End Mill?
A. Provide high surface finish
B. Engrave metal
C. Quickly remove large amounts of metal
D. Cut threads

Q29. Which tool is used to cut round corners in mold steels?
A. Bull Nose Mill
B. Slot Mill
C. Chamfer Mill
D. Face Mill

Q30. Which tool would you use to remove material from the face of a workpiece and make it plane?
A. Thread Mill
B. Face Mill
C. Taper Mill
D. Engrave Mill

Q31. What is the purpose of a Chamfer Mill tool?
A. Create undercuts
B. Add fillets to corners
C. Apply angled edges to parts
D. Create keyways

Q32. Which tool is used to create a groove in a part?
A. Face Mill
B. Radius Mill
C. Slot Mill
D. Thread Mill

Q33. What is the use of a Taper End Mill?
A. Cut flat surfaces
B. Drill holes
C. Produce walls with draft angles
D. Cut threads

Q34. Dovetail cutters can also be used for:
A. Engraving text
B. Milling bottom surface angles
C. Thread milling
D. Keyway cutting

Q35. What is another name for the Lollipop Mill?
A. Undercut Mill
B. Radius Mill
C. Ball Nose Mill
D. Bull Nose Mill

Q36. Which of the following tools can be used for artistic shading on soft materials?
A. Taper Mill
B. Chamfer Mill
C. Engrave Mill
D. Slot Mill

Q37. Why would one prefer a Thread Mill over Tapping?
A. For lower machine cost
B. For roughing operations
C. For better thread finish and less machining time
D. For creating large holes

Q38. What shape does the Barrel Mill tool have?
A. Flat cylinder
B. Hemispherical
C. Conical with radius end
D. Straight flute

Q39. Which bit removes material only from the edge to cut a disc?
A. Step drill bit
B. Twist drill bit
C. Hole Saw bit
D. Unibit

Q40. Which drill bit is best for drilling holes of multiple sizes in sheet metal?
A. Step Drill
B. Unibit
C. Hole Saw
D. Twist Drill

Q41. Which bit is primarily used for countersunk or counterbore holes?
A. Twist drill bit
B. Hole saw bit
C. Step drill bit
D. Reamer

Q42. What is the main role of a Reamer?
A. Create threads
B. Precisely finish or enlarge a hole
C. Rough cut a cavity
D. Create slots

Q43. Why would a machinist choose boring over reaming?
A. To reduce machine cost
B. To create threads
C. To achieve tight tolerance in hole location
D. To drill large diameter holes

Q44. What defines the shape of CNC lathe inserts?
A. Second letter of the nomenclature
B. First letter of the nomenclature
C. Fourth letter of the nomenclature
D. Insert material

Q45. Which shape code in turning inserts refers to a round insert?
A. R
B. V
C. C
D. T

Q46. What does the second letter in turning insert nomenclature indicate?
A. Shape
B. Material
C. Clearance angle
D. Size

Q47. What is the significance of a 0° clearance angle insert?
A. Ideal for fine profiling
B. For internal boring only
C. Used mostly for rough machining
D. Used for threading

Q48. What does the number '04' represent in insert nose radius nomenclature?
A. 0.04 mm
B. 0.8 mm
C. 4 mm
D. 0.4 mm

Q49. What is the purpose of the Stock Model tool in Mastercam?
A. Assign materials to tools
B. Create and align stock blocks
C. Define NC output
D. Export STL files

Q50. Which stock shape is selected by default in the Stock Model tool dialog?
A. Cylindrical
B. Spherical
C. Model-based
D. Rectangular

Q51. What feature must you use to define a bounding box from multiple visible bodies?
A. Convert to Mesh
B. Bounding Box Manager
C. Viewer
D. Toolpath Simulator

Q52. Which file format is supported when exporting stock models?
A. DXF
B. IGES
C. STL
D. STEP

Q53. Why would someone choose binary format over ASCII for STL export?
A. It's human-readable
B. It supports textures
C. It has smaller file size
D. It provides editable geometry

Chapter 9

Milling Toolpaths

Topics Covered

The major topics covered in this chapter are:

- ***Introduction***
- ***2D Toolpaths***
- ***Conventional and Climb Milling***
- ***Feature Based Milling***

INTRODUCTION

Milling toolpaths are generated for performing cutting operations on NC Milling machines. There are around 70 tools to generate different toolpaths for milling operations. These tools are one by one discussed in this chapter.

2D TOOLPATHS

The tools to create 2D milling toolpaths are available in the **2D** group of the **Toolpaths** tab in the **Ribbon**. Click on the **Expand gallery** button of **2D** group to access all the tools for creating 2D milling tools; refer to Figure-1.

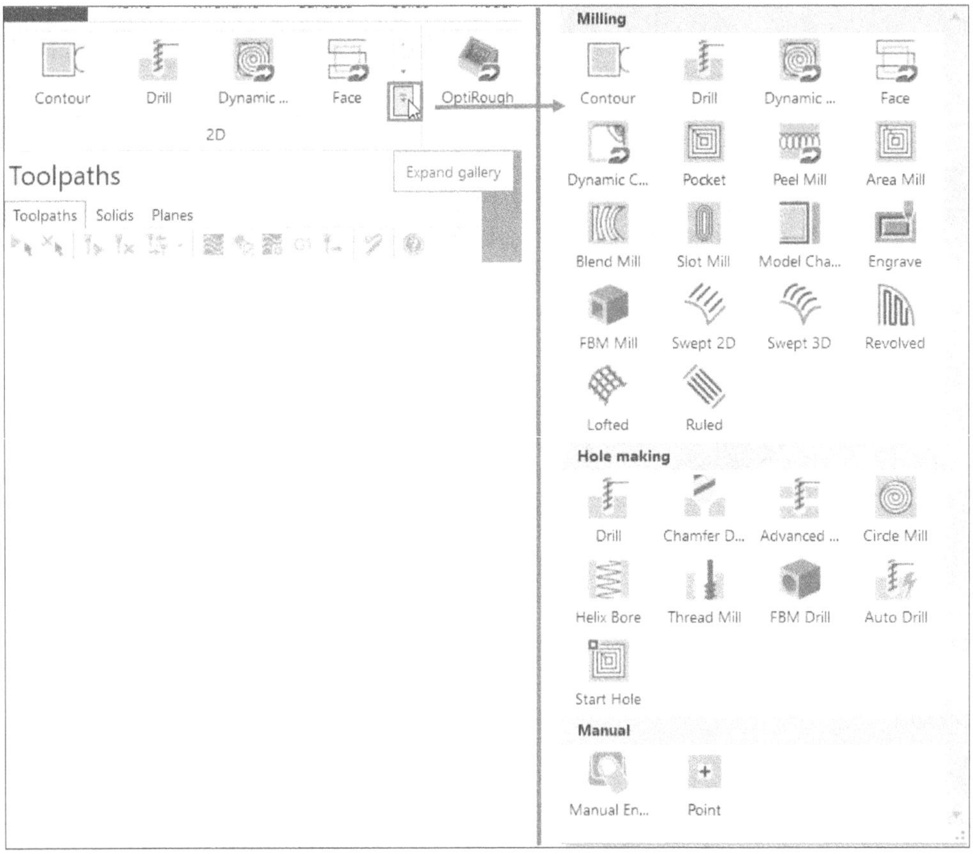

Figure-1. Expanded 2D group

Creating 2D Contour Toolpath

The Contour toolpaths are used to remove the material by following the contour of the model. This toolpath is used to remove material from the outer sides of part; refer to Figure-2. The procedure to create contour toolpaths is given next.

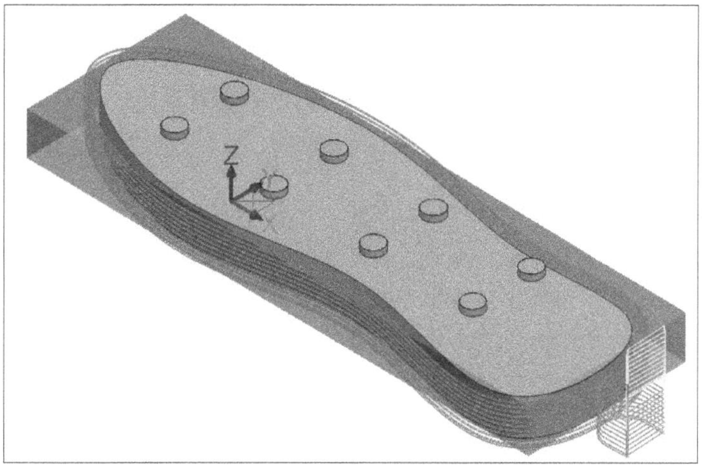

Figure-2. Contour toolpath example

- Click on the **Contour** tool from the **2D** group in the **Toolpaths** tab of the **Ribbon**. The **Wireframe Chaining** selection box will be displayed.
- Select the **Wireframe** button from the **Mode** area of selection box to select wireframe entities and select the **Solids** button from the **Mode** area to select solid faces/bodies.
- Select the faces that you want to machine using the contour milling toolpaths. Note that you need to select the outer side faces of the part to remove material at the boundaries. Click on the **OK** button from the **Wireframe Chaining** selection box. The **2D Toolpaths-Contour** dialog box will be displayed; refer to Figure-3.

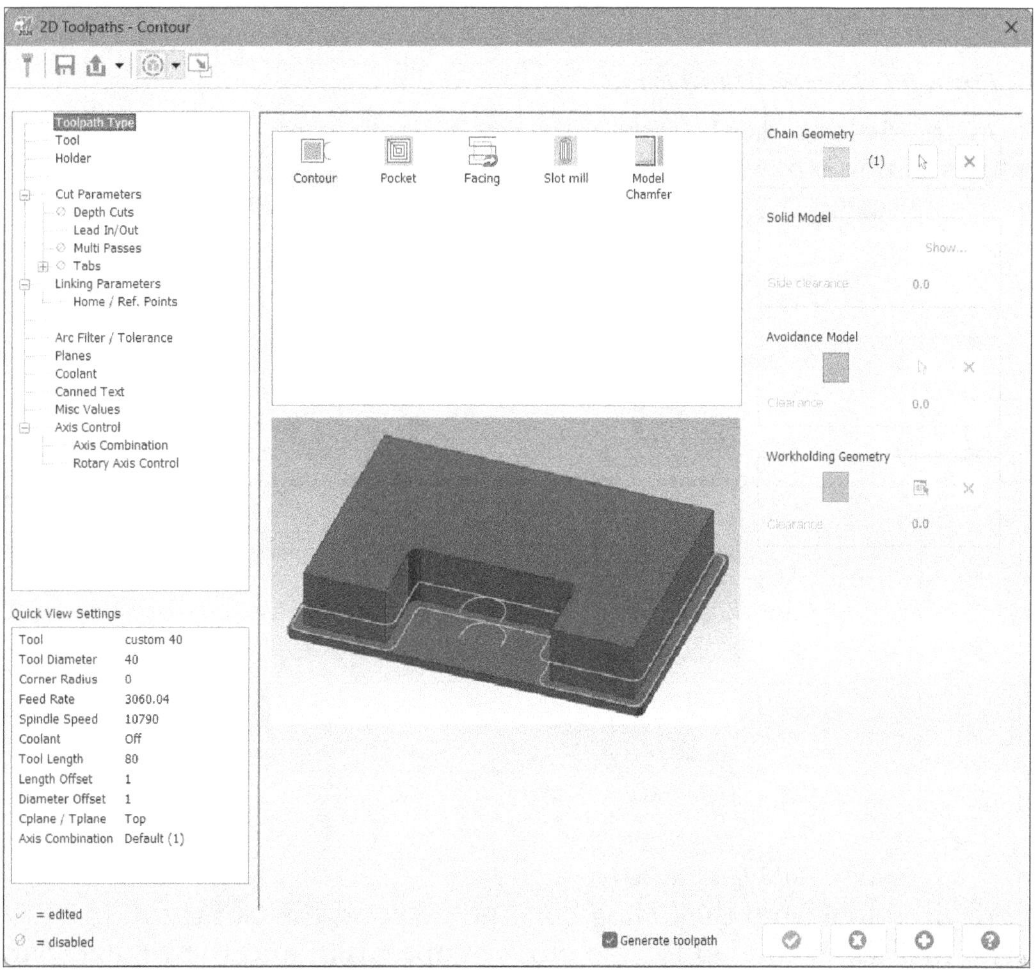

Figure-3. 2D Toolpaths-Contour dialog box

Tool Options

- Click on the **Tool** option from the left box of the dialog box. The **2D Toolpaths-Contour** dialog box will be displayed as shown in Figure-4.

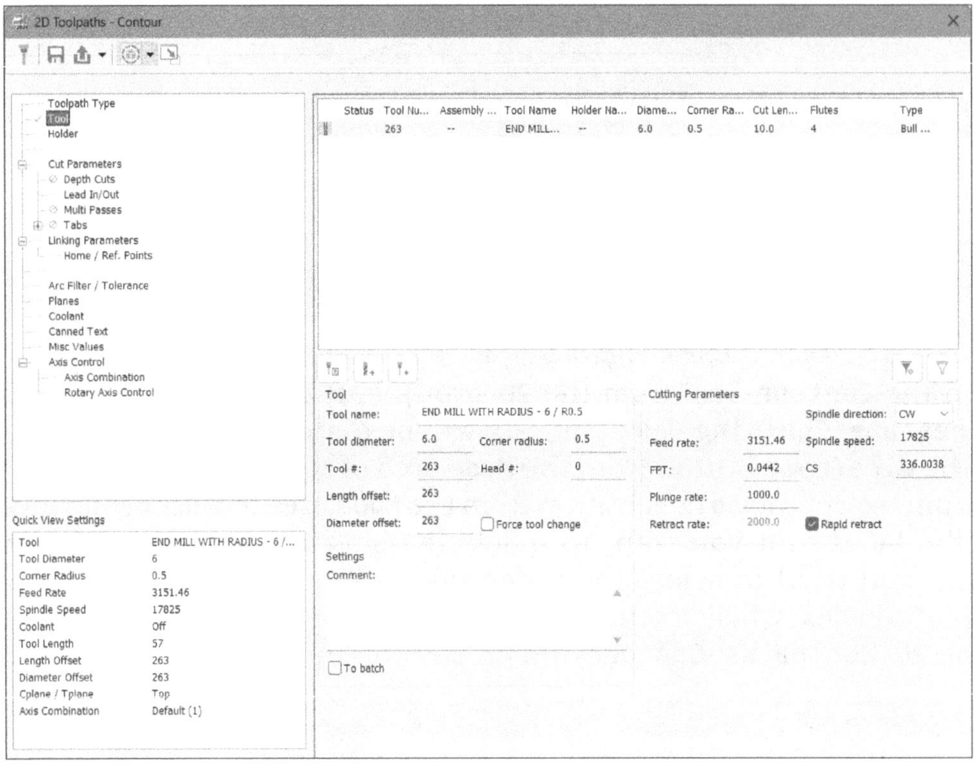

Figure-4. Tool page for 2D Toolpaths

- Click on the **Select tool from library** button from the dialog box. The **Tool Selection** dialog box will be displayed; refer to Figure-5.

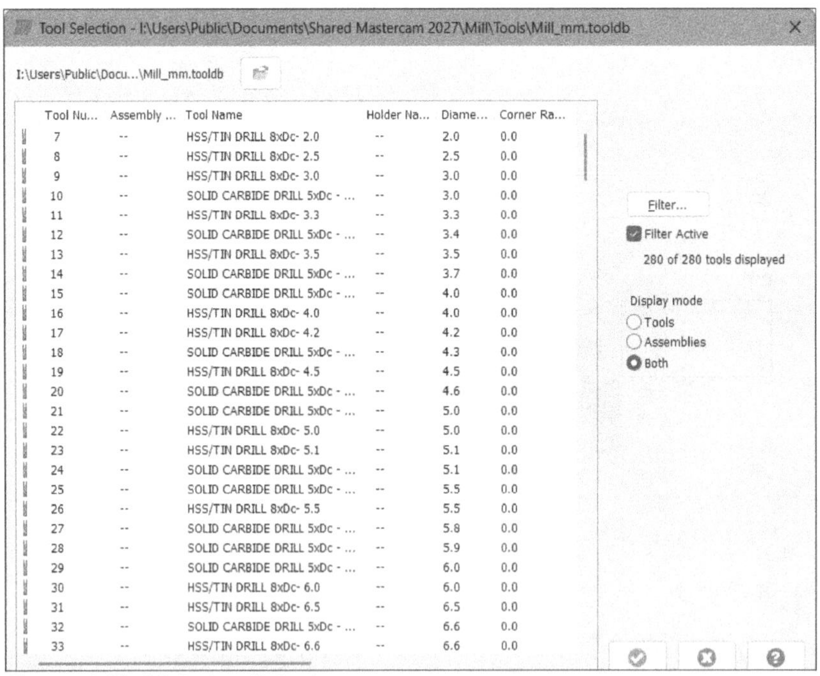

Figure-5. Tool Selection dialog box

- Select desired tool from the dialog box and click on the **OK** button from the dialog box. The tool will be added for the current operation and the related parameters will be displayed in the right of the dialog box.

- Specify desired parameters and click on the **Holder** option from the left box. The dialog box will be displayed as shown in Figure-6.

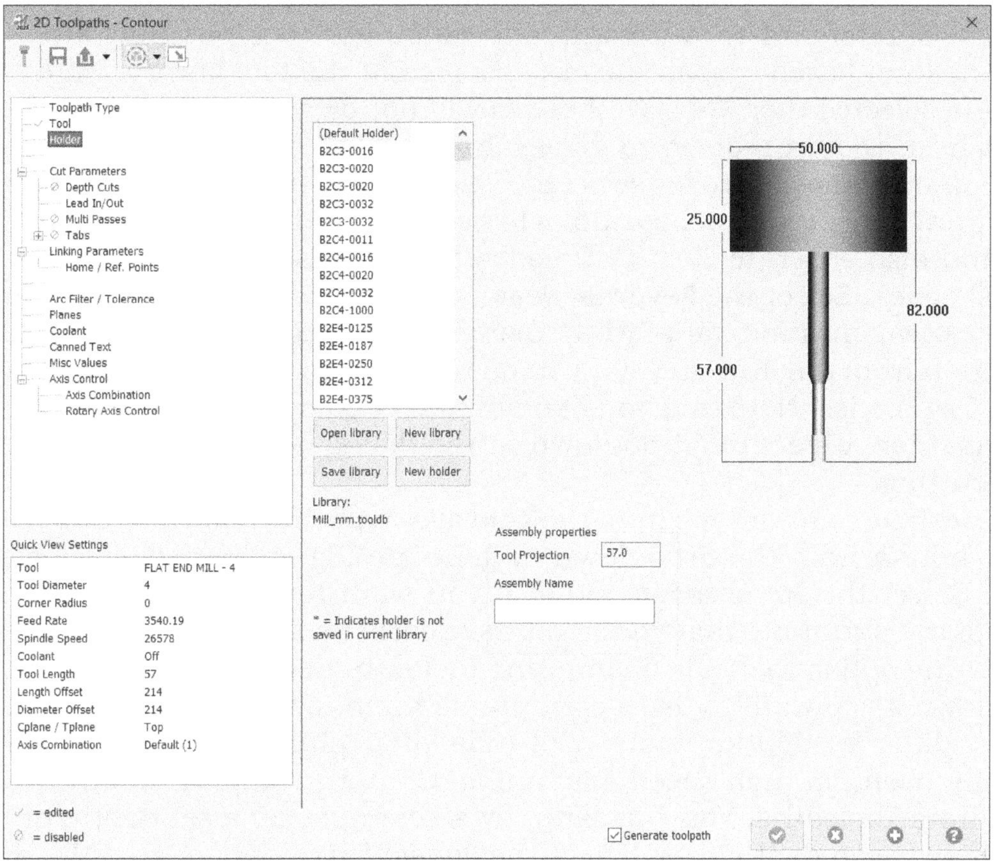

Figure-6. Holder page of 2D Toolpaths dialog box

- Click on the **Open library** button from the dialog box. The **Open** dialog box will be displayed; refer to Figure-7.

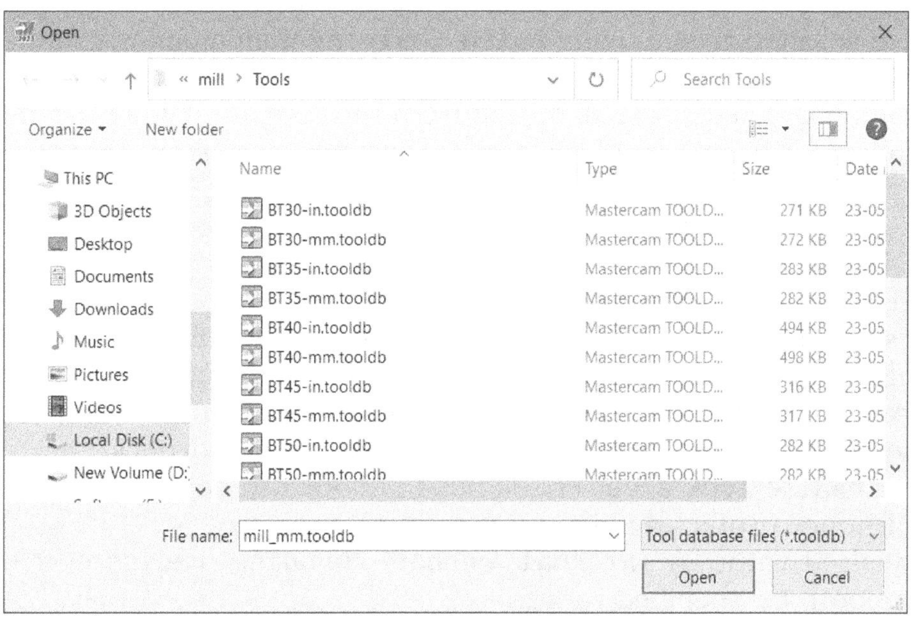

Figure-7. Open dialog box

- Select desired holder library from the dialog box and click on the **Open** button from the dialog box. The holder list will be displayed in the dialog box.
- Select desired holder and specify the related parameters.

Cut Parameters

- Click on the **Cut Parameters** option from the left and carefully define compensation direction. Select the **Computer** option from the **Compensation type** drop-down to allow Mastercam to automatically calculate tool position after applying compensation based on parameters specified in the tool library. Note that if this option is selected then G41/G42 codes will not be generated. Select the **Control** option from the drop-down to generate G41/G42 codes for tool compensation based on machine controller selected. Select the **Wear** option from the drop-down if you want to generate tool positions to be calculated based on tool compensation data and also generate G41/G42 codes to allow users to modify compensation in CNC codes. Select the **Reverse Wear** option from the drop-down to allow only positive compensation value while using the settings of **Wear** option. Select the **Off** option from the drop-down if you do not want to generate compensation data in the CNC codes. Note that you can still select compensation direction from the **Compensation direction** drop-down in the dialog box to define direction of tool while cutting.
- Select desired contour type from the **Contour Type** drop-down in this page. Select the **2D** option from the drop-down to generate 2D toolpath following the outer edges. Select the **2D chamfer** option if you want to apply chamfer at the outer edges of the part. Note that you must have earlier selected a tool according to the chamfering option to create chamfering toolpath. Select the **Ramp** option from the drop-down if you want to use a continuous ramp to transition smoothly between cuts at different depths, instead of individual plunge cuts. This technique is specially useful in high speed machining. Contour ramping is only available for 2D contour toolpaths. You can ramp by a set angle, by a set depth, or to plunge directly between depth cuts. Select the **Remachining** option from the drop-down if you want to remove material left by previous machining operations. Select the **Oscillate** option from the drop-down if you want to create an oscillating motion while cutting along the contour. Note that you need to select the depth of cut and other parameters according to the selected contour type in other pages.
- If you have selected a face using **Solid Chaining** dialog box instead of **Wireframe Chaining** dialog box then 3D options will be available in the **Contour Type** drop-down of this page. Select the **3D** option from the **Contour Type** drop-down to make the tool follow 3D trajectory of selected faces when performing contour machining instead of going in straight line. Similarly, select the **3D chamfer** option from the drop-down to create chamfer following 3D curvature of the selected faces. On selecting this option, edit boxes to define chamfer width and depth will be displayed below the drop-down.
- Select desired option from the **Roll cutter around corners** drop-down to define how corners will be created. Select the **None** option to create sharp corners. Select the **Sharp** option to roll tool around sharp corners with angle less than 135 degree. Select the **All** option to create smooth cut around all corners.
- Select the **Infinite look ahead** check box to make sure toolpath does not intersect with itself hence protecting against gouging.
- Specify desired value in **Internal corner rounding radius** edit box to make corners smooth by specified radius.
- Specify desired value in the **External corner break radius** edit box to create external corners rounded by specified radius.
- Specify the amount of stock to be left on walls and floors in the **Stock to leave on walls** and **Stock to leave on floors** edit boxes, respectively.

Depth Cuts Options

- Select the **Depth Cuts** option from left area in dialog box and then select **Depth cuts** check box to activate related parameters; refer to Figure-8. The options in this page are used to define maximum depth up to which tool can go in stock in each cutting pass and related parameters like feed rate, spindle speed, and so on.
- Specify desired depth value for each cutting pass of roughing operation in the **Maximum rough step** edit box.
- In the **Finish** area, specify the number of finishing cuts and amount of cutting depth to be achieved for finishing operation.
- If you want to change default spindle speed and feed rate for the operation then select respective check box from the **Override Feed Speed** area and type the value in edit box.
- Select the **Keep tool down** check box to reduce number of retract passes in toolpath. Note that selecting this check box will increase load on cutting tool, so make sure that your cutting tool is capable to withstand this extra load.
- Select **Subprogram** check box to detect repeating depth or hole cycles and generate subprogram for them. Select the **Absolute** radio button if subprogram will be using absolute coordinates for moving cutting tool. Select the **Incremental** radio button if subprogram will use current position of tool as reference for defining movement of tool.

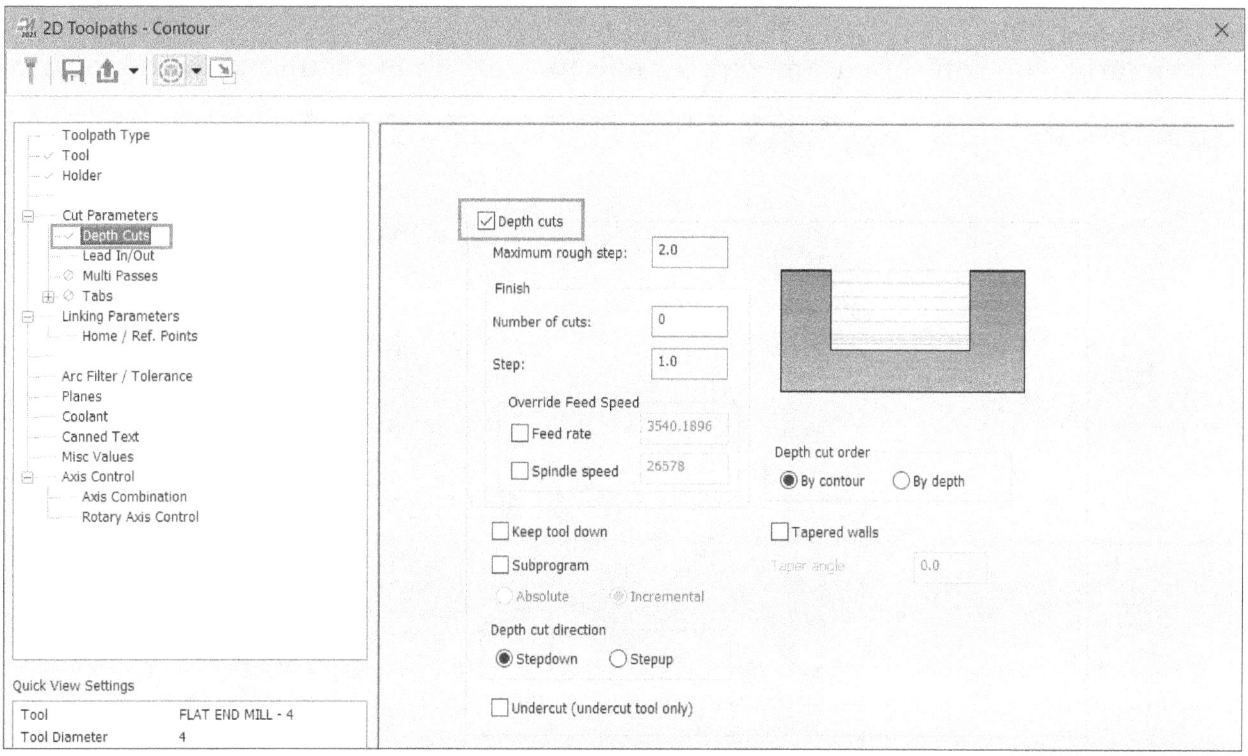

Figure-8. Depth cuts page

- Select desired radio button from the **Depth cut direction** area to define whether cutting tool will move upward or downward for next cutting pass.
- Select the **Undercut** check box if you are using undercut tool to accommodate tool compensation.
- Select desired radio button from the **Depth cut order** area to define whether tool will move equally in all cut features simultaneously (in case of **By contour**) or tool will finish one cut feature before moving to next one (in case of **By depth**).

- Select the **Tapered walls** check box if the walls of model are in taper or you want to create the toolpath in taper of specified angle. Specify desired angle value in the **Taper angle** edit box.

Lead In/Out Options

- Select the **Lead In/Out** option from **Cut Parameters** node in the left area of the dialog box to define how tool will enter or exit the workpiece while machining; refer to Figure-9. Make sure the **Lead In/Out** check box is selected to apply entry/exit parameters.
- Select the **Enter/exit at midpoint in closed contours** check box to make tool entry/exit at the mid points on contour toolpaths.
- Select the **Entry** check box to specify parameters for entry of tool in workpiece.
- Select the **Tangent** option from the **Line** drop-down to enter tool in tangent motion to contour cutting toolpath. Select the **Perpendicular** option from the **Line** drop-down to enter tool perpendicular to contour cutting toolpath. Select the **Profile Ramp** option from the **Line** drop-down to enter tool in ramp motion at the start of cutting motion.
- Specify the parameters as desired in the **Entry** area based on type of entry selected. Specify the length of entry line, ramp height, and ramp angle for line curves in entry toolpath in the **Line** area of the dialog box. Similarly, specify the radius, total sweep angle of arc, and height of helical arc in entry toolpath in **Arc** area of the dialog box.
- Similarly, you can set parameters for exit toolpath in **Exit** area of the dialog box.

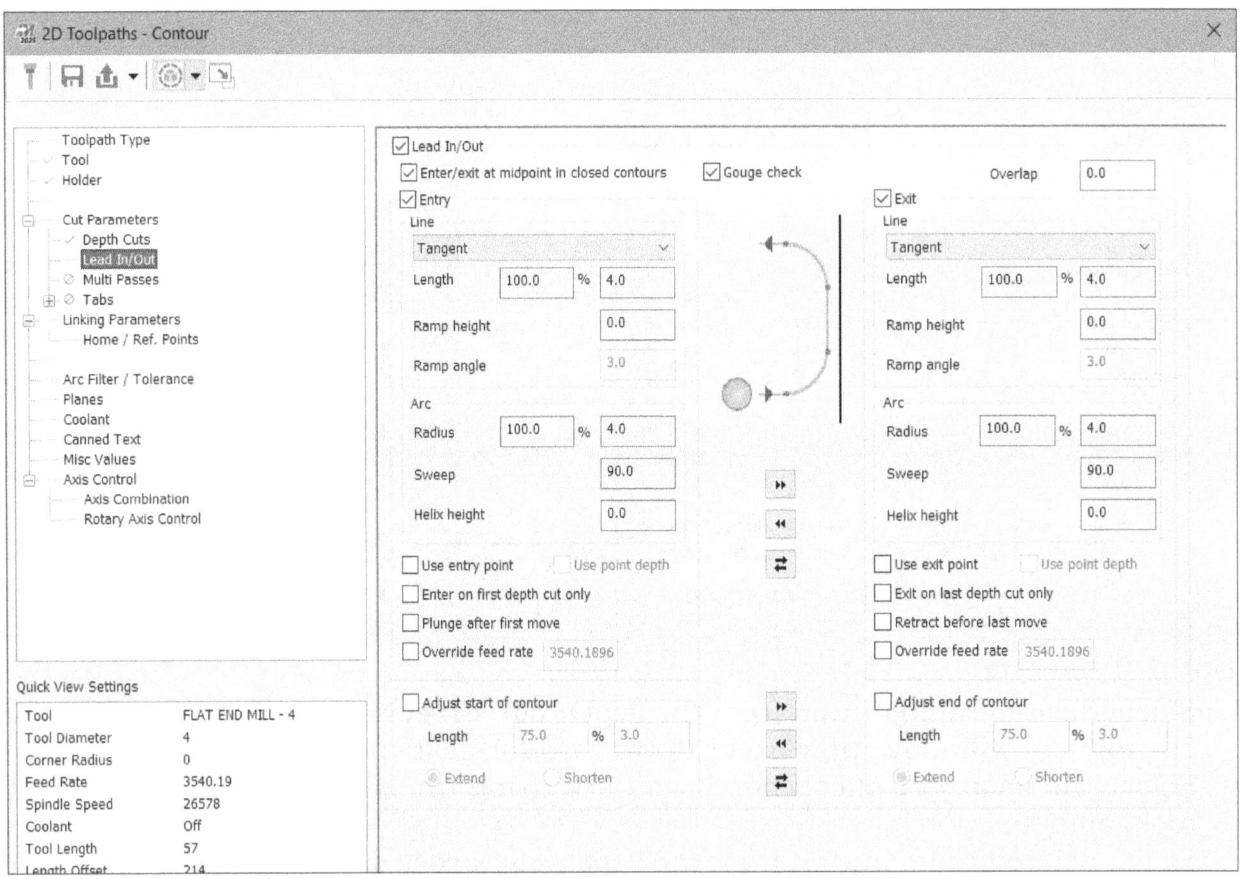

Figure-9. Lead In Out options for toolpaths

Multi Passes Options

- Select **Multi Passes** option from the left area in the dialog box if you want to specify multiple number of passes for roughing or finishing operations in the machining. After selecting this option, select the **Multi Passes** check box to activate the options; refer to Figure-10.

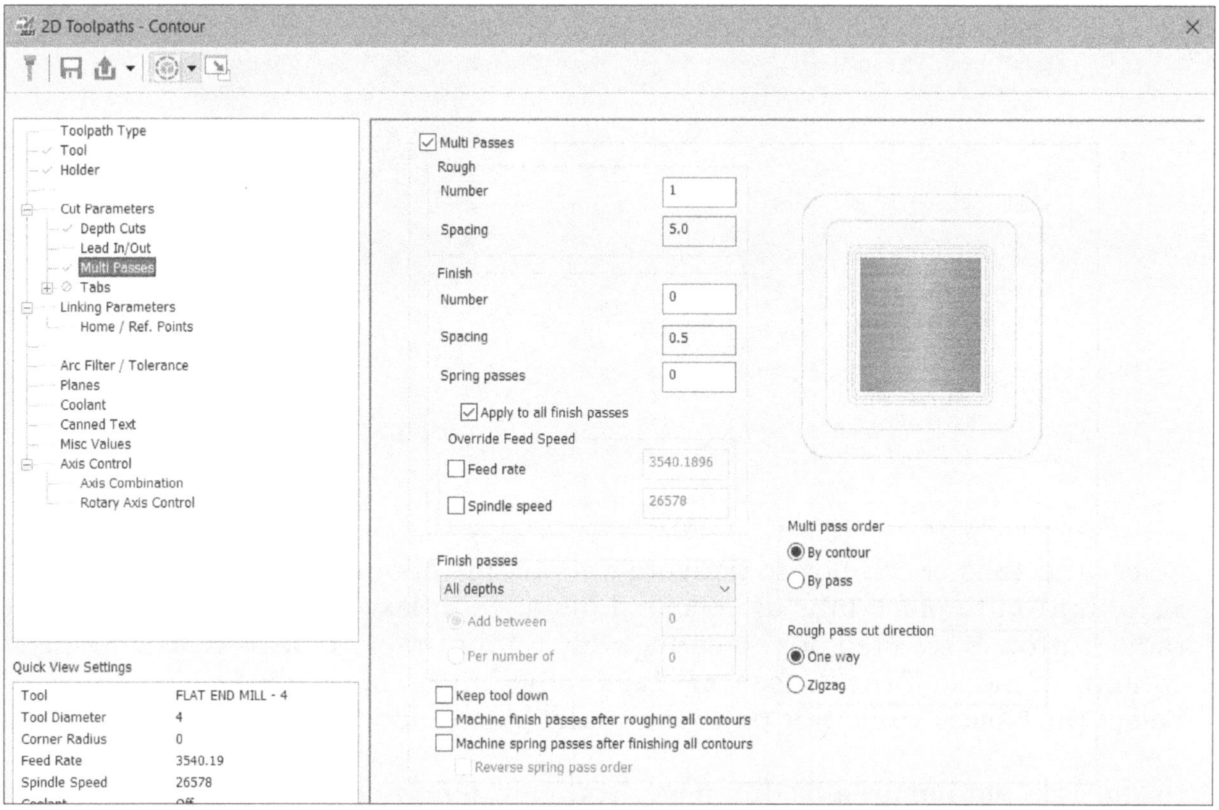

Figure-10. Multi Passes options

- Set desired number of passes and step over distance between those multiple passes in edit boxes of **Rough** and **Finish** area in the dialog box.
- Specify desired value in **Spring passes** edit box to create additional finishing passes on last cutting pass for finishing operation. This option is useful when your part is thin and flexes under load of cutting tool. Specify other parameters in this page as discussed earlier.

Tabs Options

- Select the **Tabs** option from the left area in the dialog box to define location of tabs holding the workpiece on table. The options in dialog box will be displayed as shown in Figure-11.

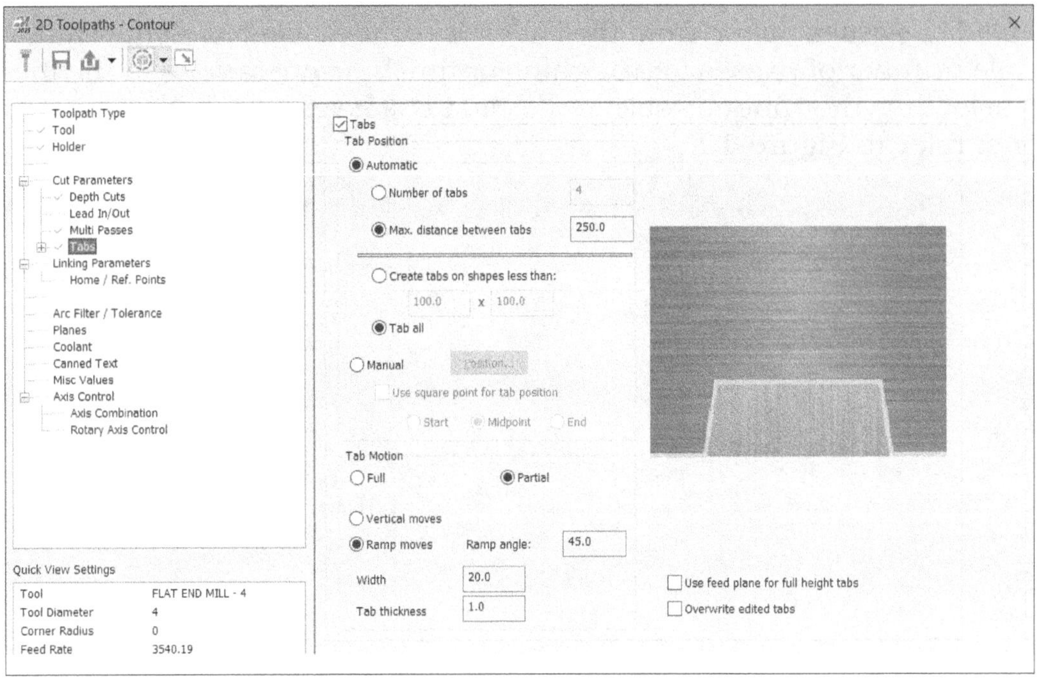

Figure-11. Tabs options

- Select the **Tabs** check box to activate options in this page. Select the **Automatic** radio button to place tabs at specified distance if **Max. distance between tabs** radio button is selected or you can specify total number of tabs placed along the contour of model if the **Number of tabs** radio button is selected.
- Select the **Manual** radio button to manually place each tab at desired location on the contour.
- In the **Tab Motion** area of this page, you can define how cutting tool will avoid hitting tabs while cutting the workpiece.
- Select the **Use feed plane for full heights tabs** check box if you want the cutting tool to retract to feed plane instead of clearance plane or retraction plane when avoiding thick tabs.
- Select the **Overwrite edited tabs** check box to ignore any changes earlier performed in tabs for machining and use settings specified in this page.
- If you want to perform a tab cutoff operation after machining rest of the model then select the **Tab Cutoff** option under **Tabs** node at the left in the dialog box and select the **Cutoff Operation** check box. The options will be displayed as shown in Figure-12. Select desired option to define sequence of tab cutoff operation.

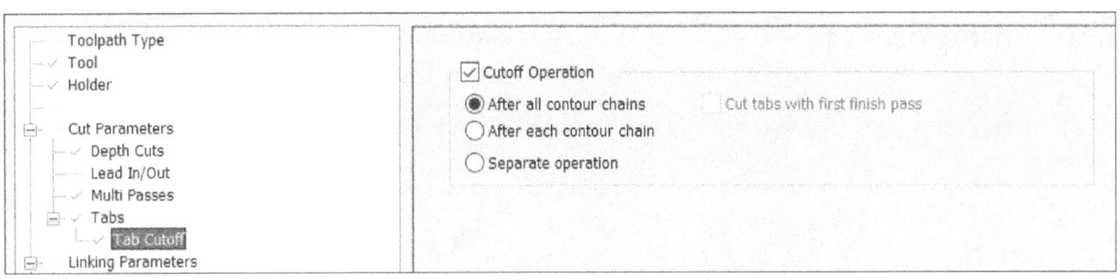

Figure-12. Tab cutoff options

Linking Parameters Options

- Select the **Linking Parameters** option from the dialog box to specify locations of various planes like retract plane, feed plane, top point of stock, and depth point of the stock up to which machining will be performed; refer to Figure-13.

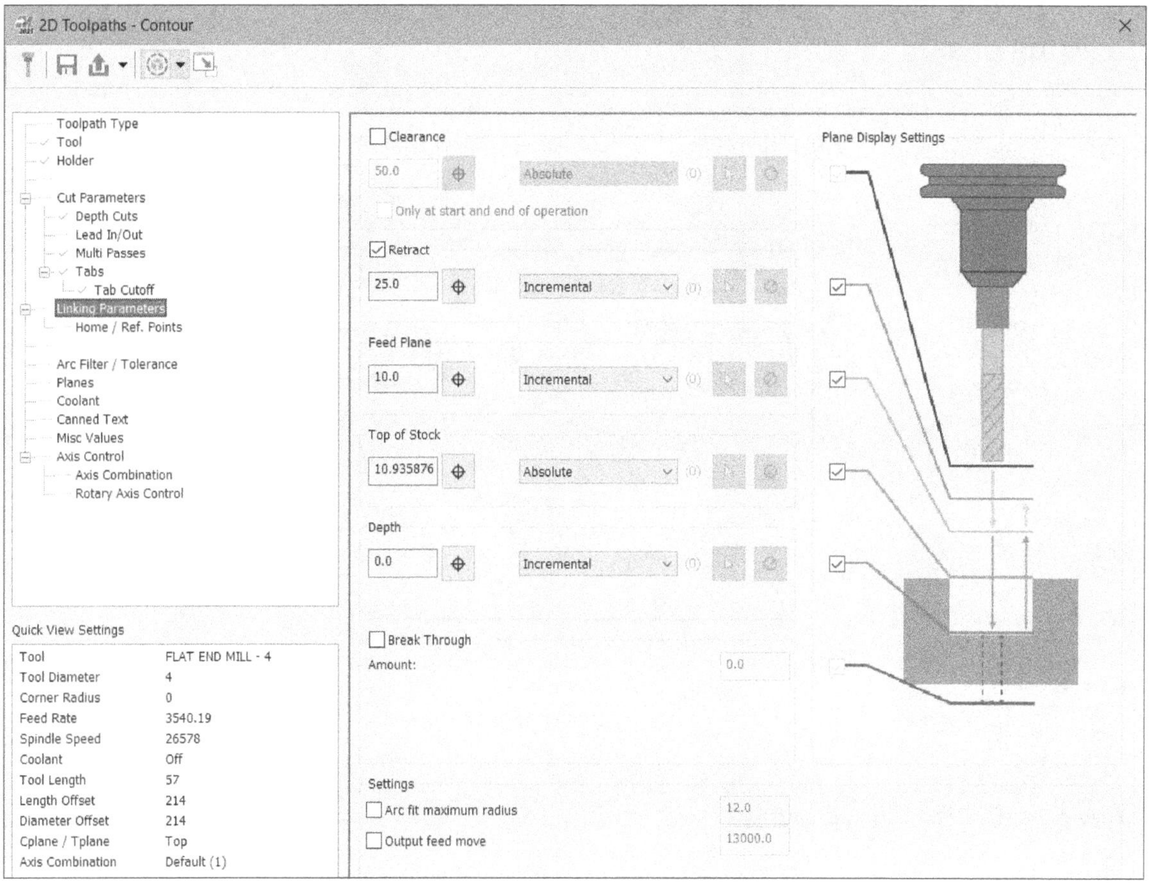

Figure-13. Linking Parameters for 2D contour toolpath

- Select the **Clearance** check box to provide clearance plane for avoiding walls of model while machining.
- Select the **Break Through** check box if you want to specify extra depth upto which the cutting tool should move at the end of cutting depth. This option is useful when you want to cut through the stock.
- Select the **Arc fit maximum radius** check box to specify the maximum radius that can be accommodated in the contour toolpath.
- Select the **Output feed move** check box to make all the rapid movements as cutting feed movements and use specified feed rate.
- Click on the **Home/Ref. Points** option from the left area of the dialog box and specify home position for machining. Select the check boxes from the **Reference points** area to set approach and retraction points at the beginning and end of cutting pass, respectively.

Arc Filter/Tolerance Options

- Select the **Arc Filter/Tolerance** option from the left area in the dialog box to define parameters related to machining precision of curves in the model. The options in the dialog box will be displayed as shown in Figure-14.
- Specify desired overall tolerance value in the **Total tolerance** edit box to define the maximum amount of deviation that can occur from original model edges/ curves when performing machining.
- Select the **Line/Arc Filtering Settings** check box to convert small consecutive lines/arcs with a bigger smooth arc; refer to Figure-15. After selecting this check box, select the **XY(G17)**, **XZ(G18)**, and **YZ(G19)** check boxes to activate arc filtering in respective planes.

- Select the **One way filtering** check box to allow small zigzags at the finishing end of cutting pass.

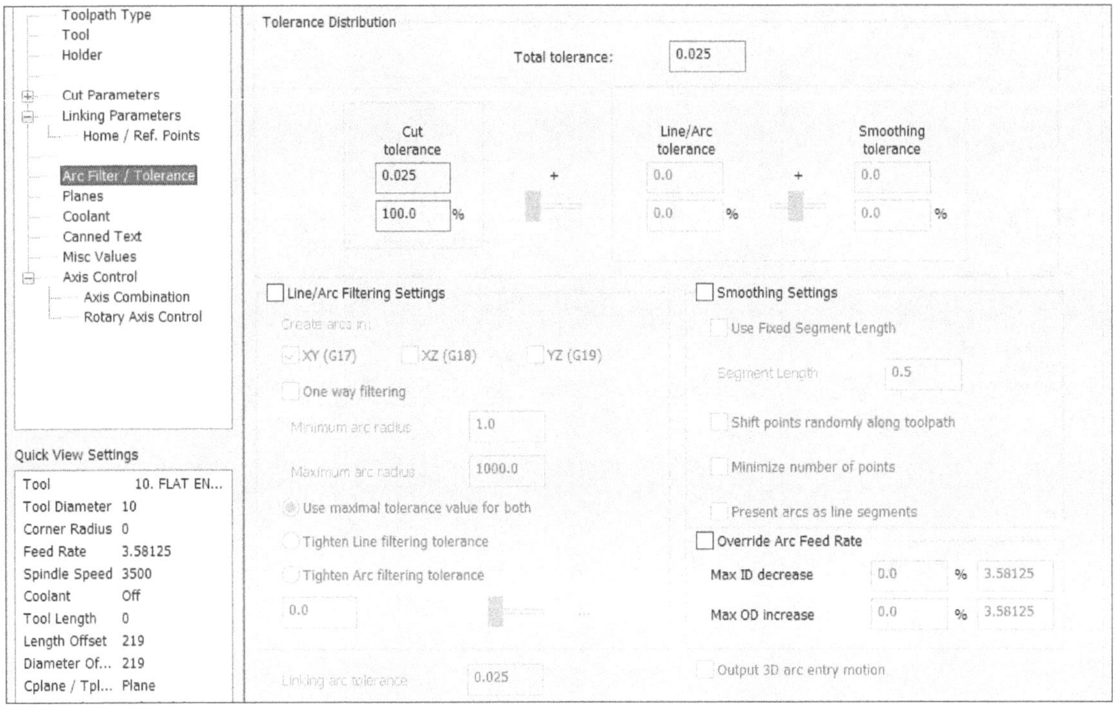

Figure-14. Arc Filter Tolerance options

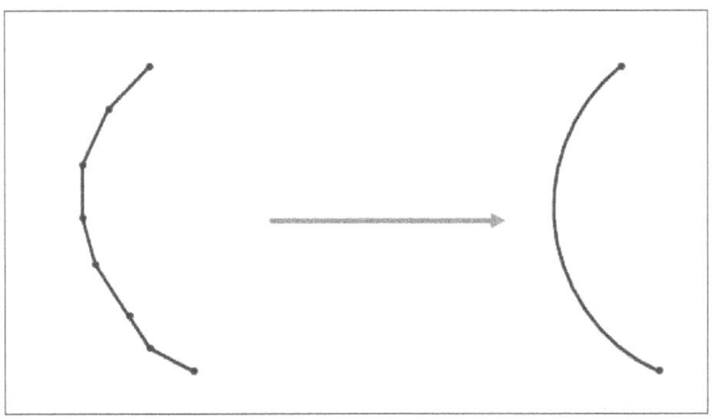

Figure-15. Arc filtering

- Specify desired values in the **Minimum arc radius** and **Maximum arc radius** edit boxes to define the minimum and maximum limits of arc radius within which Mastercam filter considers curves as arcs. If the radius of an arc is lower than minimum radius or higher than maximum radius then Mastercam will consider them as lines.
- Select **Use maximal tolerance value for both**, **Tighten Line filtering tolerance**, or **Tighten Arc filtering tolerance** radio button to define balance between line and arc tolerance for filtering.
- Select the **Smoothing Settings** check box to define parameters for smoothening lines/arcs in toolpath.
- Select the **Use Fixed Segment Length** check box to define maximum length of segments of toolpaths to be created. Generally, in parallel toolpaths, Mastercam creates non uniform segments while machining surface of model causing wavy patterns on the surface of part. In such cases, you can define a small length of segment to get smoother surface. Note that smaller segment lengths can increase length of program.

- Select the **Shift points randomly along toolpaths** check box to shift node points of toolpath backward and forward from their original positions to prevent machining impression lines generally in case of Parallel toolpaths.
- Select the **Minimize number of points** check box to exclude very close node points from toolpath hence reducing total number of points on the toolpath.
- Select the **Present arcs as line segments** check box to convert all arcs in toolpaths to small linear moves.

Planes Options

- Select the **Planes** option from the left area in the dialog box to define parameters of current toolpaths for Working coordinate system, tool plane, Comp/construction plane. By default, plane selected in **Planes Manager** is used in this page.

Coolant Options

- Select the **Coolant** option from left area in the dialog box to define how coolant will be provide while machining toolpath. The options in the dialog box will be displayed as shown in Figure-16. Select the **On** option from desired drop-down to activate respective coolant port in machine.

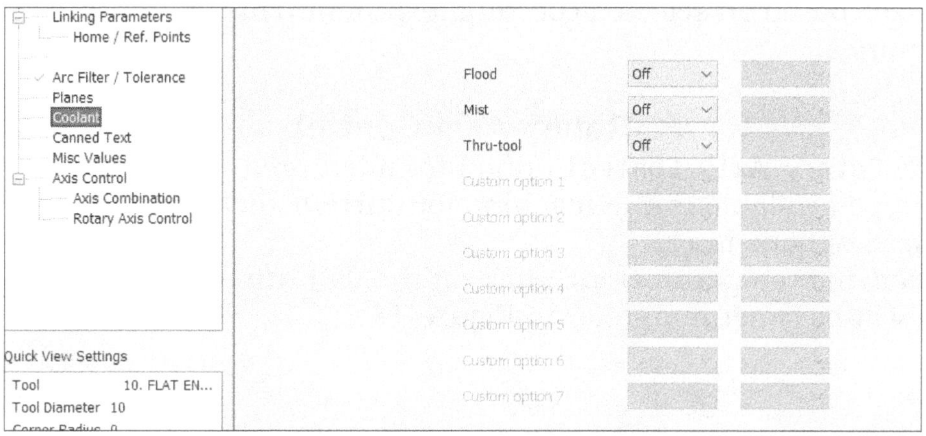

Figure-16. Coolant options

Canned Text Option

- Select the **Canned Text** option from the left area to define code blocks to be inserted before/after the tool change. Select desired code from **Canned text options** list box and click on the **Add before**, **Add with**, or **Add after** button to place the code in NC program at respective locations with tool change.

Misc Values Options

- Select the **Misc Values** option from the left area in the dialog box to set values of custom parameters created in post processor. By default, the **Automatically set to post values when posting** check box is selected. Clear this check box to change the values; refer to Figure-17.

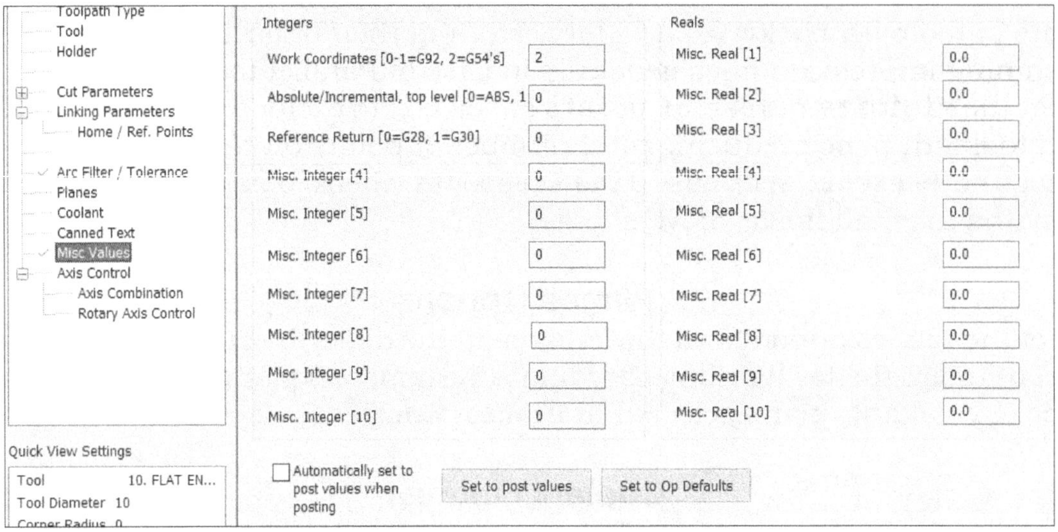

Figure-17. Misc Values options

Axis Combination

- Select the **Axis Combination** option from left area in the dialog box to choose desired axes based on selected coordinate system. This option is useful for multi-axis machines.

Rotary Axis Control

- Select the **Rotary Axis Control** option from left area to define rotation axis and rotation type available in the machine for current toolpath. You will learn more about these options later.
- After specifying the parameters, click on the **OK** button from the dialog box. The toolpath will be generated; refer to Figure-18.

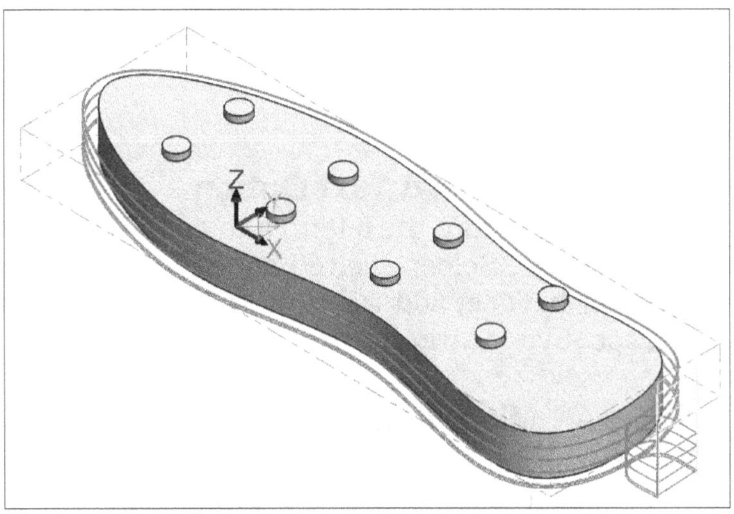

Figure-18. Toolpath generated

- To display the simulation of the material removal, click on the **Backplot selected operations** button from **Mastercam Toolpath Manager**. The **Backplot** dialog box will be displayed with the prototype of tool and model; refer to Figure-19.

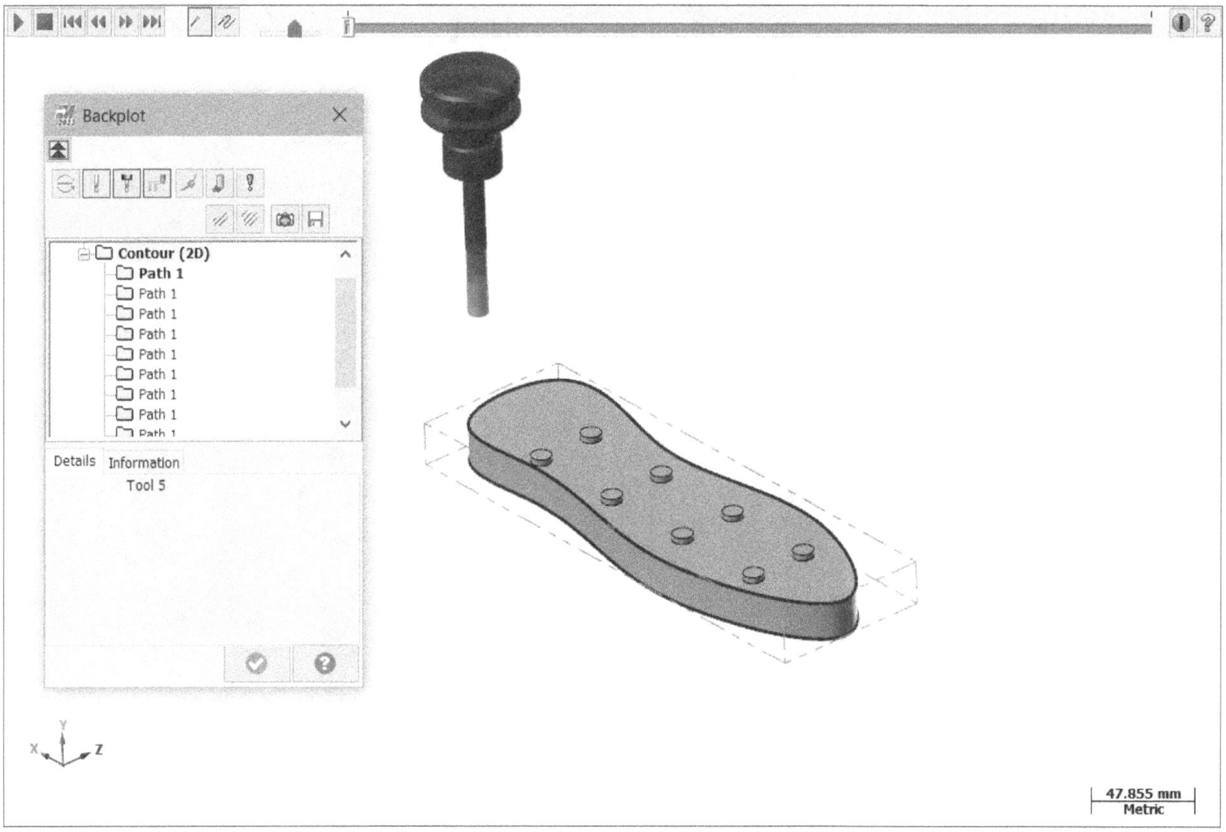

Figure-19. Backplotting a toolpath

- Click on the **Play** button from toolbar above graphics area to run the simulation. Close the **Backplot** dialog box to exit.

Creating Drill Toolpath

The **Drill** tool in the **2D** group is used to generate toolpaths for drilling holes at selected points. The procedure to create the drill toolpath is given next.

- Click on the **Drill** tool from the **2D** group in the **Toolpaths** tab of the **Ribbon**. The **Toolpath Hole Definition Manager** will be displayed as shown in Figure-20.
- Select desired points from the model where you want to drill the holes or you can select the edges of holes in your model; refer to Figure-21.

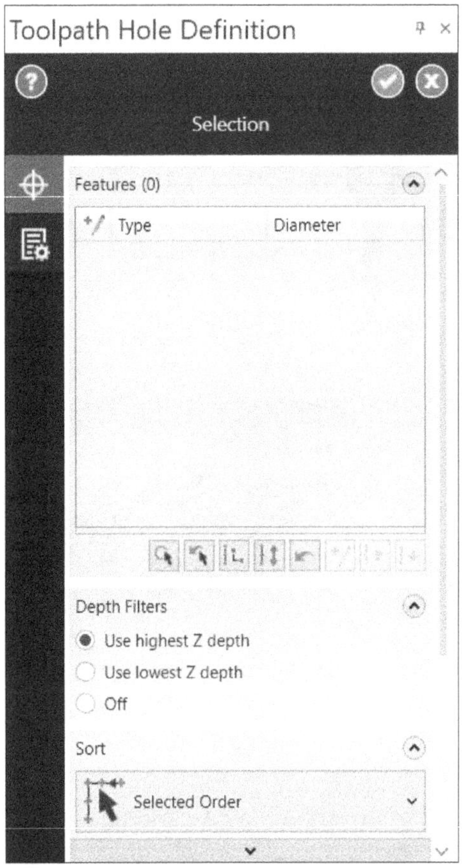

Figure-20. Toolpath Hole Definition Manager

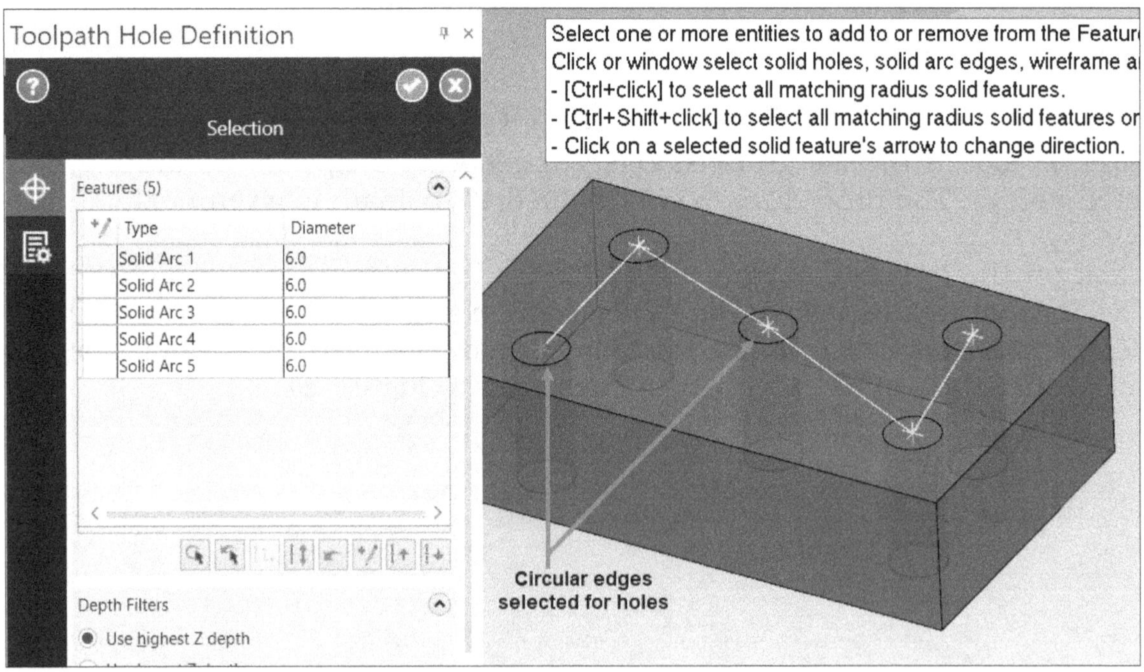

Figure-21. Selecting edges and points for hole toolpaths

- Select desired radio button from the **Depth Filters** rollout to filter the points to be used for selecting holes. For example, if **Use highest Z depth** radio button is selected then only the hole points which are at highest Z depth will be used for creating holes.
- Click on the button from the **Sort** rollout to select desired sorting method to define the order in which holes will be created; refer to Figure-22.

- Select desired option from the drop-down list to define the order of drilling holes.
- If you want to manually change the order of drilling then you can use the **Move Up** and **Move Down** buttons in the **Features** rollout of **Manager** after selecting the point/entity from the list.

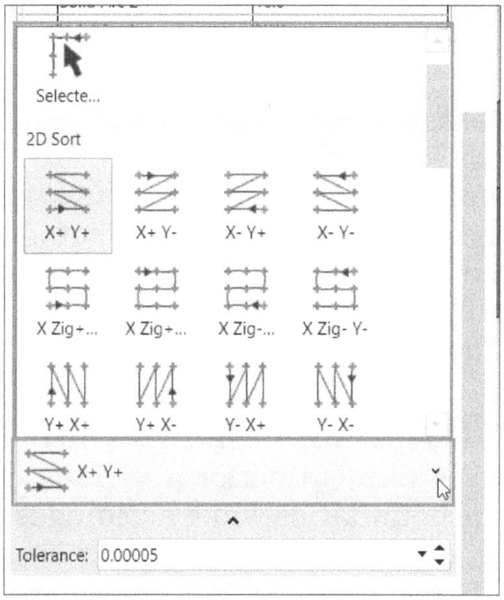

Figure-22. Sort drop-down

- Click on the **OK** button from the **Manager**. The **2D Toolpaths - Drill/Circles Simple drill** dialog box will be displayed; refer to Figure-23. Make sure the **Drill** toolpath type is selected in the dialog box.

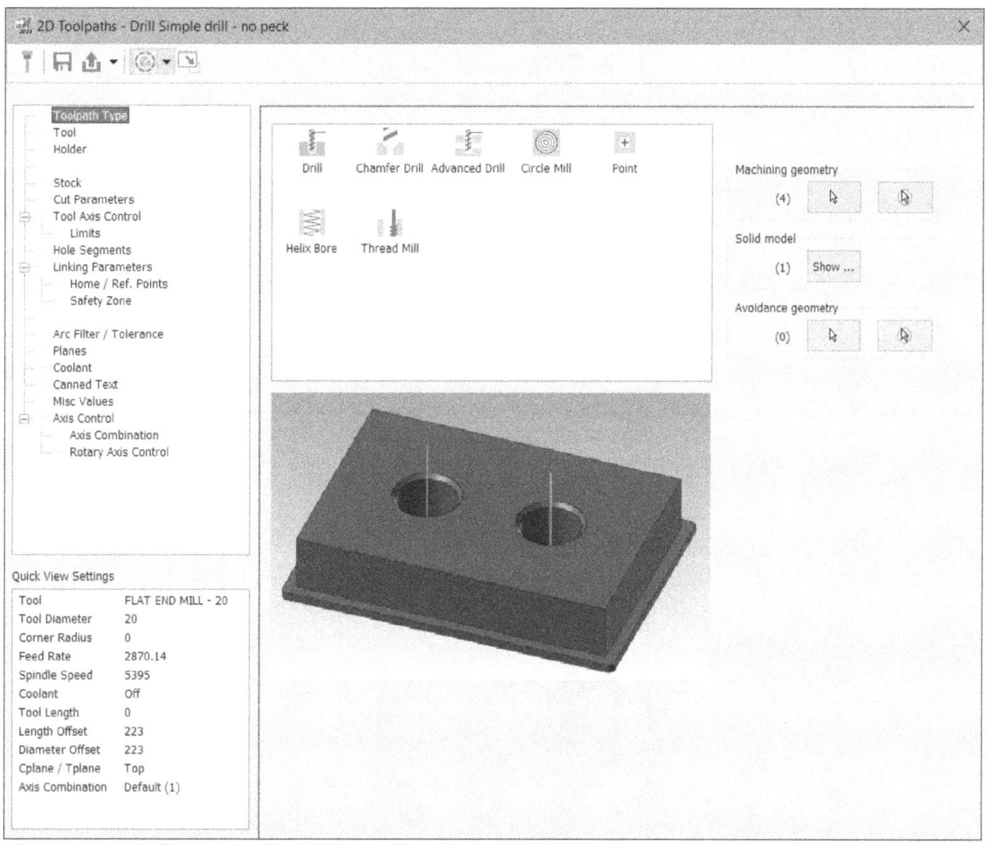

Figure-23. 2D Toolpaths-Drill/Circles Simple drill dialog box

- Click on the **Select geometry** button from the **Avoidance Model** area to select geometries to be avoided when creating toolpath.

- Click on the **Tool** option from the left box in the dialog box and select desired drill from the tool library. If desired cutting tool is not displayed in the box then click on the **Select library tool** button and select desired drill from the dialog box.
- Select desired holder by using the **Holder** option from the left box and similarly, specify the cutting parameters by using the **Cut Parameters** option. You can create a desired type of cutting cycle from the **Cycle** drop-down in **Cut Parameters** page of the dialog box.
- Click on the **Linking Parameters** option from the left box and specify the depth of the drill in the edit box for **Depth**.
- Select the **Tip Comp** check box from the page to apply drill tip compensation. Specify desired drill tip compensation value, if required.
- Set the other parameters as desired and click on the **OK** button from the dialog box to create the toolpath. You can check the toolpath by using the **Backplot** and **Verify** buttons in the **Toolpaths Manager**.

Dynamic Mill Toolpath

The Dynamic Mill toolpath is used to perform various dynamic milling tasks like removing material inside the boundaries while avoiding islands, remove material left by other tools, and removing material near the outer boundaries. The procedure to use this toolpath is given next.

Machining Inside Boundary

- Click on the **Dynamic Mill** tool from the **2D HighSpeed Toolpaths** drop-down in the **Ribbon**. The **Chain Options** dialog box will be displayed; refer to Figure-24.

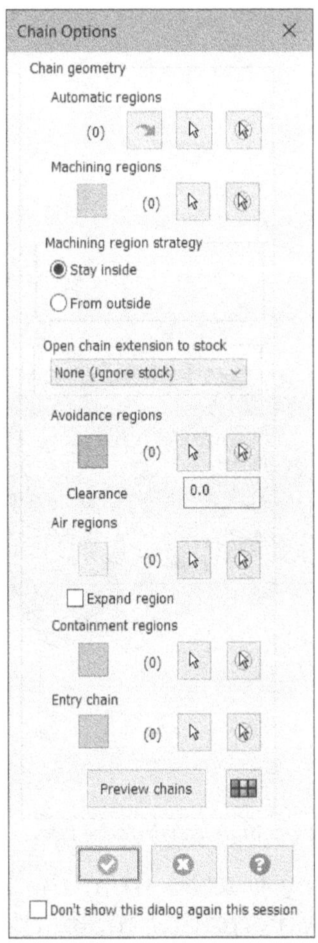

Figure-24. Chain Options dialog box

- Click on the **Select automatic regions** button from **Automatic regions** area to select faces of model to be identified automatically for machining. On selecting this button, the **Solid Chaining** selection box will be displayed. Select the faces to be machined and click on the **OK** button from selection box. The number of faces selected will be displayed in the dialog box.
- Click on the **Convert automatic regions** button to automatically categorise sections of selected faces to machining regions, avoidance regions, and air regions.
- Select **Stay inside** or **From outside** radio button from the **Machining region strategy** area to define whether you want the cutting tool to remain inside the boundaries or the cutting tool is free to move outside the boundaries of selected chains, respectively. Refer to Figure-25.

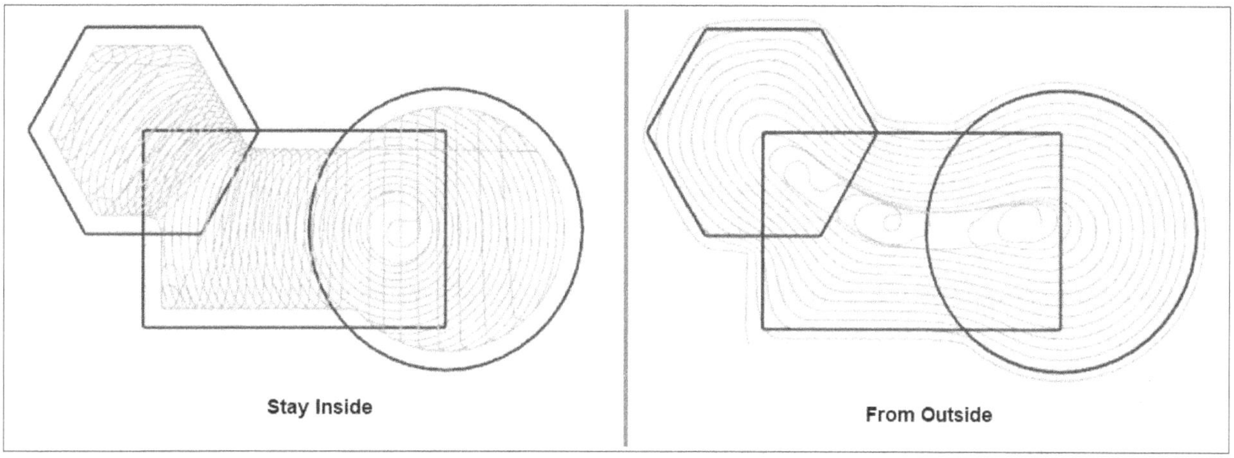

Figure-25. Stay inside and from outside options

- If you want to manually select chains for machining then click on the **Select machining chains** button from the **Machining regions** section of the dialog box. The **Wireframe Chaining** dialog box will be displayed.
- Click on the **Wireframe** button from the dialog box if you want to select wireframe entities or click on the **Solids** button from the dialog box if you want to select solid faces/bodies. Select the faces/curves that you want to machine; refer to Figure-26.

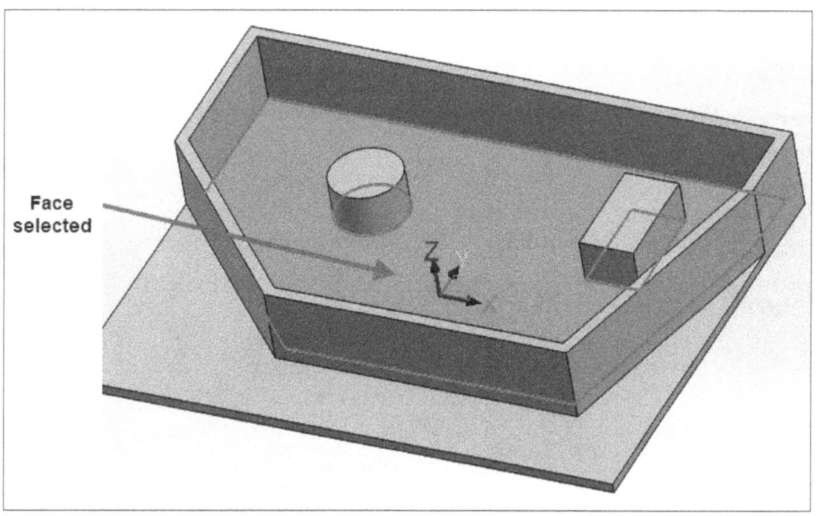

Figure-26. Face selected for dynamic mill machining

- Note that there are islands in the part which should be counted as avoidance region to dynamic mill this part. Click on the **Select avoidance chains** button from the **Avoidance regions** area of the **Chain Options** dialog box and select the faces of islands to be avoided while machining; refer to Figure-27. Specify desired value in **Clearance** edit box to give buffer around avoidance regions when machining.

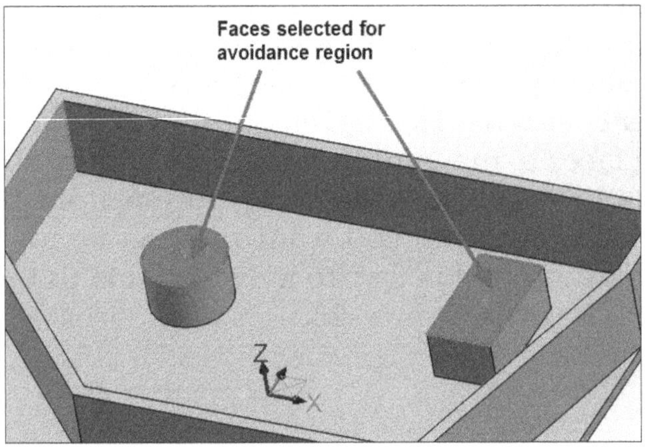

Figure-27. Avoidance region selection

- Click on the **Select air chains** button to select faces to be considered as sections for free movement of cutting tool. Note that there should be no stock material in air sections. Select the **Expand region** check box to allow free movement of cutting tool while entering material.
- Click on the **Select containment chains** selection button to define outer boundary of model to be used as limits for machining.
- Click on the **Select entry chains** selection button to define curve to be used as entry for toolpath.
- Click on the **Preview chains** button to check preview of areas to be machined, avoided, considered as air section, and containment area by current toolpath.
- Click on the **OK** button from the **Solid Chaining** dialog box and then **OK** button from the **Chain Options** dialog box. The **2D High Speed Toolpath - Dynamic Mill** dialog box will be displayed; refer to Figure-28.

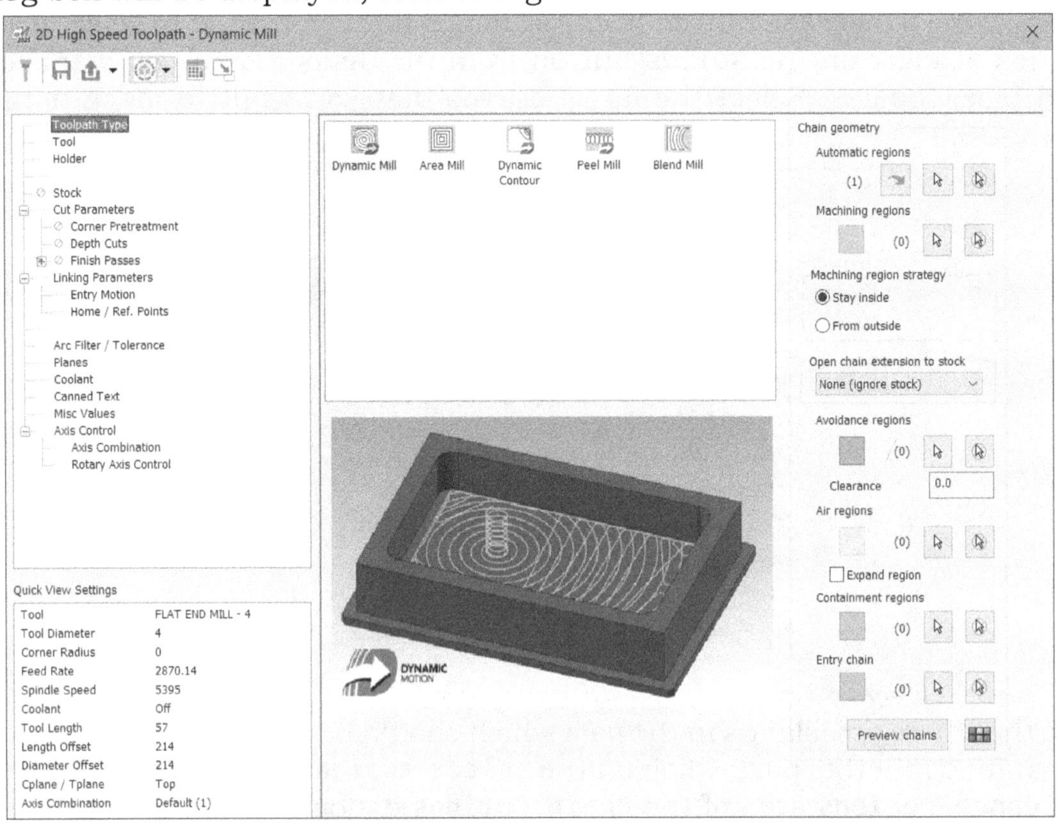

Figure-28. 2D High Speed Toolpath-Dynamic Mill dialog box

Cut Parameters

- In current example, we are creating toolpath for milling inside selected boundary so make sure the **Stay inside** radio button is selected in the **Machining region strategy** area of this page. If we need to machine a part which has open boundaries then we can select the **From outside** radio button.
- If you have selected any open chain for machining then you can select desired radio button from the **Open chain extension to stock** area to allow Mastercam to extend the chain if there is stock left nearby. By default, **None** radio button is selected, so Mastercam does not extend the open chain. If you select the **Tangent** radio button then software will extend the chain tangentially. If you select the **Shortest distance** radio button then software will extend chain to nearby shortest distance.
- If you have not selected machining regions and avoidance regions earlier then you can click on the respective selection buttons in this page and select them.
- Select the tool and tool holder from respective pages in this dialog box.
- Click on the **Cut Parameters** option from the left area. The dialog box will be displayed as shown in Figure-29.

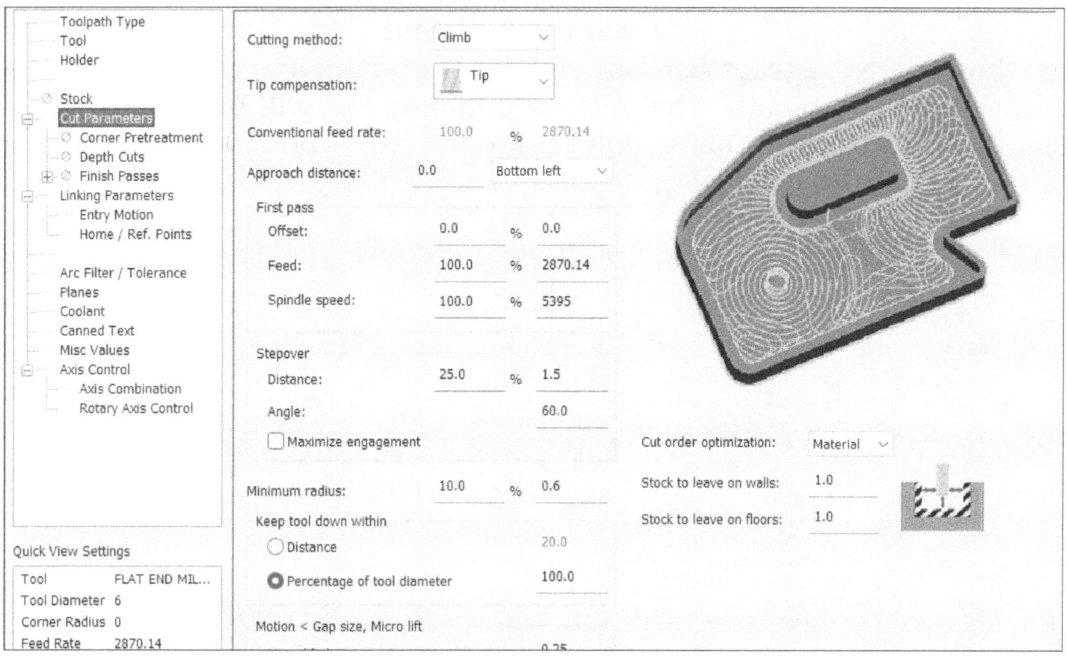

Figure-29. Cut Parameters for Dynamic Mill

- Select the cutting method and tool compensation from the respective drop-downs in the dialog box.
- In the **Approach distance** edit box, specify the distance value from which the tool will approach to the start location of cutting toolpath using cutting feed rate.
- In the **Offset** edit box of **First pass** area, specify the distance to offset toolpath from original path to reduce load on the tool during first pass.
- In the **Feed** edit box of **First pass** area, specify the reduction percentage to reduce feed rate during first pass to reduce load on tool. Similarly, specify desired value in the **Spindle speed** edit box to control speed of tool spindle during first pass.
- Specify step-over, minimum toolpath radius, gap size, and micro lift data as required in respective fields. Select the **Maximize engagement** check box from the **Stepover** section to keep the cutting tool engaged in stock while performing stepovers.

- Click on the **Cut order optimization** drop-down and select desired option to define how Mastercam selects the start point of cutting passes.
- Select desired option from the **Micro lift retract** drop-down to define the condition when cutting tool will perform small retraction before performing next cutting pass. The micro retraction distance and feed rate values can be specified in the edit boxes of **Motion < Gap size, Micro lift** area.
- Set desired values in the **Stock to leave on walls** and **Stock to leave on floors** edit boxes to define the amount of material to be left after performing the dynamic mill machining.
- Click on the **Depth Cuts** option from the left area in the dialog box and specify the depth of cut parameters as discussed in previous tools. Note that in case of Dynamic mill toolpaths, you can also perform face milling on the islands coming in toolpaths. To do so, select the **Island facing** check box in this page and specify the related parameters below it.
- Select the **Subprogram** check box in this page if you want to use sub program in NC codes. Using sub-program, we can reduce the repetition of same code at different depth levels.

Corner Pretreatment

- Select the **Corner Pretreatment** option from the left area to define how corners will be created in the toolpath. The options in dialog box will be displayed as shown in Figure-30. Select the **Corner Pretreatment** check box to activate the options.

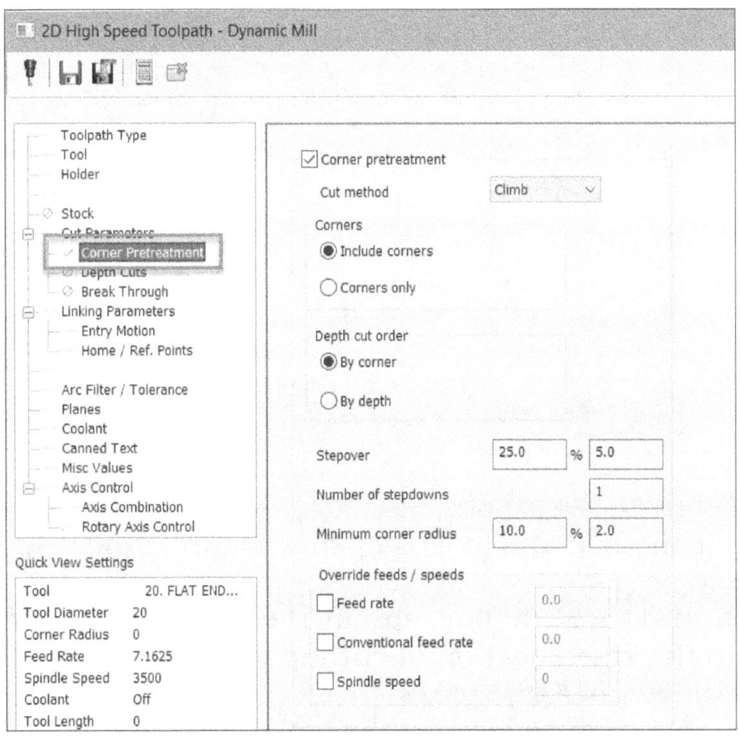

Figure-30. Corner Pretreatment options

- Select desired option from the **Cut method** drop-down to define what cutting direction will be used for machining.
- Select the **Include corners** radio button to machine corners along with other selected geometries. Select the **Corners only** radio button to machine only corners of selected geometries. Specify the other parameters in this page as discussed earlier.

- Click on the **Entry Motion** option from the left area and carefully define the motion of tool while entering in the workpiece for cutting material. If you want to change the feed rate for entry motion then you can do so by using options in **Entry feeds/ speeds** area of this page.
- Set the **Linking Parameters** as discussed earlier.

Rest Material Options

- If you want to create toolpath for rest mill then click on the **Stock** option from the left area of the **2D High Speed Toolpath - Dynamic Mill** dialog box. The options in the dialog box will be displayed as shown in Figure-31.

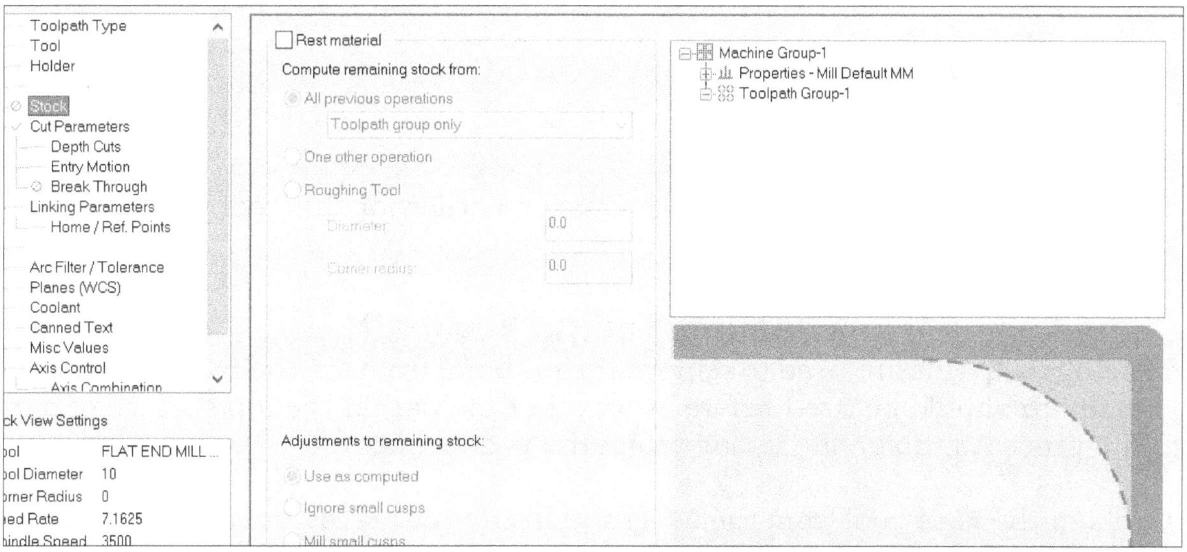

Figure-31. Rest mill options in Dynamic Mill dialog box

- Select the **Rest material** check box and then select desired option from **Compute remaining stock from** area of the dialog box. Specify the other parameters as required.
- Set the other parameters as discussed earlier.

Machining Outside Boundary

- After activating the **Dynamic Mill** tool, select the face outside the boundary as machining region; refer to Figure-32.

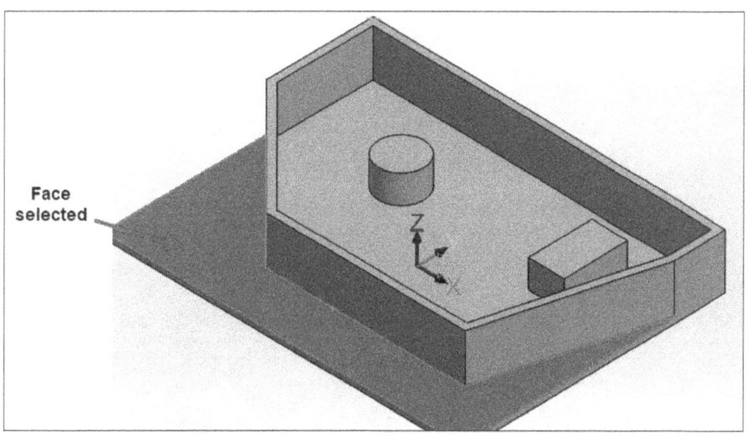

Figure-32. Face selected for machining outside with Dynamic Mill

- Click on the **OK** button from **Chain Options** dialog box. The **2D High Speed Toolpath - Dynamic Mill** dialog box will be displayed. Note that if there are islands on the face then you need to select them as avoidance region as discussed earlier.

- Select the **From outside** radio button from the **Machining region strategy** area of the dialog box; refer to Figure-33.

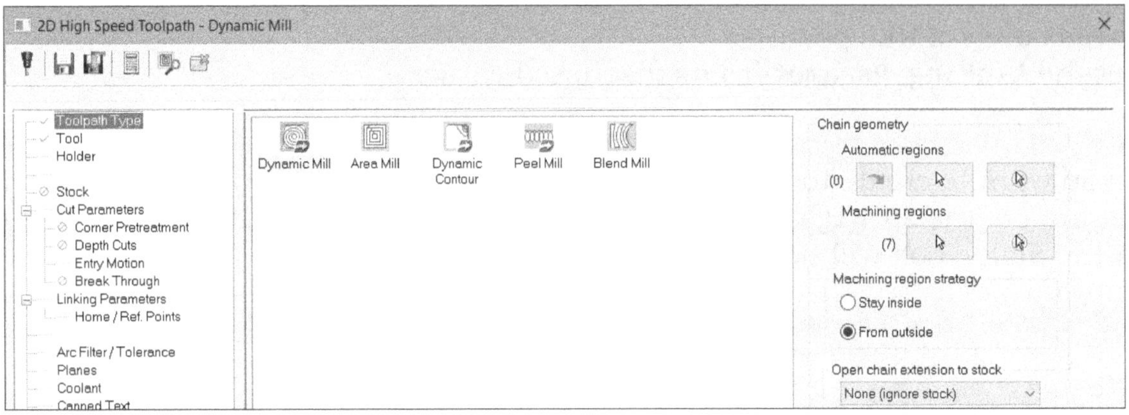

Figure-33. From outside machining region strategy

- Specify rest of the parameters as discussed earlier for this tool and click on the **OK** button to create toolpath.

Creating Facing Toolpath

The Facing toolpaths are used to remove the material from the top faces in the model. This toolpath should be used before every other toolpath if the top surface of part is flat. The procedure to create facing toolpaths is given next.

- Click on the **Face** tool from the **2D** group in the **Toolpaths** tab of the **Ribbon**. The **Solid/Wireframe Chaining** dialog box will be displayed as discussed earlier.
- Select the top face of the model on which you want to perform the facing operation. Make sure that you have selected the button from the **Chain Manager** before selecting the face to filter face selection. Also, there should be only one chain in **Chain Manager** after selecting face.
- Click on the **OK** button from the dialog box. The **2D Toolpaths - Facing** dialog box will be displayed; refer to Figure-34.

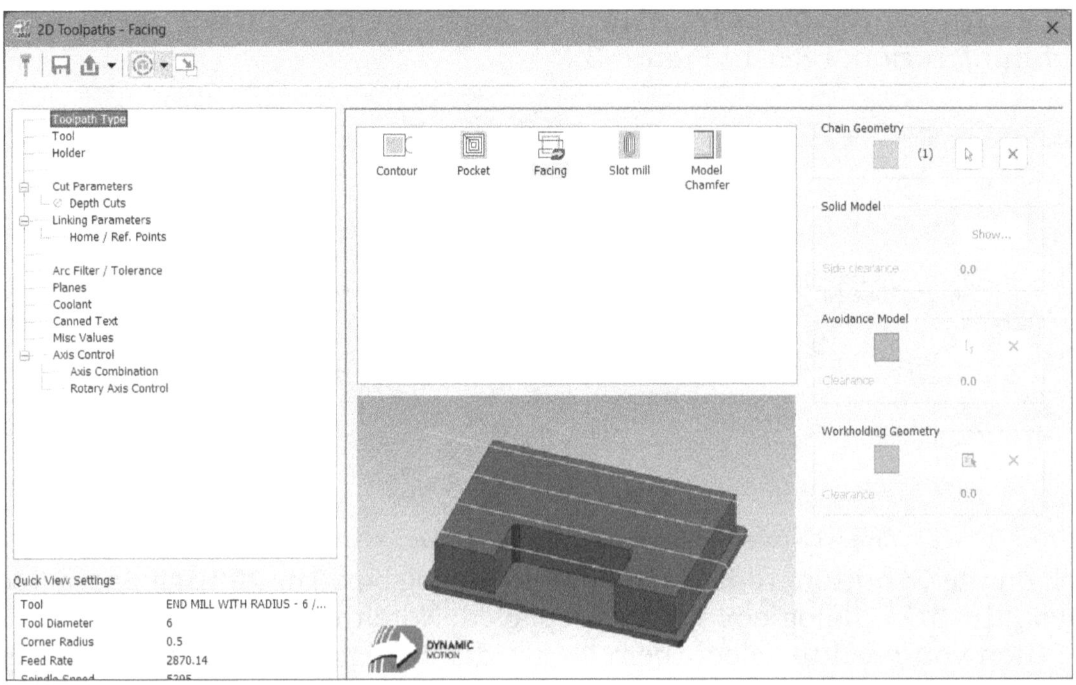

Figure-34. 2D Toolpaths-Facing dialog box

- Select the facing tool by clicking on the **Tool** option from the left box in the dialog box and similarly select desired tool holder.
- Select the **Reverse direction of last pass** check box from the **Cut Parameters** page to reverse direction of last cutting pass. Select the **Auto angle** check box to automatically set angle for cutting passes of toolpath in cutting plane of part. Select the **Roll in** check box to add arc move at the entry of toolpath in stock.
- Specify other parameters like cut parameters, depth of cuts, link parameters, and so on in the dialog box and then click on the **OK** button from the dialog box. The toolpath will be generated; refer to Figure-35.

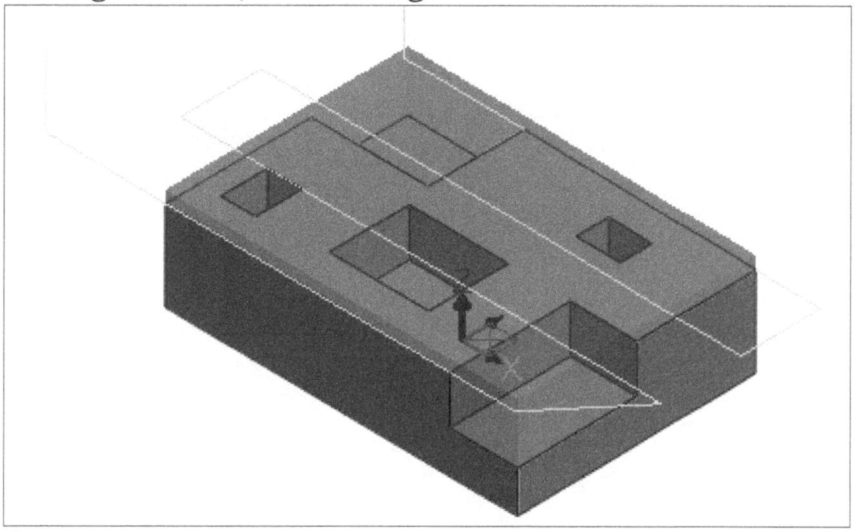

Figure-35. Toolpath for facing

- Backplot the toolpath to verify as discussed earlier.

Dynamic Contour Toolpath

The Dynamic Contour mill toolpaths are used to remove material by following the profile specified. The procedure to create this toolpath is given next.

- Click on the **Dynamic Contour** tool from the expanded **2D** group in the **Toolpaths** tab of the **Ribbon**. The **Chain Options** dialog box will be displayed as discussed earlier.
- Select the wall faces of the model to set the profile of cut; refer to Figure-36 and click on the **OK** button. The **2D High Speed Toolpath - Dynamic Contour** dialog box will be displayed; refer to Figure-37.

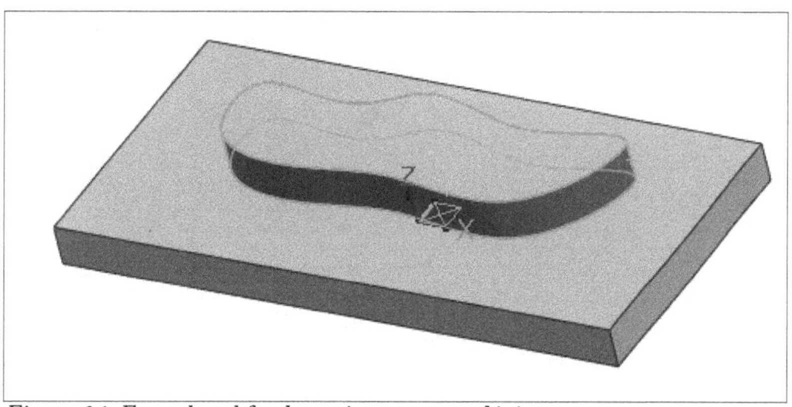

Figure-36. Face selected for dynamic contour machining

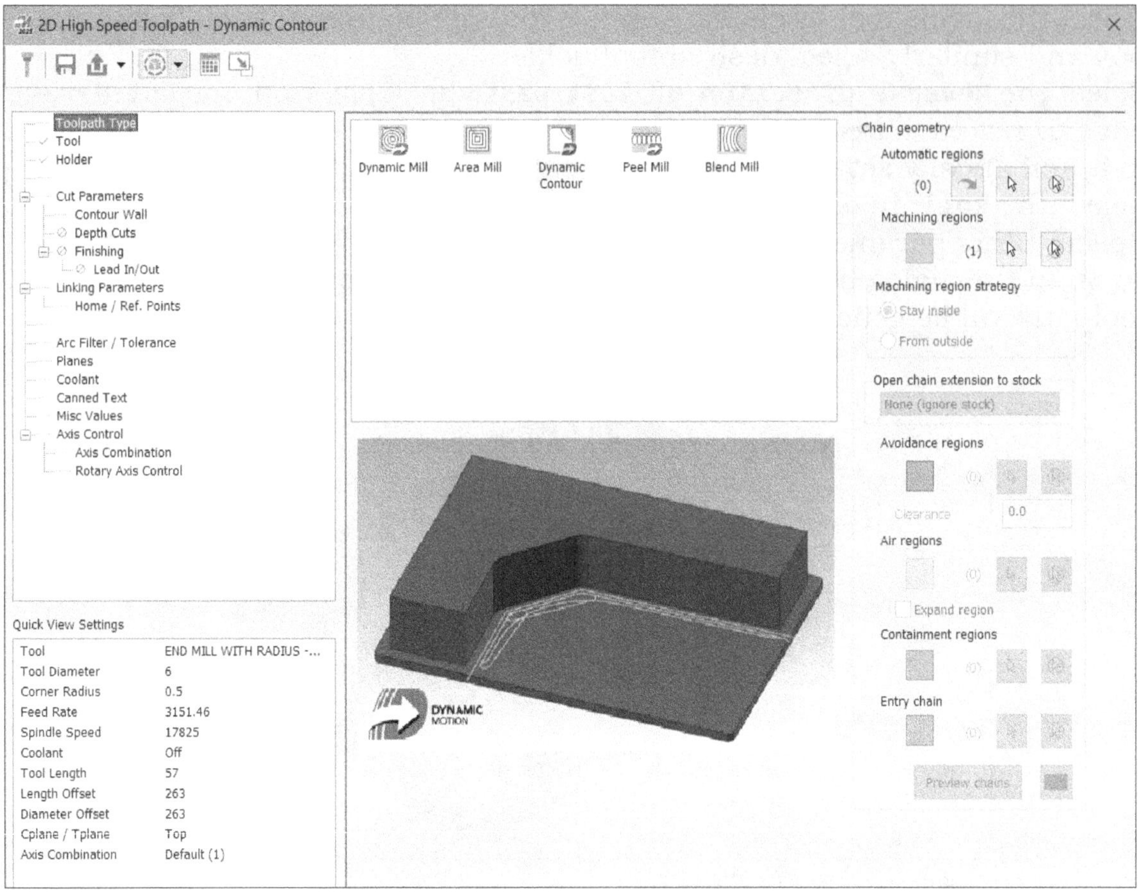

Figure-37. 2D High Speed Toolpath-Dynamic Contour dialog box

- Click on the **Contour Wall** option from the left area to specify parameters related to contour walls; refer to Figure-38. Based on the parameters specified for contour wall, dynamic toolpaths will be generated automatically by Mastercam.

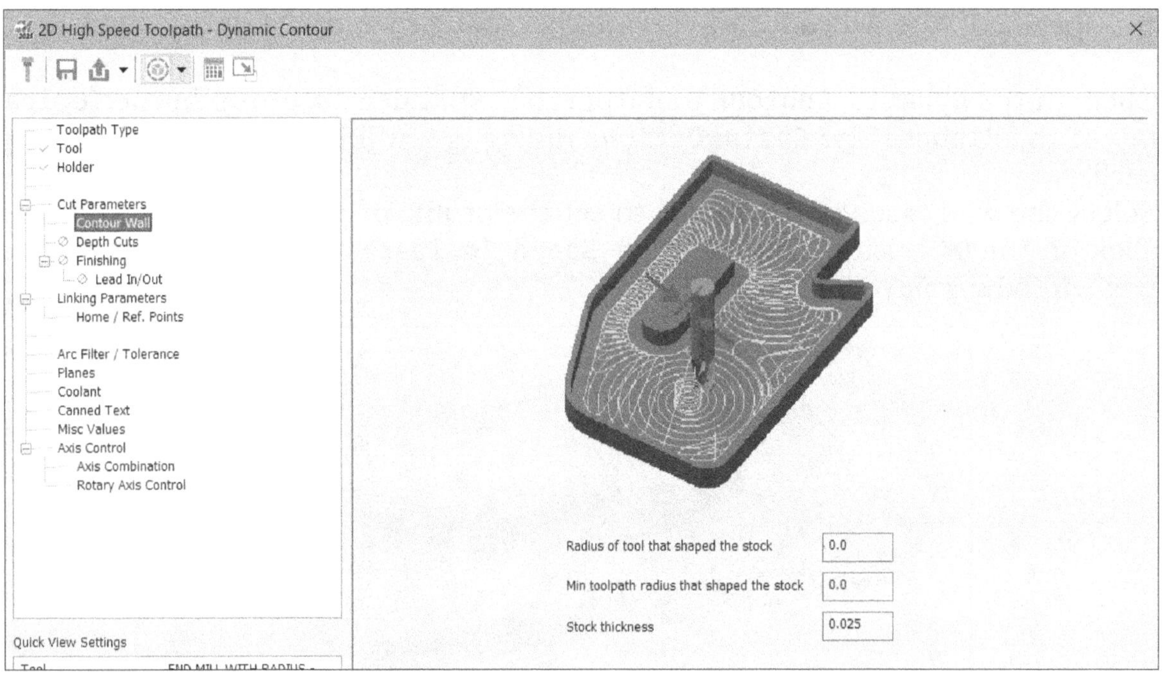

Figure-38. Dynamic contour wall options

- Specify the other parameters as discussed earlier for contour toolpath.
- Click on the **OK** button from the dialog box to generate the toolpath.

Creating Pocket Toolpath

The Pocket toolpaths are used to remove the material from the pocket in the model. The procedure to create pocket toolpaths is given next.

- Click on the **Pocket** tool from the expanded **2D** group in the **Toolpaths** tab of the **Ribbon**. The **Solid Chaining** dialog box will be displayed as discussed earlier.
- Select the bottom face of the pocket in the model; refer to Figure-39 and click on the **OK** button from the dialog box. The **2D Toolpaths-Pocket** dialog box will be displayed; refer to Figure-40.

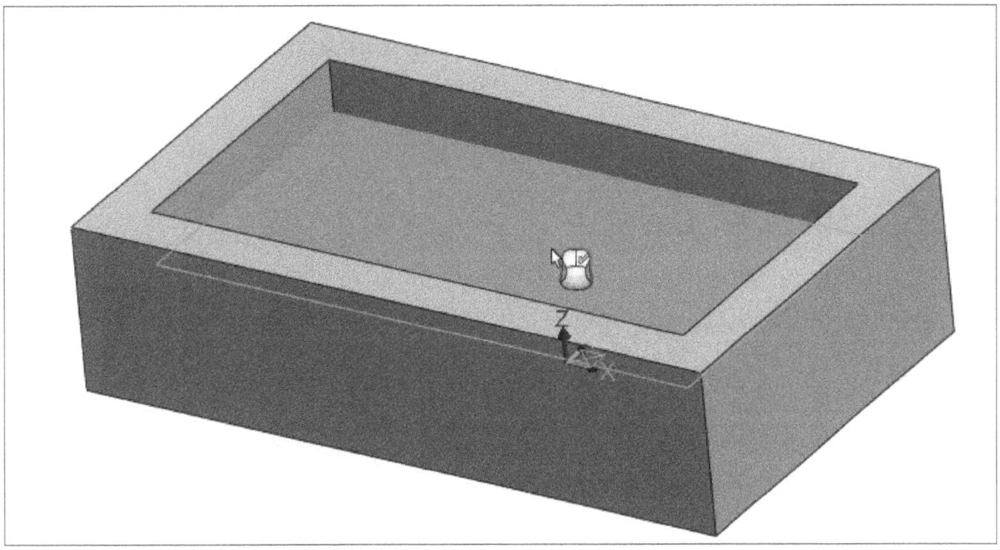

Figure-39. Pocket in the model

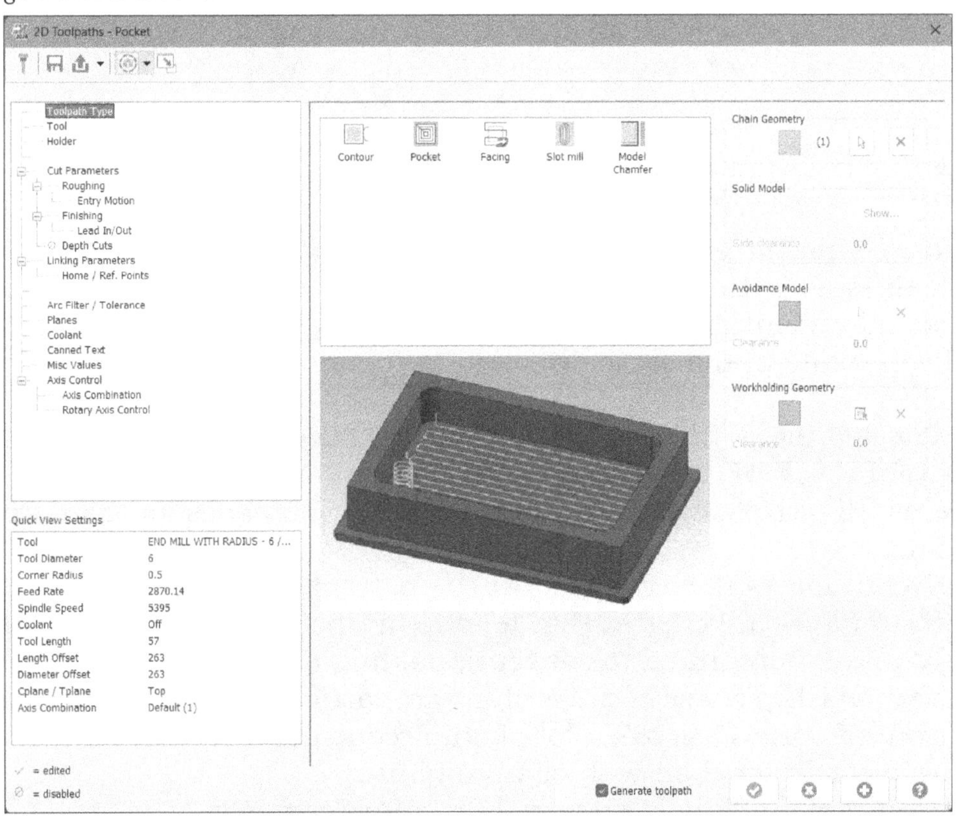

Figure-40. 2D Toolpaths-Pocket dialog box

- Click on the **Tool** option from the left box of the dialog box. The **Tool** page of the dialog box will be displayed as discussed earlier.
- Click on the **Select library tool** from the dialog box and select desired tool from the **Tool Selection** dialog box displayed. Most of the time, a flat end mill or ball end mill cutter is used for this type of toolpath.
- Click on the **OK** button from the dialog box. The tool will be added in the list. Select desired tool to apply for operation.
- Click on the **Holder** option from the left box in the **2D Toolpaths - Pocket** dialog box. The **Holder** page of the dialog box will be displayed.
- Set the holder as discussed for Contour toolpaths.
- Click on the **Cut Parameters** option from the left area. The options in the dialog box will be displayed as shown in Figure-41.

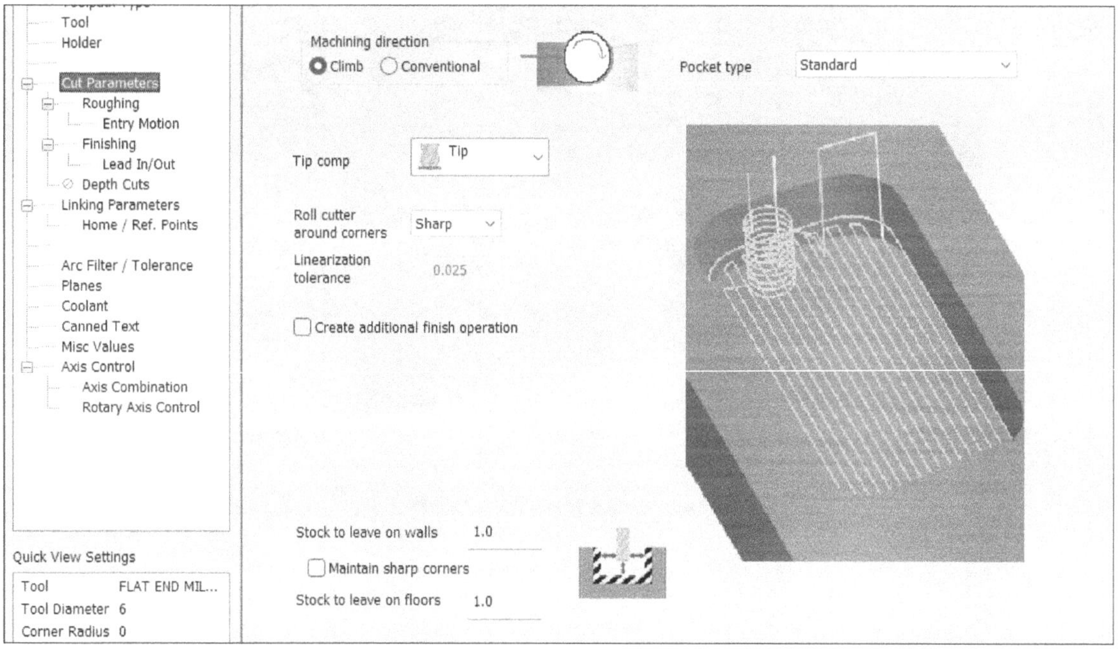

Figure-41. Cut Parameters options for pocket toolpath

- Select desired machining direction from the **Machining direction** area in the page. If the **Climb** radio button is selected then the tool will rotate in opposite direction to the tool movement direction. If the **Conventional** radio button is selected then the tool will rotate in the same direction to the tool movement direction.

Note: Conventional Milling V/S Climb Milling
Characteristics of Conventional Milling:

- The width of the chip starts from zero and increases as the cutter finishes slicing.
- The tooth meets the workpiece at the bottom of the cut.
- Upward forces are created that tend to lift the workpiece during face milling.
- More power is required to conventional mill than climb mill.
- Surface finish is worse because chips are carried upward by teeth and dropped in front of cutter. There's a lot of chip recutting. Flood cooling can help!
- Tools wear faster than with climb milling.
- Conventional milling is preferred for rough surfaces.
- Tool deflection during Conventional milling will tend to be parallel to the cut.

Characteristics of climb milling:

- The width of the chip starts at maximum and decreases.
- The tooth meets the workpiece at the top of the cut.
- Chips are dropped behind the cutter--less recutting.
- Less wear, with tools lasting up to 50% longer.
- Improved surface finish because of less recutting.
- Less power required.
- Climb milling exerts a down force during face milling, which makes work-holding and fixtures simpler. The down force may also help to reduce chatter in thin floors because it helps brace them against the surface beneath.
- Climb milling reduces work hardening.
- It can, however, cause chipping when milling hot rolled materials due to the hardened layer on the surface.
- Tool deflection during Climb milling will tend to be perpendicular to the cut, so it may increase or decrease the width of cut and affect accuracy.
- There is a problem with climb milling, which is that it can get into trouble with backlash if cutter forces are great enough. The issue is that the table will tend to be pulled into the cutter when climb milling. If there is any backlash, this allows leeway for the pulling, in the amount of the backlash. If there is enough backlash, and the cutter is operating at capacity, this can lead to breakage and potentially injury due to flying shrapnel.

Some worthwhile rules of thumb:

- When cutting half the cutter diameter or less, you should definitely perform climb mill (assuming your machine has low or no backlash and it is safe to do so!).

- Up to 3/4 of the cutter diameter, it doesn't matter which way you cut.

- When cutting from 3/4 to 1x the cutter diameter, you should prefer conventional milling.

- Specify the tool compensation parameters as required and set the value of stock to be left after machining in respective edit boxes.
- Select desired pocket type from the **Pocket type** drop-down in this page and set the related parameters as required. Note that on selecting the pocket type, preview of the selected pocket is also displayed on this page.
- Click on the **Roughing** option from the left area in the dialog box and specify the parameters like cutting speed, step over value, and so on. Select the cutting method carefully from the **Cutting method** box in this page; refer to Figure-42.

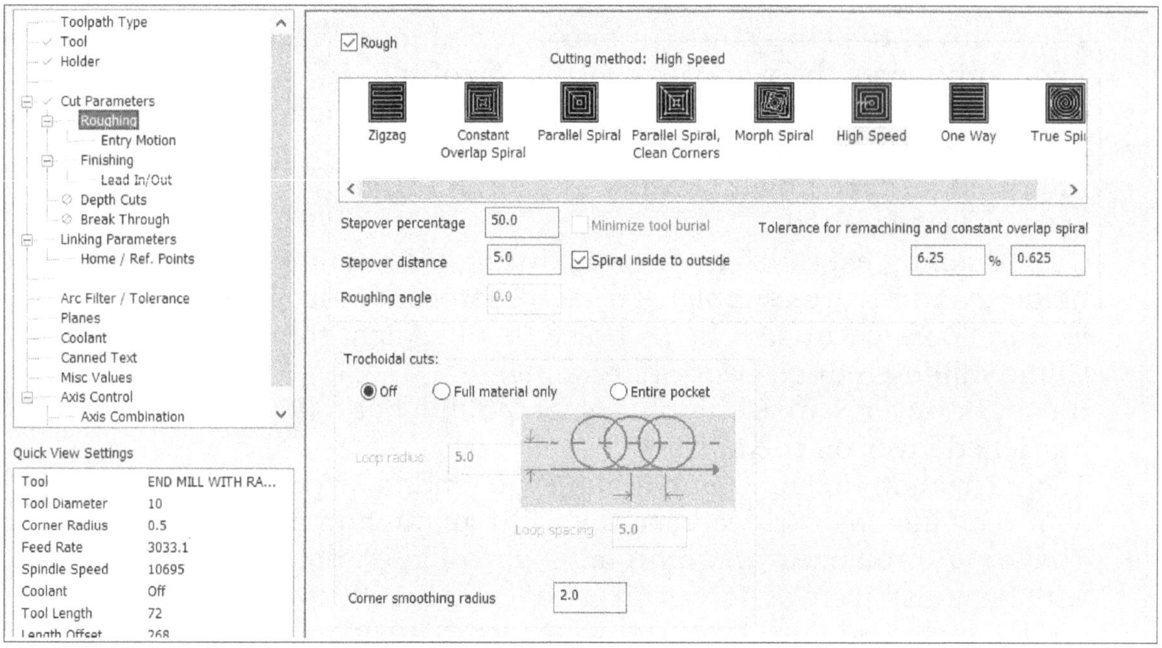

Figure-42. Roughing page in 2D Toolpath-Pocket dialog box

- For **High Speed** cutting method, you can also specify the parameters related to trochoidal cuts.
- Click on the **Entry Motion** option from the left and specify how the tool will enter while cutting material from the stock.
- Specify the other parameters as discussed in previous toolpaths like lead in/out, finishing, depth of cuts, etc.
- You can also use this toolpath for finishing operation. Select the **Finishing** option from left area in the dialog box and specify related parameters.
- Click on the **OK** button from the dialog box. The toolpaths will be generated; refer to Figure-43.

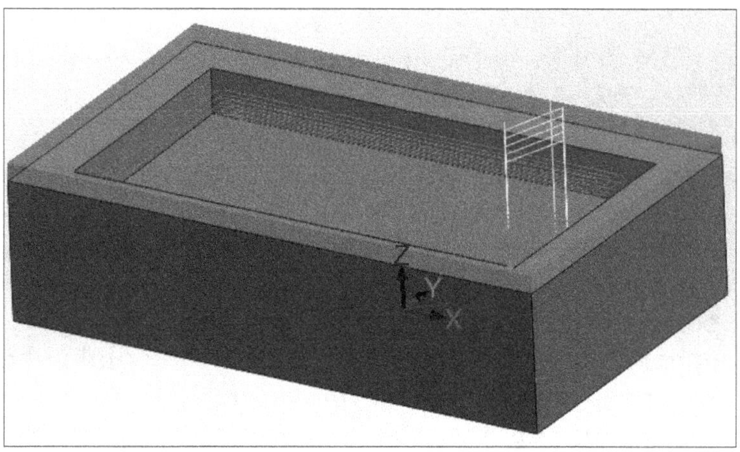

Figure-43. Pocket toolpaths generated

You can also check simulation of the tool by using the backplot option as discussed earlier. Note that sometimes, Mastercam can move the tool in stock in rapid rate, so make sure to specify adequate lead in and lead out or create start hole.

Creating Peel Mill Toolpaths

The Peel toolpath works as the name suggests. The peel toolpaths peels away the material from the workpiece along the given open boundaries. This toolpath is generally applied after contour toolpaths. The procedure to use this toolpath is given next.

- Click on the **Peel Mill** tool from the expanded **2D** group in the **Toolpaths** tab of the **Ribbon**. The **Solid Chaining** dialog box will be displayed as discussed earlier.
- Select the edges of the walls between which you want to perform the peel milling operation; refer to Figure-44.

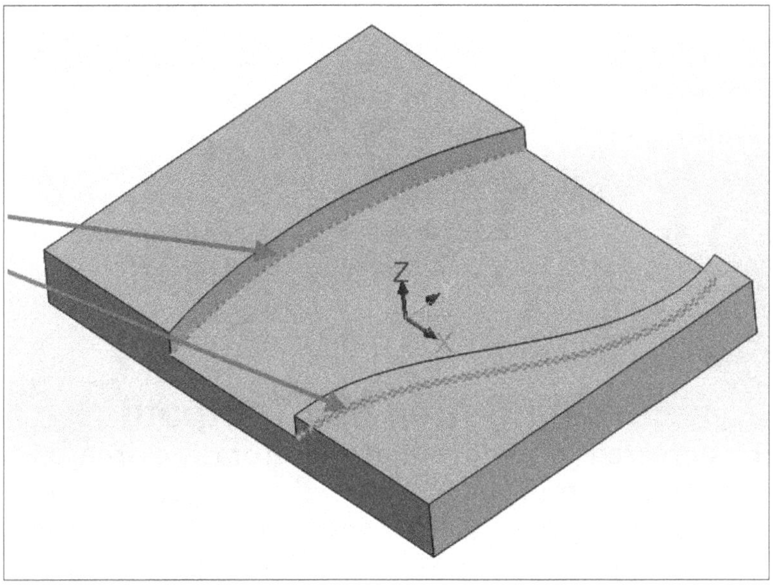

Figure-44. Edges to be selected

- Click on the **OK** button from the **Chaining** dialog box. The **2D High Speed Toolpath - Peel Mill** dialog box will be displayed; refer to Figure-45.

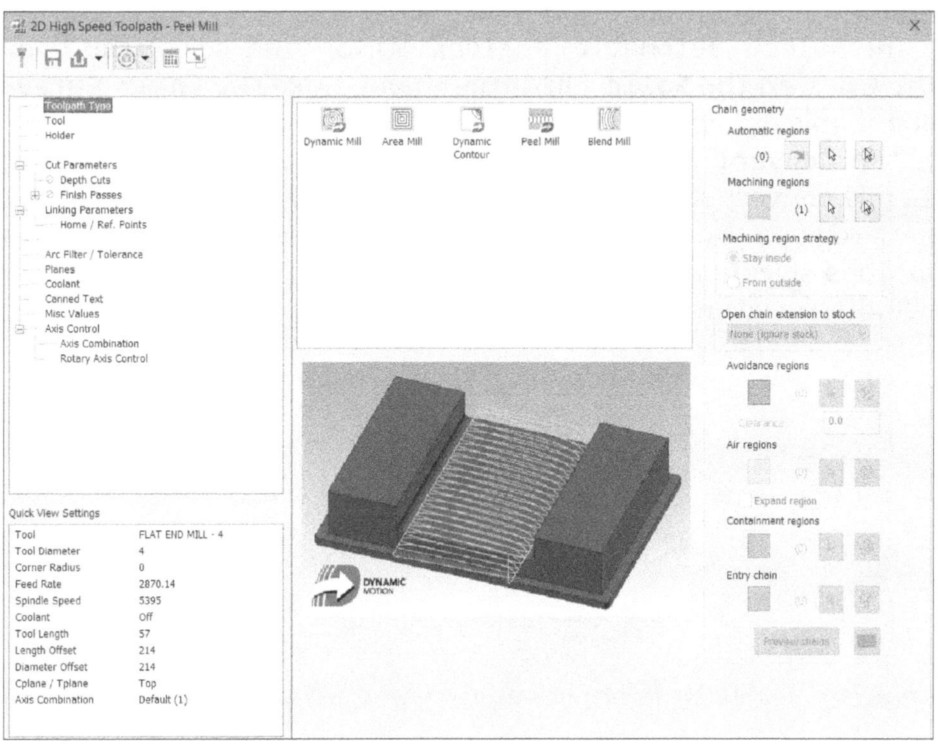

Figure-45. 2D Highspeed Toolpaths-Peel Mill

- Specify the parameters in the dialog box as discussed earlier. Note that you can extend the entry and exit path of tool by using the options in **Cut Parameters** page of this dialog box. Set desired parameters for Micro lift in cut parameters to define small distance by which tool moves upward to help clear chips and reduce heat buildup. After specifying parameters, click on the **OK** button from the dialog box. The toolpaths will be generated; refer to Figure-46.

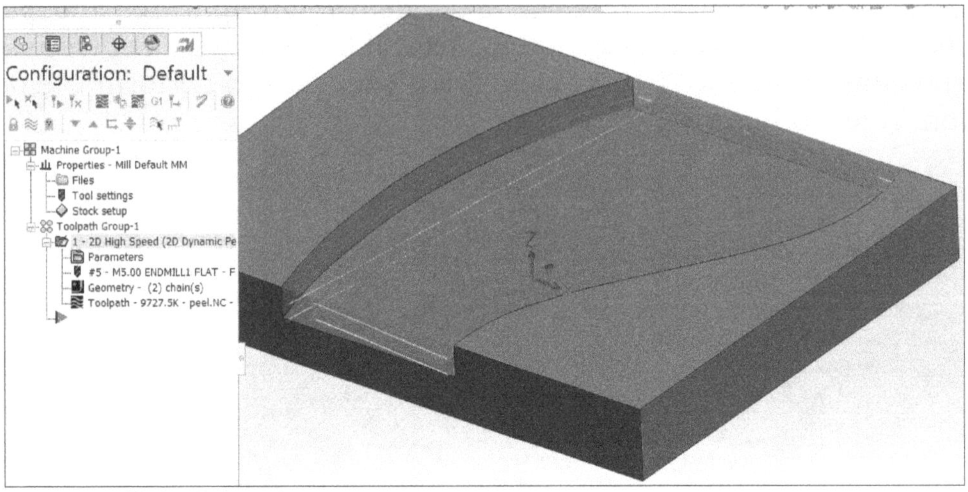

Figure-46. Toolpath for peel

Creating Area Mill Toolpath

The Area toolpath is created to remove material from the area bounded by selected boundaries. The area toolpath is generally used to machine close loops from inside or outside the selected boundaries. The **Area Mill** tool in the **2D** group of the **Toolpaths** tab in **Ribbon** is used to create area toolpath. The procedure to use this tool is discussed next.

- Click on the **Area Mill** tool from the **2D** group in the **Toolpaths** tab of **Ribbon**. The **Chain Options** selection box will be displayed.
- Click on the **Select automatic regions** button and select the floor face to be machined. Click on the **Solid Chaining** dialog box. The **Chain Options** selection box will be displayed again.
- Click on the **Convert automatic regions** button from the selection box to automatically convert selected faces to regions like machining regions, avoidance regions, air regions, and containment regions. Click on the **OK** button from the **Chain Options** selection box. The **2D High Speed Toolpath - Area Mill** dialog box will be displayed; refer to Figure-47.

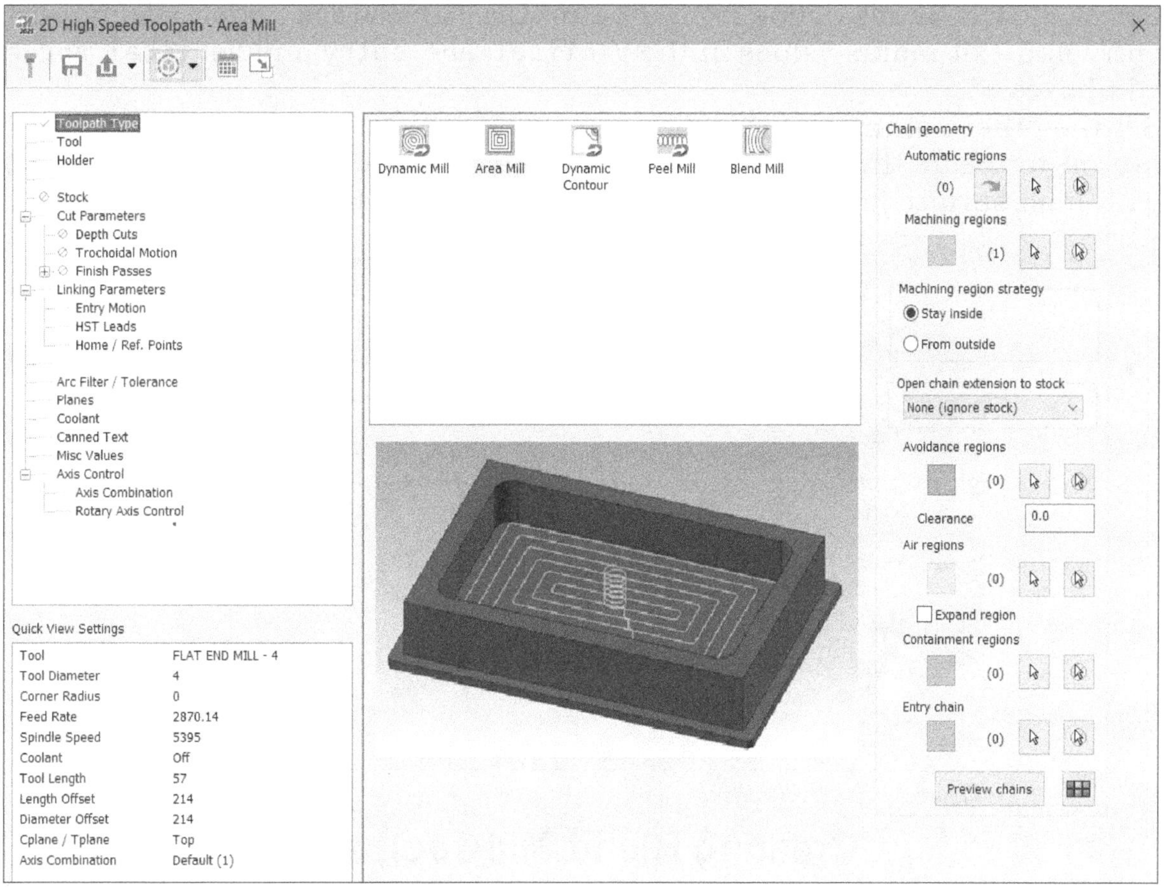

Figure-47. 2D High Speed Toolpaths-Area Mill dialog box

- Select the **Corner rounding** check box from the **Cut Parameters** page to apply rounds of specified parameters at corners in the model; refer to Figure-48. Specify desired radius value in the **Maximum radius** edit box to define maximum radius of arc by which sharp corners will be replaced in the toolpath. Specify maximum deviation from toolpath allowed in **Profile tolerance** and **Offset tolerance** edit boxes.

Figure-48. Cut Parameters for Area Mill

- Select the **HST Leads** option from the **Linking Parameters** node to define vertical entry and exit radius values in the **Vertical arc entry** and **Vertical arc exit** edit boxes.
- Set the other parameters in dialog box as discussed earlier and click on the **OK** button to create the toolpath. This toolpath is generally used to finish pockets with high surface finish due to cleaner movement of tool; refer to Figure-49.

Figure-49. Area mill toolpath

Creating Blend Mill Toolpath

The Blend mill toolpath is used to mill smoothly between two open chains of the workpiece. This toolpath is more effective when you have wall on one side and other sides are open. The procedure to use this tool is given next.

- Click on the **Blend Mill** tool from the expanded **2D** group in the **Toolpaths** tab of **Ribbon**. The **Solid Chaining** dialog box will be displayed as discussed earlier.
- Select the edges of the open chains; refer to Figure-50.

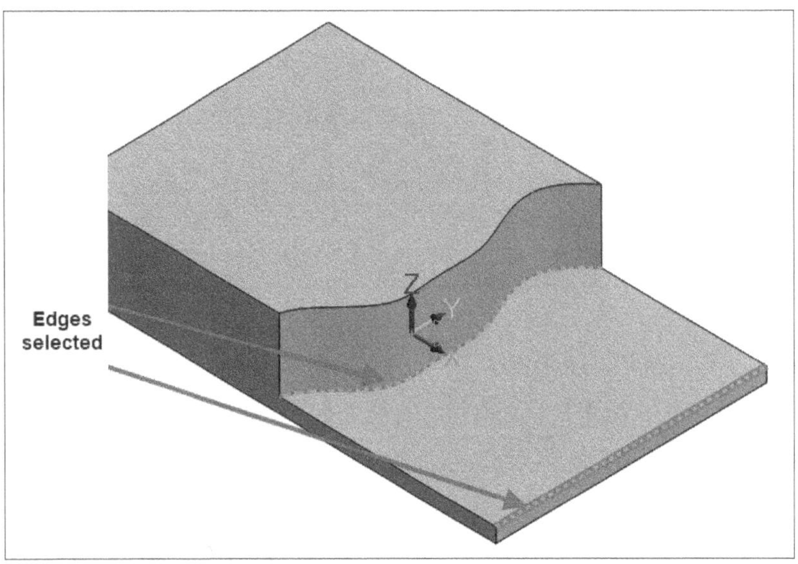

Figure-50. Edges of open chains to be selected

- Click on the **OK** button from the dialog box. The **2D High Speed Toolpath - Blend Mill** dialog box will be displayed; refer to Figure-51.

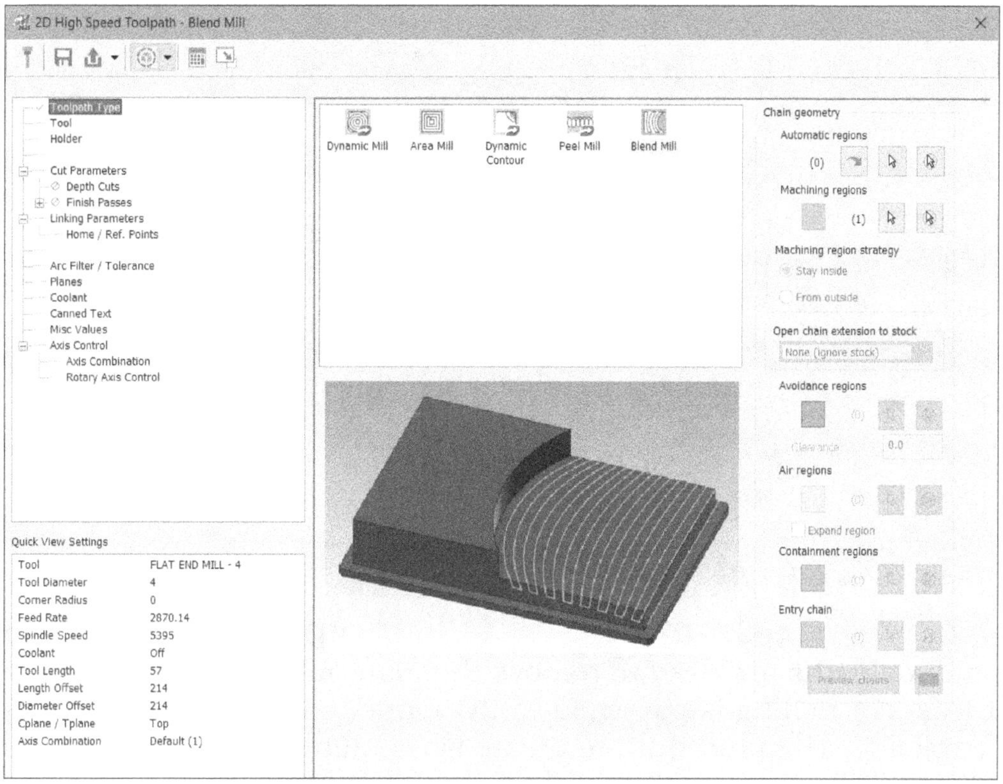

Figure-51. 2D Highspeed Toolpath-Blend Mill

- Specify the parameters as discussed earlier. Note that you need to specify the **Cut Parameters** carefully to get good surface finish; refer to Figure-52. Select the **Across** radio button or **Along** radio button depending on the shape of your model.
- After specifying the parameters, click on the **OK** button from the dialog box. The toolpaths will be generated; refer to Figure-53.

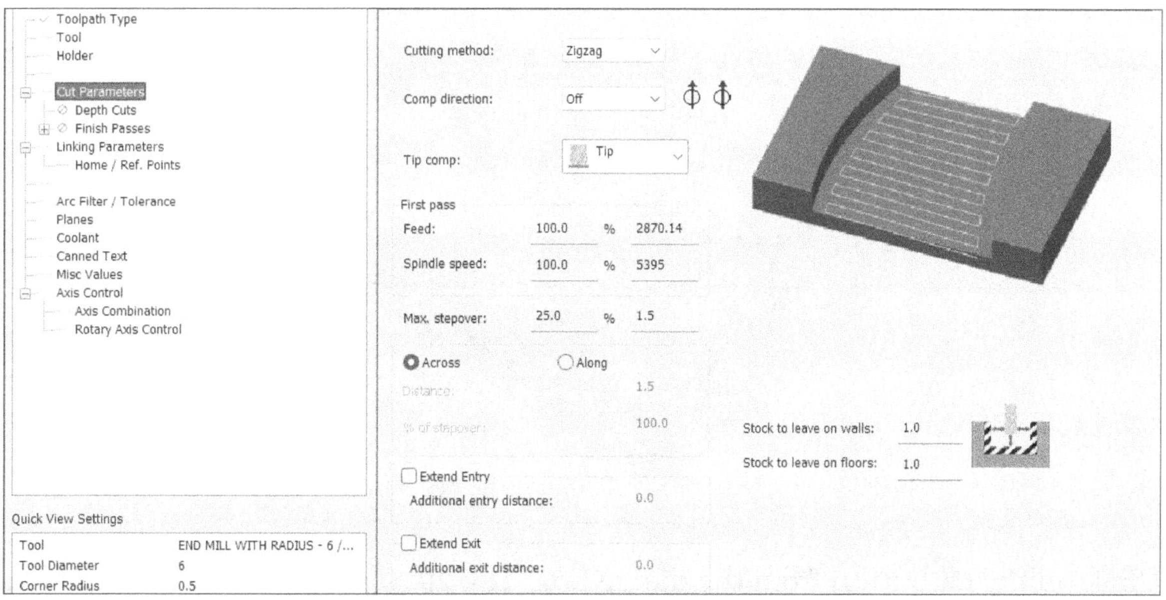

Figure-52. Cutting parameters

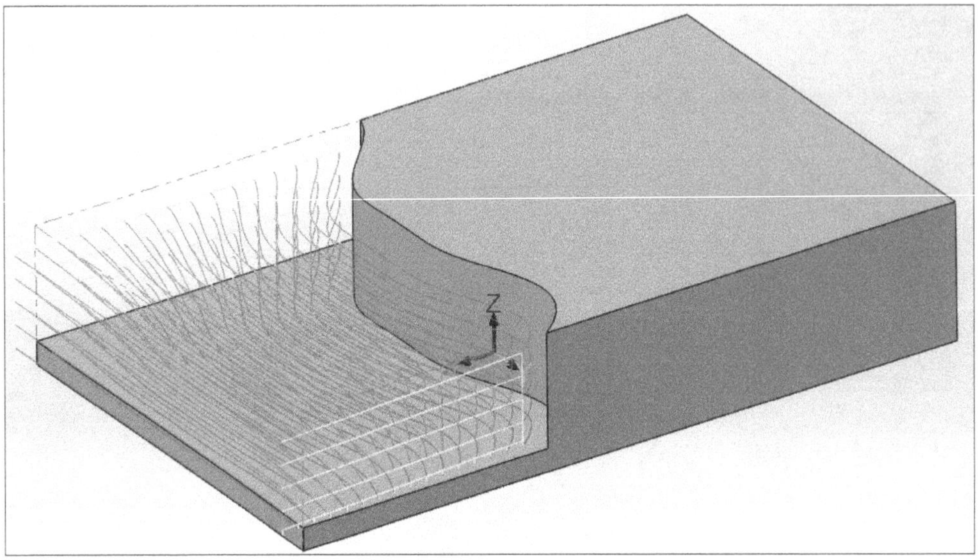

Figure-53. Toolpath for blend

Creating Slot Mill Toolpath

The Slot mill toolpaths are used to remove the material from the slots in the model. Note that this slot milling is governed in 2D plane, so the depth of cut need to be specified explicitly. The procedure to create slot milling toolpaths is given next.

- Click on the **Slot Mill** tool from the expanded **2D** group in the **Toolpaths** tab of the **Ribbon**. The **Wireframe/Solid Chaining** dialog box will be displayed as discussed earlier.
- Select the flat face of the slot; refer to Figure-54.

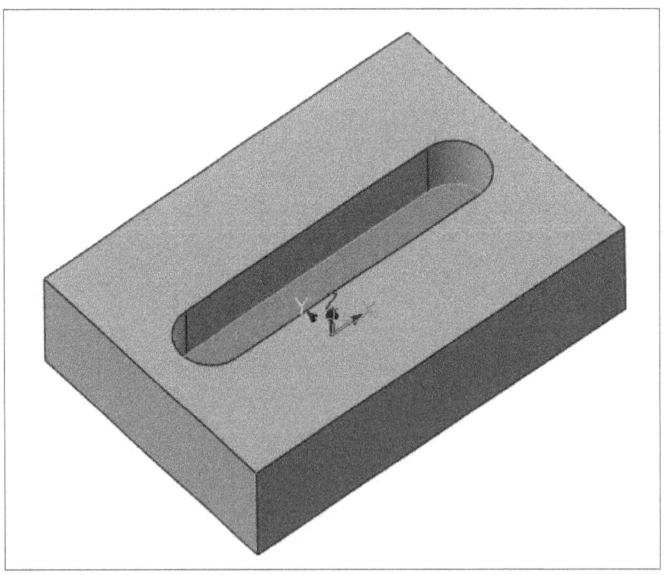

Figure-54. Flat face selected for slot

- Click on the **OK** button from the dialog box. The **2D Toolpaths - Slot Mill** dialog box will be displayed as shown in Figure-55.

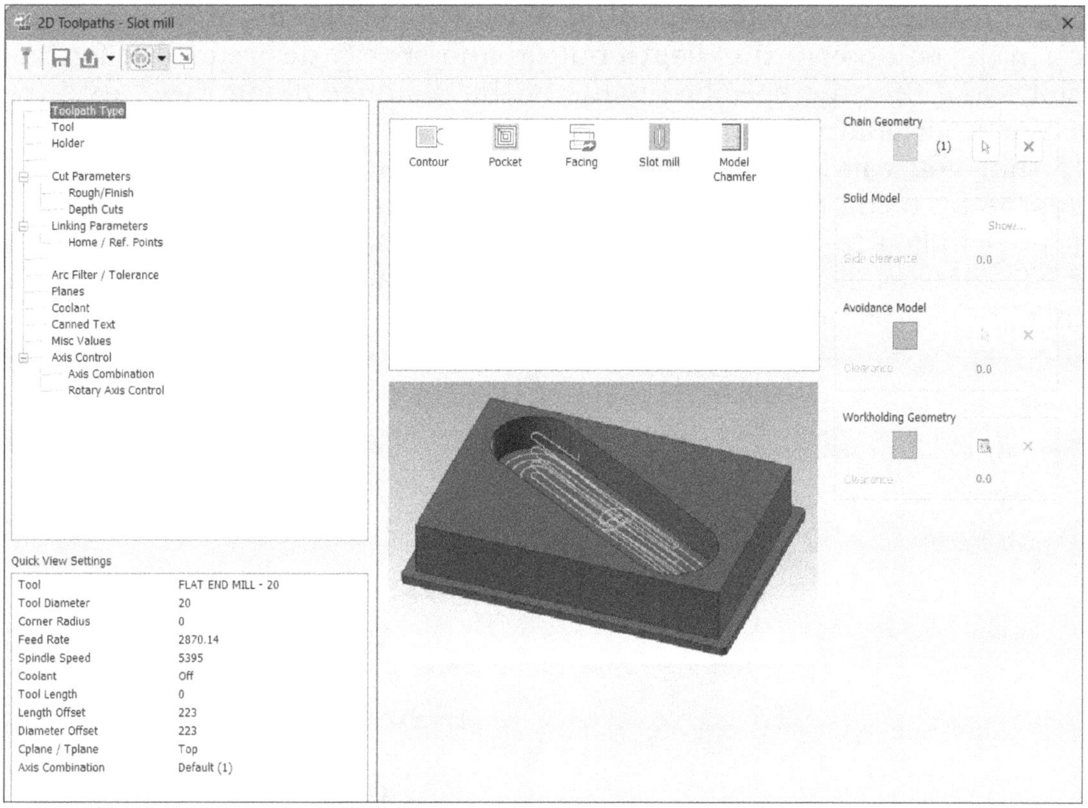

Figure-55. 2D Toolpaths-Slot Mill dialog box

- Specify the tool and the tool holder as done earlier.
- Click on the **Depth Cuts** option and specify desired depth of cuts as discussed in previous tools.
- Click on the **Linking Parameters** option. The dialog box will be displayed as shown in Figure-56.

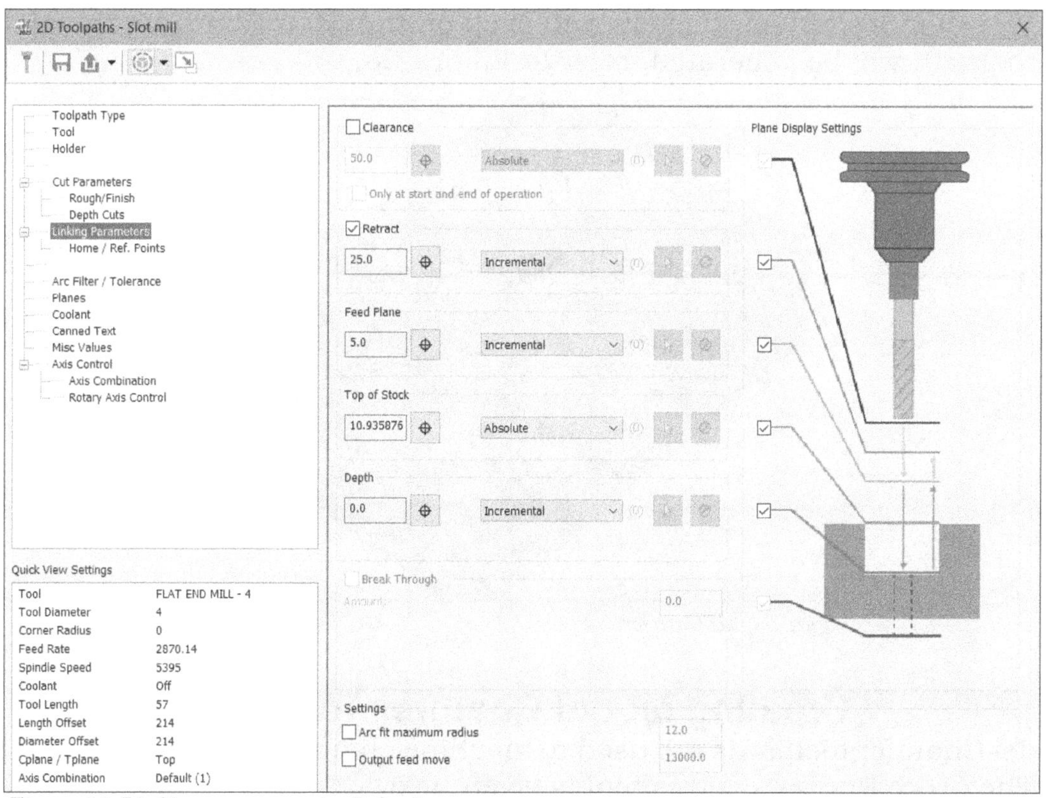

Figure-56. Linking parameters in dialog box

- Select the **Absolute** option from drop-down for the **Depth** button.
- Click in the edit box next to **Depth** button and specify desired value for the depth of slot. Note that the specified value is the distance along the Z axis from the Machine Coordinate System.
- Note that you can perform arc filtering and tolerance setting for most of the toolpaths by using the options in the **Arc Filter/Tolerance** page of the dialog box; refer to Figure-57. Although, in 2D toolpaths there is no effect of specifying plane for arcs explicitly because Mastercam will automatically create arc's plane parallel to tool-plane.

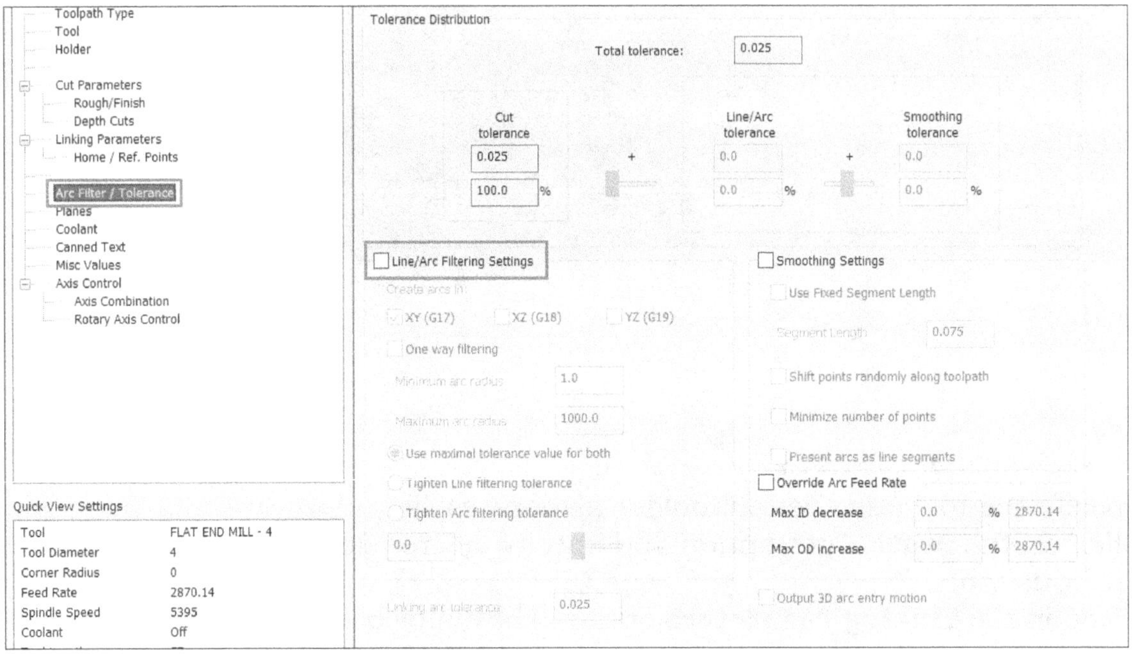

Figure-57. Arc Filter Tolerance page

- Specify other desired parameters and click on the **OK** button from the dialog box. The toolpath will be generated; refer to Figure-58.

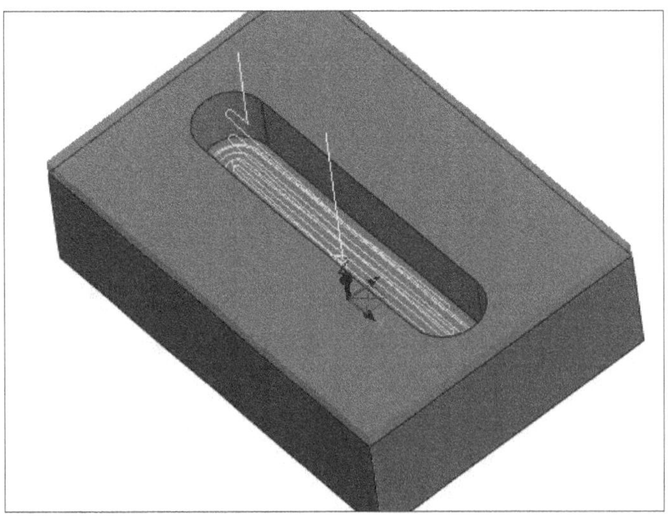

Figure-58. Toolpath for slot

Creating Model Chamfer Toolpath

The Model Chamfer toolpaths are used to machine chamfers on the edges of the solid model. The procedure to use this tool is given next.

- Click on the **Model Chamfer** tool from the expanded **2D** group in the **Toolpaths** tab of the **Ribbon**. The **2D Toolpaths - Model Chamfer** dialog box will be displayed; refer to Figure-59.

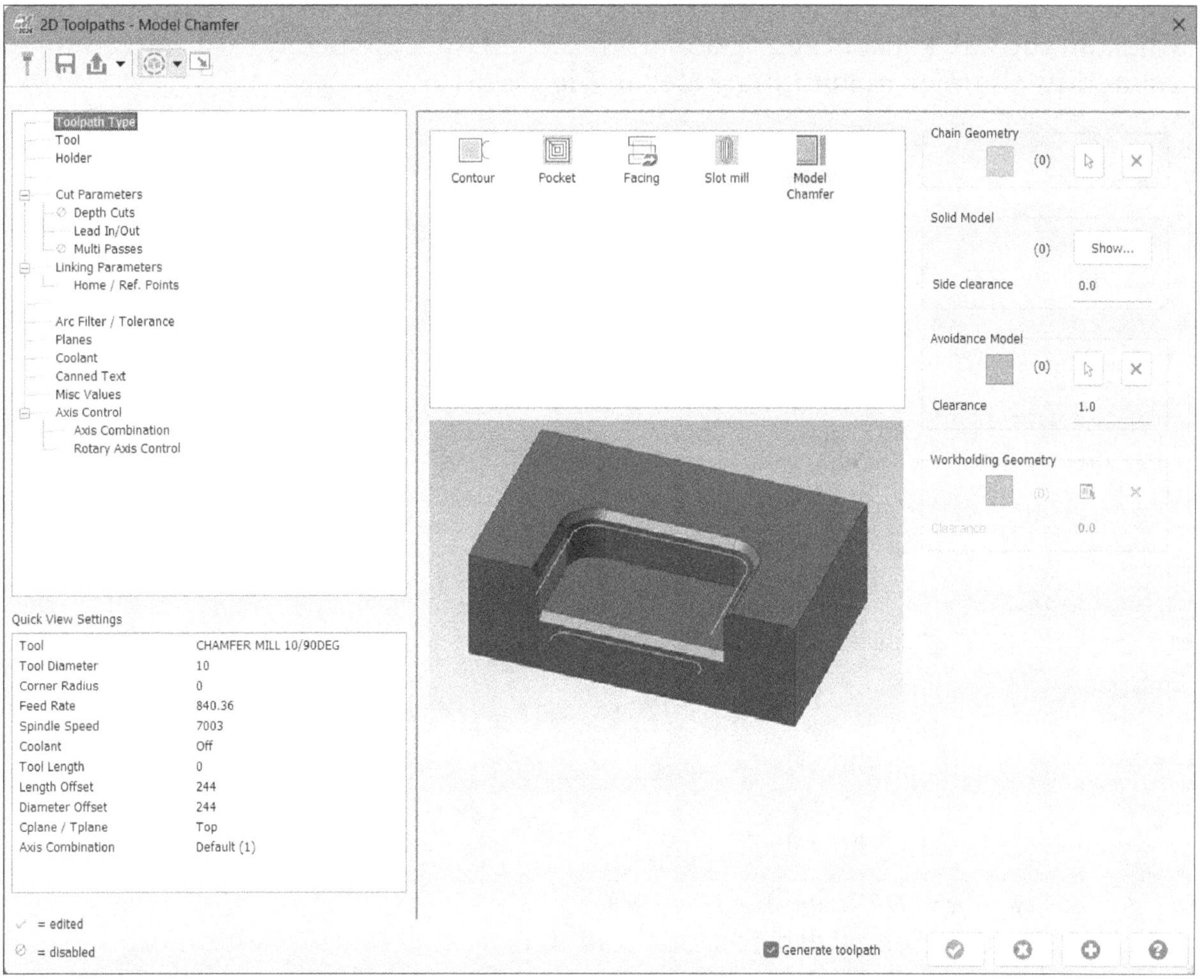

Figure-59. 2D Toolpaths-Model Chamfer dialog box

- Click on the **Select chains** button from the **Chain Geometry** area of the dialog box and select the chain of curves of chamfer to be machined; refer to Figure-60.

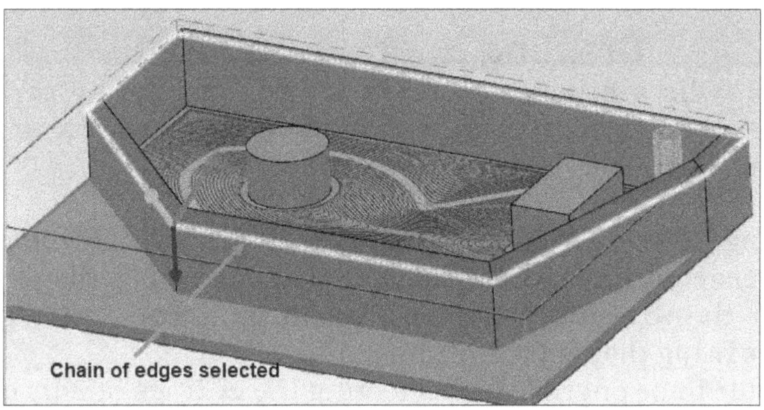

Figure-60. Chain of edges selected

- Click on the **OK** button from the **Solid Chaining** dialog box. The **2D Toolpaths - Model Chamfer** dialog box will be displayed again.
- If you want to avoid any region then click on the **Select surfaces** button from the **Avoidance model** area and select desired surfaces.

- Click on the **Tool** option from the left area of the dialog box and select desired chamfering tool using the **Select library tool** button from the dialog box as discussed earlier.
- Click on the **Holder** option from the left area and select desired cutting tool holder.
- Click on the **Cut Parameters** option from the left area to specify cutting parameters related to chamfer machining; refer to Figure-61.

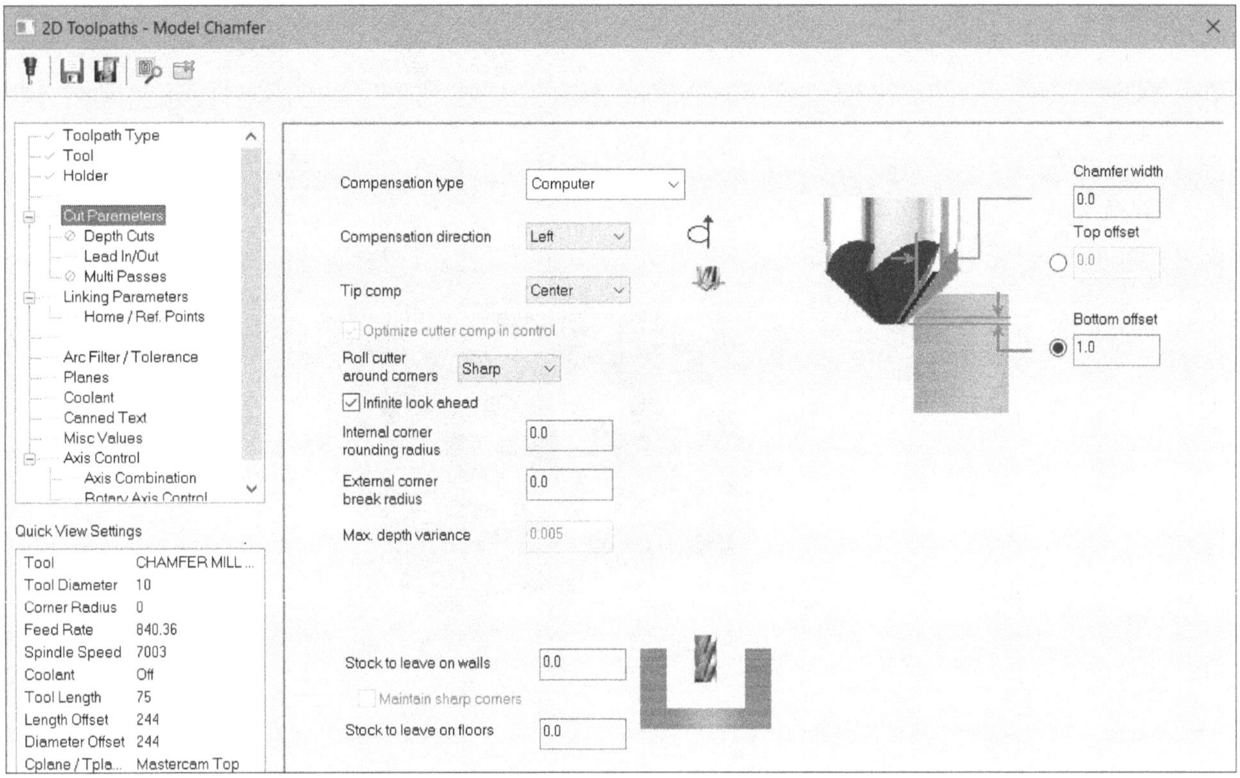

Figure-61. Cut Parameters of 2D Toolpaths-Model Chamfer dialog box

- Click in the **Chamfer width** edit box and specify the width of chamfer.
- Click in the **Bottom offset** edit box to specify the gap from bottom of chamfer where cutting tool will stop cutting.
- Set the other parameters as desired and click on the **OK** button from the dialog box. The toolpath will be created.

Creating Engrave Toolpath

The Engrave toolpaths are used to create artistic machining over the workpiece. These toolpaths are also used to print text on the press dies. The procedure to create these toolpaths is given next.

- Click on the **Engrave** tool from the expanded **2D** group of the **Toolpaths** tab in the **Ribbon**. The **Wireframe/Solid Chaining** dialog box will be displayed as discussed earlier. Select the **Wireframe** button from **Mode** area of dialog box to activate **Wireframe Chaining** dialog box.
- Select the profile to be engraved by selecting the entities one by one consecutively or select the sketch using window selection; refer to Figure-62.

Figure-62. Text entities selected for engraving

- After selecting the curves, click on the **OK** button. The **Engraving** dialog box will be displayed; refer to Figure-63.

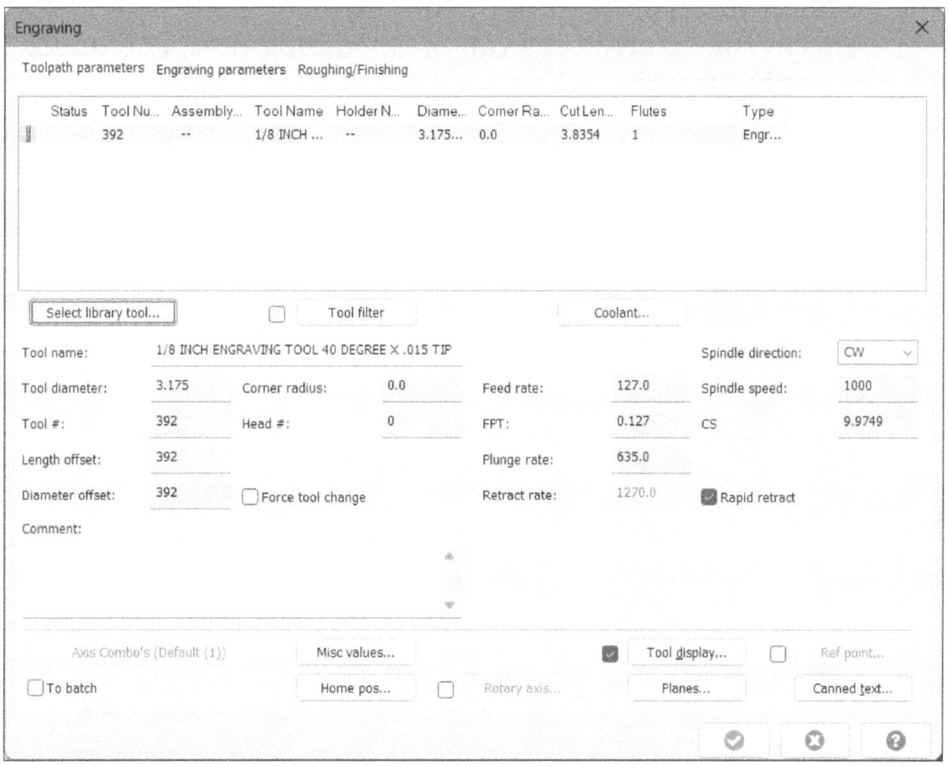

Figure-63. Engraving dialog box

- Click on the **Select library tool** button from the dialog box. The **Tool Selection** dialog box will be displayed; refer to Figure-64.

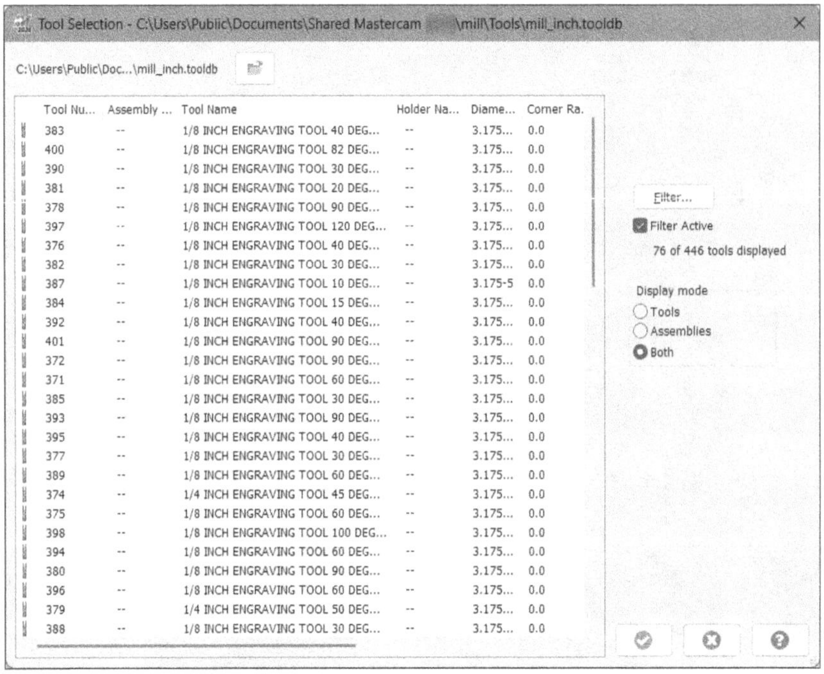

Figure-64. Tool Selection dialog box

- Select desired Engrave mill cutting tool from the list of tools and click on the **OK** button from the dialog box. Note that if you cannot find the engrave tool in list then you can create a new one as discussed earlier.
- Specify other parameters related to toolpath like feed rate, plunge rate, spindle speed, and so on in the right area of the dialog box.
- Click on the **Engraving parameters** tab of the dialog box. The dialog box will be displayed; refer to Figure-65.

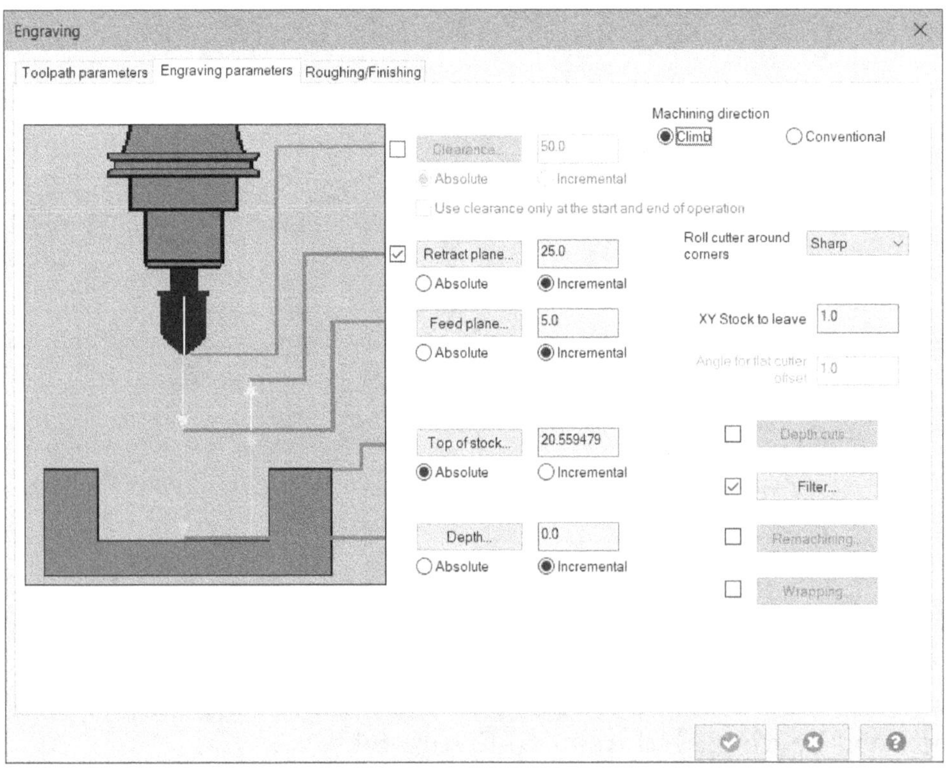

Figure-65. Engraving parameters tab

- Specify desired parameters in edit boxes. Make sure you specify correct **Top of Stock** and **Depth** values in respective edit boxes.
- Select desired radio button to specify machining direction from the **Machining direction** area.
- If you want to finish engraving in current toolpath then specify **XY Stock to leave** edit box as **0**.
- If you have a flat cutter rather than pointed engraving cutter then you can specify inclination angle of flat cutter in the **Angle for flat cutter offset** edit box. This option is generally used to perform rough V-groove machining before final engraving.
- Select the **Depth cuts** check box and then specify the depth of cuts after selecting the **Depth cuts** button to define how much material will be removed in each cutting pass.
- If you want to specify a limit on arc creation and Cut tolerance then select the **Filter** check box and specify the respective parameters by selecting the **Filter** button.
- Click on the **Roughing/Finishing** tab in the dialog box. The dialog box will be displayed as shown in Figure-66.

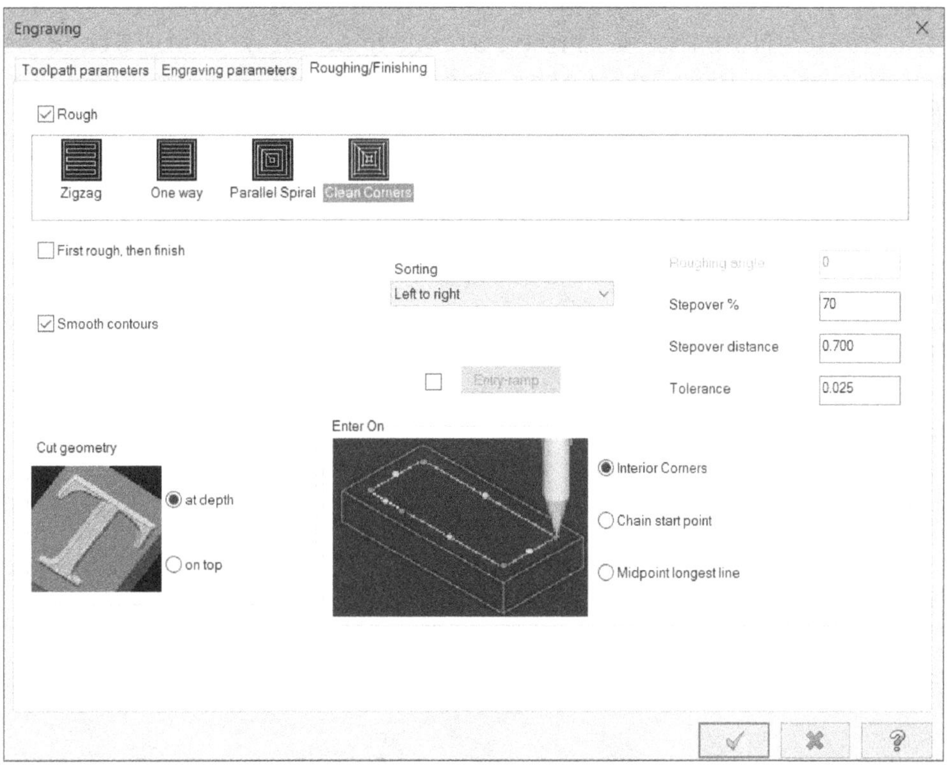

Figure-66. Roughing/Finishing tab

- Make sure that the **at depth** radio button is selected in the **Cut geometry** area of the dialog box if you want to cut the material following the inner loops of text sketch. If you want to emboss the text then select the **on top** radio button.
- Specify other parameters as required. Note that selection of cutting method can highly affect the toolpath generation and engraving quality so, you need to choose the cutting method which aligns with the text/curves to be engraved.
- Click on the **OK** button from the dialog box. The toolpath will be generated; refer to Figure-67.

Figure-67. Toolpath for engraving

Feature Based Milling

The **FBM Mill** tool is used to generate 2D milling toolpaths based on recognized features of the model. Note that you need to create stock by using **Stock setup** option from the **Properties** node in **Toolpaths Manager** to use this tool; refer to Figure-68. The procedure to use this tool is given next.

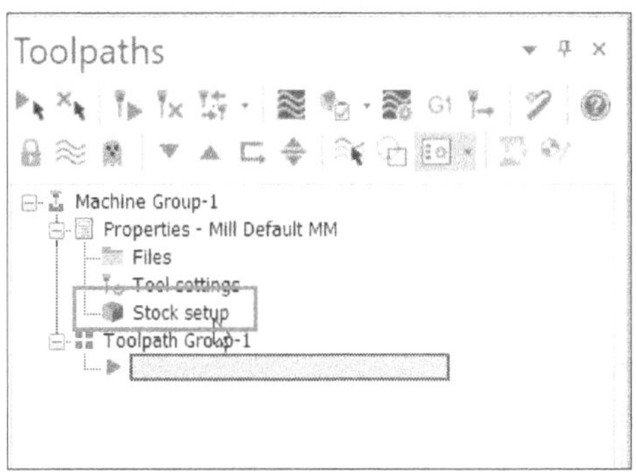

Figure-68. Stock setup option

- Open the part on which you want to perform 2D milling and create stock; refer to Figure-69.

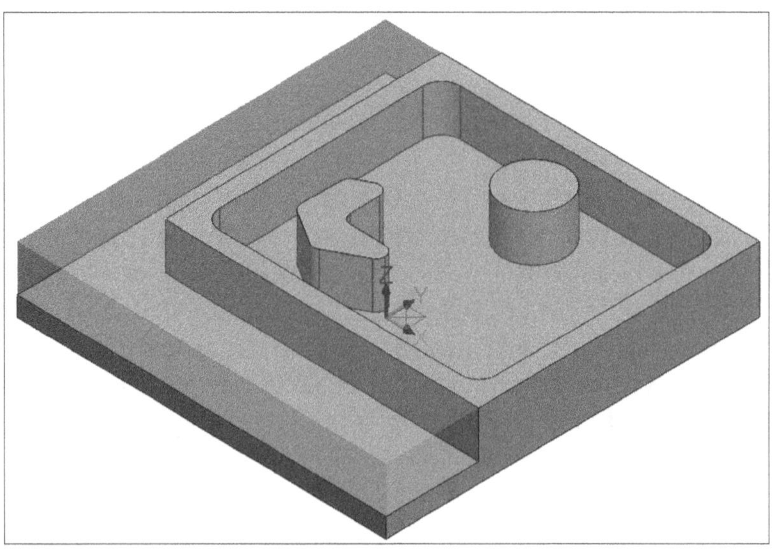

Figure-69. Model and stock for FBM

- Click on the **FBM Mill** tool from the expanded **2D** group of the **Toolpaths** tab in the **Ribbon**. The **FBM Toolpaths-Mill** dialog box will be displayed.

Setup Parameters

- Click on the **Setup** option from the left box in the dialog box. The options in dialog box will display as shown in Figure-70.

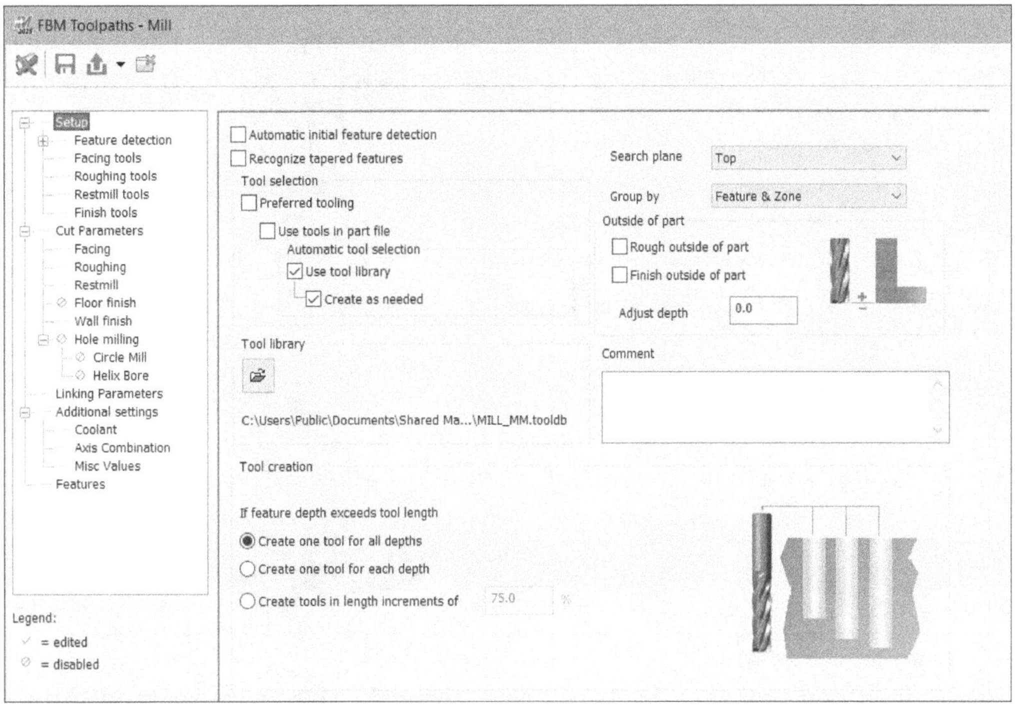

Figure-70. Setup options for FBM-Mill

- Select the **Automatic initial feature detection** check box to allow Mastercam to automatically detect initial features for the toolpaths.
- Select the **Recognize tapered features** check box if you want to include tapered features in machining.
- Select the **Preferred tooling** check box so that Mastercam searches for preferred tools of each operation (facing, roughing, etc.).
- Select the **Use tools in part file** check box if you want to restrict Mastercam to use only those tools which have been used in current file.
- Select the **Use tool library** check box so that Mastercam searches selected tool library for tools. After selecting this check box, click on the **Open** button from the **Tool library** area of the this page to select desired tool library.
- Select the **Create as needed** check box if you want Mastercam to automatically create tools as per the requirement, if tools are not available in the tool library or you have not opted to use tool library. After selecting this check box, select desired option from the **Tool creation** area of the this page to define how tool will be created. Generally, this check box is kept clear so that you can use only standard tools which are easily available in market.
- Select the check boxes in the **Outside of part** area to perform roughing and finishing operations on the part outside the boundaries.

Feature Detection Parameters

- Click on the **Feature detection** option from the left area of the dialog box. The options in the dialog box will be displayed as shown in Figure-71.

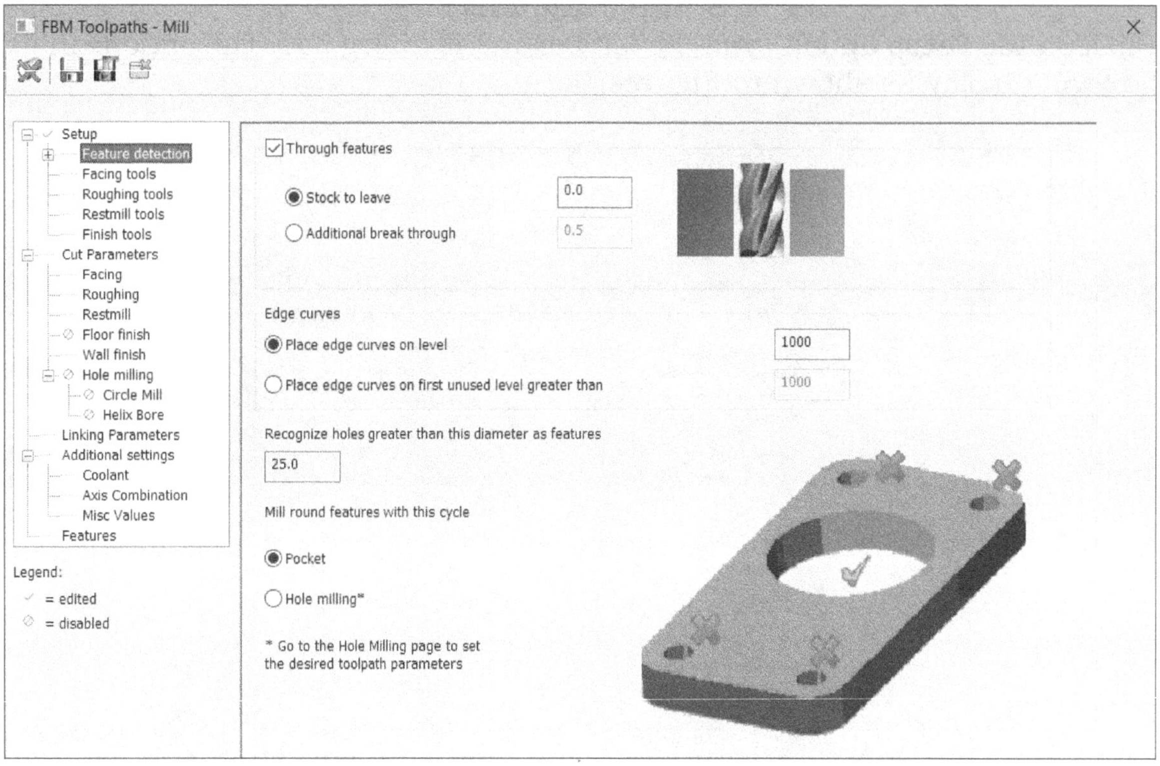

Figure-71. Feature detection options

- Specify desired parameters in the page. Specify the minimum diameter in the **Recognize holes greater than this diameter as features** edit box to make Mastercam recognise features as holes.
- Select desired milling strategy from the **Mill round features with this cycle** area of this page. If you select the **Hole milling** radio button then **Hole milling** page will also become available in this dialog box. On selecting Hole milling strategy, Circle mill and Helix bore toolpaths will be used. If you select the **Pocket** radio button then the pocket toolpaths will be used for machining.
- Select desired radio button from the **Edge curves** area to define at which level identified edge curves will be created.

Slug Cutting Options

The slug cutting is used when we have large stock of plastic or wood to be removed. In such cases, Mastercam uses Contour toolpaths in place of pocket/area toolpaths to remove material. This might be desirable when working with wood and composite materials on large vacuum table machines. Instead of pocketing the entire area, FBM Mill uses the parameters you define to generate a contour toolpath that cuts the outermost passes of the profile, leaving behind a slug that is held in place by the vacuum table.

- To enable slug cutting, click on the **Slug cutting** option from the expanded **Feature detection** node in the left of the dialog box. The options will be displayed as shown in Figure-72.

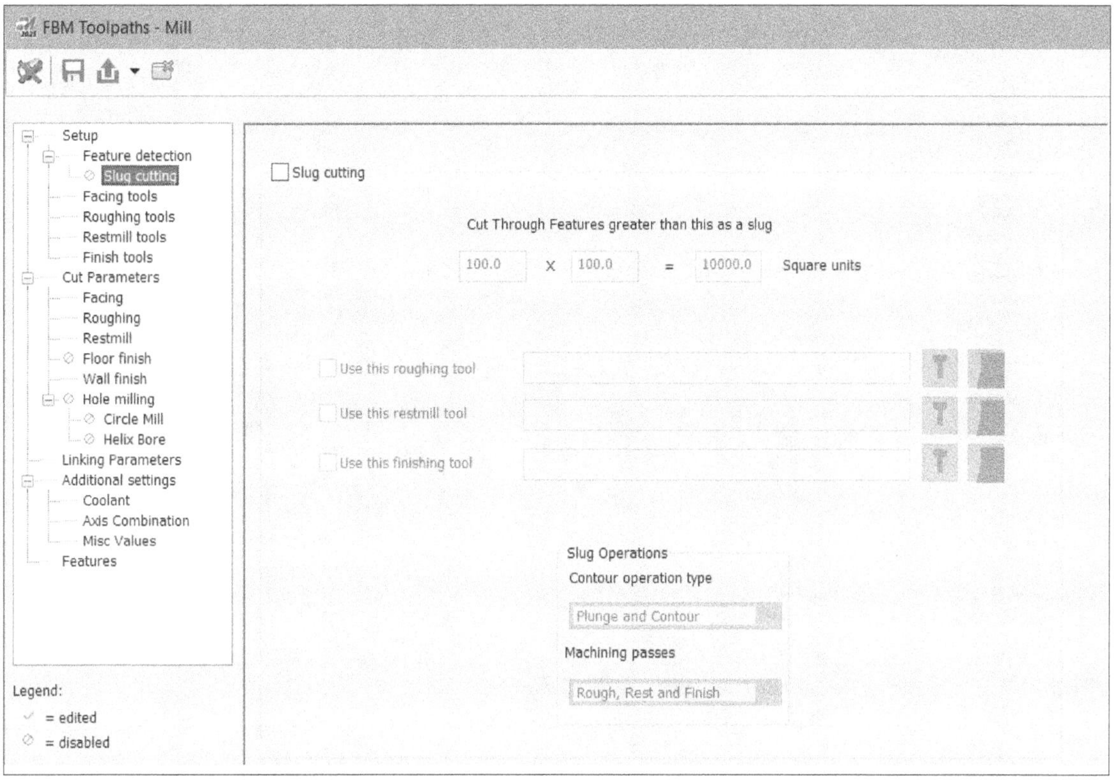

Figure-72. Slug cutting options

- Select the **Slug cutting** check box and specify related parameters to define slug cutting.
- Note that you should keep this option inactive if you are working with metals.

Facing/Roughing/Restmill/Finish Tools parameters

The options in **Facing tools**, **Roughing tools**, **Restmill tools**, and **Finish tools** pages of the dialog box are almost same. Here, we will discuss the options in the **Finish tools** page, you can apply the same knowledge on other similar pages.

- Click on the **Finish tools** option from the left area of the dialog box. The options in the dialog box will be displayed as shown in Figure-73.
- Right-click in the **Preferred tool list** box of this dialog box. A shortcut menu will be displayed; refer to Figure-74.

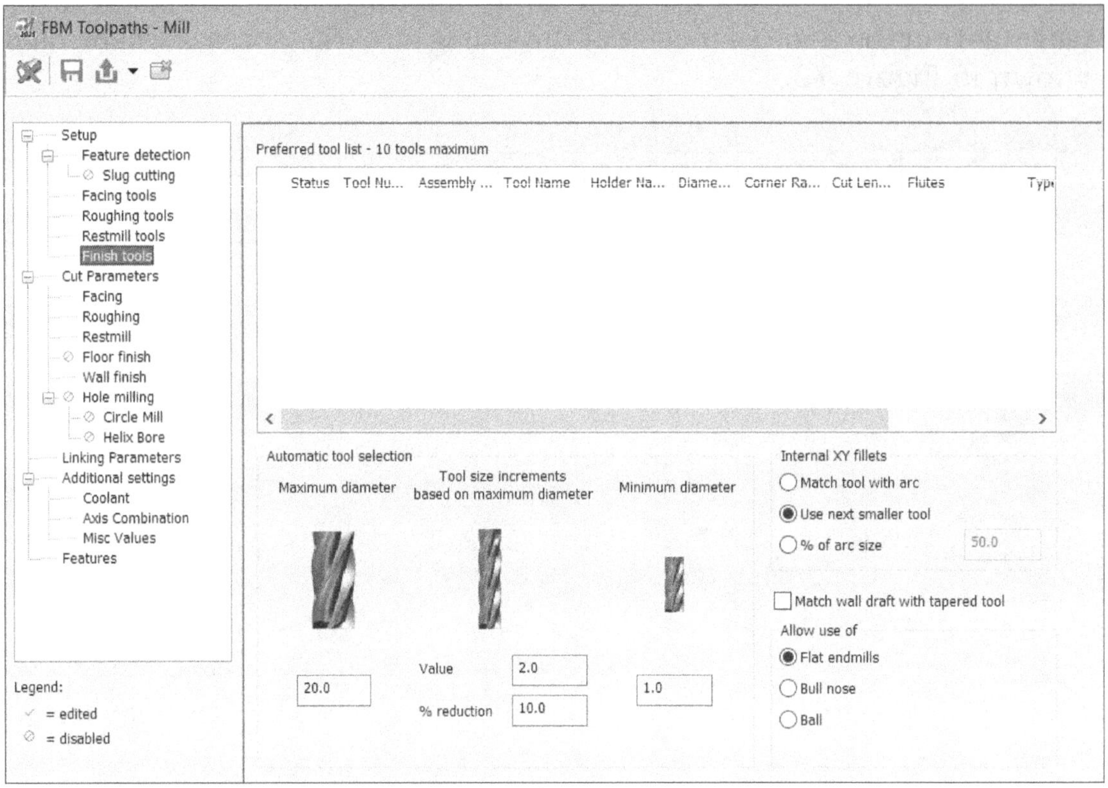

Figure-73. Finish tools page in FBM Toolpaths-Mill dialog box

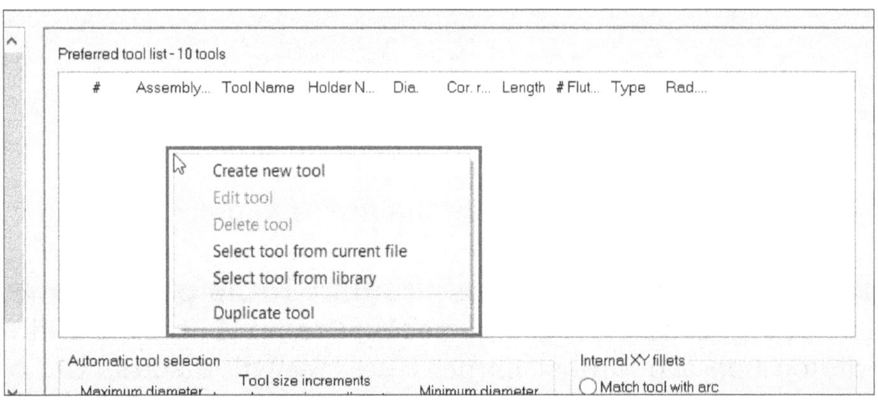

Figure-74. Shortcut menu for tool

- Create tool or select tool from the library as discussed earlier. The selected/created tools will be added in the list.
- Specify the parameters related to tool selection in the **Automatic tool selection** area of the dialog box.
- Select desired radio button from the **Allow use of** area to filter the tool types to be selected.
- Select the **Match wall draft with taper** tool check box if walls of your part are tapered.
- Select desired radio button from the **Internal XY fillets** area to set parameters for internal fillets.

Similarly, specify the parameters in other pages of this dialog box.

Features Detection

- After setting parameters, click on the **Detect** button from the toolbar in the dialog box. Mastercam will divide different regions of part into zones based on machining and the **Features** page will be displayed; refer to Figure-75.

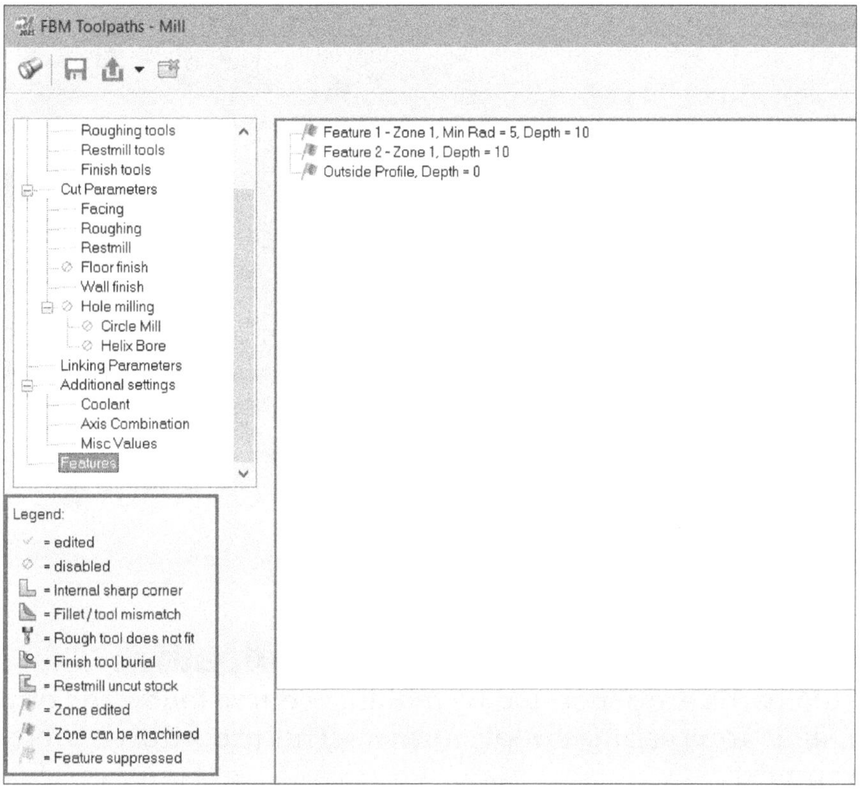

Figure-75. Options in Features page

- Check the legends on this page to know the status of various zones to be machined. For example, in Figure-75, all the zones are green flagged which means they can be machined by FBM Mill. If there is a problem in any zone and you think that it can be machined by 2D toolpaths then modify the parameters of the dialog box and click on the **Detect** button again to verify.
- Click on the **OK** button from the dialog box to generate toolpaths. The **Enter new NC name** dialog box will be displayed if this is your first toolpath. Specify desired name and click on the **OK** button. The toolpaths will be generated; refer to Figure-76.

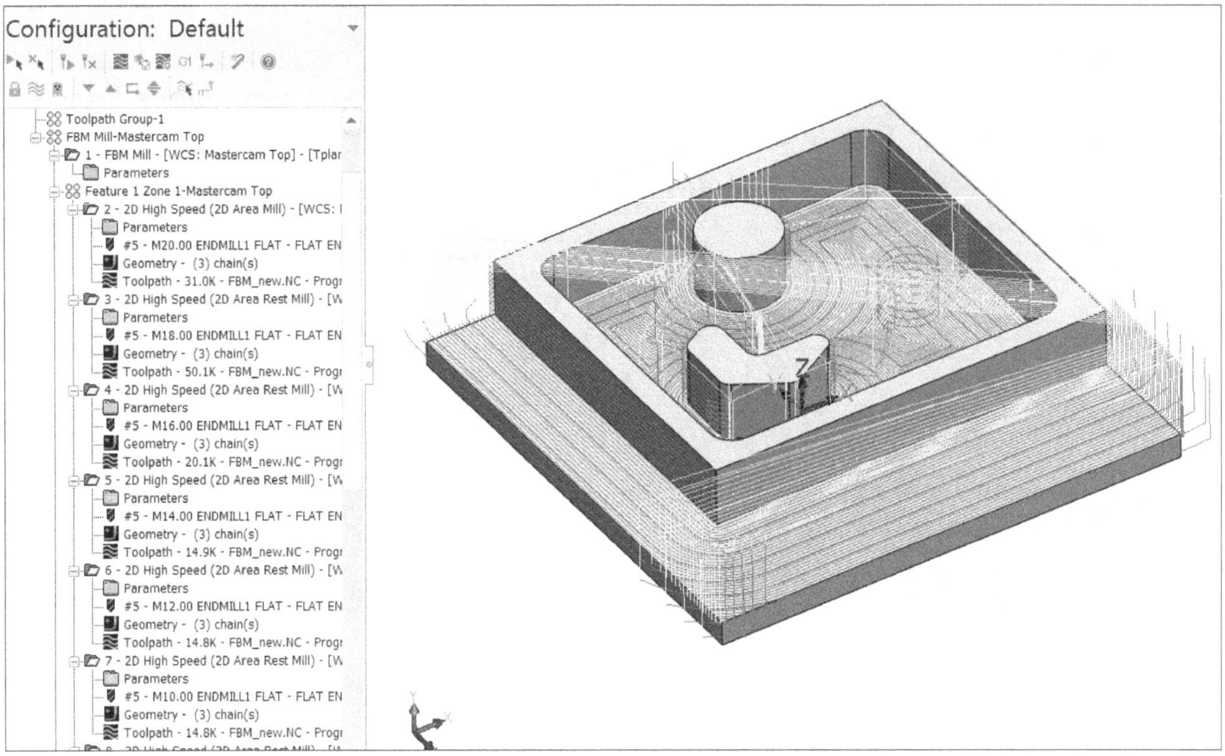

Figure-76. FBM-Mill toolpaths generated

Creating Swept 2D Toolpath

The Swept 2D toolpaths are generated by making a curve follow the other path curve. This tool is similar to creating swept surface. The procedure to create 2D swept toolpath is given next.

- Click on the **Swept 2D** tool from the expanded **2D** group in the **Toolpaths** tab of the **Ribbon**. The **Wireframe Chaining** dialog box will be displayed.
- Select the first curve for sweep path and then select the other curve used for section of sweep feature; refer to Figure-77.

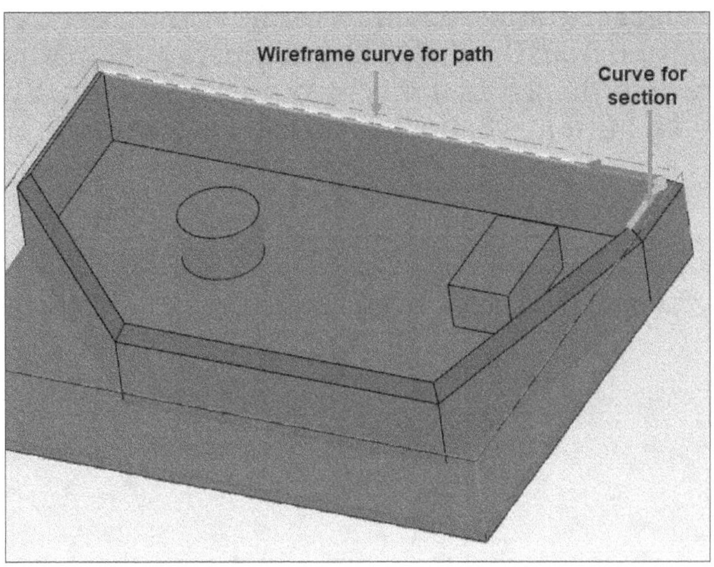

Figure-77. Curves selected for 2D sweep toolpath

- After selecting curves, click on the **OK** button from the dialog box. You will be asked to select an intersection point of path and section curves.
- Select the point of intersection of curves. The **Swept 2D** dialog box will be displayed; refer to Figure-78.

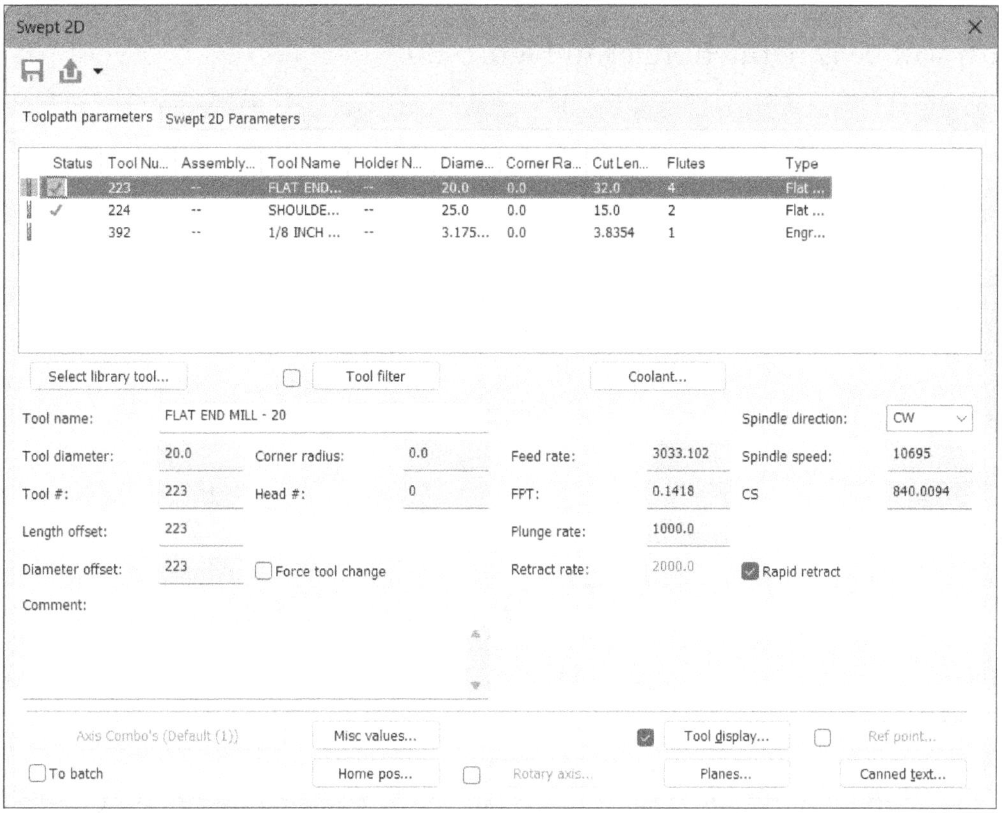

Figure-78. Swept 2D dialog box

- Select desired cutting tool and specify related parameters in the dialog box.
- Click on the **Swept 2D Parameters** tab in the dialog box to modify parameters related to swept toolpath; refer to Figure-79.

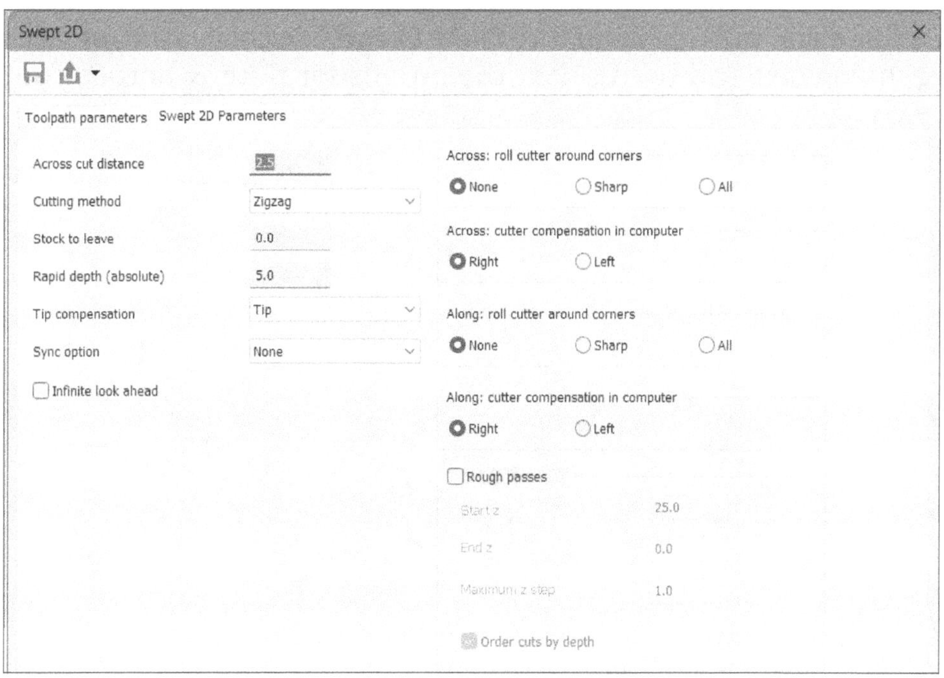

Figure-79. Swept 2D Parameters tab

- Click in the **Across cut distance** edit box and specify the distance between two across toolpath steps.
- Specify desired value in the **Rapid depth (abs)** edit box to specify the retraction height from where cutting tool plunges in the stock to perform next cutting pass.
- Set the other parameters as discussed earlier and click on the **OK** button. The toolpath will be generated; refer to Figure-80.

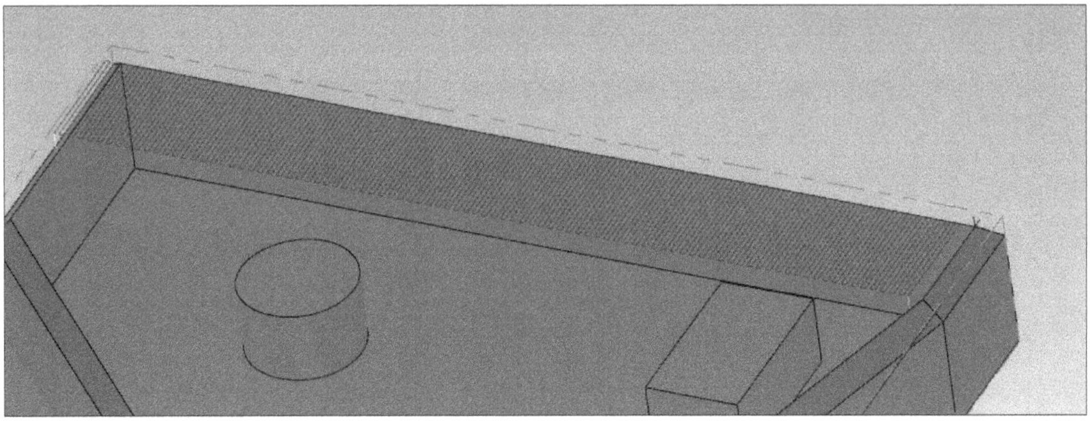

Figure-80. Swept 2D toolpath generated

Creating Swept 3D Toolpath

The swept 3D toolpath is used when you need to use multiple cross-section curves and a path curve to create a swept 3D toolpath. The procedure to create this toolpath is given next.

- Click on the **Swept 3D** tool from the expanded **2D** group in the **Toolpaths** tab of the **Ribbon**. The **Enter number of across contours** input box will be displayed.
- Specify desired value to define how many across contours will be used to define shape of the toolpaths. Note that you need to select the same number of curves that you have specified in input box for defining across contours. After specifying value, press **ENTER**. The **Wireframe Chaining** dialog box will be displayed.
- Select the **Single** button from the **Selection Method** area of the **Wireframe Chaining** dialog box and then select the curves for path & across contours; refer to Figure-81.

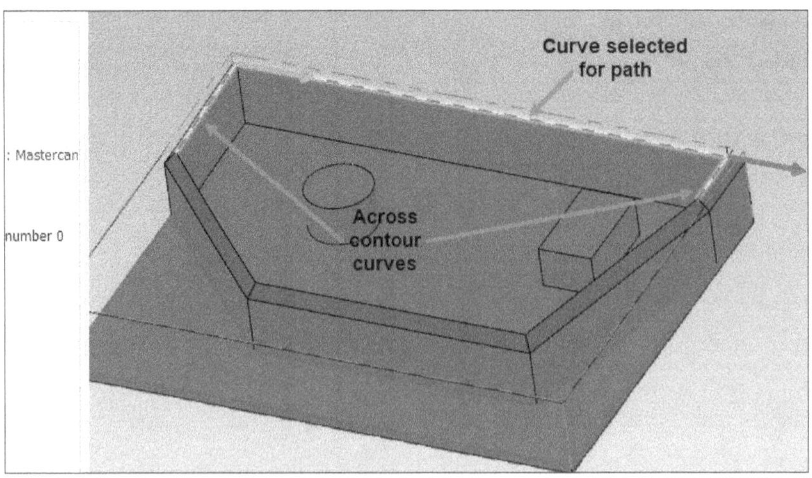

Figure-81. Wireframe curves selected for swept 3D toolpath

- After selecting the curves, click on the **OK** button from the **Wireframe Chaining** dialog box. The **Swept 3D** dialog box will be displayed; refer to Figure-82.

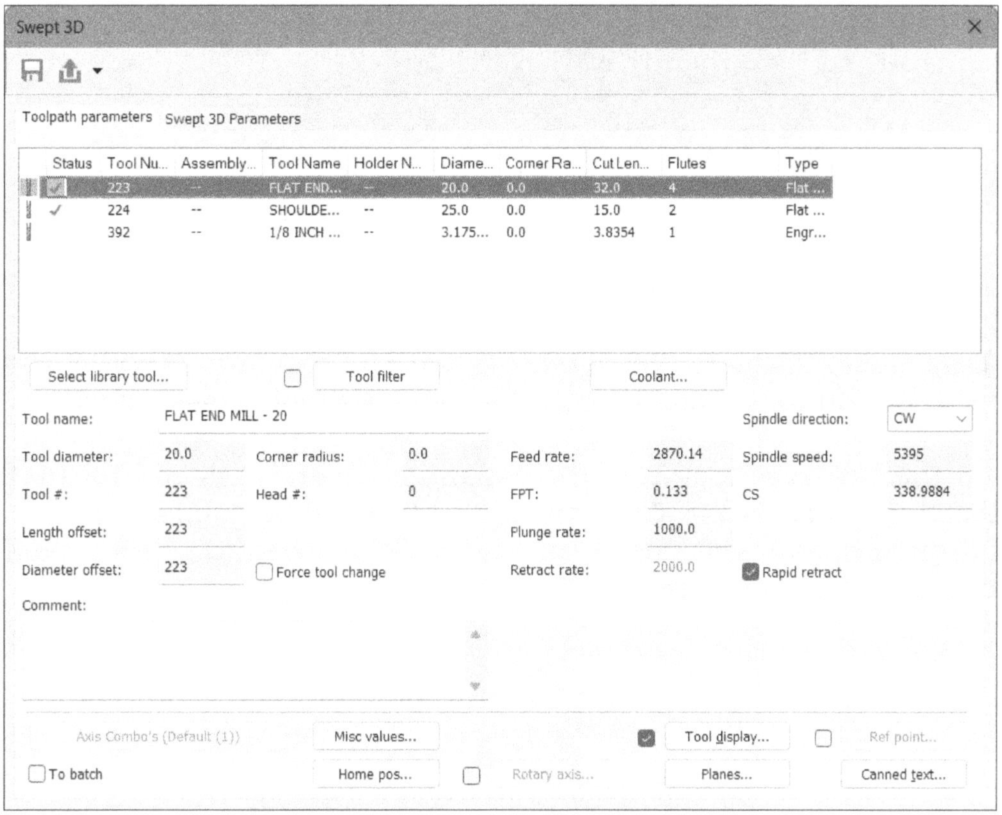

Figure-82. Swept 3D dialog box

- Select desired tool from the tool list and specify cutting parameters on the right in the dialog box.
- Click on the **Swept 3D Parameters** tab in the dialog box to specify cutting method and distance between two steps of toolpath; refer to Figure-83.

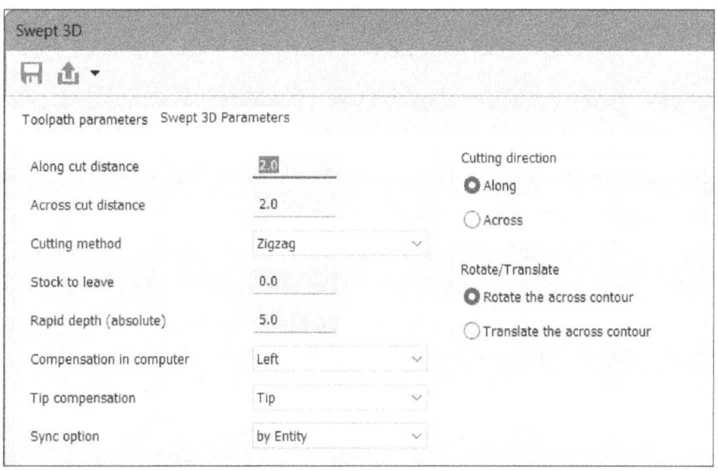

Figure-83. Swept 3D Parameters tab

- Specify the parameters as desired and click on the **OK** button from the dialog box. The toolpath will be created; refer to Figure-84.

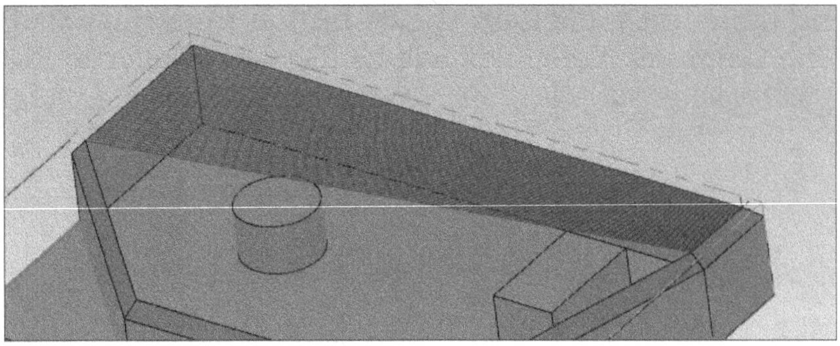

Figure-84. Swept 3D toolpath

Creating Revolve Toolpath

The **Revolved** tool in 2D toolpaths is used to create a toolpath swept by revolving an open curve about an axis. The procedure to use this tool is given next.

- Click on the **Revolved** tool from the expanded **2D** group in the **Toolpaths** tab of the **Ribbon**. The **Wireframe Chaining** dialog box will be displayed.
- Select desired open wireframe curve. You will be asked to select a point on axis of revolution; refer to Figure-85.

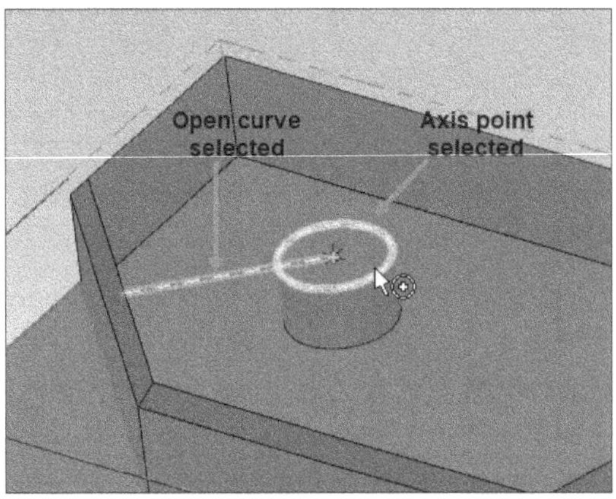

Figure-85. Wireframe curve selected for revolve toolpath

- Select desired axis point. The **Revolve** dialog box will be displayed; refer to Figure-86.
- Select desired cutting tool from the list and set the cutting parameters like feed rate, spindle speed, plunge rate, and so on.
- Click on the **Revolved parameters** tab from the dialog box to define parameters like stock to be left, axis of revolution, shape of toolpath, and so on.
- After setting desired parameters, click on the **OK** button from the dialog box. The toolpath will be created; refer to Figure-87.

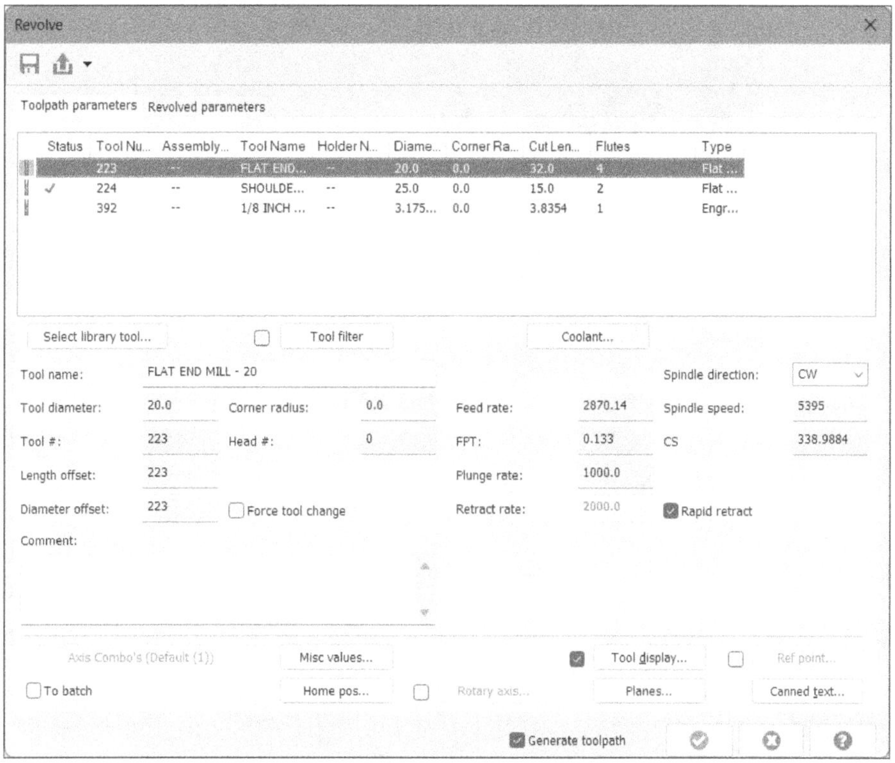

Figure-86. Revolve dialog box

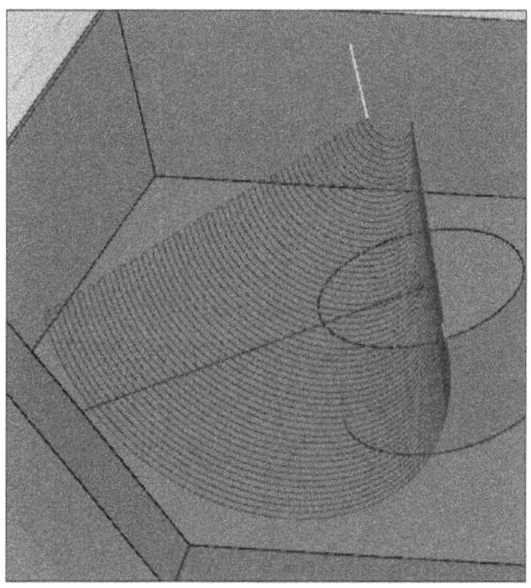

Figure-87. Revolved toolpath created

Creating Lofted Toolpath

The **Lofted** tool is used to create milling toolpath blending multiple curves. The procedure to use this tool is given next.

- Click on the **Lofted** tool from the expanded **2D** group in the **Toolpaths** tab of the **Ribbon**. The **Wireframe Chaining** dialog box will be displayed.
- Select the curves for lofted toolpath; refer to Figure-88 and click on the **OK** button from the dialog box. The **Lofted** dialog box will be displayed; refer to Figure-89.

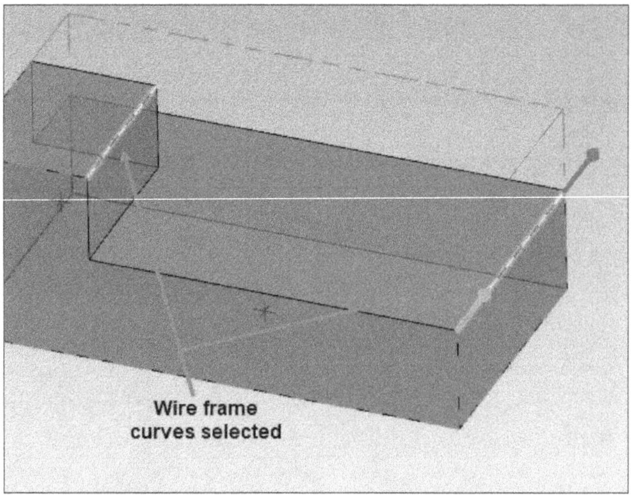

Figure-88. Wireframe curves selected for loft toolpath

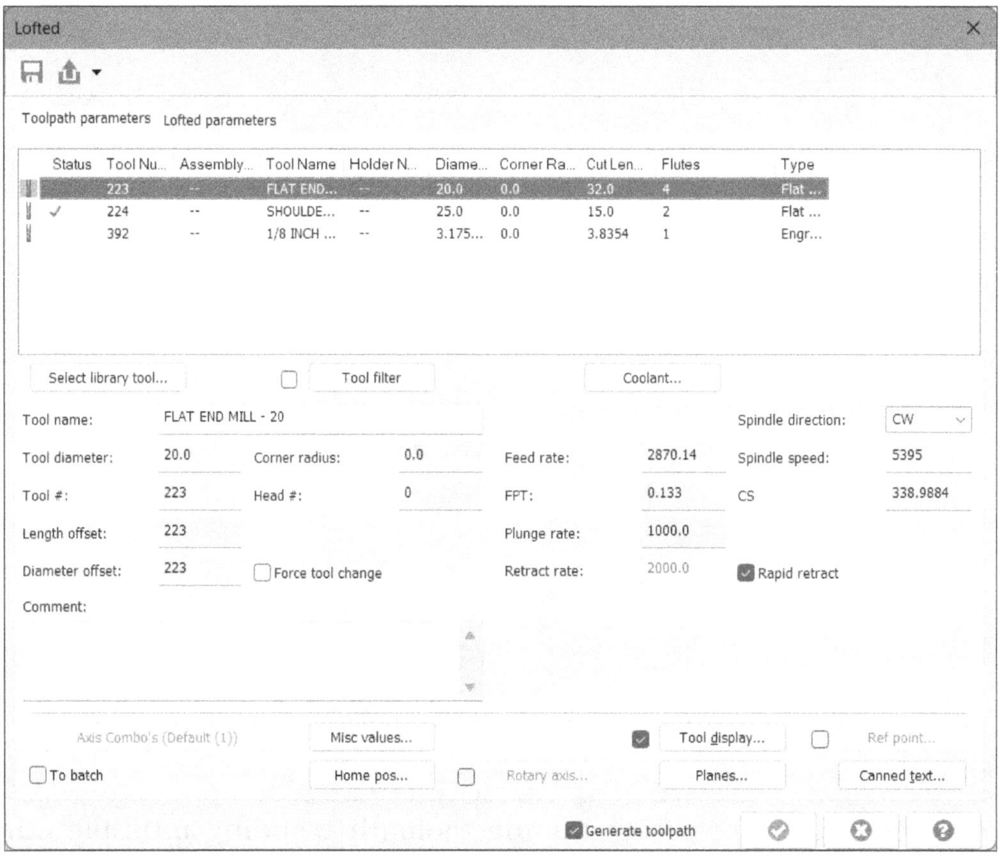

Figure-89. Lofted dialog box

- Specify the parameters as discussed earlier and click on the **OK** button. The lofted toolpath will be created; refer to Figure-90.

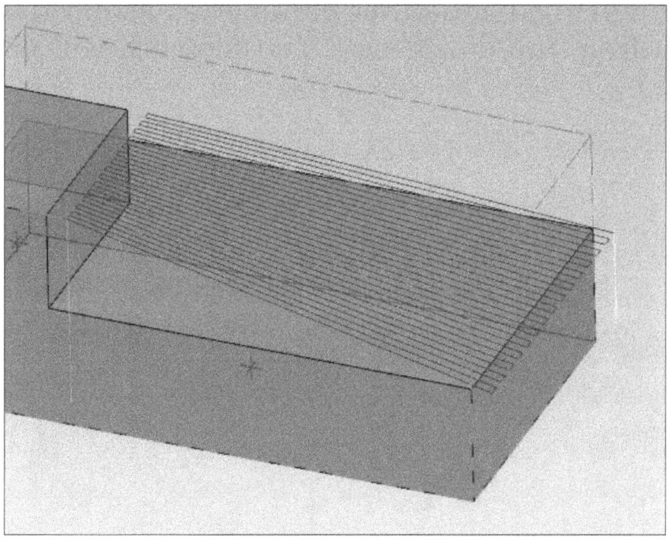

Figure-90. Lofted toolpath created

Creating Ruled Toolpath

The **Ruled** tool is used to create a toolpath blending two or more curves. Note that using this tool creates straight toolpath lines between selected curves. The procedure to use this tool is given next.

- Click on the **Ruled** tool from the expanded **2D** group in the **Toolpaths** tab of **Ribbon**. The **Wireframe Chaining** dialog box will be displayed and you will be asked to select the curves.
- Select desired chain of curves as discussed for **Ruled surface** tool earlier in the book and click on the **OK** button from the dialog box. The **Ruled** dialog box will be displayed.
- Set desired parameters in the **Toolpath parameters** tab of the **Ribbon** to define cutting tool and related parameters.
- Click on the **Ruled parameters** tab in the dialog box to specify parameters for ruled toolpath; refer to Figure-91.

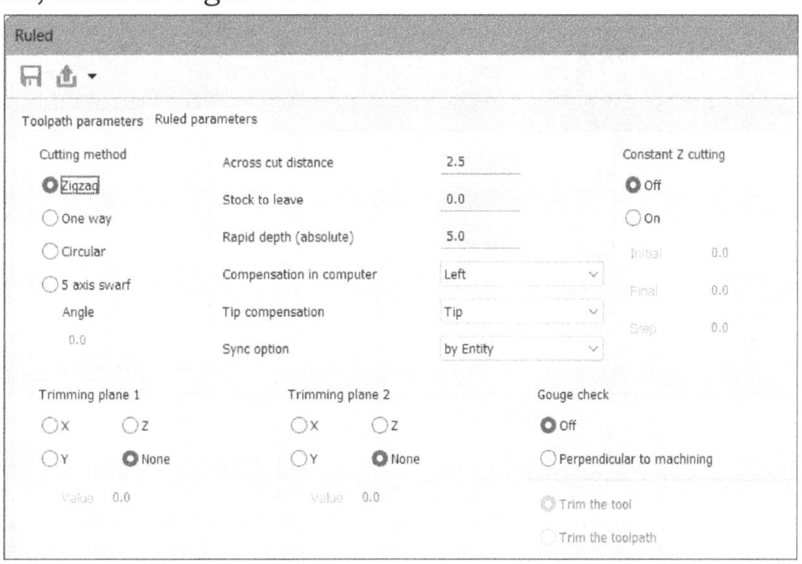

Figure-91. Ruled parameters tab

- The options in the **Trimming plane** area of the dialog box are used to define the planes in selected direction to be used for trimming the toolpath curves.

- Specify the cutting method and other parameters as discussed earlier and click on the **OK** button from the dialog box. The toolpath will be generated; refer to Figure-92.

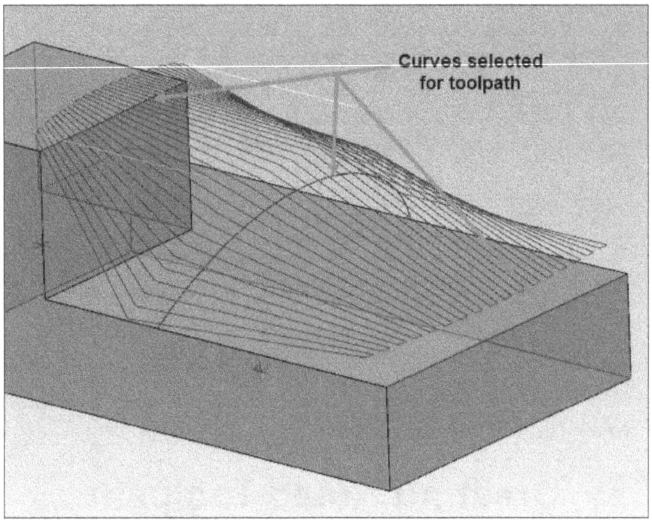

Figure-92. Ruled toolpath created

Creating Chamfer Drill Toolpath

The **Chamfer Drill** tool is used to create chamfer on the drilled holes. The procedure to use this tool is given next.

- Click on the **Chamfer Drill** tool from the expanded **2D** group in the **Toolpaths** tab of the **Ribbon**. The **Toolpath Hole Definition Manager** will be displayed; refer to Figure-93.

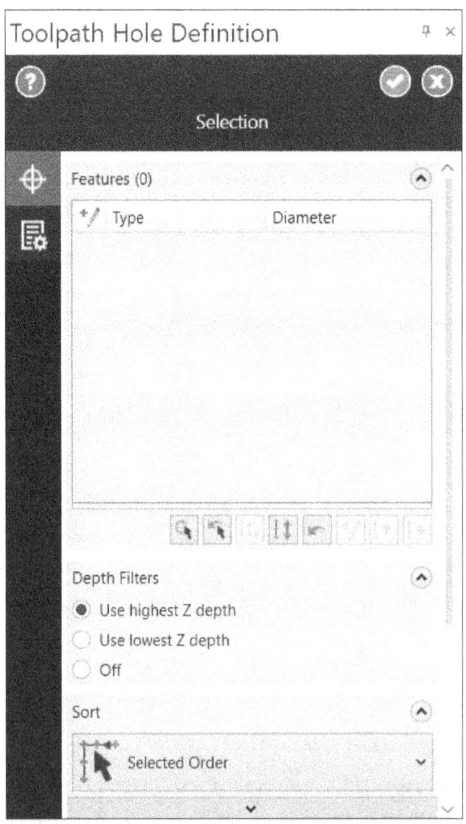

Figure-93. Toolpath Hole Definition Manager

- Select desired holes with chamfers to be machined from the model and specify the parameters as discussed earlier.
- Click on the **OK** button from the **Manager**. The **2D Toolpaths - Chamfer Drill** dialog box will be displayed; refer to Figure-94.

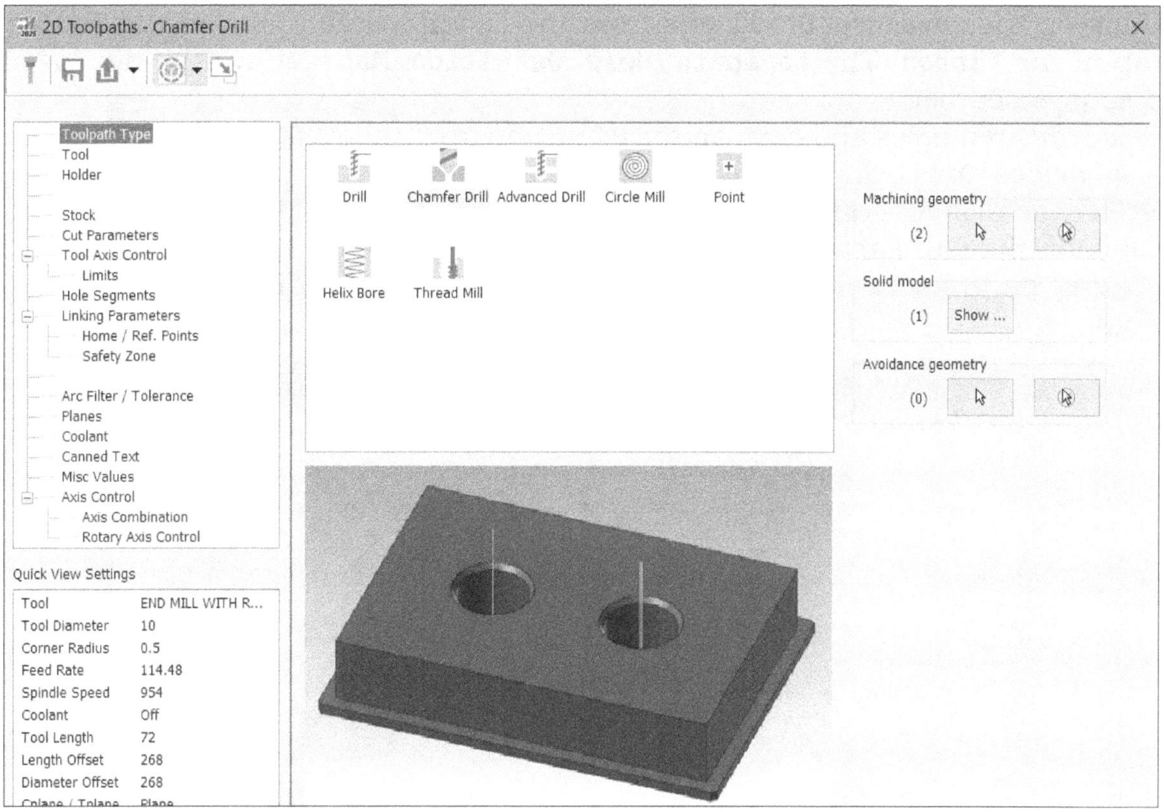

Figure-94. 2D Toolpaths-Chamfer Drill dialog box

- Select desired **Chamfer mill** tool and related tool holder from the dialog box.
- Click on the **Stock** option from the left area of the dialog box and select the stock model to be used for performing chamfer milling. Note that the stock left after performing various operations are available in the **Stock Model** drop-down of **Define stock from** area of the dialog box.
- Click on the **Cut Parameters** option from the left area of the dialog box and specify the chamfer cut depth/width.
- Set the other parameters as discussed earlier and click on the **OK** button from the dialog box. The toolpaths will be generated; refer to Figure-95.

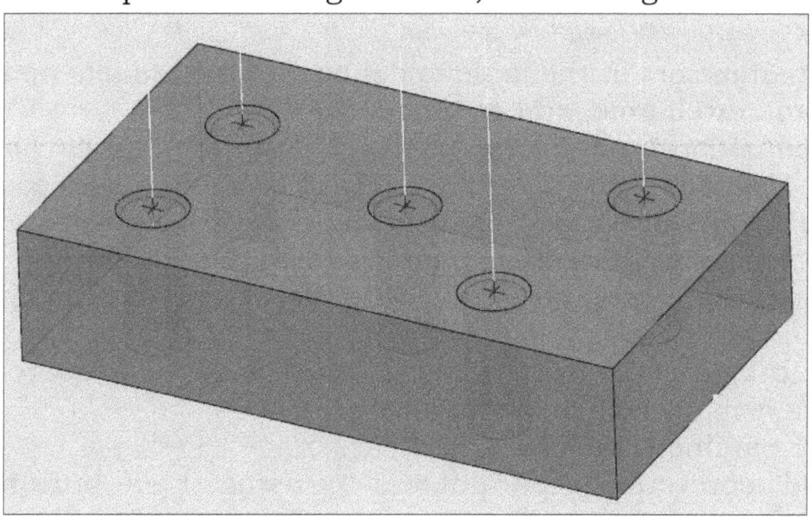

Figure-95. Chamfer drill toolpath

Creating Advanced Drill Toolpaths

The **Advanced Drill** tool is used to create advanced toolpaths with different behaviors for each toolpath segment. The procedure to use this tool is given next.

- Click on the **Advanced Drill** tool from the expanded **2D** group in the **Toolpaths** tab of the **Ribbon**. The **Toolpath Hole Definition Manager** will be displayed as discussed earlier.
- Select desired holes and click on the **OK** button from the **Manager**. The **2D Toolpaths - Advanced Drill** dialog box will be displayed.
- Select the drill tool and tool holder as discussed earlier.
- Click on the **Cut Parameters** option from the left area of the dialog box to define cutting parameters for each hole. The options will be displayed as shown in Figure-96.

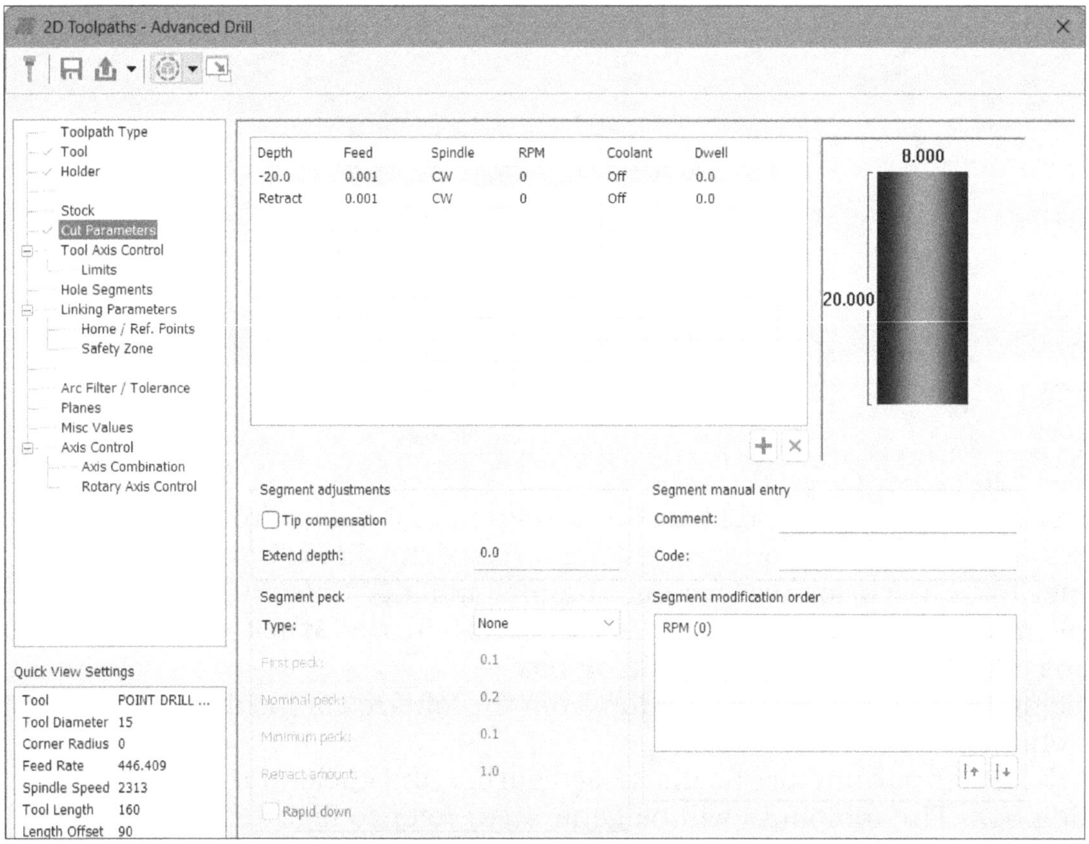

Figure-96. Cut Parameters for advanced drill operation

- Set desired parameters in the table to define parameters like depth of hole, rpm of tool, coolant, dwell time, and so on.
- Select desired option from the **Type** drop-down in the **Segment peck** area of the dialog box to define pecking parameters for chip breaking and cooling of drill bit. Select the **Full Segment** option from the drop-down if you want to create drill peck cycle for full segment. Using this option will stop the drill for specified dwell time at defined depth intervals. Select the **Chip Break** option from the drop-down if you want to create a peck cycle in which tool retracts by specified distance value after each cutting peck. Select the **Rapid down** check box to get tool down fast till the point where material has already been cut.
- Set the other parameters as discussed earlier.
- You can add more cutting parameters by using the **+** button from the **Cut Parameters** page and click on the **OK** button. The toolpath will be generated.

Creating Circular Mill Toolpath

The **Circle Mill** tool is used to machine circular pockets by moving tools in spiral motion. This toolpath is used to remove material in circular pattern with respect to the specified point. After specifying point, you need to specify diameter and depth of cut to be made. The procedure to create circular milling toolpaths is given next.

- Click on the **Circle Mill** tool from the expanded **2D** drop-down in the **Toolpaths** tab of the **Ribbon**. The **Toolpath Hole Definition Manager** will be displayed as discussed earlier.
- Select the pocket, circular arc, edge, or center point of circular pocket that you want to include for circular milling; refer to Figure-97.

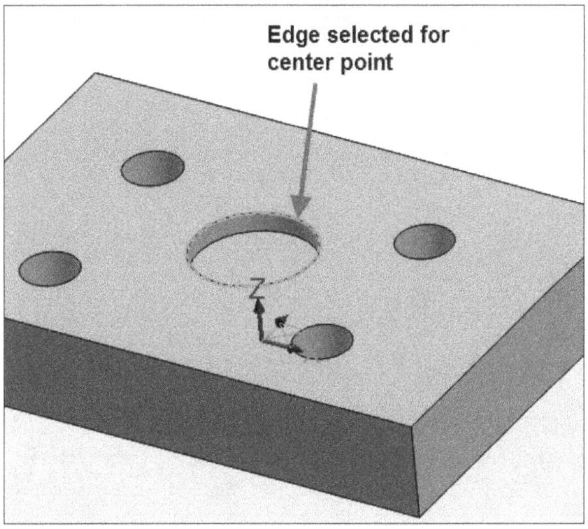

Figure-97. Points selected for circular milling

- Click on the **OK** button from the **Manager**. The **2D Toolpaths-Circle Mill** dialog box will be displayed; refer to Figure-98.

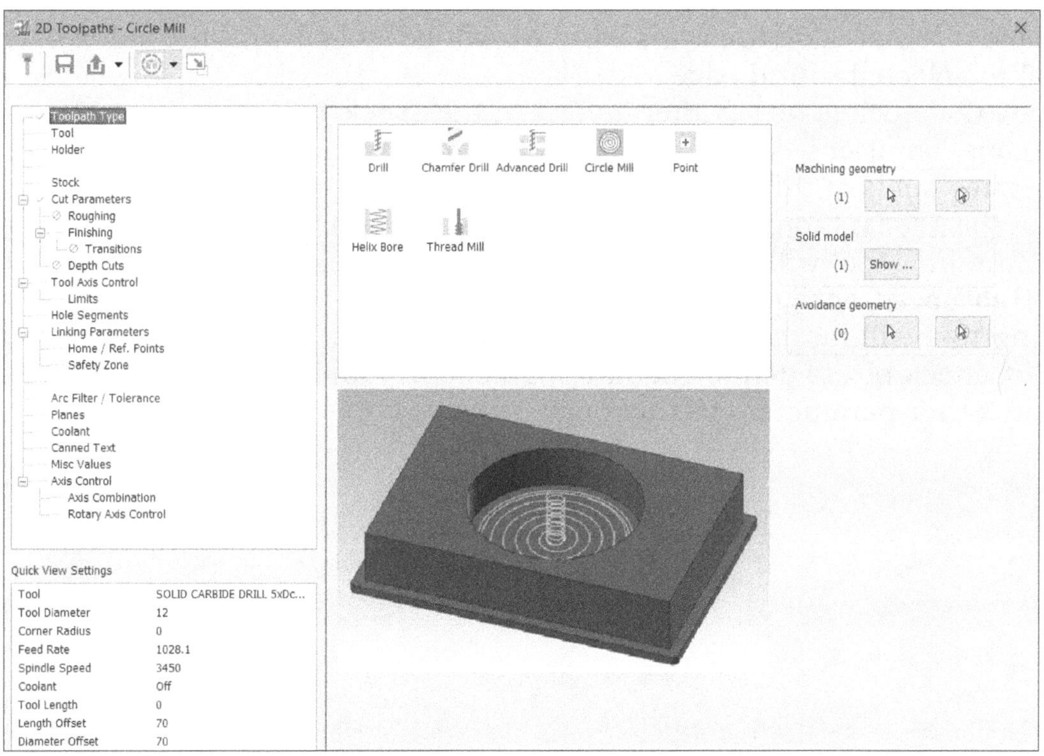

Figure-98. 2D Toolpaths-Circle Mill dialog box

- Click on the **Tool** option from the left box and specify desired tool by using the **Select library tool** button. Generally, end mill tool (with/without radius) is selected for this operation.
- Similarly, specify the holder by using the **Holder** option.
- Click on the **Cut Parameters** option from the left box. The **Cut Parameters** page of the dialog box will be displayed; refer to Figure-99.

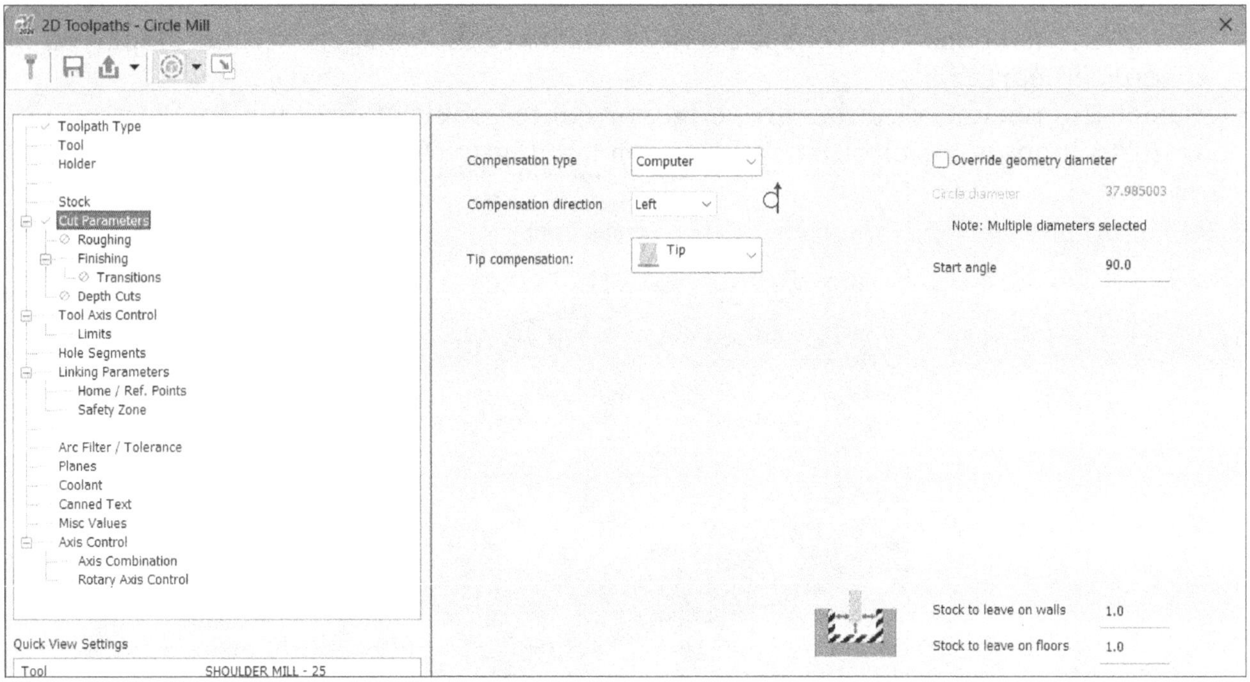

Figure-99. Cut Parameters page

- Select the **Override geometry diameter** check box to change diameter of circle for selected geometry. Click in the **Circle diameter** edit box to specify the diameter of the circular cuts being performed on the selected points. Note that if you have selected circular edge then this edit box will be locked with the value of diameter equal to selected round edge.
- Specify the stock to be left after milling in the **Stock to leave on walls** and **Stock to leave on floors** edit boxes. Set the compensation type and direction in the respective fields of this page.
- Select the **Transitions** option under **Finishing** node in left area of the dialog box to define how tool will move between cutting passes; refer to Figure-100. Select the **High speed entry** check box from **Transitions** page to define angle at which cutting tool will move with high speed between cutting passes. Select the **Lead In/Out** check box to define angular span of entry and exit of arc sweep. Similarly, specify other parameters in this page.

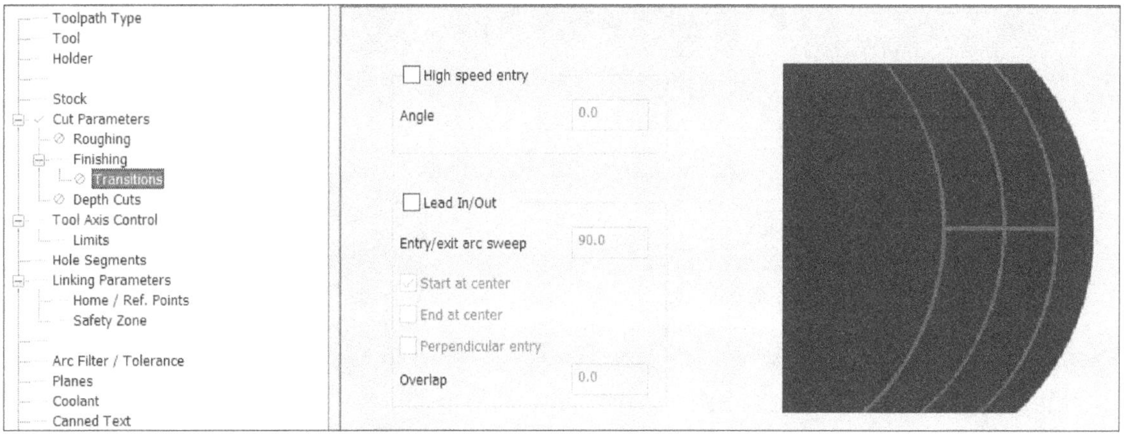

Figure-100. Transitions page for Circle Mill

- Click on the **Linking Parameters** option from the left. The options to define vertical movement of tool will be displayed.
- Specify the value of **Clearance**, **Retract plane**, and **Feed plane** as desired in the respective edit boxes. Note that clearance is the distance of tool from workpiece to avoid collision, retract plane is the location at which tool moves back after one cut operation, and feed plane is the location from where tool moves for cutting workpiece.
- Click on the **Top of stock** button and select top point of the workpiece. Be careful to specify the value manually if you have not performed facing operation on the part before using this toolpath.
- Click on the **Depth** button and select a vertex/round edge to define total depth of cut.
- If we click on the **OK** button now, then a circular cut will be made but inner material will remain intact; refer to Figure-101. This type of toolpath is useful when we need to remove large cylindrical stock from the workpiece and there is a thorough hole in the part in place of small depth cut. But this is not the requirement in our example.

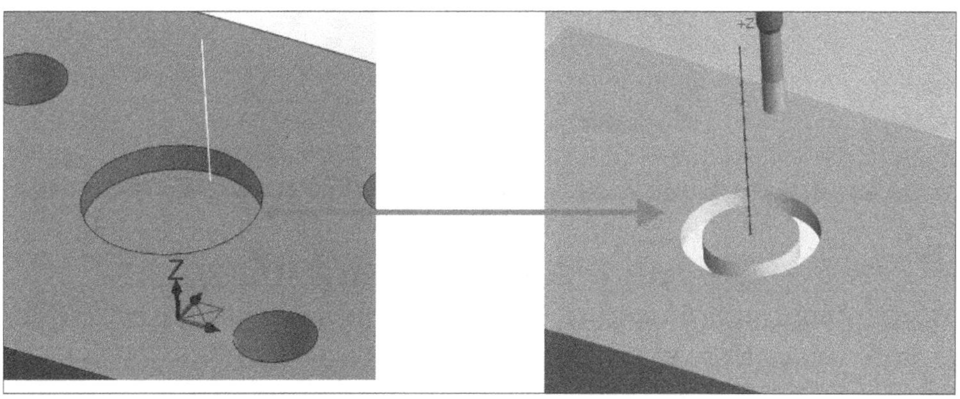

Figure-101. Circle mill toolpath without roughing and finishing steps

- Click on the **Roughing** option from the left in the **2D Toolpaths - Circle Mill** dialog box. The options will be displayed as shown in Figure-102.
- Select the **Roughing** check box from the right area of the dialog box to activate roughing options.
- Specify desired values of parameters. Note that on clicking in each edit box, function of that edit box value in toolpath is displayed in preview box. It is better to specify the value of **Stepover**, **Minimum radius**, and **Maximum radius** in percentage of your tool diameter.
- Similarly, specify the **Finishing** parameters if required.

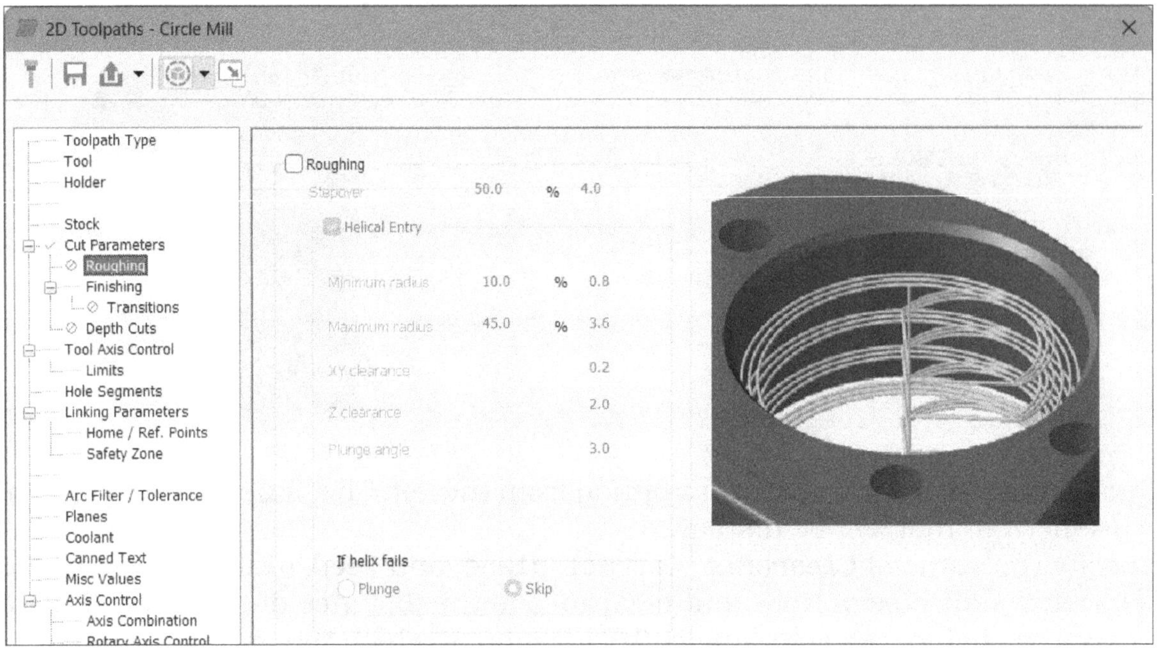

Figure-102. Options for roughing

- Specify the other related parameters like **Depth Cuts**, **Home/Ref. Points**, etc. and click on the **OK** button from the dialog box. The toolpaths will be created as shown in Figure-103.

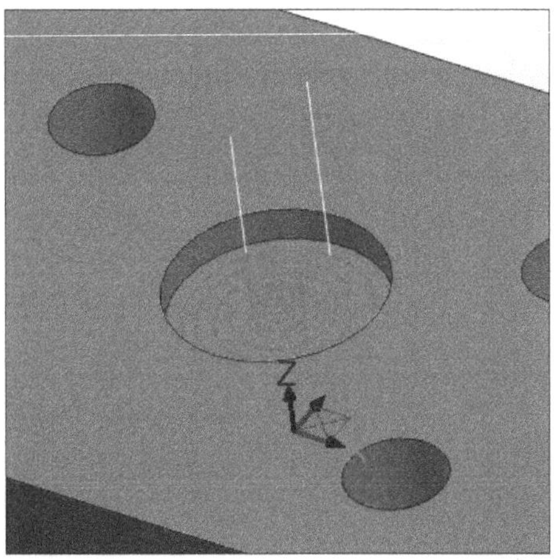
Figure-103. Circular mill toolpath generated

Note that you can cut multiple locations of same depth by using this toolpath.

Creating Helix Bore Toolpath

The Helix Bore toolpaths are used to bore a hole in a helical path. The procedure to create helix bore toolpath is given next.

- Click on the **Helix Bore** tool from the expanded **2D** group in the **Toolpaths** tab of the **Ribbon** after performing drill operation. The **Toolpath Hole Definition Manager** will be displayed and you will be asked to select the points to perform helical bore.
- Select the points at which you want to perform helical bore (you can also select edges of holes) and click on the **OK** button from the **PropertyManager**. The **2D Toolpaths - Helix Bore** dialog box will be displayed; refer to Figure-104.
- Click on the **Tools** option from the left and select desired end mill tool. Similarly, select tool holder after clicking the **Holder** option from the left.

- Click on the **Cut Parameters** option from the left. The options to specify cutting parameters will be displayed; refer to Figure-105.

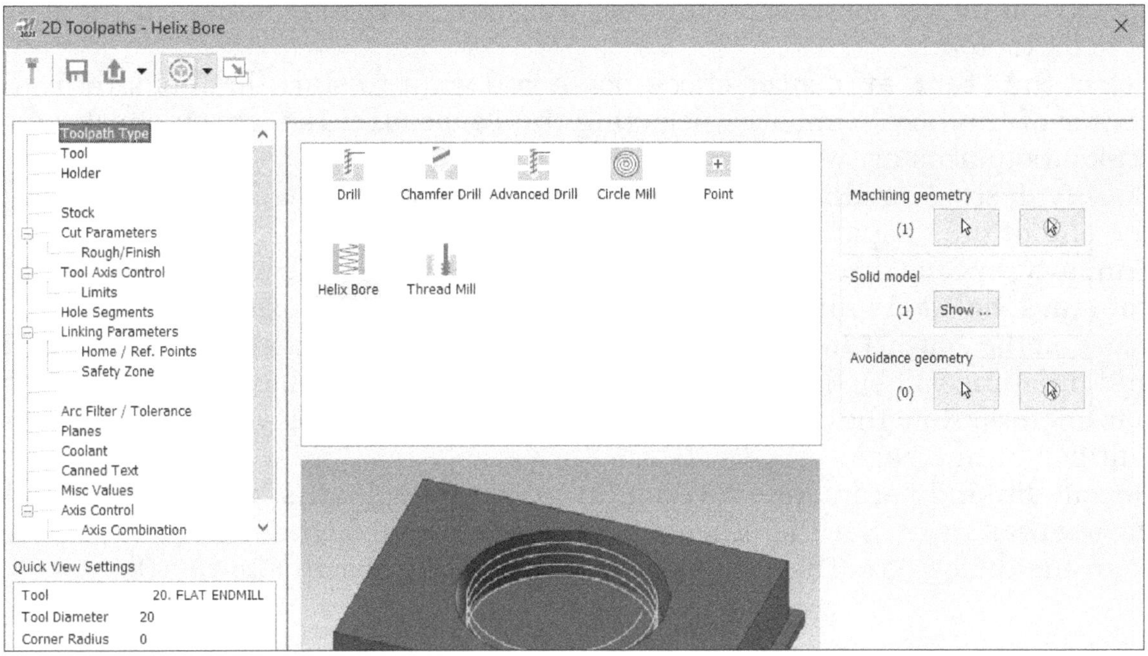

Figure-104. 2D Toolpaths-Helix Bore dialog box

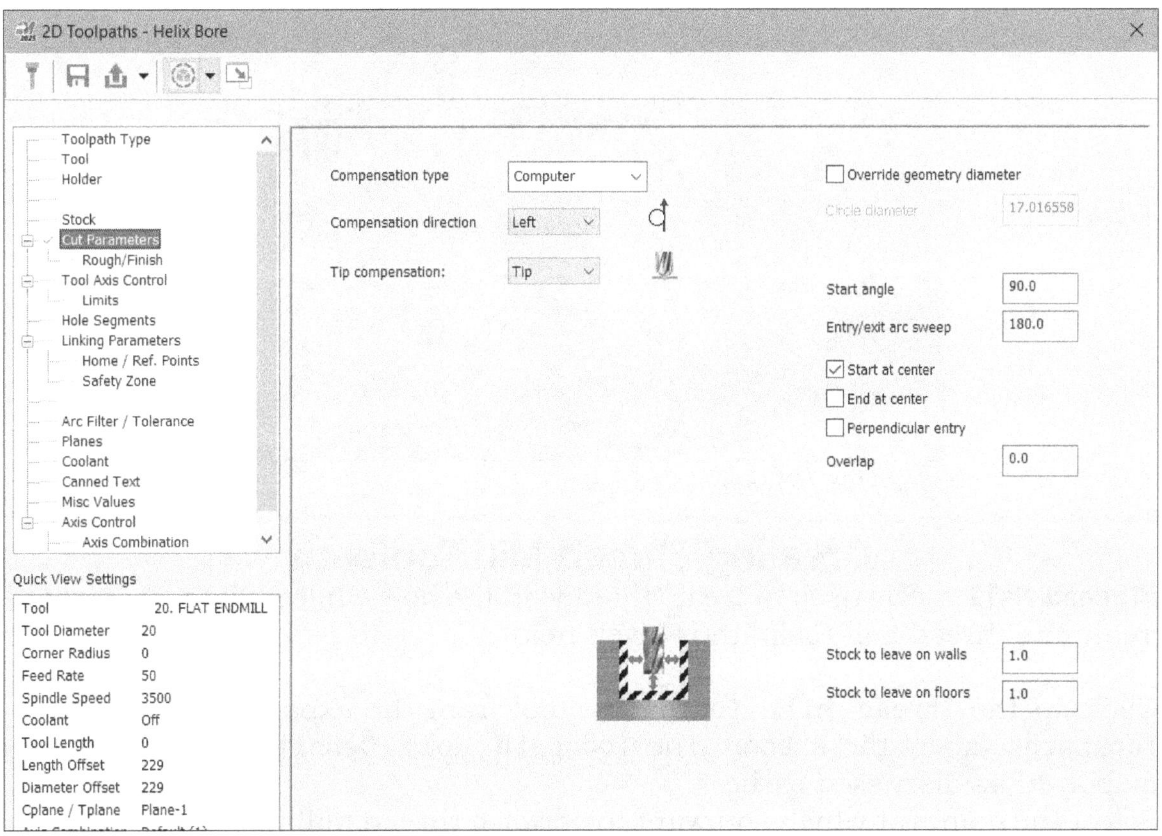

Figure-105. Cut Parameters page for helix bore toolpath

- Specify desired cutter compensation type, direction, and tool tip compensation in the respective fields of the dialog box.
- Specify desired angle value in the **Entry/exit arc sweep** edit box to define entry and exit path of tool while cutting starts and ends. If the entry/exit arc sweep is less than **180** degrees, the system applies an entry/exit line.

- Specify desired starting angle value in the **Start angle** edit box. The tool will move at this specified angle while moving for the cutting helix toolpath. If you specify 90 degree value then the tool will move perpendicularly till the starting of helix toolpath.
- Select the **Start at center** check box if you want to start the toolpath from the center of the hole. Similarly, selecting the **Perpendicular entry** check box will make toolpath start with a perpendicular line.
- Specify desired amount in the **Overlap** edit box to set how far the tool goes past the end of the toolpath before exiting for a cleaner finish.
- Similarly, specify the amount of material to be left after this operation in the **Stock to leave on walls** and **Stock to leave on floors** edit boxes.
- Click on the **Rough/Finish** option from the left box. The options related to roughing and finishing will be displayed in the right area of the dialog box. Specify desired parameters. Note that the preview of variable will be displayed as you click in an edit box of this page.
- Specify linking parameters as done in previous toolpaths by using the **Linking Parameters** page. Set the other options as required and click on the **OK** button from the dialog box. The toolpath will be created; refer to Figure-106.

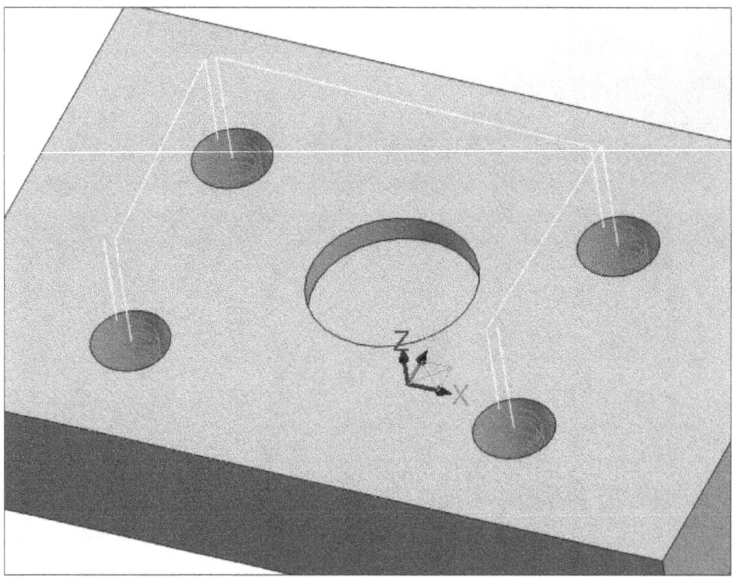

Figure-106. Helix bore toolpath created

Creating Thread Mill Toolpath

The **Thread Mill** tool is used to create threads in the hole while milling. The procedure to create the thread mill toolpath is given next.

- Click on the **Thread Mill Toolpaths** tool from the expanded **2D** group in the **Toolpaths** tab of the **Ribbon**. The **Toolpath Hole Definition Manager** will be displayed as discussed earlier.
- Select the points at which you want to perform thread milling (you can also select edges of holes in which you want to form threads) and click on the **OK** button from the **PropertyManager**. The **2D Toolpaths - Thread Mill** dialog box will be displayed; refer to Figure-107.

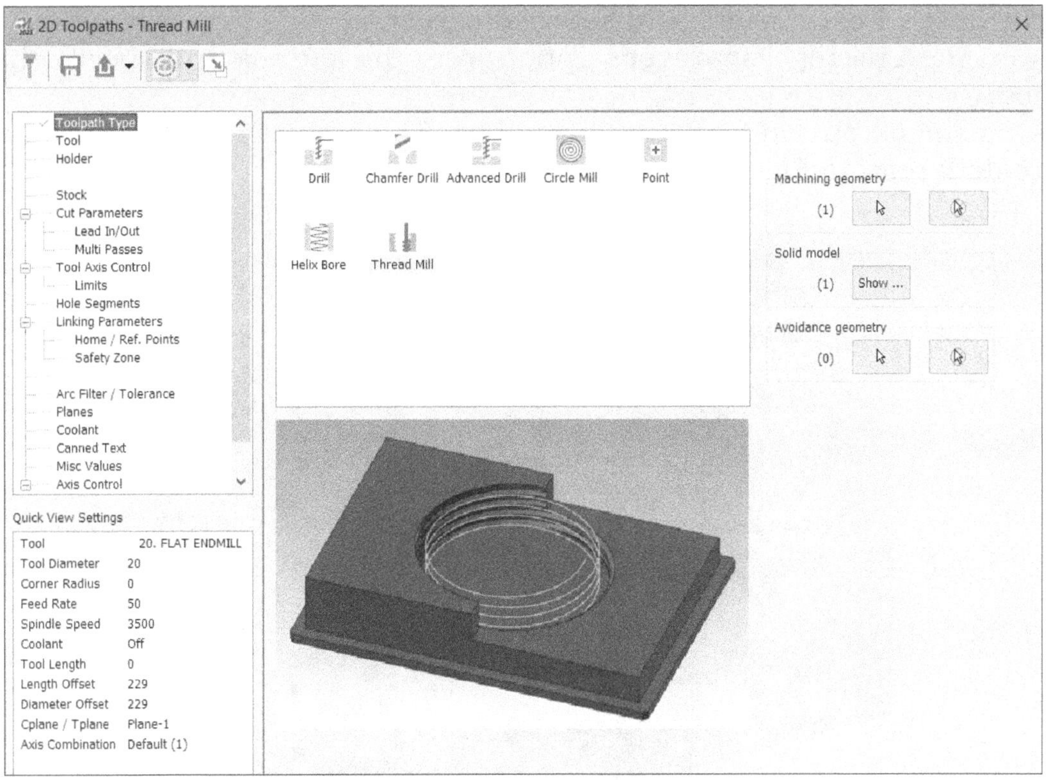

Figure-107. 2D Toolpaths-Thread Mill dialog box

- Click on the **Tool** option from the left box and select the tap of desired size. Note that in market, the tool is sold with the name thread mill cutter.
- Click on the **Holder** option from the left box and select desired holder.
- Click on the **Cut Parameters** option from the left box. The **Cut Parameters** page of the dialog box will be displayed; refer to Figure-108.

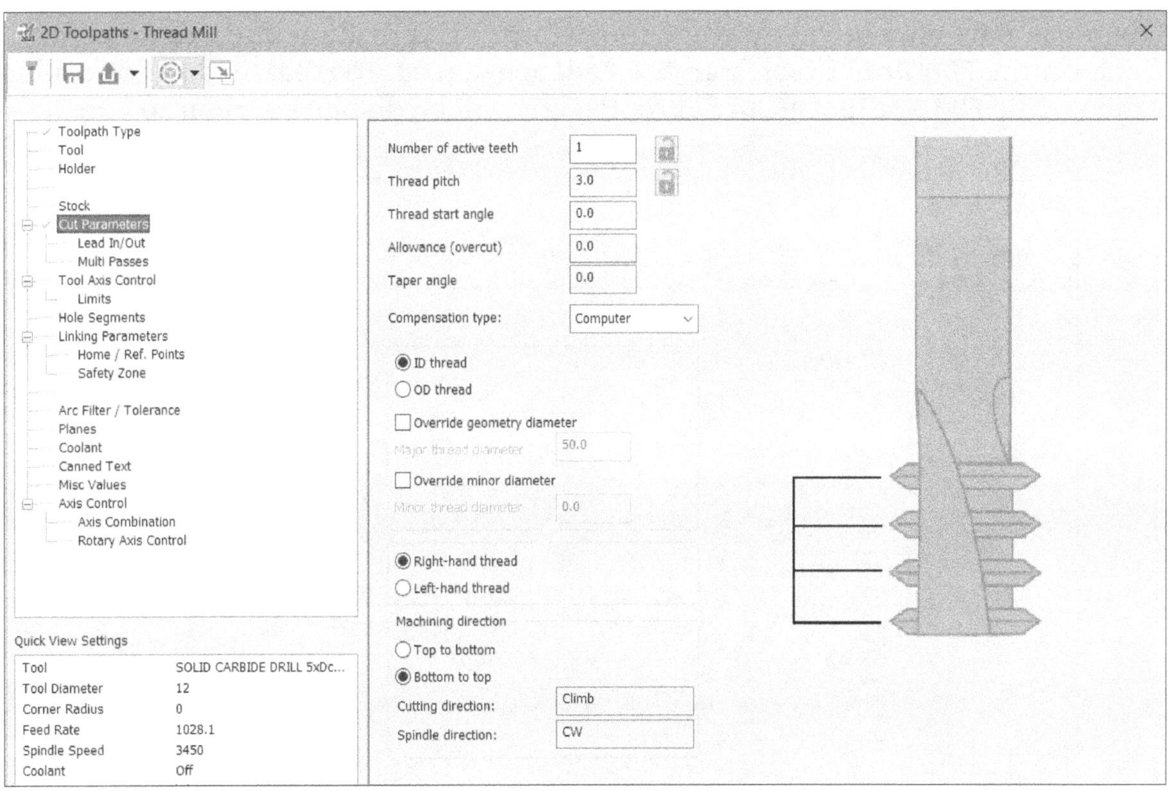

Figure-108. Thread cutting parameters page

- Specify desired parameters as discussed earlier.
- Click on the **Linking Parameters** option from the left box and specify the depth needed.
- Click on the **OK** button from the dialog box. The toolpath for thread milling will be created; refer to Figure-109.

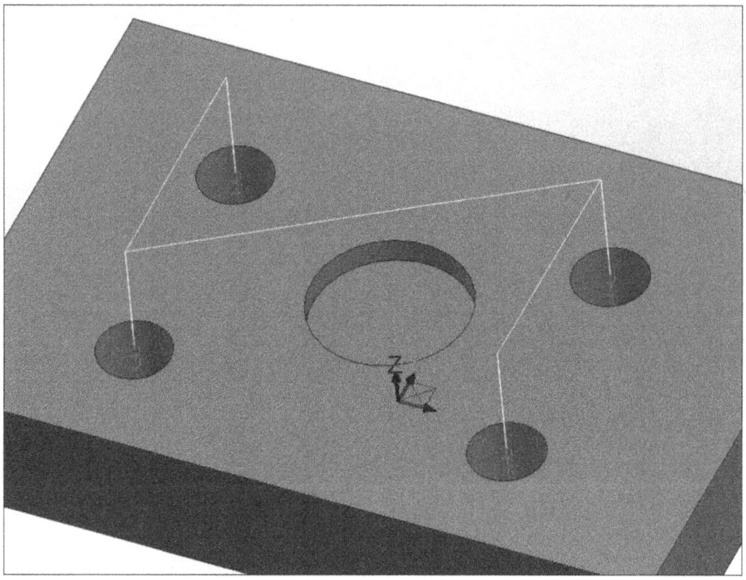

Figure-109. Toolpath for thread milling

Creating FBM Drill Toolpath

The **FBM Drill** tool is used to automatically recognize holes by depth and diameters, and automate the process of toolpath generation. The procedure to use this tool is given next.

- Open the part on which you want to perform FBM drilling and create stock.
- Click on the **FBM Drill** tool from the **Feature-Based Toolpaths** drop-down in the **Ribbon**. The **FBM Toolpaths-Drill** dialog box will be displayed; refer to Figure-110.

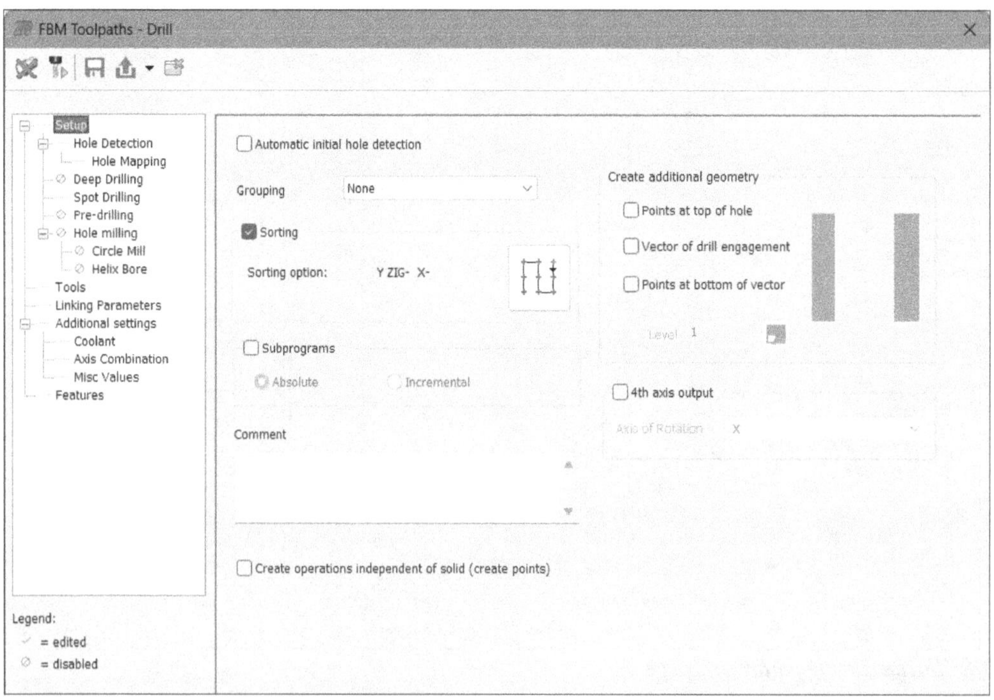

Figure-110. FBM Toolpaths-Drill dialog box

Setup Parameters

- Click on the **Setup** button from the left area of the dialog box. The options will be displayed as shown in Figure-110.
- Select the **Automatic initial hole detection** check box to let Mastercam automatically detect holes for machining.
- Select desired grouping option from the **Grouping** drop-down. Select **Tool** option if you want to group the operations based on tools used for them. Select the **Plane** option to group operations based on their planes. Select **None** if you do not want to group operations.
- Click on the **2D sort points** button from the **Sorting** area of the dialog box to sort drilling operation.
- Select the **Subprogram** check box to reduce main program length.
- If you want to create additional geometries like drill point, vector, or bottom point then select the respective check boxes from the **Create additional geometry** area of the dialog box.
- Select the **4th axis output** check box and specify desired rotation axis if your machine can rotate the part while milling.

- Set the parameters on other pages in the same way discussed earlier and click on the **Detect** button at the top in the dialog box. The holes will be detected and will be displayed in the **Features** page; refer to Figure-111.

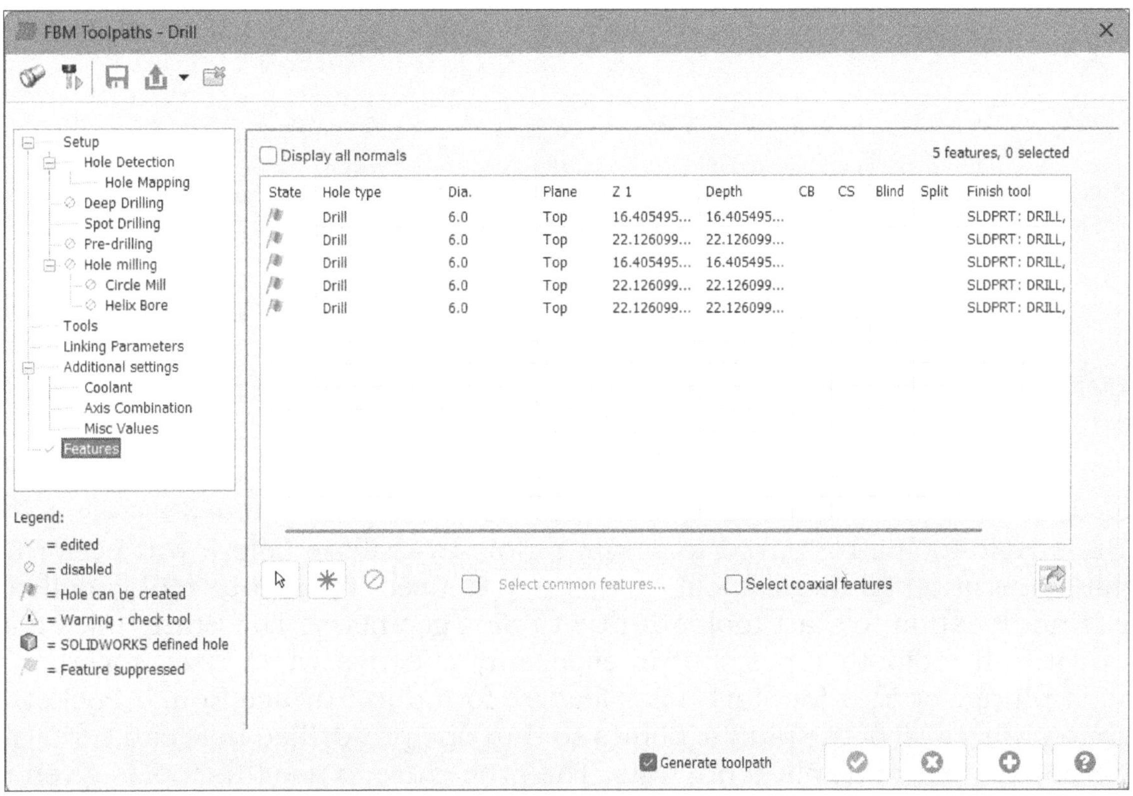

Figure-111. Drill holes detected

- Click on the **OK** button from the dialog box to create drill toolpaths.

Creating Auto Drill Toolpath

The **Auto Drill** tool works in the same way as **FBM Drill** tool but in case of **Auto Drill** tool, we need to select all the holes which we want to be machined. Mastercam will automatically define tools and toolpaths. The procedure to use this tool is given next.

- Click on the **Auto Drill** tool from the expanded **2D** group in the **Toolpaths** tab of the **Ribbon**. The **Toolpath Hole Definition Manager** will be displayed asking you to select holes.
- Select the edge, face, or walls of the holes and click on the **OK** button from the **Manager**. The **Auto Arc Drilling** dialog box will be displayed; refer to Figure-112.
- Specify the parameters as discussed earlier for drilling holes in various tabs of the dialog box and click on the **OK** button. The toolpaths will be generated.

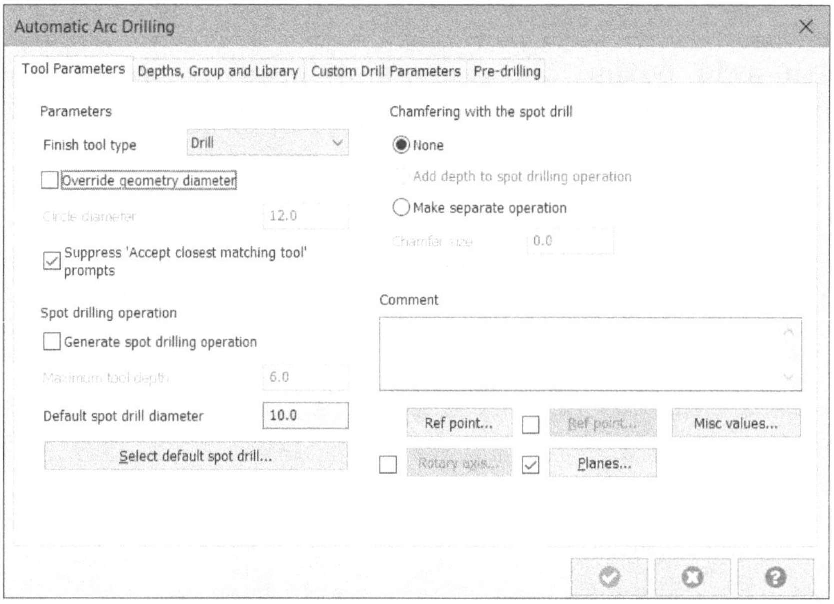

Figure-112. Automatic Arc Drilling dialog box

- Set the parameters as done for **FBM Drill** tool and click on the **OK** button. The toolpaths for drilling will be generated.

Creating Start Hole Toolpath

The Start Hole toolpath is used to create a hole by drilling before you perform any roughing operation on large stock. This option is used when your tool is delicate or there is not location to start toolpath due to part geometry. The Start Holes feature works with all toolpath types, but is especially effective when used together with the align plunge entries for start holes feature found in Surface Rough Pocket. This feature organizes all of the plunge points so that one pre-drilled hole can serve as the plunge position for multiple depth cuts. The procedure to use this tool is given next.

- Make sure you have earlier performed any milling operation before using this tool. Click on the **Start Hole** tool from the expanded **2D** group of **Toolpaths** tab in the **Ribbon**. The **Drill Start Holes** dialog box will be displayed; refer to Figure-113.

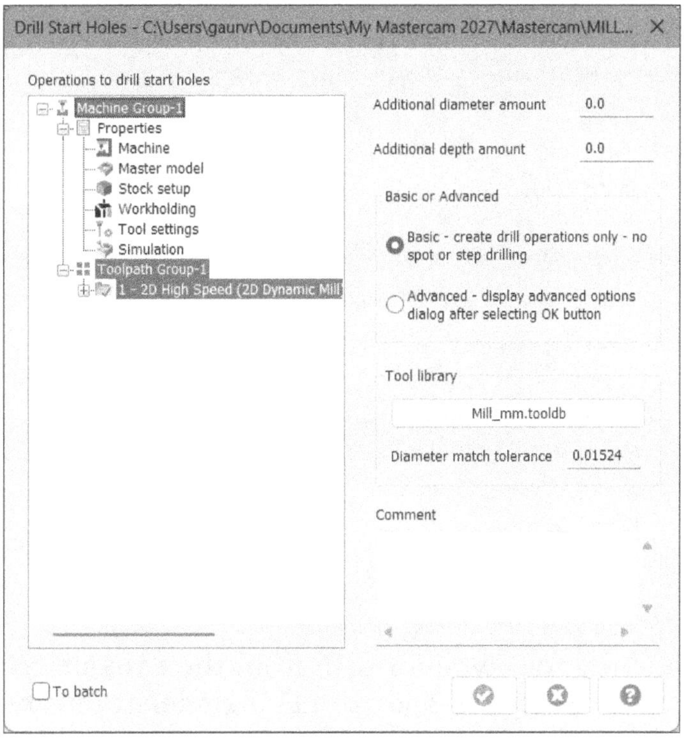

Figure-113. Drill Start Holes dialog box

- Select the operation (or operation by holding the **CTRL** key while selecting) for which you want to create starting hole. Mastercam will automatically figure out where plunge holes are required, and will calculate the dimensions of the start holes based on the sizes of the tools used in those operations.
- If you want to specify additional diameter and depth then specify the respective values in the **Additional diameter amount** and **Additional depth amount** edit boxes. Note that if mastercam has drilled a diameter of **5** mm but you want to drill **6** diameter then specify **1** in the edit box.
- Click on the button in the **Tool library** area of the dialog box to select desired library. Mastercam will choose a suitable drill from the selected tool library. Specify the tolerance value in **Diameter match tolerance** edit box. Mastercam will search in the range of specified tolerance for the drill size.
- Click on **OK** button to apply settings.
- If you want to specify advanced options related drilling like spot drilling or drilling cycle then select the **Advanced** radio button from the **Basic or Advanced** area of the dialog box and click on the **OK** button. Mastercam will start analyzing the toolpaths and in a few moments, the **Automatic Arc Drilling** dialog box will be displayed; refer to Figure-114.

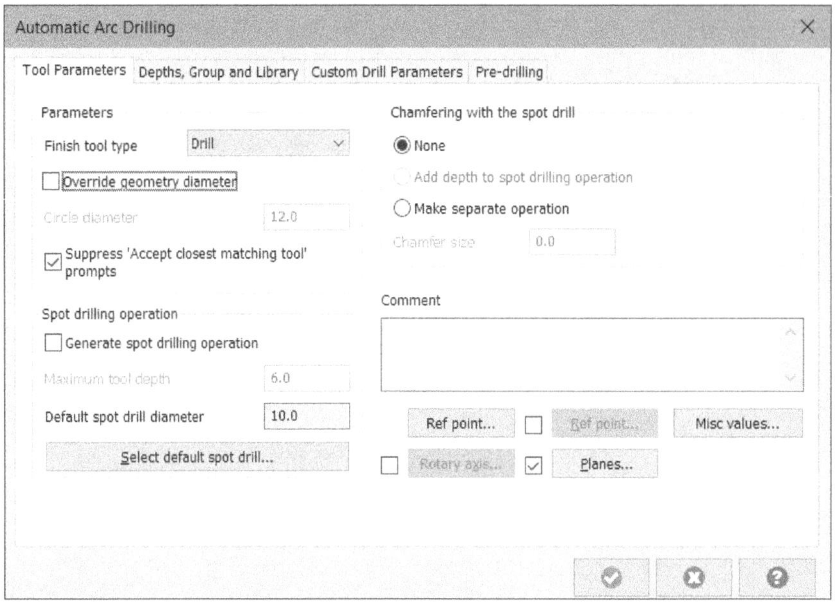

Figure-114. Automatic Arc Drilling dialog box

- Select desired finishing tool type for drill from the **Finish tool type** drop-down. To spot drill, select the **Generate spot drilling operation** check box. The options below it will become active.
- Specify the tool depth, default size, or default spot drill as required.
- Click on the **Depths, Group and Library** tab in the dialog box. The **Automatic Arc Drilling** dialog box will be displayed; refer to Figure-115.

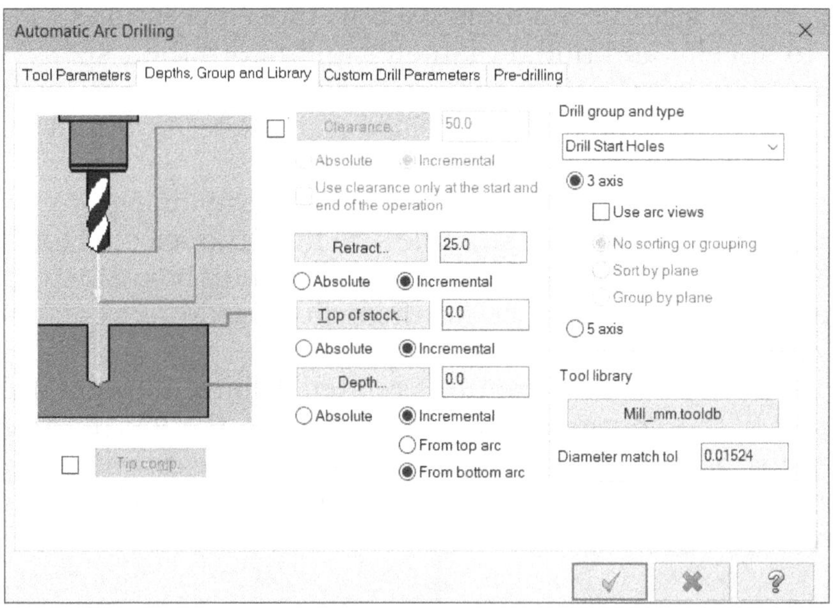

Figure-115. Depths, Group and Library tab

- Specify the retraction location, top of stock location, and depth point for drilling. Similarly, specify parameters in the other tabs and click on the **OK** button from the dialog box. The toolpaths will be created for drilling but they might be inserted after main operation, so you need to manually drag the drill toolpaths before the main operations; refer to Figure-116.

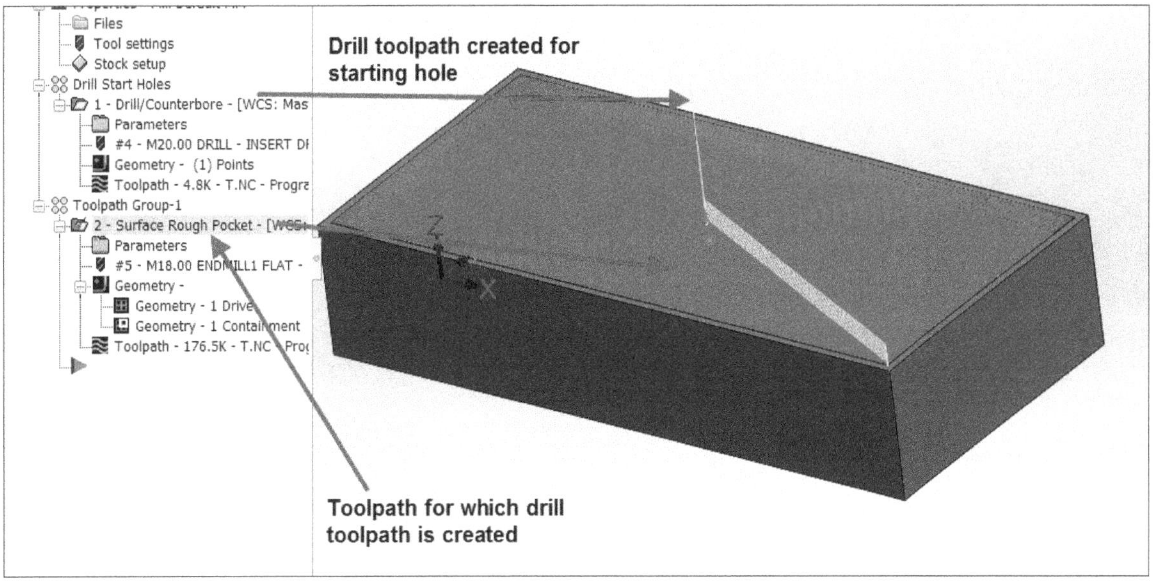

Figure-116. Start hole toolpath

Point Toolpaths

The Point toolpaths make the tool to follow the toolpaths formed by the selected points. The procedure to use this tool is given next.

- Click on the **Point** tool from the expanded **2D** group of **Toolpaths** tab in the **Ribbon**. The **Point Toolpath** dialog box will be displayed; refer to Figure-117 and you will be asked to select the points to be machined.
- Select desired radio button from the **Move type** section to define whether rapid move will be used or feed rate move will be used for cutting tool movements between points. You can use different types of movements between various points simultaneously when selecting points.

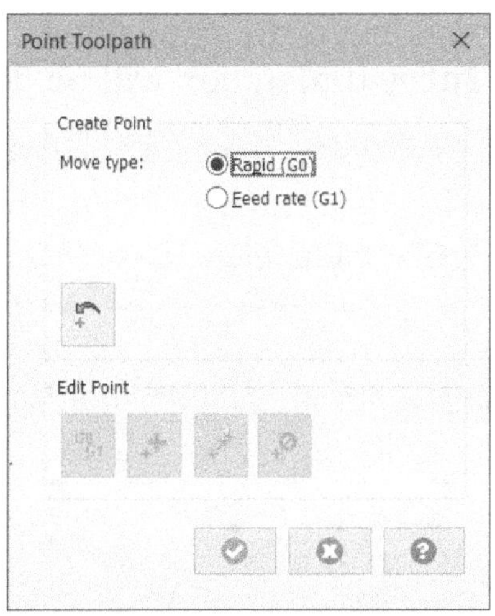

Figure-117. Point Toolpath dialog box

- Select the points and click on the **OK** button from the **Manager**. The **2D Toolpaths-Point** dialog box will be displayed; refer to Figure-118.

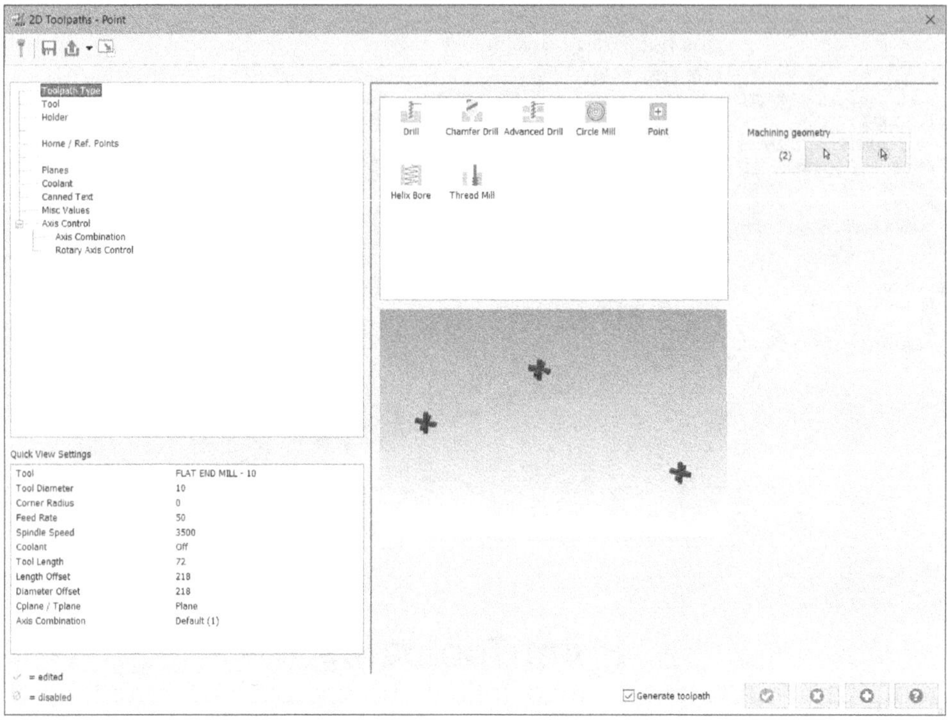

Figure-118. 2D Toolpaths-Point dialog box

- Specify the parameters as discussed earlier and click on the **OK** button from the dialog box to create the toolpaths. The tool will move straight to the selected points while cutting material.

Creating Manual Entry Toolpath

The **Manual Entry** tool is used to add desired NC codes for machining using a text file or by typing the value. The procedure to use this tool is given next.

- Click on the **Manual Entry** tool from the expanded **2D** group in the **Toolpaths** tab of the **Ribbon**. The **Manual Entry** dialog box will be displayed; refer to Figure-119.

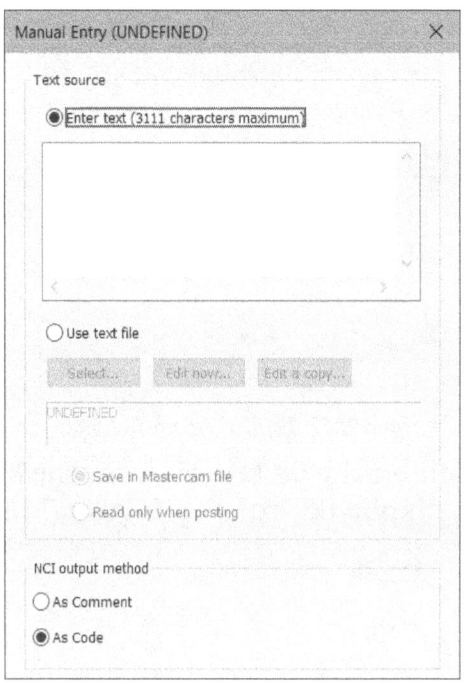

Figure-119. Manual Entry dialog box

- Select the **Enter text** radio button if you want to manually type the code/comment text. Select the **Use text file** radio button if you want to import the text from a file.
- If you have selected the **Use text file** radio button then click on the **Select** button. The **Open** dialog box will be displayed; refer to Figure-120.

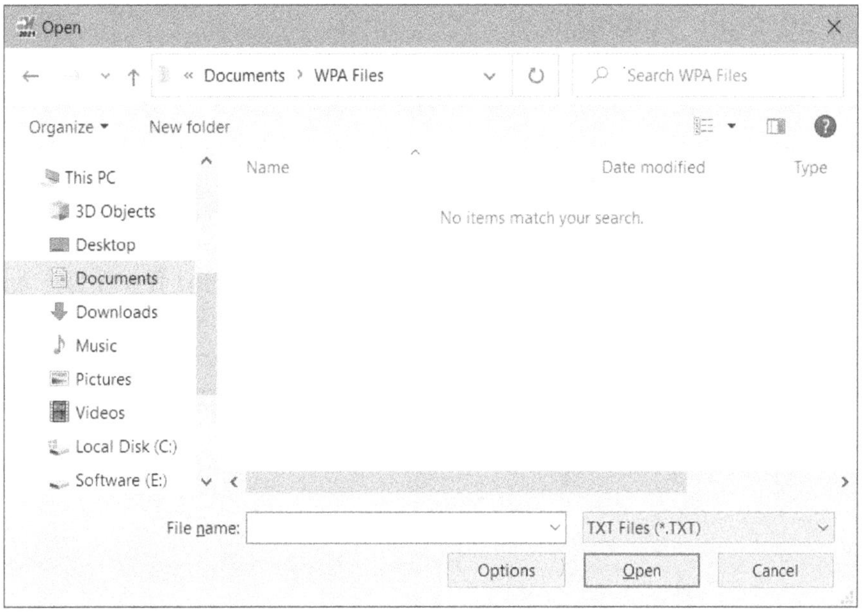

Figure-120. Open dialog box

- Select desired text file and click on the **Options** button. The **ASCII File Read parameters** dialog box will be displayed; refer to Figure-121.

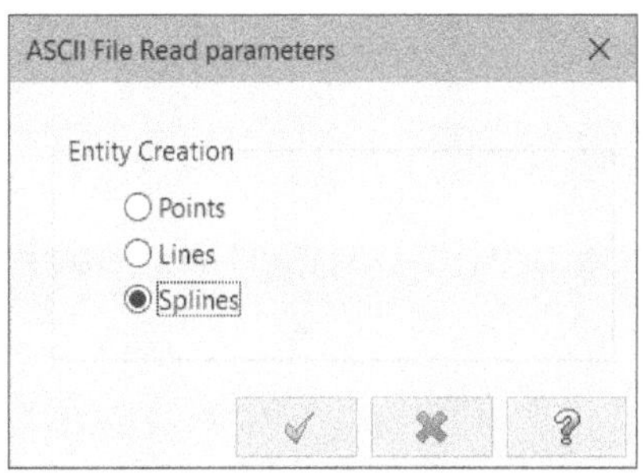

Figure-121. ASCII File Read parameters dialog box

- Select desired radio button from the dialog box to define what type of toolpath will be generated using the text in the file and click on the **OK** button.
- Click on the **Open** button from the **Open** dialog box to use the selected file. The selected file will be displayed in the **Manual Entry** dialog box.
- Select the **As Comment** radio button from the **NCI output method** area of the dialog box to use text imported from file as comment in the output file. Select the **As Code** radio button from the area to use text of selected file as NC code in output file.
- After setting desired parameters, click on the **OK** button from the dialog box.

SELF ASSESSMENT

Q1. The .... toolpaths are used to remove the material by following the contour of the model.

Q2. What is a lead-in in toolpath?

Q3. While machining a workpiece, cutting tool moves at rapid rate during lead-in. (T/F)

Q4. What is the function of clearance plane?

Q5. The .... toolpaths are used to remove the material from the top faces in the model.

Q6. Which of the following toolpaths is used to machine a large space bound by walls on its sides?
a. Pocket
b. Face
c. Contour
d. Peel

Q7. Which of the following toolpaths is used to machine a flat face at the top of a workpiece?
a. Pocket
b. Face
c. Contour
d. Peel

Q8. Which of the following toolpaths is used to machine chamfer on the edges of workpiece?
a. Pocket
b. Face
c. Contour
d. Peel

Q9. The width of the chip starts at maximum and decreases in case of Conventional Milling. (T/F)

Q10. The width of the chip starts at maximum and decreases in case of Climb Milling. (T/F)

Q11. Which of the following toolpaths is used to machine area between two open chains?
a. Pocket
b. Face
c. Contour
d. Peel

Q12. What is the difference between blend mill and peel toolpaths?

Q13. The .... tool is used to generate 2D milling toolpaths based on recognized features of the model.

Q14. The Chamfer Drill tool is used to create chamfer on the drilled holes. (T/F)

Q15. Discuss the difference between functioning of Auto Drill tool and FBM Drill tool.

REVIEW QUESTIONS

Q1. Which tab contains the tools required to create 2D milling toolpaths in Mastercam?
A. View Tab
B. Home Tab
C. Toolpaths Tab
D. Modeling Tab

Q2. What is the primary purpose of the 2D Contour toolpath?
A. Drilling holes in a part
B. Machining internal pockets
C. Following the contour of the model to remove material
D. Creating 3D chamfers

Q3. In the Contour toolpath dialog box, which button is used to select tools from the tool library?
A. Open Toolpath
B. Select library tool
C. Select tool from library
D. Load tool

Q4. What option should be selected from the Compensation type drop-down to generate G41/G42 codes based on the machine controller?
A. Computer
B. Control
C. Wear
D. Off

Q5. Which option from the Contour Type drop-down is used to generate a chamfering toolpath following 3D curvature?
A. 2D chamfer
B. Ramp
C. 3D chamfer
D. Remachining

Q6. What is the effect of selecting the Infinite look ahead checkbox?
A. Reduces tool load
B. Avoids self-intersecting toolpaths
C. Creates smooth arcs
D. Enables chamfering

Q7. What is the purpose of the Keep tool down checkbox in Depth Cuts options?
A. Increases spindle speed
B. Reduces feed rate
C. Reduces retraction passes
D. Adds roughing passes

Q8. In the Depth Cuts dialog, selecting the Subprogram checkbox allows what?
A. Increasing cutting speed
B. Using incremental coordinates only
C. Generating subprograms for repeated cycles
D. Enabling Taper angle

Q9. Which Lead In/Out option allows the tool to enter the workpiece tangentially?
A. Perpendicular
B. Profile Ramp
C. Tangent
D. Midpoint

Q10. What is the function of the Spring passes in Multi Passes options?
A. Create initial roughing passes
B. Create extra passes to ensure dimensional accuracy
C. Control entry/exit
D. Reduce step over

Q11. What does the Automatic radio button in the Tabs option allow you to do?
A. Place tabs randomly
B. Define tab size manually
C. Automatically place tabs at intervals
D. Assign tab shape

Q12. Which parameter in Linking Parameters ensures extra tool movement depth at the end of the cut?
A. Feed plane
B. Clearance
C. Break Through
D. Top of stock

Q13. What is the purpose of the Arc Filter/Tolerance page?
A. Define depth of cut
B. Define coolant usage
C. Set tool axis
D. Control precision of curves and arcs

Q14. What happens when you enable Use Fixed Segment Length in Arc Filter/Tolerance settings?
A. Toolpath segments are ignored
B. Parallel toolpaths become uniform
C. Simulation is skipped
D. Arcs are converted into tangents

Q15. Which page is used to define Working coordinate system and Tool plane for the operation?
A. Tool Options
B. Planes
C. Misc Values
D. Coolant

Q16. In Drill Toolpath creation, what is the purpose of the Depth Filters rollout?
A. Define coolant parameters
B. Sort toolpaths
C. Filter drilling points based on Z-depth
D. Select subprogram

Q17. Which drop-down in Drill toolpath allows defining the cutting cycle (like peck or deep hole drilling)?
A. Tool holder
B. Linking Parameters
C. Cycle
D. Entry

Q18. What is the function of the Dynamic Mill toolpath?
A. Cut threads
B. Apply chamfers
C. Perform high-speed material removal within boundaries
D. Drill holes in soft materials

Q19. In Dynamic Mill toolpath, which option allows selecting faces that the tool should avoid?
A. Select machining chains
B. Select containment chains
C. Select avoidance chains
D. Select air chains

Q20. What does the Stay inside option in Dynamic Mill toolpath ensure?
A. Tool cuts outside boundary
B. Tool avoids ramping
C. Tool remains within defined boundaries
D. Tool uses undercut

Q21. Which option allows Mastercam to extend open chains tangentially when using Dynamic Mill?
A. None
B. Tangent
C. Shortest distance
D. Chamfer

Q22. What is the use of Island facing in Dynamic Mill toolpath?
A. Ignore islands
B. Perform facing operations on islands
C. Cut tabs
D. Apply coolant

Q23. What does enabling Corner Pretreatment do in Dynamic Mill?
A. Skips corners
B. Creates arcs in corners
C. Allows machining corners with specific strategy
D. Applies chamfer only

Q24. In Rest Material options, which check box activates the rest mill calculation?
A. Stock to leave
B. Subprogram
C. Rest material
D. Entry motion

Q25. What must be selected when machining outside a boundary using Dynamic Mill?
A. Stay inside
B. Break through
C. From outside
D. Tapered walls

Q26. Which toolpath should be used first if the top surface of a part is flat?
A. Pocket Toolpath
B. Facing Toolpath
C. Slot Mill Toolpath
D. Blend Mill Toolpath

Q27. In a Facing toolpath, which checkbox reverses the direction of the last cutting pass?
A. Roll in
B. Auto angle
C. Reverse direction of last pass
D. Lead out

Q28. What is the purpose of selecting the "Roll in" checkbox in a Facing toolpath?
A. It increases cut depth
B. Adds arc move at toolpath entry
C. Makes passes in reverse
D. Extends tool exit

Q29. The Dynamic Contour toolpath is used primarily to:
A. Rough out cavities
B. Create decorative engraving
C. Follow a profile to remove material
D. Machine chamfered edges

Q30. In the Pocket toolpath, which cutter is most commonly used?
A. Chamfer cutter
B. Engrave mill
C. Slot cutter
D. Flat or ball end mill

Q31. In Conventional Milling, what happens to chip thickness during the cut?
A. It remains constant
B. Starts thick and reduces
C. Starts from zero and increases
D. It decreases exponentially

Q32. Which of the following is a drawback of Climb Milling?
A. Increased chip recutting
B. Shorter tool life
C. Tendency to lift workpiece
D. Problems with backlash

Q33. What defines the primary operation of Peel Mill toolpaths?
A. Milling between open boundaries
B. Creating deep pockets
C. Chamfering vertical edges
D. Finishing walls only

Q34. What is the purpose of the "Micro lift" setting in Peel Mill toolpaths?
A. Increase step-over
B. Control arc tolerance
C. Lift tool slightly to clear chips and reduce heat
D. Enable backlash control

Q35. The Area Mill toolpath is mainly used for:
A. Finishing open chains
B. Creating text engraving
C. Milling between closed loops
D. Slotting flat faces

Q36. Which checkbox in Area Mill adds rounds to sharp corners of a model?
A. Profile tolerance
B. Corner rounding
C. Arc filtering
D. Lead in/out

Q37. What is the use of the "Blend Mill" toolpath?
A. To cut narrow slots
B. To finish closed contours
C. To machine between two open chains
D. To engrave along curves

Q38. In Slot Mill toolpaths, how is depth of cut specified?
A. Automatically by tool length
B. Based on pocket height
C. Explicitly along the Z axis
D. Using the tool compensation

Q39. What is the purpose of the “Arc Filter/Tolerance” page in Slot Mill toolpath dialog box?
A. Set tool radius
B. Create planes for arcs
C. Filter out unwanted chains
D. Set tolerance for arcs and toolpath deviation

Q40. Which parameter controls the width of a chamfer in Model Chamfer toolpaths?
A. Bottom offset
B. Cut direction
C. Chamfer width
D. Tool angle

Q41. What is the effect of “Bottom offset” in a Model Chamfer toolpath?
A. Adds finishing pass
B. Sets angle of chamfer
C. Adjusts plunge rate
D. Stops tool before full chamfer depth

Q42. What is the main application of Engrave toolpaths?
A. Creating accurate bores
B. Milling flat surfaces
C. Artistic machining and text printing
D. Cutting slots through stock

Q43. In Engrave toolpath, if you want to emboss the text instead of cutting into it, which option should be selected?
A. At depth
B. On top
C. Emboss mode
D. XY Offset

Q44. What is the use of the “Angle for flat cutter offset” in Engraving toolpaths?
A. Control spindle angle
B. Used for rough V-groove machining
C. Adjust backlash
D. Sets inclination of tool holder

Q45. What does the “XY Stock to leave” parameter define in Engraving toolpaths?
A. Amount of material to retain on Z axis
B. Maximum plunge depth
C. Material to leave on sides of engraving
D. Width of toolpath

Q46. What must be done before using Feature Based Milling (FBM) in Mastercam?
A. Create an STL file
B. Define stock using Stock Setup
C. Select 3D toolpath mode
D. Enable wireframe chaining

Q47. In FBM, what is the function of the "Slug cutting" option?
A. Create pockets in wood
B. Convert chains into walls
C. Replace pocket toolpaths with contour toolpaths for stock removal
D. Increase cutter engagement

Q48. Which check box in FBM allows Mastercam to detect features automatically?
A. Recognize tapered features
B. Use tool library
C. Preferred tooling
D. Automatic initial feature detection

Q49. In the FBM Finish Tools page, which checkbox should be selected if part walls are tapered?
A. Use tool library
B. Match wall draft with taper tool
C. Allow slug cutting
D. Filter by tool type

Q50. What does the "Detect" button do in the FBM Mill dialog box?
A. Compiles all toolpaths
B. Saves toolpath under new name
C. Divides the part into zones based on machining
D. Automatically runs post-processor

Q51. Which feature in FBM Mill must be set up before toolpath generation can begin?
A. Setup Parameters
B. Tool Library
C. Stock
D. Sweep Path

Q52. What happens when you select the "Use tools in part file" checkbox in the FBM Mill tool dialog?
A. Mastercam creates new tools automatically
B. Mastercam searches the default library only
C. Only tools already in the current file are used
D. All operations use only default settings

Q53. The "Recognize tapered features" checkbox in Setup Parameters is used to:
A. Ignore features with taper
B. Enhance tool accuracy
C. Include tapered features in machining
D. Limit operations to 2D only

Q54. Which feature in Feature Detection Parameters allows you to define the cutting strategy for round features?
A. Edge Curves
B. Hole Milling
C. Mill round features with this cycle
D. Recognize holes greater than diameter

Q55. When is Slug Cutting typically used?
A. When using high-speed tools
B. When working with composite or wooden material
C. For intricate metal machining
D. For deep drilling in steel

Q56. What happens when the "Create as needed" checkbox is selected in the Setup Parameters?
A. Only existing tools are used
B. Mastercam prompts for every tool change
C. Tools are auto-created if not found in the library
D. FBM Mill is disabled

Q57. Which toolpath uses two curves—one as a sweep path and another as a section—to generate 2D toolpaths?
A. Ruled Toolpath
B. Swept 2D
C. Lofted
D. Circle Mill

Q58. Which parameter specifies the retraction height from which the tool plunges in Swept 2D Toolpath?
A. Feed Plane
B. Rapid Depth (abs)
C. Across Cut Distance
D. Start Angle

Q59. In Swept 3D Toolpaths, what must be specified before selecting curves?
A. Number of toolpaths
B. Depth of cut
C. Number of across contours
D. Starting angle

Q60. What is the Revolved toolpath used for?
A. Milling along a single curve
B. Circular milling
C. Milling by revolving a curve around an axis
D. Creating point-to-point motion

Q61. Which toolpath blends multiple curves for a smooth transition in milling?
A. Ruled
B. Lofted
C. Swept 2D
D. Circle Mill

Q62. Which toolpath is specifically designed for creating chamfers on holes?
A. Advanced Drill
B. Helix Bore
C. Chamfer Drill
D. Point Toolpath

Q63. What unique feature does the Advanced Drill toolpath offer?
A. Single-depth cuts
B. Multi-speed threading
C. Different behaviors per toolpath segment
D. Default roughing paths only

Q64. What option in Circle Mill allows changing the cutting diameter from geometry?
A. Override geometry diameter
B. Lead In/Out
C. Stepover
D. Radius Tolerance

Q65. What does the "Start at center" checkbox in Helix Bore toolpath do?
A. Begins toolpath from the edge
B. Forces tool to cut only outer edge
C. Starts the path from the center of the hole
D. Sets arc sweep angle to 0

Q66. What is the main purpose of Thread Mill toolpaths?
A. Create spiral holes
B. Drill deep pockets
C. Cut threads using milling operations
D. Perform flat surface threading

Q67. In FBM Drill toolpath, what does selecting the 'Plane' option in grouping do?
A. Organizes holes based on their axis plane
B. Sorts by tool size
C. Groups holes by geometry
D. Applies default roughing

Q68. What is the difference between Auto Drill and FBM Drill toolpaths?
A. Auto Drill requires no tool selection
B. FBM Drill detects features manually
C. Auto Drill requires manual hole selection
D. There's no difference

Q69. What is the function of the Start Hole toolpath?
A. Drills holes before final finishing
B. Starts point-based operations
C. Creates plunge entry holes before roughing
D. Adds tapping codes

Q70. Which movement types are selectable in the Point toolpath?
A. Manual feed only
B. Rapid or Feed rate
C. Lead/Out
D. Sweep Path only

Q71. What does the Manual Entry toolpath allow?
A. Automatic feature detection
B. Adding text/code to the toolpath
C. Editing imported files
D. Linking parameters manually

Chapter 10

3D Milling Toolpaths

Topics Covered

The major topics covered in this chapter are:

- ***Introduction***
- ***3D Roughing Toolpaths***
- ***3D Finishing Toolpaths***

INTRODUCTION

The toolpaths discussed in previous chapter were for 2D milling. But milling is not confined to 2D. The milling machine can cut material in 3D space along 5 different axes. In this chapter, we will discuss tools to create 3D and Multi-axis toolpaths. The tools to perform 3D milling are available in the **3D** group of **Ribbon**; refer to Figure-1. The tools to perform 3D milling are categorized in two sections: **Roughing** and **Finishing**. Note that 3D toolpaths are also called Surface toolpaths. These tools are discussed next.

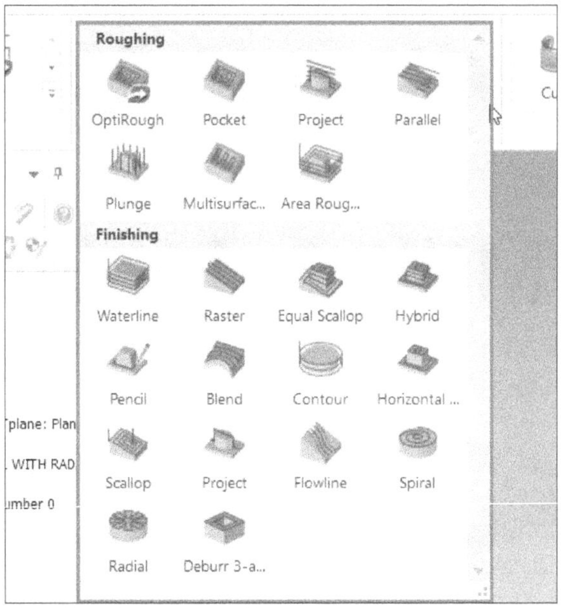

Figure-1. 3D milling toolpaths

3D ROUGHING TOOLPATHS

The 3D roughing toolpaths are used to remove large amount of material with much bigger tolerance range. Various 3D roughing toolpaths are discussed next.

OptiRough Toolpaths

The OptiRough toolpath is used to rough the part using Mastercam's optimum cutting strategy which removes large stock in single operation. The procedure to use this toolpath is given next.

- Click on the **OptiRough** tool from the **3D** group of **Toolpaths** tab in the **Ribbon**. The **3D High Speed Toolpaths-Dynamic OptiRough** dialog box will be displayed; refer to Figure-2.

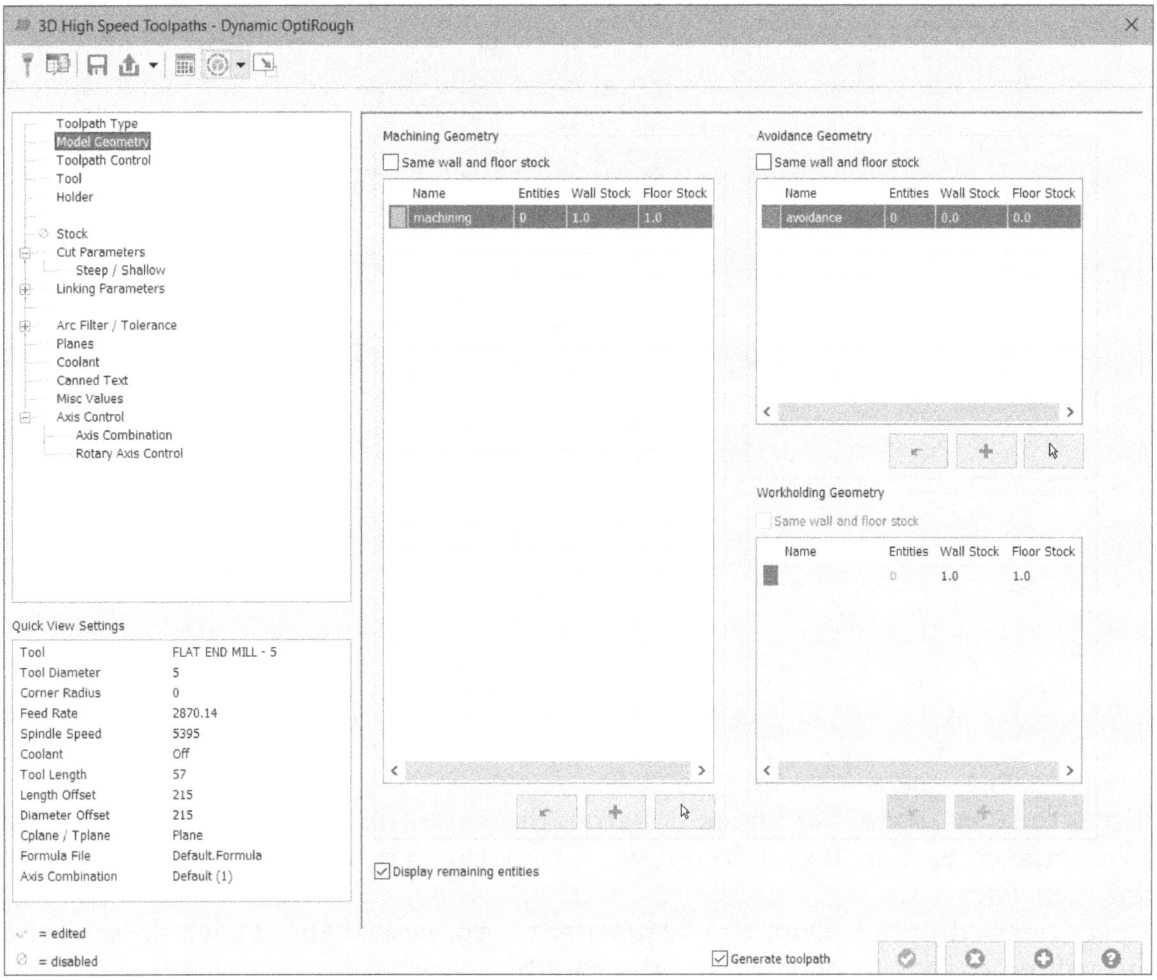

Figure-2. 3D High Speed Toolpath-Dynamic OptiRough dialog box

- Click on the **Select entities** button from the **Machining Geometry** area to select the objects for 3D machining and click on the **End Selection** button. Similarly, you can use the **Select entities** button from the **Avoidance Geometry** area of the dialog box to select objects to be avoided by 3D dynamic rough machining.
- Select the **Toolpath Type** option from the left area of the dialog box and make sure the **Roughing** radio button and the **Dynamic OptiRough** option are selected in this page. If you want to perform finishing then select the **Finishing** radio button from this page then respective toolpaths will be displayed.
- Click on the **Toolpath Control** option from the left area of the dialog box to set parameters related to containment boundary.
- In the **Containment boundary** area, there are two radio buttons: **Stay inside** and **From Outside**. Select the **Stay inside** radio button if you want to machine a pocket feature and select the **From outside** radio button if you want to machine a boss feature with open boundaries. Note that if you have a pocket with islands then you should select the **Stay inside** radio button from this area.
- Select desired tool and tool holder from the **Tool** and **Holder** pages in the dialog box as discussed earlier.
- If you want to use the dynamic optirough toolpath to remove material left by other toolpaths then select the **Stock** option from the left area. The options will be displayed as shown in Figure-3.

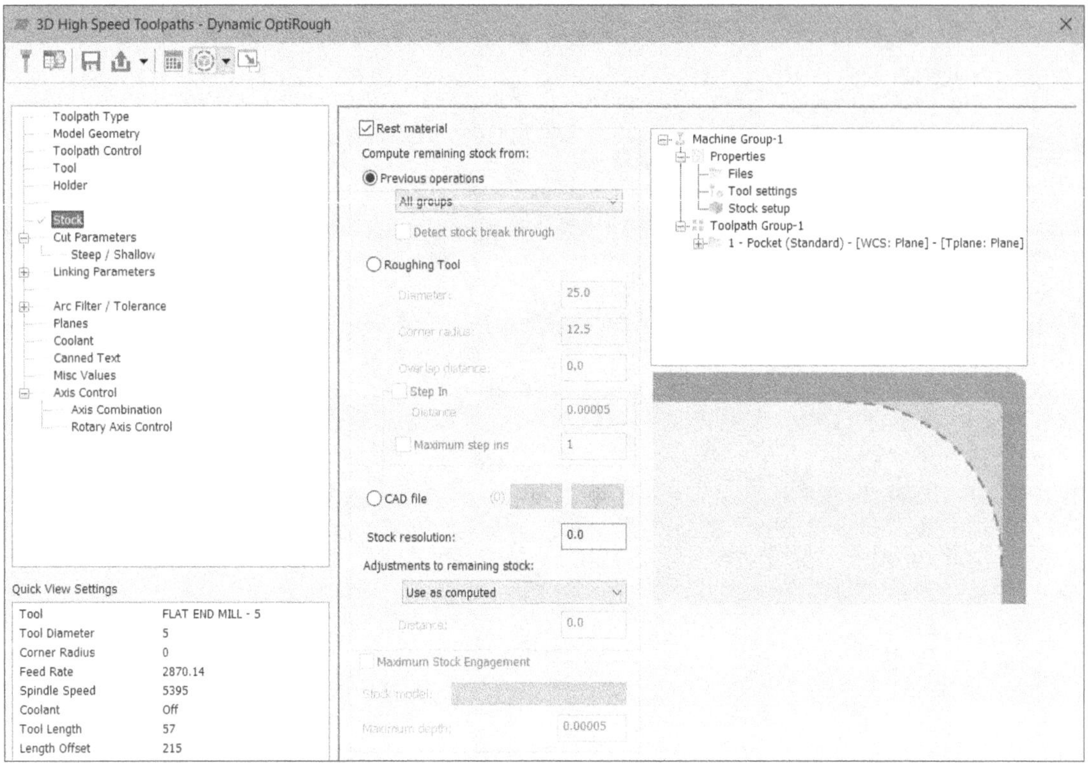

Figure-3. Stock page in the dialog box

- Select the **Rest material** check box from the page and specify desired parameters as discussed earlier. If you do not want to perform rest mill then keep this check box cleared.
- Select desired option from the **Adjustments to remaining stock** area to specify the value of stock to be left after the roughing operation.

Cut Parameters

- Click on the **Cut Parameters** option from the left area. The options will be displayed as shown in Figure-4.

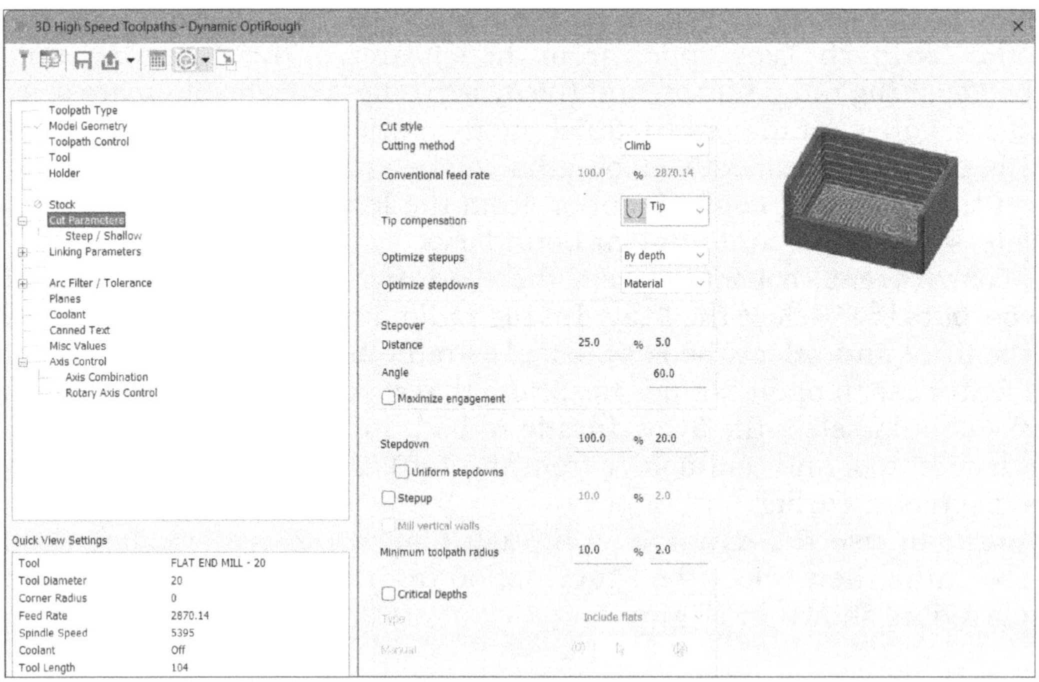

Figure-4. Cut Parameters page in Dynamic OptiRough dialog box

- Most of the parameters in this dialog box have been discussed in previous chapter, so no repetition here! Click in the **Optimize stepups** drop-down and select desired option. If you select the **By depth** option then tool will cut at equal z level in all pockets selected in the part. If you select the **Next closest** option then the tool will first perform step down operations in all the pockets at equal Z level and then it will perform step up operation in all the pockets at equal Z level. If you select the **By pocket** option then the tool will one by one rough each pocket in step down and then it will use the Next closest strategy to step up; refer to Figure-5.

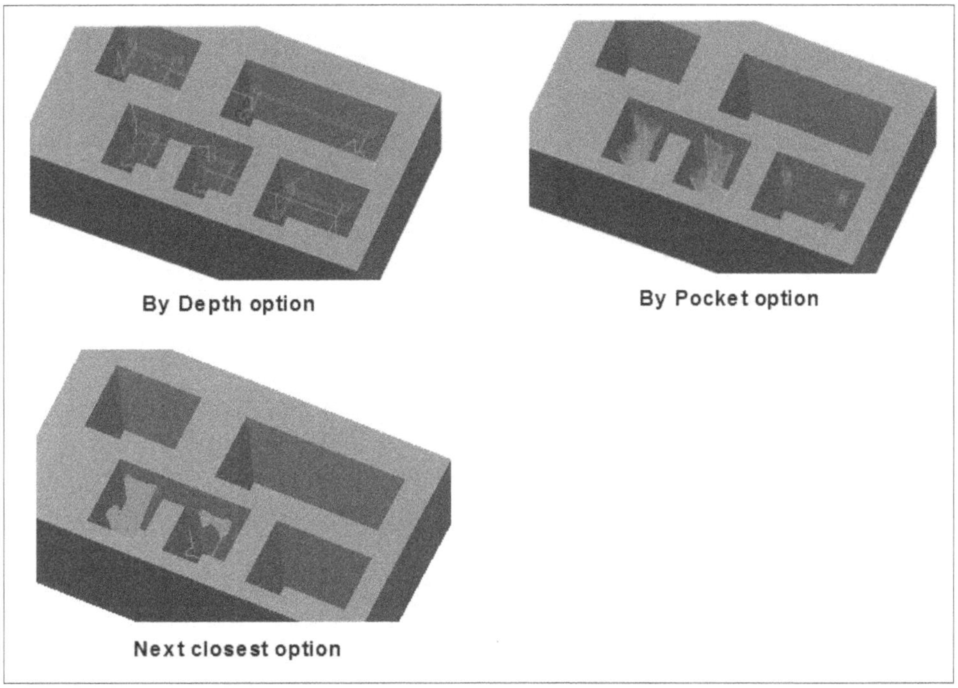

Figure-5. Optimize stepup options

- Similarly, select desired option from the **Optimize stepdowns** drop-down. Select the **Material** option to start cutting from the material near to tool. Select the **Air** option to start cutting from the lesser material area. Select the **None** option to start cutting from the location where tool of previous toolpath left cutting.
- Specify the **Stepup**, **Stepdown**, and **Stepover** values in the **Passes** area of the dialog box.
- Select the **Mill vertical walls** check box to automatically calculate material which can be spared by current operation on walls and generate extra cutting passes in waterline pattern to remove that material. Note that this will increase total machining time.
- Select the **Critical Depths** check box and select **Include flats** option from the **Type** drop-down if you want to include automatically identified flat faces in the machining passes. If you want to manually select the flat faces that are to be machined then select the **Include manual** option from the drop-down and select desired faces as discussed earlier.
- If your part has steep or shallow faces then click on the **Steep/Shallow** option from the left area and specify the depth in Z upto which your tool should machine such faces.

Toolpath Control

- The options in this page are used to specify how tool compensation will be applied with respect to containment boundary selected; refer to Figure-6.

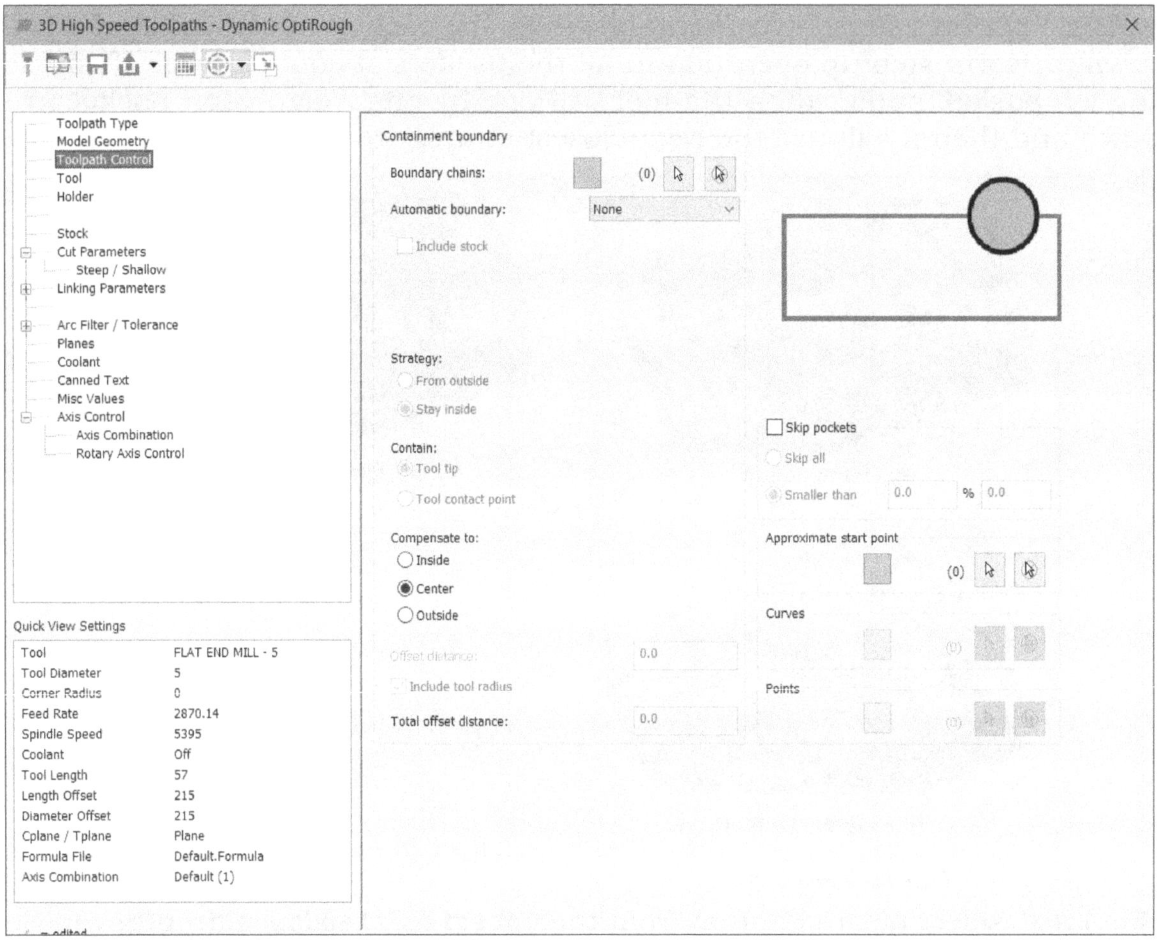

Figure-6. Tool containment page

- Select the **Inside** radio button from the **Compensate to** area to keep tool completely inside the containment boundary (generally required in pocket cuts). Select the **Outside** radio button to keep tool completely outside the containment boundary. Similarly, select the **Center** radio button to keep tool tip over the containment boundary. Note that you can also specify offset values if **Inside** or **Outside** radio button is selected.
- Specify the tool entry method in the **Transition** page of this dialog box as discussed in previous chapters.

Linking Parameters

- Click on the **Linking Parameters** option from the left area of the dialog box. The options in the page will be displayed as shown in Figure-7.

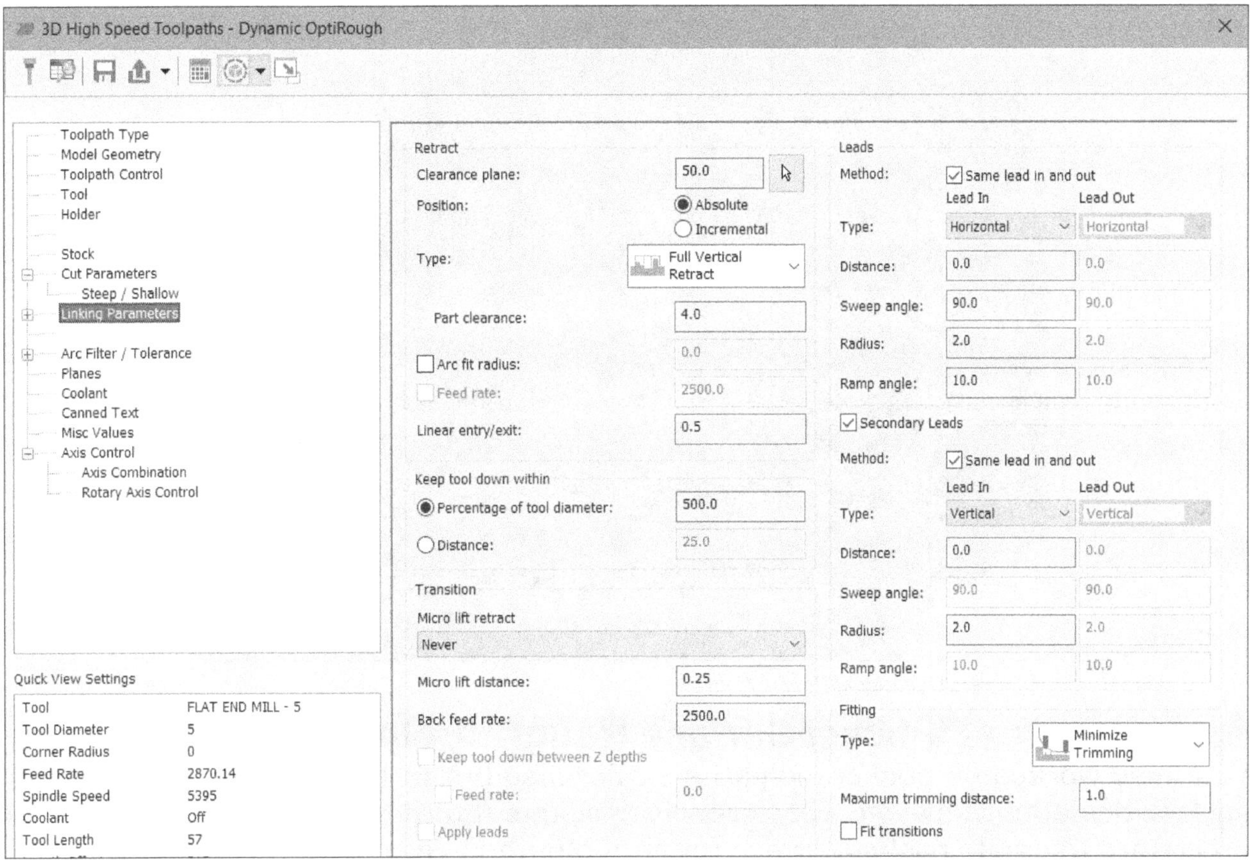

Figure-7. Linking Parameters page

- Specify the clearance plane distance in the **Clearance plane** edit box.
- Select desired option from the **Type** drop-down of **Retract** area to specify how tool will retract in non-cutting moves. On selecting the **Minimum Vertical Retract** option, the tool will retract at distance specified in **Part clearance** edit box and follow the trajectory of part edges. On selecting the **Minimum Distance** option, the tool will retract directly for larger distance but follow the trajectory of part for smaller distances. On selecting the **Full Vertical Retract** option, the cutting tool will move to retraction plane directly.
- Select the **Percent of tool diameter** radio button from the **Keep tool down within** area to define amount of material from current cutting pass to next cutting pass in percentage of tool diameter for which tool will remain invested in stock. Select the **Distance** radio button from this area if you want to specify minimum stock amount before cutting tool will retract.
- Select desired option from the **Micro lift retract** drop-down to define conditions for which cutting tool will micro lift. Specify related parameters for micro lift in the **Transition** area.
- Select the **Same lead in and out** check box to use same parameters for entering and exiting cutting passes from the **Leads** area. If you want to create secondary leads as well then select the **Secondary Leads** area. Specify the parameters in these areas as discussed earlier.
- Select desired option from the **Fitting Method** drop-down in the **Fitting** area. The options of this area are used to specify the movement of tool along the corners.
- Specify the other parameters as required and click on the **OK** button. The toolpath will be created; refer to Figure-8.

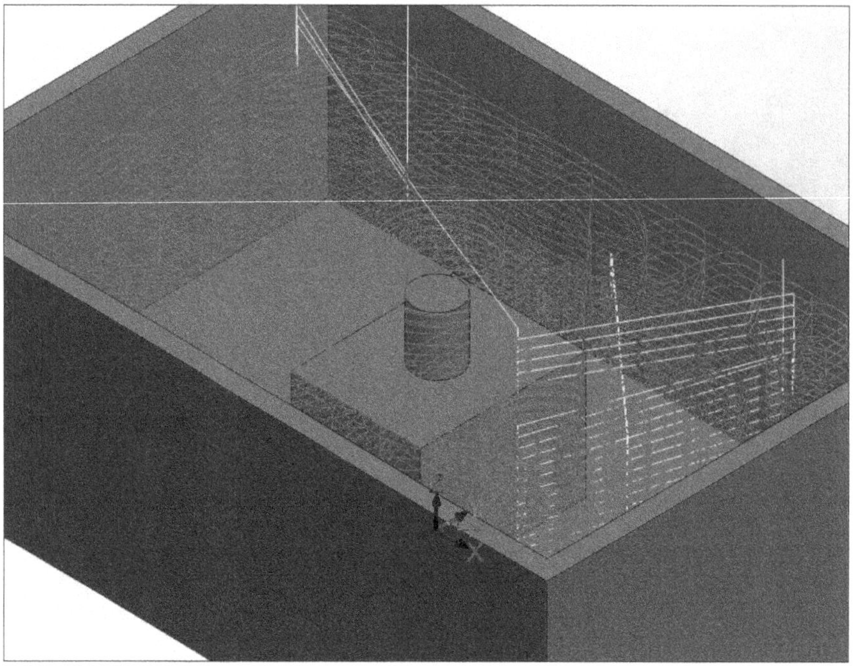

Figure-8. Dynamic optirough toolpath

Pocket Surface Rough Toolpath

You have worked on pocket toolpaths earlier also but in those cases, there was no surface deviation. Now, we will work with pockets that have irregular surfaces. The procedure to create pocket surface rough toolpath is given next.

- Click on the **Pocket** tool from the **3D** group of **Toolpaths** tab in the **Ribbon**. You will be asked to select surfaces to be machined.
- Select desired surfaces and press **ENTER**. The **Toolpath/surface selection** dialog box will be displayed; refer to Figure-9.

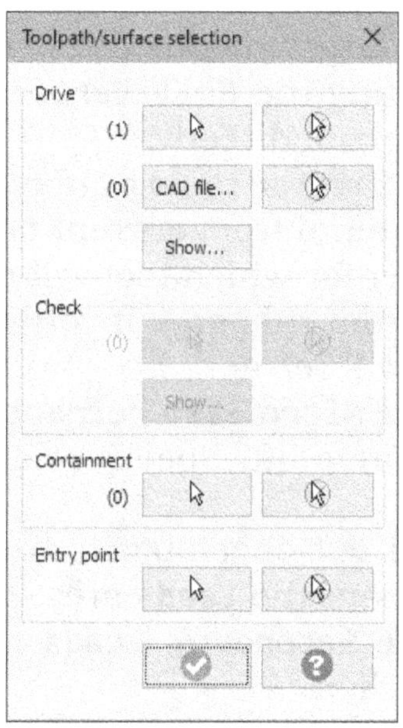

Figure-9. Toolpath/surface selection dialog box

- Click on the **Select** button from the **Containment** area of the dialog box and select the curves creating boundary of pocket. Similarly, click on the **Select** button from the **Entry point** area of the dialog box and select desired point on body to be used as start point of toolpath; refer to Figure-10.

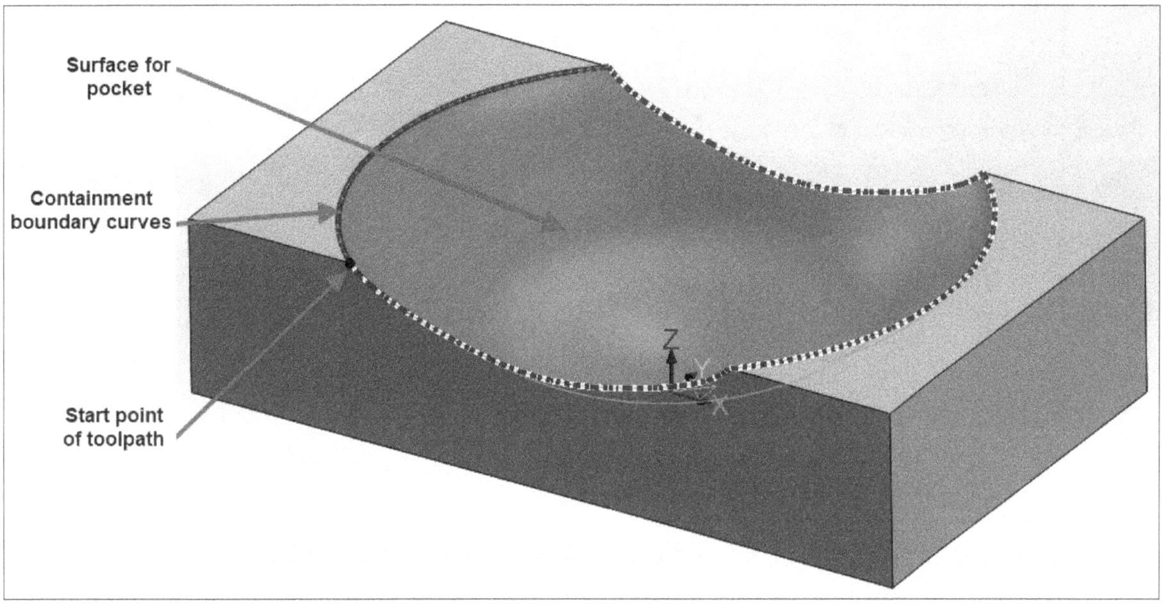

Figure-10. Selection for pocket surface rough toolpath

- After selecting desired entities, click on the **OK** button from the dialog box. The **Surface Rough Pocket** dialog box will be displayed; refer to Figure-11.

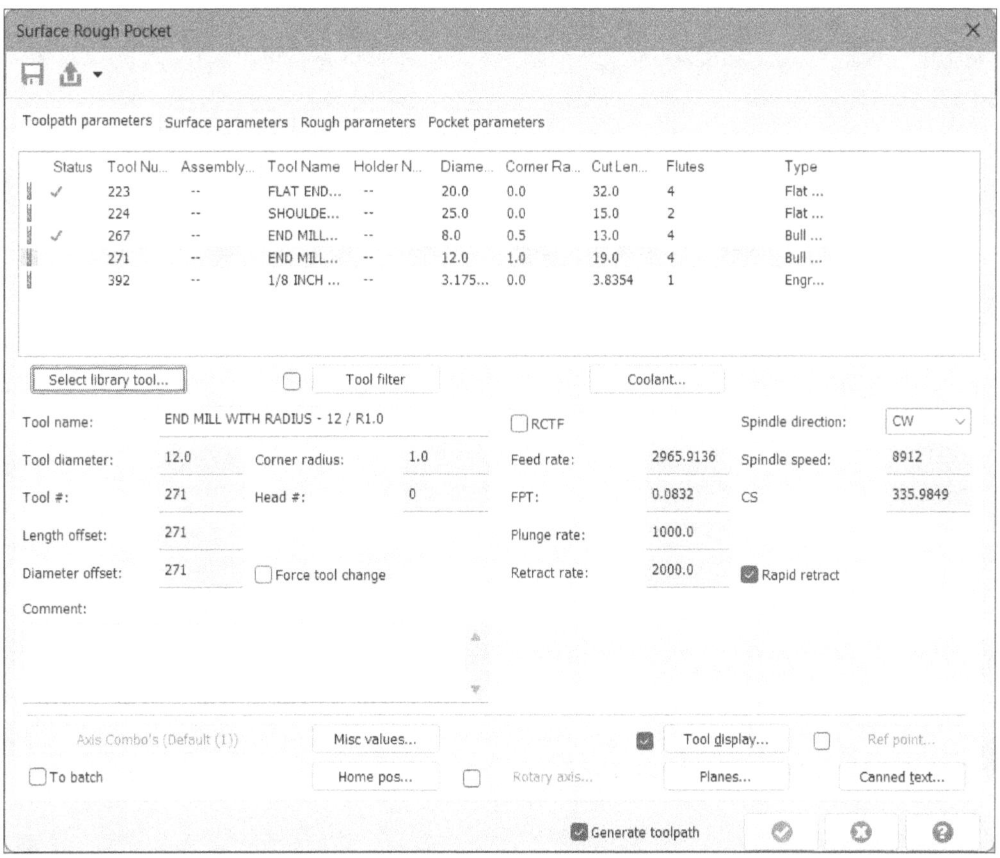

Figure-11. Surface Rough Pocket dialog box

- Specify desired parameters in **Toolpath parameters** and **Surface parameters** tabs as discussed earlier.

- Click on the **Rough parameters** tab. The options in the dialog box will be displayed as shown in Figure-12.

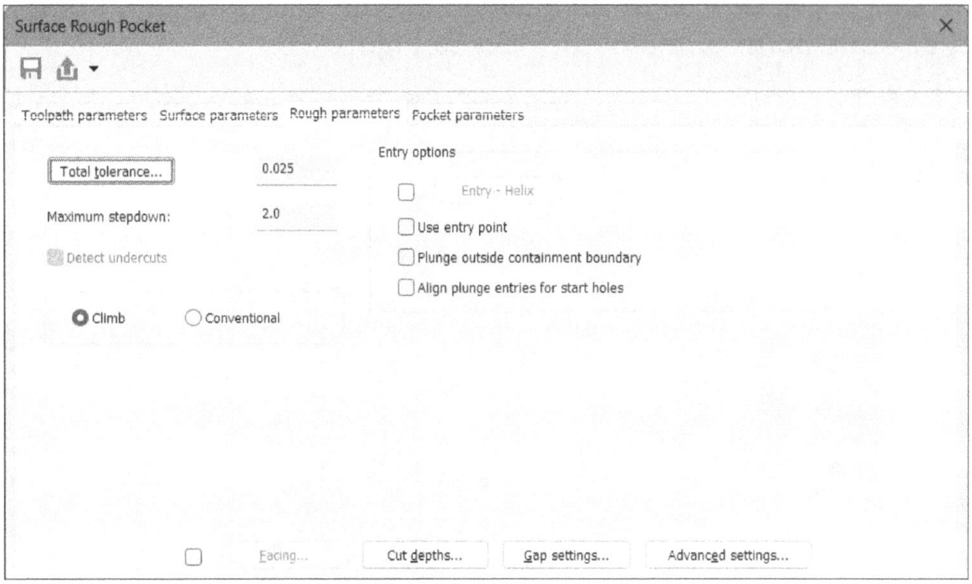

Figure-12. Options in Rough parameters tab

- From the **Entry options** area, select desired entry method for the tool. If there is a requirement of facing before pocket toolpath then select the check box before **Facing** button and click on the **Facing** button to specify parameters.
- Click on the **Pocket parameters** tab in the dialog box and select desired cutting method; refer to Figure-13.

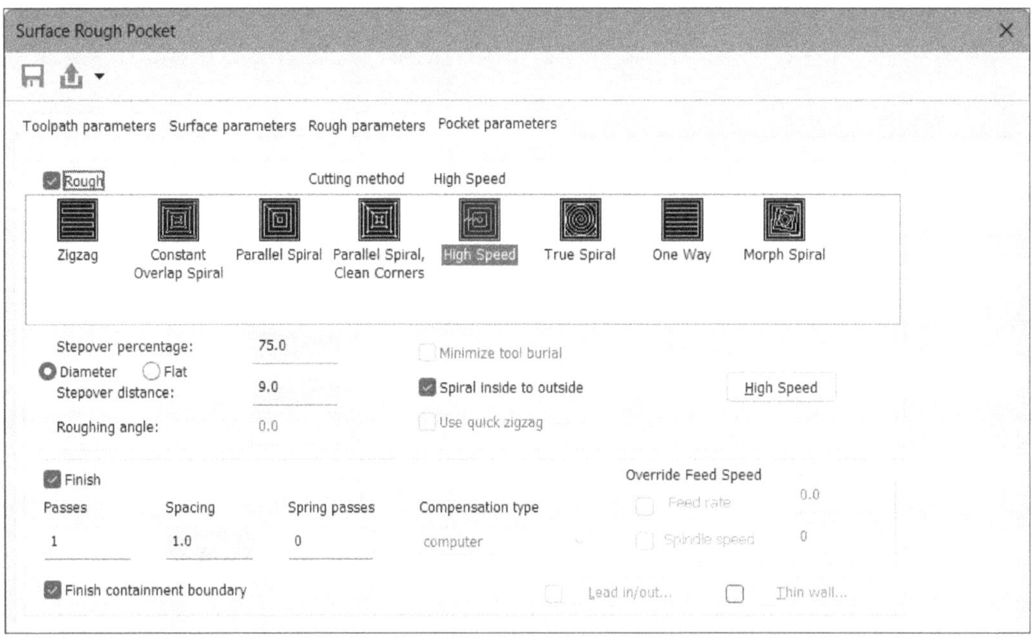

Figure-13. Pocket parameters tab

- Specify the other parameters as required and click on the **OK** button. The toolpath will be generated; refer to Figure-14.

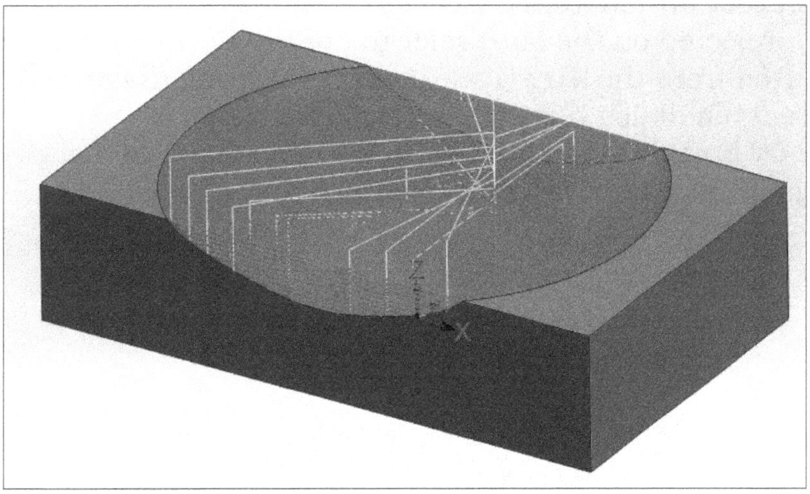

Figure-14. Pocket Surface Rough Toolpath

Project Rough Surface Toolpath

The Project Rough Surface toolpath is used to machine a toolpath projected on the surface of workpiece. You can also engrave text or curves on the face of part by using this tool; refer to Figure-15. The procedure to use this toolpath is given next.

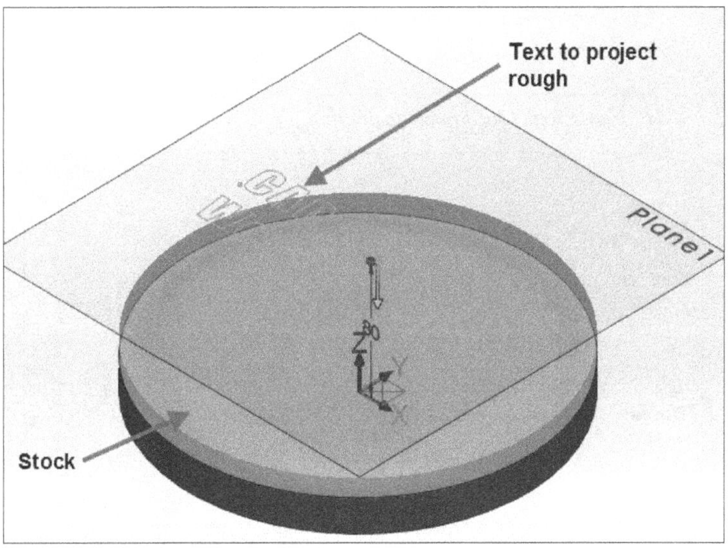

Figure-15. General arrangement for Project rough tool

- Open the model with stock and make sure that you have text or curve to be machined on the face of part. Click on the **Project** tool from the **Roughing** section of **3D** drop-down in the **Ribbon**. The **Select Boss/Cavity** dialog box will be displayed. Select the **Boss** radio button if you want to machine the surroundings of projected curves and leave the area near curves safe. Select the **Cavity** radio button from the dialog box, if you want to machine the projected curves up to specified depth.
- Select desired option as discussed earlier and click on the **OK** button. You will be asked to select the face of model on which you want to project rough surface toolpath.
- Select desired face; refer to Figure-16 and press **ENTER**. The **Toolpath/surface selection** dialog box will be displayed as discussed earlier.

- Click on the **Select** button from the **Curves** area of the dialog box and select desired curves to be projected on the face; refer to Figure-17. After selecting curves, click on the **OK** button from the **Wireframe/Solid Chaining** dialog box. The **Toolpath/surface selection** dialog box will be displayed again.
- Click on the **OK** button from the dialog box. The **Surface Rough Project** dialog box will be displayed; refer to Figure-18.

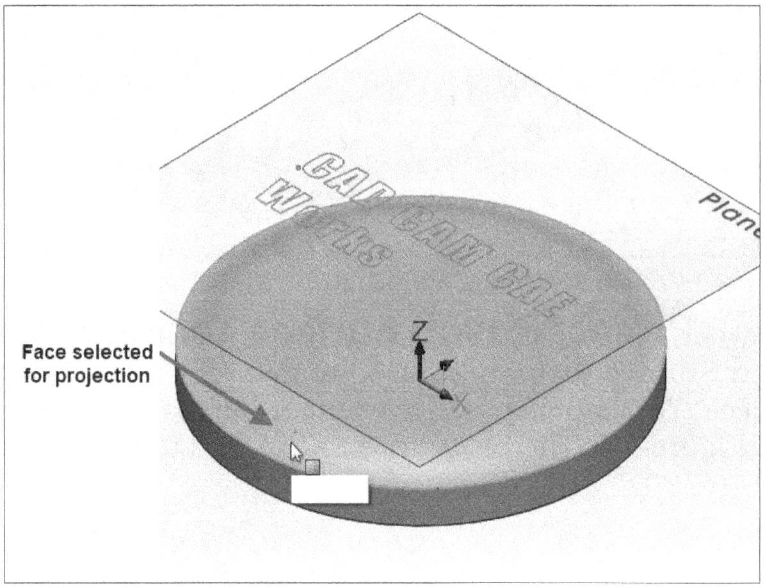

Figure-16. Face selected for project toolpath

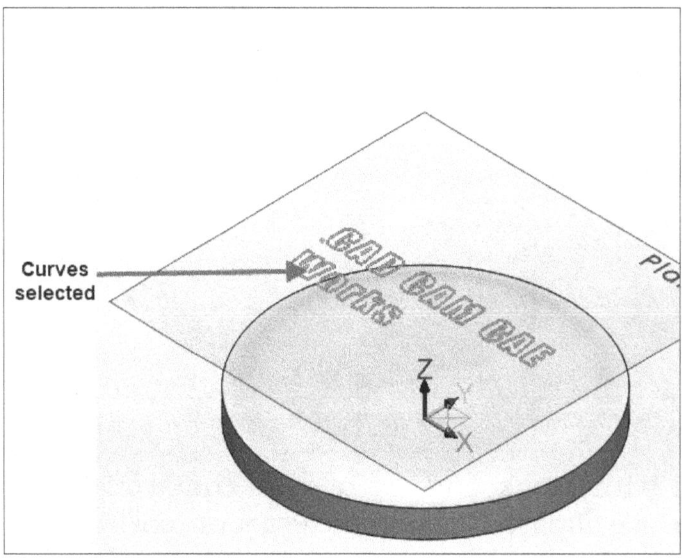

Figure-17. Sketch selected for projection

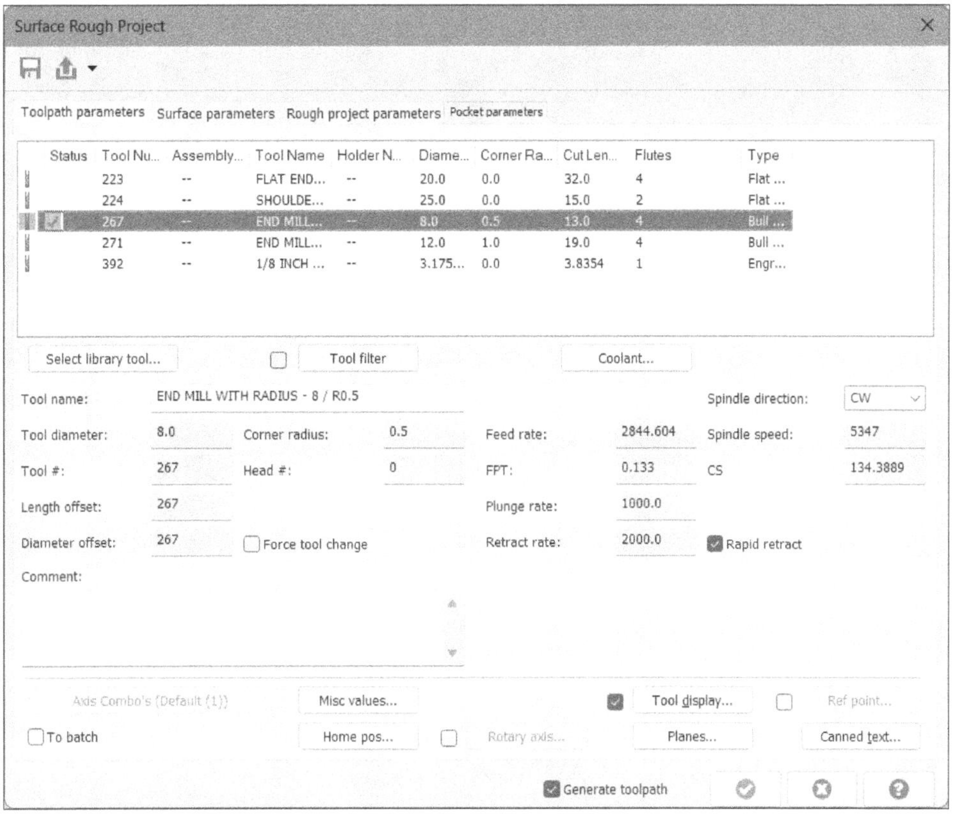

Figure-18. Surface Rough Project dialog box

- Select desired tool and specify the parameters in various tabs of this dialog box as discussed earlier. Click on the **OK** button. The toolpath will be generated; refer to Figure-19.

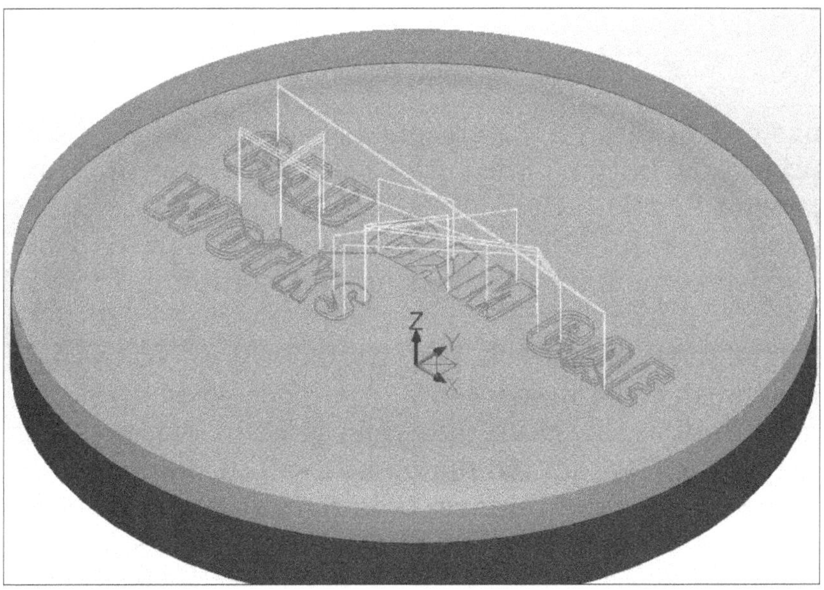

Figure-19. Toolpath generated for project rough

Parallel Rough Surface Toolpath

The Parallel Rough Surface toolpath is used when you need to remove material by parallel line motion of tool; refer to Figure-20. The procedure to use this tool is given next.

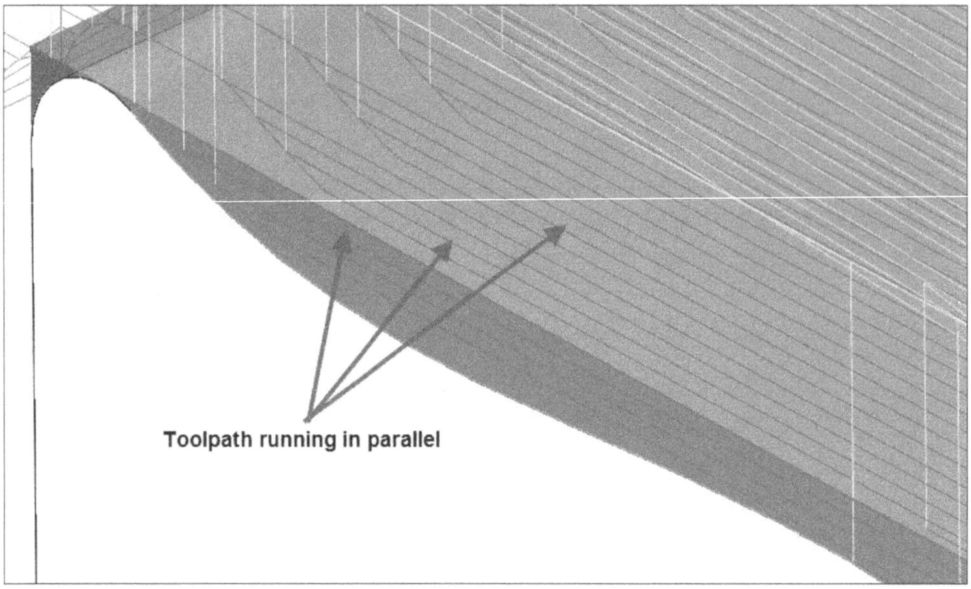

Figure-20. Parallel surface roughing

- Click on the **Parallel** tool from the **3D** group in the **Toolpaths** tab of the **Ribbon**. The **Select Boss/Cavity** dialog box will be displayed; refer to Figure-21.

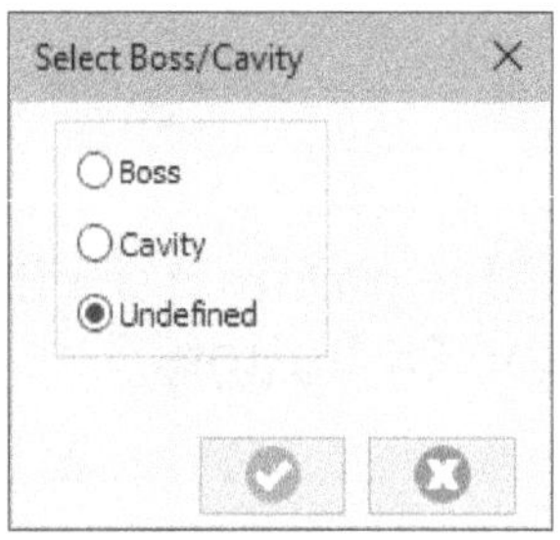

Figure-21. Select Boss/Cavity dialog box

- Select the **Boss** radio button if the surface is coming upward from the base plane. Select the **Cavity** radio button if the surface is going downward from the base plane. Select the **Undefined** radio button if you are not able to decide then Mastercam will automatically use suitable strategy. Note that there can be high difference between tool movements based on **Boss** or **Cavity** radio button selection; refer to Figure-22.
- After selecting the radio button, click on the **OK** button. You will be asked to select surfaces/faces/mesh to be machined.
- Select the faces that you want to machine; refer to Figure-23 and press **ENTER**. The **Toolpath/surface selection** dialog box will be displayed.
- If you want to avoid any feature/face/boundary then click on the **Select** button from the **Check** area of the dialog box and select the faces of the feature that you want to avoid.
- If you want to define a boundary within which tool can perform machining then click on the **Select** button from the **Containment** area and select the faces/edges/curves to define boundary.
- If you want to specifically define the approximate start point/entry point/radial point then click on the **Select** button from the **Approximate starting points** area and select desired point.
- After selecting desired entities, click on the **OK** button from the dialog box. The **Surface Rough Parallel** dialog box will be displayed; refer to Figure-24.

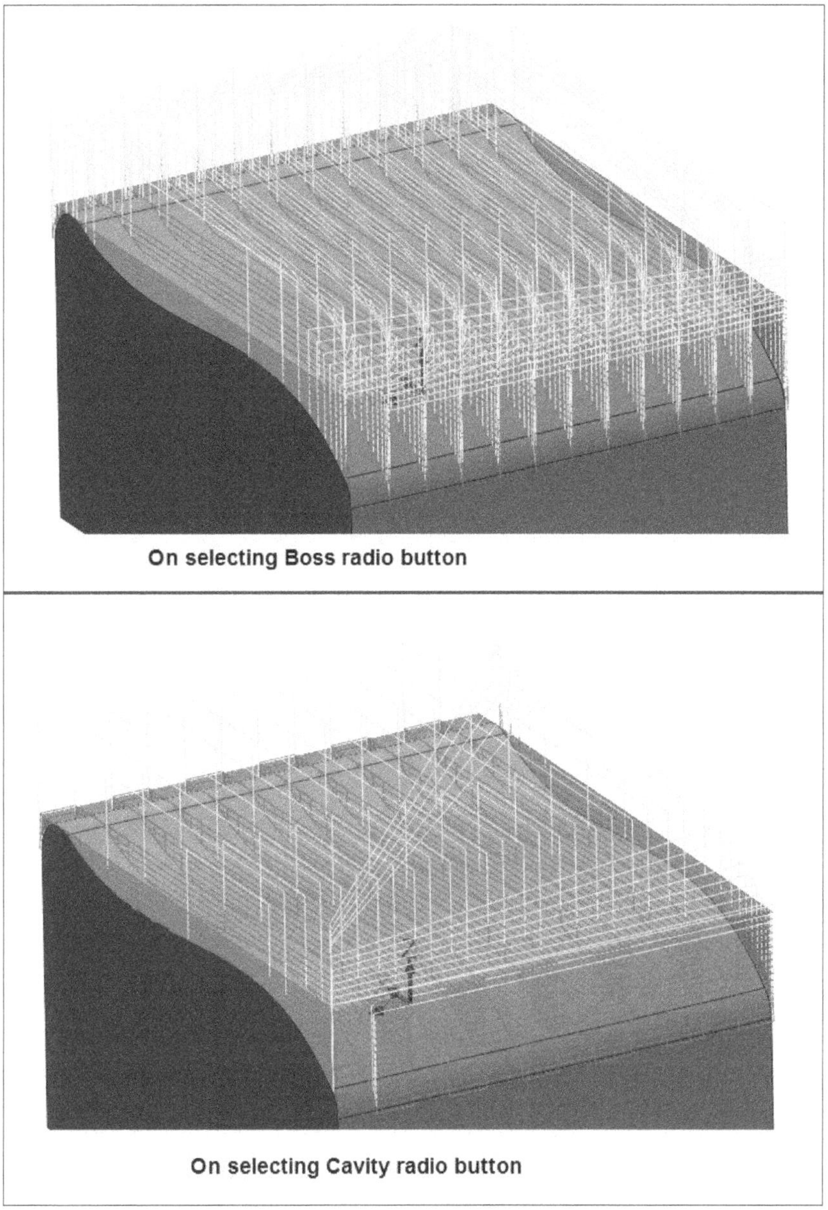

Figure-22. Difference between toolpaths on selecting Boss and Cavity radio button

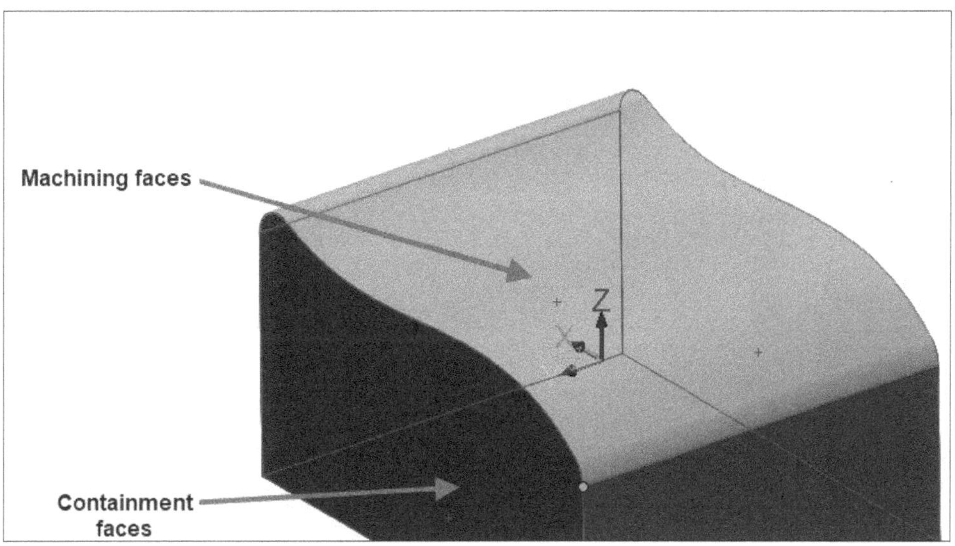

Figure-23. Faces selected for parallel rough toolpath

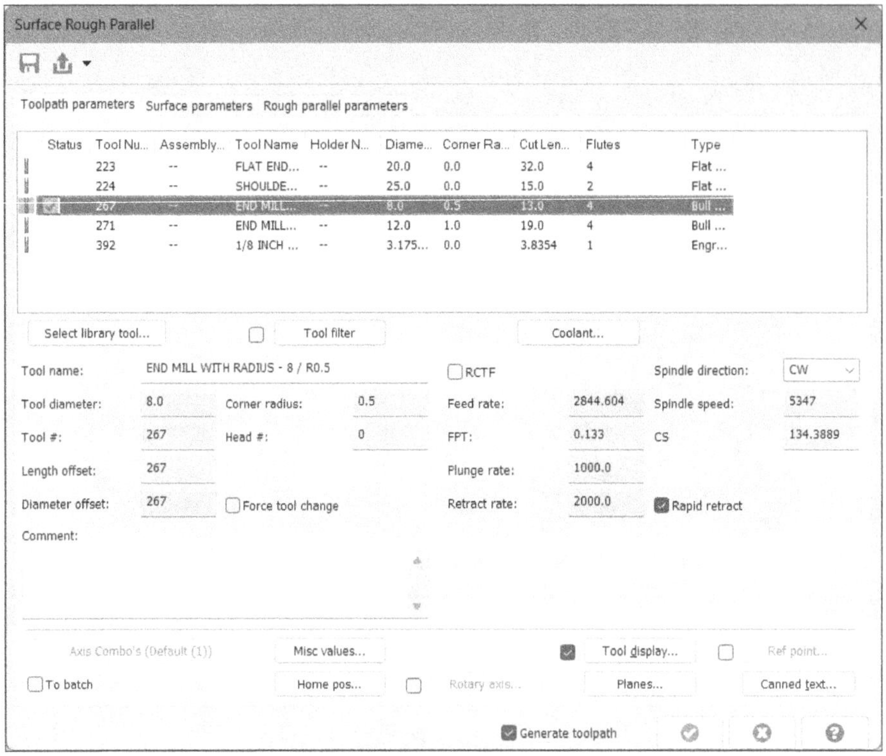

Figure-24. Surface Rough Parallel dialog box

Toolpath Parameters

- Click on the **Select library tool** button and select desired tool by double-clicking from the **Tool Selection** dialog box displayed. Generally, bull end mill or ball end mill cutter is used for surface milling.
- Select the **RCTF** check box if you want to use radial chip thinning calculations to set feed rate and spindle speed.
- Specify the other parameters in this tab as discussed earlier.

Surface Parameters

- Click on the **Surface parameters** tab in the dialog box. The options will be displayed as shown in Figure-25.

Figure-25. Surface Parameters tab

- Specify the retraction distance and feed plane distance in **Retract** and **Feed plane** edit boxes, respectively.
- Select the check box before **Clearance** button and specify desired clearance if required. Clearance is used to retract the tool at higher level to avoid collision and allow free movement of workpiece.
- Specify the amount of stock to leave on faces to be machined and check surfaces in the **Stock to leave on drive** and **Stock to leave on check** edit boxes.
- Select desired options for tool compensation and tool tip compensation from respective areas.

Rough Parallel Parameters

- Click on the **Rough parallel parameters** tab in the dialog box. The options will be displayed as shown in Figure-26.

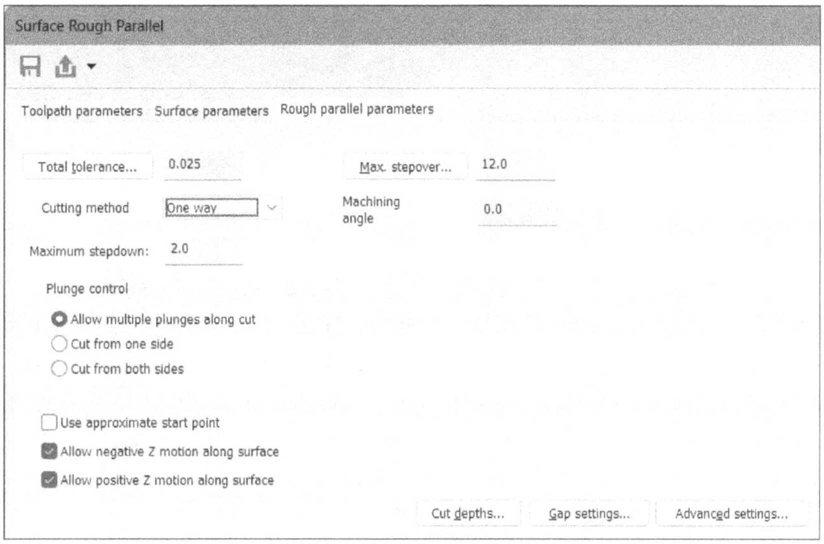

Figure-26. Rough parallel parameters tab

- Specify the cutting parameters and tolerances in this tab.
- Click on the **Cut depths** button and specify the depth of cut parameters in the **Cut Depths** dialog box displayed.
- Note that you should carefully define tolerances to get good surface finish on the part. To define tolerances, click on the **Total tolerance** button and specify parameters in the **Arc Filter/Tolerance** dialog box displayed on choosing the tool. Set desired parameters in the dialog box and click on the **OK** button.
- After specifying desired parameters, click on the **OK** button from the dialog box. The toolpath will be generated; refer to Figure-27.

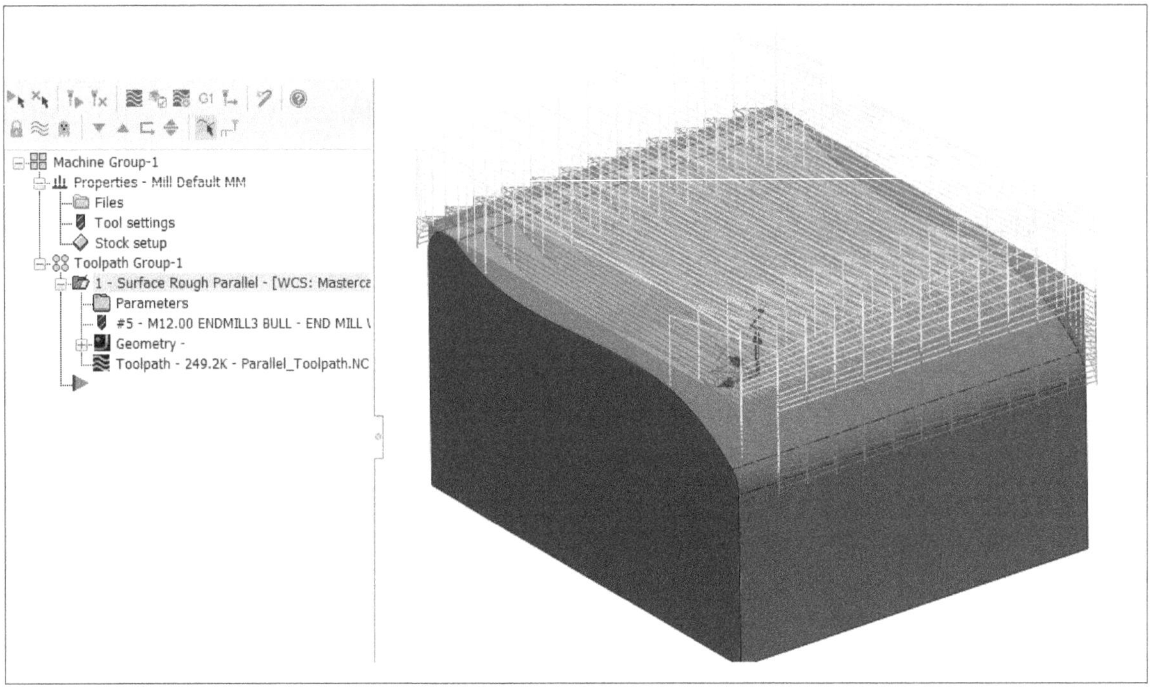

Figure-27. Toolpath generated for parallel rough

Plunge Rough Surface Toolpath

The Plunge Rough Surface toolpath works in the same way as 2D Plunge toolpath but this toolpath also considers the curvature of walls and base while cutting. Note that plunge toolpath can be beneficial if you have unstable machine and you need to machine deep slots or you need to machine corners with round. In general, plunge milling is an alternate method when side milling is not possible due to vibrations. The procedure to use this tool is given next.

- Click on the **Plunge** tool from the **3D** group of the **Toolpaths** tab in the **Ribbon**. You will be asked to select the faces/surfaces/meshes of the features to be machined.
- Select the faces/bodies/features to be machined and press **ENTER**. The **Toolpath/surface selection** dialog box will be displayed.
- Click on the **Select** button from the **Grid** area of the dialog box and select points to define grid plane for plunging; refer to Figure-28.
- Click on the **OK** button from the dialog box. The **Surface Rough Plunge** dialog box will be displayed; refer to Figure-29.

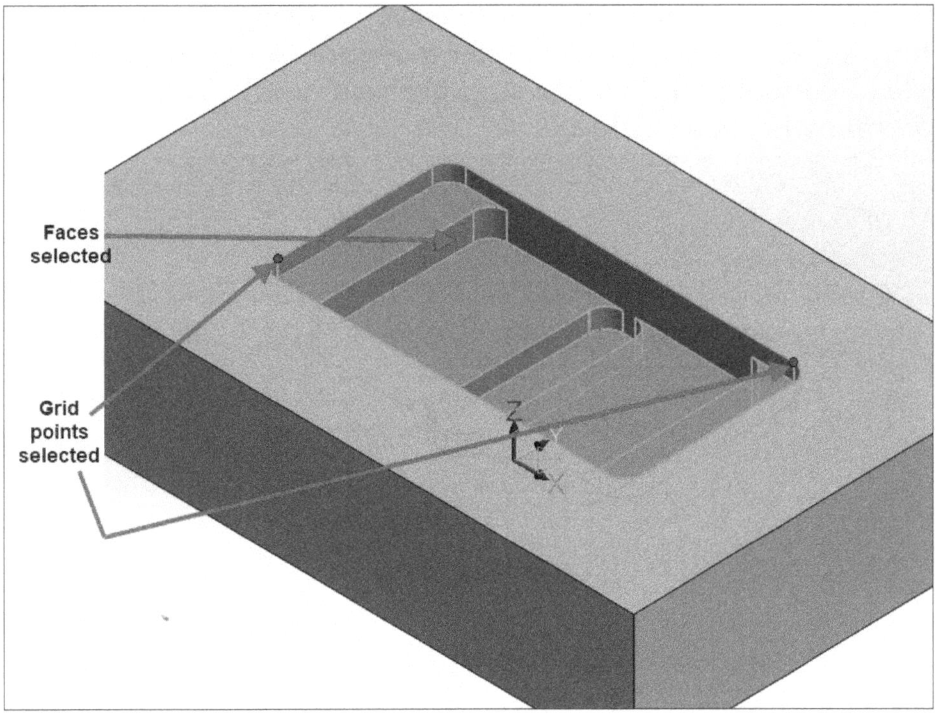

Figure-28. Features and points selected for plunge mill rough

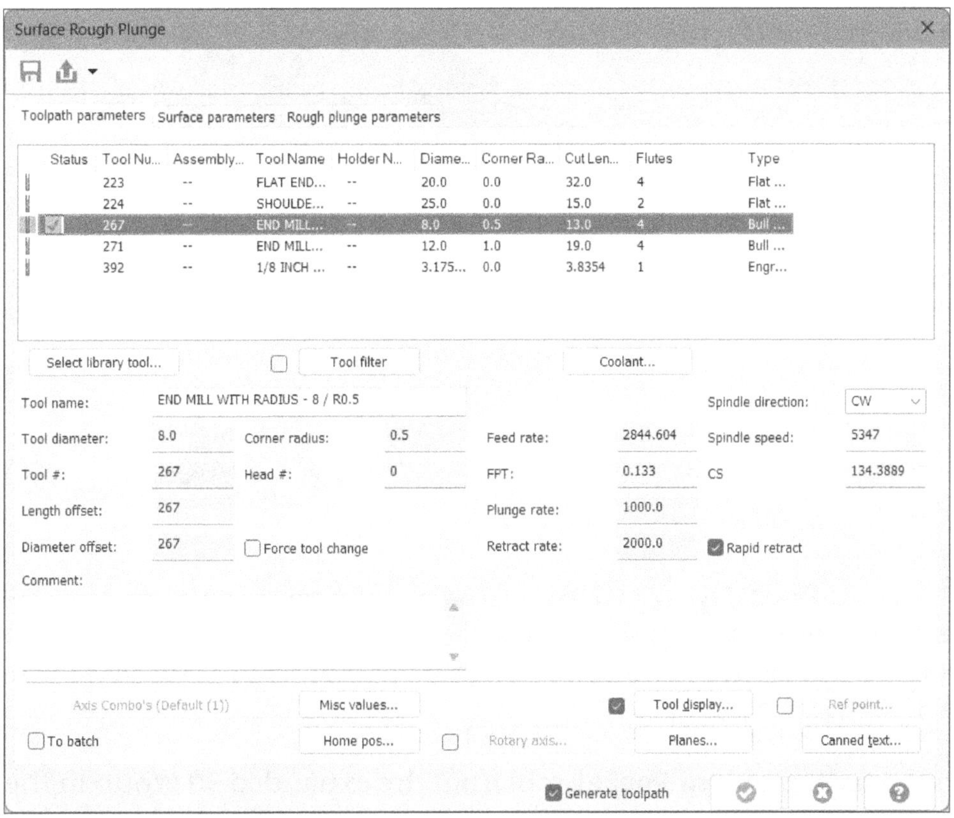

Figure-29. Surface Rough Plunge dialog box

- Specify the parameters as discussed earlier. Make sure you have a higher diameter tool selected.

- Specify the **Max stepdown** and **Maximum stepover** values in **Rough plunge parameters** tab carefully as per the tool selected; refer to Figure-30. A higher Max stepdown can increase load on tool and a higher step-over can leave the material unmachined giving you many holes as output.

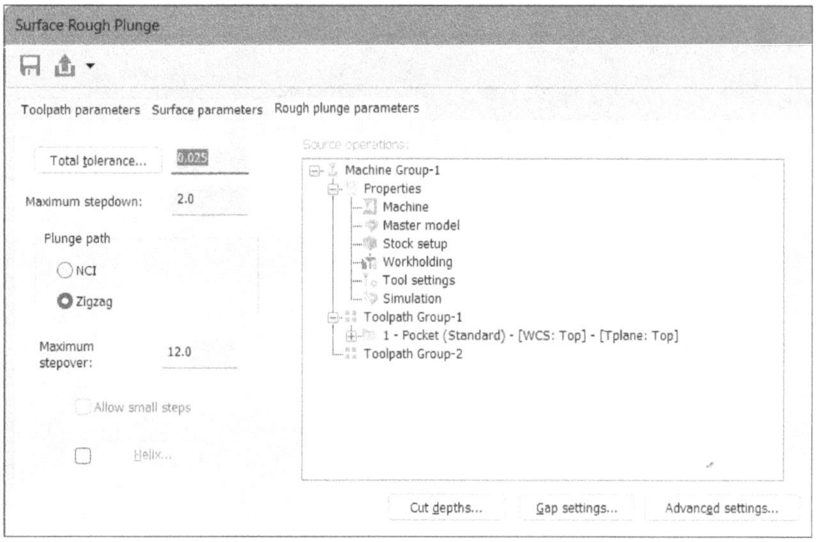

Figure-30. Rough plunge parameters tab

- After specifying parameters, click on the **OK** button. The toolpath will be generated; refer to Figure-31.

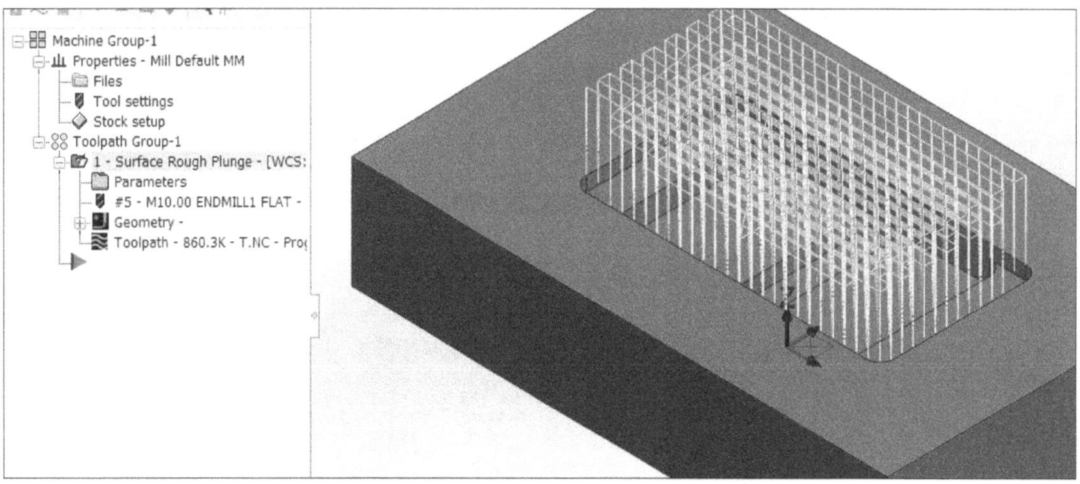

Figure-31. Plunge Surface Rough toolpath generated

Creating Multisurface Pocket Toolpath

The Multisurface pocket toolpath is used to remove large amount of stock from multiple pockets in the model with a series of planar cuts. The procedure to create this toolpath is given next.

- Click on the **Multisurface Pocket** tool from the expanded **3D** group in the **Toolpaths** tab of the **Ribbon**. You will be asked to select faces of the pockets to be machined.
- Select desired faces and press **ENTER**. The **Toolpath/surface selection** dialog box will be displayed.
- Select the containment boundary and entry point as discussed earlier and click on the **OK** button. The **Multisurface Rough Pocket** dialog box will be displayed; refer to Figure-32.

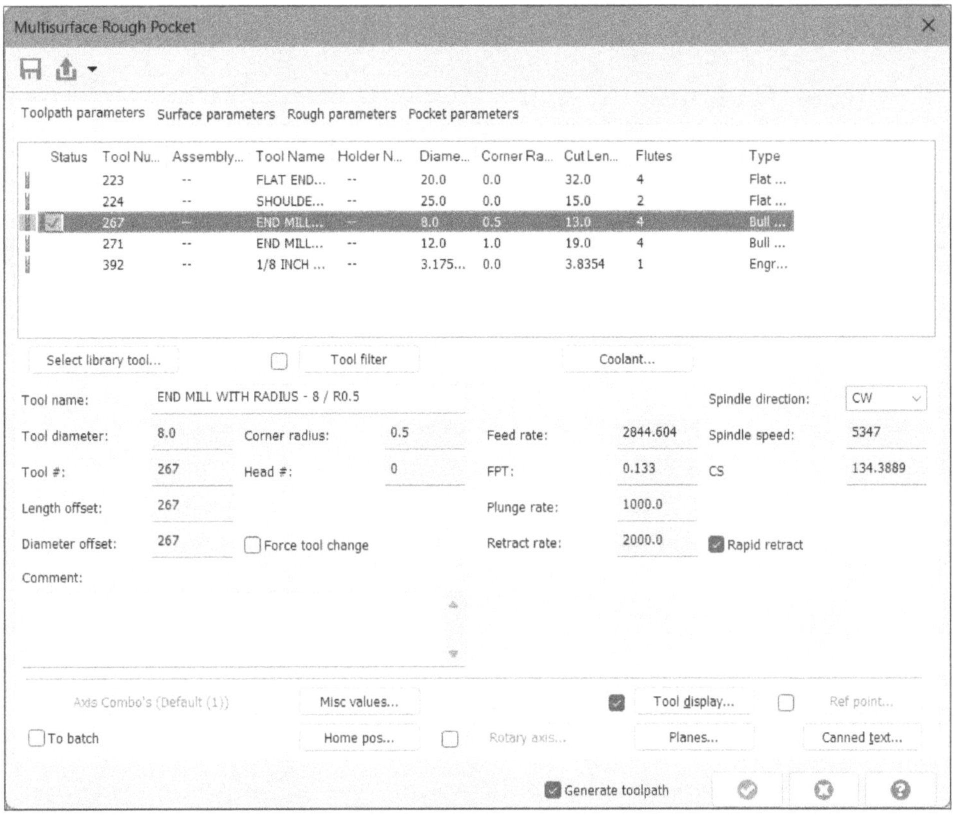

Figure-32. Multisurface Rough Pocket dialog box

- The parameters in the dialog box are similar to **Rough Pocket** dialog box discussed earlier. Set the parameters as desired and click on the **OK** button. The toolpath will be created.

Creating Area Rough Toolpath

The Area Rough toolpath is used to mill selected face area using 3D cutting paths. The most common question is asked here why area rough when dynamic rough toolpaths are available for same work. Answer is Dynamic rough toolpaths are useful when stock is similar in shape to the part but Area Rough is useful when you have a block and you want to rough machine it to get desired shape. The procedure to use this tool is given next.

- Click on the **Area Roughing** tool from the expanded **3D** group in the **Toolpaths** tab of the **Ribbon**. The **3D High Speed Toolpaths - Area Roughing** dialog box will be displayed; refer to Figure-33.

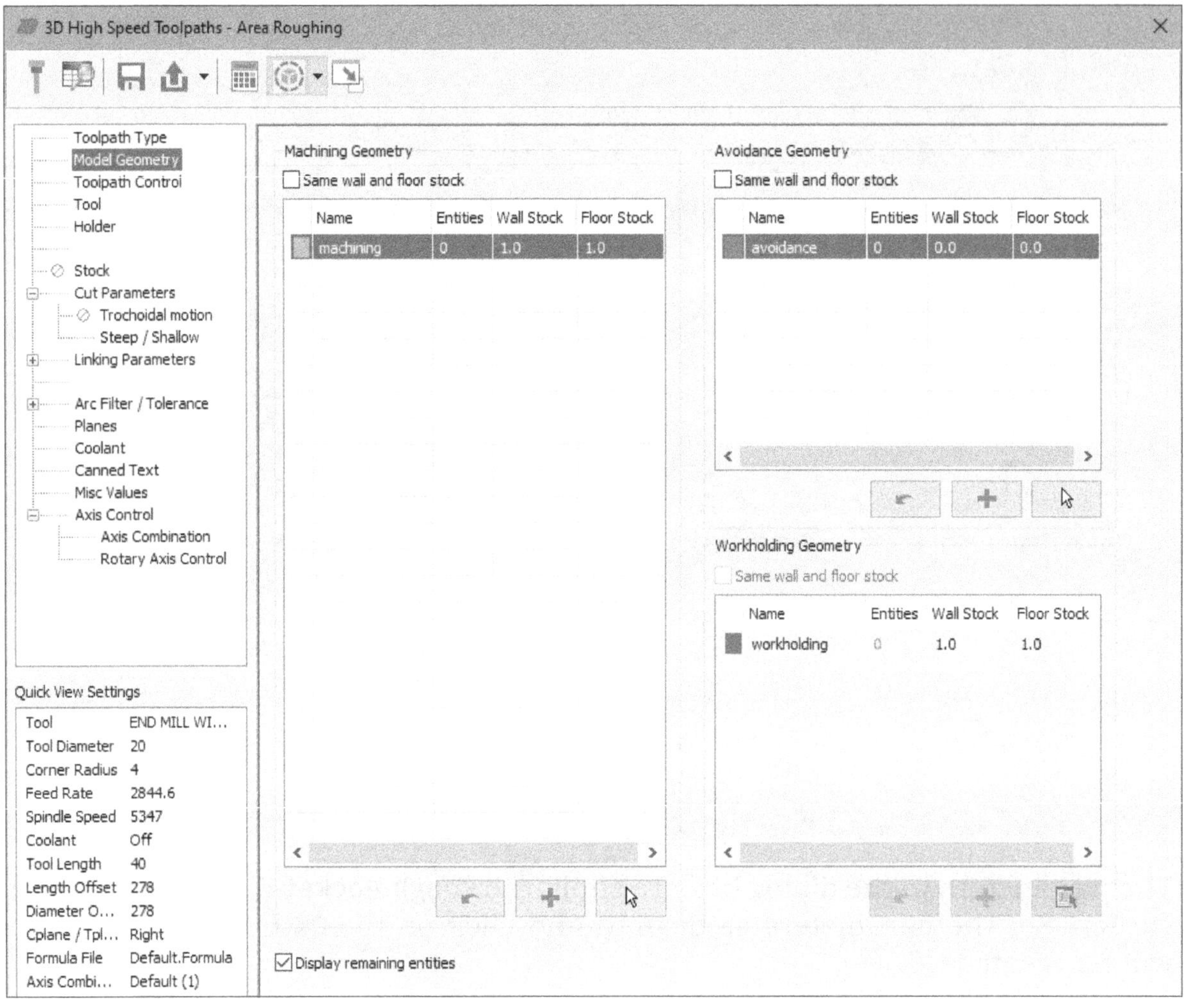

Figure-33. 3D High Speed Toolpaths-Area Roughing dialog box

- Select the faces that you want to be machined and the faces you want to avoid by using the options in the **Machining Geometry** and **Avoidance Geometry** areas respectively; refer to Figure-34 and click on the **OK** button.
- Click on the **Toolpath Control** option from the left area of the dialog box. The page in **3D High Speed Toolpaths - Area Roughing** dialog box will be displayed as shown in Figure-35.

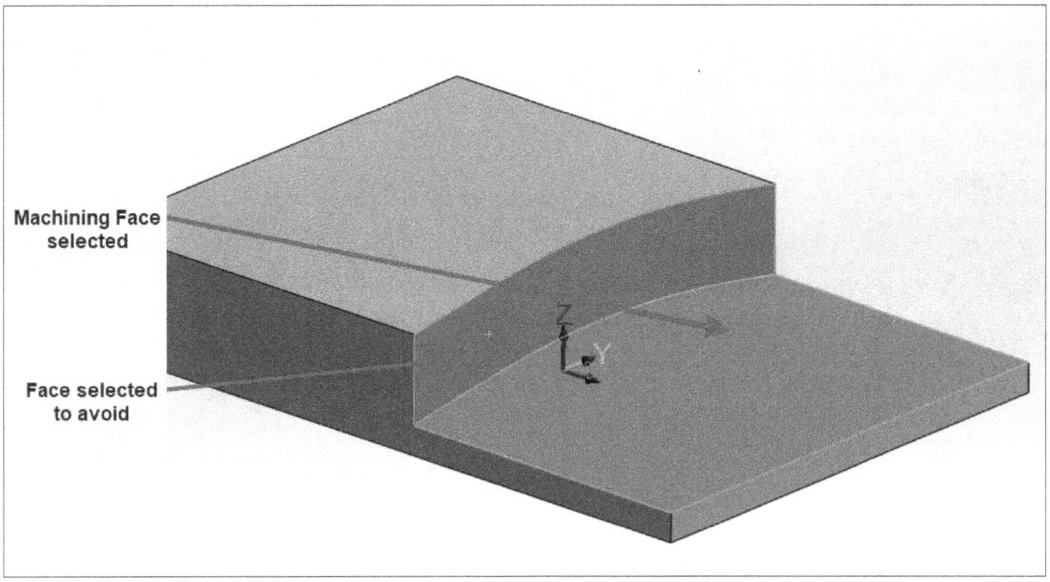

Figure-34. Faces selected for area rough

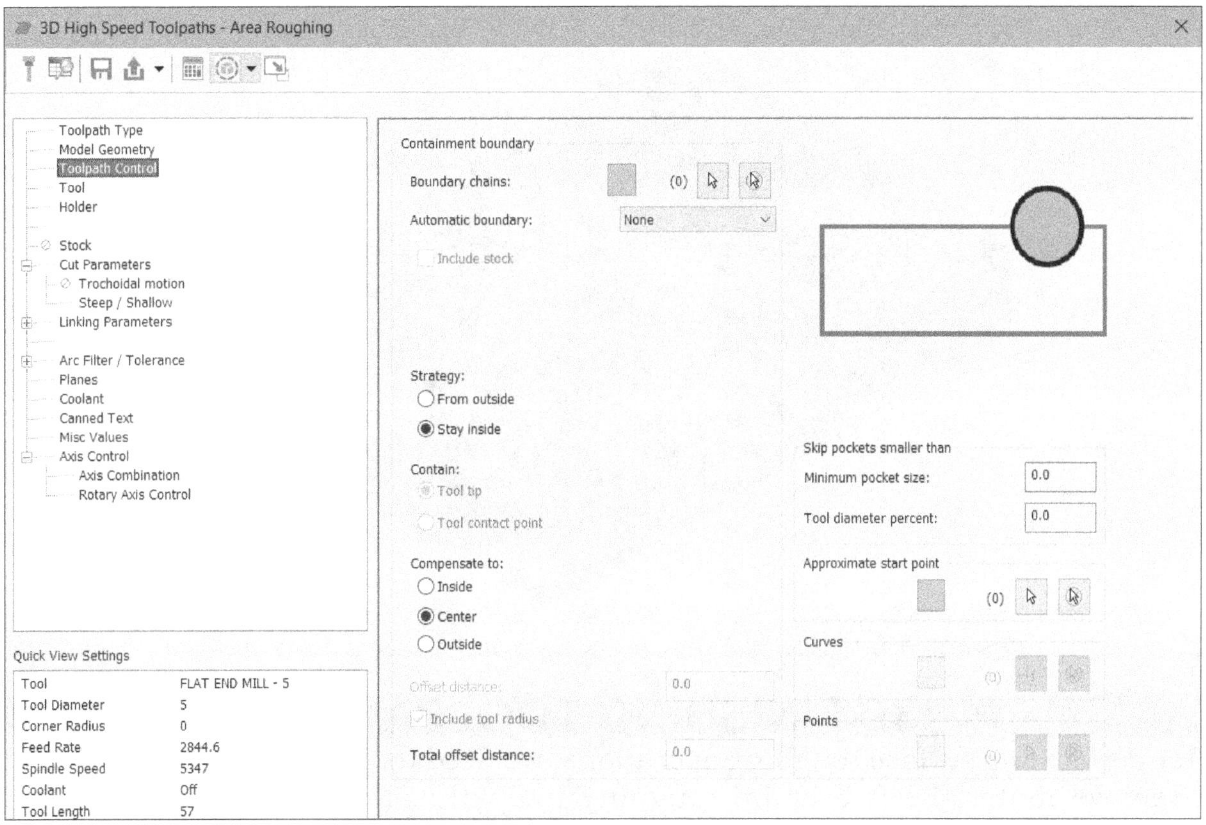

Figure-35. Surface High Speed Toolpath-Area Rough dialog box

- From the **Containment boundary** area, select the **Stay inside** radio button if you want to machine a pocket. If you want to machine a boss feature or the part has open boundary then select the **From Outside** radio button.
- Select the **Trochoidal motion** option from the left area to define the options related to motion of tool while cutting. The options in the dialog box will be displayed as shown in Figure-36. To minimize burial of tool, select the **Minimize burial** radio button from the page and specify desired parameters to create trochoidal motion of tool. Preview of the motion is displayed in right of the page.

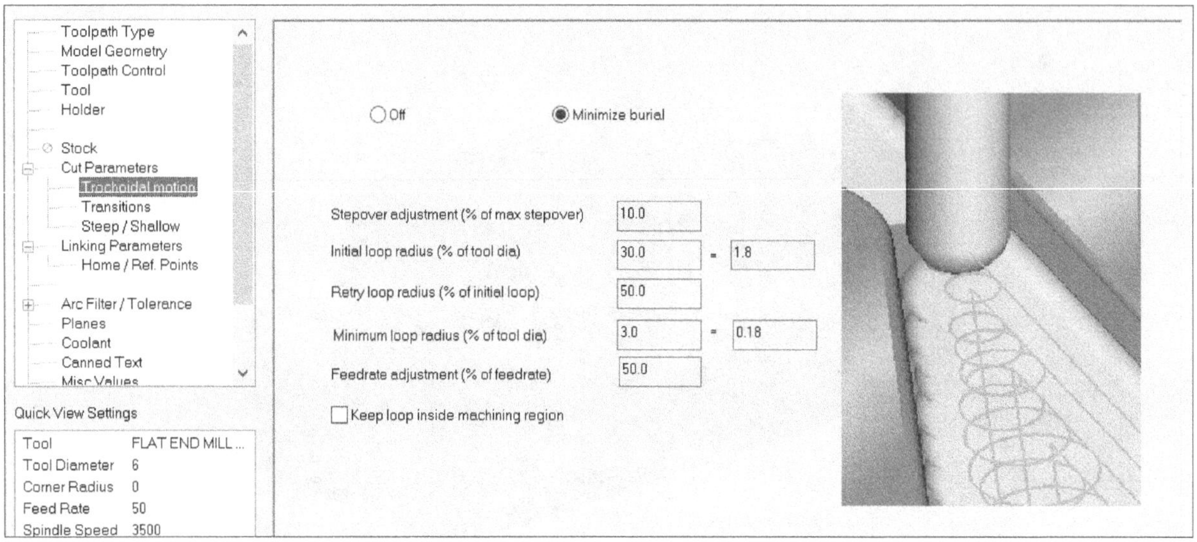

Figure-36. Trochoidal motion options

- Similarly, specify the other parameters and click on the **OK** button to create the toolpath; refer to Figure-37.

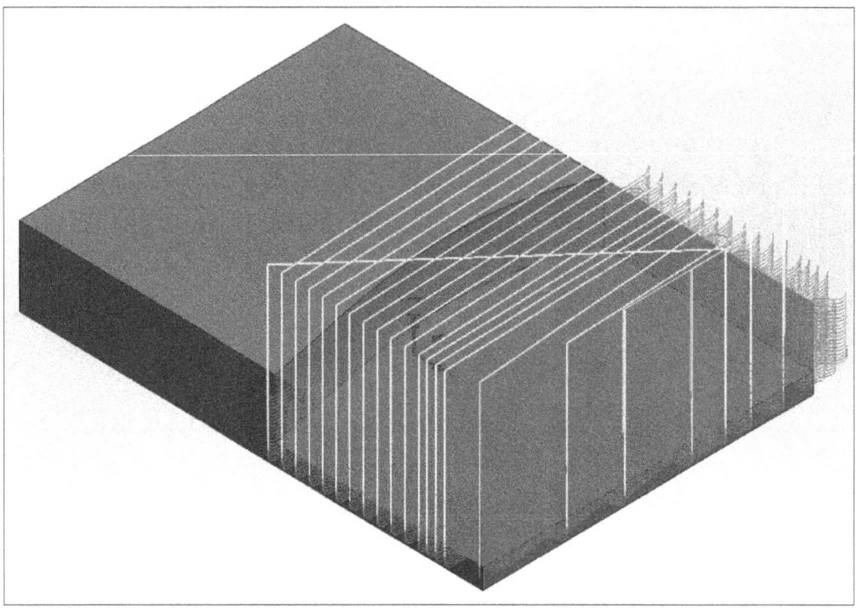

Figure-37. Area rough toolpath

3D FINISHING TOOLPATHS

After performing surface roughing operations, we need toolpaths to perform finishing to remove material left over by roughing toolpaths. Note that after performing roughing, you need a finer tool running at relatively higher speed to remove material in finishing toolpaths. These tools are available in the **Finishing** section of the expanded **3D** group; refer to Figure-38.

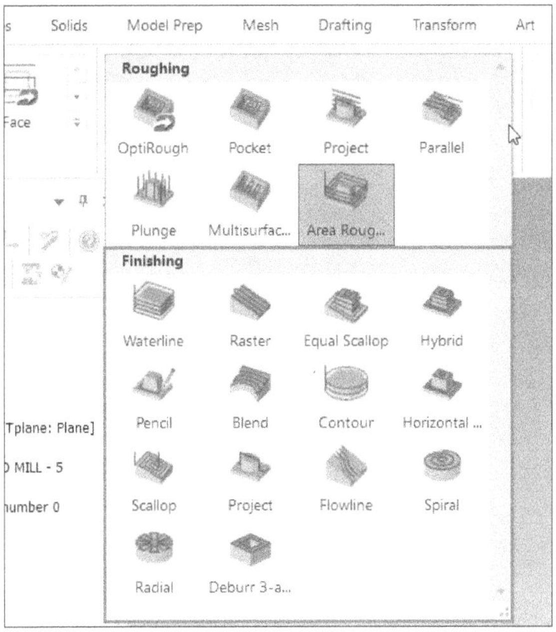

Figure-38. 3D Finishing tools

Creating Waterline Toolpath

The Waterline toolpath as the name suggests is used to create toolpath as water flows. It is used to finish the part by machining layer by layer along Z axis while following the contour of part. The Waterline toolpath is best with steeper angled surfaces. The procedure to use this tool is given next.

- After performing roughing operations, click on the **Waterline** tool from the expanded **3D** group of **Toolpaths** tab in the **Ribbon**. The **3D High Speed Toolpaths-Waterline** dialog box will be displayed; refer to Figure-39.

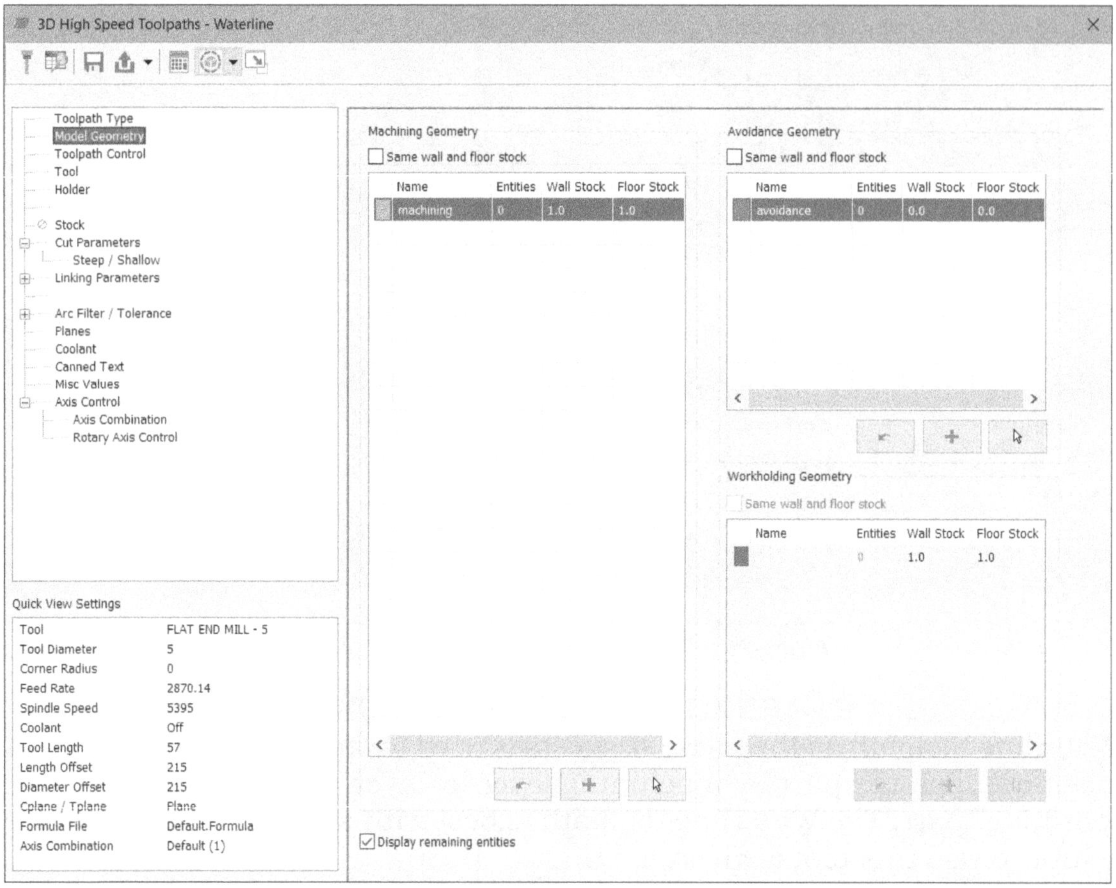

Figure-39. 3D High Speed Toolpaths-Waterline dialog box

- Click on the **Select entities** button from the **Machining Geometry** area of the dialog box. You will be asked to select the entities.
- Select the faces/features/bodies to be machined; refer to Figure-40 and press **ENTER**. The **3D High Speed Toolpaths-Waterline** dialog box will be displayed again.
- Similarly, select the avoidance geometry and work holding geometry using respective options.

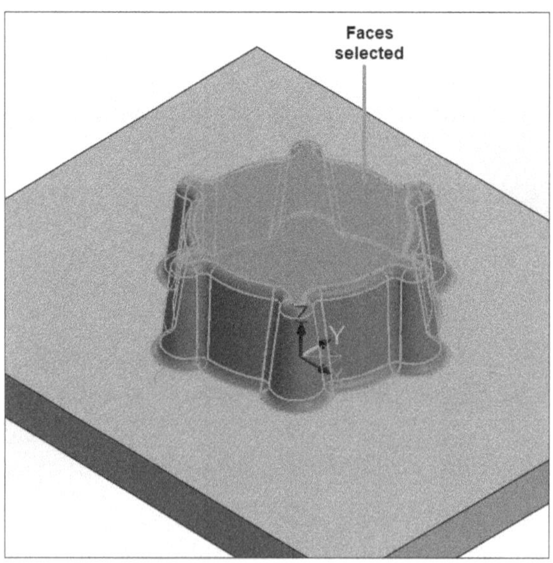

Figure-40. Features selected for machining

- Select the tool and tool holder as required from the respective pages.

Stock Options

- To define how Mastercam should calculate the stock amount, click on the **Stock** option from the left area in the dialog box. The Stock page will be displayed as shown in Figure-41.

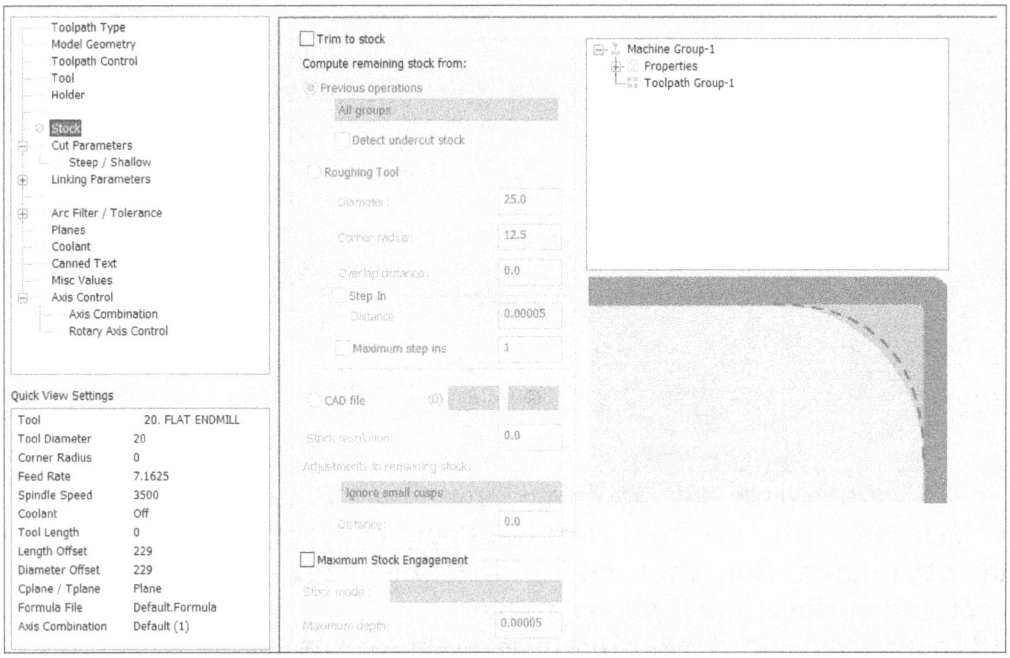

Figure-41. Stock page in 3D High Speed Toolpaths-Waterline dialog box

- Select the **Trim to stock** check box from the dialog box to define stock for current operation. On selecting this check box, the extra material left after previous operations will be assumed as stock for current operation. If you want to specifically select an operation up to which you want to trim the stock then select the **One other operation** radio button from the **Trim to stock** area and select desired operation from the operation box in the right.
- Set the other parameters like stock resolution and adjustments to remaining stock as required. Stock resolution is the accuracy value used to approximate the remaining material. Typically, stock resolution is set to 20x the total tolerance. Higher value means loose stock used for rough machining. Lower value means tight stock for finishing.
- Select the **Maximum Stock Engagement** check box if you want to keep the tool engaged in stock up to specified depth while cutting. After selecting check box, specify desired depth value in the **Maximum depth** edit box. Note that most of the time, the values specified here improve the surface quality while cutting faster.

Note that if you do not define any option in the **Stock** page, still the toolpath will be generated but Mastercam will take all the default values to perform these operations.

Cut Parameters

- Click on the **Cut Parameters** option from the left area of dialog box to display options related to cutting strategy; refer to Figure-42.

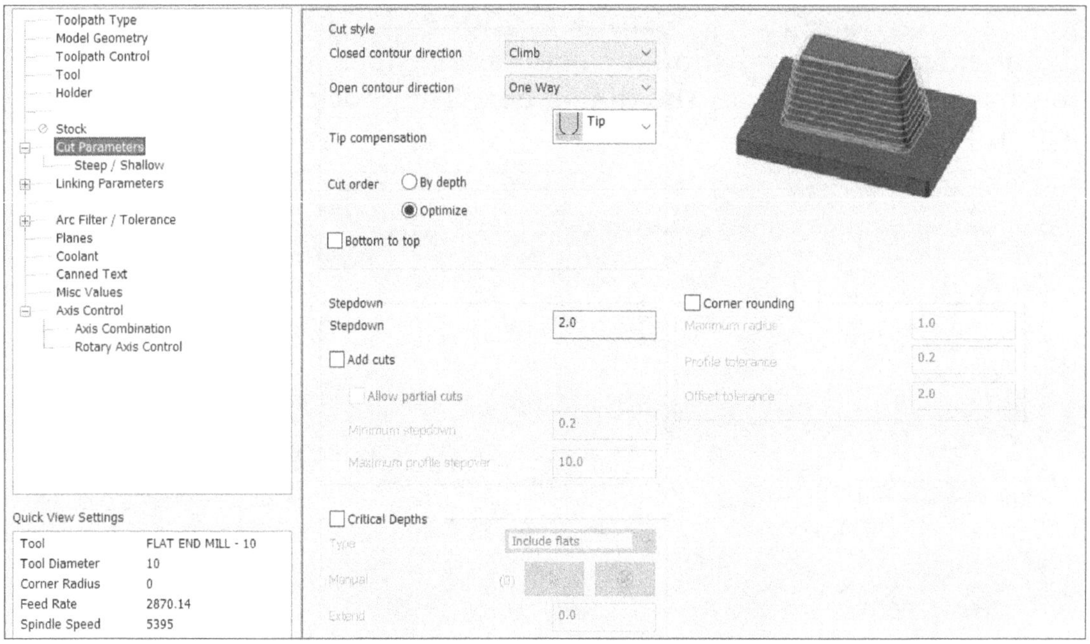

Figure-42. Cut Parameters page in 3D High Speed Toolpaths-Waterline dialog box

- Select desired cutting method from the **Open contour direction** drop-down in the **Cut style** area. Note that most of the time, **Zigzag** method is time saving if your tool and surface finish allows to use.
- In the **Closed contour direction** drop-down of **Cut style** area, you can select option to define the 3D motion and direction of cut to be generated for closed cutting passes.
- Select desired tool tip compensation option from the **Tip compensation** drop-down in the dialog box.
- From the **Cut order** area, select desired radio button to define cutting order for the operation. Select the **By depth** radio button to machine all cut passes along Z axis level by level. Select the **Optimize** radio button to keep the tool in an area and keeps it there until all cuts in that area are finished. Select **Bottom to top** radio button to machine from the bottom of the part to the top.
- Specify desired parameters in **Stepdown**, **Corner rounding**, and **Critical Depths** areas to refine surface finish.
- Set the other parameters as discussed earlier and click on the **OK** button. The toolpath will be generated; refer to Figure-43.

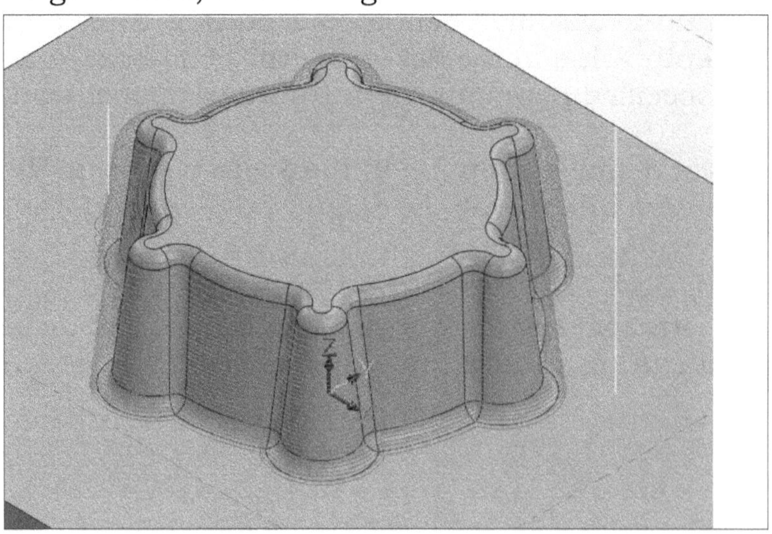

Figure-43. Waterline toolpath generated

Note that if your tool skips some area while machining then it is not fault of Mastercam. In this case, you need to change the settings and tool selected by you. Like in our example, the rounds will not be machined by 6 mm ball end mill. To finish them, we need to use a lower radius tool which needs an extra waterline toolpath. Now, you may ask why we did not use the lower radius tool at first then the answer is saving time. A lower radius tool will take more time to finish same amount of material.

Creating Raster Toolpath

The Raster toolpath is used to cut material in parallel directions. The working of this toolpath is similar to Parallel toolpath discussed earlier in this chapter; refer to Figure-44. The benefit of using this toolpath is in transition and low retraction.

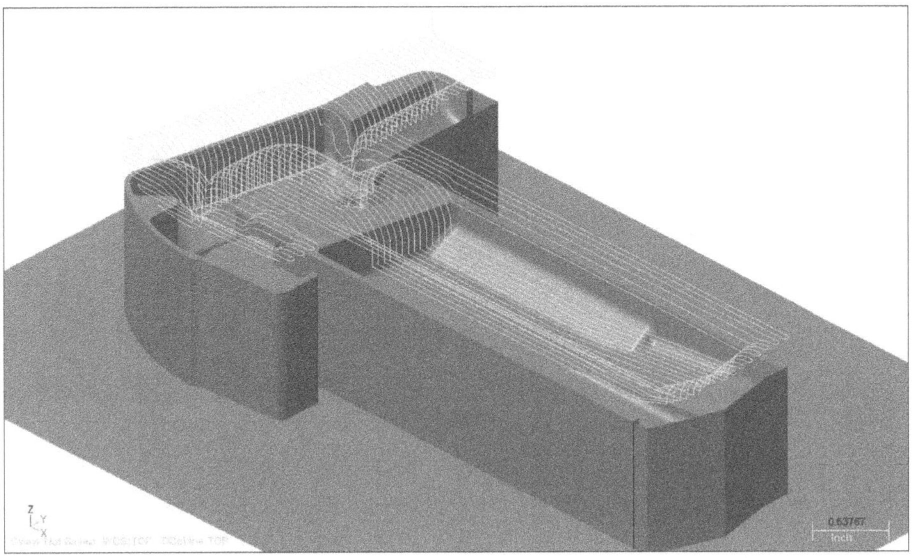

Figure-44. Raster toolpath example

Creating Scallop Surface Finish Toolpath

The Scallop Surface Finish toolpath is used to round sharp corners in the part. The procedure to create scallop surface finish toolpath is given next.

- Click on the **Scallop** tool from the **Finishing Toolpaths** drop-down in the **Ribbon**. The **3D High Speed Toolpaths-Scallop** dialog box will be displayed; refer to Figure-45. Click on the **Select entities** button from the **Machining Geometry** area to select the faces.

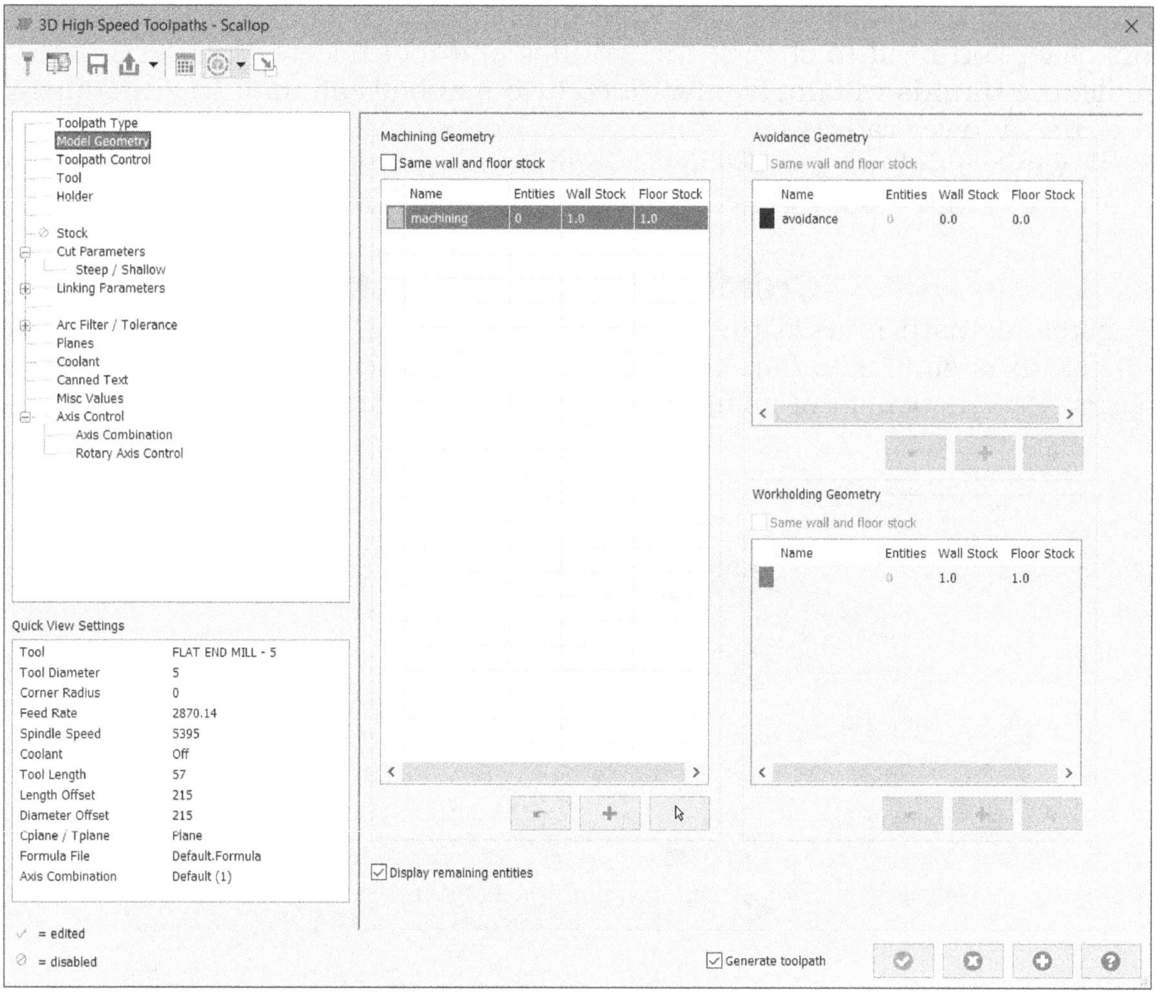

Figure-45. 3D High Speed Toolpaths-Scallop dialog box

- Select desired faces; refer to Figure-46 and press **ENTER**. The **3D High Speed Toolpaths-Scallop** dialog box will be displayed again.

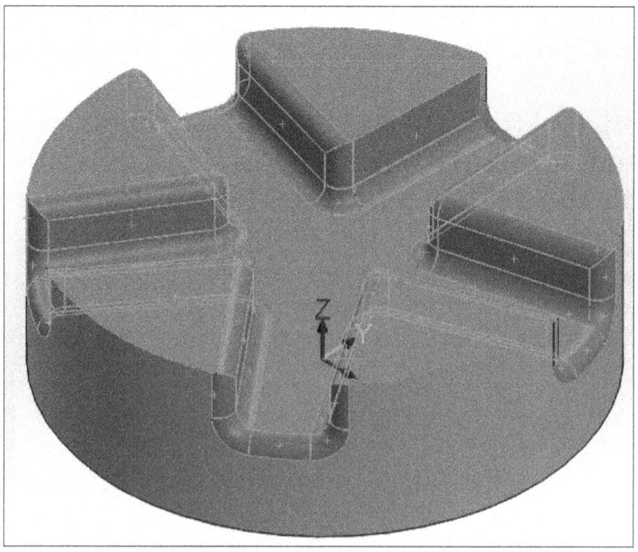

Figure-46. Faces selected for scallop toolpath

- Select desired tool (generally a ball nose cutter is used) and specify desired parameters in the **Stock** and **Cut Parameters** pages as discussed earlier.
- Select the **Steep/Shallow** option from the left area to specify how cutting tool will follow the steep/shallow surface of workpiece; refer to Figure-47.

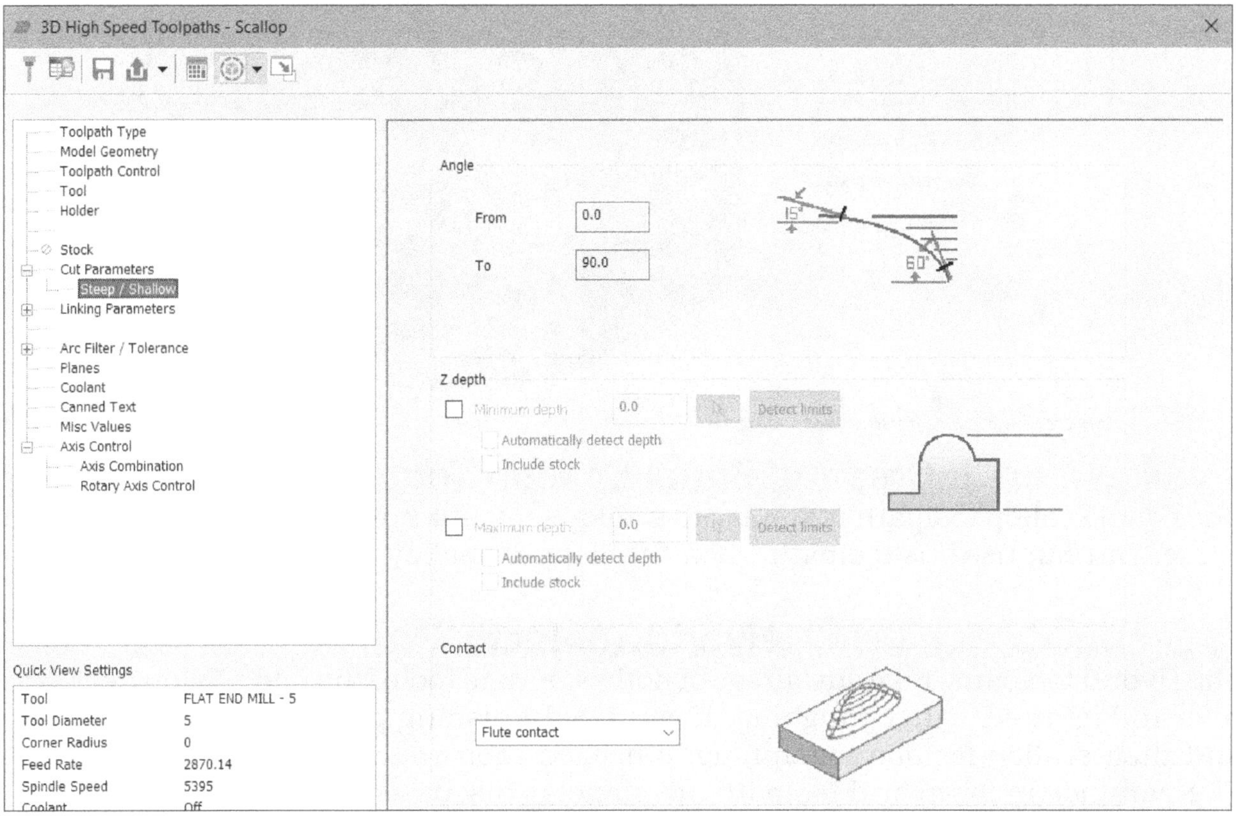

Figure-47. Steep/Shallow page

- Specify desired angle values in the **From** and **To** edit boxes of the **Angle** area to specify how cutting tool will enter and exit the steep or shallow areas of the workpiece.
- Select the **Minimum depth** and **Maximum depth** check boxes to define lowest and highest point of model up to which cutting passes will be generated. Click on the **Detect limits** button from the **Z depth** area of the dialog box to automatically set the minimum and maximum depth value for cutting toolpath. You can also specify the values manually in the respective edit boxes in the **Z depth** area. Select the **Automatically detect depth** check boxes to automatically set the limits based on selected geometries.
- Select desired option from the drop-down in the **Contact** area to set whether toolpath will be created for section of workpiece which are in contact with flute of cutting tool or the toolpath will be created for sections which are in contact with cutting tool's any length. Select the **Flute contact** option from the drop-down to use length of flute as reference for creating toolpaths. Select the **Tool assembly contact** option from the drop-down to create toolpath based on total length of cutting tool.
- Specify the other parameters as desired and click on the **OK** button. The toolpath will be created; refer to Figure-48.

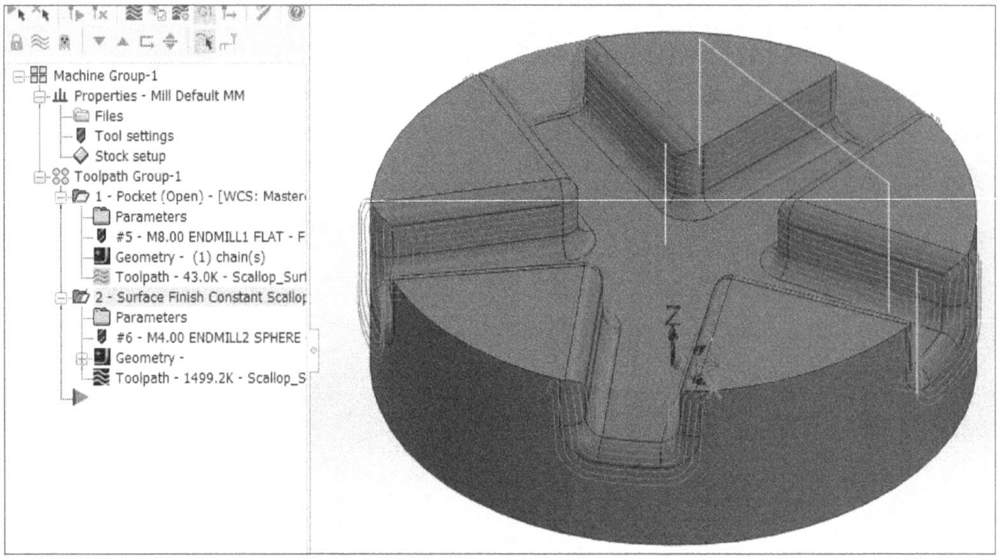

Figure-48. Surface finish scallop toolpath

Creating Equal Scallop Toolpath

The equal scallop toolpath is similar to scallop toolpath but with consistent step over value. You can use this toolpath when the slope of shallow/steep walls is consistent.

Hybrid Toolpath

The Hybrid toolpaths take advantage of both waterline toolpaths and scallop toolpaths; refer to Figure-49. After roughing, if you need finishing passes in which waterline and then scallop fashion machining is needed then you should use this toolpath. The parameters for hybrid toolpath are same as discussed earlier.

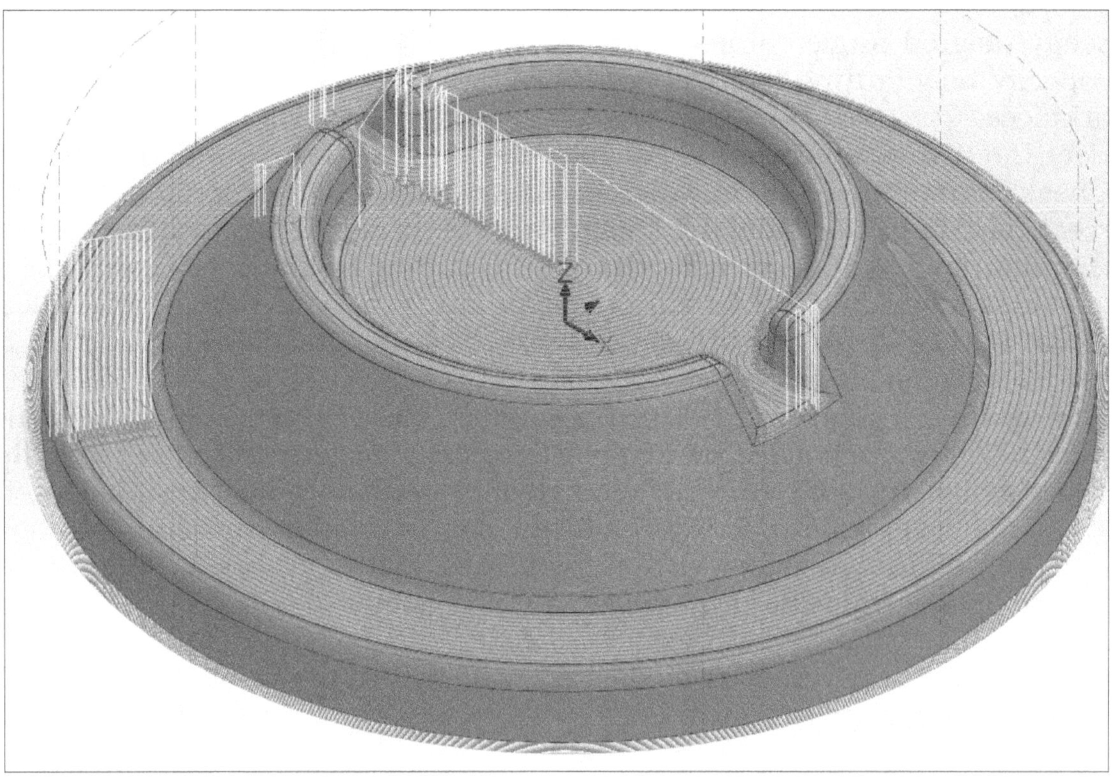

Figure-49. Hybrid High Speed Toolpath created

Pencil Surface Finish Toolpath

The Pencil Surface Finish toolpath is used to remove material at the intersection of two surfaces in the part. In this toolpath, the tool moves tangent to the intersection curve of surfaces.

Blend Surface Finish Toolpath

The Blend Surface Finish toolpath is used to remove material from the surface of part by forming a blend feature. Note that Blend is a solid/surface feature created by using boundaries of selected curves; refer to Figure-50. The procedure to create this toolpath is given next.

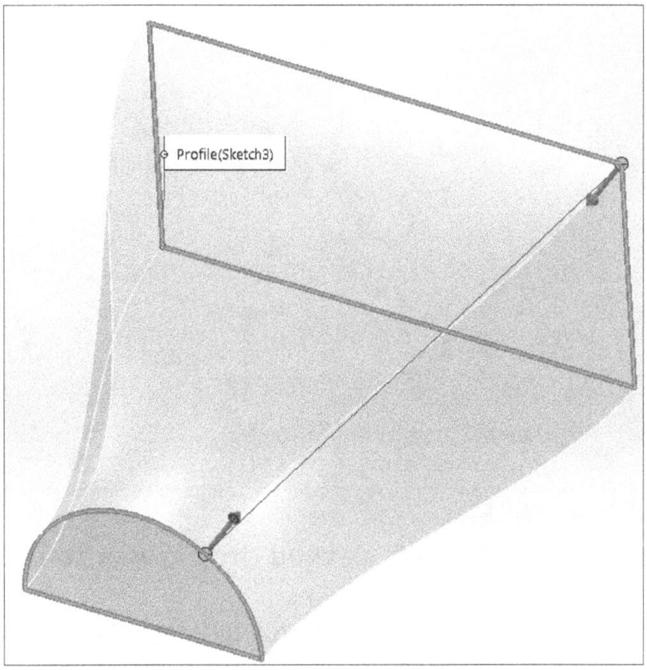

Figure-50. Blend feature example

- Click on the **Blend** tool from the expanded **3D** group of **Toolpaths** tab in the **Ribbon**. The **3D High Speed Toolpaths - Blend** dialog box will be displayed.
- Click on the **Select entities** button from the **Machining Geometry** area of the dialog box and select the faces of model to be machined; refer to Figure-51. After selecting faces, press **ENTER**. The **3D High Speed Toolpaths - Blend** dialog box will be displayed again.

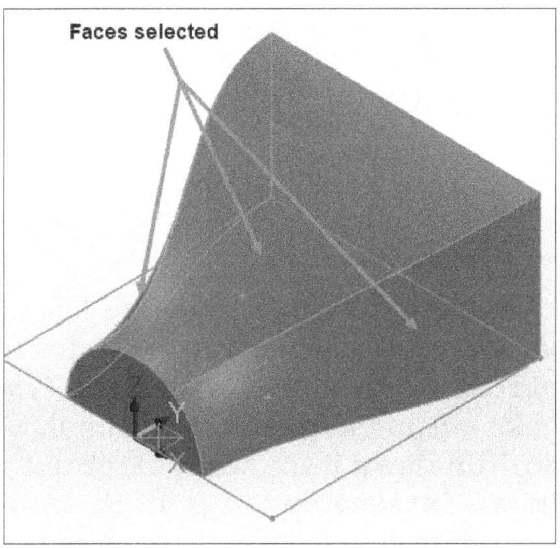

Figure-51. Faces selected for blend surface finish toolpath

- Select desired ball nose end mill and related tool holder.
- Click on the **Cut Parameters** option from the left area of the dialog box. The options in the dialog box will be displayed as shown in Figure-52.

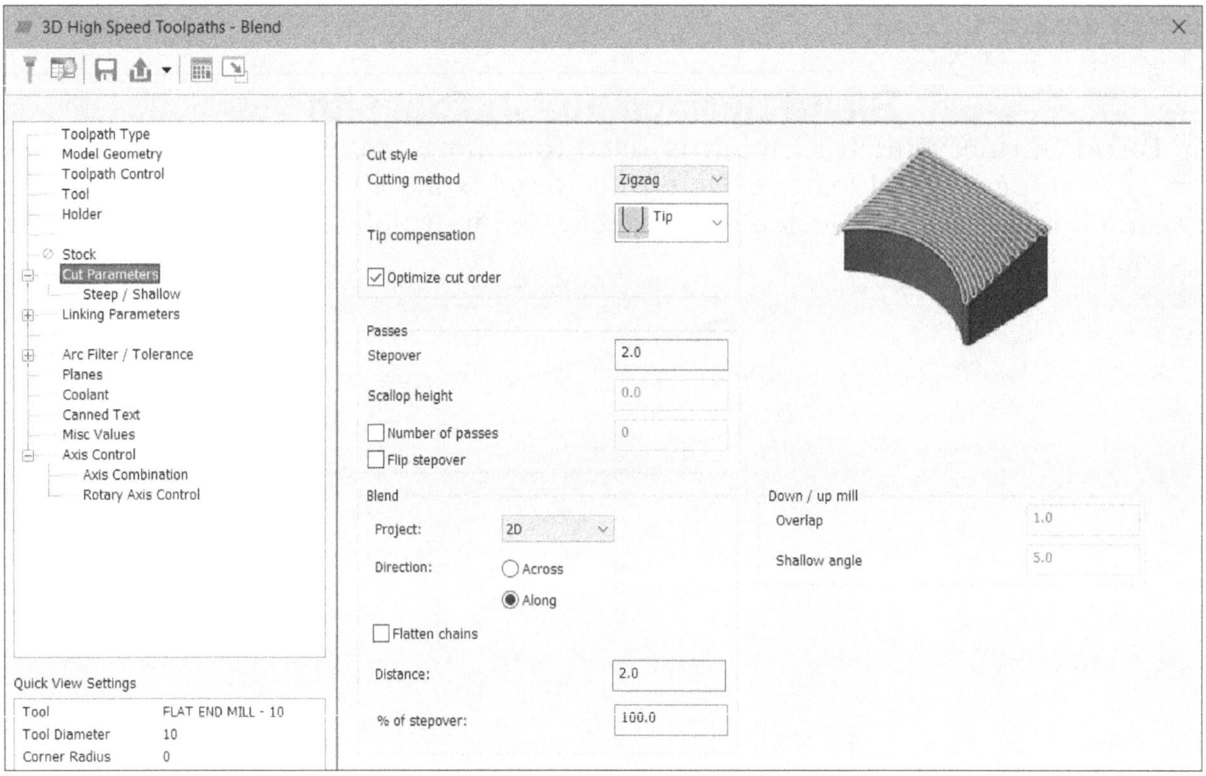

Figure-52. Cut Parameters for blend toolpath

- Select desired option from the **Cut method** drop-down to define how the tool will move while machining.
- Select desired radio button and option from the **Project** drop-down to define shape of blend toolpath. Effect of selecting different combinations is shown in Figure-53.

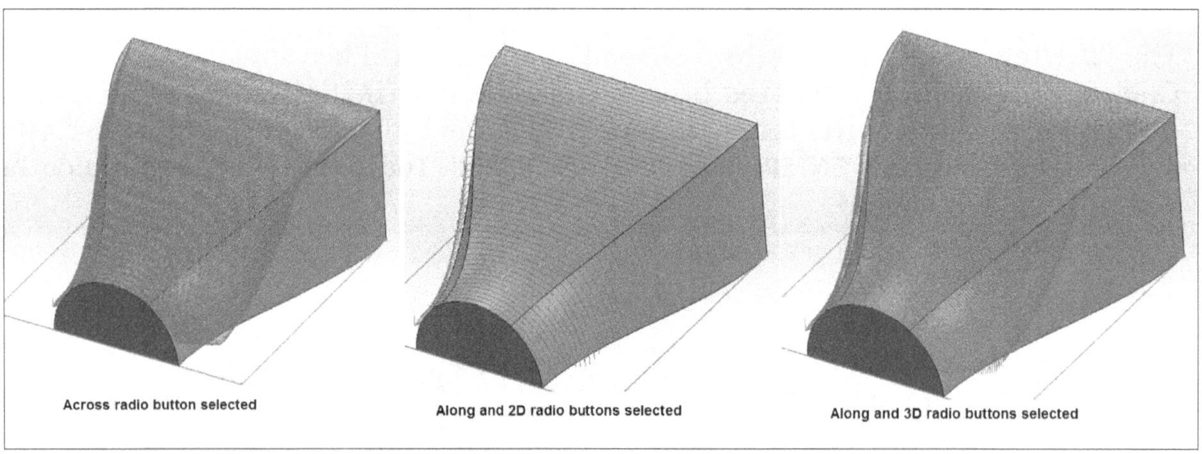

Figure-53. Selection of 2D, 3D, Across and Along toolpaths

- Click on the **Linking Parameters** option from the left area of the dialog box to specify how cutting tool will retract while cutting; refer to Figure-54.
- Select the **Minimum Vertical Retract** option from the **Type** drop-down in **Retract** area of dialog box to make cutting tool retract minimal. Select the **Full Vertical Retract** option from the drop-down if you want to retract cutting tool up to retract plane. Select the **Minimum Distance** option from the drop-down if you want the cutting tool to move in straight line from retraction plane.

- Select the **Machine Entire Pass** option from the **Type** drop-down of **Fitting** area if you want the cutting tool to exactly follow the curvature of workpiece. Select the **Minimize Trimming** option from the drop-down if you want to trim the cutting pass up to specified maximum trimming distance value while following the curvature of workpiece. Select the **Fully Trim Pass** option from the drop-down to trim the toolpath at corners to form arc of specified value.

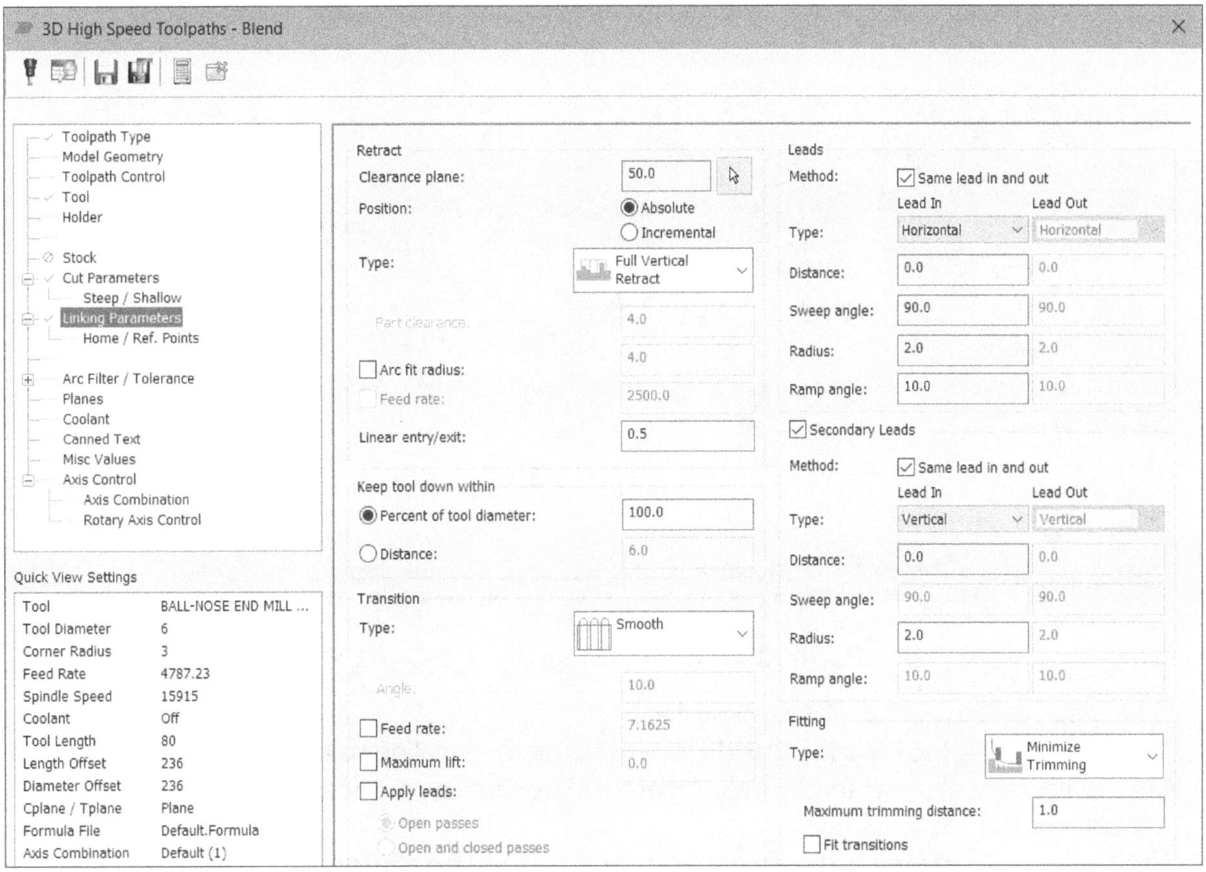

Figure-54. Linking Parameters for blend toolpath

- Specify the other parameters in this page as discussed earlier and then click on the **OK** button from the dialog box. The toolpath will be created.

Creating Surface Finish Contour Toolpath

The surface finish contour toolpath is used to finish machine walls of the workpiece in 3D. The procedure to create this toolpath is given next.

- Click on the **Contour** tool from the expanded **3D** group in the **Toolpaths** tab of the **Ribbon**. You will be asked to select faces to be finished using contour toolpath.
- Select desired faces and press **ENTER**. The **Toolpath/surface selection** dialog box will be displayed.
- Select desired entities for containment, avoidance, and start point of toolpath using the tools in the **Toolpath/surface selection** dialog box and click on the **OK** button. The **Surface Finish Contour** dialog box will be displayed; refer to Figure-55.

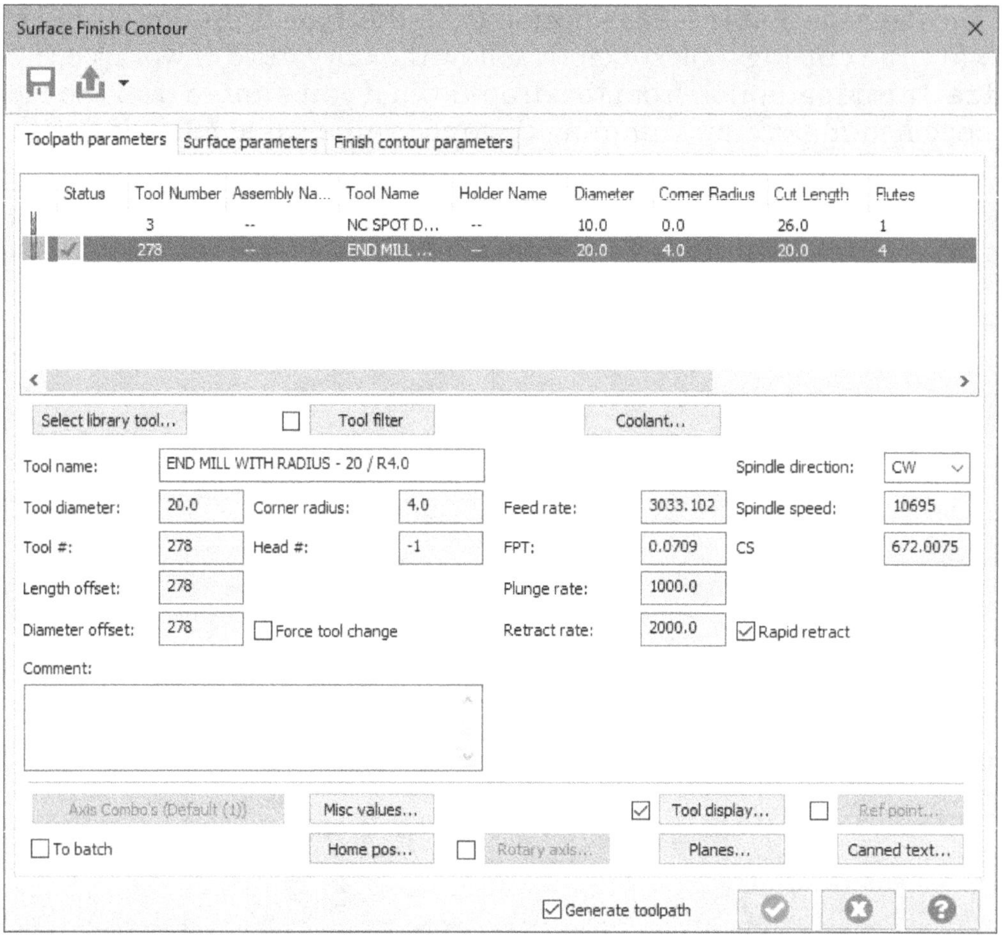

Figure-55. Surface Finish Contour dialog box

- Set the cutting tool and related parameters in the **Toolpath parameters** tab.
- Set the retraction and feed parameters in the **Surface parameters** tab of the dialog box as discussed earlier.
- Click on the **Finish contour parameters** tab of the dialog box to set the direction and transition of toolpaths. The options will be displayed as shown in Figure-56.

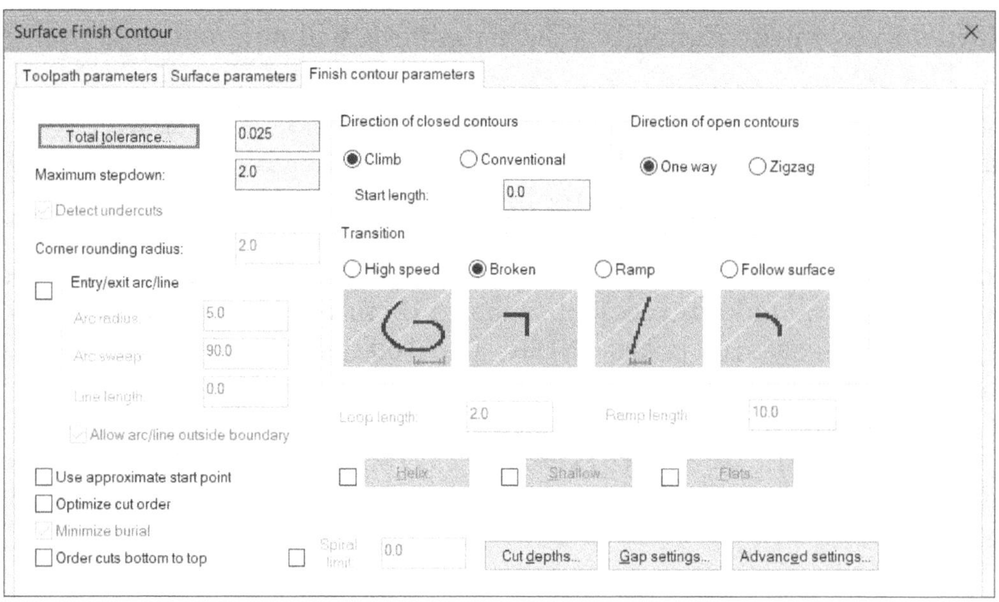

Figure-56. Finish contour parameters tab

- Most of the parameters in this dialog box have been discussed earlier. Set the other parameters and click on the **OK** button to create the toolpath.

Creating Horizontal Area Toolpath

The Horizontal Area toolpath is used to finish flat faces. This toolpath functions in the same way as Facing works in 2D Toolpaths. The procedure to create this toolpath is given next.

- After roughing, click on the **Horizontal Area** tool from the expanded **3D** group of **Toolpaths** tab in the **Ribbon**. The **3D High Speed Toolpaths-Horizontal Area** dialog box will be displayed; refer to Figure-57.
- Select the machining geometry and avoidance geometry objects as discussed earlier; refer to Figure-58.

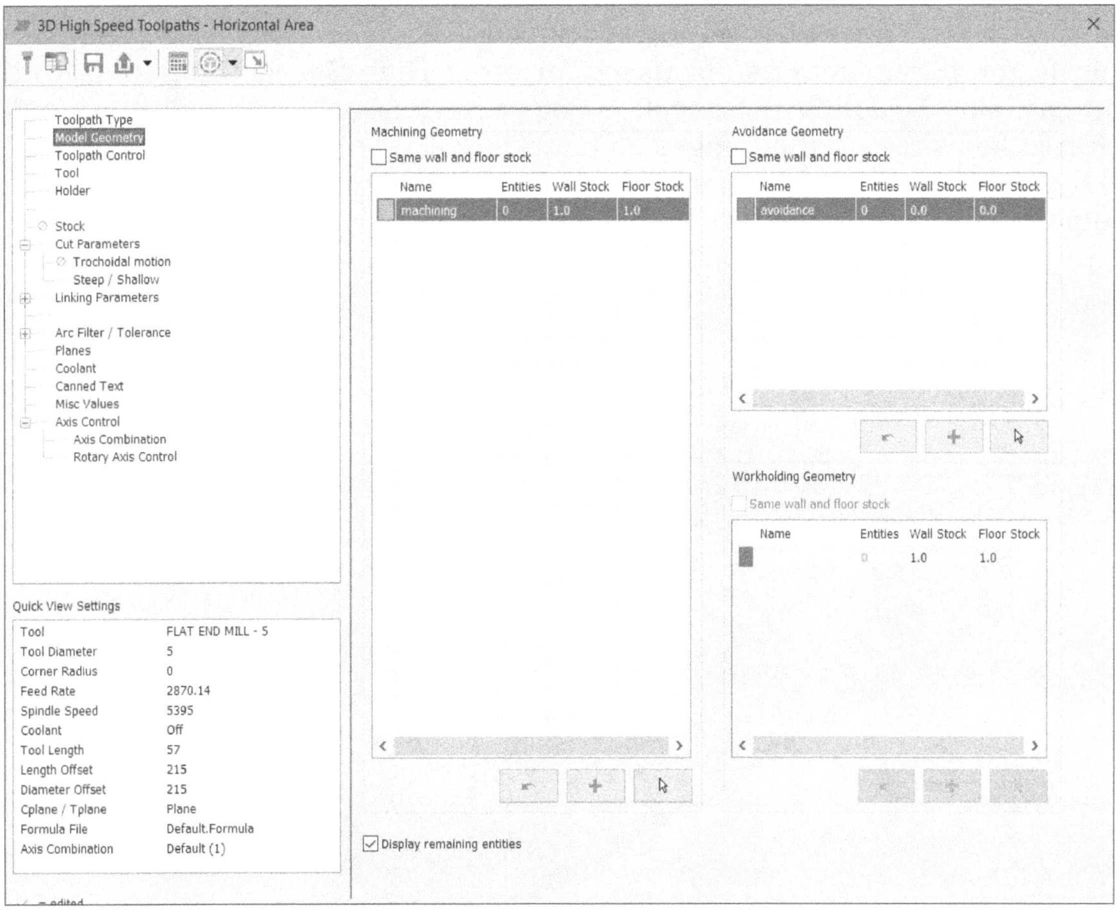

Figure-57. 3D High Speed Toolpaths-Horizontal Area dialog box

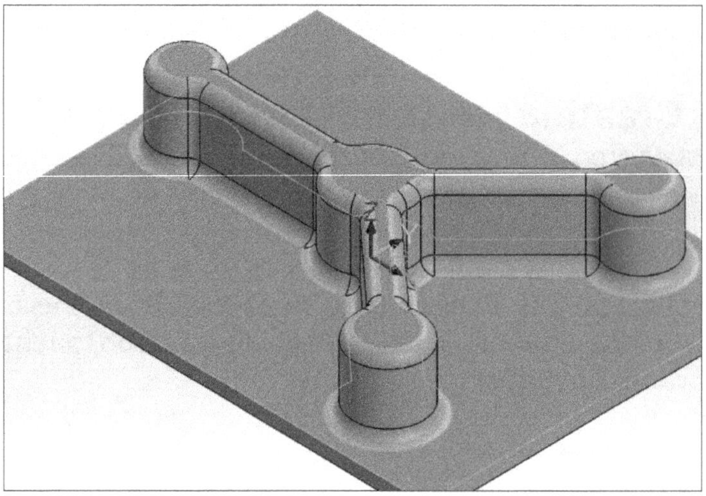

Figure-58. Faces selected for horizontal area HST

- Specify the parameters as discussed for other High Speed Toolpaths. Note that you can skip selecting the check surfaces here as toolpath will move only the selected faces taking their edges as boundaries.
- After specifying the parameters, click on the **OK** button from the dialog box. The toolpath will be generated; refer to Figure-59.

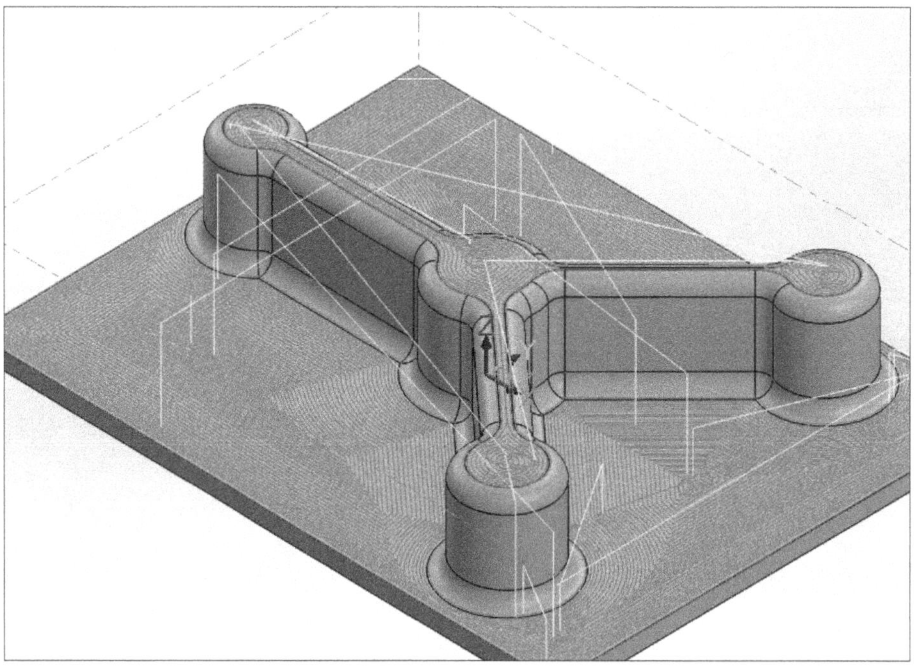

Figure-59. Toolpath for horizontal area HST

The **Project** tool in the **Finishing** section of expanded **3D** group in the **Toolpaths** tab of **Ribbon** works similar to **Project** tool discussed earlier for surface roughing toolpaths.

Flowline Surface Finish Toolpath

The Flowline Surface Finish toolpath is used when we need to remove material from channels and runner like structures of mold dies. The procedure to use this tool is given next.

- Click on the **Flowline** tool from the **Finishing** section of expanded **3D** group in the **Toolpaths** tab of the **Ribbon**. You will be asked to select faces of workpiece to be machined.
- Select the faces of the runners/channels in the part; refer to Figure-60 and press **ENTER**. The **Toolpath/surface selection** dialog box will be displayed; refer to Figure-61.
- Click on the **Flow** button from the dialog box to define parameters related to flow lines. The **Flowline data** dialog box will be displayed; refer to Figure-62.
- Click on the **Offset** button from the **Flip** rollout of dialog box to offset in/offset out the toolpath with respect to part boundaries. In this way, you can specify tool compensation left or right.
- Click on the **Cut direction** button from dialog box to change the tool's cutting direction.
- Similarly, set the step direction and flowline start corner by using the respective buttons in dialog box.
- After setting desired parameters, click on the **OK** button from **Flowline data** dialog box.
- Select the avoidance area as discussed earlier by using the options in **Check** area of the dialog box and then click on the **OK** button from the **Toolpath/surface selection** dialog box. The **Surface Finish Flowline** dialog box will be displayed; refer to Figure-63.

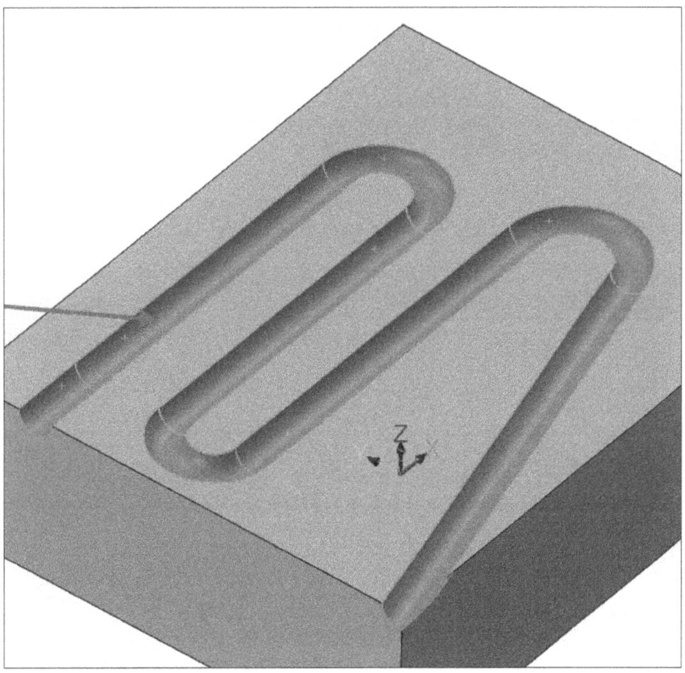

Figure-60. Faces selected for flowline toolpath

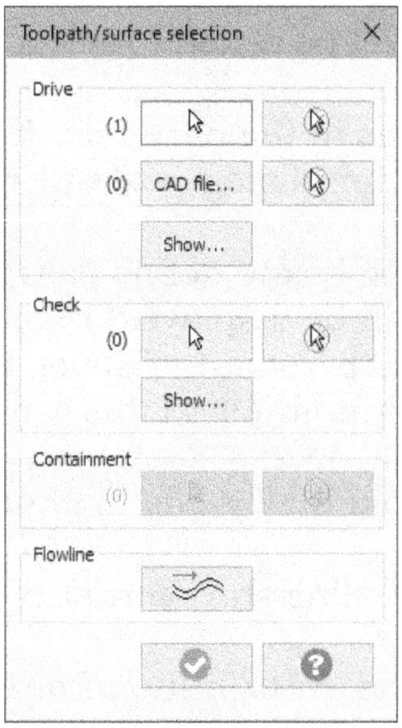

Figure-61. Toolpath surface selection dialog box

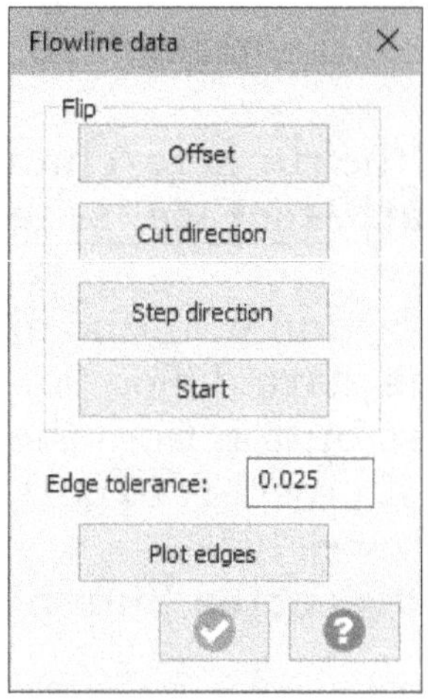

Figure-62. Flowline data dialog box

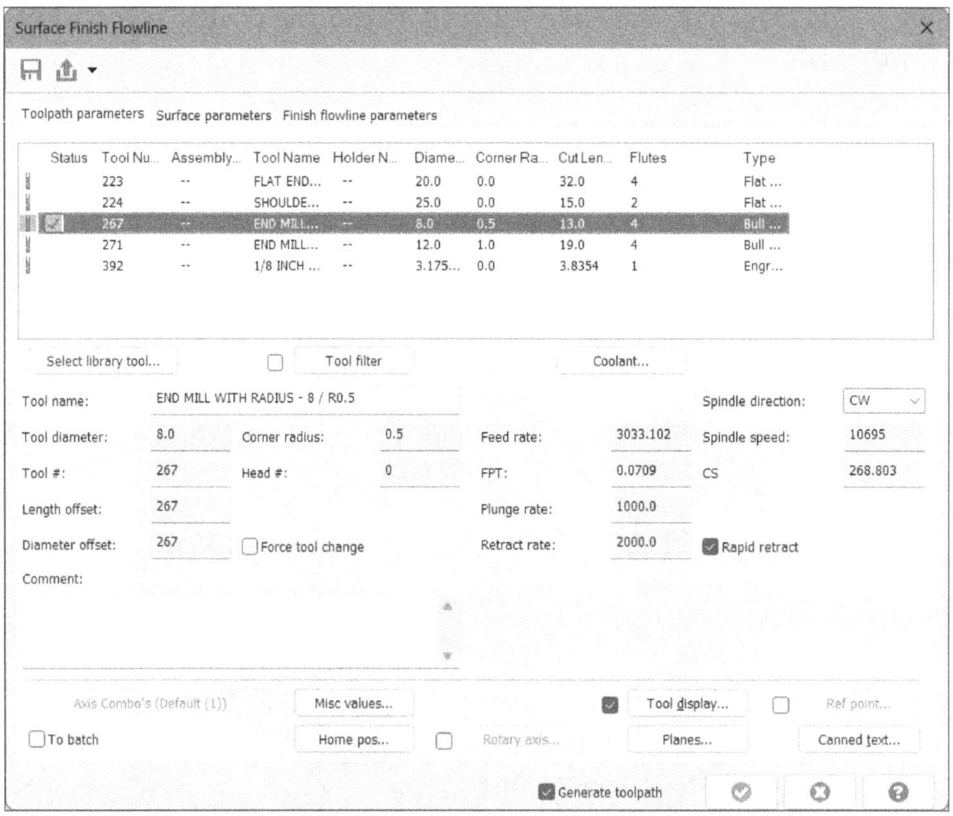

Figure-63. Surface Finish Flowline dialog box

- Select desired tool and specify related parameters in the **Toolpath parameters** and **Surface parameters** tabs of the dialog box. Note that generally, ball end mill or bull end mill cutter is used for this type of toolpath.
- Click on the **Finish flowline parameters** tab. The options in the dialog box will be displayed as shown in Figure-64.

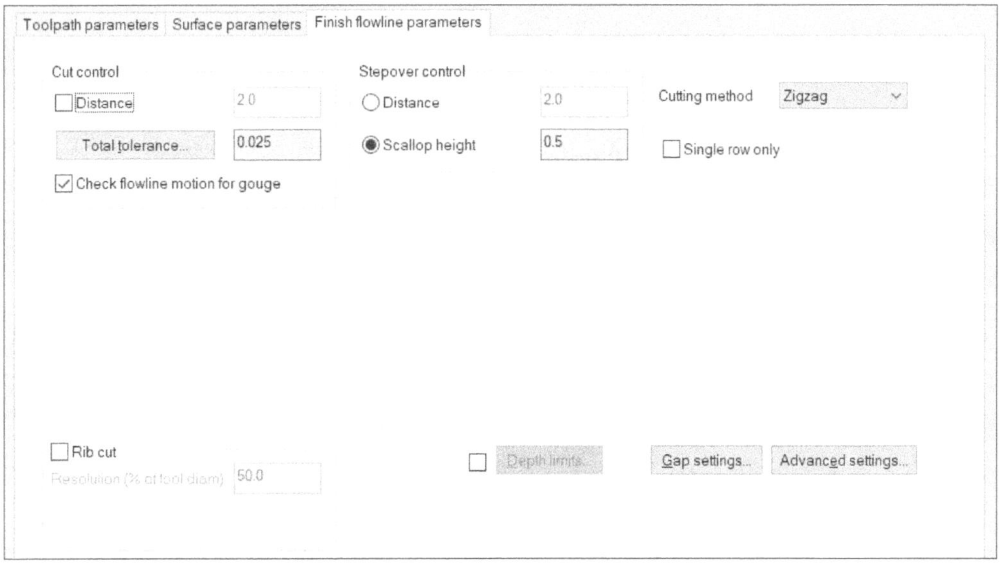

Figure-64. Rough flowline parameters tab

- Specify desired tolerance or absolute cut length in the **Cut control** area. This tolerance is range for each toolpath step within which the tool can deviate while cutting.
- Specify the other parameters in this dialog box as discussed earlier and click on the **OK** button. The toolpath will be generated; refer to Figure-65.

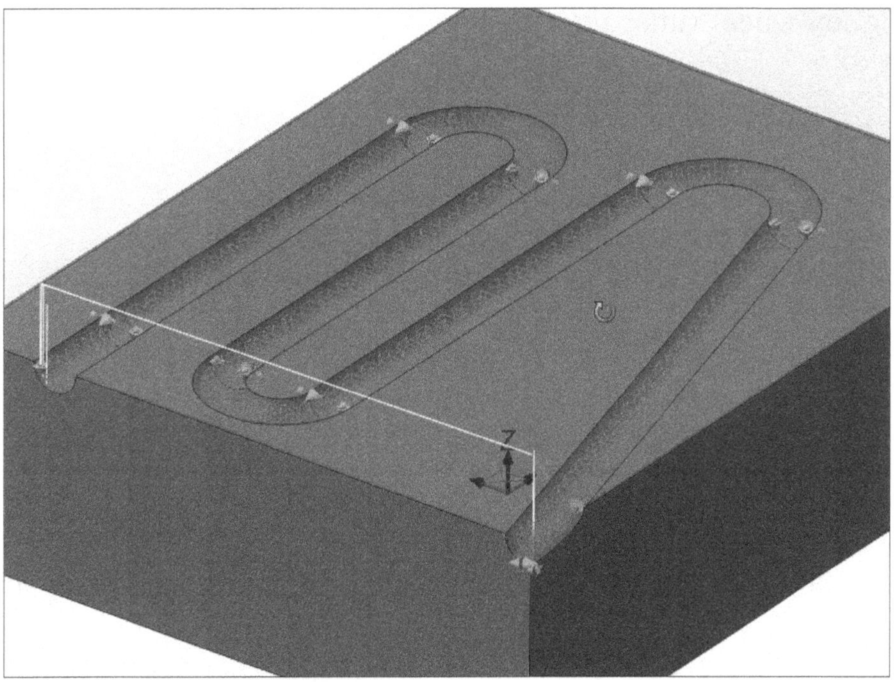

Figure-65. Surface rough flowline toolpath

Spiral Toolpath

The Spiral toolpath is used to cut material in spiral fashion. This toolpath is useful when you need to finish rough objects like shown in Figure-66. The method to use this tool is same as discussed earlier.

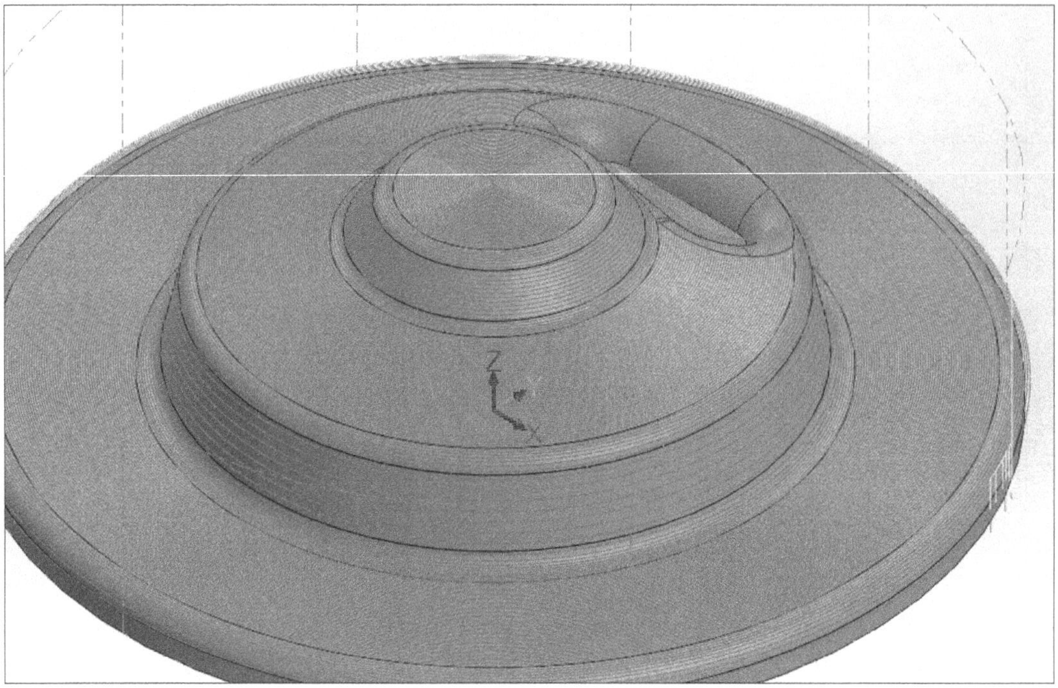

Figure-66. Spiral High Speed Toolpath

Creating Radial Surface Finish Toolpath

The Radial Surface Finish toolpath is used to create radial surface toolpaths like in spokes of alloy wheel rims; refer to Figure-67. The procedure to use this tool is given next.

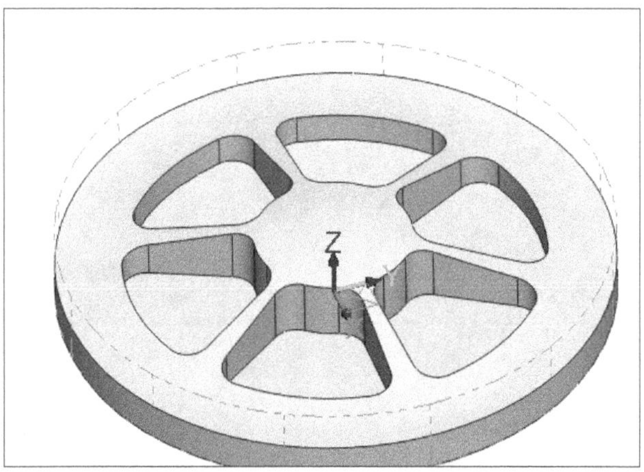

Figure-67. Model for radial rough toolpath

- Click on the **Radial** tool from the expanded **3D** group of **Toolpaths** tab in the **Ribbon**. The **3D High Speed Toolpaths - Radial** dialog box will be displayed; refer to Figure-68.

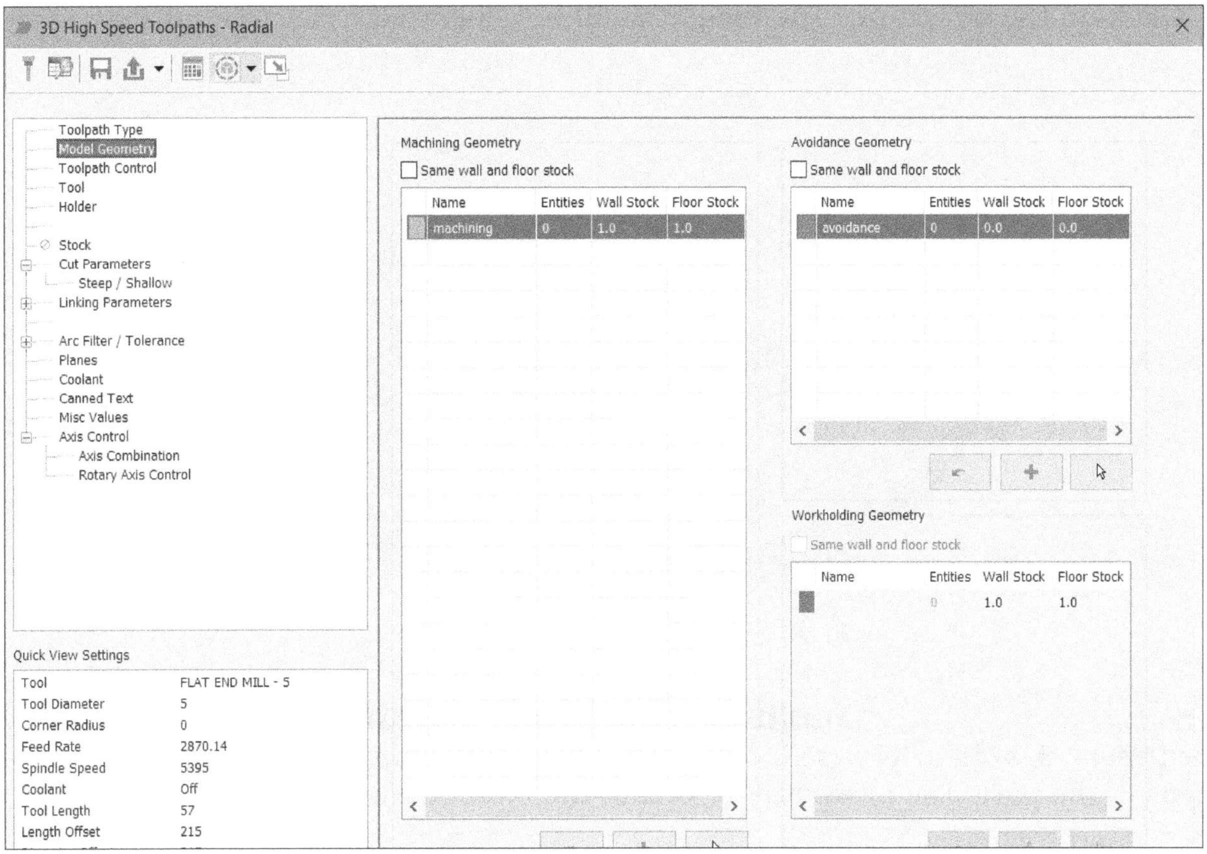

Figure-68. Surface High Speed Toolpaths-Radial dialog box

- Select desired faces for machining geometry and avoidance geometry as discussed earlier.
- Click on the **Cut Parameters** option from the left area of the dialog box to specify parameters related to Figure-69.
- Set the other parameters as discussed earlier in the dialog box.

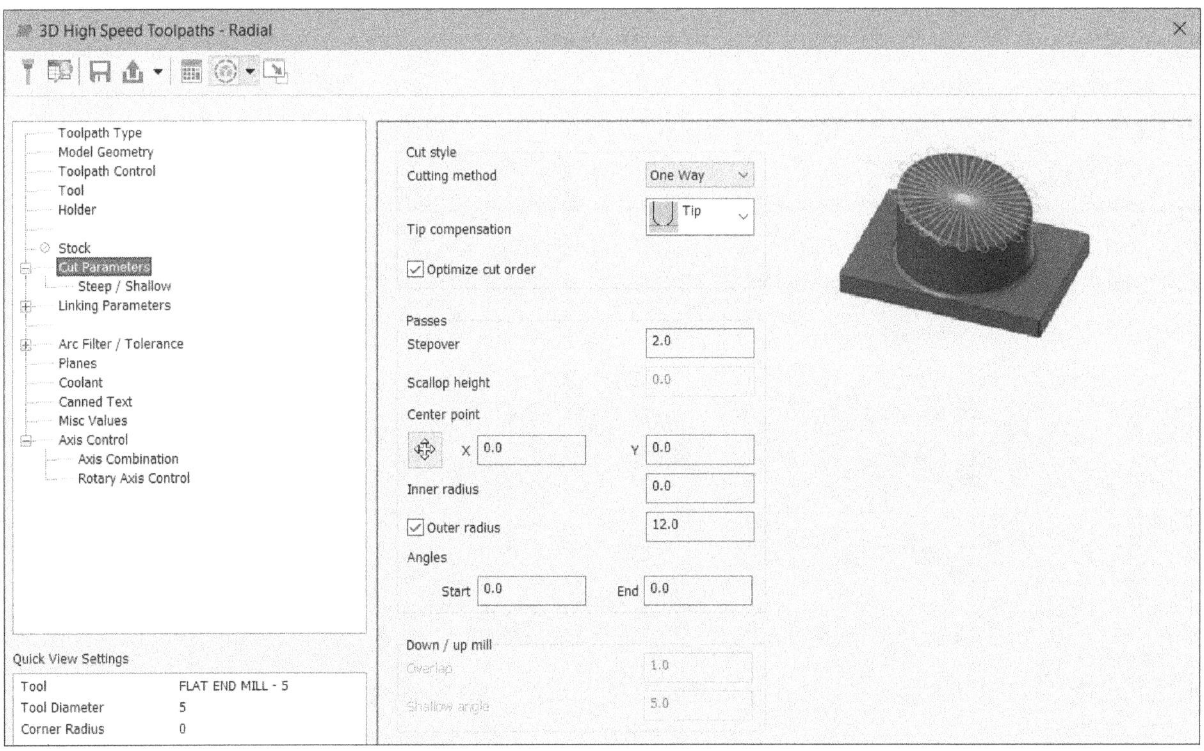

Figure-69. Cut Parameters for Radial toolpath

- Click on the **OK** button. The toolpath will be generated; refer to Figure-70.

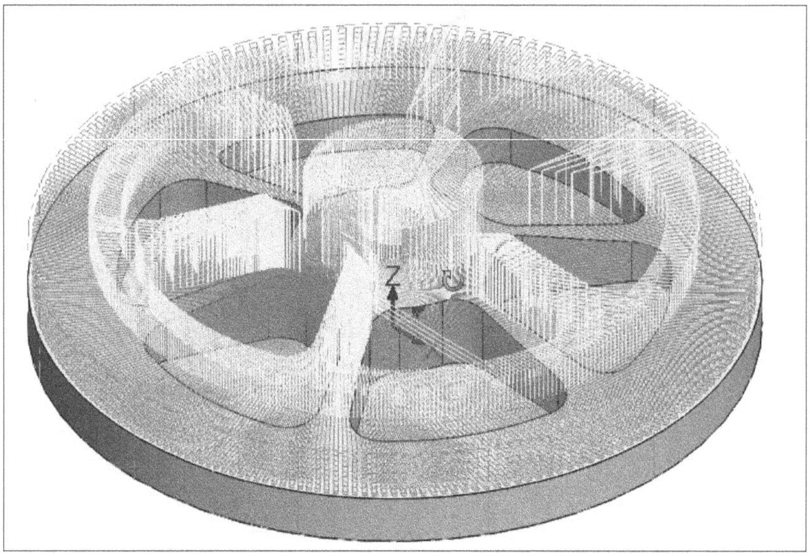

Figure-70. Surface rough radial toolpath generated

3-axis Deburring Toolpath

The **Deburr 3-axis** tool is used to create toolpath for removing burrs and break sharp edges of the part. The procedure to create the toolpath is given next.

- Click on the **Deburr 3-axis** tool from the expanded **3D** panel in the **Toolpaths** tab of the **Ribbon**. The **3D High Speed Toolpaths - Deburr 3-axis** dialog box will be displayed.
- Select the **Cut Pattern** option from the left area to specify cutting parameters for the toolpath. The options will be displayed as shown in Figure-71.

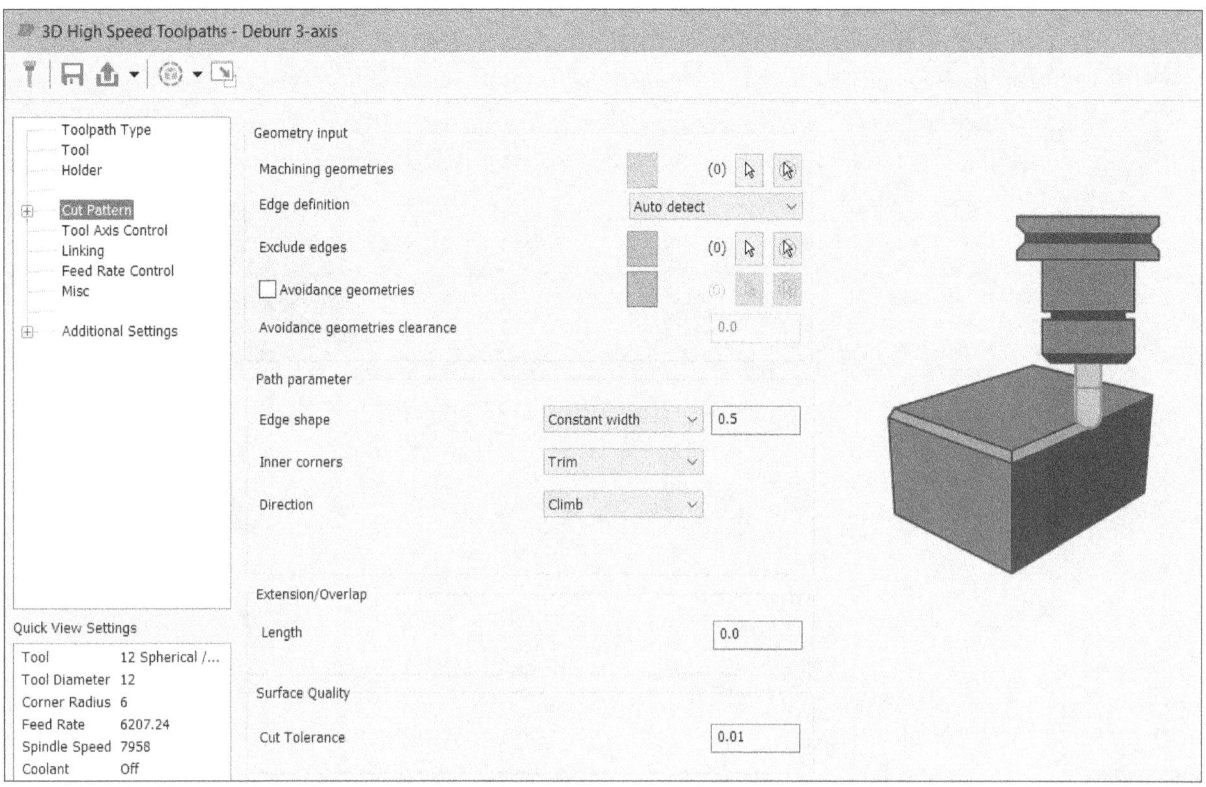

Figure-71. Cut parameters for 3-axis deburr toolpath

- Click on the **Select** button for **Machining geometries** section and select the faces of model/body whose edges are to be deburred; refer to Figure-72. Note that on triple clicking at face of body, you can select the full body. After selecting edges, click on the **End Selection** button from graphics area. The dialog box will be displayed again.

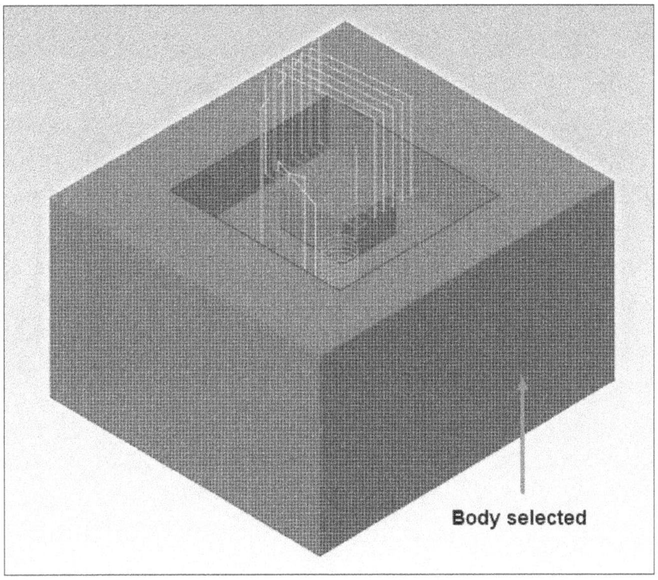

Figure-72. Faces selected for deburr

- Select desired option from the **Edge shape** drop-down to define whether you want to specify depth or width of deburred edge for the operation; refer to Figure-73 and then specify related value in the **Edge shape** edit box.

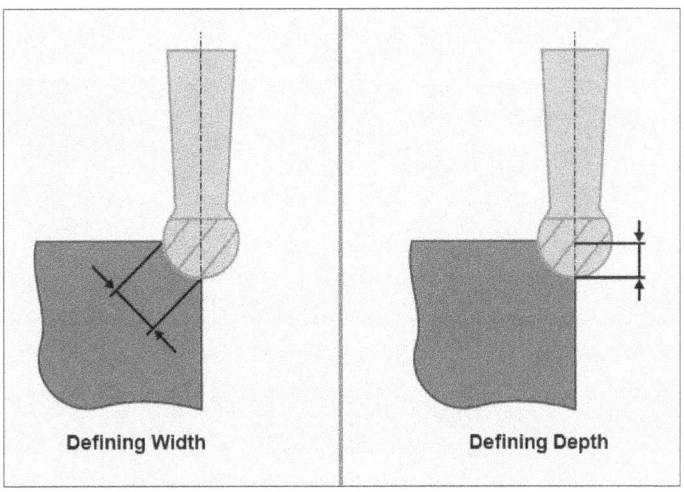

Figure-73. Edge shape options

- Select desired option from the **Inner corners** drop-down to define whether you want to create sharp corners (Trim option) or provide relief grooves (Relief option) at corners.
- Select the **Advanced Edge Options** option from left area in the dialog box. The options will be displayed; refer to Figure-74. Specify desired values to define sharp edge angle, minimum edge length, and height limits for deburred edges.

- If **Relief** option selected in the **Inner corners** drop-down of **Cut Patterns** page in the dialog box then **Advanced Relief Options** node will be displayed at the left in the dialog box. Select the **Advanced Relief Options** node from left area. The options will be displayed as shown in Figure-75.

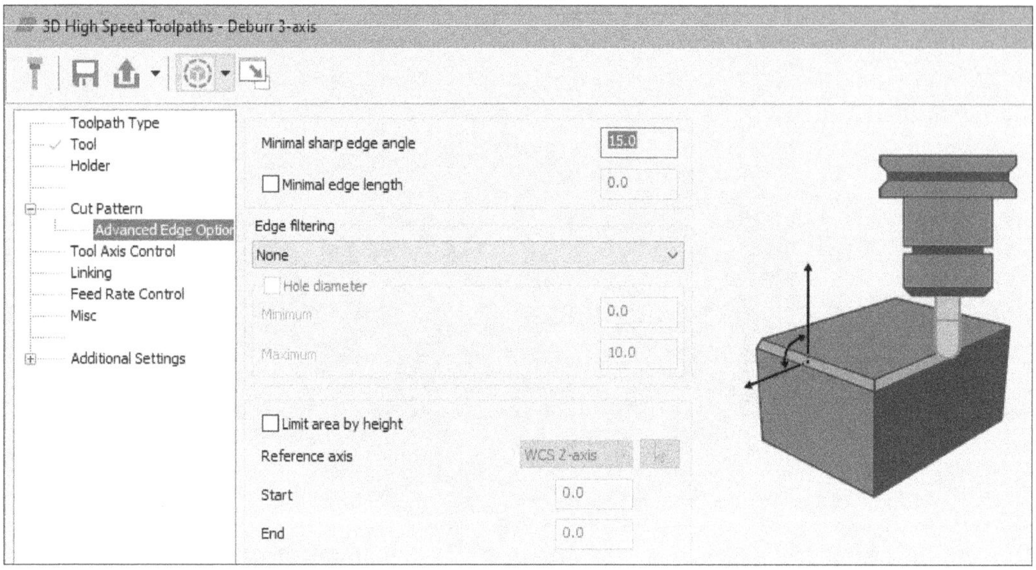

Figure-74. Advanced Edge Options

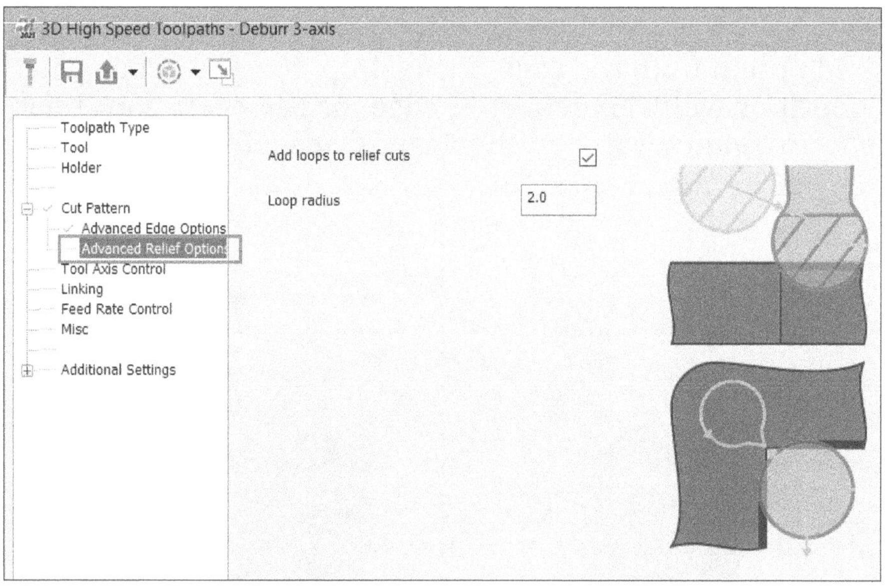

Figure-75. Advanced Relief Options

- Select the **Add loops to relief cuts** check box to add multiple loops in the toolpath for relief cuts. Specify the radius of circular loops at corners in the **Loop radius** edit box.
- Set the other parameters as discussed earlier and click on the **OK** button from the dialog box. The toolpath will be created; refer to Figure-76.

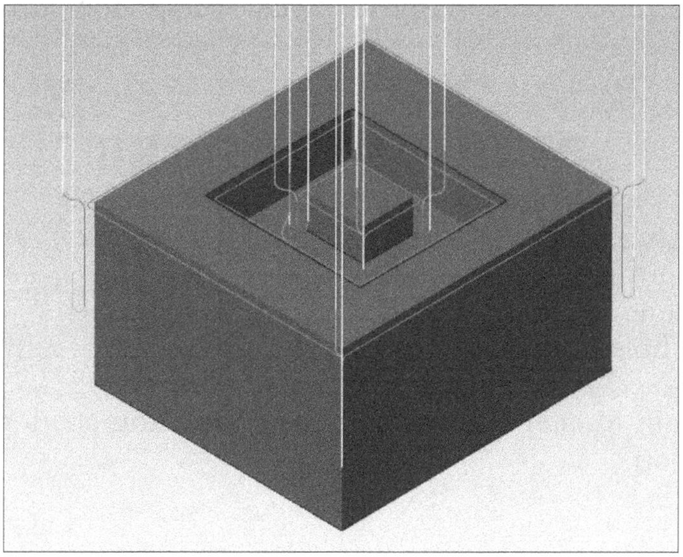

Figure-76. Deburr toolpath

SELF ASSESSMENT

Q1. Which of the following toolpaths are also called surface toolpaths?

a. 2D Toolpaths
b. 2.5D Toolpaths
c. 3D Toolpaths
d. Multi-axis toolpaths

Q2. Explain the terms Stepup, Stepover, and Stepdown.

Q3. On selecting the Minimum Distance option from Retract Method drop-down, the tool will retract directly for larger distance but follow the trajectory of part for smaller distances. (T/F)

Q4. What is the use of Project Rough Surface toolpath?

Q5. Discuss the term RCTF and its use in Mastercam.

Q6. A higher stepdown can increase load on tool. (T/F)

Q7. A higher step-over can leave the material unmachined giving you many holes as output. (T/F)

Q8. Discuss the application of waterline toolpath.

Q9. The Scallop Surface Finish toolpath is used to round sharp corners in the part. (T/F)

Q10. For 3D Blend toolpath, select the Fully Trim Pass option from the drop-down to trim the toolpath at corners to form arc of specified value. (T/F)

Q11, The Blend Surface Finish toolpath is used when we need to remove material from channels and runner like structures of mold dies. (T/F)

Q12. What is the difference between Spiral Surface Finish toolpath and Radial Surface Finish toolpath?

REVIEW QUESTIONS

Q1. What is the primary purpose of 3D roughing toolpaths?
A. Final surface finishing
B. Removing small burrs
C. Removing large amounts of material with larger tolerance
D. Drilling through holes

Q2. Which toolpath in Mastercam uses optimum cutting strategies to remove large stock in one operation?
A. Raster
B. Scallop
C. OptiRough
D. Pocket

Q3. In the OptiRough toolpath, which radio button should be selected for machining a pocket feature?
A. From Outside
B. Stay inside
C. Contour
D. Boss

Q4. What does selecting the "Mill vertical walls" checkbox do in Cut Parameters?
A. Increases spindle speed
B. Adds waterline passes for walls
C. Reduces tool wear
D. Changes tool orientation

Q5. What is the effect of selecting the "By pocket" option in Optimize stepups?
A. All pockets are cut simultaneously
B. Each pocket is rough cut and finished individually
C. The tool cuts from outside
D. The tool avoids pockets

Q6. In Toolpath Control, selecting the "Inside" radio button keeps the tool:
A. On the containment boundary
B. Outside the containment boundary
C. Completely inside the containment boundary
D. At a fixed Z level

Q7. Which retraction option keeps the tool closest to part edges during non-cutting moves?
A. Full Vertical Retract
B. Minimum Vertical Retract
C. Minimum Distance
D. Rapid Retract

Q8. What is the benefit of using the "Rest material" option in OptiRough?
A. Reduces spindle RPM
B. Allows finishing of cavities
C. Machines only uncut stock left by previous toolpaths
D. Machines sharp edges

Q9. Which toolpath is preferred for engraving text or curves on part surfaces?
A. Scallop
B. Project Rough Surface
C. Hybrid
D. Pencil

Q10. What is the key difference in selecting "Boss" or "Cavity" radio buttons in Parallel toolpath setup?
A. It changes tool selection
B. It alters surface finish type
C. It influences tool movement direction and cutting strategy
D. It controls feed rate

Q11. Which tool is generally used for Surface milling operations in Parallel Rough Surface toolpaths?
A. Flat end mill
B. Bull end mill or Ball end mill
C. Drill
D. Reamer

Q12. What is the main advantage of using Plunge Rough toolpath?
A. Reduces finishing time
B. Ideal for unstable machines or deep cuts
C. Best for flat surfaces
D. Optimized for multi-axis machining

Q13. Which 3D toolpath is specifically designed for machining multiple pockets using planar cuts?
A. Raster
B. Multisurface Pocket
C. Pencil
D. Contour

Q14. When should Area Rough toolpath be preferred over Dynamic Rough?
A. When machining curves
B. When stock is of same shape as part
C. When machining from block stock to part
D. When finishing is required

Q15. What type of geometry is most suitable for Waterline toolpath?
A. Flat surfaces
B. Horizontal surfaces
C. Steep angled surfaces
D. Undercuts

Q16. Which setting in Waterline toolpath ensures tool is always engaged in material up to a defined depth?
A. Critical Depths
B. Stepdown
C. Maximum Stock Engagement
D. Trim to stock

Q17. What does the Scallop Surface Finish toolpath primarily achieve?
A. Creates hole drilling cycles
B. Rounds sharp corners
C. Roughs material in raster pattern
D. Engraves part names

Q18. What is the key feature of Equal Scallop toolpath?
A. Used only for bosses
B. Consistent step over regardless of wall slope
C. Used only on flat surfaces
D. Engraves text

Q19. Which toolpath combines features of both Waterline and Scallop toolpaths?
A. Pencil
B. Hybrid
C. Spiral
D. Blend

Q20. Which 3D finishing toolpath is used to machine at intersections of surfaces?
A. Blend
B. Pencil
C. Scallop
D. Raster

Q21. What kind of movement does the Flowline toolpath use?
A. Waterline fashion
B. Along a blend curve
C. Along natural surface flow or channel path
D. Radial spirals

Q22. The Spiral toolpath is most useful when:
A. Machining ribs
B. Performing deep pockets
C. Finishing rounded and organic shapes
D. Milling thin walls

Q23. What is the main application of Radial toolpath?
A. Machining intersecting lines
B. Creating linear engraving
C. Machining spokes in wheel-like structures
D. Pocketing steep surfaces

Q24. Which 3D toolpath is specifically designed for deburring?
A. Waterline
B. Pencil
C. Deburr 3-axis
D. Flowline

Q25. What option in Deburr 3-axis defines whether sharp corners or relief grooves are added?
A. Edge shape
B. Inner corners
C. Transition method
D. Tool tip compensation

Q26. In the Project Rough Surface toolpath, selecting the Cavity option machines the curves:
A. Leaving area near curves safe
B. To specified depth
C. With scallop strategy
D. Using raster motion

Q27. In the Parallel Rough Surface toolpath, what happens if "Undefined" is selected instead of "Boss" or "Cavity"?
A. Toolpath will fail
B. You must select geometry manually
C. Mastercam decides best strategy automatically
D. Tool moves randomly

Q28. What is the primary function of the RCTF checkbox in Parallel toolpaths?
A. Applies automatic trochoidal motion
B. Uses radial chip thinning to calculate feed and speed
C. Enables lead-in radius
D. Allows override of plunge parameters

Q29. In Surface Parameters tab, Clearance is used to:
A. Define cutting direction
B. Avoid plunge cutting
C. Allow tool to move freely above workpiece
D. Disable compensation

Q30. Which parameter is most critical in achieving good surface finish in Rough Parallel toolpaths?
A. Tool holder type
B. Cut Depth
C. Material
D. Coolant method

Q31. In Plunge Rough toolpath, increasing Max Stepdown too much can result in:
A. Faster operation
B. Toolpath skipping features
C. Overload on tool
D. Better tool engagement

Q32. The key purpose of the Multisurface Pocket toolpath is to:
A. Perform high-speed rest finishing
B. Mill intersecting pockets
C. Rough multiple pocket surfaces using planar cuts
D. Apply simultaneous 5-axis motion

Q33. Area Rough toolpath is preferable over Dynamic OptiRough when:
A. Geometry has flat faces
B. Stock is rectangular or block shaped
C. Geometry is circular
D. Surface finish is required

Q34. In the Waterline toolpath, enabling Trim to Stock helps Mastercam to:
A. Skip toolpath generation
B. Recalculate operations based on leftover material
C. Modify cutter diameter
D. Avoid adding lead-ins

Q35. Which Waterline toolpath option defines the method of cutting open contours?
A. Tip compensation
B. Critical depths
C. Open contour direction
D. Clearance plane

Q36. When using the Raster Toolpath, the tool moves in:
A. Zigzag waterline pattern
B. Spiral format
C. Parallel linear passes
D. Trochoidal motion

Q37. What kind of tool is generally used for Scallop Surface Finish toolpaths?
A. Flat end mill
B. Tapered mill
C. Ball nose cutter
D. V-bit engraving tool

Q38. In Scallop toolpath, Flute Contact option ensures toolpath generation based on:
A. Tool shank
B. Full tool length
C. Flute length of the tool
D. Handle radius

Q39. Hybrid toolpath is a combination of:
A. Pencil and Spiral
B. Raster and Waterline
C. Scallop and Waterline
D. Blend and Radial

Q40. Which toolpath is best suited for finishing vertical walls of a 3D part?
A. Radial
B. Pencil
C. Contour
D. Area rough

Q41. Horizontal Area toolpath is functionally similar to which 2D operation?
A. Contour
B. Facing
C. Drilling
D. Thread Milling

Q42. What type of geometry is typically machined using the Flowline toolpath?
A. Flat floors
B. Channels and runners
C. Vertical bosses
D. Open pockets

Q43. In Flowline toolpath, selecting the Offset option allows:
A. Automatic stepdown
B. Tool tip compensation left/right
C. Auto scaling
D. Applying containment zone

Q44. In the Flowline toolpath, Cut direction button is used to:
A. Change vertical retraction method
B. Set the sequence of passes
C. Reverse or define tool movement direction
D. Define Z-step increment

Q45. Spiral toolpath is best used when:
A. You need planar cuts
B. Machining ribs
C. Finishing irregular organic shapes
D. Deburring hard edges

Q46. The Radial Surface Finish toolpath creates motion resembling:
A. Parallel steps
B. Circular arcs
C. Radiating spokes from center
D. Zigzag passes

Q47. What is the purpose of “Deburr 3-axis” toolpath?
A. Cut cavities
B. Machine undercuts
C. Break sharp edges and remove burrs
D. Create draft angles

Q48. In Deburr 3-axis toolpath, which option controls how sharp corners are processed?
A. Edge shape
B. Inner corners
C. Transition style
D. Pass direction

Q49. Which option in Deburr toolpath adds multiple loops for relief cuts at corners?
A. Loop radius
B. Inner corners
C. Add loops to relief cuts
D. Max edge height

Q50. What is the function of “Advanced Edge Options” in Deburr toolpath?
A. Sets spindle RPM
B. Defines geometry origin
C. Controls sharp edge angle, min length, and height limits
D. Sets backlash limits

Chapter 11

Multiaxis Milling Toolpaths

Topics Covered

The major topics covered in this chapter are:

- ***Introduction.***
- ***Curve Toolpath***
- ***Swarf Milling Toolpath***
- ***Parallel Multiaxis Toolpath***
- ***Multiaxis Along Curve Toolpath, Multiaxis Morph Toolpath, Multiaxis Flow Toolpath***
- ***Multiaxis Multisurface Toolpath, Multiaxis Port Toolpath, Multiaxis Triangular Mesh Toolpath***
- ***Deburr Toolpath***
- ***Multiaxis Pocketing Toolpath***
- ***3+2 Automatic Roughing Toolpaths, Multiaxis Project Curve Toolpath***
- ***Multiaxis Rotary Toolpath and Multiaxis Rotary Advanced Toolpath***
- ***Multiaxis Swarf Toolpath***

INTRODUCTION

In previous chapters, you have learned to create 2D and 3D toolpaths. In this chapter, you will learn to create multiaxis toolpaths for machining irregular 3D faces of the model. The tools to create multiaxis toolpaths are available in the **Multiaxis** group of **Toolpaths** tab in the **Ribbon**; refer to Figure-1. Various tools for multiaxis toolpath creation are discussed next.

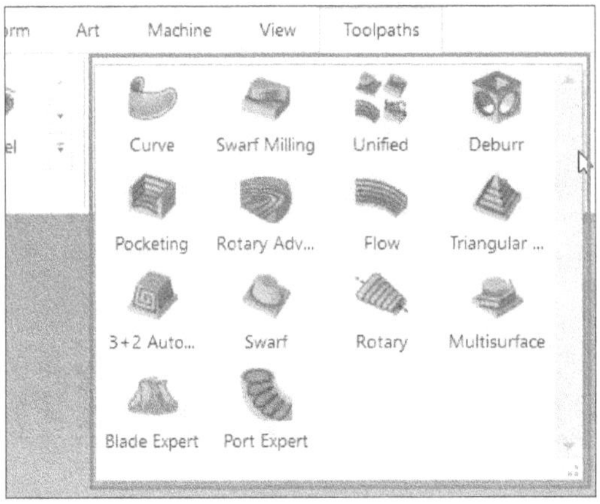

Figure-1. Multiaxis tool

CREATING CURVE TOOLPATH

The **Curve** tool is used to create toolpath for machining 3D curves. The procedure to use this tool is given next.

- Click on the **Curve** tool from the **Multiaxis** group in the **Toolpaths** tab of the **Ribbon**. The **Multiaxis Toolpath - Curve** dialog box will be displayed; refer to Figure-2.
- Select desired cutting tool and tool holder using the options in the dialog box. Generally, a ball end mill cutting tool is used to perform multiaxis milling operations.
- If you want to machine stock left from any previous operation then select the **Stock** option from the left area of the dialog box and specify related parameters.
- Click on the **Cut Pattern** option from the left area of the dialog box to define how cutting tool will move on the 3D curve path; refer to Figure-3.

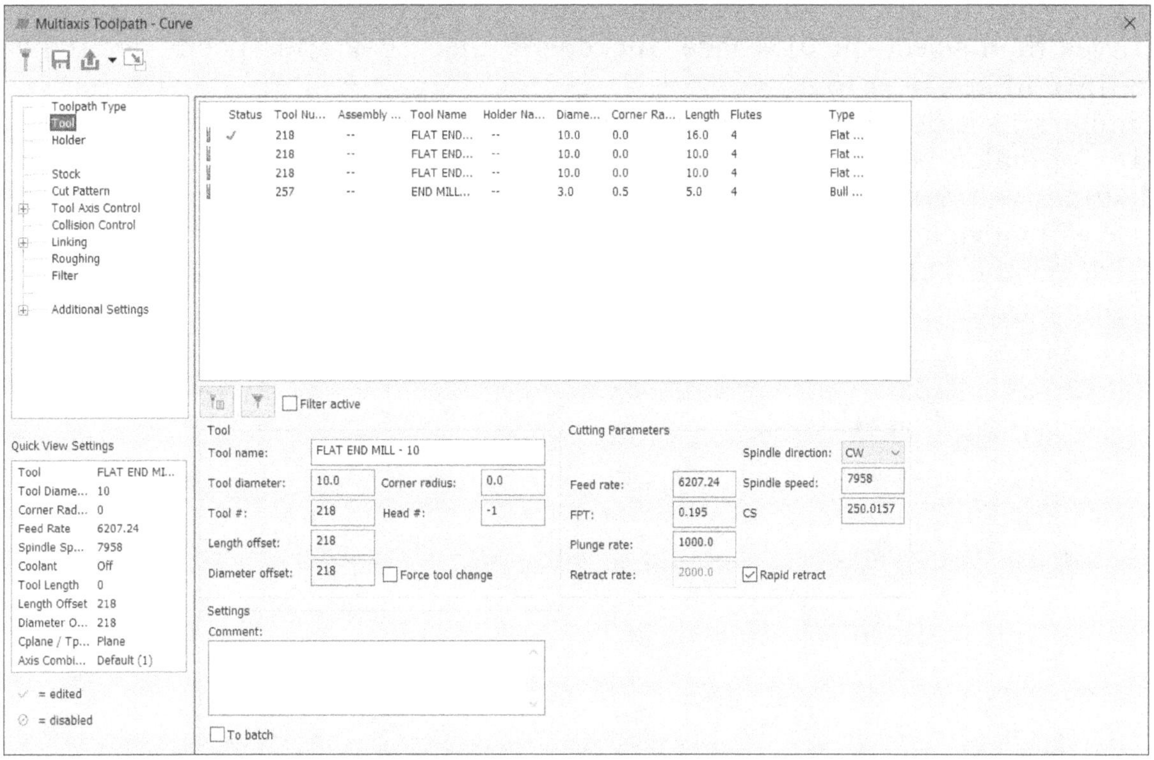

Figure-2. Multiaxis Toolpath-Curve dialog box

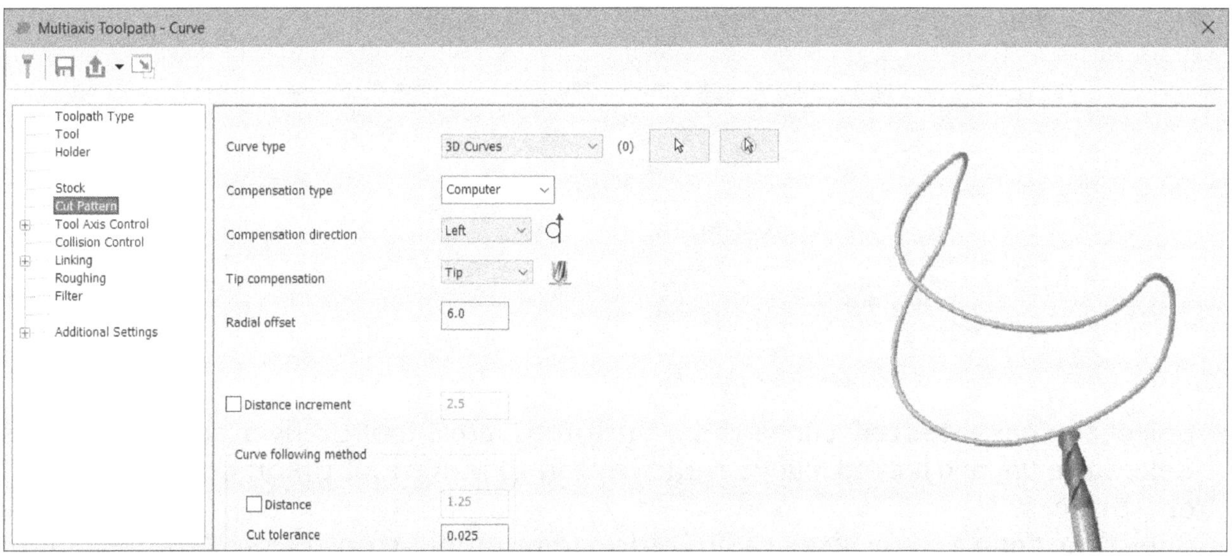

Figure-3. Cut Pattern options for 3D Curve toolpath

- Select the **3D Curves** option from the **Curve type** drop-down if you want to select 3D curves created by using selected wireframe curves or edges of the model. Select the **Surface edge - all** option from the **Curve type** drop-down if you want to select all the edges of selected surface for creating toolpath. Select the **Surface edge - single** option from the drop-down if you want to select edges one by one for defining path of curves. After selecting desired option from drop-down, click on the **Select** button next to the drop-down to select the entities.
- Set desired parameters in **Compensation type**, **Compensation direction**, and **Tip compensation** drop-downs as discussed earlier.
- Set desired value in the **Radial offset** edit box to offset cutting tool by specified value away from the selected curves.

- If you want to specify an increment value for cutting passes along the selected curves then select the **Distance increment** check box and specify desired value in the edit box next to it.
- Similarly, set desired parameters in the edit boxes of **Curve following method** area of dialog box to define how curve will be followed while cutting. Specified distance values will be considered to create imaginary control points and cutting tool will move linearly between these control points.
- Click on the **Collision Control** option from the left area of the dialog box to define parameters related to collision avoidance by cutting tool; refer to Figure-4.

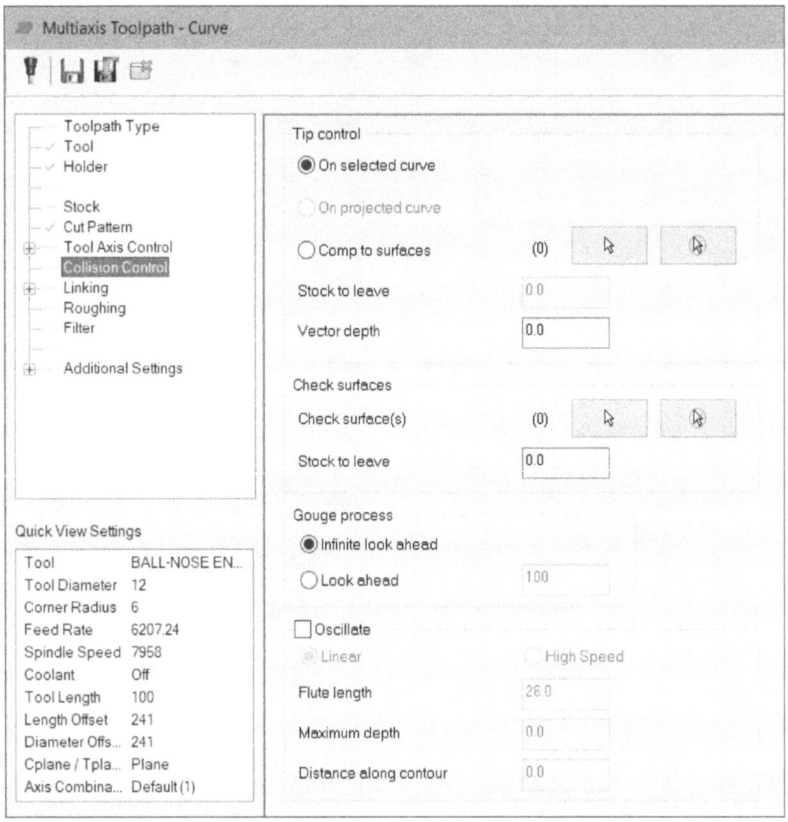

Figure-4. Collision Control options

- Select the **On selected curve** radio button to move tool tip over selected curves.
- Select the **On projected curve** radio button to move tool tip on curves projected on surfaces.
- Select the **Comp to surfaces** radio button to put tool tip on selected compensation surfaces.
- Specify desired value in **Stock to leave** edit box to define how much stock will be left after performing operation.
- Specify desired value in the **Vector depth** edit box to offset tool tip by specified value in the vector direction. A positive value in the edit box will raise the tool tip and negative value will lower the tool tip.
- Click on the **Select check surfaces** button from the **Check surfaces** area of the dialog box to specify surfaces to be avoided while machining.
- Set the other parameters as desired and click on the **OK** button to generate the toolpath. The curve toolpaths will be created; refer to Figure-5.

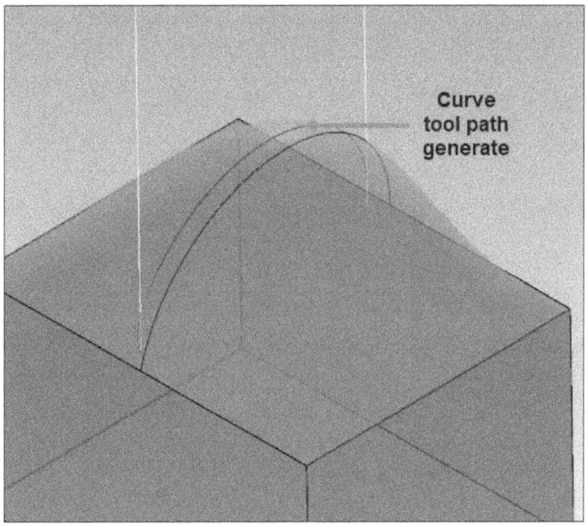

Figure-5. Curve toolpath generated

CREATING SWARF MILLING TOOLPATH

The **Swarf Milling** tool is used to machine the geometry using side edge of cutting tool. You can use this milling path to rough machine blades of turbines and other objects. The procedure to use this tool is given next.

- Click on the **Swarf Milling** tool from the **Multiaxis** group in the **Toolpaths** tab of the **Ribbon**. The **Multiaxis Toolpath - Swarf Milling** dialog box will be displayed; refer to Figure-6.

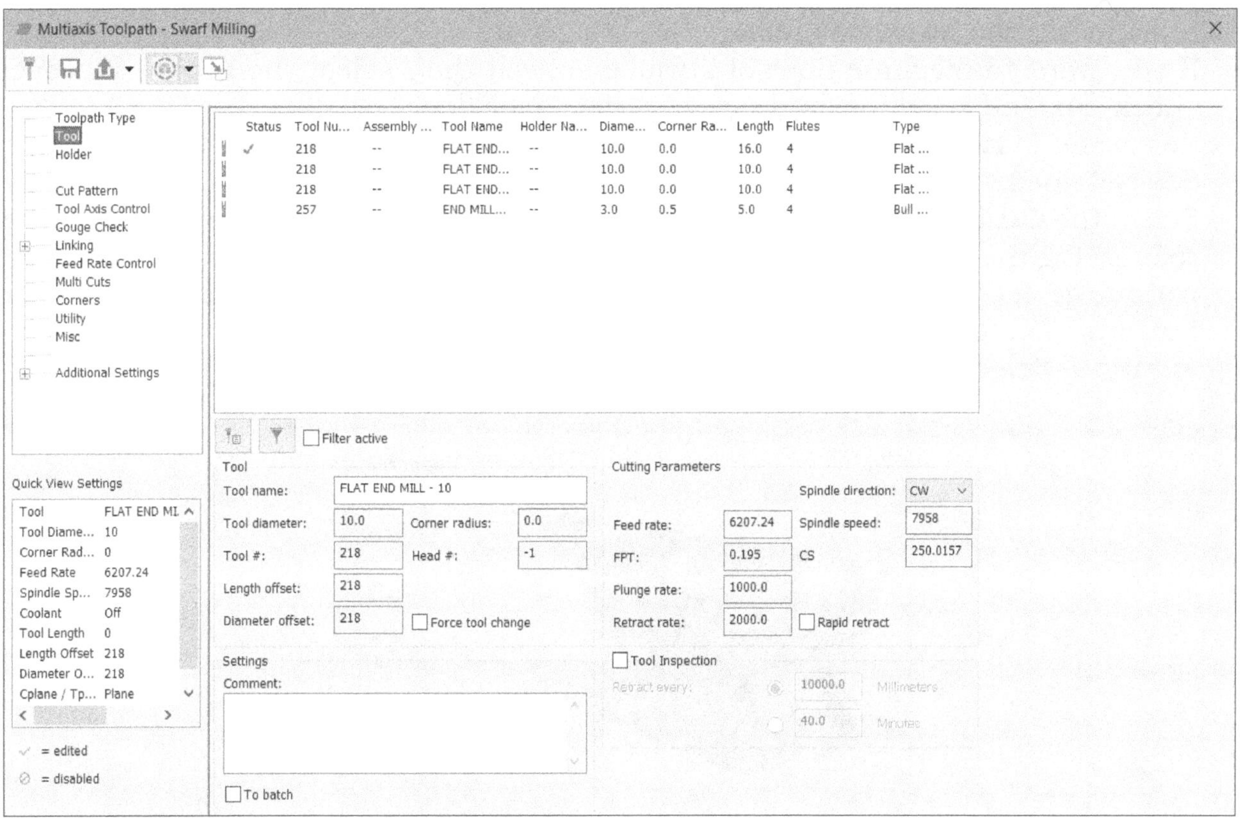

Figure-6. Multiaxis Toolpath - Swarf Milling dialog box

- Select the cutting tool and tool holder as discussed earlier.
- Click on the **Cut Pattern** option from the left area to set parameters related to cutting pattern for swarf milling; refer to Figure-7.

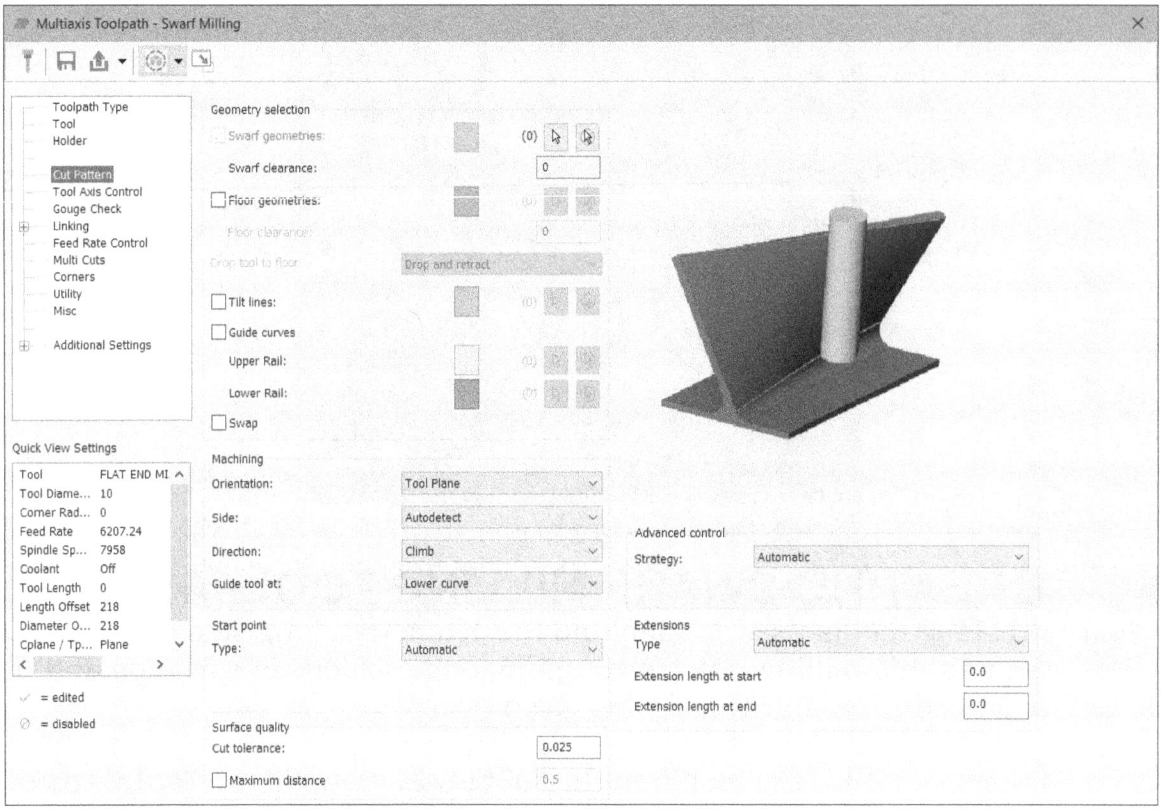

Figure-7. Cut pattern for Multiaxis Toolpath-Swarf Milling dialog box

- Click on the **Select** button for the **Swarf geometries** section and select surfaces to be machined by swarf milling.
- If you want to machine floor of surface as well then select the **Floor surfaces** check box and select desired faces/surfaces for floor.
- Select the **Tilt lines** check box to define axis direction of cutting tool and select desired lines.
- Select the **Guide curves** check box to select upper rail curve and lower rail curve; refer to Figure-8. Note that you can change the graphical representation colors of various geometric entities by using respective **Colors** buttons adjacent to selection buttons. The **Colors** dialog box will be displayed to modify the color; refer to Figure-9. Select desired color and click on the **OK** button to apply changes.

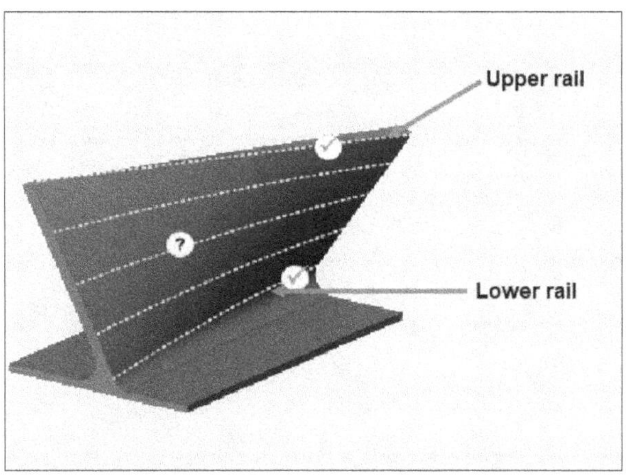

Figure-8. Rail curves for swarf toolpath

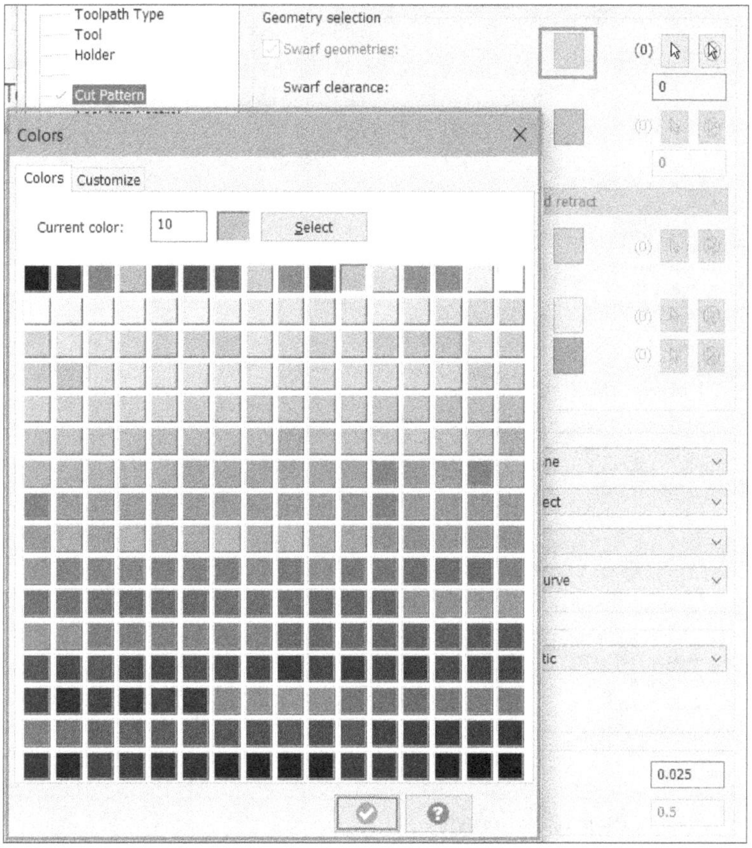

Figure-9. Colors dialog box1

- Select the **Swap** check box to switch upper rail with lower rail.
- Select desired option from the **Orientation** drop-down to define orientation of tools for operations.
- Select desired option from the **Side** drop-down to define which side of cutting tool will be used for performing milling operation.
- Set the other parameters as desired in the **Cut Pattern** page.
- Click on the **Tool Axis Control** option from the left area to specify output format for milling operation. By default, **5 axis** option is selected in the **Output format** drop-down, so cutting tool can move freely along all five axes while cutting. Select the **4 axis** option from the **Output format** drop-down to generate 4 axis toolpath output using selected tilt axis. Select the **3 axis** option from the drop-down to generate 3 axis toolpath.
- Click on the **Gouge Check** option from the left area to define parameters for avoiding collision and perform gouge check; refer to Figure-10.
- Select desired option from the **Check against** drop-down in **Gouge excess** area to define reference to be used for checking collision of tool and holder with workpiece (This collision of tool & holder with workpiece is called gouging). Select the **Guide curves only** option if you want to perform gouge check using guide curves as reference. Select the **Swarf geometries** option to perform gouge check using selected swarf geometries as reference. Select the **Additional geometries** option if you want to use additional selected geometries of the model for gouge check. Select the **Swarf and additional geometries** option if you want to use both swarf geometries and additional selected geometries for gouge check.

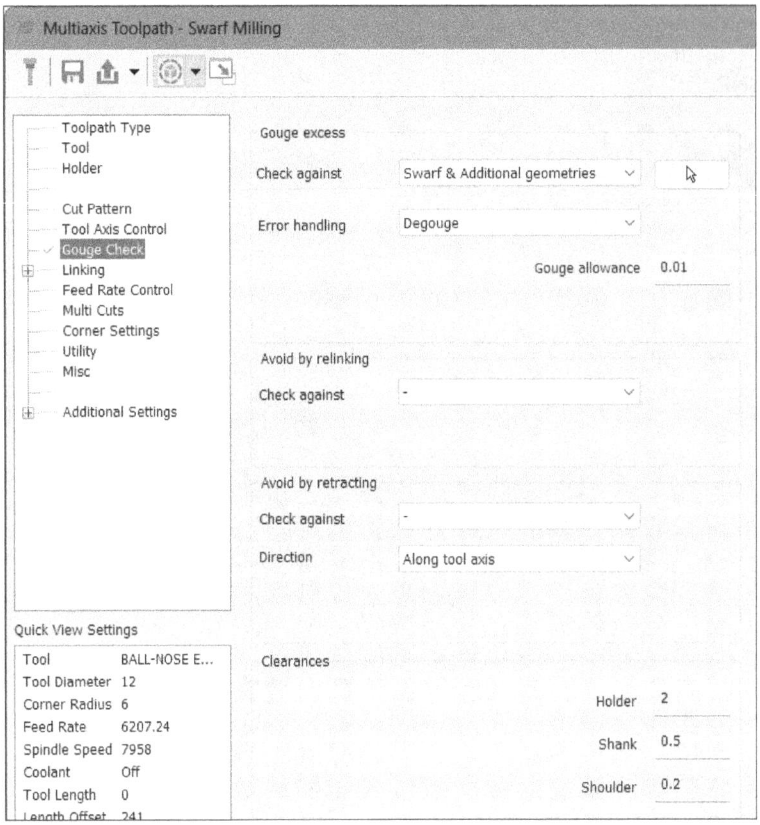

Figure-10. Gouge Check options

- If you have selected **Swarf geometries** option or **Swarf and additional geometries** option in the **Check against** drop-down then **Error handling** drop-down will be displayed in **Gouge excess** area. Select desired option from the **Error handling** drop-down to define how the tool will behave when a possible collision can occur. Select the **Degouge** option to move tool away from swarf surfaces by a small distance. Select the **Balance** option to mark gouge amount of material as rest material for next toolpath. Select the **Balance within allowance** to define the limit of material that can be marked as rest material on gouging.
- In **Gouge allowance** edit box, you can specify the amount of material that can gouge while machining. Specify the amount that you can trust, your cutting tool side edge will remove.
- Set desired options in the **Avoid by relinking** and **Avoid by retracting** drop-downs to define how the geometry of part to be avoided by respective method.
- Click on the **Linking** option from the left area in the dialog box and specify the entry/exit path for machining.
- Click on the **Feed Rate Control** option from the left area in the dialog box and set desired parameters to adjust feed rates at various critical locations like edges, blend splines, and so on.
- Click on the **Multi Cuts** option from the left area to specify the pattern in which cutting passes will be generated; refer to Figure-11.
- Specify the number of cutting passes and the cutting pattern in the dialog box.
- Select the **Corners** option from the dialog box and specify whether you want to generate sharp corners or round corners.
- Select the **Utility** option from the dialog box to set orientation of cutting tool about selected axis; refer to Figure-12. The options in this page are useful when you want to tilt the cutting tool axis about a specific coordinate system axis to machine curved surfaces usually in case of turbine blades and fins.

- After setting all desired parameters, click on the **OK** button from the dialog box. The toolpath will be generated; refer to Figure-13.

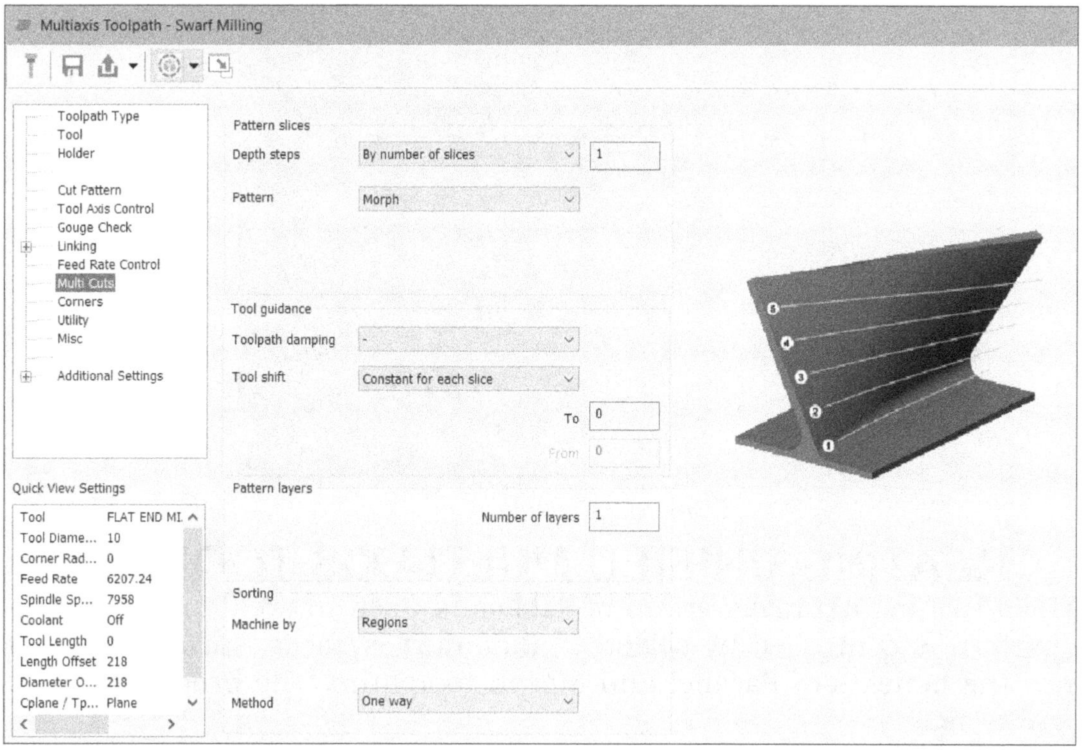

Figure-11. Multi Cuts page

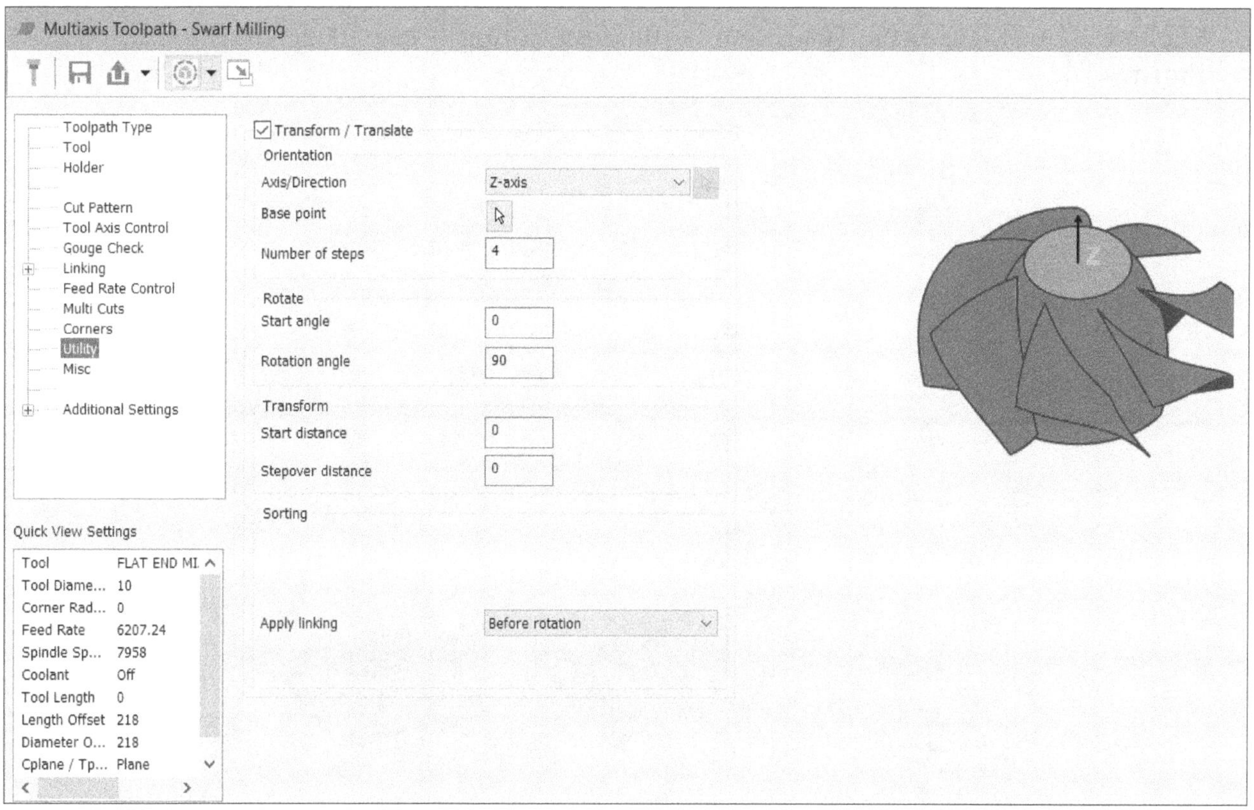

Figure-12. Utility options

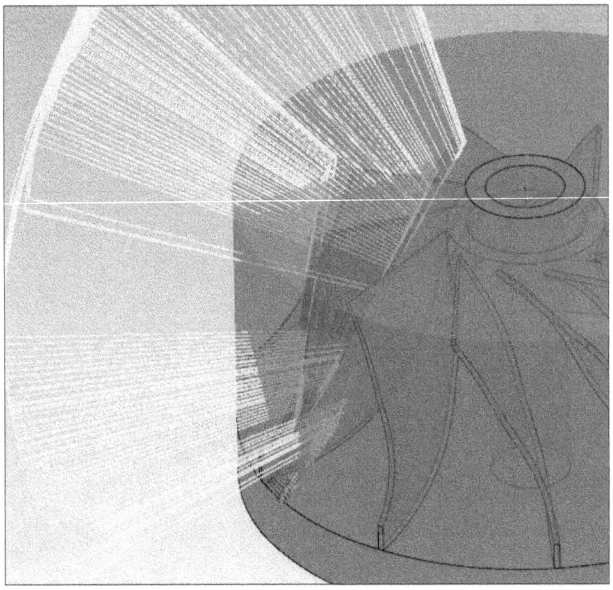

Figure-13. Swarf toolpath generated

CREATING UNIFIED MULTIAXIS TOOLPATH

The **Unified** tool in **Multiaxis** group of **Ribbon** is used to create multiaxis toolpath whose pattern is controlled by selected guide curves/faces/surface. This toolpath combines the benefits of Parallel and Morph toolpaths. The procedure to use this tool is given next.

- Click on the **Unified** tool from the **Multiaxis** group in the **Toolpaths** tab of the **Ribbon**. The **Multiaxis Toolpath - Unified** dialog box will be displayed; refer to Figure-14.

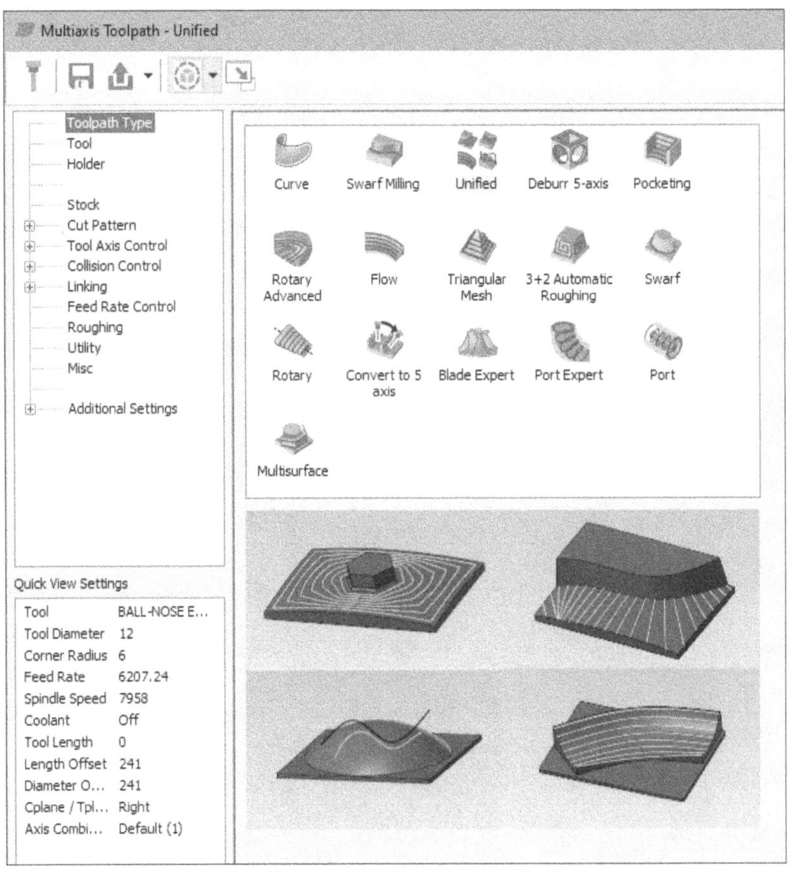

Figure-14. Multiaxis Toolpath-Unified dialog box

- Set the cutting tool, tool holder, and stock parameters as discussed earlier.
- Click on the **Cut Pattern** option from the left in the dialog box. The options in the dialog box will be displayed as shown in Figure-15.

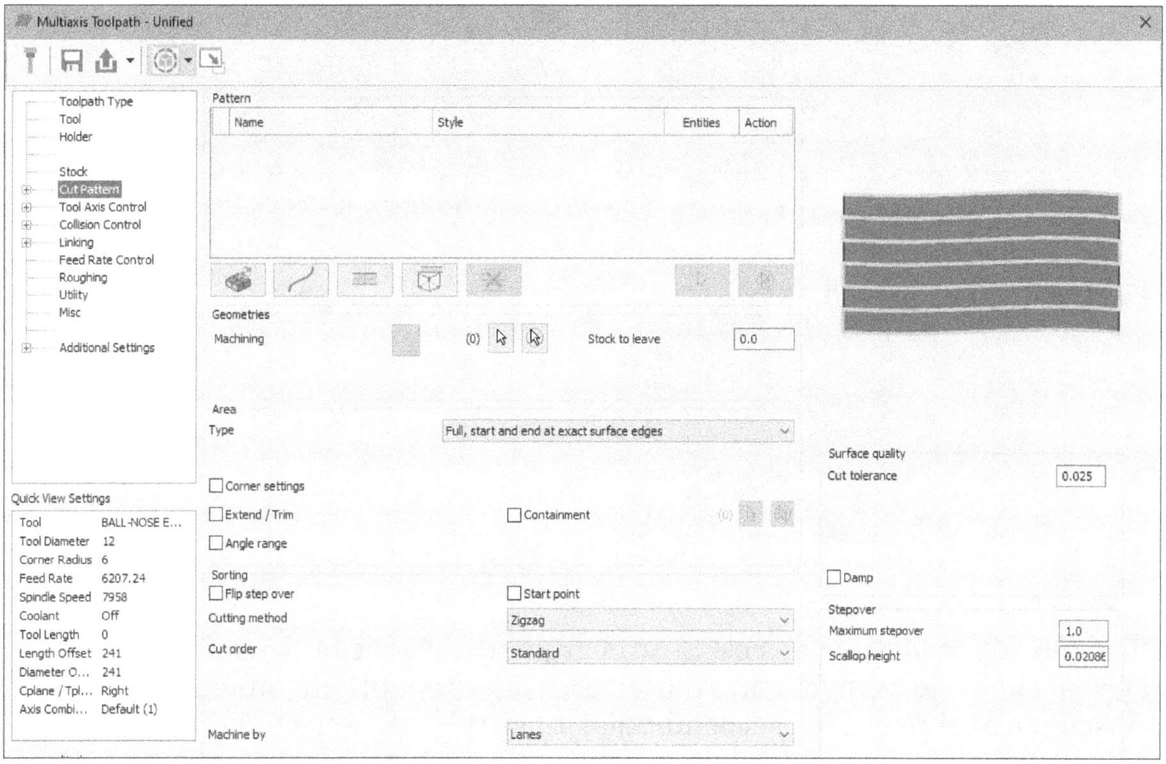

Figure-15. Cut Pattern options for Unified toolpath

- Click on the **Select** button for **Machining geometries** option in the **Machining** area of dialog box and select the entity to be machined from the model.
- Select desired button from the **Pattern** area in the dialog box to define the pattern in which toolpaths will be created. These options are discussed next.

Patterns for Unified Toolpath

- Click on the **Add Automatic row** button from the **Pattern** area to automatically generate pattern of toolpath based on selected cutting strategy. On selecting this option, an entry of Automatic pattern will be added in the table.
- Click in the **Style** drop-down to select cutting strategy; refer to Figure-16. Previews of some toolpaths for different automatic styles as shown in Figure-17.

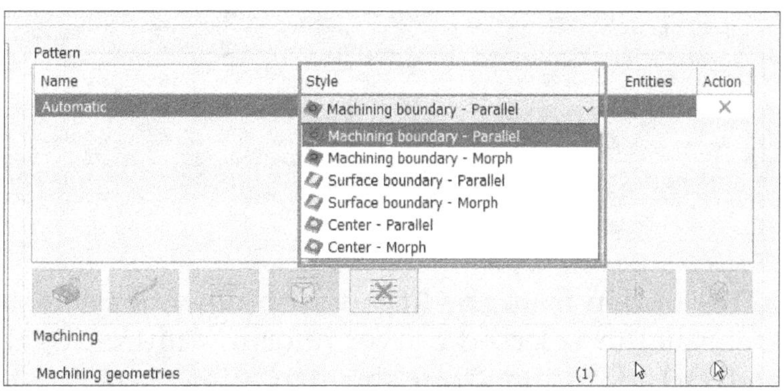

Figure-16. Style drop-down

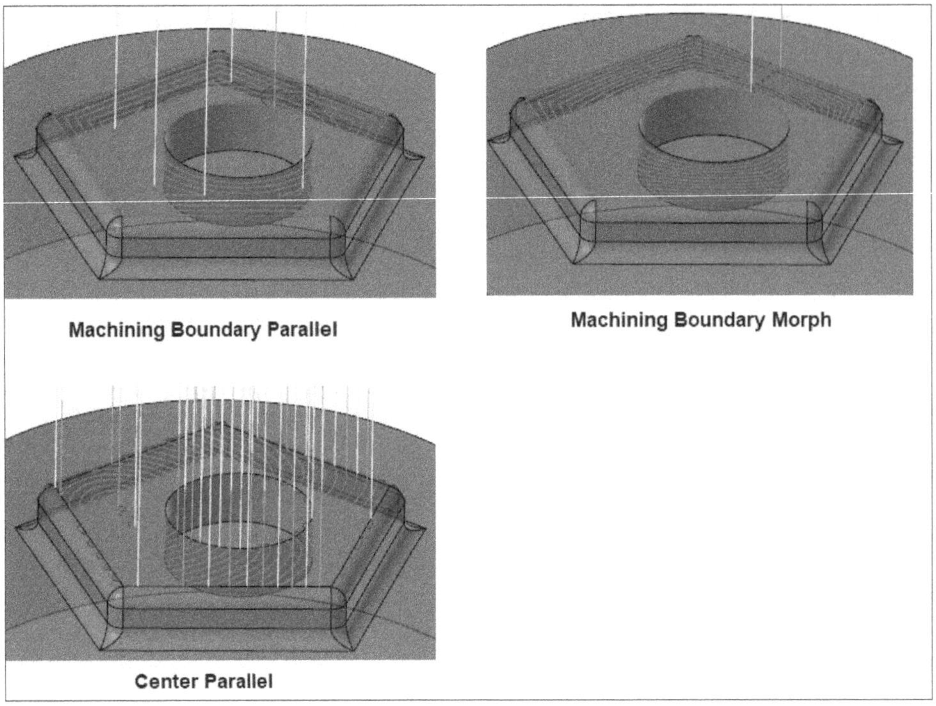

Figure-17. Preview of Automatic pattern toolpaths

- Click on the **Add Curve row** button from the **Pattern** area to use curves as references for defining cutting pattern. Using this option, you can create cutting passes parallel to curve, perpendicular to curve, use selected curve as guide, or project the curve on machining surface to cutting pass; refer to Figure-18.
- After setting desired curve options, click on the **Select** button at the bottom in **Pattern** area and select desired curve; refer to Figure-19.

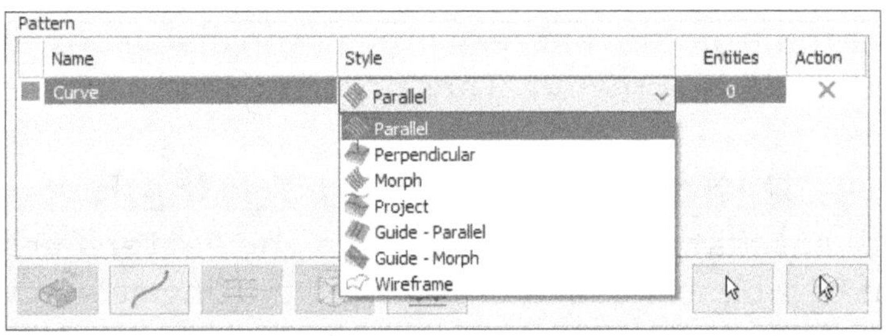

Figure-18. Style drop-down for curve

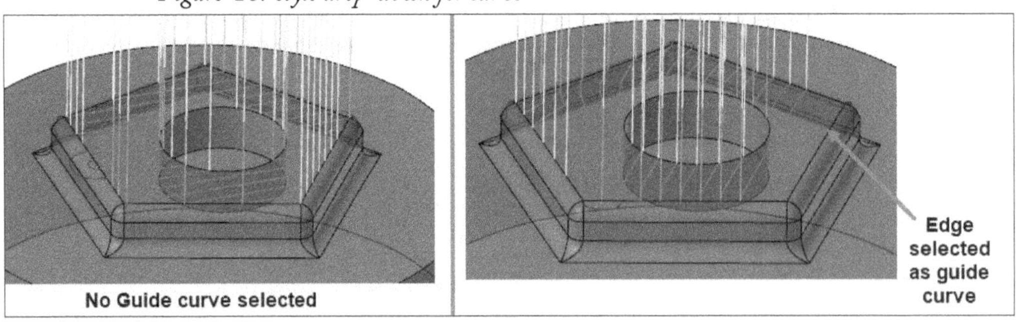

Figure-19. Using curve as guide for toolpath

- Select the **Parallel** option from the **Style** drop-down for selected curve to make cutting passes parallel to selected curve; refer to Figure-20. Similarly, you can use the **Perpendicular** option from the drop-down to create cutting passes perpendicular to selected curve. Select the **Project** option to machine only projection of selected curve of the model surface.

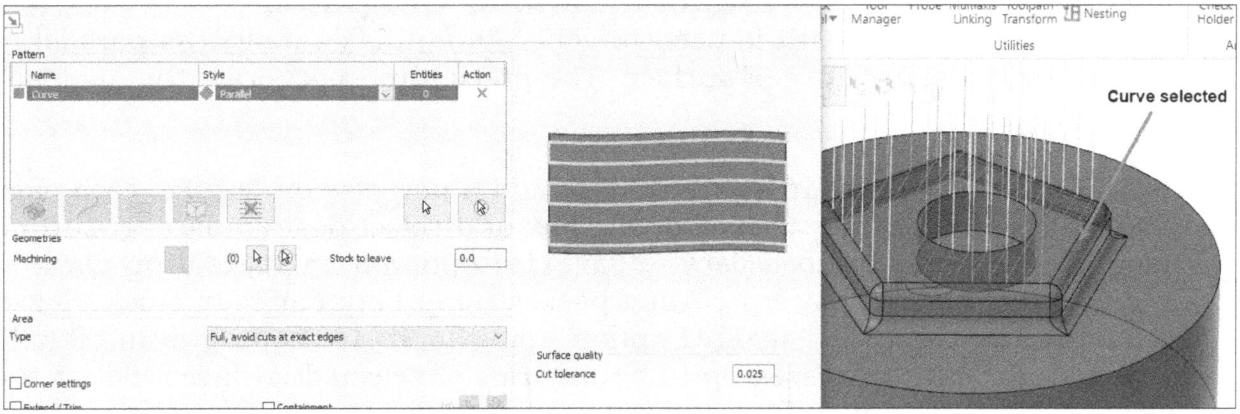

Figure-20. Cutting passes parallel to selected curve

- Select the **Add Surface row** button from the **Pattern** area to use selected surfaces for defining cutting pass pattern. You can use selected surface as guide for creating cutting passes parallel to selected surface, and create flowline along long side, short side, U, or V directions; refer to Figure-21.

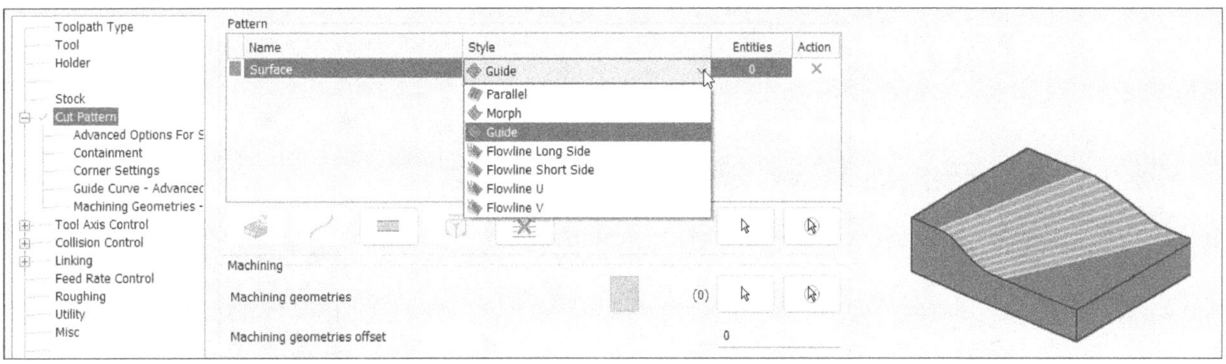

Figure-21. Using surface for cutting pattern

- Select the **Add Plane row** button to use selected plane for defining direction of cutting passes. Select desired option from the **Style** drop-down to define reference direction for cutting passes; refer to Figure-22.

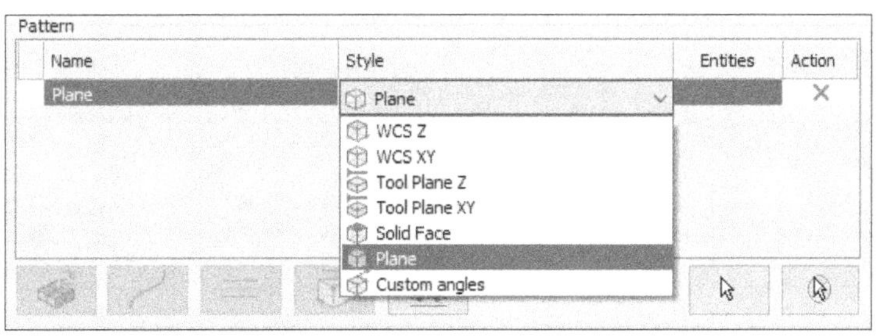

Figure-22. Style drop-down for plane

- Specify other parameters as discussed earlier and click on the **OK** button to create the toolpath.

Creating Parallel Multiaxis Toolpaths

The Parallel multiaxis toolpath is used to generate multiaxis toolpaths parallel to each other following curvature of surface. The procedure to generate this toolpath is given next.

- Click on the **Add Automatic row** button to add a new row on **Cut Pattern** page of **Multiaxis Toolpath - Unified** dialog box and select desired parallel cutting option. Select **Machining boundary - Parallel** option from **Style** drop-down in table to create parallel pattern cutting passes up to boundaries of stock. Select the **Surface boundary - Parallel** option from the **Style** drop-down in table to create parallel cutting passes up to boundaries of selected surfaces. Select the **Center - Parallel** option from the drop-down to create parallel cutting passes starting from center of selected geometry. If you want to create cutting passes parallel to selected curve then click on the **Add Curve row** button and select the **Parallel** option from the **Style** drop-down. To manually create parallel surface machining rather than using automatic option, click on the **Add Surface row** button from the **Pattern** area in the **Cut Pattern** page and select the **Parallel** option from **Style** drop-down; refer to Figure-23.

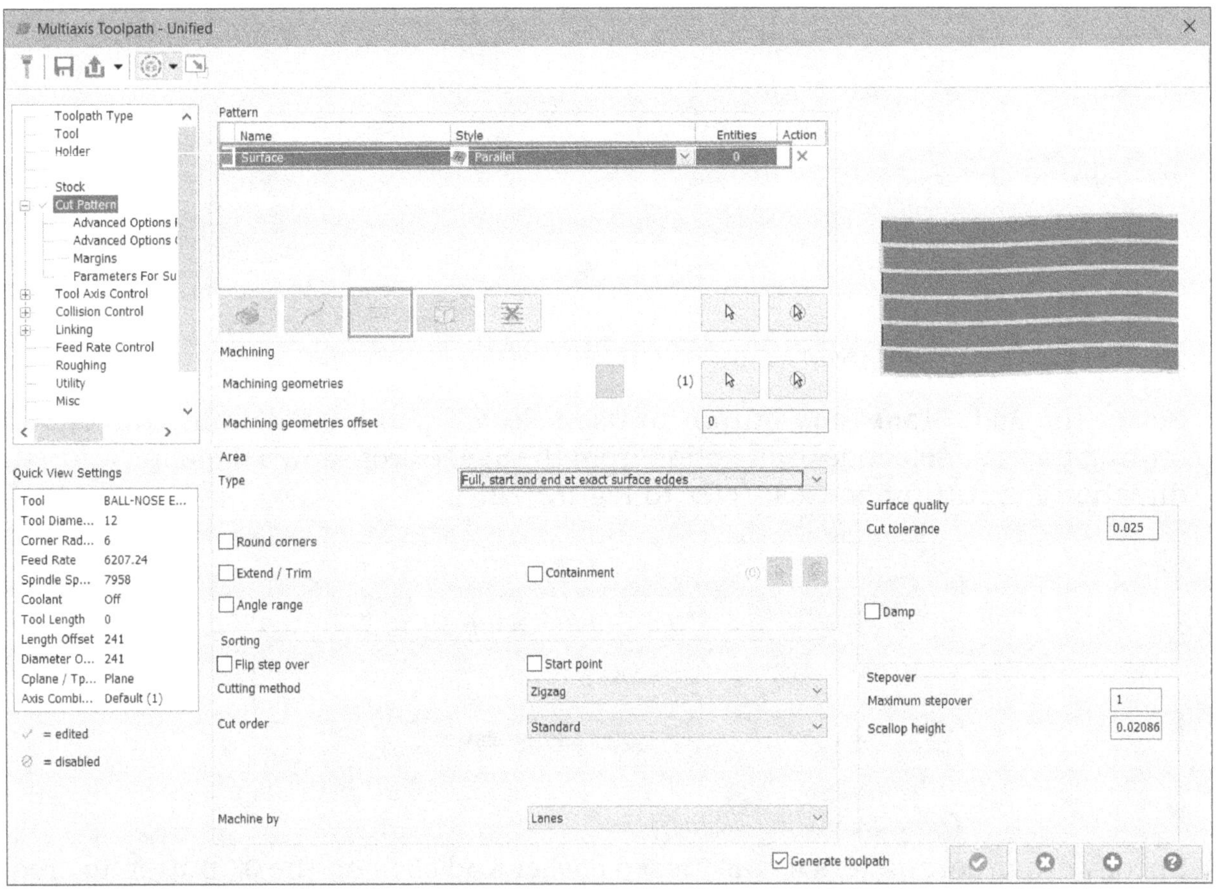

Figure-23. Surface Parallel options

- After selecting desired option for parallel toolpaths, click on the **Select** button in **Pattern** area to select related geometry. For example, if you have selected parallel to curve option then click on the **Select** button for curves from **Pattern** area and select the curves from graphics area; refer to Figure-24. If you are using surface boundary option then select the surface of model; refer to Figure-25.

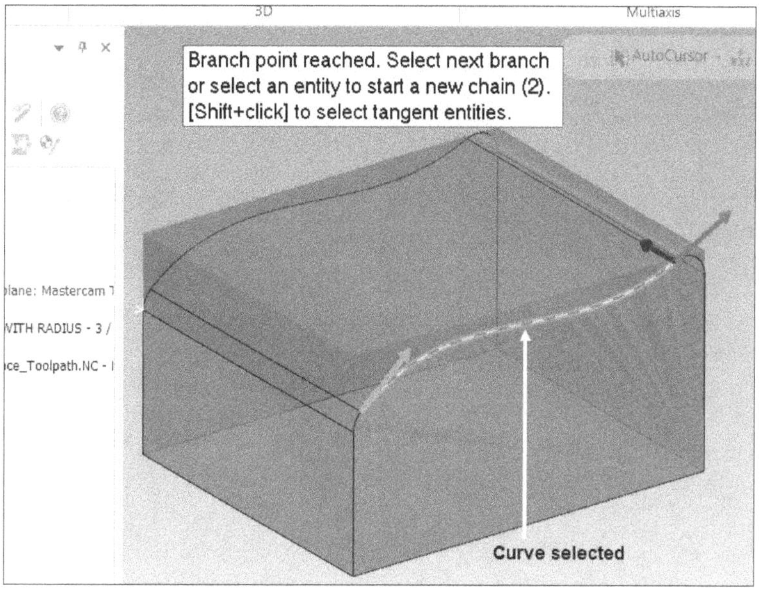

Figure-24. Curve selected for defining parallel direction

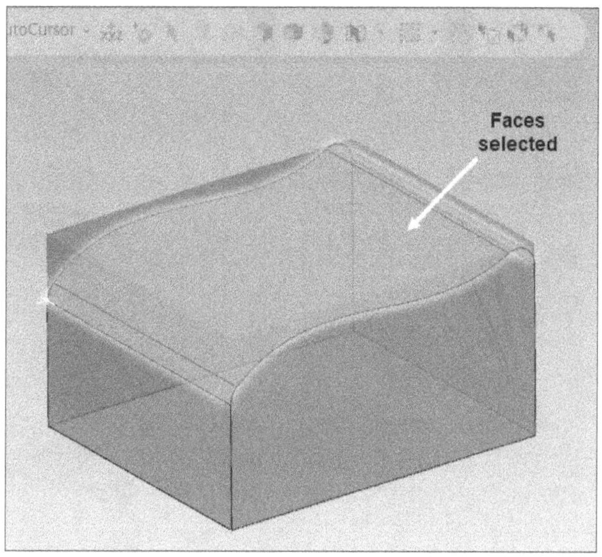

Figure-25. Drive faces selected

- Set the other parameters like cutting method, cut order, machining order, and so on as desired in this page.
- Click on the **Advanced Options For Surface Quality** option from the **Cut Pattern** node to define parameters for smoothening the toolpath. The options will be displayed as shown in Figure-26.
- Select the **Smooth toolpath** check box to smoothen sharp corners in the toolpath. After selecting the check box, specify minimum angle to be considered as sharp corner in the **Detection angle** check box and set the distance value allowed between sharp corners and toolpath spline in the **Smoothing distance** edit box.
- Select the **Parameters For Surface Edge Handling** option from the **Cut Pattern** node to smoothen abrupt changes in the edges of surface. The options will be displayed as shown in Figure-27.

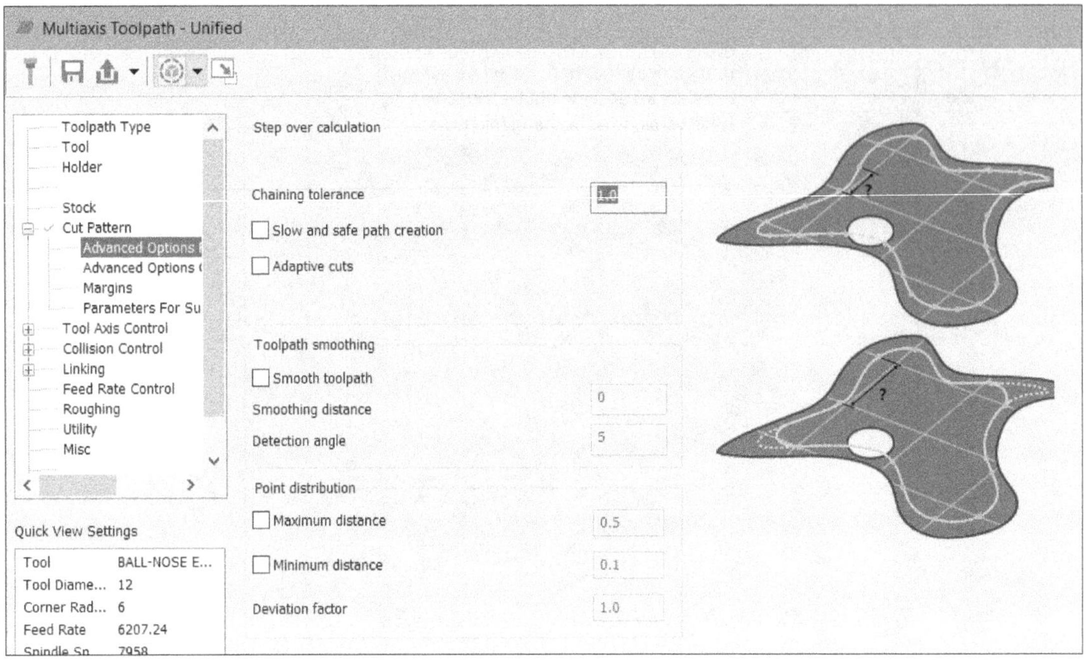

Figure-26. Advanced Options For Surface Quality page

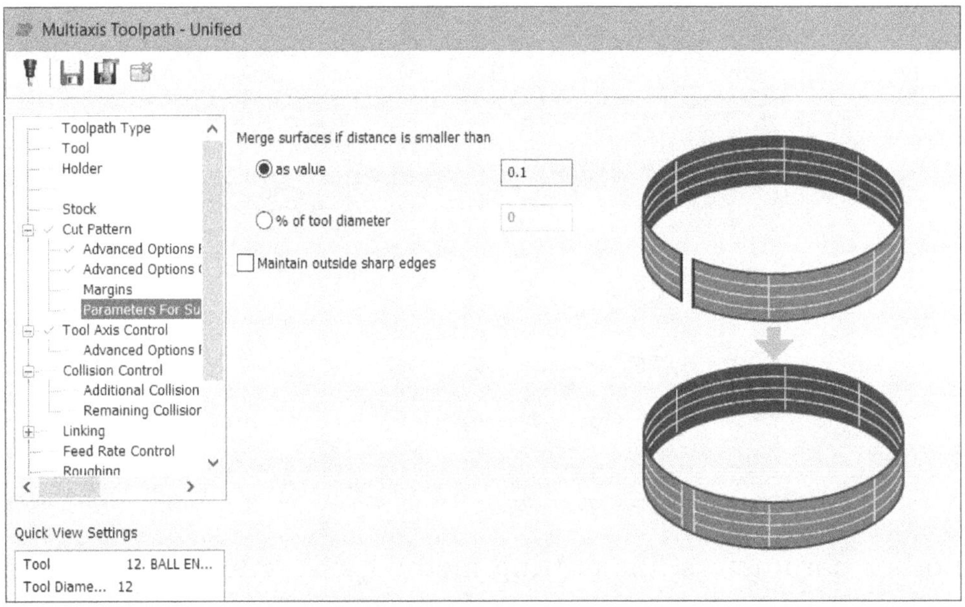

Figure-27. Parameters for Surface Edge Handling options

- Set desired value in the edit box to define minimum distance value of gap below which the gap will be merged automatically. If you want to specify gap with respect to tool diameter then select the **% of tool diameter** radio button and specify the value in respective edit box.
- Select the **Maintain outside sharp edges** check box to move tool away from sharp corner while cutting so that the sharp corners are not damaged by machining. On selecting this check box, you will be asked to specify radius of outer loop and angle value above which all corners will be considered as sharp edges
- Select the **Advanced Options Of Surface Paths Pattern** option from the left area to define how patterns will be generated for surface. Select the **Generate toolpath only at front side** check box if you do not want the toolpath to start from middle or any other location except front side. After selecting this check box, specify angle tangent to starting edge at which cutting passes will start in the **Single edge toolpath tangent angle** edit box.

- Select the **Margins** option from left area and specify the margin value by which cutting passes will be extended at the start and end of selected surface/curve boundaries. Select the **Add internal tool radius** check box to add tool radius at start and end of cutting passes.

Collision Control Options

- Select the **Collision Control** option from the left area to define parameters for avoiding collision while performing machining; refer to Figure-28.

Figure-28. Collision Control options for Unified toolpath

- Select desired check boxes from the **Check** area to define which components of cutting tool will be considered while creating strategy for avoiding collision. You can select **Flute**, **Shoulder**, **Shank**, and **Holder** check boxes to use them as reference for avoiding collision.
- Select desired options from the drop-downs in the **Strategy and parameters** area of the dialog box to define how the collision will be avoided. You can set the tool to retract, tilt, trim & relink toolpath, stop cutting, or just report collision.
- Select desired check boxes from the **Geometry** area to define which geometries will be used from the model to avoid collision. By default, the **Machining geometries** check box is selected so the faces/surfaces selected for machining are automatically avoided from collision. If you select the **Avoidance geometries** check box then you can select desired surfaces to be avoided from collision.
- Select **Cylindrical** radio button from the **Clearance type** area to define clearance distance from cylindrical components by specified values. Select the **Conical** radio button if the components are conical and you want to specify lower as well as upper offset values for clearance. After selecting the radio button, specify related parameters in the **Clearances** area of the dialog box.

- Set the other parameters as desired. Note that by default, the **1** check box is selected, so one strategy is created for avoiding collision. You can create up to 4 different strategies to avoid collision by using the options in **Additional Collision Control Strategies** page of the dialog box.
- Set the other parameters as discussed earlier and click on the **OK** button to create the toolpath. The toolpath will be generated; refer to Figure-29.

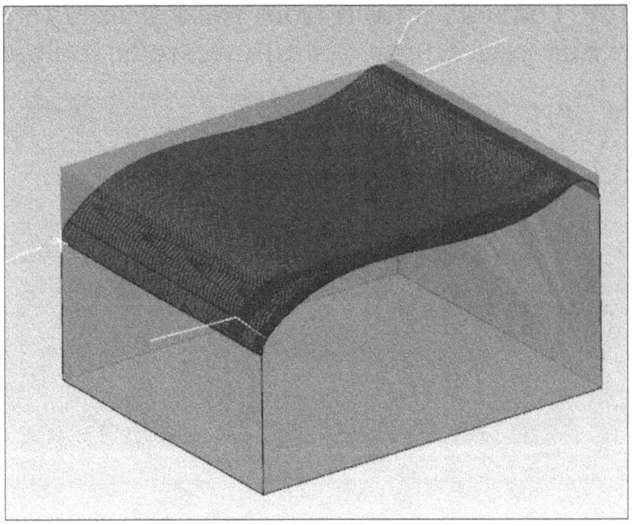

Figure-29. Parallel toolpath generated

Linking Parameters for Unified Toolpath

- Click on the **Linking** option from the left area of the dialog box to define entry and exit path for toolpath and cutting passes. The **Linking** page will be displayed in the dialog box; refer to Figure-30.

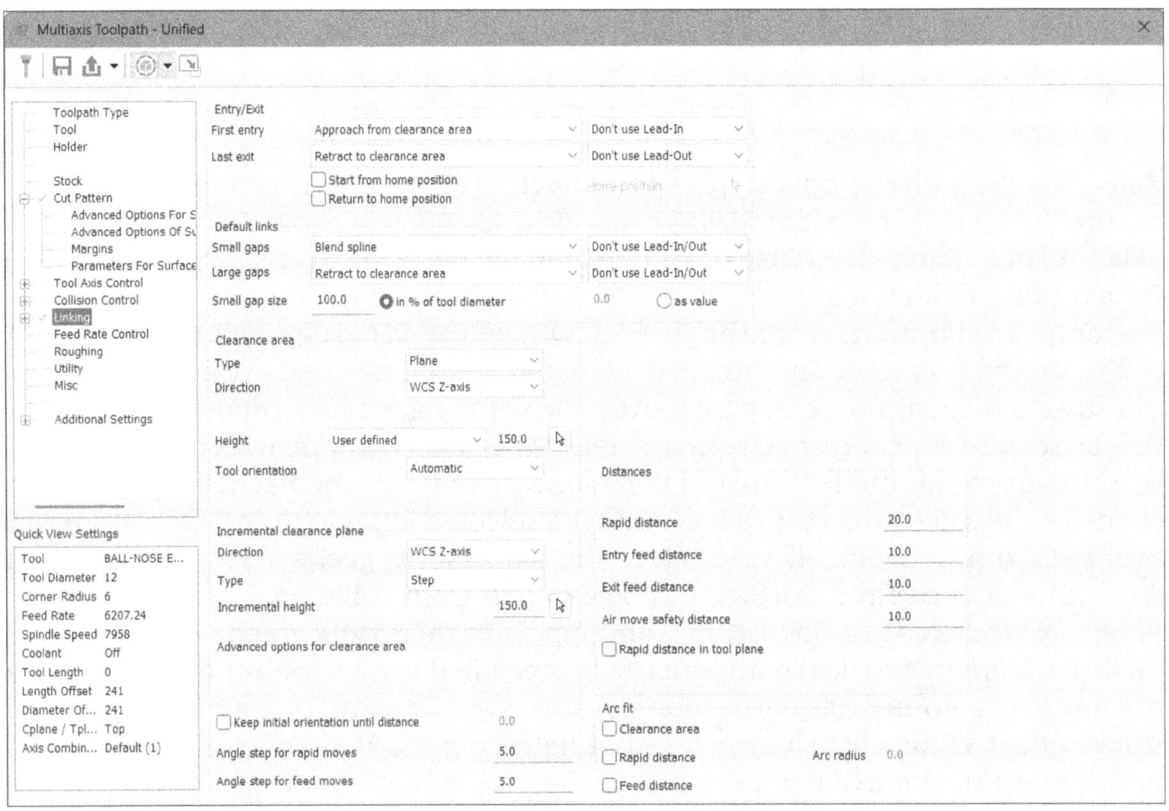

Figure-30. Linking page

- Select desired options in the **First entry** and **Last exit** drop-downs to define how cutting tools will enter the workpiece and exit the workpiece while generating toolpath.
- Select desired options from the drop-downs next to **First entry** and **Last exit** drop-downs to define whether you want to apply lead in/out curves or not. On selecting the **Use Lead-In** and **Use Lead-Out** options from the drop-downs, respective pages will be added in the dialog box.
- Select the **Start from home position** and **Return to home position** check boxes to start moving cutting tool from home position at the start of toolpath and then return the cutting tool to home position at the end of toolpath, respectively.
- The options in the **Default links** area are used to define how small and large gaps in toolpaths will be filled by linking toolpath segments. Select desired options from the **Small gaps** and **Large gaps** drop-downs to define linking segments.
- Specify desired value in the **Small gap size** edit box to define size of small gap in percentage of cutting tool diameter.
- Set the other parameters as discussed earlier and click on the **OK** button from the dialog box. The toolpath will be generated.

Creating Multiaxis Morph Toolpath

The Morph toolpath is used to perform machining on surface trapped between two leading curves. The procedure to use this tool is given next.

- Click on the **Add Automatic row** button from the **Pattern** area in the **Cut Pattern** page of **Multiaxis Toolpath - Unified** dialog box and select the **Machining boundary - Morph**, **Surface boundary - Morph**, or **Center - Morph** option from the **Style** drop-down; refer to Figure-31.

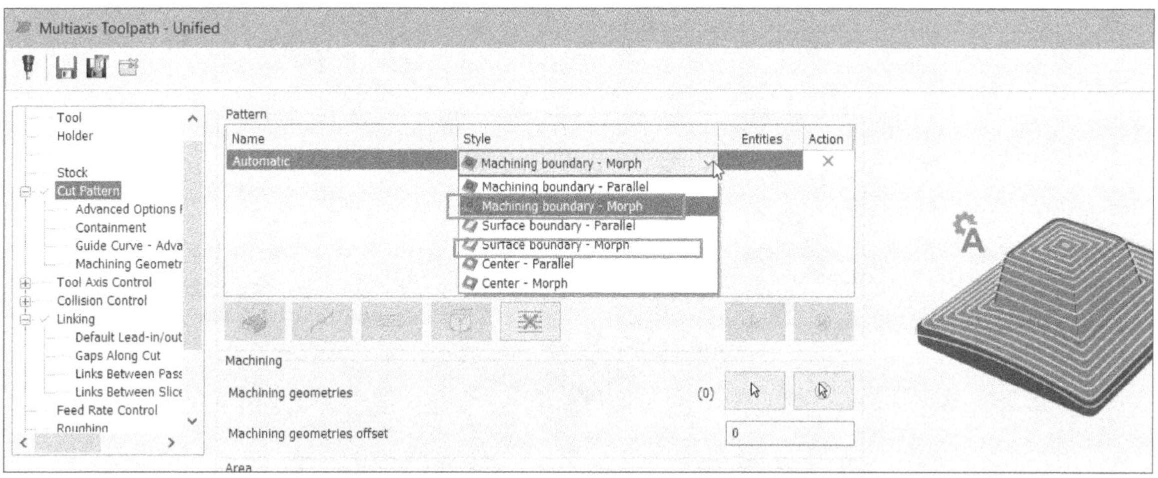

Figure-31. Morph pattern options

- Specify desired parameters in **Tool**, **Holder**, and **Stock** pages as discussed earlier.
- Select the machining geometries as discussed earlier using the selection button.
- Click on the **Containment** option from the **Cut Pattern** node at the left in the dialog box to define boundaries for morph toolpath generation. Select the User defined options from **Type** drop-down on this page to manually select boundaries for toolpath; refer to Figure-32. Click on the selection button next to drop-down and select desired geometries for defining boundary.

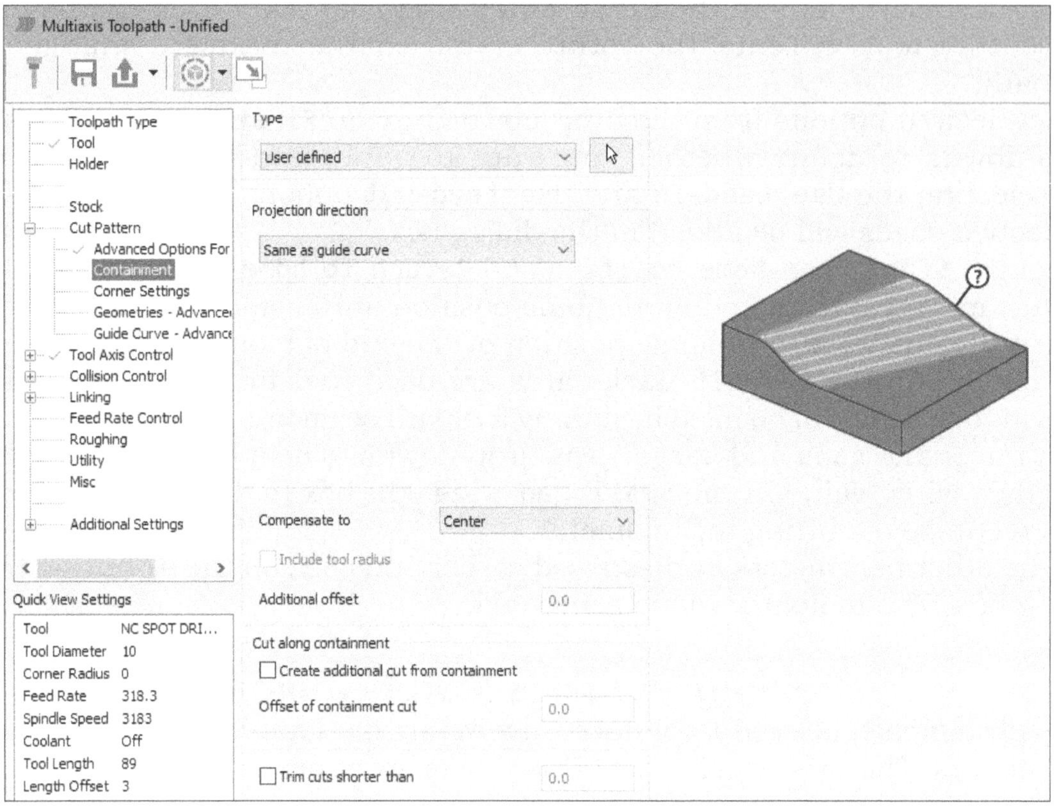

Figure-32. User defined options

- Set the other parameters in the dialog box as discussed earlier and click on the **OK** button to create the toolpath. The morph toolpath will be created; refer to Figure-33.

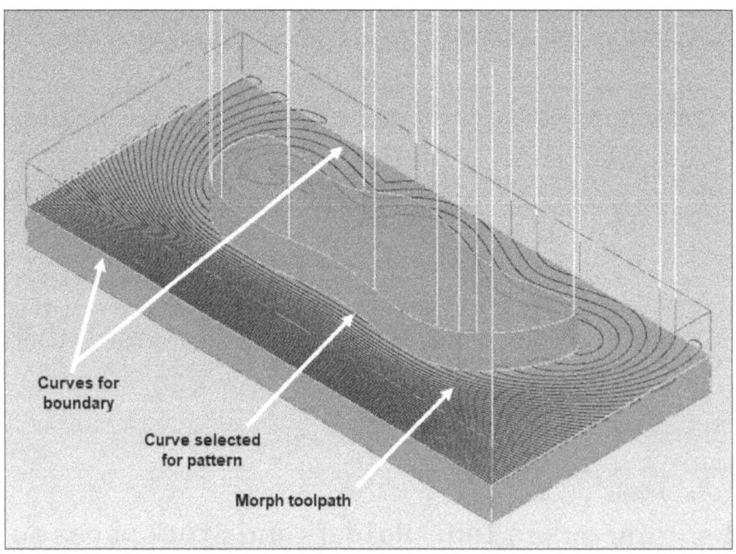

Figure-33. Morph toolpath created

CREATING MULTIAXIS FLOW TOOLPATH

The **Flow** tool is used to create toolpath on selected surfaces using U (horizontal) and V (vertical) lines as cutting passes. The procedure to generate this toolpath is given next.

- Click on the **Flow** tool from the expanded **Multiaxis** panel in the **Toolpaths** tab of the **Ribbon**. The **Multiaxis Toolpath - Flow** dialog box will be displayed; refer to Figure-34.

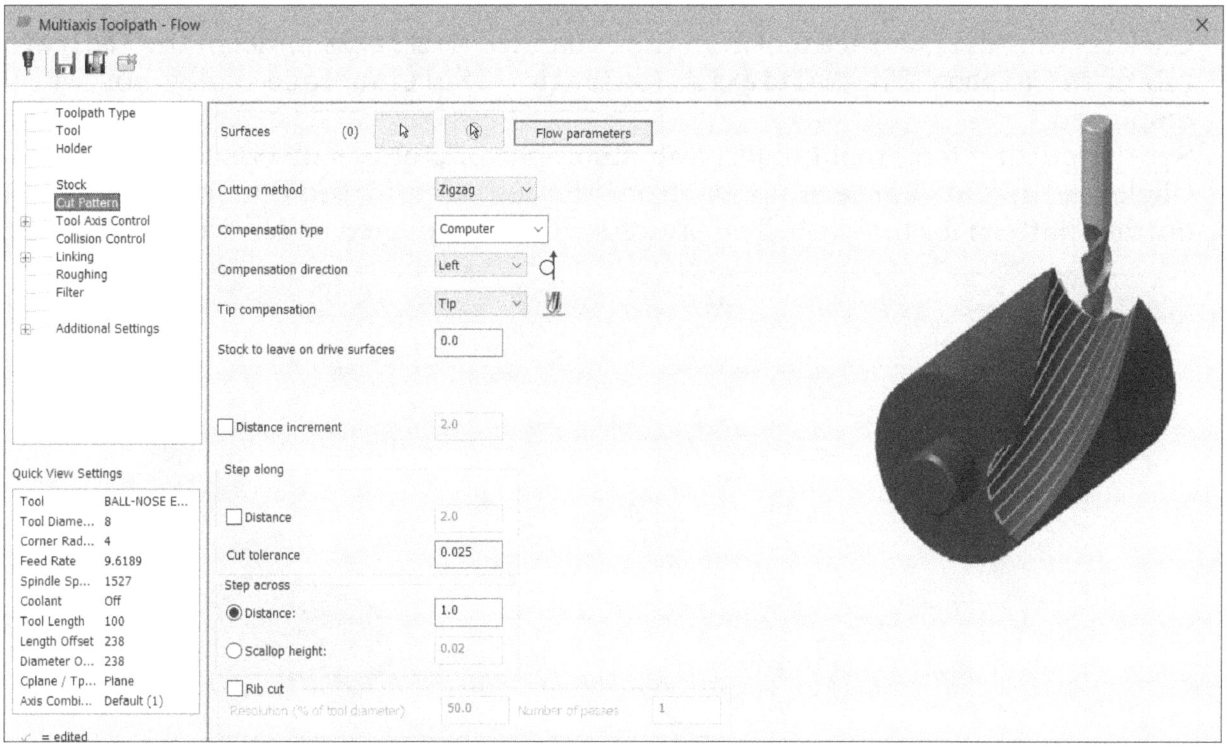

Figure-34. Multiaxis Toolpath-Flow dialog box

- Click on the **Cut Pattern** option from the left area to define cutting pattern for toolpath. Click on the **Select** button from the **Surfaces** area of the dialog box and select desired surfaces to be used for machining.
- After selecting surfaces, click on the **End Selection** button. The **Flowline data** dialog box will be displayed; refer to Figure-35.

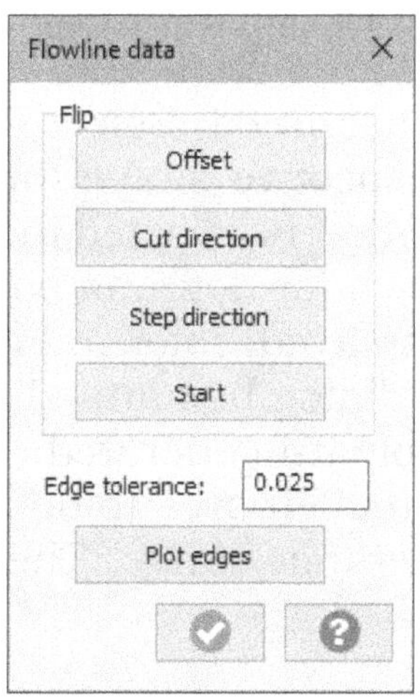

Figure-35. Flowline data dialog box

- Specify the parameters as desired in the dialog box. The options of this dialog box have been discussed earlier.
- Set the other parameters as discussed earlier and click on the **OK** button from the dialog box. The toolpaths will be generated.

CREATING MULTIAXIS MULTISURFACE TOOLPATH

The **Multisurface** tool is used to create toolpaths for machining 3D surfaces with uneven shapes. The procedure to generate multisurface toolpath is given next.

- Click on the **Multisurface** tool from the expanded **Multiaxis** panel in the **Toolpaths** tab of the **Ribbon**. The **Multiaxis Toolpath - Multisurface** dialog box will be displayed.
- Set the cutting tool, tool holder, and stock parameters as discussed earlier.
- Click on the **Cut Pattern** option from the left area in the dialog box to define cutting pattern for toolpath. The options will be displayed as shown in Figure-36.

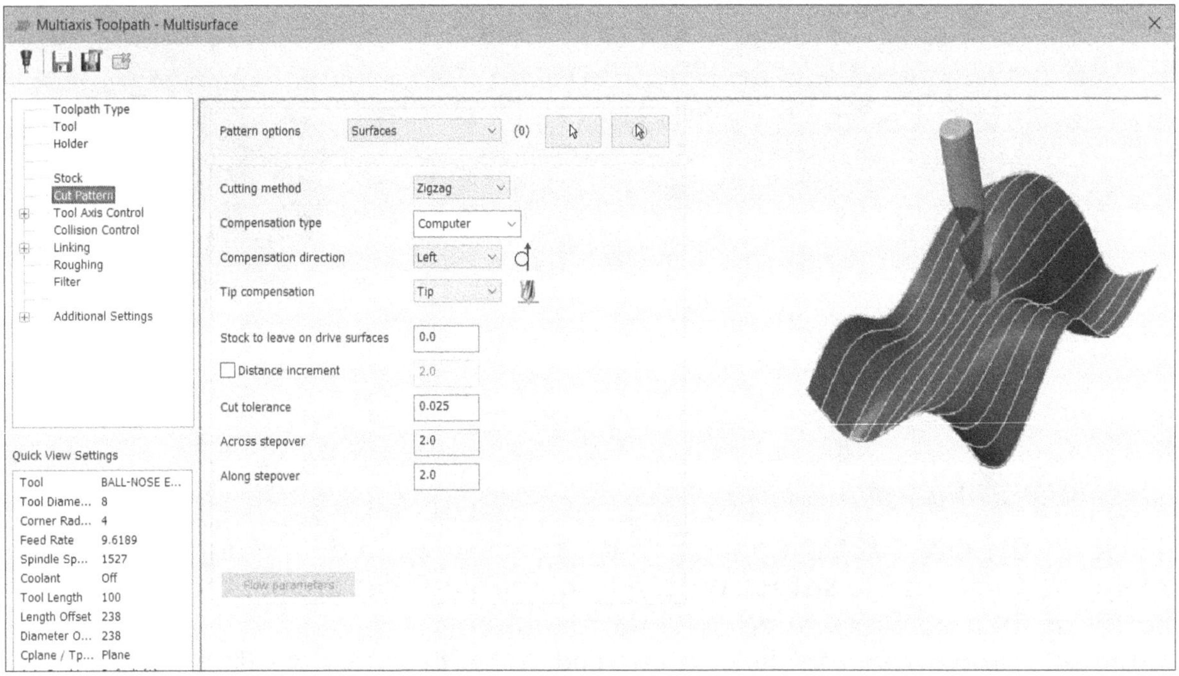

Figure-36. Multiaxis Toolpath-Multisurface dialog box

- Select desired option from the **Pattern Options** drop-down to define shape of toolpath. By default, **Surface(s)** option is selected in this drop-down, so you can select desired surfaces to be machined. Select the **Cylinder/Sphere/Box** option from the drop-down to use respective shape for generating cutting toolpath. If the **Cylinder**, **Sphere**, or **Box** option is selected in the drop-down then click on the **Select** button next to drop-down for defining parameters. The option dialog box for respective shape will be displayed; refer to Figure-37.
- Set desired parameters in the dialog box and click on the **OK** button if you want to use predefined shape for toolpath generated.
- Select the **Filter** option from the left area to define points to be filtered from the toolpath if they are within tolerance range. The **Filter** page will be displayed; refer to Figure-38.

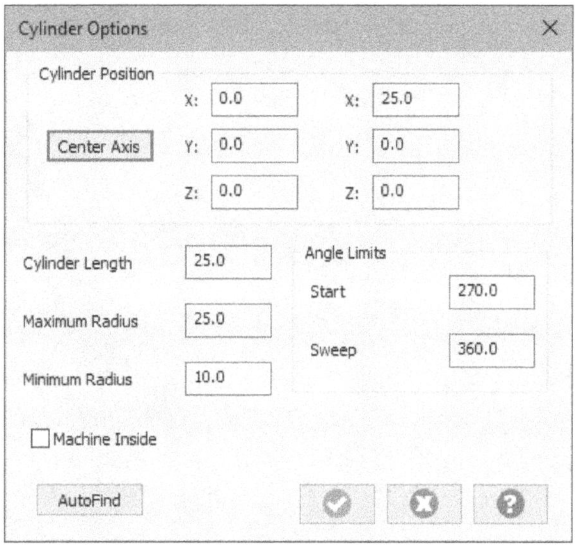

Figure-37. Cylinder Options dialog box

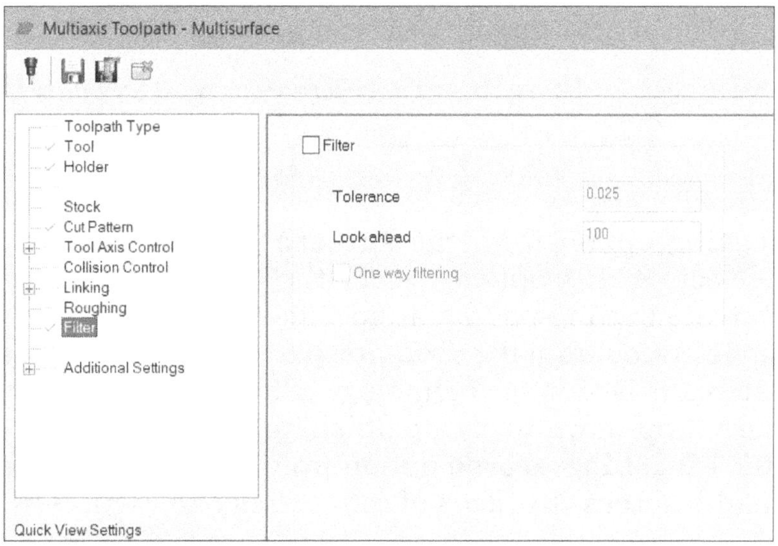

Figure-38. Filter page

- Select the **Filter** check box from the dialog box to define tolerance parameters for filtering points on toolpaths.
- Specify the distance value in **Tolerance** edit box below which the points will be filtered if distance between two points is less than tolerance value.
- Set the other parameters as desired in the **Filter** area.
- Specify other parameters as discussed earlier and click on the **OK** button to create the toolpath.

CREATING MULTIAXIS PORT EXPERT TOOLPATH

The **Port Expert** tool is used to machine inside of ports (tube like complex structures) in the model. The procedure to use this tool is given next.

- Click on the **Port Expert** tool from the expanded **Multiaxis** panel in the **Toolpath** tab of the **Ribbon**. The **Multiaxis Toolpath - Port** dialog box will be displayed; refer to Figure-39.

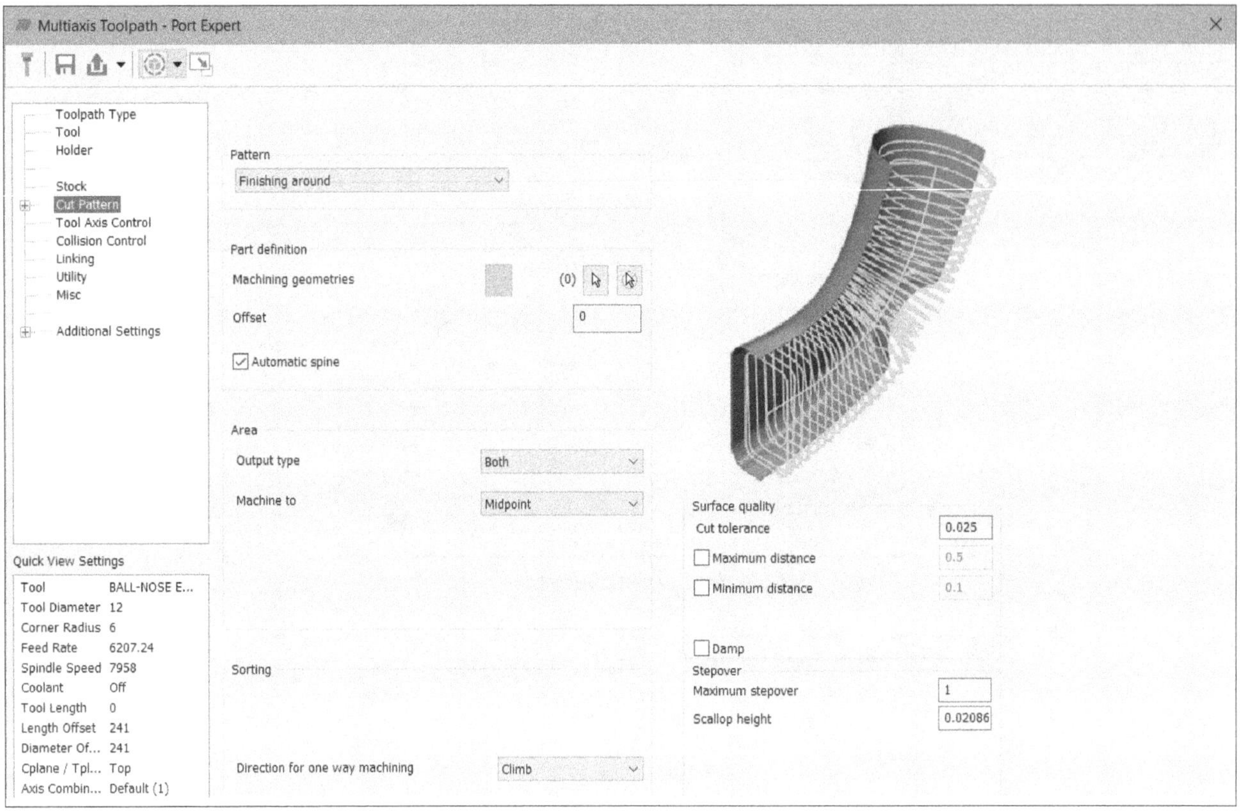

Figure-39. Multiaxis Toolpath-Port dialog box

- Select the **Roughing** option from the **Pattern** drop-down to create a roughing toolpath. On selecting this option, select the **Offset** option from the adjacent drop-down to create cutting passes at specified offset distance from each other. Select the **Dynamic** option from the drop-down to create cutting passes dynamically based on Mastercam Dynamic technology. Select the **Finishing along** option from the **Pattern** drop-down to create finishing toolpath along curves of selected faces. Select the **Finishing around** option from the **Pattern** drop-down to create finishing toolpaths across the faces of model; refer to Figure-40.

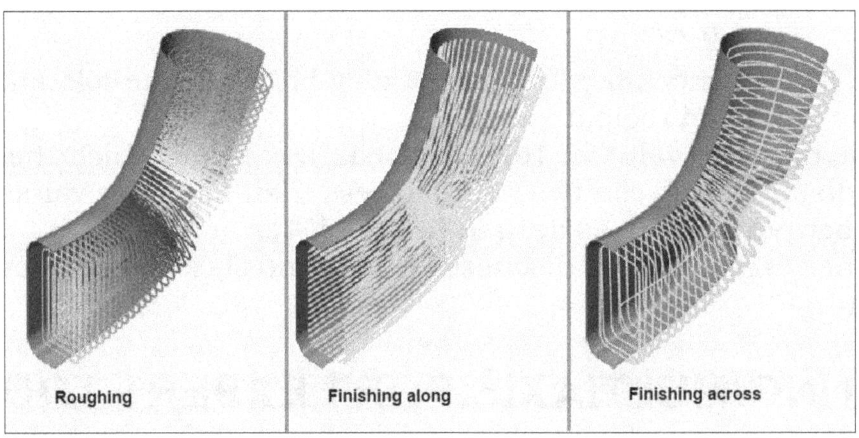

Figure-40. Port toolpath types

- Click on the **Select** button for **Machining geometries** option from the **Part definition** area of **Cut Pattern** page in the dialog box to select surfaces of the port (tube).
- After selecting faces/surfaces, click on the **End Selection** button.

- Select the **Automatic spine** check box to automatically generate center spine of tube based on selected faces. If you want to manually select the spine curve then clear this check box and select desired curve.
- If you want to create output for one side of selected tube surface then select the **Top** option or **Bottom** option from drop-down to create respective side. If you want to create both sides then select the **Both** option.
- Select desired option from the **Machine to** drop-down to specify the point on spine up to which machining will be performed.
- Specify the other parameters as discussed earlier and click on the **OK** button to generate the toolpath; refer to Figure-41.

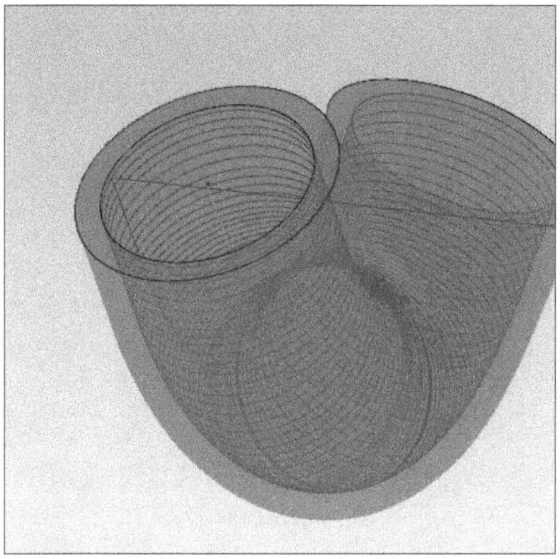

Figure-41. Port Expert toolpath generated

CREATING MULTIAXIS TRIANGULAR MESH TOOLPATH

The **Triangular Mesh** tool is used to machine objects in pyramid shapes. In this toolpath, the cutting will be in continuous contact with the body. The procedure to use this tool is given next.

- Click on the **Triangular Mesh** tool from the expanded **Multiaxis** panel in the **Toolpaths** tab of the **Ribbon**. The **Multiaxis Toolpath - Triangular Mesh** dialog box will be displayed; refer to Figure-42.

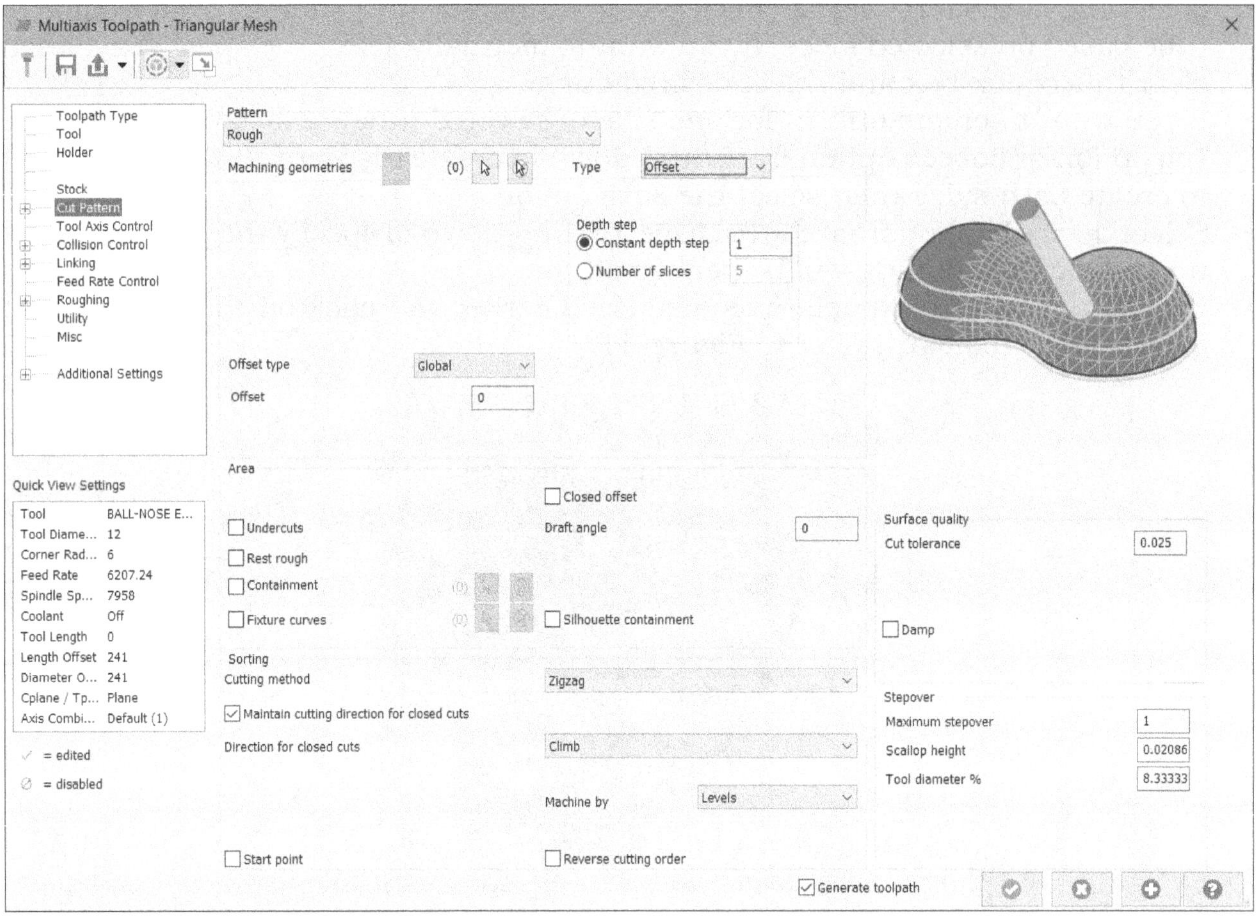

Figure-42. Multiaxis Toolpath-Triangular Mesh dialog box

- Specify the parameters related to cutting tool, tool holder, and stock as discussed earlier.
- Click on the **Cut Pattern** option from the left area of the dialog box to define parameters related to how cutting tool will move while performing machining on the model. The **Cut Pattern** page will be displayed in the dialog box; refer to Figure-42.
- Select desired option from the **Pattern** drop-down to define cutting strategies. Various cutting strategies with their related shapes are shown in Figure-43.
- Click on the **Select** button for **Machining surfaces** and select desired surfaces to be machined. Based on selected pattern type, you will be asked to select different type of curves like projection curves, drive curves, lines, and so on.
- Set the other parameters as discussed earlier and click on the **OK** button from the dialog box to create the toolpath.

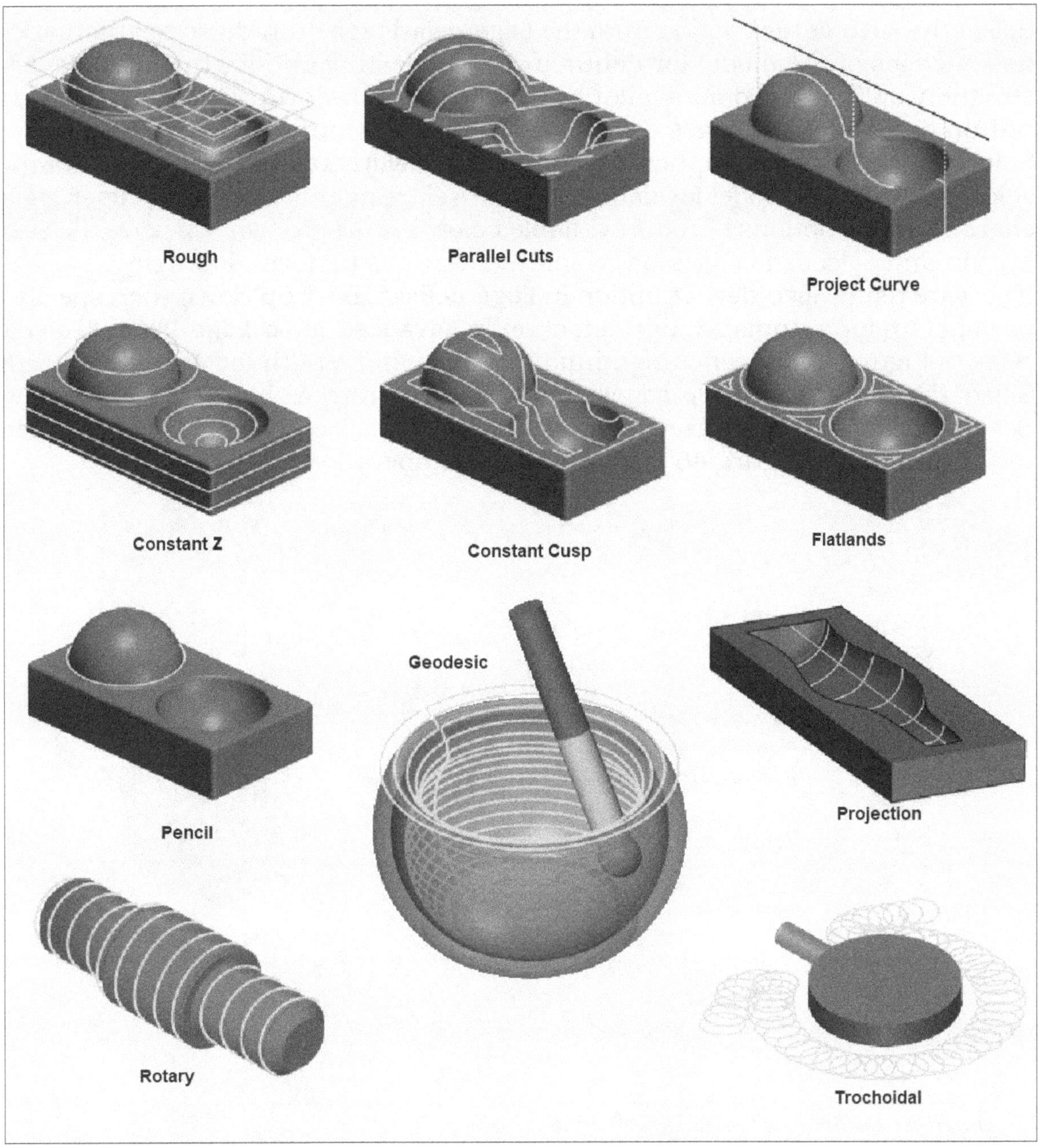

Figure-43. Triangular cut patterns

CREATING MULTIAXIS DEBURR TOOLPATH

The **Deburr 5-axis** tool is used to create toolpaths for machining edges of the model to remove burr generated by previous operations. You can also use this tool to generate chamfers at edges when using pencil shaped cutting tools. The procedure to use this tool is given next.

- Click on the **Deburr 5-axis** tool from the expanded **Multiaxis** panel of **Toolpath** tab in the **Ribbon**. The **Multiaxis Toolpath - Deburr 5-axis** dialog box will be displayed.
- Select the cutting tool and tool holder from respective pages in the dialog box.
- Click on the **Cut Pattern** option from left area. The options in this page will be displayed as shown in Figure-44.

- Select the model faces on which deburring operation is to be performed.
- Select the **Auto detect** option from the **Edge definition** drop-down to automatically detect edges of the model for deburring. On selecting option, the **Exclude edges** selection options become available below the drop-down. Click on the **Select** button and select the edges on which you do not want to perform deburring.
- Select the **User defined** option from the **Edge definition** drop-down to manually select edges of the model for deburring. On selecting this option, the **User defined edges** selection options become available below the drop-down. Click on the **Select** button and select the edges on which you want to perform deburring.
- If you are using **Auto detect** option in **Edge definition** drop-down then specify the parameters for automatic edge detection in **Advanced Auto Edge Detection** page; refer to Figure-45. Specify the minimum angle and length for detection as edge.
- Select the **Include unsharp edges** check box to deburred chamfered edges as well.
- Set the other parameters as discussed earlier and click on the **OK** button to generate toolpath; refer to Figure-46 for 5 axis deburr operation.

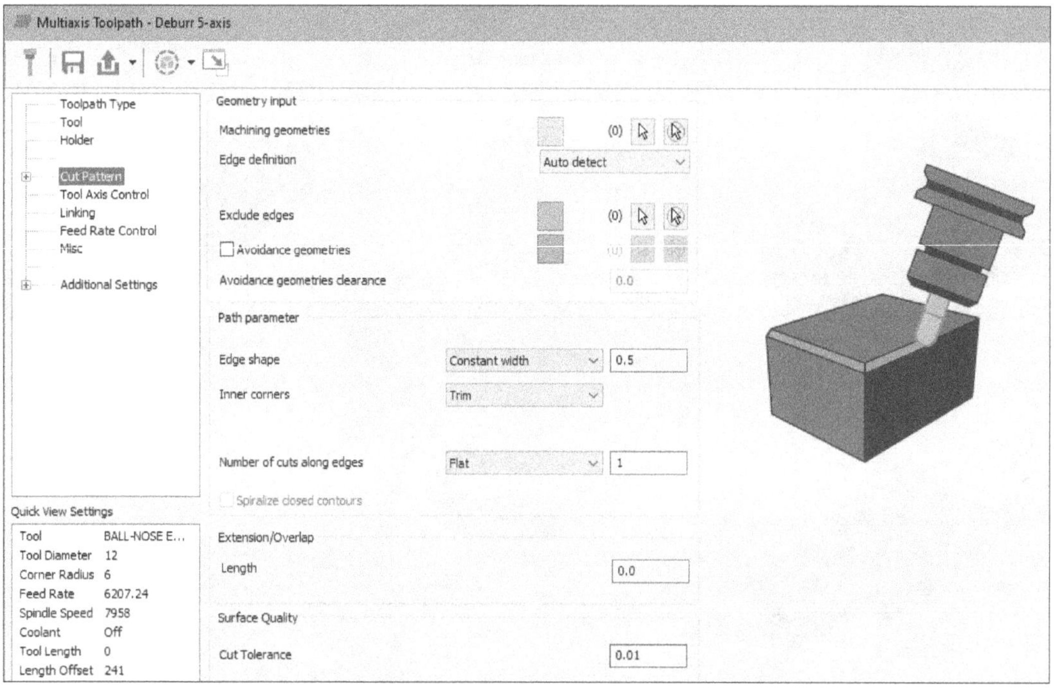

Figure-44. Cut pattern options for Deburr toolpath

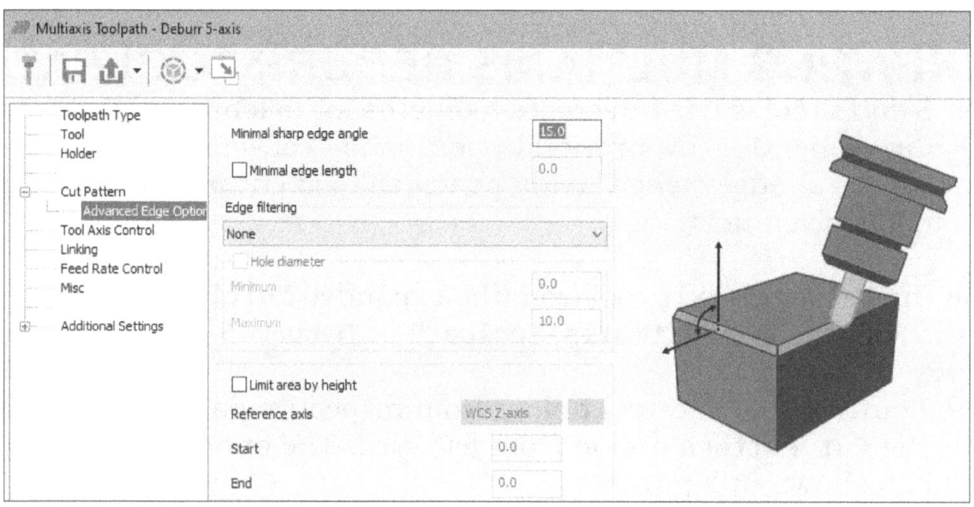

Figure-45. Advanced Auto Edge Detection page

Figure-46. Deburring shroud edges

CREATING MULTIAXIS POCKETING TOOLPATH

The **Pocketing** tool is used to machine pockets with undercuts and irregular shapes. The procedure to use this tool is given next.

- Click on the **Pocketing** tool from the expanded **Multiaxis** panel of **Toolpaths** tab in the **Ribbon**. The **Multiaxis Toolpath - Pocketing** dialog box will be displayed; refer to Figure-47.

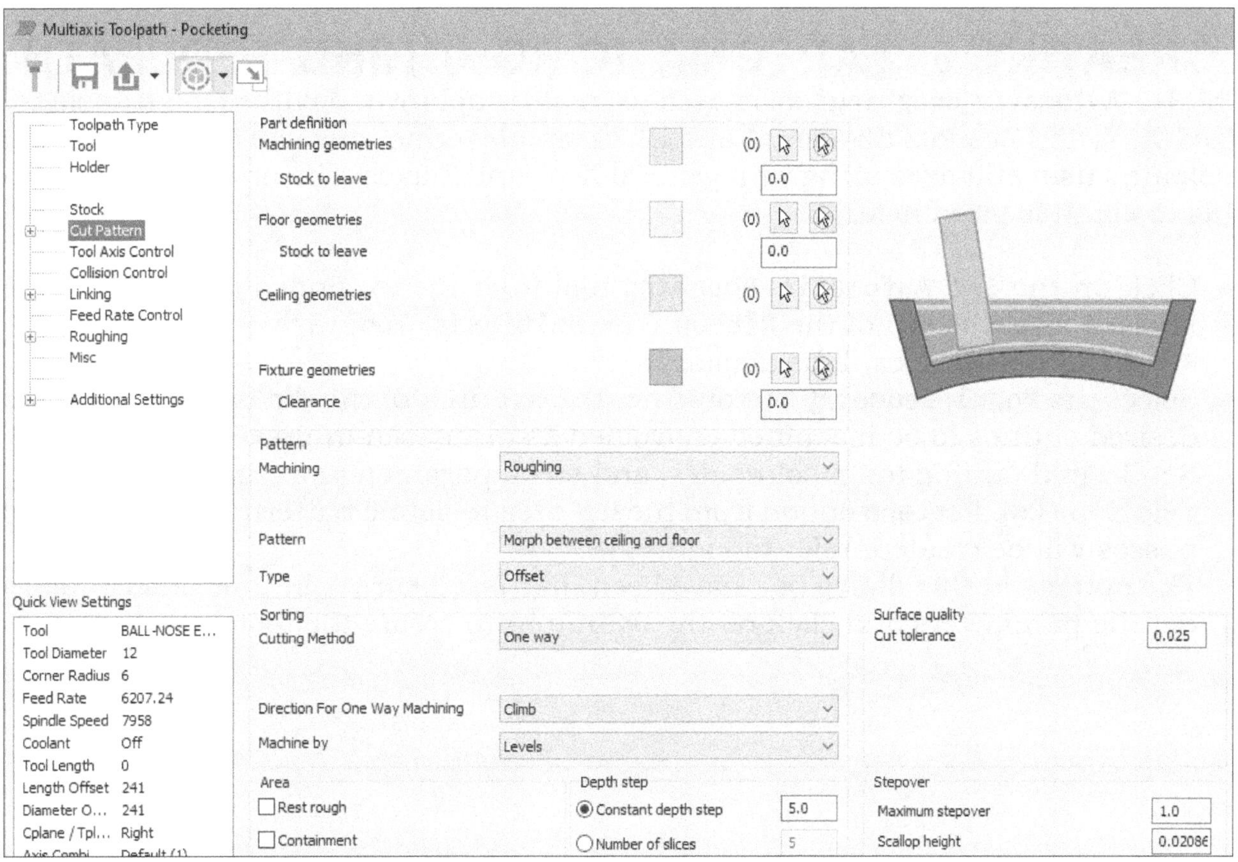

Figure-47. Multiaxis Toolpath-Pocketing dialog box

- Set desired cutting tool, tool holder, and stock parameters.

- Click on the **Cut Pattern** option from the left area to modify cutting pattern parameters. The **Cut Pattern** page will be displayed in the dialog box.
- Click on the **Select** button for **Machining geometries** option from the **Part definition** area of the dialog box and select the faces to be machined.
- Click on the **Select** button for **Floor geometries** option from the dialog box and select the faces to define floor faces up to which the machining will be performed.
- Click on the **Select** button for **Ceiling geometries** option from the dialog box and select the faces to be ceiling machined.
- Click on the **Select** button for **Fixture geometries** option from the dialog box and select the faces to define fixture machined.
- Specify desired values in the **Stock to leave** edit boxes to define amount of stock left after performing the pocketing toolpath. If **0** value is specified in the edit boxes then finishing toolpath will be performed.
- Select desired option from the **Machining** drop-down in the **Pattern** area of the dialog box to define which faces are to be machined. Select the **Roughing** option to machine both floors as well as walls in the pocket. Select the **Floor finishing** option from the drop-down if you want to machine floors only. Select the **Wall finishing** option from the drop-down to machine walls of pocket only.
- Specify desired parameters in the **Strategy** drop-down based on options selected in the **Machining** drop-down. Note that preview of toolpath will be displayed in the dialog box based on selected options in the drop-down.
- Set the other parameters as discussed and click on the **OK** button to generate toolpath.

CREATING 3+2 AUTOMATIC ROUGHING TOOLPATH

The **3+2 Automatic Roughing** tool is used to create roughing toolpaths for 3 translation axes (X, Y, and Z) and 2 tilt axes (A and B). In simple terms, this tool creates roughing toolpaths using tilt axes along with general X, Y, and Z axes. The procedure to create this toolpath is given next.

- Click on the **3+2 Automatic Roughing** tool from the expanded **Multiaxis** panel in the **Toolpaths** tab of the **Ribbon**. The **Multiaxis Toolpath - 3+2 Automatic Roughing** dialog box will be displayed.
- Select the **Model Geometry** option from the left area of the dialog box and select desired entities to be machined & avoided as discussed in previous chapters.
- Set desired cutting tool, tool holder, and stock parameters as discussed earlier.
- Select the **Cut Pattern** option from the left area to define pattern in which cutting passes will be created; refer to Figure-48.
- The options in this dialog box have been discussed earlier in previous chapters. Set the parameters and click on the **OK** button to create the toolpaths.

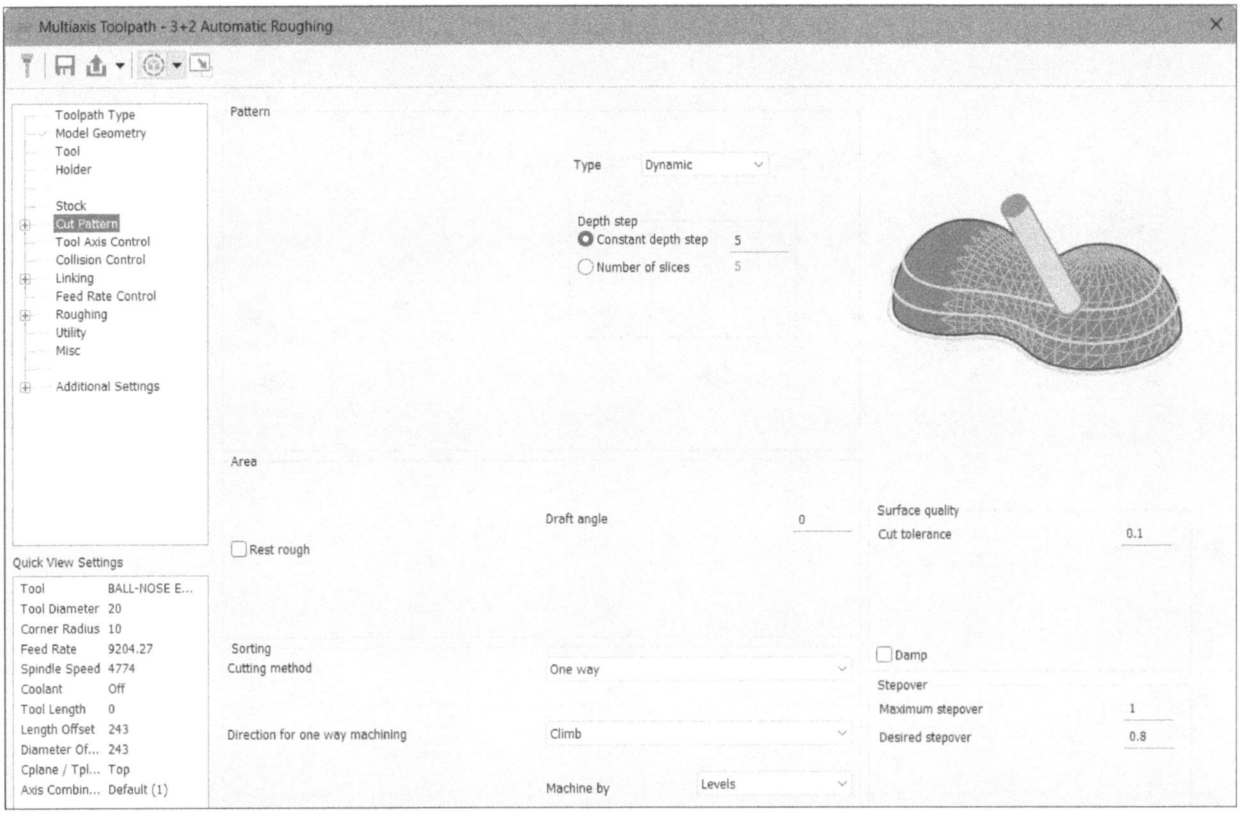

Figure-48. Cut Pattern page

CREATING MULTIAXIS PROJECT CURVE TOOLPATH

From Mastercam 2023 onwards, project curve toolpaths are now generated by **Unified** tool which was discussed earlier. This toolpath is used to machine curves projected on the 3D surface. The procedure to use this tool is given next.

- Click on the **Unified** tool from the expanded **Multiaxis** panel in the **Toolpaths** tab of the **Ribbon**. The **Multiaxis Toolpath - Unified** dialog box will be displayed.
- Select desired cutting tool, tool holder, and stock as discussed earlier.
- Select the **Cut Pattern** option from the left area. The **Cut Pattern** page will be displayed.
- Click on the **Add Curve row** button from **Pattern** area and select **Project** option from **Style** drop-down in the table; refer to Figure-49.
- Click on the **Select** button from the **Pattern** area of the dialog box and select desired curves to be projected.
- Click on the **Select** button for **Machining geometries** option and select the face(s) on which curve will be projected.
- Select the **Project Curves Options** option from left area under **Cut Pattern** node. The page will be displayed as shown in Figure-50.

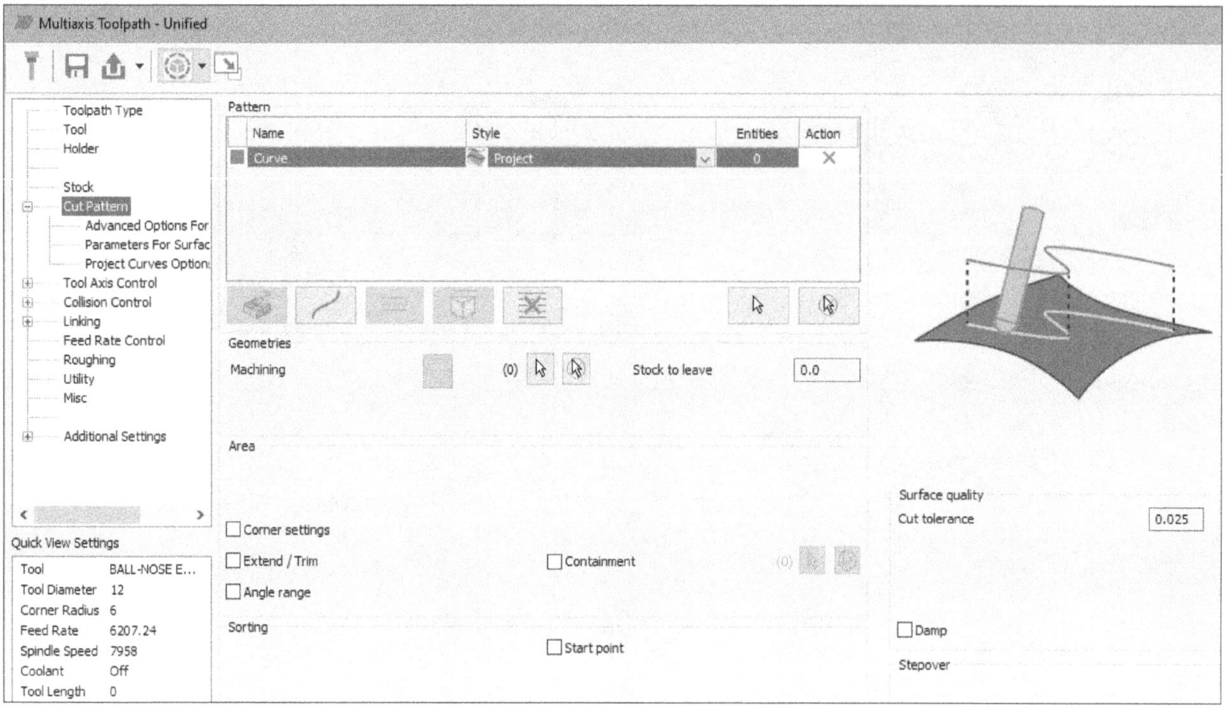

Figure-49. Project option in Style drop-down

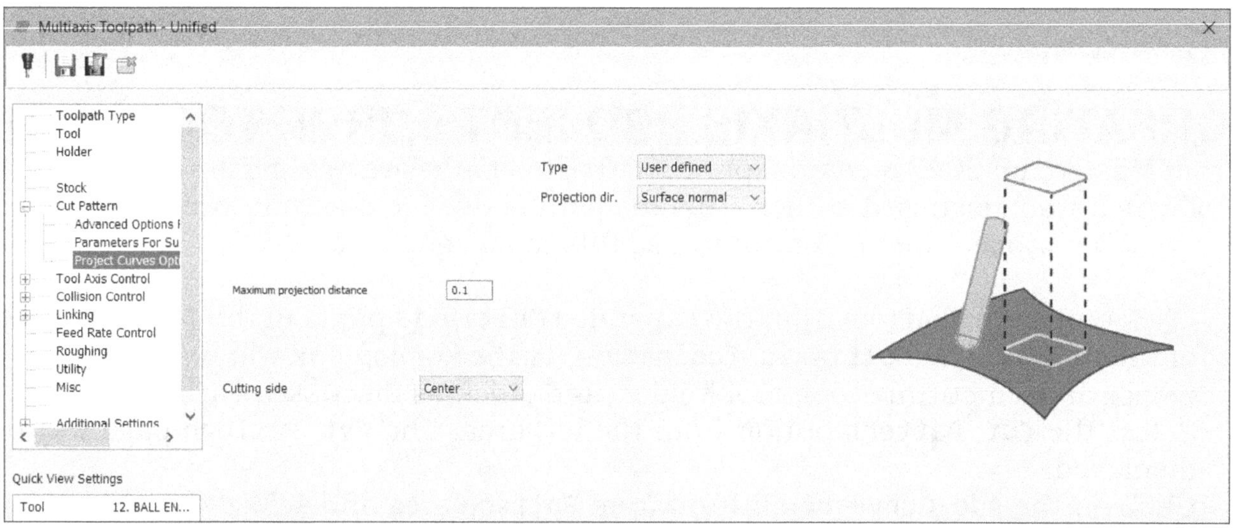

Figure-50. Project Curves Options page

- Select desired option from the **Type** drop-down to define the pattern in which curves will be projected on selected surfaces. Select the **User defined** option from the drop-down to project curves as they are created on the surface. Select the **Radial** option from the drop-down to project curves in radial pattern and set desired parameters in **Center point**, **Radius**, and **Angle** areas. Select the **Spiral** option from the drop-down to project curves in spiral motion and specify related parameters. Select the **Offset** option from the drop-down and specify offset direction with number of cuts to create offset copies of projection curves on selected drive surface.
- Specify the other parameters as discussed earlier and click on the **OK** button to create the toolpath; refer to Figure-51.

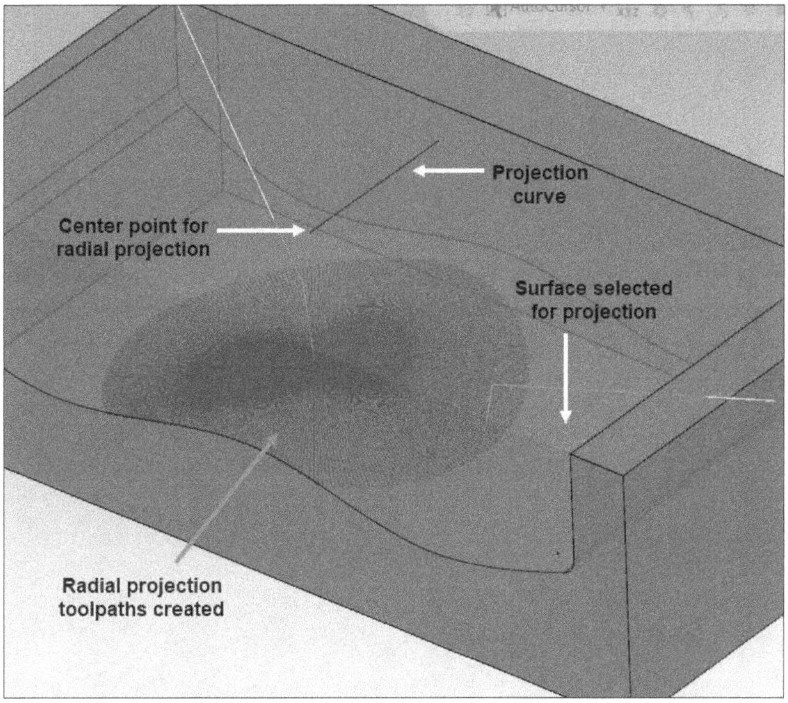

Figure-51. Projected curve toolpath created

CREATING MULTIAXIS ROTARY TOOLPATH

The **Rotary** tool is used to machine 3D models with irregular cylinder shaped surfaces. General shapes of these models is cylindrical with irregular surfacing. The procedure to use this tool is given next.

- Click on the **Rotary** tool from the expanded **Multiaxis** panel in the **Toolpaths** tab of the **Ribbon**. The **Multiaxis Toolpath - Rotary** dialog box will be displayed.
- Set desired cutting tool and tool holder parameters as discussed earlier.
- Click on the **Cut Pattern** option from the left area of the dialog box. The options to define pattern of cutting passes will be displayed in the **Cut Pattern** page of the dialog box; refer to Figure-52.
- Click on the **Select** button for **Surface** option from the dialog box and select desired faces (generally, cylindrical surfaces) of the model to be machined.
- Select desired radio button for **Cutting method** to define direction of cut. Select **Rotary cut** radio button to remove material while moving cutting tool in radial direction. Select the **Axial cut** radio button to remove material while moving cutting tool parallel to axis of cylindrical model.
- Set the other parameters as desired and click on the **OK** button. The toolpath will be created; refer to Figure-53.

Figure-52. Multiaxis Toolpath-Rotary dialog box

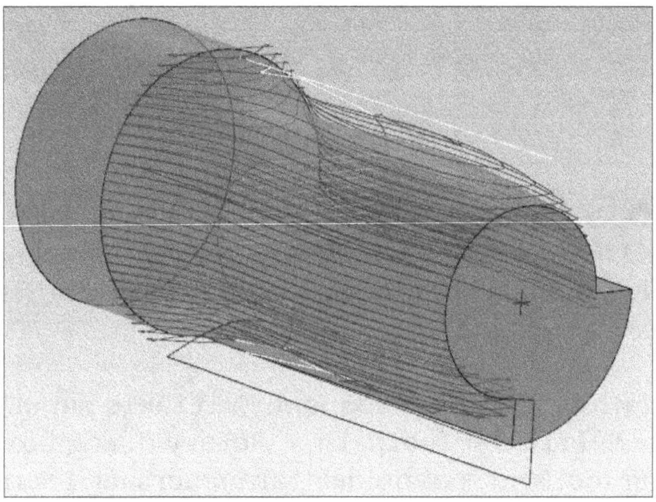

Figure-53. Rotary toolpath created

CREATING MULTIAXIS ROTARY ADVANCED TOOLPATH

The **Rotary Advanced** tool is used to create toolpaths for machining faces of helical gear like structures. The procedure to use this tool is given next.

- Click on the **Rotary Advanced** tool from the expanded **Multiaxis** panel in the **Toolpaths** tab of the **Ribbon**. The **Multiaxis Toolpath - Rotary Advanced** dialog box will be displayed.
- Select desired cutting tool, tool holder, and stock parameters in the dialog box as discussed earlier.
- Click on the **Cut Pattern** option from the left area of the dialog box to define pattern in which cutting passes will be created. The **Cut Pattern** page will be displayed in the dialog box; refer to Figure-54.
- Select desired option from the **Machining** drop-down to define whether you want to create roughing toolpath or finishing toolpath.
- Set desired option in the **Slice pattern** drop-down to define how cutting passes will be placed on the model. The **Radius constant** option will apply same radius in cutting passes.

- Set the parameters as discussed earlier in this page.

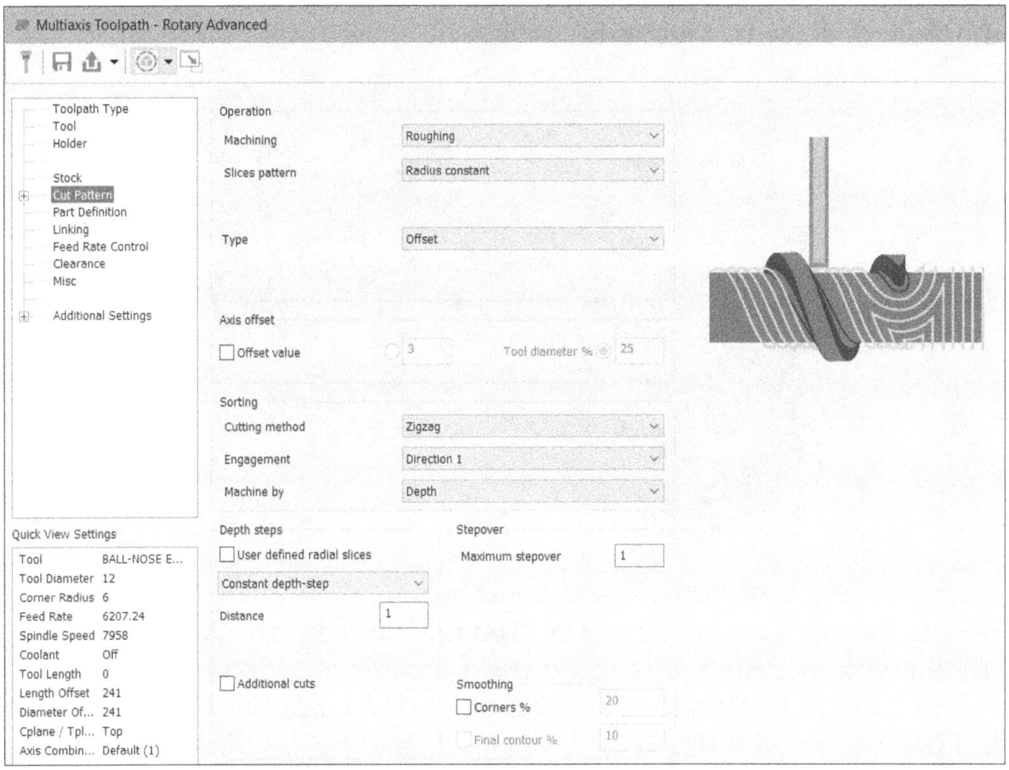

Figure-54. Multiaxis Toolpath-Rotary Advanced dialog box

- Click on the **Part Definition** option from the left area of the dialog box to select surfaces/faces to be machined. The **Part Definition** page will be displayed in dialog box; refer to Figure-55.

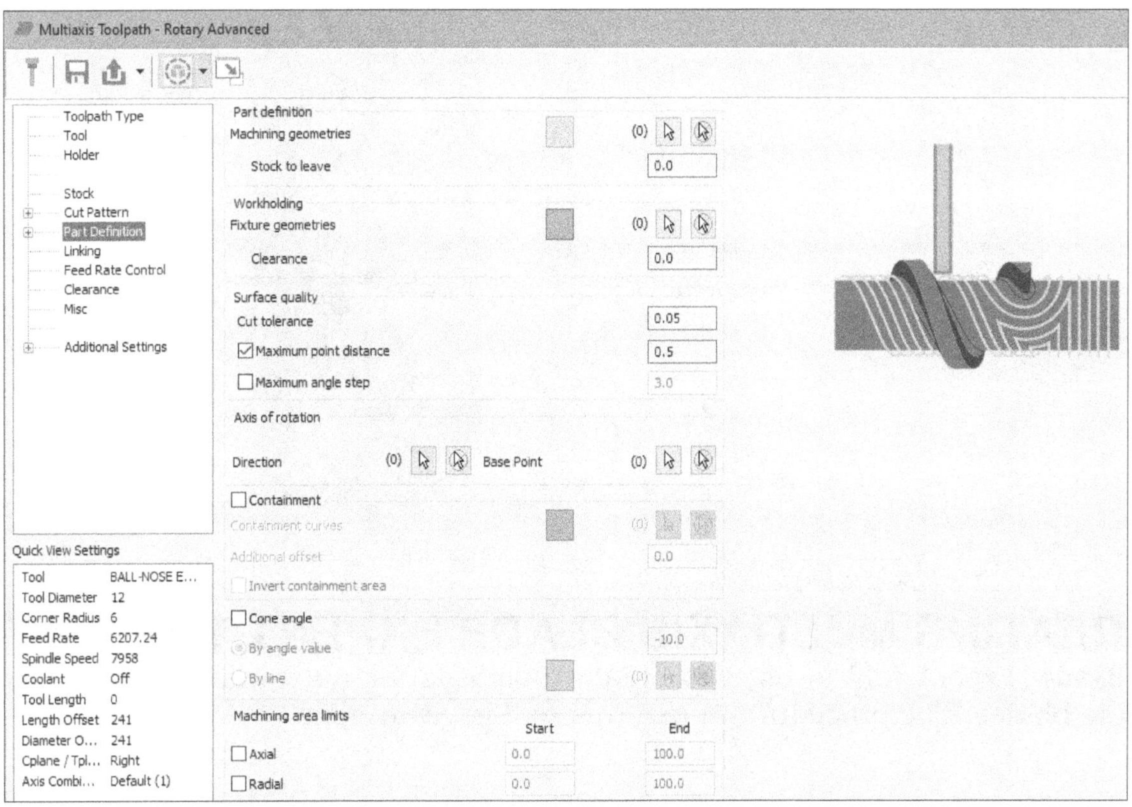

Figure-55. Part Definition page

- Click on the **Select** button for **Machining geometries** option from the **Part definition** area of the dialog box and select desired faces to define walls of part to be machined; refer to Figure-56.

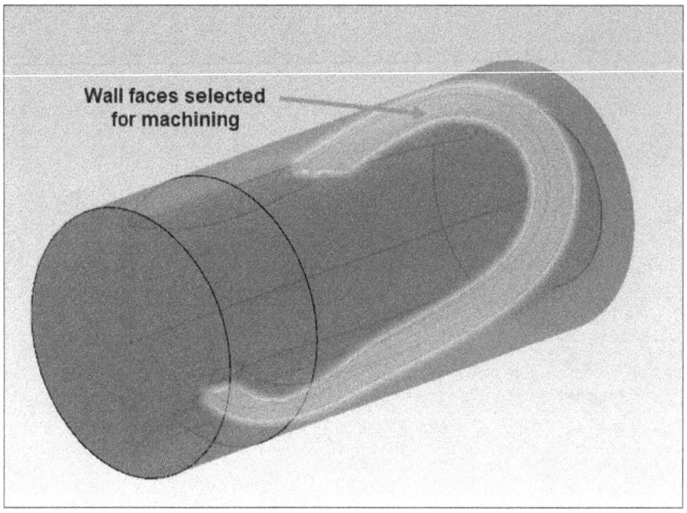

Figure-56. Wall faces selected for machining

- Click on the **Select** button for **Direction** option from the **Axis of rotation** area of the dialog box to define axis to be used for defining axis of model.
- Click on the **Select** button for **Base Point** option from the **Axis of rotation** area to define base point of axis.
- Set the other parameters as discussed earlier and click on the **OK** button to create the toolpath; refer to Figure-57.

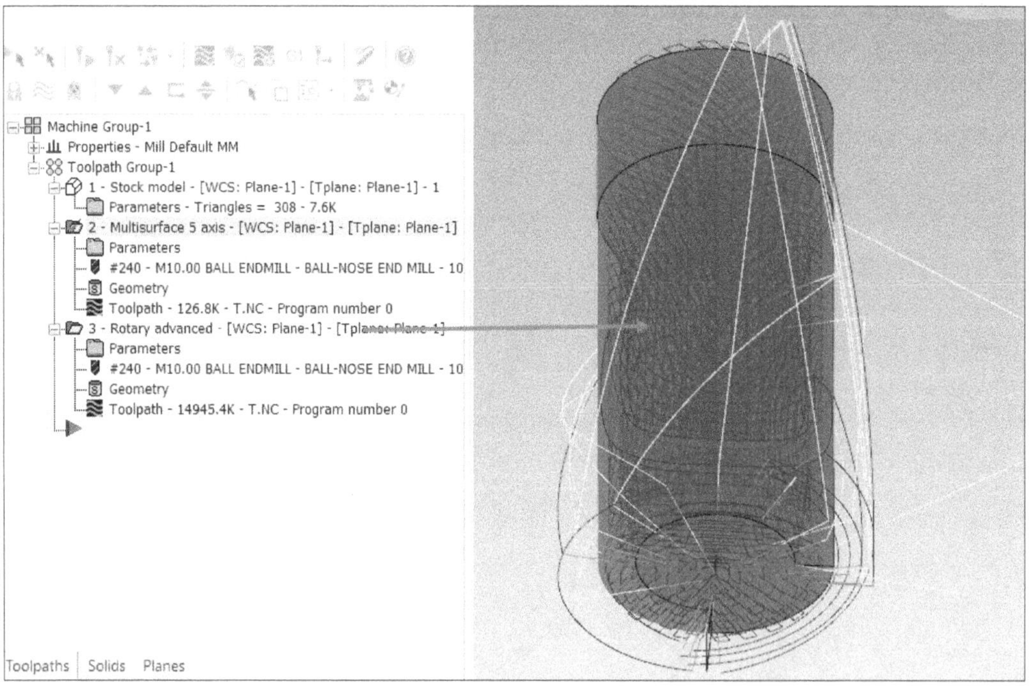

Figure-57. Advanced Rotary toolpath created

CREATING MULTIAXIS BLADE EXPERT TOOLPATH

The **Blade Expert** tool is used to create toolpaths for machining twisted faces of turbine blades. The procedure to use this tool is given next.

- Click on the **Blade Expert** tool from the expanded **Multiaxis** panel in **Toolpaths** tab of the **Ribbon**. The **Multiaxis Toolpath - Blade Expert** dialog box will be displayed.
- Select desired cutting tool and tool holder from respective pages in the dialog box as discussed earlier.
- Select the **Stock** option from left area in the dialog box. The options in the page will be displayed as shown in Figure-58. Select the **Autodetect** radio button to automatically identify stock left after previous operations.

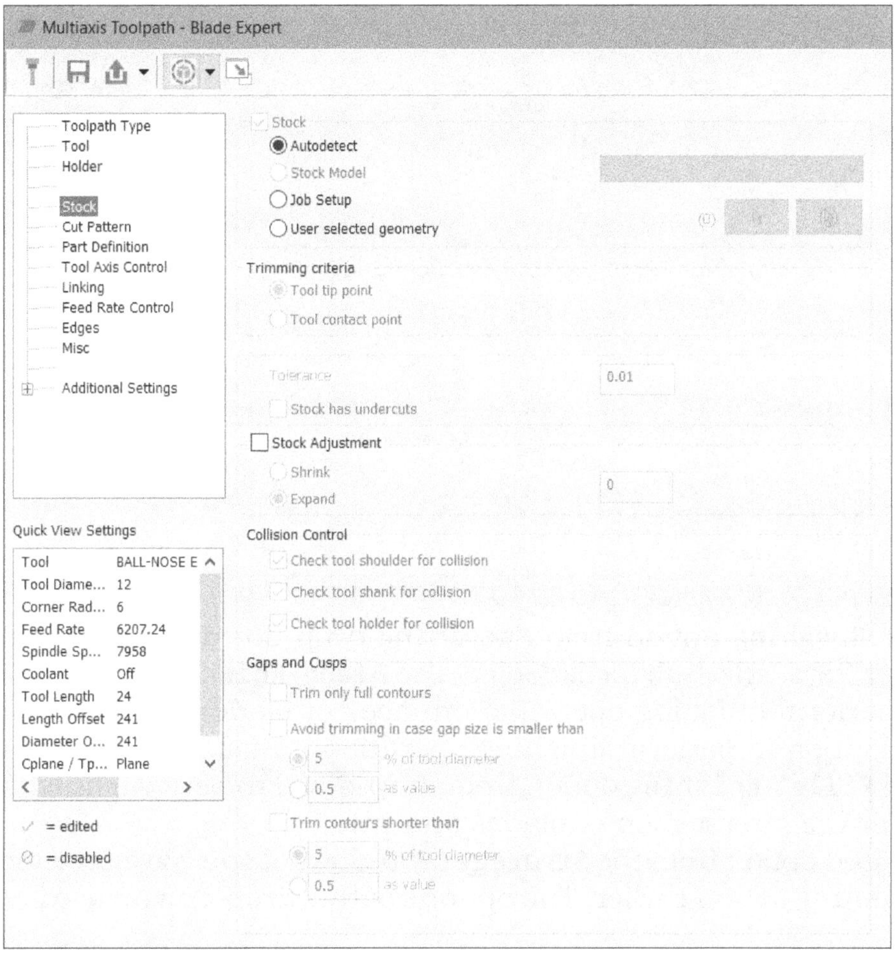

Figure-58. Stock page

- Select the **Stock Model** radio button to select desired stock model earlier created by using **Stock Model** tool. After selecting this radio button, select desired stock model from next drop-down.
- Select the **User selected geometry** radio button to manually select the solid model created for stock from graphics area.
- If you want to increase or decrease the size of stock by specified distance value then select the **Stock Adjustment** check box and select respective radio button. The edit box next to radio buttons will become active. Specify desired amount by which stock will be expanded or shrunk in all directions.
- Select the **Cut Pattern** option from left area to define the pattern in which cutting passes will be created; refer to Figure-59.

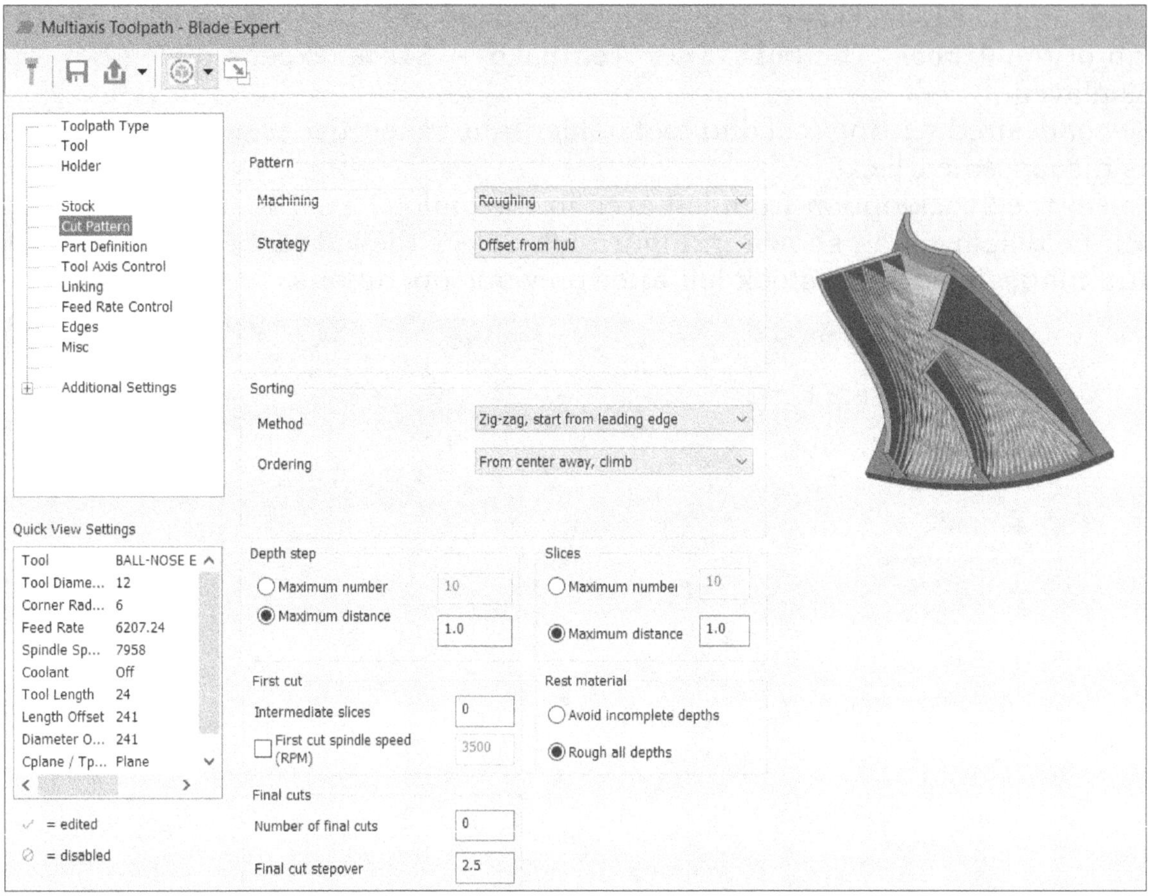

Figure-59. Cut Pattern page for Blade Expert toolpath

- Select the **Roughing** option from **Machining** drop-down to remove material from blades, splitters, and hub faces. Select the **Blade finishing** option from the drop-down to perform finishing operation on faces of blades/splitters. Select the **Hub finishing** option to perform finishing operation on faces of center hub of model. Select the **Fillet finishing** option from drop-down to perform finishing operation on fillets at the intersection of blades and hub.
- Select desired option from the **Strategy** drop-down if you have selected **Roughing** or **Blade finishing** option earlier. The options of this drop-down have been discussed earlier.
- Select desired option from the **Contour** drop-down to define which sides of selected geometries will be machined. This drop-down is available when Blade finishing or Fillet finishing operations are being performed. Specify other parameters in this page as discussed earlier.
- Select the **Part Definition** option from left area to define the geometries to be machined by toolpath. The options of **Part Definition** page will be displayed; refer to Figure-60.

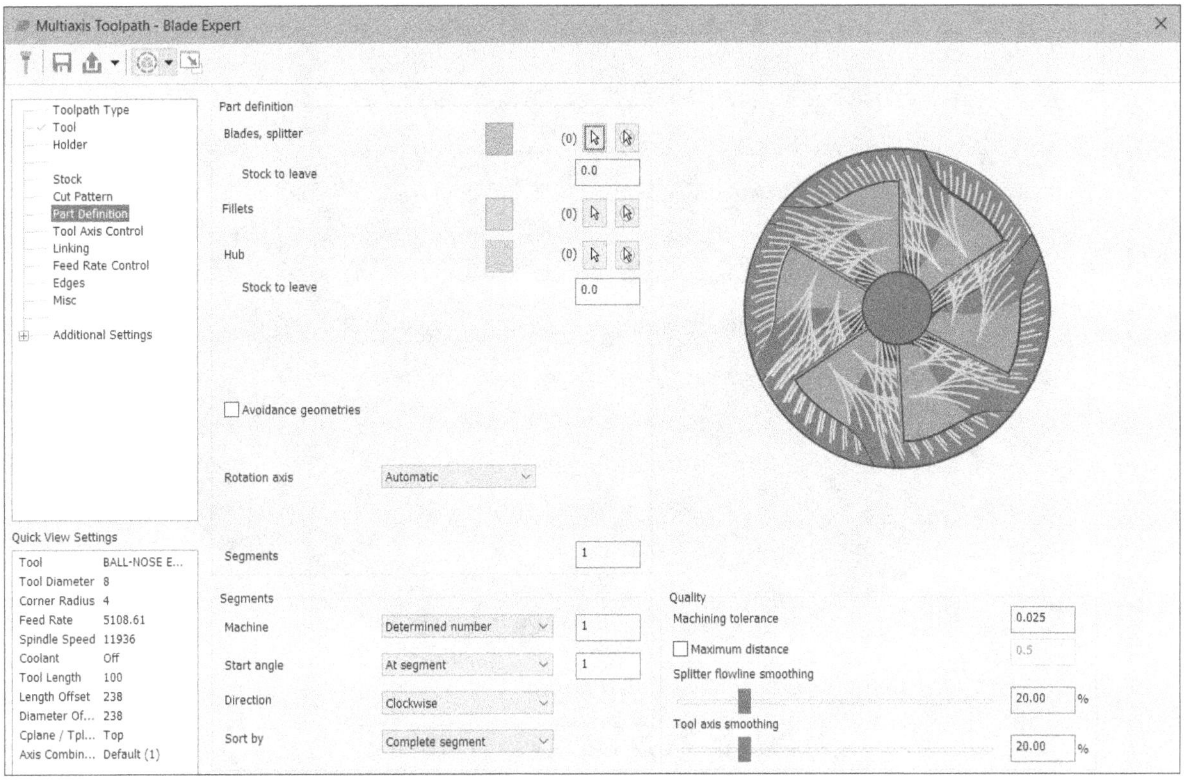

Figure-60. Part Definition page for Blade Expert

- Click on the **Select** button for desired component from **Part definition** area and select respective geometry; refer to Figure-61.

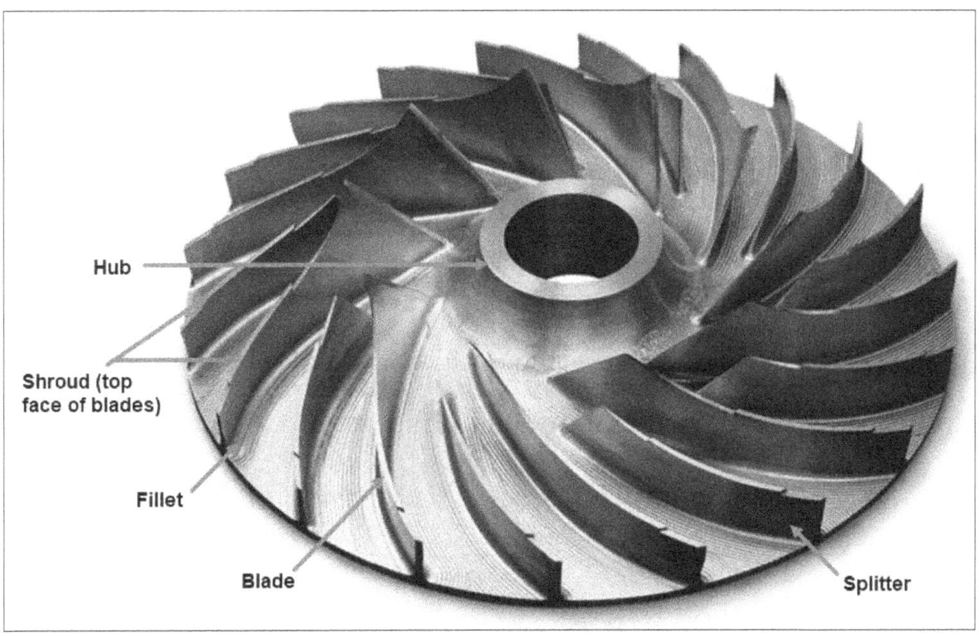

Figure-61. Blade nomenclature

- Specify other parameters in the dialog box as discussed earlier and click on the **OK** button to generate toolpath; refer to Figure-62.

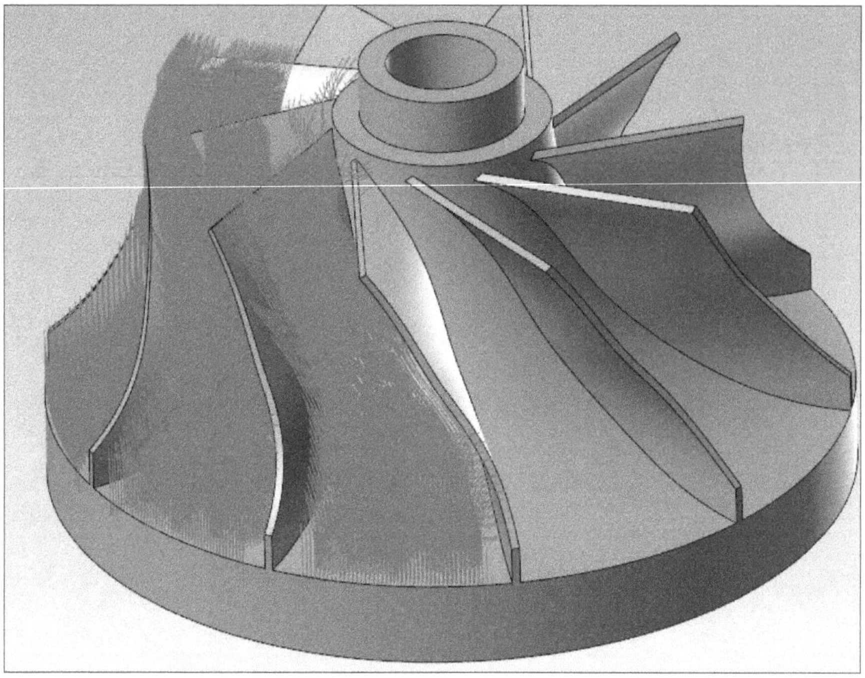

Figure-62. Cutting motion of Blade Expert toolpath

SELF ASSESSMENT

Q1. The .... Milling toolpath is used to machine the geometry using side edge of cutting tool.

Q2. The .... milling toolpath is used to rough machine blades of turbines.

Q3. What is the application of Gouge check options for swarf milling?

Q4. Selecting the Adaptive cuts check box for parallel multi-axis toolpath keeps a constant stepover irrespective of the shape of surface. (T/F)

Q5. The .... multi axis toolpath is used to perform machining on surface trapped between two leading curves.

Q6. The .... tool is used to create toolpath on selected surfaces using U (horizontal) and V (vertical) lines as cutting passes.

Q7. The .... toolpath is used to machine inside of ports (tube like complex structures) in the model.

Q8. The Triangular Mesh tool is used to machine objects in pyramid shapes. (T/F)

REVIEW QUESTIONS

Q1. What is the primary function of the Curve Tool in Mastercam's Multiaxis group?
A. To machine pockets with undercuts
B. To create toolpaths for 3D curves
C. To remove burrs from edges
D. To define stock parameters

Q2. Which cutting tool is generally used in multiaxis milling using the Curve Tool?
A. Flat end mill
B. Face mill
C. Ball end mill
D. Tapered end mill

Q3. What is the purpose of the "Distance increment" option in the Curve Tool dialog box?
A. To define the tool diameter
B. To set collision control radius
C. To specify increment value for cutting passes along curves
D. To adjust tool holder size

Q4. What does selecting the "Surface edge - all" option from the Curve type drop-down allow?
A. Selecting one edge at a time
B. Creating projection curves
C. Selecting all edges of a selected surface
D. Selecting 3D curve entities only

Q5. What is the function of the "On projected curve" option in the Collision Control page?
A. Moves tool along sharp edges
B. Moves tool tip on curves projected on surfaces
C. Prevents tool from gouging
D. Aligns tool to tool axis

Q6. In Swarf Milling, what does selecting the Guide curves checkbox allow?
A. Defines floor level of milling
B. Controls stock left on the model
C. Selects upper and lower rail curves
D. Selects edges to deburr

Q7. Which drop-down in Swarf Milling defines how tool will avoid collision with part geometries?
A. Feed Rate Control
B. Gouge Check
C. Cut Pattern
D. Tool Axis Control

Q8. What is the default output format for Swarf Milling under Tool Axis Control?
A. 2 axis
B. 3 axis
C. 4 axis
D. 5 axis

Q9. In Unified Toolpath, what does the Add Curve row button in the Pattern area allow?
A. Automatically generate cutting passes
B. Use selected curve as reference for toolpath
C. Define surface edge compensation
D. Apply random toolpath styles

Q10. What option is used to generate cutting passes parallel to selected surfaces in Unified Toolpath?
A. Add Curve row
B. Add Plane row
C. Add Surface row
D. Add Automatic row

Q11. Which feature in Parallel Multiaxis toolpath smoothens sharp corners in a toolpath?
A. Maintain outside sharp edges
B. Parameters For Surface Edge Handling
C. Advanced Options For Surface Quality
D. Generate toolpath only at front side

Q12. In Collision Control options, what does selecting the Conical radio button do?
A. Clears corners of the surface
B. Applies uniform clearance in all directions
C. Defines lower and upper offset values for clearance
D. Applies chamfering automatically

Q13. What does the "Start from home position" checkbox do in Linking parameters?
A. Enables rotary movement of tool
B. Sets tool start point to origin
C. Returns tool to selected surface
D. Starts toolpath from tool's home position

Q14. What is the function of Morph Toolpath?
A. Machine inside of tube-like structures
B. Create toolpath using U and V lines
C. Machine surface between two leading curves
D. Machine multiple uneven surfaces

Q15. What defines cutting pass direction in Flow Toolpath?
A. Edges of the surface
B. Cut Pattern and U/V lines
C. Curve orientation
D. Collision strategy

Q16. What type of surfaces are typically machined using the Multisurface tool?
A. Cylindrical surfaces
B. Flat and planar surfaces
C. 3D surfaces with uneven shapes
D. Gear-like profiles

Q17. In Port Expert Toolpath, what is the "Automatic spine" option used for?
A. Deburr edges
B. Machine only floor surfaces
C. Generate center curve of tube geometry
D. Perform radial machining

Q18. What does the Triangular Mesh toolpath maintain during cutting?
A. Tool tilt direction
B. Constant radius
C. Continuous contact with model
D. Centerline symmetry

Q19. What operation is Deburr Toolpath mainly used for?
A. Finishing turbine blades
B. Roughing undercut pockets
C. Removing burrs from model edges
D. Machining projected curves

Q20. What does the "Auto detect" option in Deburr toolpath's edge definition do?
A. Selects all model surfaces
B. Detects floor surfaces
C. Automatically finds model edges for deburring
D. Applies collision check

Q21. In Pocketing toolpath, what does selecting "Roughing" from the Machining drop-down do?
A. Machines only walls
B. Machines floors and walls
C. Machines selected edges
D. Removes fillets

Q22. What is the purpose of 3+2 Automatic Roughing toolpath?
A. To machine twisted blades
B. To finish hub and fillets
C. To create roughing toolpath using tilt axes
D. To remove burrs using pencil tools

Q23. In Project Curve Toolpath, which drop-down defines projection pattern?
A. Cut Pattern
B. Tool Axis Control
C. Project Curves Options
D. Guide Curve Styles

Q24. What does the "Spiral" option do in Project Curve Toolpath?
A. Projects curves in a radial style
B. Projects curve in circular form
C. Projects curves in spiral motion
D. Applies helix tool movement

Q25. Rotary toolpath is best suited for machining which type of model?
A. Complex turbine blades
B. Flat extrusions
C. Cylinder-shaped surfaces
D. Freeform curves

Q26. In Rotary Advanced toolpath, what is the function of the Slice pattern drop-down?
A. Defines feed rate
B. Defines surface entry point
C. Defines cutting pass layout
D. Sets edge geometry sharpness

Q27. Which toolpath is specifically used to machine turbine blade surfaces?
A. Swarf Milling
B. Curve Tool
C. Blade Expert
D. Flow Toolpath

Q28. What does selecting the "User selected geometry" radio button in Blade Expert Toolpath do?
A. Select pre-defined stock shape
B. Enables automatic tool alignment
C. Allows manual selection of stock model geometry
D. Applies smoothing spline

Chapter 12

Advanced Milling Tools

Topics Covered

The major topics covered in this chapter are:

- ***Introduction***
- ***Tool Manager***
- ***Multiaxis Linking***
- ***Toolpath Transform***
- ***Converting Toolpaths to 5-axis motion***
- ***Trimming Toolpath***
- ***Nesting Toolpaths***
- ***Checking Tool Holder for Interference***
- ***Checking Reach of Cutting Tool in Model***

INTRODUCTION

In previous chapters, you have learned to create various milling toolpaths. In this chapter, you will work on various miscellaneous tools like transforming toolpaths, trimming tools, and so on. These tools are discussed next.

Note that earlier you could access Probing tools till 2026 version of Mastercam Home Learning edition but the tools related to probe operation are not available in Home Learning Edition now and can be accessed only in commercial or educational version of the software. Also, you will need to download and install Mastercam 2027 Probing software separately as Add-on from Mastercam software download page.

MULTIAXIS LINKING

The **Multiaxis Linking** tool is used to create a toolpath at safe distance from model which links two or more toolpaths if you are using same cutting tool for two consecutive cutting strategies. The procedure to use this tool is given next.

- Click on the **Multiaxis Linking** tool from the **Utilities** panel in the **Toolpaths** tab of the **Ribbon**. The **Multiaxis Link** dialog box will be displayed; refer to Figure-1.

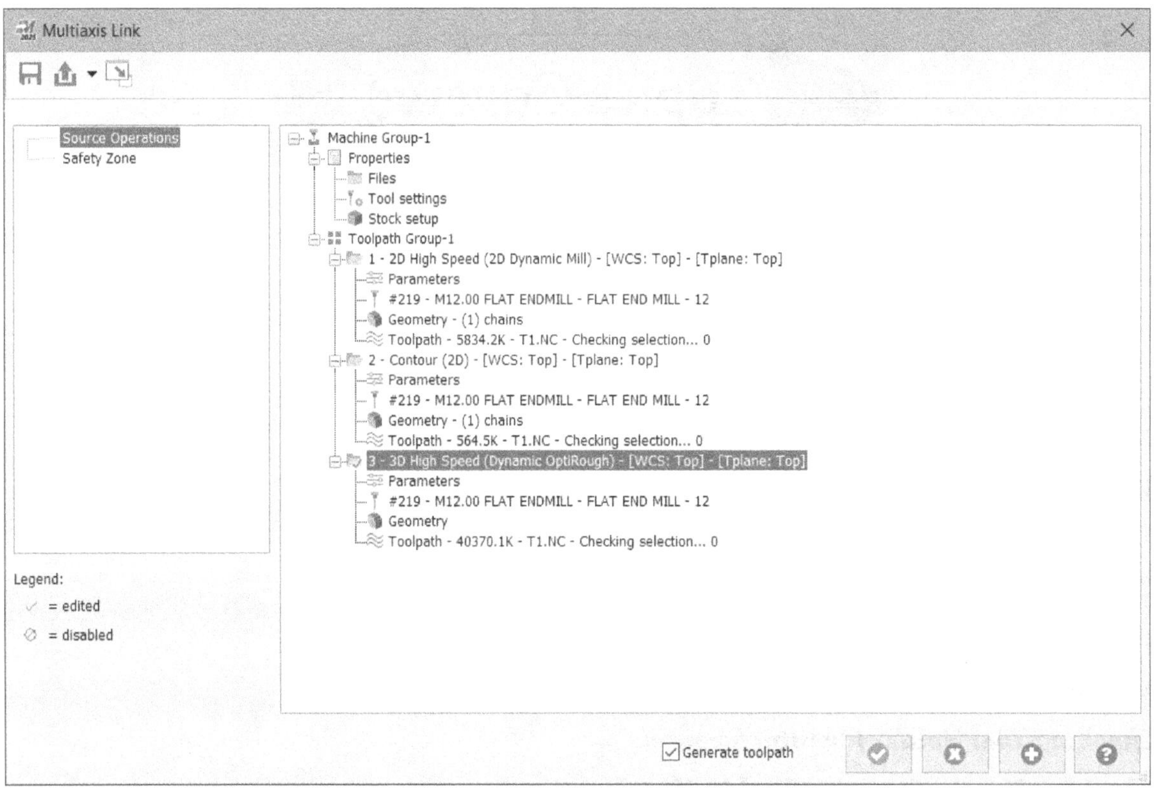

Figure-1. Multiaxis Link dialog box

- Select the toolpaths you want to link from the right area in the dialog box while holding the **CTRL** key.
- Select the **Safety Zone** option from the left area in the dialog box to define parameters related to safe distance where cutting tool will move while linking the toolpaths. The **Safety Zone** page will be displayed in the dialog box; refer to Figure-2.
- Select desired option from the **Axis of Rotation** drop-down to define axis along which cutting tool can rotate/tilt and specify related parameters in **Tool Motion** area.

- Click on the **Select Shape** button from the **Shape** area of the dialog box to define safety zone. The **Safety Zone Manager** will be displayed; refer to Figure-3 and you will be asked to select the model.

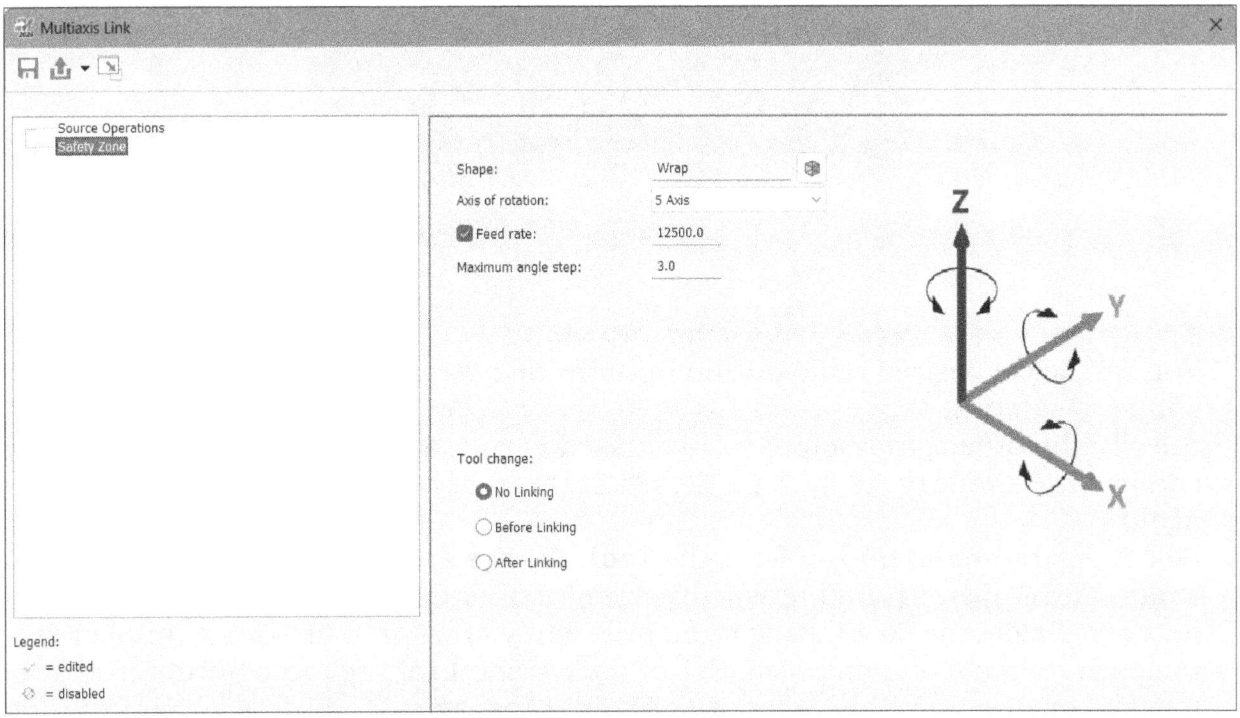

Figure-2. Safety Zone page

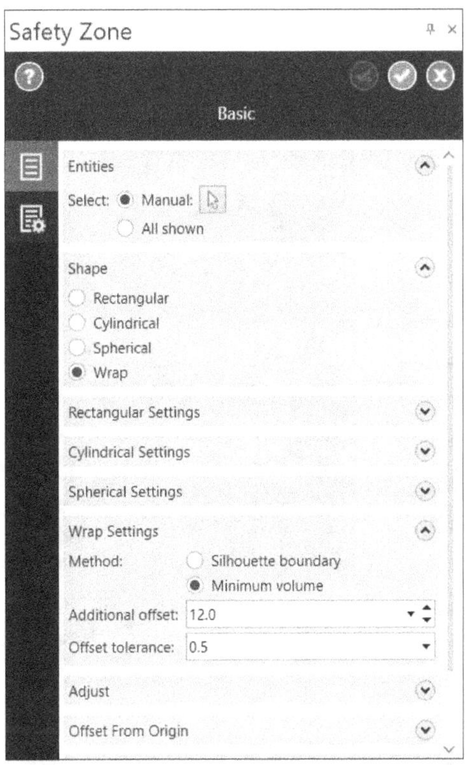

Figure-3. Safety Zone Manager

- Select the model to be used as reference for creating wrap shaped safety zone. Preview of the shape will be displayed; refer to Figure-4.

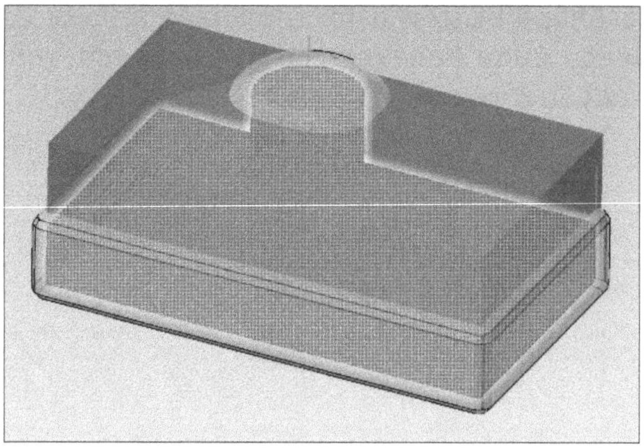

Figure-4. Preview of wrap safety zone

- You can select desired radio button from the **Shape** rollout of the **Manager** to modify shape of safety zone.
- Specify the other parameters as discussed earlier and click on the **OK** button to confirm the shape of safety zone. The **Multiaxis Link** dialog box will be displayed again.
- Select desired radio button from the **Tool Change** area of the dialog box to define what will happen to linking when cutting tool is changed from one toolpath to another. Select the **No Linking** radio button if you want to break the link between toolpaths when tool is changed. Select the **Before Linking** radio button to change tool before creating link. Select the **After Linking** radio button to perform tool change after creating link.
- After setting desired parameters, click on the **OK** button from the dialog box. The linking toolpath will be generated connecting end point of first toolpath with start point of next toolpath; refer to Figure-5.

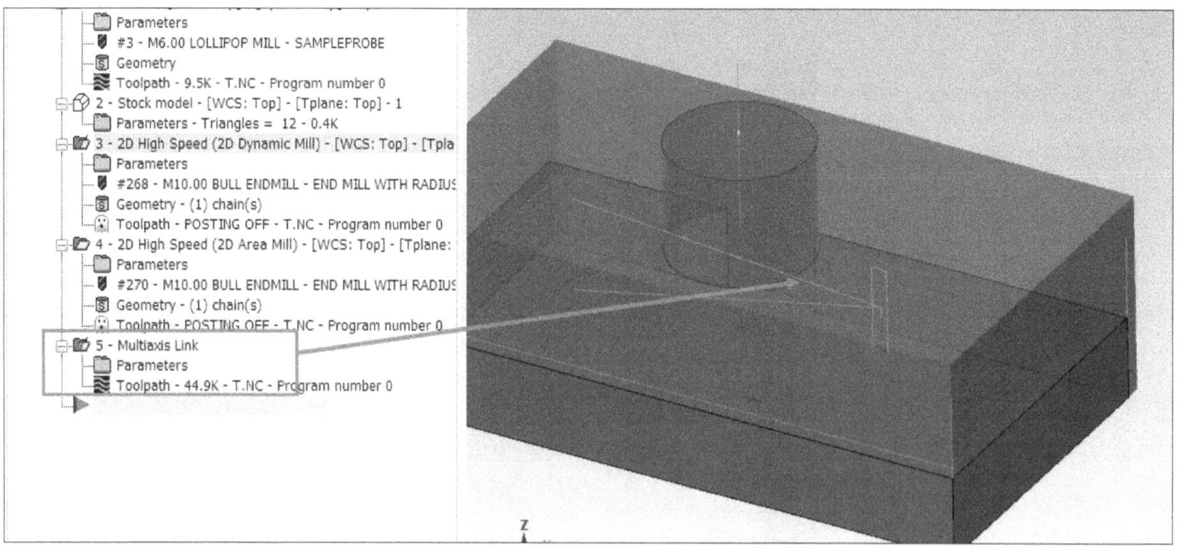

Figure-5. Multiaxis link toolpath

TOOLPATH TRANSFORMATION

The **Toolpath Transform** tool is used to translate, rotate, or mirror copy selected toolpaths. The procedure to use this tool is given next.

- After creating toolpaths for the model, click on the **Toolpath Transform** tool from the **Utilities** panel in the **Toolpaths** tab of the **Ribbon**. The **Transform Operation Parameters** dialog box will be displayed; refer to Figure-6.

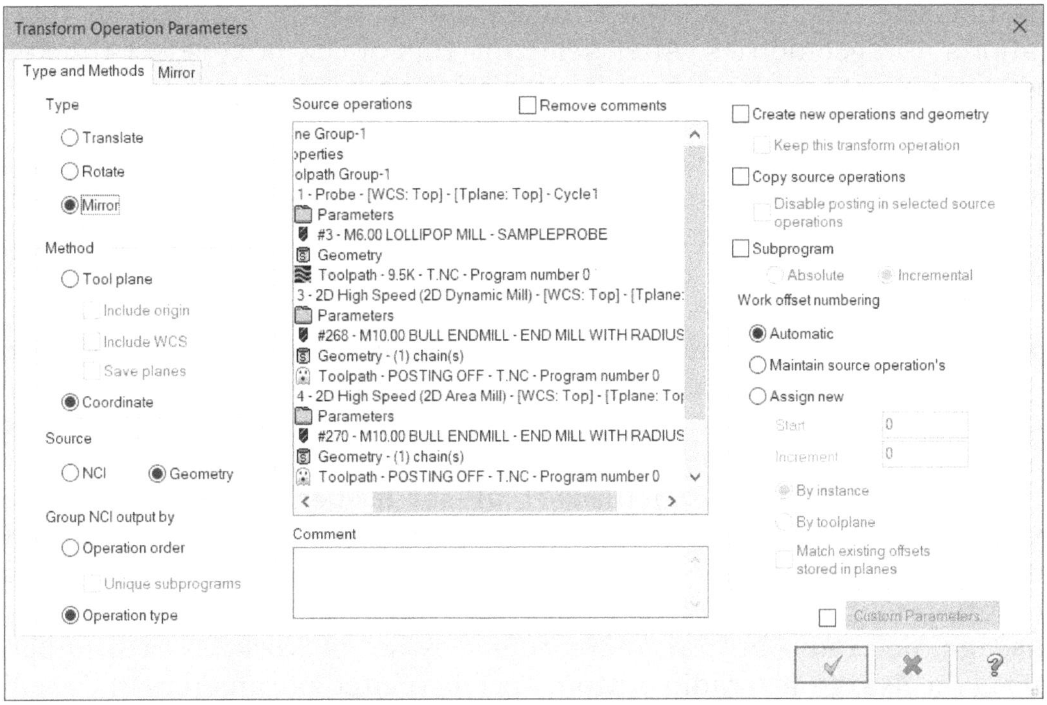

Figure-6. Transform Operation Parameters dialog box

- Select desired radio button from the **Type** area of the dialog box to define whether you want to translate, rotate, or mirror selected toolpaths. Select the **Translate** radio button if you want to move selected toolpaths to a different location. Select the **Rotate** radio button if you want to rotate selected toolpaths by specified value about an axis. Select the **Mirror** radio button if you want to create a mirror image of selected toolpaths about specified mirror plane.
- Select desired radio button from the **Method** area to define whether you want to create new tool planes and related geometries or you want to insert new coordinates in previous toolpaths. Select the **Tool plane** radio button to create a new tool plane after performing transformation operation. The **Include origin**, **Include WCS**, and **Save planes** check boxes will become available on selecting this radio button. Select the check boxes to include them with tool plane. Select the **Coordinate** radio button to copy coordinates of transformed toolpaths in original toolpath operation.
- Select desired radio button from the **Source** area of the dialog box to specify whether you want to copy only numeric codes or you want to copy geometry with toolpath. Select **NCI** radio button to copy only numeric codes generated by toolpath. Select the **Geometry** radio button to copy toolpath along with geometry while performing transformation operation.
- Select desired radio button from the **Group NCI output by** area to define how numeric codes will be grouped after transformation. Select the **Operation order** radio button to group output codes based on their operation order in original program. Select the **Operation type** radio button to group output codes based on what type of operation is being performed. For example, if there are pocket toolpaths and contour toolpaths in machining then all the pocket toolpaths will be grouped together and all the contour toolpaths will be grouped together.
- Select the **Remove comments** check box to remove comments given with toolpath after performing transformation.
- Select the **Create new operations and geometry** check box if you want to create a copy of operations and geometries after performing transformation. If this check

box is not selected then all the transformation will be applied on the original operations and geometries. After selecting this check box, select the **Keep this transform operation** check box to apply all the transformations to newly created operations and geometries while keeping the originals unchanged.

- Select the **Copy source operations** check box to create a duplicate copy of selected toolpaths directly above source. After selecting this check box, select the **Disable posting in selected source operations** check box to prevent source operations from being posted twice by disabling posting for the source operation.
- Select the **Subprogram** check box to create repeating sections of program as subprograms. Note that this option is not available if you have opted to create new operations and geometries. After selecting this check box, select the **Absolute** radio button if you want to use absolute coordinates or select the **Incremental** radio button to use incremental coordinate values when creating the program.
- Select desired radio button from the **Work offset numbering** area to define how work offset numbers will be created. Select the **Automatic** radio button to automatically assign next available offset number. Select the **Maintain source operation's** radio button to use same offset numbers as defined in source operations. Select the **Assign new** radio button to create a new set of work offset numbers. After selecting the **Assign new** radio button, specify related parameters in the edit boxes below it. Select the **Match existing offsets stored in planes** check box to match offset numbers with existing offsets associated with planes.
- Based on the radio button selected in the **Type** area of the dialog box, a new tab will be added in the dialog box. For example, if the **Mirror** radio button is selected in the **Type** area then **Mirror** tab will be added in the dialog box. The options of **Mirror**, **Rotate**, and **Translate** tabs are discussed next.

Mirror Transformation

If the **Mirror** radio button is selected then **Mirror** tab will be displayed in the dialog box. Click on the **Mirror** tab to modify parameters related to mirror transformation; refer to Figure-7. Options of this tab are discussed next.

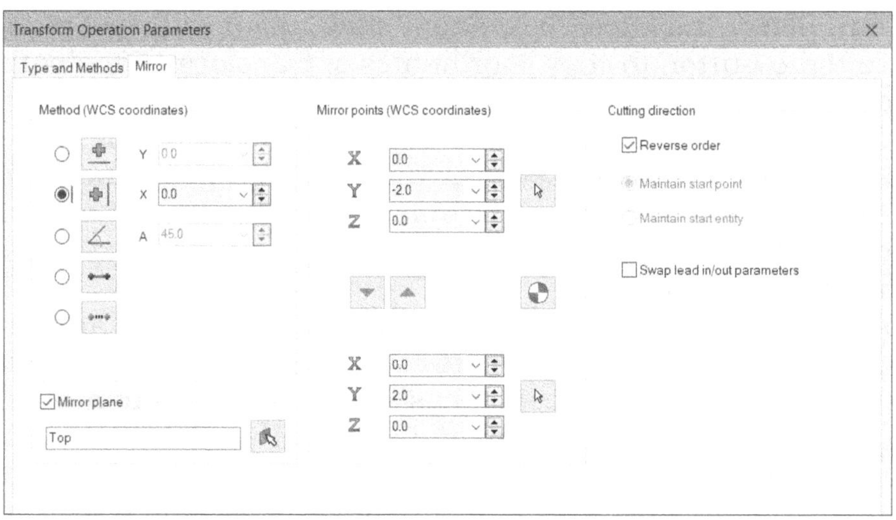

Figure-7. Mirror tab

- Select the **Mirror plane** check box from the **Mirror** tab in dialog box to use a plane as mirror reference.
- Click on the **Select Plane** button from the **Mirror plane** area of the dialog box. The **Plane Selection** dialog box will be displayed.

- Select desired plane from the dialog box and click on the **OK** button. Note that mirror plane and tool plane should be same for creating mirror copy.
- Select desired radio button from the **Method (WCS coordinates)** area of the dialog box to define location and orientation of WCS for measuring location of mirror plane/point.
- Specify desired coordinates in the **Mirror points (WCS coordinates)** area to define the start and end locations of mirror line.
- Select the **Reverse order** check box from the **Cutting direction** area to reverse the start and end points of toolpaths. Select the **Maintain start point** radio button to keep the starting point same as in original toolpath. Select the **Maintain start entity** radio button to use same geometries as selected for original toolpath.
- After setting desired parameters, click on the **OK** button to create mirror copy.

Rotation Transformation

If the **Rotate** radio button is selected in the **Type** area of the **Type and Methods** tab in the dialog box then **Rotate** tab will be displayed in the dialog box. Click on the **Rotate** tab to modify parameters related to rotate transformation; refer to Figure-8. The options of this tab are discussed next.

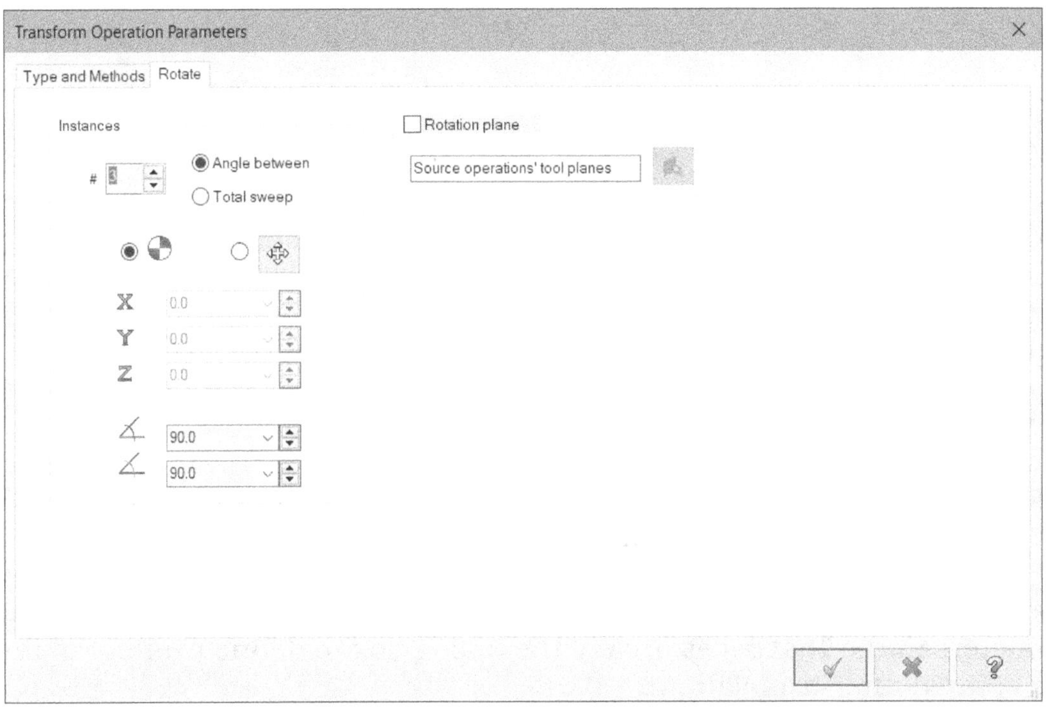

Figure-8. Rotate tab

- Specify the number of copies to be created in the **Instances** spinner.
- Select the **Angle between** radio button from the **Instances** area to define angular gap between two consecutive instances of the toolpath. Select the **Total sweep** radio button if you want to specify total angular span in which the instances will be placed equally spaced.
- Specify desired values in the first and second angle edit boxes to define angle values for both upper and lower angle ranges, respectively.
- Select the **Rotation plane** check box to use selected plane as reference for rotation. On selecting the check box, selection box below the check box will become active.
- Click on the **Select plane** button from **Rotation plane** area and select desired plane to be used for rotation.
- After setting desired parameters, click on the **OK** button to perform transformation.

Translate Transformation

If the **Translate** radio button is selected then **Translate** tab will be displayed in the dialog box. Click on the **Translate** tab to modify parameters related to translate transformation; refer to Figure-9.

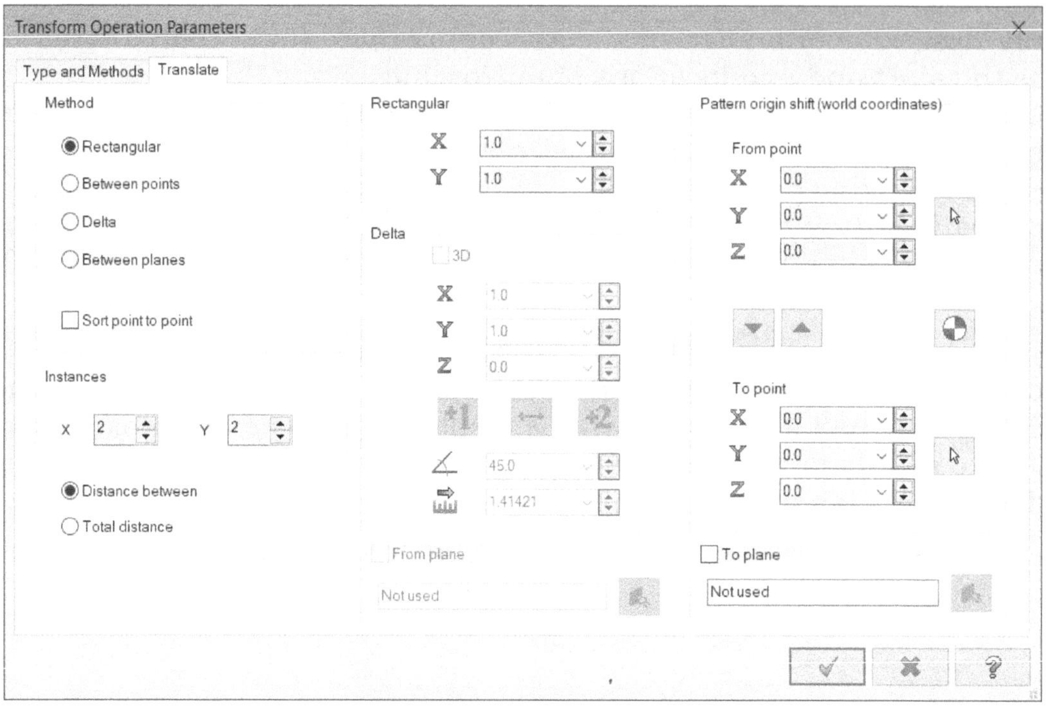

Figure-9. Translate tab

- Select desired radio button from the **Method** area to specify method to be used for moving selected toolpaths to different location. Select the **Rectangular** radio button from the **Method** area to specify distance to be moved in **X** and **Y** edit boxes of **Rectangular** area. Select the **Between points** radio button from the **Method** area to use **X**, **Y**, and **Z** edit boxes for **From point** and **To point** in the **Pattern origin shift (world coordinates)** area of the dialog box to move selected toolpaths. Select the **Delta** radio button to specify offset distance from values specified in the **Pattern origin shift (world coordinates)** area of the dialog box. Select the **Between planes** radio button from the **Method** area to use planes selected in the **From plane** and **To plane** areas of the dialog box.
- If the **Rectangular** radio button is selected in the **Method** area then specify the parameters in the **Instances** area of the dialog box to define number of instances to be created after translation.
- After setting desired parameters, click on the **OK** button to perform transformation.

CONVERTING TOOLPATH TO 5-AXIS TOOLPATH

The **Convert to 5-axis** tool is used to convert selected 2-axis or 3-axis toolpaths to 5-axis toolpaths. The procedure to use this tool is given next.

- Click on the **Convert to 5-axis** tool from the **Utilities** panel in the **Toolpaths** tab of the **Ribbon**. The **Multiaxis Toolpath - Convert to 5 axis** dialog box will be displayed; refer to Figure-10.

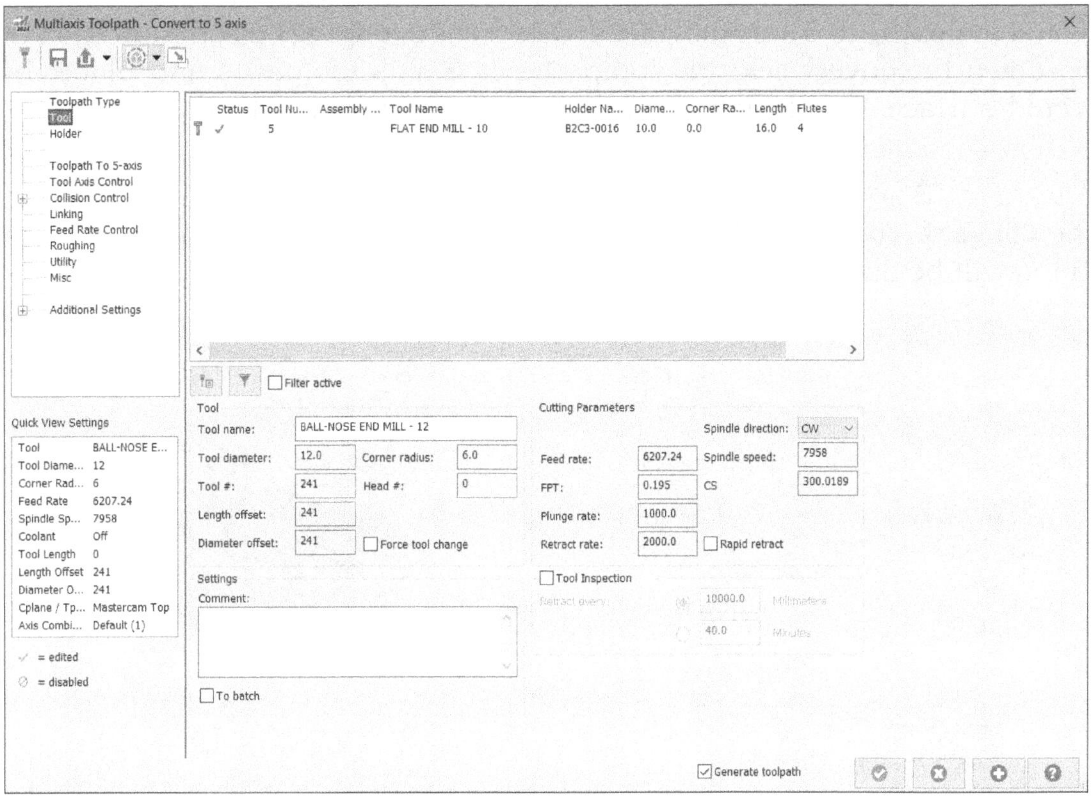

Figure-10. Multiaxis Toolpath-Convert to 5 axis dialog box

- Select desired cutting tool and tool holder to be used for converting the toolpaths to 5 axis toolpaths from respective pages in the dialog box as discussed earlier.
- Click on the **Toolpath To 5axis** option from the left area of the dialog box to specify parameters for conversion of toolpath. The options will be displayed as shown in Figure-11.

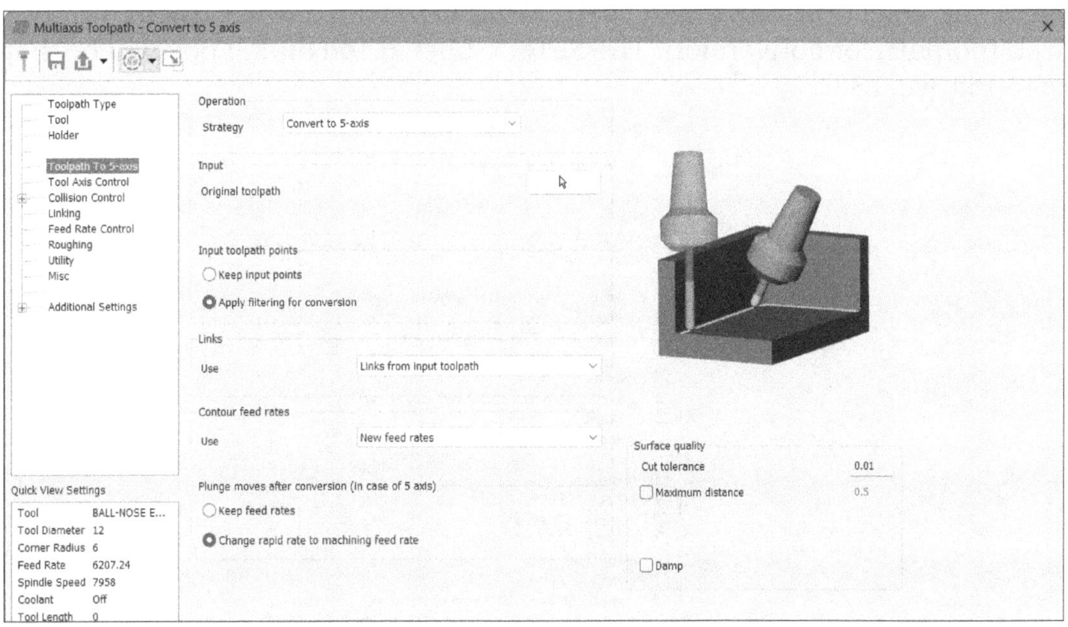

Figure-11. Toolpath To 5-axis page

- Select the **Convert to 5 axis** option from the **Strategy** drop-down to convert selected toolpaths to 5 axis toolpaths. Select the **Dropping** option from the **Strategy** drop-down to convert selected toolpaths to 5 axis toolpaths and place them on selected surface. The options for both the strategies are discussed next.

Converting to 5 axis

- If the **Convert to 5 axis** option is selected in the **Strategy** drop-down then the options will be displayed as shown in Figure-12.

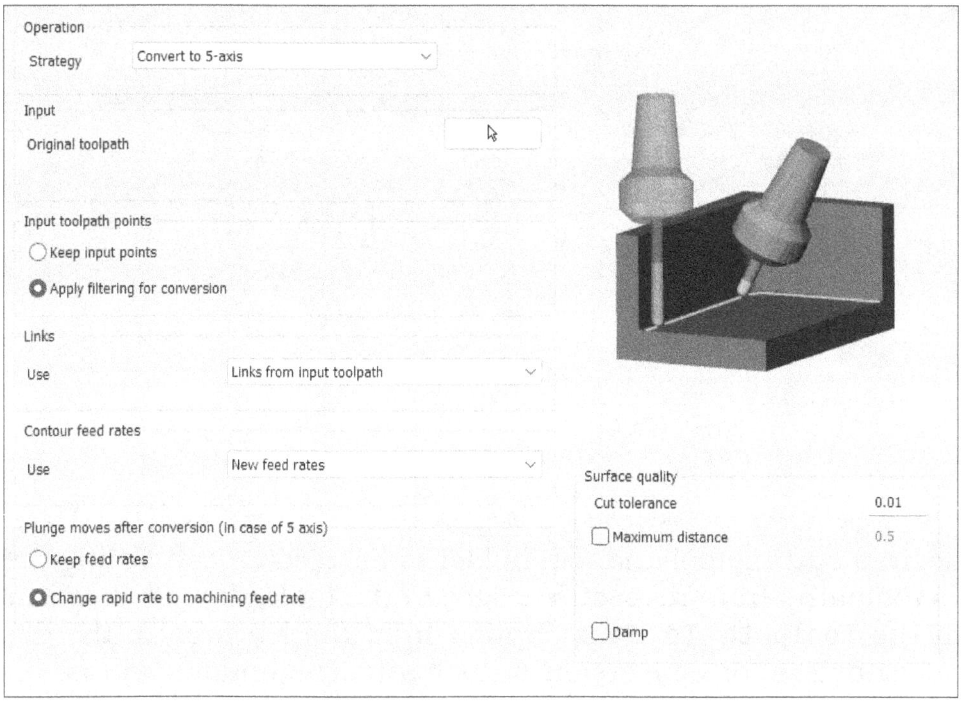

Figure-12. Convert to 5 axis options

- Click in the selection box for **Original tool path** from the **Input** area to select desired toolpath for conversion. The **Select Operation** dialog box will be displayed; refer to Figure-13.

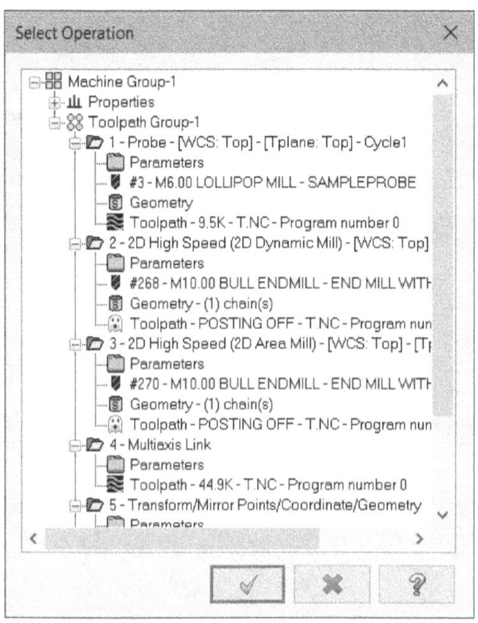

Figure-13. Select Operation dialog box

- Select desired 2D or 3D toolpath from the list to be used for conversion. Note that you can select only one toolpath at a time from the list. After selecting toolpath, click on the **OK** button from the dialog box.
- Click in the **Cut tolerance** edit box to specify maximum deviation from the toolpath that can be allowed from original toolpath.
- Select the **Keep input points** radio button from **Input toolpath points** area to keep original toolpath points as it is. Select the **Apply filtering for conversion** radio button to reduce size and noise of original toolpath.
- Select desired option from the **Use** drop-down in the **Links** area of the dialog box to define how links will be created between toolpaths. Select the **Links from input toolpath** option to create link toolpath between various toolpaths as given in input toolpaths. Select the **New links** option from the drop-down to create new links between 5 axis toolpaths being created.
- Select desired option from the **Use** drop-down of **Contour feed rates** area to define whether new feed rates specified in this dialog box will be used or feed rate values from original toolpath will be considered for contour cutting passes.
- Select desired radio button from the **Plunge moves after conversion (in case of 5 axis)** area to define how plunge moves will be converted in 5 axis toolpath. Select the **Keep feed rates** radio button to use rapid feed rate for plunge moves. Select the **Change rapid feed rate to machining feed rate** radio button to use machining feed rate instead of rapid feed rate for plunge moves in 5 axis toolpath.
- Select the **Maximum distance** check box from the **Surface quality** area of the dialog box to define maximum distance between key points of toolpath generated and specify the value of distance in the adjacent edit box.
- Select the **Damp** check box to remove abrupt tool movements by making smooth transition between cutting passes.

Dropping 5 Axis Toolpath

If you want to convert selected toolpaths into 5 axis toolpaths and place them on selected surface then select the **Dropping** option from the **Strategy** drop-down. The options will be displayed as shown in Figure-14.

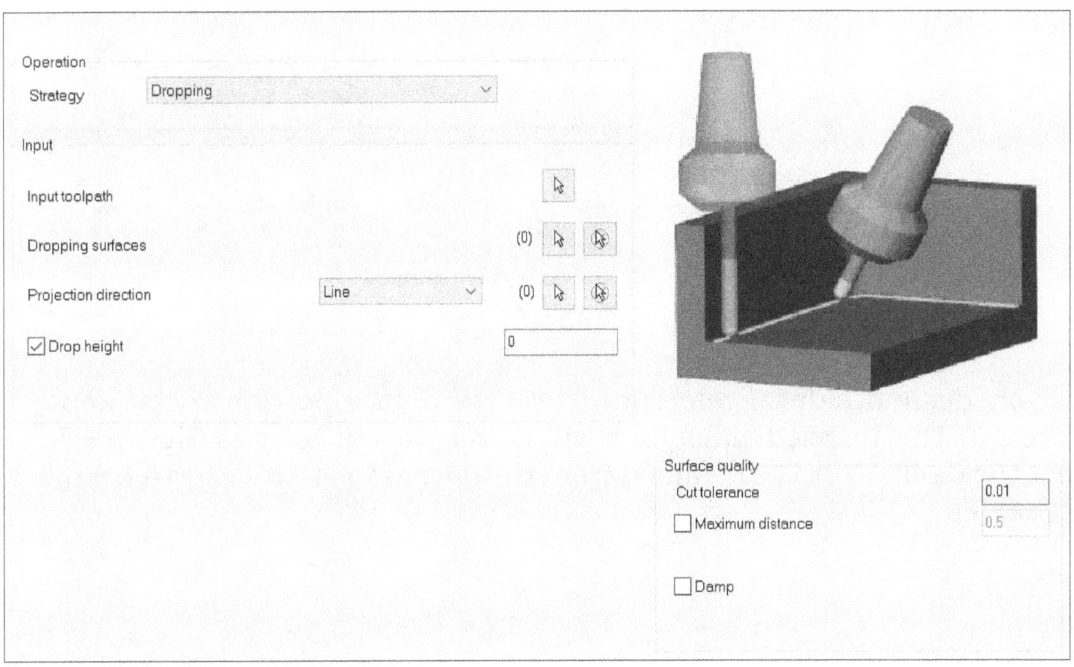

Figure-14. Dropping strategy options

- Click on the **Select** button for **Input toolpath** option and select the toolpath to be converted into 5 axis toolpath from the **Select Operation** dialog box displayed. After selecting toolpath, click on the **OK** button from the dialog box.
- Click on the **Select** button for **Dropping surfaces** option from the **Input** area and select the surface on which the 5 axis toolpath will be projected.
- Click on the **Select** button for **Projection direction** option and select desired direction reference to define projection direction for toolpaths. You can also select the **X**, **Y**, or **Z axis** option from the **Projection direction** drop-down to define projection direction.
- Select the **Drop height** check box to specify height at which toolpath will be dropped along selected direction.
- Select the **Damp** check box from **Surface quality** area to allow non-orthographic movements of cutting tool for axial movements.
- Set desired parameters in the **Surface quality** area as discussed earlier.
- The options in other pages of the dialog box have been discussed earlier. Click on the **OK** button from the dialog box to create the toolpaths.

TRIMMING A TOOLPATH

The **Trim** tool is used to trim selected portion of the toolpaths using reference geometries. Note that you need to create wireframe geometries for defining trim boundaries before using this tool. The procedure to use this tool is given next.

- Click on the **Trim** tool from the **Utilities** panel in the **Toolpaths** tab of the **Ribbon**. The **Wireframe Chaining** dialog box will be displayed as discussed earlier.
- Select desired curves to be used as reference tool for trimming; refer to Figure-15 and click on the **OK** button from the dialog box. You will be asked to select a point to define the region to be kept after deleting the other portion.

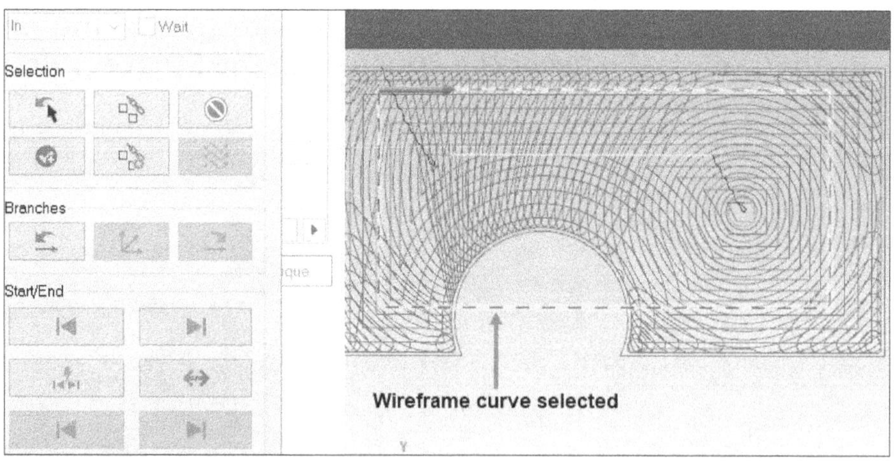

Figure-15. Wireframe curve selected for trimming

- Click on desired side of reference curve to define portion to be kept; refer to Figure-16. The **Trimmed** dialog box will be displayed; refer to Figure-17.
- Select the toolpaths to be trimmed from the **Operations to trim** area while holding the **CTRL** key.

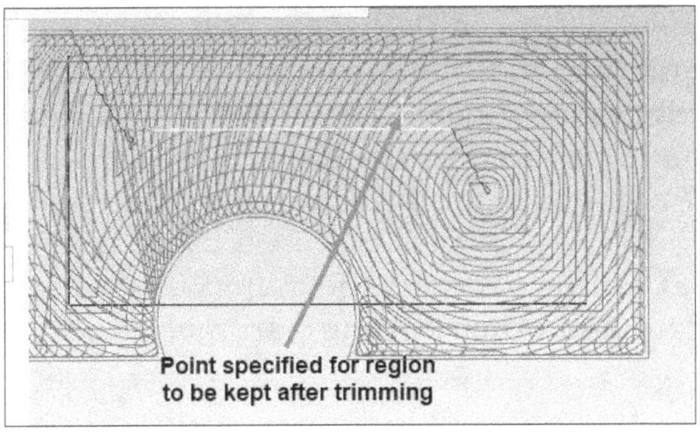

Figure-16. Specifying point for region to be kept

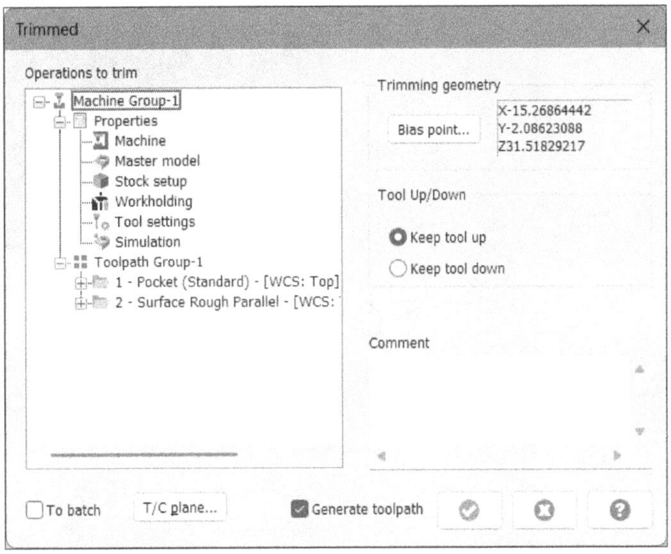

Figure-17. Trimmed dialog box

- Specify the other parameters as discussed earlier and click on the **OK** button. The toolpath will be trimmed; refer to Figure-18.

Figure-18. Trimmed toolpath

NESTING TOOLPATHS

The **Nesting** tool is used to create multiple copies of selected toolpath equally spaced at desired location. Nesting toolpath is useful when you need to machine same parts placed multiple times on same machining bed. Note that nesting can be created/ manipulated in top view only. The procedure to use this tool is given next.

- Click on the **Nesting** tool from the **Utilities** panel in the **Toolpaths** tab of the **Ribbon**. The **Nesting** dialog box will be displayed; refer to Figure-19. By default, the **Sheets** tab is selected in the dialog box. The options of this tab are discussed next.

Sheets tab

- Specify desired length and width of sheet in the **Size** edit boxes.
- Select the **Create necessary quantity** check box to automatically specify the number of toolpaths to be fitted in the sheet.
- Click in the **X** and **Y** edit boxes for **Origin** option to define location for start point of toolpaths.
- Click on the **Material** button to define the material of workpiece. Based on selected material, the feed rate and other cutting parameters will be decided.

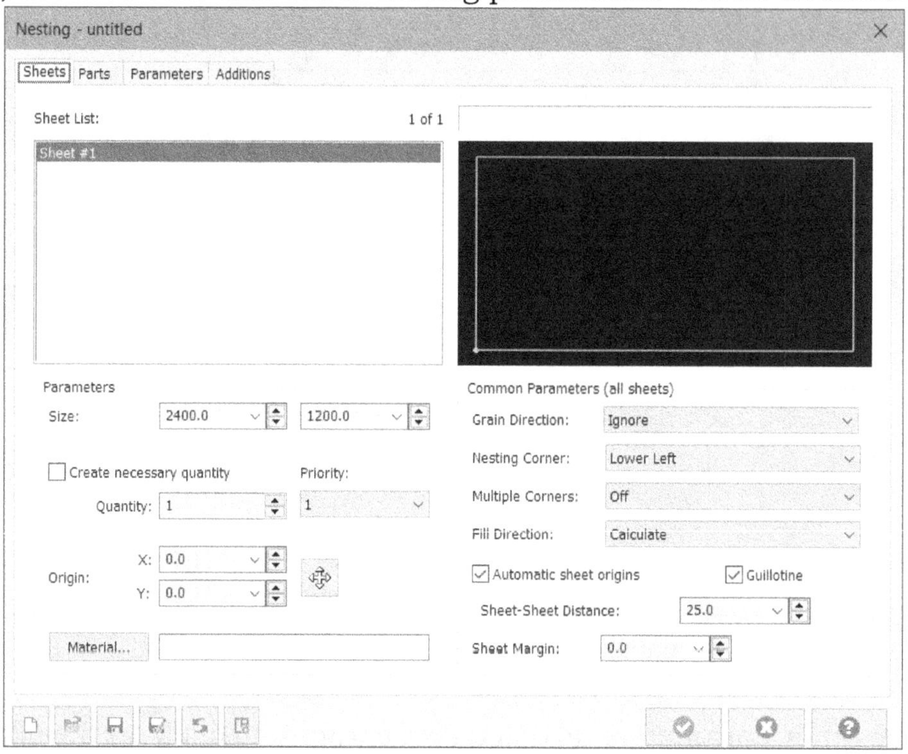

Figure-19. Nesting dialog box

- Select desired option from the **Grain Direction** drop-down to define grain direction for easy cutting of workpiece, if there is a noticeable difference in grains on surface of workpiece. Select the **Horizontal** or **Vertical** option from the drop-down to use respective direction as grain direction. Select the **Ignore** option, if grain direction does not affect cutting.
- Select desired option from the **Nesting Corner** drop-down to define start point for nesting of toolpaths.
- Select desired option from the **Multiple Corners** drop-down to define which point(s) will be used as starting reference for placing multiple parts on the sheet. After setting number of copies, you can tweak this option to find most suitable arrangement of parts on the sheet/table.
- Select desired option from the **Fill Direction** drop-down to define the direction to be used for placing instances of the toolpath. You can select **Horizontal** or **Vertical** option from the drop-down to use respective direction or you can use the **Calculate** option and let software to decide automatically the direction for nesting.
- Select the **Guillotine** check box to arrange the parts in such a way that straight cuts can be made on the workpieces.
- Select the **Automatic sheet origins** check box to allow Mastercam to place origins of multiple sheets automatically.
- Specify desired value in **Sheet-Sheet Distance** edit box to define gap between two consecutive sheets.

- Specify desired value in the **Sheet Margin** edit box to define margin gap around the sheets.

Parts tab

The options in the **Parts** tab are used to add, remove, and arrange parts; refer to Figure-20. The options of this tab are discussed next.

Figure-20. Parts tab

- Right-click in the **Part List** area to select parts/operations to be nested. A shortcut menu will be displayed; refer to Figure-21. Select the **Add operations** option from the menu to add new operations in the list. The **Select Operations** dialog box will be displayed with the list of operations applied in current file; refer to Figure-22.

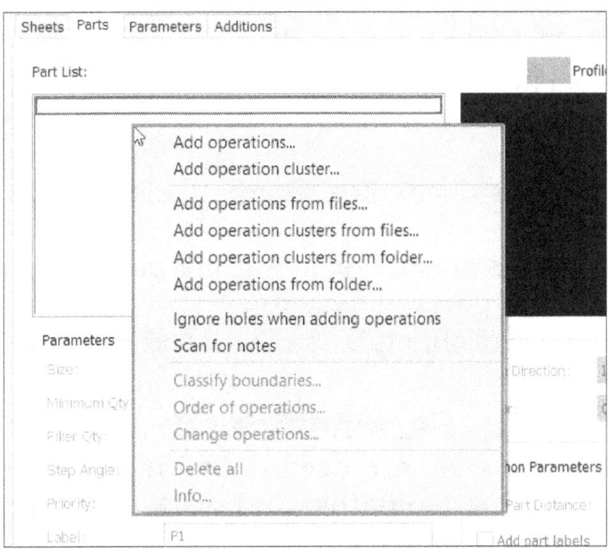

Figure-21. Shortcut menu displayed

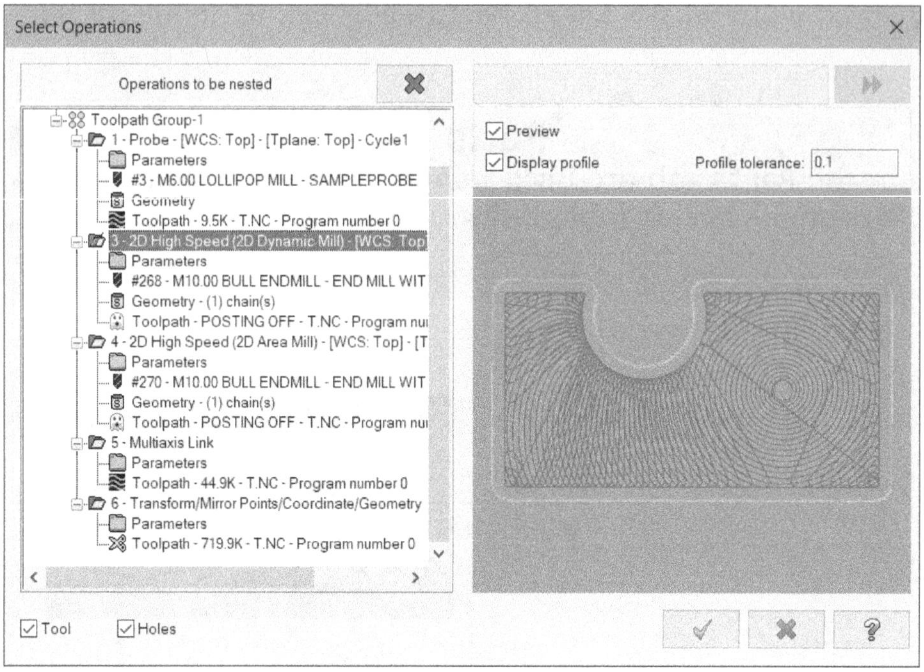

Figure-22. Select Operations dialog box

- Select desired operation(s) to be added in the part list and click on the **OK** button from the dialog box. The selected operations will be added in the list. Similarly, you can use the other options of the shortcut menu to add operations.
- Specify desired value in the **Minimum Qty** edit box to define minimum number of copies of selected operation to be added in the sheet.
- Specify desired value in the **Filler Qty** edit box to define number of filler part copies to be added in the sheet after main parts have been added.
- Specify desired value in the **Step Angle** edit box to define angle steps to be used for rotating parts when nesting.
- Select desired option from the **Priority** drop-down to define which parts will be placed on sheet for nesting. By default, larger parts are given preference in nesting.
- Select the **Use bounding box** check box to use the bounding boxes around parts to define their size on sheet.
- Select the **Use part labels** check box to place the label of part along with part on the sheet. After selecting this check box, specify the label value in **Label** edit box and height of label in the **Height** edit box below the check box. You can select the **Automatic** radio button below the check box to let Mastercam automatically decide the height of label.
- Select the **Optimize pairs** check box to create close fit pairs of parts in nesting for efficient use of space.
- Select the **Fill all sheets** check box to automatically fill the spaces in all sheets with main parts and filler parts as possible.
- Set the other parameters of this tab as discussed earlier.

Parameters tab

The options in the **Parameters** tab are used to define parameters like sorting order, conditions for stopping nesting toolpaths, and work offsets; refer to Figure-23. The options in this tab are discussed next.

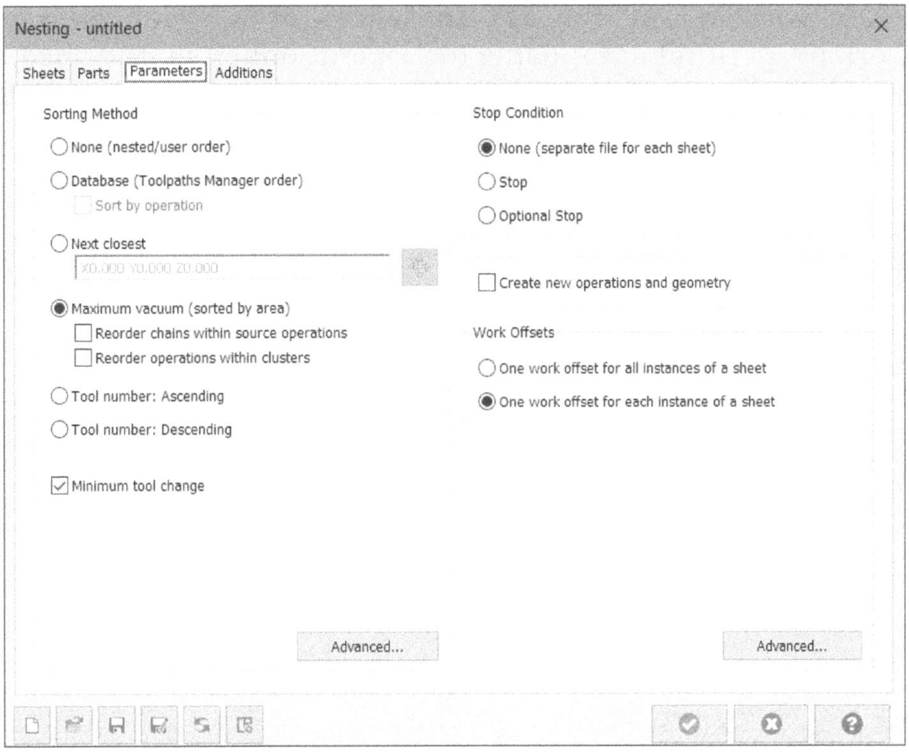

Figure-23. Parameters tab

- Select desired radio button from the **Sorting Method** area to define how operations in various sheets will be arranged for machining. Select the **None (nested/user order)** radio button to use the same order for machining as specified for nesting. Select the **Database (operation manager order)** radio button to use same order in which operation are present in the **Toolpaths Manager** (**Operations Manager**) for machining. Select the **Next closest** radio button from the **Sorting Method** area to arrange the operations as per their distance from specified point. Select the **Maximum vacuum (sorted by area)** radio button to machine those operations first which have more free area around them for operation. Select the **Tool number: Ascending** radio button from the dialog box if you want to perform operations as per the ascending number of tools used in those operations. Similarly, select the **Tool number: Descending** radio button to sort operations as per descending number of used tools.
- Select the **Minimum tool change** check box to sort the operations by tool, so that all parts using one tool are cut before changing to the next tool.
- Click on the **Advanced** button from the **Sorting Method** area to divide the sheet into regions for user defined sorting. The **Advanced Sorting** dialog box will be displayed; refer to Figure-24. Select the **Sort by region** check box and specify related parameters in the dialog box to define sorting order for regions. After setting parameters, click on the **OK** button from the dialog box.
- Select desired radio button from **Stop Condition** area of the dialog box to specify when will the machine stop for changing material. Select the **None (separate file for each sheet)** radio button to output toolpaths as per the sheets without program stops. Select the **Stop** radio button to insert program stop code (M00) at the end of each sheet. Select the **Optional Stop** radio button to insert optional stop code (M01) at the end of each sheet.
- Select the **Create new operations and geometry** check box to copy geometry and operations from original operations for each location in the nesting sheets.

- Select the **One work offset for all instances of a sheet** radio button to use a single work offset number for same tool operations in all the sheets. Select the **One work offset for each instance of a sheet** radio button to use different work offset numbers for same operations in different sheets.

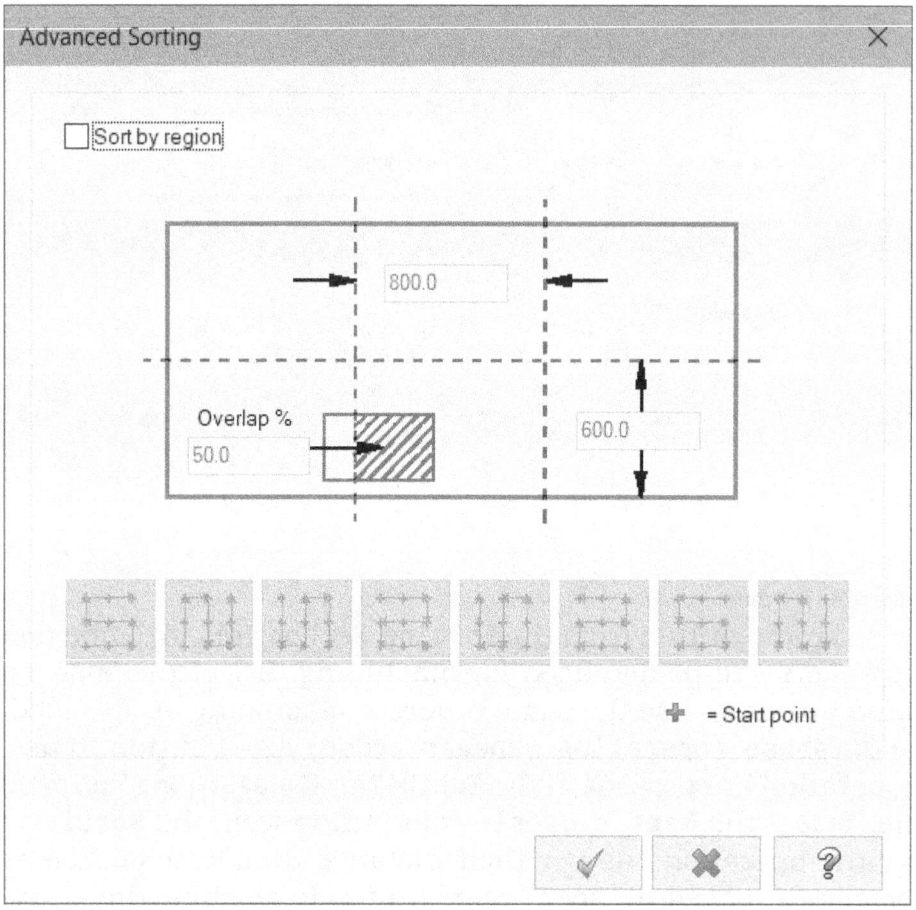

Figure-24. Advanced Sorting dialog box

- Click on the **Advanced** button from the **Work Offsets** area of the dialog box to specify advanced parameters related to work offset. The **Advanced Offsets** dialog box will be displayed; refer to Figure-25. Select the **Automatic** radio button from the dialog box to use next available work offset automatically. Select the **Maintain source operation's** radio button to use offset numbers as specified in operation data. Select the **Assign new** radio button to create a new set of offset numbers with specified increment parameters. After setting desired parameters, click on the **OK** button.

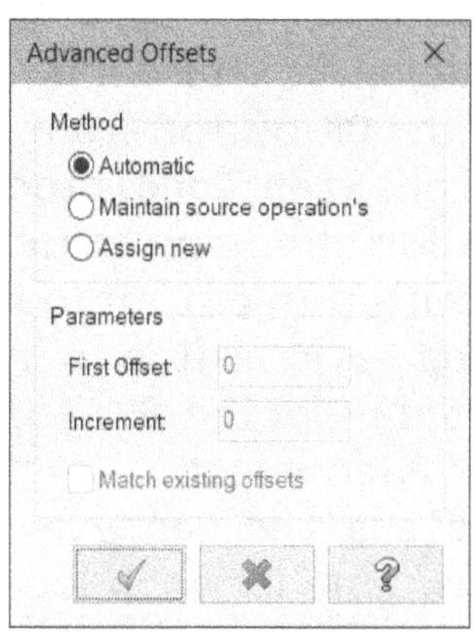

Figure-25. Advanced Offsets dialog box

Additions tab

The options in the **Additions** tab are used to specify parameters related to stock and toolpath links; refer to Figure-26. The parameters in this tab are discussed next.

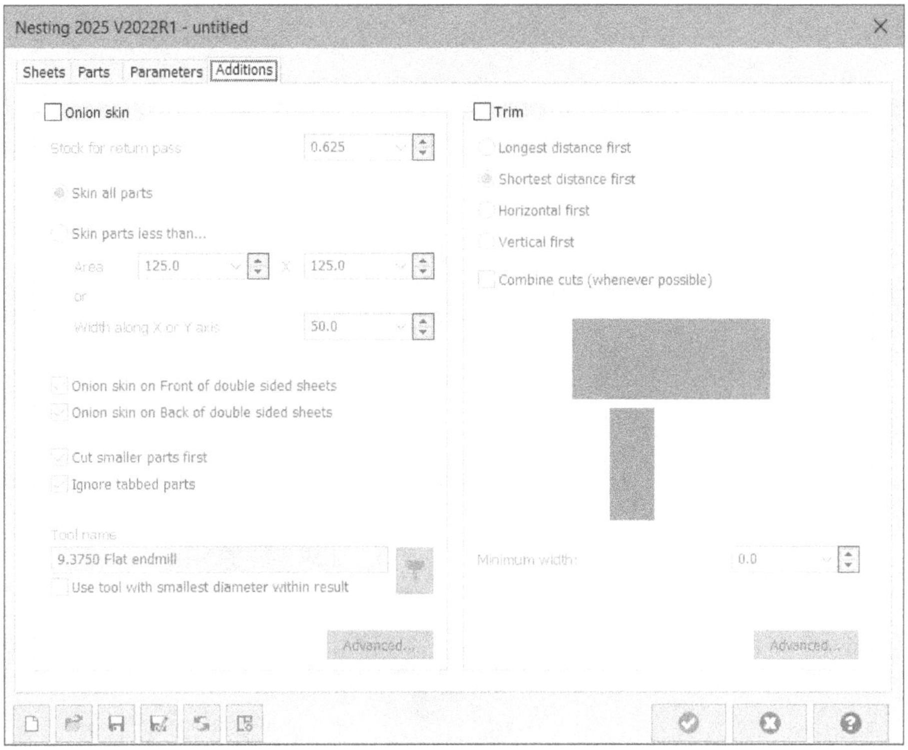

Figure-26. Additions tab

- Select the **Onion skin** check box from the dialog box to create a final return cutting pass after performing operations on all the parts of sheets. On selecting the check box, options in the **Onion skin** area will become active.
- Specify the value of stock to be removed by return pass in the **Stock for return pass** edit box.
- Select the **Skin all parts** radio button to include all the parts for performing skin contour machining operation.
- Select the **Skin parts less than** radio button to include only those parts for skin contour machining operation which have area less than values specified in the edit boxes below the radio button. You can either specify the area parameters or width parameters in these edit boxes.
- Select the **Onion skin on Front of double sided sheets** check box to create operation for front side of double sided sheets. Double sided sheets are those which have parts on their both sides.
- Select the **Onion skin on Front of double sided sheets** check box to create operation for back side of double sided sheets.
- Select the **Cut smaller parts first** check box to start cutting small size parts first and then machine larger parts. By default, the larger parts are machined first.
- Click on the **Select library tool** button next to **Tool name** edit box for selecting cutting tool to perform return cut.
- If you want to use smallest cutting tool earlier used in performing various operations on the sheet then select the **Use tool with smallest diameter within result** check box.

- Click on the **Advanced** button from the **Onion skin** area of dialog box to define advanced toolpath parameters for onion skin machining. The **2D Toolpaths - Onion skin** dialog box will be displayed; refer to Figure-27.

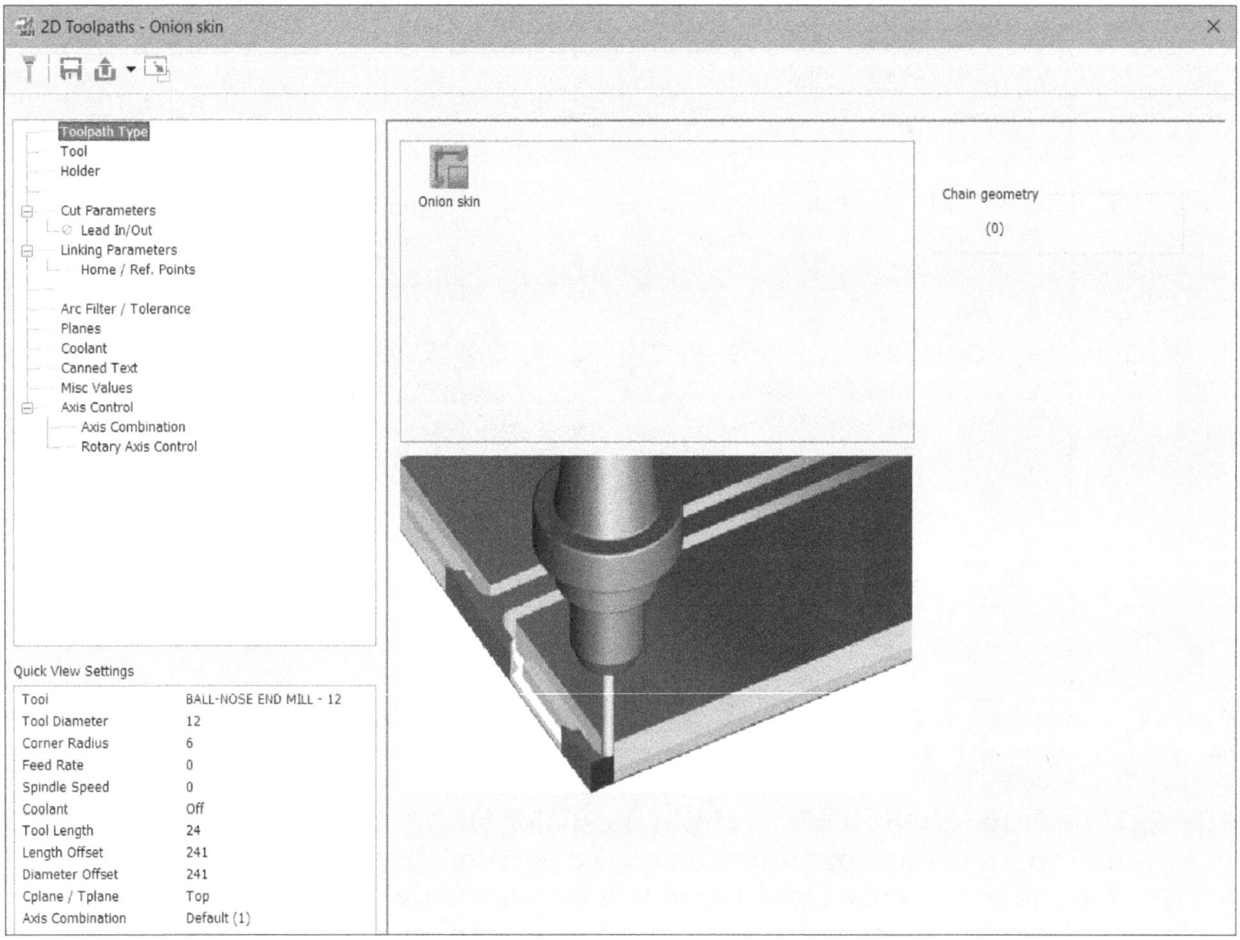

Figure-27. 2D Toolpaths-Onion skin dialog box

- The options in this dialog box are same as discussed for 2D toolpaths in previous chapters. Set the parameters as desired and click on the **OK** button.
- Select the **Trim** check box to create toolpath for machine remnants from the sheet. Note that you will need saw operation to perform trimming. On selecting this check box, the options in the **Trim** area will become active.
- Select the **Longest distance first** radio button to cut the sheet from longest side first. Select the **Shortest distance first** radio button to cut the sheet from shortest side first. Select the **Horizontal first** radio button to cut from horizontal side first. Select the **Vertical first** radio button to cut from vertical side first.
- Select the **Combine cuts (whenever possible)** check box if you want to combine different cut sides if necessary/possible for cutting sheet.
- Specify desired value in the **Minimum width** edit box to define minimum width to be considered for saw cutting.
- After setting desired parameters, click on the **OK** button from the **Nesting** dialog box. The **Nesting Results** dialog box will be displayed showing arrangement of parts in the sheet; refer to Figure-28.

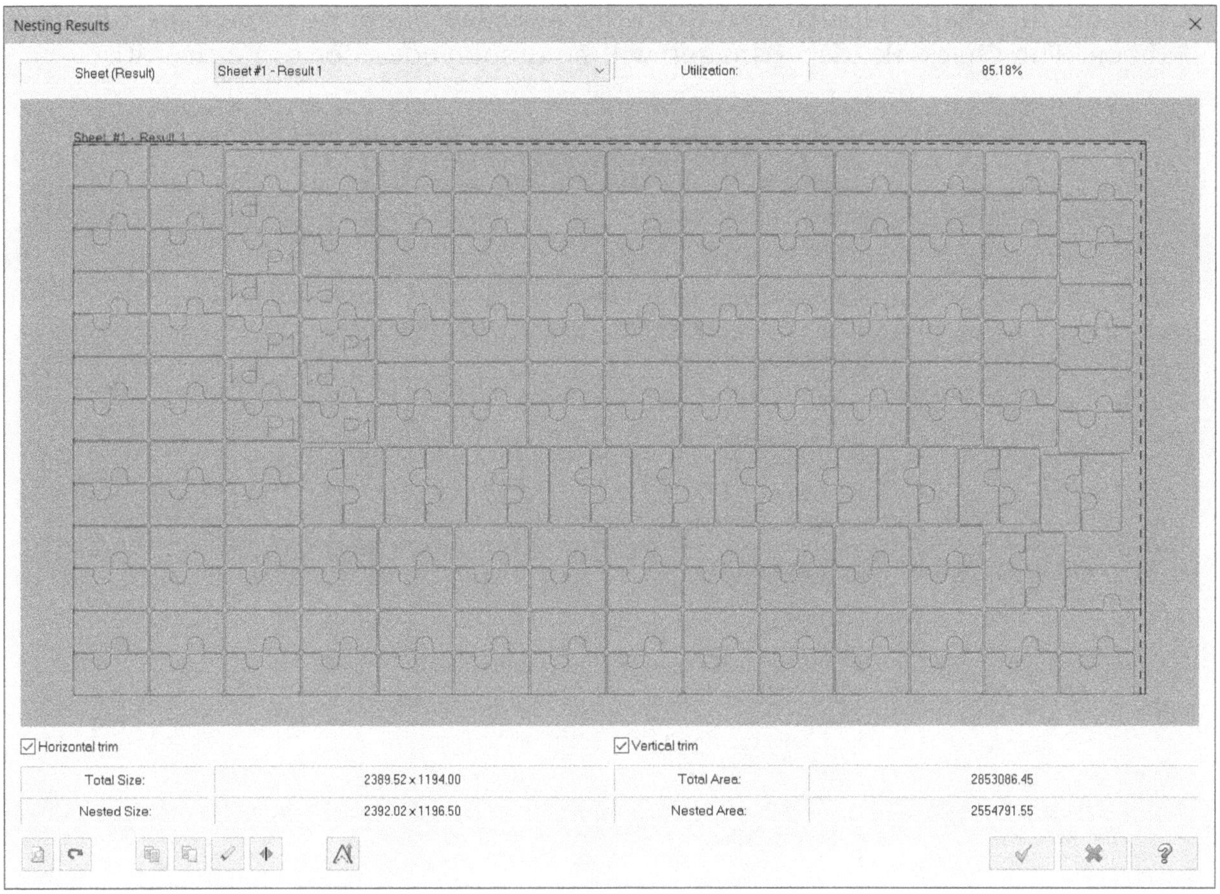

Figure-28. Nesting Results dialog box

- Using the buttons at the bottom in the dialog box, you can save, export, copy, delete, sort, and drag the report as desired. After setting desired parameters, click on the **OK** button from the dialog box. The nested toolpaths will be created; refer to Figure-29.

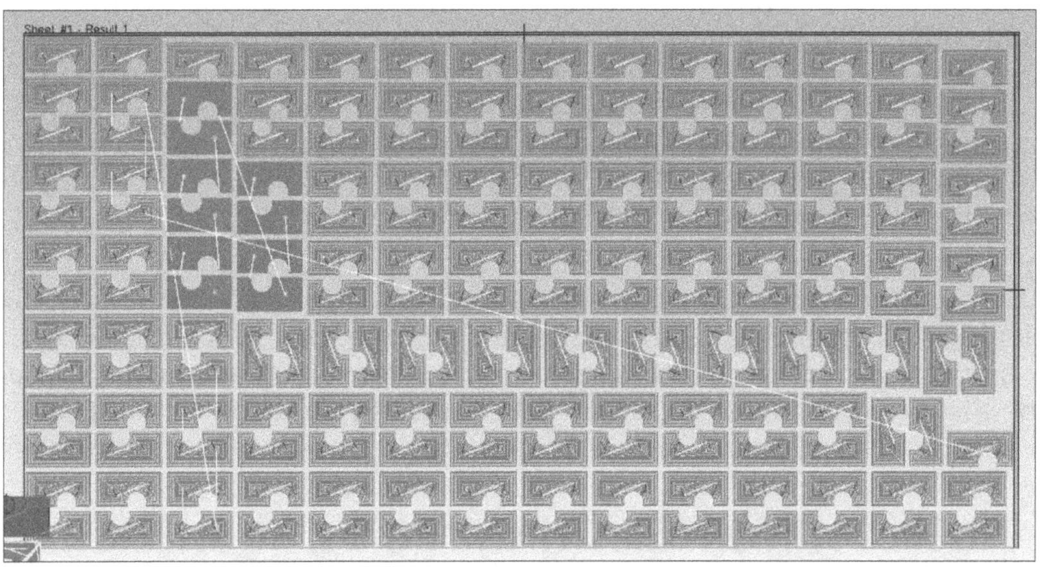

Figure-29. Nested toolpaths created

CHECKING TOOL HOLDER

The **Check Holder** tool is used to check whether tool holder makes an interference/ collision with the workpiece or other components in the machine. The procedure to use this tool is given next.

- Click on the **Check Holder** tool from the **Analyze** panel of **Toolpaths** tab in the **Ribbon**. The **Check Holder Manager** will be displayed; refer to Figure-30.

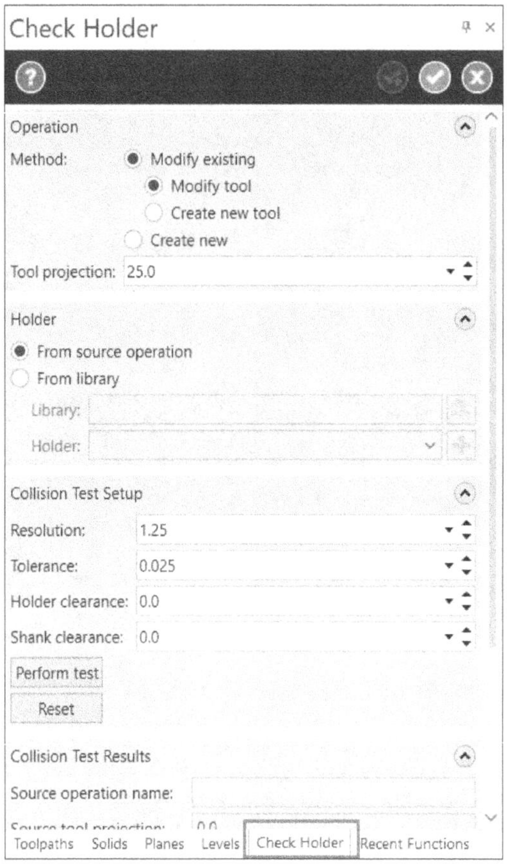

Figure-30. Check Holder Manager

- Select desired radio button for **Method** section to define whether a new tool is to be created or already available cutting tool will be modified.
- Click in the **Tool projection** edit box to define the length of cutting tool.
- Select desired radio button from the **Holder** rollout to define holder type to be used for checking collision. Select the **From source operation** radio button to use tool holder specified in operation parameters. Select the **From library** radio button to use desired tool holder selected from the **Library** and **Holder** drop-downs selected below the radio button.
- Specify desired parameters in the edit boxes of **Collision Test Setup** rollout to define spacing between grids of Mastercam for checking accurate interference, accuracy for analyzing surfaces and solids, distance around the holder to be used for clearance from the part, and clearance from tool shaft for checking collision.
- After setting desired parameters, click on the **Perform test** button. The results will be displayed in the **Collision Test Results** rollout of the **Manager**.
- After setting desired parameters, click on the **OK** button from the **Manager**.

CHECKING REACH OF TOOL IN MODEL

The **Check Tool Reach** tool is used to check whether cutting tool and tool holder can machine the geometry or it will get stuck while machining in the part. The procedure to use this tool is given next.

- Click on the **Check Tool Reach** tool from the **Analyze** panel of **Toolpaths** tab in the **Ribbon**. The **Check Tool Reach Manager** will be displayed; refer to Figure-31.

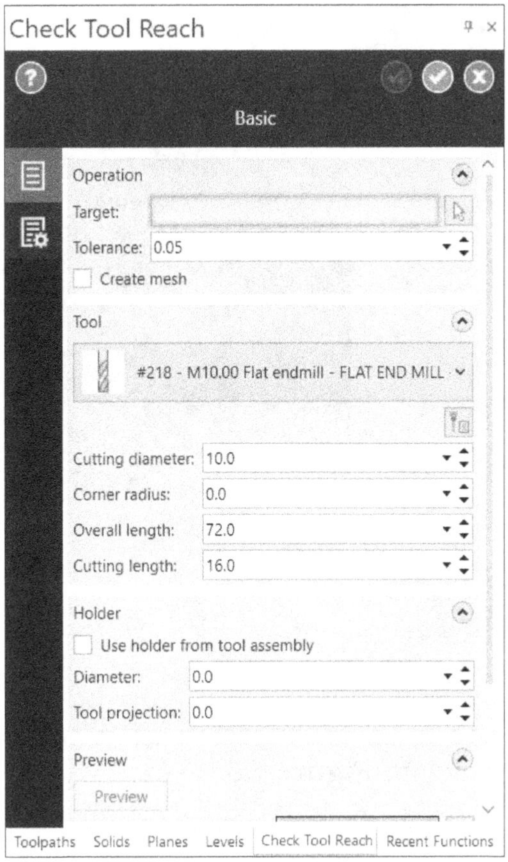

Figure-31. Check Tool Reach Manager

- Click on the **Select** button for **Target** option from the **Orientation** rollout to select the body to be checked and select desired model.
- Click in the **Tolerance** edit box and specify maximum deviation in model surface sizes.
- Select the **Create mesh** check box to display preview in the form of mesh. You can also save the mesh at different levels.
- Select desired option from the **Tool** drop-down to define the tool to be used for checking model. You can also click on the **Select** tool from library button below the **Tool** drop-down to select desired cutting tool from library. If you have selected **Manual** option in the **Tool** drop-down then you can specify the parameters for the tool in edit boxes of the **Tool** rollout.
- Similarly, specify parameters related to tool holder in the **Holder** rollout.
- After setting desired parameters, click on the **Preview** button. The preview of cutting tool reach will be displayed; refer to Figure-32.

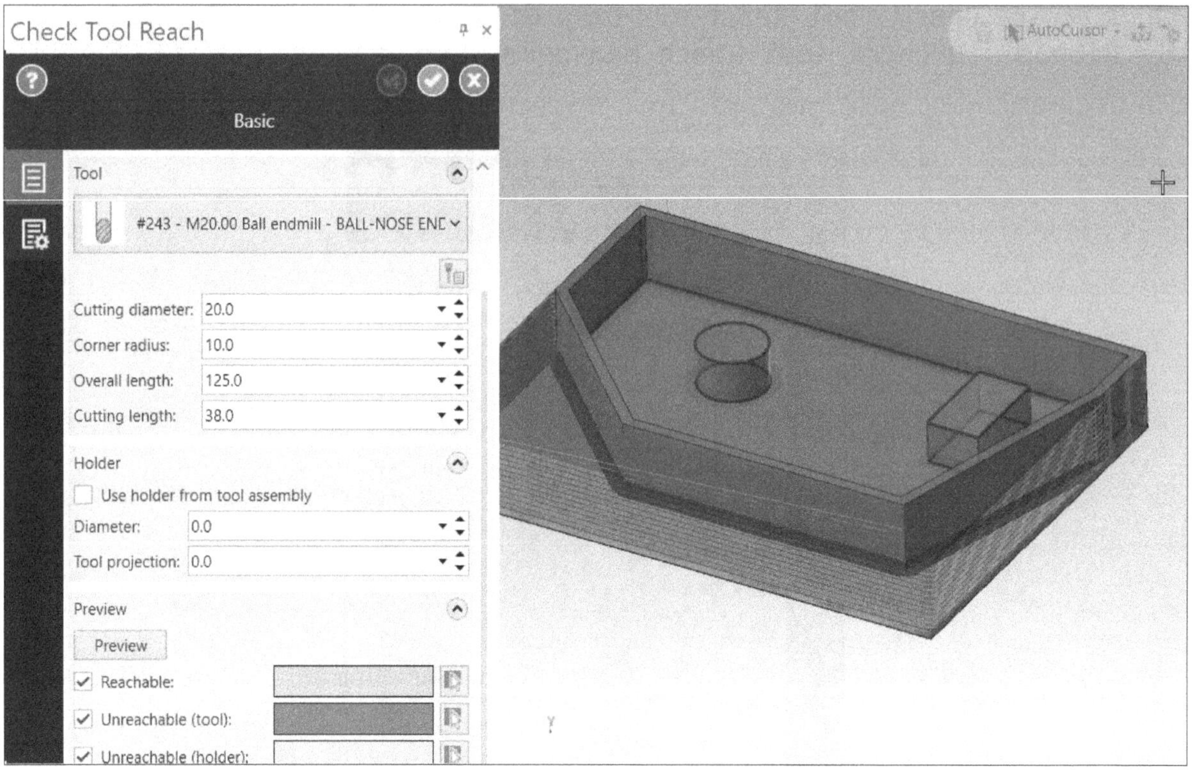

Figure-32. Preview of tool reach

- Click on the **Advanced** tab in the **Manager** to specify level on which the results of analysis will be saved; refer to Figure-33.

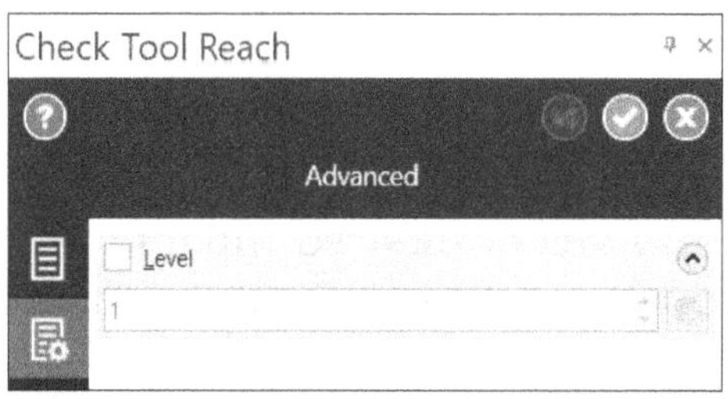

Figure-33. Advanced tab of Check Tool Reach Manager

- Select the **Level** check box and specify decided level in the drop-down on which analysis result will be saved.
- After setting desired parameters, click on the **OK** button from the **Manager**.

ART MACHINING (IMAGE BASED)

From Mastercam 2026 version onwards, Artcam addon is discontinued and this creates a vacuum to be filled by an alternative. Mastercam suggest to use Vectric Aspire which is by all means a good software. But here I would like to present another method which uses heatmap method to generate relief for images to convert them in 3D mesh. This mesh can be used as surface texture to be machined. This method uses free HMV software at link (https://procgenesis.com/SimpleHMV/simplehmv.html) to generate mesh and mesh modification tools of Mastercam to prepare it for machining. Note that this method is a simple trick to get quick artistic surface machining.

- Visit the link https://procgenesis.com/SimpleHMV/simplehmv.html in your default web browser. The interface will be displayed as shown in Figure-34.

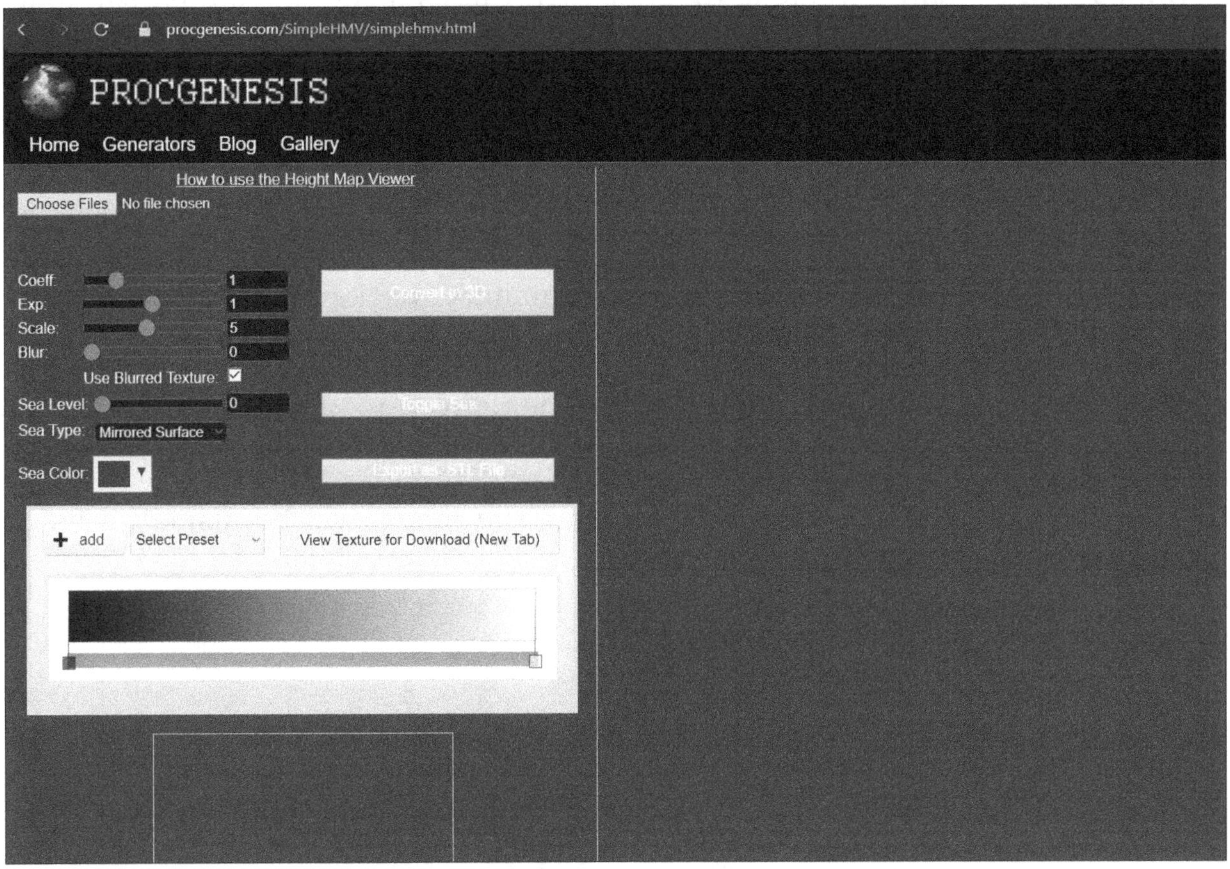

Figure-34. Heat Map Viewer page

- Click on the **Choose Files** button and using **Open** dialog box, select the image file to be used for creating art mesh. Click on the **Open** button from the dialog box. The options in webpage will become active; refer to Figure-35.

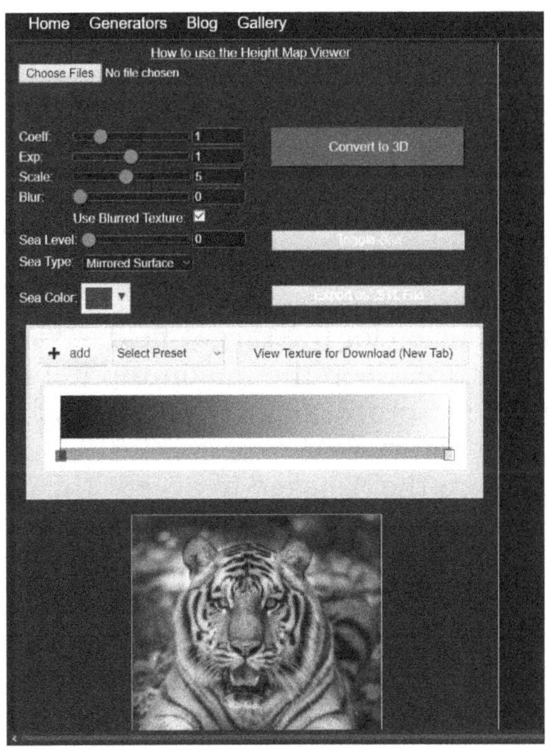

Figure-35. Interface on selecting image

- **Coefficient (Coeff)** slider defines Multiplier for all height values in 3D model.
- Use the **Exponent (Exp)** slider to control the ratio between high and low values. Values greater than 1 will tend to make high values higher in comparison to low values. Values less than 1 will make low values higher in comparison to high values.
- Use the **Scale** slider to adjust height/depth of overall 3D model. Higher scales create a more "compressed" or "flat" 3D model. Lower scales will see a greater range between high and low values.
- Use the **Blur** slider to smoothen surface in 3D model. It may also remove some fine details.
- Select the **Use Blurred Texture** check box to make background texture which is out of focus in image as blurred.
- Keep the **Sea Type** as transparent.
- After setting desired parameters, click on the Convert to 3D button from the web page and then click on the **Export as .STL File** button. The mesh file will be generated.
- Open the exported STL file in Mastercam. The model will be displayed as flat piece; refer to Figure-36.

Figure-36. STL model after importing

- Select the imported mesh model and click on the **Scale** tool from the **Size** panel in **Tools** contextual tab to resize the model. Generally a 600 mm x 600 mm model is generated.
- Now, select the mesh model again and click on the **Smooth Area** tool from the **Modify** panel of contextual tab in the **Ribbon**. The **Smooth Area Manager** will be displayed.
- Click on the **Select Mesh** button for the **Target** field in **Manager** and select the mesh body to smooth its curvature. Keep the maximum iteration value to 2 otherwise it may take very long time in processing. After processing, clear texture of image will be displayed; refer to Figure-37.
- Click on the **OK** button from the **Manager** to accept the changes.

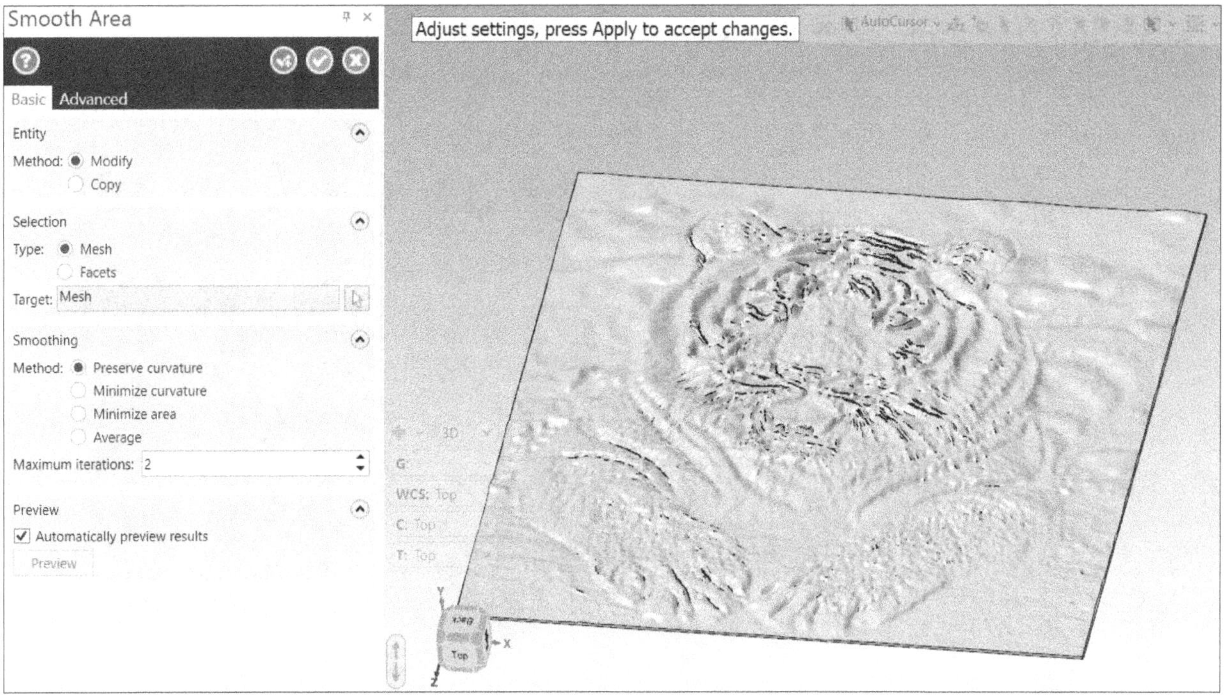

Figure-37. Preview of mesh model

- Note that model is not aligned properly with Z axis for milling so you need to rotate the model. Select the mesh model again and click on the **Dynamic** tool from the **Position** group in the **Tools** contextual tab of **Ribbon**. The **Dynamic Manager** will be displayed with gnomon attached to cursor.
- Click at the bottom left corner of the model and rotate the model by 90 degree about X axis using rotation handle; refer to Figure-38. After reaching 90 degree rotation, click to place the model.

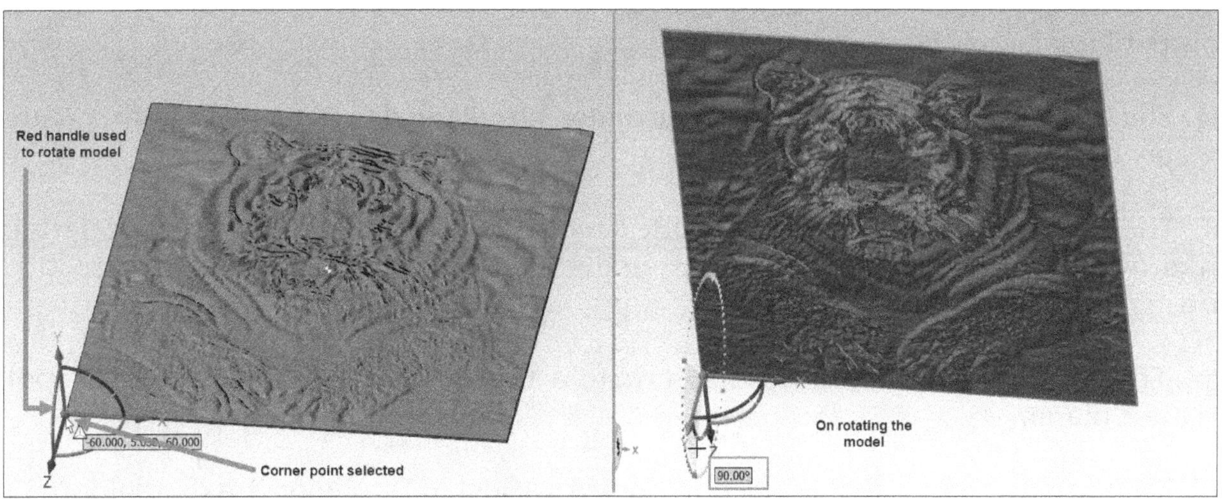

Figure-38. Rotating model

- Make sure the textured surface of model is parallel to Top plane of working environment. After performing rotation, click on the **OK** button from the **Dynamic Manager**.
- If you want to place this textured surface on another model then you can import that model using the **Merge** tool in **File** menu.

- Use the general procedure of generating toolpaths as discussed earlier to create machining program; refer to Figure-39.

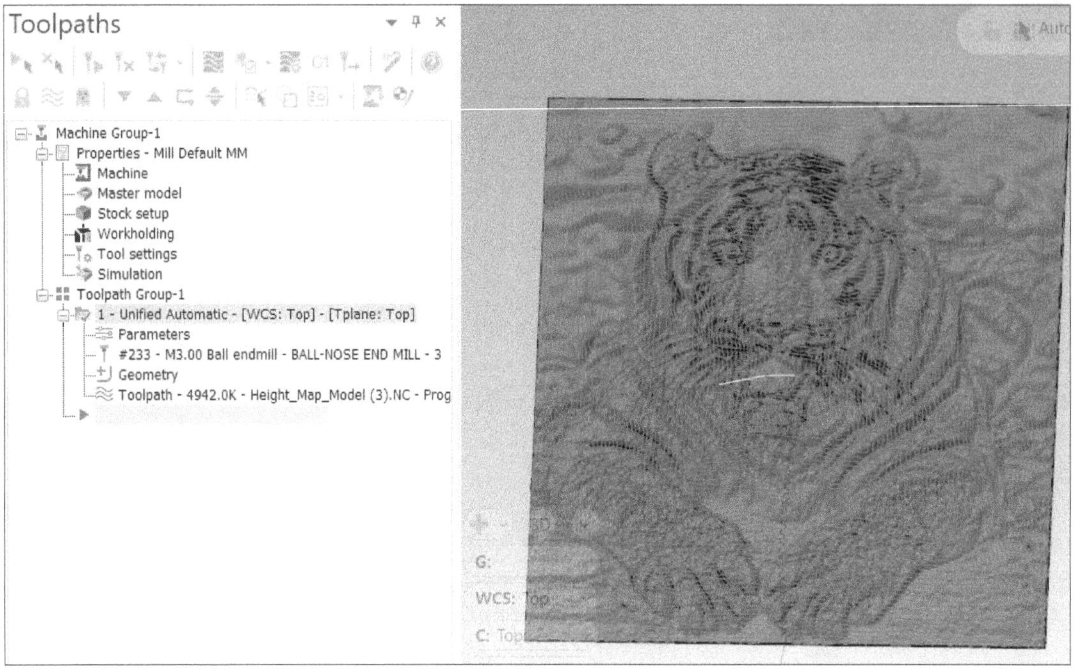

Figure-39. Toolpath generated for art model

SELF ASSESSMENT

Q1. What is the function of Probe tool?

Q2. The .... button in Probing Dialog is used to measure coordinates of selected point.

Q3. The Measure 2D Corner button is used to measure a diagonal line joining two points of a face. (T/F)

Q4. The Constructed Point button in the dialog box is used to measure a point created by specified parameters. (T/F)

Q5. The .... tool is used to create a toolpath at safe distance from model which links two or more toolpaths if you are using same cutting tool for two consecutive cutting strategies.

Q6. The .... tool is used to create a mirror copy of the selected toolpath about a plane.

Q7. The .... tool is used to convert selected 2-axis or 3-axis toolpaths to 5-axis toolpaths.

Q8. What is Cut tolerance?

Q9. The .... tool is used to remove selected portion of the toolpaths using reference geometries.

Q10. The Nesting tool is used to create multiple copies of selected toolpath non-uniformly placed throughout the sheet. (T/F)

Q11. The Check Holder tool is used to check whether tool holder makes an interference/collision with the workpiece or other components in the machine. (T/F)

Q12. The .... tool is used to check whether cutting tool and tool holder can machine the geometry or it will get stuck while machining in the part.

REVIEW QUESTIONS

Q1. What is the primary function of the Probe tool in Mastercam?
A. To perform artistic machining using images
B. To convert 3D models to 5-axis toolpaths
C. To create toolpaths for measuring coordinates, fixture offsets, and dimensions
D. To trim unwanted toolpaths using wireframes

Q2. Which button in the Select Probe dialog allows you to view advanced parameters?
A. Configure
B. Edit
C. Advanced >>
D. Settings

Q3. What does the stylus name "D6 L100 S4.5 EWL8" indicate?
A. Depth, layer, start, and end width
B. Diameter, total length, stem diameter, and holder's taper length
C. Density, length, shape, and energy level
D. None of the above

Q4. What is the function of the Safety Plane parameter in the Probe Configuration dialog?
A. Specifies the start point of the toolpath
B. Defines the plane below which no measurements occur
C. Sets the distance from the model's top to the safety clearance
D. Adjusts angle of rotation of probe

Q5. Which option measures a diagonal line between two face points in the model?
A. Measure 2D Corner
B. Measure Plane
C. Measure Line
D. Constructed Line

Q6. What is the purpose of the Constructed Point button?
A. To measure a point based on three selected face intersections
B. To create and measure a user-defined point with offsets
C. To select predefined geometry points from mesh
D. To delete unnecessary measurement points

Q7. What tool would you use to connect the endpoints of two toolpaths using the same tool?
A. Toolpath Transform
B. Machine Update
C. Multiaxis Linking
D. Nesting

Q8. What does the "Translate" option under Toolpath Transform do?
A. Converts 2D toolpath to 5-axis toolpath
B. Moves toolpaths to a different location
C. Converts toolpath into geometry
D. Adds tolerance to toolpaths

Q9. When performing a Mirror transformation, which selection is necessary?
A. Material direction
B. Safety plane location
C. Mirror plane
D. Label height

Q10. Which method allows you to convert a toolpath to 5-axis and project it onto a surface?
A. Translate
B. Mirror
C. Dropping
D. Nesting

Q11. Which check box in the Toolpath Transform dialog lets you retain original operations and create transformed copies?
A. Subprogram
B. Include WCS
C. Create new operations and geometry
D. Reverse order

Q12. What does the Trim tool require before being used?
A. STL model
B. Wireframe geometry as trimming boundary
C. Probe calibration
D. Safety zone selection

Q13. Which of the following is not required in the Nesting > Sheets tab?
A. Grain direction
B. Sheet size
C. Part labels
D. Origin location

Q14. In the Nesting > Parts tab, what does the "Step Angle" define?
A. Toolpath depth increment
B. Angle step for part rotation during nesting
C. Taper angle of stylus
D. Safe clearance angle

Q15. What does the "Use bounding box" checkbox do in the Nesting dialog?
A. Ensures only rectangular parts are nested
B. Uses a bounding box to define part size
C. Limits total nesting area
D. Creates G-code for all toolpaths

Q16. What is the Onion skin feature used for in the Nesting dialog?
A. Cutting only internal corners
B. Roughing pass before main cut
C. Return pass after machining all parts
D. Ignoring surface finish

Q17. Which tool checks whether a tool holder collides with a workpiece or machine?
A. Check Tool Reach
B. Check Holder
C. Machine Update
D. Probe Calibration

Q18. What function does the "Create mesh" option serve in the Check Tool Reach dialog?
A. Optimizes G-code
B. Converts toolpath to 5-axis
C. Displays a visual preview of reach in mesh form
D. Creates safety zones

Q19. Which free online tool is suggested for generating 3D meshes from images in Art Machining?
A. Fusion Mesh Generator
B. Vectric Aspire
C. SimpleHMV
D. Mesh Lab

Q20. Which step is essential after importing the STL for art machining in Mastercam?
A. Apply G-code block
B. Toolpath trimming
C. Rotate the model to align with Z-axis
D. Export as DXF

Q21. What is the function of the Machine Update tool in the Probing dialog?
A. To update inspection parameters
B. To modify WCS, tool length, and tool diameter
C. To calibrate machine axes
D. To define point approach distance

Q22. What does the G-Code Block button allow the user to do?
A. Automatically generate G-code for nesting
B. Insert pre-defined macros
C. Manually insert G-code in the probing cycle
D. Display previously executed G-codes

Q23. In probe calibration, which parameter defines vertical clearance from the workpiece?
A. Artefact diameter
B. Center location
C. Tolerance value
D. Safety plane height

Q24. What is the purpose of the Safety Zone option in the Multiaxis Linking dialog?
A. To define a no-cutting area
B. To determine start and end points of probing
C. To define safe tool motion distance when linking toolpaths
D. To restrict rotation of tool holder

Q25. In Toolpath Transform, what does the Subprogram check box do?
A. Converts toolpaths to probing cycles
B. Creates repeating sections of toolpath as subprograms
C. Posts G-code blocks as tool comments
D. Inserts a probing loop

Q26. Which tool helps in grouping NCI output codes by operation order or type?
A. Check Tool Reach
B. Toolpath Transform
C. Machine Update
D. Trim

Q27. What happens when you select "Keep input points" in Convert to 5-axis dialog?
A. Keeps stylus at same tilt
B. Maintains original toolpath points
C. Projects path onto model's bottom surface
D. Filters the input path

Q28. The "Damp" check box in the Dropping toolpath method allows:
A. Creating sharp internal corners
B. Removing rapid movements
C. Smooth axial movements for better surface quality
D. Setting drop height

Q29. Before using the Trim tool, what must be prepared?
A. STL mesh
B. Probe stylus
C. Wireframe geometry for trimming
D. Tool holder template

Q30. In Nesting > Parameters tab, which option defines machining sequence based on free area?
A. Tool number: Ascending
B. Maximum vacuum
C. Database order
D. Sorting by regions

Q31. What is the role of the "Use part labels" check box in the Nesting > Parts tab?
A. Sorts parts based on label
B. Applies different offsets per label
C. Displays part label with each part on sheet
D. Prevents part rotation

Q32. What does the "Optimize pairs" option do during nesting?
A. Rotates toolpaths
B. Maximizes tool change frequency
C. Places matching parts closely to minimize waste
D. Hides filler parts

Q33. In the Check Holder tool, what does the Holder rollout define?
A. Safety margin height
B. Holder type and source
C. X and Y projections
D. Path for output files

Q34. Which option is used to define collision clearance from tool shaft?
A. Holder diameter
B. Accuracy tolerance
C. Shaft clearance
D. Model deviation

Q35. What feature of Check Tool Reach creates a 3D visual of reachable areas?
A. Projection toolpath
B. Safety zone
C. Mesh preview
D. STL alignment

Q36. What is the default alignment issue after importing mesh for art machining?
A. Orientation to X-axis
B. Mesh too thick
C. Not aligned to Z-axis
D. Texture not loaded

Q37. Which tool is used to rotate the mesh model for Z-axis alignment?
A. Mirror
B. Dynamic
C. Scale
D. Check Holder

Q38. What is the main purpose of the Smooth Area tool in mesh post-processing?
A. Trim unwanted protrusions
B. Reduce file size
C. Improve surface clarity by smoothing curvature
D. Apply textures

Q39. In the Art Machining workflow, what effect does the Exponent (Exp) slider have?
A. Compresses mesh layers
B. Adjusts feed rate
C. Alters contrast between high and low relief
D. Sets the cutting direction

Q40. Which operation is necessary before machining the art mesh?
A. Probe calibration
B. Mesh refinement
C. Rotation alignment
D. Nesting toolpath

Chapter 13

Milling Operations Practical and Practice

Topics Covered

The major topics covered in this chapter are:

- ***Practical***
- ***Practice***

PRACTICAL 1

Machine the part as given in Figure-1. The stock for the part is a rectangular boundary block.

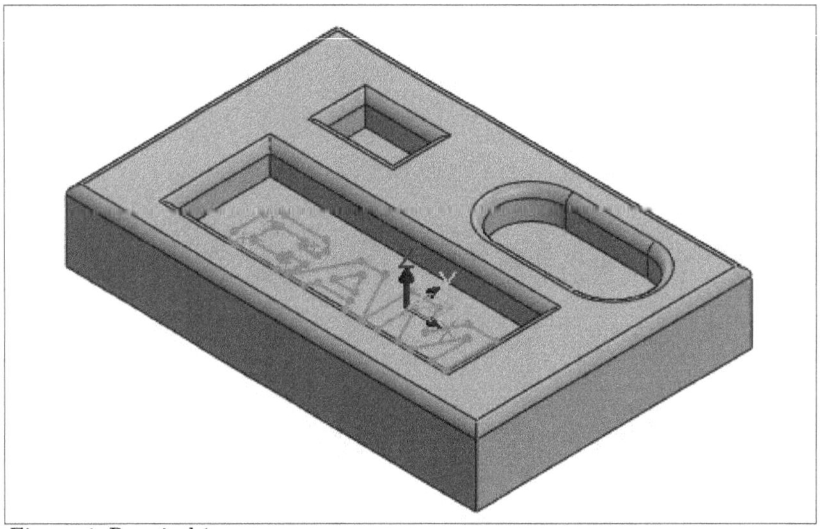

Figure-1. Practical 1

Opening the Model

- Download the files of resource kit from website.
- Start Mastercam application and click on the **Open** button from the top in the **Quick Access Toolbar**. The **Open** dialog box will be displayed.
- Select the model file for this practical and click on the **Open** button. The model will open in Mastercam.

Machining Plane setup

- Click on the **From solid face** option from the **Create a new plane** drop-down in the **Planes Manager**. You will be asked to select face of the model.
- Select the bottom face of the model and click on the **OK** button from the **Select plane** dialog box after switching to desired orientation; refer to Figure-2. The **New Plane Manager** will be displayed. Note that Z axis should be pointing upward.

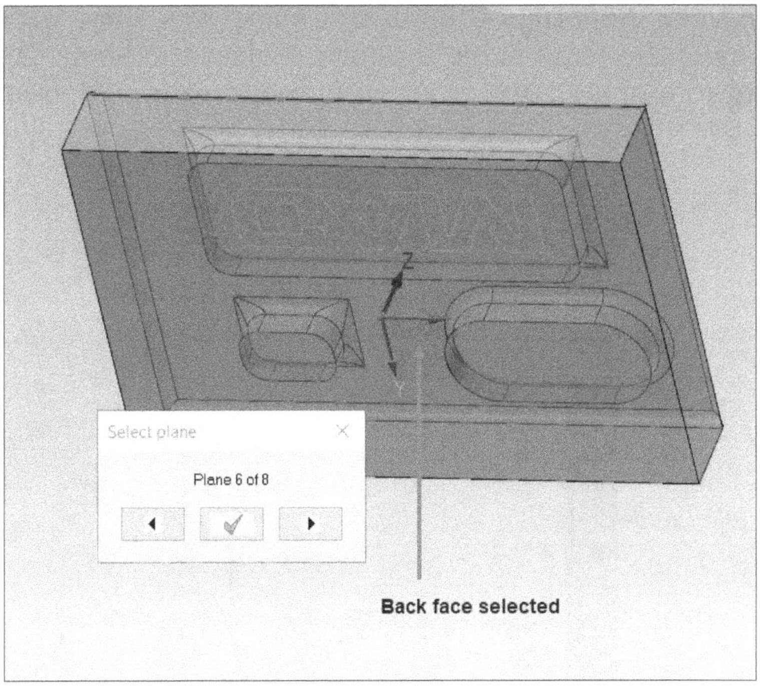

Figure-2. Back face selected

- Specify desired name for plane, here we are specifying Mastercam Top as the plane's name and click on the **OK** button in the **New Plane Manager**.
- Set the Mastercam Top plane as construction plane and tool plane in the **Planes Manager**.

Creating the Stock

- Select **Default** option from the **Mill** drop-down in the **Machine** tab of **Ribbon** to use default milling machine.
- Click on the **Toolpath** tab from the **Manager**. The **Toolpaths Manager** will be displayed; refer to Figure-3.

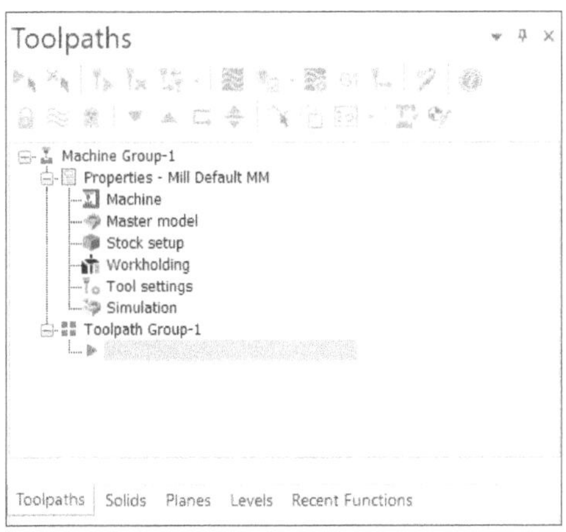

Figure-3. Mastercam Toolpath Manager

- Click on the **+** sign next to **Properties** option and click on the **Stock setup** option. The **Machine Group Setup Manager** will be displayed with the **Stock Setup** tab selected; refer to Figure-4.
- Scroll down in the **Manager**, expand the **Stock Plane Transformation** rollout in **Manager** and select the **MASTERCAM TOP** plane in the **Current** drop-down of the **Manager** to define orientation of plane.

- Expand the **Preview Settings** rollout and select the **Show wireframe entities** check box to make the text visible in stock. Select the **Show stock plane** option from the rollout to display current stock plane in graphics area.

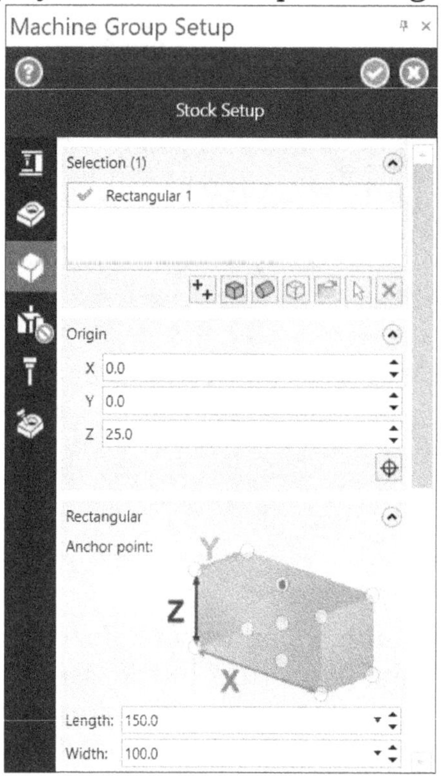

Figure-4. Machine Group Properties dialog box with Stock setup page

- Click on the **Add from a bounding box** button from **Selection** rollout at the top in **Manager** to create bounding box stock for the model. The **Bounding Box Manager** will be displayed and you will be asked to select the model; refer to Figure-5. Click on the **Manual** selection button if not asking to select model by default.

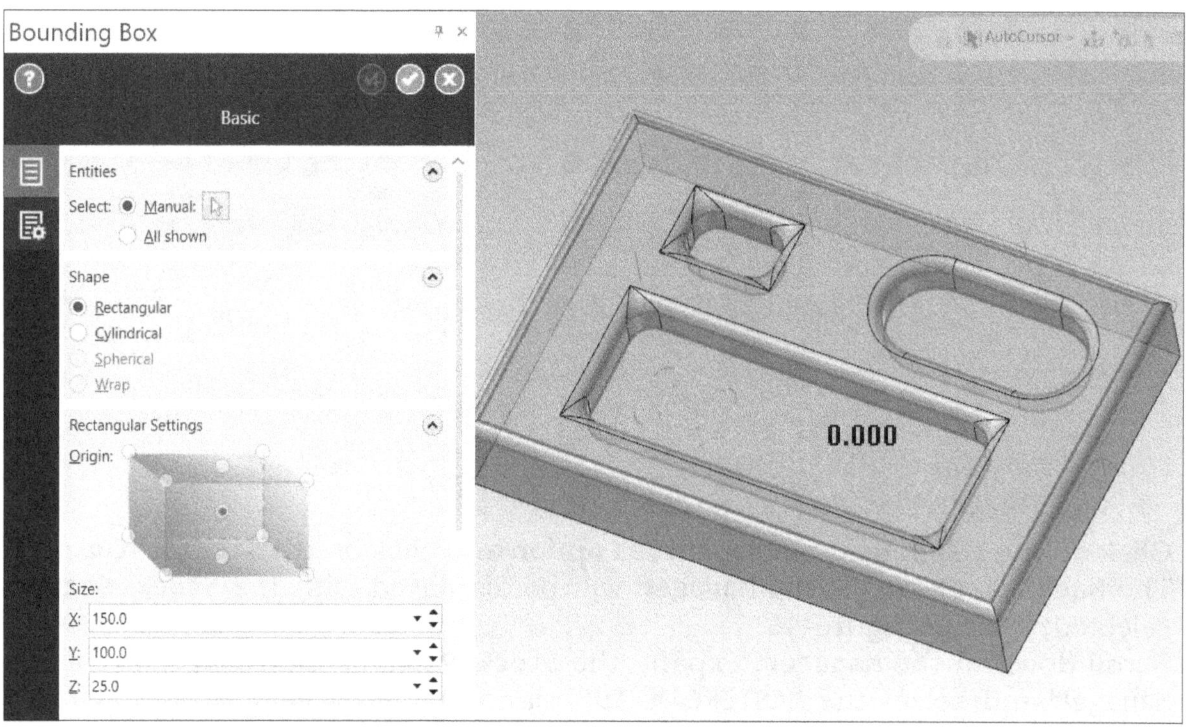

Figure-5. Creating stock

- Select the model and click on the **End Selection** button or you can select the **All shown** radio button from the **Entities** rollout to select model visible in graphics area. Preview of the stock will be displayed.
- Select the bottom center radio button from **Rectangular Settings** rollout to use it as reference for measuring stock size; refer to Figure-6.

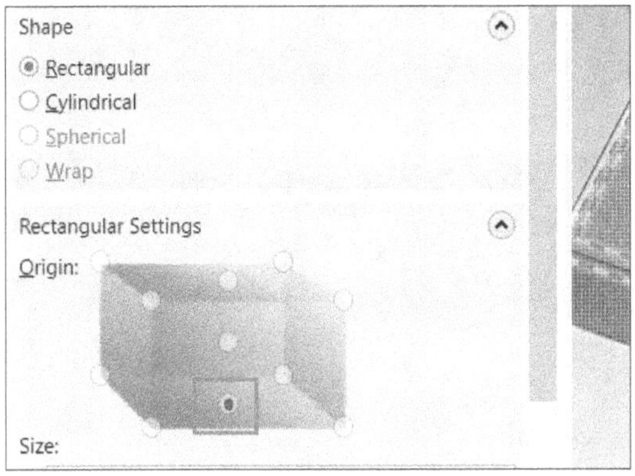

Figure-6. Reference point to be selected

- Increase the value in the **Z** spinner of **Size** section by **1** and click on the **OK** button from the **Manager**. The **Machine Group Properties** dialog box will be displayed again.
- Click on the **OK** button from the dialog box. The stock will be created; refer to Figure-7.

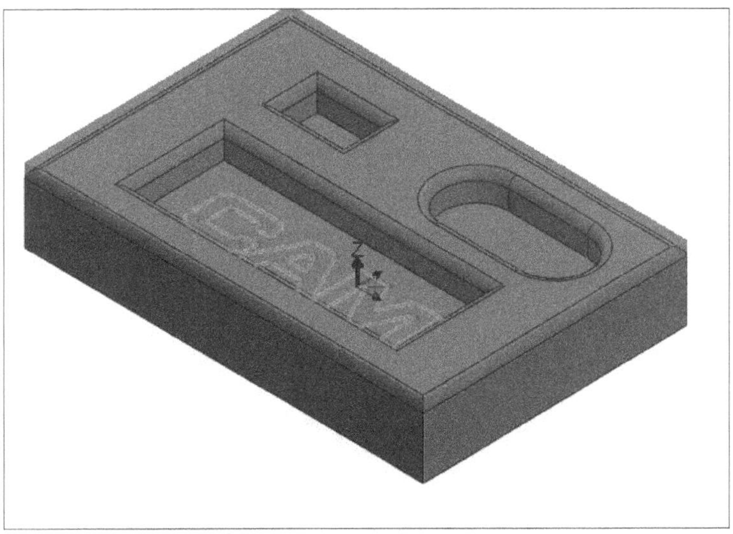

Figure-7. Stock created

Performing the Facing Operation

- Click on the **Face** tool from the **2D** panel in the **Toolpaths** tab of the **Ribbon**. The **Wireframe/Solid Chaining** dialog box will be displayed and you will be asked to select the entities for facing operation.
- Select the outer edges of the model or top flat face of model as shown in Figure-8.

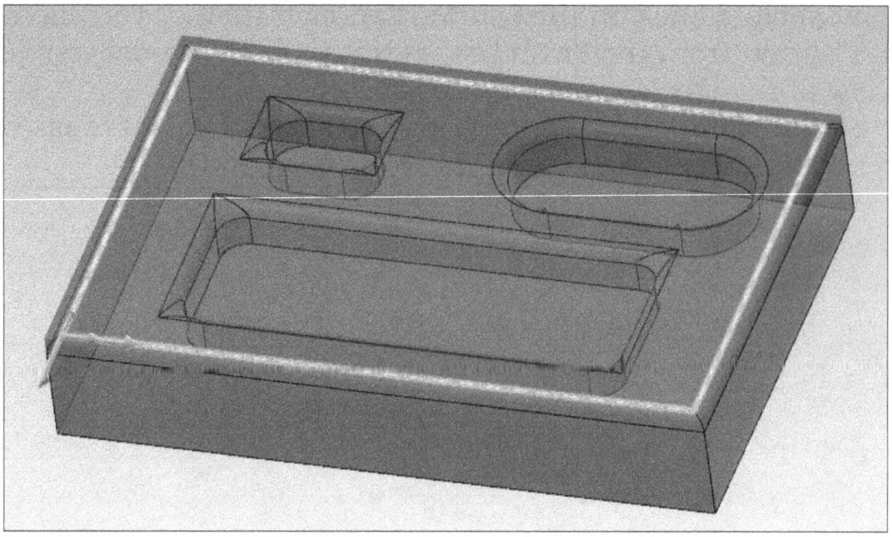

Figure-8. Edge chain selected

- Click on the **OK** button from the **Solid Chaining** dialog box. The **2D Toolpaths-Facing** dialog box will be displayed; refer to Figure-9.
- Click on the **Tool** option from the left list box in the dialog box. The options related to tool will be displayed; refer to Figure-10.

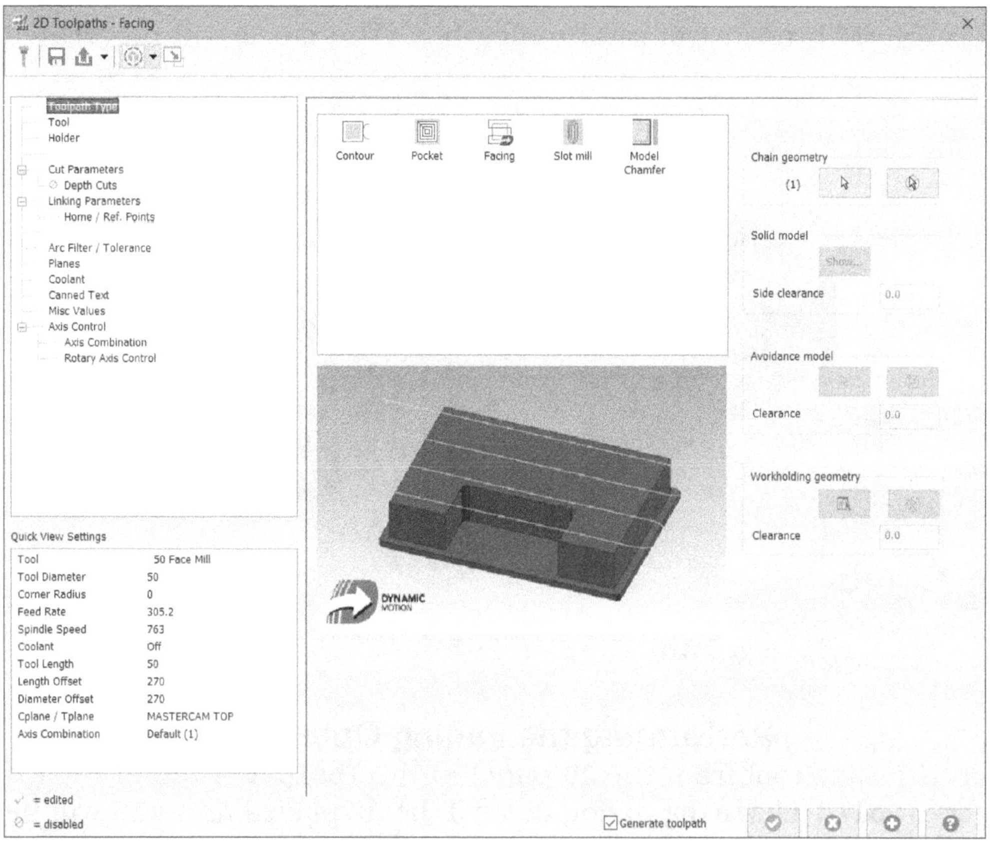

Figure-9. 2D Toolpaths-Facing dialog box

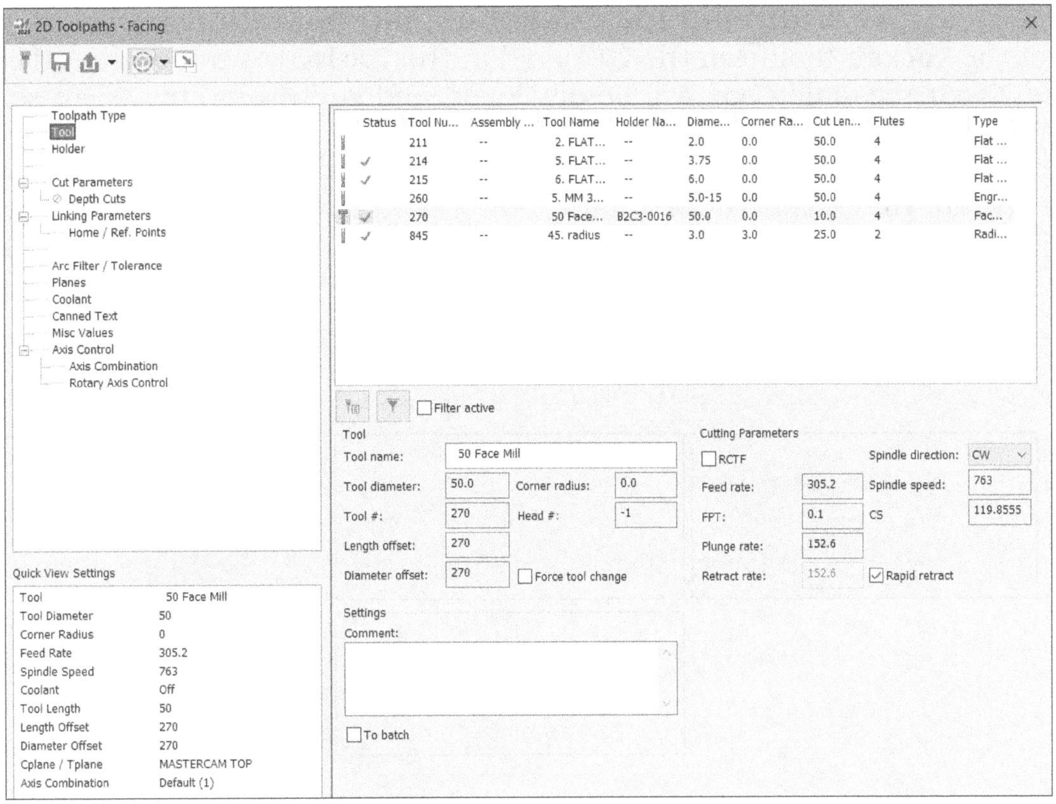

Figure-10. Tool page for Facing Toolpaths

- Click on the **Select library tool** button from the dialog box. The **Tool Selection** dialog box will be displayed.
- Select the **50 diameter face mill** tool from the dialog box and click on the **OK** button from the dialog box.
- Click on the **Holder** option from the left list box and select desired tool holder.
- Click on the **Linking Parameters** option from the left list box in the dialog box.
- Select the **Incremental** radio button next to the **Depth** button and specify the value as **-1** in the **Depth** edit box.
- Click on the **OK** button from the dialog box. The toolpath will be generated; refer to Figure-11.

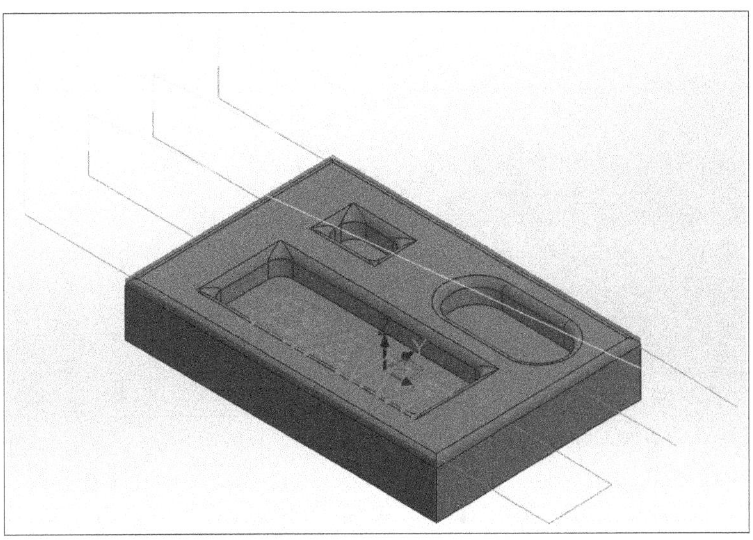

Figure-11. Facing toolpaths generated

Performing the pocket milling operation

- Select the **Pocket** tool from the **2D** panel in the **Toolpaths** tab of the **Ribbon**. The **Solid Chaining** dialog box will be displayed and you are prompted to select the faces for pocket milling.
- Select the faces as shown in Figure-12 and click on the **OK** button from the dialog box. The **2D Toolpaths-Pocket** dialog box will be displayed; refer to Figure-13.

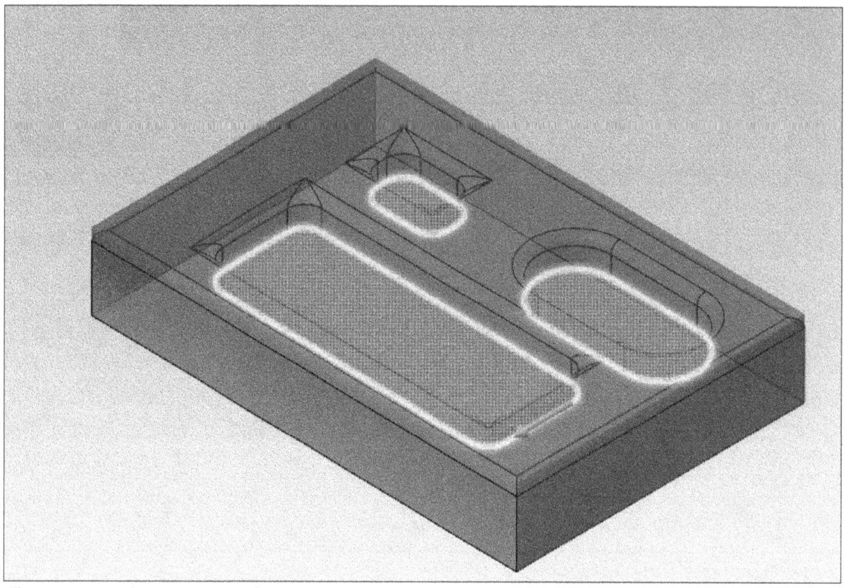

Figure-12. Faces selected for pocket milling

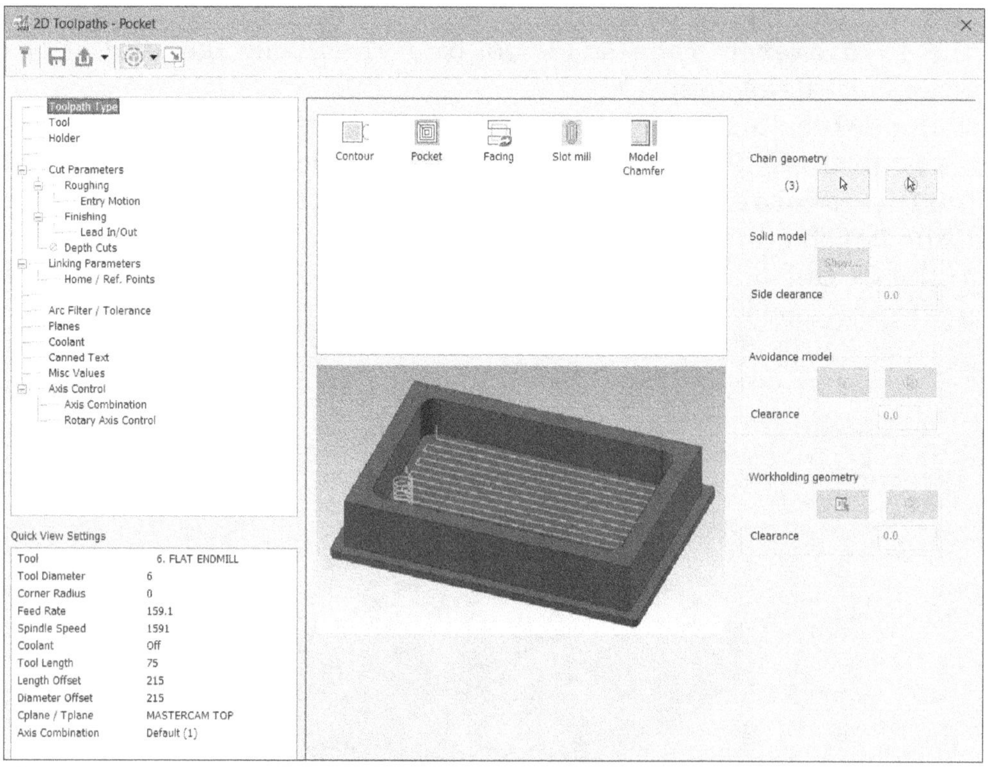

Figure-13. 2D Toolpaths-Pocket dialog box

- Click on the **Tool** option from the left box and click on the **Select library tool** button from the dialog box. The **Tool Selection** dialog box will be displayed.

- Select the **6 mm Flat Endmill** tool from the tool list and click on the **OK** button from the **Tool Selection** dialog box.
- Select desired tool holder by using the **Holder** option from the left box.
- Click on the **Linking Parameters** option from the left box.
- Select the **Absolute** radio button below the **Depth** button and then select the **Depth** button. You will be asked to select a point to specify the depth.
- Select the point as shown in Figure-14. The dialog box will be displayed again and the value in the **Depth** edit box will be changed automatically.

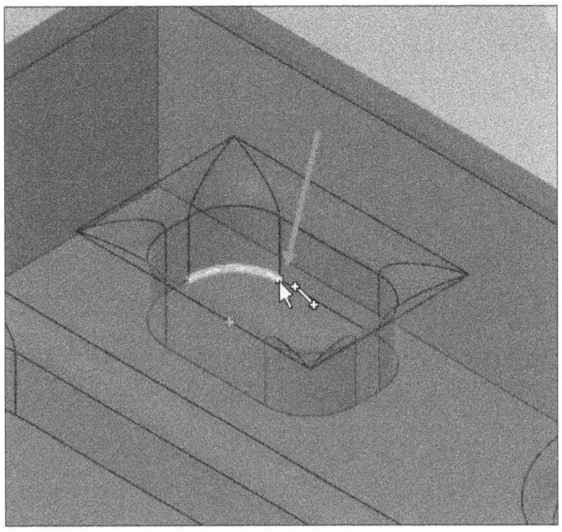

Figure-14. Point to be selected

- Click on the **OK** button from the **2D Toolpaths-Pocket** dialog box. The toolpath will be generated; refer to Figure-15.

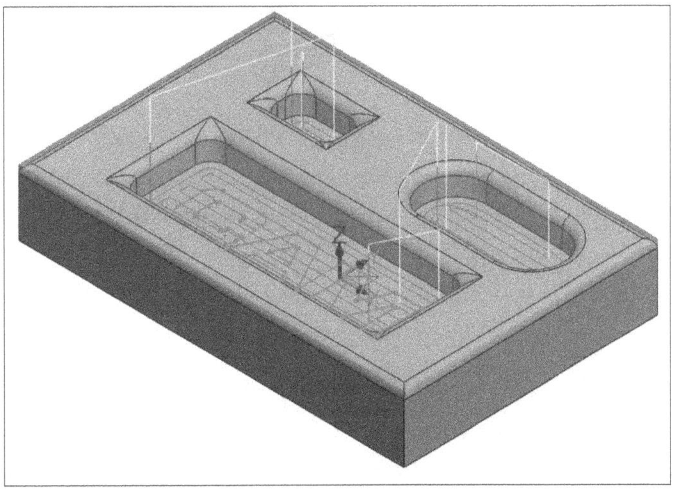

Figure-15. Pocket toolpaths generated

Performing the Engraving operation

- Click on the **Engrave** tool from the **2D** panel in the **Toolpaths** tab of the **Ribbon**. The **Solid Chaining** dialog box will be displayed.
- Click on the **Wireframe** button from **Mode** area of the dialog box. The **Wireframe Chaining** dialog box will be displayed.
- Select the text by window selection and click on desired point of text to specify start point for toolpath; refer to Figure-16.

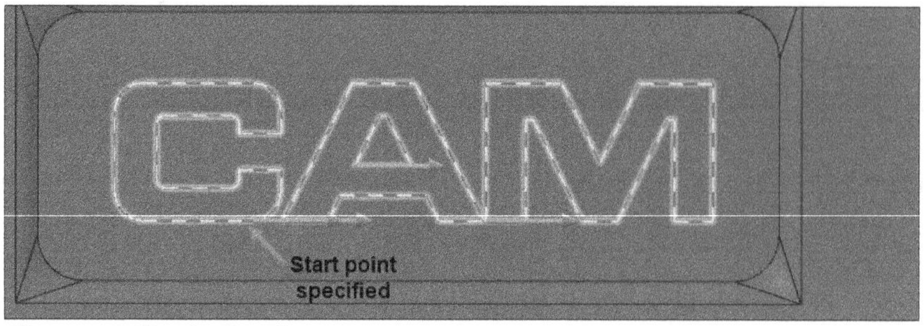

Figure-16. Sketch selected

- Click on the **OK** button from the dialog box. The **Engraving** dialog box will be displayed; refer to Figure-17.

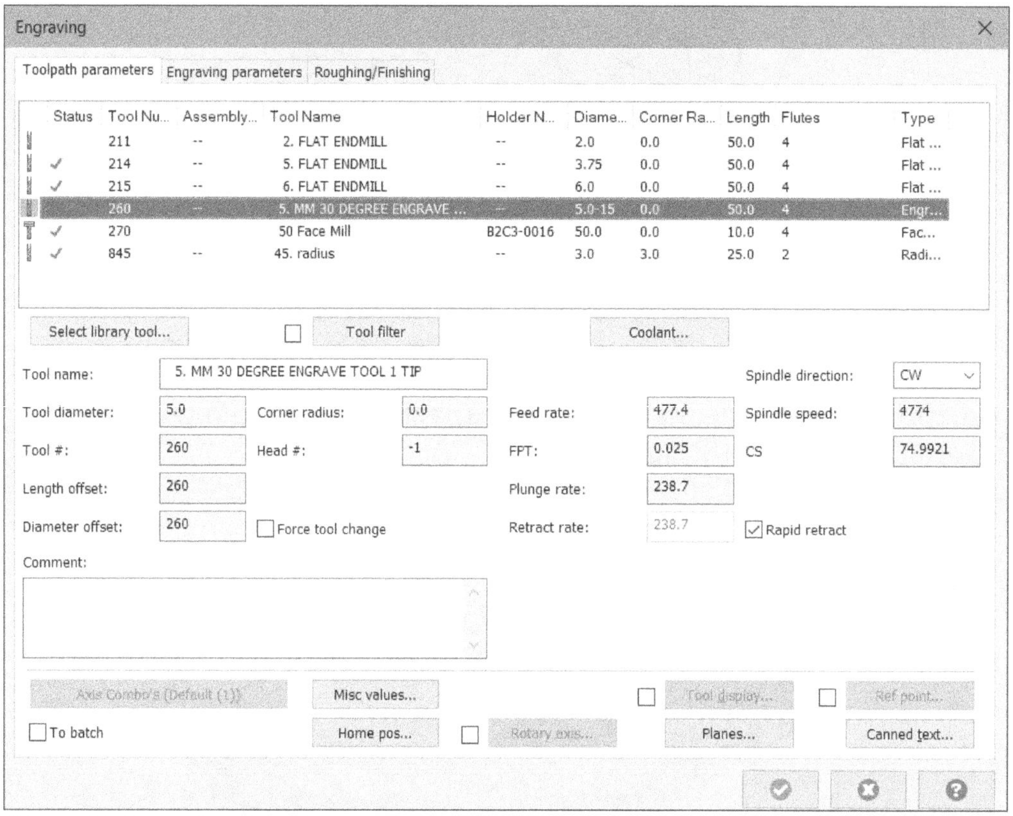

Figure-17. Engraving dialog box

- Click on the **Select library tool** button from the dialog box and select **5 mm 30 degree Engrave** tool from the list.
- Click on the **OK** button from **Tool Selection** dialog box displayed.
- Click on the **Engraving parameters** tab from the dialog box. The parameters related to engraving will be displayed.
- Select the **Incremental** radio button for the depth and specify **-1** in the **Depth** edit box.
- Click on the **Roughing/Finishing** tab and select the **at depth** radio button from the **Cut geometry** area of the dialog box.
- Click on the **OK** button from the **Engraving** dialog box. The toolpath will be generated; refer to Figure-18.

Figure-18. Engraving toolpath generated

Creating rounds on the edges

- Click on the **Contour** tool from the **2D** panel in the **Toolpaths** tab of the **Ribbon**. The **Wireframe Chaining** dialog box will be displayed.
- Click on the **Solids** button from the **Mode** area of dialog box and select the edges of the model that are to be rounded; refer to Figure-19. Note that for the boundary of model, you need to select outer edges and for pockets, you need to select inner boundaries.

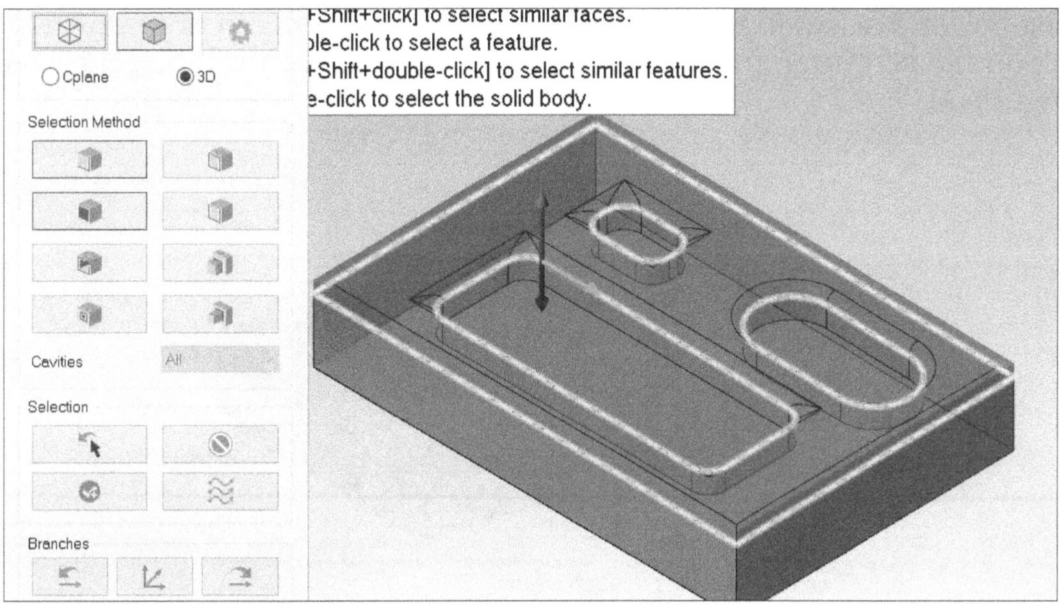

Figure-19. Edges selected for round

- Click on the **OK** button from the dialog box. The **2D Toolpaths-Contour** dialog box will be displayed.
- Select a tool for rounding having round radius of **3** mm. Note that you can create your own round tool by using the procedure explained earlier or by modifying the existing tool; refer to Figure-20.

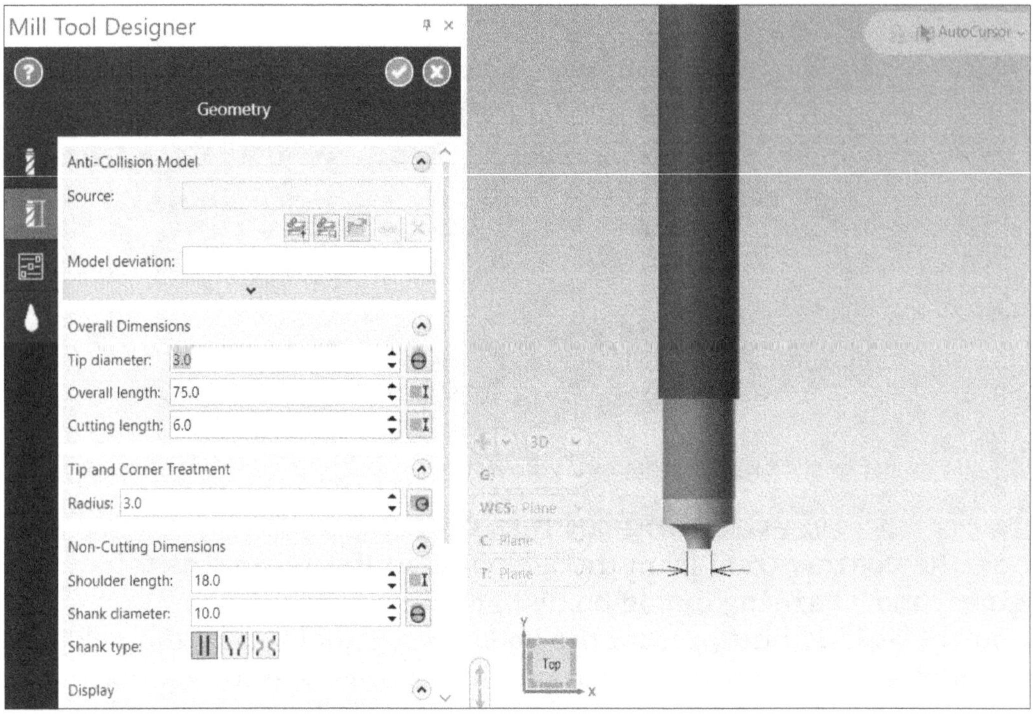

Figure-20. Edit Tool dialog box

- Click on the **Cut Parameters** option from the left box in the **2D Toolpaths-Contour** dialog box and select **Right** in the **Compensation direction** drop-down.
- Click on the **OK** button from the dialog box. The toolpath will be generated; refer to Figure-21.

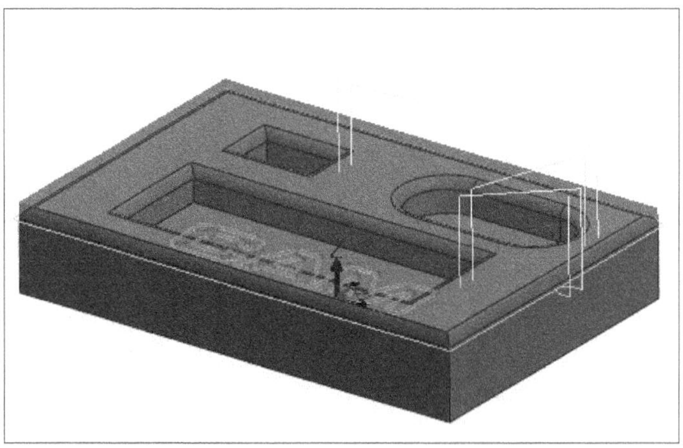

Figure-21. Toolpath for radius creation

Note that in this tutorial, we have not changed the **Depth Cuts** parameter and we have machined each operation in single pass but in real-machining, you need to set depth of each pass as per your tool catalog.

PRACTICE 1

Machine the part given in Figure-22. Stock for the part is a bounding cylinder. Use a Mill-Turn machine to do turning as well as milling. You will learn about turning toolpaths later in the book. So, you can come back to this practical after taking next chapters.

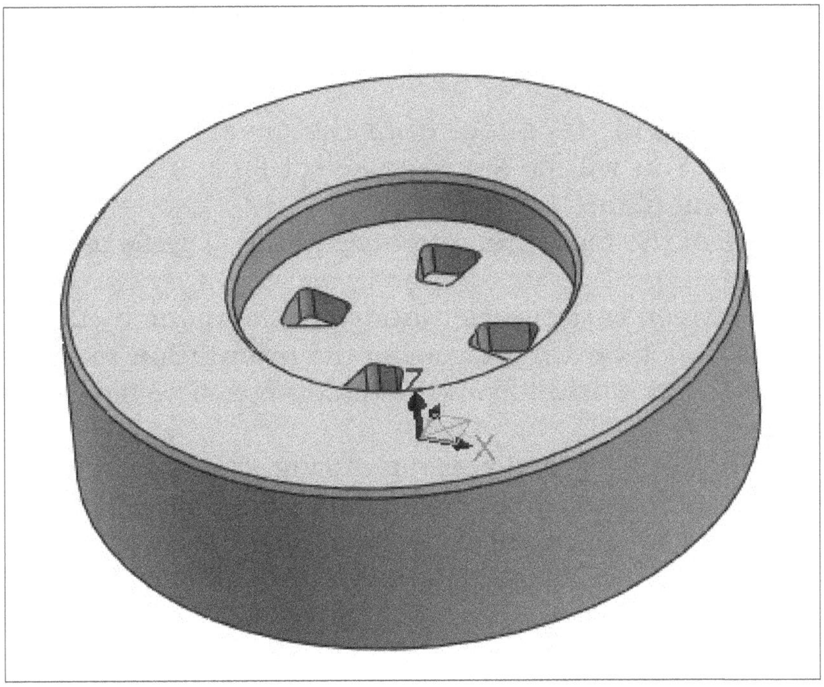

Figure-22. Practice 1

PRACTICAL 2

Create a machining program for part given in Figure-23. The stock of part is a block of size 170x120x42. The controller for machine is Haas.

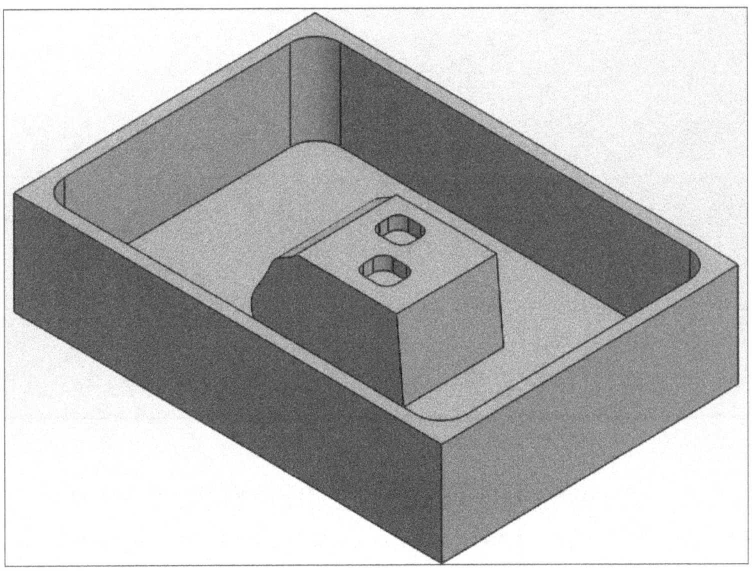

Figure-23. Part for Practical

Steps:

Identifying toolpath strategies

We need to perform facing operation to make surface of part even. Next, we need to perform pocket toolpath with bigger tool for roughing and then smaller tool for finishing. We also need to perform surface rough and surface finish parallel to machine boss feature in the middle of part. In the end, perform pocket finish for small pockets at the top of boss feature. Let us begin with setting up the job.

Preparation for Machining

- Open the part for Practical 2 of this chapter from the resource kit. The part should display as shown in Figure-23.
- Click on the **From solid face** tool from the **Create a new plane** drop-down of **Planes Manager**. You will be asked to select face of the model to be used as reference for creating plane.
- Select the top face of the model as reference plane. The **Select plane** dialog box will be displayed.
- You can switch between various orientations of the plane by using the buttons in the **Select plane** dialog box. After getting the orientation in which Z axis points upward, click on the **OK** button from the dialog box. The **New Plane Manager** will be displayed.
- Specify the name of plane as **Top Face**; refer to Figure-24 and click on the **OK** button from the **Manager**. The plane will be created and displayed in the **Planes Manager**.
- Set the new plane as WCS, C, and T plane as discussed earlier.

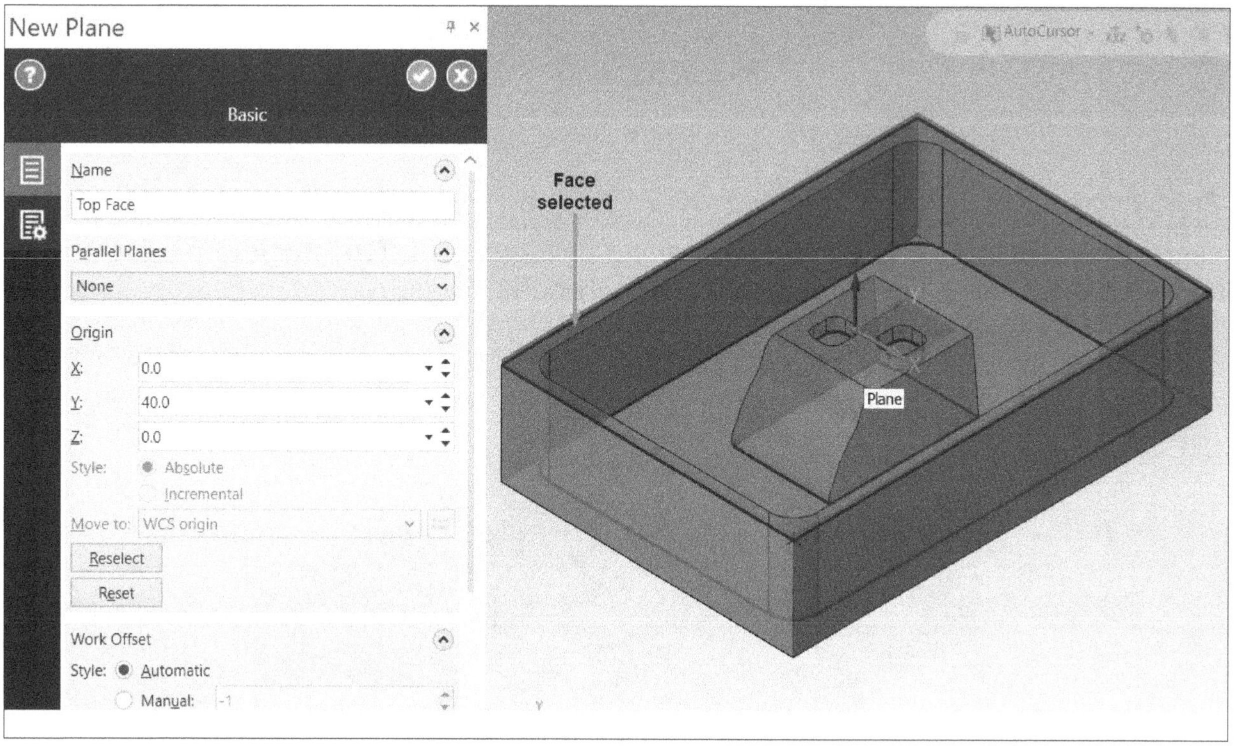

Figure-24. Defining new plane

Setting Up Haas 3X Mill Machine

- Select **Default** option from the **Mill** drop-down in **Machine** tab of **Ribbon**.
- Click on the **Machine** option in the expanded **Properties** node of **Machine** group in the **Mastercam Toolpath Manager**; refer to Figure-25. The **Machine Group Setup Manager** will be displayed; refer to Figure-26.

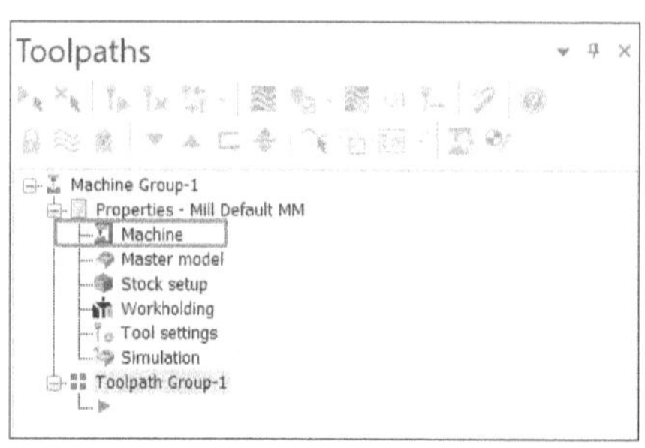

Figure-25. Files option in Mastercam Toolpath Manager

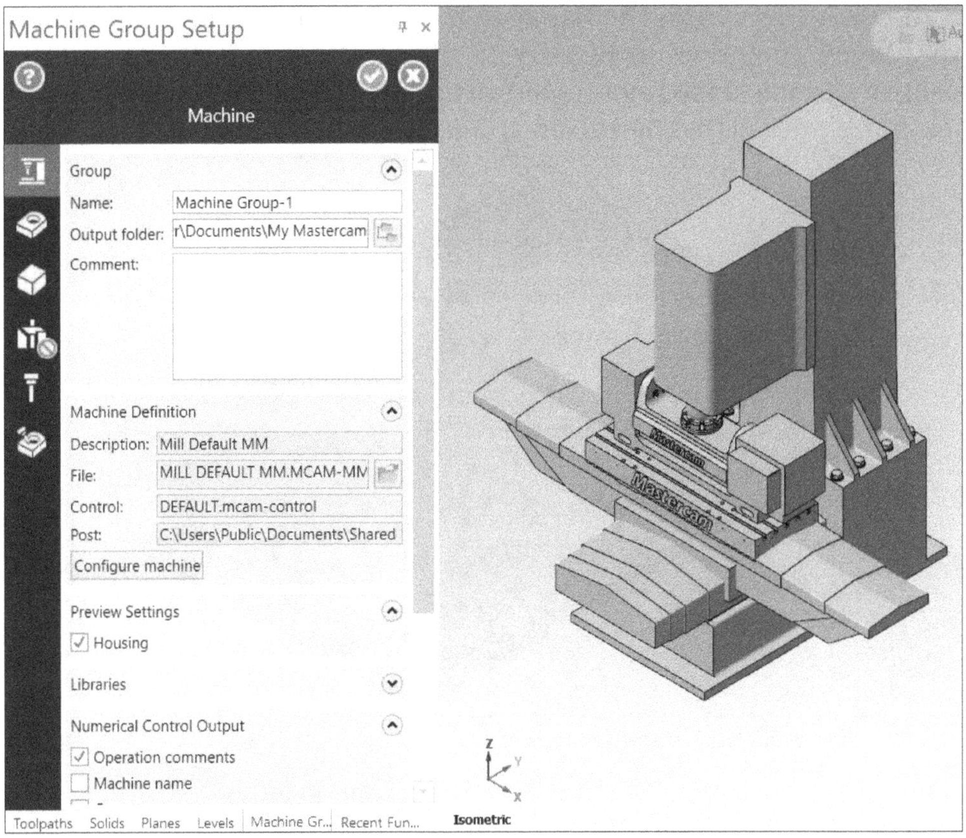

Figure-26. Files tab in Machine Group Properties dialog box

- Click on the **Select machine definition** button next to **File** field of **Machine Definition** rollout in the **Manager**. The **Open Machine Definition File** dialog box will be displayed.
- Select the **GENERIC HAAS 3X MILL MM.MCAD-MMD** file from the dialog box and click on the **Open** button to load Haas machine definition. The Haas 3X mill will be loaded with post processor and controller definitions. You can use default definitions as well for this tutorial.

Setting Tool Parameters and Stock

- Click on the **Tool** tab in the Manager and select the **Assign tool numbers sequentially** check box from **Toolpath Configuration** rollout. Also, select the **Warn of duplicate tool numbers** check box, so that a single tool number is not assigned to two different tools.
- Click on the **Stock Setup** tab in the **Manager**. The stock setup options will be displayed.
- Expand the **Stock Plane Transformation** rollout. The options to select plane will be displayed.
- Select the newly created plane from **Current** drop-down and click on the **Add from a bounding box** button from the **Selection** rollout in the **Manager**. The **Bounding Box Manager** will be displayed.
- Select the **Rectangular** radio button from the **Shape** area of the dialog box and bottom center radio button from the **Rectangular Settings** rollout.
- Select the **All shown** radio button from **Entities** rollout and click on the **OK** button from the **Manager**. The **Machine Group Setup Manager** will be displayed again.

- Click on the **OK** button from the **Manager** to create the stock. The model with stock will be displayed as shown in Figure-27. If the stock is not displaying by default, then select the **Stock Display** toggle button and then **Stock Shading** button from the **Stock** panel of **Toolpaths** tab in the **Ribbon**.

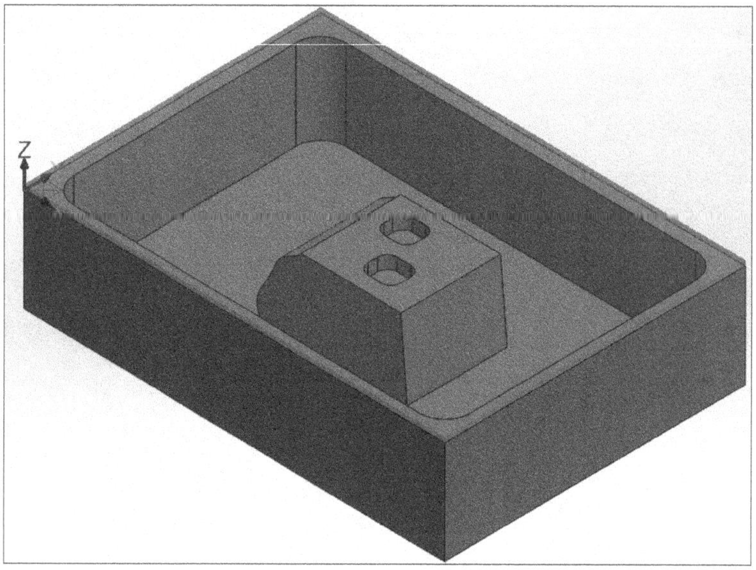

Figure-27. Stock created for practical 2

Facing

- Click on the **Face** tool from the **2D** panel of **Toolpaths** tab in the **Ribbon**. The **Wireframe/Solid Chaining** dialog box will be displayed.
- Select the **Outer open edges** button from the **Select Method** area in the dialog box and select the top face of model, so that only one chain is formed; refer to Figure-28. Click on the **OK** button from the dialog box. The **2D Toolpaths-Facing** dialog box will be displayed.

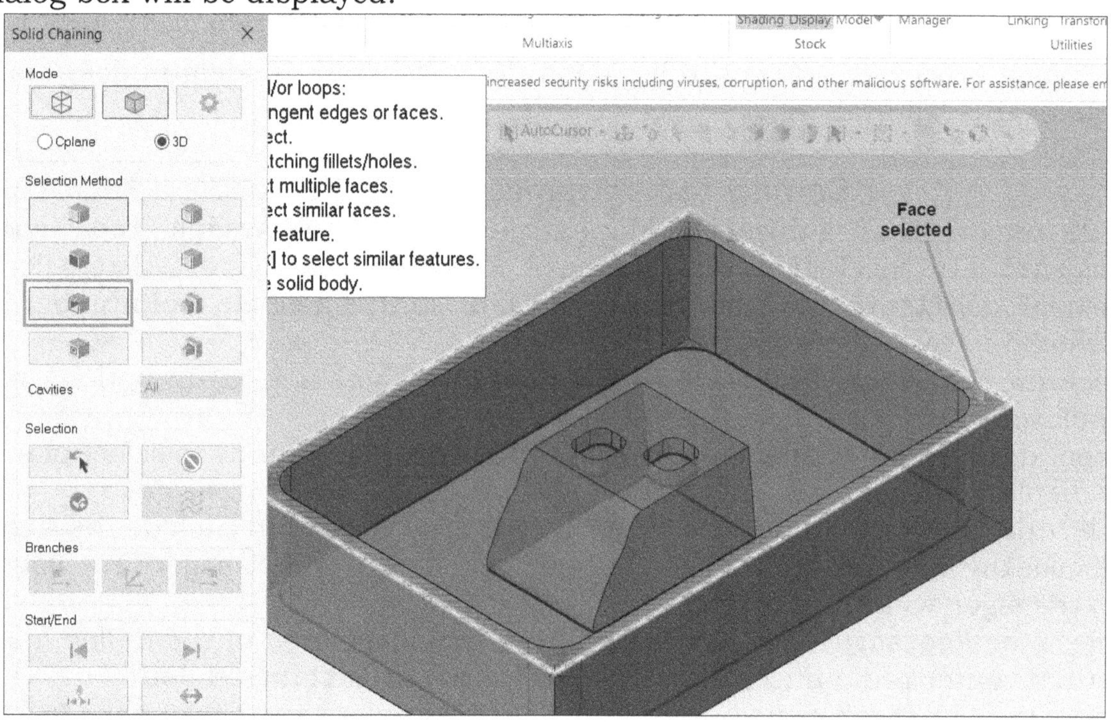

Figure-28. Edges selected for facing boundary

- Click on the **Tool** option from the left area and then click on the **Select library tool** button from the **Tool** page in the dialog box. The **Tool Selection** dialog box will be displayed.

- Select the **FACE MILL-50/58** tool from the list; refer to Figure-29 and click on the **OK** button. The tool will get selected for operation.
- Click on the **Cut Parameters** option from the left area and set the cutting style as **Zigzag** in the **Style** drop-down of the page. Also, set the **Stock to leave on floors** as **0** in this page.
- Click on the **Linking Parameters** option from the left area and set the total cutting depth as absolute **0** in the **Depth** edit box of the page.
- Click on the **OK** button from the dialog box to create toolpath.

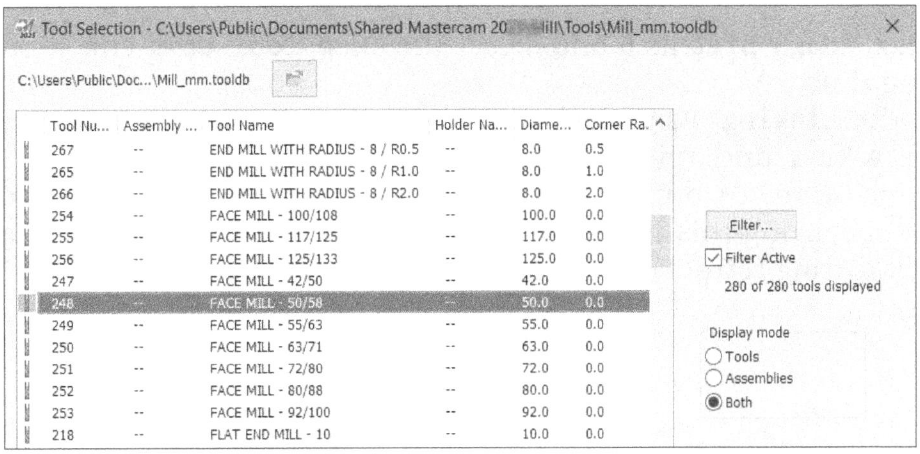

Figure-29. Face mill tool to be selected

2D Pocket Toolpath

2D toolpaths take relatively less time when we need to remove large stock. So, we will now remove extra material of pocket from the stock.

- Click on the **Pocket** tool from the **2D** drop-down in the **Ribbon**. The **Solid Chaining** dialog box will be displayed.
- Select the **Face** button from the **Selection Method** area of the dialog box and select the bottom face of the part to be machined; refer to Figure-30.
- Click on the **OK** button from the dialog box. The **2D Toolpaths-Pocket** dialog box will be displayed.

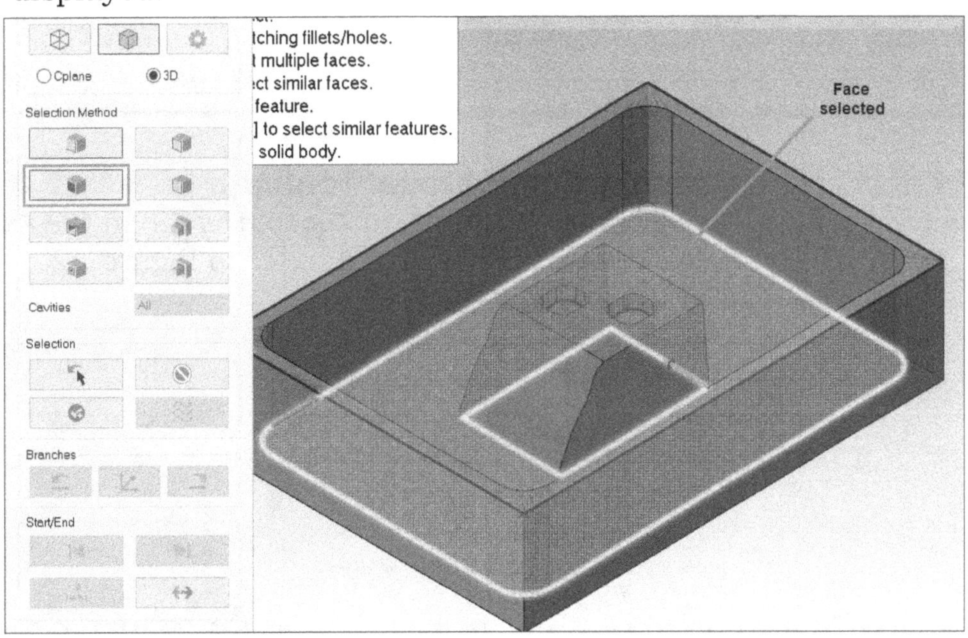

Figure-30. Face selected for 2D pocket

- Click on the **Tool** option from the left and select the **Flat End Mill** of **10** mm diameter as tool. Set desired tool holder for this tool.
- In the **Cut Parameters** page, specify the stock to leave values as **0** in both **Stock to leave on walls** and **Stock to leave on floors** edit boxes.
- Click on the **Roughing** option from the left and select **Zigzag** as the cutting method from the respective page to smoothen cutting based on our model.
- Click on the **Depth Cuts** option from the left area to specify maximum depth limit for each cut and select the **Depth cuts** check box. The options in the page will become active.
- Set the **Max Rough Step** as **6** and select the **Keep tool down** check box to reduce machining time.
- Click on the **Linking Parameters** option from the left area to specify total cut depth, retraction, and other parameters. Select the **Retract** value as incremental **35** and click on the **OK** button. The toolpath will be generated; refer to Figure-31. Note that specifying this retract value will make sure that the tool do not collide with stock during retraction.

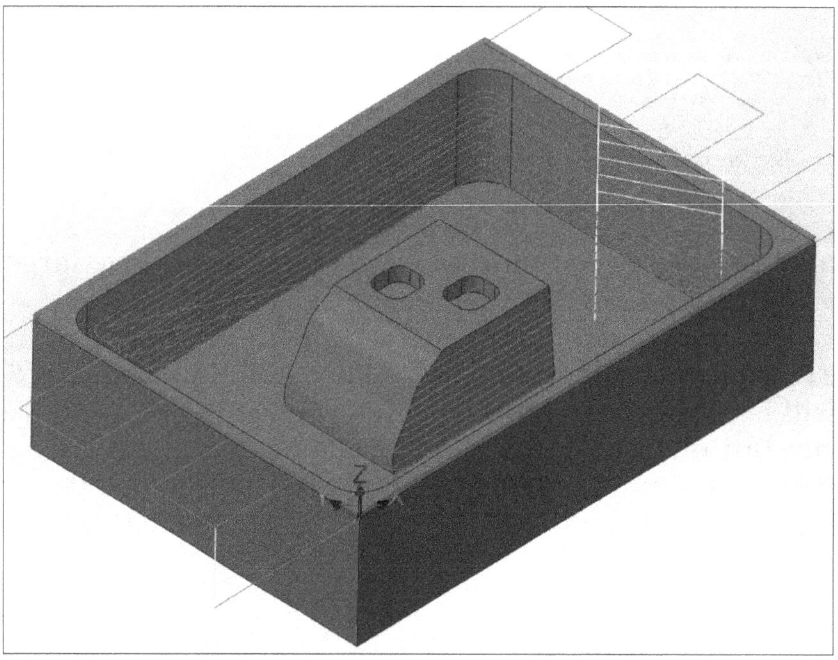

Figure-31. 2D Pocket toolpath created

Surface Rough Parallel Toolpath

- Click on the **Parallel** tool from the **3D** panel of **Toolpaths** tab in the **Ribbon**. The **Select Boss/Cavity** dialog box will be displayed; refer to Figure-32.

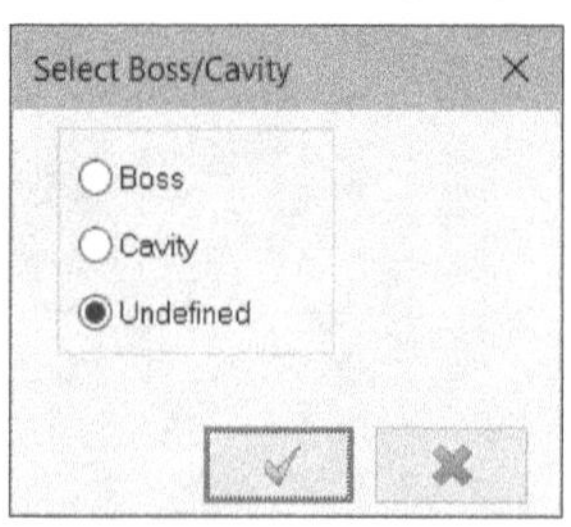

Figure-32. Select Boss/Cavity dialog box

- Select the **Boss** radio button from the dialog box and click on the **OK** button. You will be asked to select the faces of the model to be machined.

- Select the faces/features of the model to be machined; refer to Figure-33 and click on the **End Selection** button. The **Toolpath/surface selection** dialog box will be displayed.
- Click on the **OK** button from the dialog box. The **Surface Rough Parallel** dialog box will be displayed; refer to Figure-34.

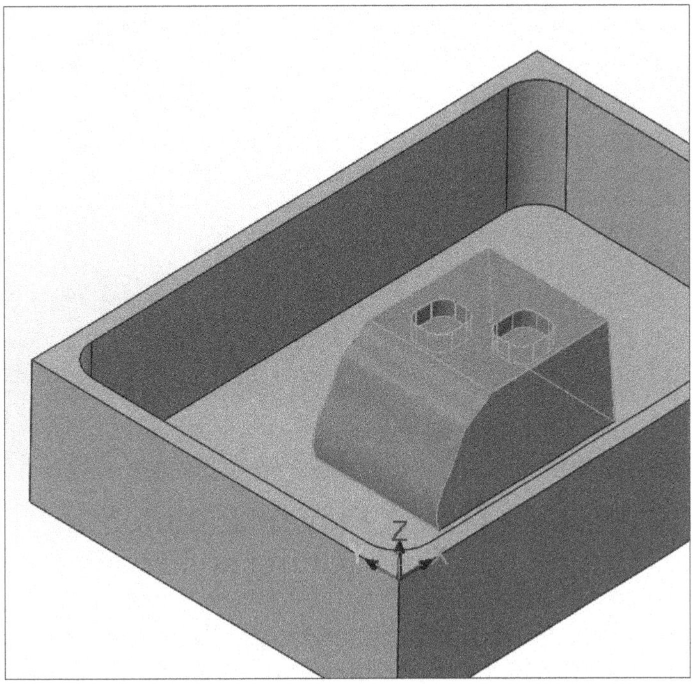

Figure-33. Faces and features selected for parallel rough

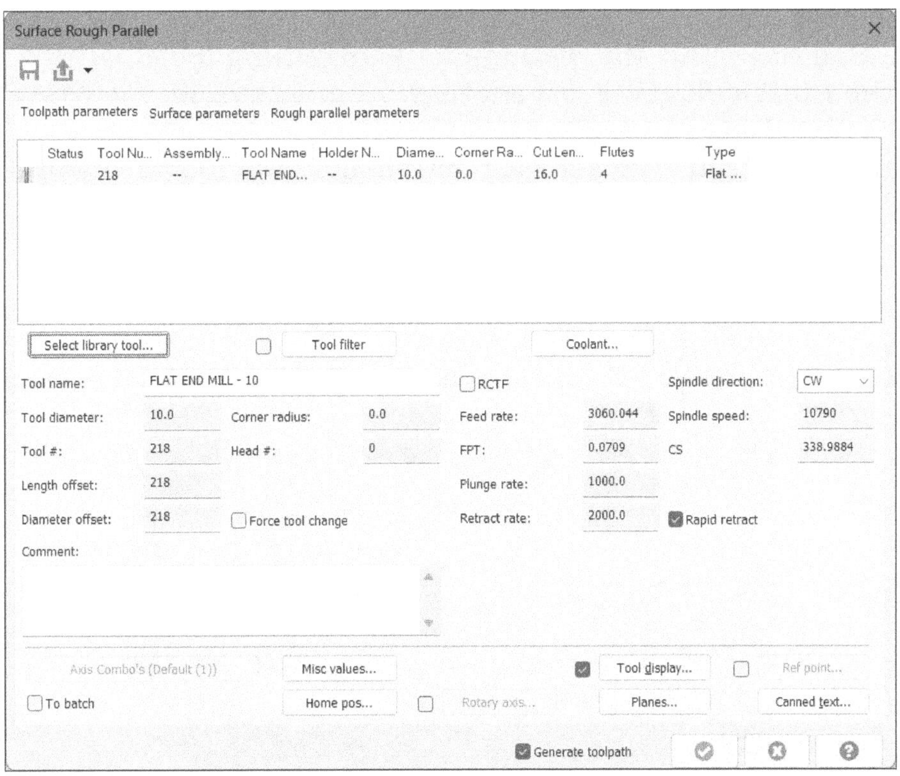

Figure-34. Surface Rough Parallel dialog box

- Select the Ball Nose end mill of **8** diameter as tool.
- Click on the **Rough parallel parameters** tab and specify **Max stepdown** as **2** and **Max stepover** as **4** in respective edit boxes in this tab.

- Click on the **OK** button from the dialog box. The toolpath will be generated; refer to Figure-35.

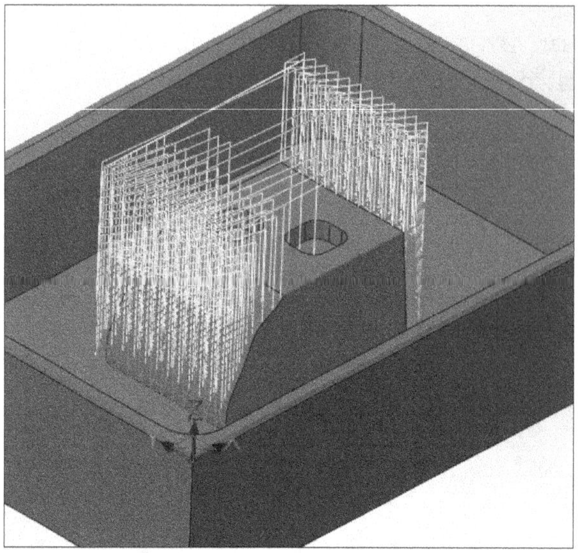

Figure-35. Surface parallel rough toolpath generated

Surface Finish Flowline Toolpath

- Click on the **Flowline** tool from the **Finishing** section of expanded **3D** panel in the **Toolpaths** tab of the **Ribbon**. You will be asked to select the faces to be machined.
- Select the faces earlier selected for surface parallel operation and click on the **End Selection** button. The **Toolpath/surface selection** dialog box will be displayed.
- Click on the **OK** button from the dialog box. The **Surface Finish Flowline** dialog box will be displayed.
- Select the Ball Nose End Mill of diameter **6** as cutting tool.
- Click on the **Finish flowline parameters** tab and specify the **Distance** value in **Stepover control** area as **1**.
- Click on the **OK** button. The **Surface finish flowline** toolpath will be generated; refer to Figure-36.

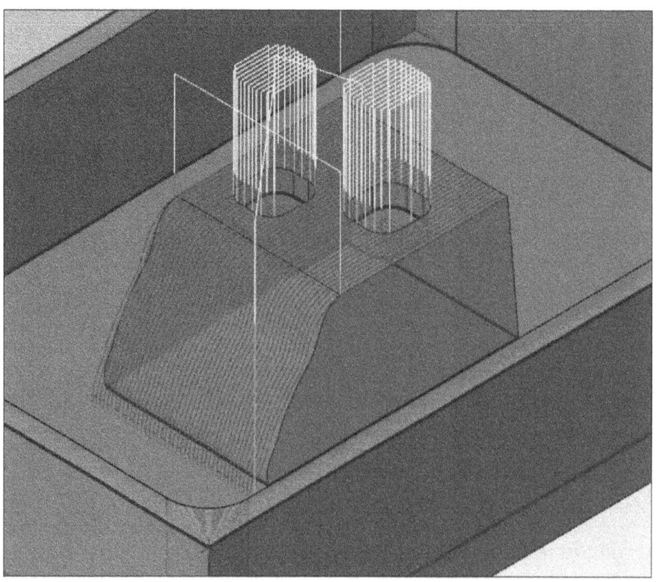

Figure-36. Surface finish flowline toolpath

Pocket Toolpath

Create a 2D pocket toolpath for small pockets at the top face of boss feature using **3** mm diameter flat end mill; refer to Figure-37.

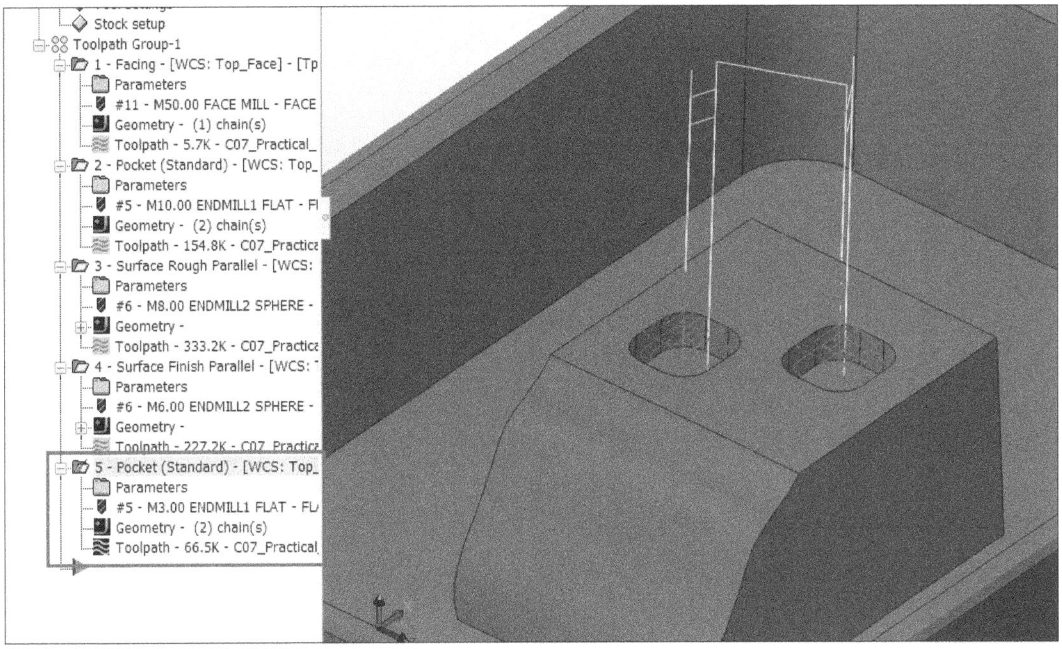

Figure-37. Toolpath for small pockets

Generate the numeric codes by selecting the toolpath group and then clicking on the **Post selected operations** button from the **Toolpaths Manager**. You verify the toolpaths by using the **Verify selected operations** button from the **Toolpaths Manager**.

PRACTICE 2

Create NC program for both sides of the model shown in Figure-38. The dimensions of stock for model are: **Diameter = 700 mm and Length of cylinder = 270 mm**; refer to Figure-39.

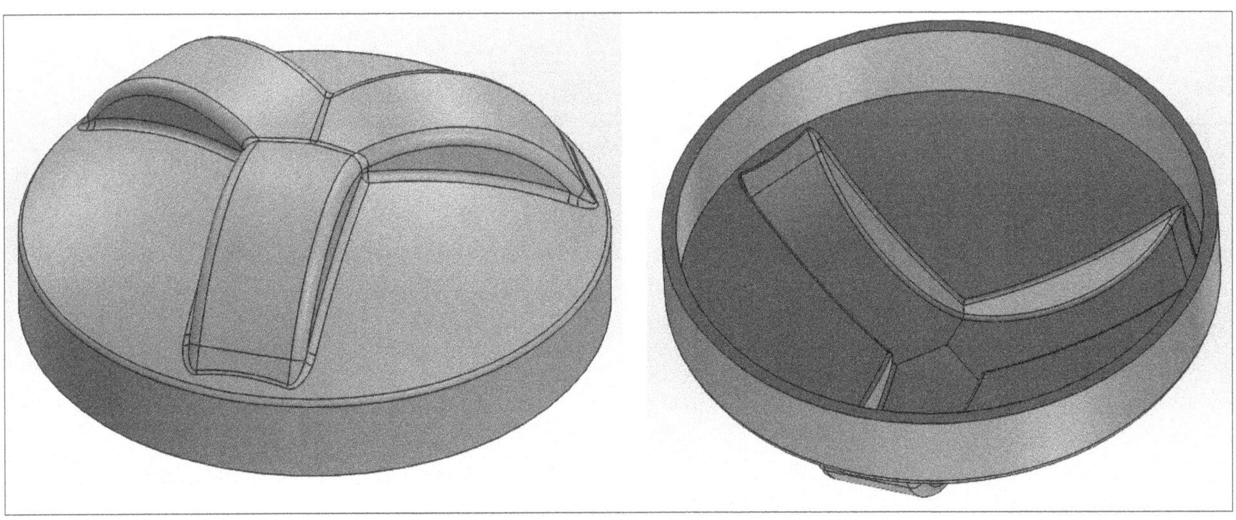

Figure-38. Practice Model

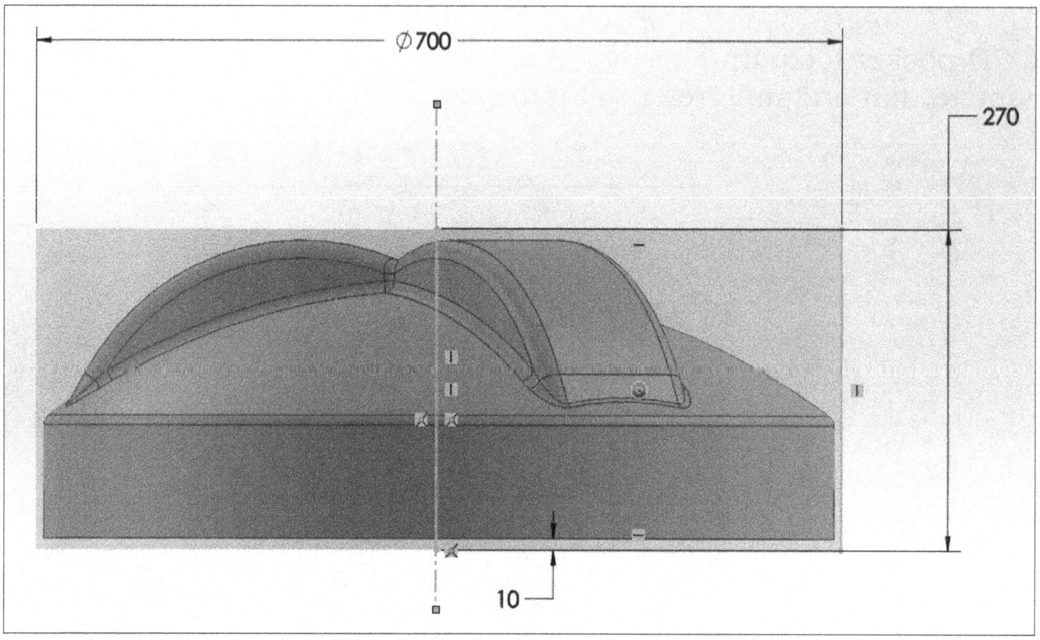

Figure-39. Stock dimensions for Practice

Chapter 14

Lathe Machining and Toolpaths

Topics Covered

The major topics covered in this chapter are:

- ***Introduction***
- ***Lathe Machine Setup***
- ***Defining Stock for Lathe Operation***
- ***Lathe Tool Manager***
- ***Creating Turn Profile***
- ***General Lathe Toolpaths***
- ***Rough Machining Toolpath, Finishing Toolpaths, Lathe Drill Operations, Face Toolpath***
- ***Lathe Cutoff Toolpath, Groove Toolpath, Dynamic Rough Toolpath, Thread Toolpath***
- ***Plunge Turn Toolpath, Contour Rough Toolpath, Prime Turning Toolpaths***
- ***Custom Threads, Toolpath Through Points, Canned Toolpaths***
- ***Practical***

INTRODUCTION

Lathe toolpaths are used to perform various turning operations like facing, roughing, cutting off, drilling, and so on. To create toolpaths related to lathe machining, you need to first setup a lathe machining. The procedure to setup a lathe machine is discussed next.

LATHE MACHINE SETUP

Lathe toolpaths are meant for machining a work piece on lathe or CNC turning machine. By default, the Lathe Toolpaths are deactivated. To activate these tool paths, you need to select a lathe machine. The procedure is given next.

- Click on the down arrow below **Lathe** tool in the **Machine Type** panel of the **Machine** tab in the **Ribbon**. The list of available turning machines will be displayed; refer to Figure-1.

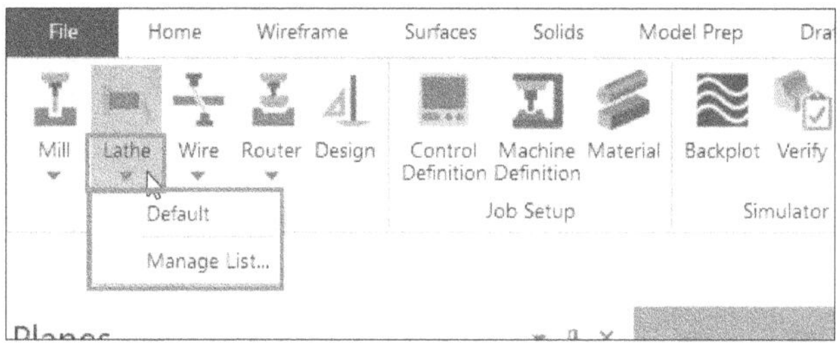

Figure-1. List of lathe machines

- Select **Manage List** option from the list. The **Machine Definition Menu Management** dialog box will be displayed.
- Select desired lathe machine and click on the **Add** button. The selected machine will be added in the list.
- Click on the **OK** button from the dialog box to add the machine. The machine will be added in the list.
- Click on the down arrow below **Lathe** tool again and select desired turning machine from the list. The tools to create lathe machining toolpaths will be displayed in the **Ribbon**; refer to Figure-2.

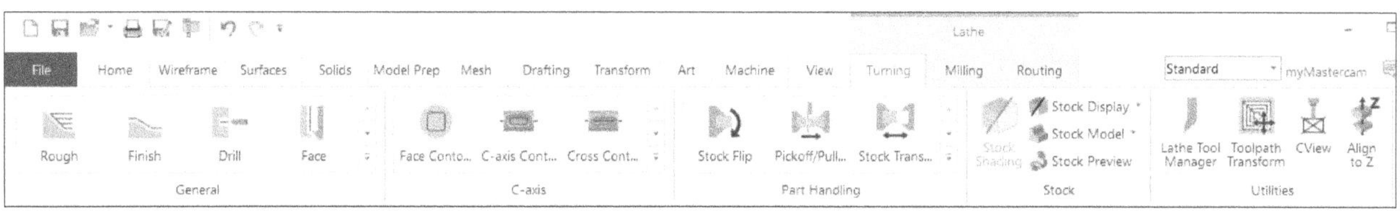

Figure-2. Turning toolpaths

DEFINING STOCK FOR LATHE OPERATION

The stock for turning operations is created by using the stock setup option for machine in the **Toolpaths Manager**. Before creating stock, it is important to align the model with WCS of machining plane. The procedures to align model and create stock are given next.

Aligning Model with Machining Plane

- After creating model and setting up a lathe machine, various planes are added in the **Planes Manager**; refer to Figure-3.

- Set the **+D+Z** plane as WCS, C, and T plane in the **Planes Manager** by clicking in respective columns next to the plane; refer to Figure-4.

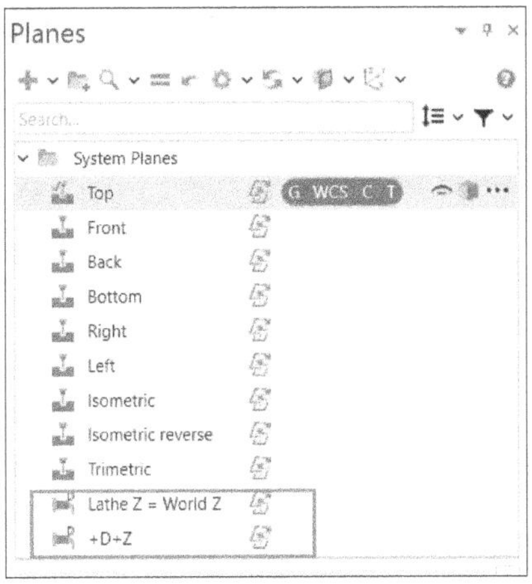

Figure-3. Planes added for lathe machining

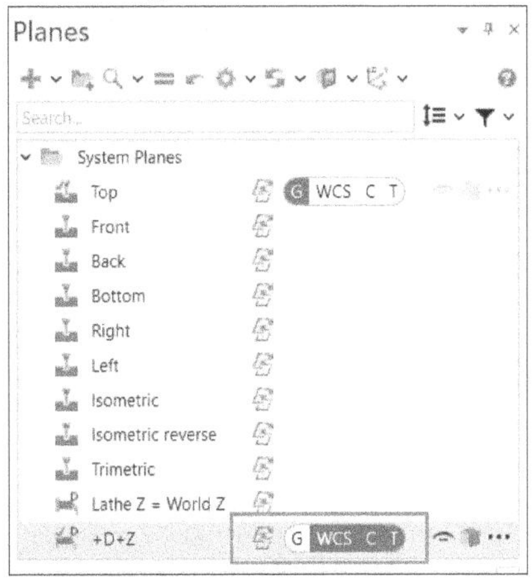

Figure-4. Setting plane as WCS, construction, and tool plane

- Note that most of the time, the model is not oriented to the plane used for machining. Click on the **Align to Z** tool from the **Layout** panel in the **Model Prep** tab of the **Ribbon**; refer to Figure-5. The **Align to Z Manager** will be displayed; refer to Figure-6.

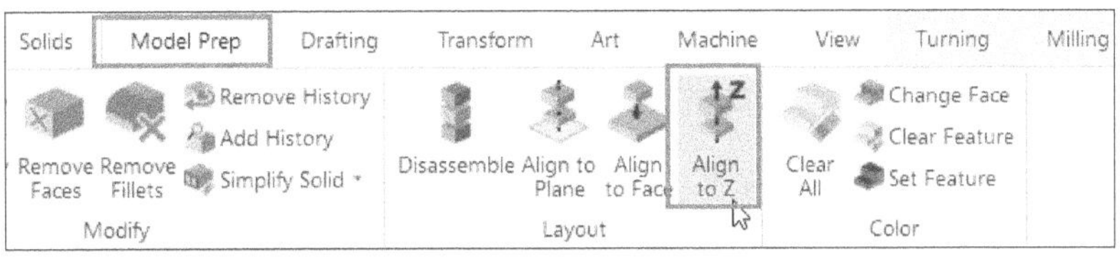

Figure-5. Align to Z tool

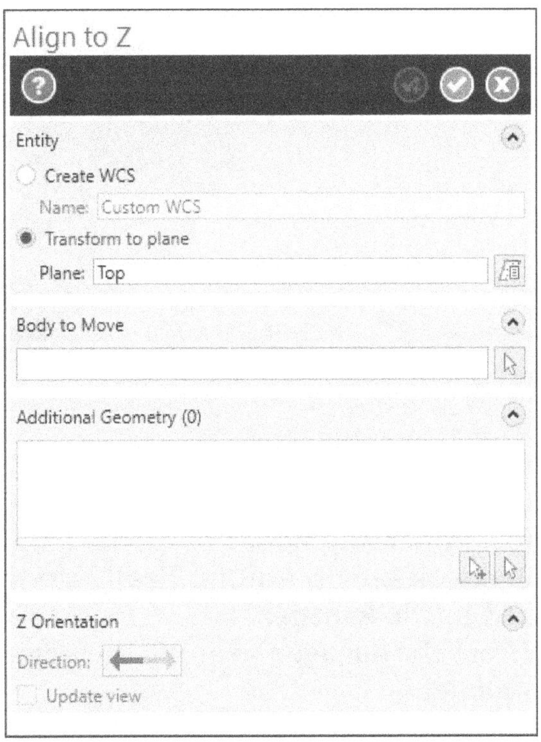

Figure-6. Align to Z Manager

- Select the **Transform to plane** radio button from the **Manager** to set selected plane as turning machine plane. After selecting radio button, click on the **Select destination plane** button next to the radio button. The **Plane Selection** dialog box will be displayed; refer to Figure-7.

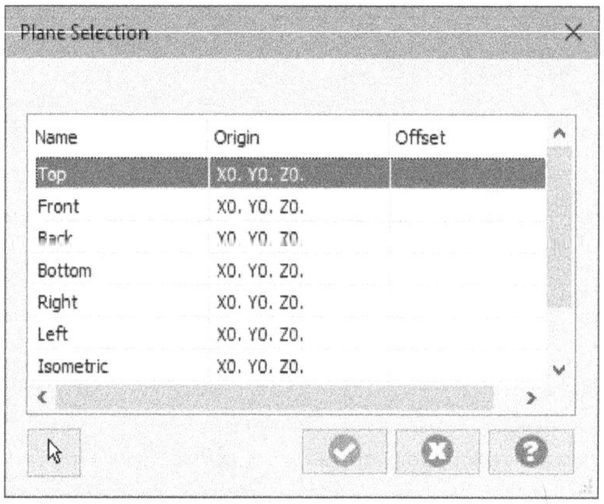

Figure-7. Plane Selection dialog box

- Select the **+D+Z** plane from the list in the dialog box and click on the **OK** button.
- Click on the **Reselect** button for **Body to Move** selection box and select the model to be machined at location where you want to place coordinate system. Preview of alignment will be displayed; refer to Figure-8.

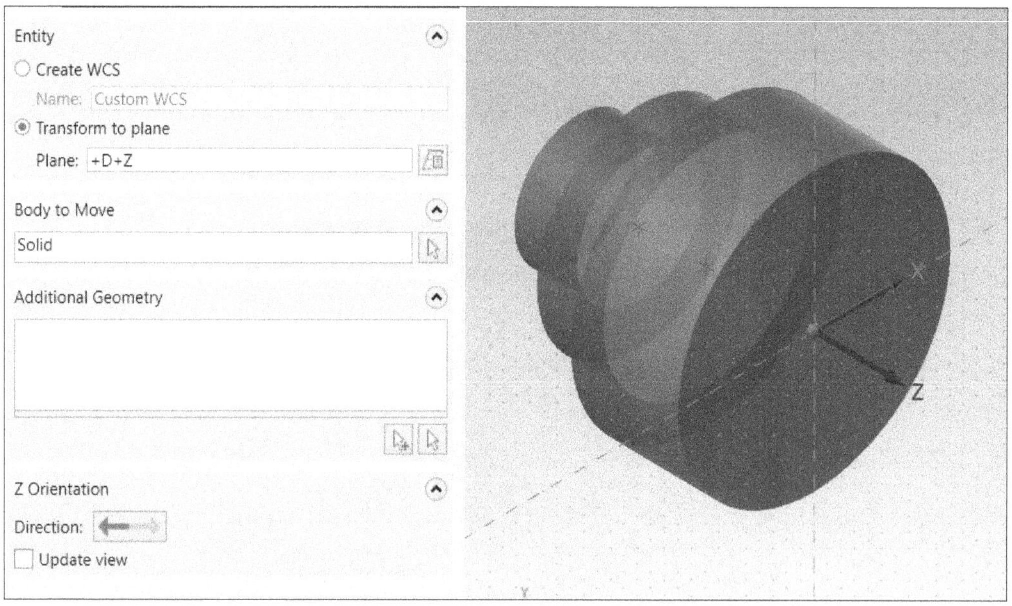

Figure-8. Preview of alignment

- Click on the **Reverse Direction** button from the **Z Orientation** rollout to reverse Z direction if needed for proper alignment of model as in our case.
- Select the **Update view** check box to automatically update isometric view as per the parameters specified in the **Manager**.
- Click on the **OK** button from the **Manager** to apply the alignment. Now, we are ready to create stock for the model.

Creating Stock of Model

- Expand the **Properties** node of **Machine Group** in the **Toolpaths Manager** and click on the **Stock setup** option; refer to Figure-9. The **Stock Setup** tab will be displayed in the **Machine Group Properties** dialog box; refer to Figure-10.

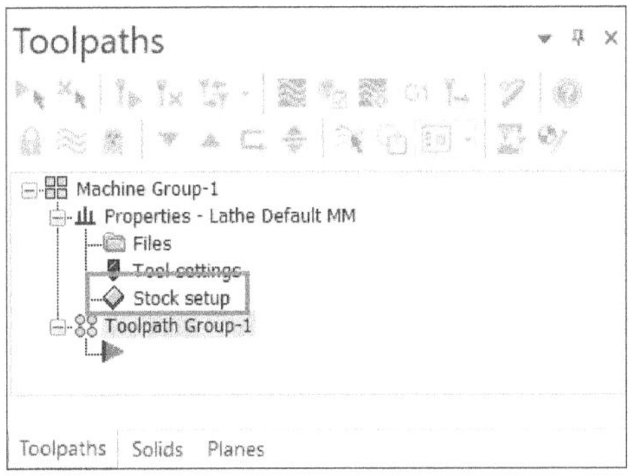

Figure-9. Stock setup option

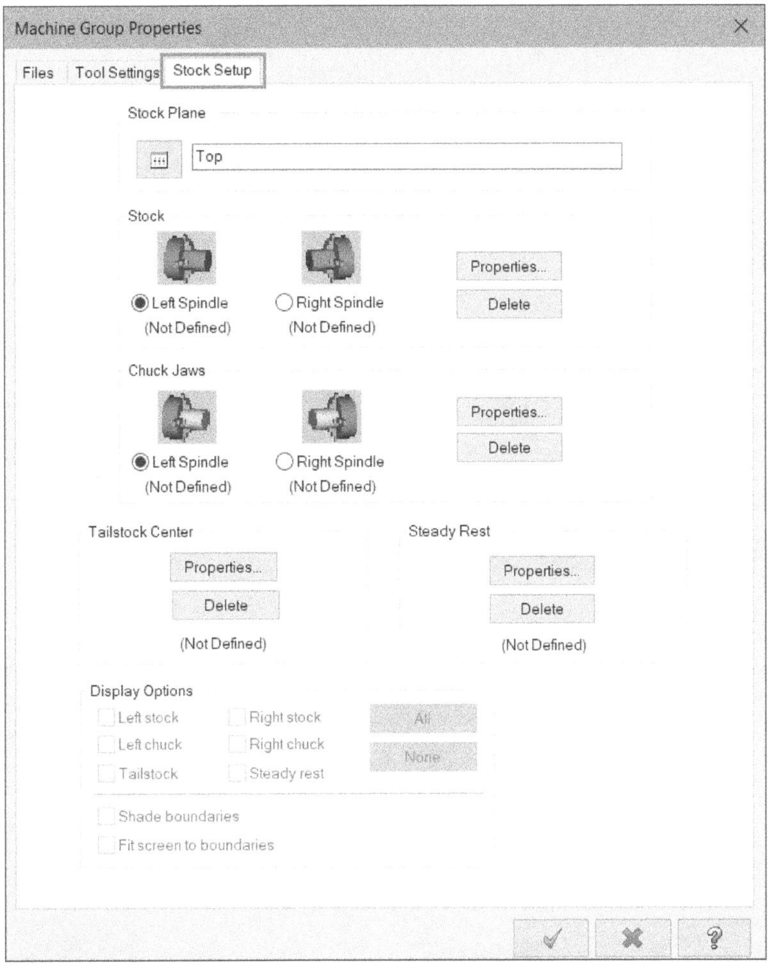

Figure-10. Stock Setup tab

- Click on the **Select Plane** button from the **Stock Plane** area at the top in the dialog box to define the plane in which stock will be created. Note that the stock plane and cutting tool plane should be same.
- Click on the **Properties** button from **Stock** area of the dialog box. The **Machine Component Manager - Stock** dialog box will be displayed; refer to Figure-11.
- Specify desired values in the OD, Length, and other edit boxes to define values for stock; refer to Figure-12. Specify desired value in **OD** edit box to define outer diameter of stock. If there is a hole in the stock then select the **ID** check box and specify desired value in **ID** edit box. Specify the total length of stock bar in the **Length** edit box. Click on the **Select** button from **Position Along Axis** area of the dialog box to define start point of stock. You will be asked to specify base point for cylinder. Select the surface point of model to define base point for cylinder; refer to Figure-13.

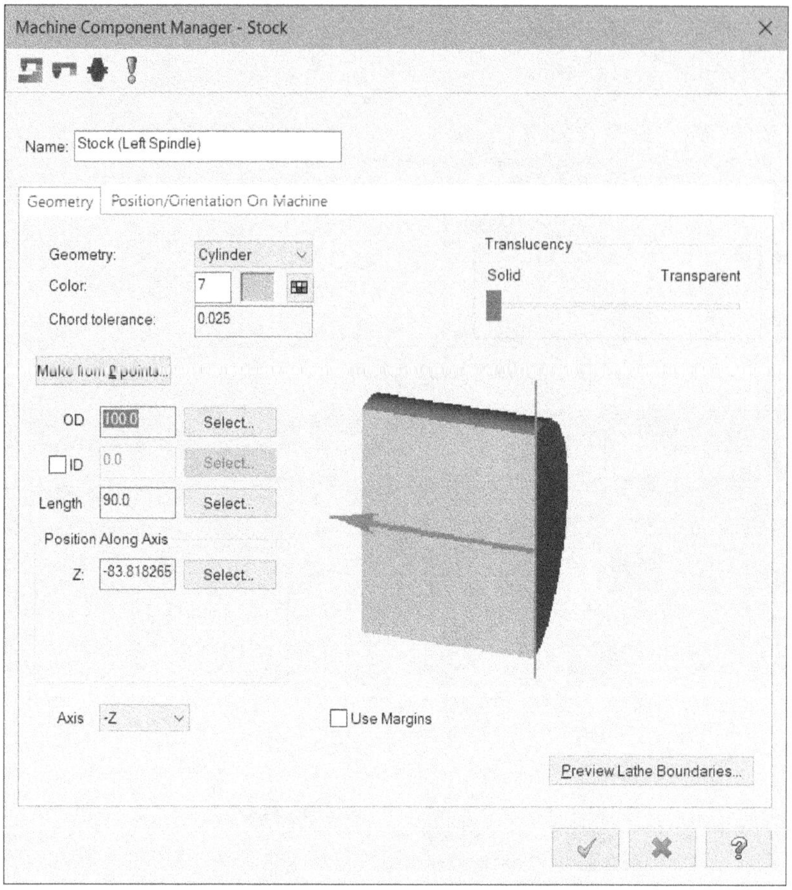

Figure-11. Machine Component Manager-Stock dialog box

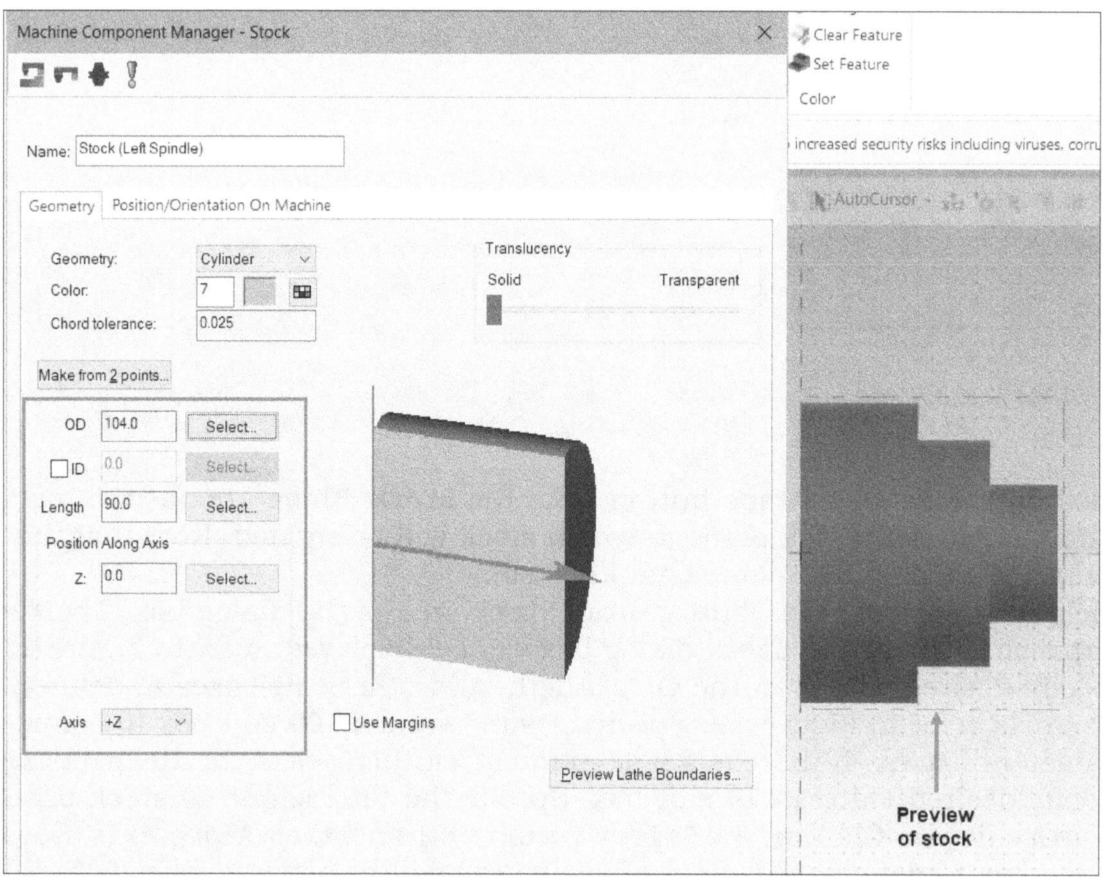

Figure-12. Preview of stock created

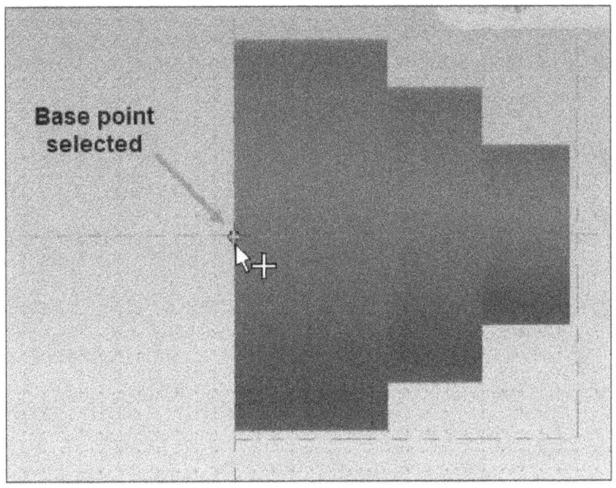

Figure-13. Selecting base point of model

Use Margins options

The **Use Margins** options are applicable when you have set the OD, ID, and Length values exactly matching to the finished part. In that case, you can specify the extra material to be removed from stock by using the margin values. These margin values give dimensions of stock.

- Select the **Use Margins** check box from the dialog box. The options for specifying margins will be displayed in the dialog box.
- Specify desired values of margins, preview of the stock will be modified accordingly; refer to Figure-14.

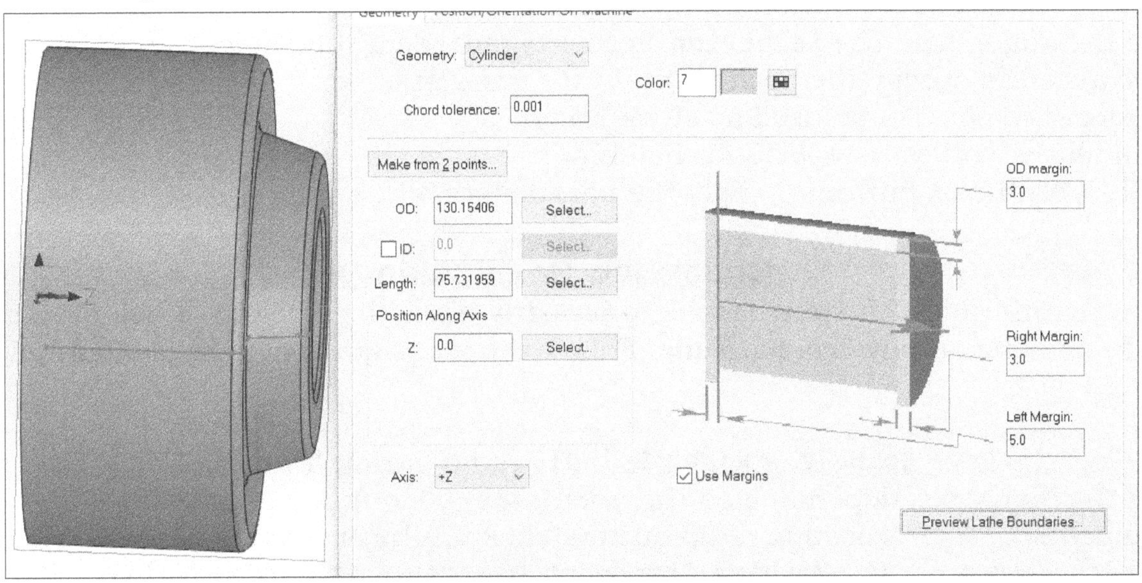

Figure-14. Specifying margin values

- Click on the **Preview Lathe Boundaries** button to check the preview of stock and click **OK** button from the **PropertyManager** to exit the preview.

Position/Orientation On Machine

The options in the **Position/Orientation On Machine** tab are used to set the WCS on Stock and Machine. Note that all the dimensions in the NC codes will be calculated based on these WCS. The options are discussed next.

- Clear the **Stock is drawn in position on the machine** check box if the origin is not placed as per your requirement in stock preview. The options in the dialog box will be displayed as shown in Figure-15.

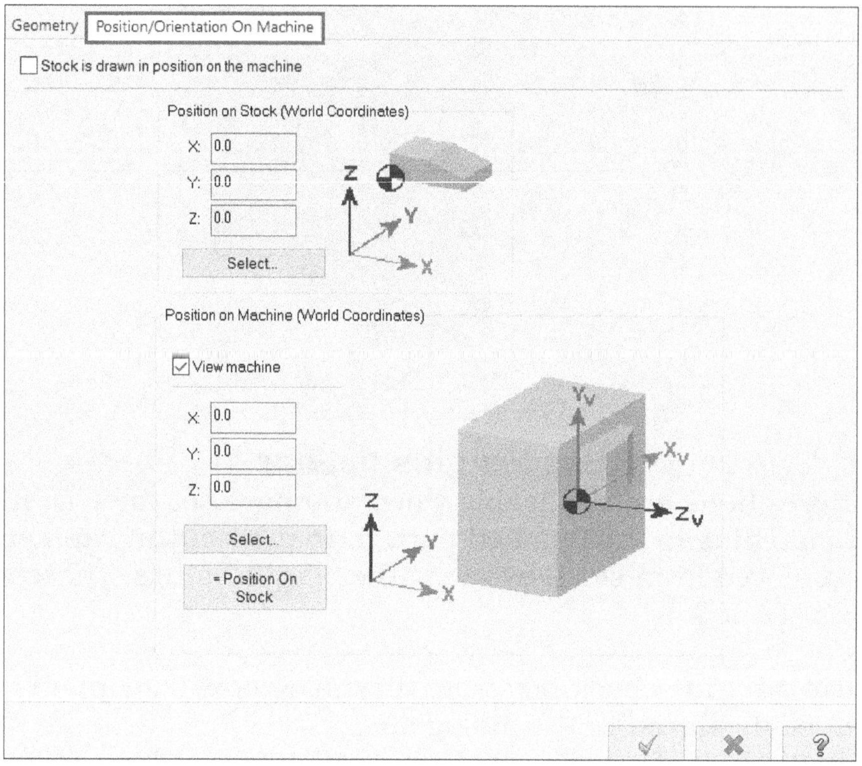

Figure-15. Position Orientation On Machine tab in dialog box

- Click on the **Select** button in the **Position on Stock (World Coordinates)** area of the dialog box. The **Selection PropertyManager** will be displayed and you will be asked to specify the position of WCS for stock.
- Select the point to be used as stock origin.
- Similarly, you can set WCS for machine.
- Click on the **OK** button to apply the parameters.

Chuck Jaw Positioning

After creating stock, the next step is to properly place the stock in chuck of lathe as it is to be done on physical machine. Follow the steps given next to position part in chuck.

- Select the **Left Spindle** or **Right Spindle** radio button from the **Chuck Jaws** area of the dialog box depending on the orientation of your part to specify chuck jaws to be used. After selecting radio button, click on the **Properties** button from the **Chuck Jaws** area. The **Machine Component Manager - Chuck Jaws dialog box** will be displayed; refer to Figure-16.

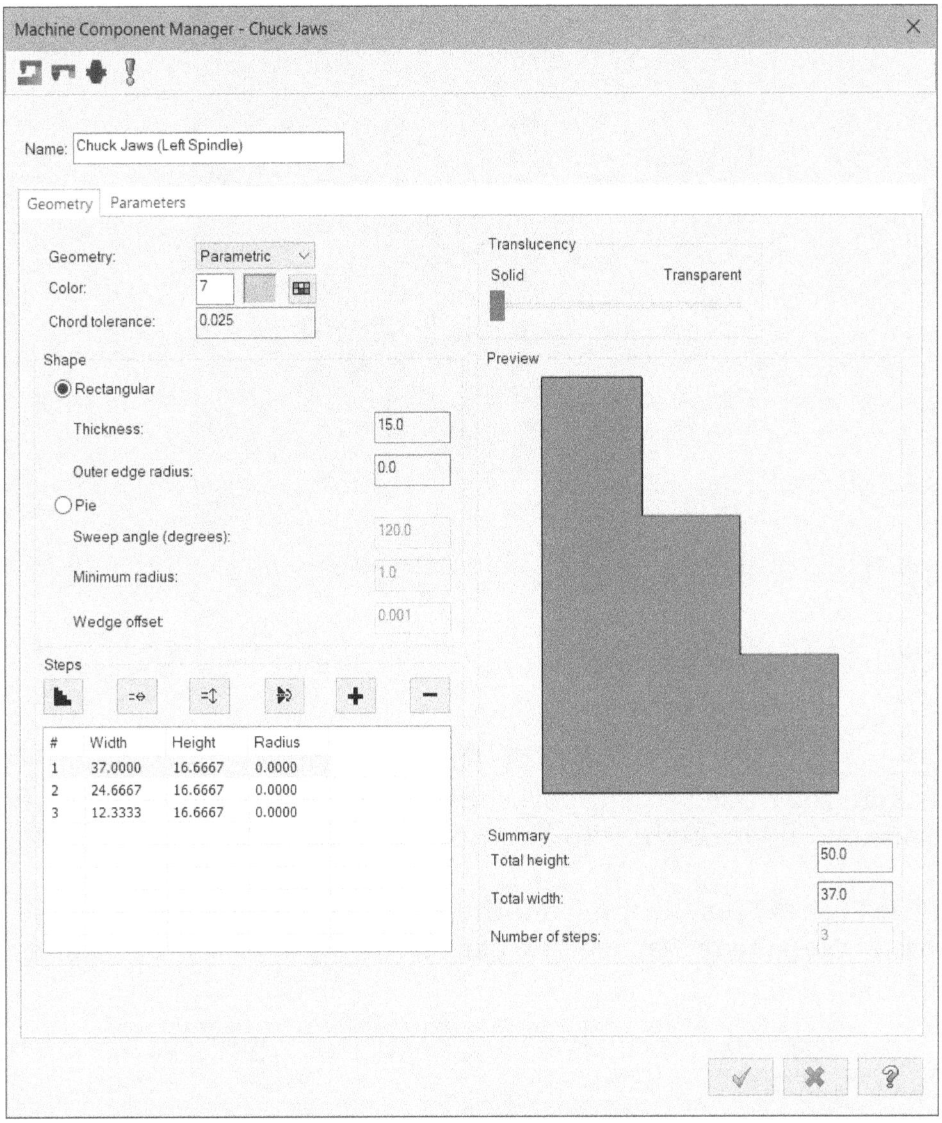

Figure-16. Machine Component Manager-Chuck Jaws dialog box

- Select desired radio button from the **Shape** area and specify various size parameters for components of chuck. By default, the **Rectangular** radio button is selected so, rectangular chucks are created. Select the **Pie** radio button if you want to create radial jaws with specified sweep angle. Note that if the sweep angle is less than 360/number jaws value then there will be gap between jaws.
- Using the buttons and parameters in the **Step** area, you can specify individual jaw size.
- Click on the **Parameters** tab of the dialog box to specify clamping method and position of clamps. Select the **Outside diameter (OD)** radio button if the clamps are to be placed on outer diameter of stock. Select the **Inside diameter (ID)** radio button if the clamps are to be placed at the inside of stock.
- Select the **From stock** check box to automatically place the jaws at start points of stock.
- Click on the **Preview Lathe Boundaries** button to check preview of jaws; refer to Figure-17. After checking preview, press **ENTER** to return to the dialog box.
- Click on the **OK** button from the dialog box to create the jaws.

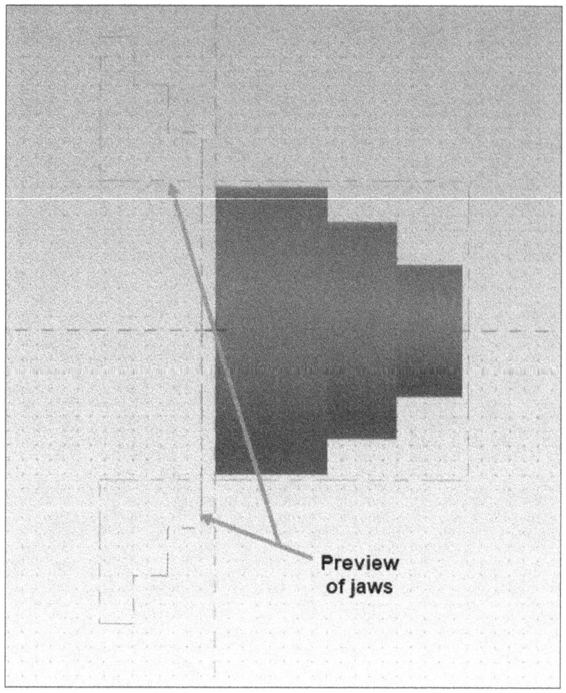

Figure-17. Preview of jaws

Tail Stock Positioning

Tail stock is generally used to support long cylindrical parts that can bend during turning operation. The procedure to add tail stock in machining setup is given next.

- Click on the **Properties** button from the **Tailstock Center** area of the dialog box. The **Machine Component Manager - Center** dialog box will be displayed; refer to Figure-18.

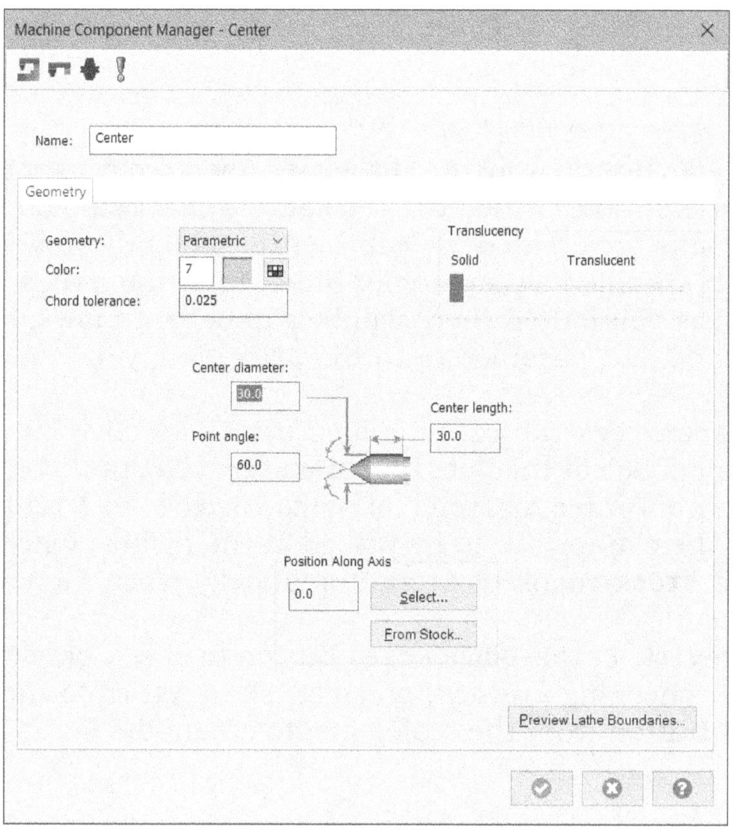

Figure-18. Machine Component Manager-Center dialog box

- By default, the **Parametric** option is selected in the **Geometry** drop-down of the dialog box. Select the **Cylinder** or **Solid entity** option if you want different geometry of tail stock. The options for these parameters have already been discussed. (We will continue with **Parametric** option in the drop-down.)
- Specify the parameters of tail stock in the edit boxes of dialog box.
- Click on the **From Stock** button to automatically place the tail stock at the end of stock or specify desired position in the **Position Along Axis** edit box.
- Click on the **Preview Lathe Boundaries** button to check the preview of tail stock.
- Click on the **OK** button to apply the settings.

Steady Rest Positioning

- Click on the **Properties** button from the **Steady Rest** area of the dialog box. The **Machine Component Manager - Steady Rest** dialog box will be displayed; refer to Figure-19. Note that you must have a closed sketch in the graphics area to define shape of steady rest before using this option; refer to Figure-20.

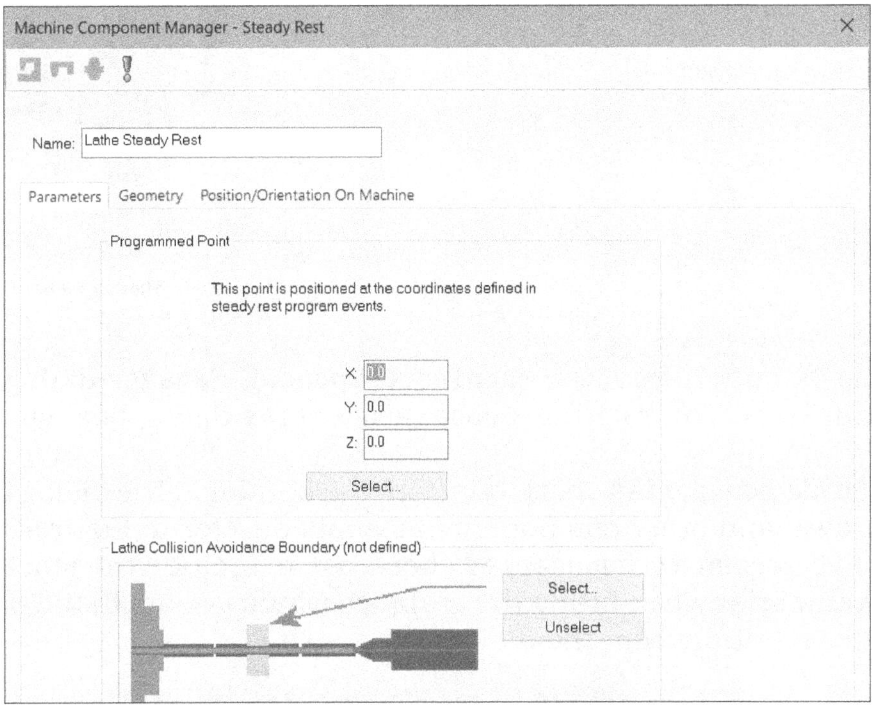

Figure-19. Machine Component Manager-Steady Rest dialog box

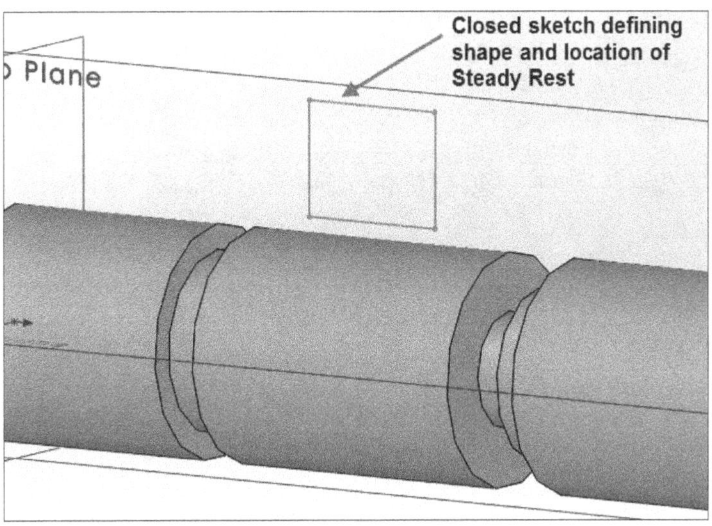

Figure-20. Sketch created for Steady Rest

- Click on the **Select** button from the **Lathe Collision Avoidance Boundary** area of the dialog box. The **Chain Manager** will be displayed and you will be asked to select the sketch defining boundary of Steady Rest.
- Select the sketch and click on the **OK** button from the **Chain Manager**. Click on the **OK** button from the **Machine Component Manager** dialog box. Preview of the Steady Rest component will be displayed; refer to Figure-21. Note that we have selected the **Shade boundaries** check box in the **Machine Group Properties** dialog box, so that all the components are displayed as shaded.

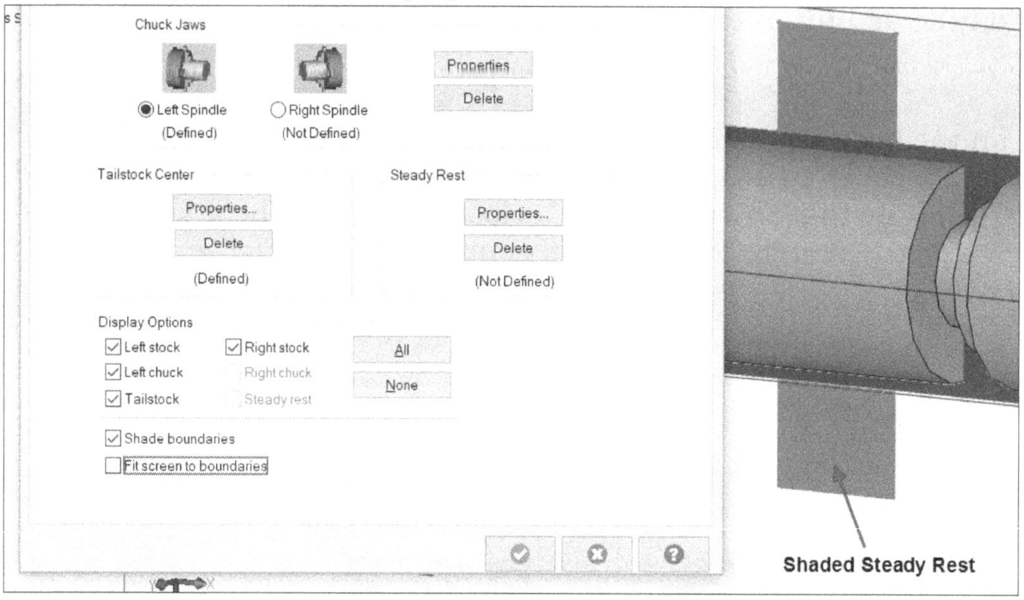

Figure-21. Preview of Steady Rest

- Click on the **OK** button from the **Machine Component Manager** dialog box to apply all the parameters. The **Machine Group Properties** dialog box will be displayed again.
- Select the **Shade boundaries** check box from the bottom in the dialog box to display the stock, jaws, and other components as shaded; refer to Figure-22.
- Select the **Fit screen to boundaries** check box to include the stock, chuck, and tailstock boundaries when fitting the graphics window zoom to the part geometry.
- Click on the **OK** button from the dialog box to exit.

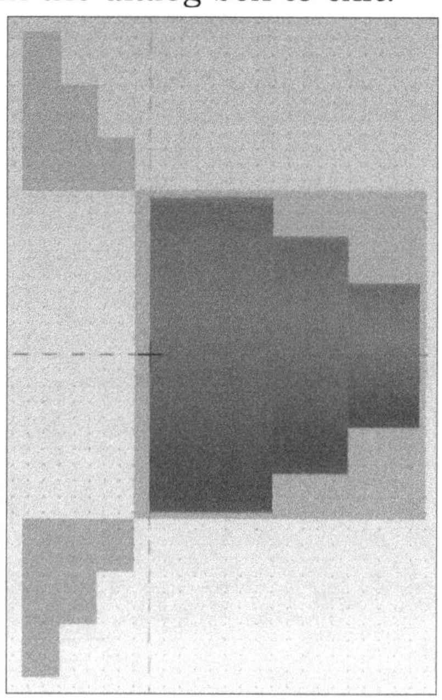

Figure-22. Shaded stock and jaws

LATHE TOOL MANAGER

The **Lathe Tool Manager** is used to create and manage cutting tools for lathe machining. The procedure to use this tool is given next.

- Click on the **Lathe Tool Manager** tool from the **Utilities** panel of **Turning** tab in the **Ribbon**. The **Tool Manager** dialog box will be displayed; refer to Figure-23.

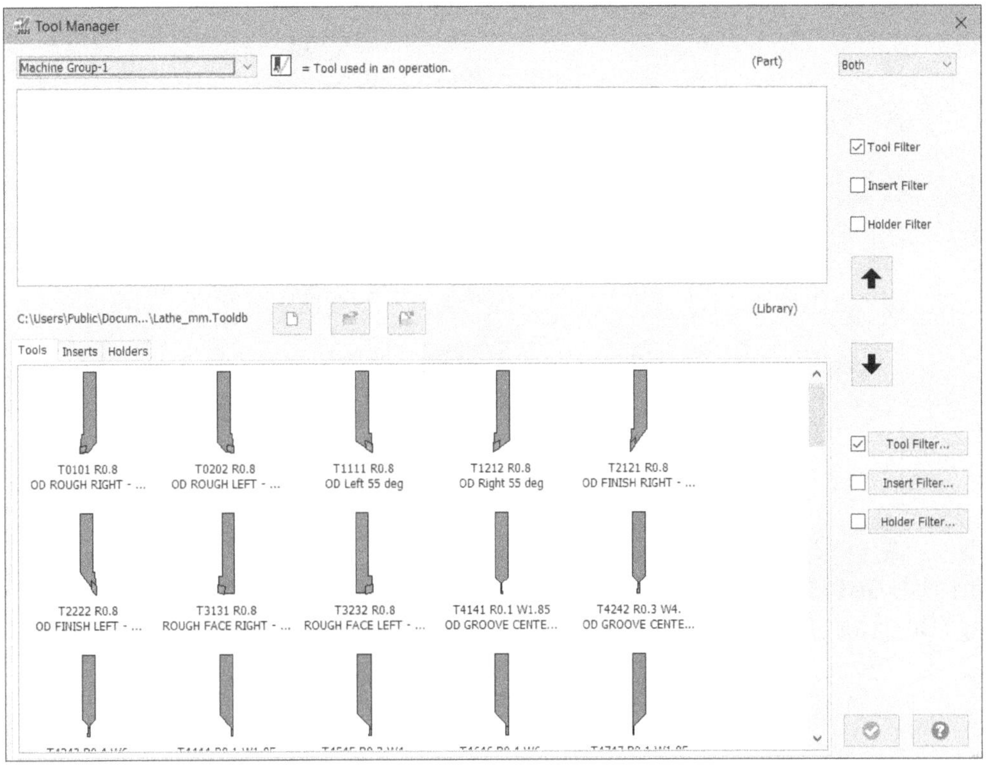

Figure-23. Tool Manager dialog box

- Double-click on the tool to be added in the machine group from the bottom list. The selected tool will be added to machine group and displayed in the upper list of dialog box.
- Now, double-click on the tool that you want to edit from the top box. The **Define Tool** dialog box will be displayed; refer to Figure-24.
- There are four tabs in the dialog box to edit 4 different sections of the tool. By default, the **Inserts** tab is selected in the dialog box. The options are as follows:

Inserts tab

- Click on the **Select Catalog** button and select desired catalog file by using the dialog box displayed. On selecting the catalog, the related inserts will be displayed in the **Define Tool** dialog box.

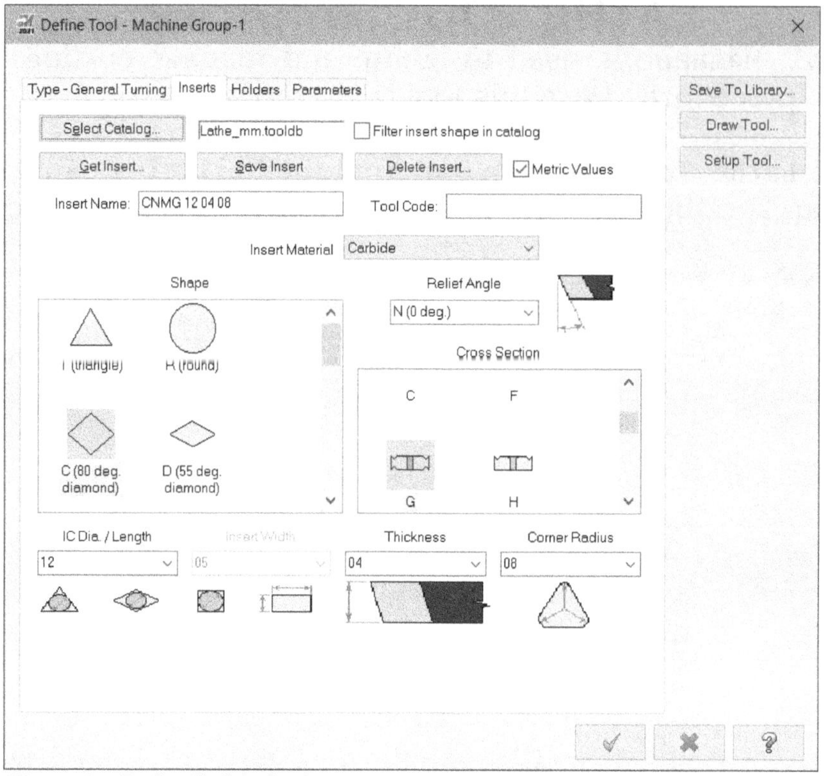

Figure-24. Define Tool dialog box

- Click on the **Get Insert** button to display the list of the tool inserts. The **General Turning/Boring Inserts** dialog box will be displayed; refer to Figure-25.

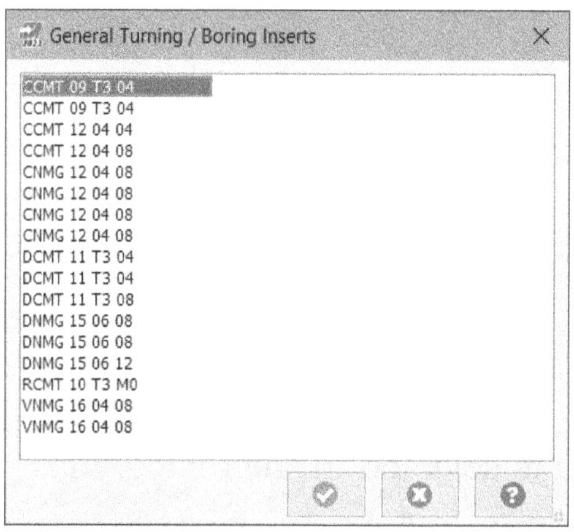

Figure-25. General Turning or Boring Inserts dialog box

- Select desired tool insert from the dialog box and click on the **OK** button. The shape and other parameters of the tool will be automatically decided on the basis of manufacturer's catalog.
- To change the parameters like **IC Diameter**, **Thickness**, and so on; click in the respective edit box and specify desired value.
- To specify the tool direction and machine assembly parameters, click on the **Setup Tool** button. The **Lathe Tool Setup** dialog box will be displayed; refer to Figure-26.

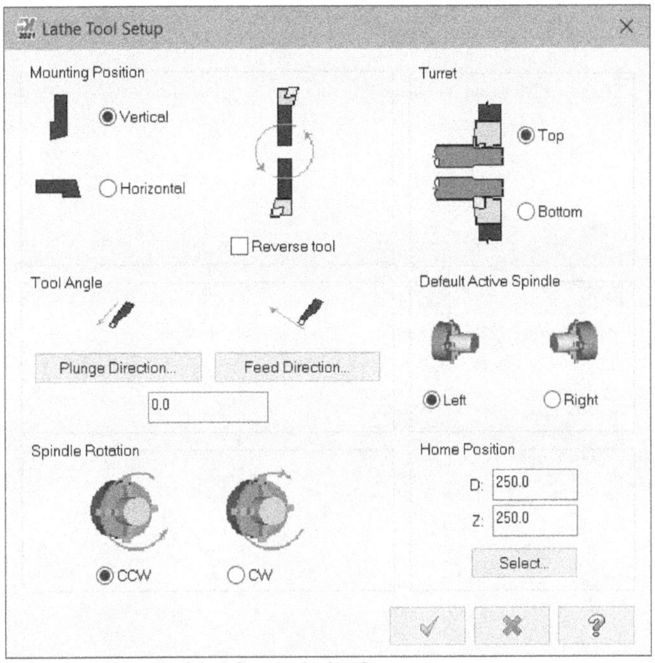

Figure-26. Lathe Tool Setup dialog box

- The radio buttons in the **Mounting Position** area are used to specify the direction in which the tool holder will be placed.
- The radio buttons in the **Turret** area are used to specify whether the tool insert will be facing downward or upward.
- Select the **Plunge Direction** or **Feed Direction** button from the **Tool Angle** area to specify the direction in which the tool will be aligned while cutting the workpiece.
- Similarly, select the radio buttons from the **Spindle Rotation** and **Default Active Spindle** areas as required.
- Click in the edit boxes in **Home Position** area and specify the home position of the tool tip. **Note that specifying correct home position of tool is important to avoid early collision of cutting tool with stock.** Sometimes, you may get warning at the start of toolpath telling you that there is a collision of cutting tool with stock, in those cases you need to change this value.
- Click on the **OK** button from the dialog box.

Type tab

- Click on the **Type** tab from the dialog box. The **Define Tool** dialog box will be displayed as shown in Figure-27.
- Select desired button to change the tool type if the tool you want to use is not displayed in the **Inserts** tab.
- On selecting desired button, the respective parameters will be displayed in the **Inserts** tab which have been discussed earlier.

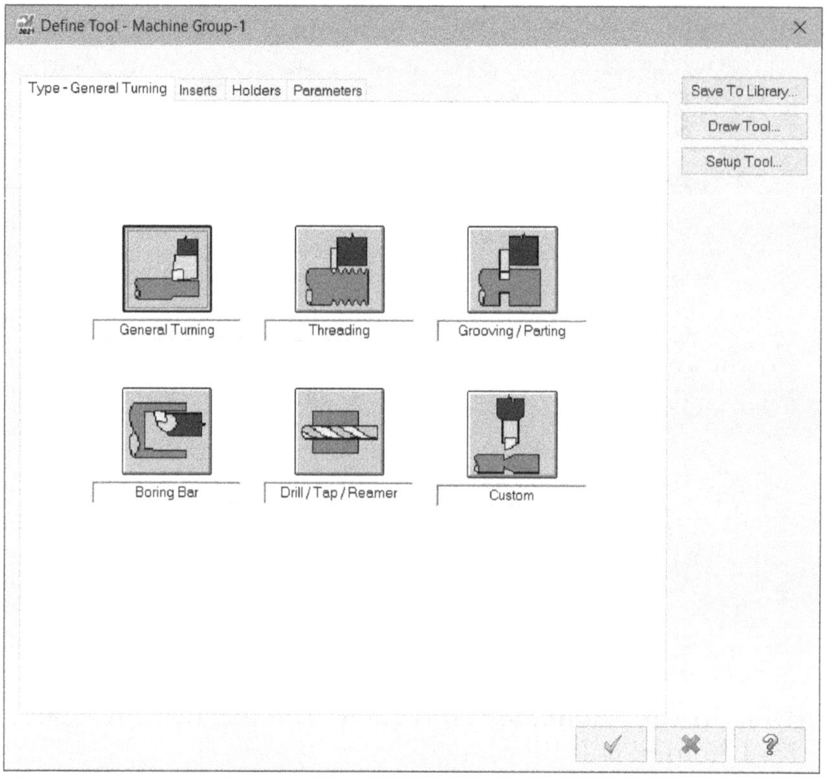

Figure-27. Define Tool dialog box with tool types

Holders tab

The options in the **Holders** tab are used to specify the size and shape of the tool holders. The steps to modify these options are given next.

- Click on the **Holders** tab in the **Define Tool** dialog box. The dialog box will be displayed as shown in Figure-28.

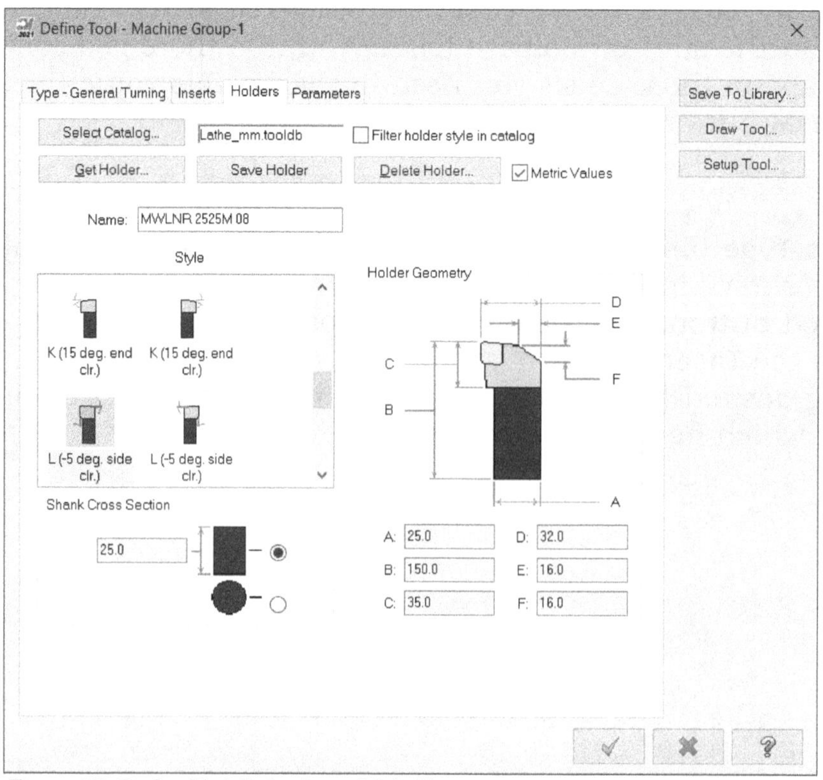

Figure-28. Define Tool dialog box with holder parameters

- Click on the **Select Catalog** button. The **New Holder Catalog** dialog box will be displayed; refer to Figure-29.
- Select desired catalog and click on the **Open** button from the dialog box.
- Click on the **Get Holder** button from the **Define Tool** dialog box. The **General Turning Holders** dialog box will be displayed; refer to Figure-30.

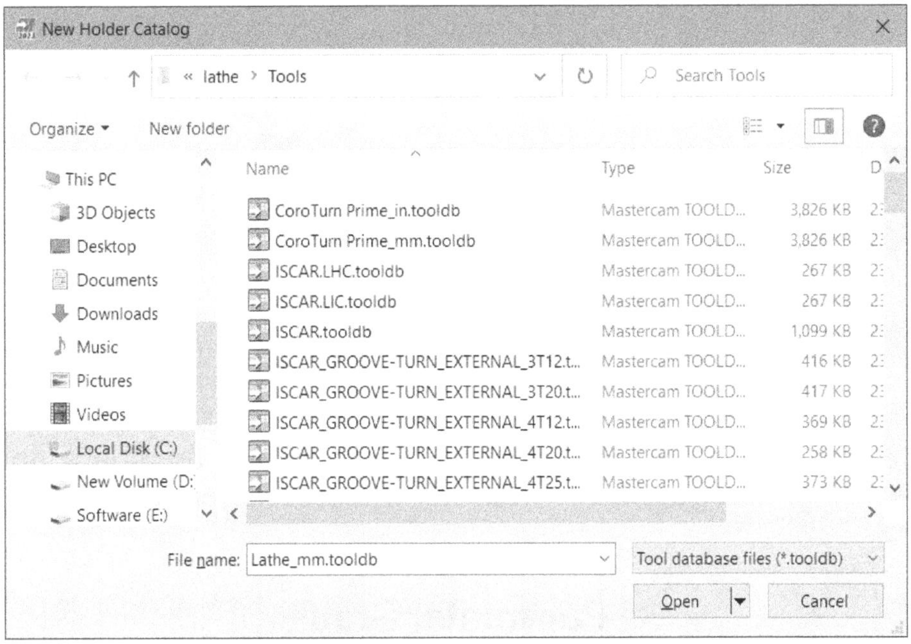

Figure-29. New Holder Catalog dialog box

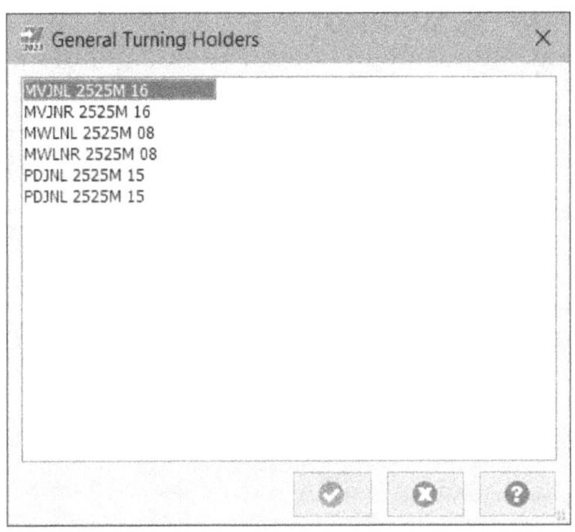

Figure-30. General Turning Holders dialog box

- Select desired holder from the dialog box and click on the **OK** button. The parameters related to the selected holder will be displayed; refer to Figure-31.

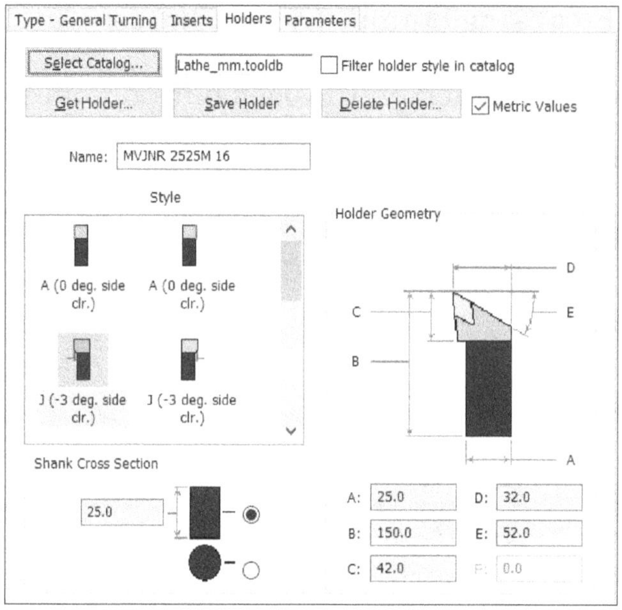

Figure-31. Parameters for selected tool holder

- Specify desired parameters in the dialog box to specify the shape and size of the tool holder. Note that you need to specify the parameters as per the insert used for cutting.

Parameters tab

- Click on the **Parameters** tab to specify the cutting parameters of the tool. The **Define Tool** dialog box will be displayed as shown in Figure-32.

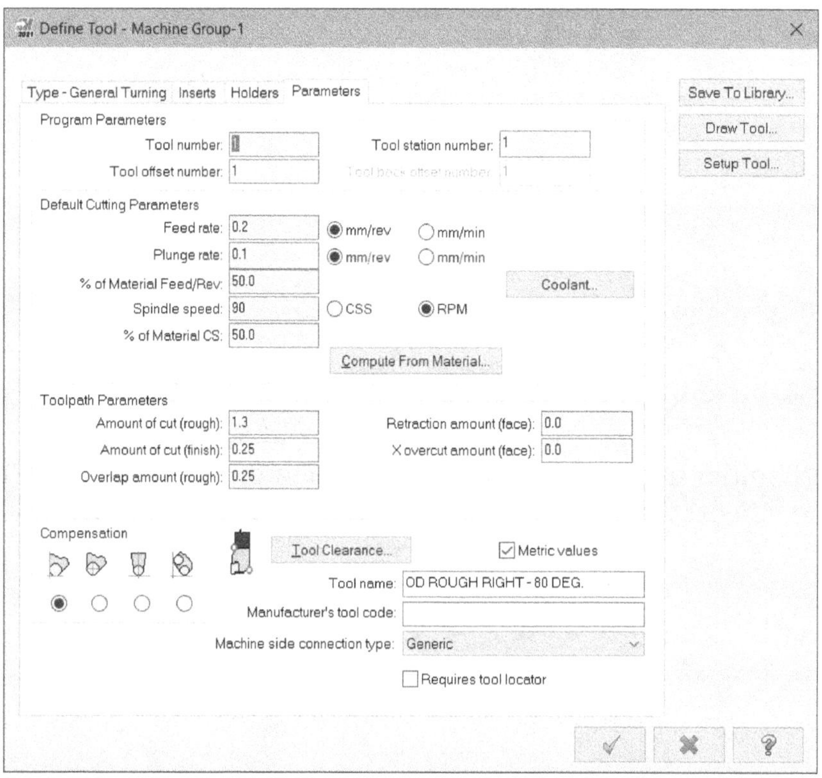

Figure-32. Define Tool dialog box with tool parameters

- Specify the parameters as per the requirement and click on the **OK** button from the dialog box. The **Tool Manager** dialog box will be displayed again.
- After adding desired tools, click on the **OK** button from the dialog box.

CREATING TURN PROFILE

The turn profile is used to define shape of part to be machined using turning toolpaths. For performing turning operations, we need wireframe curves to be followed by cutting tool. The procedure to create turning profile is given next.

- Open the **Plane Manager** and select the plane which splits part into two; refer to Figure-33.
- Click in the fields under column C, T, and WCS next to the plane to set this plane as construction plane, tool plane, and world coordinate system.

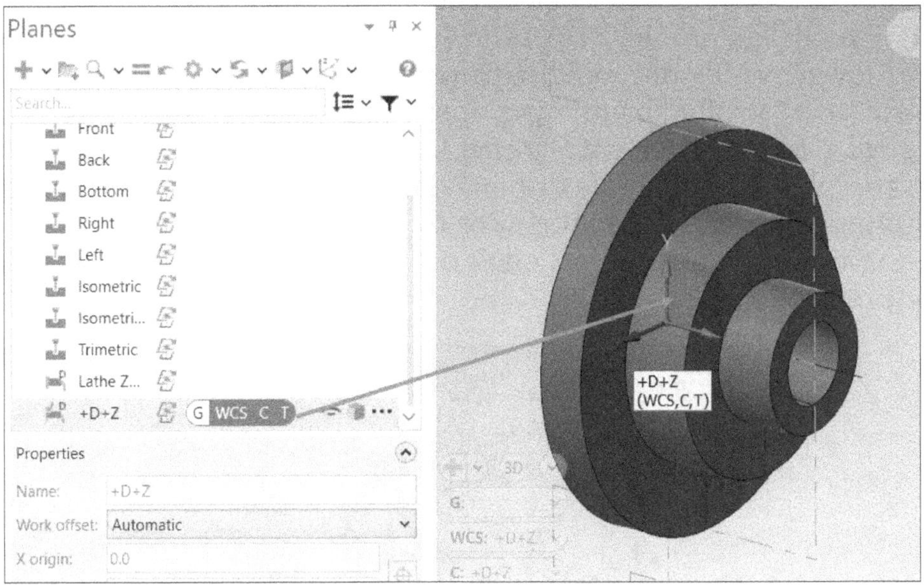

Figure-33. Front plane selected

- Click on the **Turn Profile** tool from the **Shapes** panel in the **Wireframe** tab of the **Ribbon**. The **Turn Profile Manager** will be displayed; refer to Figure-34.

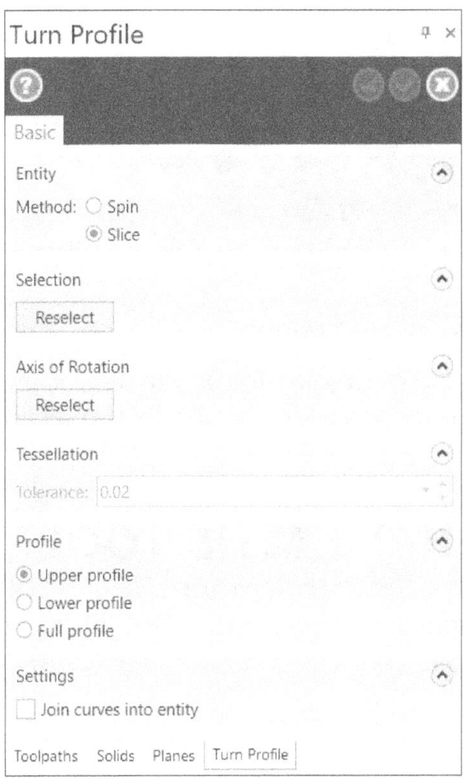

Figure-34. Turn Profile Manager

- Select the **Spin** radio button to create profile of solid body by revolving it about selected axis. Note that when this option is selected then undercuts are not included in the profile. Select the **Slice** radio button to create a profile by using section plane. The profile will be created at intersection of plane and part. Note that the plane used for slicing is currently selected as construction plane.
- Click on the **Reselect** button from **Axis of Rotation** rollout to define axis of rotation for spinning the model to generate profile.
- Select desired radio button from the **Profile** rollout to define which portion of part will be generated as profile. Select the **Upper profile** radio button to generate upper half of model as profile. Select the **Lower profile** radio button to generate lower half of model as profile. Select the **Full profile** radio button to generate both upper and lower profile of model with respect to construction plane. Generally, we generate lower profile for turning operations.
- Select the **Join curves into entity** check box to join all the individually generated curves in the profile as a single curve. Note that using this check box can cause irregular shaped splines, so make sure to check the preview.
- After setting desired parameters, click on the **OK** button. The turn profile will be generated; refer to Figure-35.

Figure-35. Turn profile generated

Note that we will use this turn profile for various toolpaths generated for turning operations. Note that you can also use tools in **Wireframe** tab of **Ribbon** to create desired profile.

GENERAL LATHE TOOLPATHS

The tools to perform various lathe operations are available in the **General** panel of **Turning** tab in the **Ribbon**; refer to Figure-36. The procedures to create various toolpaths are discussed next.

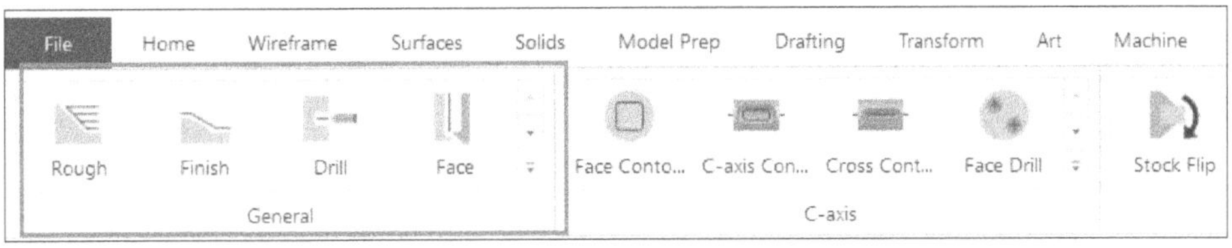

Figure-36. General panel

CREATING ROUGH MACHINING TOOLPATH

The rough turning operation is performed to remove large stock of material from the part. The procedure to create rough turning operation is given next.

- After creating stock of the part and generating turn profile, click on the **Rough** tool from the **General** panel in the **Turning** tab of the **Ribbon**. The **Wireframe Chaining** dialog box will be displayed as discussed earlier.
- Select desired wireframe chain to be used for turning operation; refer to Figure-37.

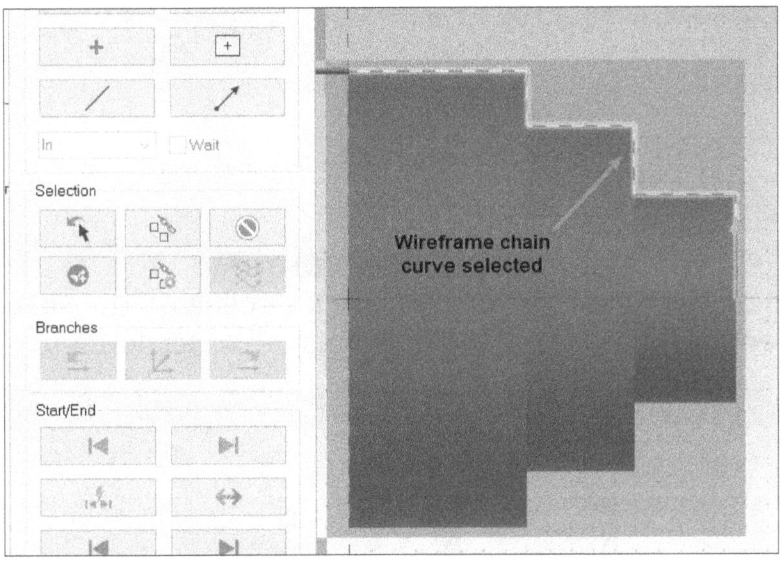

Figure-37. Wireframe chain selected for rough machining

- After selecting desired chain, click on the **OK** button from the **Wireframe Chaining** dialog box. The **Lathe Rough** dialog box will be displayed; refer to Figure-38.

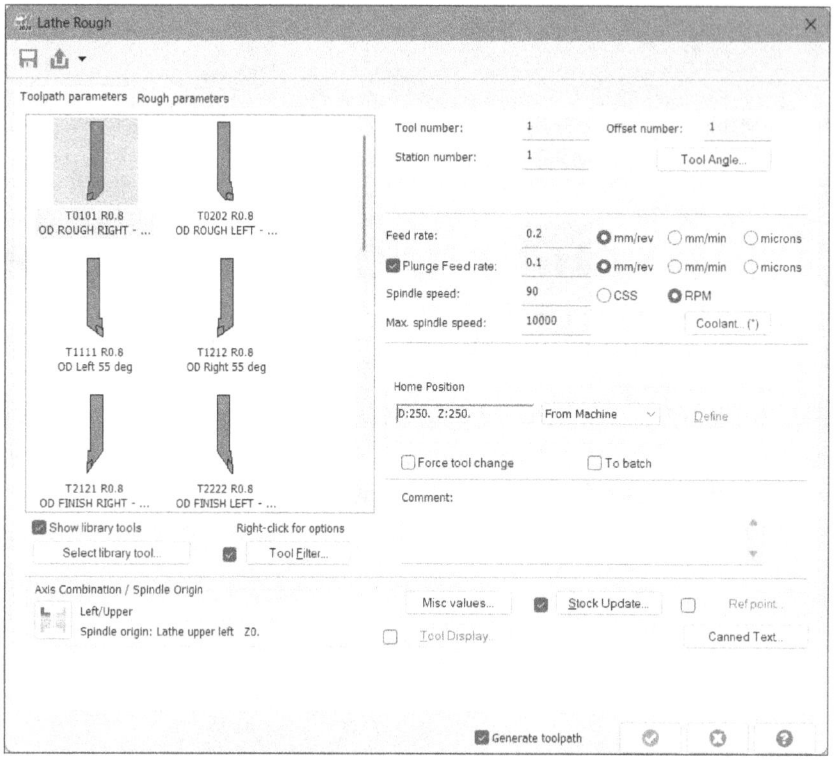

Figure-38. Lathe Rough dialog box

Toolpath parameters

- Select desired tool from the list box in the left or click on the **Select library** tool, the **Tool Selection** dialog box will be displayed; refer to Figure-39.

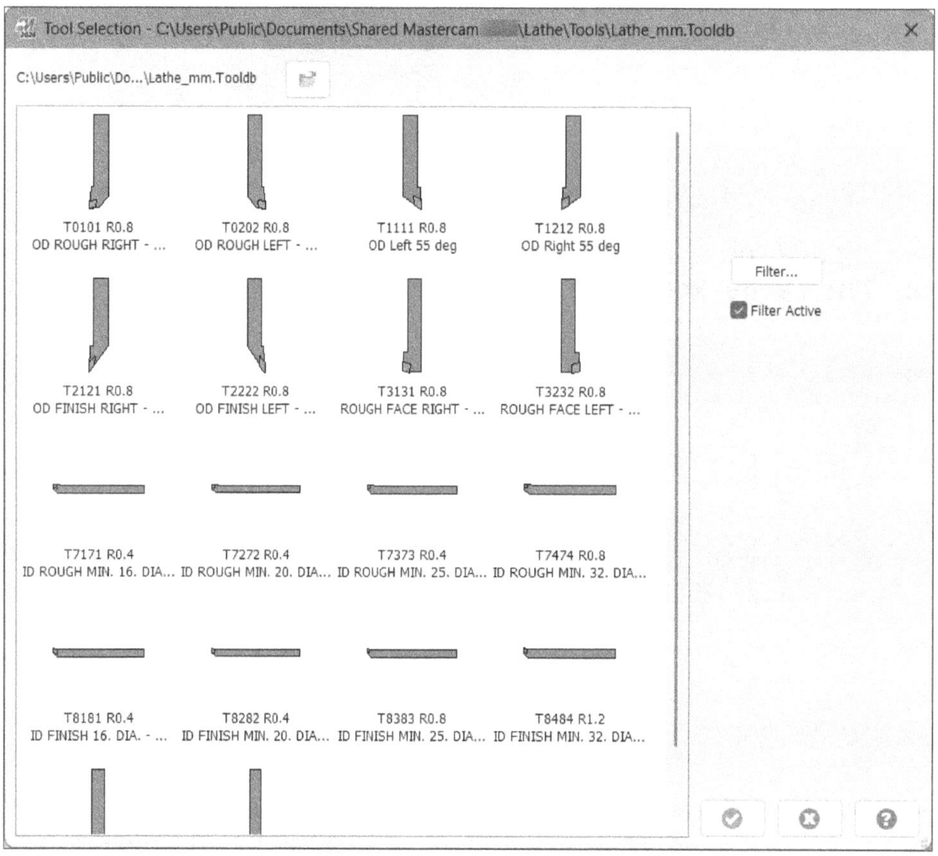

Figure-39. Tool Selection dialog box

- Select desired tool to add it in the list box and click on the **OK** button.
- Now, select the tool from the list box in the **Lathe Rough Properties** dialog box. The respective feed rate and speed parameters will be displayed at the right in the dialog box.
- Specify desired parameters at the right area in the dialog box. These parameters are discussed next.

Tool number, Offset Number, and Station Number

As the name suggests, these are the numbers that correspond to specific entities. The **Tool number** edit box of this dialog box is used to specify the tool number according to the turret. If this number is specified wrong then a wrong tool will be used in the machining as per the NC program.

The **Offset number** edit box is used to set an offset number for the tools that wear by same amount. For example, you have two tools that wear by same amount then to compensate for the wear, you need to specify the offset number for the tools. This offset number is linked to values in X and Z coordinates that positions the tool accordingly for machining.

The **Station number** edit box is used to set the station number of the tool. A machine can have multiple station of tools (turrets). For example, a machine can have a tools turret system instead of tail stock and a general tool turret. In such cases, we need to specify the station numbers.

Tool Angle

The **Tool Angle** button is used to change the angle of the tool for machining. This button is active in case of milling operations. For Lathe tools, the similar function regarding the angle is discussed later.

Feed Rate

The **Feed rate** options are used to specify the speed by which the tool will move while cutting material. Select desired radio button to specify the unit and specify the speed in edit box.

Plunge Feed rate

The **Plunge feed rate** options are used to specify the speed by which the tool will be plunged in the workpiece. Select desired radio button to specify the unit and specify the speed in edit box.

Spindle Speed

The **Spindle Speed** option is used to specify the spindle rotation speed while performing cutting operations. It can be specified in constant surface speed(CSS) or rounds per minute (RPM).

Home Position

- Click on the **Define** button in the **Home Position** area of the dialog box to define the home position of the tool if **User define** option is selected in the drop-down. The **Home Position - User Defined** dialog box will be displayed; refer to Figure-40.

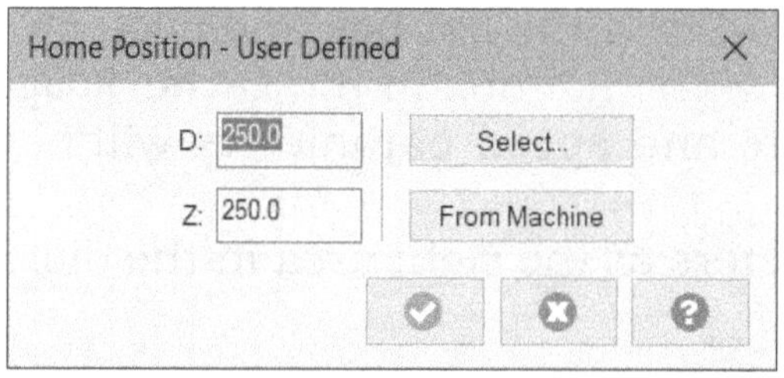

Figure-40. Home Position User Defined dialog box

- Specify desired values or use the **Select** button to specify the position.
- Click on the **OK** button from the **Home Position - User Defined** dialog box.
- To set the angle of tool in lathe, click on the **Tool Angle** button from the dialog box. The **Tool Angle** dialog box will be displayed; refer to Figure-41.
- Set desired direction of tool using the options and click on the **OK** button from the dialog box. Note that the angle specified in **Tool Orientation on Machine** area of the dialog box is used to specify the angle of tool about its own axis. You can use this option if your machine allows to place tool at rotated position.

Rough parameters

- Click on the **Rough parameters** tab to display the parameters related to cutting. Refer to Figure-42.

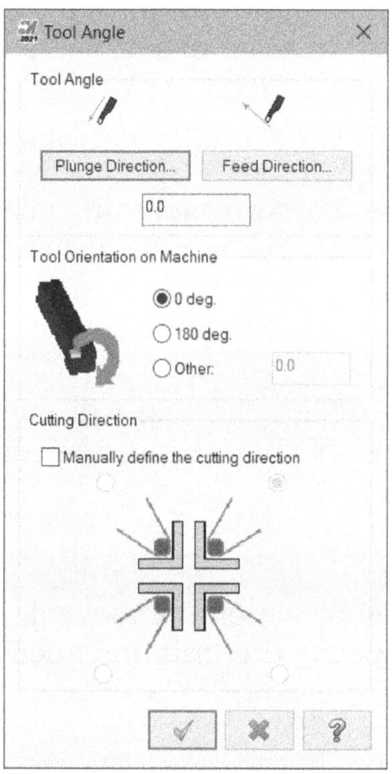

Figure-41. Tool Angle dialog box

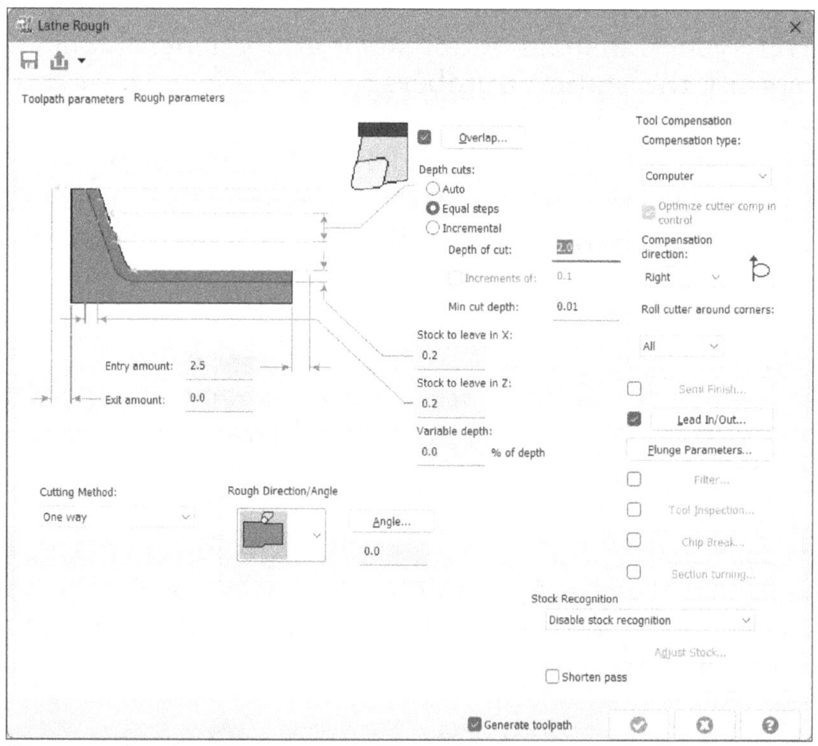

Figure-42. Rough parameters tab of Lathe Rough Properties dialog box

- Select desired cutting method from the **Cutting Method** drop-down. Figure-43 shows difference between various cutting methodologies available in the drop-down.
- Select the direction of roughing from the drop-down in the **Rough Direction/ Angle** area of the dialog box; refer to Figure-44. Set the tool cutting edge angle in the **Angle** edit box of this area.
- Specify the data related to cutting like; Depth of cut, minimum cut depth, cutting method, and so on.

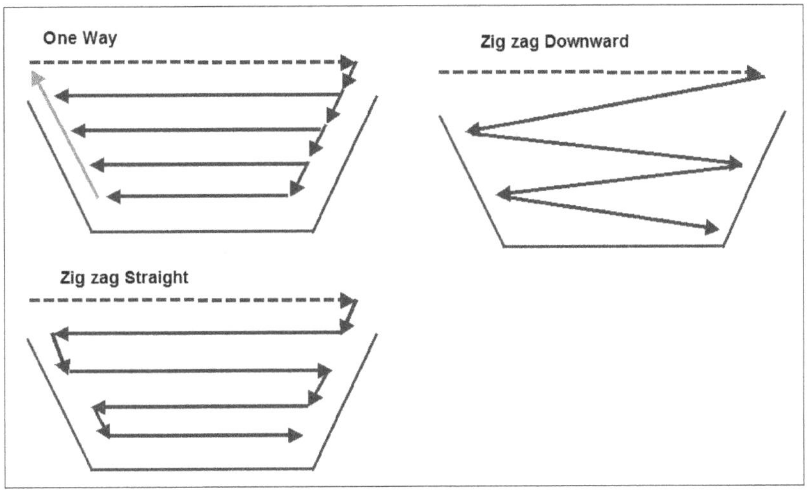

Figure-43. Cutting Methods on lathe

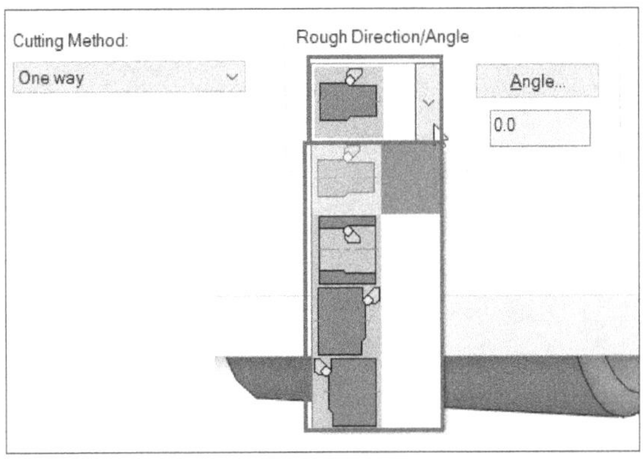

Figure-44. Rough Direction drop-down

Tool Compensation

- The options in the **Tool Compensation** area are used to adjust toolpath to allow for the cutting tool's radius. When we perform machining by a cutting tool, its cutting edge gets worn. To compensate for this wear, we apply tool compensation. Select desired option from the **Compensation type** drop-down in the dialog box. If you select the **Computer** option then tool compensation will be added in the coordinates of NC program by Mastercam but G41/G42 codes will not be generated and hence you will not be able to control compensation by machine panel. If you select the **Control** option then G41/G42 codes will be generated in the NC program and you will be able to control tool compensation using the machine panel. If you select the **Wear** option then Mastercam will calculate the compensated tool positions as if **Computer** is selected, but it will also outputs the G41/G42 codes. This lets the operator adjust for tool wear at the control panel also. If you select the **Reverse Wear** option then it will work in the same way as **Wear** option but you need to enter the positive compensation value in place of negative value. If you select the **Off** option then Mastercam will neither apply compensation in NC program nor it will create G41/G42 codes.
- Select the tool compensation direction from the **Compensation direction** drop-down in the **Tool Compensation** area of the dialog box. Select desired option from the **Roll cutter around corners** drop-down to define shape at corners.

Semi Finish Options

- Select the **Semi Finish** check box if you want to apply extra cutting pass for semi finishing the component during roughing. Click on the **Semi Finish** button after selecting the check box. The **Semi Finish Parameters** dialog box will be displayed; refer to Figure-45. Specify the parameters like number of semi-finishing passes, stepover, stock to be left in X direction, and stock to be left in Z direction.
- Specify the feed rate and spindle speed parameters as discussed earlier. Click on the **OK** button from the dialog box to apply the parameters.

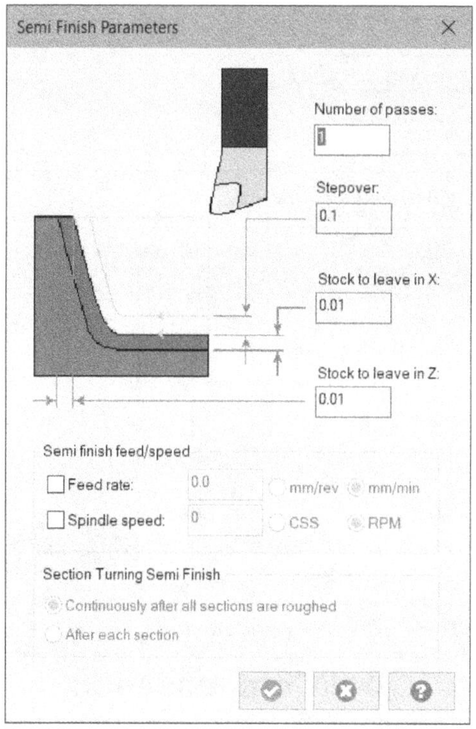

Figure-45. Semi Finish Parameters dialog box

Lead In/Out Options

- To specify the parameters related to entry and exit of tool in cutting toolpath, select the **Lead In/Out** check box and click on the **Lead In/Out** button. The **Lead In/Out** dialog box will be displayed; refer to Figure-46.

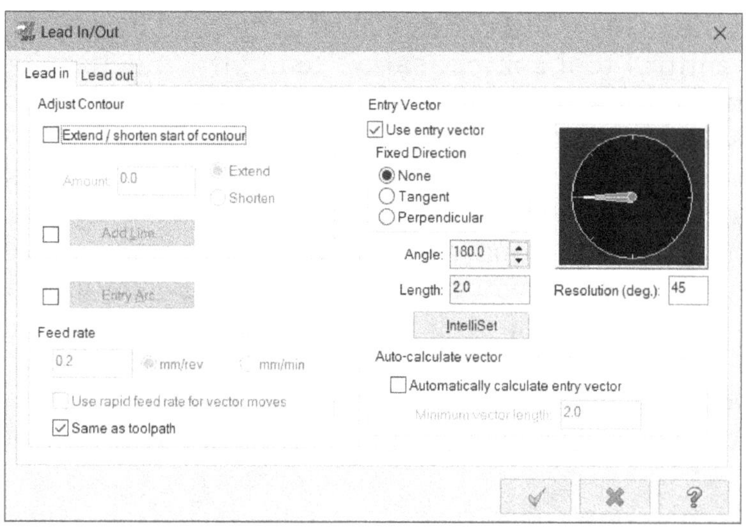

Figure-46. Lead In/Out dialog box

- Select the **Extend/shorten start of contour** check box if you want to specify desired value of extension or shortening in the contour when tool is entering the workpiece. After selecting check box, select the **Extend** or **Shorten** radio button and specify desired value.
- If you want to add a straight line to the cutting toolpath at beginning then select the check box before **Add Line** button and then click on the **Add Line** button. The **New Contour Line** dialog box will be displayed; refer to Figure-47. Specify the length of line and angle in the respective edit boxes and click on the **OK** button. Note that you can specify the same value in **Angle** and **Length** edit boxes of the **Entry Vector** area of the dialog box. If you want to use tangential or perpendicular direction of the toolpath to add **Lead In** then select the respective radio button from the **Entry Vector** area.

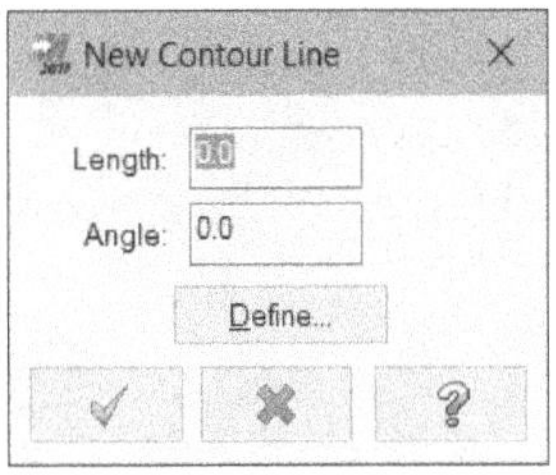

Figure-47. New Contour Line dialog box

- Similarly, you can set arc lead in by selecting the **Entry Arc** check box and clicking on the **Entry Arc** button.
- You can let Mastercam decide the **Lead In** for you by selecting the **Automatically calculate entry vector** check box from the **Auto-Calculate vector** area of the dialog box. Specify the minimum vector length in the next edit box. Note that on selecting this option, Mastercam calculates entry or exit vectors based on the stock, chuck, and tailstock information, along with related parameter values, and calculates entry and/or exit vectors that begin outside the stock boundary and end at the start/finish of the toolpath.
- To specify the parameters for lead out, click on the **Lead Out** tab of the dialog box. The parameters in this tab are same as discussed for **Lead In** tab. Click on the **OK** button to apply lead in/out.

Plunge Parameters

Plunge parameters are used to define the method by which tool will plunge in the workpiece.

- Click on the **Plunge Parameters** button from the dialog box. The **Plunge Cut Parameters** dialog box will be displayed as shown in Figure-48.

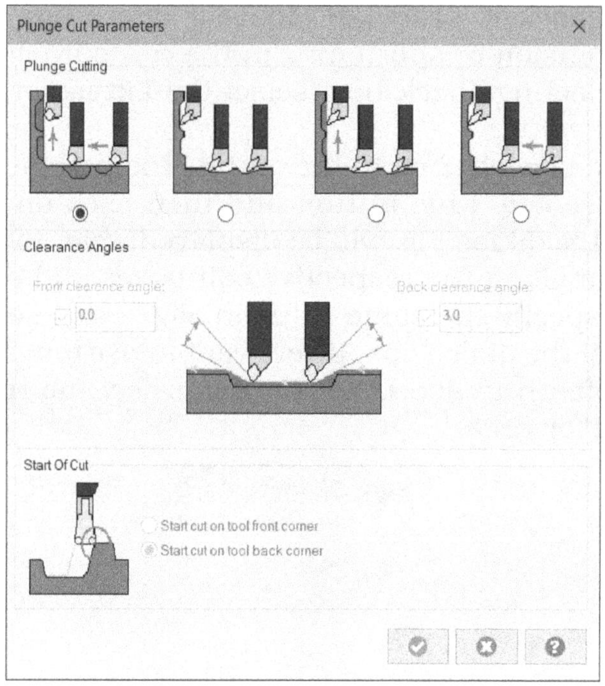

Figure-48. Plunge Cut Parameters dialog box

- Select desired radio button to specify plunging criteria and set required values for them in respective edit boxes. Click on the **OK** button from the dialog box.
- Similarly, you can use **Filter**, **Tool Inspection**, **Chip Break**, and **Section Turning** options.

Stock Recognition Options

Stock Recognition drop-down lets you choose from three options that control how the stock boundary is used for computing the toolpath. These options are available only if all of the following conditions are true:

- Only one contour is chained.
- Stock for the current active spindle is defined in the Stock Setup.
- The chained contour lies at least partially within the stock boundary.

There are three options which let you decide how Mastercam will use the stock boundary to compute the toolpath:

- **Use stock for outer boundary** - The stock is used as the outer boundary for roughing. If the ends of the chained contour lie within the stock, the chain is linearly extended to the stock using the parameters set on the **Adjust Stock toolbar** (Displayed on clicking **Adjust Stock** button; refer to Figure-49). This eliminates the need to create the (usually vertical) line added to the end of the inner-chained boundary to indicate the height of the stock.

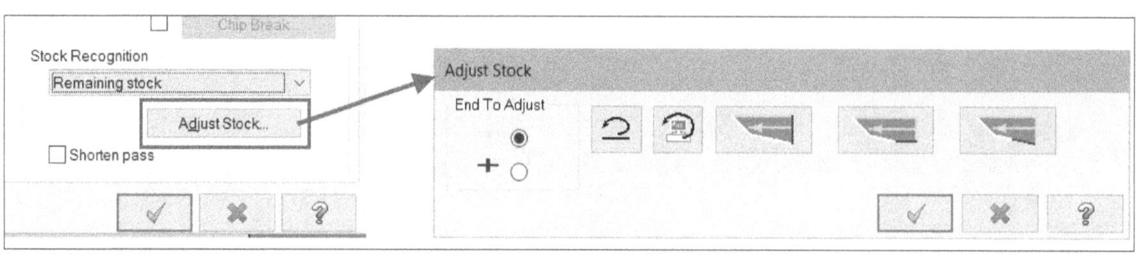

Figure-49. Adjust Stock toolbar

- **Extend contour to stock only** - The chained contour is linearly extended to the stock using the parameters set using the **Adjust Stock** toolbar if the endpoints are inside the stock boundary.
- **Remaining stock** - Uses only stock remaining from previous operations.
- **Disable stock recognition** - The roughing toolpath is computed as if the stock does not exist. You must chain the outer boundary for roughing between boundaries.

The first two options eliminate the need to chain the outer boundary for roughing between boundaries since Mastercam determines the stock to be removed.

You should select **Extend contour to stock** only for zigzag roughing of pocket/ groove geometry. If you are using zigzag rough to remove stock, you should select **Use stock for outer boundary**.

When stock recognition is enabled, the following things happen:

- The chained contour is linearly extended to the stock boundary using the methods selected on the **Adjust Stock toolbar**.
- If no entry amount is set and no lead-in parameters are defined, the chained contour is extended past the stock boundary by the entry/exit tool clearance defined in **Stock Setup**. Mastercam also adds the tool nose radius to this amount if it is required.
- When roughing a depression, such as in zigzag roughing, and no lead-in parameters are defined and extend contour is disabled for the lead out, the chained contour is extended past the stock boundary by the entry/exit tool clearance defined in **Stock Setup**. The software also adds the tool nose radius to this amount if it is required.

Note: For finish toolpaths, canned rough, and pattern repeat toolpaths, the only option is **Extend contour to stock**.

- Click on the **OK** button from the dialog box to apply the specified parameters. Preview of the toolpath will be displayed; refer to Figure-50. If the specified parameters are incorrect, then the **Click OK or Cancel to continue PropertyManager** will be displayed if tool is colliding with jaws or stock directly. Apply the changes accordingly to rectify error.

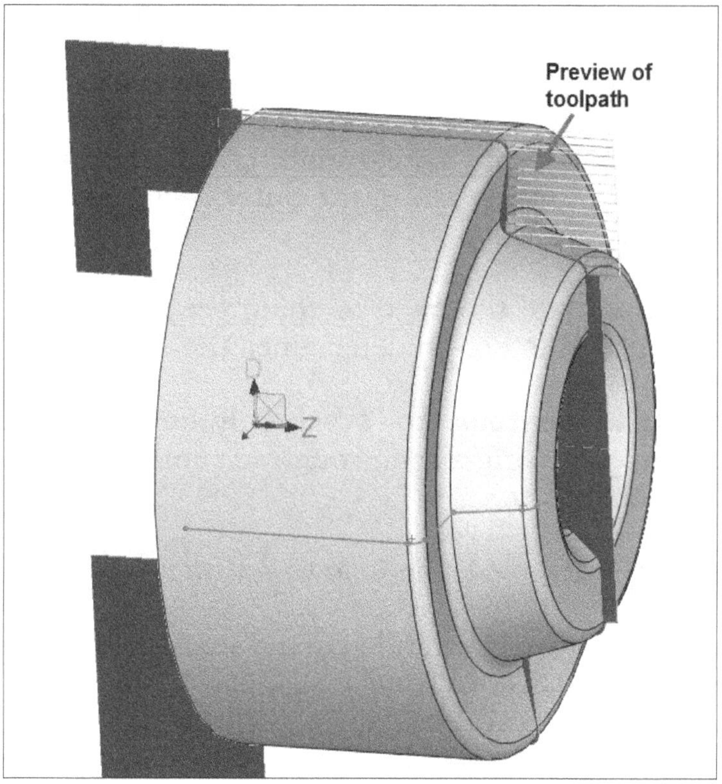

Figure-50. Preview of rough toolpath

FINISH TOOLPATH ON LATHE

The **Finish** tool in the **General** panel of **Turning** tab in the **Ribbon** is used to machine the stock left on the workpiece. The procedure to use this tool is given next.

- Click on the **Finish** tool from the **General** panel in the **Turning** tab of **Ribbon**. The **Wireframe Chaining** dialog box will be displayed as discussed earlier.
- Select the sketch or faces that you earlier selected for rough cutting and click on the **OK** button from the **Wireframe Chaining** dialog box. The **Lathe Finish** dialog box will be displayed similar to **Lathe Rough** dialog box; refer to Figure-51.

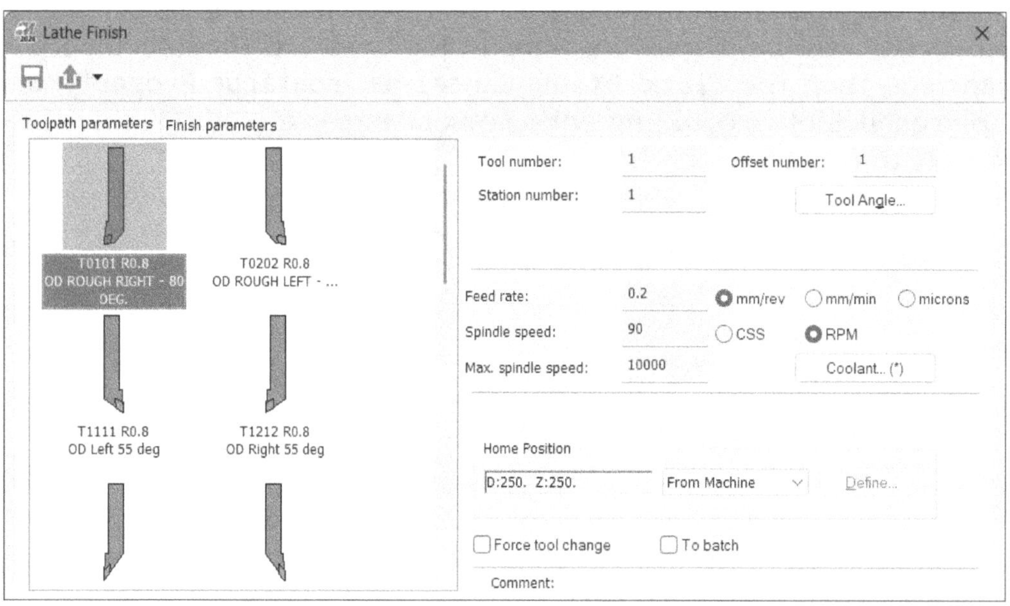

Figure-51. Lathe Finish dialog box

- Select desired tool and specify the related parameters.
- Click on the **Finish parameters** tab and make sure the stock to leave in X and Z directions is **0**.
- Click on the **OK** button from the dialog box. The toolpath will be created.

LATHE DRILL

The **Drill** tool is used to generate toolpaths for drilling holes in the workpiece. The procedure to use this tool is given next.

- Click on the **Drill** tool from the **General** panel in the **Turning** tab of the **Ribbon**. The **Lathe Drill** dialog box will be displayed; refer to Figure-52.
- Select desired drill and specify the related parameters for drilling.
- Click on the **Simple drill-no peck** tab. The dialog box will be displayed as shown in Figure-53.

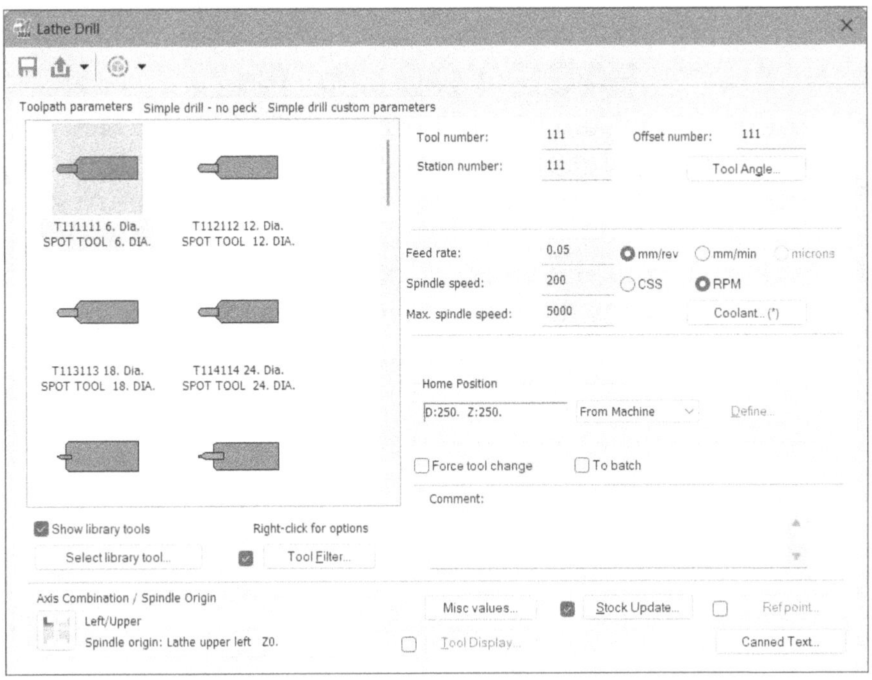

Figure-52. Lathe Drill dialog box

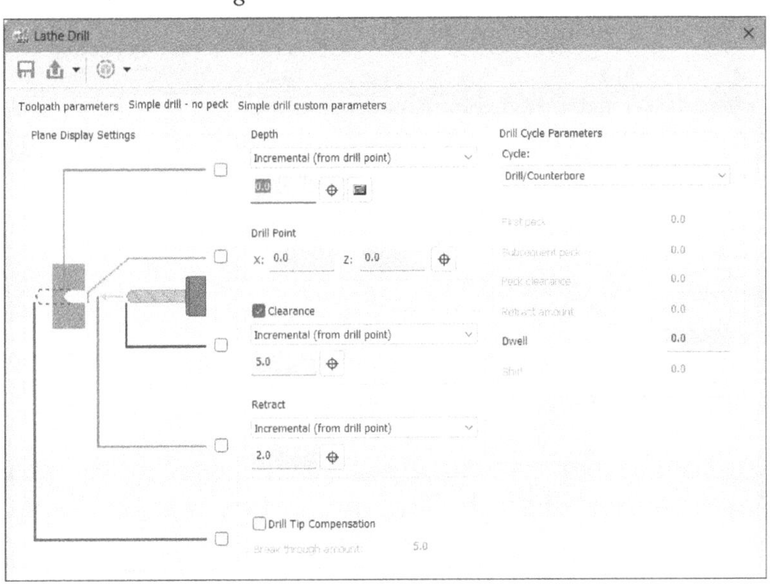

Figure-53. Simple drill page of Lathe Drill Properties dialog box

- Click on the **Drill Point** button and specify the starting point of the drill.
- Click in the edit box next to **Depth** button and specify desired value of depth for the drilling or click on the **Depth** button and select a point up to which you want to drill the hole.
- Specify the tool clearance value in the **Clearance** edit box and retraction distance in the **Retract** edit box.
- If you want to create a peck drill cycle, chip break cycle, or any other drilling cycle then click in the **Cycle** drop-down and select the respective option. The related parameters in the **Drill Cycle Parameters** area of the dialog box will become active. Set desired values in edit boxes of this area.
- If you want to specify any custom parameter for drill then click on the **Simple drill custom parameters** tab and specify the parameters. Note that the name of this tab will change based on the option selected in the **Cycle** drop-down of previous tab.
- Click on the **OK** button from the dialog box. The drilling toolpath will be created.

FACE TOOLPATH

The facing toolpaths are generated to remove material from the face of the workpiece. In any machining sequence, this is generally the first toolpath to be generated for flat head work-pieces. The steps to generate the face toolpath are given next.

- Click on the **Face** tool from the **General** panel in the **Turning** tab of the **Ribbon**. The **Lathe Face** dialog box will be displayed; refer to Figure-54.

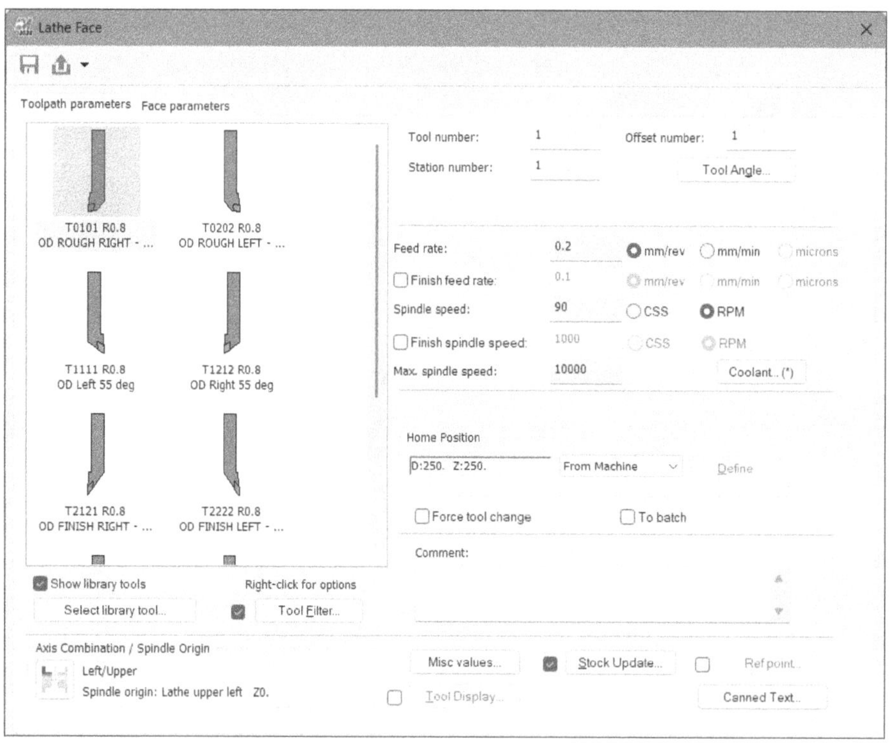

Figure-54. Lathe Face dialog box

- Select the facing tool as per the requirement and specify the related parameters.
- Click on the **Face parameters** tab. The dialog box will be displayed as shown in Figure-55.

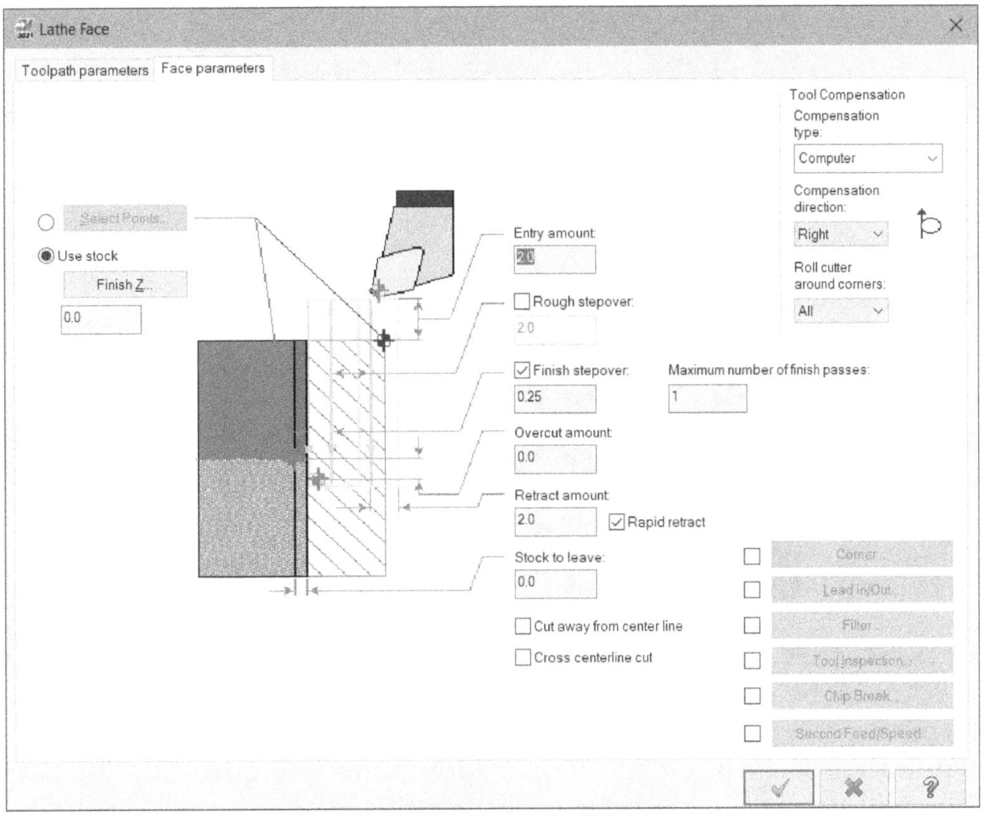

Figure-55. Face parameters page of Lathe Face Properties dialog box

- Specify the parameters related to material to be removed.
- Click on the **Finish Z** button to specify the depth to which the material is to be removed from the face and then select the edge of the model up to which you want the material to be removed from the stock; refer to Figure-56.

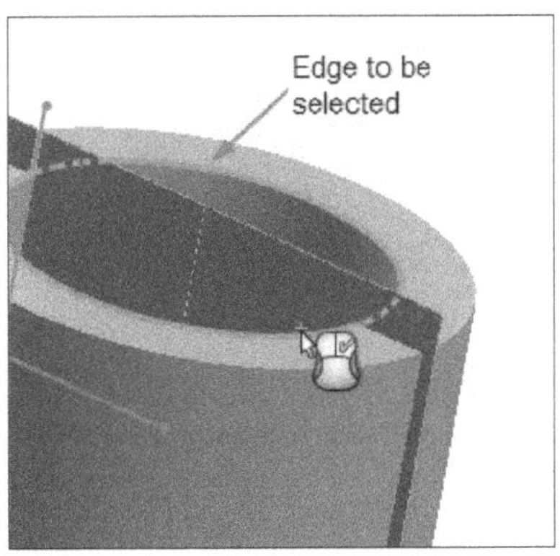

Figure-56. Edge to be selected

- Click on the **OK** button from the dialog box. Simulation of cutting will run and the tool path will be created.

LATHE CUTOFF TOOLPATH

We generate the Lathe Cutoff toolpath to cut the stock in two parts; refer to Figure-57. The procedure to generate this tool path is given next.

Figure-57. Cut off operation

- Click on the **Cutoff** tool from the expanded **General** panel in **Turning** tab of the **Ribbon**. You will be asked to select a point from where the cutoff operation is to be performed.
- Select a point for performing cutoff operation; refer to Figure-58. The **Lathe Cutoff** dialog box will be displayed; refer to Figure-59.

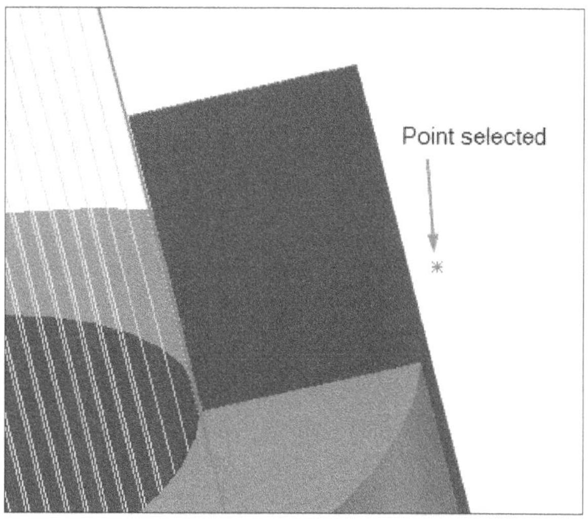

Figure-58. Point selected for cutoff

- Select the cutoff tool (OD CUTOFF Tool in our case) from the tool list box and specify the related parameters in the dialog box.
- Set desired parameters in the **Cutoff parameters** tab of the dialog box like retract radius, corner geometry, tool compensation etc.
- Click on the **OK** button from the dialog box. The simulation of cutoff operation will run and the output will be displayed; refer to Figure-60.

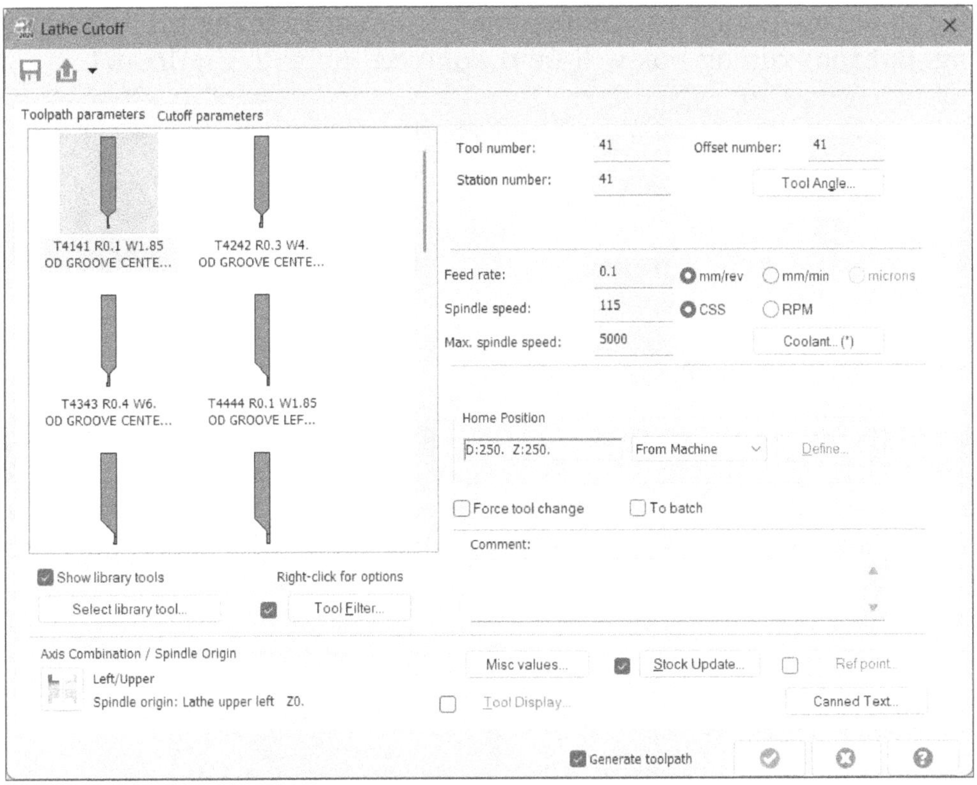

Figure-59. Lathe Cutoff Properties dialog box

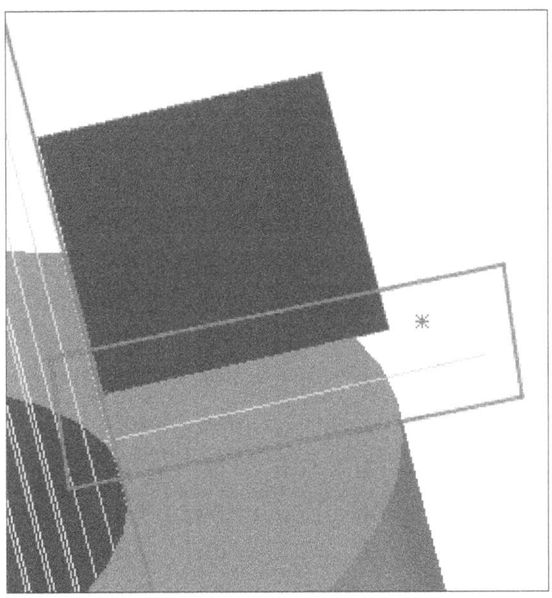

Figure-60. Output of cutoff operation

GROOVE TOOLPATH

The next toolpath that can be created on lathe is Groove. The **Groove** tool is used to create groove toolpaths in the workpiece. The procedure to use this tool is given next.

- Click on the **Groove** tool from the **General** panel of **Turning** tab in the **Ribbon**. The **Grooving Options** dialog box will be displayed; refer to Figure-61.

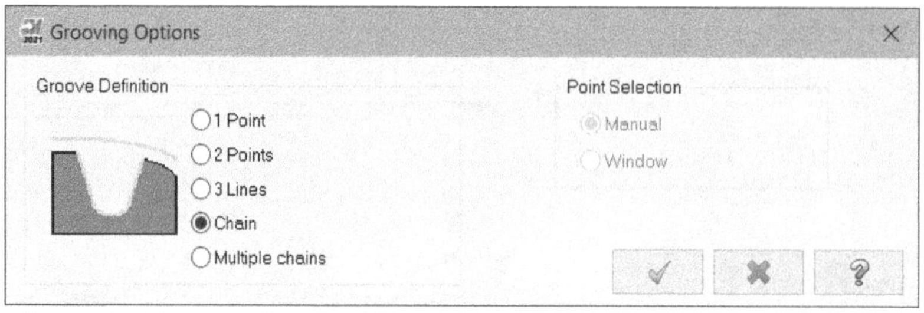

Figure-61. Grooving Options dialog box

- Select desired radio button from the dialog box and then click on the **OK** button from it. Note that if you select the **Multiple chains** radio button in the dialog box then you can select multiple grooves to generate toolpaths; refer to Figure-62. The **Wireframe Chaining** dialog box will be displayed as discussed earlier.

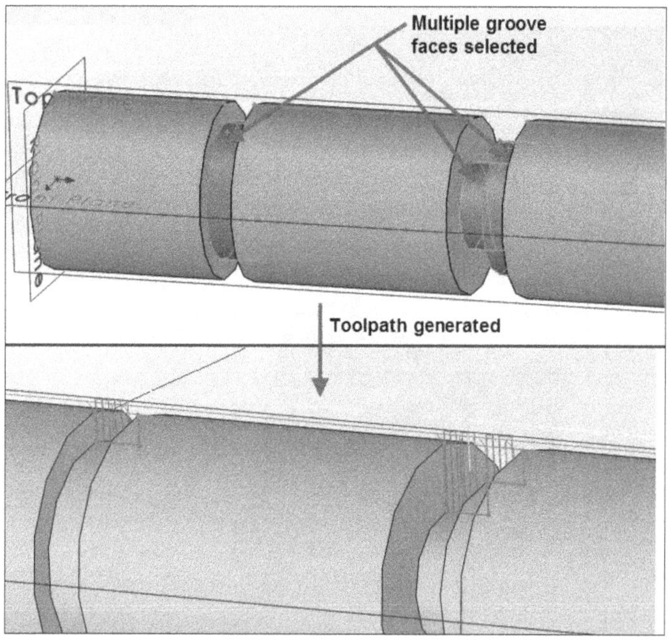

Figure-62. Multiple faces selected for groove toolpath

- Select desired entities and then click on the **OK** button from the dialog box. The **Lathe Groove** dialog box will be displayed, refer to Figure-63.

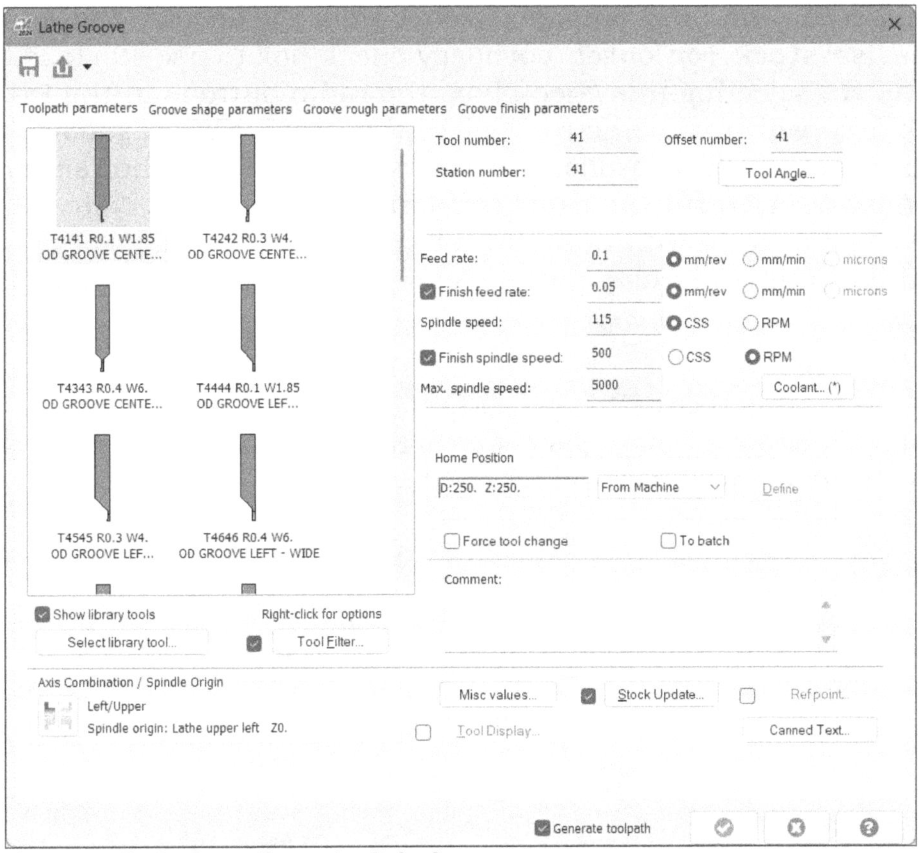

Figure-63. Lathe Groove Properties dialog box

- Select desired tool and specify the related parameters in the **Toolpath parameters** tab of the dialog box.

Groove shape parameters tab

- Click on the **Groove shape parameters** tab to specify parameters related to groove shape; refer to Figure-64 if 1 Point, 2 Points, or 3 Lines option is selected in the **Grooving Options** dialog box earlier. Otherwise, options to define shape/radius of groove will not be displayed in the dialog box.

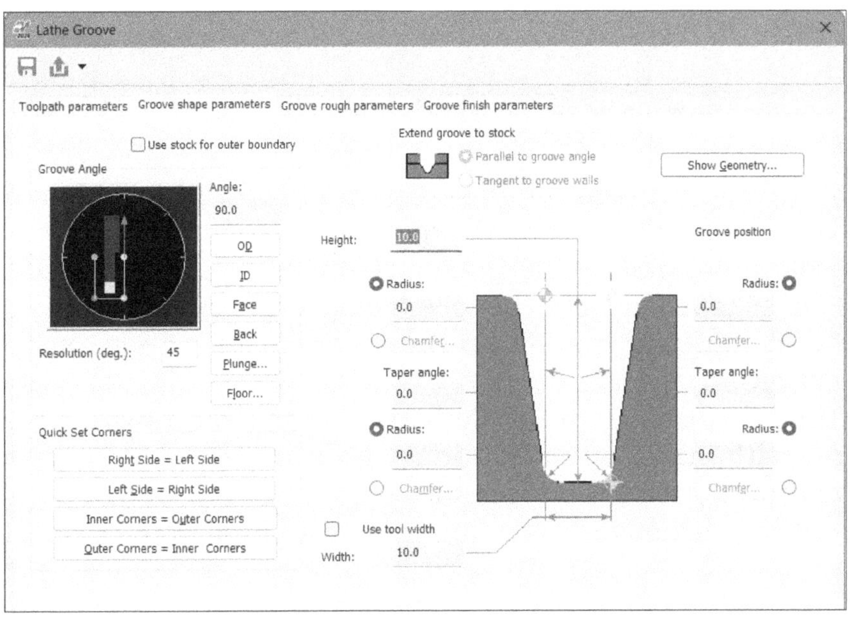

Figure-64. Groove shape parameters tab

- Select desired button to set angle of groove from the **Groove Angle** area.
- Select the **Use stock for outer boundary** check box to use stock as boundary of the groove. On selecting this check box, the radio buttons in the **Extend groove to stock** area will become active. Select the **Parallel to groove angle** radio button to cut the stock in parallel direction to groove. Select the **Tangent to groove walls** radio button to cut the stock tangent to groove walls. Note that preview of the groove is displayed with radio button in the dialog box.
- Specify the radius and angle parameters of groove in related edit boxes of the dialog box.

Groove rough parameters tab

The options in the **Groove rough parameters** tab are used to specify the parameters for roughing of the groove; refer to Figure-65.

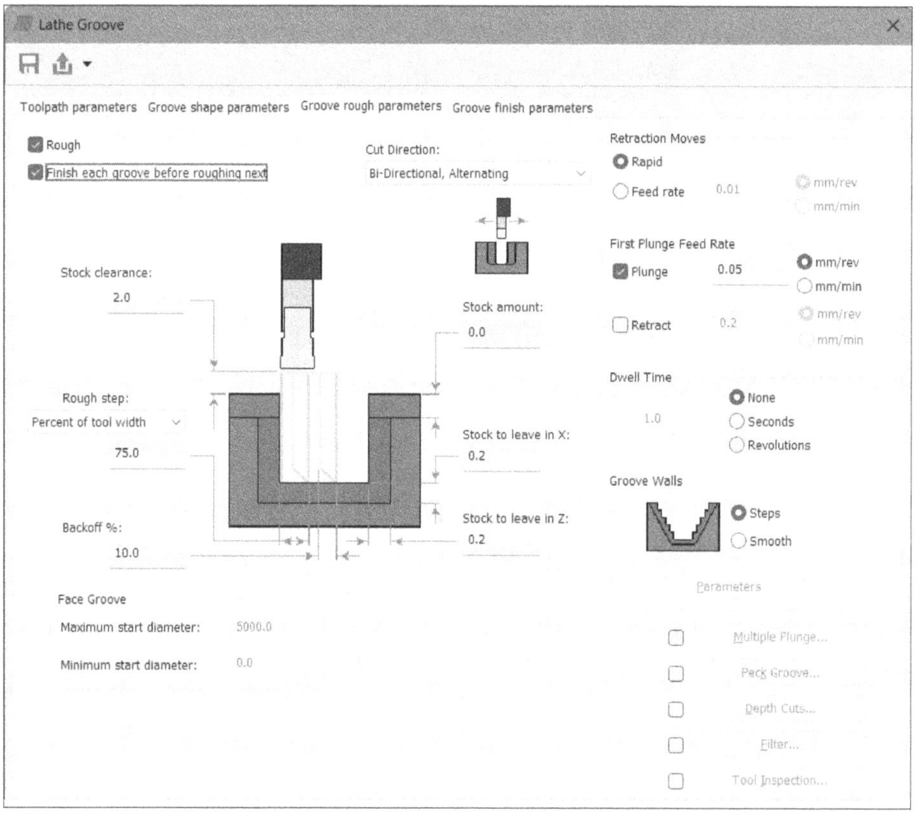

Figure-65. Groove rough parameters tab

- If you do not want to perform roughing operations for groove then clear the **Rough** check box, all the options in the tab will become inactive.
- To perform roughing, make sure the **Rough** check box is selected.
- Select the **Finish each groove before roughing next** check box to make sure one groove is completely machined by roughing operation before cutting tool moves to next groove.
- Set the cutting direction from the **Cut Direction** drop-down. Chain direction is available only with inner/outer boundary grooves. For canned groove toolpaths, only positive and negative are available.
- Specify the cutting parameters as required for roughing in the respective edit boxes.

Groove finish parameters tab

The options in the **Groove finish parameters** tab are used to specify parameters related to finishing groove; refer to Figure-66.

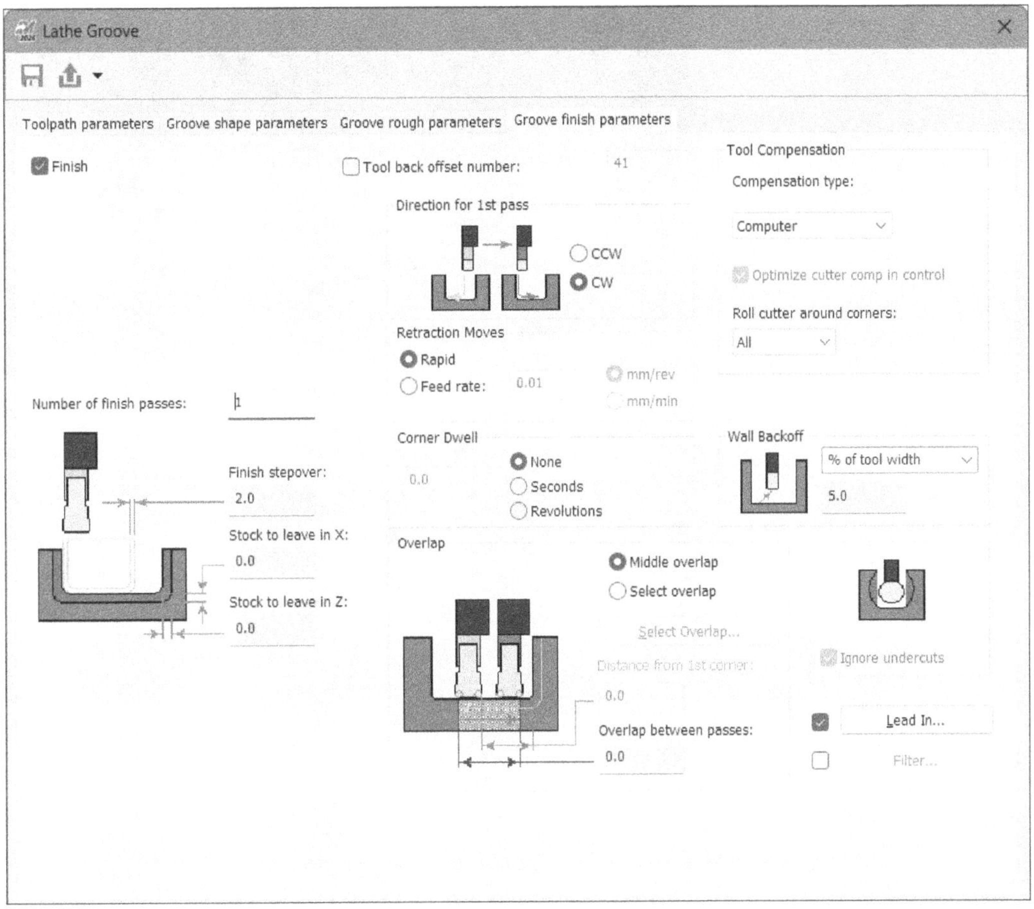

Figure-66. Groove finish parameters tab

- Clear the **Finish** check box from the tab if you do not want to perform finishing cut otherwise specify the finishing parameters as required in respective edit boxes.
- Make sure you specify correct lead in for finishing pass using the **Lead In** button in the dialog box.
- Click on the **OK** button, the tool path will be created automatically.

DYNAMIC ROUGH TOOLPATH

The dynamic rough toolpath is designed to cut hard materials with button inserts (i.e. radius or ball). The dynamic motion allows the toolpath to cut gradually, remain engaged in the material more effectively, and use maximum cutting surface of your insert, while extending the tool life and increasing the cutting speed. Note that you should use the **Rough** tool and **Face** tool before using the **Dynamic Rough** tool if there are grooves left in the dynamic rough toolpath then tool can collide with stock; refer to Figure-67. The steps to create this toolpath are given next.

- Click on the **Dynamic Rough** tool from the **General** panel in the **Turning** tab of the **Ribbon**. The **Wireframe Chaining** dialog box will be displayed as discussed earlier. Select the faces/lines/sketch for toolpath; refer to Figure-68.

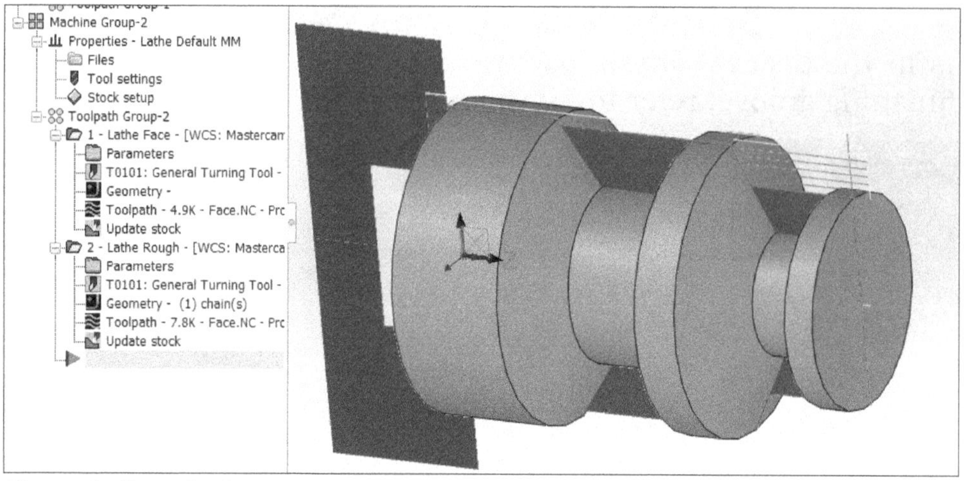

Figure-67. Part after facing and rough machining

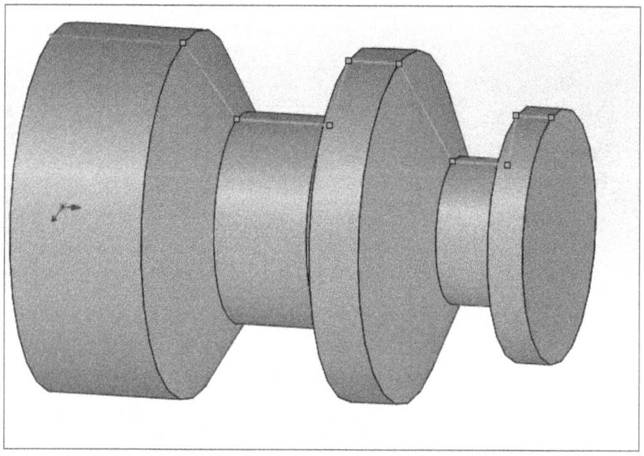

Figure-68. Sketch selected for dynamic rough machining

- Click on the **OK** button from the **Wireframe Chaining** dialog box. The **Lathe Dynamic Rough** dialog box will be displayed; refer to Figure-69.

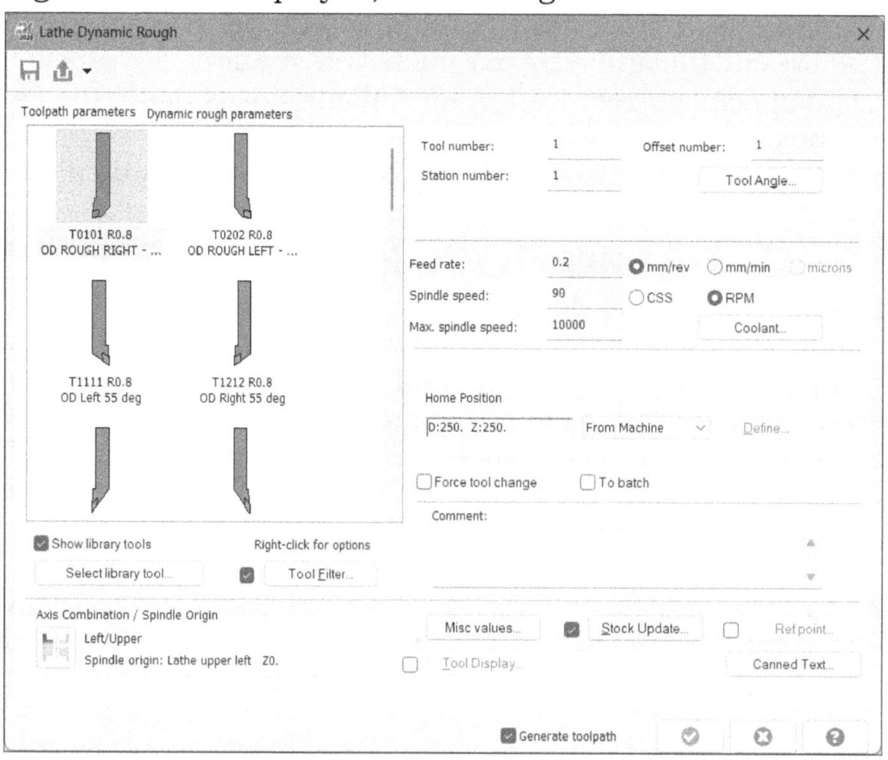

Figure-69. Lathe Dynamic Rough dialog box

- Select a tool that has Button insert (Round or Ball shaped) from the tool list. Specify the other parameters as discussed earlier in the **Toolpath parameters** tab of the dialog box.
- Click on the **Dynamic rough parameters** tab in the dialog box. The options in the dialog box will be displayed as shown in Figure-70.

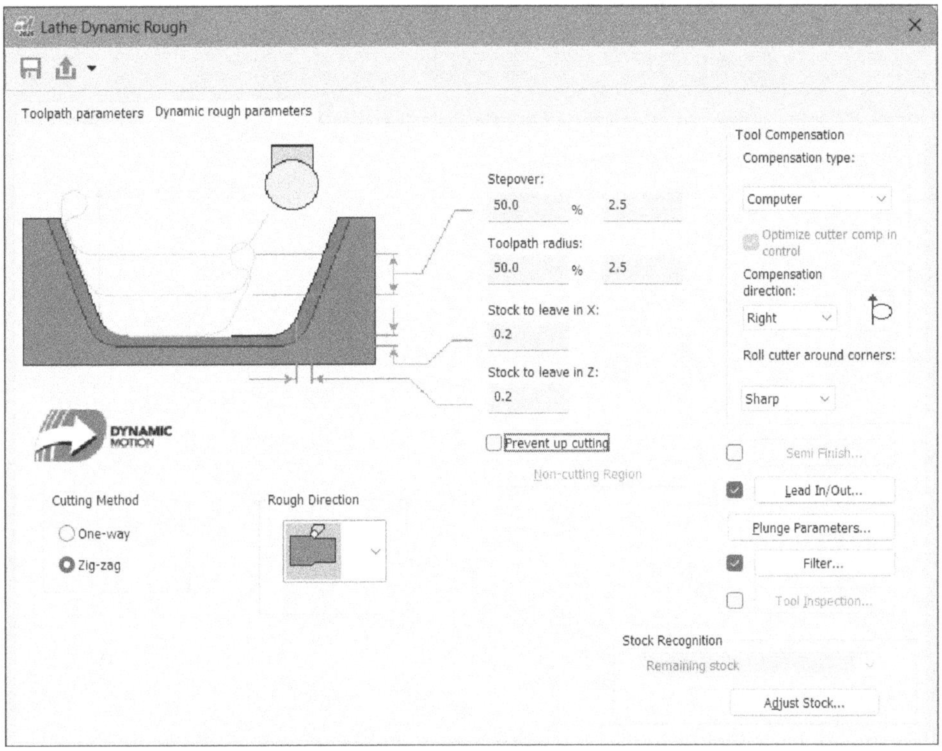

Figure-70. Dynamic rough parameters tab

- Specify the step-over percentage and toolpath radius with respect to tool tip radius in the **Stepover** and **Toolpath radius** edit boxes, respectively.
- Set the cutting method and direction in the **Cutting Method** drop-down and **Rough Direction** drop-down, respectively. Similarly, specify the other parameters. (OK! You are machinist, set the other parameters by yourself!!)
- Click on the **OK** button from the dialog box to create toolpath. The toolpath will be displayed as shown in Figure-71.

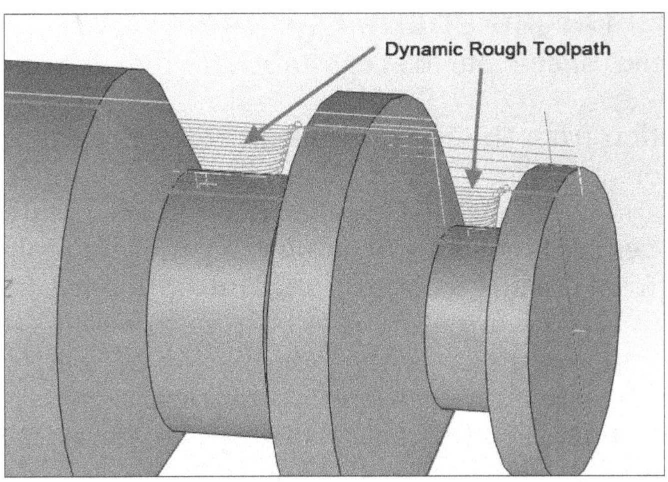

Figure-71. Dynamic rough toolpath created

THREAD TOOLPATH

The thread toolpath is used to create internal threads in a hole or external threads on a shaft. The steps to create thread toolpath are given next.

- Click on the **Thread** button from the expanded **General** panel in the **Turning** tab of the **Ribbon**. The **Lathe Thread** dialog box will be displayed; refer to Figure-72.

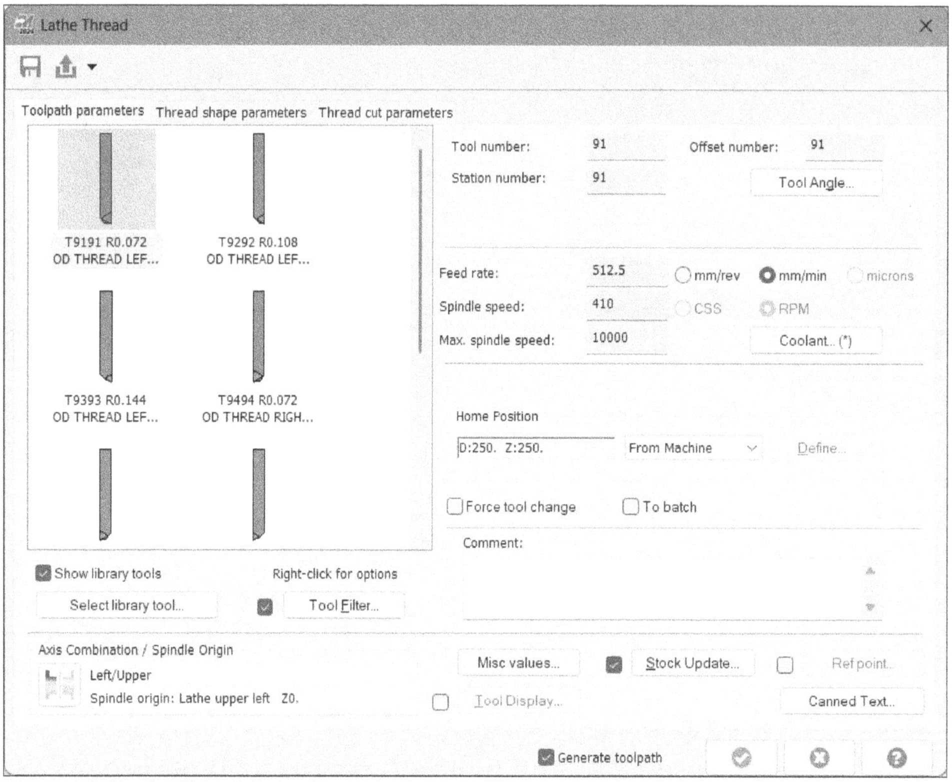

Figure-72. Lathe Thread dialog box

- Specify the parameters in the **Toolpath parameters** tab. Note that you need to specify either feed rate or spindle speed in this tab. The other value will be automatically decided based on the shape of thread specified in the **Thread shape parameters** tab.

Thread shape parameters tab

- Click on the **Thread shape parameters** tab. The dialog box will be displayed as shown in Figure-73.
- Select desired option from the **Thread orientation** drop-down in the dialog box. Selecting **OD** option will create external threads, selecting **ID** option will create internal threads, and selecting the **Face/Back** option will create threads on the face.
- Select the **Cross centerline cut** check box to generate toolpath on the opposite side of centerline from cutting tool position. This option is generally selected when you do not want to flip the orientation of cutting tool and geometry of workpiece demands it. Here we will discuss the options for **OD**, you can create the other threads by using the respective options by yourself.
- Click on the **Start Position** button to specify the start point for the threading. You will be prompted to specify the start point.
- Click at desired point on the model to specify the start point; refer to Figure-74.

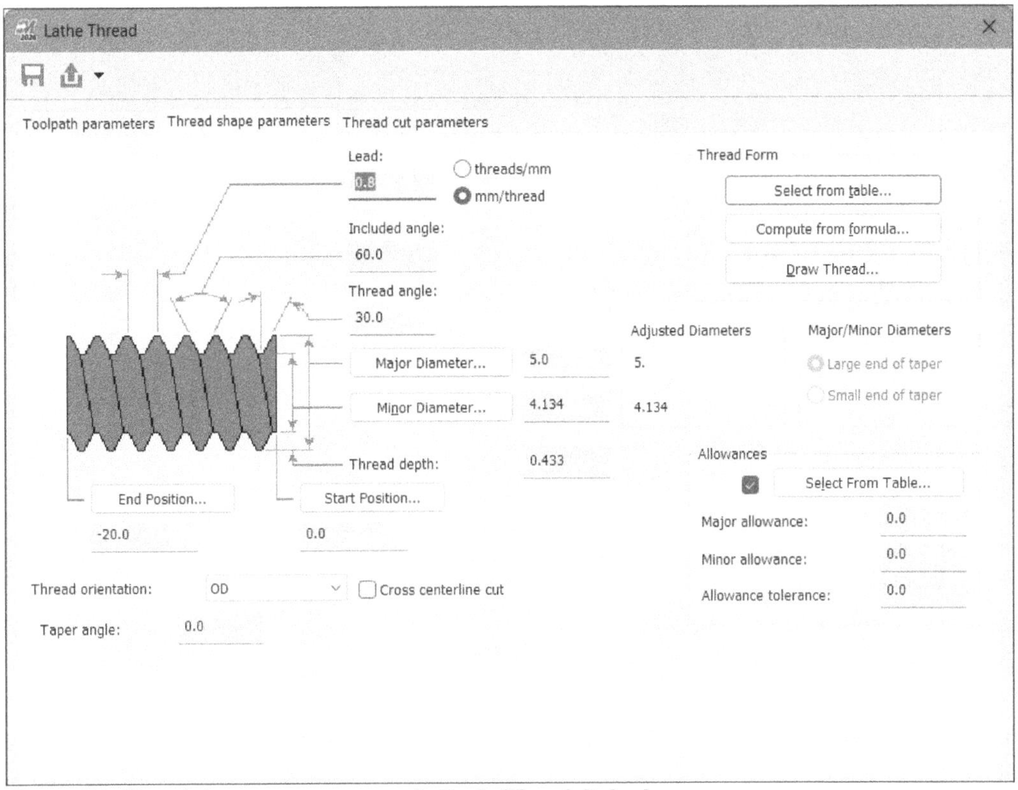

Figure-73. Thread shape parameters page in Lathe Thread dialog box

- Similarly, click on the **End Position** button from the dialog box and select the end position of the thread.
- Click on the **Major Diameter** button to define major diameter of thread. You will be asked to select a point defining the major diameter.
- Select a point on hole/shaft surface; refer to Figure-75. The value of major diameter will be displayed in the adjacent edit box.
- Similarly, set the value of minor diameter or enter the value directly in the edit box.

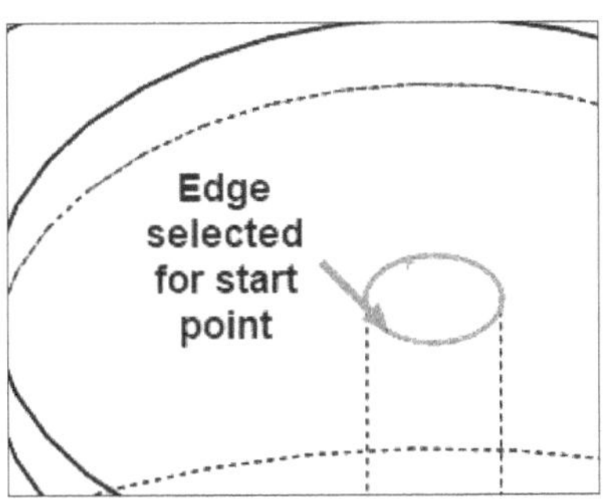

Figure-74. Start point for threading

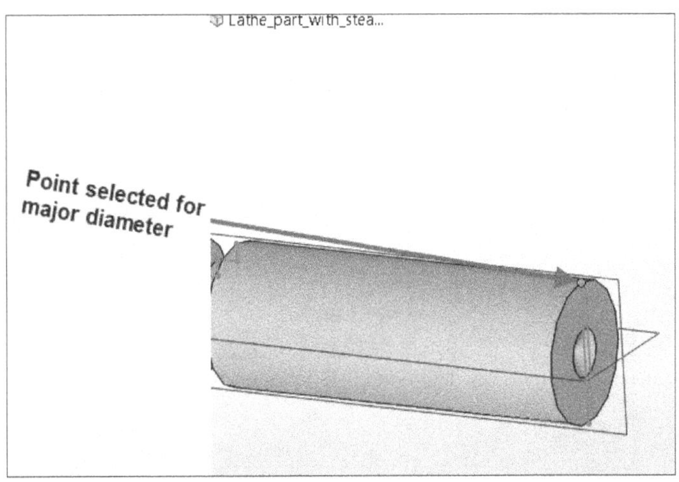

Figure-75. Point selected for major diameter

- If you want to create standard thread form then click on the **Select from table** button from the **Thread Form** area of the dialog box. The **Thread Table** dialog box will be displayed; refer to Figure-76. Select desired profile from the **Thread form** drop-down and double-click on desired thread from the table. The parameters of selected thread will automatically be reflected in the dialog box. Similarly, you can use other options in the **Thread Form** area.

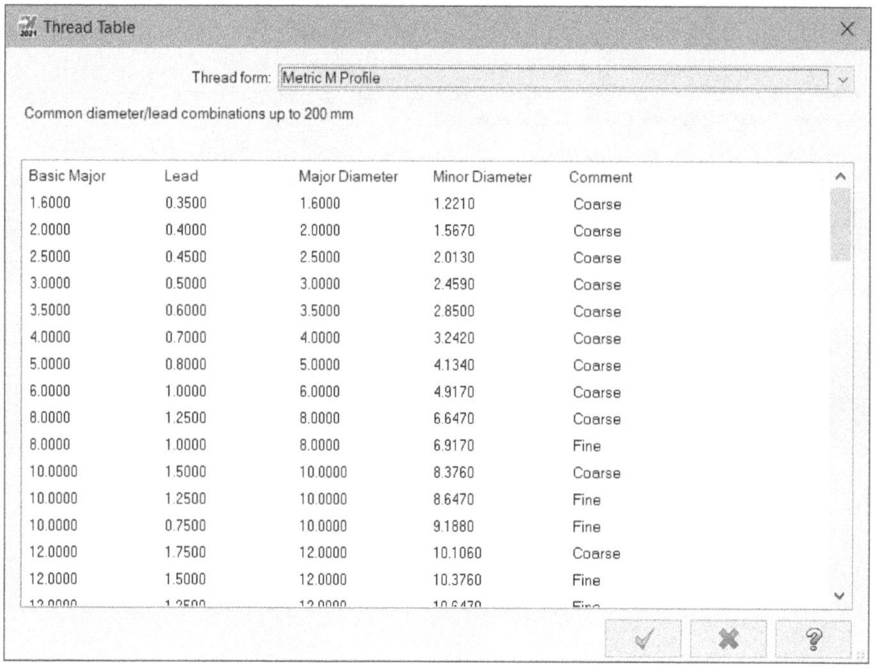

Basic Major	Lead	Major Diameter	Minor Diameter	Comment
1.6000	0.3500	1.6000	1.2210	Coarse
2.0000	0.4000	2.0000	1.5670	Coarse
2.5000	0.4500	2.5000	2.0130	Coarse
3.0000	0.5000	3.0000	2.4590	Coarse
3.5000	0.6000	3.5000	2.8500	Coarse
4.0000	0.7000	4.0000	3.2420	Coarse
5.0000	0.8000	5.0000	4.1340	Coarse
6.0000	1.0000	6.0000	4.9170	Coarse
8.0000	1.2500	8.0000	6.6470	Coarse
8.0000	1.0000	8.0000	6.9170	Fine
10.0000	1.5000	10.0000	8.3760	Coarse
10.0000	1.2500	10.0000	8.6470	Fine
10.0000	0.7500	10.0000	9.1880	Fine
12.0000	1.7500	12.0000	10.1060	Coarse
12.0000	1.5000	12.0000	10.3760	Fine

Figure-76. Thread Table dialog box

- Select the **Allowances** check box and specify desired values to set allowances in thread form.

Thread cut parameters

- Click on the **Thread cut parameters** tab in the dialog box. The dialog box will be displayed as shown in Figure-77.

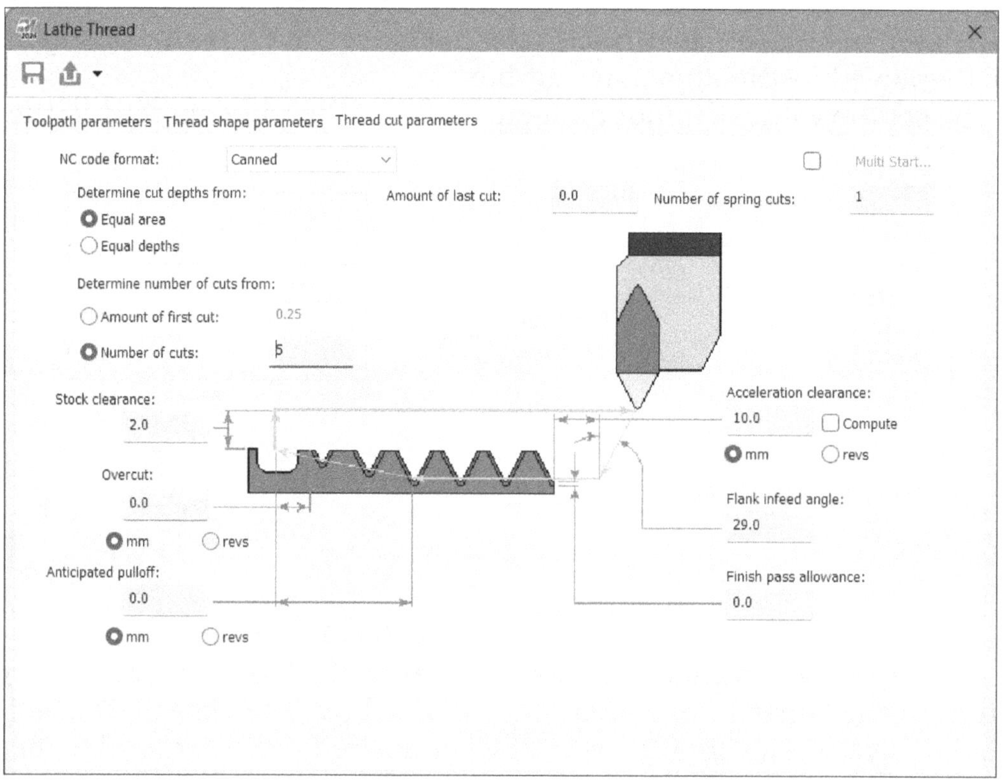

Figure-77. Thread cut parameters page in Lathe Thread Properties dialog box

- Specify the parameters of the thread cut as required by your manufacturing drawing.
- If you want to create multi start threads then select the check box adjacent to **Multi Start** button and click on the **Multi Start** button; refer to Figure-78.

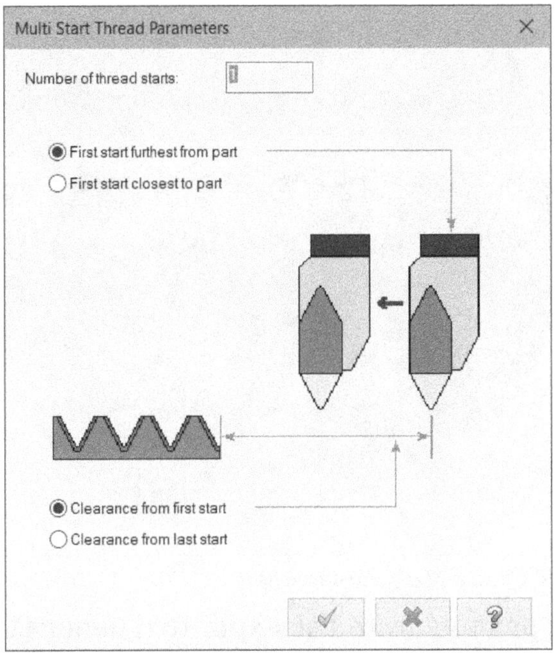

Figure-78. Multi Start Thread Parameters dialog box

- Specify the number of thread starts in the **Number of thread starts** edit box of the dialog box. Set the other parameters and click on the **OK** button.
- Click on the **OK** button from the dialog box. The toolpath will be created automatically.

PLUNGE TURN TOOLPATH

The Plunge Turn toolpath is generated to remove the material from workpiece when there is no option left except plunging the tool in the workpiece. We say it as a last option because there are high chances of breaking tool or machine if this toolpath is not generated correctly. Make sure to select a tool specifically designed for this type of toolpath (Mastercam suggests using the ISCAR tools designed for plunge turn). Using a cutting tool not designed for plunge turning could damage the tool and/or the part. In plunge turn toolpath, the tool plunges in the stock and moves laterally to cut material which is not in case of other toolpaths. Figure-79 shows a case where we need plunge turn toolpath. In this case, we have done facing, rough turning, and finish turning of part. Now, we need to remove material of the taper face and inner groove using the plunge turning. The procedure to generate this tool path is given next.

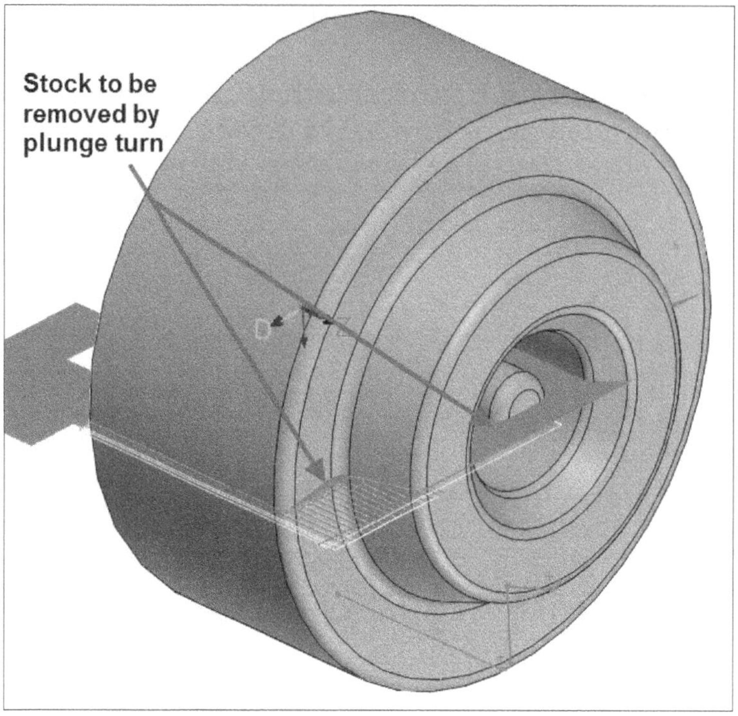

Figure-79. Case for plunge turn toolpath

- Click on the **Plunge Turn** tool from the expanded **General** panel of **Turning** tab in the **Ribbon**. The **Grooving Options** dialog box will be displayed; refer to Figure-80.

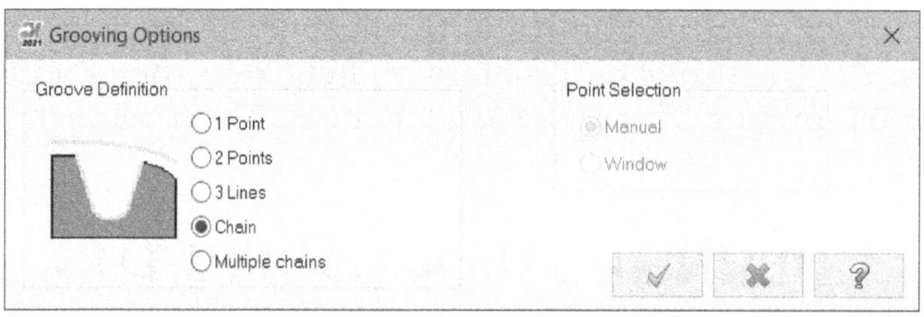

Figure-80. Grooving Options dialog box

- Select desired option and click on the **OK** button from the dialog box. (In our case, its **Multiple Chains** radio button). The **Wireframe Chaining** dialog box will be displayed and you will be prompted to select the chain of sketch entities.
- Select the sketch curves/faces for plunge turning; refer to Figure-81.

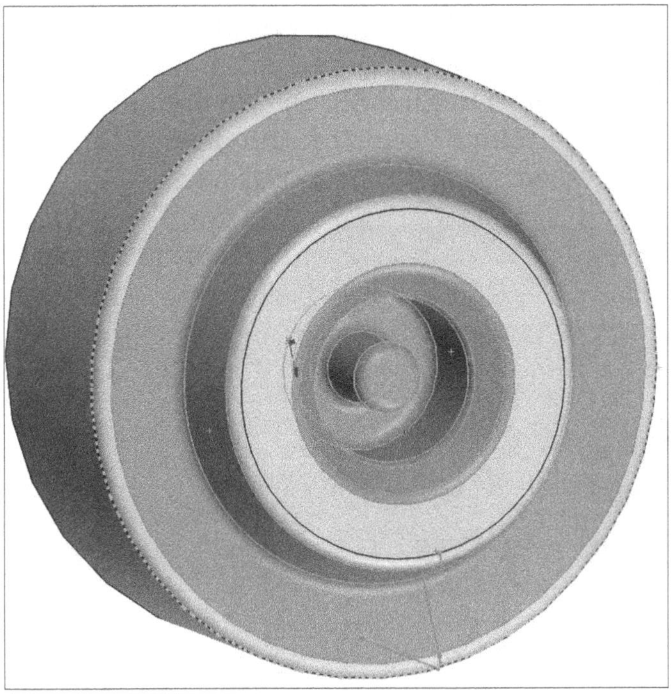

Figure-81. Faces selected for plunge turning

- Click on the **OK** button from the dialog box. The **Plunge Turn** dialog box will be displayed; refer to Figure-82.

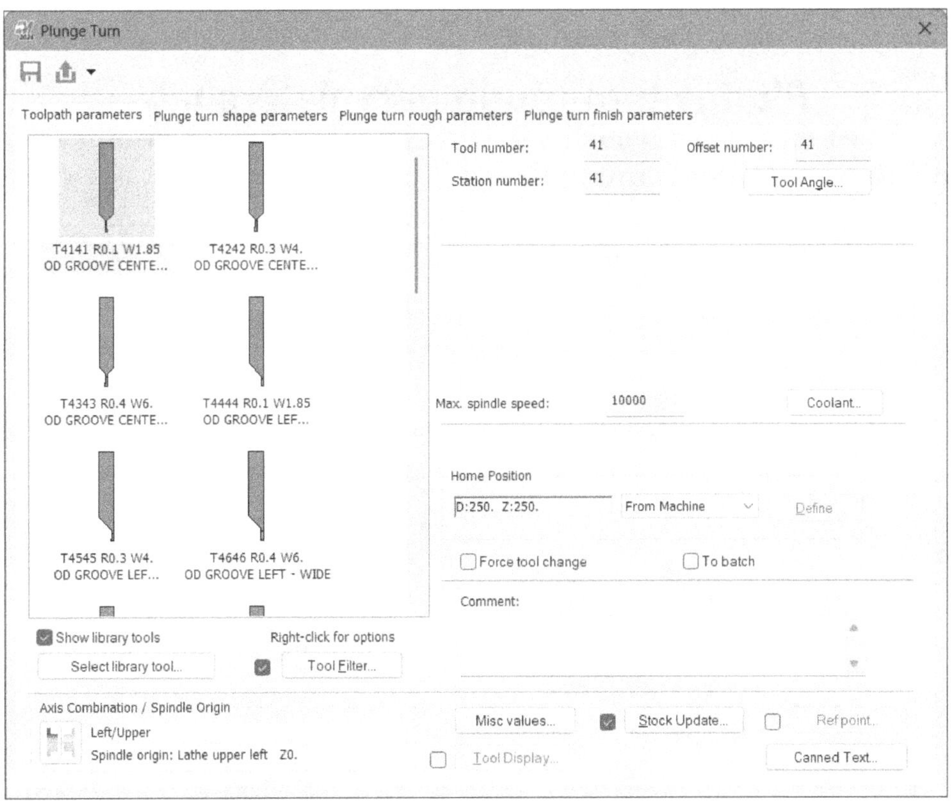

Figure-82. Plunge Turn dialog box

- Select a grooving tool with insert specially design for plunge turn machining.
- Click on the **Tool Angle** button and set the plunge direction normal to the stock face. Make sure the home position is set correctly in the **Home Position** edit box.

Plunge turn shape parameters tab

- Click on the **Plunge turn shape parameters** tab in the dialog box. The dialog box will be displayed as shown in Figure-83. Set desired angle if the groove is inclined otherwise groove will be created based on the plunge direction earlier set. Set the other options as discussed for groove toolpath.

Figure-83. Plunge turn shape parameters tab

Plunge turn rough parameters tab

- Click on the **Plunge turn rough parameters** tab. The options in the dialog box will be displayed as shown in Figure-84.

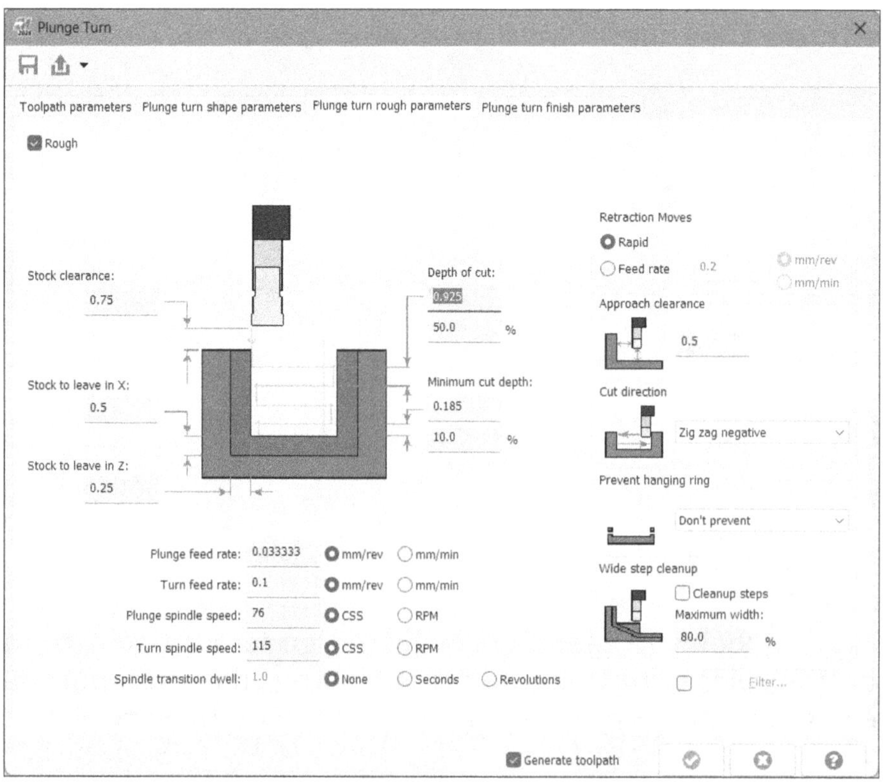

Figure-84. Plunge turn rough parameters tab

- Specify the **Stock clearance** value carefully (wrong value can cause collision). Specify the values in other edit boxes in the dialog box as required or allowed by tool specifications.
- If there are multiple grooves and there is a change of collision between tool and stock then make sure you select the **Finish each groove before roughing next** check box in this tab.
- Specify desired value in **Approach clearance** edit box to define the distance from stock, the tool will move before making the next cut in part. This option is similar to stock clearance for grooves.
- Select desired cutting direction in the drop-down of **Cut direction** area. Preview of the cutting direction is displayed in the **Cut direction** area on selecting an option in this drop-down.
- The options in the drop-down of **Prevent hanging ring** area are used to set the prevention of hanging rings generated after cutting step. A hanging ring occurs when the tool pushes off a small piece of material from the edge of the cut rather than cutting. With **Prevent hanging ring** enabled, the toolpath includes plunge moves to remove this extra material properly. Selecting :

    - Don't prevent - Hanging ring prevention is off.
    - Bi-Directional - Removes possible burrs from both sides of the cut.
    - Positive - Removes a possible burr from the positive side of the cut.
    - Negative - Removes a possible burr from the negative side of the cut.

- Select the **Cleanup steps** check box from **Wide step cleanup** area to turn on this function, which helps remove steps that are too large to remove on a finish cut. Such large steps can remain when the width of the cut is wider than the width of the insert. Wide step cleanup removes steps that are wider than a user definable width, based on the width of the tool's flat. Smoothing will take multiple passes if the extra width is more than the specified maximum percent of tool width.
- Similarly, specify the parameters as required in the **Plunge turn finish parameters** tab and click on the **OK** button from the dialog box. The simulation of machining will run and the toolpath will be generated; refer to Figure-85.

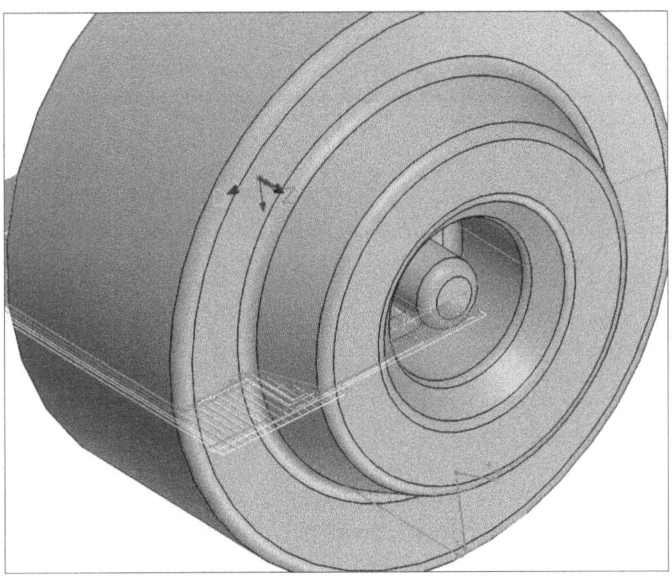

Figure-85. Toolpath generated by plunge turn

CONTOUR ROUGH TOOLPATH

The Contour rough toolpath is used to create toolpath following the contour of workpiece. This toolpath is useful for parts where the initial stock shape is similar to the final part shape, such as using a casting for stock; refer to Figure-86. Note that this toolpath does not support collision detection on the holder, so it is now your duty to verify path of tool holder. The procedure to create this toolpath is given next.

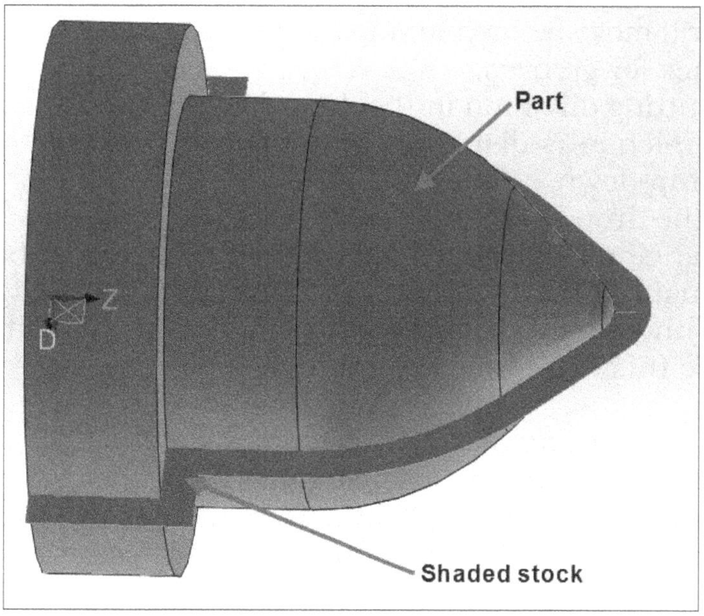

Figure-86. Part with stock of same shape

- Click on the **Contour Rough** tool from the expanded **General** panel of **Turning** tab in the **Ribbon**. The **Wireframe Chaining** dialog box will be displayed.
- Select the faces to be machined; refer to Figure-87 and click on the **OK** button from the dialog box. The **Lathe Contour Rough** dialog box will be displayed.

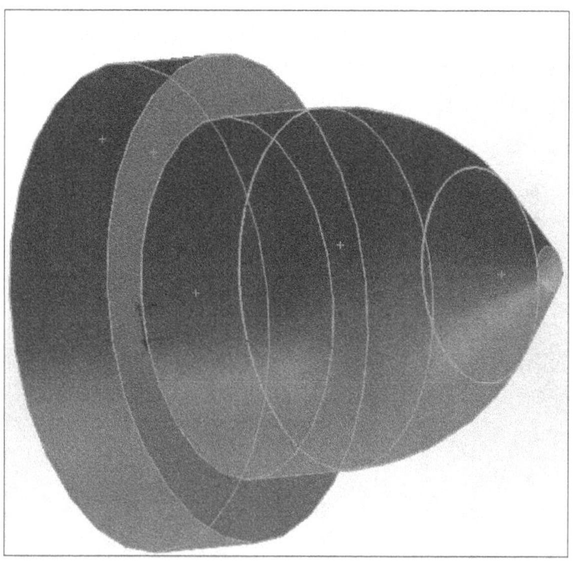

Figure-87. Faces selected for contour rough toolpath

- Select any OD or ID roughing tool based on faces selected and set desired parameters in the dialog box as discussed earlier.
- Click on the **Contour rough parameters** tab in the dialog box. The dialog box will be displayed as shown in Figure-88.

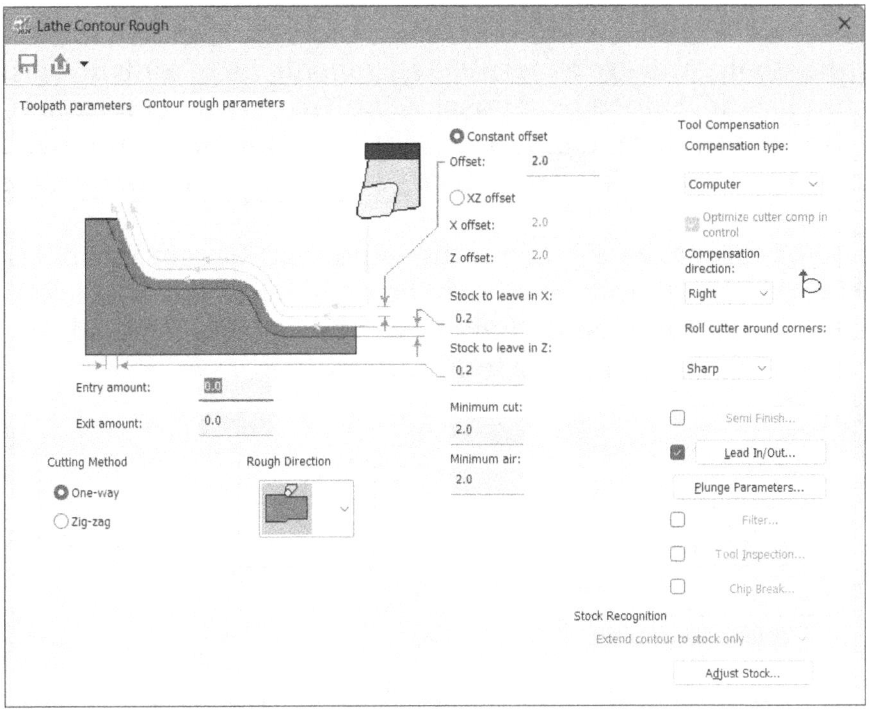

Figure-88. Lathe Contour Rough dialog box

- Set desired entry and exit distance values in the **Entry amount** and **Exit amount** edit boxes, respectively.
- Set the cutting method and cutting direction as required by using the **Cutting Method** area and **Rough Direction** drop-down, respectively.
- Select the **Constant offset** radio button and specify the constant depth of cut in **Offset** edit box or select the **XZ offset** radio button and specify different values of depth of cut in X offset and Z offset edit boxes.
- Set the stock to be left after roughing in the **Stock to leave in X** and **Stock to leave in Z** edit boxes.
- Define the value of smallest cut to be made in the **Minimum cut** edit box. Similarly, define the value of minimum distance required for a rapid move in the **Minimum air** edit box.
- Set the other parameters as discussed earlier. Make sure to specify correct **Lead In/Out** parameters to create accident free toolpath.
- After specifying desired parameters, click on the **OK** button to create toolpath; refer to Figure-89.

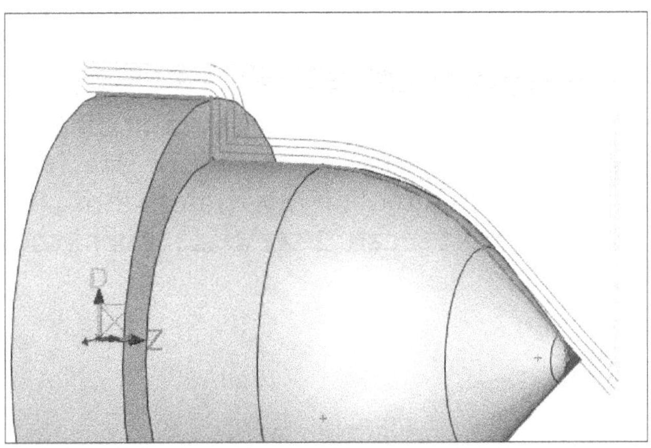

Figure-89. Lathe contour rough toolpath

PRIMETURNING TOOLPATH

The PrimeTurning toolpaths are generated specifically for Sandvik Coromant cutting tools. Mastercam has developed best possible cutting strategies for fast and accurate cutting operations using these tools. Note that this toolpath is not available in home learning edition of software. The procedure to generate this toolpath is given next.

- Click on the **PrimeTurning** tool from the expanded **General** panel in the **Turning** tab of the **Ribbon**. The **Wireframe Chaining** dialog box will be displayed. Select the geometries to be machined and click on the **OK** button. The **Lathe PrimeTurning** dialog box will be displayed; refer to Figure-90.

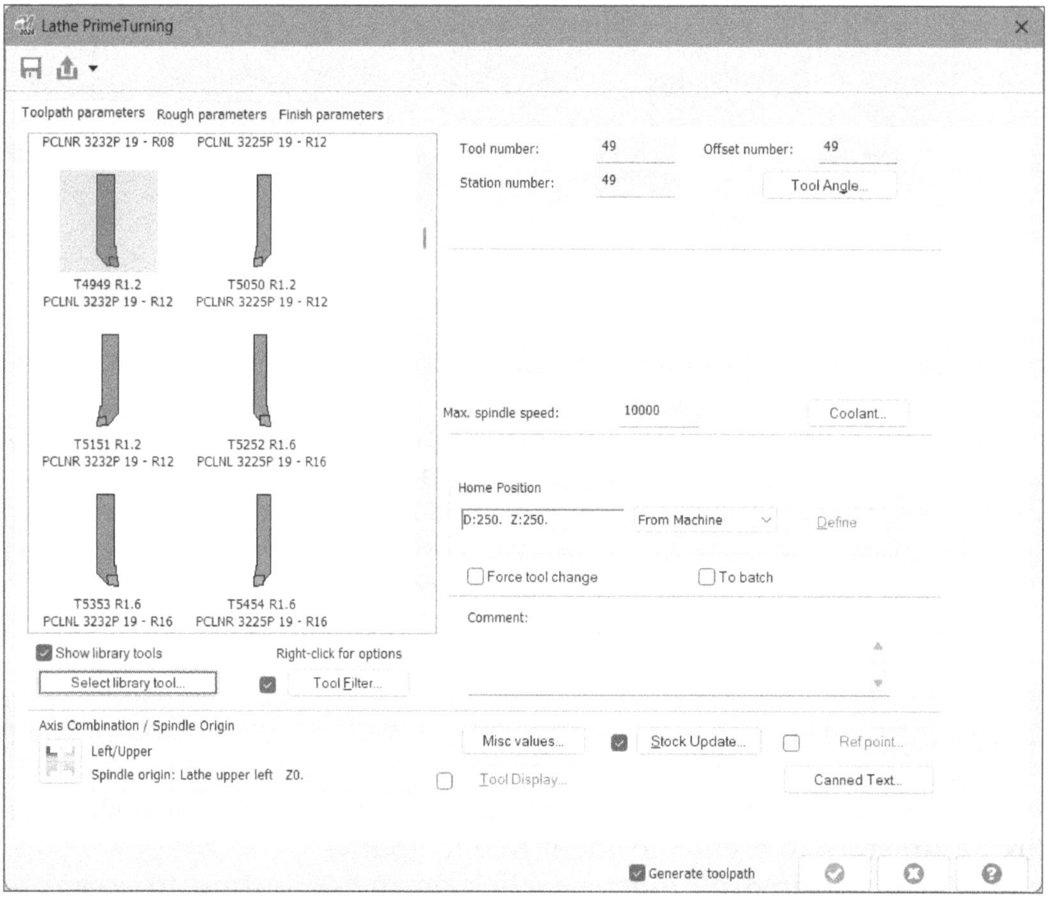

Figure-90. Lathe PrimeTurning dialog box

- Select desired cutting tool from the list. Note that you need to select **CoroTurn Prime** library to select related tools. To do so, click on the **Select library tool** button from the dialog box. The **Tool Selection** dialog box will be displayed. Click on the **Open** button at the top in the **Tool Selection** dialog box. The **Select tool library** dialog box will be displayed; refer to Figure-91. Select the **CoroTurn Prime mm.tooldb** file if you want to use tools in **mm** dimensions. (Generally in **C:\Users\Public\Documents\Shared Mastercam 20xx\Mill Turn\tools** folder)

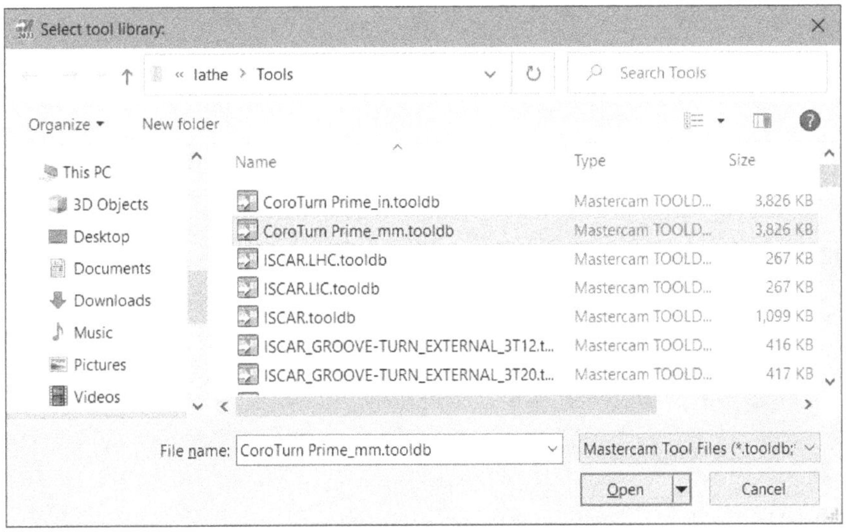

Figure-91. Select tool library dialog box

- After selecting the library file, click on the **Open** button from the dialog box. The tools related to selected library will be displayed in the **Tool Selection** dialog box; refer to Figure-92.

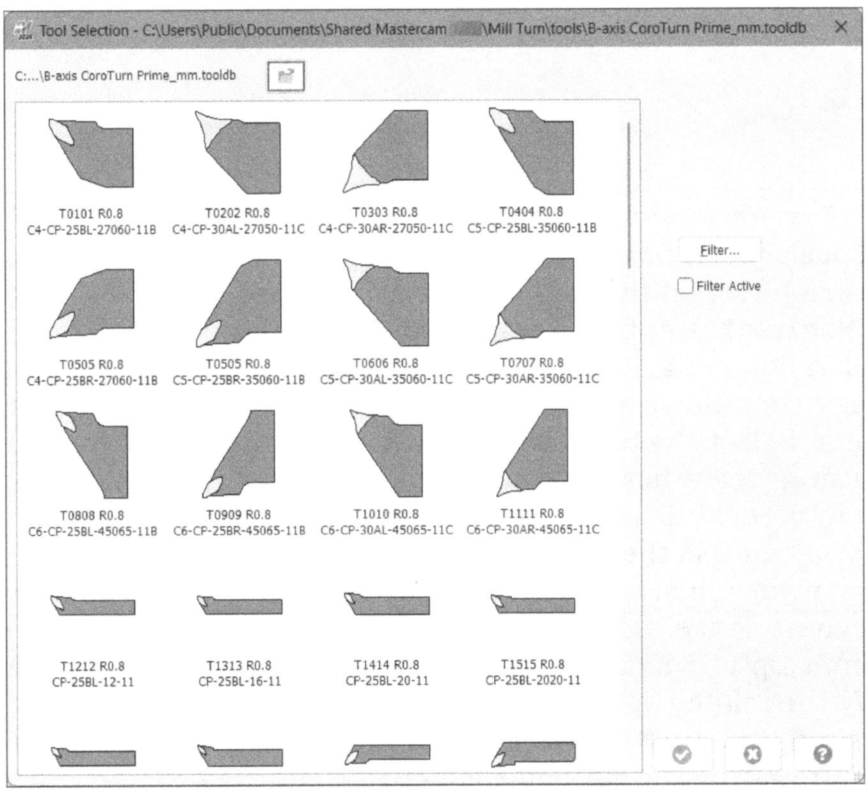

Figure-92. Tool Selection dialog box

- Click on the **OK** button from the dialog box. The list of related tools will be displayed in the **Lathe PrimeTurning** dialog box.
- Select desired cutting tool and specify related parameters as discussed earlier.

Rough Parameters Tab

The options in the **Rough Parameters** tab are used to define strategy for removing large stock of material from the workpiece; refer to Figure-93.

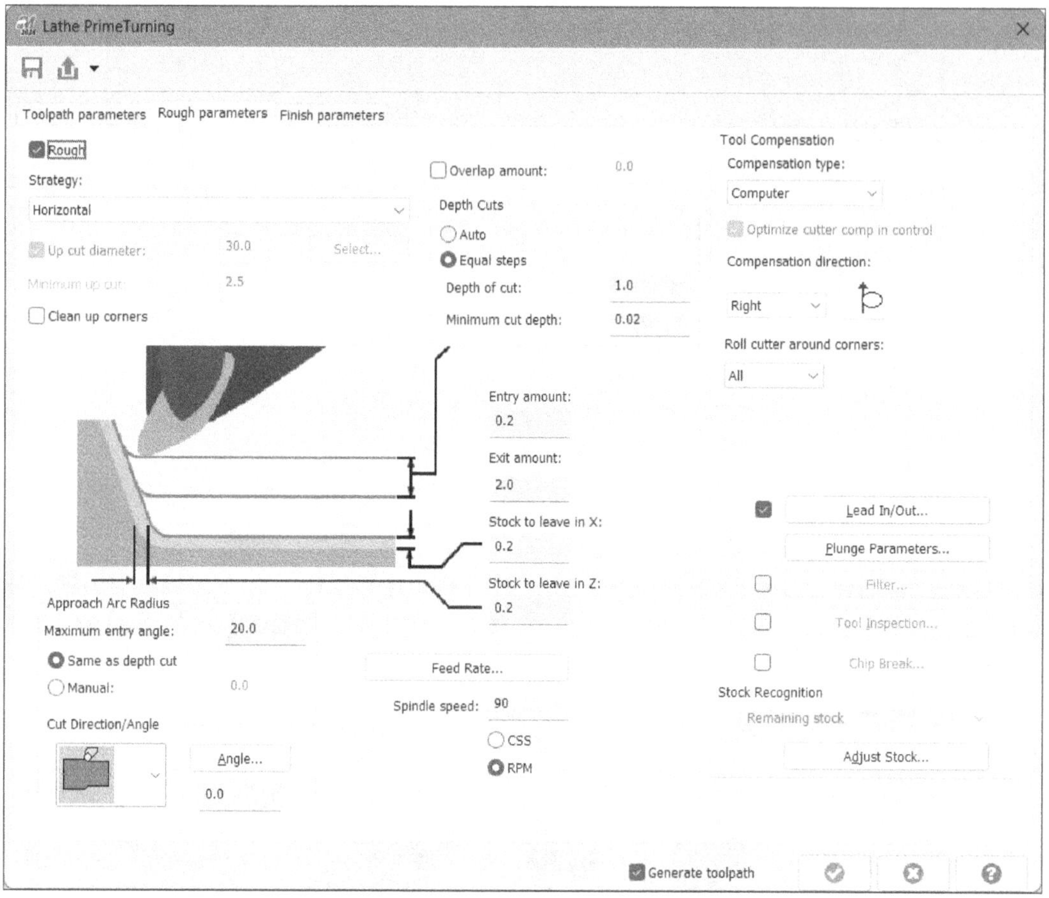

Figure-93. Rough parameters tab

- Clear the **Rough** check box if you do not want to perform roughing operation. On doing so, the options in this tab will get deactivated.
- Select the **Horizontal** option from the **Strategy** drop-down if you want to move cutting tool in horizontal direction while cutting. Select the **Vertical** option from the **Strategy** drop-down if you want to move cutting tool in vertical direction while cutting. Select the **Horizontal then vertical** option from the drop-down to move cutting tool in horizontal direction first and make all the necessary cuts, after move in vertical direction and remove rest of the material for better finish. Similarly, you can use the other strategies from the drop-down.
- If a strategy involving vertical direction is selected then **Up cut diameter** check box will become active. Select the **Up cut diameter** check box to specify upper diameter limit up to which the vertical cuts will be made. After selecting check box, specify the related value in edit box next to the check box.
- Specify desired value in **Minimum up cut** edit box to define the distance moved by cutting tool upward after making each cut.
- Select the **Clean up corners** check box to remove material from sharp edges of the workpiece.
- Specify desired parameters in the **Approach arc radius** area to define how cutting tool will approach the arc like shapes in workpiece.
- Click in the **Entry amount** edit box to specify the approach distance from where cutting tool will start cutting passes.
- Specify desired value in **Exit amount** edit box to specify the distance from workpiece up to which the cutting tool will move using cutting feed rate.

- The other parameters of this tab has been discussed earlier. Similarly, specify the parameters in **Finish parameters** tab of the dialog box and click on the **OK** button. The toolpath will be generated.

The **Manual Entry** tool in expanded **General** panel works in the same way as it does for Milling operations discussed earlier.

CUSTOM THREADING TOOLPATH

The **Custom Thread** tool is used to create machining toolpath for generating custom threads like square threads, trapezoidal threads, and so on. The procedure to use this tool is given next.

- Open the model on which you want to create custom thread machining and after setting up machine and other parameters, click on the **Custom Thread** tool from the expanded **General** panel in the **Turning** tab of the **Ribbon**. The **Custom Thread Manager** will be displayed; refer to Figure-94.

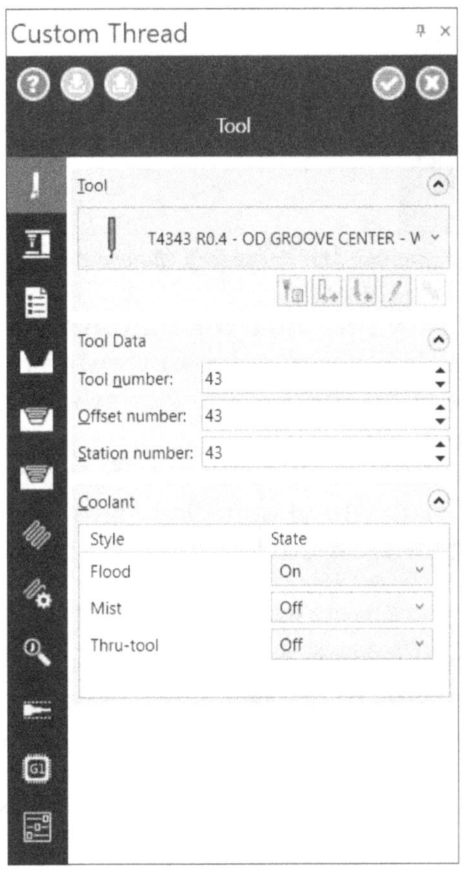

Figure-94. Custom Thread Manager

- Select desired cutting tool from the **Tool** drop-down. If no tool is available in this drop-down then click on the **Select library** tool button from **Tool** rollout and select desired tool from library.
- Set the coolant conditions in the drop-downs of **Coolant** rollout depending on type of your machine.
- Click on the **Machine** option from left side in the **Manager** to display options related to machine setup. The options will be displayed as shown in Figure-95.

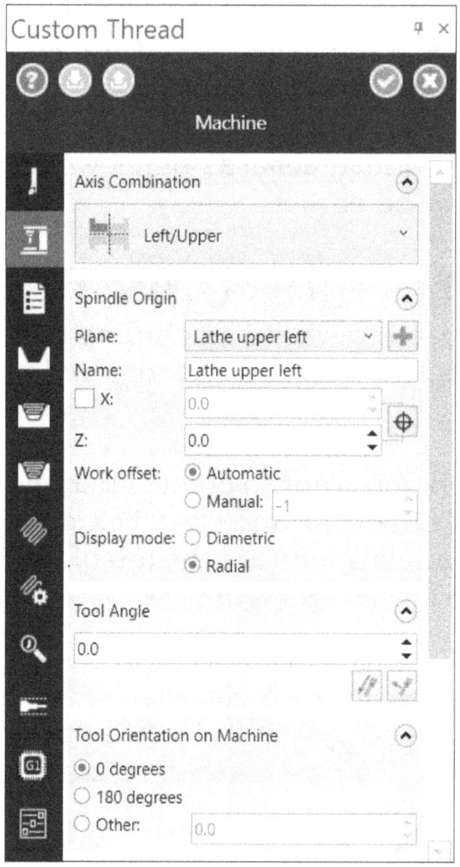

Figure-95. Machine page in Custom Thread Manager

- Select the orientation of your part on machine using the options in **Axis Combination** drop-down. For example, if you want to machine using upper section of part and your spindle is on the left of your stock then select the **Lathe upper left** option from this drop-down.
- Specify the location of spindle origin with respect to part face in the **Z** edit box. If you want to specify X coordinate of spindle origin as well then select the **X** check box. Click on the **Select origin** button next to edit boxes for selecting the point from graphics area.
- Specify desired angle value in the **Tool Angle** edit box if you want to create taper threads. Set the other parameters in this page as discussed earlier.
- Parameters in **Operation** page of the **Manager** are used to define home position and references points for retraction/approach. Specify these parameters as discussed earlier in the book.
- Click on the **Shape** option from left area to define the shape and size of custom thread; refer to Figure-96.
- Select the **Parametric** radio button from the **Shape Type** rollout to create thread profile based on parameters specified in the **Shape Style** table at the bottom in this page; refer to Figure-97. You can check the preview of thread profile by selecting the **Preview** button; refer to Figure-98.

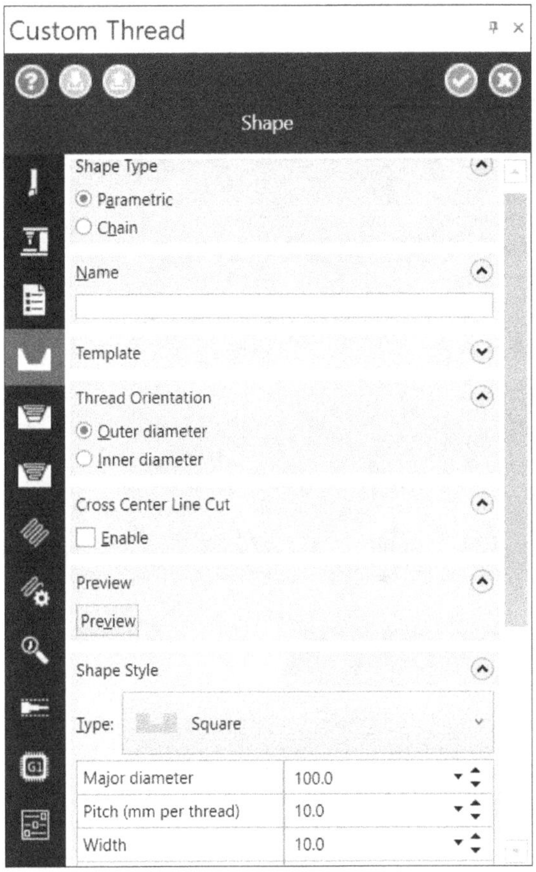

Figure-96. Shape page

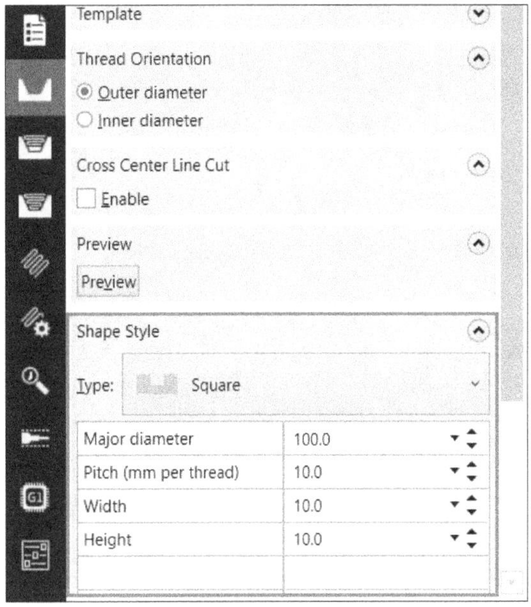

Figure-97. Shape Style table

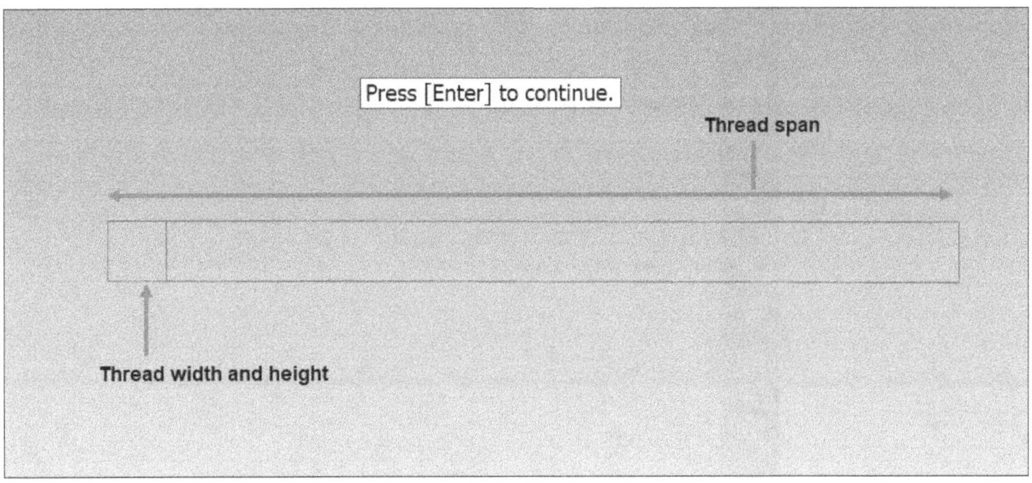

Figure-98. Square thread profile preview

- You can change the shape of thread from **Type** drop-down in **Shape Style** rollout at the bottom in the **Manager**.
- Select the **Chain** radio button from the **Shape Type** rollout at the top in **Manager** if you want to select profile of thread from the model and click on the **Select Chain** button. You will be asked to select the wireframe chain. Select desired wireframe chain; refer to Figure-99 and click on the **OK** button from **Wireframe Chaining** dialog box.
- Select the **Outer diameter** or **Inner diameter** radio button from **Thread Orientation** rollout to define whether threads are internal or external.
- Click on the **Rough Motion Control** option from left area to define parameters for rough cutting passes. The page will be displayed as shown in Figure-100.

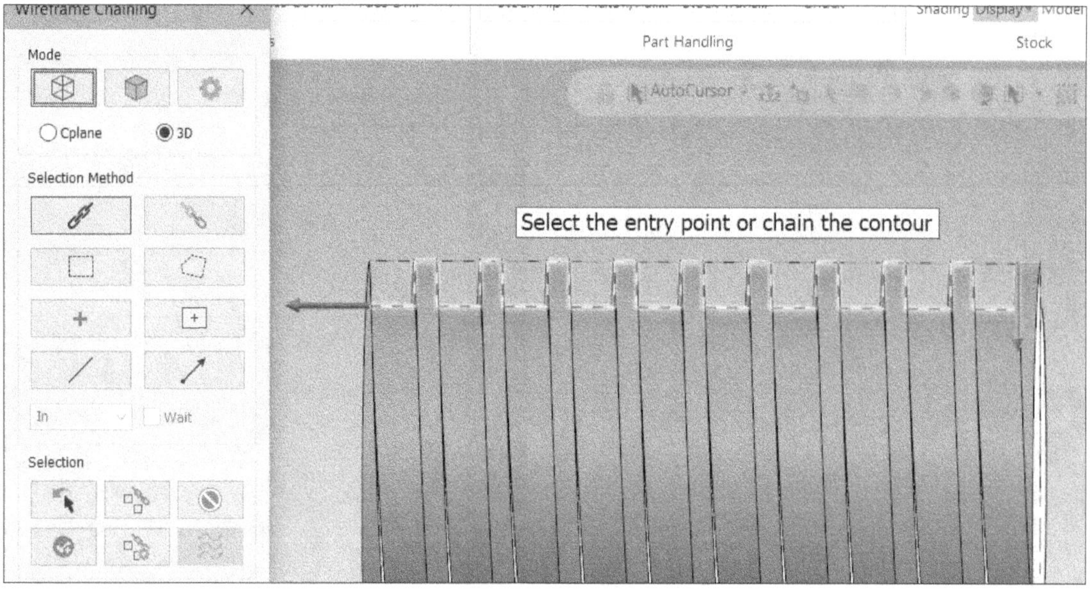

Figure-99. Chain selected for thread

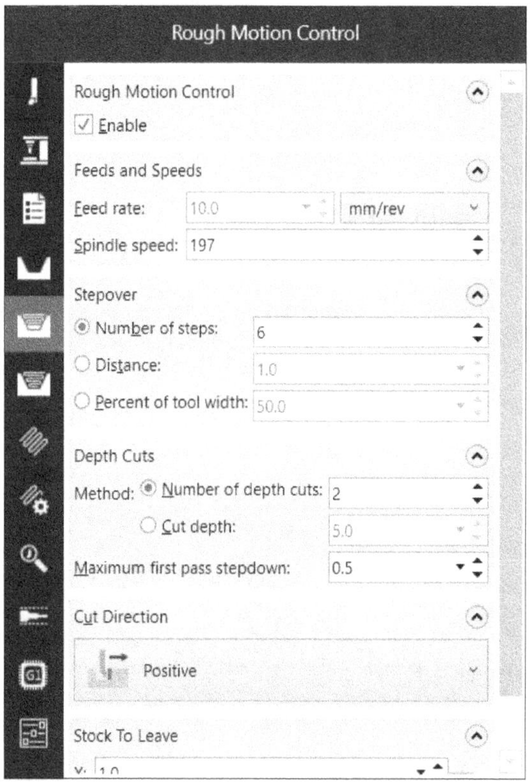

Figure-100. Rough Motion Control page

- Select the **Enable** check box to enable roughing operation and specify the cutting parameters of roughing operation as discussed earlier. Similarly, you can specify parameters in **Finish Motion Control** page and other pages of the **Manager**. Generally, default parameters in these pages are fine if there is no further variation in the threads.
- Click on the **OK** button from the **Manager** to create the toolpath; refer to Figure-101.

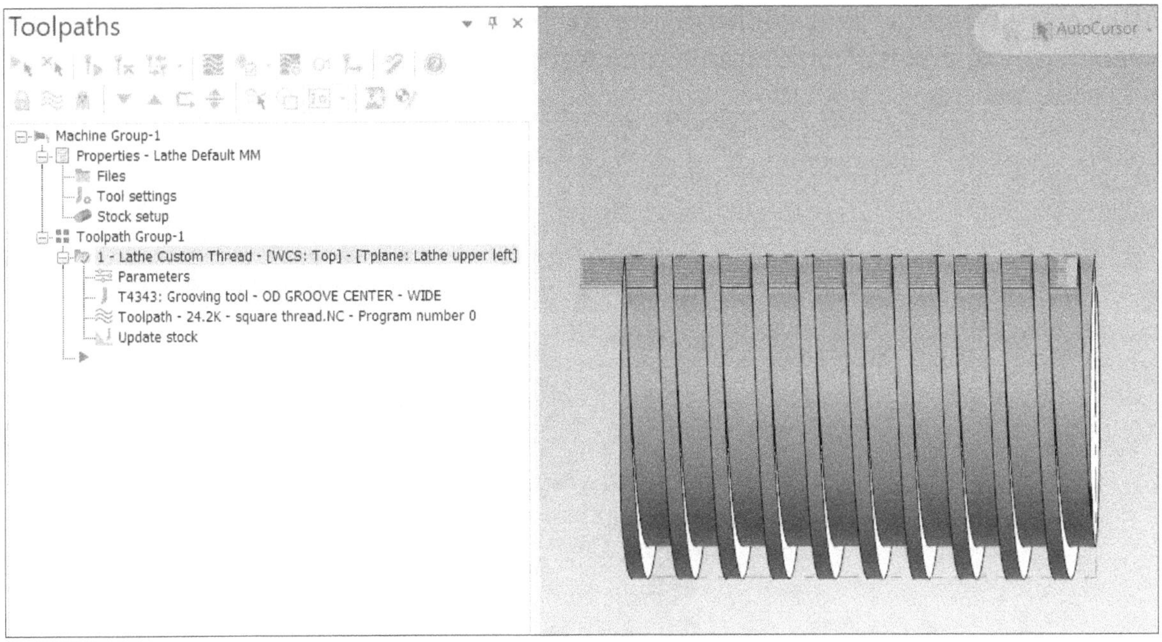

Figure-101. Custom thread toolpath

TOOLPATH THROUGH POINTS

The **Point** tool is used to create machining toolpaths with the help of points. Select the points as per their order of cutting and tool will move accordingly to generate the toolpath. The steps to perform the operation are given next.

- Click on the **Point** tool from the expanded **General** panel in the **Turning** tab of **Ribbon**. The **Lathe Point Toolpath** dialog box will be displayed; refer to Figure-102.

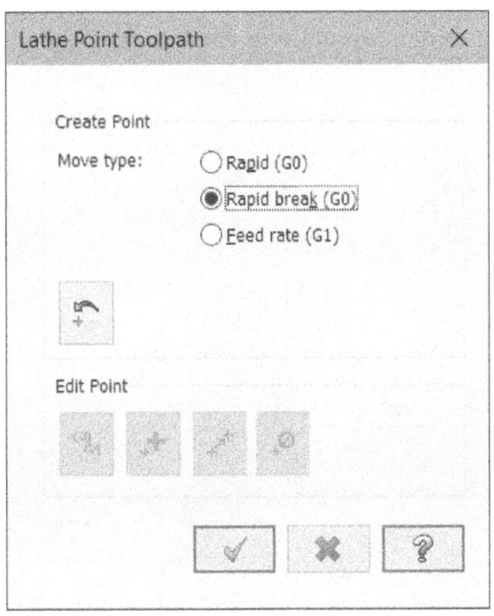

Figure-102. Lathe Point Toolpath dialog box

- Select desired radio button for **Move type** from **Create Point** area of the dialog box. Select the **Rapid(G0)** radio button to rapidly move cutting tool for non-cutting passes. Select the **Rapid break (G0)** radio button to perform non-cutting pass movement of tool at the end of which a cutting pass will start. Select the **Feed rate (G1)** radio button to create cutting pass movement.
- After selecting desired radio button, click in the drawing area to specify points; refer to Figure-103. You can specify the points in continuation while selecting different radio buttons from the dialog box.

- After specifying points, click on the **OK** button from the dialog box. The **Lathe Point** dialog box will be displayed as shown in Figure-104.

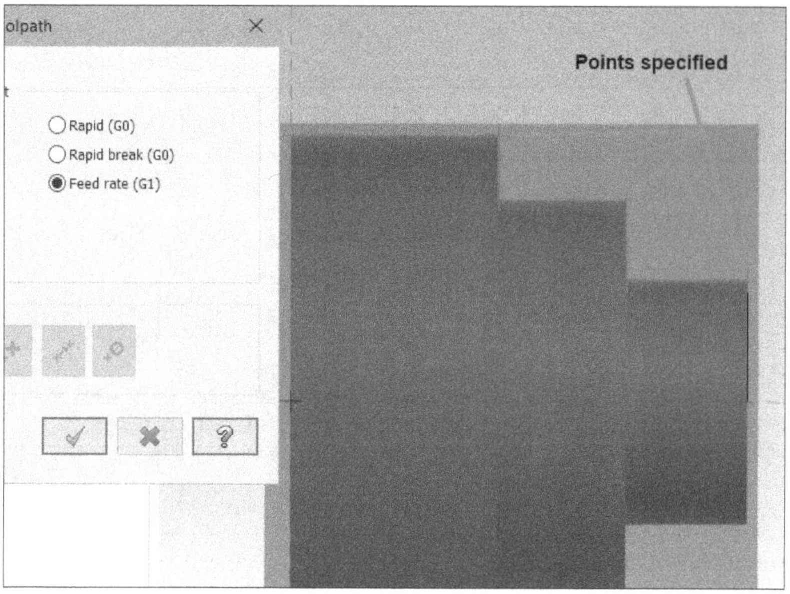

Figure-103. Points specified for toolpath

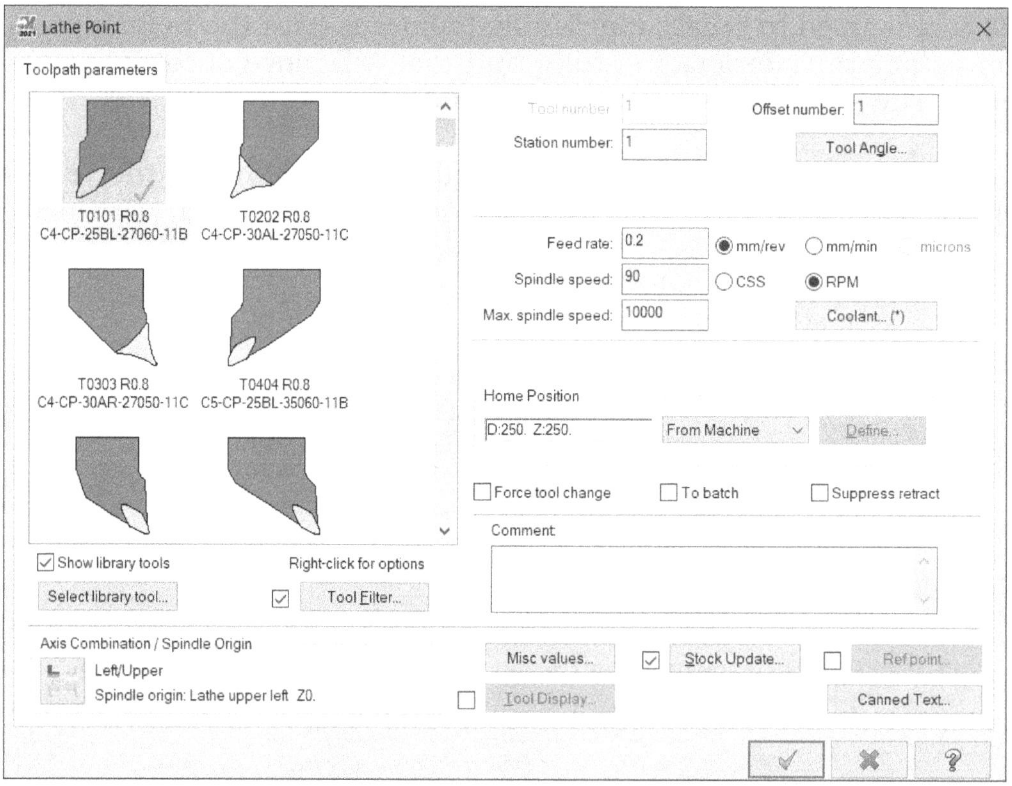

Figure-104. Lathe Point dialog box

- Specify desired parameters and then click on the **OK** button. The toolpath will be generated accordingly.

CANNED TOOLPATHS

Some of you might be aware of canned cycles used in various machines for cutting workpiece. The canned cycles are repetitive cutting steps with specified depth increment. For example, if you want to remove 50 mm of stock by roughing operation then you need to use the canned roughing cycle to remove this much amount of material. For this cycle, you will specify start point, end point, and number of steps required. There are four tools to generate canned cycles for various cutting operations:

- Canned Rough Toolpath
- Canned Finish Toolpath
- Canned Groove Toolpath
- Canned Pattern Repeat Toolpath

We will discuss the Canned Rough Toolpath and the other tools work in the same way.

Canned Rough Toolpath

The canned rough toolpath is used in the same way as the rough toolpaths are used. The steps to create canned rough toolpaths are given next.

- Click on the **Canned Rough** tool from the expanded **General** panel in the **Turning** tab of the **Ribbon**. The **Wireframe Chaining** dialog box will be displayed as discussed earlier.
- Select the sketched chain for toolpath and click on the **OK** button from the dialog box. The **Lathe Canned Rough** dialog box will be displayed; refer to Figure-105.

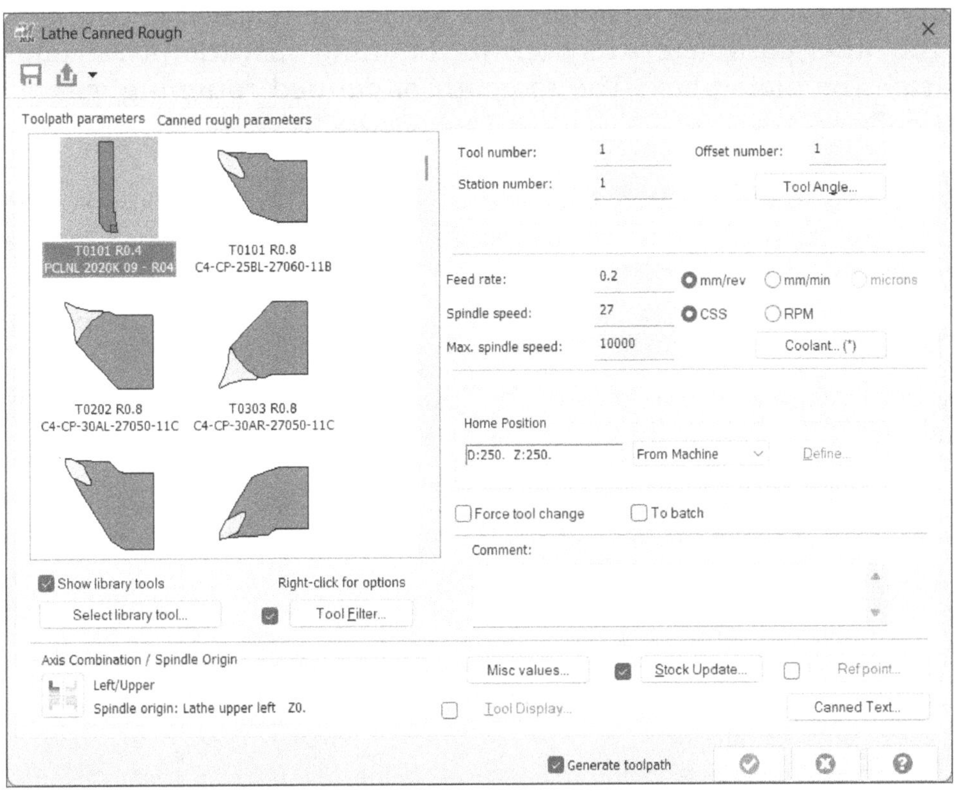

Figure-105. Lathe Canned Rough dialog box

- Select desired tool and specify the cutting parameters.
- Click on the **Canned Rough Parameters** tab in the dialog box to define toolpath parameters; refer to Figure-106.

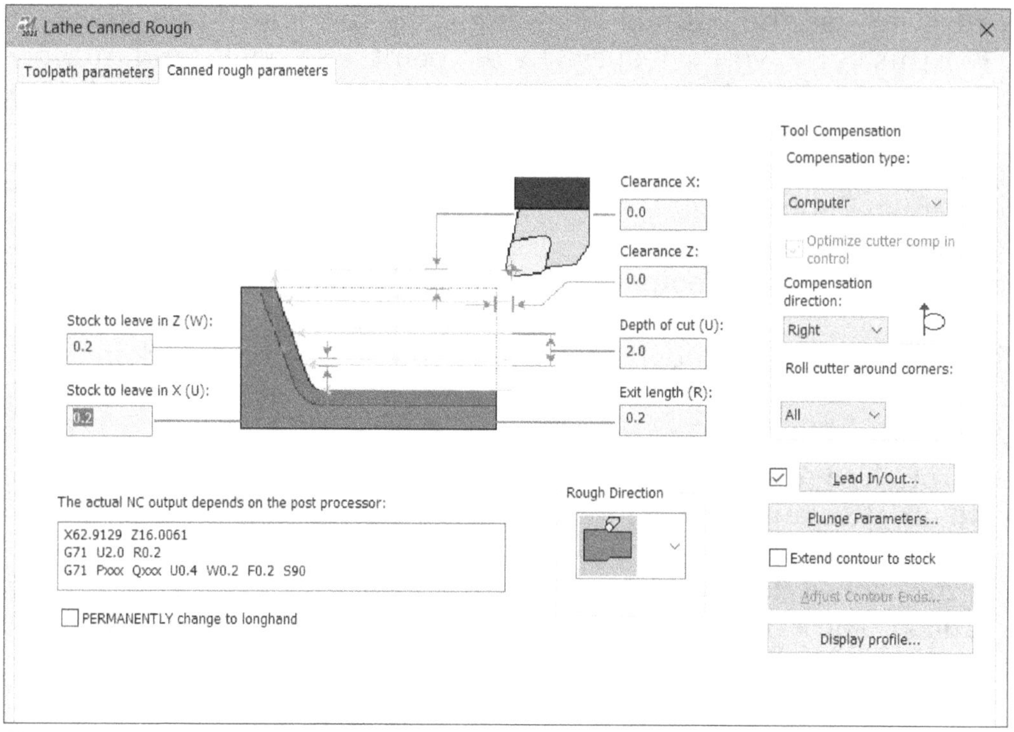

Figure-106. Canned rough parameters tab

- Specify the depth of cut and stock to be left in the respective edit boxes.
- Specify the other parameters as done in roughing operations and click on the **OK** button from the dialog box. The toolpath of canned roughing will be generated automatically.

In this chapter, we have worked with various toolpaths and tools related to Lathe machining. In the next chapter, we will work with some advanced lathe machining tools and toolpaths.

PRACTICAL 1

In this practical, we will create toolpaths for the given model; refer to Figure-107. The dimensions of stock are shown in Figure-108.

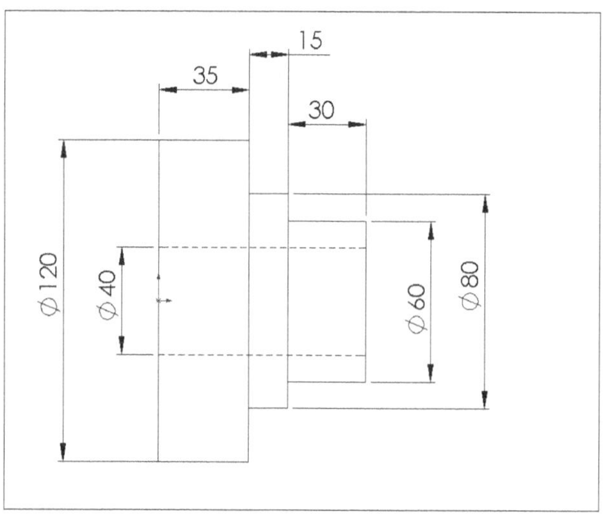

Figure-107. Practical 1

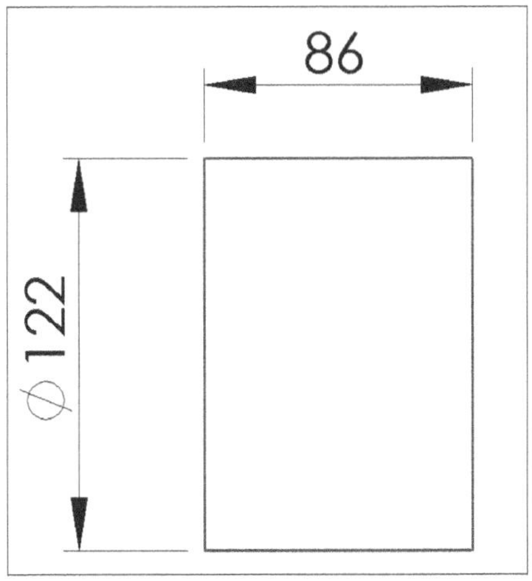

Figure-108. Stock dimension for Practical

The first step before we start machining is to identify the operations that are required to machine the part. We can identify from the part that there is facing operation, one drilling operation, one boring operation to get good finish of hole, and rough turning with finish turning operation. Note that these basic machining operations can be sub-divided into multiple operations based on the capabilities of the CAM software. We will start one by one for various operations to be performed.

Preparing the model

- Start Mastercam and click on the **Open** button from the **Quick Access** toolbar displayed at top in the Application window. The **Open** dialog box will be displayed; refer to Figure-109.

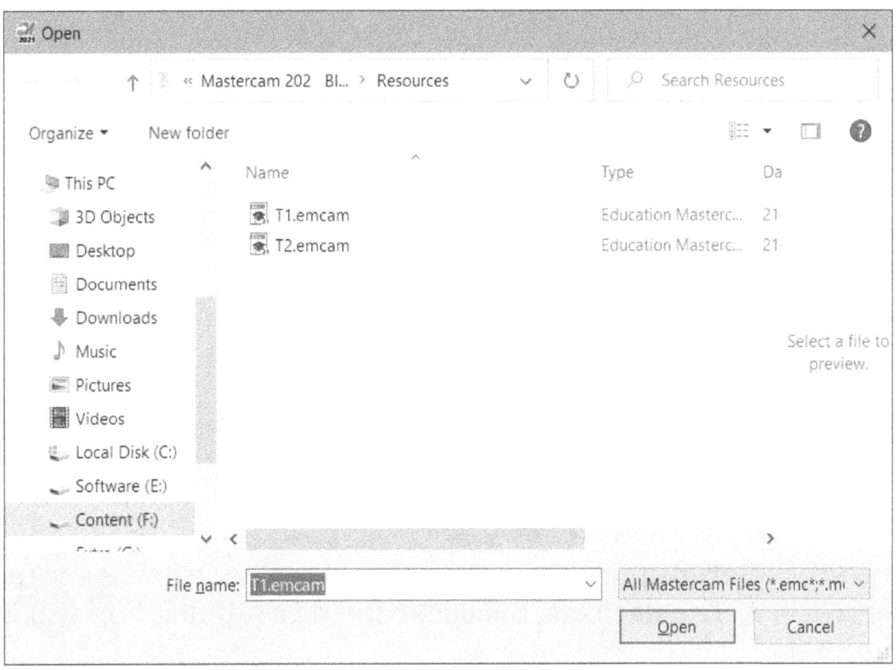

Figure-109. Open dialog box

- Select the model file provided for Practical of Chapter 13 in the Resources (ask at our Email address if do not have part files) and click on the **Open** button from the dialog box. The model will be displayed as shown in Figure-110.

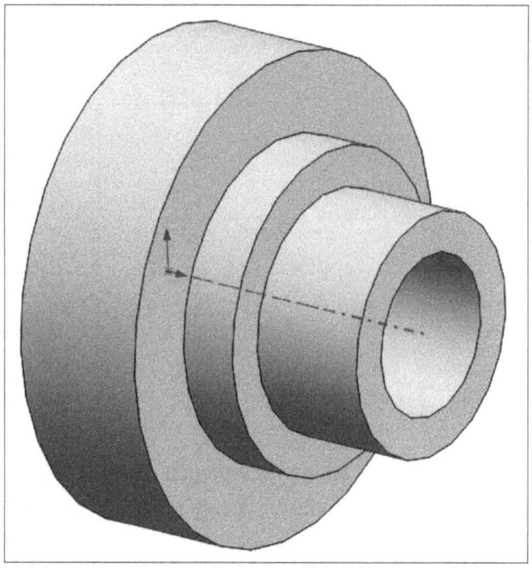

Figure-110. Model for Practical 1

- Select the **Lathe Default MM.MCAD-LMD** machine from the **Lathe** drop-down in the **Machine Type** panel of **Machine** tab in the **Ribbon**. If not available then add it as discussed earlier.

Creating Stock

- Set the **+D+Z** plane as WCS, construction, and tool plane in the **Planes Manager**; refer to Figure-111.

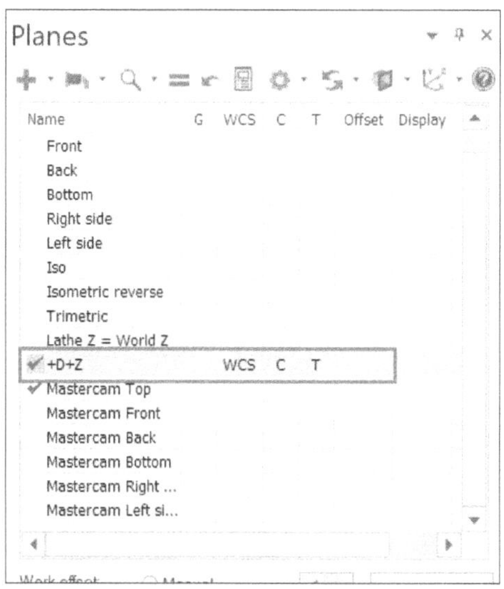

Figure-111. Setting plane

- Click on the **Stock Setup** option from the **Properties** node in the **Toolpath Manager**; refer to Figure-112. The **Machine Group Properties** dialog box will be displayed; refer to Figure-113.

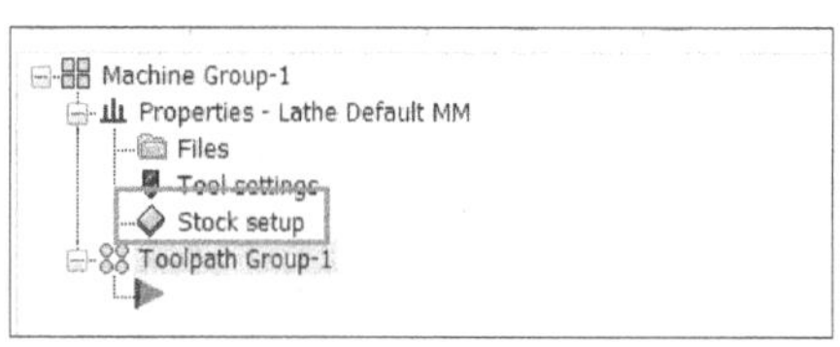

Figure-112. Stock setup option

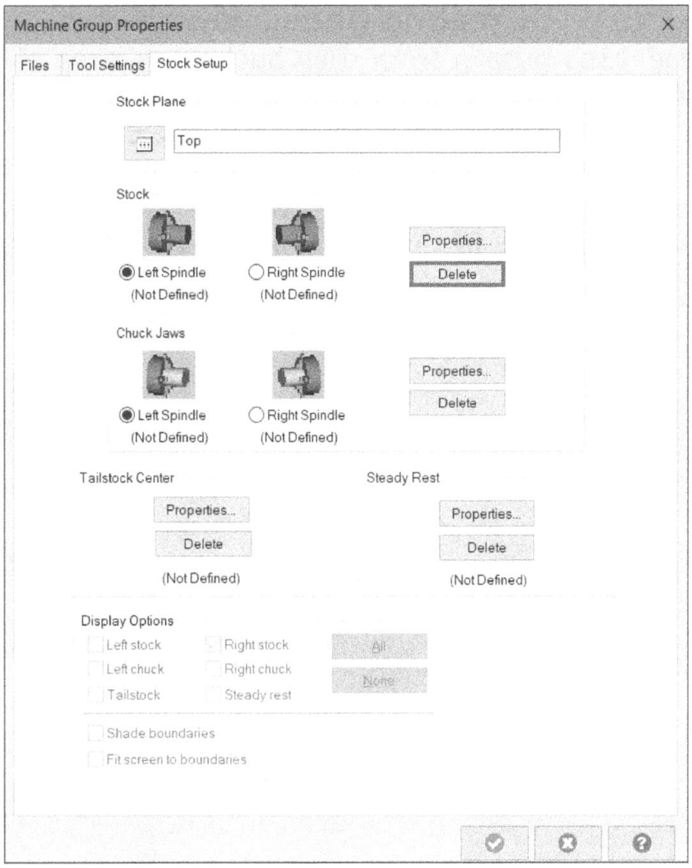

Figure-113. Machine Group Properties dialog box

- Click on the **Plane select** button and select **+D+Z** plane as stock plane.
- Make sure the **Left Spindle** radio buttons are selected in the dialog box and then click on the **Properties** button in the **Stock** area of the dialog box. The **Machine Component Manager-Stock** dialog box will be displayed. Specify the **OD** as **120** and **Length** as **80** in respective edit boxes. Select **+Z** option from the **Axis** drop-down and select the **Use Margins** check box.
- Specify **OD Margin** as **2.0**, **Right Margin** as **3.0**, and **Left Margin** as **3.0** in respective edit boxes; refer to Figure-114.
- Click on the **OK** button from the dialog box.

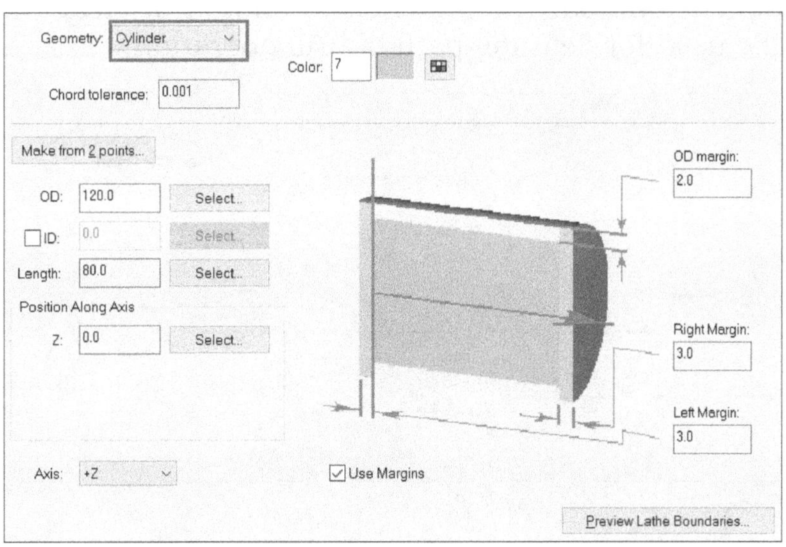

Figure-114. Margins and parameters for stock

Creating Chuck Jaws

- Click on the **Properties** button from the **Chuck Jaws** area of the dialog box. The **Machine Component Manager - Chuck Jaws** dialog box will be displayed.
- Select the **Outer diameter (OD)** check box from the **Clamping Method** area in the dialog box. Select the **From Stock** check box and **Grip on maximum diameter** check box from the **Position** area of the dialog box.
- Specify the **Grip length** as **6** in the edit box; refer to Figure-115.

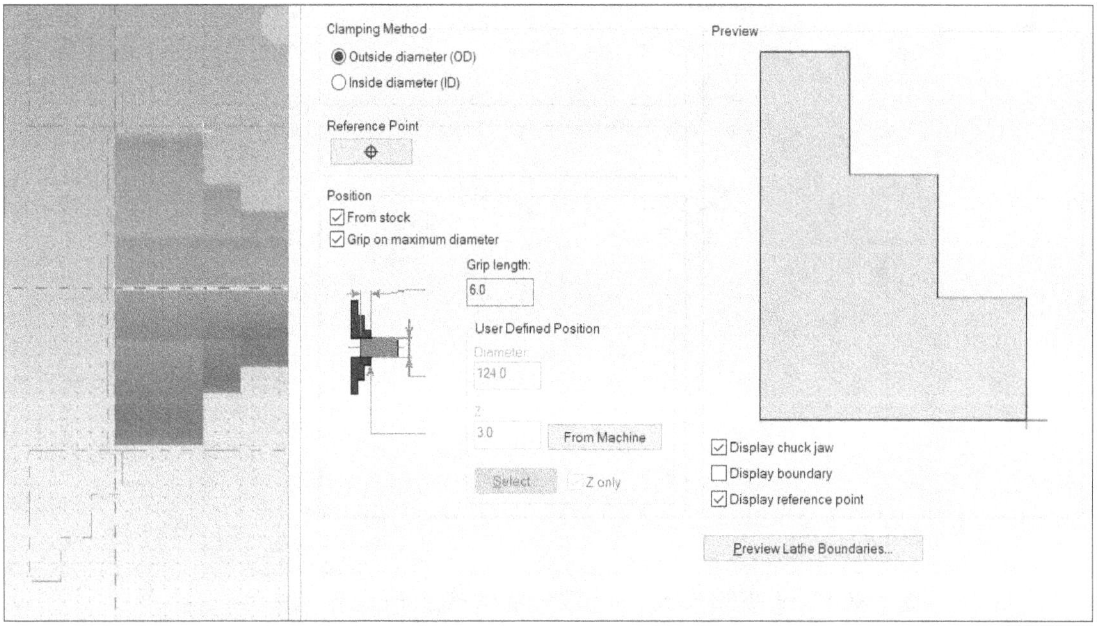

Figure-115. Parameters for chuck jaws

- Click on the **OK** button from the dialog box. The **Machine Group Properties** dialog box will be displayed again. Select the **Shade boundaries** check box and click on the **OK** button from the dialog box to exit.

Creating Sketch for Toolpaths

- Click on the **Line Endpoints** tool from the **Lines** panel of **Wireframe** tab in the **Ribbon** and create a sketch line as shown in Figure-116. Note that you do not need to get exact dimensions but the dimensions should be near the shown values. This line will be used for defining path of drill operation.

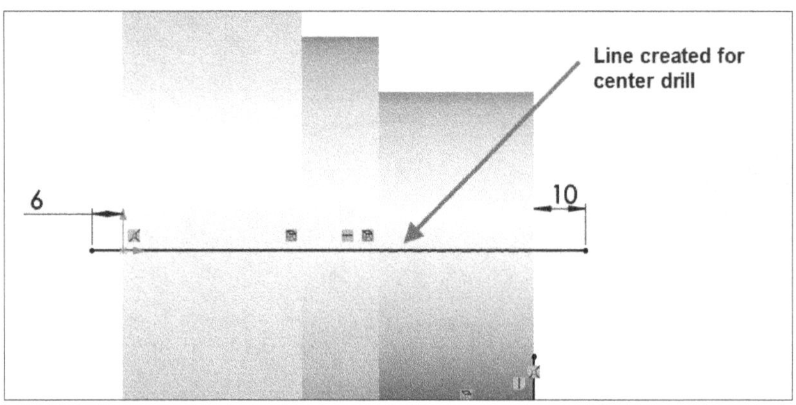

Figure-116. Sketch for toolpath of Practical 1

Performing Facing Operation

- Click on the **Face** tool from the **General** panel of the **Turning** tab in the **Ribbon**. The **Lathe Face** dialog box will be displayed.
- Select the **T3131 R0.8 ROUGH FACE RIGHT -80 DEG** tool from the tool list. The parameters as per the tool will be displayed on the right area in the dialog box.
- Select the **Finish feed rate** and **Finish spindle speed** check boxes from the right area.
- Set the values as per your machine and tool capabilities in the right area (We will continue with default values).
- Click on the **Face parameters** tab in the dialog box.
- Click on the **Finish Z** button in the dialog box. You will be asked to select a point.
- Select the edge of model as shown in Figure-117. The value of finish Z will be reflected automatically in the **Finish Z** edit box in the dialog box.

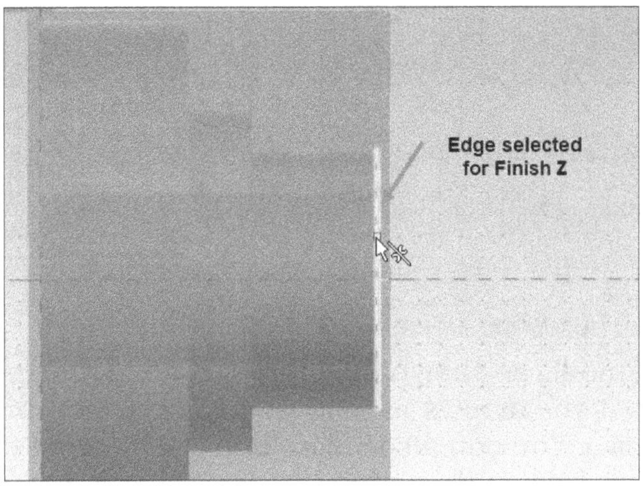

Figure-117. Edge selected for Finish Z

- Specify the other parameters as shown in Figure-118 and click on the **OK** button to generate toolpath.

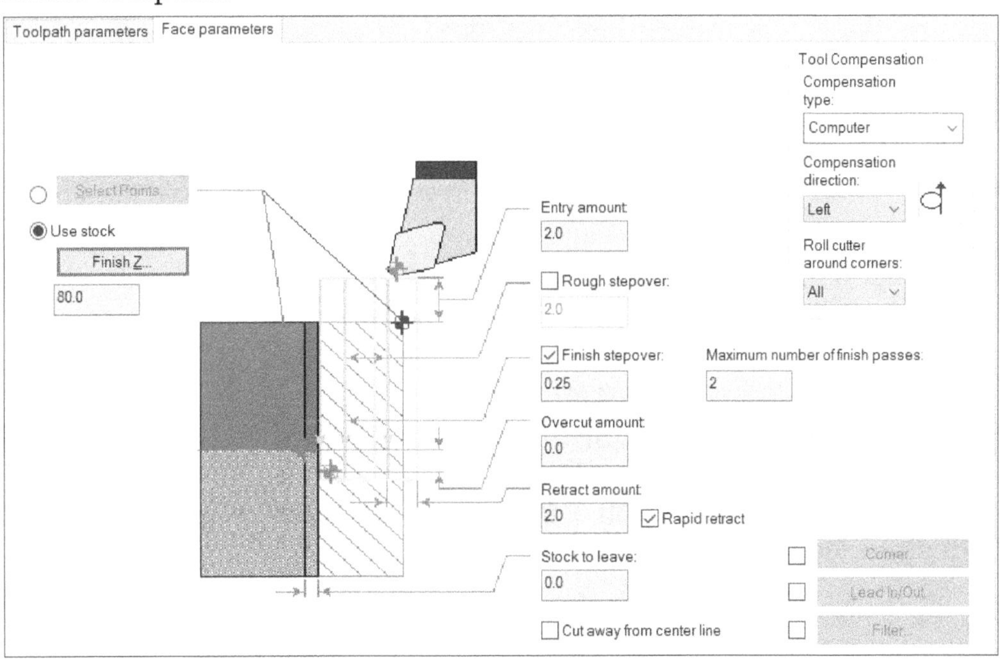

Figure-118. Parameters for facing

Performing OD Rough & OD Finish

- Click on the **Rough** tool from the **General** panel in the **Ribbon**. The **Wireframe Chaining** dialog box will be displayed asking you to select geometries for toolpath.
- Select the **Solids** button from the **Mode** area of the dialog box. The options of **Solid Chaining** will be displayed as shown in Figure-119 with model in wireframe style.

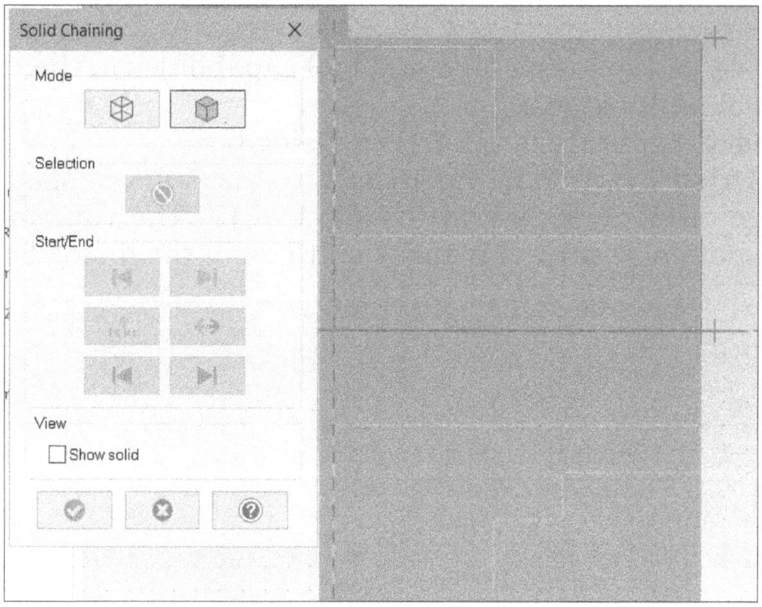

Figure-119. Solid Chaining dialog box

- Select the edges of model as shown in Figure-120, to define path for rough turning operation. Note that the arrows should point in correct direction to define how cutting tool will move. You can also create line chain using tools in **Wireframe** tab to define path for tool if you do not get full profile curves for toolpath.

Figure-120. Selecting edges to define path

- After selecting the edges, click on the **OK** button from the dialog box. The **Lathe Rough** dialog box will be displayed.
- Select the **T0101 R0.8 OD ROUGH RIGHT - 80 DEG** tool from the tool list box and specify desired feed rate parameters.

- Click on the **Rough parameters** tab and specify **0.5** in both **Stock to leave in X** and **Stock to leave in Z** edit boxes. If we run this toolpath then the tool is going to hit chuck and may kill the machine. We need to adjust the end contour of toolpath.
- Click on the **Lead In/Out** button and then click on the **Lead Out** tab in the **Lead In/Out** dialog box. Select the **Extend/shorten end of contour** check box from the **Adjust Contour** area of the dialog box. The related options will become active.
- Select the **Shorten** radio button and specify the amount as **4.0** in the edit box; refer to Figure-121.

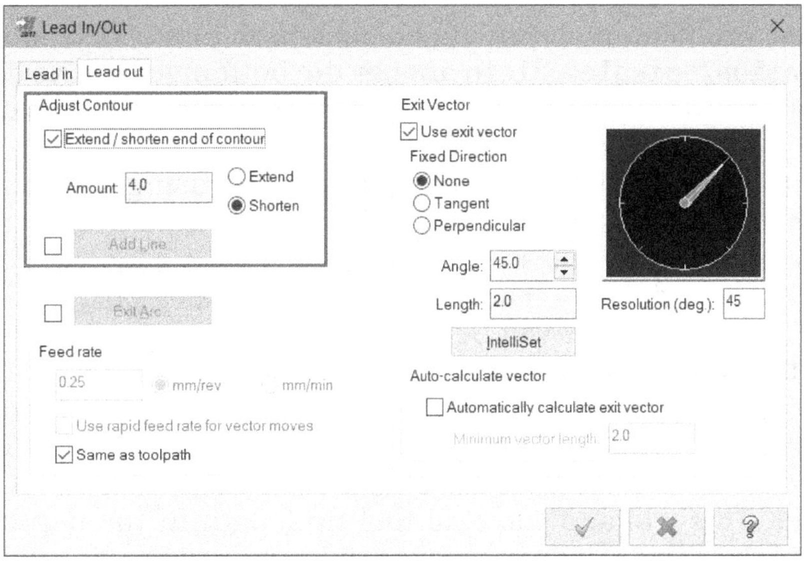

Figure-121. Adjusting contour to save tool and chuck

- Click on the **OK** button from the dialog box and then click on the **OK** button from the **Lathe Rough** dialog box. The toolpath will be generated; refer to Figure-122.

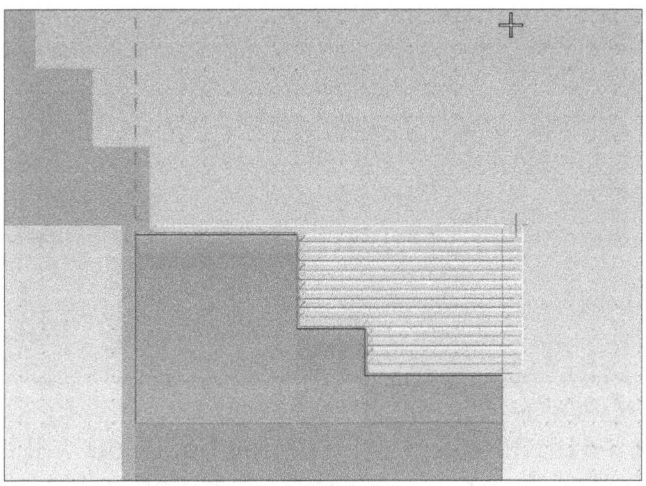

Figure-122. Lathe rough toolpath generated

Similarly, you perform the OD finish by using the **Finish** tool in the **General** panel of **Ribbon**.

Performing Drilling

To get a better accuracy in center hole, we can plan to perform drilling with lesser diameter and then perform boring with exact diameter. The steps are given next.

- Click on the **Drill** tool from the **General** panel of **Turning** tab in the **Ribbon**. The **Lathe Drill** dialog box will be displayed.
- Select the **T129129 35 DIA DRILL** from the tool list box. The related parameters will be displayed on the right in the dialog box. Again, set the parameters as per your machine and tool capabilities (We are continuing with default values).
- Sometimes, axis and spindle origin do not align automatically with default origins and can cause problem in specifying hole position of tool. Click on the button in **Axis Combination/Spindle Origin** area at the bottom left in the dialog box. Don't change anything and click on the **OK** button from the dialog box. This will align current tool plane with default WCS.
- Specify a suitable home position for cutting tool by using the options in the **Home Position** area as the default drill and drill holders in the application are bigger in size compared to other tools.
- Click on the **Simple drill - no peck** tab in the dialog box. The options related to drill depth and drill point will be displayed.
- Click on the **Depth** button and select the end point of centerline we created earlier in sketch; refer to Figure-123. The **Lathe Drill** dialog box will be displayed again with depth value reflected in **Depth** edit box. Click on the **Depth Calculator** button next to the edit box and click on the **OK** button from the **Depth Calculator** dialog box displayed. This will add the drill tool tip length in the depth if you want to create a through all hole.

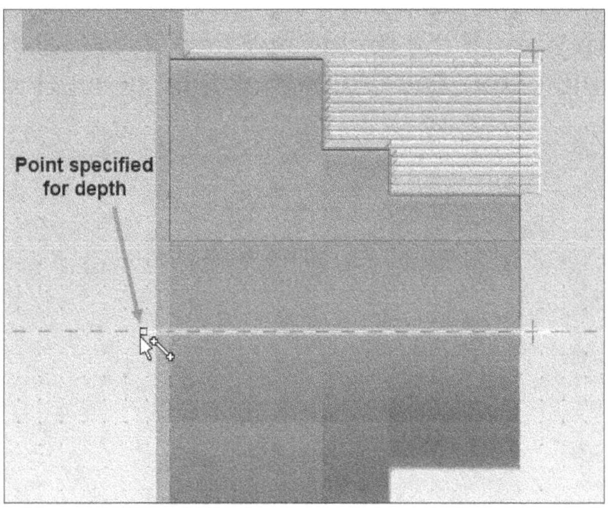

Figure-123. Drill depth point selected

- Click on the **Drill Point** button in the dialog box. You will be asked to select the starting point of drill toolpath. Select the other end point of the same line.
- Click on the **OK** button from the dialog box to create the toolpath.

Performing Boring Operation

No! this operation is not that much 'boring (dull)'. This operation is performed to increase the diameter of hole in tight tolerance.

- Click on the **Finish** tool from the **Lathe Toolpaths** drop-down in the **Ribbon**. The **Wireframe Chaining** dialog box will be displayed and you will be asked to select geometry for finishing operation.
- Select the inner edge of the model as shown in Figure-124 and click on the **OK** button from the dialog box. The **Lathe Finish** dialog box will be displayed.
- Select the **T8383 R0.8 ID FINISH MIN 25 DIA - 55 DEG** tool from the tool list box. Specify the feed parameters as per your machine and tool capabilities. Note that you need to modify or create new tools in Mastercam if you have different tools in your workshop. Otherwise, the NC program generated here will not be useful on your machine.

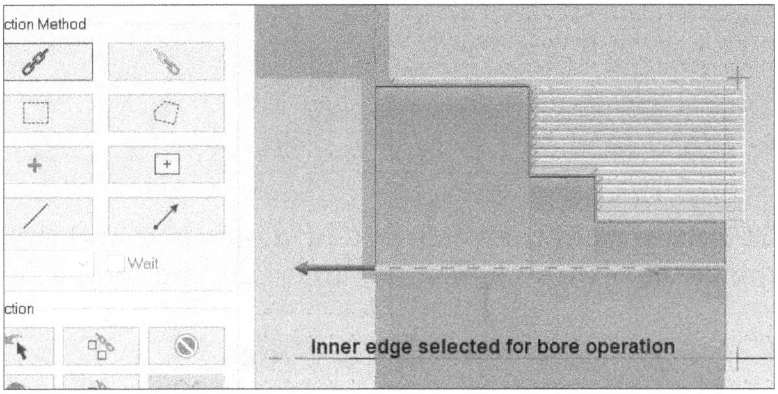

Figure-124. Edge selected for bore finishing

- Click on the **Finish parameters** tab in the dialog box. The options related to finish toolpath will be displayed.
- Set the **Finish stepover** value as **1** and **Number of finish passes** as **2** in respective edit boxes.
- If you click on **OK** button and create the toolpath now, then there will be some material left at the back face which need boring operation; refer to Figure-125. To solve this problem, we will set some extra lead out in the toolpath.

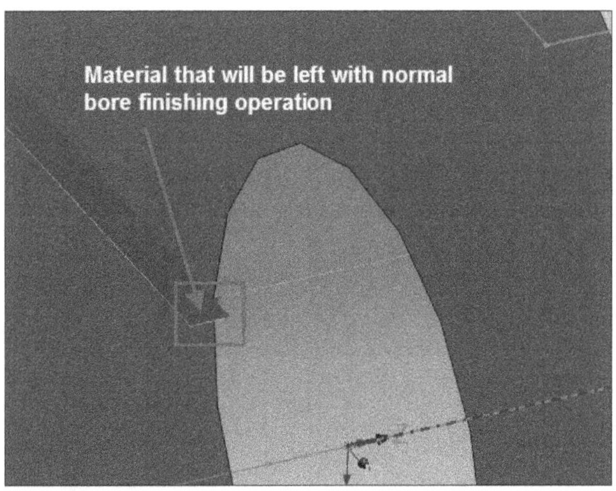

Figure-125. Material that could be left after boring

- Click on the **Lead In/Out** button from the dialog box. The **Lead In/Out** dialog box will be displayed.
- Click on the **Lead out** tab in the dialog box and extend the contour by **5**; refer to Figure-126 (Options marked in boxes).

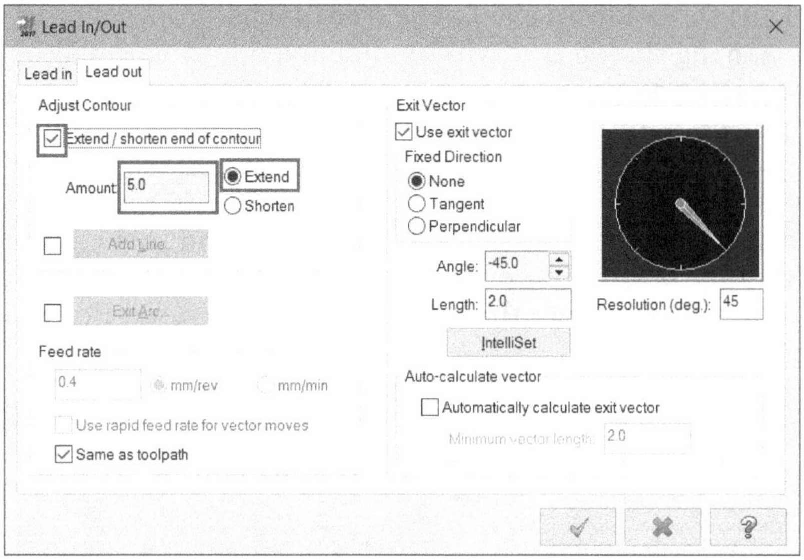

Figure-126. Options to extend contour

- Click on the **OK** button from the **Lead In/Out** dialog box and then click on the **OK** button from the **Lathe Finish** dialog box to create the toolpath.

Generating G-codes

- Select the specific operation like **Lathe Rough** from the **Mastercam Toolpath Manager** if you want to generate G codes for any specific operation; refer to Figure-127. If you want to generate G codes for all the operations in current toolpath group then select the group from the **Mastercam Toolpath Manager**.

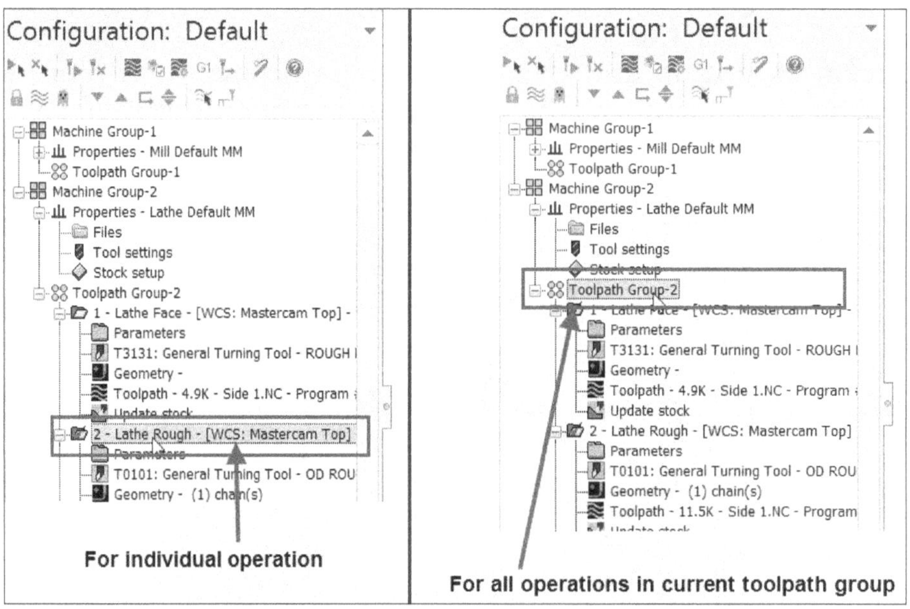

Figure-127. Operation to be selected

- Click on the **Post selected operations** button  from the toolbar in the **Toolpaths Manager**. The **Post processing** dialog box will be displayed; refer to Figure-128. Note that this option is not available in learning edition of software.

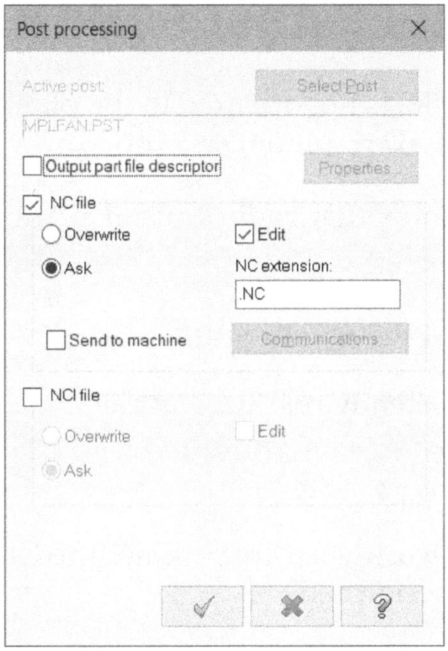

Figure-128. Post processing dialog box

- If you have a machine connected to the system then you can select the **Send to machine** check box and communicate the program directly to machine.
- Click on the **OK** button from the dialog box. Note that the post processor selected in Machine definition will be used to output G codes. The **Save As** dialog box will be displayed; refer to Figure-129.

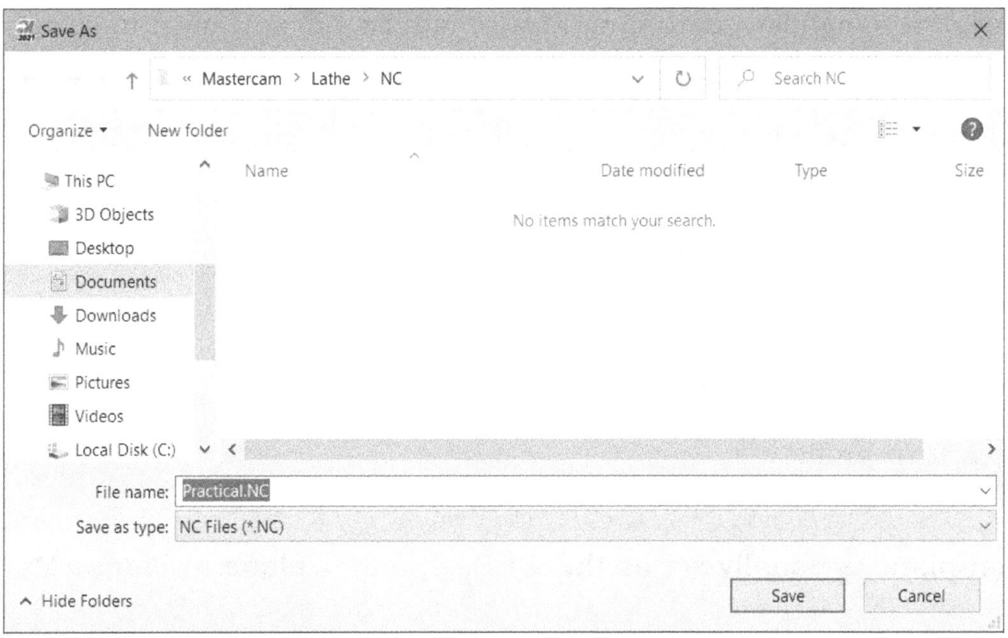

Figure-129. Save As dialog box

- Click on the **Save** button and save the file with desired name. The **Mastercam Code Expert** application will open. Verify the codes and close the application if you find the codes satisfactory. Otherwise, you can edit the code file.

In this chapter, we have discussed the procedure to create toolpaths for lathe machines. We have worked on a real model for lathe machining. In the next chapter, we will discuss some more lathe machining tools and practical exercises.

SELF ASSESSMENT

Q1. Most of the time, the model is not oriented to the plane used for turning operation, to align the model face with +D+Z plane, use the .... tool.

Q2. Select the Inside diameter (ID) radio button if the stock is placed inside the chuck jaws. (T/F)

Q3. What is the function of tailstock in lathe?

Q4. What is the function of steady rest in a lathe?

Q5. What is spindle speed?

Q6. If there is a flat head workpiece to be machined then which of the following toolpaths is the first to be performed?

a. Facing
b. Roughing
c. Drilling
d. Finishing

Q7. The Lathe Cutoff toolpath is used to cut the stock in two parts. (T/F)

Q8. To perform dynamic roughing in Mastercam Lathe, you need to select a button insert (round or ball shaped). (T/F)

Q9. The PrimeTurning toolpaths are generated specifically for ISCAR cutting tools. (T/F)

REVIEW QUESTIONS

Q1. What must be done first to activate Lathe Toolpaths in Mastercam?

A. Select a coordinate system
B. Select a lathe machine from the machine type panel
C. Create a turn profile
D. Set the stock dimensions

Q2. Which plane is usually set as the WCS, C, and T plane in Planes Manager for turning?

A. +X+Y
B. +D+Z
C. +Y+Z
D. +Z-X

Q3. What tool is used to orient the model correctly with the machining plane?

A. Align to X
B. Rotate 90
C. Align to Z
D. Flip Plane

Q4. In stock setup, which value defines the outer diameter of the stock?

A. ID
B. Z-depth
C. OD
D. Margin

Q5. What does selecting the “Use Margins” option allow you to define?

A. Tool diameter
B. Minimum cut depth
C. Extra material to be removed from stock
D. Feed rate

Q6. What is the function of the “Stock is drawn in position on the machine” checkbox?

A. To hide the stock
B. To place the origin manually
C. To automatically center stock
D. To switch machine origin

Q7. Which component is positioned using the “Left Spindle” or “Right Spindle” option?

A. Tool
B. Tailstock
C. Chuck jaws
D. Steady rest

Q8. What is required before using the Steady Rest setup?

A. WCS alignment
B. A closed sketch in the graphics area
C. Spindle speed setup
D. OD and ID settings

Q9. Which catalog is accessed first when creating a tool in Lathe Tool Manager?

A. Inserts
B. Holders
C. Parameters
D. Type

Q10. What is set in the "Home Position" area of the Define Tool dialog?

A. Tool shape
B. Insert catalog
C. Tool direction
D. Tool tip position

Q11. What is the function of the "Turn Profile" tool?

A. To cut grooves
B. To define part shape using wireframe curves
C. To set plunge speed
D. To create facing toolpaths

Q12. Which profile option creates the upper half of the model as a profile?

A. Full profile
B. Slice profile
C. Upper profile
D. Spin profile

Q13. Which toolpath operation is used to remove large stock of material?

A. Face
B. Finish
C. Rough
D. Cutoff

Q14. What is the purpose of the "Offset Number" in roughing?

A. Tool change delay
B. Feed rate calculation
C. Compensation for tool wear
D. Chuck position

Q15. If "Control" is selected in tool compensation type, what happens?

A. Tool path is ignored
B. Mastercam does not apply compensation
C. G41/G42 codes are generated in NC program
D. Insert is replaced

Q16. Which option must be selected to apply a semi-finishing pass during roughing?

A. Apply Facing
B. Use Margins
C. Semi Finish
D. Profile Join

Q17. What is the purpose of the "Lead In/Out" parameters?

A. Set stock length
B. Set entry and exit of toolpath
C. Define cutting depth
D. Align tool rotation

Q18. Which option allows you to plunge the tool using a specific method?

A. Feed Angle
B. Entry Vector
C. Plunge Parameters
D. Setup Tool

Q19. What is a requirement for stock recognition to be available?

A. At least two contours
B. No spindle stock defined
C. Only one contour chained and stock defined
D. Roughing tool not selected

Q20. Which Finish toolpath parameter must be set to zero to ensure final dimensions?

A. Feed rate
B. OD and ID
C. Stock to leave in X and Z
D. Station number

Q21. What is the main purpose of the Lathe Drill operation?

A. Remove burrs
B. Perform finishing
C. Drill holes in the workpiece
D. Define turn profile

Q22. Which dialog box is used to specify parameters like retract radius and tool compensation in Cutoff operation?

A. Finish parameters tab
B. Cutoff parameters tab
C. Holder dialog box
D. Stock setup dialog box

Q23. Which toolpath is used to create grooves in a workpiece in lathe operations?
A. Dynamic Rough
B. Groove
C. Contour Rough
D. Thread

Q24. What happens if the Multiple chains radio button is selected in the Grooving Options dialog box?
A. Only internal grooves can be selected
B. Only external grooves can be selected
C. Multiple grooves can be selected
D. One groove must be selected at a time

Q25. In the Groove shape parameters tab, what option allows the groove to cut in parallel direction to the groove angle?
A. Tangent to groove walls
B. Perpendicular to groove walls
C. Parallel to groove angle
D. Axial direction

Q26. In Groove rough parameters, which cutting directions are available for canned groove toolpaths?
A. Chain only
B. Positive and negative
C. Clockwise and counter-clockwise
D. Up and down

Q27. What is used in Dynamic Rough toolpath to extend tool life and cutting speed?
A. Grooving inserts
B. Multiple start passes
C. Button inserts
D. Diamond inserts

Q28. Before using Dynamic Rough toolpath, which tools are recommended to be used first?
A. Thread and Groove
B. Point and Contour
C. Rough and Face
D. Groove and Plunge Turn

Q29. In Thread shape parameters, selecting the Cross centerline cut checkbox allows:
A. Creating square threads
B. Generating toolpath on the opposite side of centerline
C. Flipping the orientation of cutting tool
D. Ignoring the toolpath for opposite side

Q30. What is used to automatically populate standard thread data in Thread toolpath?
A. Custom thread generator
B. Manual feed rate input
C. Thread Form table
D. Toolpath radius dialog

Q31. What precaution is necessary when using Plunge Turn toolpath?
A. Use finishing tool only
B. Ensure holder collision detection is off
C. Use tool designed specifically for plunge turning
D. Only use for threading

Q32. What is a “hanging ring” in Plunge Turn operations?
A. An additional clearance cut
B. A small burr left after cut
C. An oversized groove
D. A skipped toolpath

Q33. Which option in Plunge Turn rough parameters helps avoid burrs on both sides of a cut?
A. Don’t prevent
B. Positive
C. Bi-Directional
D. Negative

Q34. The Contour Rough toolpath is best suited for:
A. Turning large shafts
B. Face finishing
C. Machining similar stock and part profiles
D. Custom thread machining

Q35. Which offset option in Contour Rough parameters allows setting different cut depths in X and Z directions?
A. Constant offset
B. Bi-directional offset
C. XZ offset
D. Chain offset

Q36. What is a key limitation of Contour Rough toolpath?
A. Does not allow lead-in
B. No support for ID machining
C. No collision detection on holder
D. Cannot rough threads

Q37. PrimeTurning toolpaths are developed specifically for:
A. ISCAR inserts
B. Mastercam default tools
C. Sandvik Coromant tools
D. Custom inserts

Q38. To use PrimeTurning, which library should be selected?
A. Generic Lathe
B. CoroTurn Prime
C. ISO Metric
D. Canned Tool Library

Q39. In PrimeTurning Rough Parameters, which strategy performs horizontal cuts followed by vertical cuts?
A. Horizontal
B. Vertical
C. Horizontal then vertical
D. Spiral

Q40. What is the function of the Clean up corners checkbox in PrimeTurning?
A. Sharpens thread forms
B. Improves tool radius
C. Removes sharp edge material
D. Adjusts coolant settings

Q41. What type of threads can be created using the Custom Thread toolpath?
A. Only V-threads
B. Only square threads
C. Custom threads like square and trapezoidal
D. Only internal threads

Q42. In Custom Thread Manager, what does selecting the Chain radio button under Shape Type allow?
A. Selecting preloaded thread profiles
B. Drawing custom thread manually
C. Selecting thread profile from model geometry
D. Adjusting thread pitch

Q43. Which tab in Custom Thread Manager is used to define custom thread shapes based on parameters?
A. Machine
B. Shape
C. Operation
D. Rough Motion Control

Q44. Which tool is used to generate toolpaths based on specific point selections?
A. Groove
B. Custom Thread
C. Point
D. Contour Rough

Q45. What does selecting Rapid break (G0) in Point toolpath dialog box do?
A. Makes a rapid pass without cutting
B. Starts a cutting pass after a rapid move
C. Only allows tool retraction
D. Prevents tool engagement

Q46. What are canned toolpaths primarily used for?
A. Simulating rough passes
B. Generating automatic finishing passes
C. Performing repetitive cutting operations
D. Threading and grooving only

Q47. In Canned Rough Parameters tab, which two values are primarily required?
A. Tool number and holder type
B. Step-over and relief
C. Depth of cut and stock to be left
D. Diameter and thread pitch

Chapter 15

Advanced Lathe Tools and Toolpaths

Topics Covered

The major topics covered in this chapter are:

- ***Introduction***
- ***Stock Pickoff, Pull, and Cutoff Operations***
- ***Stock Transfer***
- ***Stock Flip***
- ***Stock Advance***
- ***Undoing Stock related operations***
- ***Chuck and Tailstock movement code generation***
- ***Face Contouring***
- ***Cross Contouring***
- ***Back Plot and Verifying Toolpaths***
- ***Practical and Practice***

INTRODUCTION

In the previous chapter, you have learned about the basic operations that are performed on simple 2 axis lathe. But, the CNC turning machines are not confined to 2 axis lathe. The turning machine can be of as many as 4 axis. Note that we have left the back face of model un-machined in Practical of previous chapter. But in real machining, we will open the chuck and reverse the side of part to get back face machined. We will learn about such operations in this chapter. We will also learn about bar pulling or cutoff operations, C axis operations, and face contouring operations that can be performed on advanced lathe machines. In the end, we will simulate the process of machining in real-time.

FACE CONTOUR

The **Face Contour** tool is used to draw a toolpath for machining curves on face of part; refer to Figure-1.

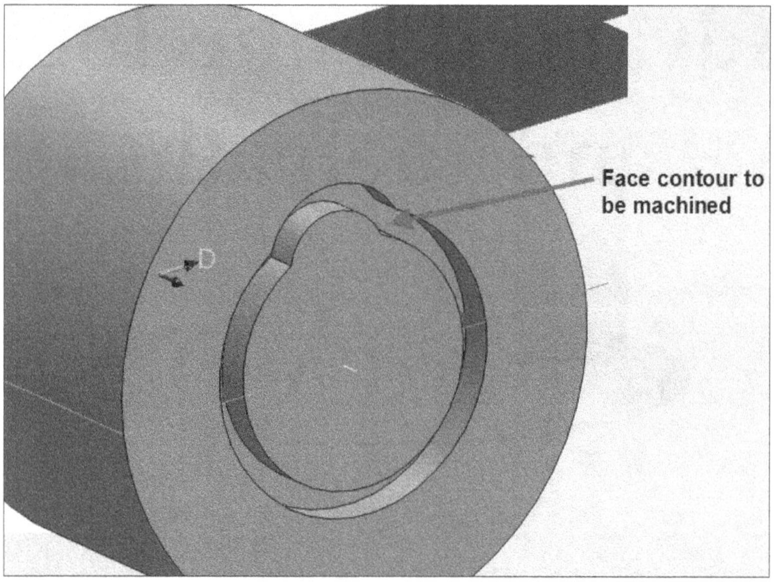

Figure-1. Face contour to be machined

Note that you should use this toolpath after you have done facing and roughing operation, so that there is a low amount of stock left on the face. The procedure to create a face contour toolpath is given next.

- Click on the **Face Contour** tool from the **C-axis** panel of **Turning** tab in the **Ribbon**. The **Solid Chaining** dialog box will be displayed.
- Select the faces on the front face of part to be machined; refer to Figure-2. Click on the **OK** button from the dialog box to apply selection. The **C-Axis Toolpath - C-Axis Face Contour** dialog box will be displayed; refer to Figure-3.

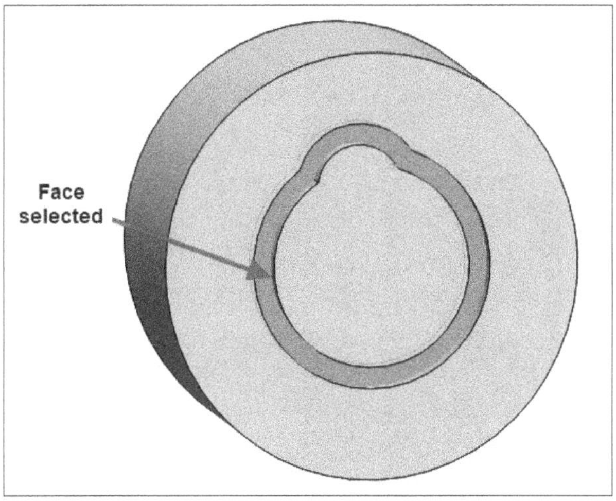

Figure-2. Face selected for face contouring

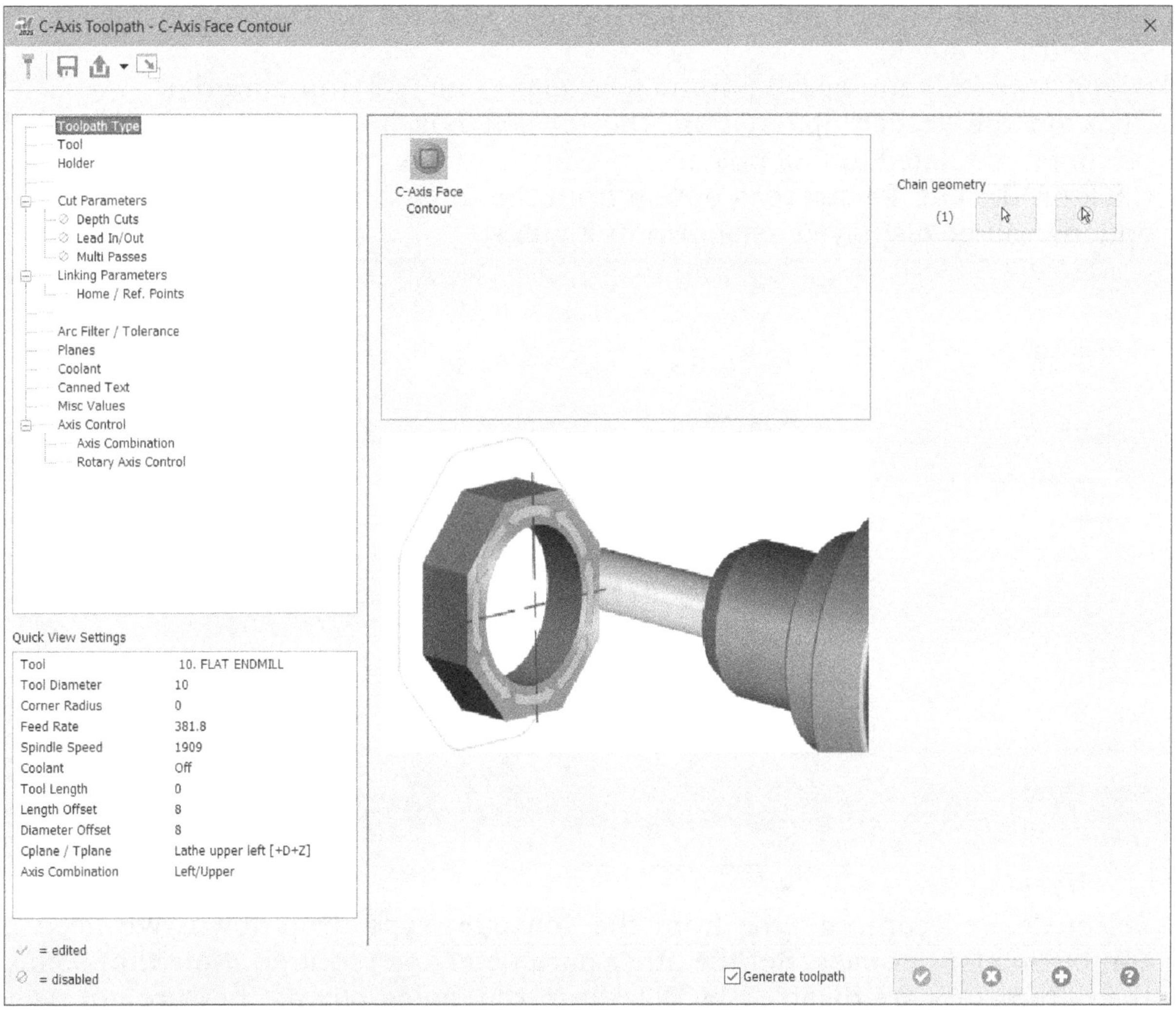

Figure-3. C-Axis Toolpath-C-Axis Face Contour dialog box

- Click on the **Tool** option from the top left box in the dialog box. The options related to tool selection will be displayed. Click on the **Select library** tool from the right area. The **Tool Selection** dialog box will be displayed; refer to Figure-4.

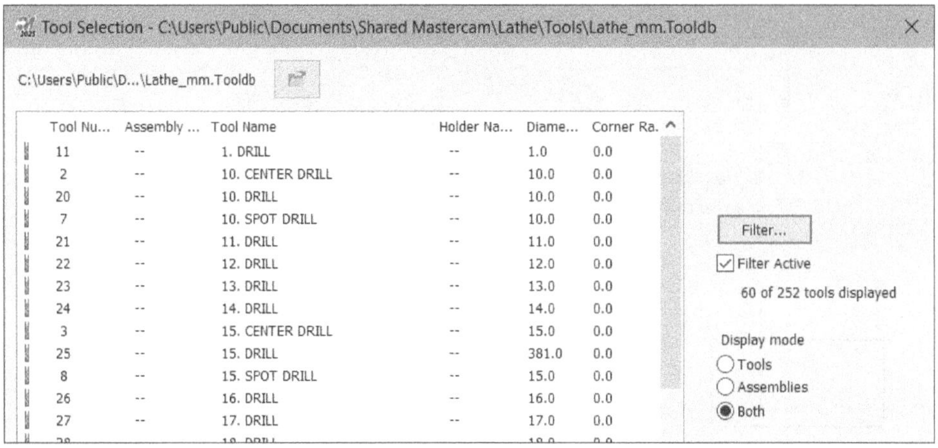

Figure-4. Tool Selection dialog box

- Select desired tool from the list and click on the **OK** button. (In our case, we have selected **3 mm** flat end mill because the face selected for contour is flat and the slot width is small).
- Specify the feed and speed parameters as per the tool and material.
- Click on the **Holder** option from the top left box in the dialog box to set the parameters related to tool holder.
- Click on the **Cut Parameters** option from the top left box in the dialog box. The options will be displayed as shown in Figure-5.

Figure-5. Cut Parameters page for face contour tool

- Select desired contour type from the **Contour type** drop-down. We need 2D contouring for our case. Set the other parameters as required. Note that some of the parameters are disabled by default in the dialog box as they are not useful for current toolpath. If you still need to specify any disable parameters then click on it from the top left box and select the related check box from the right area to activate the options.
- After specifying desired parameters, click on the **OK** button from the dialog box. The toolpath will be generated.

CROSS CONTOUR

The **Cross Contour** tool is used to create toolpath for contour along C axis; refer to Figure-6. The procedure to use this tool is given next.

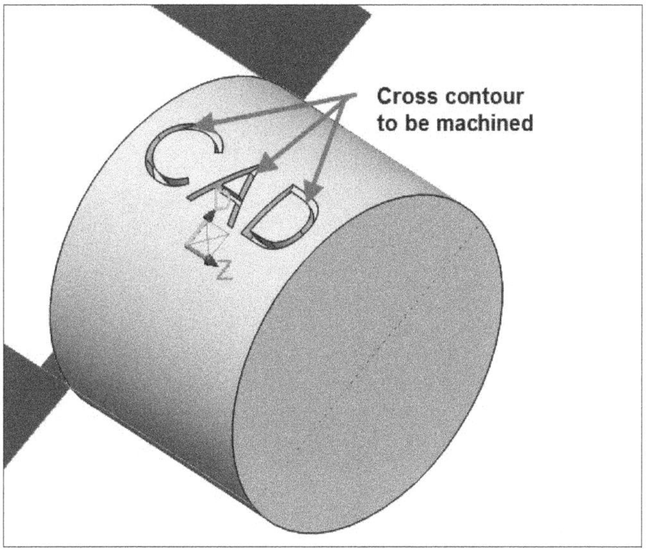

Figure-6. Cross contour to be machined

- Click on the **Cross Contour** tool from the **C-axis** panel of **Turning** tab in the **Ribbon**. The **Solid Chaining** dialog box will be displayed.
- Select the faces that you want to be machined; refer to Figure-7 and click on the **OK** button from the dialog box. The **C-Axis Toolpath - C-Axis Cross Contour** dialog box will be displayed; refer to Figure-8.

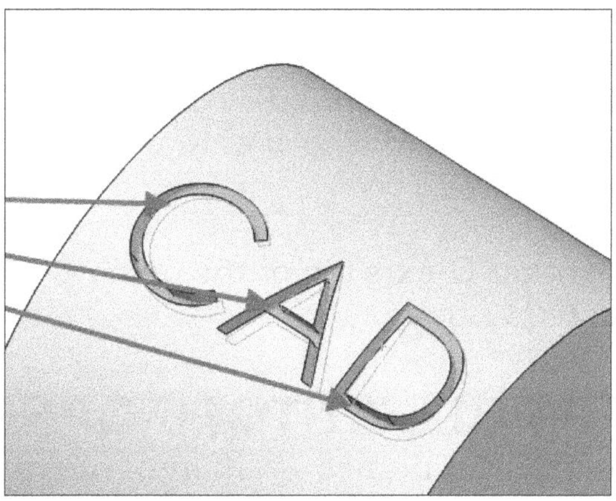

Figure-7. Faces selected for cross contour

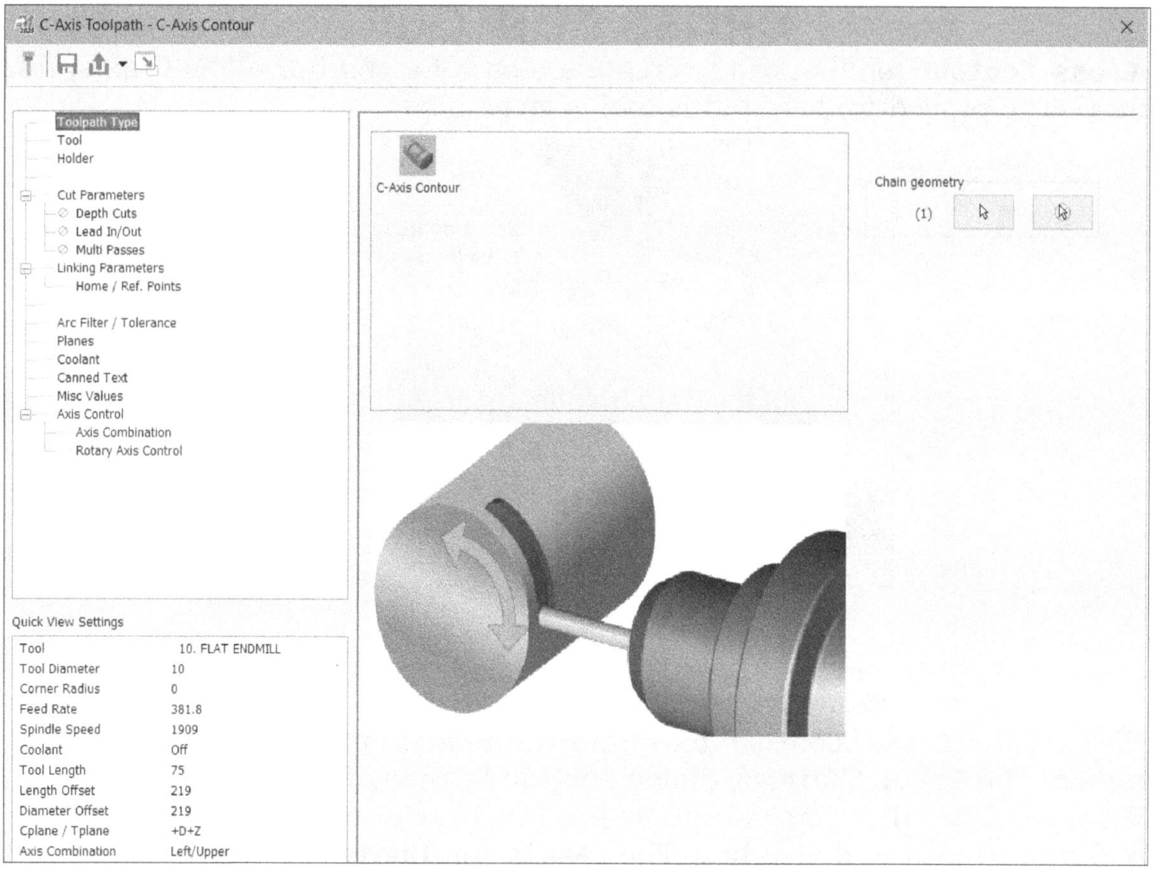

Figure-8. C-Axis Toolpath-C-Axis Cross Contour dialog box

- Select desired tool after clicking on the **Tool** option from the top left box in the dialog box as discussed in previous tool description.
- Specify the other parameters as required.
- Click on the **OK** button from the dialog box to create the toolpath. The toolpath will be displayed.

Similarly, you can use the other C-axis toolpaths using **C-Axis Contour**, **Face Drill**, **Cross Drill**, and **C-Axis Drill** tools.

PICKOFF/PULL/CUTOFF OPERATION

Although, these are three different names of different operations but the mechanism behind them is same. Till now, we have worked with single chuck. If we have two chucks and other chuck can move back and forth then we can unclamp the first chuck and clamp the part in other chuck to perform back face machining, bar pulling, or cutoff operations. The procedure to perform these operations is given next.

Preparing for Pickoff/Pull/Cutoff Operation

Preparation can have different meaning to different people but here by preparation we mean, selecting the machine or post processor which is capable of creating codes for such operations and creating secondary chuck which can move back and forth in machine. Note that the default Lathe machine in Mastercam is capable of performing these operations. The steps to prepare model for part handling operations are given next.

- Click on the **Stock setup** option from the **Properties** node of the newly added machine in **Mastercam Toolpath Manager**.
- Define stock and left spindle of chuck jaws for the part; refer to Figure-9.

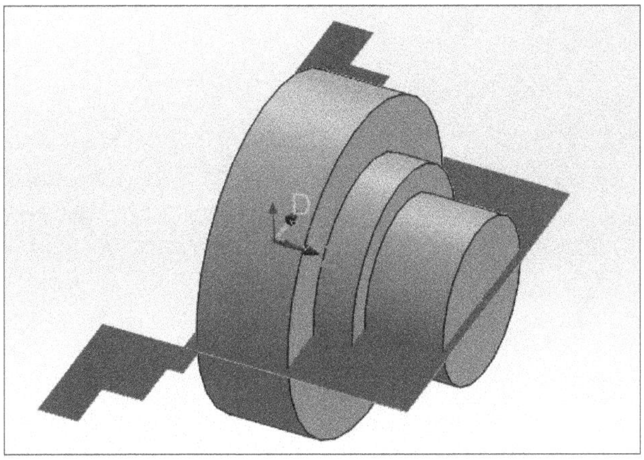

Figure-9. Left chuck and stock created

- Select the **Right Spindle** radio button from the **Chuck Jaws** area of the **Machine Group Properties** dialog box and click on the **Properties** button. The **Machine Component Manager - Chuck Jaws** dialog box will be displayed as discussed earlier.
- Select desired clamping method from the **Clamping Method** area in **Parameters** tab of the dialog box.
- Specify the diameter of the shaft/boss which you want to clamp in jaws in the **Diameter** edit box and specify desired distance from the coordinate system in **Z** edit box to place the secondary chuck jaws. Preview of the chuck will be displayed; refer to Figure-10. Click on the **OK** button from the **Machine Component Manager - Chuck Jaws** dialog box and then from the **Machine Group Properties** dialog box to create chuck.

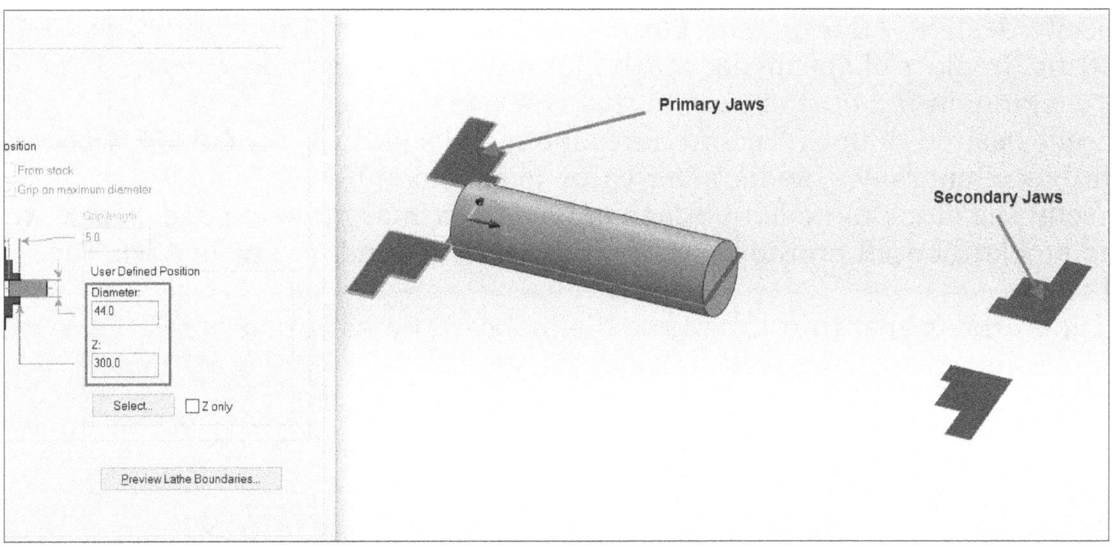

Figure-10. Preview of secondary jaws

Performing Pickoff, bar pull, cutoff Operation

- Click on the **Pickoff/Pull/Cutoff** tool from the **Part Handling** panel of **Turning** tab in the **Ribbon**. The **Pickoff / Bar Pull / Cutoff** dialog box will be displayed; refer to Figure-11.

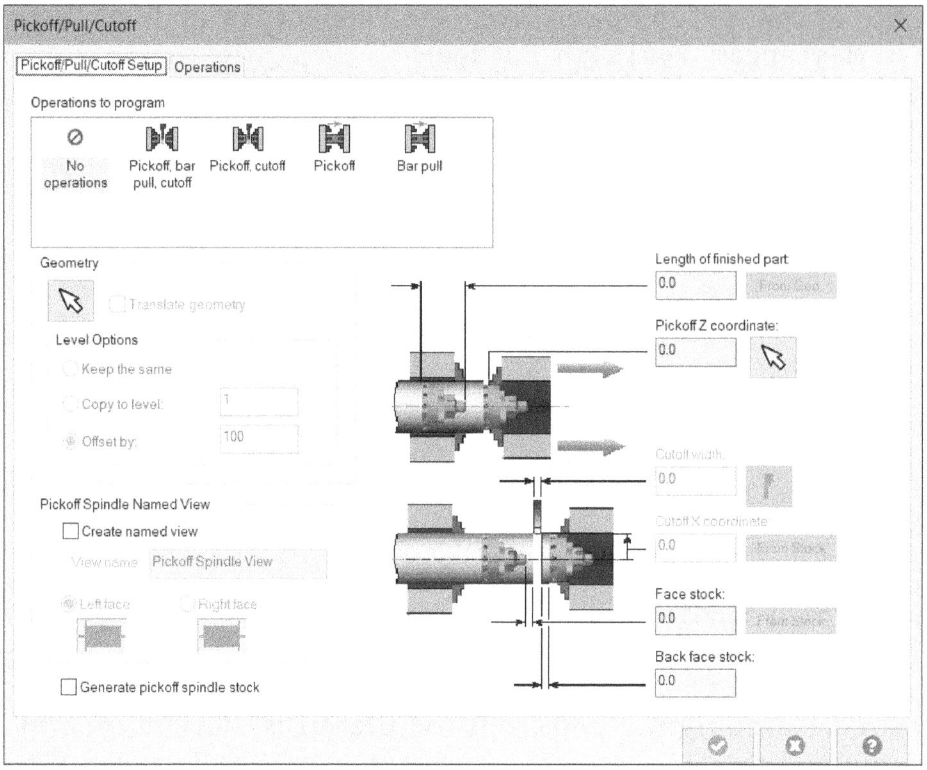

Figure-11. Pickoff / Bar Pull / Cutoff dialog box

- Select the **Pickoff, bar pull, cutoff** option from the **Operations to program** box.
- Specify the parameters like length of finished part in the **Length of finished part** edit box. Once the part will cutoff, the specified length of part will remain in primary chuck.
- Specify desired value in the **Pickoff Z coordinate** edit box. The value specified here is the location at which secondary jaw will hold the cut off portion of part.
- Specify desired value in the **Cutoff width** edit box. This width will be lost in cutting. In place of specifying width manually, you can choose desired cut off tool by clicking on the button next to this edit box.
- Specify desired value of X coordinate for cut off location in the **Cutoff X coordinate** edit box. Generally, the diameter value is specified here.
- Specify the stock to be left on face of part in primary jaw in **Face stock** edit box and stock to be left on the back face of part in secondary jaw in **Back face stock** edit box.
- Click on the **Operations** tab in the dialog box. The parameters related to various operations will be displayed; refer to Figure-12.

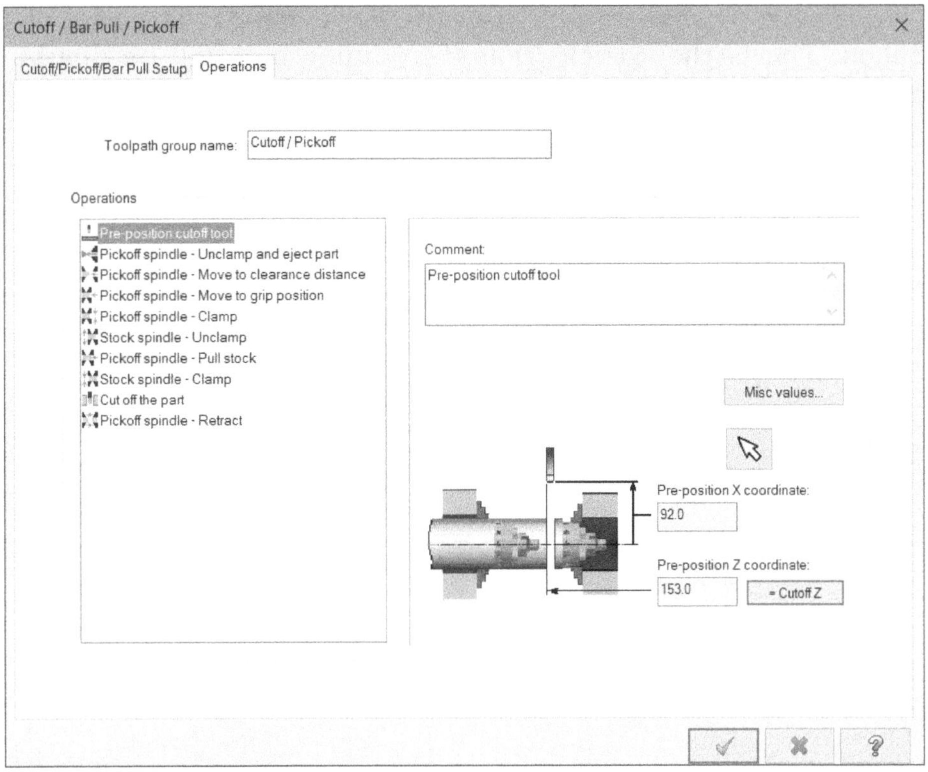

Figure-12. Operations tab

- Set desired parameters in the tab and click on the **OK** button. The process of cutting bar, pulling it out, and taking away by secondary spindle will happen automatically. The related codes will be generated accordingly.

STOCK TRANSFER

The **Stock Transfer** tool is used to transfer stock from one chuck to another (sub-spindle). This tool is useful when you want to machine back face of part after machining the front side; refer to Figure-13. The procedure to use this tool is given next.

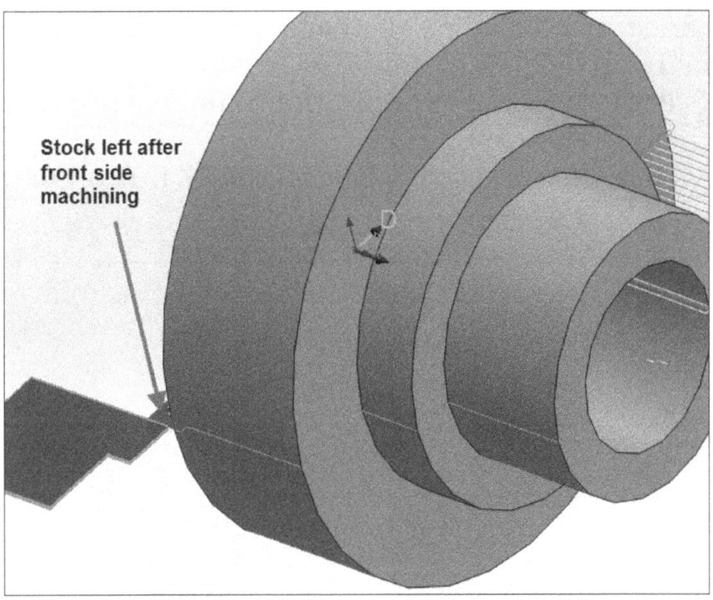

Figure-13. Stock left after front side machining

- Click on the **Stock Transfer** tool from the **Part Handling** panel of **Turning** tab in the **Ribbon**. The **Lathe Stock Transfer** dialog box will be displayed; refer to Figure-14.

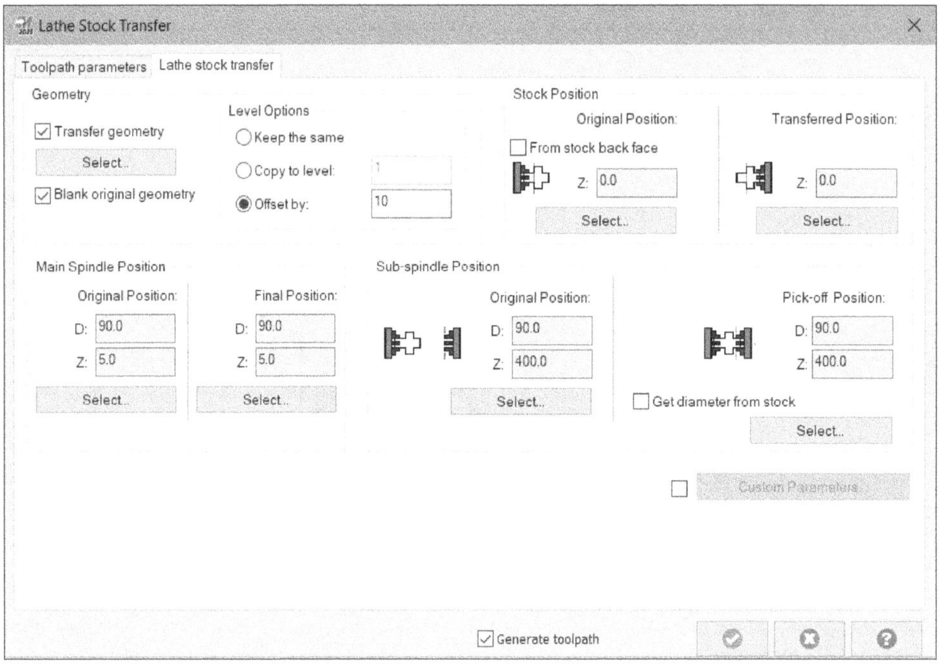

Figure-14. Lathe Stock Transfer dialog box

- Click on the **Select** button from the **Geometry** area of the dialog box. You will be asked to select the geometry to be transferred.
- Select the geometry to be transferred. The parameters in the dialog box will be modified according to geometry selected. In most of the cases, you can directly hit **OK** button to transfer the geometry but if you need to modify parameters then details are given next.
- Specify the distance of a reference point which you want to be shifted in the **Z** edit box of **Original Position** area. Like, you can specify the position of back face point.
- Specify the distance in **Z** edit box of **Transferred Position** area to which you want to move the back face point earlier selected.
- In the **Pick-off Position** area, specify the diameter and **Z** value at which you want to clamp the part in sub-spindle.
- After specifying desired parameters, click on the **OK** button to transfer stock; refer to Figure-15.

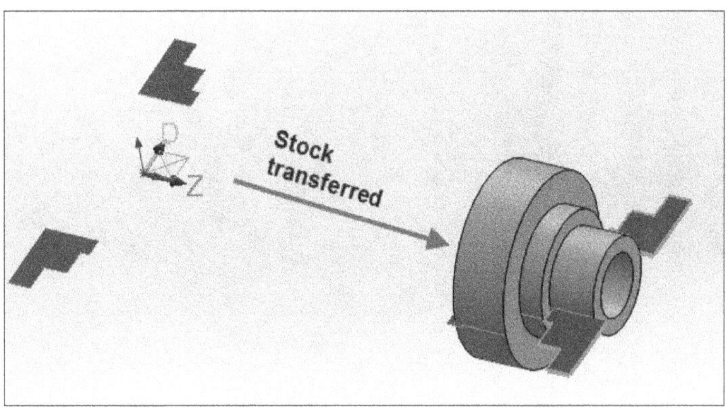

Figure-15. Stock transferred

STOCK FLIP

The **Stock Flip** tool is used to reverse the face of model so that you can perform back face machining and other operations; refer to Figure-16. The procedure to use this tool is given next.

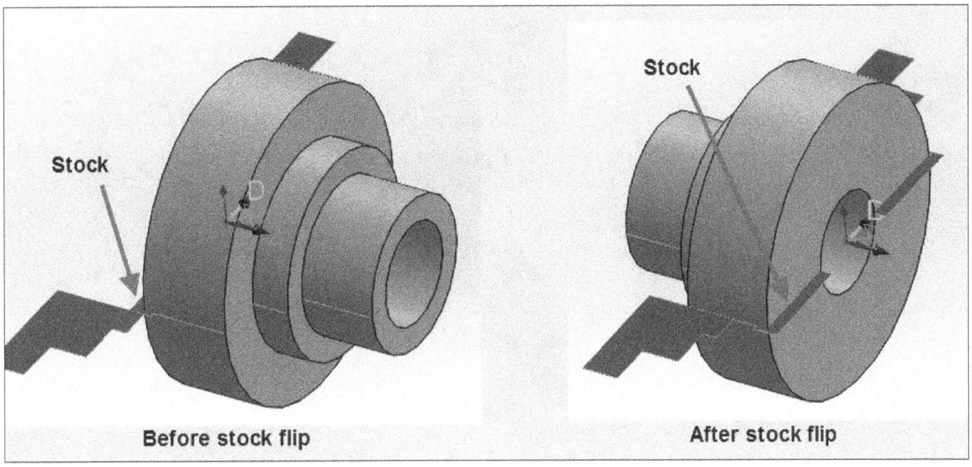

Figure-16. Model before and after stock flip

- Click on the **Stock Flip** tool from the **Part Handling** panel of **Turning** tab in the **Ribbon**. The **Lathe Stock Flip** dialog box will be displayed; refer to Figure-17.

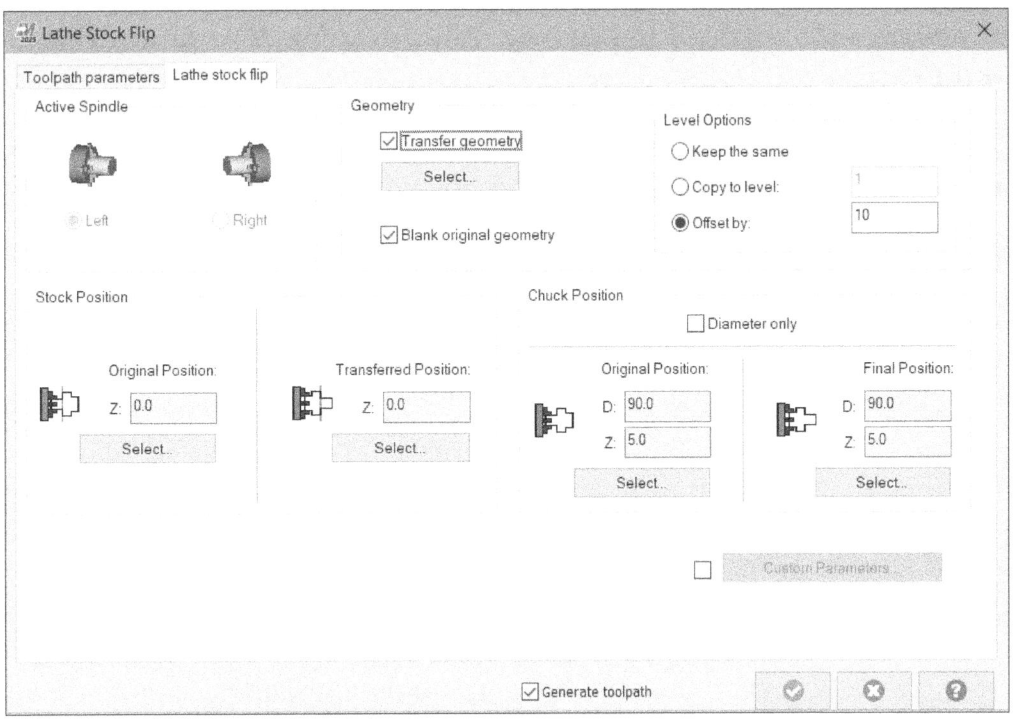

Figure-17. Lathe Stock Flip dialog box

- Click on the **Select** button from the **Geometry** area of the dialog box. You will be asked to select the model to be flipped.
- Select the model to be flipped and click on the **OK** button from the **Selection PropertyManager**.
- In the **Final Position** edit boxes, specify the diameter value and **Z** position where chuck should hold the part. Note that when part will be flipped, the back face of the model will be at new Z=0 position. So, you may need to specify a negative **Z** value to hold the part; refer to Figure-18.

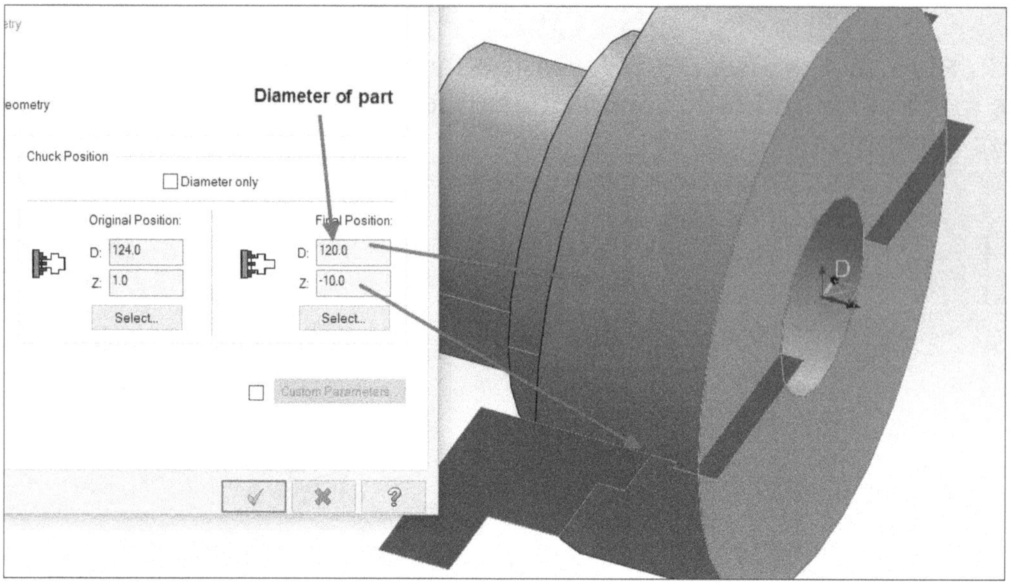

Figure-18. Model after stock flip

- After specifying desired parameters, click on the **OK** button to create stock flip. Now, you can perform machining on back face of the model.

STOCK ADVANCE

The **Stock Advance** tool is used to push or pull the stock. The procedure to use this tool is given next.

- Click on the **Stock Advance** tool from the **Part Handling** panel of **Turning** tab in the **Ribbon**. The **Lathe Stock Advance** dialog box will be displayed; refer to Figure-19.

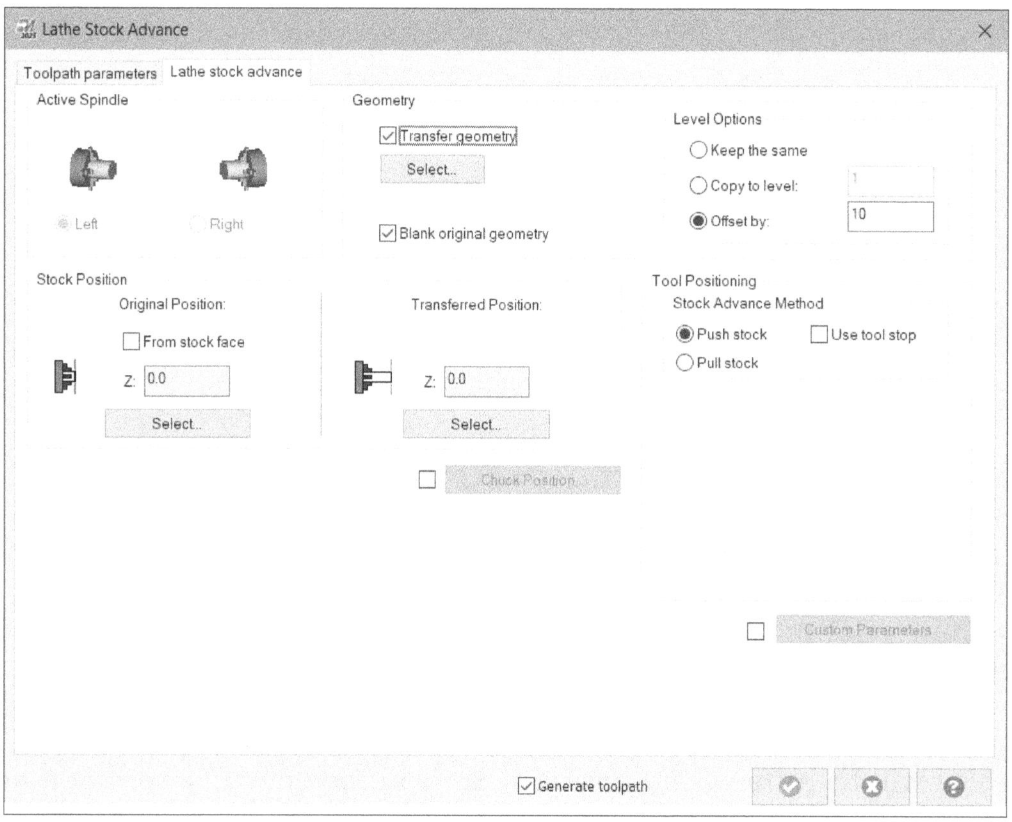

Figure-19. Lathe Stock Advance dialog box

- Click on the **Select** button from the **Geometry** area of the dialog box and select the part you want to move.
- If you select the **Transfer geometry** check box then the part will also move by specified distance along with stock. (We recommend you to select this check box.)
- If the **Blank original geometry** check box is selected then the original part will get hidden and only the moved part will be displayed.
- Specify the original position of stock in the **Original Position** edit box of **Stock Position** area in the dialog box or you can select the **From stock face** check box to automatically take the Z value of front face of stock.
- In the **Transferred Position** edit box, specify desired value of Z for front face of stock after moving it.
- Select the **Push stock** or **Pull stock** radio button to use the respective method for stock advance. Specify the related parameters in the edit boxes below the radio buttons.
- Click on the **OK** button from the dialog box to create the feature.

UNDOING STOCK RELATED OPERATIONS IN MASTERCAM

This topic is more of a case rather than tool procedure. One simple question: What if you have performed stock advance and later you realize that you do not need it. What will you do? One answer will come as delete the operation from the **Toolpath Manager**. Figure-20 shows a case where we have done stock advance operation but now we want to reverse it. The steps are given next.

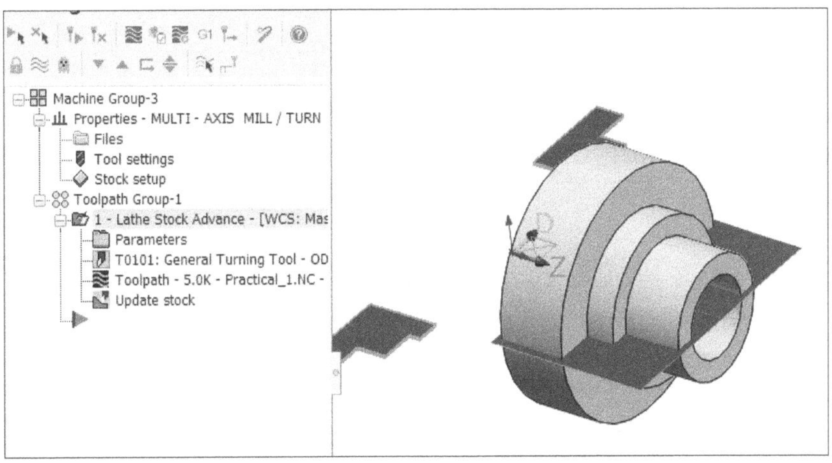

Figure-20. Lathe stock advance done on part

- Select the stock operation that you want to reverse from the **Toolpath Manager** and right-click on it. A shortcut menu will be displayed.
- Select the **Delete** option from the shortcut menu; refer to Figure-21. The stock will move back to chuck but the model will not move back.

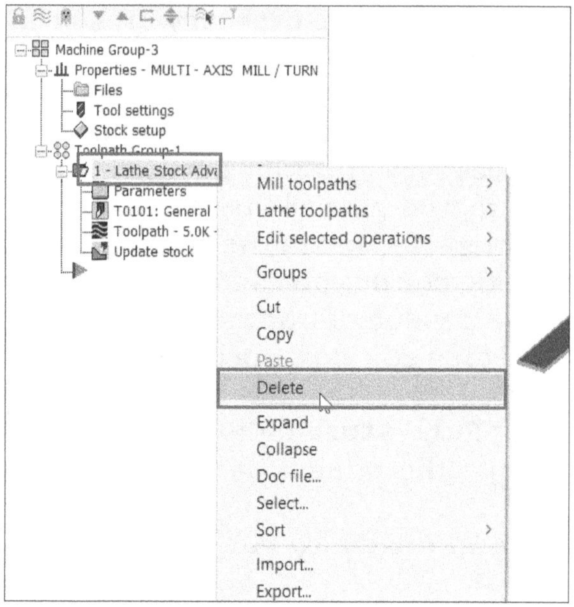

Figure-21. Delete option in shortcut menu

- Click on the **Solids** tab in the **Manager** and delete the body created after stock handling operation; refer to Figure-22.

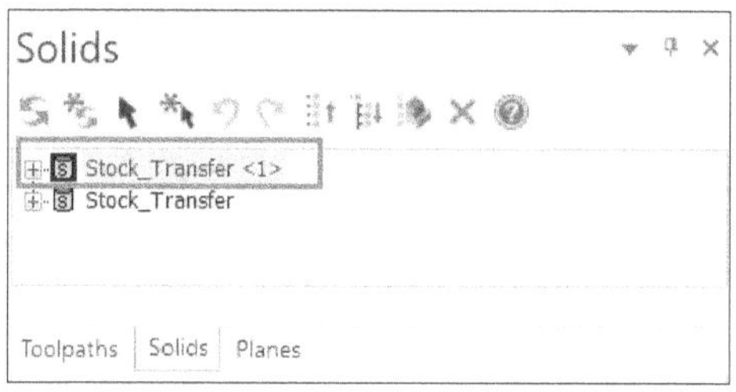

Figure-22. Body to be deleted

- Now, click on the **Toolpath Manager** button from the left pane and remove stock as well as clamp by using the **Machine Group Properties** dialog box discussed earlier.

CHUCK

The **Chuck** tool is used to output M codes for clamping and de-clamping of the chuck. The procedure to use this tool is given next.

- Click on **Chuck** tool from the **Part Handling** panel in the **Turning** tab of the **Ribbon**. The **Lathe Chuck** dialog box will be displayed; refer to Figure-23.

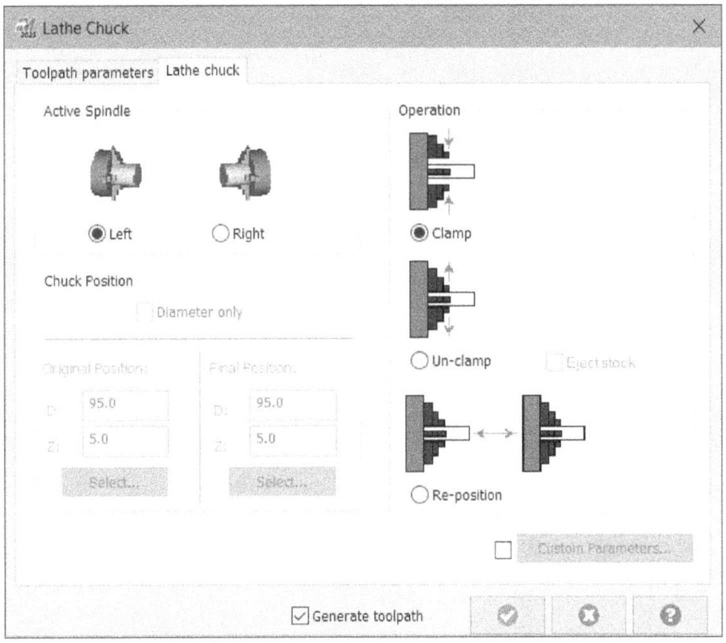

Figure-23. Lathe Chuck dialog box

- Select desired radio button from the **Active Spindle** area to perform operations on that spindle.
- Select desired operation like, clamp, un-clamp, or re-position from the **Operation** area of the dialog box and click on the **OK** button.

TAIL STOCK

The **Tail Stock** tool in **Lathe Toolpaths** drop-down is used to manage operations related to tail stock. To use this tool, you must have already defined tailstock in machine definition. The procedure to add tail stock has been discussed in previous chapter. The procedure to use **Tail Stock** tool is discussed next.

- Click on the **Tail Stock** tool from the **Part Handling** panel of **Turning** tab in the **Ribbon**. The **Lathe Tailstock** dialog box will be displayed; refer to Figure-24.
- Select desired operation from the **Operation** area of the dialog box. If you want to move the tailstock towards the part then select the **Advance** radio button. If you want to move the tailstock away from part then select the **Retract** radio button.
- Specify the parameters related to selected operation in the **Tailstock Position** area of the dialog box.
- Click on the **OK** button to perform the operation and add codes in NC program.

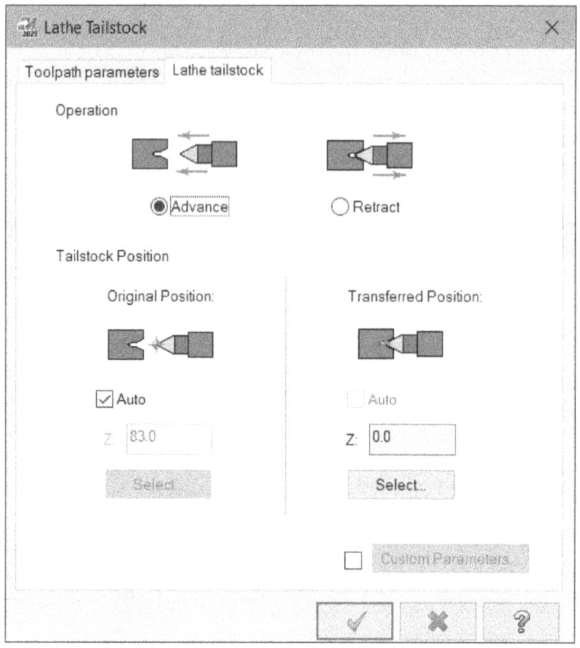

Figure-24. Lathe Tailstock dialog box

Similarly, you can use the **Steady Rest** tool to manage operations related to steady rest.

Note that the operations discussed in this chapter are not available in all the machines, so you should check your machine manual before programming. Like, the operations to flip stock or stock advance are not available in general turning machines.

BACKPLOT AND VERIFYING TOOLPATH

Till now, we have created many toolpaths for CNC turning machines but we have not verified them in simulation environment. Here, we will discuss the options to graphically verify toolpaths created earlier.

Back plotting Toolpath

The **Backplot** button in **Toolpaths Manager** is used to check movement of the tool for selected toolpaths. The procedure to use this tool is given next.

- Select the toolpath group or toolpath which you want to check and click on the **Backplot selected operations** button from the **Toolpaths Manager**; refer to Figure-25. The **Backplot** dialog box will be displayed with the preview of tool and **Backplot VCR** bar; refer to Figure-26.

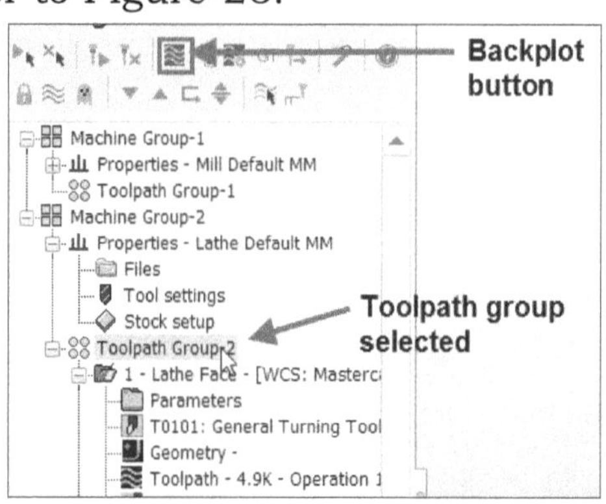

Figure-25. Backplotting toolpath group

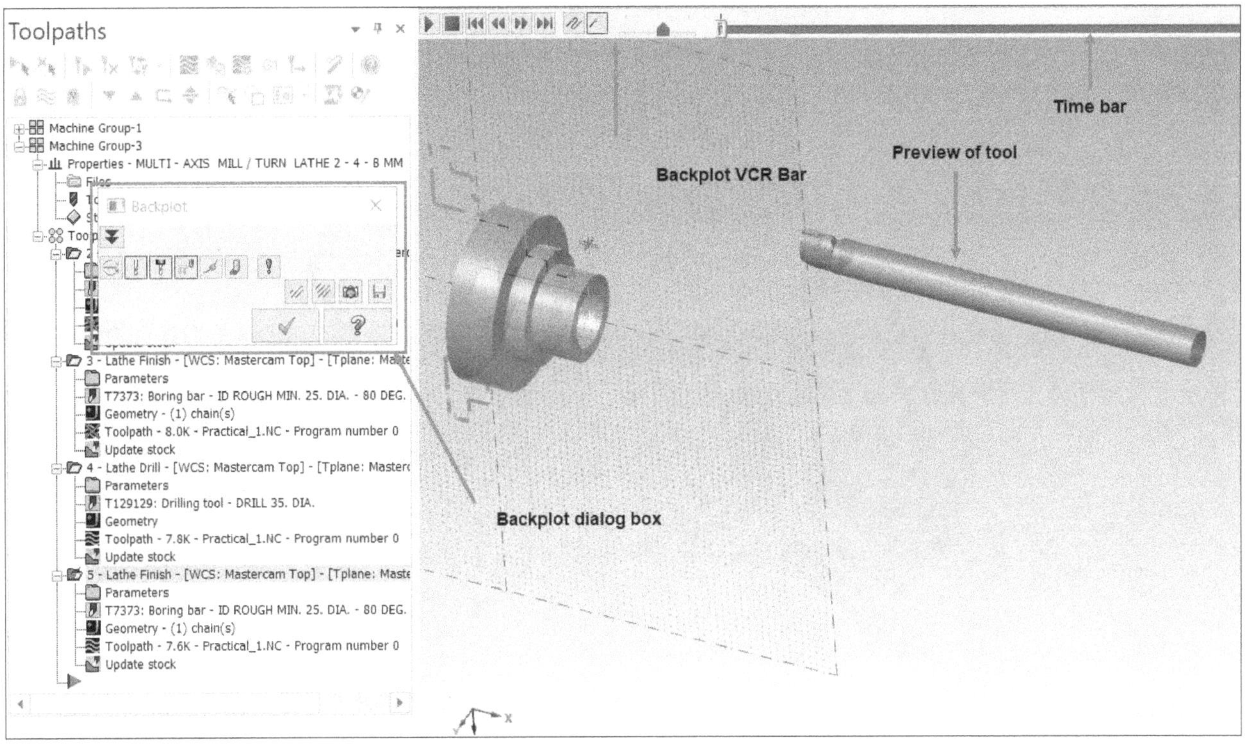

Figure-26. Backplot PropertyManager with Backplot VCR bar

- Click on the **Play** button from the **Backplot VCR Bar** to play simulation of tool path generation. Select desired filters from the **Backplot** dialog box to display or hide elements in the simulation. Click on the **OK** button from the dialog box to exit the tool.

Verifying Toolpaths

The **Verify** tool is used to verify the toolpath in 3D dynamic environment. The procedure is given next.

- Select the operations to be verified and click on the **Verify selected operations** button from the **Toolpaths Manager**. The **Mastercam Simulator** window will be displayed; refer to Figure-27.
- Select the parameters as required and then click on the **Play** button to run the dynamic simulation. Use this simulator to verify tool collisions. You can record the simulation using the **Record** button in the **Ribbon**.
- Close the dialog box after verifying toolpath.

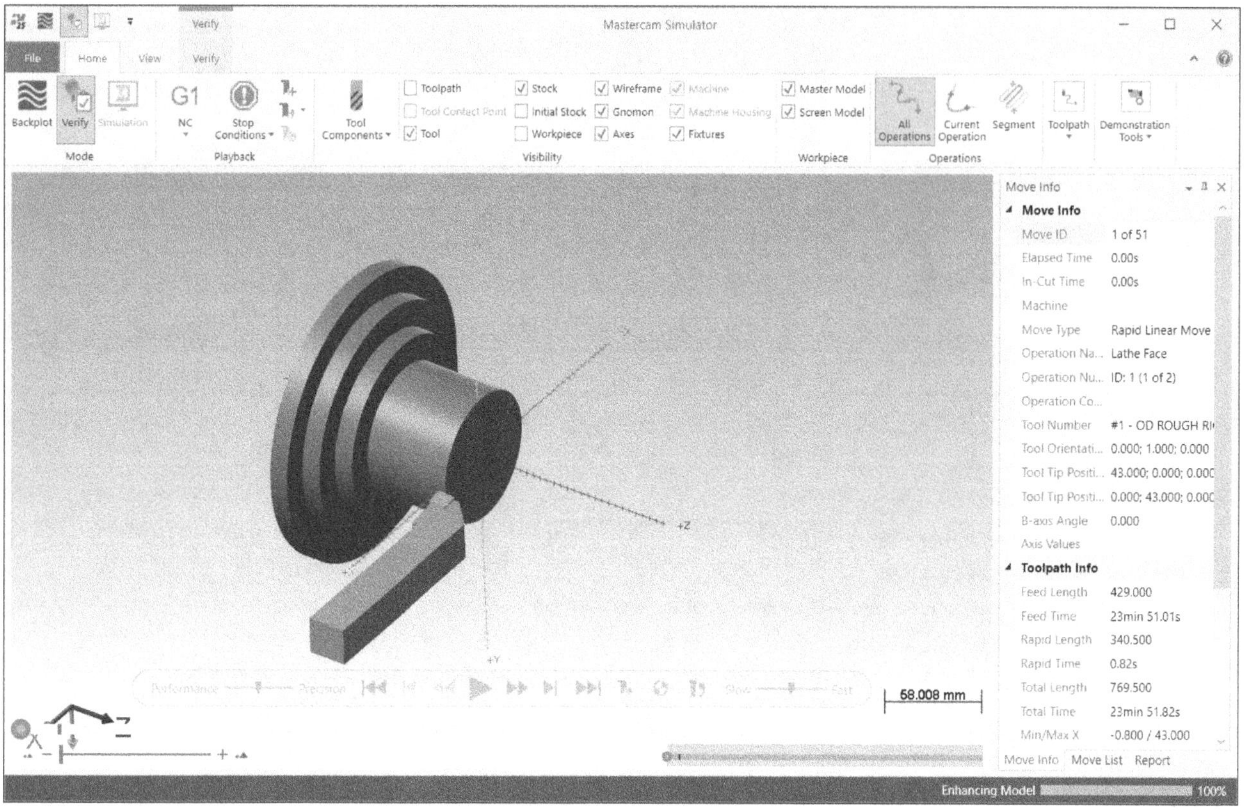

Figure-27. Mastercam Simulator window

PRACTICAL 1

Create an NC program for part shown in Figure-28. The stock dimensions are given in Figure-29. Note that the SolidWorks part file for model is available in the resources of this book.

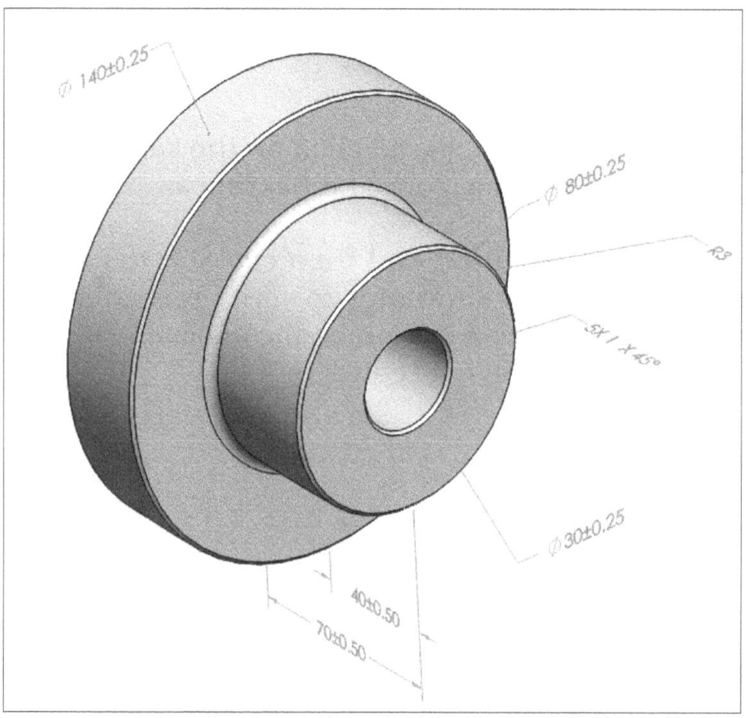

Figure-28. Model for Practical 1

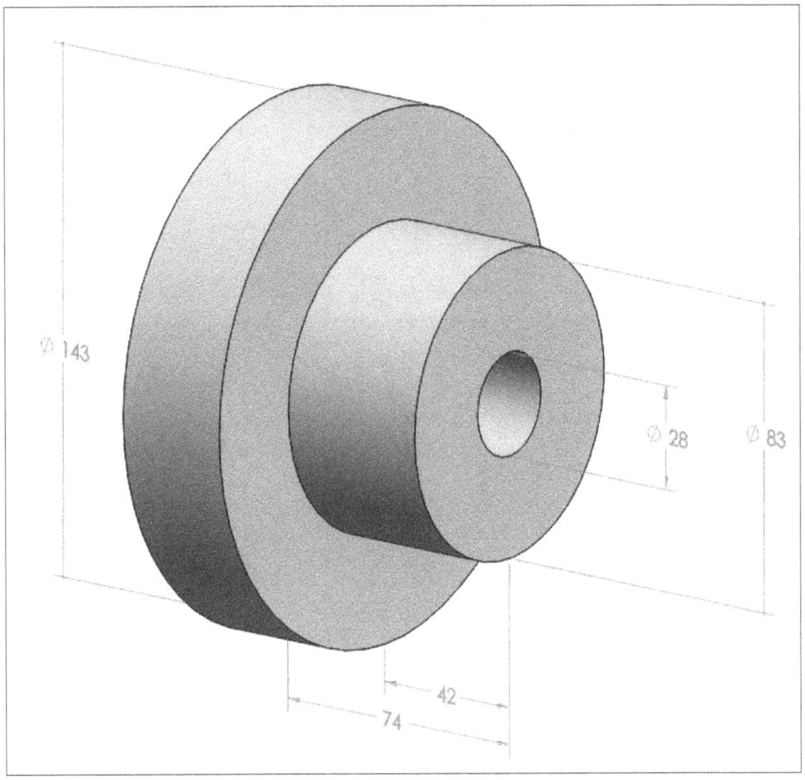

Figure-29. Dimensions of stock for gear blank

Opening Part and Setting Lathe Machine

- Start Mastercam if not started yet.
- Open the **Gear blank for practical.sldprt** file from the resources folder of the book. The model will open.
- Click on the **Default** option from the **Lathe** drop-down in **Machine Type** panel of **Machine** tab in the **Ribbon**. A new machine group will be added with lathe machine settings; refer to Figure-30.

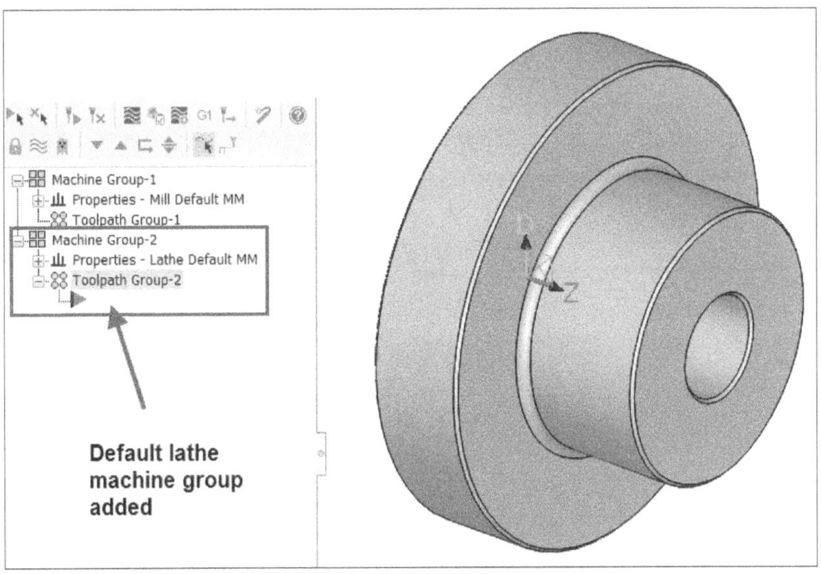

Figure-30. Default lathe machine group added

- Now, we will import a part to create stock. Click on the **File -> Merge** tool from the menu bar. The **Open** dialog box will be displayed.

- Select the **IGES** format from the **File Type** drop-down and select the stock for practical gear blank file from book resources; refer to Figure-31.

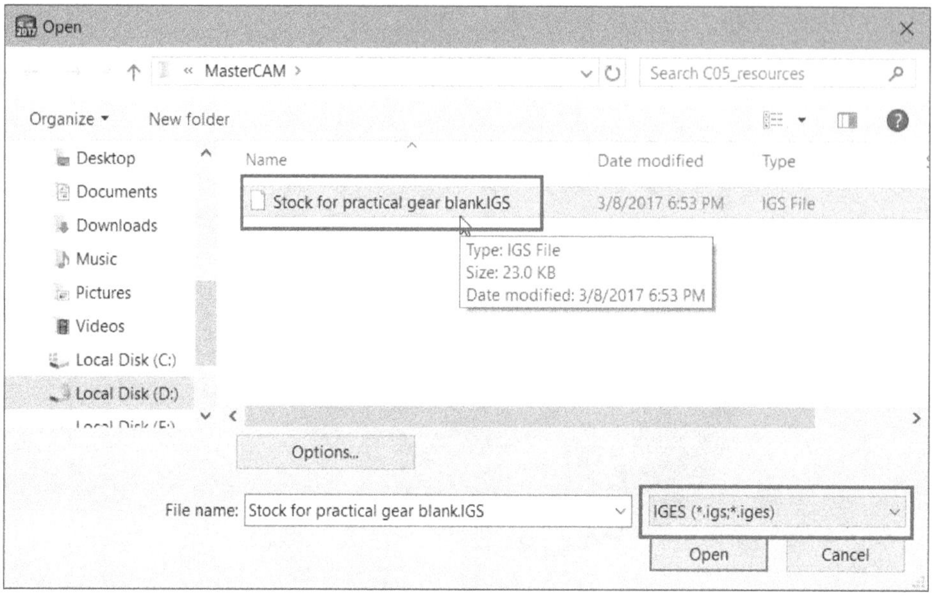

Figure-31. Open dialog box for imported files

- After selecting file, click on the **Open** button from the dialog box. Preview of imported file will be displayed in the drawing area with **Merge Pattern Manager**; refer to Figure-32.

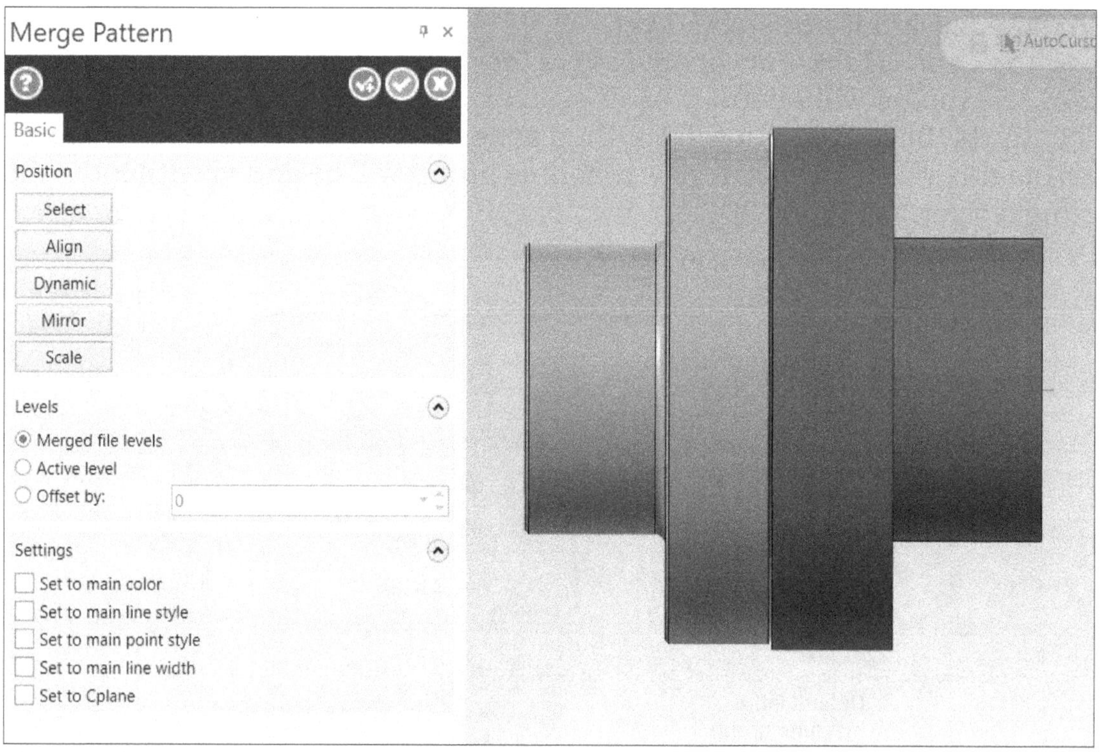

Figure-32. Preview of imported model

- Select the **Front** tool from the **Graphics View** panel in **View** tab of the **Ribbon**; refer to Figure-33 or press **ALT+2** to orient the model in front view.

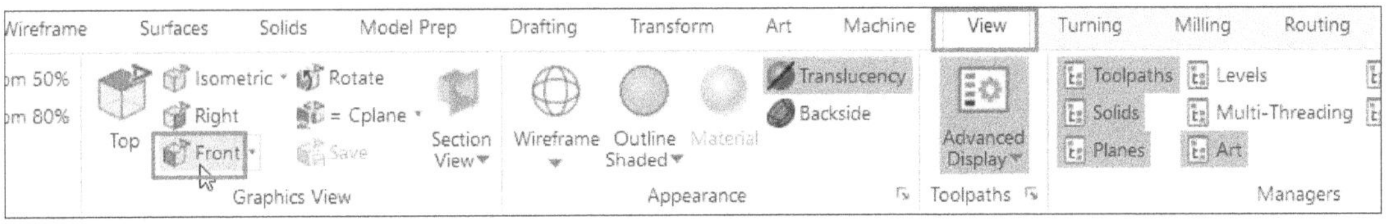

Figure-33. Selecting front view

- Click on the **OK** button as the file imported is a surface model and it is better to convert it into solid before performing proper positioning of model.
- Click on the **Solids from Surfaces** tool from the **Create** panel in the **Solids** tab of the **Ribbon**. You will be asked to select the surfaces to be used for creating solid and **From Surfaces Manager** will be displayed.
- Select the surfaces of imported model to be used for creating solid; refer to Figure-34. Note that you can also use solid model created in Mastercam to define stock for the model.

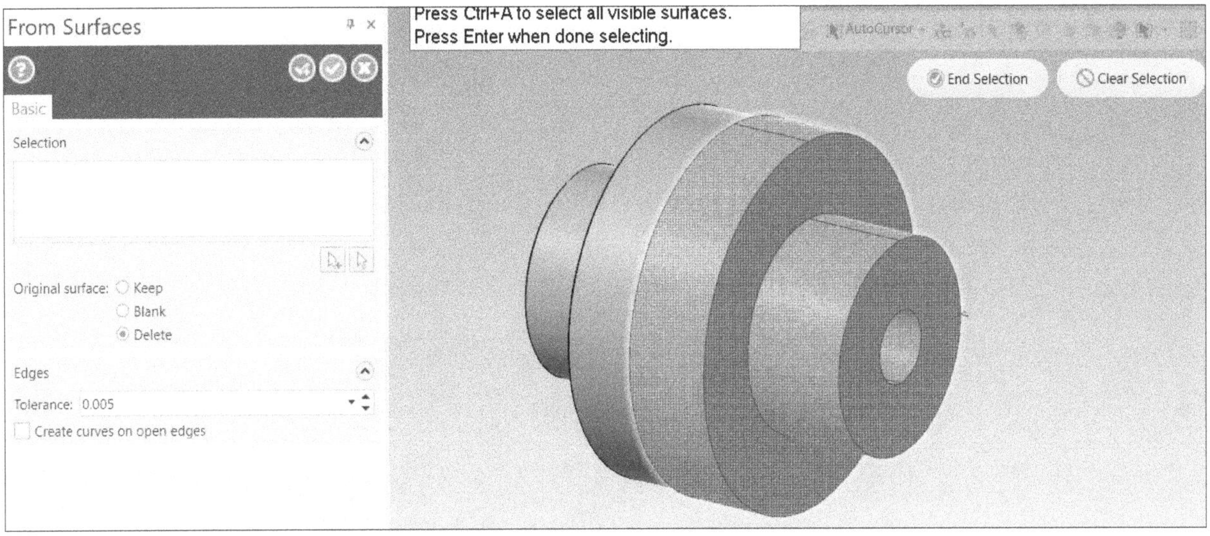

Figure-34. Surfaces selected for converting to solid

- After selecting surfaces, click on the **End Selection** button. The options in the **From Surfaces Manager** will become active.
- Select the **Delete** radio button from **Original surface** section and click on the **OK** button from the **Manager**.
- Orient to Front view and select the original model to be achieved after machining. The **Tools** contextual tab will be displayed in the **Ribbon**.
- Click on the **Mirror** tool from the **Position** panel in the **Tools** contextual tab of the **Ribbon**. The preview of mirror feature will be displayed with **Mirror Manager**; refer to Figure-35.
- Select the **Move** radio button for **Method** section to move the original body at mirror location.
- Select the **Vector** radio button from the **Axis** rollout and click on the **Selection** button to select desired mirror axis. You will be asked to specify two points for defining axis.
- Select the top and bottom point on back face of model; refer to Figure-36. Preview of mirror feature will be displayed.

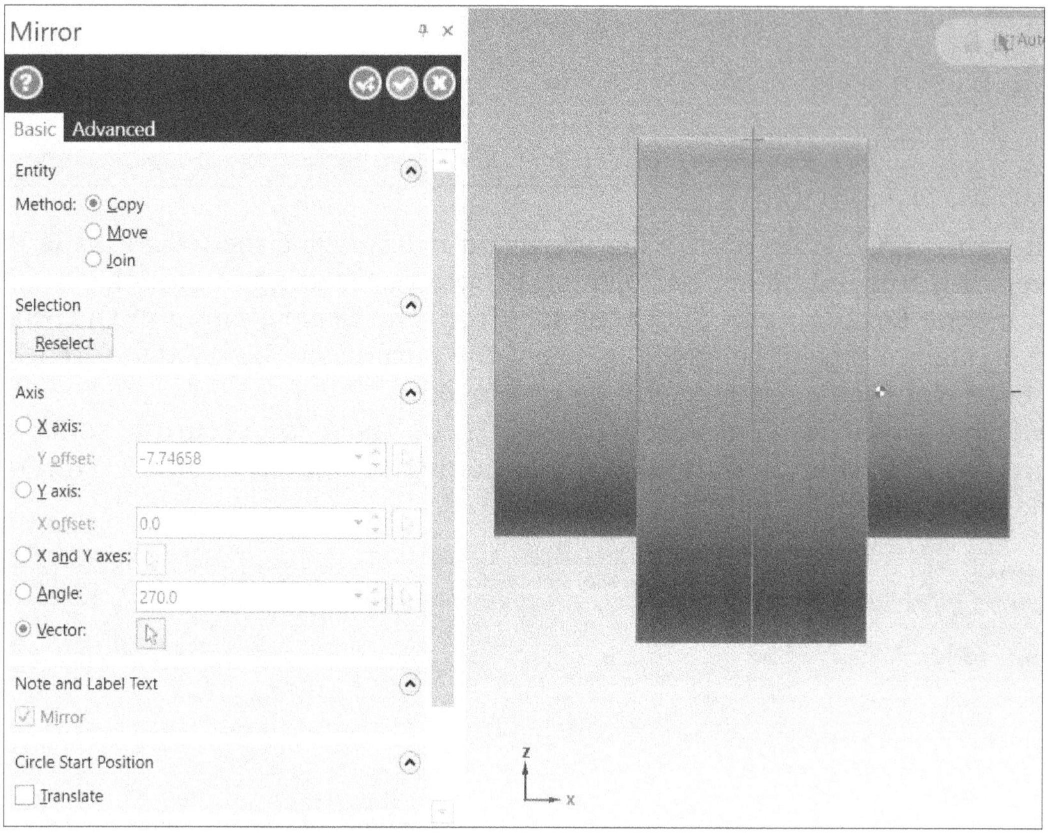

Figure-35. Preview of mirror feature

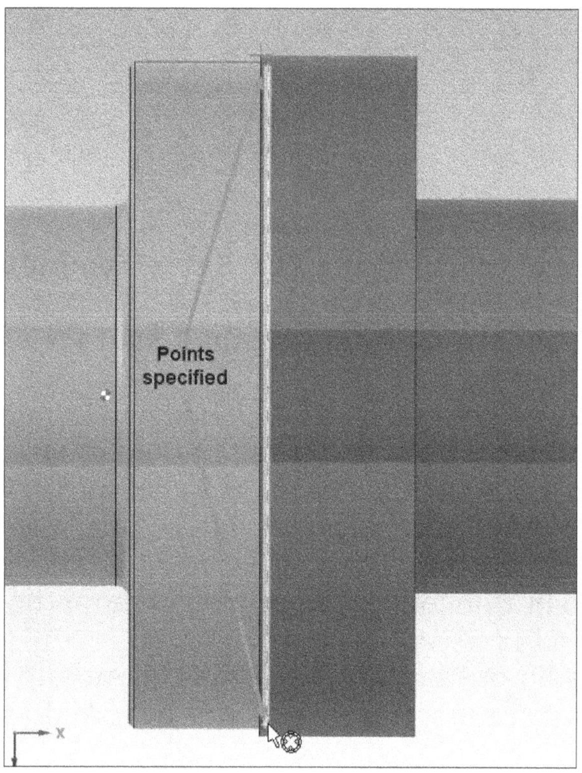

Figure-36. Specifying point for mirror axis

- Click on the **OK** button from the **Manager** to create the mirror copy. Select the **Translucency** button from the **Appearance** panel in the **View** tab of the **Ribbon**. The model will be displayed; refer to Figure-37.

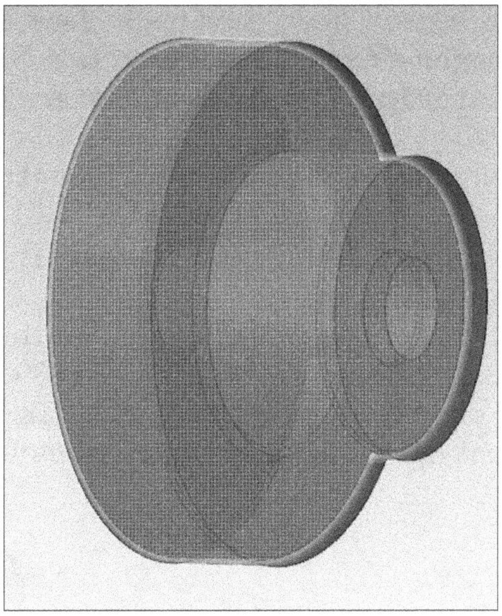

Figure-37. Model after mirror copy

Defining Stock and Chuck Jaws

- Click on the **Stock setup** option from the **Properties** node in the **Mastercam Toolpath Manager**. The **Machine Group Properties** dialog box will be displayed with **Stock Setup** tab selected.
- Make sure the **Left Spindle** radio buttons are selected in **Stock** and **Chuck Jaws** areas of the dialog box and then click on the **Properties** button from the **Stock** area in the dialog box. The **Machine Component Manager - Stock** dialog box will be displayed.
- Select the **Solid entity** option from the **Geometry** drop-down in the dialog box. The options in the dialog box will be displayed as shown in Figure-38.

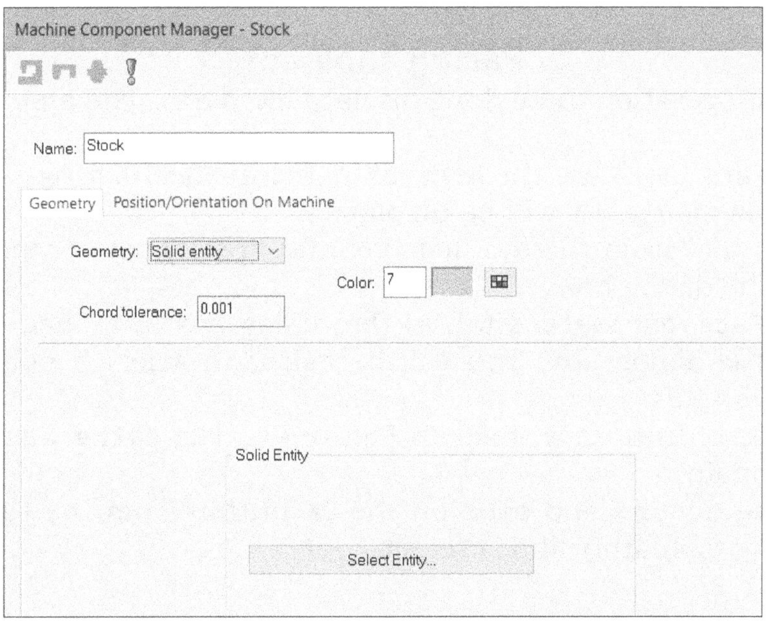

Figure-38. Machine Component Manager-Stock dialog box partial view

- Click on the **Select Entity** button in the **Solid Entity** area of the dialog box. You will be asked to select a body to be used as stock.
- Select the imported model and click on the **OK** button from the dialog box. The **Machine Group Properties** dialog box will be displayed again.

- Click on the **Properties** button from the **Chuck Jaws** area of the dialog box. The **Machine Component Manager-Chuck Jaws** dialog box will be displayed.
- Select the **From Stock** and **Grip on maximum diameter** check boxes in the **Position** area.
- Enter the value of grip length as **6** in the **Grip Length** edit box of the **Position** area of the dialog box.
- Click on the **OK** button from the dialog box. The **Machine Group Properties** dialog box will be displayed again.
- Select the **Shade boundaries** check box and click on the **OK** button from the dialog box. The model will be displayed as shown in Figure-39. Note that you need to hide the imported model for checking the stock model. To do so, select the imported model and select the **Blank** option from the **Display** panel in **Home** tab of the **Ribbon**.

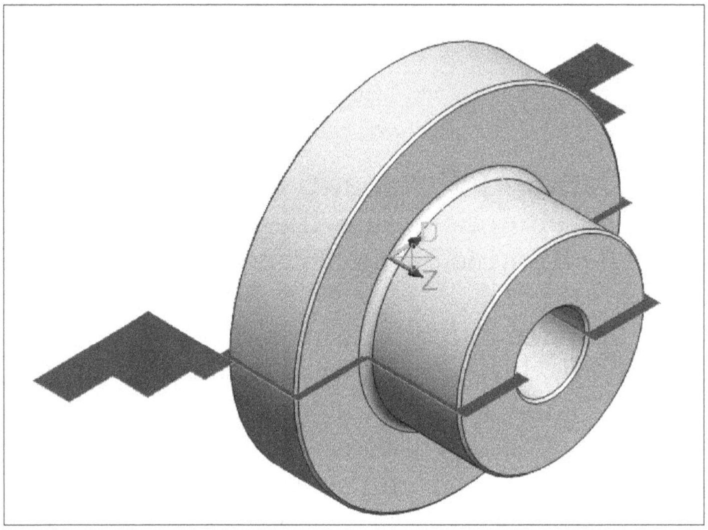

Figure-39. Model after applying stock and chuck jaws

Facing Toolpath

Facing is the first operation to be done on flat face parts. The steps are given next.

- Click on the **Face** tool from the **General** panel in the **Turning** tab of the **Ribbon**. The **Lathe Face** dialog box will be displayed.
- Select desired tool from the tool list box and specify related parameters in the right area of the dialog box.
- Click on the **Face parameters** tab in the dialog box and click on the **Finish Z** button from the dialog box. You will be asked to select a point to specify the location of finish Z.
- Select the edge of front face; refer to Figure-40. The **Lathe Face** dialog box will be displayed again.
- Set desired parameters and click on the **OK** button from the **Lathe Face** dialog box. The facing toolpath will be created.

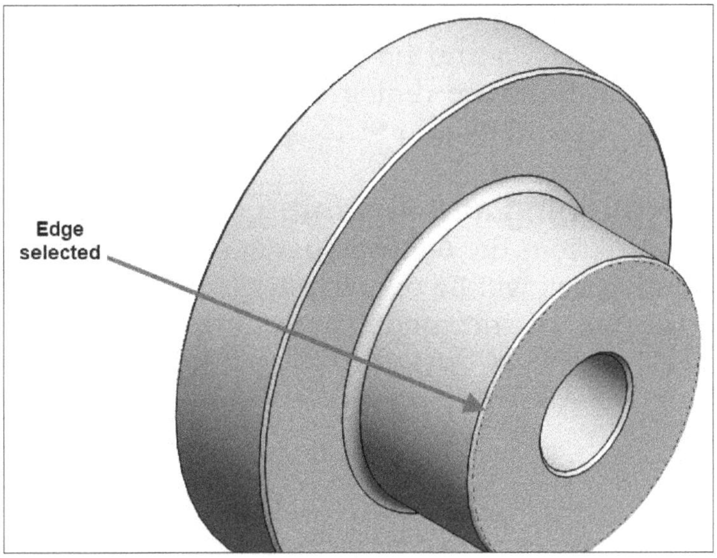

Figure-40. Edge selected for facing

ID Finish

- Click on the **Finish** tool from the **Lathe Toolpaths** drop-down. The **Wireframe Chaining** dialog box will be displayed.
- Click on the **Solids** button from the top in the dialog box and select the face curves as shown in Figure-41.

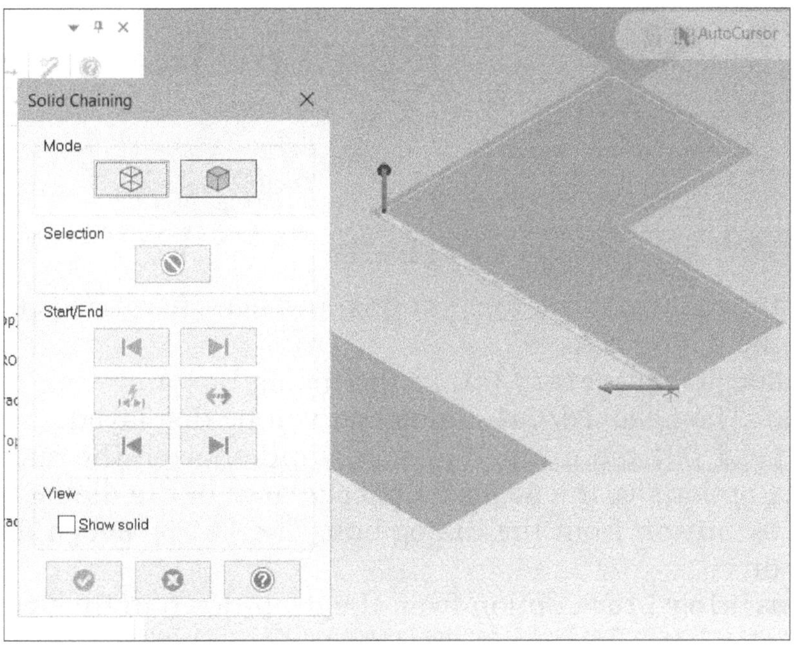

Figure-41. Chain curves selected for ID finish

- Click on the **OK** button from the dialog box. The **Lathe Finish** dialog box will be displayed.
- Select the **T8181 R0.4 ID FINISH 16 DIA- 55 DEG** tool from the tool list box and specify the related parameters in the right area of the dialog box.
- Click on the **Finish Parameters** tab in the dialog box and click on the **Lead In/Out** button. The **Lead In/Out** dialog box will be displayed.
- Click on the **Lead Out** tab and select the **Extend/shorten end of contour** check box. The options below it will become active.

- Select the **Extend** radio button and specify the value **5** in the **Amount** edit box. (We are extending the contour, so that no material of hole is left on the back face.)
- Click on the **OK** button from the dialog box. Specify desired parameters in the **Lathe Finish** dialog box and click on the **OK** button.

Roughing and Finishing Outer faces

- Click on the **Rough** tool from the **General** panel of **Turning** tab in the **Ribbon**. The **Solid Chaining** dialog box will be displayed.
- Select the outer curves of the model including chamfer and round; refer to Figure-42 and click on the **OK** button from the **Solid Chaining** dialog box. The **Lathe Rough** dialog box will be displayed.

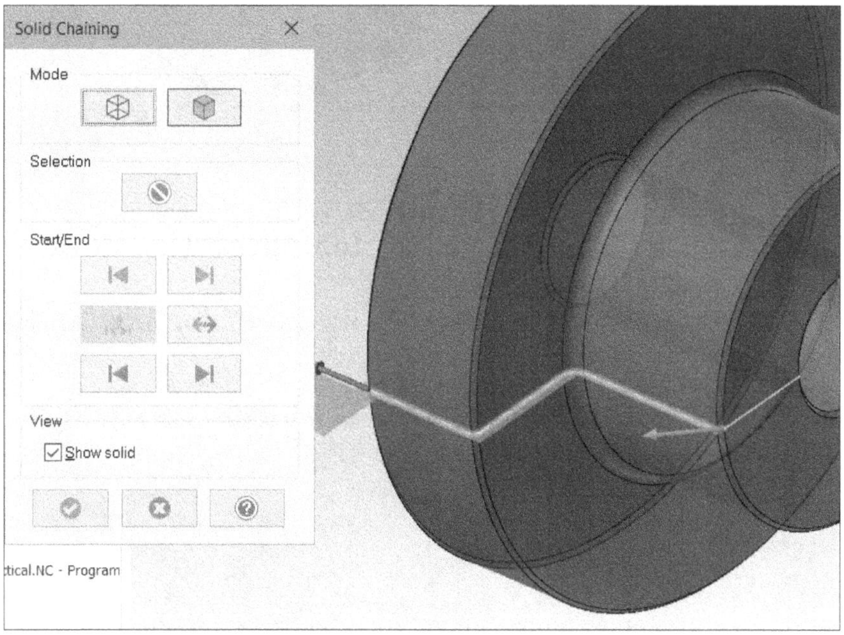

Figure-42. Entities selected for roughing operation

- Select the **T0101** tool from the tool list box and specify related parameters in the right area of the dialog box.
- Click on the **Rough parameters** tab in the dialog box and then click on the **Lead In/Out** button. The **Lead In/Out** dialog box will be displayed.
- Click on the **Lead Out** tab in the dialog box and shorten the end of contour by **7** mm using the options in the **Adjust Contour** area of the dialog box.
- Click on the **OK** button from the dialog box. The **Lathe Rough** dialog box will be displayed again.
- Select the **Remaining Stock** option from the drop-down in the **Stock Recognition** area of the dialog box and specify the other parameters as required.
- Click on the **OK** button to create toolpath.

Similarly, click on the **Finish** tool from the **Lathe Toolpaths** drop-down and create the finish toolpath using the same faces and **T2121** tool. Make sure you specify the same **Lead out** for finish tool path as you have specified for rough toolpath.

Performing Stock Flip

- Click on the **Stock Flip** tool from the **Lathe Toolpaths** drop-down in the **Ribbon**. The **Stock Flip** dialog box will be displayed.

- Make sure **Transfer geometry** and **Blank original geometry** check boxes are selected in the **Geometry** area of the dialog box and then click on the **Select** button. You will be asked to select the geometry to be flipped.
- Select the part from graphics area and click on the **OK** button from **Selection PropertyManager**.
- Specify the diameter as **80** and **Z** value as **-50** in the **D** and **Z** edit boxes of **Final Position** in the **Chuck Position** area of the dialog box, respectively.
- Click on the **OK** button from the dialog box. The part will flip with stock; refer to Figure-43.

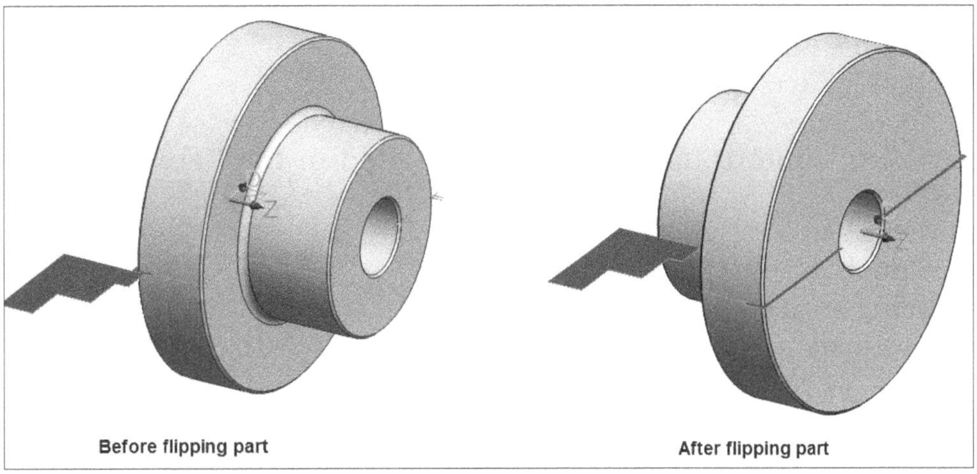

Figure-43. Flipping stock

Now, create the facing and finishing tool path for the remaining stock as discussed earlier. Save the file at desired location and generate NC file using the button in **Toolpath Manager** as discussed earlier.

SELF ASSESSMENT

Q1. Face Contour toolpath should be used before performing facing and roughing operations. (T/F)

Q2. What is C axis in Mastercam Lathe machining?

Q3. To perform Pickoff /Pull/Cutoff Operation on CNC lathe, we need both left and right chucks to be defined. (T/F)

Q4. The Stock Transfer tool is used to unclamp the chuck so that side of workpiece can be manually changed. (T/F)

Q5. The .... tool is used to reverse the face of model so that you can perform back face machining.

Q6. The .... button in Toolpaths Manager is used to check movement of the tool for selected toolpaths.

REVIEW QUESTIONS

Q1. When should the Face Contour tool be used in the machining process?
A. Before the roughing operation
B. After the finishing operation
C. Before facing
D. After facing and roughing

Q2. Which dialog box appears when you click on the Face Contour tool?
A. Lathe Toolpath - Face Cut
B. C-Axis Toolpath - C-Axis Face Contour
C. Solid Selection - Face Chain
D. Tool Manager - Face Setup

Q3. Which type of contouring is generally required in the Face Contour operation for flat faces?
A. 3D contouring
B. Spiral contouring
C. 2D contouring
D. Radial contouring

Q4. Which tool was selected for the Face Contour example in the content?
A. 5 mm ball end mill
B. 4 mm slot drill
C. 3 mm flat end mill
D. 2 mm radius cutter

Q5. What does the Cross Contour tool create?
A. Toolpath for X-axis machining
B. Toolpath for Z-axis profiling
C. Toolpath along the C-axis
D. Toolpath for roughing

Q6. What is the common use of the Pickoff/Pull/Cutoff operation?
A. Cutting internal threads
B. Milling slots
C. Back face machining, bar pulling, or cutoff
D. Creating internal cavities

Q7. In Pickoff operations, which machine component must be movable?
A. Primary chuck
B. Spindle motor
C. Secondary chuck
D. Turret

Q8. Which edit box allows specifying where the secondary jaw will hold the part in Z direction during Pickoff?
A. Cutoff X coordinate
B. Pickoff Z coordinate
C. Back face stock
D. Face stock

Q9. What is the function of the Stock Transfer tool?
A. Moves tool from spindle to turret
B. Transfers material to the toolpath
C. Transfers stock from primary to sub-spindle
D. Shifts the part within the same chuck

Q10. In Stock Flip, where does the back face of the model end up after flipping?
A. At X=0
B. At Y=0
C. At new Z=0
D. At original Z=0

Q11. What is the purpose of the "Transfer geometry" checkbox in Stock Advance?
A. Only moves geometry
B. Moves both geometry and stock
C. Changes orientation of part
D. Activates tool holder setup

Q12. How do you undo a stock handling operation like stock advance in Mastercam?
A. Change the simulation settings
B. Reset the post processor
C. Delete the stock operation and body created
D. Press Ctrl+Z in simulation window

Q13. What does the Chuck tool control in Mastercam?
A. Tailstock pressure
B. Tool spindle alignment
C. M codes for chuck clamping/unclamping
D. Tool offset positions

Q14. Which area in the Tailstock dialog lets you move the tailstock forward?
A. Retract area
B. Advance area
C. Toolpath area
D. Final Position

Q15. Which tool is used for verifying toolpath movement in a dynamic 3D simulation?
A. Tool Holder Analyzer
B. Cross Contour Simulator
C. Verify selected operations
D. Toolpath Setup Assistant

Q16. What does the Backplot feature primarily help with?
A. Programming M-codes
B. Selecting cutting tools
C. Checking toolpath movement visually
D. Designing tool geometry

Q17. What happens if a stock operation is deleted but the model remains changed?
A. Stock returns, model also reverts
B. Model stays shifted, stock returns
C. Both model and stock revert
D. Nothing changes

Q18. What is required to use the Tailstock tool in Mastercam?
A. A completed simulation
B. An added secondary chuck
C. A defined tailstock in machine definition
D. A roughing operation beforehand

Q19. What happens when the "Blank original geometry" checkbox is selected in Stock Advance?
A. The part becomes transparent
B. Original geometry is hidden
C. New geometry is disabled
D. Nothing is visible in simulation

Q20. Which tools are located under the Part Handling panel in the Turning tab?
A. Chamfer, Grooving, Contour
B. Chuck, Stock Transfer, Tail Stock
C. Facing, Roughing, Cross Drill
D. Tool Library, Holder, Coolant

Index

Symbols

2D chamfer option 9-6
2D High Speed Toolpath - Blend Mill dialog box 9-34
2D High Speed Toolpath - Dynamic Mill dialog box 9-23
2D High Speed Toolpath - Peel Mill dialog box 9-31
2D Toolpaths-Contour dialog box 9-4
2D Toolpaths - Model Chamfer dialog box 9-39
2D Toolpaths - Pocket dialog box 9-28
2D Toolpaths-Pocket dialog box 9-27
3+2 Automatic Roughing tool 11-30
3D Curves option 11-3
= Cplane tool 7-12
+D+Z plane 14-4

A

Add Automatic row button 11-11
Add Component button 8-11
Add group tool 4-10
Add History tool 5-12
Add Plane row button 11-13
Add Section button 4-46
Add Surface row button 11-13
Add To Existing tool 6-12
Add view button 4-45
Adjust Stock toolbar 14-28
Advanced Display button 7-14
Advanced Drill tool 9-60
Advanced Toolpath Display Options 7-14
Align button 1-36
Align Note tool 6-21
Align to Face tool 5-17
Align tool 6-14
Align to Plane tool 5-15
Align to Z tool 5-18, 14-3
Along option 1-20
Analyze option 1-42
Angular tool 6-8
Anti-Collision Model rollout 8-22
Appearance group 7-13
Approach distance edit box 9-21
Arc 3 Points tool 2-12
Arc Center option 1-18
Arc Endpoints tool 2-16
Arc Filter/Tolerance option 9-11
Arc Polar Endpoints tool 2-18
Arc Polar tool 2-17
Arc Tangent tool 2-13
Area Rough tool 10-21
Area tool 9-32
Associative tool 6-20
AutoCursor Fast Point tool 1-22
Auto-highlight of level entities check box 1-23
Automatic button 6-20
AutoSave tool 1-33
Axis Combination option 9-14
Axis Combinations tab 8-12

B

Backplot button 15-16
Backplot selected operations button 9-14
Backplot VCR bar 15-17
Ball Nose Mill 8-25
Barrel Mill 8-28
Baseline tool 6-10
Blade Expert tool 11-37
Blend Mill tool 9-34
Blend Surface Finish toolpath 10-33
Blend tool 10-33
Block tool 3-3
Bolt Circle tool 2-5
Boolean tool 4-18
Bore Bar 8-30
Bounding Box/Cylinder PropertyManager 8-39
Bounding Box tool 2-31
Break at Intersection tool 2-46
Break at Points tool 2-47
Break Circles tool 2-59
Break Into Lines tool 6-22
Break Many tool 2-46
Break Two Pieces drop-down 2-45
Break Two Pieces tool 2-45
Bull Nose Mill 8-25

C

CAD option 1-42
Canned Rough tool 14-61
Canned Text option 9-13
Center - Parallel option 11-14
Chained tool 6-10
Chaining Options 1-43

Chamfer Drill tool 9-58
Chamfer Entities tool 2-53
Chamfer Mill 8-26
Change Face tool 5-19
Change Recognition tool 1-31
Change tool 3-42
Check Holder tool 12-21
Check Tool Reach tool 12-22
Chuck Jaws area 14-8
Chuck tool 15-14
Circle Center Point tool 2-11
Circle Edge Point tool 2-15
Circmill Toolpaths tool 9-61
Circular Pattern tool 4-25
Circular tool 6-7
Clear All tool 5-18
Clearance check box 9-11
Climb Milling 9-28
Close Arc tool 2-58
Collision Control option 11-17
Color group 5-18
Colors option 1-44
Combine Views tool 2-59
Communication option 1-44
Community menu 1-41
Cone tool 3-5
Configuration tool 1-41
Constant Fillet drop-down 4-27
Constant Fillet tool 4-27
Contour Rough tool 14-50
Contour tool 10-35
Contour Toolpaths tool 9-3
Contour Type drop-down 9-6
Contour Wall option 9-26
Control Definition Files dialog box 8-12
Control Definition tab 8-12
Control Definition tool 8-17
Conventional Milling 9-28
Convert cascading menu 1-39
Converters option 1-45
Convert to 5-axis tool 12-8
Convert to PMesh tool 8-41
Coolant option 9-13
Corner Pretreatment option 9-22
CoroTurn Prime library 14-52
Cplane 2D/3D button 1-29
CPLANE button 1-29
Create Letters tool 2-29
Create new tool option 8-20
Cross Contour tool 15-5
Cross Hatch tool 6-17
Curve tool 11-2
Customize Ribbon option 1-14
Custom Thread tool 14-55
Cutoff tool 14-34
Cut Parameters option 9-6, 10-27
Cylinder tool 3-2, 4-2, 5-20

D

Deburr 3-axis tool 10-44
Deburr tool 11-27
Decimation tool 5-26
Depth Cuts option 9-7, 9-22
Detect button 9-49
Detect limits button 10-31
Dimmed tool 7-13
Disassemble tool 5-14
Display options drop-down 4-11
Distance and Angle Chamfer tool 4-34
Distribute tool 7-8
Divide tool 2-47
Door Geometry tool 2-37
Dove Mill 8-27
Draft Edge tool 4-37
Draft Extrude tool 4-38
Draft Face tool 4-36
Draft Plane tool 4-40
Draft tool 3-15
Drill Bit 8-29
Drilling machine 1-4
Drill Start Holes dialog box 9-70
Drill tool 9-15, 14-31
Dropping 5 Axis Toolpath 12-11
Dynamic button 1-37
Dynamic Contour tool 9-25
Dynamic Mill tool 9-18
Dynamic Rough tool 14-39
Dynamic tool , 4-9
Dynamic Trim tool 2-41

E

Edit control definition button 8-13
Edit Global tool 8-5
Edit Local tool 8-5
Edit Spline tool 2-61
Edit Surface tool 3-39

Edit tool option 8-23
Edit UV tool 3-40
Electric Discharge Machine 1-4
Electro Chemical Machine 1-5
Ellipse tool 2-26
Enable power keys check box 1-22
End Mill 8-24
Endpoint option 1-18
Engrave Mill 8-27
Engrave Toolpaths tool 9-40
Entity tool 2-55
Entry Motion option 9-23
Explode Mesh tool 5-27
Export as STL tool 8-40
Extend tool 3-27
Extend Trimmed Edges tool 3-28
Extrude tool 3-11, 4-2

F

Face Center option 1-18
Face Contour tool 15-2
Face Mill 8-26
Face to Face Fillet tool 4-28
Face tool 14-32
Facing tool 9-24
FBM Drill tool 9-68
FBM Mill tool 9-44
Feature detection option 9-46
Feed rate options 14-23
Fence tool 3-19
File menu 1-30
Fillet Chains tool 2-51
Fillet Entities tool 2-50
Fillet to Curves tool 3-33
Fillet to Plane tool 3-32
Fillet to Surfaces tool 3-29
Fill Holes tool 3-26, 5-23
Find Holes tool 5-10
Finishing process 1-3
Finish tool 14-30
Finish tools option 9-47
Fit tool 7-11
Flat Boundary tool 3-9
Flowline tool 10-39
Flow tool 11-20
Follow rules drop-down 4-13
Freeform radio button 2-7
From entity normal tool 4-6
From geometry tool 4-5, 4-10
From Gview tool 4-6
From solid face tool 4-6
From Surfaces tool 4-27

G

General Turning/Boring Inserts dialog box 14-14
Geometry display drop-down 1-32
Get Insert button 14-14
Global Machine Definition Manager 8-16
Graphics View group 7-11
Grid group 7-18
Grid Settings 7-18
Groove tool 14-36
Grooving Options dialog box 14-36
Groups Manager 7-16

H

Helix Bore tool 9-64
Helix tool 2-27
Help menu 1-41
Holders tab 14-16
Hole Axis tool 5-2
Hole Table tool 6-16
Hole tool 4-21
Home Position area 14-23
Horizontal Area tool 10-37
Horizontal tool 6-6, 6-11
HST Leads option 9-34
Hybrid toolpaths 10-32

I

Import tool 4-8
Impression tool 4-19
Insert Holders 8-31
Intersection option 1-18
Invert Selection tool 1-25

J

Join Entities tool 2-48

K

Kinematic Tree rollout 8-8

L

Laser Beam Machine 1-5
Lathe Canned Rough dialog box 14-61
Lathe Contour Rough dialog box 14-50
Lathe Cutoff Properties dialog box 14-34

Lathe Drill dialog box 14-31
Lathe Dynamic Rough dialog box 14-40
Lathe Finish Properties dialog box 14-30
Lathe Insert 8-33
Lathe PrimeTurning dialog box 14-52
Lathe Rough dialog box 14-21
Lathe Stock Advance dialog box 15-12
Lathe Thread dialog box 14-42
Lathe Tool Manager tool 14-13
Layout tool 4-43
Leader tool 6-18
Lead In/Out option 9-8
Lead In/Out Options 14-26
Levels Manager 7-16
Line Bisect tool 2-10
Line Closest tool 2-10
Line Endpoints tool 2-7
Line Parallel tool 2-8
Line Perpendicular tool 2-9
Lofted tool 9-55
Loft tool 3-10, 4-15
Lollipop Mill 8-27

M

Machine Component Manager-Linear Axis dialog box 8-8
Machine Component Manager - Rotary Axis dialog box 8-9
Machine Component Manager - Stock dialog box 14-5
Machine Component Manager - Tool Spindle dialog box 8-10
Machine Configuration area 8-10
Machine Definition drop-down 8-5
Machine Definition Menu Management dialog box 14-2
Machine Group Properties dialog box 14-4
Machining boundary - Parallel option 11-14
Manage List option 8-4
Managers 1-26
Managers group 7-15
Manual Entry tool 9-74
Manual Pattern tool 4-26
Mask area 1-43
Mastercam Simulation window 15-17
Material button 7-14
Material tool 8-18
MCO radio button 8-16
Merge tool 1-36
Mesh Conversion rollout 8-16
Meshes from Entities tool 5-20
Mesh radio button 8-16
Midpoint 2 Points option 1-19
Midpoint option 1-19
Migration Wizard tool 1-39
Mill drop-down 8-4
Milling machine 1-4
Minimize burial radio button 10-23
Mirror plane check box 12-6
Mirror tool 7-6
Misc Values option 9-13
Model Chamfer tool 9-39
Modify at Intersection tool 2-44
Modify Feature tool 5-7
Modify Fillet tool 5-7
Modify Length tool 2-49
Modify Mesh Facets tool 5-27
Morph tool 11-19
Move tool 5-4
Move to Origin tool 7-6
Multiaxis group 11-2
Multiaxis Linking tool 12-2
Multiaxis Toolpath - 3+2 Automatic Roughing dialog box 11-30
Multiaxis Toolpath - Blade Expert 11-37
Multiaxis Toolpath - Convert to 5 axis dialog box 12-8
Multiaxis Toolpath - Curve dialog box 11-2
Multiaxis Toolpath - Flow dialog box 11-21
Multiaxis Toolpath - Multisurface dialog box 11-22
Multiaxis Toolpath - Pocketing dialog box 11-29
Multiaxis Toolpath - Port dialog box 11-23
Multiaxis Toolpath - Project Curve dialog box 11-31
Multiaxis Toolpath - Rotary Advanced dialog box 11-34
Multiaxis Toolpath - Rotary dialog box 11-33
Multiaxis Toolpath - Swarf Milling dialog box 11-5
Multiaxis Toolpath - Triangular Mesh dialog box 11-25
Multiaxis Toolpath - Unified dialog box 11-10
Multi-Edit tool 6-21
Multi Passes option 9-9
Multi Start button 14-45
Multisurface Pocket tool 10-20
Multisurface tool 11-22

Multi-Threading Manager 7-16

N

NC Machines 1-5
Nearest option 1-20
Nesting tool 12-13
Net tool 3-16
New tool 1-34
No Hidden tool 7-13
Note tool 6-14

O

Offset Mesh tool 5-21
Offset number edit box 14-23
Offset tool 3-17
One Distance Chamfer drop-down 4-31
One Distance Chamfer tool 4-32
Open in Editor tool 1-35
Open library button 9-5
Open tool 1-34
Optimize tool 5-13
OptiRough tool 10-2
Ordinate group 6-11
Oscillate option 9-6
Outline Shaded tool 7-13

P

Parallel multiaxis toolpath 11-14
Parallel tool 10-14
Peel tool 9-31
Pencil Surface Finish toolpath 10-33
Perpendicular tool 6-9
Pickoff/Pull/Cutoff tool 15-7
Planer 1-4
Plane Selection dialog box 4-45
Planes Manager 7-16, 4-4
Planes option 9-13
Plunge feed rate options 14-23
Plunge Parameters button 14-27
Plunge Rough Surface toolpath 10-18
Plunge tool 10-18
Plunge Turn tool 14-46
Pocketing tool 11-29
Pocket tool 10-8
Pocket Toolpaths tool 9-27
Point Dynamic tool 2-3
Point Endpoints tool 2-4
Point Nodes tool 2-5
Point option 1-20
Point Position drop-down 2-2
Point Position tool 2-2
Point Segment tool 2-4
Point Small Arcs tool 2-5
Point tool 6-8, 14-59
Point toolpaths 9-73
Polygon tool 2-25
Port tool 11-23
Position/Orientation On Machine tab 14-7
Power Surface tool 3-20
PrimeTurning tool 14-52
Printer drop-down 1-40
Print tool 1-40
Profile Ramp option 9-8
Project Manager tool 1-30
Project tool 2-56, 7-5, 10-11, 10-38
Push-Pull tool 5-3

Q

Quadrant option 1-20
Quick Access Toolbar 1-13
Quick Cplane tool 4-8
Quick Masks Toolbar 1-25

R

Radial tool 10-42
Radius Mill 8-26
Raster toolpath 10-29
Raster to Vector tool 2-33
Reamer 8-30
Recent Functions Manager 7-17
Rectangle tool 2-23
Rectangular Pattern tool 4-23
Rectangular Shapes tool 2-24
Refine tool 5-25
Refit Spline tool 2-59
Reflow UV tool 3-42
Regenerate group 6-20
Relative option 1-21
Relative to WCS cascading menu 4-7
Reload tool 8-17
Remachining option 9-6
Remove Boundary tool 3-37
Remove Faces tool 5-8
Remove Fillets tool 5-9
Remove History tool 5-11
Repair File tool 1-33
Repair Small Faces tool 5-13
Replace tool 8-17

Reverse Wear option 9-6
Revolved tool 9-54
Revolve tool 3-14, 4-13
Ribbon 1-17
Roll tool 7-7
Rotary Advanced tool 11-34
Rotary Axis Control option 9-14
Rotary tool 11-33
Rotate radio button 12-7
Rotate tool 7-4, 7-11
Rotation Position tool 7-19
Rough Direction/Angle area 14-24
Roughing process 1-2
Rough parallel parameters tab 10-17
Rough parameters tab 14-24
Rough tool 14-21
Ruled tool 9-57

S

Save Some tool 1-38
Save tool 1-38
Scale tool 7-10
Scallop tool 10-29
Section View button 7-13
Section view status area 1-29
Selected entities status area 1-29
Selection Filters 1-23
Selection Method drop-down 1-24
Selection Mode drop-down 1-24
Selection Settings tool 1-22
Selection Toolbar 1-17
Select Last tool 1-25
Semi Finish Options 14-26
Shaded tool 7-13
Shaper 1-4
Shell tool 4-35
Show Axes drop-down 7-17
Show Gnomons drop-down 7-18
Show Grid toggle button 7-18
Simplify Solid tool 5-13
Simplify Spline tool 2-60
Sinker EDM 1-5
Slot Mill 8-26
Slotmill tool 9-36
Slug cutting option 9-47
Smart Dimension tool 6-2
Smooth Area tool 5-24
Smooth dialog box 2-35
Smooth Free Edges tool 5-22
Smooth Geometry dialog box 2-36
Smooth more button 2-35
Snap to Grid toggle button 7-18
Solid Selection dialog box 4-19
Solids Manager 7-16
Sphere tool 3-4
Spindle Speed option 14-23
Spiral tool 2-28
Spiral toolpath 10-41
Spline Automatic tool 2-22
Spline Blended tool 2-20
Spline Convert to NURBS tool 2-23
Spline From Curves tool 2-21
Spline Manual tool 2-19
Split Solid Faces tool 5-5
Split tool 3-38
Stair Geometry tool 2-36
Start Hole tool 9-70
Station number edit box 14-23
Status Bar 1-29
Steady Rest area 14-11
Steady Rest tool 15-16
Steep/Shallow option 10-31
Stock Advance tool 15-12
Stock Flip tool 15-11
Stock Model tool 8-36
Stock Recognition drop-down 14-28
Stock setup option 14-4
Stock Transfer tool 15-9
Stretch tool 7-9
Style drop-down 11-11
Surface boundary - Parallel option 11-14
Surface Finish Contour dialog box 10-35
Surface Modeling 1-2
Surface parameters tab 10-16
Surface Rough Flowline dialog box 10-39
Swarf Milling tool 11-5
Sweep tool 3-13, 4-16
Sweep Twist check box 4-17
Swept 2D Parameters tab 9-51
Swept 2D tool 9-50
Swept 3D Parameters tab 9-53
Swept 3D tool 9-52

T

Tail stock 8-3
Tailstock Center area 14-10
Tail Stock tool 15-15
Tangent tool 6-11

Taper Mill 8-27
Thicken tool 4-35
Thread button 14-42
Thread Form area 14-43
Thread Mill 8-28
Threadmill Toolpaths tool 9-66
Three Fillet Blend tool 3-36
Three Surface Blend tool 3-35
Toggle AutoCursor Lock 1-21
Tool Angle button 14-23
Tool Angle dialog box 14-24
Tool Changer 8-3
Tool Compensation area 14-25
Tool Manager 8-18
Tool Manager dialog box 8-18
Tool number edit box 14-23
Toolpaths Manager 7-16
Toolpath Transform tool 12-4
Tool Spindle 8-2
Torus tool 3-7
TPLANE button 1-29
Track Changes drop-down 1-32
Track Changes tool 1-32
Transform tab 7-2
Translate radio button 12-8
Translate tool 7-3
Translate to Plane tool 7-4
Translucency button 7-14
Triangular Mesh tool 11-25
Trim by Plane tool 4-41
Trim Many tool 2-43
Trim to Chain tool 5-30
Trim to Curves drop-down 3-21
Trim to Entities drop-down 2-42
Trim to Entities tool 2-42
Trim tool 12-12
Trim to Plane tool 3-25, 5-28
Trim to Point tool 2-43
Trim to Surface/Sheet tool 4-42, 5-29
Trim to Surfaces tool 3-23
Trochoidal motion option 10-23
Turning machine 1-3
Turn Profile tool 14-19
Turret 8-3
Two Distance Chamfer tool 4-33
Two Surface Blend tool 3-34

U

U flowlines 3-11
Unified tool 11-10
Untrim Spline tool 2-60
Untrim tool 3-37
Unzooming 7-11
Use Margins options 14-7

V

Variable fillet rollout 3-31
Variable Radius Fillet tool 4-31
Verify Selection check box 1-23
Verify tool 15-17
Vertical tool 6-7, 6-12
V flowlines 3-11
Viewsheets 1-27
Viewsheets group 7-19
View tab 7-11
Visual styles area 1-29

W

Waterline tool 10-25
WCS button 1-29
Wear option 9-6
Window tool 6-13
Wire-cut EDM 1-5
Wireframe tool 7-13
Witness Line tool 6-19
Wizard Holes tool 9-70

Z

Zip2Go tool 1-39
Zoom group 7-11
Zooming 7-11

Ethics of an Engineer

- Engineers shall hold paramount the safety, health, and welfare of the public and shall strive to comply with the principles of sustainable development in the performance of their professional duties.
- Engineers shall perform services only in areas of their competence.
- Engineers shall issue public statements only in an objective and truthful manner.
- Engineers shall act in professional manners for each employer or client as faithful agents or trustees, and shall avoid conflicts of interest.
- Engineers shall build their professional reputation on the merit of their services and shall not compete unfairly with others.
- Engineers shall act in such a manner as to uphold and enhance the honor, integrity, and dignity of the engineering profession and shall act with zero-tolerance for bribery, fraud, and corruption.
- Engineers shall continue their professional development throughout their careers, and shall provide opportunities for the professional development of those engineers under their supervision.

www.ingramcontent.com/pod-product-compliance
Lightning Source LLC
LaVergne TN
LVHW082001200926
848481LV00010B/2786
* 9 7 8 1 7 7 4 5 9 2 3 0 4 *